ADVANCED ACCOUNTING

ACCOUNTING TEXTBOOKS FROM WILEY

Arpan and Radebaugh: **International Accounting and Multinational Enterprises, 2nd**
Burch and Grudnitski: **Information Systems: Theory and Practice, 5th**
Cloud, Cook, and Waters: **College Accounting Procedures, 2nd, Chapters 1–12, 1–16, 1–24**
DeCoster, Schafer, and Ziebell: **Management Accounting: A Decision Emphasis, 4th**
Defliese, Jaenicke, Sullivan, and Gnospelius: **Montgomery's Auditing, Revised College Version**
Delaney, Adler, Epstein, and Foran: **GAAP, Interpretation and Application 1989 Edition**
Delaney and Gleim: **CPA Examination Review—Auditing**
Delaney and Gleim: **CPA Examination Review—Business Law**
Delaney and Gleim: **CPA Examination Review—Theory and Practice**
Gleim and Delaney: **CPA Examination Review—Volume I Outlines and Study Guide**
Gleim and Delaney: **CPA Examination Review—Volume II Problems and Solutions**
Guy and Carmichael: **Audit Sampling: An Introduction to Statistical Sampling in Auditing, 2nd**
Haried, Imdieke, and Smith: **Advanced Accounting, 4th**
Helmkamp: **Managerial Accounting**
Helmkamp, Imdieke, and Smith: **Principles of Accounting, 3rd**
Imdieke: **Financial Accounting**
Kam: **Accounting Theory**
Kell, Boynton, and Ziegler: **Modern Auditing, 4th**
Kemp and Phillips: **Advanced Accounting**
Kieso and Weygandt: **Intermediate Accounting, 6th**
Magee: **Advanced Managerial Accounting**
Moriarity and Allen: **Cost Accounting, 2nd**
Moscove and Simkin: **Accounting Information Systems, 3rd**
Newell and Kreuze: **College Accounting, Chapters 1–10, 1–15, 1–27**
Ramanathan: **Management Control in Nonprofit Organizations, Text and Cases**
Robinson, Davis, and Alderman: **Accounting Information Systems, 2nd**
Romney, Cherrington, and Hansen: **Casebook in Accounting Information Systems**
Schroeder, McCullers, and Clark: **Accounting Theory: Text and Readings, 3rd**
Solomon, Vargo, and Walther: **Accounting Principles, 2nd**
Solomon, Vargo, and Walther: **Financial Accounting, 2nd**
Taylor and Glezen: **Auditing: Integrated Concepts and Procedures, 4th**
Taylor, Glezen, and Ehrenreich: **Case Study in Auditing, 4th**
Weygandt, Kieso, and Kell: **Accounting Principles**
Wilkinson: **Accounting and Information Systems, 2nd**
Wilkinson: **Accounting Information Systems: Essential Concepts and Applications**

ADVANCED ACCOUNTING

PATRICK S. KEMP Ph.D., CPA
MARY ELLEN PHILLIPS MBA, CPA

Oregon State University
Corvallis, Oregon

WILEY

JOHN WILEY & SONS
New York · Chichester · Brisbane · Toronto · Singapore

Library of Congress Cataloging in Publication Data.

Kemp, Patrick S. (Patrick Samuel), 1932-
    Advanced accounting / Patrick S. Kemp, Mary Ellen Phillips.
        p. cm.

    Bibliography: p.
    Includes index.
    ISBN 0-471-62647-3
    1. Accounting.   I. Phillips, Mary Ellen.   II. Title.

HF5635.K353   1989
657'.046--dc 19   88-32124
                                             CIP

Printed in the United States of America

10 9 8 7 6 5 4 3 2 1

Dedicated to

Carol Kemp
Bob Kemp   *Jeanette Phillips*
and to   *Robert Phillips*
the memory of   *Vickie Scott*
Cathy Kemp

ABOUT THE AUTHORS

Patrick S. Kemp, Ph.D., CPA, received his doctorate in accountancy from the University of Illinois. He has served as Chairman of the Department of Accounting and is Professor of Accounting at Oregon State University. He has public accounting experience with Arthur Young & Company (Houston) and Ernst & Whinney (Winston-Salem, North Carolina). Professor Kemp is the author of other accounting books and is a member of the American Accounting Association, the American Institute of Certified Public Accountants, the National Association of Accountants, and the Oregon Society of Certified Public Accountants. He is a past President of the local chapter of the Oregon Society of Certified Public Accountants and is currently serving on the board of directors of the Society's Educational Foundation. Professor Kemp is a frequent instructor in continuing professional education courses for accountants. Professor Kemp's publications deal primarily with financial accounting and reporting issues.

Mary Ellen Phillips, MBA, CPA, is Assistant Professor of Accounting at Oregon State University. She has public accounting experience with Touche Ross & Company (Portland, Oregon) and Deloitte Haskins & Sells (Portland, Oregon and Seattle, Washington). Professor Phillips is a recipient of the Byron Newton Award for Excellence in Teaching awarded annually by the Oregon State University College of Business. Professor Phillips is a member of the American Accounting Association, the American Institute of Certified Public Accountants, and the Oregon Society of Certified Public Accountants. She has held numerous positions of leadership in the Oregon Society of Certified Public Accountants and is currently serving on the Ethics Committee, the Personal Financial Planning Committee, and the Estate Planning Committee, and is Treasurer of the local chapter of the Oregon Society of Certified Public Accountants. Professor Phillips has served as a consultant to a local accounting firm on accounting and reporting issues for a number of years. Professor Phillips' publications deal with a number of financial accounting and reporting issues.

PREFACE

Advanced Accounting is intended for use in financial accounting courses beyond the intermediate level. It is written at a level appropriate for senior students majoring in accounting and provides in-depth coverage of consolidated financial statements, foreign operations, partnerships, interim and segment reporting, estates and trusts, corporate dissolutions, nonbusiness accounting, sole proprietorships, and personal financial statements. The book incorporates all relevant recent pronouncements on financial accounting and reporting in both the private and public sectors.

The book begins with a theoretical discussion of entities and the theories of equity, which are then applied to the various entities discussed throughout the text. Alternative methods and supplementary information are presented in appendices to the chapters. The book provides sufficient material for a two-quarter or two-semester advanced accounting course. It is flexible enough, however, to be adapted to a one-quarter or one-semester course through careful selection of topics by the instructor.

The book is written clearly and concisely, with an appropriate balance between theory and applications. The text of each chapter introduces the main topics, covers the theory and procedures applicable to each topic, presents complete and understandable illustrative problems applying the theory and procedures, and concludes with a summary of the important points of the chapter. One or more review problems covering major points in the chapter follow the summary. Solutions to the review problems follow the end-of-chapter materials.

ORGANIZATION

Chapter 1 discusses the nature of entities and the theories of equity, providing a foundation for the treatment of various entities in subsequent chapters. In addition, Chapter 1 covers other comprehensive bases of accounting (cash and modified cash bases), sole proprietorship accounting, and personal financial statements (including current value concepts).

Partnership accounting is presented in Chapters 2 through 4. The topics covered include formation of partnerships, partnership income allocation, admission of new partners, withdrawal of partners, dissolution of partnerships, and entities similar to partnerships. The Uniform Partnership Act is included as an appendix to Chapter 2.

Chapters 5 through 14 cover corporate combinations, consolidated financial statements, and foreign operations. Our treatment of consolidated financial statements differs from most advanced accounting books in two ways. First, we use an adjusted trial balance worksheet format instead of the format arranged in financial statement sections that is used in most advanced accounting books. We have found this format to be superior both pedagogically and pragmatically. Second, we present all worksheet adjustments and eliminations in labeled schedules that balance in terms of debits and credits instead of the common practice of showing them in the form of journal entries. We have found that this approach makes it clear to the student that worksheet adjustments and eliminations are not recorded in the accounting records, thus avoiding the typical confusion of worksheet adjustments and eliminations with actual journal entries. In these chapters, we discuss and illustrate both the equity and cost methods of accounting for investments in subsidiaries. Because the two methods result in identical consolidated financial statements, either could be used. We emphasize the equity method, however, because it facilitates the consolidation process. A comprehensive illustrative problem in Chapters 7 through 11 covering each of five successive years reinforces the student's understanding of the continuity of the consolidation process.

The topics of interim financial statements and reporting segment information are covered in Chapter 15. The discussion of interim financial statements includes the treatment of both state and federal income taxes.

Chapters 16 and 17 contain a review of revenue recognition concepts and methods for both products and services. These chapters use accounting for real estate sales, including conversion between the methods, to illustrate these revenue recognition concepts and methods.

Chapters 18 provides a conventional treatment of estates and trusts. The discussion of accounting and reporting for estates includes recording the initial inventory, accounting for the transactions of an estate, distributions to legatees and devisees, and the fiduciary's report.

Chapter 19 deals with the accounting problems of financially troubled businesses. In addition to corporate liquidations, it includes troubled debt restructurings and quasi-reorganizations.

Chapters 20 through 23 cover accounting and reporting for nonbusiness entities. We begin with accounting for not-for-profit hospitals (which are most like business entities), followed by voluntary health and welfare organizations, not-for-profit colleges and universities, and finally governmental units (which are least like business entities). This progression allows us to introduce new concepts, terminology, and procedures gradually in an orderly manner, rather than all at once. A summary at the end of Chapter 22 compares the accounting for the different not-for-profit entities. A summary at the end of Chapter 23 compares the accounting for the different funds of governmental units. The appendix to Chapter 23 contains the complete set of financial statements for the city of Albany, Oregon.

SUPPLEMENTS

The Solutions Manual contains solutions to all chapter-end materials. It identifies the subject matter of each exercise and problem. A Test Bank containing multiple choice questions and exercises for each chapter is provided. Microcomputer spreadsheet (Lotus 1-2-3) templates for selected consolidation worksheet and other worksheet problems are available.

ACKNOWLEDGMENTS

We wish to thank the many people who have contributed to this book. Special thanks go to our colleague at Oregon State University, Mary Alice Seville, who reviewed intensively the chapters on nonbusiness entities. We appreciate the aid and support of Lucille Sutton, Deborah Herbert, Sheila Granda, and Suzanne Hendrickson of John Wiley & Sons, Inc. and of Bernice

Pettinato and Mary Dorian of Beehive Production Services. Thanks also go to our reviewers: Manuel A. Tipgos of the University of Kentucky, Abo Habib of the University of Central Arkansas, Ali A. Peyvandi of California State University—Fresno, and Mary Maury of St. John's University.

We appreciate the cooperation of the American Institute of Certified Public Accountants and the Financial Accounting Standards Board in permitting us to quote from their pronouncements. We also acknowledge permission from the American Institute of Certified Public Accountants to adapt questions and problems from the Uniform CPA Examinations.

Finally, we are grateful to the hundreds of Oregon State University students who participated in the class testing of the book.

Patrick S. Kemp
Mary Ellen Phillips

CONTENTS

1

ENTITY AND EQUITY THEORIES, SOLE PROPRIETORSHIPS, AND PERSONAL FINANCIAL STATEMENTS

T his chapter provides the theoretical foundation of equity and entity theories that are used throughout the text and also covers the accounting and reporting for sole proprietorships and individuals. The topics included are

- The definitions of entity and the relationship of these definitions to the various entities discussed in the text
- The definition of equity
- The proprietary, entity, and fund theories of equity
- The accounting and reporting for a sole proprietorship with emphasis on the conversion of accounting records kept on either the cash basis or modified cash basis to the accrual basis
- The preparation of personal financial statements incorporating the illustration of sole proprietorship accounting from the previous section

ENTITIES

The accounting and reporting in introductory and intermediate financial accounting courses is that of a **business entity,** which is defined as a business unit separate and distinct from the owners of the business. This definition establishes the boundaries or limits for events to be included, thus allowing us to decide which events to ignore in the financial accounting and reporting process. In our society, the existing entities are a much broader range of groups and organizations than just business entities, ranging from natural persons to legally created enterprises.

Statement of Financial Accounting Concepts No. 6 states that an entity may be a business enterprise, an educational or charitable organization, a natural person, or the like; an entity may comprise two or more affiliated entities and does not necessarily correspond to a legal entity.[1] These entities include not only business units such as sole proprietorships, general partnerships, limited partnerships, joint ventures, S corporations, professional corporations, regular corporations, and consolidated groups of corporations, but also entities such as individuals, family units, estates, trusts, receiverships, not-for-profit organizations, and governmental units.

An entity can be very simple, such as an individual or a sole proprietorship, or it can be a very complex organization, such as a corporate conglomerate or a university. Within each type of entity, there are enterprises that are quite small and others that are very large. For example, a partnership can consist of two partners who own equal shares of equity in a one-office accounting firm, or it can consist of hundreds of partners with different shares of ownership and different levels of responsibility in an international accounting firm with hundreds of offices in all parts of the world. Within each type of entity there can be enterprises with very simple capital structures or very complex capital structures. For example, a corporation can have three shares of stock that are owned by three shareholders and are not traded or a corporation can be a multinational business with thousands of shares of different types of publicly traded stock outstanding.

The entitites covered in this text range from the smallest and simplest to the largest and most complex, and also include some entities quite different from those discussed in other financial accounting courses. Chapter 1 begins with the smallest and simplest, a natural person or persons, and the financial accounting and reporting for a sole proprietorship and for an individual or family unit. Chapters 2 through 4 cover the accounting and reporting for partnerships, which are generally a group of natural persons. Chapters 5 through 13 discuss some of the largest and most complex entities, corporations related through ownership of the stock of one corporation by another corporation. These legally separate entities' financial information is combined and reported as a single consolidated entity.

Chapters 14 through 17 discuss accounting and reporting issues applicable to entities that can be large or small, and/or simple or complex. Chapter 14 covers foreign operations and Chapters 16 and 17 discuss revenue and expense recognition for a variety of special situations. These topics are applicable to all types of business enterprises. In addition, Chapters 14 and 15 cover three topics related to large corporations: consolidated financial statements when a company has foreign subsidiaries, interim reporting, and segment reporting. Chapters 18 through 23 deal with a wide range of entities with similar characteristics, and very different accounting and reporting from the other entities covered in the text. These chapters cover estates, trusts, troubled debt restructurings, corporate liquidations, not-for-profit hospitals, voluntary health and welfare organizations, not-for-profit colleges, and governmental units.

---

[1] *Statement of Financial Accounting Concepts No. 6, Elements of Financial Statements* (Stamford, Conn.: FASB, 1985), paragraph 24.

EQUITY AND EQUITY THEORIES

Equity is the residual interest in the assets of an entity remaining after deducting the liabilities.[2] The **assets** are the probable future economic benefits obtained or controlled by a particular entity as a result of past transactions or events.[3] The **liabilities** are sacrifices of economic benefits arising from present obligations to transfer assets or provide services to another entity in the future as a result of past transactions or events.[4] Therefore, all the transactions and events that increase or decrease assets and liabilities by different amounts change the balance of equity. Or viewed from the income statement point of view, equity is the result of the entity's operations and other events and circumstances that change the balances of the assets and liabilities.

BUSINESS ENTITIES

In a business entity, equity comes from two sources: net assets contributed or invested by the owners, and income earned and not distributed to the owners. Equity represents ownership interest in the net assets of the entity. Owners can also be employees, suppliers of goods and services, customers, borrowers, or lenders of the business entity. The ownership equity does not come from these relationships that owners might have with the business entity, but is restricted to their role as owners.

The equity of a sole proprietorship is accounted for and reported as a single amount on the balance sheet and the distinction between invested (contributed) capital and earnings retained in the business is not maintained. In a partnership the equity is reported as a single amount for each partner. The investment by the owners of a corporation is divided into the various types of securities issued for the assets invested, such as preferred and common stock. The amount of the investment received from the issuance of corporate stock can be further delineated as the amount related to the par or stated value and the amount received in excess of the par or stated value. In addition, the amount of earnings retained in the corporation is reported separately from the amounts invested by the owners.

Equity is increased by investments of assets by owners in their role as owners, and may also be increased by provision of services or satisfaction of business obligations by the owners. Equity is decreased by distributions of assets to owners, as owners, and may also be decreased by the entity rendering services or incurring liabilities for the owners, as separate entities. Equity sets the limits, often legal limits, on the distributions to the owners, as owners. Generally, a business entity does not have to distribute assets to owners except when the entity is being dissolved or liquidated.

In a not-for-profit organization, there is no investment by owners or distributions to owners, because no owners exist and the general purpose is not profit making but provision of goods and services either for a fee that approximates cost or without cost to the recipients. Equity is a residual interest (the difference between assets and liabilities) but does not represent

[2] *SFAC No. 6,* paragraph 49.

[3] *SFAC No. 6,* paragraph 25.

[4] *SFAC No. 6,* paragraph 35.

ownership interest as in a business enterprise. Equity is increased by contributions or receipts of assets and decreased by the use of assets either for the payment of liabilities or for the provision of goods and services to the beneficiaries.

EQUITY THEORIES

After defining entity and equity as the basis for accounting, and before discussing the accounting and reporting for the various entities covered in the text, a theoretical framework is needed from which to view the equity of the various entities. The definition of equity indicates that it is a residual, the difference between assets and liabilities, but the definition does not suggest the manner or approach to be taken in determining the equity. Should the equity of an entity be viewed strictly from the point of view of the owners, or only from the point of view of the entity itself as separate and distinct from the owners, or as a restriction on the use of assets? The entities covered in the text are viewed all three ways, and a single approach is not sufficient to describe the equity of each of the various entities discussed.

PROPRIETARY THEORY

Under the **proprietary theory** of equity, equity is from the owners' point of view, as the proprietary theory does not separate the business entity from the natural person(s). Thus, changes in equity are viewed from the perspective of their change in the wealth of the individual owner(s), regardless of the form of business, whether it is a sole proprietorship, a partnership, or a corporation. If equity is viewed this way, the assets are considered as belonging to the owners. Therefore, the liabilities incurred to obtain those assets are the obligations of the owners. The proprietary theory suggests that the balance sheet is the most important of the financial statements, and the income statement and the statement of changes in owners' (stockholders') equity are of lesser importance because they do not measure changes in owners' wealth. If change in owners' wealth is the emphasis, it follows that the balance sheet equation should emphasize this change in wealth. Therefore, the balance sheet equation is

$$\text{Assets} - \text{Liabilities} = \text{Equity (proprietorship)}$$

This is one of the oldest theories of equity, probably stemming from the trading ventures of the fourteenth and fifteenth centuries, when wealthy individuals financed expeditions to the Orient and the New World. The financier provided the ships, provisions, and necessary funds for the voyage in return for the goods brought back by the explorer. The explorer made the voyage, brought back the cargo acquired, and was paid for his daring. The financier's wealth was changed by the difference between the initial investment in the voyage and the selling price of the cargo brought back. This theory is also discussed in accounting texts of the eighteenth and nineteenth centuries when proprietorships and partnerships were the predominant form of business.

The proprietary theory is still evident in present-day accounting for sole proprietorships and partnerships. Regardless of the nomenclature attached to the allocation of income to the owners, such as interest, bonuses, or salaries, it is considered an increase in owners' wealth. Any distribution of assets to the owners is treated as a reduction of the owners' equity or wealth. In corporate accounting, when the equity method is used to account for long-term investments, the increase in wealth of the corporate owners is measured and recorded by the income earned by their investment, and not by the increase in assets received from the investment in the form of dividends.

ENTITY THEORY

The most prevalent theory in financial accounting for business enterprises is the **entity theory** of equity. The entity theory views the business as being separate and distinct from the owners. This theory, which is the direct opposite of the proprietary theory, implies that the assets are the business entity's assets and the liabilities are the obligations of the business entity. Thus, from the entity theory viewpoint, equity measures the share of the business entity's assets provided by the owners. Because the assets are the business entity's assets, the balance sheet should reflect the sources of the assets of the firm, the liabilities and the owners' (stockholders') share. The appropriate balance sheet equation is

$$\text{Assets} = \text{Liabilities} + \text{Owners' Equity}$$

The change in the net assets provided by owners becomes the important measurement, and this change is reflected in the net income of the business entity and the distributions of profits to the owners. Thus, the income statement, which measures the items that increase and decrease net income (revenues, expenses, gains, and losses), and the statement of changes in owners' or stockholders' equity, which summarizes the types of changes, become the most important financial statements. The balance sheet is secondary.

With some exceptions, the accounting for corporations is viewed from the entity theory perspective. For example, a corporate investor cannot be held liable for the debts of the corporation. The entity theory is also used in the accounting for sole proprietorships and partnerships. When an owner enters into transactions on behalf of the business, the assets purchased become the assets of the business, and any liabilities incurred become the liabilities of the firm.

FUND THEORY

The last of the three theories of equity, the **fund theory** is most applicable to entities covered in the last part of the text: estates, trusts, businesses in receivership, not-for-profit hospitals, voluntary health and welfare organizations, not-for-profit colleges and universities, and governmental units. The elements that these entities have in common are custodianship of assets, responsibility for the uses of the assets, accountability for the assets the entity has not disbursed, and restrictions on the uses of the assets. Therefore, the emphasis in these entities is on the sources of assets, the uses of assets, and the balance of assets remaining. This emphasis indicates that the balance sheet equation is

$$\text{Assets} = \text{Equities (restrictions on assets)}$$

The most important financial statement is a sources and uses of funds (resources) statement.

The emphasis on sources, uses, and remaining assets is seen in the charge and discharge statements for estates and trusts, the realization and liquidation accounts for companies in receivership, and the statements of changes in fund balances used by not-for-profit entities and governmental units.

SOLE PROPRIETORSHIPS

The discussion of accounting and reporting for sole proprietorships covers the conversion of cash basis records to the accrual method of accounting, the differences between the financial statements of a sole proprietorship and those of a corporation, and the financial reporting on the accrual basis. Generally accepted accounting principles apply to all forms of business entities, and therefore, are applicable to sole proprietorships as well as partnerships and corporations.

Frequently, a sole proprietorship is a small business without the accounting personnel or accounting expertise found in large businesses. The owner often operates from the **proprietary theory** of entity perspective, viewing the assets and liabilities of the business as personal assets and liabilities. This point of view means that the proprietor may not see any distinction between the business entity and the personal entity, may not maintain this division within the accounting records, and may not see any need to separate the two entities. Therefore, the preparation of financial statements is frequently more difficult, because is it necessary to sort out business transactions from personal transactions. The personal transactions recorded in the records of a business become assets added or withdrawn from the business by the owner. The business assets and liabilities that the sole proprietor treats as personal assets and liabilities need to be recorded in the records of the business. Any unrecorded assets will increase the sole proprietor's equity in the business and any additional liabilities will decrease the owner's equity.

In addition, the approach taken by the sole proprietor is frequently one of cash flows, with little interest or concern for the tenets of accrual accounting. These conditions can result in poor and/or inadequate accounting records that are often maintained on a cash or modified cash (tax) basis, rather than on an accrual accounting basis. In both a modified cash and tax basis, only some of the assets and liabilities that would be recognized using accrual accounting are recorded. However, generally accepted accounting principles require the use of accrual accounting to recognize and measure all the elements included in a set of financial statements.[5] Accrual accounting recognizes that operations and other events that affect an entity during a period often do not coincide with the cash receipts and disbursements of the period.[6] Accrual accounting attempts to recognize noncash events when they occur, which results in accruals, allocations, and amortizations.[7] By including credit transactions, changes in prices, changes in the form of assets and liabilities, and other transactions that have cash consequences but do not presently involve cash, accrual accounting provides information about an entity's assets and liabilities and changes in the assets and liabilities that cannot be obtained from a cash basis of accounting.[8]

---

[5] *SFAC No. 6*, paragraph 134.

[6] *Statement of Financial Accounting Concepts No. 1, Objectives of Financial Reporting by Business Enterprises* (Stamford, Conn.: FASB, 1978), paragraph 44.

[7] *SFAC No. 6*, paragraph 141.

[8] *SFAC No. 6*, paragraph 140.

PREPARATION OF ACCRUAL BASIS DATA FROM CASH BASIS RECORDS

The accounting for a sole proprietorship is identical to the accounting for a corporation with the exception of the owner's equity. All assets invested by the owner are credited to an account called **Owner's Equity,** which replaces all the shareholders' equity accounts of a corporation. Any withdrawals of assets by the owner are usually debited to an account called **Owner's Drawings,** which is comparable to a Dividends Declared account. It is possible for the proprietor to lend money to the business entity and to borrow money from the business entity. If these transactions have the usual business rates of interest, terms of repayment, and maturity, they are considered arm's-length transactions and are recorded as either loans to or from the owner.

As previously mentioned, sole proprietorships often keep their records on either a cash or a tax (modified cash) basis, because the owner tends to measure success of the business by the amount of cash available for personal use. If financial statements are to be prepared according to generally accepted accounting principles, the cash basis records need to be converted into accrual basis information. If records are truly on the cash basis, the only asset that is recorded in the accounting records is cash, and no liabilities are recorded.

When the true cash basis of accounting is used, the only entries recorded are those that alter cash. No adjusting entries are prepared, because the only changes in assets of interest are the changes in the cash balance that come entirely from transaction entries. Frequently, the records may not be completely on a cash basis but will have one or more elements of accrual accounting. This is often referred to as a **modified** cash basis of accounting. The most commonly capitalized (recorded) assets are inventory and operating assets (property, plant, and equipment) because accounting for these assets is necessary for the determination of income for income taxing purposes. If the operating assets are recorded, any debt incurred to acquire the assets is also recorded.

CONVERSION TO ACCRUAL BASIS ACCOUNTING

In order to convert to the accrual basis accounting records maintained either on the true cash basis or on the modified cash basis, the amounts of both the beginning and the ending balances of the unrecorded balance sheet accounts must be known and used in the conversion. The beginning balances need to be included in order to report the correct amount of income for the period. These amounts, which should have been recorded at the beginning of the period, are adjustments of the income of prior periods and, therefore, change beginning owner's equity.

If assets were not recorded at the beginning of the period, the net income of prior years was understated because either revenues were understated or expenses were overstated. If liabilities were not recorded at the beginning of the period, income of the prior periods was overstated because expenses were understated or revenues were overstated. The ending balances need to be recorded to have a balance sheet prepared on the accrual basis. The effects on income from not recording the ending balances are the opposite of not recording beginning balances. If assets are not recorded at the end of the period, income is understated because either revenues are understated or expenses are overstated. If liabilities are not recorded, income is overstated because either expenses are understated or revenues are overstated.

The following discussion illustrates the effects of unrecorded assets and liabilities at the beginning and the end of the period. Illustrative Problem 1.1 then uses these examples to convert the true cash basis records of Bolts' Hardware Store to the accrual basis using a worksheet. These adjustments could be recorded in the records of the business or a worksheet might be used. Accountants will frequently use the worksheet approach for the conversion to the accrual basis, because to convert the accounting records would create a bookkeeping system that the business lacks the accounting expertise to maintain.

UNRECORDED ASSETS AND ADJUSTMENTS TO REVENUES

If the sales revenue recorded for the year using the cash basis is $115,000, which is the total amount of cash received from the customers during the year, what should sales revenue be on the accrual basis? First, a portion of the cash recorded as sales revenue represents the collection of amounts due at the beginning of the year. Therefore, sales revenue is overstated by the amount of the beginning accounts receivable collected during the year. Second, the accounts receivable at the end of the year have not been recorded. Therefore, sales revenue is understated by the amount of ending accounts receivable. If beginning accounts receivable was $14,000 and ending accounts receivable is $20,200, the computation of sales revenue on the accrual basis is

Cash Basis Sales Revenue	$ 115,000
Beginning Accounts Receivable	(14,000)
Ending Accounts Receivable	20,200
Accrual Basis Sales Revenue	$ 121,200

The adjusting journal or worksheet entries to make the conversion from the cash basis to the accrual basis for sales revenue and accounts receivable are

Sales Revenue	14,000	
Owner's Equity		14,000
Accounts Receivable	20,200	
Sales Revenue		20,200

The two entries reflect the effect of not recording the accounts receivable as assets on the income of prior periods and the current year. The two entries could be combined into one entry as follows, but the single entry does not as clearly reflect the effects of not recording either the beginning or ending balance of accounts receivable:

Accounts Receivable	20,200	
Sales Revenue		6,200
Owner's Equity		14,000

UNCOLLECTIBLE ACCOUNTS RECEIVABLE

The previous example of sales and accounts receivable ignored the possibility of uncollectible accounts receivable. If either a portion of the beginning accounts receivable and/or a portion of the ending accounts receivable were not collectible, additional adjustments are necessary to establish the Allowance for Uncollectible Accounts and to record the bad debt expense for the period. For example, if $1,000 of the beginning accounts receivable were deemed uncollectible, $700 of accounts actually defaulted during the year, and $1,200 of the ending accounts receivable are considered uncollectible, the Allowance for Uncollectible Accounts on the accrual basis is

Beginning Allowance for Uncollectible Accounts	$ 1,000
Accounts Written Off During the Period	(700)
Bad Debt Expense of the Period (1)	900
Ending Allowance for Uncollectible Accounts	$ 1,200

(1) $1,200 - ($1,000 - $700) = $900

If we assume that the ending balance of accounts receivable of $20,200, does not include the $700 of accounts that were written off during the year, the computation converting sales revenue from the cash basis to the accrual basis has understated sales revenue on the accrual basis by the amount of the accounts receivable written off during the period. The adjusting journal or worksheet entries to convert from the cash basis to the accrual basis are

Owner's Equity	1,000	
Allowance for Uncollectible Accounts		300
Sales Revenue		700
Bad Debt Expense	900	
Allowance for Uncollectible Accounts		900

The first entry adjusts sales revenues and establishes the balance of the allowance account after the write-off of the uncollectible accounts for the period, and the last entry records the expense of the year.

UNRECORDED ASSETS AND ADJUSTMENTS TO EXPENSES

The failure to record the asset, supplies inventory, is an example of an unrecorded asset affecting expenses. The cash basis records show supplies expense of $2,700, which is the amount of supplies purchased for cash during the year. If the beginning supplies inventory was $500, and the supplies on hand at the end of the year are $800, the expense of prior periods was overstated by $500 and the expense of the current year is understated by $500. The expense of the current year is overstated by the unrecorded asset of $800. The amount of supplies expense for the year on the accrual basis is

Cash Basis Supplies Expense	$ 2,700
Beginning Inventory of Supplies	500
Ending Inventory of Supplies	(800)
Accrual Basis Supplies Expense	$ 2,400

The adjusting journal or worksheet entries to convert from the cash basis to the accrual basis are

Supplies Expense	500	
Owner's Equity		500
Supplies Inventory	800	
Supplies Expense		800

This same analysis could be applied to inventory and cost of goods sold except that some of the ending inventory may have been purchased on account.

When assets are apportioned to expense over several periods, the analysis becomes a little more complex, but follows the same line of reasoning. For example, if a company purchased a three-year insurance policy for $5,400 on April 1, 1989, the expense from the policy would be $150 per month ($5,400 ÷ 36), and the expense by year on the accrual basis is

$$
\begin{array}{lll}
1989: & \$150 \times \;9 \text{ months} = & \$1,350 \\
1990: & \$150 \times 12 \text{ months} = & 1,800 \\
1991: & \$150 \times 12 \text{ months} = & 1,800 \\
1992: & \$150 \times \;3 \text{ months} = & 450 \\
& & \overline{4,050} \\
& \text{Total} & \$5,400
\end{array}
$$

On the cash basis, the entire $5,400 would have been reported as expense in 1989, thus understating 1989 income by $4,050, the amount that should be expense in 1990, 1991, and 1992. The income of the following three years is overstated by the amount that should be expense of those years. If the year being converted from the cash basis to the accrual basis is 1990, the journal entries are

Prepaid Insurance	4,050	
Owner's Equity		4,050
Insurance Expense	1,800	
Prepaid Insurance		1,800

The first entry adjusts the beginning owner's equity for the understatement of income (overstatement of expense) for 1989. The second entry is the usual adjusting entry made when accounting for insurance using the accrual basis of accounting.

UNRECORDED LIABILITIES AND ADJUSTMENTS TO EXPENSES

An example of the effect of unrecorded liabilities on expenses can be illustrated with a number of different liability accounts. The following example uses an unpaid payroll at year end to illustrate the effects of not recording a liability. A company pays its employees on the fifth of the month for wages earned during the prior month. The payroll information for the beginning and end of the year is

	Beginning	Ending
Wages Earned	$5,000	$5,800
State and Federal Income Taxes Withheld	800	1,000
FICA Taxes Withheld	400	600
Wages Due Employees	$3,800	$4,200
Employer's Portion of FICA Taxes Payable	$ 400	$ 600

The wages and payroll tax expenses from the beginning of the year have been recorded as expenses of the current year and should be expenses of the prior year. The wages expense and payroll tax expense at the end of the year have not been included as expenses, and the liabilities for the payroll have not been recorded. The journal or worksheet entries to convert to the accrual method are

Owner's Equity	5,400	
Wages Expense		5,000
Payroll Tax Expense		400
Wages Expense	5,800	
Payroll Tax Expense	600	
State and Federal Income Taxes Withheld		1,000
FICA Taxes Payable		1,200
Wages Payable		4,200

UNRECORDED ASSETS, UNRECORDED LIABILITIES AND ADJUSTMENTS TO EXPENSE

Assets are often purchased on credit rather than for cash. Inventory is an example of an asset typically purchased on credit. When current assets are acquired on credit, three different types of accounts are involved in converting from the cash to the accrual basis: the unrecorded asset, the unrecorded liability, and the expense. For example, in converting from the cash to the accrual basis for inventory, the cash basis records show $48,000 of purchases that represent the cash payments for the acquisition of inventory. On a strictly cash basis of accounting, the purchases are recorded as cost of goods sold, since inventory is not recorded. If the modified cash basis is used, generally cost of goods sold has been adjusted for the difference between beginning and ending inventory.

For example, the counting and pricing on a FIFO basis showed $29,400 of inventory on hand at year end. The ending inventory of the previous year was $24,200. A review of the payments to suppliers of inventory showed that the accounts payable for inventory at year end totaled $6,700 and the unpaid accounts payable at the beginning of the year were $7,100. The cost of goods sold on the accrual basis is

Beginning Inventory		$ 24,200
Purchases		
Cash Basis Cost of Goods Sold	$ 48,000	
Beginning Accounts Payable	(7,100)	
Ending Accounts Payable	6,700	
Accrual Basis Purchases		47,600
Accrual Basis Goods Available for Sale		71,800
Ending Inventory		(29,400)
Accrual Basis Cost of Goods Sold		$ 42,400

Cash basis cost of goods sold was overstated by beginning accounts payable and understated by ending accounts payable. The cost of goods sold of the prior year was understated by the beginning accounts payable. In addition, the cash basis cost of goods sold was understated by the amount of beginning inventory and overstated by the amount of ending inventory. The cost of goods sold of the prior year was overstated by the amount of beginning inventory.

The adjusting journal entries to adjust cash basis cost of goods sold for both inventory and accounts payable are

Owner's Equity	7,100	
Cost of Goods Sold		7,100
Cost of Goods Sold	24,200	
Owner's Equity		24,200
Cost of Goods Sold	6,700	
Accounts Payable		6,700
Inventory	29,400	
Cost of Goods Sold		29,400

Proof: $48,000 − $7,100 + $24,200 + $6,700 − $29,400 =
   $42,400 cost of goods sold

The first two entries can be combined into one entry and the last two entries could be combined into one entry. If the accountant has a good understanding of the effects, the four entries can be combined into one journal entry. All accomplish the same purpose of converting cash basis of goods sold to the accrual basis, recording the unrecorded asset and liability, and adjusting beginning owner's equity for the effect of the unrecorded beginning asset and liability.

UNRECORDED OPERATING ASSETS AND RELATED LIABILITIES, AND ADJUSTMENTS TO EXPENSE

When the true cash basis is used, neither the operating assets nor any liabilities incurred for the acquisition of the operating assets are recorded. The cash amounts paid each year for the operating assets are treated as an expense of the current period. Frequently, a sole proprietor will treat these operating assets as personal assets, because the depreciation of the assets will appear on the sole proprietor's personal tax return since the income of the business is taxed on the sole proprietor's personal tax return and no return is filed for the business entity. The following example illustrates both cases: treating cash payments for the asset as an expense of the period, and the sole proprietor treating the assets and the related liabilities as personal assets and liabilities.

As an example, assume that a sole proprietor purchased land and a store building for $50,000 and incurred a mortgage of $35,000. The land was worth $10,000 when the purchase was initially made and the building was worth $40,000. The owner's tax return indicates the building is being depreciated over a 20-year life using the straight-line method of depreciation and has been depreciated for 8 years prior to the current year. The balance of the mortgage payable at the beginning of the year is $25,000. During the year, $3,600 of mortgage payments were made including $2,400 of interest expense. The $1,200 of principal payments were recorded as land and building expense. The asset and liability accounts should have the following balances at year end:

Land		$ 10,000
Building	$ 40,000	
Less: Accumulated Depreciation (1)	18,000	22,000
Mortgage Payable (2)		23,800

(1) $40,000 ÷ 20 = $2,000 × 9 years = $18,000
(2) $25,000 − $1,200 = $23,800

In addition, the expenses of the year should include $2,000 of depreciation expense and should not include the $1,200 of land and building expense from principal debt payments. The following journal entry records the correct asset and liability balances and the correct amount of expense for the year:

Land	10,000	
Building	40,000	
Depreciation Expense	2,000	
Accumulated Depreciation		18,000
Mortgage Payable		23,800
Owner's Equity		9,000
Land and Building Expense		1,200

The $9,000 credit to owner's equity represents the amount by which the principal portion of the cash payments of prior years exceeded the depreciation expense that should have been recorded for prior years ($25,000 − $16,000).

If the owner has considered the land and building personal assets and has been making the mortgage payments from personal cash, then the accountant must decide if the asset is a business asset or a personal asset. If the business had been paying rent to the owner, no adjustments would be made because the entity—the sole proprietorship—is a tenant and the entity—the owner—is the landlord. If, however, the proprietorship has not paid any rent to the owner, and the land, building, and mortgage are all in the name of the business, then the assets, the liability, and the current year's expense should be recorded on the sole proprietorship's books. The adjusting journal entry to convert the asset, liability, and expense to a business asset is similar to the conversion to the accrual method of the previous example, except that the cash payments in the current year as well as any expenses of the current period must also be included in the entry. The adjusting journal entry is

Land	10,000	
Building	40,000	
Depreciation Expense	2,000	
Interest Expense	2,400	
Accumulated Depreciation		18,000
Mortgage Payable		23,800
Owner's Equity		12,600

This entry, and the previous one to convert from the cash to the accrual basis, illustrate incorporating several interrelated items into a single adjusting journal entry. The following analysis of the events over time demonstrates the correctness of the amount credited to the owner's equity account:

Additions to Equity	
Cash Paid for the Land and Building Initially	$ 15,000
Principal Paid by the Owner Prior to the Current Year ($35,000 − $25,000)	10,000
Principal Paid by the Owner in the Current Year	1,200
Interest Paid by the Owner in the Current Year	2,400
Total	28,600
Reductions of Equity	
Depreciation of Prior Years ($2,000 × 8 years)	16,000
Change in Owner's Equity	$ 12,600

The payment of an expense of the current year by an owner is an additional contribution of capital to the business. The depreciation expense of the current year will reduce the owner's equity through the closing journal entry process. The interest expense of the prior years that the owner paid would have increased the owner's equity, and the interest expense that should have been recorded would have reduced the net income, and thus the owner's equity. Therefore, the effect on the owner's equity account is zero.

ILLUSTRATIVE PROBLEM 1.1: CONVERSION FROM THE CASH BASIS TO THE ACCRUAL BASIS OF ACCOUNTING

Illustrative Problem 1.1 uses all of the previous adjusting entries for current assets and liabilities and the adjusting journal entry that assumed the land and building were treated as personal assets by the owner even though they were in fact business assets. The cash basis trial balance, the beginning and ending balances of the unrecorded assets and liabilities, and the unrecorded depreciation expense and interest expense for the land and the building used in the previous discussion are restated below. Exhibit 1-2 of this problem demonstrates the use of a worksheet to convert accounting records maintained on the true cash basis to accrual basis values. Because the owner, Harry Bolts, lacks the accounting knowledge to maintain an accrual basis set of records, a worksheet is being prepared. In Exhibit 1-1, the entries developed in the prior discussion have been rewritten as one single entry for each topic to illustrate the net effect on each ledger account.

BOLTS' HARDWARE STORE
Cash Basis Trial Balance
December 31, 1990

	Debit	Credit
Cash	$ 15,600	
Owner's Equity: Harry Bolts		$ 30,000
Owner's Drawings: Harry Bolts	45,000	
Sales Revenue		115,000
Cost of Goods Sold	48,000	
Wages Expense	29,600	
Payroll Tax Expense	4,100	
Supplies Expense	2,700	
Totals	$145,000	$145,000

BOLTS' HARDWARE STORE
Unrecorded Assets, Liabilities, and Expenses

	1/1/90	12/31/90
Accounts Receivable	$ 14,000	$ 20,200
Allowance for Uncollectible Accounts	1,000	1,200
Inventory	24,200	29,400
Supplies	500	800
Prepaid Insurance	4,050	2,250
Land	10,000	10,000
Building	40,000	40,000
Accumulated Depreciation: Building	16,000	18,000

	1/1/90	12/31/90
Accounts Payable	7,100	6,700
Wages Payable	3,800	4,200
State and Federal Income Taxes Withheld	800	1,000
FICA Taxes Payable	800	1,200
Mortgage Payable	25,000	23,800
Depreciation Expense	–0–	2,000
Interest Expense	–0–	2,400

The entries to convert the cash basis trial balance to the accrual basis are as follows in Exhibit 1-1.

EXHIBIT 1-1

Illustrative Problem 1.1
Conversion Journal Entries
BOLTS' HARDWARE STORE

(a) Accounts Receivable	20,200	
Sales Revenue		6,200
Owner's Equity: Harry Bolts		14,000
(b) Bad Debt Expense	900	
Owner's Equity: Harry Bolts	1,000	
Allowance for Uncollectible Accounts		1,200
Sales Revenue		700
(c) Supplies Inventory	800	
Supplies Expense		300
Owner's Equity: Harry Bolts		500
(d) Prepaid Insurance	2,250	
Insurance Expense	1,800	
Owner's Equity: Harry Bolts		4,050
(e) Owner's Equity: Harry Bolts	5,400	
Wages Expense	800	
Payroll Tax Expense	200	
State and Federal Income Taxes Withheld		1,000
FICA Taxes Payable		1,200
Wages Payable		4,200
(f) Inventory	29,400	
Cost of Goods Sold		5,600
Accounts Payable		6,700
Owner's Equity: Harry Bolts		17,100
(g) Land	10,000	
Building	40,000	
Depreciation Expense	2,000	
Interest Expense	2,400	
Accumulated Depreciation: Building		18,000
Mortgage Payable		23,800
Owner's Equity: Harry Bolts		12,600

Exhibit 1-2 illustrates the worksheet prepared to convert the cash basis records of Bolts' Hardware Store to the accrual basis for the preparation of financial statements.

EXHIBIT 1-2

Illustrative Problem 1.1
BOLTS' HARDWARE STORE
Worksheet to Convert to the Accrual Basis of Accounting
December 31, 1990
Dr (Cr)

	Cash Basis Balance	Adjustments Debits	Adjustments Credits	Accrual Basis Balance
Cash	15,600			15,600
Accounts Receivable		20,200 (a)		20,200
Allowance for Uncollectible Accounts			1,200 (b)	(1,200)
Inventory		29,400 (f)		29,400
Supplies Inventory		800 (c)		800
Prepaid Insurance		2,250 (d)		2,250
Land		10,000 (g)		10,000
Building		40,000 (g)		40,000
Accumulated Depreciation: Building			18,000 (g)	(18,000)
Accounts Payable			6,700 (f)	(6,700)
Wages Payable			4,200 (e)	(4,200)
State and Federal Income Taxes Withheld			1,000 (e)	(1,000)
FICA Taxes Payable			1,200 (e)	(1,200)
Mortgage Payable			23,800 (g)	(23,800)
Owner's Equity: Harry Bolts	(30,000)	1,000 (b) 5,400 (e)	14,000 (a) 500 (c) 4,050 (d) 17,100 (f) 12,600 (g)	(71,850)
Owner's Drawings: Harry Bolts	45,000			45,000
Sales Revenue	(115,000)		6,200 (a) 700 (b)	(121,900)
Cost of Goods Sold	48,000		5,600 (f)	42,400
Wages Expense	29,600	800 (e)		30,400
Payroll Tax Expense	4,100	200 (e)		4,300
Supplies Expense	2,700		300 (c)	2,400
Insurance Expense		1,800 (d)		1,800
Bad Debt Expense		900 (b)		900
Depreciation Expense		2,000 (g)		2,000
Interest Expense		2,400 (g)		2,400
Totals	–0–	114,050	114,050	–0–

FINANCIAL REPORTING FOR A SOLE PROPRIETORSHIP

The reporting of net income for a sole proprietorship is identical to reporting for a corporation except for income taxes. A sole proprietorship is a **tax pass-through entity,** meaning that it pays no income taxes; therefore, the income statement does not contain any income tax expense. The income statement of Bolts' Hardware Store is illustrated in Exhibit 1-3. As the income earned by the sole proprietorship is taxed on the sole proprietor's personal tax return, no tax liability appears on the balance sheet. The proprietary theory suggests that we are interested in changes in owner's wealth and not in sources of assets; therefore, the complex shareholders' equity section of a corporate balance sheet is replaced by a single line item, owner's equity. The balance sheet of Bolts' Hardware Store is illustrated in Exhibit 1-5.

The linking statement between the income statement and the balance sheet is a statement of changes in owner's equity rather than a statement of changes in retained earnings. This statement is very similar in format to a statement of changes in retained earnings and is illustrated in Exhibit 1-4 for Bolts' Hardware Store. If the assets withdrawn are other than cash, then details of the various types of assets withdrawn could be included in the statement of changes in owner's equity. If the other assets are material in amount, they are reported as separate line items.

The statement of cash flows for Bolts' Hardware Store, prepared using the direct method, is presented in Exhibit 1-6. Because the records of Bolts' Hardware Store are maintained on the cash basis, the direct method can be used easily. Exhibits 1-3 through 1-6 present the financial statements of the sole proprietorship, Bolts' Hardware Store, using the accrual basis trial balance developed in Exhibit 1-2.

EXHIBIT 1-3

Illustrative Problem 1.1
BOLTS' HARDWARE STORE
(A Sole Proprietorship)
Income Statement
Year Ended December 31, 1990

Sales Revenue		$ 121,900
Cost of Goods Sold		42,400
Gross Profit		79,500
Expenses		
Wages	$ 30,400	
Payroll taxes	4,300	
Supplies	2,400	
Insurance	1,800	
Bad Debts	900	
Depreciation	2,000	
Interest	2,400	44,200
Net Income		$ 35,300

EXHIBIT I-4

Illustrative Problem 1.1
BOLTS' HARDWARE STORE
(A Sole Proprietorship)
Statement of Changes in Owner's Equity
Year Ended December 31, 1990

Balance January 1, 1990	$ 71,850
Net Income for 1990	35,300
Withdrawals of Assets	(45,000)
Balance December 31, 1990	$ 62,150

EXHIBIT I-5

Illustrative Problem 1.1
BOLTS' HARDWARE STORE
(A Sole Proprietorship)
Balance Sheet
December 31, 1990

Assets

Current Assets			
Cash			$ 15,600
Accounts Receivable		$ 20,200	
Less: Allowance for Uncollectible Accounts		1,200	19,000
Inventory			29,400
Supplies			800
Prepaid Insurance			2,250
Total Current Assets			67,050
Property			
Land		10,000	
Building	$ 40,000		
Less: Accumulated Depreciation	18,000	22,000	32,000
Total Assets			$ 99,050

Liabilities and Owner's Equity

Current Liabilities	
Accounts Payable	$ 6,700
Wages Payable	4,200
State and Federal Income Taxes Withheld	1,000
FICA Taxes Payable	1,200
Total Current Liabilities	13,100
Long-Term Debt: Mortgage Payable	23,800
Total Liabilities	36,900
Owner's Equity	62,150
Total Liabilities and Owner's Equity	$ 99,050

EXHIBIT 1-6

Illustrative Problem 1.1
BOLTS' HARDWARE STORE
Statement of Cash Flows
Year Ended December 31, 1990

Cash Flows from Operating Activities		
Cash Received from Customers		$115,000
Cash Paid to Suppliers	$ 48,000	
Cash Paid to Employees	29,600	
Cash Paid for Payroll Taxes	4,100	
Cash Paid for Supplies	2,700	
Cash Paid for Interest	2,400	86,800
Net Cash Provided by Operating Activities		28,200
Cash Flows from Investing Activities		
Cash Contributed by Owner		3,600
Cash Flows from Financing Activities		
Mortgage Principal Payments	1,200	
Owner's Drawings	45,000	(46,200)
Net Decrease in Cash		14,400
Cash at the Beginning of the Year		30,000
Cash at the End of the Year		$ 15,600

Reconciliation of Net Income to Net Cash Provided by Operating Activities

Net Income		$ 35,300
Additions to Reconcile Net Income to Net Cash Provided by Operating Activities		
Depreciation	$ 2,000	
Decrease in Prepaid Insurance	1,800	
Increase in Wages Payable	400	
Increase in State and Federal Income Taxes Withheld	200	
Increase in FICA Taxes Payable	400	4,800
Deductions to Reconcile Net Income to Net Cash Provided by Operating Activities		
Increase in Accounts Receivable: Net	6,000	
Increase in Inventory	5,200	
Increase in Supplies	300	
Decrease in Accounts Payable	400	(11,900)
Net Cash Provided by Operating Activities		$ 28,200

In addition to the cash flows recorded in the records of Bolts' Hardware Store, the cash paid by Harry Bolts as principal and interest payments on the mortgage must be included as both a cash inflow from investing activities and a cash outflow as the payments were trans- actions of Bolts' Hardware Store.

PERSONAL FINANCIAL STATEMENTS

This part of the chapter discusses and illustrates the preparation of personal financial statements. The discussion includes a history of the generally accepted accounting principles for personal financial statements; the steps in the preparation of financial statements, including a discussion of determining estimated current values and income tax liabilities; and the actual financial statements and reporting requirements.

In the 1964 presidential election campaign, some of the candidates prepared their financial statements on the cost basis and some of the candidates used current values. President Lyndon Johnson chose to use the cost basis, and there was speculation in the news media regarding the current value of the television stations owned by the first lady, Lady Bird Johnson. This speculation brought to the public's and the profession's attention the lack of generally accepted accounting principles for the preparation of personal financial statements. As a result, in 1968 the American Institute of Certified Public Accountants issued an Industry Audit Guide, *Audits of Personal Financial Statements*. This guide required personal financial statements to be prepared using cost values and recommended that current values be presented as supplementary information.[9]

In 1982, the AICPA issued a statement of position covering the accounting and financial reporting for personal financial statements. Unlike its predecessor, this pronouncement requires assets and liabilities to be reported at their **estimated current values** and permits the presentation of historical cost values or tax base values as supplementary information.[10] The following reasons were given for reversing the position of the previous standard and changing to current values:

- The primary focus of personal financial statements is a person's assets and liabilities, not the person's income.
- The primary users believe that current values are more relevant than cost values.
- Lenders require current values to assess the collateral and debt-paying ability of the person.
- Current values are needed for estate, gift, and income tax planning.
- Current value financial information is often required of candidates for public office.[11]

The first reason indicates that the approach to the preparation of personal financial statements is based on the proprietary theory of equity with emphasis on balance sheet items. The only financial statement required to be prepared is a statement of financial condition (balance sheet). This statement can be supplemented by a statement of changes in net worth (statement of changes in equity). Personal financial statements can be prepared for an individual, a married couple, or a family group. The financial statements of a married couple and a family group are prepared because accountants believe that combined financial information for legally related entities is more meaningful than reporting the entities separately.

---

[9] *Industry Audit Guide, Audits of Personal Financial Statements* (New York: AICPA, 1968), paragraph 9.

[10] *Statement of Position 82-1, Accounting and Financial Reporting for Personal Financial Statements* (New York: AICPA, 1982), paragraph 4.

[11] *SOP 82-1*, paragraph 3.

PREPARATION STEPS

Because most individuals do not maintain formal accounting records, the first step is to determine the assets and the liabilities of the personal entity: an individual, a married couple, or a family group. A variety of information sources, including the individual, may be used to ascertain the statement of financial condition items. For example, an accountant might use an individual's bank statements, brokerage statements, tax returns, insurance policies, property tax statements, payroll information, will, divorce decree, and inventory of safety deposit box. In addition, the financial statements of other entities in which the person has an ownership interest could be used by the accountant. Once a complete list of the assets and liabilities is obtained, the second step is to determine the estimated current values of the assets and the liabilities.

ESTIMATED CURRENT VALUES

Theoretically the estimated current value is the value a willing buyer and a willing seller would agree is a fair and reasonable price when each is well informed, willing, and not compelled to buy or sell. In other words, it is the fair market value from an unforced arm's-length transaction. A variety of techniques can be used to estimate the current value. These techniques include

- Recent transactions of similar assets, which is the preferable method
- Capitalization of past or prospective earnings
- Liquidation values
- Specific price indexing of the historical cost of certain assets
- Appraisals by real estate brokers, insurance estimators, and property tax assessors
- Discounted cash flows using market rates of interest for assets and transaction rates for liabilities
- Valuations by specialists and experts for unusual or unique assets

More than one technique can be used to value some assets, and more than one technique might be computed in order to verify the reasonableness of the estimated current value. Therefore, there is no **one** right way to determine the estimated current value of assets and liabilities, although *Statement of Position 82-1* presents specific recommendations for certain assets and liabilities. Remember that the current values are simply **estimates** of current values, and the benefit of a good estimate must be more than the cost of obtaining the estimate.

Techniques for Estimating Current Value. To illustrate the various techniques for estimating current values, assume we are estimating the current value of Mr. Bolts' equity in his sole proprietorship, Bolts' Hardware Store, from Illustrative Problem 1.1. The historical cost of his equity is $62,150 as shown on the accrual basis balance sheet in Exhibit 1-5. If a similar hardware store in a neighboring town was recently sold for $225,000, the $225,000 would represent a recent transaction and could be used on Mr. Bolts' statement of financial condition, and is considered to be the preferable value assuming good comparability between the two businesses.

Second, estimated current value could be determined by capitalizing past or future earnings. If hardware stores typically sell for the book value of net assets plus five times current earnings, the value of Bolts' Hardware Store is

Net Assets of Bolts' Hardware Store	$ 62,150
Capitalized Earnings ($35,300 × 5 years)	176,500
Value of Bolts' Hardware Store	$ 238,650

The capitalization of earnings could have used an average of the earnings of prior years, or could also be computed by using estimates of future earnings.

Another alternative is to estimate the liquidation value: the amount of cash that could be generated if all the assets were sold and the liabilities were satisfied. Mr. Bolts believes that all the accounts receivable can be collected, the inventory can be sold for an average price of 150% of book value, the supplies can be sold for book value, and the balance of prepaid insurance can be recovered. In addition, Mr. Bolts is confident that the land and store building could be sold for $150,000, net of the selling costs. Based on these facts, the liquidation value of the hardware store is computed as follows:

Asset Liquidation Values	
Cash	$ 15,600
Accounts Receivable	19,000
Inventory ($29,400 × 150%)	44,100
Supplies	800
Prepaid Insurance	2,250
Property Valued at Mr. Bolts' Estimate	150,000
Total Proceeds	231,750
Less: Liabilities	36,900
Liquidation Value of Bolts' Hardware Store	$ 194,850

Instead of using the estimated liquidation values, specific price indices can be used to revalue the undervalued assets. For example, Bolts' Hardware Store uses the FIFO method of inventory; therefore, the inventory value is assumed to be a close approximation of the estimated current value. The land and buildings were purchased nine years ago when the specific price index for real estate in the area of Bolts' Hardware Store was 125. The current price index for comparable real estate is 425. The information indicates that the two undervalued assets of Bolts' Hardware Store are the land and the building. The normal selling costs for commercial real estate in the area of Bolts' Hardware Store are 10%. The estimated current value of Mr. Bolts' equity using the specific price indices is

Net Assets		$ 62,150
Increase in Value of Land and Buildings		
Specific Price Indexed Value ($50,000 × 425/125)	$ 170,000	
Less: Normal Selling Costs	17,000	
Estimated Current Value	153,000	
Less: Net Book Value Included in Net Assets	32,000	121,000
Value of Bolts' Hardware Store		$ 183,150

The price indices should be applied to the original purchase price and not to the net book value of the asset, as the objective is to determine an estimate of the current value of the land

and the store building. When selling costs are material, the determination of the estimated current value must consider the effect of those costs.[12] In the liquidation technique illustrated above, Mr. Bolts' estimate of the selling price of the land and buildings was net of the selling costs. In the above example, the estimate of current value was reduced by the selling costs because the 10% selling costs were assumed to be material in amount.

If a real estate broker, who is an expert in commercial businesses, estimates the selling price of Bolts' Hardware Store to be $220,000, net of selling costs, this estimate is an example of an appraisal value that can be used as an estimated current value.

Another alternative would be to discount the expected cash generated by Bolts' Hardware Store to the present. For example, if $40,000 of the $45,000 of assets withdrawn by Mr. Bolts were cash withdrawals, and Mr. Bolts estimates that the business will generate at least $40,000 cash for each of the next 10 years, and the current market rate of interest is 12%, the value of Bolts' Hardware Store would be $226,008 [$40,000 × 5.6502 (the present value of an annuity for 10 years at 12%)].

These examples have demonstrated the various techniques that can be used to determine the estimated current values of assets and liabilities. The following discussion and examples cover the more common assets and liabilities included in personal financial statements.

Estimating the Current Values of Specific Assets and Liabilities. Marketable securities are reported at their closing market prices or estimates of the closing prices if not actively traded. Receivables are reported at the amount of cash expected to be collected, discounted to the statement of financial condition date at the current market rate of interest. Life insurance is reported at the cash surrender value, net of any loans against the cash value. Determining the value of a closely held business is difficult because of the lack of a ready market. The previous examples for Bolts' Hardware Store demonstrate the fact that different estimating techniques will result in different estimated current values. The problem is deciding which of the values is the best estimate of current value. The Bolts' Hardware Store example also shows that a variety of estimates are possible for real estate, and the same techniques used for Bolts' Hardware Store, as an entity, can be used for real estate. Intangibles and rights to receive cash in the future are valued by discounting the projected cash receipts at the market rate of interest.

Individuals frequently have rights to receive future sums of cash. These rights might include vested pension benefits, vested profit-sharing benefits, deferred compensation contracts, beneficial interests in trusts or estates, remainder interests in estates or trusts, annuities, or fixed amounts of alimony for a fixed period of time. All of these rights are nonforfeitable—the individual is guaranteed receipt of the asset at some future time. These rights have the following characteristics:

- They are for specific or determinable amounts.
- They are not contingent on the disability or death of an individual.
- The person does not have to perform any additional services to receive the benefits.

When future interests have these characteristics they are included in the assets of the individual, and the estimated current value is the amount of projected cash receipts, discounted to the present at the current market rate of interest. Rights to future sums of cash that do not have the above characteristics are omitted from the statement of financial condition.

Because a statement of financial condition is prepared on the accrual basis, all liabilities

---

[12] *SOP 82-1*, paragraph 12.

need to be accrued and included in the statement. Liabilities are presented using the cash outflows necessary to satisfy the debt, discounted to the present at the rate of interest specified in the debt contract. Assets are discounted using the current market rates of interest, but liabilities are discounted using the rate of interest specified by the transaction. The most complex part of liabilities is the amount of federal and state income taxes payable, and future liability for federal and state income taxes to be reported on the statement of financial condition. Three types of income taxes are possible: income taxes payable, income taxes estimated to be payable for the current year, and an estimate of income taxes to be paid in the future on the unrealized appreciation in net assets.

The first two types of income taxes are reported as one amount in the liability section of the statement. The first is the unpaid portion of the liability for income taxes already determined by tax returns filed or to be filed with the Internal Revenue Service and state income taxing authorities. The second is an estimate of the income taxes on income earned in the current year to the statement of financial condition date net of any amounts already paid either through withholdings from wages or by the individual having made estimated income tax payments. The formula used to compute the estimate is

$$\left[\frac{\text{Taxable Income Earned in Current Year to Financial Statement Date}}{\text{Expected Taxable Income for the Current Year}} \times \begin{array}{c}\text{Expected}\\ \text{Income Taxes}\\ \text{for the}\\ \text{Current Year}\end{array}\right] - \begin{array}{c}\text{Amounts Paid by}\\ \text{Withholding From Wages}\\ \text{and/or Estimated Income}\\ \text{Tax Payments}\end{array} = \begin{array}{c}\text{Estimated}\\ \text{Income}\\ \text{Taxes}\\ \text{Payable}\end{array}$$

ILLUSTRATIVE PROBLEM 1.2: COMPUTATION OF ESTIMATED INCOME TAXES PAYABLE

Assume that Mr. and Mrs. Bolts have asked their accountant to prepare financial statements for them as of March 31, 1991. The Bolts' tax return for 1990 shows an unpaid balance due of $8,000. In addition, Mr. Bolts has earned taxable income of $20,000 for the first three months of 1991. Mrs. Bolts has earned $10,000 and has had $2,500 of federal income taxes withheld from her salary. The Bolts expected their total estimated taxable income for 1991 to be $90,000 and the expected income taxes on that income to be $27,000. The computation of the income tax liability to be included in the financial statements is in Exhibit 1-7.

EXHIBIT 1-7

Illustrative Problem 1.2
Computation of Estimated Income Taxes Payable
MR. AND MRS. BOLTS
March 31, 1991

Balance Due on 1990 Tax Return		$ 8,000
Estimated Income Taxes on Income Earned in 1991		
Tax Liability $\dfrac{\$30,000}{\$90,000} \times \$27,000$	$ 9,000	
Less: Federal Income Taxes Withheld	2,500	6,500
Total Estimated Income Tax Liability		$14,500

The third type of tax liability is the most complex of the three types and represents an estimate of income taxes that may be paid in the future based on the difference between (a) the estimated current values of assets and estimated current amounts of liabilities and (b) the tax bases of assets and liabilities at the statement of financial condition date. The assets and the liabilities are reported at their estimated current values, which can be substantially in excess of the bases of the assets and the liabilities for income tax purposes. A positive difference between the estimated current values and the tax bases of the assets and liabilities represents **unrealized appreciation** in value, and a negative difference represents **unrealized depreciation** in value. If unrealized depreciation is present, no asset is recorded because no tax refund is possible, only loss carry forwards to offset against future gains, which are assumed to be zero.

When the assets are sold or the liabilities are satisfied, the individual will pay income taxes on the positive difference between the selling price and the tax bases on those elements **subject to income taxes.** Items subject to tax are items that would be reported on the tax return of the individual, which include revenues, expenses, gains, and losses. The financial statement is being prepared on the accrual basis; therefore, it is necessary to estimate the amount of income taxes the individual would pay if all the assets were sold at their estimated current values and all the liabilities were satisfied at their estimated current amounts. The income tax rules used to make the computations are the federal tax laws and the **effective tax rate** used is based on the combined potential liability for both federal and state income taxes at the statement of financial condition date. This estimate is similar in nature to the deferred tax liability that is reported by corporations and appears on the financial statement between liabilities and the net worth of the individual.

ILLUSTRATIVE PROBLEM 1.3: COMPUTATION OF FUTURE INCOME TAXES PAYABLE

Assume that the estimated current values of Mr. and Mrs. Bolts' assets total $801,100 and the tax bases of those assets is $375,000, and $7,100 of net unrealized appreciation in value is not subject to tax. When items are **not subject to tax,** they are neither reported as revenues or gains, nor are they allowed as expenses or losses on the income tax return. For the Bolts, who are over age 55, the gain on their personal residence of $33,500 is not subject to tax. The tax code provides that only gains on the sales of personal residences in excess of $125,000 are taxable when the individuals are over 55 years of age. In addition, the tax law does not allow the taxpayer to deduct losses on personal assets. The personal assets typically found in personal financial statements are household effects and automobiles that have not been used as business assets. The Bolts have a loss in the amount of $26,400 on their personal effects that is not subject to tax. Therefore the total amount not subject to tax is $7,100 ($33,500 − $26,400).

The estimated current amount of the liabilities totals $150,000 and the tax bases of the liabilities are $160,000. This difference indicates that the Bolts can satisfy their liabilities at the present time for $150,000, although the accrual and tax base amount of the debt is $160,000; therefore, the Bolts would have $10,000 of gain subject to tax. Based on the present federal tax code, the effective tax rate of Mr. and Mrs. Bolts is 30%. The computation of the estimated income taxes on the differences between the estimated current values of assets and the estimated current amounts of liabilities and their tax bases is presented in Exhibit 1-8.

EXHIBIT 1-8

Illustrative Problem 1.3
Computation of Estimated Income Taxes on the Excess
of Estimated Current Values Over the Tax Bases
MR. AND MRS. BOLTS
March 31, 1991

Assets		
Estimated Current Values of Assets		$ 801,100
Less: Tax Bases		375,000
Unrealized Appreciation in Value		426,100
Less: Amounts Not Subject to Tax		7,100
Unrealized Appreciation in Value Subject to Income Tax		419,000
Liabilities		
Tax Bases of Liabilities	$ 160,000	
Estimated Current Amounts	150,000	
Unrealized Appreciation in Value Subject to Income Tax		10,000
Total Unrealized Appreciation Subject to Tax		429,000
Effective Tax Rate		30.0%
Estimated Income Taxes on the Excess of Estimated Current Values of Assets and Estimated Current Amounts of Liabilities Over Their Tax Bases		$ 128,700

PREPARATION OF THE STATEMENT OF FINANCIAL CONDITION

The statement of financial condition is prepared on the accrual basis as required by generally accepted accounting principles. The equity theory applied to personal financial statements is the proprietary theory and only a statement comparable to a balance sheet is prepared. No income statement is included; therefore, personal financial statements can be prepared at any point in time. Because the objective of personal financial statements is the reporting of assets and liabilities at a point in time with no emphasis on income or need to delineate working capital, the statement of financial condition is not presented in a classified format. Instead the assets and liabilities are presented in order of liquidity and maturity.[13]

An individual's equity interest in a closely held business is reported as a line item in the statement of financial condition. The individual business assets and liabilities are not reported in the statement because they are the assets and liabilities of the business entity, not the separate entity, the person. The disclosure rules for personal financial statements require

[13]SOP 82-1, paragraph 8.

summarized balance sheet and income statement information for the most recent full year of the business to be reported in the notes to the financial statements. For example, in the statement of financial condition of Mr. and Mrs. Bolts, the estimated current value of Bolts' Hardware Store is included, and the notes will contain summarized information taken from the financial statements presented in Exhibits 1-3, 1-4, and 1-5 of Illustrative Problem 1.1. Illustrative Problem 1.4 demonstrates the preparation of a statement of financial condition for Mr. and Mrs. Bolts. The facts presented previously regarding the assets and liabilities of the Bolts are used in the example.

ILLUSTRATIVE PROBLEM 1.4: PERSONAL FINANCIAL STATEMENTS

After an analysis of a variety of sources of information, including discussions with Mr. and Mrs. Bolts, the following list of the assets and liabilities was compiled as of March 31, 1991. This example assumes the tax bases of assets and liabilities are equal to their costs, except for the IRAs, which have a zero tax base and a cost of $10,000. Some assets will have cost equal to tax base and others may not. This difference can also exist for the same assets held by different individuals. Additional information needed in the preparation of financial statements for Mr. and Mrs. Bolts is also included in the following list:

	Tax Base and Cost
Assets	
Mr. Bolts' personal money market checking account	$ 15,150
Mrs. Bolts personal checking account	2,400
IRA accounts of Mr. and Mrs. Bolts cost $10,000; current value $11,000.	–0–
Marketable securities	
500 shares of Xerox Corp.	15,000
Closing market price $68 per share on March 31, 1991.	
1,000 shares of Toys Unlimited	10,000
Traded over the counter, the bid and ask prices on the last day traded were $15 and $17, respectively.	
Stock options	–0–
Mrs. Bolts has options to purchase 2,000 shares of Toys Unlimited; the market price of the options is $8 and the exercise price is $6.	
Investment in Bolts' Hardware Store	62,150
After a discussion with Mr. Bolts, a decision was made to use the recent sale in the neighboring community of $225,000 as the estimated current value.	
Pension and profit-sharing plan	–0–
Mrs. Bolts has been employed for the past 15 years by Toys Unlimited, which has an employee pension and profit-sharing plan. The total of Mrs. Bolts' share is $94,500, which is 60% vested, and the remainder will become vested after 20 years of employment.	
Remainderman interest in a trust	–0–
Mrs. Bolts is the only child of Mr. and Mrs. Nuts. Mr. Nuts died several years ago and the assets of his estate were placed in a trust. Mrs. Nuts is	

	Tax Base and Cost

to receive the income from the trust for her lifetime, and Mrs. Bolts is to receive the trust assets upon the death of her mother. On March 31, 1991, the assets of the trust totaled $400,000. The life expectancy of Mrs. Nuts is 10 years and the current market rate of interest is 12%.

Life insurance	38,000
Mr. Bolts' policies	
Face value $100,000, cash surrender value $80,000, and Mr. Bolts has borrowed $42,000 against the policies.	
Mrs. Bolts' policies	25,000
Face value $100,000, cash surrender value $25,000.	
Residence	141,500
The house was recently appraised for insurance purposes at $175,000.	
Personal effects, exclusive of antiques	39,400
A recent appraisal established a replacement cost of $68,000, but if sold, the maximum selling price is $13,000.	
Antiques	26,400
Mrs. Bolts has inherited a number of family heirlooms, and has added to the collection by purchases of her own. An expert recently appraised the antiques at $57,050.	
Total Assets	**$ 375,000**

Liabilities	
Personal debts	$ 14,000
Income tax liability (Exhibit 1.7)	14,500
Home mortgages	
First mortgage: Home Savings and Loan	94,000
The interest rate is only 6% and Home Savings has offered to accept $84,000 in full settlement of the mortgage.	
Second mortgage: Heritage Bank	37,500
The money was used to remodel the residence to make room for Mrs. Bolts' antique collection.	
Total liabilities	**$ 160,000**

Tax liability on the excess of estimated current values of assets and the estimated current amounts of liabilities over their tax bases (Exhibit 1-8)	$ 128,700

Exhibit 1-9 illustrates the statement of financial condition for Harry and Henrietta Bolts as of March 31, 1991, prepared from the above information, including an explanation of the computations.

EXHIBIT 1-9

Illustrative Problem 1.4
HARRY AND HENRIETTA BOLTS
Statement of Financial Condition
March 31, 1991

Assets

Cash		$ 17,550
Investments		
IRAs	$ 11,000 (1)	
Marketable Securities	50,000 (2)	
Stock Options	4,000 (3)	
Investment in Bolts Hardware Store	225,000	290,000
Vested Interest in Pension and Profit-Sharing Plan of Toys Unlimited		56,700 (4)
Remainder Interest in Testamentary Trust Established by the Will of Mr. Nuts		128,800 (5)
Cash Surrender Value of Life Insurance $105,000 Less Loans of $42,000		63,000
Residence		175,000
Personal Effects		13,000 (6)
Antiques		57,050
Total Assets		$ 801,100

Liabilities and Net Worth

Liabilities	
Personal Debts	$ 14,000
Income Taxes Payable	14,500
First Mortgage Payable: Home Savings and Loan	84,000 (7)
Second Mortgage Payable: Heritage Bank	37,500
Total Liabilities	150,000
Estimated Income Taxes on the Difference Between the Estimated Current Values of Assets and the Estimated Current Amounts of Liabilities and Their Tax Bases	128,700
Net Worth	522,400
Total Liabilities and Net Worth	$ 801,100

Computations of Estimated Current Values and Estimated Current Amounts

(1)	Market value = $11,000	
(2)	Xerox Corp. (500 shares at $68)	$ 34,000
	Toys Unlimited [1,000 shares at ($15 + $17) ÷ 2]	16,000
	Total	$ 50,000

When a closing price is not available an average of the bid and ask prices is used.

(3) [2,000 options × ($8 − $6)] = $4,000
The difference between exercise price and option price is the current value.

(4) ($94,500 × 60%) = $56,700
   Only the vested portion is a nonforfeitable right. The balance requires continuing service by Mrs. Bolts and therefore is forfeitable.

(5) [$400,000 × .3220 (present value of $ in 10 years)] = $128,800
   Mrs. Bolts can anticipate receiving the assets of the trust in 10 years. Assets are discounted at the market rate of interest.

(6) Personal effects are valued at the amount they can currently be sold at and not their replacement cost. An estimated current value is the amount a willing buyer and a willing seller would agree is a fair transaction price.

(7) The bank will accept $84,000 in full settlement of the balance due. Even though the Bolts may not be able or willing to pay the balance of the mortgage, its estimated current amount is the price the bank is willing to accept in full settlement of the balance of the mortgage.

The statement of financial condition could have been prepared in a comparative format with the estimated current values at March 31, 1990 also included in the statement, and the statement could have presented both the estimated current value and the cost or tax base for each of the items on the statement of financial condition. In addition to the statement of financial condition, a statement of changes in net worth can be presented, but it is not required. This statement provides information about the major sources that increased and decreased net worth. No attempt is made to determine the net income of the individuals. The determination of net income is inappropriate because the business affairs of individuals do not constitute a business enterprise with profit making as the objective. Also, the reporting of income is not important when viewing the financial statements of individuals from the proprietary theory of equity, because the concern is not with income, but rather with the changes in net worth of the individuals.

The sources of increases and decreases in net worth presented in the statement of changes in net worth are divided into two categories, sources that are **realized** and sources that are **unrealized.** The combining of realized and unrealized sources is deemed to be appropriate because of the mix of business and personal assets and liabilities reported on the statement of financial condition.[14] The **realized increases** are the sources of revenue and income of the individuals. The realized increases can include salaries and wages earned; income of businesses the individuals have an interest in, such as sole proprietorships and partnerships; interest and dividends earned; rental income from real estate holdings; income received from estates and trusts; and gains from the sale of assets. The **realized decreases** are the expenses incurred during the year. Personal expenditures are generally reported as one amount.

The **unrealized increases** are the increases in the estimated current values of the assets, decreases in the estimated current amounts of liabilities, and decreases in the estimated income taxes on the differences between the estimated current values of assets and the estimated current amounts of liabilities and their tax bases. The **unrealized decreases** are decreases in the estimated current values of assets, increases in the estimated current amounts of liabilities, and increases in the estimated income taxes on the differences in current values of assets and liabilities over their tax bases.

In order to present this statement, the estimated current values of all the assets and

---

[14] *SOP 82-1*, paragraph 6.

liabilities at the end of the prior year must be known so that it is possible to compute the unrealized increases and decreases. In addition, the beginning balance of the estimated income taxes on the unrealized gains and losses must be known, indicating that a statement of financial condition at the end of the prior year is necessary, or that all the information required for the preparation of the statement must be determined. The need for this information is the reason the statement is optional. In addition, the data may not be readily available, as a statement of financial condition can be prepared at any point in time with regard to a calendar or fiscal year. If Harry and Henrietta Bolts want a statement of changes in net worth to accompany their statement of financial condition in Exhibit 1.9 of Illustrative Problem 1.4, the statement could be presented as shown in Exhibit 1-10 (this is simply an example of the statement of changes in net worth and no computations have been presented to substantiate the information contained in the statement).

DISCLOSURE REQUIREMENTS

Personal financial statements, like financial statements for any entity, require a complete set of notes to further explain and clarify the information contained in the statements. The disclosures include

- The names and relationships of the individuals making up the reporting entity
- A statement indicating assets and liabilities are valued at estimated current values
- The methods used to determine the current values of assets and the current amounts of liabilities
- The differences between the estimated current values and the tax bases of major assets
- The methods and assumptions used to compute the estimated income taxes on the unrealized gains and losses
- Descriptions of the maturities, interest rates, and collateral for receivables and debt
- Descriptions of all intangible assets and their estimated useful lives

If an individual has major investments in stocks and bonds, the details of the holdings are disclosed. If an individual jointly owns assets with another entity, the nature of the joint ownership is disclosed. If an individual has a material investment in a closely held business, such as Harry Bolts' hardware store, the following information is required:

- Name of company and percentage of ownership
- Nature of the business
- Summarized financial information, both income statement and balance sheet data for the most recent year
- Basis of accounting (cash, modified cash, tax, accrual)
- Significant loss contingencies

The note to accompany the Bolts' statement of financial condition for the investment in the hardware store could be written as follows:

> Bolts' Hardware Store, a general-purpose neighborhood store, is wholly owned by Harry Bolts. At December 31, 1990, the accrual basis financial statements of Bolts' Hardware Store reported net income of $35,300 on sales of $121,900. The summarized balance sheet information is

EXHIBIT 1-10

Illustrative Problem 1.4
HARRY AND HENRIETTA BOLTS
Statement of Changes in Net Worth
Year Ended March 31, 1991

Realized Increases in Net Worth	
Income of Bolts' Hardware Store	$ 41,000
Salary of Mrs. Bolts	38,000
Dividends from Marketable Securities	3,000
Total Realized Increases	82,000
Realized Decreases in Net Worth	
Income Taxes	25,500
Interest Expense	15,750
Real Estate Taxes	2,500
Personal Expenditures	45,700
Total Realized Decreases	89,450
Net Realized Decrease in Net Worth	(7,450)
Unrealized Increases in Net Worth	
Stock Options	4,000
Bolts' Hardware Store	15,000
Pension and Profit-Sharing Plan	5,400
Life Insurance	5,000
Remainder Interest in Trust	4,400
Residence	33,500
Antiques	11,050
Mortgage Payable: Home Savings and Loan	10,000
Total Unrealized Increases	88,350
Unrealized Decreases in Net Worth	
Marketable Securities	6,000
Estimated Income Taxes on the Differences Between the Estimated Current Values of Assets and the Estimated Current Amounts of Liabilities and Their Tax Bases	22,500
Total Unrealized Decreases	28,500
Net Unrealized Increase in Net Worth	59,850
Net Increase in Net Worth	52,400
Net Worth at the Beginning of the Year	470,000
Net Worth at the End of the Year	$ 522,400

BOLTS' HARDWARE STORE
Balance Sheet
December 31, 1990

Current Assets	$ 67,050	Current Liabilities	$ 13,100
Property	32,000	Long-term Debt	23,800
		Owner's Equity	62,150
Total Assets	$ 99,050	Total Equities	$ 99,050

In addition, the following information, which is not reported in the statement of financial condition, is required to be reported in the notes accompanying the financial statements:

- The face amount of the life insurance policies the individuals own. The cash surrender value is on the statement.
- Forfeitable rights and commitments that are not for fixed or determinable amounts, or are contingent on some future event, or require the future performance of service.

In the Bolts example, they would report the face amount of their life insurance policies of $200,000, and Mrs. Bolts' 40 percent unvested pension and profit-sharing plan of $37,800. Any major contingencies or material related-party transactions are required to be discussed in the notes.[15]

SUMMARY

The entity theory allows us to decide which events to include and exclude in recording the financial transactions and events affecting an entity because it establishes the assets and liabilities to be recorded. An entity is a business enterprise, a nonbusiness enterprise, a natural person, or a consolidation of two or more entities. The equity of an entity is the difference between assets and liabilities—a residual interest.

Three theories are used to provide an approach to determining equity: the proprietary theory, the entity theory, and the fund theory. The proprietary theory approaches equity from the owner's point of view. The assets and liabilities are considered the owner's assets and liabilities, and the approach is one of measurement of changes in owner's wealth. The balance sheet is the most important financial statement and uses the equation, assets minus liabilities equals owners equity.

The entity theory approaches equity from the entity's point of view. The assets and liabilities are considered the entity's assets and liabilities, and the approach is one of measurement of changes in assets. The income statement and the statement of changes in owner's equity are the most important financial statements. The balance sheet equation is assets equal liabilities plus owner's equity.

The fund theory approaches equity from the restrictions on assets point of view. The approach is one of the measurement of sources of assets, the uses of assets within their restrictions, and the accountability for assets. The most important financial statement is the

---

[15] *SOP 82-1*, paragraphs 31 and 32.

statement that reports sources and uses of assets. The balance sheet equation is assets equal restrictions on assets (equity).

Sole proprietorships are the simplest form of business, often operated from a proprietary point of view without accounting expertise or personnel. The records frequently are maintained on the cash or modified cash basis rather than on the accrual basis. In addition, because the owner approaches the business from the proprietary point of view, some assets and liabilities that are personal are treated as business assets and some assets and liabilities that belong to the business are treated as personal.

Generally accepted accounting principles require that all financial accounting and reporting use the accrual basis of accounting. The cash or modified cash records must be converted to the accrual basis to prepare the financial statements and the conversion is frequently accomplished by using a worksheet. In order to convert to the accrual basis, both the beginning of the period and the end of the period balances of all assets and liabilities must be determined. The only difference between the financial statements of a sole proprietorship and a corporation is the lack of income taxes as a sole proprietorship is a tax pass-through entity, meaning the tax is passed on to the individual.

Financial statements are prepared for legally related individuals under the accrual basis of accounting at any point in time using estimated current values for assets and estimated current amount for liabilities. The techniques that can be used to estimate the current values of assets and the current amounts of liabilities are recent transactions of similar assets, which is the preferable method; capitalization of past or prospective earnings; liquidation values; specific price indexing of the specific assets; appraisals by real estate brokers, insurance estimators, and property tax assessors; discounted cash flows using the market rates of interest for assets, and transaction rates of interest for liabilities; and valuations by specialists and experts for unusual or unique assets.

The financial statements consist of a statement of financial condition with an optional statement of changes in net worth. No income statement is prepared because of the mixture of business and personal revenues and expenses. The statement of financial condition presents the estimated current values of assets and the estimated current amounts of liabilities on the accrual basis in the order of liquidity and maturity. The statement may present the cost basis or the tax base of assets and liabilities as supplemental information to the current values and amounts.

REVIEW PROBLEMS

CONVERSION TO THE ACCRUAL BASIS OF ACCOUNTING

June Blossom owns and operates a local garden store. The accounting records of the garden store are maintained on the tax basis. The only assets besides cash that are recorded are inventory and operating assets. The following unadjusted trial balance as of September 30, 1990, was prepared from the accounts of Blossom Garden Store:

BLOSSOM GARDEN STORE
Unadjusted Trial Balance
September 30, 1990

	Debit	Credit
Cash	$ 16,200	
Inventory, 9/30/89	21,300	
Land	18,000	
Store Building	57,500	
Accumulated Depreciation: Store Building		$ 22,500
Equipment and Store Fixtures	22,400	
Accumulated Depreciation: Equipment and Store Fixtures		10,100
Notes Payable: Equipment		4,000
Mortgage Payable: Land and Buildings		41,700
Owner's Equity: June Blossom, 9/30/89		67,200
Owner's Drawings: June Blossom	38,900	
Sales Revenue		94,250
Purchases	40,625	
Supplies Expense	3,175	
Salaries and Wages Expense	16,450	
Insurance Expense	4,200	
Interest Expense	3,200	
Gain on Sale of Equipment		2,200
Totals	$241,950	$241,950

The following information for conversion to the accrual basis of accounting has been determined:

1. All sales are for cash.
2. The inventory on hand at September 30, 1990 totaled $27,650.
3. Blossom Garden Store owed $8,950 of accounts payable at the beginning of the year, and the amount of unpaid bills at September 30, 1990 totaled $7,240. Blossom Garden Store only purchases inventory on credit.
4. The supplies on hand at October 1, 1989 were $690 and the supplies on hand at September 30, 1990 totaled $540.
5. The insurance expense is the total premium on a two-year policy issued on April 1, 1990. The policy replaced a previous $6,000 three-year policy that expired on March 31, 1990.
6. The building is being depreciated by the straight-line method over 20 years, with an estimated salvage value of $7,500.
7. The gain on the sale of equipment is the total price received from the sale of an old tractor with a cost of $6,500 and accumulated depreciation of $6,000. Equipment and store fixtures are depreciated at the rate of 10% per year. A full year's depreciation is taken in the year of acquisition and none in the year of sale.
8. During the year June Blossom landscaped her new home with shrubbery from the garden store. The total cost of the shrubbery was $3,800. The drawing account only includes the cash June Blossom has withdrawn from the business.
9. The note payable requires annual payments every March 31 of $1,000 principal plus 10% interest on the outstanding balance.

Required

1. Prepare a worksheet to convert the records of Blossom Garden Store from the tax basis of accounting to the accrual basis of accounting as of September 30, 1990. Support your worksheet with the journal entries including adjusting journal entries. Cost of goods sold should be determined as an adjusting journal entry.
2. Prepare the financial statements for Blossom Garden Store on the accrual basis as of September 30, 1990.

PERSONAL FINANCIAL STATEMENTS

June Blossom is a widow with two children, April, age 14, and May, age 16. She has asked you to help her prepare a statement of financial condition for her and her daughters as of September 30, 1990. After reviewing her and her children's tax returns and other pertinent information, and discussing their assets with her, you determine the following information to be used in the preparation of the statement of financial condition:

	Tax Base
Cash in money market checking account: June	$ 13,265
Cash in savings account at Superior Savings: April	21,300
Cash in savings account at Superior Savings: May	22,350
IRA account at Wise Investment Brokerage: June	–0–
Current market value is $11,400.	
Blossom Garden Store	55,100
June believes the garden store is worth $240,000. A call to a real estate broker determined that similar small businesses usually sell for a total price of 5 times earnings. The real estate broker also noted that the land and building were more valuable than most because of the excellent location; therefore, she would add an additional $25,000 to the 5 times earnings.	
Interest in testamentary trust	–0–
Mr. Blossom died five years ago and left his estate in trust for the benefit of his daughters and his wife. The terms of the trust specify that the daughters are to each receive one-third of the income of the trust until April is 25 years old. June Blossom is to receive the remaining one-third of the income. When April is 25 years old, the trust will be terminated. April and May will each receive $75,000 from the trust, and June is to receive the balance of the trust assets. The trust assets consist of high-grade securities, totaling $500,000. The trust has earned an average of $50,000 a year.	
Life insurance (cash value less loans equals tax base)	$ 31,475

Insured	Face Value	Cash Value	Loans
June	$100,000	$29,000	$8,500
April	25,000	6,200	–0–
May	25,000	5,900	–0–

	Tax Base
Apartment house, purchased in 1980	102,800

Apartment house, purchased in 1980

> June Blossom believes she can sell the property, net of selling costs, for $400,000. The most recent property tax statement has a value of $270,000, which is 90% of market value. A 10% mortgage with a balance of $81,250 is owed to Security Savings on the property at September 30, 1990.

Personal residence, purchased six months ago — **132,500**

> Property values have been staying at a constant level in the Blossoms' town. June Blossom has spent $10,000 on decks, patios, and an outdoor spa, in addition to the $3,800 of shrubbery from her business. June Blossom owes Home Savings and Loan $51,400 on the mortgage.

Automobiles

  BMW driven by June Blossom — **4,200**

> June uses this car in her business, and the tax base reflects depreciation. June believes she can sell the car for $22,000. A call to the local auto dealer revealed that the top Blue Book price for a similar BMW is $18,750. (Blue Book is a listing of automobiles by make and model that gives the current selling prices based on the condition of the car.)

  1984 Ford Mustang — **4,900**

> Given to May by her grandfather on her sixteenth birthday on September 25, 1990. The grandfather paid $4,900 for the car.

Household furnishings — **21,700**

> Used furnishings typically sell for 20% of cost.

Liabilities

> In addition to the liabilities listed above, June owes $4,200 for the spa and decks, and $1,750 in household bills.

Income taxes

> June has just settled a dispute with the Internal Revenue Service regarding her 1986, 1987, and 1988 tax returns, agreeing to a settlement of $3,100. June estimates her taxable income for 1990 will be $80,000. Her taxable income for the period 1/1/90 through 9/30/90 totaled $60,000. June's tax is estimated to be $24,000 for 1990, and she has made $13,400 of estimated income tax payments. The tax payments of the daughters are equal to their tax liability at September 30, 1990. The effective tax rate for the family is estimated to be 25%. The loss on the household furnishings is the only asset that is not subject to tax.

Required

1. Prepare a statement of financial condition for the Blossom family as of September 30, 1990, showing both the estimated current values and amounts and their tax bases, assuming the market rate of interest is 12%.
2. Prepare a footnote to accompany the statement of financial condition to disclose the required information for the Blossom Garden Store.

QUESTIONS

1. Describe the type of groups or organizations that can be entities according to *Statement of Financial Accounting Concepts No. 6.*
2. Define equity and explain the events that cause equity to change over time.
3. Describe the types of transactions that increase and decrease equity in a business enterprise and in a not-for-profit organization.
4. Describe the three theories of equity, including the approach taken and the balance sheet equation.
5. Describe the reasons it may be more difficult to prepare financial statements according to generally accepted accounting principles for sole proprietorships than for other forms of business.
6. Describe accrual accounting and give the reasons it is considered preferable to other basis of accounting.
7. Describe the differences in the equity accounts of a sole proprietorship and a corporation.
8. Describe the information that is needed to convert a completely cash basis set of records to the accrual basis.
9. Describe the differences between the financial statements of corporations and sole proprietorships.
10. List the reasons given by the AICPA for changing from the use of historical cost values to estimated current values in the preparation of personal financial statements.
11. Describe the entities that can be included in personal financial statements.
12. Describe the various techniques that can be used to estimate current values.
13. Describe the values to be used to report the following assets on a statement of financial condition: marketable securities, receivables, life insurance, intangibles, and payables other than income taxes.
14. Describe the characteristics that the rights to receive future sums of cash must have to be included as assets in personal financial statements, and give examples of the rights that are included.
15. Describe the three types of income taxes that could be reported in a statement of financial condition.
16. Write the formula for estimating the amount of unpaid taxes for the current year.
17. Explain how the estimate of income taxes, based on the difference between the estimated current values of assets and the estimated current amounts of liabilities and their tax bases, is computed. How and where is this amount reported in the statement of financial condition?
18. How do personal financial statements differ from the financial statements of a business entity?
19. Describe the alternative ways a statement of financial condition can be prepared.
20. Describe the types of sources of changes in net worth, and give examples of each type of source that would be reported on a statement of changes in net worth.
21. Explain why a statement of changes in net worth does not show the net income of the individuals.
22. Explain why a statement of changes in net worth is not a required financial statement.

EXERCISES

EXERCISE 1-1

A Co. maintains its records on a strictly cash basis. During 1991, A Co. received $89,760 in cash from the sales of merchandise. At the beginning of the year, customers owed A Co. $13,460, and at the end of the year, the total of uncollected accounts receivable was $15,290.

Required

Determine (1) the amount of sales revenue to be reported on an accrual basis income statement, and (2) write the journal entry to convert the cash basis records to the accrual basis.

EXERCISE 1-2

Acorn Company maintains its records on the cash basis. During 1992, Acorn reported sales revenue of $100,000 on the cash basis. The accounts receivable at January 1, 1992 were $20,000 and the accounts receivable at December 31, 1992 were $24,000. Acorn Company estimates that $1,500 of beginning accounts receivable are not collectible and $2,000 of ending accounts receivable are not collectible. Accounts receivable in the amount of $1,700 were written off during the period.

Required

Prepare the journal entry to convert Acorn Company's sales to the accrual basis.

EXERCISE 1-3

B. Co. leases a portion of its warehouse to C Co. for $1,200 per month. On November 1, 1991, C Co. paid six months rent in advance. On July 1, 1990, B Co. loaned D Co. $25,000 for five years at 10% interest. The terms of the loan require D Co. to pay $5,000 of principal plus interest on the unpaid balance each July 1.

Required

1. Determine the revenue from the lease and the loan to be reported for 1991, if B Co. uses (1) the cash basis of accounting, and (2) the accrual basis of accounting.
2. Prepare the journal entries to convert (1) the accrual basis revenue to cash basis revenue, and (2) the cash basis revenue to accrual basis revenue.

EXERCISE 1-4

F Co. purchased $3,145 of supplies for cash during the year, their first year of operations. At the end of the year, F Co. has unpaid invoices for supplies of $428 and unused supplies of $820.

Required

1. Determine the supplies expense on (1) the cash basis, and (2) the accrual basis.
2. Write the journal entry to convert (1) from the cash basis to the accrual basis, and (2) from the accrual basis to the cash basis.

EXERCISE 1-5

G Co. purchased $87,920 of inventory for cash during the year. At the beginning of the year, G Co. had unpaid invoices for purchases of inventory totaling $13,460, and at the end of the year the unpaid invoices totaled $12,790. The inventory on hand at the beginning of the year totaled $15,780, and the value of the inventory on hand at the end of the year was $14,210.

Required

1. Determine the cost of goods sold if (1) the cash basis is used, (2) the modified cash basis is used and inventory but not accounts payable is recorded, and (3) the accrual basis of accounting is used.
2. Write the journal entry to convert to the accrual basis from (1) the cash basis, and (2) the modified cash basis.

EXERCISE 1-6

H Co. purchased a three-year insurance policy on May 1, 1990 for $7,200 cash and recorded the entire amount as insurance expense.

Required

Prepare the journal entry to convert to the accrual basis as of the end of (1) 1990, (2) 1991, and (3) 1992.

EXERCISE 1-7

R. Storekeeper operates a men's clothing store. R. Storekeeper purchased the land and the store building on January 1, 1986 for $50,000; at that time the building was estimated to be worth $42,500. R. Storekeeper financed the purchase with a 10-year, $40,000 contract at 12% interest. The contract requires annual principal payments of $4,000 and interest on the unpaid balance each December 31. The building is estimated to have a useful life of 20 years and a salvage value of $2,500. R. Storekeeper considers the land and building his personal assets and has made all the mortgage payments.

Required

1. Determine the assets and liabilities that should be on the balance sheet of the clothing store at December 31, 1990, if the assets and the mortgage are in the name of the business.
2. Determine the amount of expense that should be on the income statement of the clothing store for the year 1990 from the assets and the mortgage.
3. Write a single journal entry to record the assets, liabilities, and expense.
4. Prove that the amount credited to Owner's Equity in (3) above is correct.

EXERCISE 1-8

1. During 1990, Kew Company, a service organization, had $200,000 in cash sales and $3,000,000 in credit sales. The accounts receivable balances were $400,000 and $485,000 at December 31, 1989 and 1990, respectively. If Kew desires to prepare a cash basis income statement, how much should be reported as sales revenue for 1990 on a cash basis?

a. $ 3,285,000
b. $ 3,200,000
c. $ 3,115,000
d. $ 2,915,000

2. Hall Company owns an office building and leases the offices under a variety of rental agreements involving rent paid monthly in advance and rent paid annually in advance. Not all tenants make timely payments of their rent. During 1992, Hall reported rental revenue of $40,000 on the cash basis. The following data has been determined:

	1991	1992
Rentals Receivable	$ 4,800	$ 6,200
Unearned Rentals	16,000	12,000

Rental revenue for 1992 on the accrual basis is?

a. $ 34,600
b. $ 37,400
c. $ 42,600
d. $ 45,400

3. James Lee, M.D. keeps his accounting records on a cash basis. During 1991, Dr. Lee collected $100,000 in fees from his patients. At December 31, 1990, Dr. Lee had accounts receivable of $20,000. At December 31, 1991, Dr. Lee had accounts receivable of $30,000 and unearned fees of $1,000. On an accrual basis, how much was Dr. Lee's patient service revenue for 1991?

a. $ 111,000
b. $ 109,000
c. $ 90,000
d. $ 89,000

4. The following information is available for Bart Company for 1990.

Cost of Goods Sold on the Cash Basis	$ 580,000
Increase in Accounts Payable	50,000
Decrease in Inventory	20,000

Cost of goods sold for 1990 on the accrual basis is?

a. $ 650,000
b. $ 610,000
c. $ 550,000
d. $ 510,000

5. Lane Company acquired copyrights from authors, paying advance royalties in some cases, and in others, paying royalties within 30 days of year end. Lane reported royalty expense of $375,000 on the accrual basis for the year ended December 31, 1991. The following data are included in Lane's December 31 balance sheets:

	1990	1991
Prepaid Royalties	$ 60,000	$ 50,000
Royalties Payable	75,000	90,000

The royalty expense for 1991 on the cash basis is?

a. $ 350,000
b. $ 370,000
c. $ 380,000
d. $ 400,000

6. Clay Company borrows money under various loan agreements involving notes discounted and notes requiring interest payments at maturity. During the year ended December 31, 1991, Clay reported interest expense on the cash basis of $100,000. The following asset and liability balances were determined for converting to the accrual basis:

	1990	1991
Prepaid Interest	$ 23,500	$ 18,000
Interest Payable	45,000	53,500

How much interest expense should Clay report for 1991 on the accrual basis?

a. $ 86,000
b. $ 97,000
c. $ 103,000
d. $ 114,000

(AICPA adapted)

EXERCISE 1-9

1. Personal financial statement should present

a. Assets and liabilities at their historical cost
b. Assets at their estimated current values and liabilities at their estimated current amounts at the date of the financial statements

c. Assets at their estimated current values at the date of the financial statements and liabilities at their historical cost
d. Assets and liabilities at their historical cost and, as additional information, at their estimated current values

2. Personal financial statements consist of a statement of financial condition and a(an) optional

	Income Statement	Statement of Changes in Net Worth
a.	No	No
b.	No	Yes
c.	Yes	Yes
d.	Yes	No

(AICPA adapted)

EXERCISE 1-10

Alfred and Alma Bates have asked you to help them prepare their personal statement of financial condition as of June 30, 1990. The Bates own an apartment building and provide you with the following information regarding the building and its operations:

Initial cost June 30, 1984	$ 120,000
Depreciation per year on their tax return	4,000
Gross annual rentals received in cash	47,500
Net income	20,500
Property tax appraisals at 80% of market, net of selling costs	164,000
Insurance appraisal at replacement cost	200,000
Current selling price appraisal by real estate broker	205,000
Real estate selling costs	6.0%
Real estate price indices	
At time of purchase	180
At June 30, 1990	320

Required

1. Determine the estimated current value of the apartment building to be used on the Bates' statement of financial condition using
   1) The various appraisals
   2) Discounted cash flows for 20 years, assuming a 10% market rate of interest
   3) Earnings capitalized for 10 years
   4) Specific price index
   5) Net book value of property plus 5 years of cash flows discounted at 10%
2. Which value would you use on their personal statement of financial condition?

EXERCISE 1-11

Jeffrey and Joanne Kyle have investments in the following assets:

	Cost	Market Value
250 shares of United Airlines	$22 share	$31 share
200 shares of Big Bend Mining Company	$5 share	Bid $8 1/4
		Ask $9 1/2
150 shares of Two Rivers Market	$12 share	$9 share

Required

Determine the estimated current value of the securities to be reported on the Kyles' statement of financial condition.

EXERCISE 1-12

Mary and Melissa Marble are the remainderwomen of a trust established by their grandfather. A remainderwoman is a person who is entitled to receive a portion of the assets remaining in a trust at a specific point in time or after a specific event. Upon the death of their grandmother they will receive 60% of the assets of the trust, and upon the death of their mother they will receive the remainder of the assets. Their mother, Marilyn, and their grandmother, Maybell, are the income beneficiaries of the trust. Maybell receives 60% of the income of the trust and Marilyn receives the remaining 40%. Maybell is 70 years old with a life expectancy of 8 years. Marilyn is 38 years old with a life expectancy of 40 years. The trust has assets totaling $1,800,000 and has earned an average rate of return of 10% for several years. The current market rate of interest is 12%.

Required

1. Determine the estimated current value of the future rights (to the nearest dollar) to be reported on the statement of financial condition for
   1) Marilyn
   2) Marilyn, Mary, and Melissa
   3) The entire family group
2. What market rate of interest would make the estimated current value of the nonforfeitable rights of the entire family group equal to the face value of the assets of the trust?

EXERCISE 1-13

Robert and Rachelle Clark have the following rights:

	Cost
Pension and profit-sharing plan, 100% vested	$ 72,000
Pension and profit-sharing plan, 65% vested	41,000
25 lottery tickets. Robert estimates their chances are 1 in 100 of winning $50,000.	50
Rachelle is the beneficiary of a $35,000 life insurance policy on the life of her father who is 81.	
Rachelle is receiving alimony in the amount of $600 per quarter. She is guaranteed 20 payments.	

Required

Determine the amount of the rights to receive future sums of cash that should be included in the Clarks' statement of financial condition if the market rate of interest is 12%.

EXERCISE 1-14

Brad and Brenda Lake have asked you to prepare their statement of financial condition as of March 31, 1992. You determine the following information regarding their federal income taxes:

Balance owing on their 1991 federal income tax return paid on April 15, 1992	$ 6,000
Taxable income earned to date in 1992	12,000
1992 federal withholding to date	3,200
1992 estimated taxable income	72,000
1992 effective tax rate	28.0%

Required

Determine the amount of income taxes payable to be reported on the Lakes' statement of financial condition at March 31, 1992.

EXERCISE 1-15

Carl and Caroline Olson have assets with a total estimated current value of $625,000. The estimated current amount of their liabilities is $230,000. The tax bases of their assets totals $265,000 and the tax bases of their liabilities are $250,000. The Olsons' effective tax rate is 33% and $65,000 of unrealized appreciation in assets is not subject to tax.

Required

Determine the estimated income taxes on the excess of the estimated current values of assets and the estimated current amounts of liabilities over their tax bases.

EXERCISE 1-16

1. Mr. and Mrs. Carson are applying for a bank loan and the bank has requested a personal statement of financial condition as of December 31, 1992. Included in their assets at this date are the following:

- 1,000 shares of Alden Corporation common stock purchased in 1988 at a cost of $50,000. The quoted market value of the stock was $75 per share on December 31, 1992.
- A residence purchased in 1989 at a cost of $120,000. Improvements costing $15,000 were made in 1991. Unimproved similar homes in the area are currently selling at approximately the same price levels as in 1989.

In the Carsons' December 31, 1992, personal statement of financial condition, the above assets should be reported at a total amount of

a. $ 170,000
b. $ 185,000
c. $ 195,000
d. $ 210,000

2. Mr. and Mrs. Dean require a personal statement of financial condition as of December 31, 1992. Included in their assets at this date are the following:

- A $300,000 whole life insurance policy (on Mr. Dean) having a cash value of $43,000 at December 31, 1992, subject to a $37,000 loan payable to the insurance company.
- A residence purchased in 1986 at a cost of $150,000. Similar homes in the area are currently selling at approximately $175,000.

In the Deans' December 31, 1992, personal statement of financial condition, the above assets should be reported at a total amount of

a. $ 218,000
b. $ 193,000
c. $ 181,000
d. $ 156,000

Questions 3 and 4 are based on the following information.

Mr. and Mrs. Taft are applying for a bank loan and the bank has requested a personal statement of financial condition as of December 31, 1992. Included in their assets and liabilities at this date are the following.

Assets

Mr. Taft owns 50% of the common stock of Dee Corporation. A shareholders' agreement restricts the sale of the stock and, under certain circumstances, requires Dee to repurchase the stock based on the book value of the net assets, plus an agreed amount for goodwill. At December 31, 1992, the buy-out value of Taft's stock is $675,000. Mr. Taft's tax basis for his Dee stock is $430,000.

Mrs. Taft owns jewelry appraised on December 31, 1992, at $70,000 by an independent appraiser for insurance purposes. The jewelry, acquired by purchases and gifts over a 10-year period, has a total tax basis of $40,000.

Liabilities

The Taft residence is encumbered by a mortgage payable in monthly installments of $1,000 through December 1998. Interest at 10% a year is included in the $1,000 monthly payment. The balance of the mortgage principal is $58,000 at December 31, 1992.

Mr. Taft has guaranteed the payment of loans of Dee Corporation under a $300,000 line of credit. The loan balance is $200,000 at December 31, 1992. Dee's financial condition at December 31, 1992, is such that its repayment of the loan balance is reasonably assured.

3. In the Tafts' December 31, 1992, personal statement of financial condition, the Dee Corporation investment and the jewelry should be reported at a total amount of

a. $ 470,000
b. $ 500,000
c. $ 715,000
d. $ 745,000

4. In the Tafts' December 31, 1992, personal statement of financial condition, the liabilities listed above should be reported at a total amount of

a. $ 58,000
b. $ 72,000
c. $ 258,000
d. $ 272,000

5. Leslie Shaw's personal statement of financial condition at December 31, 1991, shows net worth of $400,000 before consideration of employee stock options owned on that date. Information relating to the stock options is as follows:

- Options are to purchase 10,000 shares of Korn Corporation stock.
- Option exercise price is $10 a share.
- Options expire on June 30, 1992.
- Market price of the stock is $25 a share at December 31, 1991.
- Assume that exercise of the options in 1992 would result in ordinary income taxable at 35%.

After giving effect to the stock options, Shaw's net worth at December 31, 1991, would be

a. $ 497,500
b. $ 550,000
c. $ 562,500
d. $ 650,000

6. Included in W. Cody's assets at December 31, 1991, are the following:

- 2,000 shares of Dart Corporation common stock purchased in 1988 for $100,000. The market value of the stock was $80 per share at December 31, 1991.

- A $500,000 whole life insurance policy having a cash value of $72,000 at December 31, 1991, subject to a $30,000 loan payable to the insurance company.

In Cody's December 31, 1991, personal statement of financial condition, the above assets should be reported at

a. $ 232,000
b. $ 202,000
c. $ 172,000
d. $ 142,000

7. Jay Dunn owns 50% of the common stock of Nolan Corp. Jay paid $10,000 for this stock in 1985. At December 31, 1990, it was ascertained that Jay's 50% stock ownership in Nolan had a current value of $90,000. Nolan's cumulative net income and cash dividends declared for the 5 years ending December 31, 1990, were $150,000 and $20,000 respectively. In Jay's personal statement of financial condition at December 31, 1990, how much should be shown as his net investment in Nolan?

a. $ 90,000
b. $ 85,000
c. $ 75,000
d. $ 10,000

(AICPA adapted)

PROBLEMS

PROBLEM 1-1
J. Carter owns and operates a wholesale peanut butter business, Carter Foods. The warehouse needs modernizing and J. Carter has asked the local bank for a loan to purchase new equipment. The bank requires a complete set of financial statements prepared on the accrual basis. The records of Carter Foods are kept on the cash basis. The cash basis records show the following totals for 1991:

Cash	$ 24,100
Sales Revenue	157,600
Cost of Peanuts Purchased	38,750
Wages Paid to Employees	42,200
Cost of Supplies	12,000
Cost of Shipping	6,230
Cost of Rent of Land and Building	15,000
Cost of Advertising	8,900
Cash Withdrawals	20,000

The following information is obtained from the records and information supplied by J. Carter:

1. The accounts receivable at the beginning of the year were $32,560 and at the end of the year totaled $40,640.
2. The amounts owed for peanuts at the beginning of the year were $21,400 and totaled $17,500 at the end of the year.
3. The inventory of peanuts on hand at the beginning of the year was $6,540 and at the end of the year the value of the inventory was $7,890. In addition, J. Carter took home $1,000 worth of peanuts during the year.

4. The beginning balance of supplies was $2,340 and the ending balance of supplies was $2,965.
5. Three months of rent totaling $3,000 is owed to J. L. Bean for the land and factory building at the end of the year. The amount of rent paid in the current year included $6,000 of rent from the prior year.
6. The employees had earned $2,100 in the prior year that was unpaid as of the beginning of the year. At the end of the year, $3,400 had been earned but not paid.
7. Carter Foods owes $1,600 for federal withholding from employees' wages, and $560 for FICA taxes, one-half of which was withheld from the employees' wages. At the beginning of the year, the company owed $1,400 for federal withholding and $480 for FICA taxes.
8. An analysis of the advertising account showed that $1,790 of bills for new clothes for J. Carter had been debited to that account.
9. The factory equipment was acquired 7 years ago for $63,000. The tax returns of J. Carter show that the equipment was being depreciated on the straight-line basis over 10 years with an estimated salvage value of $1,500.

Required

1. Prepare a worksheet to convert the cash basis information to the accrual basis for preparation of the annual financial statements for the year ended December 31, 1991 for Carter Foods. Support your worksheet amounts with journal entries.
2. Prepare the income statement and the statement of changes in owner's equity on the accrual basis for the year ended December 31, 1991 for Carter Foods. Prepare the statement of cash flows using the direct method for the year ended December 31, 1991, for Carter Foods. Prepare the balance sheet on the accrual basis as of December 31, 1991 for Carter Foods.

PROBLEM 1-2

Mary Canter owns and operates a paint and wallpaper store, Colorful Paint and Wallpaper. Mary has been renting the store building, but would like to purchase the building. First Federal Bank is willing to loan Mary the necessary funds if she will present them with an income statement prepared on the cash basis for the past two years so they can assess her debt-paying ability. The adjusted trial balances for the years 1989, 1990, and 1991 were taken from the ledger of Colorful Paint and Wallpaper.

COLORFUL PAINT AND WALLPAPER
Adjusted Accrual Basis Trial Balances
Years Ending December 31
Dr. (Cr.)

	1989	1990	1991
Cash	$ 28,100	$ 21,505	$ 13,835
Accounts Receivable	13,560	16,420	14,270
Inventory	21,570	22,350	21,980
Supplies	2,120	1,740	1,820
Prepaid Insurance	2,100	4,900	3,200
Prepaid Rent	1,500	1,800	1,200
Store Fixtures	12,000	13,600	14,400
Accumulated Depreciation: Store Fixtures	(6,200)	(7,500)	(8,400)
Accounts Payable: Inventory	(6,530)	(10,240)	(8,760)
Utility Bills Payable	(425)	(370)	(310)
Wages Payable	(1,650)	(2,400)	(2,140)
Owner's Equity	(66,705)	(66,145)	(61,805)

	1989	1990	1991
Owner's Drawings			
Cash	18,000	21,000	24,080
Merchandise	540	–0–	–0–
Sales Revenue	(61,300)	(59,730)	(61,230)
Cost of Goods Sold	26,900	25,100	29,400
Wages Expense	3,600	3,620	4,260
Supplies Expense	1,300	1,550	1,700
Insurance Expense	3,600	4,200	4,200
Rent Expense	6,000	6,300	6,600
Depreciation Expense	1,200	1,300	900
Utilities Expense	720	1,000	800
Totals	$ –0–	$ –0–	$ –0–

During 1990 and 1991 no store fixtures were sold or scraped.

Required

1. Prepare a worksheet to convert the accrual basis trial balance at December 31, 1990 to the cash basis.
2. Prepare schedules to determine the revenue and expense amounts for 1991 on the cash basis.
3. Prepare a comparative cash basis income statement for the years 1990 and 1991.
4. Determine if Colorful Paint and Wallpaper has sufficient cash flow to support Mary Canter, based on her drawings for 1991, and to make mortgage payments totaling $7,200 a year and property taxes estimated to be $1,800. (*Hint:* She will no longer be paying rent.)

PROBLEM 1-3

The Short and Tall Shop, a sole proprietorship owned by Elmer Gentry, sells business clothing to men and women who are shorter than five foot three inches and taller than six feet. The accounting records have been maintained on the modified cash basis for a number of years. The only assets the shop records are store fixtures and inventory. Elmer Gentry wants to move the Short and Tall Shop to a newly developed shopping center and replace the old store fixtures that were purchased for cash 15 years ago. The shopping center requires an accrual basis set of comparative financial statements for the past 2 years before it will lease the space to ensure that the businesses who rent have sufficient income to make the lease payments and sufficient cash or borrowing power to purchase new store fixtures. The following information has been determined regarding the assets and liabilities of the Short and Tall Shop at the end of the prior 3 years:

	1989	1990	1991
Cash	$ 14,600	$ 10,500	$ 6,210
Accounts Receivable	21,400	19,560	22,350
Inventory	34,500	37,200	39,100
Prepaid Insurance	2,400	2,600	3,200
Prepaid Rent	1,200	1,400	1,700
Store Fixtures	18,000	18,000	18,000
Accumulated Depreciation: Store Fixtures	13,000	14,000	15,000
Accounts Payable	10,340	9,520	12,860
Wages and Payroll Taxes Payable	2,300	4,700	3,300
Owner's Drawings			
Cash	20,000	25,000	28,000
Merchandise	2,200	3,150	2,700

The income statements of the Short and Tall Shop prepared on the modified cash basis for 1990 and 1991 are

SHORT AND TALL SHOP
Income Statements
For the Year Ended December 31

	1990	1991
Sales Revenue	$ 122,400	$ 130,800
Cost of Goods Sold	50,100	53,200
Gross Margin	72,300	77,600
Expenses		
Wages and Payroll Taxes	36,400	38,600
Utilities	2,750	2,890
Insurance	2,800	3,600
Rent	3,600	4,200
Depreciation	1,000	1,000
Total Expenses	46,550	50,290
Net Income	$ 25,750	$ 27,310

Required

1. Prepare comparative schedules to convert the modified cash basis income statement information to the accrual basis.
2. Prepare comparative financial statements for the Short and Tall Shop on the accrual basis for the years 1990 and 1991.
3. If you are the landlord of the shopping center and expect to charge the Short and Tall Shop $6,000 rent per year, and you estimate the new fixtures will cost $22,000, would you sign a lease with the Short and Tall Shop? If not, explain your reasons.

PROBLEM 1-4

Presented below is information pertaining to Ward Specialty Foods, a calendar-year sole proprietorship that maintains its books on the cash basis during the year. At year-end, however, Mary Ward's accountant adjusts the books to the accrual basis only for sales, purchases, and cost of sales, and records depreciation to more clearly reflect the business income for income tax purposes.

WARD SPECIALTY FOODS
Trial Balance
December 31, 1991

	Debit	Credit
Cash	$ 18,500	
Accounts Receivable, 12/31/90	4,500	
Inventory, 12/31/90	20,000	
Equipment	35,000	
Accumulated Depreciation, 12/31/90		$ 9,000
Accounts Payable, 12/31/90		4,800
Payroll Taxes Withheld		850
Mary Ward, Capital, 12/31/90		33,650

	Debit	Credit
Mary Ward, Drawings	24,000	
Sales Revenue		187,000
Purchases	82,700	
Salaries Expense	29,500	
Payroll Tax Expense	2,900	
Rent Expense	8,400	
Miscellaneous Expense	3,900	
Insurance Expense	2,400	
Utilities Expense	3,500	
Totals	$235,300	$235,300

During 1991, Mary Ward signed a new eight-year lease for the store premises and is in the process of negotiating a loan for remodeling purposes. The bank requires Mary Ward to present financial statements for 1991 prepared on the accrual basis. Mary Ward's accountant obtained the following additional information:

1. Amounts due from customers totaled $7,900 at December 31, 1991.
2. A review of the receivables at December 31, 1991, disclosed that an allowance for doubtful accounts of $1,100 should be provided. Mary Ward had no bad debt losses from the inception of the business through December 31, 1991.
3. The inventory amounted to $23,000 at December 31, 1991, based on physical count of goods priced at cost. No reduction to market was required.
4. On signing the new lease on October 1, 1991, Mary Ward paid $8,400, representing one year's rent in advance for the lease year ending October 31, 1992. The $7,500 annual rental under the old lease was paid on October 1, 1990, for the lease year ended October 31, 1991.
5. On April 1, 1991, Mary Ward paid $2,400 to renew the comprehensive insurance coverage for one year. The premium was $2,160 on the old policy that expired on April 1, 1991.
6. Depreciation on equipment was computed at $5,800 for 1991.
7. Unpaid vendors' invoices for food purchases totaled $8,800 at December 31, 1991.
8. Accrued expenses at December 31, 1990 and December 31, 1991 were

	12/31/90	12/31/91
Payroll Taxes	$ 250	$ 400
Salaries	375	510
Utilities	275	450

Required

1. Prepare a worksheet to convert the trial balance of Ward Specialty Foods to the accrual basis for the year ended December 31, 1991, supporting your adjustments with computations and/or explanations. Cost of goods sold should be an adjustment.
2. Prepare the Statement of Changes in Mary Ward, Capital, for the year ended December 31, 1991.

(AICPA adapted)

PROBLEM 1-5

On December 31, 1990, the Owner's Equity account of Brian's Barber shop totaled $39,600 on the cash basis. During 1991, the following cash transactions were entered in the records of Brian's Barber Shop:

	Debit	Credit
Service Revenue		$ 76,300
Salaries Expense	$ 33,500	
Payroll Tax Expense	4,900	
Rent Expense	6,000	
Supplies	7,400	
Insurance Expense	1,800	
Utilities Expense	2,300	
Owner's Drawings	19,200	

If the records had been maintained on the accrual basis, the other asset and the liability accounts would have had the following balances:

	12/31/90	12/31/91
Accounts Receivable	$ 3,100	$ 2,900
Supplies	2,400	1,700
Prepaid Insurance	400	900
Prepaid Rent	1,000	–0–
Wages Payable	1,100	1,400
Payroll Taxes Payable	350	520
Utilities Payable	320	140
Rent Payable	–0–	1,000

Required
1. Prepare a schedule to convert the cash basis income of Brian's Barber Shop for the year ended December 31, 1991 to the accrual basis.
2. Prepare a schedule to determine Brian's equity in Brian's Barber Shop at December 31, 1991 on the accrual basis.

PROBLEM 1-6
Presented below is information pertaining to Cox Stationery Supply, a calendar-year sole proprietorship owned by John Cox. The business maintains its books on the cash basis except that, at year end, the closing inventory and depreciation are recorded. On December 31, 1989, after recording inventory and depreciation, and closing the nominal accounts, Cox Stationery Supply had the following general ledger trial balance:

COX STATIONERY SUPPLY
Trial Balance
December 31, 1989

	Debit	Credit
Cash	$ 16,500	
Merchandise Inventory	39,000	
Equipment	52,500	
Accumulated Depreciation		$ 20,500
Note Payable: Bank		10,000
Payroll Taxes Withheld		1,300
Cox, Capital		76,200
	$108,000	$108,000

During the last quarter of 1989, John Cox and Mary Rice, an outside investor, agreed to incorporate the business under the name Cox Stationers, Inc. Cox will receive 1,000 shares for his business, and Rice will pay $86,000 cash for her 1,000 shares. On January 1, they received the certificate of incorporation for Cox Stationers, Inc., and the corporation issued 1,000 shares of common stock each to Cox and Rice for the above consideration. The agreement between Cox and Rice requires that the December 31, 1989 balance sheet of the proprietorship should be converted to the accrual basis, with all assets and liabilities stated at current fair values, including Cox's goodwill implicit in the terms of the common stock issuance.

Additional Information

1. Amounts due from customers totaled $23,500 at December 31, 1989. A review of collectibility disclosed that an allowance for doubtful accounts of $3,300 is required.
2. The $39,000 merchandise inventory is based on a physical count of goods priced at cost. Unsalable damaged goods costing $2,500 are included in the count. The current fair market value of the total merchandise inventory is $45,000.
3. On July 1, 1989, Cox paid $3,800 to renew the comprehensive insurance coverage for one year.
4. The $10,000 note payable is dated July 1, 1989, bears interest at 12%, and is due July 1, 1990.
5. Unpaid vendor's invoices totaled $30,500 at December 31, 1989.
6. During January 1990, final payroll tax returns filed for Cox Stationery Supply required remittances totaling $2,100.
7. Not included in the trial balance is the $3,500 principal balance at December 31, 1989, of the three-year loan to purchase a delivery van on December 31, 1987. The debt was assumed by the corporation on January 1, 1990. The current fair value of the used equipment is $40,000, including the delivery van.
8. Cox Stationers, Inc. has 7,500 authorized shares of $50 par value common stock.

Required
1. Prepare a schedule to compute Cox's capital on the accrual basis.
2. Prepare a schedule to compute Cox's goodwill implicit in the issuance to him of 1,000 shares of common stock for his business.
3. Prepare a formal balance sheet of Cox Stationers, Inc. immediately after the issuance of common stock to Cox and Rice.

(AICPA adapted)

PROBLEM 1-7
1. Alfred's Auto Body Shop maintains its records on the modified cash basis, recording inventory, prepaid insurance, and plant assets. For the year ended December 31, 1990, the modified cash financial statements showed net income of $42,600, beginning owner's equity of $40,000, and withdrawals of $34,000 cash and $1,800 of painting supplies for personal use. If the accrual basis had been used, the following additional assets and liabilities would have been recorded:

	12/31/89	12/31/90
Accounts Receivable	$ 14,750	$ 18,960
Supplies	2,300	1,500
Accounts Payable	12,350	9,370

Required
Prepare the statement of changes in owner's equity for Alfred's Auto Body Shop on the accrual basis for the year 1990.

2. Alfred and his wife Althea would like you to prepare a statement of financial condition for them as of December 31, 1990. You have just completed their 1990 income tax return that shows a total tax liability for 1990 of $21,000. The following payments were made on their 1990 income tax liability:

Income Taxes Withheld, 1990	$ 3,000
Estimated Income Tax Payments	
April 15, 1990	3,500
June 15, 1990	3,500
September 15, 1990	3,500
January 13, 1991	3,500
Balance Due on Tax Return, April 15, 1991	4,000

Required
Prepare a schedule to determine the amount of income taxes payable that should be reported on their statement of financial condition as of December 31, 1990.

3. You determine the following information regarding the potential taxes that Alfred and Althea might pay in the future:

	Financial Statement Value	Tax Base
Assets	$ 625,000	$ 390,000
Liabilities	225,000	240,000

You also determine that $20,000 of current value will not be subject to tax and that their effective tax rate will be 28%.

Required
a. Prepare a schedule to determine the potential tax liability that will be reported on Alfred and Althea's statement of financial condition at December 31, 1990, labeling your answer with the description that would appear on the statement.
b. Explain where the potential liability is reported on the statement of financial condition.

PROBLEM 1-8
Bob and Vickie Stewart are applying for a bank loan to purchase their first home. Freedom Savings & Loan requires a statement of financial condition. After a discussion with the Stewarts, you determine they have the following assets and liabilities at June 30, 1991.

1. Cash in checking and savings accounts of $13,200.
2. Pension and profit-sharing plans.
  1) Bob has $32,100 in a pension and profit-sharing plan that is 40% vested. Bob has made contributions of $10,400 to the plan and his employer has contributed the balance.
  2) Vickie has $35,400 in a pension and profit-sharing plan; the fully vested amount is $10,000 and the remainder will not become vested for another 5 years. Vickie's employer has made all the contributions to the plan.
3. Automobiles.
  1) 1989 Honda purchased for $8,000. The current selling price is $5,000 and the current replacement cost is $9,500.
  2) 1991 Ford Pickup purchased for $9,200. The current selling price is $8,000 and the current replacement cost is $9,500.

4. Home furnishings were purchased over several years at a cost of $6,800. The current selling price is $1,800.

5. Other personal effects consist of jewelry, sterling, china, and cameras with a cost of $8,500. These items were recently appraised for insurance purposes at $11,400.

6. Liabilities.
   1) Contract for the purchase of the Ford pickup of $6,400.
   2) Master Charge account balance of $940 and $300 of utility bills are outstanding.
   3) The Stewarts' withholding is estimated to be adequate to cover their current income tax liability.

7. Gifts received that are not included in the above assets and whose basis is zero.
   1) Bob received a grand piano from his parents. The replacement cost of the piano, which is approximately equal to the market value, is $10,000.
   2) Vickie received a metal sculpture from her grandmother. The sculpture was recently appraised by a reputable art dealer at $4,500.

Required

Prepare a statement of financial condition for the Stewarts, showing both the current values and the tax bases, assuming the cost basis of their assets is equal to the their tax base and their effective tax rate is 28%. The losses on the automobiles and the furnishings are not subject to tax.

PROBLEM 1-9

Betty Block and her roommate Jim Corner want to purchase a motor home that is selling for $25,000 and to borrow $20,000 to finance the purchase. Square County Bank requires personal financial statements from borrowers before they will make loans in excess of $10,000. Betty and Jim provide you with the following information regarding their financial affairs as of April 1, 1992:

1. Cash in Betty's checking account $6,400.

2. Cash in Jim's checking account $4,400.

3. Jim has a pension and profit-sharing plan with assets totaling $105,000. Jim's employer pays all the payments. The plan is 25% vested after 5 years, 50% vested after 10 years, and fully vested after 20 years. Jim has been employed for 12 years by the company.

4. Betty's employer does not have a pension plan, but Betty has invested $12,000 in an IRA account that has earned $4,650. Betty has received the full tax benefit of her contributions; therefore, her tax base is zero.

5. Betty has a $50,000 face value whole life insurance policy with a cash surrender value of $16,000 on which she has borrowed $6,000. Betty has paid premiums of $5,000.

6. Jim owns a 1990 Buick that cost $13,400; he owes $6,000 on the contract. The current selling price of a comparable car is $9,700.

7. Betty owns a 1989 Pontiac that cost $11,100, which is paid for. The Blue Book price for a comparable car is $7,800.

8. Apartment furnishings costing $7,000 were jointly purchased by Betty and Jim. The insurance appraisal on the furnishings is $10,000. A used furniture dealer has offered them $2,500 for the furnishings.

9. Income taxes.
   1) Betty owes $1,200 on her 1991 income tax return. She estimates her 1992 income will be $36,000 and her 1992 tax will be $9,000. Betty has earned $8,000 to date this year and has had income tax withheld of $1,500. Her effective tax rate is 25%.
   2) Jim's tax return shows a refund due of $800, which is not subject to tax. Jim estimates his 1992 income will be $30,000 and his 1992 tax will be $6,000. Jim has earned $7,000 to date in 1992 and has had tax withheld of $1,200. Jim's effective tax rate is 20%.

Required

1. Would it be in accordance with *Statement of Position 82-1* to prepare a joint statement of financial condition for Betty Block and Jim Corner? If not, explain your reasons.
2. Assume that their costs equal their tax bases, except for the IRA account. Prepare the statement(s) of financial condition presenting both the current values and the tax bases to be presented to Square County Bank. If the current values of the automobiles and the household furnishings are less than their tax bases, the losses are not subject to tax.

PROBLEM 1-10

Brad and Barbara Cline have an apartment house and a number of rights to receive future sums of cash. They have asked you to assist them in preparing their statement of financial condition that they have completed except for the apartment house, the rights, and the computation of their estimated income tax liability. The Clines provide you with the following information regarding these items:

- Apartment House. The land and building were purchased 8 years ago for $169,000. The Clines' tax return shows that $150,000 was allocated to the building and $19,000 of the purchase price was allocated to the land. The tax return shows depreciation of $6,000 per annum and accumulated depreciation of $48,000. In addition, the tax return shows building improvements totaling $23,000 purchased at the beginning of the current year, and depreciation of $2,300 for the year. Exclusive of depreciation, the tax return shows rental income of $27,300. A recent tax appraisal at 80% of market value showed an assessed valuation of $160,000. A real estate agent has indicated that apartment houses typically sell for 10 times earnings. A comparable apartment house in the neighborhood was recently sold for $210,000.

- Rights to Receive Future Sums of Cash.
  1) Brad had the winning number in the state's lottery game, and today received the first of 20 annual installments of $120,000, which is after the withholding of $30,000 of federal income taxes. Brad spent $1 for the winning ticket.
  2) Barbara is receiving alimony in the amount of $500 per month and she is guaranteed an additional 11 payments.
  3) Barbara is the beneficiary of a $500,000 insurance policy on the life of her father. Barbara's father has a life expectancy of 15 years.
  4) Brad is the remainderman beneficiary of a trust established by his father. Upon the death of Brad's mother, Brad will receive the assets of trust, which at present total $450,000. Brad's mother has a life expectancy of 18 years.
  5) Barbara has purchased $100 worth of lottery tickets and estimates her chances of winning $100,000 are 1 in 100,000.

- Income Taxes. The Clines estimate their effective tax rate will be 33% for the current year. The only payments they have made are the $30,000 withheld from the lottery winnings. Their earnings to date in the current year totaled $8,000 from the apartment house, their only source of income prior to winning the lottery. The estimated current value of the Clines' other assets is $17,500 with a tax base of $10,000, which are all subject to tax. The estimated current amounts of their liabilities are equal to their tax base of $115,000.

Required

1. Determine all the different various current values that can be ascertained from the information presented for the apartment house. Which of the values is the preferable one to use?
2. Determine the estimated current value of the Clines' rights to receive future cash if the current market rate of interest is 10%. If you omitted any items, explain why you omitted them.

3. Determine the amount of the Clines' income taxes payable, and the amount of potential income taxes on the excess of the estimated current values of assets and the estimated current amounts of liabilities over their tax bases.

PROBLEM 1-11

Ben and Barbara Henry have asked you to prepare a statement of financial condition for them as of August 31, 1991, to be used for income tax and estate planning. After reviewing their tax returns and other financial information, and having several discussions with the Henrys, you determine the following is a complete list of all their assets and liabilities and sufficient information to determine the tax bases and estimated current values of the assets and liabilities:

1. Cash in checking and savings accounts is $17,320.
2. Marketable Securities.
   1) 250 shares of Pacific Utilities, originally purchased for $31 per share. The current market price is $28 per share.
   2) 1,000 shares of Sunshine Mixing Co., originally purchased at $4 per share. The stock has not been traded in three months. A call to a broker who makes a market in the stock indicated he would purchase the shares for $3.50 per share.
3. Closely Held Businesses.
   1) 500 shares of Ben's Brewery, inherited from Ben Henry Sr. The shares were valued at $387 per share when inherited, which is Ben's tax base. The current market value of the Brewery is estimated to be $825,000 for 1,000 total shares outstanding. The remaining 500 shares are owned by Ben's mother and sister.
   2) Barbara's Beanery is a coffee house owned and operated by Barbara who is famous for her giant size muffins. Barbara has a tax base of $22,600 in the Beanery. Barbara recently received an offer to purchase the Beanery for $55,000 if she would include her muffin recipes. Barbara declined the offer.
4. Retirement Assets.
   1) Ben, who is president of Ben's Brewery, has a pension and profit-sharing plan. He can receive the assets contributed totaling $86,900 if he leaves the employ of the Brewery. If he stays until age 60, he will receive a monthly retirement of $2,000 for life. Ben is 45 years of age, is tired of the beer business, and is contemplating resigning as the president of Ben's Brewery. Ben has not paid income taxes on the contributions to the pension plan and, therefore, his tax base in the pension plan is zero.
   2) Barbara has an IRA account in which she has deposited $10,000, and the account has earned $3,250 to date. Her tax base in the IRA account is zero.
5. Residences and Personal Effects.
   1) Home in Portland purchased 10 years ago for $60,000. A current real estate tax appraisal, which is at 75% of net market price, valued the home at $135,000. During the 10 years the Henrys have owned the home, they have spent $30,000 in remodeling and updating. The Henrys owe Security Bank $41,200 on the 12% mortgage.
   2) Vacation cabin purchased 3 years ago for $72,000. A friend of the Henrys' has offered them $100,000 for the cabin. The cabin next door, which is comparable, recently sold for $85,000 net of the selling costs. The Henrys owe $49,600 on the contract of purchase, which has a 6% interest rate and requires principal payments of $3,200 per year. The developer of the vacation resort where the cabin is located has offered to accept $44,000 in full settlement of the contract balance. The offer is good until December 31, 1991.
6. Speed boat purchased two years ago for $21,000. A recent insurance appraisal valued the boat at $15,000.

7. Automobiles.
   1) Ben drives a four-wheel Jeep with a cost of $14,000 and a current Blue Book value of $9,800.
   2) Barbara drives an Oldsmobile station wagon that cost $16,500. The Blue Book value is $11,000.
8. Household effects were purchased over a period of years for a cost of $33,400. A current appraisal established the cost to replace at $68,750. Except for one oil painting originally purchased for $2,100 and recently appraised at $5,000, the balance of the furnishings are ordinary and could be sold for 20% of their original cost.
9. Outstanding personal bills totaled $4,560 at August 31, 1991.
10. The estimate of the Henry's 1991 tax liability is $36,000 on taxable income of $90,000. The Henrys have earned $60,000 to date in the current year. Ben's withholding for the year totaled $19,000 and the Henrys have made no estimate payments. The Henrys' effective tax rate is estimated to be the same as their current rate of tax for 1991.

Required

Prepare a statement of financial condition for Ben and Barbara Henry as of August 31, 1991, assuming that any anticipated losses on the speed boat, the automobiles, and the household furnishings are not subject to tax and the market rate of interest is 10%.

PROBLEM 1-12

On December 31, 1992, David Jensen retired as a senior pilot for Delta Airlines. Donna retired two years ago from Boeing where she had been an engineer. The Jensens have asked you to help them prepare a statement of financial condition and to assist them in their tax and retirement planning. In preparation for retirement, the Jensens have sold their personal residence and plan to use their vacation home as their permanent residence. The tax bases of the assets and liabilities of the Jensens at December 31, 1992, are

	Tax Base
Cash in 6% Money Market Checking Accounts	$ 22,400
Six-month, 10% Time CDs. Maturity Date March 31, 1993	175,000
Investments in Stocks and Bonds	
$20,000 face value, 12% Seattle School District bonds, paying interest semiannually, on June 30 and December 31. Maturity date, June 30, 1993. The current market price is 96.	19,000
$50,000 face value, 10% Washington Water Power bonds, paying interest semiannually, on March 31 and September 30. Maturity date, March 31, 1994. The current market price is 101.	46,850
$40,000 face value, 9% City of Portland bonds, paying interest semiannually, on April 30 and October 31. Maturity date, April 30, 1994. The current market price is 99.	38,600
$250 shares of Safeway stores. Current market price 60. Annual dividend received $2.50 per share.	7,500
Stocks Purchased Through Employee Stock Option Plans	
1,000 shares of Delta Airlines. The current market price is 48. Annual dividend received $3.50 per share.	18,000
2,000 shares of Boeing. The current market price is 65. Annual dividend received $4.00 per share.	75,000
Pensions	
David is to receive a pension of $18,000 per year from Delta Airlines. The pension terms state that David or his heirs are guaranteed at least 10 years of payments.	—0—

	Tax Base
Donna is receiving a pension from Boeing. Her pension is $14,400 per year and will continue for her lifetime. Donna is 64 and has a life expectancy of 14 years.	
Vacation home. Estimated current value is $100,000	80,000
Automobiles. Blue Book value $19,000	36,500
Liabilities	22,400
The Jensens have personal debts of	2,008
The Jensens owe $19,000 of federal income taxes for the year just ended. Their estimated effective tax rate is 28%.	19,000

Required

Prepare a statement of financial condition for David and Donna Jensen as of December 31, 1991 showing both the estimated current values and the tax bases of assets and liabilities, assuming a market rate of interest of 10% and any losses on the disposal of the automobiles are not subject to tax.

SOLUTIONS TO REVIEW PROBLEMS

CONVERSION TO THE ACCRUAL BASIS OF ACCOUNTING

1.

BLOSSOM GARDEN STORE
Worksheet to Convert from the Tax Basis to the Accrual Basis of Accounting
September 30, 1990
Dr. (Cr.)

	Tax Basis	Adjustments Debits	Adjustments Credits	Accrual Basis
Cash	16,200			16,200
Inventory	21,300	27,650 (b)	21,300 (b)	27,650
Supplies		540 (c)		540
Prepaid Insurance		3,150 (d)		3,150
Land	18,000			18,000
Store Building	57,500			57,500
Accumulated Depreciation: Store Building	(22,500)		2,500 (e)	(25,000)
Equipment and Store Fixtures	22,400		6,500 (f)	15,900
Accumulated Depreciation: Equipment and Store Fixtures	(10,100)	6,000 (f)	1,590 (g)	(5,690)
Accounts Payable			7,240 (a)	(7,240)
Interest Payable			200 (i)	(200)
Notes Payable: Equipment	(4,000)			(4,000)
Mortgage Payable	(41,700)			(41,700)
Owner's Equity	(67,200)	{ 8,950 (a) } { 250 (i) }	{ 690 (c) } { 1,000 (d) }	(59,690)
Owner's Drawings	38,900	3,800 (h)		42,700
Sales Revenue	(94,250)			(94,250)

	Tax Basis	Adjustments Debits	Adjustments Credits	Accrual Basis
Cost of Goods Sold		32,565 (b)	⎰ 3,800 (h) ⎱	28,765
Purchases	40,625		⎱ 1,710 (a) ⎰	–0–
			38,915 (b)	
Supplies Expense	3,175	150 (c)		3,325
Salaries and Wages Expense	16,450			16,450
Insurance Expense	4,200		2,150 (d)	2,050
Depreciation Expense		⎰ 2,500 (e) ⎱		4,090
		⎱ 1,590 (g) ⎰		
Interest Expense	3,200		50 (i)	3,150
Gain on Sale of Equipment	(2,200)	500 (f)		(1,700)
Totals	–0–	87,645	87,645	–0–

Conversion and Adjusting Entries

(a) Owner's Equity 8,950
        Accounts Payable 7,240
        Purchases 1,710
    To record the ending accounts payable and adjust purchases for the beginning and ending accounts payable

(b) Inventory 27,650
    Cost of Goods Sold 32,565
        Inventory 21,300
        Purchases (1) 38,915
    To record cost of goods sold

    (1) ($40,625 − $1,710)

(c) Supplies Inventory 540
    Supplies Expense 150
        Owner's Equity 690
    To adjust supplies expense to the accrual basis and record the ending balance of supplies

(d) Prepaid Insurance (1) 3,150
        Owner's Equity 1,000
        Insurance Expense (2) 2,150
    To convert insurance expense to the accrual basis and record the ending balance of prepaid insurance

    $6,000 × 6/36 = $1,000
    $4,200 × 6/24 = 1,050
      Total $2,050

    (1) $4,200 − $1,050 = $3,150
    (2) $4,200 − $2,050 = $2,150

(e) Depreciation Expense 2,500
        Accumulated Depreciation: Building 2,500
    To record the depreciation expense on the building

    $57,500 − $7,500 = $50,000
    $50,000/20 years = $ 2,500

(f) Accumulated Depreciation: Equipment and Store Fixtures   6,000
     Gain on the Sale of Equipment   500
             Equipment and Store Fixtures   6,500
     To adjust the gain on the sale of equipment

     Cash Received $ 2,200
     Less Net Book Value of Tractor   500
     Gain on the Sale   1,700

(g) Depreciation Expense   1,590
             Accumulated Depreciation: Equipment and Store
                 Fixtures   1,590
     To record the depreciation on equipment and store fixtures

             $22,400 − $6,500 = $15,900
             $15,900 × 10% = $1,590

(h) Owner's Drawings   3,800
             Cost of Goods Sold   3,800
     To record the cost of inventory withdrawn by the owner

Note: This entry could have been made prior to making the entry for
     cost of goods sold. If previously recorded, the credit would be
     to Purchases.

(i) Owner's Equity   250
             Interest Payable   200
             Interest Expense   50
     To adjust interest expense to the accrual basis and record interest
     payable

     $5,000 × 10% × 6/12 = $ 250
     $4,000 × 10% × 6/12 =   200
     Total Expense   450
     Expense Recorded   500 (1)
     Overstatement $ 50

     (1) $5,000 × 10%)

2.

BLOSSOM GARDEN STORE
(A Sole Proprietorship)
Income Statement
Year Ended September 30, 1990

Sales Revenue		$ 94,250
Cost of Goods Sold		28,765
Gross Margin		65,485
Expenses		
Supplies	$ 3,325	
Salaries and Wages	16,450	
Insurance	2,050	
Depreciation	4,090	25,915
Operating Income		39,570
Other Revenue and (Expense)		
Interest Expense	(3,150)	
Gain on Sale of Equipment	1,700	1,450
Net Income		$ 38,120

BLOSSOM GARDEN STORE
(A Sole Proprietorship)
·Statement of Changes in Owner's Equity
Year Ended September 30, 1990

Owner's Equity, October 1, 1989		$ 59,690
Net Income		38,120
Drawings		
Cash	$ 38,900	
Inventory	3,800	(42,700)
Owner's Equity, September 30, 1990		$ 55,110

BLOSSOM GARDEN STORE
(A Sole Proprietorship)
Balance Sheet
September 30, 1990

Assets

Current Assets			
Cash			$ 16,200
Inventory			27,650
Supplies			540
Prepaid Insurance			3,150
Total Current Assets			47,540
Property, Plant, and Equipment			
Land		$ 18,000	
Store Building	$ 57,500		
Less: Accumulated Depreciation	25,000	32,500	
Equipment and Store Fixtures	15,900		
Less: Accumulated Depreciation	5,690	10,210	60,710
Total Assets			$ 108,250

Liabilities and Owner's Equity

Current Liabilities			
Accounts Payable			$ 7,240
Interest Payable			200
Total Current Liabilities			7,440
Long-Term Debt			
Notes Payable: Equipment		$ 4,000	
Mortgage Payable		41,700	45,700
Total Liabilities			53,140
Owner's Equity: June Blossom			55,110
Total Liabilities and Owner's Equity			$ 108,250

PERSONAL FINANCIAL STATEMENTS

1.

JUNE, APRIL, AND MAY BLOSSOM
Statement of Financial Condition
September 30, 1990

	Estimated Current Value	Tax Base
Assets		
Cash		
Money Market Checking Account	$ 13,265	$ 13,265
Savings Accounts	43,650	43,650
Investments		
IRA Account	11,400 (1)	–0–
Investment in Blossom Garden Store	215,600 (2)	55,110
Trust Established by Will of Mr. Blossom		
Income Beneficiary Interests	296,885 (3)	–0–
Remainderman Interest	143,750 (4)	–0–
Cash Surrender Value of Life Insurance $41,100 Less		
Loan of $8,500	32,600	31,475
Apartment House	300,000 (5)	102,800
Residence	146,300 (6)	146,300
Automobiles		
BMW	18,750 (7)	4,200
Ford Mustang	4,900	4,900
Personal Effects	4,340 (8)	21,700
Total Assets	$1,231,440	$ 423,400

Liabilities and Net Worth		
Liabilities		
Personal Debts	$ 5,950 (9)	$ 5,950
Income Taxes Payable	7,700 (10)	7,700
10% Mortgage Payable: Apartment House	81,250	81,250
11% Mortgage Payable: Home	51,400	51,400
Total Liabilities	146,300	146,300
Estimated Income Taxes on the Difference Between the Estimated Current Values of Assets and the Estimated Current Amounts of Liabilities and Their Tax Bases	206,350 (11)	–0–
Net Worth	878,790	277,100
Total Liabilities and Net Worth	$1,231,440	$ 423,400

Computations:

(1) $11,400 market value
(2) ($38,120 × 5) + $25,000 = $215,600
(3) [$50,000 × 5.9377 (present value of an annuity for 11 years at 12%)] = $296,885

(4) $500,000 × .2875 (present value of a $ in 11 years)]

(5) $270,000 ÷ .90 = $300,000. *SOP 82-1* requires that debt on major investments, other than closely held businesses, be reported as a liability and not netted against the asset.

(6) $132,500 + $3,800 (shrubbery) + $10,000 = $146,300. This assumes that the decks, patios, and spa have added to the selling price.

(7) The Blue Book price of an automobile is considered the best estimate of a car's value, unless the car is customized or very unique.

(8) $21,700 × 20% = $4,340

(9) $4,200 + $1,750 = $5,950

(10) $3,100 + \left[\left(\dfrac{\$60,000}{\$80,000} \times \$24,000 \right) - \$13,400 \right] = \$7,700$

(11) Estimated Income Taxes

Estimated Current Value of Assets	$ 1,231,440
Less: Tax Basis of Assets	423,400
Excess of Current Values Over Tax Bases	808,040
Add: Losses Not Allowable	17,360
Excess of Current Values Over Tax Bases Subject to Tax	825,400
Effective Tax Rate	25.0%
Total Estimated Income Taxes	$ 206,350

2. Note to Financial Statements: Blossom Garden Store

June Blossom operates Blossom Garden Store as a sole proprietorship. Ms. Blossom is a certified nurserywoman and the store specializes in landscape designs and shrubbery. The following summarized financial information is prepared on the accrual basis of accounting according to generally accepted accounting principles as of September 30, 1990.

Current Assets	$ 47,540
Property, Plant, and Equipment	60,710
Total Assets	$ 108,250
Current Liabilities	$ 7,440
Long-Term Debt	45,700
Total Liabilities	53,140
Owner's Equity: June Blossom	55,110
Total Liabilities and Owner's Equity	$ 108,250

Net sales revenue for the year ended September 30, 1990, totaled $94,250 and net income was $38,120.

2

PARTNERSHIP FORMATION
AND NET INCOME ALLOCATION

C hapter 2 is the first of three chapters dealing with the accounting and reporting for partnerships. This chapter explains the formation and net income allocation in partnerships, Chapter 3 deals with changes in the partners, and Chapter 4 covers the liquidation and dissolution of partnerships. The topics of this chapter include

- The characteristics of partnerships
- The relationships of the partners
- The elements of partnership agreements
- The equity theories that apply to partnerships
- The three methods of recording the formation of a partnership: the net investment method, the bonus method, and the goodwill method by the contribution of net assets and the contribution of an existing business entity
- The operations of a partnership including partners' equity accounts, the differences between the determination of corporate income and partnership income, and the allocation of net income to the various partners
- The financial statements of partnerships
- Other business entities that are similar to partnerships

CHARACTERISTICS OF PARTNERSHIPS

A partnership is a group of two or more people who have voluntarily agreed to operate a business entity as co-owners for a profit. Professionals, such as accountants, often use the partnership form of business. The members of a partnership can establish each partner's share

65

of the initial investment and the division of net income to suit themselves, in contrast to a corporation, which has a formal capital structure and methods of distributing earnings to stockholders prescribed by law. In 48 states, the Uniform Partnership Act, with some modifications, governs those partnerships that do not have formal partnership agreements or whose agreement fails to cover a specific issue.

Legally a partnership is dissolved whenever a change in the partners occurs. If a new partner joins the partnership or an existing partner withdraws or dies, the legal entity ceases to exist. Thus, a partnership has a limited life in contrast to a corporation, which has an unlimited life. Partners can override the limited life of the partnership by specifying in their partnership agreement that the business entity is to continue without interruption when a change in the partners occurs. Many partnerships of professionals, including accountants, have been in operation for a number of years, although the partners of the entity have changed many times.

RELATIONSHIP OF THE PARTNERS

Partners are co-owners of the assets, liabilities, and net income of the partnership. The assets and liabilities that partners contribute to the partnership, as well as the assets acquired, and the liabilities incurred during the operation of the partnership, are the joint property of all the partners. The earnings of the partnership are also jointly owned. This co-ownership is called **joint tenancy** or **tenancy in partnership.**

A partner can act for the partnership, committing the group to transactions and obligations—even transactions that not all partners may agree are sound. Thus, the partners are the **mutual agents** of each other. The partnership is bound to honor the transactions and obligations that a partner has made on behalf of the partnership, unless they are outside the scope of the business purpose as specified in the partnership agreement or unless they are illegal.

The partners are jointly and individually liable for the debts of the partnership. Partners have **unlimited liability** because the creditors of the partnership can demand payment from the partners' personal assets when the partnership is unable to pay its debts. When forming a partnership, it is wise to determine if your partners are prudent in their business dealings and if they have sufficient personal assets to pay their share of the liabilities should a partnership become bankrupt.

PARTNERSHIP AGREEMENTS

Partnership agreements can be either verbal or written. A written partnership agreement is preferable. If the partnership does not have an agreement or the agreement does not cover a specific area, the Uniform Partnership Act would prevail in those states where it has been enacted. The two states that have not adopted the Uniform Partnership Act have similar partnership acts. The Uniform Partnership Act is in Appendix 2.A following this chapter.

The basic points to be covered in a partnership agreement are

- The basis to be assigned to the net assets when the partnership is formed
- The business activities the partnership will engage in
- The duties and responsibilities of the partners
- The accounting methods to be used in the determination of net income
- The formula to be used in the allocation of profits and losses
- The rules for admission of new partners and withdrawal of existing partners
- The manner of dissolution

The most important areas that should be in a partnership agreement are changes in partners and the conditions of dissolution. Because a partnership is made up of people who usually are friends when they begin a partnership, but who after being in business for a while may not be, the terms of buying one another out or dissolution are critical. Disagreements can arise between partners because partners are co-owners of net assets and net income and can all bind the partnership to agreements and transactions. The most common problems to surface are who is the boss and who is right. The partners may begin a partnership in full agreement as to the division of responsibilities between them, the amount of time and effort each will contribute, and the division of net income. As time passes and the activities of the business evolve, and the personal lives of the partners change, they may no longer agree.

For example, three partners begin a partnership agreeing to put equal time and effort into the partnership and share profits equally. As time passes one of the partners becomes deeply involved in a hobby and is no longer willing to spend the amount of time the other two are giving to the business, but the partner is still receiving one-third of the income. If the partnership agreement has not provided for a method of resolving the inequity that has arisen, friction exists between the partners. If the partnership agreement provides for a means of mediating the problem or of altering the agreement, the problem can be solved without dissolution of the entity. A good partnership agreement covers most of the potential problems that can arise when a group of people join together for their common benefit with joint ownership of net assets and net income. In addition, it provides a mechanism for altering the provisions of the partnership agreement as the business evolves and changes through time.

THE EQUITY THEORIES THAT APPLY TO PARTNERSHIPS

A partnership has some of the attributes that would result if the proprietary theory of equity, assets − liabilities = proprietors' equity, were ascribed to the entity. A partnership also has some of the attributes of the entity theory of equity, assets = liabilities + proprietors' equity. When the partnership form of business first began during the era of trading voyages to the Far East, an investor or benefactor would enter into an agreement to finance a voyage for a share of the assets brought back at the end of the journey. These short-term partnerships are more like the joint ventures formed today with their limited life. The proprietary theory was the only one applicable as profits were the difference between the net initial investment and the value of the net assets at the end of the voyage. As business evolved over time and the corporate form of business came into being, the character and complexity of the partnership form of business changed. Modern partnerships have some of the characteristics indicative of the entity theory as well as the proprietary theory.

The proprietary theory is evident in the following characteristics of a partnership:

- Distributions of partnership assets to partners are allocations of income, regardless of the descriptive titles given to the components in the computation of a partner's share of the profit or loss.
- The equity accounts of a partnership do not make a distinction between the sources of equity, investment and earnings.
- The partnership technically ceases to exist when a change in the partners occurs.
- A partner is liable for the debts incurred by the partnership that the partnership cannot pay.
- Partners can revalue the assets when a change in the partners occurs, which suggests a new entity has been formed.
- The partnership is not a taxable entity, but a **tax pass-through entity,** in which the income of the partnership is taxed to the individual partners and not to the partnership.

The following characteristics would suggest that the entity theory of equity also applies to partnerships:

- The assets the partners contributed to the partnership and the assets acquired by the partnership are the property of the partnership.
- The liabilities contributed to the partnership by the partners become the liabilities of the partnership.
- The partnership can enter into contracts in the name of the partnership.
- The partners can override the limited life of the partnership by specifying an ongoing life in the partnership agreement.

FORMATION OF A PARTNERSHIP

A partnership is formed when two or more people contribute assets and/or liabilities to start a new business.[1] For financial accounting purposes, the assets are recorded at their **fair market value** when contributed, and any liabilities assumed by the partnership are also recorded at their **fair market value.** The partnership is considered to be a separate and distinct entity from the partners. The transfer of net assets to the partnership is treated as an arm's-length transaction; thus, the amounts assigned to the assets and liabilities are their fair market values.

Three alternative ways exist to record the contribution of net assets to a partnership by the partners. The simplest way is the **net investment method.** In the net investment method, each partner's capital account is credited with the fair market value of the net assets contributed. The second way is called the **bonus method.** In the bonus method, the partners have entered into an agreement to credit a specific amount to one of the partner's capital accounts, which is different from the fair market value of the net assets contributed. Thus, one partner is receiving credit for more capital than the amount of net assets contributed, while the other

---

[1] An entity other than a natural person can be a partner in a partnership. For instance, it could be another partnership or a corporation.

partner is receiving less credit. The partner receiving less credit is said to be giving a bonus to the partner who receives more capital.

The third way is called the **goodwill method.** In the goodwill method the partners agree to an amount of goodwill, an unidentified intangible asset, that they believe a partner is contributing to the firm in excess of the fair market value of the net assets being contributed. The goodwill is recorded as an asset and the increase in net assets is effectively credited to the capital account of the partner who has brought the intangible asset to the partnership. The above discussion is based on just two partners forming a partnership, but several partners can be involved with bonuses or goodwill to more than one partner.

ILLUSTRATIVE PROBLEM 2.1: FORMATION OF A PARTNERSHIP

On January 1, 1990, K and P formed a partnership and agreed to divide profits and losses equally. The following facts relate to the net assets contributed by K and P:

	Market Value January 1, 1990
K's Contribution	
Cash	$ 30,000
Store Fixtures	10,000
K's Net Investment	$ 40,000
P's Contribution	
Land	$ 15,000
Store Bulding	60,000
Mortgage Payable	(25,000)
P's Net Investment	$ 50,000

Case 1: Net Investment Method.   The journal entry to record the formation of the partnership, using the fair market values of the net assets is

Cash	30,000	
Land	15,000	
Building	60,000	
Store Fixtures	10,000	
Mortgage Payable		25,000
Capital, Partner K		40,000
Capital, Partner P		50,000

The partners profit- and loss-sharing ratio does not affect the amounts recorded in the capital accounts.

Case 2: Bonus Method.   The partners could have agreed to begin the partnership with equal capital accounts. Effectively P is giving a bonus of $5,000 to K for agreeing to enter the partnership. The journal entry under this agreement is

Cash	30,000	
Land	15,000	
Building	60,000	
Store Fixtures	10,000	
Mortgage Payable		25,000
Capital, Partner K		45,000
Capital, Partner P		45,000

Case 3: Goodwill Method.   Another approach to recording this same transaction is to assume that the partnership is worth $100,000 (twice P's net investment) and to treat the difference of $10,000 between K's net investment and P's net investment as goodwill. This treatment assumes that K is contributing an intangible asset to the business, such as previous business reputation or special skills, that is not specifically identifiable. The difference between the identifiable net assets contributed by the partners is used to assign a dollar value to the goodwill brought to the partnership by K. If the partners elected to record goodwill, the entry to record the formation of the partnership is

Cash	30,000	
Land	15,000	
Building	60,000	
Store Fixtures	10,000	
Goodwill	10,000	
Mortgage Payable		25,000
Capital, Partner K		50,000
Capital, Partner P		50,000

COMPARISON OF THE BONUS AND GOODWILL METHODS

The amortization of the goodwill will eventually affect the capital balances of the partners. If partners K and P share profits and losses equally, then after the amortization of the goodwill, each will have $45,000 [$50,000 − (1/2 × $10,000)] of capital. The results are the same as if the partners had recorded their initial investment by the bonus method. Any other profit and loss ratio will yield different results from the bonus method. The partners could have assigned a value to the goodwill that partner K is bringing to the business rather than using the difference between their capital accounts. If they had decided on some other value, then after amortization of goodwill, their capital accounts would not be the same as in the bonus method (unless the combination of the amount of goodwill and the profit- and loss-sharing ratio just happened to create the same results). When the goodwill method is used, the amortization will not result in capital balances that are equal to the fair market value of the net assets contributed.

The justification given for using the goodwill method is that a new business is being formed. The definition of goodwill, the amount by which the price paid for a business entity exceeds the fair market value of net assets acquired, indicates that goodwill arises only when an entire business is being purchased. When partners each contribute some assets, but not an existing business, to form a partnership, the recording of goodwill does not agree with this definition and is questionable.

FORMING A PARTNERSHIP FROM SOLE PROPRIETORSHIPS

Illustrative Problem 2.1 is based on forming a partnership to which each partner contributes net assets, but not a complete business entity. Sometimes partnerships are the result of a sole proprietor inviting another person to join the business and form a partnership. The partnership does not result from each partner contributing net assets, but from one or more of the partners contributing an existing business entity. This often happens when an accountant, practicing alone, joins with another sole practitioner to form a partnership.

ILLUSTRATIVE PROBLEM 2.2: FORMATION OF A PARTNERSHIP FROM SOLE PROPRIETORSHIPS

On October 1, 1990, two certified public accountants, L and M, decide to combine their practices and form a partnership. The partnership is to assume all the liabilities of the sole proprietorships. The following are the fair market values of the assets and liabilities of each of their individual accounting firms that will become the assets and liabilities of the partnership, L & M, CPAs:

	L, CPA	M, CPA	Total
Assets			
Cash	$ 5,000	$ 7,000	$ 12,000
Accounts Receivable	15,000	12,000	27,000
Work In Process	14,000	17,000	31,000
Office Furniture	5,000	8,000	13,000
Computer System	9,000		9,000
Total Assets	48,000	44,000	92,000
Liabilities			
Accounts Payable	3,000	4,000	7,000
Loan Payable: Computer	9,000		9,000
Total Liabilities	12,000	4,000	16,000
Net Investment	$ 36,000	$ 40,000	$ 76,000

Case 1: Net Investment Method.   Each partner's capital account is credited with the net investment contributed to the new partnership.

Cash	12,000	
Accounts Receivable	27,000	
Work In Process	31,000	
Office Furniture	13,000	
Computer System	9,000	
Accounts Payable		7,000
Loan Payable: Computer		9,000
Capital, Partner L		36,000
Capital, Partner M		40,000

Case 2: Bonus Method.   L and M agree to begin the partnership with equal capital balances. Each partner's capital account is credited with $38,000 as M is effectively giving a bonus of $2,000 to L for forming the partnership.

Cash	12,000	
Accounts Receivable	27,000	
Work In Process	31,000	
Office Furniture	13,000	
Computer System	9,000	
Accounts Payable		7,000
Loan Payable: Computer		9,000
Capital, Partner L		38,000
Capital, Partner M		38,000

Case 3: Goodwill Method.   L is bringing several new clients to the partnership and M has agreed that L's capital account should be $50,000 to reflect the value of those new clients. The journal entry to record the formation of the partnership, L & M CPAs, is

Cash	12,000	
Accounts Receivable	27,000	
Work In Process	31,000	
Office Furniture	13,000	
Computer System	9,000	
Goodwill from Clientele Credit	14,000	
Accounts Payable		7,000
Loan Payable: Computer		9,000
Capital, Partner L		50,000
Capital, Partner M		40,000

In Illustrative Problem 2.2, the partners have arrived at a value for the intangible asset, goodwill from clientele credit, that L has contributed to the new partnership. If Partners L and M agree to share profits and losses equally, the amortization of the $14,000 of goodwill will result in L's contribution being $43,000 [$50,000 − (1/2 × $14,000)] and M's contribution being $33,000. M has effectively paid L $7,000 ($40,000 − $33,000) for the revenue from the clients brought to the partnership by Partner M. If M's share of the profit and loss is more than 50%, M would pay more than $7,000 for the new clients L contributed to the partnership.

In Illustrative Problem 2.1, the recording of goodwill did not agree with the definition of goodwill—the excess of the price paid for a business over the fair market value of net assets acquired. In Illustrative Problem 2.2, where two existing business entities are joined together to form a single business entity, goodwill from clientele credit agrees with the accounting definition of goodwill. The new partnership is combining two existing business entities and forming a new entity. The goodwill does reflect the potential business that L has contributed to the partnership, which was not recorded in the books of L's sole proprietorship. When at least one of the partners is contributing an existing business to a partnership, the recording of goodwill makes sense, given the accounting definition of goodwill and the criteria for recording goodwill.

OPERATIONS OF A PARTNERSHIP

Generally accepted accounting principles apply to all forms of business entities including partnerships. Therefore, the recording of transactions is the same as in corporate accounting, except for transactions with the partners. If a partner borrows money from the partnership or lends money to the partnership under normal lending and borrowing terms (interest rate, manner of repayment, and time to maturity), the loans are recorded either as a loan receivable from a partner or a loan payable to a partner. The loans are recorded in separate ledger accounts in order to distinguish them from normal trade transactions. If the loans do not contain normal lending terms, they are recorded as permanent withdrawals of assets or contributions of assets.

PARTNER'S EQUITY ACCOUNTS

A partnership's general ledger typically contains two partner's equity accounts for each partner: a capital account and a drawing account. The drawing account is debited for withdrawals of assets (cash, other assets, or the payment of personal liabilities) that are considered normal. The sum of the drawing accounts of all the partners is comparable to the Dividends Declared account of a corporation. Each partner's drawing account is usually closed to the partner's capital account at the end of the year. The capital account is credited with the fair market value of the net assets contributed to start the partnership, any additional contributions of assets, and the partner's share of net income. The partner's capital account is reduced by the partner's share of net losses, the closing of the drawing account, and any excess withdrawals. An alternative approach is to close the Income Summary account to the partner's drawing accounts and then close the drawing accounts to the capital accounts. This approach causes the drawing accounts to reflect the events for the period similar to the ones reflected in the Retained Earnings account of a corporation. The examples and text material are based on closing of Income Summary to the partners' capital accounts.

EXCESS DRAWINGS

A partnership agreement may limit the amount of drawings of the partners to a specific amount per month, quarter, or year in order to ensure that a partner does not withdraw more from the partnership than the partner's share of net income and to discourage the depletion of the assets of the partnership. If the partnership agreement contains such a provision, drawings that exceed the limit are classified as **excessive** and are debited directly to the partner's capital account. Some partnership agreements may require that all the partners must consent to excess drawings, particularly when capital is critical to the business. Excess drawings are considered a reduction of the capital investment of the partner and not a withdrawal of net income. Excess drawings are also important when capital investment enters into the determination of a partner's share of net income or loss. The total of all the partner's capital accounts, after closing, is comparable to the sum of Common Stock, Additional Paid-in Capital, and Retained Earnings of a corporation.

DIFFERENCES BETWEEN THE DETERMINATION OF CORPORATE INCOME AND PARTNERSHIP INCOME

A partnership's net income differs from the net income of a corporation in several respects. A partnership is not subject to income tax, but functions as a **tax pass-through entity** with the various categories of income and losses for tax purposes retaining their character. For example, ordinary income to the partnership would be ordinary income to the partners, while a capital gain to the partnership would be a capital gain to the partners for tax purposes. A partnership files an income tax return that is informational in nature, which describes the various types of taxable income and the amount of each type of taxable income that is allocated to each partner. The partners report their proportionate shares of all the various types of taxable income and losses reported on the partnership tax return on their individual tax returns.

Partners are **not considered employees** of the partnership, but are viewed as owners. Any payments of cash to partners, regardless of the names given to the payments ("salaries," "bonuses," or "interest on capital investment"), are withdrawals of partnership assets and are treated as drawings and **not** as expenses. These withdrawals are debited to the partners' drawing accounts when paid. The only payments to partners that are considered expenses and not drawings are the payments of interest on legitimate loans made by a partner to a partnership. A partner may also withdraw assets that are not designated as "salaries," "bonuses," or "interest on capital investment" and these are also debited to the drawing account unless specified as excessive by the partnership agreement.

The partners use the terms "salaries," "bonuses," and "interest on capital investment" to designate the factors that are used in the allocation of net income (profit and loss). These factors are not included as expenses in the determination of partnership net income.

ALLOCATION OF NET INCOME

Partners can agree to share net income (profits and losses) in any manner that they believe is fair and reasonable. The Uniform Partnership Act states that in the absence of an agreement the partners are to share profits and losses equally.[2] Partners contribute both capital and time and effort to a partnership and expect to be compensated for both their investment and their labor. Therefore, a portion of the profit or loss (net income) allocated to each partner may be interest on some measure of capital investment or may be designated as salaries or bonuses. When capital is the critical factor, such as in a partnership investing in real estate, using a measure of capital investment is appropriate. The simplest case is the use of a ratio that reflects both the capital and labor of the partners.

Partnership agreements can have a single basis for distribution of profits and losses, for example, a ratio; or the partners may agree to a combination of several allocation factors. Allocations are computed in the order that they appear in the partnership agreement when a combination of factors is to be used to determine the distribution of profits and losses. A partnership may have one set of factors for the allocation of net income and another set of factors for net loss.

---

[2]Uniform Partnership Act, Section 18.

Some of the common ways that partners could agree to share profits and losses (net income) are

1. In a specific ratio
2. In the ratio of a measure of their capital investment
3. A salary allocation, and the balance in a specific ratio
4. A salary allocation, a bonus allocation, and the balance in a specific ratio
5. Interest on a measure of their capital investment, a salary allocation, a bonus allocation, and the balance in a specific ratio

ILLUSTRATIVE PROBLEM 2.3: ALLOCATION OF NET INCOME

Case 1: Allocation of Profit Using a Ratio.   The partnership of K and P earned net income of $63,000 for the year 1990. The partners have agreed to share profits and losses in the ratio of 6:4, respectively. The journal entry for the allocation of the partnership profit of $63,000 is

Income Summary	63,000	
Capital, Partner K (1)		37,800
Capital, Partner P (2)		25,200

(1) 60% × $63,000 = $37,800
(2) 40% × $63,000 = $25,200

Case 2: Allocation of Profit Using Capital Ratios.   The partners could agree to share profits and losses in the ratio of their beginning capital balances, their ending capital balances, or a weighted average of their capital balances. The capital accounts of Partners K and P for 1990 are

Capital, Partner K				*Capital, Partner P*		
8/1/90	16,500	1/1/90	40,000		1/1/90	50,000
		4/1/90	12,500		4/1/90	7,000
	16,500		52,500		8/1/90	3,000
		12/31/90	36,000		10/1/90	4,000
					12/31/90	64,000

Note: The debit of $16,500 in the capital account of the Partner K indicates the partnership agreement of K and P had set a limit on the amount of assets that could be withdrawn in any month. These drawings were considered excessive withdrawals of assets according to their agreement and, therefore, were debited to Partner K's capital account rather than to Partner K's drawing account.

Case 2a: Ratio of Beginning Capital balances.   If the partners have agreed to allocate profit and loss on the basis of their beginning capital balances, the allocation of the partnership profit of $63,000 is

Partner K	($40,000/$90,000) × $63,000 =	$28,000
Partner P	($50,000/$90,000) × $63,000 =	$35,000
Total		$63,000

Case 2b: Ratio of Ending Capital Balances.   If the partners have agreed to allocate profit and loss on the basis of their ending capital balances, the allocation of $63,000 of profit is

Partner K	($36,000/$100,000) × $63,000 =	$22,680
Partner P	($64,000/$100,000) × $63,000 =	40,320
Total		$63,000

Case 2c: Ratio of Weighted Average Capital Balances.   The computation of the weighted average multiplies each successive balance in the capital account by the fractional portion of the year the balance is invested. The weighted averages of the capital investments of Partners K and P are

Partner K	$40,000 ×	3/12 =	$10,000		Partner P	$50,000 ×	3/12 =	$12,500
	$52,500 ×	4/12 =	17,500			$57,000 ×	4/12 =	19,000
	$36,000 ×	5/12 =	15,000			$60,000 ×	2/12 =	10,000
						$64,000 ×	3/12 =	16,000
		12/12	$42,500				12/12	$57,500

An alternative way to compute the weighted average is to multiply each balance by the number of months and then divide the total by 12. If the investments do not divide readily by 12, the following method is easier to use. These examples have used months as an illustration, but in actual practice the weighted average may be computed using weeks or days. The weighted averages of the net investments of K and P are

Partner K	$40,000 ×	3 =	$120,000		Partner P	$50,000 ×	3 =	$150,000
	$52,500 ×	4 =	210,000			$57,000 ×	4 =	228,000
	$36,000 ×	5 =	180,000			$60,000 ×	2 =	120,000
						$64,000 ×	3	192,000
		12	$510,000				12	$690,000
	$510,000 ÷ 12 =		$ 42,500			$690,000 ÷ 12 =		$ 57,500

The allocation of the partnership profit of $63,000 is

Partner K	($42,500/$100,000) × $63,000 =	$26,775
Partner P	($57,500/$100,000) × $63,000 =	36,225
Total		$63,000

Case 3: Allocation of Profit Using Salaries and a Ratio.   If the partnership agreement of K and P specifies that K is to receive a salary of $13,000 and P is to receive a salary of

$17,000, with the remainder of the profit or loss in the ratio of 6:4 respectively, the allocation of the partnership profit of $63,000 is

K AND P PARTNERSHIP
Profit Allocation Schedule
Year Ended December 31, 1990

Allocation Factor	Partner K	Partner P	Total
Salaries	$ 13,000	$ 17,000	$ 30,000
Remainder 6:4	19,800 (1)	13,200 (2)	33,000
Total	$ 32,800	$ 30,200	$ 63,000

(1) $33,000 × .6 = $19,800
(2) $33,000 × .4 = $13,200

Case 4: Allocation of Profit Using Salaries, Bonus, and a Ratio. The partnership agreement could specify that in addition to the salaries in Case 3 above, P is to receive a bonus equal to 10% of the net income after the salaries and bonus. The bonus computation is

$$Bonus = .10[Net\ Income - Salaries - Bonus]$$
$$Bonus = .10[\$63,000 - \$30,000 - Bonus]$$
$$Bonus = .10[\$33,000 - Bonus]$$
$$Bonus = \$3,300 - .10(Bonus)$$
$$1.10\ Bonus = \$3,300$$
$$Bonus = \$3,000$$

The allocation of the partnership profit of $63,000 is

K AND P PARTNERSHIP
Profit Allocation Schedule
Year Ended December 31, 1990

Allocation Factor	Partner K	Partner P	Total
Salaries	$ 13,000	$ 17,000	$ 30,000
Bonus		3,000	3,000
	$ 13,000	$ 20,000	$ 33,000
Remainder 6:4	18,000 (1)	12,000 (2)	30,000
Total	$ 31,000	$ 32,000	$ 63,000

(1) $30,000 × .6 = $18,000
(2) $30,000 × .4 = $12,000

Case 5: Allocation of Profit Using Interest, Salaries, Bonus, and a Ratio. The partnership agreement of K and P specified the following factors for the allocation of profits and losses:

1. Interest of 10% on their average capital balances
2. Salaries of $13,000 and $17,000, respectively

3. A bonus to P equal to 10% of the partnership's net income reduced by the allocation factors for salaries and bonus

4. The remainder in the ratio of 6:4, respectively

Case 5a: Income Sufficient to Cover Allocation Factors.   If the net income of the partnership is $63,000, the allocation of profit is

K AND P PARTNERSHIP
Profit Allocation Schedule
Year Ended December 31, 1990

Allocation Factor	Partner K	Partner P	Total
Interest on Average Capital	$ 4,250 (1)	$ 5,750 (2)	$ 10,000
Salaries	13,000	17,000	30,000
Bonus		3,000	3,000
	$ 17,250	$ 25,750	$ 43,000
Remainder 6:4	12,000 (3)	8,000 (4)	20,000
Total	$ 29,250	$ 33,750	$ 63,000

(1) $42,500 × .1 = $ 4,250
(2) $57,500 × .1 = $ 5,750
(3) $20,000 × .6 = $12,000
(4) $20,000 × .4 = $ 8,000

Case 5b: Income Not Sufficient to Cover Allocation Factors.   If the allocation factors, exclusive of the remainder, total more than the net income, the remainder to be allocated is negative rather than positive. If the net income of the partnership of K and P is only $36,600, the allocation of profit is

K AND P PARTNERSHIP
Profit Allocation Schedule
Year Ended December 31, 1990

Allocation Factor	Partner K	Partner P	Total
Interest on Average Capital	$ 4,250	$ 5,750	$ 10,000
Salaries	13,000	17,000	30,000
Bonus		600 (1)	600
	$ 17,250	$ 23,350	$ 40,600
Remainder 6:4	(2,400) (2)	(1,600) (3)	(4,000)
Total	$ 14,850	$ 21,750	$ 36,600

(1) Bonus = .10[$36,600 − $30,000 − B]
     Bonus = $660 − .10B
     Bonus = $600
(2) $4,000 × .6 = $(2,400)
(3) $4,000 × .4 = $(1,600)

OTHER ALTERNATIVES FOR NET INCOME ALLOCATION

A partnership agreement could require that net losses be distributed differently from net profits. If the partnership agreement of K and P in Illustrative Problem 2.3, Case 5b specified that if the partnership did not have sufficient income to cover interest, salaries, and bonus, the negative remainder is to be allocated equally rather than in the ratio of 6:4; the allocation of the partnership net profit of $36,600 is

K AND P PARTNERSHIP
Profit Allocation Schedule
Year Ended December 31, 1990

Allocation Factor	Partner K	Partner P	Total
Interest on Average Capital	$ 4,250	$ 5,750	$ 10,000
Salaries	13,000	17,000	30,000
Bonus		600	600
	$ 17,250	$ 23,350	$ 40,600
Remainder Equally	(2,000)	(2,000)	(4,000)
Total	$ 15,250	$ 21,350	$ 36,600

A partnership agreement could specify that the allocation of profit be only **to the extent possible** rather than **fully** as in Illustrative Problem 2.3. In this case, net income is allocated by each factor in the order listed in the partnership agreement until the net income is exhausted, and then the allocation ceases. If the income is not sufficient to cover a profit allocation factor, each partner is assigned a proportionate share of the factor. Assume the partnership agreement of K and P is as presented in Case 5 of Illustrative Problem 2.3, except that the agreement stated that net income is to be allocated only to the extent possible, and the net income of the partnership of K and P is $36,600. The profit allocation becomes

K AND P PARTNERSHIP
Profit Allocation Schedule
Year Ended December 31, 1990

Allocation Factor	Partner K	Partner P	Total
Interest on Average Capital	$ 4,250	$ 5,750	$ 10,000
Salaries	11,527 (1)	15,073 (2)	26,600
Total	$ 15,777	$ 20,823	$ 36,600

(1) ($13,000/$30,000) × $26,600 = $11,527
(2) ($17,000/$30,000) × $26,600 = $15,073

The previous examples are just a few of the ways that partners can agree to share profits and losses. An unlimited number of alternatives exist that partners can employ for the distribution of partnership profits and losses. When computing the allocations of partnership profits and losses, we should read the partnership agreement and follow the allocation factors that the partners have devised in the order prescribed using either the fully or to the extent possible methods.

FINANCIAL STATEMENTS OF PARTNERSHIPS

Generally accepted accounting principles apply to partnerships as well as to corporations. Therefore, a partnership's financial statements are similar to those of a corporation, with a few exceptions. The income statement of a partnership is comparable to the income statement of a corporation, except that profit allocation factors of salaries, bonuses, and interest on capital investments are not included in the determination of net income. In addition, no income tax expense is reported on the partnership's income statement.

A partnership's financial statements usually include a schedule of profit allocation and a statement of changes in the partners' capital accounts. The schedule of profit allocation is similar to the earnings per share figure and/or the footnote covering earnings per share in public corporations as it shows the amount of profit allocated to each partner, rather than to each share. The statement of changes in the partners' capital accounts is comparable to a statement of changes in stockholders' equity of a corporation.

The balance sheet of a partnership reports assets and liabilities in the same manner as a corporation does, except that loans to partners and loans from partners are separate line items. The stockholders' equity section of a corporation's balance sheet is replaced with the ending balances of the partners' capital accounts. If a partnership has a large number of partners, only the total of all the partners' equity is reported on the balance sheet to prevent the equity section from becoming too long. Because no limit exists to the number of partners that can be in a partnership, the number could be in the hundreds, such as with the large international accounting firms. The balance is referenced to the statement of changes in the partners' capital accounts.

A complete set of financial statements also includes a statement of cash flows that is identical to a statement prepared for a corporation except that partners' drawings of cash, both normal and excessive, are reported as a cash flow from financing activities in lieu of dividends paid. The text material and problems in the chapters on partnerships omit this statement to reduce the length of the examples and homework problems, but you should keep in mind that generally accepted accounting principles do require the inclusion of the statement of cash flows when presenting a set of financial statements.

The financial statements for the K and P Partnership as presented in Exhibits 2-1 through 2-4 are based on the formation of the partnerships as presented in Illustrative Problem 2.1, Case 1 and the profit allocation from Illustrative Problem 2.3, Case 5a. This example assumes the partners have been paid the salaries, the bonus, and the interest on their capital accounts. The salaries, bonus, and interest payments have been debited to the partners' respective drawing accounts. The $16,500 debited to Partner K's capital account is treated as an excess withdrawal of assets as in the previous illustration.

OTHER BUSINESS ENTITIES THAT ARE SIMILAR TO GENERAL PARTNERSHIPS

The partnerships discussed in this chapter are **general partnerships** and the partners are called **general partners.** A general partner contributes capital, acts on behalf of the partnership, enters into transactions on behalf of all the partners, and has unlimited liability.

If a partnership has some partners whose activities, liability, and income are restricted,

EXHIBIT 2-1

K AND P PARTNERSHIP
Statement of Income
Year Ended December 31, 1990

Sales Revenue		$ 250,000
Cost of Goods Sold		150,000
Gross Margin		100,000
Other Expenses		
Wages of Employees	$ 25,500	
Utilities	5,000	
Depreciation	4,000	
Interest on Mortgage	2,500	37,000
Net Income		$ 63,000

EXHIBIT 2-2

K AND P PARTNERSHIP
Profit Allocation Schedule
Year Ended December 31, 1990

Allocation Factor	Partner K	Partner P	Total
Interest on Average Capital	$ 4,250	$ 5,750	$ 10,000
Salaries	13,000	17,000	30,000
Bonus		3,000	3,000
	$ 17,250	$ 25,750	$ 43,000
Remainder 6:4	12,000	8,000	20,000
Total	$ 29,250	$ 33,750	$ 63,000

EXHIBIT 2-3

K AND P PARTNERSHIP
Statement of Changes in Partners' Capital Accounts
Year Ended December 31, 1990

	Partner K	Partner P	Total
Beginning Capital, 1/1/90	$ 40,000	$ 50,000	$ 90,000
Capital Contributed in 1990	12,500	14,000	26,500
Excess Withdrawals	(16,500)		(16,500)
Net Income	29,250	33,750	63,000
Drawings	(17,250)	(25,750)	(43,000)
Ending Capital, 12/31/90	$ 48,000	$ 72,000	$ 120,000

EXHIBIT 2-4

K AND P PARTNERSHIP
Balance Sheet
December 31, 1990

Assets

Current Assets			
Cash		$ 14,000	
Accounts Receivable: Net		25,000	
Inventory		40,000	$ 79,000
Property, Plant, and Equipment			
Land		15,000	
Building	$ 60,000		
Less: Accumulated Depreciation	3,000	57,000	
Store Fixtures	10,000		
Less: Accumulated Depreciation	1,000	9,000	81,000
Total Assets			$ 160,000

Liabilities and Partners' Equity

Current Liabilities			
Accounts Payable		$ 15,000	
Wages Payable		2,000	$ 17,000
Long-Term Debt: Mortgage Payable			23,000
Total Liabilities			40,000
Partners' Equity			
Capital, K		48,000	
Capital, P		72,000	120,000
Total Liabilities and Partners' Equity			$ 160,000

that partnership is called a **limited partnership** and the partners are **limited partners.** A limited partner contributes capital, but is not allowed to enter into transactions on behalf of the partnership or to participate in the management of the partnership. The limited partner's liability is set at a specific amount, which generally does not exceed the partner's net investment in the partnership. A limited partner's share of net income is generally a specified percentage. A limited partner is similar to a preferred stockholder of a corporation, and has many of the characteristics of a creditor. Every limited partnership must have at least one general partner. Limited Partnerships are governed by the Uniform Limited Partnership Act or similar state laws.

Joint ventures are partnerships of individuals or other business entitites who have banded together for a specific purpose or project. Joint ventures are formed for the completion of a single project such as the development of real estate, the construction of a pipeline, or the building of a bridge, or for a single purpose such as the removal of timber from a given tract. The intent of a joint venture is for the entity to exist only until the purpose or project is completed. Joint ventures have a limited life and a limited purpose. The partners can commit the partnership only to agreements and transactions that fit within the scope of the business purpose or project of the joint venture. The operation and accounting for a joint venture is the same as for a general partnership.

Another form of business that is used by professionals, such as accountants, in those states where permitted by law is the **professional corporation** (PC). Professional corporations have most of the characteristics of ordinary corporations except that the stockholders do not have limited liability. The professionals cannot shield their professional liability to their patients or clients by being in a professional corporation. If the professional is sued for malpractice, the injured party may have access to the personal assets of the professional when the PCs assets are not adequate to cover the settlement or judgment depending on the state's laws.

Stockholders in a professional corporation are restricted to those people who have the appropriate licenses to practice the profession of the corporation. The stockholders of a professional corporation can sell their shares, but only to other professionals licensed to practice that profession. The difficulties of transfer of ownership that exist with partnerships is partially overcome by a professional corporation. Initially when states enacted their professional corporation laws, significant income tax advantages existed relative to pension and profit-sharing plans. Changes in the tax laws have eliminated most of the advantages. Today, most professional corporations operate like partnerships except the professional is an employee and a stockholder rather than a partner.

Another form of corporation, created by the tax code, that is similar to a general partnership is called an **S corporation.** An S corporation is limited to a maximum of 35 stockholders who are individuals. Unlike the stockholders in an ordinary corporation, who receive dividends from a corporation that has paid tax on its income and who also pay tax on the dividends received, the stockholders of an S corporation are taxed on their share of the income, as if they were partners. The S corporation does not pay income taxes except on very limited types of income. The S corporation is a tax pass-through entity as are general and limited partnerships and joint ventures. The S corporation is comparable to an ordinary corporation, except for the limitation on the number of stockholders, who must be individuals, and the manner in which income is taxed. Accounting and reporting for S corporations is the same as for ordinary corporations.

SUMMARY

A partnership is a group of two or more people who join together to operate a business. The partnership is legally dissolved whenever a partner is admitted or withdraws from the partnership. The partners may override this dissolution by the use of an ongoing business clause in their partnership agreement. Partners are co-owners of the assets, liabilities, and profits of the partnership, and are jointly and individually liable for the debts of the partnership. The partners are mutual agents of each other binding the partnership to any contracts or agreements entered into by one of the partners. A partnership has characteristics indicating that both the proprietary and entity theories of equity apply to partnerships.

When a partnership is formed, the assets and liabilities contributed are recorded at their fair market value. Three methods, net investment, bonus, and goodwill, are used to record the formation of a partnership. When the net investment method is used, the partners are credited with the fair market value of the net assets contributed. When the bonus method is used, one or more partners are credited with more than the fair market value of the net assets contributed and one or more other partners with less. When the goodwill method is used, the intangible asset, goodwill, is recorded and allocated to the partners. Theoretically the recording of goodwill can only be defended when one or more or the partners contributes an entire business to the partnership.

Accounting and reporting for partnerships is similar to corporations with some exceptions. The partners can allocate profits or losses among themselves in any manner that they believe to be fair and equitable. Profit allocation factors, such as salaries, bonuses, and interest, are not expenses of the partnership, but are simply a means of describing the methods used to divide profits and losses between the partners. A partnership is a tax pass-through entity; therefore, income taxes are not reported on the financial statements of the partnership. The complex stockholders' equity accounts of a corporation are replaced with partners' capital and drawing accounts. Except for income taxes and the simple capital structure, the financial statements of a partnership are comparable to the financial statements of a corporation.

REVIEW PROBLEM

On January 1, 1990, A and B formed a partnership. The partners have agreed to contribute the following assets to the partnership:

	Market Value January 1, 1990
A's Contribution	
Cash	$ 16,000
Inventory	25,000
Accounts Payable: Inventory	(5,000)
A's Net Investment	$ 36,000
B's Contribution	
Cash	$ 15,000
Equipment	9,000
B's Net Investment	$ 24,000

On February 1, 1990, Partner A contributed an additional $12,000 to the partnership and on August 1, 1990, Partner A withdrew $6,000 that the partnership agreement classified as excess drawings. On May 1, 1990, Partner B contributed additional equipment with a fair market value of $8,000. Partner B had originally purchased the equipment for $12,000 and it had a net book value of $6,000 when contributed. On November 1, 1990, Partner B contributed an additional $4,000 to the partnership. The partnership agreement of A and B has the following terms for the allocation of net profit or loss to the partners:

1. Interest of 12% on the average capital balance
2. Salaries of $900 per month to each partner
3. Bonus of 8% of net income after the bonus to A
4. Remainder to be divided in the ratio of 7:3, respectively

Required
1. Prepare the journal entry for the formation of the partnership assuming the partnership agreed to be responsible for the $5,000 of accounts payable and decided to record (1) neither a bonus nor goodwill, (2) a bonus, and (3) goodwill.
2. Prepare a schedule showing the allocation of $48,600 of net income, assuming the partners recorded the formation of the partnership by the bonus method.
3. Show how your solution to (2) above would be different if net income were only $22,950.
4. Show how your solution to (3) above would be different if the partnership agreement stated that the factors were to be allocated only to the extent possible.
5. Prepare a statement of changes in partners' capital accounts, assuming the partners elected to record the formation of the partnership using the bonus method, the income is $48,600, which is to be allocated fully, and the only drawings were the payments of the monthly salaries.

QUESTIONS

1. Describe the various relationships of partners.
2. Describe the major points that should be covered in a partnership agreement.
3. Describe the three ways that can be used to record the formation of a partnership.
4. Discuss when it might be appropriate to record goodwill in the formation of a partnership and when it would not be appropriate.
5. Describe the conditions necessary for loans to and from partners to a partnership to be recorded as loans. If not recorded as loans, how are they recorded?
6. Describe the equity accounts of a partner and the items that are debited and credited to the equity accounts.
7. Describe the differences between the net income of a partnership and a corporation.
8. Describe the differences between the fully and to the extent possible methods of allocating partnership profit.
9. Describe the differences between the financial statements of a partnership and a corporation.
10. Contrast a limited partnership and a joint venture with a general partnership.
11. Describe the characteristics of a professional corporation and an S corporation and contrast them with an ordinary corporation.

EXERCISES

EXERCISE 2-1
A and B have decided to form a partnership. A contributes cash of $20,000 and B contributes land with a fair market value of $6,000 and a building with a fair market value of $30,000. B purchased the land and building five years ago for $25,000. B's book value of the land is $3,500 and the book value of the building is $18,500. The partners agree to share profits and losses in the ratio of 4:6, respectively.

Required

Prepare the journal entries to record the formation of the partnership under the following assumptions:

1. The partners have agreed to record their contributions by the net investment method.
2. The partners have agreed to share initial capital equally.
3. The partners have agreed to record goodwill equal to the difference in their capital accounts and to share capital equally.

EXERCISE 2-2

C and D have decided to form a partnership. C contributes cash of $10,000 and inventory of $12,000. D contributes store fixtures with a net book value of $12,000 and a fair market value of $18,000, and cash of $6,000. D owes City Bank $8,000 on a note for the purchase of the store fixtures.

Required

Prepare the journal entries for the formation of the partnership, if the partnership assumes the note payable to City Bank under each of the following assumptions:

1. The partners have agreed to record their contributions by the net investment method.
2. The partners have agreed to share capital equally.
3. The partners have agreed to record goodwill equal to the difference in their capital accounts and D is to have $20,000 of capital.

EXERCISE 2-3

Dr. E has been practicing medicine as a sole proprietor. Dr. E and Dr. G have decided to form a medical partnership. The assets and liabilities of E's practice are to become the assets and liabilities of the new partnership. Dr. G will contribute $13,000 cash to the partnership, for a one-third interest in capital and a one-third interest in the profits and losses. The trial balance of Dr. E's sole proprietorship is

	Debits	Credits
Cash	$ 8,000	
Accounts Receivable: Net	15,000	
Medical Equipment	21,000	
Accumulated Depreciation: Medical Equipment		$ 9,000
Note Payable: Medical Equipment		7,000
Capital, Dr. E		28,000

The partners have determined that the net realizable value of the accounts receivable is correct. An appraisal of the medical equipment determined that its fair market value is $25,000.

Required

1. Prepare the journal entry for the formation of the partnership of Dr. E and Dr. G under each of the following assumptions:
   1) Dr. E is giving a bonus to Dr. G.
   2) The partners have agreed to record goodwill of $9,000.
2. Ignoring other factors, after the amortization of the goodwill, how will the partners' capital accounts differ from what they would be if the bonus method had been used to record the formation of the partnership.

EXERCISE 2-4

1. A partnership is formed by two individuals who were previously sole proprietors. Property other

than cash that is part of the initial investment in the partnership is recorded for financial accounting purposes at the

a. Proprietors' book values or the fair value of the property at the date of the investment, whichever is higher.
b. Proprietors' book values or the fair value of the property at the date of the investment, whichever is lower.
c. Proprietors' book values of the property at the date of the investment.
d. Fair market value of the property at the date of the investment.

2. On July 1, 1988, Motta and Puleo formed a partnership, agreeing to share profits and losses in the ratio of 4:6, respectively. Motta contributed a parcel of land that cost him $25,000. Puleo contributed $50,000 cash. The land was sold for $50,000 on July 1, 1988, four hours after formation of the partnership. How much should be recorded in Motta's capital account on the formation of the partnership?

a. $ 10,000
b. $ 20,000
c. $ 25,000
d. $ 50,000

3. Cody and Paul formed a partnership on April 1, 1988, and contributed the following assets:

	Cody	Paul
Cash	$ 150,000	$ 50,000
Land		310,000

The land was subject to a mortgage of $30,000, which was assumed by the partnership. Under the partnership agreement, Cody and Paul will share profit and loss in the ratio of one-third and two-thirds, respectively. Paul's capital account on April 1, 1988 should be

a. $ 300,000
b. $ 330,000
c. $ 340,000
d. $ 360,000

Data for Questions 4, 5, and 6

Derby and Elder form a partnership and agree to share profit and losses in the ratio of 6:4, respectively. The partners contribute the following assets and liabilities to the partnership

	Historical Cost	Fair Market Value
Derby		
Cash	$ 30,000	$ 30,000
Inventory	25,000	40,000
Accounts Payable: Inventory	10,000	10,000
Elder		
Cash	20,000	20,000
Land and Building	65,000	110,000
Mortgage Payable: Building	40,000	40,000

4. If the partners agree that the partnership will assume the liabilities related to the assets contributed, the amount credited to Derby's capital account on the formation of the partnership is

a. $ 45,000
b. $ 54,000
c. $ 60,000
d. $ 90,000

5. If Derby and Elder agree that the amount credited to Derby's capital account should be $70,000 and no goodwill is to be recorded, the amount of the bonus and the partner receiving the bonus is

a. A bonus of $10,000 to Derby
b. A bonus of $20,000 to Elder
c. A bonus of 16,000 to Derby
d. A bonus of $5,000 to Elder

6. If the partners agree that Elder is bringing an intangible asset to the partnership that they have agreed to record as goodwill in the amount of $20,000, the amount credited to the capital account of Elder is

a. $ 65,000
b. $ 98,000
c. $ 102,000
d. $ 110,000

(Questions 1, 2, and 3 AICPA adapted)

EXERCISE 2-5

The partnership of G and H had net income of $30,000 for 1992.

Required

Prepare the journal entry to record the allocation of profit to G and H under each of the following assumptions:

1. G and H share profits equally.
2. G and H have no partnership agreement.
3. G and H share profits and losses in the ratio of 4:2, respectively.

EXERCISE 2-6

The partnership agreement of I and J states that the partners are to share profits and losses in the ratio of the weighted average of their capital investments.

Capital I				*Capital J*			
1990		1990		1990		1990	
5/1	5,000	1/1	20,000	8/1	6,000	1/1	18,000
		2/1	8,000			4/1	4,000
		9/1	6,000			10/1	10,000

Required

Determine each partner's share of the net income of $23,500 for 1990 based on the entries in their capital accounts.

EXERCISE 2-7

The partnership agreement of K and L specifies that K is to receive a salary of $12,000 per year and L is to receive a salary of $18,000. L is also to receive a bonus of 5% of net income after salaries and bonus for managing the partnership. Any remainder is to be divided in the ratio of 3:2, respectively.

Required

Prepare a profit allocation schedule to allocate the net income of $61,500 for the year ended December 31, 1991.

EXERCISE 2-8

The partnership agreement of M and N contained the following provisions:

1. Interest of 8% on beginning capital balances
2. Salary of $12,000 to M and salary of $20,000 to N
3. Remainder in the ratio of 6:4, respectively

The beginning capital of M was $30,000 and the beginning capital of N was $45,000.

Required

Prepare a profit allocation schedule for the M and N Partnership for the year ended December 31, 1990 under each of the following assumptions:

1. Net income is $41,000.
2. Net income is $32,000 and is to be allocated fully.
3. Net income is $32,000 and is to be allocated to the extent possible.

EXERCISE 2-9 (CONTINUATION OF EXERCISE 2-8)

Partners M and N had the following transactions in their capital accounts during 1990:

Capital M				*Capital N*			
1990		1990		1990		1990	
4/1	4,000	1/1	30,000	8/1	6,000	1/1	45,000
		2/1	6,000			4/1	6,000
		9/1	7,000			10/1	10,000

The partners used the profit allocation from Exercise 2-8 (1) and the only amounts debited to their drawing accounts were their salaries.

Required

Prepare a statement of changes in partners' capital accounts for the year ended December 31, 1990.

EXERCISE 2-10

1. The partnership agreement for the partnership of Mayo and Pack provided for salary allowances of $45,000 to Mayo and $35,000 to Pack, and the residual profit was allocated equally. During 1991, Mayo and Pack each withdrew cash equal to 80 percent of their salary allowances. If during 1991, the partnership had profits in excess of $100,000 without regard to salary allowances and withdrawals, Mayo's equity in the partnership would

a. Increase more than Pack's
b. Decrease more than Pack's
c. Increase the same as Pack's
d. Decrease the same as Pack's

2. The partnership agreement of Jones, King, and Lane provides for annual distribution of profit or loss in the following order:

- Jones, the managing partner, receives a bonus of 20% of profit.
- Each partner receives 15% interest on average capital investment.
- Residual profit or loss is divided equally.

The average capital investments for 1991 were

Jones	$ 100,000
King	200,000
Lane	300,000

How much of the $90,000 partnership profit for 1991 should be distributed to Jones?

a. $ 15,000
b. $ 27,000
c. $ 30,000
d. $ 33,000

3. Fox, Greg, and Howe are partners with average capital balances during 1991 of $120,000, $60,000 and $40,000, respectively. Partners receive 10% interest on their average capital balances. After deducting salaries of $30,000 to Fox and $20,000 to Howe, the residual profit or loss is divided equally. In 1991, the partnership sustained a $33,000 loss before interest and salaries to partners. By what amount should Fox's capital account change?

a. $ 7,000 increase
b. $ 11,000 decrease
c. $ 35,000 decrease
d. $ 42,000 increase

(AICPA adapted)

PROBLEMS

PROBLEM 2-1

Able and Baker have agreed to form a partnership and each is to contribute the following assets and liabilities:

	Historical Cost	Fair Market Value
Able		
Cash	$ 10,000	$ 10,000
Inventory	35,000	50,000
Equipment	15,000	25,000
Accounts Payable: Inventory	12,000	12,000
Notes Payable: Equipment	18,000	18,000
Baker		
Cash	20,000	20,000
Land and Building	65,000	90,000
Mortgage Payable: Building	40,000	40,000

Required

1. Determine the amount to be credited to each partner's capital account if the partners agree to use the net investment method.
2. Determine the amount to be credited to each partner's capital account if they agree to equal capital balances and if they elect to use (1) the bonus method, (2) the goodwill method.
3. What are the arguments for and against using the goodwill method in recording the formation of a partnership?

PROBLEM 2-2

Dr. O has been practicing dentistry for several years. Dr. O and Dr. T, who just graduated from dental school, have agreed to form a partnership. Dr. O will contribute his practice and Dr. T will contribute cash of $15,000. Dr. T will also sign a 10-year, 12% note payable to the partnership in the amount of $60,000. Dr. T has agreed to pay the interest quarterly from her personal assets and 20% of the principal each year out of her earnings. Dr. T's drawings are restricted to the amount of her salary. If her income, net of salary, in any year is not sufficient to pay the loan principal due, Dr. T must pay the partnership any remainder due out of her personal assets. The partnership agreement of Drs. O and T specifies that they will each receive 9% interest on their beginning net capital investment (capital accounts reduced by any loans payable to the partnership), salaries of $30,000 each, and the remainder is to be divided in the ratio of 6:4, respectively. On January 1, 1990, the trial balance of Dr. O's practice prior to the formation of the partnership in both book values and fair market values is

	Net Book Value	Fair Market Value
Cash	$ 17,000	$ 17,000
Accounts Receivable	25,000	19,000
Allowance for Uncollectible Accounts	(3,000)	
Supplies	2,500	3,000
Land	12,000	20,000
Building	40,000	60,000
Accumulated Depreciation: Building	(15,000)	
Dental Equipment	20,000	12,000
Accumulated Depreciation: Equipment	(9,000)	
Office Furniture	6,000	3,000
Accumulated Depreciation: Furniture	(4,000)	
Wages Payable	(2,000)	(2,000)
Note Payable: Dental Equipment	(4,000)	(4,000)
Mortgage Payable: Land and Building	(18,000)	(18,000)
Total Investment	$ 67,500	$ 110,000

Required

1. What conditions are necessary for the note from Dr. T to be recorded as a loan receivable from a partner?
2. Prepare the journal entry for the formation of the partnership assuming that the dentists have agreed to share capital equally.
3. How would your journal entry in (2) above be different if Dr. O's capital account is credited with an additional $20,000 of capital in excess of his net investment for the patient base of his existing practice?
4. How would your journal entry in (2) above be different if the dentists had agreed to record goodwill of $20,000 in recognition of the patient base of Dr. O's existing practice?

5. Prepare the journal entry to allocate $84,000 of practice income earned in 1990, assuming that the partners had elected to record the initial capital investment by the goodwill method.

6. Prepare the journal entry to record the allocation of Dr. T's income in excess of her salary as payment on the loan.

PROBLEM 2-3

Mr. S has been operating a successful flower shop, Lasting Blooms, Florists, for a number of years. Ms. W has been an employee of the flower shop for several years and she and Mr. S have decided to form a partnership and open a branch in a new shopping center. The partners have agreed that Mr. S will manage the existing flower shop and Ms. W will manage the new location. The partners have agreed to keep their books on the accrual basis. Mr. S has been using the cash basis of accounting, except for the recording of operating assets, liabilities for the purchase of operating assets, and depreciation expense. The trial balance of Lasting Blooms, Florists on January 1, 1990 prior to the formation of the partnership is

	Debit	Credit
Cash	$ 8,000	
Land	10,000	
Building	25,000	
Accumulated Depreciation: Building		$ 12,000
Refrigeration Units	15,000	
Accumulated Depreciation: Refrigeration Units		7,500
Store Fixtures	8,000	
Accumulated Depreciation: Store Fixtures		4,500
Loan Payable: Refrigeration Units		3,000
Mortgage Payable: Building		10,000
Capital, Mr. S		29,000
Totals	$ 66,000	$ 66,000

The following information has been determined to convert the accounting records of Lasting Blooms from the modified cash basis to the accrual basis as of January 1, 1990:

1. Mr. S allows some customers to charge orders. The records indicate $4,100 of unpaid accounts receivable. Mr. S has estimated that only $3,300 of the accounts receivable will be collected and the partners have agreed to establish an allowance for doubtful accounts for the difference.

2. Lasting Blooms specializes in artificial flower arrangements and also sells cut flowers. An inventory of the flower arrangements, taken at selling price, indicates $6,020 of arrangements on hand. Mr. S has been using a 40% markup on cost to price the dried arrangements. Because of the perishable nature of the cut flowers, the inventory on hand at cost is only $1,200.

3. Lasting Blooms has supplies on hand of florist tape, ribbon, and vases that cost $1,700.

4. An appraisal of the land, building, refrigeration units, and store fixtures showed the following:

	Fair Market Value	Remaining Life in Years
Land	$ 15,000	
Store Building	40,000	20
Refrigeration Units	10,000	5
Store Fixtures	4,000	8

5. Mr. S has determined that Lasting Blooms owes payroll taxes of $900 and suppliers $3,100 for fresh flowers and the materials for making artificial arrangements.

Required

1. Prepare a worksheet to convert the trial balance of Lasting Blooms, Florists to fair market values using the accrual basis of accounting as of January 1, 1990.
2. The partners will sign a lease for the new shop. The lease requires a year's rent of $6,000 in advance. The partners estimate that refrigeration units will cost $18,000 and the store fixtures will cost $7,000. The new shop will need $5,000 of inventory and $1,200 of supplies. Determine the amount of cash necessary to meet the cost of setting up the new shop.
3. The agreement between Mr. S and Ms. W required Ms. W to contribute cash sufficient to pay for the establishment of the branch and an additional amount to bring her equity to 40% of the total equity. Determine the amount of cash Ms. W needs to have a 40% investment.
4. Determine the amount to be credited to each partner's capital account if the new partnership is to assume all the liabilities of Lasting Blooms and Ms. W invests $49,500 for a 40% interest in the initial capital of the partnership.

PROBLEM 2-4 (CONTINUATION OF PROBLEM 2-3)

On January 1, 1990, Mr. S and Ms. W formed a partnership. Mr. S contributed the assets and the liabilities of Lasting Blooms and Ms. W contributed $49,500 for a 40% interest in the initial capital. The following transactions were entered into by the partnership during 1990:

1. The new shop was outfitted for business as follows:

One-year's lease	$ 6,000
Refrigeration units	18,000
Store fixtures	7,000
Inventory	5,000
Supplies	1,200

All of the above were purchased on January 2, 1990 for cash.
2. Sales on account totaled $21,000 and purchases on account were $19,000.
3. Cash receipts were

Cash Sales	$ 43,000
Collections of Accounts Receivable	20,000

Cash disbursements were

Payments of Accounts Payable	$ 17,000
Purchases of Supplies	5,000
Payments of Wages and Payroll Taxes (including $900 accrual)	8,000
Drawings, Mr. S	18,000
Drawings, Ms. W	12,000

4. The partnership paid a total of $2,500 of interest on the note and the mortgage and $1,000 of principal on each debt.
5. During the year, $500 of accounts receivable were determined to be uncollectible and were written off.

The following information was determined for the preparation of the year-end adjustments:

6. At the end of the year, the inventory at cost totaled $6,700 and the supplies on hand totaled $2,000.

7. The partners estimated the life of the new refrigeration units and store fixtures to be 10 years. The building contributed by Mr. S has a remaining life of 20 years, the refrigeration units 5 years, and the store fixtures 8 years. All assets are assumed to have no salvage value and are to be depreciated using the straight-line method.
8. The partners estimate that 2% of accounts receivable are not collectible.

Required

1. Set up a worksheet with the initial trial balance of the partnership, enter the transactions and adjustments for 1990, assuming a periodic inventory system and determining cost of goods sold with an adjusting journal entry, and prepare the adjusted trial balance on the worksheet.
2. Prepare the financial statements for the Lasting Blooms partnership assuming that the partnership agreement states that Mr. S is to receive a salary of $18,000 and Ms. W is to receive a salary of $12,000. Any remaining profit and loss is to be divided in the ratio of 6:4, respectively.
3. Prepare the journal entries to close the income summary and the drawing accounts at year end.

PROBLEM 2-5

P, Q, and R have decided to form a partnership to provide financial planning services to individuals and pension plans. The partners have agreed that Q has exceptional business experience and they anticipate that Q's contribution will add significantly to the net income of the partnership. Each partner has both assets and liabilities to contribute to the partnership. The partners have agreed that the partnership will assume the liabilities. The partnership agreement of P, Q, and R Investment Counselors states that the partners are to share profits and losses to the extent possible, in the following order:

1. Interest of 9% on beginning capital balances net of the average monthly withdrawals during the year.
2. A salary based on 40% of their net billings to clients for the year, not to exceed $25,000.
3. Any excess over $25,000 is to be allocated at the reduced rate of 20% of remaining net billings.
4. A bonus of 10% of net income after interest, salaries, and bonus to P for managing the business.
5. The remainder in the ratio of 3:5:2, respectively.

The following assets at their fair market values were contributed by P, Q, and R to form the partnership:

	Partner P	Partner Q	Partner R
Cash	$ 5,000	$ 14,000	$ 6,000
Land	20,000		
Office Building	65,000		
Office Furniture			12,000
Computer System		13,000	
Computer Software			2,000
Telephone System			5,000
Note Payable: Computer		(7,000)	
Mortgage Payable: Building	(30,000)		
Net Investment	$ 60,000	$ 20,000	$ 25,000

During 1990, the first year of operations, the net billings and the drawings of the partners were

	Partner P	Partner Q	Partner R	Total
Net Billings to Clients	$ 50,000	$ 82,500	$ 60,000	$ 192,500
Total Drawings	30,000	48,000	20,400	98,400

Required

1. Prepare a journal entry to record the formation of the partnership, P, Q, and R Investment Counselors, assuming that the partners have agreed that Q is to have a capital balance of $40,000 to reflect the special skills he brings to the partnership. The special skills are to be considered goodwill.
2. Prepare a schedule to allocate net income of $116,512 for 1990.
3. How would your solution to (2) above be different if the partners had net income of $50,512.
4. Prepare a statement of the changes in the partners' capital accounts for 1990, assuming net income was $116,512.

PROBLEM 2-6

Campbell, Heinz, and Progresso have a complex partnership agreement that contains the following provisions:

1. Interest of 12% on the average capital invested in the business, using 30-day months
2. Salaries of $3,500 per month to each partner
3. A bonus to Heinz of 10% of net income after interest, salaries, and bonus
4. The remainder in the ratio of 3:4:3, respectively, if positive, and equally, if negative

During the three months ended, September 30, 1990, the following entries were made in the capital accounts of the partners:

Capital: Campbell				Capital: Heinz				Capital: Progresso		
8/1	9,000	7/1	30,000	9/1	6,000	7/1	42,000		7/1	39,000
		9/1	3,000			8/1	12,000		8/1	4,300
									9/1	4,600

Required

1. Prepare a schedule to determine the amount of income to be credited to each partner's capital account if the net income of the partnership for the quarter ended September 30, 1990, is $67,992.
2. Determine the amount to be credited to each partner's capital account if the agreement said to allocate to the extent possible and the net income for the quarter ended September 30, 1990, is $30,492.

PROBLEM 2-7

The partnership agreement of X, Y, and Z, CPAs contains the following provisions:

1. *Determination of net income.* Net income is to be determined using the accrual method of accounting, except that bad debt expense, determined under the direct write-off method because of its immaterial nature, is to be omitted in the determination of income for profit and loss allocation. The actual bad debt expense is assigned to the partner whose client defaulted, and is charged to the partner's share of profits and losses.
2. *Profit and loss allocation.* Profits and losses are to be allocated quarterly using the following allocation factors:
   1) Interest of 3.0% on the weighted average capital balances, computed daily using 30-day months.
   2) Salaries to be computed based on the average billing rate charged to customers during the quarter times the number of hours worked to a maximum of 500 hours per quarter. Hours in excess of 500 are to count as half an hour.
   3) A bonus to Y of 1.0% of net income not to exceed $1,500 for acting as the managing partner.
   4) Any remainder to a limit of $15,000 is to be divided equally. Any remainder in excess of $15,000 is to be allocated based on the ratio of 3:3:2, respectively.

5) Each partner's share of profits and losses is to be reduced by any bad debts that come from that partner's client base.

3. *Normal and excess drawings.* Each partner will be paid a monthly cash advance of $2,000 on his share of profits and losses. Any drawings in excess of $2,000 will be treated as excess drawings for the purposes of computing the weighted average capital balance to be used in the profit and loss allocation calculations.

In addition to the normal monthly cash advances of $2,000, the following drawings were made by the partners:

Partner X: 5/11/92   Cash of $5,000 for down payment on a new car
            6/ 9/92   Extra computer desk, net book value $500
Partner Y: 4/13/92   Check in the amount of $6,000 payable to the IRS for payment
                      of Y's personal income taxes
Partner Z: 4/22/92   Cash of $3,000 to pay daughter's college tuition
            5/16/92   Calculator, net book value $200

The following additional information has been determined from the records of the firm:

	Partner X	Partner Y	Partner Z
Chargeable Hours	400	460	510
Office Hours	60	120	40
Total Hours Worked	460	580	550
Total Billings to Clients	$20,000	$28,520	$35,700
Beginning Capital Balances	$18,000	$22,000	$24,400
Bad Debts from Clients	$ 880	–0–	$ 1,100

Required

Prepare a profit and loss allocation schedule for the partnership of X, Y, and Z, CPAs for the quarter ending June 30, 1992, assuming that the net income for the quarter as reported on the accrual basis income statement was $115,320.

PROBLEM 2-8

The partnership of A, B, and C has the following partnership agreement for the allocation of profits and losses:

1. Interest of 7% on beginning capital balances.
2. Salaries of $12,000, $15,000, and $18,000, respectively.
3. C is to receive a bonus of 10% of net income after interest, salaries, and C's bonus.
4. B is to receive a bonus of 20% of net income after interest, salaries, and C's bonus.
5. Any remaining profits are to be divided in the ratio of 3:3:2, respectively.
6. If the partnership's net income is not sufficient to cover interest and salaries, the negative remainder is to be shared equally.

The beginning capital balances of the partners were

Capital, A	$ 23,500
Capital, B	31,600
Capital, C	27,800

Required

Prepare a profit and loss allocation schedule if net income for the year ended March 31, 1991 is (1) $83,803 and (2) $34,000.

UNIFORM PARTNERSHIP ACT

Part I **Preliminary Provisions**

Sec. 1.   (Name of Act.) This act may be cited as Uniform Partnership Act.

Sec. 2.   (Definition of Terms.) In this act, "Court" includes every court and judge having jurisdiction in the case.

"Business" includes every trade, occupation, or profession.

"Person" includes individuals, partnerships, corporations, and other associations.

"Bankrupt" includes bankrupt under the Federal Bankruptcy Act or insolvent under any state insolvent act.

"Conveyance" includes every assignment, lease, mortgage, or encumbrance.

"Real property" includes land and any interest or estate in land.

Sec. 3.   (Interpretation of Knowledge and Notice.)

(1) A person has "knowledge" of a fact within the meaning of this act not only when he has actual knowledge thereof, but also when he has knowledge of such other facts as in the circumstances shows bad faith.

(2) A person has "notice" of a fact within the meaning of this act when the person who claims the benefit of the notice.

(a) States the fact to such person, or

(b) Delivers through the mail, or by other means of communication, a written statement of the fact to such person or to a proper person at his place of business or residence.

Sec. 4.   (Rules of Construction.)

(1) The rule that statutes in derogation of the common law are to be strictly construed shall have no application to this act.

(2) The law of estoppel shall apply under this act.

(3) The law of agency shall apply under this act.

(4) This act shall be so interpreted and construed as to effect its general purpose to make uniform the law of those states which enact it.

(5) This act shall not be construed so as to impair the obligations of any contract existing when the act goes into effect, nor to affect any action or proceedings begun or right accrued before this act takes effect.

Sec. 5.   (Rules for Cases Not Provided for in this Act.) In any case not provided for in this act the rules of law and equity, including the law of merchant, shall govern.

Part II **Nature of Partnership**

Sec. 6.   (Partnership Defined.)

(1) A partnership is an association of two or more persons to carry on as co-owners a business for profit.

(2) But any association formed under any other statute of this state, or any statute adopted by authority, other than the authority of this state, is not a partnership under this act, unless such association

would have been a partnership in this state prior to the adoption of this act; but this act shall apply to limited partnerships except in so far as the statutes relating to such partnerships are inconsistent herewith.

Sec. 7. (Rules for Determining the Existence of a Partnership.) In determining whether a partnership exists, these rules shall apply.

(1) Except as provided by Section 16 persons who are not partners as to each other are not partners as to third persons.

(2) Joint tenancy, tenancy in common, tenancy by the entireties, joint property, common property, or part ownership does not of itself establish a partnership, whether such co-owners do or do not share any profits made by the use of the property.

(3) The sharing of gross returns does not of itself establish a partnership, whether or not the persons sharing them have a joint or common right or interest in any property from which the returns are derived.

(4) The receipt by a person of a share of the profits of a business is prima facie evidence that he is a partner in the business, but no such inference shall be drawn if such profits were received in payment

(a) As a debt by installments or otherwise,

(b) As wages of an employee or rent to a landlord,

(c) As an annuity to a widow or representative of a deceased partner,

(d) As interest on a loan, though the amount of payment vary with the profits of the business,

(e) As the consideration for the sale of goodwill of a business or other property by installments or otherwise.

Sec. 8. (Partnership Property.)

(1) All property originally brought into the partnership stock or subsequently acquired by purchase or otherwise, on account of the partnership, is partnership property.

(2) Unless the contrary intention appears, property acquired with partnership funds is partnership property.

(3) Any estate in real property may be acquired in the partnership name. Title so acquired can be conveyed only in the partnership name.

(4) A conveyance to a partnership in the partnership name, though without words of inheritance, passes the entire estate of the grantor unless a contrary intent appears.

Part III **Relations of Partners to Persons Dealing with the Partnership**

Sec. 9. (Partner Agent of Partnership as to Partnership Business.)

(1) Every partner is an agent of the partnership for the purpose of its business, and the act of every partner, including the execution in the partnership name of any instrument, for apparently carrying on in the usual way the business of the partnership of which he is a member binds the partnership, unless the partner so acting has in fact no authority to act for the partnership in the particular matter, and the person with whom he is dealing has knowledge of the fact that he has no such authority.

(2) An act of a partner which is not apparently for the carrying on of the business of the partnership in the usual way does not bind the partnership unless authorized by the other partners.

(3) Unless authorized by the other partners or unless they have abandoned the business, one or more but less than all the partners have no authority to

(a) Assign the partnership property in trust for creditors or on the assignee's promise to pay the debts of the partnership,

(b) Dispose of the goodwill of the business,

(c) Do any other act which would make it impossible to carry on the ordinary business of a partnership,

(d) Confess a judgment,

(e) Submit a partnership claim or liability to arbitration or reference.

(4) No act of a partner in contravention of a restriction on authority shall bind the partnership to persons having knowledge of the restriction.

Sec. 10.   (Conveyance of Real Property of the Partnership.)

(1) Where title to real property is in the partnership name, any partner may convey title to such property by a conveyance executed in the partnership name; but the partnership may recover such property unless the partner's act binds the partnership under the provisions of paragraph (1) of section 9 or unless such property has been conveyed by the grantee or a person claiming through such grantee to a holder for value without knowledge that the partner, in making the conveyance, has exceeded his authority.

(2) Where title to real property is in the name of the partnership, a conveyance executed by a partner, in his own name, passes the equitable interest of the partnership, provided the act is one within the authority of the partner under the provisions of paragraph (1) of section 9.

(3) Where title to real property is in the name of one or more but not all the partners, and the record does not disclose the right of the partnership, the partners in whose name the title stands may convey title to such property, but the partnership may recover such property if the partners' act does not bind the partnership under the provisions of paragraph (1) of section 9, unless the purchaser or his assignee, is a holder for value, without knowledge.

(4) Where the title to real property is in the name of one or more or all the partners, or in a third person in trust for the partnership, a conveyance executed by a partner in the partnership name, or in his own name, passes the equitable interest of the partnership, provided the act is one within the authority of the partner under the provisions of paragraph (1) of section 9.

(5) Where the title to real property is in the names of all the partners a conveyance executed by all the partners passes all their rights in such property.

Sec. 11.   (Partnership Bound by Admission of Partner.) An admission or representation made by any partner concerning partnership affairs within the scope of his authority as conferred by this act is evidence against the partnership.

Sec. 12.   (Partnership Charged with Knowledge of or Notice to Partner.) Notice to any partner of any matter relating to partnership affairs, and the knowledge of the partner acting in the particular matter, acquired while a partner or then present to his mind, and the knowledge of any other partner who reasonably could and should have communicated it to the acting partner, operate as notice to or knowledge of the partnership, except in the case of a fraud on the partnership committed by or with the consent of that partner.

Sec. 13.   (Partnership Bound by Partner's Wrongful Act.) Where, by any wrongful act or omission of any partner acting in the ordinary course of the business of the partnership or with the authority of his copartners, loss or injury is caused to any person, not being a partner in the partnership, or any penalty is incurred, the partnership is liable therefor to the same extent as the partner so acting or omitting to act.

Sec. 14.   (Partnership Bound by Partner's Breach of Trust.) The partnership is bound to make good the loss

(a) Where one partner acting within the scope of his apparent authority receives money or property of a third person and misapplies it; and

(b) Where the partnership in the course of its business receives money or property of a third person and the money or property so received is misapplied by any partner while it is in the custody of the partnership.

Sec. 15. (Nature of Partner's Liability.) All partners are liable

(a) Jointly and severally for everything chargeable to the partnership under sections 13 and 14.

(b) Jointly for all other debts and obligations of the partnership; but any partner may enter into a separate obligation to perform a partnership contract.

Sec. 16. (Partner by Estoppel.)

(1) When a person, by words spoken or written or by conduct, represents himself, or consents to another representing him to any one, as a partner in an existing partnership or with one or more persons not actual partners, he is liable to any such person to whom such representation has been made, who has, on the faith of such representation, given credit to the actual or apparent partnership, and if he has made such representation or consented to its being made in a public manner he is liable to such person, whether the representation has or has not been made or communicated to such person so giving credit by or with knowledge of the apparent partner making the representation or consenting to its being made.

(a) When a partnership liability results, he is liable as though he were an actual member of the partnership.

(b) When no partnership liability results, he is liable jointly with the other persons, if any, so consenting to the contract or representation as to incur liability, otherwise separately.

(2) When a person has been thus represented to be a partner in an existing partnership, or with one or more persons not actual partners, he is an agent of the persons consenting to such representation to bind them to the same extent and in the same manner as though he were a partner in fact, with respect to persons who rely upon the representation. Where all the members of the existing partnership consent to the representation, a partnership act or obligation results; but in all other cases it is the joint act or obligation of the person acting and the persons consenting to the representation.

Sec. 17. (Liability of Incoming Partner.) A person admitted as a partner into an existing partnership is liable for all the obligations of the partnership arising before his admission as though he had been a partner when such obligations were incurred, except that this liability shall be satisfied only out of partnership property.

Part IV **Relations of Partners to One Another**

Sec. 18. (Rules Determining Rights and Duties of Partners.) The rights and duties of the partners in relation to the partnership shall be determined, subject to any agreement between them, by the following rules.

(a) Each partner shall be repaid his contributions, whether by way of capital or advances to the partnership property and share equally in the profits and surplus remaining after all liabilities, including those to partners, are satisfied; and must contribute toward the losses, whether of capital or otherwise, sustained by the partnership according to his share in the profits.

(b) The partnership must indemnify every partner in respect of payments made and personal liabilities reasonably incurred by him in the ordinary and proper conduct of its business, or for the preservation of its business or property.

(c) A partner, who in aid of the partnership makes any payment or advance beyond the amount of capital which he agreed to contribute, shall be paid interest from the date of the payment or advance.

(d) A partner shall receive interest on the capital contributed by him only from the date when repayment should be made.

(e) All partners have equal rights in the management and conduct of the partnership business.

(f) No partner is entitled to remuneration for acting in the partnership business, except that a surviving partner is entitled to reasonable compensation for his services in winding up the partnership affairs.

(g) No person can become a member of a partnership without the consent of all the partners.

(h) Any difference arising as to ordinary matters connected with the partnership business may be decided by a majority of the partners; but no act in contravention of any agreement between the partners may be done rightfully without the consent of all the partners.

Sec. 19.   (Partnership Books.) The partnership books shall be kept, subject to any agreement between the partners, at the principal place of business of the partnership, and every partner shall at all times have access to and may inspect and copy any of them.

Sec. 20.   (Duty of Partners to Render Information.) Partners shall render on demand true and full information of all things affecting the partnership to any partner or the legal representative of any deceased partner or partner under legal disability.

Sec. 21.   (Partner Accountable as a Fiduciary.)

(1) Every partner must account to the partnership for any benefit, and hold as trustee for it any profits derived by him without the consent of the other partners from any transaction connected with the formation, conduct, or liquidation of the partnership or from any use by him of its property.

(2) This section applies also to the representatives of a deceased partner engaged in the liquidation of the affairs of the partnership as the personal representatives of the last surviving partner.

Sec. 22.   (Right to an Account.) Any partner shall have the right to a formal account as to partnership affairs

(a) If he is wrongfully excluded from the partnership business or possession of its property by his copartners,

(b) If the right exists under the terms of any agreement,

(c) As provided by section 21,

(d) Whenever other circumstances render it just and reasoanble.

Sec. 23.   (Continuation of Partnership Beyond Fixed Term.)

(1) When a partnership for a fixed term or particular undertaking is continued after the termination of such term or particular undertaking without any express agreement, the rights and duties of the partners remain the same as they were at such termination, so far as is consistent with a partnership at will.

(2) A continuation of the business by the partners or such of them as habitually acted therein during the term, without any settlement or liquidation of the partnership affairs, is prima facie evidence of a continuation of the partnership.

Part V **Property Rights of a Partner**

Sec. 24.   (Extent of Property Rights of a Partner.) The property rights of a partner are (1) his rights in specific partnership property, (2) his interest in the partnership, and (3) his right to participate in the management.

Sec. 25.   (Nature of a Partner's Right in Specific Partnership Property.)

(1) A partner is co-owner with his partners of specific partnership property holding as a tenant in partnership.

(2) The incidents of this tenancy are such that

(a) A partner, subject to the provisions of this act and to any agreement between the partners, has an equal right with his partners to possess specific partnership property for partnership purposes; but he has no right to possess such property for any other purpose without the consent of his partners.

(b) A partner's right in specific partnership property is not assignable except in connection with the assignment of rights of all the partners in the same property.

(c) A partner's right in specific partnership property is not subject to attachment or execution, except on a claim against the partnership. When partnership property is attached for a partnership debt the partners, or any of them, or the representatives of a deceased partner, cannot claim any right under the homestead or exemption laws.

(d) On the death of a partner his right in specific partnership property vests in the surviving partner or partner's except where the deceased was the last surviving partner, when his right in such property vests in his legal representative. Such surviving partner or partners, or the legal representative of the last surviving partner, has no right to possess the partnership property for any but a partnership purpose.

(e) A partner's right in specific partnership property is not subject to dower, curtesy, or allowances to widows, heirs, or next of kin.

Sec. 26. (Nature of Partner's Interest in the Partnership.) A partner's interest in the partnership is his share of the profits and surplus, and the same is personal property.

Sec. 27. (Assignment of Partner's Interest.)

(1) A conveyance by a partner of his interest in the partnership does not of itself dissolve the partnership, nor, as against the other partners in the absence of agreement, entitle the assignee, during the continuance of the partnership to interfere in the management or administration of the partnership business or affairs, or to require any information or account of partnership transactions, or to inspect the partnership books; but it merely entitles the assignee to receive in accordance with his contract the profits to which the assigning partner would otherwise be entitled.

(2) In case of a dissolution of the partnership, the assignee is entitled to receive his assignor's interest and may require an account from the date only of the last account agreed to by all the partners.

Sec. 28. (Partner's Interest Subject to Charging Order.)

(1) On due application to a competent court by any judgment creditor of a partner, the court which entered the judgment, order, or decree, or any other court, may charge the interest of the debtor partner with payment of the unsatisfied amount of such judgment debt with interest thereon; and may then or later appoint a receiver of his share of the profits, and of any other money due or to fall due to him in respect of the partnership, and make all other orders, directions, accounts and inquiries which the debtor partner might have made, or which the circumstances of the case may require.

(2) The interest charged may be redeemed at any time before foreclosure, or in case of a sale being directed by the court may be purchased without thereby causing a dissolution

(a) With separate property, by any one or more of the partners, or

(b) With partnership property, by any one or more of the partners with the consent of all the partners whose interests are not so charged or sold.

(3) Nothing in this act shall be held to deprive a partner of his right, if any, under the exemption laws, as regards his interest in the partnership.

Part VI **Dissolution and Winding up**

Sec. 29. (Dissolution Defined.) The dissolution of a partnership is the change in the relation of the partners caused by any partner ceasing to be associated in the carrying on as distinguished from the winding up of the business.

Sec. 30. (Partnership Not Terminated by Dissolution.) On dissolution the partnership is not terminated, but continues until the winding up of partnership affairs is completed.

Sec. 31. (Causes of Dissolution.) Dissolution is caused

(1) Without violation of the agreement between the partners,

(a) By the termination of the definite term or particular undertaking specified in the agreement,

(b) By the express will of any partner when no definite term or particular undertaking is specified,

(c) By the express will of all the partners who have not assigned their interests or suffered them to be charged for their separate debts, either before or after the termination of any specified term or particular undertaking.

(d) By the expulsion of any partner from the business bona fide in accordance with such a power conferred by the agreement between the partners;

(2) In contravention of the agreement between the partners, where the circumstances do not permit a dissolution under any other provision of this section, by the express will of any partner at any time;

(3) By any event which makes it unlawful for the business of the partnership to be carried on or for the members to carry it on in partnership;

(4) By the death of any partner;

(5) By the bankruptcy of any partner or the partnership;

(6) By decree of court under section 32.

Sec. 32. (Dissolution by Decree of Court.)

(1) On application by or for a partner the court shall decree a dissolution whenever

(a) A partner has been declared a lunatic in any judicial proceeding or is shown to be of unsound mind,

(b) A partner becomes in any other way incapable of performing his part of the partnership contract,

(c) A partner has been guilty of such conduct as tends to affect prejudicially the carrying on of the business,

(d) A partner willfully or persistently commits a breach of the partnership agreement, or otherwise so conducts himself in matters relating to the partnership business that it is not reasonably practicable to carry on the business partnership with him,

(e) The business of the partnership can only be carried on at a loss,

(f) Other circumstances render a dissolution equitable.

(2) On the application of the purchaser of a partner's interest under sections 27 or 28

(a) After the termination of the specified term or particular undertaking,

(b) At any time if the partnership was a partnership at will when the interest was assigned or when the charging order was issued.

Sec. 33. (General Effect of Dissolution on Authority of Partner.) Except so far as may be necessary to wind up partnership affairs or to complete transactions begun but not then finished, dissolution terminates all authority of any partner to act for the partnership,

(1) With respesct to the partners,

(a) When the dissolution is not by the act, bankruptcy, or death of a partner; or

(b) When the dissolution is by such act, bankruptcy, or death of a partner, in cases where section 34 so requires.

(2) With respect to persons not partners, as declared in section 35.

Sec. 34. (Right of Partner to Contribution From Copartners After Dissolution.) Where the dissolution is caused by the act, death, or bankruptcy of a partner, each partner is liable to his copartners for his share of any liability created by any partner acting for the partnership as if the partnership had not been dissolved unless

(a) The dissolution being by act of any partner, the partner acting for the partnership had knowledge of the dissolution, or

(b) The dissolution being by the death or bankruptcy of a partner, the partner acting for the partnership had knowledge or notice of the death or bankruptcy.

Sec. 35. (Power of Partner to Bind Partnership to Third Persons After Dissolution.)

(1) After dissolution a partner can bind the partnership except as provided in paragraph (3)

(a) By any act appropriate for winding up partnership affairs or completing transactions unfinished at dissolution;

(b) By an transaction which would bind the partnership if dissolution had not taken place, provided the other party to the transaction

(I) Had extended credit to the partnership prior to dissolution and had no knowledge or notice of the dissolution; or

(II) Though he had not so extended credit, had nevertheless known of the partnership prior to dissolution, and, having no knowledge or notice of dissolution, the fact of dissolution had not been advertised in a newspaper of general circulation in the place (or in each place if more than one) at which the partnership business was regularly carried on.

(2) The liability of a partner under paragraph (1b) shall be satisfied out of partnership assets alone when such partner had been prior to dissolution.

(a) Unknown as a partner to the person with whom the contract is made; and

(b) So far unknown and inactive in partnership affairs that the business reputation of the partnership could not be said to have been in any degree due to his connection with it.

(3) The partnership is in no case bound by any act of a partner after dissolution

(a) Where the partnership is dissolved because it is unlawful to carry on the business, unless the act is appropriate for winding up partnership affairs; or

(b) Where the partner has become bankrupt; or

(c) Where the partner has no authority to wind up partnership affairs; except by a transaction with one who

(I) Had extended credit to the partnership prior to dissolution and had no knowledge or notice of his want of authority; or

(II) Had not extended credit to the partnership prior to dissolution, and, having no knowledge or notice of his want of authority, the fact of his want of authority has not been advertised in the manner provided for advertising the fact of dissolution in paragraph (1bII).

(4) Nothing in this section shall affect the liability under section 16 of any person who after dissolution represents himself or consents to another representing him as a partner in a partnership engaged in carrying on business.

Sec. 36. (Effect of Dissolution of Partner's Existing Liability.)

(1) The dissolution of the partnership does not of itself discharge the existing liability of any partner.

(2) A partner is discharged from any existing liability upon dissolution of the partnership by an agreement to that effect between himself, the partnership creditor, and the person or partnership continuing the business; and such agreement may be inferred from the course of dealing between the creditor having knowledge of the dissolution and the person or partnership continuing the business.

(3) Where a person agrees to assume the existing obligations of a dissolved partnership, the partners whose obligations have been assumed shall be discharged from any liability to any creditor of the partnership who, knowing of the agreement, consents to a material alteration in the nature or time of payment of such obligations.

(4) The individual property of a deceased partner shall be liable for all obligations of the partnership incurred while he was a partner but subject to the prior payment of his separate debts.

Sec. 37.   (Right to Wind Up.) Unless otherwise agreed the partners who have not wrongfully dissolved the partnership or the legal representative of the last surviving partner, not bankrupt, has the right to wind up the partnership affairs; provided, however, that any partner, his legal representative or his assignee, upon cause shown, may obtain winding up by the court.

Sec. 38.   (Rights of Partners to Application of Partnership Property.)

(1) When dissolution is caused in any way, except in contravention of the partnership agreement, each partner as against his copartners and all persons claiming through them in respect of their interests in the partnership, unless otherwise agreed, may have the partnership property applied to discharge its liabilities, and the surplus applied to pay in cash the net amount owing to the respective partners. But if dissolution is caused by expulsion of a partner, bona fide under the partnership agreement and if the expelled partner is discharged from all partnership liabilities, either by payment or agreement under section 36(2), he shall receive in cash only the net amount due him from the partnership.

(2) When dissolution is caused in contravention of the partnership agreement the rights of the partners shall be as follows.

(a) Each partner who has not caused dissolution wrongfully shall have,

    (I) All the rights specified in paragraph (1) of this section, and

    (II) The right, as against each partner who has caused the dissolution wrongfully, to damages for breach of the agreement.

(b) The partners who have not caused the dissolution wrongfully, if they all desire to continue the business in the same name, either by themselves or jointly with others, may do so, during the agreed term for the partnership and for that purpose may possess the partnership property, provided they secure the payment by bond approved by the court, or pay to any partner who has caused the dissolution wrongfully, the value of his interest in the partnership at the dissolution, less any damages recoverable under clause (2aII) of the section, and in like manner indemnify him against all present or future partnership liabilities.

(c) A partner who has caused the dissolution wrongfully shall have

    (I) If the business is not continued under the provisions of paragraph (2b) all the rights of a partner under paragraph (1), subject to clause (2aII), of this section.

    (II) If the business if continued under paragraph (2b) of this section the right as against his copartners and all claiming through them in respect of their interests in the partnership, to have the value of his interest in the partnership, less any damages caused to his copartners by the dissolution, ascertained and paid to him in cash, or the payment secured by bond approved by the court, and to be released from all existing liabilities of the partnership; but in ascertaining the value of the partner's interest the value of the goodwill of the business shall not be considered.

Sec. 39.   (Rights Where Partnership is Dissolved for Fraud or Misrepresentation.) Where a partnership contract is rescinded on the ground of the fraud or misrepresentation of one of the parties thereto, the party entitled to rescind is, without prejudice to any other right, entitled,

(a) To a lien on, or right of retention of, the surplus of the partnership property after satisfying the partnership liabilities to third persons for any sum of money paid by him for the purchase of an interest in the partnership and for any capital or advances contributed by him; and

(b) To stand, after all liabilities to third persons have been satisfied, in the place of the creditors of the partnership for any payments made by him in respect of the partnership liabilities; and

(c) To be indemnified by the person guilty of the fraud or making the representation against all debts and liabilities of the partnership.

Sec. 40.   (Rules for Distribution.) In settling accounts between the partners after dissolution, the following rules shall be observed, subject to any agreement to the contrary.

(a) The assets of the partnership are
>   (I) The partnership property,
>   (II) The contributions of the partners necessary for the payment of all the liabilities specified in clause (b) of this paragraph.

(b) The liabilities of the partnership shall rank in order of payment, as follows.
>   (I) Those owing to creditors other than partners,
>   (II) Those owing to partners other than for capital and profits,
>   (III) Those owing to partners in respect to capital,
>   (IV) Those owing to partners in respect of profits.

(c) The assets shall be applied in the order of their declaration in clause (a) of this paragraph to the satisfaction of the liabilities.

(d) The partners shall contribute, as provided by section 18(a) the amount necessary to satisfy the liabilities; but if any, but not all, of the partners are insolvent, or, not being subject to process, refuse to contribute, the other parties shall contribute their share of the liabilities, and, in the relative proportions in which they share the profits, the additional amount necessary to pay the liabilities.

(e) An assignee for the benefit of creditors or any person appointed by the court shall have the right to enforce the contributions specified in clause (d) of this paragraph.

(f) Any partner or his legal representative shall have the right to enforce the contributions specified in clause (d) of this paragraph, to the extent of the amount which he has paid in excess of his share of the liability.

(g) The individual property of a deceased partner shall be liable for the contributions specified in clause (d) of this paragraph.

(h) When partnership property and the individual properties of the partners are in possession of a court for distribution, partnership creditors shall have priority on partnership property and separate creditors on individual property, saving the rights of lien or secured creditors as heretofore.

(i) Where a partner has become bankrupt or his estate is insolvent the claims against his separate property shall rank in the following order.
>   (I) Those owing to separate creditors,
>   (II) Those owing to partnership creditors,
>   (III) Those owing to partners by way of contribution.

Sec. 41.   (Liability of Persons Continuing the Business in Certain Cases.)

(1) When any new partner is admitted into an existing partnership, or when any partner retires and assigns (or the representative of the deceased partner assigns) his rights in partnership property to two or more of the partners, or to one or more of the partners and one or more third persons, if the business is continued without liquidation of the partnership affairs, creditors of the first or dissolved partnership are also creditors of the partnership so continuing the business.

(2) When all but one partner retire and assign (or the representative of the deceased partner assigns) their rights in partnership property to the remaining partner, who continues the business without liquidation of partnership affairs, either alone or with others, creditors of the dissolved partnership are also creditors of the person or partnership so continuing the business.

(3) When any partner retires or dies and the business of the dissolved partnership is continued as set forth in paragraphs (1) and (2) of this section, with the consent of the retired partners or the representative of the deceased partner, but without any assignment of his right in partnership property, rights of creditors of the dissolved partnership and of the creditors of the person or partnership continuing the business shall be as if such assignment had been made.

(4) When all the partners or their representatives assign their rights in partnership property to one or more third persons who promise to the debts and who continue the business of the dissolved

partnership, creditors of the dissolved partnership are also creditors of the person or partnership continuing the business.

(5) When any partner wrongfully causes a dissolution and the remaining partners continue the business under the provisions of section 38(2b), either alone or with others, and without liquidation of the partnership affairs, creditors of the dissolved partnership are also creditors of the person or partnership continuing the business.

(6) When a partner is expelled and the remaining partners continue the business either alone or with others, without liquidation of the partnership affairs, creditors of the dissolved partnership are also creditors of the person or partnership continuing the business.

(7) The liability of a third person becoming a partner in the partnership continuing the business, under this section, to the creditors of the dissolved partnership shall be satisfied out of partnership property only.

(8) When the business of a partnership after dissolution is continued under any conditions set forth in this section the creditors of the dissolved partnership, as against the separate creditors of the retiring or deceased partner or the representative of the deceased partner, have a prior right to any claim of the retired partner or the representative of the deceased partner against the person or partnership continuing the business, on account of the retired or deceased partner's interest in the dissolved partnership or on account of any consideration promised for such interest or for his right in partnership property.

(9) Nothing in this section shall be held to modify any right of the creditors to set aside any assignment on the ground of fraud.

(10) The use by the person or partnership continuing the business of the partnership name, or the name of a deceased partner as part thereof, shall not of itself make the individual property of the deceased partner liable for any debts contracted by such person or partnership.

Sec. 42.   (Rights of Retiring or Estate of Deceased Partner When the Business is Continued.) When any partner retires or dies, and the business is continued under any of the conditions set forth in section 41(1, 2, 3, 5, 6), or section 38(2b), without any settlement of accounts as between him or his estate and the person or partnership continuing the business, unless otherwise agreed, he or his legal representative as against such persons or partnership may have the value of his interest at the date of dissolution ascertained, and shall receive as an ordinary creditor an amount equal to the value of his interest in the dissolved partnership with interest, or, at his option or at the option of his legal representative, in lieu of interest, the profits attributable to the use of his right in the property of the dissolved partnership; provided that the creditors of the dissolved partnership as against the separate creditors, or the representative of the retired or deceased partner, shall have priorty on any claim arising under this section, as provided by section 41(8) of this act.

Sec. 43.   (Accrual of Actions.) The right to an account of his interest shall accrue to any partner, or his legal representative, as against the winding up partners or the surviving partners or the person or partnership continuing the business, at the date of dissolution, in the absence of any agreement to the contrary.

SOLUTION TO REVIEW PROBLEM

1.	(1) Cash		31,000	
	Inventory		25,000	
	Equipment		9,000	
		Accounts Payable		5,000
		Capital, Partner A		36,000
		Capital, Partner B		24,000

(2)	Cash	31,000	
	Inventory	25,000	
	Equipment	9,000	
	Accounts Payable		5,000
	Capital, Partner A		30,000
	Capital, Partner B		30,000
(3)	Cash	31,000	
	Inventory	25,000	
	Equipment	9,000	
	Goodwill	12,000	
	Accounts Payable		5,000
	Capital, Partner A		36,000
	Capital, Partner B		36,000

2.

Partner A	Partner B
$30,000 × 1 = $ 30,000	$30,000 × 4 = $120,000
$42,000 × 6 = 252,000	$38,000 × 6 = 228,000
$36,000 × 5 = 180,000	$42,000 × 2 = 84,000
12 $462,000	12 $432,000
$462,000 ÷ 12 = $38,500	$432,000 ÷ 12 = $ 36,000

Bonus = .08 (Net Income − Bonus)
Bonus = .08 ($48,600 − Bonus)
Bonus = $3,888 − .08(Bonus)
1.08 Bonus = $3,888
Bonus = $3,600

A AND B PARTNERSHIP
Profit Allocation Schedule
Year Ended December 31, 1990

Allocation Factor	Partner A	Partner B	Total
Interest on Average Capital	$ 4,620 (1)	$ 4,320 (2)	$ 8,940
Salaries	10,800 (3)	10,800	21,600
Bonus	3,600		3,600
	19,020	15,120	34,140
Remainder 7:3	10,122 (4)	4,338 (5)	14,460
Total	$ 29,142	$ 19,458	$ 48,600

(1) $38,500 × .12 = $4,620
(2) $36,000 × .12 = $4,320
(3) $900 × 12 = $10,800
(4) $14,460 × .7 = $10,122
(5) $14,460 × .3 = $ 4,338

3.

A AND B PARTNERSHIP
Profit Allocation Schedule
Year Ended December 31, 1990

Allocation Factor	Partner A	Partner B	Total
Interest on Average Capital	$ 4,620	$ 4,320	$ 8,940
Salaries	10,800	10,800	21,600
Bonus	1,700 (1)		1,700
	17,120	15,120	32,240
Remainder 7:3	(6,503) (2)	(2,787) (3)	(9,290)
Total	$ 10,617	$ 12,333	$ 22,950

(1)   Bonus = .08 (Net Income − Bonus)
         Bonus = .08 ($22,950 − Bonus)
         Bonus = $1,836 − .08(Bonus)
   1.08 Bonus = $1,836
         Bonus = $1,700
(2) $9,290 × .7 = $6,503
(3) $9,290 × .3 = $2,787

4.

A AND B PARTNERSHIP
Profit Allocation Schedule
Year Ended December 31, 1990

Allocation Factor	Partner A	Partner B	Total
Interest on Average Capital	$ 4,620	$ 4,320	$ 8,940
Salaries	7,005	7,005	14,010
Total	$ 11,625	$ 11,325	$ 22,950

(1) $22,950 − $8,940 = $14,010
    $14,010 ÷ 2 = $7,005

5.

A AND B PARTNERSHIP
Statement of Changes in Partners' Capital Accounts
Year Ended December 31, 1990

	Partner A	Partner B	Total
Beginning Capital, 1/1/90	$ 30,000	$ 30,000	$ 60,000
Capital Contributed in 1990	12,000	12,000	24,000
Excess Withdrawals	(6,000)		(6,000)
Net Income	29,142	19,458	48,600
Drawings	(10,800)	(10,800)	(21,600)
Ending Capital, 12/31/90	$ 54,342	$ 50,658	$ 105,000

CHAPTER
3

CHANGES IN PARTNERS

 partnership is legally dissolved whenever a new partner is admitted or an original partner withdraws from the partnership. Partners can override the legal dissolution of their partnership by having an ongoing business clause in their partnership agreement. The ongoing business clause allows the partnership to operate as a going concern. The discussion of the admission and withdrawal of partners includes the following topics:

- The admission of a partner who contributes net assets to the partnership
- The admission of a partner who purchases an interest from the partners as individuals
- The admission of a new partner who buys out the partnership share of an original partner, which results in simultaneous admission and withdrawal
- The withdrawal of a partner whose interest is purchased by the partners as individuals and by the partnership
- The effects of the partners changing their relative shares of capital by buying and selling to and from each other as individuals

The three methods—the net investment approach, the bonus method, and the recognition of goodwill—discussed in Chapter 2 for the formation of a partnership can also be used when a new partner is admitted to a firm or when a partner withdraws. All three methods are presented for both the admission and withdrawal of partners, but you should keep in mind the discussion in Chapter 2 regarding the propriety of using the goodwill method if a new partner does not contribute an existing business or when an original partner withdraws from the partnership.

ADMISSION AND WITHDRAWAL METHODS

A partnership is legally dissolved whenever a change in the partners occurs. As discussed in Chapter 2, partners can override this limited life by specifying in the partnership agreement that the business entity is to continue without interruption when a change in the partners occurs. The alternative methods that can be used to record the formation of a partnership also can be used in recording the admission and withdrawal of partners.

The process used to allocate profits and losses to partners in a manner that the partners consider fair and reasonable also affects the admission and withdrawal of partners. Therefore, no precise rules exist for admission or withdrawal of partners; instead, admission and withdrawal terms are the result of what the partners believe to be just and equitable. A partnership can specify the manner in which new partners are to be admitted and present partners are allowed to withdraw either in the partnership agreement or by the partners simply reaching a decision.

If the partnership agreement does not contain provisions for admission and withdrawal of partners, or if the partners cannot agree on the terms, the Uniform Partnership Act is applied. The Uniform Partnership Act states that when a partner assigns an interest in a partnership to another person, the new partner can only receive the existing partner's share of the profits, but cannot participate in the operations or management of the partnership.[1]

ADMISSION METHODS

If the net investment is used, the new partner's capital account is credited with the fair market value of the assets contributed, or if the new partner purchases the partnership interest from the existing partners, the new partner is credited with the net book value of the equity of the original partners' share purchased. If the bonus method is used to record the admission of a partner, the bonus can be granted either to the original partners or to the new partner. If the bonus method is used to record the withdrawal of a partner, the bonus can be granted either to the remaining partners or to the withdrawing partner. If the goodwill method is selected for the admission of a partner, the goodwill may be credited either to the original partners or to the new partner.

WITHDRAWAL METHODS

When a partner withdraws from a partnership, two possible approaches can be taken to determine the amount of goodwill. One approach is to base the amount of the goodwill on the amount actually purchased by the partnership. The goodwill recorded is only the amount of goodwill attributable to the interest being acquired. The alternative way is to consider the price a partner accepts for a percentage of the firm as a valid measure of the fair market value of the entire partnership. In this approach the amount of the goodwill is the increase in value of the whole partnership. The arguments proposed in Chapter 2 for deciding if the recording

---

[1]Uniform Parternship Act, Section 27.

of goodwill has authoritative support are equally applicable to the recording of admission and withdrawal of partners.

If a partner brings an existing business to the partnership, such as a sole practitioner merging an accounting practice with an existing accounting partnership, the goodwill recorded meets the definition of the excess of the price paid over the fair market value net assets acquired. If the admission of a partner is viewed as the formation of a new business, with the original partners contributing the existing partnership's net assets and the new partners contributing assets, the recording of goodwill also is appropriate. The recording of goodwill, when a partner withdraws either by selling of a partnershp interest to a new partner or by being bought out by the remaining partners, is similar to the admission of a new partner.

ADMISSION OF A PARTNER WHO CONTRIBUTES NET ASSETS

A new partner can be admitted to an existing partnership by contributing net assets. This contribution can be cash, a group of net assets, or an existing business. If an existing business is contributed, a merger has taken place and the recording of goodwill can be justified according to generally accepted accounting principles. The assets contributed by the new partner and any liabilities assumed by the partnership are recorded at their fair market values. Both the increase in net assets and the percentage of capital the new partner is to receive must be considered in determining the amount of capital to credit to the new partner's capital account. Illustrative Problem 3.1 discusses and presents an example of each of the three methods— net investment, bonus, and goodwill—and then presents a comparison of the methods.

ILLUSTRATIVE PROBLEM 3.1: ADMISSION OF A PARTNER WHO CONTRIBUTES NET ASSETS TO THE PARTNERSHIP

If the net investment method is used to record the admission of a new partner, the assets contributed are debited with their fair market values and any liabilities assumed by the partnership are also recorded at their fair market value. The fair market value of the net assets contributed is credited to the new partner's capital account.

The partners of the A and B Partnership agree to admit C as a partner. Prior to the admission of C, Partners A and B had the following capital balances, shares of capital, and shares of profit and loss:

	Partner A	Partner B	Total
Capital Balance	$ 15,000	$ 35,000	$ 50,000
Share of Capital	30%	70%	
Share of Profit and Loss (2:3)	2/5	3/5	

Case 1: Net Investment Method.   C contributes $11,667 cash and office furniture with a fair market value of $5,000 for a one-fourth interest in capital and net income. The new partnership has net assets of $66,667 ($50,000 from the existing partnership and $16,667 of assets contributed by C). C contributed an amount exactly equal to one-fourth of the new

capital. The journal entry to record the admission of C is

Cash	11,667	
Office Furniture	5,000	
Capital, Partner C		16,667

The original partners and the new partner may agree to record an initial capital balance for the new partner that is different from the fair market value of the net assets contributed. If the amount of capital allocated to the new partner is less than the net assets contributed, the new partner is granting a bonus to the original partners, or if the amount of capital is greater, the original partners are granting a bonus to the new partner. The bonus is recorded in the original partners' capital accounts based on their preadmission profit- and loss-sharing ratio on the assumption that any gains or losses from the sale of the partnership would have affected their capital accounts in that ratio.

A transaction that results in a bonus to the original partners implies either undervalued assets or the existence of unrecorded assets, such as goodwill, or both. If the bonus method is used, the partners have decided not to record the goodwill, but to allocate additional capital to the partners who have generated the unrecorded assets. In accounting firms and other professional partnerships, in addition to the fair market value of the net assets contributed by the new partner, a value for clientele credit (goodwill) is determined as a basis for establishing the price to a new partner. This is usually computed as a percentage of the prior year's gross or net revenues, or an average of several prior years may be used. In addition, the amount is usually adjusted for the loss or acquisition of any major customers or clients. If the transaction results in a bonus to the new partner, it implies that the new partner has brought an unidentifiable intangible asset to the partnership or the assets of the partnership are overvalued, or a combination of the two causes.

The partners of the A and B Partnership agree to admit C as a partner. Prior to the admission of C, Partners A and B had the following capital balances, shares of capital, and shares of profit and loss

	Partner A	Partner B	Total
Capital Balance	$ 15,000	$ 35,000	$ 50,000
Share of Capital	30%	70%	
Share of Profit and Loss (2:3)	2/5	3/5	

Case 2: Bonus to Original Partners.   C contributes cash of $17,000 and office furniture with a fair market value of $5,000 for a one-fourth interest in the equity of the partnership. The total capital is $72,000 ($50,000 + $17,000 + $5,000) and C is credited with one-fourth of $72,000 or $18,000. The remaining $4,000 is a bonus to the existing partners and is recorded in their profit- and loss-sharing ratio of 2:3, respectively. The journal entry to record the admission of C is

Cash	17,000	
Office Furniture	5,000	
Capital, Partner A		1,600
Capital, Partner B		2,400
Capital, Partner C		18,000

After the admission of C, the partners' capital accounts and capital shares are

	Partner A	Partner B	Partner C	Total
Capital Balance	$ 16,600	$ 37,400	$ 18,000	$ 72,000
Share of Capital	23.06%	51.94%	25.00%	

Case 3: Bonus to New Partner. C contributes $7,000 cash and office furniture with a fair market value of $5,000 for a one-fourth interest in capital and profits. The total capital is $62,000 ($50,000 + $12,000) and C's one-fourth is $15,500. The difference between the $15,500 credited to C's capital account and the $12,000 of assets invested is a $3,500 bonus to C from Partners A and B, and is debited to their capital accounts in their profit- and loss-sharing ratio of 2:3, respectively. The journal entry to record the admission of C is

Cash	7,000	
Office Furniture	5,000	
Capital, Partner A	1,400	
Capital, Partner B	2,100	
Capital, Partner C		15,500

After the admission of C, the partners' capital accounts and capital shares are

	Partner A	Partner B	Partner C	Total
Capital Balance	$ 13,600	$ 32,900	$ 15,500	$ 62,000
Share of Capital	21.94%	53.06%	25.00%	

If the partners view this transaction as the formation of a new business entity, they can decide to revalue undervalued or overvalued assets and to record goodwill. The revaluation of assets and the goodwill recognized are credited to the original partners' capital accounts in their profit and loss ratio because, if the partners had sold the partnership, any gains or losses would be shared using that ratio. The agreement between the partners may result in the amount of goodwill that is recorded being credited either to the capital accounts of the original partners or to the capital account of the new partner.

If the fair market value of the net assets that the new partner is contributing is assumed to represent the fair market value of the share of capital that the new partner is to receive, this indicates that the original partners are to receive goodwill. The goodwill is the excess of the total fair market value of the partnership, as determined by the value of the net assets that the new partner is willing to contribute, less the sum of the fair market values of the recorded net assets of the present partnership and the contribution of the new partner. Conversely, if the amount being contributed by the new partner is less than the fair market value of the share being allocated, this indicates that the new partner is bringing goodwill to the partnership.

The first step in recording the admission of the new partner if the original partners are to receive goodwill is to adjust the book values of the partnership's net assets to their fair market values and record the goodwill indicated by the transaction price for the new partner's share of capital. The admission of the new partner is then recorded by crediting the new partner with initial capital equal to the value of the net assets contributed.

The partners of the A and B Partnership agree to admit C as a partner. Prior to the admission of C, Partners A and B had the following capital balances, shares of capital, and shares of profit and loss:

	Partner A	Partner B	Total
Capital Balance	$ 15,000.	$ 35,000	$ 50,000
Share of Capital	30%	70%	
Share of Profit and Loss (2:3)	2/5	3/5	

Case 4: Goodwill to Original Partners.   C agrees to invest $22,000 cash for a one-fourth interest in the partnership. The partners agree that $22,000 represents a valid measure of the fair market value of a 25% share and to record goodwill. The partners also agree that the fair market value of the net assets of the A and B Partnership, prior to the admission of C, is $60,000 and the only undervalued asset is the buiding, which has a fair market value $10,000 higher than its net book value. If the new partner is willing to invest $22,000, the value of the partnership is $88,000 ($22,000 ÷ .25). The building is increased by the $10,000 of excess of fair market value over its net book value and goodwill of $6,000 [$88,000 − ($60,000 + $22,000)] is recorded. The increase in net assets is credited to the original partners in their profit and loss ratio. The journal entries to revalue the building and record the goodwill of the existing partnership, and to record the admission of C are

Building	10,000	
Goodwill	6,000	
Capital, Partner A		6,400
Capital, Partner B		9,600
Cash	22,000	
Capital, Partner C		22,000

After the admission of C, the partners' capital accounts and capital shares are

	Partner A	Partner B	Partner C	Total
Capital Balance	$ 21,400	$ 44,600	$ 22,000	$ 88,000
Share of Capital	24.32%	50.68%	25.00%	

If the fair market value of the net assets of an existing partnership is divided by the percentage of ownership the original partners will have after the admission of a new partner, the fair market value of the new partnership is determined. In effect, the fair market value of the present assets is being used to establish the fair market value of the new partnership. If the amount being contributed by the new partner is less than the fair market value of the share being allocated, this indicates the new partner is bringing goodwill to the partnership.

To determine if a new partner is bringing goodwill to the partnership, we can compare the fair market value of the net assets being invested to the new partner's percentage of ownership of the fair market value of the partnership as a whole. If the original partners agree to admit the new partner for an investment that is less than the percentage of capital being given, this indicates that the new partner is bringing goodwill to the partnership. The amount of the goodwill is the difference between the new partner's percentage of ownership and the amount being invested. The fair market value of the net assets of the partnership before the admission of the new partner will equal the percentage of ownership equity of the original partners after the admission. The first step in recording the admission of the new partner is to record any differences between the net book value of the assets and their fair market values. The increases or decreases are recorded in the original partners' capital accounts. Then the amount of the goodwill plus the value of the net assets contributed is recorded as the capital of the new partner.

The partners of the A and B Partnership agree to admit C as a partner. Prior to the admission of C, Partners A and B had the following capital balances, shares of capital, and shares of profit and loss:

	Partner A	Partner B	Total
Capital Balance	$ 15,000	$ 35,000	$ 50,000
Share of Capital	30%	70%	
Share of Profit and Loss (2:3)	2/5	3/5	

Case 5: Goodwill to New Partner.   C agrees to invest $12,000 for a one-fourth interest in the partnership and the partners agree that the partnership's building is undervalued by $10,000. If the original partnership is 75% of the new partnership, the value of the new partnership is $80,000 ($60,000 ÷ .75). If C is credited with 25% of $80,000, or $20,000, and only contributed $12,000 of assets, this indicates that C brought an intangible asset to the partnership that is worth $8,000 [$80,000 − ($60,000 + $12,000)]. Because the partners are unable to identify this asset, the $8,000 difference is recorded as goodwill. The journal entries to record the increase in the book value of the building and the admission of C are

Building	10,000	
Capital, Partner A		4,000
Capital, Partner B		6,000
Cash	12,000	
Goodwill	8,000	
Capital, Partner C		20,000

After the admission of C, the partners' capital accounts and capital shares are

	Partner A	Partner B	Partner C	Total
Capital Balance	$ 19,000	$ 41,000	$ 20,000	$ 80,000
Share of Capital	23.75%	51.25%	25.00%	

COMPARISON OF THE METHODS

The capital balances of the partners under the various assumptions and methods are summarized as follows:

	Case 1 Net Investment Method	Case 2 Bonus Original Partners	Case 3 Bonus New Partner	Case 4 Goodwill Original Partners	Case 5 Goodwill New Partner
Partner A	$ 15,000	$ 16,600	$ 13,600	$ 21,400	$ 19,000
Partner B	35,000	37,400	32,900	44,600	41,000
Partner C	16,667	18,000	15,500	22,000	20,000
Total	$ 66,667	$ 72,000	$ 62,000	$ 88,000	$ 80,000

The depreciation of the increase in the carrying value of the building and the amortization of goodwill recorded in Cases 4 and 5 will affect the capital balances of the partners over time. In Case 4, Partner C was credited with 25% of the capital. If Partner C receives the same share of profits as the initial capital share, and Partners A and B share the remaining 75% in their former profit- and loss-sharing ratio of two-fifths and three-fifths the effect of the depreciation of the building and the amortization of goodwill over time, ignoring all other transactions, on the capital balances of the partners is

	Capital A	Capital B	Capital C	Total
Case 4 Balance	$ 21,400	$ 44,600	$ 22,000	$ 88,000
Depreciation of the Building	(3,000) (1)	(4,500) (2)	(2,500)	(10,000)
Amortization of Goodwill	(1,800)	(2,700)	(1,500)	(6,000)
Balance	$ 16,600	$ 37,400	$ 18,000	$ 72,000

(1) 2/5 × 75% = 30%
(2) 3/5 × 75% = 45%

The depreciation of the building and the amortization of goodwill result in the same capital balances as the bonus to original partners in Case 2. In Cases 2 and 4, the new partner invested the same amount of assets and received the same share of capital. Only if Partner C's share of profit and loss is equal to the share of the initial capital received, and Partners A and B continue to share the remaining profit and loss in their profit ratio, will the depreciation and amortization over time reduce the capital balances to the amounts that are recorded under the bonus method. Any other profit- and loss-sharing ratio used by the partnership of A, B, and C will have different results. For example, if Partner C receives only 20% of the net income and Partners A and B continue their 2 : 3 relationship of the remaining 80%, the effect of the depreciation of the increase in the carrying value of the building and the amortization of goodwill is

	Capital A	Capital B	Capital C	Total
Case 4 Balance	$ 21,400	$ 44,600	$ 22,000	$ 88,000
Depreciation of the Building	(3,200) (1)	(4,800) (2)	(2,000)	(10,000)
Amortization of Goodwill	(1,920)	(2,880)	(1,200)	(6,000)
Balance	$ 16,280	$ 36,920	$ 18,800	$ 72,000

(1) 2/5 × 80% = 32%
(2) 3/5 × 80% = 48%

Alternatively, if Partner C receives a one-fourth interest in profits, which is the same as the initial capital share, but Partners A and B each receive one-half of the remaining 75%, or 37.5%, the effect on their capital accounts over time is

	Capital A	Capital B	Capital C	Total
Case 4 Balance	$ 21,400	$ 44,600	$ 22,000	$ 88,000
Depreciation of the Building	(3,750)	(3,750)	(2,500)	(10,000)
Amortization of Goodwill	(2,250)	(2,250)	(1,500)	(6,000)
Balance	$ 15,600	$ 38,600	$ 18,000	$ 72,000

In Case 5, the effect of increased depreciation of the building and the amortization of goodwill over time on the balances of the capital accounts of the partners has the same results as in Case 3 above. If the new partnership of A, B, and C agrees that Partner C receive 25% of the profit and loss, and Partners A and B continue in their 2:3 relationship as in the original partnership (30:45:25), the following occurs:

	Capital A	Capital B	Capital C	Total
Case 5 Balance	$ 19,000	$ 41,000	$ 20,000	$ 80,000
Depreciation of the Building	(3,000)	(4,500)	(2,500)	(10,000)
Amortization of Goodwill	(2,400)	(3,600)	(2,000)	(8,000)
Balance	$ 13,600	$ 32,900	$ 15,500	$ 62,000

In this example, the results are the same as in Case 3 in which the original partners granted a bonus to the new partner. In both Cases 3 and 5, Partner C invested the same amount for the same share of capital. These results, like the effects in Case 4, occur only if the new partner's share of profits and losses is the same as the share of initial capital and if the original partners share the remaining profits in their old profit- and loss-sharing ratio. Neither the bonus method nor the goodwill method result in capital balances that are the same as the net investment method.

The partners may select a method that they wish to use, or if they decide to rely on us to make the choice, the choice of the method to use for recording the admission of a new partner depends on our interpretation of the substance of the transaction and the fair market value of the net assets in relation to their net book value of the existing partnership. If we believe that the partnership, after the admission of a new partner, is simply an ongoing business entity, we will use either the net investment method or the bonus method. We are viewing this transaction as being similar to a corporation issuing new shares. The corporation has more equity and the share of equity of the original shareholders has decreased, but the corporation is still the same business entity.

Some accountants would argue that the original partnership has ceased to exist and a new business entity has been formed; thus, the original partnership should be revalued and any goodwill either from the original partnership or brought to the partnership by the new partner should be recorded. Some accountants would argue that the establishment of the entry price for the new partner is not an arm's-length transaction and, therefore, the recording of goodwill is not justified. Other accountants would disagree, stating that the new partner and the original partners arrived at a purchase price prior to the formation of the new partnership and that they were unrelated parties at the time of the agreement on the acquisition price. Thus, whether or not we believe that goodwill should be recorded when a new partner is admitted to a partnership depends on how we view the effect of changes in partners on the partnership.

ADMISSION OF A PARTNER WHO PURCHASES AN INTEREST DIRECTLY FROM THE ORIGINAL PARTNERS

A new partner can be admitted to a partnership by purchasing an interest from one or more of the original partners as individuals. The new partner may purchase all of an original partner's interest or may purchase a portion of one or more of the original partners' share of partnership capital. If a new partner purchases the entire partnership interest of an original partner, there is simultaneous admission and withdrawal of partners. No new assets are contributed to a partnership if a new partner purchases an interest from one or more of the original partners or a retiring partner.

When a new partner is admitted to a partnership that provides services, the new partner is often an employee who has been promoted to partner and who does not have substantial cash resources. Becoming a partner is effectively the admission to ownership and not the promotion of an employee. Often a CPA is admitted as a partner in an accounting firm by purchasing an interest directly from the present partners. The interest purchased is usually paid for out of the new partner's future earnings. This is generally accomplished by debiting the new partner's capital account for his payment and crediting the capital accounts of the selling partners as the new partner receives a share of income, thus effecting a shift of future income. In some accounting firms, particularly the large ones, the amounts paid out of earnings by the new partners for their share of capital are used to provide payments to the retiring partners for their share of the partnership's equity.

The journal entries for the admission of a partner who purchases an interest directly from a partner or partners are similar to those for the admission of a partner who contributes net assets, except that no new assets are added to the partnership. The share of capital purchased from the original partners is a reduction of their capital balances. Either the net investment method or the goodwill method can be used for the admission of a partner who purchases an interest directly from the partners as individuals. The bonus method is not used because the share purchased is transferred from the selling partners' capital accounts to the buying partner's capital account. Any bonus between the new and original partners is reflected in the price the partners accepted for their partnership interest, which is not a transaction of the partnership. The following example is based on the same original partnership as presented in Illustrative Problem 3.1.

ILLUSTRATIVE PROBLEM 3.2: ADMISSION OF A PARTNER WHO PURCHASES AN INTEREST DIRECTLY FROM THE PARTNERS

The partners of the A and B Partnership agree to admit C to the partnership with a one-fourth interest in capital and profits. Partners A and B agree that C will buy two-fifths of the interest from A and three-fifths from B. Prior to the admission of C, Partners A and B had the following capital balances, shares of capital, and shares of profit and loss:

	Partner A	Partner B	Total
Capital Balance	$ 15,000	$ 35,000	$ 50,000
Share of Capital	30%	70%	
Share of Profit and Loss	2/5	3/5	

Case 1: Net Investment Method.   C agrees to pay $16,500 for a one-fourth interest and will pay $6,600 to A and $9,900 to B. The price paid by C does not enter into the recording of the capital interest purchased by C. The total equity of the firm is the same as no new assets are added to the partnership.

Capital, Partner A	5,000 (1)	
Capital, Partner B	7,500 (2)	
Capital, Partner C		12,500

(1) $50,000 × 1/4 = $12,500 capital to C
    $12,500 × 2/5 = $5,000 from A
(2) $12,500 × 3/5 = $7,500 from B

Case 2: Goodwill to Original Partners.   The partners agree that the $16,500 C is willing to pay them for a one-fourth interest in the capital of the partnership is a valid measure of the fair market value of the partnership. The fair market value of the firm is $66,000 ($16,500 ÷ .25). The partners determine that the only undervalued asset is the building. The fair market value of the building is $10,000 more than the book value. The journal entries to record the increase in assets of the present partnership and the admission of C are

Building	10,000	
Goodwill	6,000 (1)	
Capital, Partner A		6,400
Capital, Partner B		9,600

(1) $66,000 − Partnership capital $50,000 − increase in building $10,000
    = $6,000 of goodwill

Capital, Partner A	6,600	
Capital, Partner B	9,900	
Capital, Partner C		16,500

After the admission of C, the partners' capital balances are

	Partner A	Partner B	Partner C	Total
Original Capital	$ 15,000	$ 35,000		$ 50,000
Increased in Value	6,400	9,600		16,000
Allocation to C	(6,600)	(9,900)	$ 16,500	–0–
New Capital	$ 14,800	$ 34,700	$ 16,500	$ 66,000

Case 3: Goodwill to the New Partner.   The partners agree that the fair market value of the net assets of the firm is $60,000 and to increase the basis of the building by $10,000. C is bringing expert skills to the partnership that Partners A and B believe are worth $8,000. Therefore, they agree to sell portions of their capital interest to C for a total price of $9,000 and to record goodwill of $8,000 all allocable to C. C is to receive a one-fourth interest, purchased from A and B in the ratio of 2:3.

Building	10,000	
Capital, Partner A		4,000
Capital, Partner B		6,000
Goodwill	8,000	
Capital, Partner A	3,600	
Capital, Partner B	5,400	
Capital, Partner C		17,000

After the admission of C, the partners' capital accounts are

	Partner A	Partner B	Partner C	Total
Original Capital	$ 15,000	$ 35,000		$ 50,000
Increase in Value	4,000	6,000		10,000
Admission of C	(3,600)	(5,400)	17,000	8,000
New Capital	$ 15,400	$ 35,600	$ 17,000	$ 68,000

COMPARISON OF THE METHODS

If the new partnership of A, B, and C agree that Partner C is to receive 25% of the profits, Partner A is to receive 30%, and Partner B is to receive 45%, which maintains the same relative shares for Partners A and B, the depreciation of the building and the amortization of goodwill over time effects the capital balances of the partners as follows:

	Capital A	Capital B	Capital C	Total
Case 2 Balance	$ 14,800	$ 34,700	$ 16,500	$ 66,000
Depreciation of the Building	(3,000)	(4,500)	(2,500)	(10,000)
Amortization of Goodwill	(1,800)	(2,700)	(1,500)	(6,000)
Balance	$ 10,000	$ 27,500	$ 12,500	$ 50,000

	Capital A	Capital B	Capital C	Total
Case 3 Balance	$ 15,400	$ 35,600	$ 17,000	$ 68,000
Depreciation of the Building	(3,000)	(4,500)	(2,500)	(10,000)
Amortization of Goodwill	(2,400)	(3,600)	(2,000)	(8,000)
Balance	$ 10,000	$ 27,500	$ 12,500	$ 50,000

The effect on the balances in the partners' capital accounts is the same as if the partners had used the net investment method. These results occur only because (1) Partners A and B sold capital to C in their profit- and loss-sharing ratio, (2) the new profit- and loss-sharing ratio gave Partner C the same percentage as the percentage of initial capital purchased, and (3) Partners A and B maintained their relative shares of profit and loss. If any other allocation of capital to C is used, or if any other profit and loss-sharing ratio is used after the admission of Partner C, the results are not equal to those occurring when the net investment method is used. The discussion following Illustrative Problem 3.1 demonstrates the effects of alternatives (2) and (3). If Partners A and B agree to selling equal shares of capital to C, the effect on the capital balances of the partners in Case 2 above and the effect of depreciation and amortization over time is

	Partner A	Partner B	Partner C	Total
Original Capital	$ 15,000	$ 35,000		$ 50,000
Increase in Value	6,400	9,600		16,000
Allocation to C	(8,250)	(8,250)	16,500	–0–
New Capital Case 2	$ 13,150	$ 36,350	$ 16,500	$ 66,000

	Capital A	Capital B	Capital C	Total
Case 2 Balance	$ 13,150	$ 36,350	$ 16,500	$ 66,000
Depreciation of the Building	(3,000)	(4,500)	(2,500)	(10,000)
Amortization of Goodwill	(1,800)	(2,700)	(1,500)	(6,000)
Balance	$ 8,350	$ 29,150	$ 12,500	$ 50,000

If the net investment method is used, Partner A would give C $6,250 of capital, leaving Partner A with a capital balance of $8,750, and Partner B would give C $6,250 of capital, reducing Partner B's capital to $28,750. Therefore, the results are not the same, because the relative percentages of capital sold to Partner C are not the same as the new profit- and loss-sharing ratio between A and B. However, if after the admission of C, Partners A and B share profit and loss in the same percentage as the percentage of capital given to C, the results are the same as the net investment method. The $400 shift between A and B is caused by A giving new Partner C 50% of the capital to be received, yet in the profit and loss allocation, Partner A's capital is reduced by only 40% of the remaining 75% of profit and loss.

SIMULTANEOUS ADMISSION AND WITHDRAWAL

A partner can withdraw from a partnership by selling all of a capital share of a partnership to an outside party with the permission of the remaining partners. If the net investment method is used, the amount of capital in the selling partner's capital account is transferred to the capital account of the new partner. The transaction price for the partnership interest does not affect the entry. No new assets have been contributed and total partnership equity is unchanged. If the remaining partners agree to credit the new partner's capital account with an amount that is greater than the capital of the withdrawing partner, they are granting a bonus to the new partner, or if the new partner is credited with less capital than the withdrawing partner had, the new partner agrees to give a bonus to the remaining partners.

As with the admission of a partner, the partners can use the value that the new partner is willing to pay the withdrawing partner for the entire share of a capital as a measure of the value of the firm and elect to revalue assets and/or record goodwill. The new partner also can be granted goodwill. The most common method used in practice is simply to transfer the capital balance of the retiring partner to the new partner. Illustrative Problem 3.3 covers all the above possibilities as each of the alternatives can be used.

ILLUSTRATIVE PROBLEM 3.3: SIMULTANEOUS ADMISSION AND WITHDRAWAL OF A PARTNER

Partners D, E, and F agree to the retirement of Partner E and the purchase of Partner E's interest by N, who will be admitted to the partnership to replace Partner E. Prior to the admission of N and the retirement of Partner E, the partners had the following capital balances and shares of profit and loss:

	Partner D	Partner E	Partner F	Total
Capital Balance	$ 45,000	$ 25,000	$ 30,000	$100,000
Profit and Loss Share (2:1:1)	50%	25%	25%	

Case 1: Net Investment Method.   The balance of Partner E's capital is transferred to N's capital account. The price that N agrees to pay Partner E for the interest does not affect this entry. Total partners' equity is unchanged as no new assets are added to the partnership.

Capital, Partner E	25,000	
Capital, Partner N		25,000

Case 2: Bonus to Remaining Partners.   The partners agree that N is to have $22,000 of capital. N is granting a bonus of $3,000 to Partners D and F that is shared in their profit- and loss-sharing ratio of 2:1. The journal entry for the admission of N is

Capital, Partner E	25,000	
Capital, Partner D		2,000
Capital, Partner F		1,000
Capital, Partner N		22,000

After recording the admission of N and the withdrawal of Partner E, the capital balance of Partner D is $47,000 and Partner F's capital is $31,000.

Case 3: Bonus to New Partner.   The partners agree that N is to have $29,500 of capital. Partners D and F are granting a $4,500 bonus to N. The journal entry for the admission of N is

Capital, Partner D	3,000	
Capital, Partner E	25,000	
Capital, Partner F	1,500	
Capital, Partner N		29,500

The capital balance of Partner D is $42,000 and Partner F's balance is $28,500.

Case 4: Goodwill to Remaining Partners. The partners agree that the $27,000 that Partner E and N have established as the price for transfer of 25% of the partnership equity is a valid measure of the net assets (equity) of the original partnership. They also agree that the net book value of the assets is approximately equal to the fair market value. The fair market value of the partnership should be $108,000 ($27,000 ÷ .25). The journal entries to record the revaluation of the partnership, and the withdrawal of Partner E and the admission of N are

Goodwill	8,000 (1)	
Capital, Partner D		4,000
Capital, Partner E		2,000
Capital, Partner F		2,000

(1) $108,000 − $100,000 = goodwill of $8,000

Capital, Partner E	27,000	
Capital, Partner N		27,000

Partner D has $49,000 of capital, Partner E has $27,000, and Partner F has $32,000. If Partner E's percentage of capital was not equal to E's percentage of profits, then after the recording of goodwill, E's percentage of capital would not be 25% of the total. Several approaches could be used to solve the inequity. Partner E and N might agree to a change in the price to bring the cost to N equal to the capital balance or the partners could agree to a shift of capital between them—in effect, a bonus.

Case 5: Goodwill to New Partner. The partners agree that N is bringing an intangible asset to the partnership that is worth $6,000 and to record goodwill, all allocable to N. The journal entry is

Goodwill	6,000	
Capital, Partner E	25,000	
Capital, Partner N		31,000

The effect of the amortization of goodwill over time on the capital accounts of the partners will vary, depending on the profit and loss ratio used in the new partnership. If the partners agree that Partner N will receive the same share of profits and losses that Partner E received, and Partner D continues to receive 50% and Partner F continues to receive 25% (2:1:1 ratio), the amortization of goodwill has the following effect on the capital balances of the partners:

	Capital D	Capital N	Capital F	Total
Case 4 Capital	$ 49,000	$ 27,000	$ 32,000	$ 108,000
Amortization of Goodwill	(4,000)	(2,000)	(2,000)	(8,000)
Balance	$ 45,000	$ 25,000	$ 30,000	$ 100,000

The partners have maintained the same profit and loss ratio and Partner N has the same ratio of profit and loss as initial capital; therefore, the amortization of goodwill has the same result as the net investment method. If the original partners had agreed to any other division of profits, the result is not equal to the net investment method. In Case 5, Partner N received all of the goodwill, but his capital account will be reduced by only 25% of the amortization. The effect of the amortization of the goodwill over time on the capital balances of the partners is

	Capital D	Capital N	Capital F	Total
Case 5 Capital	$ 45,000	$ 31,000	$ 30,000	$ 106,000
Amortization of Goodwill	(3,000)	(1,500)	(1,500)	(6,000)
Balance	$ 42,000	$ 29,500	$ 28,500	$ 100,000

The results are the same as Case 3 where the partners granted a bonus of $4,500 to N.

WITHDRAWAL OF A PARTNER

An existing partner can withdraw from a partnership by selling an interest to an outside party with the agreement of the remaining partners or by selling an interest to the remaining partners. The withdrawal of a partner can be voluntary or can be caused by a mandatory retirement age in the partnership agreement. The death of a partner will cause automatic withdrawal unless the estate of the individual is permitted to replace the deceased partner. If the partnership agreement does not specify the terms of buying out the interest of the deceased partner, the Uniform Partnership Act states that the estate of the partner is to receive the balance of the capital account plus any share of profits earned to the date of death.[2] Partnerships often ensure the lives of the partners to provide the partnership with sufficient cash to purchase the interest of a deceased partner. Regardless of the reason for the withdrawal of a partner, the accounting for the withdrawal does not change. A well-constructed partnership agreement provides the terms under which a partner may withdraw and the amount and manner of payment to the withdrawing partner.

The purchase of a present partner's interest by the remaining partners as individuals is usually recorded by the net investment method. The partners are not unrelated parties and therefore the transaction is not an arm's-length one. The capital of the withdrawing partner is transferred to the remaining partners based on the portion purchased. Any bonus received or given is reflected in the transaction price, which is not a transaction of the partnership. For example, if Partners D, E, and F in Illustrative Problem 3.3 agree that Partners D and F as individuals will each purchase one-half of E's capital, the journal entry to record the withdrawal of E is

[2]Uniform Partnership Act, Section 42.

Capital, Partner E	25,000	
Capital, Partner D		12,500
Capital, Partner F		12,500

The remaining partners could approach the withdrawal of Partner E as ending the existing partnership and a new partnership being formed by the remaining partners. If this is the case, they may elect to revalue the partnership and record any goodwill, with the price paid to the withdrawing partner establishing the value of the new partnership. Sometimes due to conflicts between partners, a partner is bought out as a means of allowing the partnership to continue without friction. The price paid may not reflect the fair market value of the partnership, but the price paid for resolution of conflict. If this is the reason for paying a price in excess of the capital account, it is hard to justify the recording of goodwill. The price does not reflect the fair market value of the partnership, but the price paid to maintain a going concern. If the partners choose to revalue the business, the journal entry is exactly like the entry to revalue the partnership when goodwill is allocated to the original partners.

When the partnership purchases the capital interest of a withdrawing partner, any of the three methods may be used. In both the bonus method and the goodwill method, either the withdrawing partner or the remaining partners may receive the bonus or the goodwill. The allocation of bonuses and goodwill to the remaining partners is in their profit- and loss-sharing ratio. The recording of goodwill when a partner withdraws may be based either on the amount paid for the interest alone or on a revaluation of the partnership as a whole. The previous discussion regarding goodwill upon the admission of a partner is equally applicable to the recording of goodwill when a partner withdraws from a partnership.

ILLUSTRATIVE PROBLEM 3.4: WITHDRAWAL OF A PARTNER

The partners of D, E, and F Partnership agree to the retirement of Partner E and the purchase of E's share of capital by the partnership. Prior to the retirement of Partner E, the capital balances and profit- and loss-sharing percentages were

	Partner D	Partner E	Partner F	Total
Capital Balance	$ 35,000	$ 25,000	$ 40,000	$ 100,000
Profit and Loss Share (5:2:3)	50%	20%	30%	

Case 1: Net Investment Method.   Partner E agrees to accept a payment of $10,000 in cash plus a 10%, three-year note receivable in the amount of $15,000 from the partnership. The journal entry to record the retirement of Partner E is

Capital, Partner E	25,000	
Cash		10,000
Note Payable: E		15,000

Case 2: Bonus to Retiring Partner.   Partner E agrees to accept a payment of $10,000 in cash plus a 10%, three-year note receivable in the amount of $19,000 from the partnership.

The journal entry to record the retirement of E is

Capital, Partner E	25,000	
Capital, Partner D	2,500 (1)	
Capital, Partner F	1,500 (2)	
Cash		10,000
Note Payable: E		19,000

(1) $29,000 - $25,000 = $4,000 bonus to E
    $4,000 \times [5/(5 + 3)] = $2,500
(2) $4,000 \times 3/8 = $1,500

The remaining partners share the bonus to E in their remaining profit and loss ratio of 5:3. The balance in Partner D's capital account after the retirement of Partner E is $32,500 and Partner F's capital account balance is $38,500.

Case 3: Bonus to Remaining Partners.   Partner E agrees to accept a payment of $10,000 in cash plus a 10%, three-year note receivable in the amount of $11,000 from the partnership. The journal entry to record the retirement of Partner E is

Capital, Partner E	25,000	
Capital, Partner D		2,500 (1)
Capital, Partner F		1,500 (2)
Cash		10,000
Note Payable: E		11,000

(1) $25,000 - $21,000 = $4,000 bonus to remaining partners
    $4,000 \times 5/8 = $2,500
(2) $4,000 \times 3/8 = $1,500

Case 4: Goodwill Only to Extent of Amount Paid to Retiring Partner.   Partner E agrees to accept a payment of $10,000 in cash plus a 10%, three-year note receivable in the amount of $19,000 from the partnership. The journal entry to record the retirement of Partner E is

Capital, Partner E	25,000	
Goodwill	4,000	
Cash		10,000
Note Payable: E		19,000

If Partners D and F agree to continue to share profits in the ratio of 5:3, the amortization of goodwill results in exactly the same amounts in their capital balances as the bonus method. Partner D's capital is reduced by $2,500 (5/8 of $4,000) and Partner F's capital is reduced by $1,500 (3/8 of $4,000). These are the same amounts as the reduction of capital balances when they recorded a bonus to Partner E.

Case 5: Goodwill For the Partnership as a Whole Based on the Amount Paid to the Retiring Partner.   Partner E agrees to accept a payment of $10,000 in cash plus a 10%, three-year note receivable in the amount of $19,000 from the partnership. The journal entry to record the retirement of Partner E is

Capital, Partner E	25,000	
Goodwill	16,000 (1)	
Cash		10,000
Note Payable: E		19,000
Capital, Partner D		7,500 (2)
Capital, Partner F		4,500 (3)

(1) $29,000 - $25,000 = $4,000$ of goodwill for 1/4 of the capital of the partnership
    Total partnership value is $116,000 ($29,000 \div .25$)

(2) $16,000 - 4,000 = $12,000$
    $12,000 \times 5/8 = $7,500$

(3) $12,000 \times 3/8 = $4,500$

In Case 5, the entire firm was revalued. If the remaining partners continue to share profits and losses in the ratio of 5:3, the effect of amortizing the goodwill over time on the capital balances of the remaining partners is

	Partner D	Partner E	Total
Balance before Retirement	$ 35,000	$ 40,000	$ 75,000
Addition from Goodwill	7,500	4,500	12,000
Amortization of Goodwill	(10,000)	(6,000)	(16,000)
Balance	$ 32,500	$ 38,500	$ 71,000

The results are again the same as the bonus method. Some accountants would argue that the amount of the goodwill should be only the amount purchased from the existing partner, and others would contend that a new entity has been created and it should be revalued.

In all of the examples for the admission and withdrawal of partners presented in this chapter, the new partner received the same share of profit as initial capital, the amount of interest sold was divided among the original partners in their original profit- and loss-sharing relationship, and the remaining partners shared profits and losses in the same relative proportion. Only under these conditions will comparability of methods result. If any of these conditions does not exist, the results are not the same, which is why some accountants will not use the goodwill method, and prefer to use either the net investment or the bonus method.

CHANGE IN THE PARTNERS' PROPORTIONATE SHARES OF CAPITAL

During the operation of the partnership, the partners may want to alter their relative shares of the capital of the partnership. The partners may also change their profit- and loss-sharing ratios, or if the partnership has a complex partnership agreement, it may be changed. Thus, without changing the existing partners, one or more partners may sell or purchase a portion of the interest of one or more of the other partners.

The partner purchasing an additional interest in capital acquires that interest by purchasing a portion of an existing partner's capital directly from that partner as an individual, although as previously discussed, the payment may be made out of future earnings. If the partners in a partnership change their relative proportion of ownership without any change in partners, the net investment method is usually used to record the shift in capital because the transaction is not an arm's-length transfer as the partners are the same individuals. The price paid does not affect the capital transferred from one partner to another partner.

   The partners of the D, E, and F Partnership agree to Partner E's purchasing $15,000 of Partner D's capital. The partners also agree to change their profit- and loss-sharing ratio to reflect the purchase. Prior to the shift, the capital balances and profit shares are

	Partner D	Partner E	Partner F	Total
Capital Balance	$ 35,000	$ 25,000	$ 40,000	$ 100,000
Profit and Loss Share (5:3:2)	50%	20%	30%	

If Partner E pays Partner D $20,000 for 15% of the partnership's capital, the journal entry to record the shift is

Capital, Partner D	15,000	
Capital, Partner E		15,000

The transaction is outside the partnership and the price paid does not affect the entry.

SUMMARY

A partner can be admitted to a partnership by contributing net assets to the partnership or by buying an interest directly from the partners as separate entities. A partner can withdraw from a partnership by having the partnership interest purchased by the partnership or by selling the interest to either the existing partners or a new partner. The admission and withdrawal of partners from a partnership can be recorded by the net investment, the bonus, or the goodwill methods.

   If a partner contributes net assets to the partnership and the net investment method is used, the new partner's capital account is credited with the fair market value of net assets contributed. If the bonus method is used, the new partner's capital account is credited with the percentage of capital being purchased. If the amount credited to the new partner's capital account is more than the fair market value of new assets contributed, the original partners are giving a bonus to the new partner and, if the amount is less, the new partner is giving a bonus to the original partners. If the goodwill method is used, goodwill is recorded and assigned either to the original partners, the new partner, or to both the original and the new partners.

   If a new partner purchases an interest from the original partners as separate entities, the new partner's capital account is credited with the percentage of ownership purchased and the selling partners capital accounts are reduced by the percentage of equity sold. The bonus method is not used as any bonus to either the original partners or the new partner is reflected in the price paid, which is not a transaction of the partnership. If the partner's believe a new business has been formed, they may record goodwill and assign it to either the original partners, the new partner, or to both the original and new partners.

   If a partner withdraws from a partnership and the interest is purchased by the partnership for a price that is more than or less than the withdrawing partner's capital account, either the bonus method or the goodwill method can be used. The bonus method results in a bonus to remaining partners if the price paid is less than the balance of the withdrawing partner's capital account and a bonus to the withdrawing partner if the price is more. If the goodwill method is used, the goodwill recorded can be either the amount paid for the withdrawing partner's share in excess of the partner's capital account, or the entire firm can be revalued.

If a partner withdraws by selling the partnership interest to a new partner, the capital account of the withdrawing partner is credited to the new partner. The bonus method can be used if the partners all agree that the new partner is to receive more or less than the percentage of capital purchased from the withdrawing partner. The partners may agree to record goodwill of the existing partnership or to record goodwill attributable to the new partner.

REVIEW PROBLEMS

The accounting firm of K, L, and M, CPAs has been operating as a partnership for a number of years. The capital balances, the capital shares, and the profit and loss shares at December 31, 1989, are

	Partner K	Partner L	Partner M	Total
Capital Balance	$ 12,000	$ 24,000	$ 48,000	$ 84,000
Capital Share	1/7	2/7	4/7	
Profit and Loss Share (1:3:6)	1/10	3/10	6/10	

1. On January 1, 1990, the partners of K, L, and M, CPAs agree to admit N to the partnership for a contribution of $10,000 of cash and a computer system with a fair market value of $8,000 on which N still owes $2,000 to City Bank. The partnership will assume responsibility for paying the balance due City Bank. N is to receive 20% of the profits and the existing partners will maintain their proportionate share of profits.

Required
Prepare the journal entry for the admisson of new partner N for each of the following assumptions.

1) Net investment method is used.
2) N is to have a 9% interest in the capital of the partnership.
3) N is to have a 23% interest in the capital of the partnership.
4) N's payment of $16,000 is a valid measure of 12.5% of the fair market value of the new partnership and N is to receive a 12.5% interest in capital.
5) N is bringing new clients to the partnership that the partners agree to value at $7,000 and N is to receive credit for the goodwill brought to the firm.

2. Ignore part 1. above. N will be admitted to the partnership by purchasing a one-fourth interest in capital directly from the partners as individuals. The partners agree to sell capital to N in the ratio of 1:2:4, respectively.

Required
Prepare the journal entries for the admission of N for each of the following assumptions:

1) N will pay the partners as individuals $24,500.
2) The partners agree to revalue the firm based on the $24,500 N is willing to pay for a one-fourth interest. The partners believe that the fair market value of the firm is approximately the same as the book value.
3) The partners believe that N is bringing an excellent client base to the partnership and agree to give N credit of $10,000 for the potential increase in revenue.

3. Ignore parts 1. and 2. above. Partner K has reached the mandatory retirement age of 70 as specified in the partnership agreement. Five years ago, he sold 20% of his partnership interest to Partner M and gradually has been withdrawing from the activities of the partnership. Partners L and M agree that the partnership will purchase Partner K's interest until they are able to find another partner to join the firm.

Required

1) Prepare the journal entry for the withdrawal of Partner K, if K agrees to accept from the partnership
    (a) $12,000 cash.
    (b) $5,000 cash and a 12%, five-year, $16,000 note.
    (c) $9,000 cash.
    (d) $21,000 cash and the remaining partners record goodwill for Partner K's portion only.
    (e) $15,000 cash and the partnership is revalued.
2) Prepare the journal entries for the withdrawal of Partner K using the possible alternative methods if Partners L and M together purchase K's capital for $15,000. Partner L purchases one-third and Partner M purchases two-thirds.

QUESTIONS

1. What will be the duties and responsibilities of a new partner who has purchased an interest from an existing partner under the Uniform Partnership Act?
2. Describe the two ways that a new partner can purchase an interest in an existing partnership.
3. Describe the three methods that can be used to record the admission or withdrawal of a partner.
4. Describe the conditions that will result in a bonus to (1) original partners (2) a new partner.
5. Describe the conditions that will result in goodwill to (1) original partners (2) a new partner.
6. Describe the two approaches that can be used to recording goodwill when a partner retires.
7. Present the arguments for and against recording goodwill when a change in the partners occurs. Do you believe goodwill should be recorded?
8. Describe the conditions that must exist after the admission or withdrawal of a partner that will cause the goodwill method to ultimately bring the partner's capital balances to those that the bonus method records, ignoring other conditions.
9. When a partner purchases an interest directly from the partners rather than investing new assets in the partnership, explain why only the net investment and the goodwill methods are used.

EXERCISES

EXERCISE 3-1

The partners of the U and V Partnership agree to admit W to the partnership with a one-fifth interest in capital and profits. The partners agree that the fair market value of the net assets of the U and V Partnership is approximately equal to the book value. Prior to the admission of W, Partner U had a capital balance of $20,000 and Partner V had a capital balance of $30,000. U and V's partnership agreement provides for the sharing of profits and losses in the ratio of 3:5, respectively.

Required

Prepare the journal entry for the admission of W under each of the following assumptions:

1. W contributes cash of $12,500.
2. W contributes cash of $16,500.

3. W contributes cash of $9,500.
4. W contributes cash of $16,500 and the partners agree that W's contribution is a fair measure of the net worth of the new partnership and to record goodwill.
5. W contributes cash of $9,500 and the partners agree that W is bringing new business to the partnership and to record goodwill.

EXERCISE 3-2

The partners of the R and S Partnership agree to admit T to a one-third interest in capital and profits. T will purchase the interest directly from the original partners as individuals, purchasing 40% from Partner R and 60% from Partner S. The partners also agree that the fair market value of the partnership's assets is approximately equal to the book value. Prior to the admission of T, Partner R had a capital balance of $42,000 and Partner S had a capital balance of $63,000. Partners R and S share profits and losses in the ratio of 2:3, respectively.

Required

Prepare the journal entry for the admission of T for each of the following assumptions:

1. T pays Partners R and S a total of $40,000.
2. The partners agree that the $40,000 price T is willing to pay for the one-third interest is a fair measure of the value of the partnership and to record goodwill.
3. Partners R and S agree to sell the portions of their interests to T for a price that is less than book value because they believe that T is bringing special skills to the business that will have a substantial impact on the partnership. The total price T will pay is $30,000 and the partners agree to value the goodwill T is bringing to the business at $7,500.

EXERCISE 3-3

Partners O, P, and Q agree that Partner Q will sell his interest directly to N for $22,000. Prior to the sale, Partner O had $14,000 of capital, Partner P had $18,000, and Partner Q had $16,000. Partners O, P, and Q share profits and losses equally.

Required

Prepare the journal entry for the withdrawal of Partner Q and the admission of N under the following conditions

1. N is to receive Q's share of the capital.
2. N is to receive credit for $20,000 of capital.
3. N is to receive credit for $13,000 of capital.
4. Partners O, P, and N agree to record goodwill based on the price Q accepted for his partnership interest.
5. Partners O, P, and N agree that N is bringing goodwill to the partnership and to value that goodwill at $5,000.

EXERCISE 3-4

The partners of A, B, and C Partnership agree to the withdrawal of C. Partners A and B will each purchase one-half of C's interest for $12,500. Prior to the withdrawal of Partner C, the partners had the following capital balances: Partner A $16,000, Partner B $24,000, and Partner C $20,000. Prior to the withdrawal of Partner C, the partners shared profits and losses equally.

Required

Prepare the journal entry for the withdrawal of Partner C for the following assumptions:

1. The net investment method is used.
2. The remaining partners decide to revalue the firm. The only undervalued asset is land with a book value of $8,000 and a fair market value of $14,000.

EXERCISE 3-5

Refer to Exercise 3-4. Assume that the partnership agrees to purchase Partner C's interest, record the withdrawal of C if the cash paid to C is (1) $16,000, and (2) $23,000.

EXERCISE 3-6

In 1991, Z was admitted to the partnership of X and Y with a 10% interest in capital and profits. On December 31, 1992, the capital balances, capital ratios, and profit- and loss-sharing ratios were as follows:

	Partner X	Partner Y	Partner Z	Total
Capital Balance	$ 24,000	$ 32,000	$ 8,000	$ 64,000
Percentage of Capital	3/8	4/8	1/8	
Profit and Loss Share	40%	50%	10%	

Partners X and Y each agree to sell one-half of their interest in capital to Partner Z. Partner Z will pay Partner X $16,500 for half of X's interest and will pay Partner Y $22,000 for half of Y's interest in the X, Y, and Z Partnership.

Required

Prepare the journal entry for the transfer of interest between the partners.

EXERCISE 3-7

1. Cicci and Arias are partners who share profits and losses in the ratio of 7:3, respectively. On October 5, 1991, their respective capital accounts were

Cicci	$ 35,000
Arias	30,000
Total	$ 65,000

On that date they agreed to admit Soto as a partner with a one-third interest in the capital and profits and losses, upon his investment of $25,000. The new partnership will begin with a total capital of $90,000. Immediately after Soto's admission, what are the capital balances of the partners?

	Cicci	Arias	Soto
a.	$ 30,000	$ 30,000	$ 30,000
b.	$ 31,500	$ 28,500	$ 30,000
c.	$ 31,667	$ 28,333	$ 30,000
d.	$ 35,000	$ 30,000	$ 25,000

2. The following balance sheet is presented for the partnership of Cooke, Dorry, and Evans, who share profits and losses in the ratio of 4:3:3, respectively:

Cash	$ 90,000
Other Assets	820,000
Cooke, Loan	30,000
Total	$ 940,000

Accounts Payable	$ 210,000
Evans, Loan	40,000
Cooke, Capital	300,000
Dorry, Capital	200,000
Evans, Capital	190,000
Total	$ 940,000

Assume that the assets and the liabilities are fairly valued on the balance sheet and the partnership decides to admit Fisher as a new partner with a one-fourth interest. No goodwill or bonus is to be recorded. How much should Fisher contribute in cash or other assets?

a. $ 172,500
b. $ 170,000
c. $ 230,000
d. $ 233,333

3. Ames and Buell are partners who share profits and losses in the ratio of 3:2, respectively. On August 31, 1992, their capital accounts were

Ames	$ 70,000
Beull	60,000
	$ 130,000

On that date they agreed to admit Carter as a partner with a one-third interest in the capital and profits and losses, for an investment of $50,000. The new partnership will begin with a total capital of $180,000. Immediately after Carter's admission, what are the capital balances of the partners?

	Ames	Buell	Carter
a.	$ 60,000	$ 60,000	$ 60,000
b.	$ 63,333	$ 56,667	$ 60,000
c.	$ 64,000	$ 56,000	$ 60,000
d.	$ 70,000	$ 60,000	$ 50,000

4. At December 31, 1991, Arno and Dey are partners with capital balances of $80,000 and $40,000, and they share profit and loss in the ratio of 2:1, respectively. On this date, West invests $36,000 cash for a one-fifth interest in the capital and profit of the new partnership. The partners agree that the implied partnership goodwill is to be recorded simultaneously with the admission of West. The total implied goodwill of the firm is

a. $ 4,800
b. $ 6,000
c. $ 24,000
d. $ 30,000

5. At December 31, 1992, Reed and Quinn are partners with capital balances of $40,000 and $20,000, and they share profit and loss in the ratio of 2:1, respectively. On this date, Poe invests $17,000 cash for a one-fifth interest in the capital and profit of the new partnership. Assuming that goodwill is *not* recorded, how much should be credited to Poe's capital account on December 31, 1992?

a. $ 12,000
b. $ 15,000
c. $ 15,400
d. $ 17,000

6. The following condensed balance sheet is presented for the partnership of Lever, Polen, and Quint, who share profits and losses in the ratio of 4:3:3, respectively:

Cash	$ 90,000
Other Assets	830,000
Lever, Loan	20,000
	$ 940,000
Accounts Payable	$ 210,000
Quint, Loan	30,000
Lever, Capital	310,000
Polen, Capital	200,000
Quint, Capital	190,000
	$ 940,000

Assume that the assets and liabilities are fairly valued on the balance sheet and that the partnership decides to admit Fahn as a new partner, with a 20% interest. No goodwill or bonus is to be recorded. How much should Fahn contribute in cash or other assets?

a. $ 140,000
b. $ 142,000
c. $ 175,000
d. $ 177,500

(AICPA adapted)

EXERCISE 3-8

1. When Dee retired from the partnership of Dee, Ken, and Ned, the final settlement of Dee's partnership interest exceeded Dee's capital balance. Under the bonus method, the excess

a. reduced the capital balances of Ken and Ned.
b. had *no* effect on the capital balances of Ken and Ned.
c. was recorded as goodwill.
d. was an expense.

2. On June 30, 1991, the balance sheet for the partnership of Coll, Maduro, and Prieto, together with their respective profit and loss ratios, were

Assets, at cost	$ 180,000
Coll, Loan	$ 9,000
Coll, Capital (20%)	42,000
Maduro, Capital (20%)	39,000
Prieto, Capital (60%)	90,000
Total	$ 180,000

Coll has decided to retire from the partnership. By mutual agreement, the assets are to be adjusted to their fair value of $216,000 at June 30, 1991. The partners agreed that the partnership would pay Coll $61,200 in cash for Coll's partnership interest, including Coll's loan, which is to be repaid in full. No goodwill is to be recorded. After Coll's retirement, what is the balance of Maduro's capital account?

a. $ 36,450
b. $ 39,000
c. $ 45,450
d. $ 46,200

Information for Questions 3, 4, 5, and 6

The partnership of Meg, Betty, and June has reached an impass as June is no longer willing to contribute the amount of time and effort to the partnership that she has previously given. The partners share profits and losses in the ratio of 3:3:4, respectively. The partners have the following capital balances just prior to June's withdrawal from the partnership:

Meg	$ 45,000
Betty	35,000
June	20,000

3. If Betty purchases June's interest from June for $32,000 and *no* goodwill is recorded, the balance of Betty's capital account immediately after the withdrawal of June is

a. $ 67,000
b. $ 61,000
c. $ 60,250
d. $ 55,000

4. The partners agree that the partnership will purchase June's interest for $32,000 and *no* goodwill is to be recorded. The balance of Meg's capital account immediately after the withdrawal of June is

a. $ 41,400
b. $ 39,600
c. $ 39,000
d. $ 38,250

5. The partners agree that the partnership will purchase June's interest for $32,000 and will record goodwill to the extent paid to June. The balance of Betty's capital account immediately after the withdrawal of June is

a. $ 35,000
b. $ 38,600
c. $ 39,200
d. $ 41,000

6. The partners agree that the partnership will purchase June's interest for $32,000 and will revalue the partnership based on the price June is willing to accept for her interest in the partnership. The balance of Meg's capital account immediately after the withdrawal of June is

a. $ 39,000
b. $ 63,000
c. $ 69,000
d. $ 72,000

(Questions 1 and 2 AICPA adapted)

PROBLEMS

PROBLEM 3-1
The partnership of H, I, and J has been in business for a number of years operating a very successful chain of delicatessens called The Wine Depot and Deli. In addition to the deli items, the stores also carry an extensive selection of wines. The wines are purchased when they are first released and stored in a carefully controlled wine cellar until mature and drinkable. The partners agree to admit K to the partnership on January 1, 1992. K will have a 15% share of capital and the partners will share profts and losses in the ratio of 7:5:5:3, respectively, after the admission of K.

1. The partners feel that due to the increase in value from aging, the inventory of wine is undervalued by $19,500. In addition, the partners believe that net book value of the remaining assets is approximately equal to their fair market value. At December 31, 1991, the capital balances and profit shares are

	Partner H	Partner I	Partner J	Total
Capital Balance	$ 60,000	$ 34,000	$ 31,000	$ 125,000
Profit and Loss Share	40%	30%	30%	

Required
Prepare the journal entry to revalue the existing partnership and determine the balances of the partners' capital accounts.

2. The partners agree to revalue the wine inventory regardless of the method selected for the admission of K.

Required
Prepare schedules showing the balances of the partners' capital accounts after the admission of K for each of the following independent situations:

1) K purchases the interest directly from Partner H for $24,000. The partners agree that the price paid by K represents a valid measure of the fair market value of the partnership.
2) The partners, as individuals, agree to each sell K equal portions of the existing capital. K agrees to pay each partner $8,000 and the partners agree to only revalue the wine inventory.
3) K has been a wine connoisseur for many years and has an extensive collection of wine that is kept in the cellar of K's home. K will purchase the interest by contributing wine with a fair market value of $20,000 to the partnership and a promise to pay $7,000 plus interest at 10% out of K's share of

future profits. The partners agree that the fair market value of the partnership before the admission of K is $160,000.
  a. The bonus method is used to record the admission of K.
  b. The goodwill method is used to record the admission of K.
4) The partners agree that K, because of K's long-standing interest in wine, is bringing needed knowledge to the partnership. K agrees to contribute wine with a fair market value of $20,000.
  a. The bonus method is used to record the admission of K.
  b. The goodwill method is used to record the admission of K.

3. *Required*
1) For alternatives (3) and (4) of part 2, state what conditions are necessary for the goodwill and the bonus methods to eventually have the same effect on the capital balances of the partners.
2) For the same alternatives, demonstrate the effect of the amortization of goodwill on the capital accounts of the partners and explain why the results are different from the bonus method, if they are.

PROBLEM 3-2
The partnership of A and B has successfully operated a men's clothing store, Clothes for All Occasions, for a number of years. The manufacturers supplying the store with suits and other business clothing are touting the excellent lines of professional clothes for women they now produce. Partners A and B decide to expand their business to women's wear and to admit Ms. C to their partnership because of her knowledge of professional dress for women and her clientele. Partners A and B feel that the fair market value of their partnership is greater than the book value of net assets. Ms. C feels that she is bringing special skills to the business as well as an established clientele from the dress shop where she has been an employee, which will make the women's department a success. Partners A and B and Ms. C agree to consult the accountant of the A and B partnership to determine how to record the formation of their new partnership to reflect the values that all of the parties are bringing to the partnership. The balance sheet of Clothes for All Occasions in book values and fair market values is

CLOTHES FOR ALL OCCASIONS
Balance Sheet
January 31, 1991

	Book Value	Fair Market Value
Assets		
Cash	$ 7,000	$ 7,000
Accounts Receivable	48,000	48,000
Inventory	30,000	35,000
Land	10,000	12,000
Store Building: Net	31,000	40,000
Store Fixtures: Net	10,000	6,000
Total Assets	$ 136,000	$ 148,000

	Book Value	Fair Market Value
Liabilities and Partners' Equity		
Accounts Payable	$ 16,000	$ 16,000
Mortgage Payable	27,000	27,000
Total Liabilities	43,000	43,000
Partners' Equity		
Partner A	46,000	?
Partner B	47,000	?
Total Partners' Equity	93,000	105,000
Total Liabilities and Partners' Equity	$ 136,000	$ 148,000

Partners A and B have been sharing profits and losses in the ratio of 45:55, respectively. The partners and Ms. C agree that the clientele she is bringing from the dress shop should provide approximately $40,000 of annual sales for the ladies department, which they expect to continue for at least five years.

Required
1. Prepare the journal entry to revalue the partnership of A and B.
2. Determine the amount of cash that Ms. C will have to invest in Clothes for All Occasions to have a 30% share of capital and profits for each of the following assumptions, and prepare the journal entry for the admission of Ms. C to the partnership:
   1) The partners elect to use the bonus method to record the change in the value of the partnership's net assets.
   2) The partners agree to revalue the net assets and to give Ms. C credit for her clientele at the rate of 10% of the annual sales for each of the five years and record Ms. C's goodwill.
   3) The parties agree that the established clientele of the existing business generates approximately $160,000 of sales per year. The value of the new partnership is to be the fair market value of the net assets of the partnership of A and B, plus the value of the partnership's clientele capitalized at 7% of present annual sales for three years. Ms. C's clientele is to be valued in the same manner as the original partnership's clientele. Ms. C is to be given credit for her clientele and Partners A and B for theirs.

PROBLEM 3-3
The partners of the A, B, and C Partnership agree to admit D to their partnership. D is to receive a 25% interest in capital and a 35% share of profits and losses. Partners A, B, and C have been sharing profits and losses as follows:

	Partner A	Partner B	Partner C	Total
Salaries	$ 13,250	$ 18,250	$ 13,500	$ 45,000
Bonus			5,000	5,000
Remainder	20%	30%	50%	100%

The condensed balance sheet of the A, B, and C Partnership prior to the admission of D is

A, B, AND C PARTNERSHIP
Condensed Balance sheet
December 31, 1990

Current Assets	$ 60,000	Liabilities	$ 59,000
Property, Plant, and Equipment	95,000	Partners' Equity	
		Partner A	18,000
		Partner B	33,000
		Partner C	45,000
Total Assets	$ 155,000	Total Equities	$ 155,000

Required

1. Determine an overall profit and loss ratio for the partners, assuming the net income was $65,000.
2. Prepare journal entries for the admission of D for each of the following independent assumptions and using the overall profit ratio from 1. above.
   1) D will invest $30,000. The partners agree that the fair market value of the net assets of the partnership after the admission of D should be $136,000 and the book value of the net assets approximates their fair market value.
   2) D will invest $36,000. The net assets are correctly valued.
   3) D will invest $36,000 and the partners agree the partnership has generated goodwill.
   4) D will invest $22,500. The partners agree D is bringing goodwill to the firm and the net assets of the partnership are correctly valued.

PROBLEM 3-4

The partnership of Maples and Oaks began operations on January 1, 1989. Maples contributed net assets of $50,000 and Oaks contributed net assets of $40,000 to begin the business. Maples and Oaks share profits and losses equally after salaries of $30,000 and $28,000, respectively to the partners. The business is in need of capital for expansion and the partners agree to admit Pines to the partnership on January 1, 1992 for a contribution of cash. Pines is to contribute cash equal to 50% of the partnership's capital for a one-third interest in capital and profits and losses.

Pines will join the partnership provided that the partners agree to correct the errors Pines' accountant found in the records of the partnership.

Pines agrees with Maples and Oaks contention that the partnership has generated goodwill during its operation and agrees to goodwill being recorded. The goodwill is to be the excess of net income over the partners' salary allocations for the past three years capitalized at a 10% annual rate.

The following errors and omissions were discovered by Pines' accountant:

1. Unrecorded items.

	December 31		
Item	1989	1990	1991
Prepaid Expenses	$ 3,100	$ 4,500	$ 3,900
Unearned Revenues	4,200	3,200	5,600
Interest Receivable	2,200	1,800	3,300

2. The partnership uses the direct write-off method for bad debts. During 1989, $2,100 of accounts were written off; in 1990, $1,700 were written off; and in 1991, $2,400 were written off. Sales for

the prior three years were $215,000 for 1989, $232,000 for 1990, and $256,000 for 1991. Bad debt expense is estimated at 1% of sales.

3. The inventory at December 31, 1991, contains obsolete merchandise totaling $13,200. The partners agree that the selling price is only 20% of cost.

The net income as determined by the partnership and the drawings of the partners were

	Year Ended December 31		
Item	1989	1990	1991
Net Income	$ 80,000	$ 90,000	$ 100,000
Partners' Drawings			
Maples	42,000	51,000	57,000
Oaks	34,000	36,000	38,000

Required

1. Prepare a schedule to determine the correct amount of income for the years 1989, 1990, and 1991.
2. Prepare a schedule to determine the amount of goodwill to be assigned to the original partnership.
3. Prepare a schedule to determine the correct balance of the partners' capital accounts at December 31, 1991.
4. Determine the amount of cash that Pines will contribute to the partnership to become a member of the firm.
5. Write the correcting journal entries at December 31, 1991, assuming the books are closed.
6. Write the journal entries on January 1, 1992, to record goodwill and the admission of Pines to the partnership.

PROBLEM 3-5

The partnership of Campbell, Heinz, and Progresso has reached an impass as they cannot agree on how new business should be generated or existing business should be served. Heinz agrees to withdraw from the partnership and sell his interest to Lipton for $60,000. Prior to the withdrawal of Heinz, the partners had the following capital balances and profit- and loss-sharing relationship:

	Campbell	Heinz	Progresso	Total
Capital Balance	$ 60,000	$ 40,000	$ 50,000	$ 150,000
Profit and Loss Share (3:4:3)	30%	40%	30%	

Required

Determine the balance in the partners' capital accounts after the admission of Lipton and the withdrawal of Heinz for each of the following:

1. Lipton paid Heinz $60,000 for his interest. No goodwill is recorded.
2. The partners agree that Lipton is to have a capital balance of $52,000.
3. The partners agree that Lipton is to have a capital balance of $34,000.
4. The partners agree that the price Lipton is willing to pay Heinz represents the fair market value of Heinz's interest and the only undervalued asset is the building whose fair market value is $25,000 more than its book value.
5. The partners agree that Lipton is bringing goodwill to the partnership with a value of $15,000, and that the price paid by Lipton represents the undervaluation of the building in the amount of $25,000, and the balance is goodwill of the existing partnership.

PROBLEM 3-6

The partnershp of H, I, J, and K has been in operation for two years with the partners sharing profits and losses in the ratio of 7:5:5:3, respectively. During the past year it has become apparent that Partners K and J are not compatible and J has decided to withdraw from the partnership as of the end of the year at the urging of Partners H and I. Partner J wants $45,000 for his share of capital. The balances in the capital accounts at the end of the year are

	Partner H	Partner I	Partner J	Partner K	Total
Capital	$ 51,000	$ 30,000	$ 35,000	$ 24,000	$ 140,000

Required

1. Discuss why using the $45,000 Partner J wants for his capital interest may not be a valid measure of the fair market value of J's share of the partnership.
2. Prepare the journal entry for the withdrawal of Partner J for each of the following assumptions:
   1) The partners agree to Partner K purchasing Partner J's interest.
   2) The partnership will acquire Partner J's interest for $45,000 and will use the bonus method.
   3) The partnership will acquire Partner J's interest for $45,000, which will be paid in five annual installments of $9,000 plus interest at 10%. The partners feel that the price Partner J will accept for the share capital is a fair measure of the equity of the business.

PROBLEM 3-7

On January 1, 1988, Able, Baker, Crumbs, and Dough formed a partnership. At the time of formation the partners agreed to the following amount of investment, division of profits and losses, and drawings:

Partner	Initial Investment	Profit and Loss Ratio	Annual Withdrawals 1988	1989	1990
Able	$ 18,000	15%	$ 7,200	$ 9,600	$ 12,300
Baker	28,000	30	7,200	9,600	12,300
Crumbs	30,000	35	7,200	9,600	15,000
Dough	20,000	20	7,200	9,600	12,300
Total	$ 96,000	100%	$ 28,800	$ 38,400	$ 51,900

The partnership agreement also states that a partner cannot withdraw any additional assets without the permission of the other partners. During the following three years, the partnership earned $65,000 in 1988, $78,000 in 1989, and $86,000 in 1990. During this same period, each partner withdrew exactly the amount in cash and assets as the partners had initially agreed were normal drawings.

The partnership agreement contains a clause that allows a partner to withdraw from the partnership after giving at least six months notice to the other partners. The withdrawing partner is to receive the balance of her capital account plus her share of the goodwill. Goodwill is to be determined by capitalizing, at a 10% annual rate, the excess of the annual earnings over a 20% return on beginning capital for a period of three years. On June 15, 1990, Crumbs notified the other partners of her intention to withdraw at the end of 1990.

Required

1. Determine the balances in the capital accounts of the partners at the end of 1988, 1989, and 1990.
2. Determine the amount of goodwill for each of the three years.
3. Determine the amount that Crumbs is to be paid upon her withdrawal at December 31, 1990.

4. Prepare the journal entry for the withdrawal of Crumbs for each of the following situations:
   1) No goodwill is recorded.
   2) Only the goodwill attributable to Crumbs is recorded.
   3) The total goodwill as determined under the partnership agreement is recorded.

PROBLEM 3-8

Partners Jim, Kelly, and Marion had capital balances of $60,000, $35,000, and $40,000, respectively on December 31, 1992. The partners share profits and losses in the ratio of 3:2:5, respectively. During 1993, the partnership suffered a loss of $16,000 and each partner had withdrawn $12,000 in cash from the partnership. Kelly is unhappy with the operations of the partnership and has decided to withdraw as of January 1, 1994.

Required

1. Determine the balance of the partners' capital accounts prior to the withdrawal of Kelly.
2. Kelly will accept $15,000 for her partnership interest from the partnership. Prepare the journal entry for the withdrawal of Kelly if the reason for Kelly being willing to accept less than her capital balance is that the inventory of the partnership is overvalued.
3. The partners agree to the partnership buying Kelly's interest for $24,000. Prepare journal entries for the withdrawal of Kelly under each of the following independent situations:
   1) Only the goodwill attributable to Kelly is recorded.
   2) The goodwill attributable to the firm as a whole is recorded.
   3) Kelly is receiving a bonus.

PROBLEM 3-9

The partnership of Early, Faith, and Good, Attorneys at Law has been in operation for several years. On June 30, 1992, Faith died suddenly. The partnership agreement of Early, Faith, and Good Attorneys at Law stated that upon the death of a partner, the estate of the deceased partner is to be paid the fair market value of the partner's share of the net assets plus any share of profits earned during the current year, net of any drawing of current year's profits. The partnership is to pay all undistributed profits plus 40% of the fair market value of the capital share within 60 days of death. The remainder of the capital share is to be paid in four annual installments payable on the anniversary of the date of death. Interest at 10% per year is to be paid at the time of capital share payments on the unpaid balance of the capital share.

Partners Early and Good and the executrix of the estate of Faith cannot agree on the fair market value of Faith's share or on the amount of earned income that has not been withdrawn. The parties have asked you to resolve the conflict. Partners Early and Good present you with the following information.

1. The partnership agreement contains the following profit and loss allocation:
   1. Salaries equal to 30% of gross billings to clients.
   2. A bonus to Early for managing the practice equal to 5% of net income.
   3. Interest on monthly average capital balances of 10%.
   4. Any remainder to be shared equally.
2. Any drawings in excess of $2,000 per month are considered excessive for the computation of average capital balances. Every January and July, additional drawings are permitted to the limit of the amount earned in the prior six months, except that they may not reduce the partnership's cash balance below $15,000.
3. Operating activities for the six months ended June 30, 1992, were

Gross Billings to Clients	
Partner Early	$ 50,000
Partner Faith	60,000
Partner Good	90,000
Employees of the Firm	70,000
	$ 270,000
Cash Expenditures	
Salaries and Wages	$ 96,000
Payroll Taxes	18,000
Utilities	16,000
Property Taxes	5,000
Law Books	4,000
Payments on Computer Loan	
Principal	2,000
Interest	500
Mortgage Payments on Building	
Principal	800
Interest	2,200
	$ 144,500

4. The balance sheet at December 31, 1991, was

EARLY, FAITH, AND GOOD, ATTORNEYS AT LAW
Balance Sheet
December 31, 1991

Cash	$ 43,000	Loan Payable: Computer	$ 8,000
Accounts Receivable: Net	35,000	Mortgage Payable	45,000
Land	20,000	Partners' Equity	
Depreciable Assets: Net	117,000	Early	51,000
		Faith	56,000
		Good	55,000
Total Assets	$ 215,000	Total Equities	$ 215,000

5. The partners' drawings for the period January 1, 1992, through June 30, 1992 were

Date	Early	Faith	Good
January 1	$ 12,000	$ 10,000	$ 6,000
January 31	2,000	1,800	2,400
February 28	2,000	2,000	2,000
March 31	4,000	2,000	2,000
April 30	2,000	2,000	2,800
May 31	2,000	2,000	2,000
June 30	2,000	2,000	3,000
Total	$ 26,000	$ 23,800	$ 20,200

6. The partnership has $93,000 of outstanding accounts receivable at June 30, 1992, which are estimated to be 90% collectible.
7. It has been the firm's policy to depreciate the assets for a full year in the year of acquisition and to record no depreciation in the year of sale. Depreciable assets at December 31, 1991 consisted of

Asset	Cost	Salvage Value	Life in Years	Depreciation Method	Accumulated Depreciation	Net Book Value
Building	$ 98,000	$ 8,000	25	Straight-line	$ 18,000	$ 80,000
Law Library	28,000	–0–	10	Straight-line	10,000	18,000
Computer System	16,000	–0–	8	200% Declining Balance	4,000	12,000
Office Furniture	10,000	1,000	5	Straight-line	3,000	7,000

The executor of the estate of Faith presented the following information:

1. The drawings on January 1, 1992, were drawings of income earned in the prior year.
2. The fair market value of the land and the buildings is $140,000.
3. A local attorney is willing to pay the estate $81,000 for Faith's share so the value of Faith's equity in the partnership should be $81,000.

The partners agree that the value of the land and the building exceeds the net book value and agree to the $140,000 valuation. The partners, however, question the $81,000 fair market value of Faith's equity in the partnership. The parties agree to let you decide regarding the drawings.

Required

1. Determine, based on the terms of the partnership agreement, if the drawings of January 1 are excessive drawings of the period or drawings of prior period's profits.
2. Prepare a worksheet for determining the net income for the period, January 1, 1992 through June 30, 1992, and the balance sheet at June 30, 1992 using a single account for expenses.
3. Determine the profit allocation for the six months ended June 30, 1992.
4. Determine the capital balances of the partners at June 30, 1992.
5. Determine the value of the partnership based on
   1) Revaluing the land and the building
   2) Using the $81,000 offer for Faith's share. Was the offer a fair one?
6. Assuming the $81,000 value is correct, prepare a schedule for the executor showing the dates and amounts of all payments to be received including both principal and interest.

SOLUTION TO REVIEW PROBLEM

1.
1) Net Investment Method

Cash	10,000	
Computer System	8,000	
Loan Payable City Bank		2,000
Capital, Partner N		16,000

2) Bonus to Existing Partners

Cash	10,000	
Computer System	8,000	
Loan Payable City Bank		2,000
Capital, Partner K (1)		700
Capital, Partner L (2)		2,100
Capital, Partner M (3)		4,200
Capital, Partner N (4)		9,000

  (1) $84,000 + $16,000 = $100,000
     ($100,000 \times 9\%) = $9,000
     $16,000 - $9,000 = $7,000 bonus to existing partners
     $7,000 \times 10\% = $700
  (2) $7,000 \times 30\% = $2,100
  (3) $7,000 \times 60\% = $4,200
  (4) $100,000 \times 9\% = $9,000

3) Bonus to New Partner

Cash	10,000	
Computer System	8,000	
Capital, Partner K	700	
Capital, Partner L	2,100	
Capital, Partner M	4,200	
Loan Payable City Bank		2,000
Capital, Partner N (1)		23,000

  (1) 23\% \times ($84,000 + 16,000) = $23,000

4) Goodwill to Existing Partners

Cash	10,000	
Computer System	8,000	
Goodwill (1)	28,000	
Loan Payable City Bank		2,000
Capital, Partner K (2)		2,800
Capital, Partner L (3)		8,400
Capital, Partner M (4)		16,800
Capital, Partner N		16,000

  (1) $16,000 \div .125 = $128,000
     $128,000 - ($84,000 + 16,000) = $28,000 of goodwill to existing partners
  (2) $28,000 \times 10\% = $ 2,800
  (3) $28,000 \times 30\% = $ 8,400
  (4) $28,000 \times 60\% = $16,800

5) Goodwill to New Partner

Cash	10,000	
Computer System	8,000	
Goodwill	7,000	
Loan Payable City Bank		2,000
Capital, Partner N		23,000

2.

1) Direct Purchase from the Partners as Individuals (the price paid does
   not affect the entry)

Capital, Partner K (1)	3,000	
Capital, Partner L (2)	6,000	
Capital, Partner M (3)	12,000	
Capital, Partner N		21,000

   (1) N purchased a one-fourth interest in capital or $21,000
       ($84,000 × 1/4)
     K's share = 1/7 × $21,000 = $ 3,000
   (2) L's share = 2/7 × $21,000 = $ 6,000
   (3) M's share = 4/7 × $21,000 = $12,000

2) Revaluation of Firm to Reflect Goodwill

Goodwill (1)	14,000	
Capital, Partner K (2)		1,400
Capital, Partner L (3)		4,200
Capital, Partner M (4)		8,400

   (1) $24,500 ÷ .25 = $98,000 value of partnership
      $98,000 − $84,000 = $14,000 of goodwill
   (2) $14,000 × 1/10 = $1,400
   (3) $14,000 × 3/10 = $4,200
   (4) $14,000 × 6/10 = $8,400

Capital, Partner K (1)	3,500	
Capital, Partner L (2)	7,000	
Capital, Partner M (3)	14,000	
Capital, Partner N		24,500

   (1) $24,500 × 1/7 = $ 3,500
   (2) $24,500 × 2/7 = $ 7,000
   (3) $24,500 × 4/7 = $14,000

3) Goodwill Brought by New Partner

Goodwill	10,000	
Capital, Partner K (1)	1,929	
Capital, Partner L (2)	3,857	
Capital, Partner M (3)	7,714	
Capital, Partner N		23,500

$84,000 + $10,000 goodwill = $94,000
$94,000 × 25% = $23,500 to N
$23,500 − $10,000 goodwill = $13,500 of capital from existing partners

   (1) $13,500 × 1/7 = $1,929
   (2) $13,500 × 2/7 = $3,857
   (3) $13,500 × 4/7 = $7,714

3.

1) (a) Net Investment Method

Capital, Partner K	12,000	
Cash		12,000

1) (b) Bonus to Retiring Partner

Capital, Partner K	12,000	
Capital, Partner L (1)	3,000	
Capital, Partner M (2)	6,000	
Cash		5,000
Note Payable to K		16,000

(1) $5,000 + $16,000 = $21,000 - $12,000 = $9,000 bonus to retiring partner
$9,000 \times [30\%/(30\% + 60\%)] = $3,000
(2) $9,000 \times [60\%/(30\% + 60\%)] = $6,000

1) (c) Bonus to Remaining Partners

Capital Partner K	12,000	
Capital, Partner L (1)		1,000
Capital, Partner M (2)		2,000
Cash		9,000

(1) $12,000 - $9,000 = $3,000 bonus to remaining partners
$3,000 \times [30\%/(30\% + 60\%)] = $1,000
(2) $3,000 \times [60\%/(30\% + 60\%)] = $2,000

1) (d) Goodwill to Extent of Amount Purchased from Retiring Partner

Capital, Partner K	12,000	
Goodwill (1)	9,000	
Cash		21,000

(1) $21,000 - $12,000 = $9,000

1) (e) Goodwill from Revaluing Entire Partnership

Capital, Partner K	12,000	
Goodwill	21,000	
Cash		15,000
Capital, Partner L (2)		6,000
Capital, Partner M (3)		12,000

(1) $15,000/(1/7) = $105,000 value of partnership
$105,000 - $84,000 = $21,000 of goodwill
(2) $21,000 - ($15,000 - $12,000) = $18,000 goodwill to remaining partners
$18,000 \times [.30/(.30 + .60)] = $ 6,000
(3) $18,000 \times [.60/(.30 + .60)] = $12,000

2) A Transfer of Capital Only

Capital, Partner K	12,000	
Capital, Partner L		4,000
Capital, Partner M		8,000

3) Revaluation of the Firm Based on the Price Paid to K

Capital, Partner K	12,000	
Capital, Partner L		4,000
Capital, Partner M		8,000
Goodwill (1)	21,000	
Capital, Partner L		7,000
Capital, Partner M		14,000

(1) $15,000 \div 1/7 = $105,000 = value of firm
$105,000 - $84,000 = $21,000 of goodwill

4

LIQUIDATING A PARTNERSHIP

C hapter 4 concludes the discussion of partnerships. The chapter discusses the voluntary and forced liquidation of partnerships both when the partners are solvent and when they are insolvent. The topics of this chapter are

- The voluntary liquidation of a partnership via a simple partnership liquidation with the complete conversion of all noncash assets to cash before distribution is made to the partners
- The treatment of loans receivable from partners and loans payable to partners
- The treatment of debit balances in partners' capital accounts as a result of losses from the realization of the assets
- The voluntary installment liquidation of a partnership in which partners withdraw cash periodically as the assets are realized
- The preparation of a predistribution plan for the disbursement of cash in an installment liquidation
- The problems and accounting for partnerships that are bankrupt as well as partnerships forced into liquidation by bankrupt partners

Partners of a solvent partnership may go out of business voluntarily by either selling the partnership as a business entity, or dissolving the partnership, or by liquidating the partnership. When they choose to dissolve the partnership, the liabilities are either satisfied or assumed by the partners, and the assets or assets net of liabilities assumed are divided between the partners according to their capital balances. For example, a partnership of two CPAs may decide to dissolve their partnership and practice as sole proprietors. They would pay the creditors and divide the assets between them, which they would then use to form their sole proprietorships.

When partners elect to liquidate their partnership, the assets are sold, the liabilities are satisfied, and the remainder of the cash is distributed to the partners according to their capital balances. In a voluntary liquidation, partners can choose to receive one or more of the partnership's assets in lieu of cash; therefore, all the assets do not have to be converted into cash. Partners may be forced to liquidate their partnership because either the partnership is bankrupt or one or more of the partners has declared personal bankruptcy or both. In a forced liquidation all the assets must be converted to cash to satisfy the creditors of the partnership and/or the partners unless the asset is taken by a creditor in satisfaction of part or all of a liability. As one might expect, the liquidation of a solvent partnership and that of a bankrupt partnership present different accounting problems.

UNIFORM PARTNERSHIP ACT

Section 40 of the Uniform Partnership Act pertains to the distribution of assets when a partnership is liquidated. It states that a partnership's assets are to be used to satisfy the equities of the partnership in the following order:

1. The liabilities to outside creditors
2. The partners' loans
3. The partners' capital
4. The partners' profit share[1]

The act also requires the partners to contribute their personal assets to the partnership to satisfy all of the equities.[2] This means that partners who have negative capital balances must contribute sufficient assets to bring their capital balance to zero. If a partner is bankrupt or unwilling to pay, the other partners are responsible for the partnership's obligations in their profit- and loss-sharing relationship. The act also states that the personal assets of a bankrupt partner must be applied first to the partner's separate creditors, then to the partnership's creditors, and last to amounts owed to other partners.

VOLUNTARY LIQUIDATION OF A PARTNERSHIP

The simplest way for partners to liquidate the partnership is to convert all noncash assets into cash, to satisfy all the liabilities, and then to distribute the remaining cash to the partners— a **simple liquidation.** Or, once the liabilities are satisfied, the partners can decide to distribute cash periodically as it becomes available from the realization of the noncash assets—an **installment liquidation.**

LIQUIDATING INDIVIDUAL ASSETS

When a partnership is liquidated, the emphasis shifts from the measurement of income and its effect on partners' capital to the effect of the realization of assets on the partners' capital

---

[1]Uniform Partnership Act, Section 40, parts a, b, and c.

[2]Uniform Partnership Act, Section 40, part a.

accounts. All gains and losses from the realization of assets and the satisfaction of liabilities, as well as any costs (expenses) of liquidation, are entered directly in the partners' capital accounts instead of using the income statement accounts of the partnership. Therefore, for purposes of liquidation no distinction exists between capital and income, and so Priorities (3) and (4) of the Uniform Partnership Act, the capital share of the partners and the profit share, are treated as one in the liquidation schedules.

DISTRIBUTING GAINS AND LOSSES

A partnership agreement may specify that in liquidation, gains and losses from the realization of assets are to be shared differently than the profit- and loss-sharing ratio used while the partnership was a going concern. This specification may be based on substantial differences between the partners' capital investment and their time and effort spent in operating the partnership. That is, the partners who contributed the majority of the assets may want to receive the full benefit of the gains and losses on disposition of those assets. But if the partnership agreement does not contain such a provision, the gains and losses from liquidation are allocated to the partners in their profit- and loss-sharing ratio.

If the partners have a complex partnership agreement, the remainder ratio is used, because the partnership is no longer a profit-making entity but is a liquidating entity. Using the remainder ratio treats the gains and losses on disposal of the assets as an adjustment of the income of prior periods. Any costs incurred during the partnership's liquidation or any adjustments of the balances of the liabilities are treated as reductions of the partners' capital accounts and shared in the profit- and loss-sharing ratio.

If a partner's capital account becomes negative as a result of losses from the conversion of assets to cash, or additions to liabilities, or liquidation costs, the partner is required to contribute enough cash to bring to zero the balance of his or her capital account. If a partner also has lent assets to the partnership, the partner's negative capital balance will first be offset against the partner's loan payable balance. This offset is made because the partner's loan balance has priority over the partner's capital balance and so it prevents the payment of the loan balance when the partner still owes assets to the partnership for the negative capital balance. If the loan balance is not sufficient to cover the negative capital balance, the partner is required to contribute cash or other assets to bring the balance to zero.

Although the Uniform Partnership Act ranks a loan payable to a partner ahead of a partner's capital balance, this loan is usually not paid until all of the partnership's assets have been realized and the final balances in the capital accounts have been determined. If the loan is paid ahead of the final determination, the partner may receive cash that should not be distributed as the liquidation could result in a negative balance in the partner's capital account. Therefore, the simplest and safest solution is to add the loan payable to the capital account in order to determine the net capital investment before the liquidation process begins. If a partner is unable or unwilling to contribute cash or assets to cover the deficit in the capital account, the other partners absorb the debit balance in their profit- and loss-sharing ratio. The partners, who share the deficit, have a claim against the deficient partner for the amount of the debit balance they absorb.

If a partner has borrowed money from the partnership, the partner may repay this loan as part of the realization of the partnership's assets. Or the loan may simply be offset against the partner's capital account, thereby reducing this partner's capital account. The reduction of the capital balance is the safest treatment as it prevents the payment of a positive capital balance when a partner owes money to the partnership. This treatment of loans payable to the partners and loans receivable from the partners is particularly important when accounting for installment liquidations and bankruptcy situations.

Illustrative Problem 4.1 demonstrates the preparation of a schedule of partnership liquidation. The worksheet is a simple tool to illustrate the effects of the liquidation process on the capital accounts of the partners and is often used as a planning device when liquidation is contemplated. When the transactions actually occur, they are recorded in the balance sheet accounts of the partnership. The first worksheet, Exhibit 4-1, shows the amount of cash to be allocated to the partners when all the partners have positive capital balances. Exhibits 4-2 and 4-3 illustrate the treatment of a partner's capital balance that becomes negative as a result of the liquidation. Exhibit 4-4 illustrates the correct treatment of a loan payable to a partner, and Exhibit 4-5 shows the correct treatment of a loan receivable from a partner who cannot repay the balance owing to the partnership.

ILLUSTRATIVE PROBLEM 4.1: DISTRIBUTION IN A VOLUNTARY LIQUIDATION AFTER ALL ASSETS HAVE BEEN REALIZED—A SIMPLE LIQUIDATION

The partners of the M, N, and P Partnership, who share profits in the ratio of 4:3:3, respectively, have agreed to liquidate the business by selling all the assets, paying the liabilities, and then distributing the remaining cash to the partners. The balance sheet of the partnership prior to liquidation is

M, N, AND P PARTNERSHIP
Balance Sheet
December 31, 1990

Assets			Equities		
Cash	$ 10,000		Liabilities		$ 110,000
Noncash Assets	220,000		Capital		
			Partner M		30,000
			Partner N		40,000
			Partner P		50,000
Total Assets	$ 230,000		Total Equities		$ 230,000

Case 1: A Simple Liquidation With No Complications (Exhibit 4-1).   The partnership realizes $150,000 in total for the noncash assets.

When all the assets have been sold or liquidated, first the creditors are satisfied, then the remainder of the cash is distributed to the partners based on the balances in their capital accounts.

Case 2a: One Partner's Capital Balance Becomes Negative, and Partnership Receives Cash from Deficient Partner (Exhibit 4-2).   The partnership realizes $130,000 from the sale of the partnership's assets and Partner M remits cash for the deficit capital balance.

EXHIBIT 4-1

Illustrative Problem 4.1
M, N, and P Partnership
Schedule of Partnership Liquidation
Dr. (Cr.)

	Assets		Liabilities	Partners' Capital		
	Cash	Noncash		Partner M	Partner N	Partner P
Profit and Loss Ratio				40%	30%	30%
Preliquidation Balances	$ 10,000	$ 220,000	$(110,000)	$(30,000)	$(40,000)	$(50,000)
Realization of Assets	150,000	(220,000)		28,000	21,000	21,000
Predistribution Balances	160,000	$ −0−	(110,000)	(2,000)	(19,000)	(29,000)
Cash Distribution						
Liabilities	(110,000)		110,000			
Partners' Capital	(50,000)			2,000	19,000	29,000
Final Balances	$ −0−		$ −0−	$ −0−	$ −0−	$ −0−

EXHIBIT 4-2

Illustrative Problem 4.1
M, N, and P Partnership
Schedule of Partnership Liquidation
Dr. (Cr.)

	Assets		Liabilities	Partners' Capital		
	Cash	Noncash		Partner M	Partner N	Partner P
Profit and Loss Ratio				40%	30%	30%
Preliquidation Balances	$ 10,000	$ 220,000	$(110,000)	$(30,000)	$(40,000)	$(50,000)
Realization of Assets	130,000	(220,000)		36,000	27,000	27,000
Balance After Realization	140,000	$ −0−	(110,000)	6,000	(13,000)	(23,000)
Cash Received from M	6,000			(6,000)		
Predistribution Balances	146,000		(110,000)	$ −0−	(13,000)	(23,000)
Cash Distribution						
Liabilities	(110,000)		110,000			
Partners' Capital	(36,000)				13,000	23,000
Final Balances	$ −0−		$ −0−		$ −0−	$ −0−

If a partner's capital balance becomes negative, the partner with the negative capital balance must contribute assets to the partnership in the amount of the negative balance. The partner with the deficit balance has effectively borrowed from the partners with positive capital balances. The cash (assets) contributed to cover the deficit capital balance is the amount that partner owes the other partners, as Partner M has done in Exhibit 4-2. The creditors are always satisfied before payments are made to partners with positive capital balances.

Case 2b: One Partner's Capital Balance Becomes Negative, and Deficient Partner Cannot Pay the Partnership (Exhibit 4-3).   The partnership realizes $130,000 from the sale of the partnership's assets and Partner M cannot pay the partnership for the deficit capital balance.

If a partner cannot or will not pay the partnership an amount sufficient to cover the deficit balance in the partner's capital account, the deficit is allocated to the other partners using their remaining relative profit and loss ratios. For example, in Exhibit 4-3 Partner N's share is 50 percent [30%/(30% + 30%)]. The partners have a claim against the partner for the amount of the loss absorbed as they have lent capital to the partner with a negative capital balance. In Exhibit 4-3 Partners N and P each have a claim against Partner M for $3,000, representing the losses of Partner M that they absorbed.

EXHIBIT 4-3

Illustrative Problem 4.1
M, N, and P Partnership
Schedule of Partnership Liquidation
Dr. (Cr.)

	Assets			Partners' Capital		
	Cash	Noncash	Liabilities	Partner M	Partner N	Partner P
Profit and Loss Ratio				40%	30%	30%
Preliquidation Balances	$ 10,000	$ 220,000	$(110,000)	$(30,000)	$(40,000)	$(50,000)
Realization of Assets	130,000	(220,000)		36,000	27,000	27,000
Balance After Realization	140,000	$ −0−	(110,000)	6,000	(13,000)	(23,000)
Absorption of Debit Balance (3:3)				(6,000)	3,000	3,000
Predistribution Balances	140,000		(110,000)	$ −0−	(10,000)	(20,000)
Cash Distribution						
Liabilities	(110,000)		110,000			
Partners' Capital	(30,000)				10,000	20,000
Final Balances	$ −0−		$ −0−		$ −0−	$ −0−

Case 3: Partner Has a Loan Payable to the Partnership (Exhibit 4-4).   Assume that included in the $110,000 liabilities is a loan payable to Partner M in the amount of $20,000. The realization of the noncash assets results in cash of $130,000.

The debit balance of a partner is first offset against any loans payable to that partner as in Exhibit 4-4. Alternatively, the loan payable could have been added to the capital balance before preparing the worksheet. Only after the balance of the loan payable to the partner is reduced to zero will a partner need to contribute assets to the partnership to cover the deficit balance in that partner's capital account because the partner has a positive net investment in the partnership. The liabilities are satisfied first, then loans payable to partners, and last the positive capital balances of partners.

EXHIBIT 4-4

Illustrative Problem 4.1
M, N, and P Partnership
Schedule of Partnership Liquidation
Dr. (Cr.)

	Assets			Note Payable	Partners' Capital		
	Cash	Noncash	Liabilities	M	Partner M	Partner N	Partner P
Profit and Loss Ratio					40%	30%	30%
Preliquidation Balances	$ 10,000	$ 220,000	$(90,000)	$(20,000)	$(30,000)	$(40,000)	$(50,000)
Realization of Assets	130,000	(220,000)			36,000	27,000	27,000
Balance After Realization	140,000	$ −0−	(90,000)	(20,000)	6,000	(13,000)	(23,000)
Offset of Debit Balance Against Loan Payable				6,000	(6,000)		
Predistribution Balances	140,000		(90,000)	$(14,000)	$ −0−	(13,000)	(23,000)
Cash Distribution							
Liabilities	(90,000)		90,000				
Partner's Loan	(14,000)			14,000			
Partners' Capital	(36,000)					13,000	23,000
Final Balances	$ −0−		$ −0−	$ −0−		$ −0−	$ −0−

Case 4: Loan Receivable from Partner That Partner Cannot Pay (Exhibit 4-5). Assume that included in the assets is a loan receivable from Partner N in the amount of $27,000. Partner N does not have cash to pay the partnership for this loan. The partnership realizes $103,000 from the disposition of the noncash assets.

A loan receivable from a partner should be offset against that partner's capital account in order to determine the partner's net investment, unless the partner can repay the loan to the partnership. If the partner cannot pay the partnership and the losses incurred cause that partner's capital account to become negative, that partner's deficit balance is allocated to the other partners in their remaining profit- and loss-sharing ratio. The partners who share the loss have a claim against the partner whose deficit balance they absorbed. In Exhibit 4-5 Partners M and P have a claim against Partner N for $14,000. Partner M's share is $8,000 [$14,000 × 40%/(40% + 30%)] and Partner P's share is $6,000.

EXHIBIT 4-5

Illustrative Problem 4.1
M, N, and P Partnership
Schedule of Partnership Liquidation
Dr. (Cr.)

	Cash	Noncash	Receivable N
		Assets	
Profit and Loss Ratio			
Preliquidation Balances	$ 10,000	$ 193,000	$ 27,000
Realization of Assets	103,000	(193,000)	
Balance After Realization	113,000	$ −0−	$ 27,000
Offset of Loan Receivable Against Capital Account			(27,000)
Balance After Offset	113,000		$ −0−
Absorption of Debit Capital Balance (4:3)			
Balance After Absorption	113,000		
Offset of Debit Balance Against Loan Payable			
Predistribution Balances	113,000		
Cash Distribution			
Liabilities	(90,000)		
Partner's Loan	(6,000)		
Partner's Capital	(17,000)		
Final Balance	$ −0−		

INSTALLMENT LIQUIDATIONS

The process of realization of the noncash assets can extend over several months or even years, during which time the partners may desire to receive cash. In order to determine both the partners that should receive cash and the amount of cash that can safely be distributed, a predistribution plan can be formulated prior to the actual liquidation. The predistribution plan provides the partners with planning information for the liquidation. The predistribution plan is based on the maximum amount of loss that the partnership can incur before a partner's capital account becomes zero. As we discussed earlier, the loans receivable from the partners and loans payable to the partners are combined with their capital accounts to determine the partners' net capital investment. The loans receivable from the partners are subtracted from their capital accounts and the loans payable to partners are added to their capital accounts.

Liabilities	Note Payable M	Partners' Capital		
		Partner M	Partner N	Partner P
		40%	30%	30%
$(90,000)	$(20,000)	$(30,000)	$(40,000)	$(50,000)
		36,000	27,000	27,000
(90,000)	(20,000)	6,000	(13,000)	(23,000)
			27,000	
(90,000)	(20,000)	6,000	14,000	(23,000)
		8,000	(14,000)	6,000
(90,000)	(20,000)	14,000	$ −0−	(17,000)
	14,000	(14,000)		
(90,000)	(6,000)	$ −0−		(17,000)
90,000				
	6,000			
				17,000
$ −0−	$ −0−			$ −0−

PREDISTRIBUTION PLAN

When formulating the predistribution plan the first step is to compute the maximum loss absorbable for each partner as illustrated in Exhibit 4-6. The maximum loss absorbable is the total amount of partnership loss that would make a partner's capital account have a zero balance. The maximum loss absorbable is computed by dividing the partner's net capital investment by that partner's share of profits and losses. If the partners anticipate that the partnership will incur liquidation costs, the costs are subtracted from the net investment before determining the maximum loss absorbable, because they will reduce the partner's capital balances when paid. The partners are then ranked from the least absorbable loss to the most absorbable loss. This ranking allows us to determine the order of elimination of the partners in the schedule of loss absorption.

After ranking the partners, a liquidation schedule, called a **schedule of loss absorption,** is prepared. This schedule is similar to the examples in Illustrative Problem 4.1 except that the schedule uses the amount of loss that would eliminate a partner instead of the realization of assets as illustrated in Exhibit 4-7. The loss used for the partner with the least absorption is the first one entered on the schedule, and uses the loss computed in the schedule of maximum loss absorbable. When determining the loss that would eliminate the remaining partners, a new amount of loss must be computed, because the loss is only being shared by the partners with positive capital balances. After the elimination of each partner a new loss amount must be determined.

When all the partners but one have been eliminated, a schedule called a **cash predistribution plan** as demonstrated in Exhibit 4-8 is prepared that shows the order of payment of cash as the noncash assets are realized. The order of cash payments and the amount of the cash payment is provided by the schedule of loss absorption. The bottom line of the schedule shows the amount owed to creditors, and the first partner who will receive cash and the amount of cash to be received. The next previous line shows the amount of cash to be received and the partners who will receive the cash. In preparing the cash predistribution plan, you continue working upward through the schedule until you reach the first partner that was eliminated. Remember that when preparing this schedule the creditors must be paid first before any distributions to the partners, as indicated by the priority of payments specified in the Uniform Partnership Act.

ILLUSTRATIVE PROBLEM 4.2: PREPARATION OF A PREDISTRIBUTION PLAN

The partners of the A, B, C, and D Partnership have decided to liquidate their partnership. Prior to the liquidation, the partnership's balance sheet was

A, B, C, AND D PARTNERSHIP
Balance Sheet
December 31, 1990

Assets		Equities	
Cash	$ 30,000	Liabilities	$ 110,000
Noncash Assets	220,000	Loan Payable: Partner D	10,000
Loan Receivable: Partner B	20,000	Capital	
		Partner A	30,000
		Partner B	40,000
		Partner C	40,000
		Partner D	40,000
Total Assets	$ 270,000	Total Equities	$ 270,000

The partners feel that they can take sufficient time to receive the maximum possible price for the partnership's noncash assets, but they want to have cash paid to them as it becomes available. Partners A, B, C, and D have been sharing profits and losses in the ratio of 4:2:2:2, respectively. Exhibit 4-6 contains the maximum loss absorbable schedule and Exhibit 4-7 is the schedule of loss absorption.

The amounts of loss that will eliminate Partners B and C when added to the amount of loss that eliminated Partner A does not add up to the maximum loss absorbable. This difference

EXHIBIT 4-6

Illustrative Problem 4.2
A, B, C, and D Partnership
Schedule of Maximum Loss Absorbable

Partner	Net Capital Balance[a]		Profit and Loss Ratio		Maximum Loss Absorbable	Sequence of Elimination
A	$ 30,000	÷	4/10	=	$ 75,000	1
B	20,000	÷	2/10	=	100,000	2
C	40,000	÷	2/10	=	200,000	3
D	50,000	÷	2/10	=	250,000	4

[a]Capital account adjusted for loans receivable from partners and loans payable to partners. If these adjustments are not included, a partner could receive cash from the partnership that should be distributed to other partners.

EXHIBIT 4-7

Illustrative Problem 4.2
A, B, C, and D Partnership
Schedule of Loss Absorption
Dr. (Cr.)

	Assets	Liabilities	Partners' Net Capital			
			A	B	C	D
Profit and Loss Ratio			40%	20%	20%	20%
Preliquidation Balances	$ 250,000	$(110,000)	$(30,000)	$(20,000)	$(40,000)	($50,000)
Loss That Would Eliminate A	(75,000)		30,000	15,000	15,000	15,000
Balance	175,000	(110,000)	$ –0–	(5,000)	(25,000)	(35,000)
Loss That Would Eliminate B	(15,000)			5,000	5,000	5,000
Balance	160,000	(110,000)		$ –0–	(20,000)	(30,000)
Loss That Would Eliminate C	(40,000)				20,000	20,000
Balance	$ 120,000	$(110,000)			$ –0–	$(10,000)

in loss absorbable occurs because once Partner A is eliminated, only Partners B, C, and D will be left, and in this illustration, they share profits and losses equally. The same situation will occur once B is eliminated.

Exhibit 4-8, the cash predistribution plan, is prepared by reading upward through the schedule of loss absorption.

EXHIBIT 4-8

Illustrative Problem 4.2
A, B, C, and D Partnership
Cash Predistribution Plan

		Creditors	Partner A	Partner B	Partner C	Partner D
Cash on Hand	$ 30,000	All				
Cash Realized from Sales of Noncash Assets						
First	80,000	All				
Next	10,000					All
Next	40,000				1/2	1/2
Next	15,000			1/3	1/3	1/3
Any Amounts Over	$ 175,000		4/10	2/10	2/10	2/10

SOME CAUTIONS REGARDING THE PREDISTRIBUTION PLAN

The predistribution plan does not allow for any costs of liquidation that might occur during the liquidation process. Therefore, if the partnership anticipates that it will incur expenses, the partners' net capital balances are adjusted for the expenses before determining the maximum loss absorbable. If expenses are incurred during liquidation that have not been anticipated, the schedules need to be recomputed or else incorrect amounts of cash will be distributed to the partners. It is also possible that during the liquidation process, additional liabilities that were not recorded may surface. These will also invalidate the schedules. As the partnership realizes cash from the disposition of the noncash assets, the gains and losses will alter the partners' capital accounts. The predistribution plan assumes that all assets will be sold at losses. An alternative to using a predistribution plan is to prepare an installment liquidation worksheet, as illustrated in Exhibit 4-9, for the realization events. Each time the partners want to distribute cash, a schedule of safe payments, as illustrated in Exhibit 4-10, is prepared to determine the amount of cash that each partner will receive, if any.

PREPARING AN INSTALLMENT LIQUIDATION WORKSHEET

A worksheet similar to the one prepared in Illustrative Problem 4.1 is constructed. The first step is to combine the loans receivable from the partners and the loans payable to partners with the partners' capital account balances, as demonstrated in Illustrative Problem 4.2. If the net investment of the partners is not determined, the schedule of safe payments can show distributions of cash to the wrong partners, because a partner with a loan to the partnership may have a deficit capital balance, or a partner with a loan receivable may have a positive capital balance yet owe the partnership for the loan.

The next step is to enter each transaction or set of transactions for the period between cash distributions, and to record the effect of the transactions on the partners' net capital balances. The external creditors of the partnership must first be paid before a determination of the amount of cash to distribute to the partners is computed using a schedule of safe payments. In Illustrative Problem 4.3, as in Illustrative Problem 4-1, all of the noncash assets have been added together. If the process of liquidation makes several dispositions of the same asset (for example, accounts receivable or inventory), using a separate column for each of the different assets rather than totaling all of the noncash assets together is helpful.

After the creditors have been paid, the partners may elect to periodically distribute the cash as it is realized from the sale of the noncash assets. A schedule of safe payments is prepared each time a distribution of cash is desired by the partners. The schedule assumes that all noncash assets are worthless so that no cash will be realized upon their disposition. The remaining noncash assets are eliminated and the loss deducted from the partners' net capital balances in their profit- and loss-sharing ratio. If the partnership anticipates additional expenses during the realization process, these are also deducted from the net capital balances in the profit- and loss-sharing ratio.

If a partner or partners have negative capital balances, these are allocated to the partners with positive balances in their profit- and loss-sharing relationship. The absorption of the debit balance of one or more partners may cause the positive net capital balance of another partner or partners to become negative. If the allocation of a debit balance makes another partner's capital account negative, that debit balance must be absorbed by the partners whose capital balances are still positive. The process continues until only those partners with positive balances remain. The positive balances show which partners will receive the cash and the amount of cash for each. If no additional liquidation costs are incurred or unrecorded liabilities are discovered, the results of the schedule of safe payments and the cash predistribution plan are the same. For an example of an installment liquidation worksheet, the partnership of A, B, C, and D from Illustrative Problem 4.2 is used.

ILLUSTRATIVE PROBLEM 4.3: INSTALLMENT LIQUIDATION WORKSHEET

The partners of the A, B, C, and D Partnership, who share profits and losses in the ratio of 4:2:2:2, respectively, have agreed to liquidate their partnership over a span of time. The balance sheet of the partnership prior to its liquidation was

A, B, C, AND D PARTNERSHIP
Balance Sheet
December 31, 1990

Assets			Equities	
Cash	$ 30,000		Liabilities	$ 110,000
Noncash Assets	220,000		Loan Payable: Partner D	10,000
Loan Receivable: Partner B	20,000		Capital	
			Partner A	30,000
			Partner B	40,000
			Partner C	40,000
			Partner D	40,000
Total Assets	$ 270,000		Total Equities	$ 270,000

The following events occurred during the liquidation.

Month of 1991	Costs Paid	Cash from Assets Sold	Net Book Value of Assets Sold
January	$3,000	$94,000	$135,000
February	7,000	45,000	30,000
March	–0–	50,000	55,000

They have also decided to distribute cash once a month after their creditors have been satisfied. Exhibits 4-9 and 4-10 present the installment liquidation schedule and the schedule of safe payments for the A, B, C, and D Partnership. In addition to the partnership's existing liabilities, the partners anticipate that the costs of liquidation will total $8,000.

EXHIBIT 4-9

Illustrative Problem 4.3
A, B, C, and D Partnership
Installment Liquidation Schedule
Dr. (Cr.)

	Assets			Partners' Net Capital			
	Cash	Noncash	Liabilities	A	B	C	D
Profit and Loss Ratio				40%	20%	20%	20%
Preliquidation Balances	$ 30,000	$ 220,000	$(110,000)	$(30,000)	$(20,000)	$(40,000)	$(50,000)
Payment of Expenses	(3,000)			1,200	600	600	600
Sale of Assets	94,000	(135,000)		16,400	8,200	8,200	8,200
Payment of Liabilities	(110,000)		110,000				
Balance January 31, 1991	11,000	85,000	$ –0–	(12,400)	(11,200)	(31,200)	(41,200)
Distribution of Cash (1)	(6,000)						6,000
Payment of Expenses	(7,000)			2,800	1,400	1,400	1,400
Sale of Assets	45,000	(30,000)		(6,000)	(3,000)	(3,000)	(3,000)
Balance February 28, 1991	43,000	55,000		(15,600)	(12,800)	(32,800)	(36,800)
Distribution of Cash (2)	(43,000)					19,500	23,500
Sale of Assets	50,000	(55,000)		2,000	1,000	1,000	1,000
Balance March 31, 1991	50,000	$ –0–		(13,600)	(11,800)	(12,300)	(12,300)
Final Cash Distribution	(50,000)			13,600	11,800	12,300	12,300
Balance	$ –0–			$ –0–	$ –0–	$ –0–	$ –0–

FORCED LIQUIDATION OF A PARTNERSHIP

The operations of a partnership can result in the partnership's bankruptcy or in one or more of the partners' personal bankruptcy, thereby forcing the liquidation of the partnership. Both the partnership and one or more of the partners may be bankrupt. The Uniform Partnership

EXHIBIT 4-I0

Illustrative Problem 4.3
Schedule of Safe Payments
January 31, 1991
Dr. (Cr.)

(1)

	Partners' Net Capital				
	A	B	C	D	Total
Capital Balances	$(12,400)	$(11,200)	$(31,200)	$(41,200)	$(96,000)
Anticipated Expenses[a]	2,000	1,000	1,000	1,000	5,000
Noncash Assets	34,000	17,000	17,000	17,000	85,000
Adjusted Balances	23,600	6,800	(13,200)	(23,200)	(6,000)
Allocation of Debit Balances (2:2)	(23,600)	(6,800)	15,200	15,200	–0–
Adjusted Balances	$ –0–	$ –0–	2,000	(8,000)	(6,000)
Allocation of Debit Balance			(2,000)	2,000	–0–
Cash to be Paid			$ –0–	$(6,000)	$(6,000)

[a]Anticipated Expenses $8,000 − Expenses Paid $3,000 = Expenses Expected to Be Paid in the Future $5,000. The $7,000 of actual expenses for February is not used because the partners would not know on January 31, 1991, that the estimate of liquidation expenses is incorrect.

(2)

Schedule of Safe Payments
February 28, 1991
Dr. (Cr.)

	Partners' Net Capital				
	A	B	C	D	Total
Capital Balances	$(15,600)	$(12,800)	$(32,800)	$(36,800)	$(98,000)
Noncash Assets	22,000	11,000	11,000	11,000	55,000
Adjusted Balances	6,400	(1,800)	(21,800)	(25,800)	(43,000)
Allocation of Debit Balance (2:2:2)	(6,400)	2,134	2,133	2,133	–0–
Adjusted Balances	$ –0–	334	(19,667)	(23,667)	(43,000)
Allocation of Debit Balance (2:2)		(334)	167	167	–0–
Cash to Be Paid		$ –0–	$(19,500)	$(23,500)	$(43,000)

Act specifies that when a partner is bankrupt, the partner's personal assets must be used first to satisfy the partner's separate creditors, second to satisfy the partnership's creditors, and last to satisfy the amounts owed to other partners who covered the deficit in the bankrupt partner's capital account.[3]

[3]Uniform Partnership Act, Section 40, part (i).

The liquidation of a bankrupt partnership is similar to the problem discussed in Illustrative Problem 4.1 except that the partnership's assets are not sufficient to cover its liabilities, thus indicating that one or more of the partners have a debit capital balance. Some of the partners may also be personally bankrupt, which can reduce the amount of assets that the partnership can collect to cover the deficit in the partner's capital account. Illustrative Problem 4.4 demonstrates the effect of the liquidation of a bankrupt partnership when one of the partners also is bankrupt. The problem shows that if a partner is bankrupt, the status of that partner's personal assets and liabilities must also be considered when preparing the liquidation schedule.

ILLUSTRATIVE PROBLEM 4.4: BANKRUPT PARTNERSHIP

The R, S, and T Partnership has operated at a loss for the past two years and its liabilities exceed its assets. The partnership's creditors are demanding payment. Partner T is also bankrupt as a result of making unwise investments. Partners R, S, and T share profits and losses equally. The balance sheet of the R, S, and T Partnership and the balance sheets of the individual partners, prior to liquidation, were

R, S, AND T PARTNERSHIP
Balance Sheet
December 31, 1990

Assets		Equities	
Cash	$ 5,000	Liabilities	$ 110,000
Noncash Assets	90,000	Capital	
		Partner R	8,000
		Partner S	12,000
		Partner T	(35,000)
Total Assets	$ 95,000	Total Equities	$ 95,000

PARTNERS R, S, AND T
Schedule of Separate Assets and Liabilities
December 31, 1990

	Partner R	Partner S	Partner T
Personal Assets	$ 100,000	$ 165,000	$ 65,000
R, S, and T Partnership Capital Account	8,000	12,000	(35,000)
Total Assets	108,000	177,000	30,000
Personal Liabilities	35,000	80,000	50,000
Personal Net Worth	$ 73,000	$ 97,000	$(20,000)

The R, S, and T Partnership realizes $72,000 from the liquidation of the noncash assets. Exhibit 4-11 shows the schedule of partnership liquidation.

EXHIBIT 4-11

Illustrative Problem 4.4
R, S, and T Partnership
Schedule of Partnership Liquidation
Dr. (Cr.)

	Assets			Partners' Capital		
	Cash	Noncash	Liabilities	Partner R	Partner S	Partner T
Profit and Loss Ratio				1/3	1/3	1/3
Preliquidation Balances	$ 5,000	$ 90,000	$(110,000)	$(8,000)	$(12,000)	$ 35,000
Realization of Assets	72,000	(90,000)		6,000	6,000	6,000
Prepayment Balances	77,000	$ –0–	(110,000)	(2,000)	(6,000)	41,000
Cash from Partner T[a]	15,000					(15,000)
Allocation of Debit Balance				13,000	13,000	(26,000)
Cash from Partners R and S	18,000			(11,000)	(7,000)	
Payment of Liabilities	(110,000)		110,000			
Final Balances	$ –0–	$ –0–	$ –0–	$ –0–	$ –0–	$ –0–

[a]Personal assets $65,000 − personal liabilities $50,000 = $15,000 available to satisfy the partnership's creditors

Just as with a voluntary liquidation, the partners with positive capital balances absorb the debit balances of the partners with deficit capital balances. However, unlike a voluntary liquidation, the partners will not have a claim against the bankrupt partner except as general creditors.

SUMMARY

The liquidation of a partnership can be either a voluntary liquidation or a forced liquidation. When a business is being liquidated the emphasis shifts from the measurement of net income to the balances in the partners' capital accounts, thus all expenses, gains, and losses are recorded in the capital accounts of the partners. In a voluntary liquidation, the partners decide to sell the assets of the partnership, to satisfy the creditors, and to distribute the remaining cash to the partners. In a forced liquidation, the liquidation occurs as creditors are demanding satisfaction because either the partnership is bankrupt and/or one or more of the partners are personally bankrupt.

A simple voluntary liquidation is one in which all the noncash assets are sold or liquidated, the creditors are satisfied, and the remaining cash (assets) is distributed to the partners based on the balances in their capital accounts. If partners have lent assets to the partnership, their net investment is the sum of their capital and loan accounts and the loan accounts can be used to absorb any deficit in their capital accounts. If partners have borrowed assets from the partnership, their net investment is their capital balances net of the loans receivable. In accounting for a liquidation, the loans receivable are offset against the partners' capital accounts if not repaid to the partnership, so that assets are not distributed to the wrong partners. The loans payable can be added to the partners' capital accounts.

A voluntary installment liquidation is one in which the assets are sold over time and cash or assets are distributed to the partners periodically during the period of the liquidation. A predistribution plan can be prepared prior to the liquidation to determine the amount of assets and the partners who will receive the assets as the liquidation progresses. The first step in preparing a cash predistribution plan is to determine the maximum loss absorbable by each partner. The maximum loss absorbable is computed by dividing the net investment of a partner by the partner's profit and loss ratio. If the partnership anticipates liquidation expenses, these are also subtracted from the net investment before determining the maximum loss absorbable. The maximum loss absorbables are used to rank the partners in the order that partnership losses would bring their capital balances to zero.

The second step is to prepare a schedule of loss absorption. This schedule uses the losses that would eliminate a partner, rather than expected losses from the sales of assets starting with the partner with the least absorbable loss from the maximum loss absorbable schedule, and ending with the partner with the most absorbable loss. As each partner is eliminated, the loss must be recomputed as only the remaining partners share the loss. When the schedule is complete, it lists the amount and the order in which cash can safely be distributed to the partners after the creditors are satisfied.

The last step is to prepare the actual cash predistribution plan. This schedule is prepared using the amounts and order established by the schedule of loss absorption.

A worksheet can be prepared to illustrate an actual installment liquidation, although the transactions are recorded in the balance sheet accounts of the partnership rather than using a worksheet. The net investment of the partners is used in this schedule. The transactions of the liquidation are entered on the worksheet and the partners' capital accounts are adjusted for the expenses, gains, or losses that occurred. At each interval in which a distribution of cash is desired, a schedule of safe payments is prepared that assumes all the noncash assets have a zero value. If the partners anticipate additional liquidation expenses, these are also subtracted from the partners' capital balances.

If the elimination of the noncash assets and the anticipated liquidation expenses makes a partner's capital balance negative, the negative balance is allocated to the partners with positive capital balances in the remaining profit- and loss-sharing ratio. This allocation may cause other partners' capital balances to become negative, and then the allocation process is repeated. If the actual expenses are equal to the anticipated expenses and no gains on the sale of assets occur, the schedule of safe payments shows the same distributions as the cash predistribution plan; if not, the results are different.

A forced liquidation is accounted for in the same manner as a voluntary liquidation, except that the personal assets and liabilities of the partners must be considered in determining whether or not partners with negative capital balances will be able to pay the partnership for those negative balances. Negative capital balances are loans from the partnership to the partners with negative capital balances. The personal creditors of a partner have preference over the partnership for the partner's personal assets. If the partnership is bankrupt, the liabilities of the partnership exceed the assets. The creditors of the partnership will receive all the cash generated by the liquidation and then will have a claim against the partners as individuals for any unpaid amounts.

REVIEW PROBLEM

The partners of the K, L, and M Partnership have reached retirement age and have agreed to liquidate their partnership over time rather than to sell the business entity. The partners share profits and losses in the ratio of 4:3:3, respectively. The partnership's condensed balance sheet before the assets were sold was

K, L, AND M PARTNERSHIP
Balance Sheet
June 30, 1990

Assets			Equities		
Current Assets			**Liabilities**		
Cash	$ 10,000		Accounts Payable	$ 60,000	
Accounts			Loan Payable:		
Receivable: Net	50,000		Partner L	50,000	
Loan Receivable:			Total Liabilities	110,000	
Partner M	30,000		**Partners' Capital**		
Inventory	100,000		Partner K $ 20,000		
Total Current			Partner L 30,000		
Assets	190,000		Partner M 70,000	120,000	
Store Fixtures: Net	40,000				
Total Assets	$ 230,000		Total Equities	$ 230,000	

1. The partners have agreed to pay the liabilities as cash becomes available. The partners also have decided to distribute cash to the partners at the end of every month. The lease on the store building requires that the partnership restore the building to its original condition. The partners estimate that the restoration will cost $9,000.

Required

1) Determine the maximum loss absorbable for each partner.
2) Prepare a cash predistribution plan for the partnership.
3) Discuss the events that might invalidate the cash predistribution plan.

2. The partnership entered into the following liquidating transactions during the three months ended September 30, 1990:

July 1	Paid an attorney $2,500 to resolve a dispute with the landlord regarding the restoration of the store building. The partners believe their estimate of $9,000 is still accurate.
July 8	Sold inventory, with a book value of $60,000, for $50,000.
Month of July	Collected $20,000 of the accounts receivable. The partners have agreed that $15,000 of the accounts receivable are uncollectible.
August 5	Sold inventory with a book value of $20,000 for $12,000.
August 20	Sold all of the store fixtures for $28,000.
Month of August	Collected an additional $10,000 of the accounts receivable.

September 4	Sold the remaining inventory for 60 cents on the dollar.
September 24	Paid a contractor $8,500 to restore the rental building according to the agreement arranged by the attorney.
Month of September	Collected $8,000 of the accounts receivable, which included $4,000 previously written off. The remaining receivables are deemed uncollectible.
September 30	Final distribution is made to the partners.

Required

1) Assume all partners are solvent. Prepare an installment liquidation schedule for the K, L, and M Partnership. (The use of separate columns for each of the assets will be helpful.)
2) Explain why the monthly cash payments do not agree with your cash predistribution plan from Part 1.

3. *Required*

1) Describe what recourse Partners L and M have with regard to Partner K's debit capital balance if K will not pay and K is (1) solvent and (2) bankrupt.
2) If Partner K has $113,000 in personal assets, exclusive of his interest in the K, L, and M Partnership, and owes his personal creditors $120,000, show how your solution to Part 2 (1) is different.

QUESTIONS

1. Describe how loans receivable from partners and loans payable to partners are treated in a liquidation and why that treatment is necessary.
2. What is the order of payment of the equities as specified in the Uniform Partnership agreement?
3. If a partner is bankrupt, what is the order of payment of the partner's obligations as specified in the Uniform Partnership Act? What affect does the order have on the liquidation of a partnership? If a partner is bankrupt, will liquidation of the partnership result?
4. Why is it necessary to include the loans receivable from partners, the loans payable to partners, and the anticipated liquidation costs in determining a cash predistribution plan?
5. What factors can cause the cash distribution from an installment liquidation to be different from a previously calculated cash predistribution plan?
6. Describe how noncash assets and expected liquidation costs are treated in a schedule of safe payments.
7. Describe how debit balances in partners' capital accounts are treated in a schedule of safe payments.

EXERCISES

EXERCISE 4-1

The partners of the A, B, and C Partnership have agreed to liquidate their partnership. The partnership has cash of $8,000, noncash assets of $81,000, and liabilities of $27,000. The capital accounts of the partners are: Partner A $6,000, Partner B $29,000, and Partner C $27,000. The partners share profits and losses in the ratio of 3:3:2, respectively. The partnership was able to sell all the noncash assets for $63,400 and paid $2,400 of liquidation expenses.

Required

Prepare a liquidation schedule for the partnership, assuming all partners are solvent and can pay the partnership for any capital deficit.

EXERCISE 4-2

Refer to Exercise 4-1. The liabilities of $27,000 include a $7,000 note payable to Partner A.

Required

Prepare a liquidation schedule for the partnership.

EXERCISE 4-3

Refer to Exercise 4-1. The noncash assets of $81,000 include a note receivable from Partner B in the amount of $11,000. The liabilities of $27,000 include a note payable to Partner A of $7,000.

Required

Prepare a liquidation schedule, assuming the noncash assets were sold for $52,400 instead of $63,400.

EXERCISE 4-4

Refer to Exercise 4-1. Partner A is bankrupt. Partner A has personal assets of $37,000 exclusive of Partner A's interest in the partnership, and personal liabilities of $36,000.

Required

Prepare a liquidation schedule for the partnership.

EXERCISE 4-5

On January 1, 1990, the partners of the D, E, and F Partnership decide to liquidate the partnership. Prior to the liquidation, the partnership had cash of $6,000, noncash assets of $73,000, liabilities to outsiders of $18,000, and a note payable to Partner F of $7,000. The capital balances of the partners were: Partner D $18,000, Partner E $27,000, and Partner F $9,000. The partners share profits and losses in the ratio of 3:3:4, respectively.

Required

1. Determine the maximum loss absorbable for the partners.
2. Prepare a cash predistribution plan for the partnership.

EXERCISE 4-6

Refer to Exercise 4-5. During January 1990, the partnership received cash of $15,000 from the sale of assets with a book value of $19,000 and paid $1,800 of liquidation expenses. During February, the partnership realized $22,000 from the sale of assets with a book value of $17,500 and paid liquidation expenses of $4,200. During March, the remaining assets were sold for $18,000. The partners desire to distribute cash at the end of each month.

Required

1. Prepare an installment liquidation schedule for the partnership, assuming all the partners are solvent.
2. Why are the cash payments different from the cash predistribution plan of Exercise 4-5?

EXERCISE 4-7

The G and H Partnership has not been profitable and the creditors of the partnership are demanding payment. The partnership has cash of $2,000, noncash assets of $29,000, and liabilities of $35,000. Partner G has a positive capital balance of $11,000 and Partner H has a negative capital balance of $15,000. Partner G has $41,000 of personal assets, exclusive of his capital balance, and personal liabilities of $16,400. Partner H has $43,000 of personal assets, exclusive of her interest in the partnership, and personal liabilities of $37,300. Partners G and H share profits and losses equally.

Required

Prepare a liquidation schedule for the G and H Partnership, assuming the noncash assets are sold for $21,200.

EXERCISE 4-8

1. The following condensed balance sheet is presented for the partnership of Alexander, Bell, and Graham, who share profits and losses in the ratio of 6:2:2, respectively:

Cash	$ 80,000
Other Assets	280,000
Total	$ 360,000
Liabilities	$ 140,000
Alexander, Capital	100,000
Bell, Capital	100,000
Graham, Capital	20,000
Total	$ 360,000

The partners agreed to liquidate the partnership after selling the other assets. If the other assets are sold for $160,000, how much should Alexander receive upon liquidation, assuming all the partners are solvent?

a. $ 25,000
b. $ 26,000
c. $ 28,000
d. $ 100,000

2. The following condensed balance sheet is presented for the partnership of Cooke, Dorry, and Evans, who share profits and losses in the ratio of 4:3:3, respectively:

Cash	$ 90,000
Other Assets	820,000
Cooke: Loan	30,000
Total	$ 940,000
Accounts Payable	$ 210,000
Evans: Loan	40,000
Cooke, Capital	300,000
Dorry, Capital	200,000
Evans, Capital	190,000
Total	$ 940,000

The partners decide to liquidate the partnership. If the other assets are sold for $600,000, how much of the available cash should be distributed to Cooke?

a. $ 170,000
b. $ 182,000
b. $ 212,000
d. $ 300,000

3. The following condensed balance sheet is presented for the partnership of Lever, Polen, and Quint, who share profits and losses in the ratio of 4:3:3, respectively:

Cash	$ 90,000
Other Assets	830,000
Lever: Loan	20,000
Total	$ 940,000

Accounts Payable	$ 210,000
Quint: Loan	30,000
Lever, Capital	310,000
Polen, Capital	200,000
Quint, Capital	190,000
Total	$ 940,000

The partners decide to liquidate the partnership. If the other assets are sold for $700,000, how much of the available cash should be distributed to Lever?

a. $ 230,000
b. $ 238,000
c. $ 258,000
d. $ 310,000

4. On January 1, 1991, the partners of Cobb, Davis, and Eddy Partnership, who share profits and losses in the ratio of 5:3:2, respectively, decided to liquidate their partnership. On this date the partnership's condensed balance sheet was

Assets

Cash	$ 50,000
Other Assets	250,000
	$ 300,000

Liabilities and Capital

Liabilities	$ 60,000
Capital, Cobb	80,000
Capital, Davis	90,000
Capital, Eddy	70,000
	$ 300,000

On January 15, 1991, the first cash sale of other assets with a carrying amount of $150,000 realized $120,000. Safe installment payments to the partners were made on the same date. How much cash should be distributed to each partner?

	Cobb	Davis	Eddy
a.	$ 15,000	$ 51,000	$ 44,000
b.	$ 40,000	$ 45,000	$ 35,000
c.	$ 55,000	$ 33,000	$ 22,000
d.	$ 60,000	$ 36,000	$ 24,000

(AICPA adapted)

PROBLEMS

PROBLEM 4-1

The partners of the Q, R, and S Partnership have decided to liquidate their partnership. Prior to liquidation, the partnership balance sheet is

Assets

Cash	$ 12,600
Noncash Assets	91,100
	$ 103,700

Liabilities and Capital

Liabilities	$ 61,700
Capital, Partner Q	18,000
Capital, Partner R	18,000
Capital, Partner S	6,000
	$ 103,700

The noncash assets include a note receivable from Partner Q in the amount of $15,000. The liabilities include a note payable to Partner R of $8,000, and a note payable to Partner S of $12,000. The partners share profits and losses in the ratio of 2:2:1, respectively.

Required

1. Determine the amount of cash each partner will receive for each of the following independent situations:
   1) The noncash assets are sold for $60,000 and all the partners are solvent.
   2) The noncash assets are sold for $54,000 and Partner Q is bankrupt. Partner Q's net worth, exclusive of his interest in the partnership, is $2,000.
   3) The noncash assets are sold for $54,000 and $4,975 of liquidation expenses are paid. Partner Q is bankrupt and his personal liabilities exceed his personal assests, exclusive of his interest in the partnership.
2. If the partners receive an offer of $28,000 for the business, exclusive of the cash, would they be better off accepting the offer or liquidating under the conditions or 1 (3) above?

PROBLEM 4-2

The partners of the D, E, and F Partnership share profits in the ratio of 4:3:3, respectively. Prior to the closing of the books on December 31, 1991, the condensed trial balance of the partnership is

	Debit	Credit
Cash	$ 14,500	
Noncash Assets	81,000	
Loan Receivable: Partner E	11,000	
Drawings, Partner D	15,000	
Drawings, Partner E	17,000	
Drawings, Partner F	17,500	
Liabilities		$ 46,300
Loan Payable: Partner D		5,000
Loan Payable: Partner F		7,500

	Debit	Credit
Capital, Partner D		18,000
Capital, Partner E		27,000
Capital, Partner F		22,200
Income Summary		30,000
Totals	$ 156,000	$ 156,000

The partners liquidated the business during January 1992 and Partner E paid $4,300 in cash to cover the negative balance in his captial account.

Required

1. Prepare a schedule to determine the net investment of the partners in the partnership.
2. Determine the amount of loss the partnership incurred on the disposal of the partnership assets.
3. Prepare a liquidation schedule to support your answer to 1 above.

PROBLEM 4-3

The H, I, J, and K Partnership has been operating a building supply business for over 25 years. When the partnership was initially formed, Partner J contributed the land and the building and most of the operating capital. The partners share profits and losses in the ratio of 2:2:3:3, respectively. The partners were unable to find a buyer for the business, and on March 31, 1990 decided to liquidate the partnership over time. The partnership agreement contains the following provisions regarding liquidation:

1. Any liquidation expenses are to be shared in the profit and loss ratio.
2. Any gains or losses from the sale of current assets are to be shared in the profit and loss ratio.
3. Any gains and losses from the sale of noncurrent assets are to be shared in the ratio of 1:1:6:2, respectively.

The balance sheet of the partnership, prior to liquidation is

H, I, J, AND K PARTNERSHIP
Balance Sheet
March 31, 1990

Assets			Equities		
Current Assets			**Current Liabilities**		
Cash		$ 23,500	Accounts Payable		$ 51,400
Accounts Receivable: Net		47,600	Loan Payable: Partner K		8,000
Inventory		92,200	Total Current		
Loan Receivable: Partner I		24,000	Liabilities		59,400
Total Current Assets		187,300	Mortgage Payable:		
Plant and Equipment			Land and Building		57,600
Land	$ 15,000		Total Liabilities		117,000
Building: Net	61,000		**Partners' Capital**		
Equipment: Net	29,200	105,200	Partner H	$ 46,300	
			Partner I	34,500	
			Partner J	75,300	
			Partner K	19,400	175,500
Total Assets		$ 292,500	Total Equities		$ 292,500

The partners agreed that they will be able to find a buyer for the land and the building. The partners have determined that based on current real estate values the expected selling price of the land and building will be approximately $100,000. The partners also believe the market value of the equipment to be $15,200. The partners anticipate the liquidation expenses could be as high as $14,000.

Required

1. Determine the maximum loss absorbable, assuming the plant and equipment will be sold at the profit estimated by the partners.
2. Prepare a cash predistribution plan assuming that the partnership will realize the partners' estimates of the market values of the assets and incur their estimate of expenses.
3. Draft a memo to the partners explaining the methods used to prepare a cash predistribution plan and explaining the causes that can result in the actual cash distribution being different than the cash predistribution plan.

PROBLEM 4-4 (CONTINUATION OF PROBLEM 4-3)

Refer to Problem 4-3. The partners decide to liquidate the partnership over time and to distribute cash monthly as it is available. The following transactions occurred during the installment liquidation:

April 1	Sold the land and building for $95,000 and paid the balance owing on the mortgage.
April 10	Sold equipment with a cost of $22,000 and accumulated depreciation of $8,900 for $9,000.
Month of April	Collected $21,200 of accounts receivable and determined that $1,400 were uncollectible.
Month of April	Sold $38,600 of inventory for $31,120 of which $6,240 of the sales were on credit and the remainder were for cash.
Month of April	Paid $5,400 of liquidation expenses.
May 7	Sold the remaining equipment for $7,300.
May 14	Received a bill from a supplier in the amount of $3,700, which had not been previously recorded.
Month of May	Sold inventory with a cost of $26,300 for $17,100. Sales totaling $9,250 were on account and the remainder were for cash.
Month of May	Collected $24,300 of accounts receivable and determined that $2,360 of accounts receivable were not collectible.
Month of May	Paid $6,220 of liquidation expenses. The partners believe that the remaining costs of liquidation could be as high as $7,500.
June 6	Sold the remaining inventory for 40 cents on the dollar.
Month of June	Collected $12,400 of accounts receivable and determined that the remainder are uncollectible.
Month of June	Paid the remaining liquidation expenses of $9,100.

Required

Prepare an installment liquidation schedule for the partnership assuming all the partners are solvent and can contribute cash to cover any deficit in their capital accounts.

PROBLEM 4-5

The partners of the A, B, C, and D Partnership who share profits and losses in the ratio of 2:1:1:2, respectively, have decided to liquidate the business. The partnership's balance sheet prior to liquidation was

A, B, C, AND D PARTNERSHIP
Balance Sheet
December 31, 1990

Assets		Equities		
Cash	$ 13,000	Accounts Payable		$ 40,500
Accounts Receivable	29,000	Loan Payable: Partner B		9,000
Inventory	36,000	Loan Payable: Partner C		12,000
Supplies	3,000	Partners' Capital		
Note Receivable: Partner A	20,000	Partner A	$ 26,000	
Goodwill	9,000	Partner B	6,000	
		Partner C	9,000	
		Partner D	7,500	48,500
Total Assets	$ 110,000	Total Equities		$ 110,000

1. The partners estimate that the liquidation costs will be $3,600.

Required

Determine the maximum loss absorbable by the partners and prepare a cash predistribution plan. (*Hint:* If a business is not sold as an entity, what could you sell the goodwill for?)

2. The partners entered into the following transactions during the course of the installment liquidation of the partnership. The partners decided to distributed cash after each sale of inventory.

1. Collected $14,000 of account receivable and wrote off $1,800 of receivables.
2. Paid $2,400 of liquidation expenses and anticipate $1,200 additional liquidation expenses.
3. Sold all the supplies for $2,100 and $22,800 of inventory for $19,800.
4. Collected $9,000 of accounts receivable and wrote off $2,100 of receivables.
5. Paid $1,500 of liquidation expenses and anticipate an additional $600 of expenses.
6. Sold $10,000 of inventory for $11,500.
7. Paid an additional $600 of liquidation expenses.
8. Collected $1,800 of additional receivables and determined the remaining receivables are uncollectible.
9. Sold the remaining inventory for $2,900.

Required

1) Prepare an installment liquidation schedule assuming all the partners are solvent.
2) How would the solution to 1 above be different, if the partners with debit capital balances were insolvent?
3) Explain why the cash payments do not agree with the predistribution plan of Part 1.

PROBLEM 4-6

The partners of the Able, Baker, and Carter Partnership have decided to liquidate the partnership. The partners share profits and losses in the ratio of 2:3:5, respectively. Prior to liquidation, the condensed trial balance of the partnership is

	Debit	Credit
Cash	$ 20,000	
Other Current Assets	70,000	
Note Receivable: Baker	30,000	
Property, Plant and Equipment: Net	120,000	
Accounts Payable		$ 32,000
Note Payable: Able		40,000
Mortgage Payable: Land and Building		52,000
Capital, Able		20,000
Capital, Baker		46,500
Capital, Carter		49,500
	$ 240,000	$ 240,000

1. The partners estimate that the liquidation expenses will be $15,000.

Required
Prepare a cash predistribution plan.

2. The partners decided to liquidate the partnership over time, and to distribute the available cash at the end of each month. The following events occurred during the installment liquidation of the Able, Baker, and Carter Partnership. All the partners are solvent and can pay any amount needed to cover a negative capital balance.

First Month
1. Sold $50,000 worth of current assets for $40,000.
2. Paid liquidation expenses of $6,000 for selling the current assets.
3. Paid the accounts payable.

Second Month
1. Sold the equipment, which has a net book value of $40,000, for $25,000.
2. Sold the remainder of the current assets for $12,000.
3. Paid liquidation expenses of $2,000.

Third Month
1. Sold the land and the building for $95,000 and paid the balance owing on the mortgage.
2. Paid liquidation costs of $10,000.

Required
Prepare an installment liquidation worksheet supported by schedules of safe payments. (*Hint:* The mortgage should be netted against the land and building in the schedules of safe payments as it is a secured claim.)

PROBLEM 4-7
On January 1, 1991, the partners of the Allen, Brown, and Cox Partnership, who share profits and losses in the ratio of 5:3:2, respectively, decided to liquidate their partnership. The partnership trial balance at this date is

	Debit	Credit
Cash	$ 18,000	
Accounts Receivable	66,000	
Inventory	52,000	
Machinery and Equipment: Net	189,000	
Allen: Loan	30,000	
Accounts Payable		$ 53,000
Brown: Loan		20,000
Allen, Capital		118,000
Brown, Capital		90,000
Cox, Capital		74,000
	$ 355,000	$ 355,000

The partners plan a program of piecemeal conversion of assets in order to minimize liquidation losses. All available cash, less an amount retained to provide for future expenses, is to be distributed to the partners at the end of each month. A summary of the liquidation transactions is

January 1991
1. $51,000 was collected on accounts receivable; the balance is uncollectible.
2. $38,000 was received for the entire inventory.
3. $2,000 of liquidation expenses were paid.
4. $50,000 was paid to outside creditors, after an offset of a $3,000 credit memorandum received on January 11, 1991.
5. $10,000 cash was retained in the business at the end of the month for potential unrecorded liabilities and anticipated expenses.

February 1991
6. $4,000 liquidation expenses were paid.
7. $6,000 cash was retained in the business at the end of the month for potential unrecorded liabilities and anticipated expenses.

March 1991
8. $146,000 was received on sale of all items of machinery and equipment.
9. $5,000 liquidation expenses were paid.
10. No cash was retained in the business.

Required
Prepare an installment liquidation worksheet and a schedule of safe payments as of January 31, 1991.

(AICPA adapted)

PROBLEM 4-8
The partnership of Tom, Dick, and Mary has not been successful and the creditors are demanding that the partnership be liquidated. In addition, the business failure has resulted in both Dick and Mary being personally bankrupt. The partnership has assets of $87,000 that include a loan receivable from Tom in the amount of $9,000. The liabilities of the partnership total $71,000 and include a $14,000 note payable to Dick. The balances in the partners' capital accounts are Tom $17,000 credit, Dick $4,900 debit, and Mary $3,900 credit. The partners share profits and losses in the ratio of 4:2:2, respectively. The partners have the following personal assets and liabilities including their partnership interest:

	Tom	Dick	Mary
Assets	$ 42,000	$ 37,500	$ 41,000
Liabilities	21,000	34,200	39,400

Required

1. Determine the net investment of each of the partners in the partnership.
2. Determine the personal net worth of the partners exclusive of their interest in the partnership.
3. Determine the amount available to satisfy the personal creditors of Dick and Mary if the assets of the partnership were sold for $64,000, an unrecorded liability of $2,400 was discovered, and $3,200 of liquidation costs were paid.

PROBLEM 4-9

Audi, Tor, Kant, and Count have been partners in a CPA firm for a number of years. Kant and Count have reached retirement age and the partners are trying to decide whether to sell the accounting practice or to continue the business. The partnership agreement contains the following provisions regarding retirement and liquidation:

1. The remaining partners may purchase the retiring partner's share of the firm for 75% of the partner's client base plus the book value of the partner's share of net assets.
2. The client base is to be computed as the average billings to clients for the past three years that were the partner's primary responsibility.
3. In the event that the remaining partners are unwilling to purchase the interest, either the entire firm or the client base of the retiring partner is to be sold for the best available price.
4. The remaining partners are to pay for the partnership interest over a period of 10 years with interest at 10% on the unpaid balance.

Audi and Tor are willing to purchase Count's partnership interest, but they are not willing to purchase Kant's interest. Kant has been the audit partner of the firm with primary responsibility for the major audit clients. During the past three years, the firm has lost five major audit clients due to mergers and business failures. Audi and Tor are only willing to pay for the remaining client base of Kant and not for the client base, which includes the five clients that the firm no longer services. Kant finds this arrangement unsatisfactory and is demanding that the firm be sold or that her client base be sold as specified in the partnership agreement. The gross billings of the partners for the past three years were

Year	Audi	Tor	Kant	Count	Total
1989	$ 80,000	$ 65,000	$ 137,000	$ 120,000	$ 402,000
1990	90,000	71,000	124,000	123,000	408,000
1991	94,000	74,000	111,000	132,000	411,000
Total	$ 264,000	$ 210,000	$ 372,000	$ 375,000	$ 1,221,000

Kant's gross billings without the five major audit clients the firm has lost total $300,000 (1989—$106,000, 1990—$101,000, and 1991—$93,000). The partners have been sharing profits and losses in the ratio of 2:2:3:3, respectively. The balance sheet of the partnership at December 31, 1991 is

AUDI, TOR, KANT, AND COUNT, CPAs
Balance Sheet
December 31, 1991

Assets		Equities	
Cash	$ 26,300	Wages Payable	$ 24,700
Accounts Receivable: Net	72,600	Payroll Taxes Payable	7,800
Work in Process	61,400	Note Payable: Tor	16,000
Professional Library: Net	14,900	Note Payable: Kant	14,000
Note Receivable: Count	19,500	Partners' Capital	
Goodwill: Net	42,000	Audi	33,000
		Tor	36,500
		Kant	54,600
		Count	50,100
Total Assets	$ 236,700	Total Equities	$ 236,700

The goodwill is from the admission of Kant to the partnership five years ago.

An accounting firm in the neighboring town, Can and Able, CPAs, has offered to purchase the entire firm, exclusive of the cash, for $230,000, or to purchase the clients of Kant for $75,000.

Required

1. Prepare a schedule to determine the amount each partner will receive if the partners agree to accept the offer from Can and Able to purchase the entire firm.
2. Prepare a schedule to determine the effect on the capital accounts of the partners if the partnership sells Kant's client base to Can and Able for $75,000. Is the contention of the remaining partners regarding the value of Kant's client base a valid one? Why or why not?
3. Prepare a schedule to determine the amount that will have to be paid to Kant and Count under the partnership agreement.
4. Determine the amount that would be paid to Kant if she would accept 75% of her client base determined without the five audit clients.
5. If you were Kant, which of the above possibilities would you prefer? Why?
6. Discuss the problems that Audi and Tor will have if they purchase the partnership interests of Kant and Count.

SOLUTION TO REVIEW PROBLEM

1. 1)

K, L, AND M PARTNERSHIP
Schedule of Partners' Adjusted Capital Balances
June 30, 1990

Partner	Capital Balance		Adjustment For Loans		Liquidation Expenses		Adjusted Capital Balance
K	$ 20,000		–0–	–	$ 3,600	=	$ 16,400
L	30,000	+	$ 50,000	–	2,700	=	77,300
M	70,000	–	30,000	–	2,700	=	37,300

K, L, AND M PARTNERSHIP
Schedule of Maximum Loss Absorbable

Partner	Adjusted Capital Balance		Profit and Loss Ratio		Maximum Loss Absorbable	Sequence of Elimination
K	$ 16,400	÷	4/10	=	$ 41,000	1
L	77,300	÷	3/10	=	257,667	3
M	37,300	÷	3/10	=	124,333	2

1. 2)

K, L, AND M PARTNERSHIP
Schedule of Loss Absorption
June 30, 1990
Dr. (Cr.)

	Assets	Liquidation Expenses	Accounts Payable	Partners' Adjusted Capital		
				K	L	M
Profit and Loss Ratio				40%	30%	30%
Preliquidation Balances	$ 200,000	$(9,000)	$(60,000)	$(16,400)	$(77,300)	$(37,300)
Loss That Would Eliminate K	(41,000)			16,400	12,300	12,300
Balance	159,000	(9,000)	(60,000)	$ –0–	(65,000)	(25,000)
Loss That Would Eliminate M	(50,000)				25,000	25,000
Balance	$ 109,000	$(9,000)	$(60,000)		$(40,000)	$ –0–

The $9,000 of expected liquidation expenses are shown as liabilities to maintain the equality of debits and credits. An alternative is to subtract the $9,000 from total assets.

K, L, AND M PARTNERSHIP
Cash Predistribution Plan
June 30, 1990

	Amount	Creditors	Partner K	Partner L	Partner M
Cash on Hand	$ 10,000	All			
Cash Realized from Sales of Noncash Assets					
First	59,000	All			
Next	40,000			All	
Next	50,000			1/2	1/2
Any Amounts Over	$ 159,000		4/10	3/10	3/10

1. 3)

Any change in the expected liquidation expenses, or gains on the sales of assets, or any undisclosed liabilities will cause the predistribution plan to be in error. If changes occur, a revised schedule should be prepared using the new information.

2. 1)

K, L, AND M PARTNERSHIP
Installment Liquidation Schedule
Dr. (Cr.)

	Assets					Partners' Net Capital		
	Cash	Accounts Receivable	Inventory	Store Fixtures	Liabilities	K	L	M
Profit and Loss Ratio						40%	30%	30%
Preliquidation Balances	$ 10,000	$ 50,000	$ 100,000	$ 40,000	$(60,000)	$(20,000)	$(80,000)	$(40,000)
Payment of Attorney's Fees	(2,500)					1,000	750	750
Sale of Inventory	50,000		(60,000)			4,000	3,000	3,000
Collection of Receivables	20,000	(20,000)						
Write-off of Receivables		(15,000)				6,000	4,500	4,500
Payment of Liabilities	(60,000)				60,000			
Balance July 31, 1990	17,500	15,000	40,000	40,000	$ —0—	(9,000)	(71,750)	(31,750)
Cash Distribution (1)	(8,500)						8,500	
Sale of Inventory	12,000		(20,000)			3,200	2,400	2,400
Sale of Store Fixtures	28,000			(40,000)		4,800	3,600	3,600
Collection of Receivables	10,000	(10,000)						
Balance August 31, 1990	59,000	5,000	20,000	$ —0—		(1,000)	(57,250)	(25,750)
Cash Distribution (2)	(50,000)						40,750	9,250
Sale of Inventory	12,000		(20,000)			3,200	2,400	2,400
Payment of Expenses	(8,500)					3,400	2,550	2,550
Collection and Write-off of Receivables	8,000	(5,000)				(1,200)	(900)	(900)
Balance September 30, 1990	20,500	$ —0—	$ —0—			4,400	(12,450)	(12,450)
Cash from Partner K	4,400					(4,400)		
Payment of Cash	(24,900)						12,450	12,450
Final Balances	$ —0—					$ —0—	$ —0—	$ —0—

(1)   SCHEDULE OF SAFE PAYMENTS
                                        July 31, 1990
                                          Dr. (Cr.)

	Partner K	Partner L	Partner M	Total
Profit and Loss Ratio	40%	30%	30%	
Balance July 31, 1990	$(9,000)	$(71,750)	$(31,750)	$(112,500)
Anticipated Expenses	3,600	2,700	2,700	9,000
Noncash Assets	38,000	28,500	28,500	95,000
Balance	32,600	(40,550)	(550)	(8,500)
Allocation of K's Debit Balance	(32,600)	16,300	16,300	–0–
Balance	$ –0–	(24,250)	15,750	$(8,500)
Allocation of M's Debit Balance		15,750	(15,750)	–0–
Cash Payment		$(8,500)	$ –0–	$(8,500)

(2)   SCHEDULE OF SAFE PAYMENTS
                                      August 31, 1990
                                          Dr. (Cr.)

	Partner K	Partner L	Partner M	Total
Profit and Loss Ratio	40%	30%	30%	
Balance Aug. 31, 1990	$(1,000)	$(57,250)	$(25,750)	$(84,000)
Anticipated Expenses	3,600	2,700	2,700	9,000
Noncash Assets	10,000	7,500	7,500	25,000
Balance	12,600	(47,050)	(15,550)	(50,000)
Allocation of K's Debit Balance	(12,600)	6,300	6,300	–0–
Cash Payment	$ –0–	$(40,750)	$(9,250)	$(50,000)

2.   2) The total liquidation expenses were $11,000 ($2,500 legal fees and $8,500 restoration costs). The legal fees were not anticipated and the restoration costs were $500 less than expected. This $2,000 of additional expenses reduced Partner K's capital by $800 more than initially anticipated. It also reduced the capital accounts of the other partners by $600 more than anticipated.

3.   1) The partners have a legal claim against Partner K for the $4,400. If Partner K is bankrupt, the partners have a claim against Partner K for $4,400, but can only collect to the extent of the assets remaining after Partner K's personal creditors have been satisfied.

3.   2)   K, L, AND M PARTNERSHIP
                                 Installment Liquidation Schedule
                                          Dr. (Cr.)

	Cash		Partners' Net Capital	
		K	L	M
Balance September 30, 1990	$ 20,500	$ 4,400	$(12,450)	$(12,450)
Allocation of Debit Balance		(4,400)	2,200	2,200
Payment of Cash	(20,500)		10,250	10,250
Final Balances	$ –0–	$ –0–	$ –0–	$ –0–

5

INTRODUCTION TO CONSOLIDATED FINANCIAL STATEMENTS

O ne corporation can gain control over the affairs of another corporation in either of two ways. One way is to acquire the net assets of the other corporation: that is, to acquire its assets and assume its liabilities; the other way is to acquire a controlling interest in the voting common stock of the other corporation. In this chapter, we examine the appropriate accounting for each of these types of corporate combinations under each of two accounting methods: the purchase method and the pooling of interests method. In addition, in the case of a corporate combination effected through a common stock acquisition, we discuss and illustrate the preparation of consolidated financial statements at the date on which the controlling interest is acquired.

More specifically, this chapter deals with the following topics:

- Reasons for corporate combinations
- Means of attaining control
- Conditions for preparing consolidated financial statements
- The purchase method of accounting
- The pooling of interests method of accounting
- Net asset acquisitions
- Common stock acquisitions
- The consolidation process

REASONS FOR CORPORATE COMBINATIONS

Corporate combinations may occur for a variety of reasons. Broadly stated, expansion of operations through acquisition of another company, rather than through internal growth, is a major motivating factor. Different types of expansion through combinations are possible.

One of these is vertical expansion. For example, one corporation may wish to gain control over another in order to assure a source of supply of a raw material or to secure an outlet for its products. Horizontal expansion involves growth within the same industry category. For example, a department store chain that wishes to add additional stores may find it advantageous to acquire another company rather than to construct new stores itself. This approach can aid in geographical expansion or entering new markets. On the other hand, it may merely be a way to eliminate a competitor.

Corporate combinations also provide a ready means of diversifying into completely different industries. The modern phenomenon of the conglomerate usually is the result of one or more corporate combinations. Other motivations for corporate combination include executive prestige and certain income tax advantages. Sometimes, the officers of one corporation wish to acquire other corporations simply to be able to administer a larger organization. Income tax advantages include gaining access to operating loss carryovers and tax credits.

MEANS OF ATTAINING CONTROL

As noted earlier, one corporation can gain control over the affairs of another corporation either by acquiring the net assets of the other corporation or by acquiring a controlling interest in its voting common stock.

The direct asset acquisition results in a legal combination. The assets and liabilities of the acquired corporation are merged with those of the acquiring corporation and the two formerly separate legal entities become a single, combined legal entity. (Although the acquired corporation conceivably could continue in existence, typically it would be dissolved.) Subsequent financial statements of the acquiring corporation would portray a single legal entity composed of the elements of the two formerly separate legal entities.

When one corporation acquires a controlling interest in the voting common stock of another, the two corporations remain separate legal entities, although they may, and usually do, begin to operate as a combined economic entity. The acquiring corporation is known as the **parent** company, while the corporation whose stock has been acquired by the parent is called a **subsidiary** company. Thus, a parent–subsidiary relationship has been established, which leads to the presumption that **consolidated financial statements** should be prepared.[1] Throughout most of this book, we are concerned with parent–subsidiary relationships, although we do consider direct corporate combinations briefly in this chapter.

Theoretically, separate financial statements could be prepared for the parent company in which its investment in the subsidiary would be reported as an asset in the balance sheet and its share of the subsidiary's net income as an income element in the income statement. These financial statements would respect the legal boundaries of the two corporations and treat them as separate accounting entities. Consolidated financial statements, in contrast, "present, primarily for the benefit of the shareholders and creditors of the parent company, the results of operations and the financial position of a parent company and its subsidiaries essentially as if the group were a single company with one or more branches or divisions."[2] This quotation acknowledges that a parent may have more than one subsidiary.

---

[1] *Accounting Research Bulletin No. 51, Consolidated Financial Statements* (New York: AICPA, 1959), paragraph 1.

[2] *ARB No. 51,* paragraph 1.

CONDITIONS FOR PREPARING CONSOLIDATED FINANCIAL STATEMENTS

Until recently, according to *Accounting Research Bulletin No. 51*, the presumption that consolidated financial statements are preferable to separate parent company financial statements rested on the presence of three conditions.

- Effective parent company control over the subsidiary
- Related activities
- Resulting fair presentation[3]

Parent company control is defined for this purpose as ownership of more than 50 percent of the voting common stock of the subsidiary. If such a controlling interest exists, but is not really effective, however, we would be led away from consolidated financial statements and toward separate parent company financial statements.

The effectiveness of parent company control would tend to be limited if that control were only temporary. For example, the parent might buy and sell shares of subsidiary stock frequently, so that its percentage of ownership moves back and forth across the 50 percent line. The fact that it happens to be greater than 50 percent at a given balance sheet date would not be sufficient to support the preparation of consolidated financial statements.

Financial difficulties also could limit the effectiveness of parent company control. For example, if the subsidiary were in legal reorganization or bankruptcy, real control might be in the hands of a court-appointed trustee, regardless of majority ownership. Again, the presumption that consolidated financial statements are appropriate would not apply.

Foreign subsidiaries present a special problem with regard to the effectiveness of parent company control because of the uncertainties and restrictions that often occur. Thus, according to Chapter 12 of *Accounting Research Bulletin No. 43*, the question of whether or not to include foreign subsidiaries in consolidated financial statements (other than as investments) should be carefully considered.[4]

In recent years, many diversified corporations have used the related activities criterion as a basis for not including one or more subsidiaries from their consolidated financial statements. For example, financing subsidiaries frequently have not been consolidated, but have been reported as investments. In contrast, other diversified corporations have included all majority-owned investees in the consolidated financial statements. This disparity has raised questions of comparability between and among reporting entities, as well as charges that not consolidating majority-owned investees may result in misleading financial statements.

In 1987, the Financial Accounting Standards Board addressed these questions by issuing *Statement of Financial Accounting Standards No. 94, Consolidation of All Majority-owned Subsidiaries*, which became effective at the end of 1988. This pronouncement amends *ARB No. 51* to remove from it the discretionary exceptions to the general presumption of consolidation. Coordinately, *SFAS No. 94* deletes from Chapter 12 of *Accounting Research Bulletin No. 43* the discretionary guidance in regard to foreign subsidiaries cited above. The result is to require consolidation

---

[3] *ARB No. 51*, paragraphs 1–3.

[4] *Accounting Research Bulletin No. 43, Restatement and Revision of Accounting Research Bulletins* (New York: AICPA, 1953), Chapter 12, paragraphs 8–9.

of all majority-owned subsidiaries, domestic and foreign, over which the parent company has effective control.[5]

The only remaining exceptions to this general rule are those circumstances in which control (a) is likely to be temporary, or (b) does not rest with the majority owner. The latter category includes, in addition to the subsidiary's being in legal reorganization or bankruptcy, its operating "under foreign exchange restrictions, controls, or other governmentally imposed uncertainties so severe that they cast significant doubt on the parent's ability to control the subsidiary."[6]

The original third criterion, resulting fair presentation also is limited by the issuance of *SFAS No. 94* through its elimination of the discretionary guidance originally given in *ARB No. 51*. Certainly, fair presentation in the consolidated financial statements continues to be an important goal. It is no longer possible, however, to justify the exclusion of a majority-owned subsidiary from consolidation on this basis.

CIRCUMSTANCES OF ACQUISITION

A parent company may acquire its ownership interest in a subsidiary under varying circumstances with regard to

- the percentage of ownership acquired, and
- the cost of the investment relative to the book value of the underlying net assets.

The cost versus book value consideration also applies to the direct acquisition of the net assets of one corporation by another.

PERCENTAGE OF OWNERSHIP ACQUIRED

The parent may acquire either 100 percent or less than 100 percent of the subsidiary's voting common stock. In the first case, the subsidiary is called a **wholly owned** subsidiary; in the second case, it is called a **partially owned** subsidiary. Any stockholders of a partially owned subsidiary other than the parent company or other affiliated companies are called the **minority interest** or **minority stockholders.** The term **minority interest** (or **external interest**) also is used to refer to the percentage of the subsidiary's voting common stock held outside the affiliated group, as well as to the dollar amount of such an interest.

Because the acquired corporation in a direct asset acquisition typically is dissolved and its assets and liabilities are merged with those of the acquiring company, the matter of minoritiy or external interest does not apply.

---

[5] *Statement of Financial Accounting Standards No. 94, Consolidation of All Marjority-Owned Subsidiaries* (Stamford, Connecticut: FASB, 1987), paragraph 13.

[6] *SFAS No. 94,* paragraph 13.

COST OF INVESTMENT VERSUS BOOK VALUE OF NET ASSETS

A parent company may acquire its investment in a subsidiary's voting common stock from retiring subsidiary stockholders (or one corporation may acquire the net assets of another) at one of the following values:

- At book value
- At a cost that is greater than book value
- At a cost that is less than book value

In the parent–subsidiary context, **book value** is the parent's ownership interest in the net assets (assets minus liabilities) of the subsidiary, measured in terms of the aggregate value at which those net assets are carried on the subsidiary's books. For both practical and problem-solving purposes, book value can be calculated as [a] the parent's percentage of ownership in the subsidiary multiplied by [b] the subsidiary's total stockholders' equity. In the case of a direct net asset acquisition, book value is the net carrying value of the assets and liabilities of the acquired company on its books.

When cost and book value are different in either a common stock acquisition or a net asset acquisition, it is necessary to

1. identify the transaction as being either a **purchase** or a **pooling of interests,** and
2. adopt the corresponding accounting method.

Accounting Principles Board Opinion No. 16, Business Combinations, issued in 1970, governs both the identification of the transaction and the application of the appropriate accounting method.

ACCOUNTING FOR THE COMBINATION

In brief, a purchase combination is one in which one corporation buys (or buys out) another; a pooling of interests combination is one in which the ownership interests of two or more corporations are combined. Either type of combination can be accomplished either directly, through acquisition of net assets, or indirectly, through acquisition of common stock. A purchase combination can be effected by payment of cash or other assets, or by issuing common stock. A pooling of interests combination, however, is possible (with minor exceptions) only through the issuance of voting common stock.

THE PURCHASE METHOD OF ACCOUNTING

The purchase method of accounting reflects the substance of a transaction in which one corporation buys another. This type of combination is an exchange transaction between independent parties—the acquiring corporation and either the acquired corporation (in a net asset acquisition) or the common stockholders of the acquired corporation (in a common stock acquisition). The essential features of the purchase method are the following.

First, a new basis of accountability arises for the acquired net assets; that is, they are recorded on the acquiring company's books (or reported in the consolidated financial statements) at the acquiring company's cost, which is presumed to represent the aggregate fair market value of those net assets. In essence, the purchase of a collection of assets is being recorded on the same basis as the purchase of a single asset would be—at the purchaser's cost. Direct costs of acquisition, such as registration, legal, and accounting fees, are treated as part of the cost of acquisition, whereas related indirect expenses are treated as expenses of the period. The discussion in Chapter 6 regarding assignment of the difference between cost and book value is applicable to any purchase combination, direct or indirect.

Second, no part of the stockholders' equity of the acquired company is carried forward after the combination, except as minority interest in consolidated financial statements. Under the purchase assumption, the acquiring company literally has *purchased* the acquired company, either directly or indirectly. If the acquiring company issues either common or preferred stock in exchange, an increase would be recorded in the balance of that class of stock and, if appropriate, the related additional paid-in capital, on the acquiring company's books. These increased balances are the only possible effect of the purchase transaction on the stockholders' equity reported in subsequent acquiring company financial statements (in a net asset acquisition) or consolidated financial statements (in a common stock acquisition).

Finally, if the acquisition occurs during an accounting period, the net income of the acquired company is apportioned between segments of that period, as discussed and illustrated in Chapter 7. The effect of this apportionment is to include only net income of the acquired company from the date of acquisition to the end of the year in the acquiring company financial statements (in a net asset acquisition) or consolidated financial statements (in a common stock acquisition).

THE POOLING OF INTERESTS METHOD OF ACCOUNTING

The pooling of interests method of accounting reflects the substance of a transaction in which ownership interests are combined. In contrast to the purchase method, this type of combination is not viewed as an exchange transaction between independent parties. Instead, the common stockholders of the two companies are combining their ownership interests, and thus their assets and liabilities, to form a single entity. Thus, a pooling of interests always is effected through the issuance of common stock by one company for either the net assets or substantially all of the common stock of another company. The essential features of the pooling of interests method parallel those of the purchase method.

First, no new basis of accountability arises. Instead, the assets and liabilities of an acquired company are recorded on the acquiring company's books (or reported in the consolidated financial statements) at their previous carrying values on the books of the acquired company. Because no exchange transaction between independent parties has occurred, restatement of carrying values to fair market value would be inappropriate. Thus, the two sets of book values are combined, either on the acquiring company's books (in a net asset acquisition) or in the consolidated financial statements (in a common stock acquisition). Accordingly, expenses related to the combination are treated as expenses of the combined entity for the period in which the combination occurs.

The retained earnings balances of the combining companies as of the time of the combination are carried forward, either on the books of the acquiring company or in the consolidated financial statements, to the extent permitted by the resulting capital structure. Because a pooling of interests involves a combination of common stock ownership interests to form a single entity rather than an exchange transaction, the economic histories of the combining entities, as reflected in their respective retained earnings balances, also are combined. The common stock issued to effect the combination, of course, must be recorded at par value on the books of the issuing corporation. If the total par value of the stock issued is greater than the combined common stock and additional paid-in capital balances of the acquired company, however, it may not be possible to carry forward the total amount of the combined retained earnings balances. This matter is illustrated in Case 2 of Illustrative Problem 5.1, which appears later in this chapter and is discussed more thoroughly at that point.

The income statement of the combined entity, or the consolidated income statement, for the period in which the combination occurs reflects the results of operations as if the companies had been combined for the entire period, regardless of when during the period the combination actually occurs. Again, because a pooling of interests involves a combination of common stock ownership interests to form a single entity, the economic histories of the combining entities (in this case, very recent histories) are combined.

Conditions for Using the Pooling of Interests Method.   *APB Opinion No. 16* specifies twelve conditions that must be present in order for the pooling of interests method to be used. They are

Combining companies.

a. Each of the combining companies is autonomous and has not been a subsidiary or division of another corporation within two years before the plan of combination is initiated.
b. Each of the combining companies is independent of the other combining companies.[7]

Combining of interests.

a. The combination is effected in a single transaction or is completed in accordance with a specific plan within one year after the plan is initiated.
b. A corporation offers and issues only common stock with rights identical to those of the majority of its outstanding voting common stock in exchange for substantially all of the voting common stock of another company at the date the plan of combination is consummated.
c. None of the combining companies changes the equity interest of the voting common stock in contemplation of effecting the combination either within two years before the plan of combination is initiated or between the dates the combination is initiated and consummated; changes in contemplation of effecting the combination may include distributions to stockholders and additional issuances, exchanges, and retirements of securities.
d. Each of the combining companies reacquires shares of voting common stock only for purposes other than business combinations, and no company reacquires more than a normal number of shares between the dates the plan of combination is initiated and consummated.
e. The ratio of the interest of an individual common stockholder to those of other common stockholders in a combining company remains the same as a result of the exchange of stock to effect the combination.
f. The voting rights to which the common stock ownership interests in the resulting combined corporation are entitled are exercisable by the stockholders; the stockholders are neither deprived of nor restricted in exercising those rights for a period.

---

[7] *Accounting Principles Board Opinion No. 16, Business Combinations* (New York: AICPA, 1970), paragraph 46.

g. The combination is resolved at the date the plan is consummated and no provisions of the plan relating to the issue of securities or other consideration are pending.[8]

Absence of planned transactions.

a. The combined corporation does not agree directly or indirectly to retire or reacquire all or part of the common stock issued to effect the combination.
b. The combined corporation does not enter into other financial arrangements for the benefit of the former stockholders of a combining company, such as a guaranty of loans secured by stock issued in the combination, which in effect negates the exchange of equity securities.
c. The combined corporation does not intend or plan to dispose of a significant part of the assets of the combining companies within two years after the combination other than disposals in the ordinary course of business of the formerly separate companies and to eliminate duplicate facilities or excess capacity.[9]

These conditions are considered restrictive, not permissive. "A business combination which meets *all* of the conditions specified and explained in paragraphs 46 to 48 should be accounted for by the pooling of interests method."[10] "All other business combinations should be treated as the acquisition of one company by another and accounted for by the purchase method."[11]

Both methods are discussed and illustrated in the following sections, with respect to both net asset acquisitions and common stock acquisitions. Because compliance with the conditions specified in *APB Opinion No. 16* is rather difficult, however, pooling of interests combinations are rare relative to purchase combinations. Therefore, after Chapter 5, all combinations are considered to be purchases unless otherwise indicated.

NET ASSET ACQUISITIONS

A business combination in which one corporation acquires the assets and assumes the liabilities of another corporation can be treated as a purchase regardless of the consideration given by the acquiring company (provided, of course, that it does not meet all of the conditions specified for a pooling of interests). Such a combination can be treated as a pooling of interests only if it meets all of the specified conditions, one of which is the exchange of voting common stock. The acquiring company must issue voting common stock and, ultimately, the stockholders of the acquired company must receive the stock and become stockholders of the acquiring company. Appropriate accounting for net assets acquisitions under both the purchase method and the pooling of interests method is shown in Illustrative Problem 5.1.

NET ASSET ACQUISITION RECORDED AS A PURCHASE

As noted earlier, one of the features of the purchase method is that because an exchange transaction has occurred, a new basis of accountability arises for the acquired assets. In a net

---

[8] *APB Opinion No. 16,* paragraph 47.

[9] *APB Opinion No. 16,* paragraph 48.

[10] *APB Opinion No. 16,* paragraph 45.

[11] *APB Opinion No. 16,* paragraph 44.

asset acquisition, assets are recorded on the acquiring company's books at that company's cost, which is presumed to represent the aggregate fair market value of those net assets. An excess of that cost over the book value of the net assets acquired might be attributed to a variety of causes or combinations thereof, including errors on the books of either company, undervaluation of the acquired company's assets, and unrecorded assets of the acquired company. Each of these causes is discussed in some detail in Chapter 6.

A second feature of the purchase method is that no part of the stockholders' equity of the acquired company is carried forward after the combination. Thus, if the combination is accomplished through issuance of common stock, only Common Stock and Additional Paid-in Capital are credited on the acquiring company's books in recording the transaction.

Because we will deal with business combinations in this chapter only at the date of acquisition, the third feature of the purchase method, the apportionment of the acquired company's net income, is inapplicable. This process is discussed and illustrated in detail in Chapter 7.

NET ASSET ACQUISITION RECORDED AS A POOLING OF INTERESTS

As noted earlier, under the pooling of interests method, no new basis of accountability arises for the acquired assets because no exchange transaction has occurred. In a net asset acquisition, acquired assets are recorded at their previous book values on the acquiring company's books.

A second feature of the pooling of interests method is that the retained earnings balances of all combining companies as of the time of the combination are carried forward, to the extent permitted by the resulting capital structure. The total stockholders' equity of the acquiring company immediately after the combination *must* equal the sum of the total stockholders' equities of the combining companies immediately before the combination. If the total par value of the stock issued is greater than the combined common stock and additional paid-in capital balances of the acquired company, however, it may not be possible to carry forward the total amount of the combined retained earnings balances. In effect, part of the combined retained earnings is converted to common stock.

When this happens, the acquiring company's Additional Paid-in Capital account can be debited to provide additional credit "space" to use in recording the acquired company's Retained Earnings balance. Sometimes, this procedure still may not enable the acquiring company to carry forward the full amount of the combined Retained Earnings balances, but no more than that amount can ever be carried forward. This approach is explained more fully in Case 2 of Illustrative Problem 5.1.

The third feature of the pooling of interests method, the reflection in the income statement of the combined entity of the results of operations as if the companies had been combined for the entire period in which the combination occurs, is inapplicable to this chapter.

ILLUSTRATIVE PROBLEM 5.I: NET ASSET ACQUISITION

Company A issues 8,000 shares of its previously unissued common stock, which has a market value of 80, and acquires the net assets of Company B. The condensed trial balances of

Company A and Company B immediately before their combination on November 30, 1990 are shown below.

	Company A	Company B
Current Assets	$ 250,000	$ 200,000
Plant and Equipment	870,000	480,000
	$1,120,000	$ 680,000
Accumulated Depreciation	$ 320,000	$ 180,000
Liabilities	175,000	130,000
Common Stock ($25 par)	300,000	100,000
Additional Paid-in Capital	50,000	40,000
Retained Earnings	275,000	230,000
	$1,120,000	$ 680,000

Case 1: The Purchase Method.   The cost of Company B's net assets to Company A is the aggregate market value of the stock issued, $640,000. The book value of the net assets acquired can be calculated as Company B's total assets, $500,000, minus its total liabilities, $130,000, or $370,000. The excess of cost over book value, therefore, is $270,000.

Company B's plant and equipment is determined to have a fair market value of $570,000, as opposed to its net book value of $300,000. Attributing the excess of cost over book value to that undervaluation of Company B's assets, Company A records the combination as follows.

Plant and Equipment is debited for $570,000. The other assets and liabilities acquired are recorded at their previous book values. The newly issued Company A common stock is recorded at par value of $25 per share, with the excess $55 per share credited to Additional Paid-in Capital, as shown in the following journal entry:

Current Assets	200,000	
Plant and Equipment	570,000	
Liabilities		130,000
Common Stock		200,000
Additional Paid-in Capital		440,000

The effects of this journal entry on Company A's precombination account balances are shown below.

	Before Combination	Journal Entry	After Combination
Current Assets	$ 250,000	200,000	$ 450,000
Plant and Equipment	870,000	570,000	1,440,000
	$1,120,000		$1,890,000
Accumulated Depreciation	$ 320,000		$ 320,000
Liabilities	175,000	(130,000)	305,000
Common Stock ($25 par)	300,000	(200,000)	500,000
Additional Paid-in Capital	50,000	(440,000)	490,000
Retained Earnings	275,000		275,000
	$1,120,000		$1,890,000

Company B most likely is dissolved, with the new Company A common stock being issued to the Company B stockholders in exchange for their Company B common stock. Company A, the surviving entity, would present the balance sheet shown in Exhibit 5-1 immediately after the combination.

EXHIBIT 5-1

Illustrative Problem 5.1, Case 1
Purchase Method Balance Sheet

COMPANY A
Balance Sheet
November 30, 1990

Assets

Current Assets		$ 450,000
Plant and Equipment	$1,440,000	
Less: Accumulated Depreciation	320,000	1,120,000
Total Assets		$1,570,000

Liabilities and Stockholders' Equity

Liabilities		$ 305,000
Stockholders' Equity		
Common Stock ($25 par)	$ 500,000	
Additional Paid-in Capital	490,000	
Retained Earnings	275,000	1,265,000
Total Liabilities and Stockholders' Equity		$1,570,000

Case 2: The Pooling of Interests Method. Under the pooling of interests method, the combination is recorded on Company A's books in the following manner. Because no new basis of accountability arises in a pooling of interests, the assets and liabilities acquired are recorded at their previous carrying values on Company B's books. The newly issued Company A common stock, of course, is recorded at par value of $25 per share, or $200,000. A "trial" journal entry to record this information is

Current Assets	200,000	
Plant and Equipment	300,000	
Liabilities		130,000
Common Stock		200,000
Retained Earnings		170,000

Because the total par value of the Company A common stock issued, $200,000, is greater than the combined common stock and additional paid-in capital balances (or net assets) of Company B immediately before the combination, $140,000, it is not possible to credit Retained

Earnings for the full amount of Company B's balance immediately before the combination, $230,000, unless $60,000 can be debited to another stockholders' equity account. The only such account available is Company A's Additional Paid-in Capital account, which has a balance of only $50,000. By debiting Company A's Additional Paid-in Capital account $50,000, we become able to credit Retained Earnings for $220,000, as shown in the journal entry below.

Current Assets	200,000	
Plant and Equipment	300,000	
Additional Paid-in Capital	50,000	
Liabilities		130,000
Common Stock		200,000
Retained Earnings		220,000

The net amount credited to stockholders' equity must equal the net amount debited to assets and liabilities. (In this case, both are $370,000.) The question is how this total amount is to be allocated among the stockholders' equity accounts. As noted earlier, Common Stock must be credited for the aggregate par value of the shares issued. As a result, it may or may not be possible to achieve the goal of recording the total amount of the acquired company's Retained Earnings balance.

The critical constraint here is Company A's Additional Paid-in Capital balance immediately before the combination. Because it is only $50,000, we are able to credit Retained Earnings for only $220,000, thus enabling us to carry forward Retained Earnings of only $495,000 rather than $505,000. In effect, part of the combined retained earnings is converted to common stock. If Company A's Additional Paid-in Capital balance had been at least $60,000, we could have credited Retained Earnings for the full amount of Company B's precombination Retained Earnings balance of $230,000, but no more.

In a pooling of interests, Company B would be dissolved, with the new Company A common stock being issued to the Company B stockholders in exchange for their Company B common stock. Company A, the surviving entity, would present the balance sheet shown in Exhibit 5-2 immediately after the combination.

Examination of this balance sheet enables us to look at the combination of retained earnings balances from a different perspective. As noted earlier, the total stockholders' equity of the acquiring company immediately after the combination *must* equal the sum of the total stockholders' equities of the combining companies immediately before the combination. In this case, the balance sheet immediately after the combination reports total stockholders' equity of $995,000, which is the sum of the total stockholders' equities of the combining companies immediately before the combination, as detailed below.

	Company A	Company B
Common Stock ($25 par)	$ 300,000	$ 100,000
Additional Paid-in Capital	50,000	40,000
Retained Earnings	275,000	230,000
	$ 625,000	$ 370,000

The sum of the two Retained Earnings balances is $505,000. The total par value of the Company A common stock issued, $200,000, is $60,000 greater than the sum of Company B's Common Stock and Additional Paid-in Capital balances immediately before the combi-

EXHIBIT 5-2

Illustrative Problem 5.1, Case 2
Pooling of Interests Method Balance Sheet

COMPANY A
Balance Sheet
November 30, 1990

Assets

Current Assets		$ 450,000
Plant and Equipment	$1,170,000	
Less: Accumulated Depreciation	320,000	850,000
Total Assets		$1,300,000

Liabilities and Stockholders' Equity

Liabilities		$ 305,000
Stockholders' Equity		
Common Stock ($25 par)	$ 500,000	
Retained Earnings	495,000	995,000
Total Liabilities and Stockholders' Equity		$1,300,000

nation, $140,000. Company A's precombination Additional Paid-in Capital balance of $50,000 offsets all but $10,000 of that difference, enabling us to carry forward Retained Earnings of $495,000, but not the full $505,000. In effect, the remaining $10,000 is converted to common stock.

The full $505,000 of postcombination retained earnings could have been achieved if either

- the total par value of the Company A common stock issued had been equal to or less than the $140,000 sum of Company B's Common Stock and Additional Paid-in Capital balances immediately before the combination, or
- Company A's Additional Paid-in Capital balance had been at least $60,000.

COMMON STOCK ACQUISITIONS

When one corporation acquires a controlling interest in the voting common stock of another corporation, consolidated financial statements can be prepared under the purchase method regardless of the consideration given by the acquiring company (provided, of course, that the combination does not meet all of the conditions specified for a pooling of interests). Consolidated financial statements can be prepared under the pooling of interests method only if the combination meets all of the specified conditions, including that of the exchange of voting common stock. The acquiring company must issue voting common stock in exchange for substantially all of the voting common stock of the acquired company.

COMMON STOCK ACQUISITION TREATED AS A PURCHASE

Because a new basis of accountability arises for the acquired assets under the purchase method, the parent's investment in the common stock of the subsidiary is recorded at the parent's cost. As in the case of a direct asset acquisition, an excess of cost over book value might be attributed to a variety of causes or combinations thereof, including errors on the books of either company, undervaluation of the acquired company's assets, and unrecorded assets of the acquired company, which are discussed in Chapter 6. Until we reach that point, however, we will designate any excess of cost over book value in the consoliated financial statements as **goodwill from consolidation,** an amount in excess of the going concern value of the subsidiary paid by the parent to gain the advantages of control over the subsidiary. The parent company's recording of its investment in a subsidiary under the purchase method is presented in Case 1 of Illustrative Problem 5.2.

An excess of book value over cost also might be attributed to a variety of causes or combinations thereof, including errors on the books of either company, and overvaluation of the acquired company's assets, which are discussed in Chapter 6. Temporarily, we will designate any excess of book value over cost in the consolidated financial statements as *an aggregate overvaluation of subsidiary net assets.*

The designation of any excess of cost over book value as goodwill from consolidation and any excess of book value over cost as an aggregate overvaluation of subsidiary net assets is admittedly arbitrary. It is done at this point in order to simplify the introduction of the consolidation process.

A second feature of the purchase method is that no part of the stockholders' equity of the acquired company is carried forward after the combination. This is accomplished through the eliminations made in preparing the consolidated financial statements, as shown in Case 1 of Illustrative Problem 5.2.

Because we deal with business combinations in this chapter only at the date of acquisition, the third feature of the purchase method, the apportionment of the acquired company's net income, is inapplicable. As indicated earlier, this process is discussed and illustrated in detail in Chapter 12.

COMMON STOCK ACQUISITION TREATED AS A POOLING OF INTERESTS

Because no new basis of accountability arises for the acquired assets in a pooling of interests, both the parent's investment in the subsidiary's common stock and the issuance of the parent's common stock are recorded in terms of the aggregate book value of the underlying net assets on the subsidiary's books. The parent company's recording of its investment in a subsidiary under the pooling of interests method is presented in Case 2 of Illustrative Problem 5.2.

The second feature of the pooling of interests method, that the retained earnings balances of all combining companies as of the time of the combination are carried forward to the extent permitted by the resulting capital structure, is accomplished through the eliminations made in preparing the consolidated financial statements. Again, the parent's Additional Paid-in Capital account can be debited to provide "space" to carry forward the full amount of the combined Retained Earnings balances, but no more than that amount can ever be carried forward. These eliminations are shown in Case 2 of Illustrative Problem 5.2.

The third feature of the pooling of interests method, the reflection in the income statement of the combined entity of the results of operations as if the companies had been combined for the entire period in which the combination occurs, is inapplicable to this chapter.

CONSOLIDATED BALANCE SHEET AT THE DATE OF ACQUISITION

When one corporation acquires the assets and assumes the liabilities of another corporation, the acquired corporation usually is dissolved and the acquiring company emerges as the surviving entity. In subsequent financial statements, the assets, liabilities, revenues, and expenses of the two formerly separate companies are combined. The stockholders' equity balances, of course, are those of the acquiring company.

When one corporation acquires a controlling interest in the voting common stock of another corporation, establishing a parent–subsidiary relationship, we can accomplish essentially the same result by preparing consolidated financial statements. These consolidated financial statements represent two (or more) separate legal entities as a single economic entity.

In order to prepare consolidated financial statements, it is necessary to eliminte all **intercompany balances** and combine those that remain. Intercompany balances are account balances, or portions thereof, on the two sets of books that offset each other, either in whole or in part. Although these balances are valid with respect to each affiliate individually, they are superfluous from the standpoint of the consolidated entity. If they are not eliminated, these intercompany balances either will result in double-counting or will inflate the consolidated financial statements.

At the date on which the parent acquires its investment in the subsidiary, the **date of acquisition,** one set of intercompany balances always will be present—the subsidiary's stockholders' equity balances versus the balance of the parent's Investment in Subsidiary account. To the extent of the parent's percentage of ownership in the subsidiary, both sides of this set of intercompany balances represent the majority ownership interest in the subsidiary's net assets. Thus, they must be eliminated to permit the assets and liabilities of the subsidiary to be combined with the corresponding assets and liabilities of the parent, so that the two separate legal entities can be represented as a single economic entity.

If the subsidiary has **treasury stock,** it must be taken into account both in determining the parent's percentage of ownership and as a component of the subsidiary's stockholders' equity. First, percentage of ownership is based on the number of shares of common stock *outstanding,* rather than merely the number of shares issued. Thus, the number of treasury shares must be subtracted from the total number of shares issued in determining the parent's percentage of ownership. Second, treasury stock is a negative stockholders' equity balance, which must be eliminated along with the other subsidiary stockholders' equity balances, as described above.

To facilitate the preparation of a consolidated balance sheet at the date of acquisition, we will use a **consolidation worksheet** that includes a column for each affiliate's trial balance, a column for eliminations, and a column for the resulting consolidated balance sheet amounts. (In Chapter 7, we will expand this worksheet to include income statement information as well.) The format of the worksheet is shown in Exhibit 5-4. The consolidation worksheet is supported by a series of schedules, as described in the following sections.

THE CONSOLIDATION PROCESS

Many complex tasks can be made easier by establishing and following a working routine. Basically, this involves breaking the complex task down into individual steps and then following those steps in the same sequence each time the task is performed. This is different from merely memorizing the steps and their sequence; this is learning to do by doing. This technique is quite useful in preparing consolidated financial statements. The routine begun here in Chapter 5 is used throughout the book, with new steps added as new elements of the parent–subsidiary relationship are introduced.

SCHEDULE OF THE DIFFERENCE BETWEEN COST AND BOOK VALUE

We will begin the consolidation routine by preparing a schedule that compares the cost of the parent's investment in the subsidiary with the book value of that investment at the date of acquisition. The difference between these two quantities is the excess of cost over book value or the excess of book value over cost, as the case may be. This schedule is used only when the consolidated financial statements are being prepared under the purchase method. Because no new basis of accountability arises in a pooling of interests, no comparison of cost and book value can be made. Indeed, in a pooling of interests, the parent's "cost" *is* book value.

As noted earlier, for purposes of this chapter, we will treat any excess of cost over book value as goodwill from consolidation and any excess of book value over cost as an aggregate overvaluation of subsidiary net assets.

In Chapters 6 and 7, we will expand this schedule to allow for other interpretations of the difference between cost and book value, as well as to provide for amortization thereof. For the time being, however, the difference between cost and book value at the date of acquisition, as determined in this schedule, provides us with a target figure for goodwill from consolidation or overvaluation of subsidiary assets. That is, we can expect this amount to emerge in the Balance Sheet column of the consolidation worksheet as the residual balance of the parent's Investment in Subsidiary account. This schedule is illustrated in Exhibit 5-3.

SCHEDULES OF ELIMINATIONS

The next step in the consolidation routine is to prepare a schedule of each set of eliminations of intercompany balances. Eliminations that reduce credit balances are, of course, effectively debits, whereas those that reduce debit balances are effectively credits. The eliminations are expressed in terms of debits and credits in both the schedules of eliminations and the consolidation worksheet itself. Debit eliminations are shown "plain" (without notation) and credit eliminations are shown in parentheses.

Each set of eliminations must balance in terms of debits and credits; that is, the total of the debit eliminations must equal the total of the credit eliminations. In this respect, each set of eliminations resembles a journal entry. Indeed, many textbooks present sets of eliminations in journal entry form. One critical difference exists, however, between worksheet adjustments and journal entries. Unlike journal entries, worksheet adjustments are *not* recorded on the books of either the parent or the subsidiary. They are entered only on the consolidation worksheet. Thus, they must be repeated in each successive year. We find that presenting the sets of eliminations in the form of supporting schedules helps students to avoid confusion between actual journal entries and worksheet eliminations. For this reason, they are used consistently throughout this text.

Thus far, we have encountered only one set of intercompany balances—the subsidiary's stockholders' equity balances versus the parent's Investment in Subsidiary balance. The eliminations with respect to these balances, which we will refer to as the Intercompany Ownership Interests set of eliminations, are made somewhat differently, depending on whether the consolidated financial statements are being prepared under the purchase method or under the pooling of interests method.

Under the Purchase method, the Intercompany Ownership Interests set of eliminations is constructed as follows:

1. Eliminate the balance of each subsidiary stockholders' equity account, multiplied by the parent's percentage of ownership, from that account by debiting it. (Remember the possible effect of subsidiary treasury stock.)
2. Eliminate the total of the above eliminations from the parent's Investment in Subsidiary account by crediting it.

As noted above, we can expect the difference between cost and book value to emerge in the Balance Sheet column of the consolidation worksheet as the residual balance of the parent's Investment in Subsidiary account. These eliminations are illustrated in Exhibit 5-3.

Under the pooling of interests method, the Intercompany Ownership Interests eliminations are made in a manner compatible with two of the features of that method—that no new basis of accountability arises and that the combined Retained Earnings balances should be carried forward to the extent possible.

1. Eliminate the balance of the parent's Investment in Subsidiary account from that account by crediting it.
2. Eliminate the balance of each subsidiary stockholders' equity account other than Retained Earnings, multiplied by the parent's percentage of ownership, from that account by debiting it.
3. Eliminate as much of the balance of the parent's Additional Paid-in Capital account, by debiting it, as necessary to avoid eliminating any part of the subsidiary's Retained Earnings balance, if possible. (This may require elimination of the entire balance.)
4. Eliminate as much of the subsidiary's Retained Earnings balance, by debiting it, as is necessary to balance the set of eliminations in terms of debits and credits. This amount is the portion of the subsidiary's Retained Earnings balance that cannot be carried forward. (If the parent's Additional Paid-in Capital balance is large enough, this elimination may not be necessary.)

A special set of eliminations, unique to the pooling of interests method, is necessary to combine the Retained Earnings balances. In this Retained Earnings Combination set of eliminations, the subsidiary's Retained Earnings is debited and the parent's Retained Earnings is credited for [a] the parent's percentage of ownership, multiplied by [b] the subsidiary's Retained Earnings balance remaining after the Intercompany Ownership Interests set of eliminations. The pooling of interests eliminations are illustrated in Exhibit 5-8.

In subsequent chapters, we will encounter many additional sets of intercompany balances, requiring additional sets of eliminations. As the number of eliminations grows, it becomes increasingly useful to have a means of cross-reference between the schedules of eliminations and the consolidation worksheet. This is accomplished by numbering the eliminations sequentially as the schedules of eliminations are prepared and then labeling each elimination by number as it is entered in the worksheet.

THE CONSOLIDATION WORKSHEET

The consolidation worksheet used to prepare a consolidated balance sheet at the date of acquisition contains a column for each affiliate's trial balance, a column for eliminations, and a column for the resulting consolidated balance sheet information. (See Exhibit 5-4.) The trial balance columns are arranged in the "over and under" format, listing for each affiliate all debit balances and their total, followed by all credit balances and their total. The Balance Sheet column is arranged in the same manner.

The Eliminations column contains the elimination amounts transferred, or posted, from the supporting schedules of eliminations, each appearing opposite the account to which it applies. Both the cross-reference numbers and the debit-credit notations described above are carried over into the worksheet. Debit eliminations are shown without notation; credit eliminations are shown in parentheses.

Each set of asset and liability balances is combined and the total, plus or minus any applicable eliminations, is extended to the Balance Sheet column. Any given asset or liability, of course, might be present in only one trial balance. The parent company's Investment in Subsidiary account is a good example.

The stockholders' equity balances of the parent, however, are not combined with their counterparts in the subsidiary's trial balance. As indicated earlier in this chapter, consolidated financial statements are intended for the use of parent company stockholders and creditors (and, of course, other parties interested in the parent company). Thus, the parent's stockholders' equity balances become those of the consolidated entity, while those of the subsidiary either are eliminated entirely or yield minority interest residuals, as described below. To facilitate this different treatment of the parent's and the subsidiary's stockholders' equity balances, they are entered on separate lines in the trial balance columns of the worksheet.

The balances emerging in the Balance Sheet column of the worksheet as residuals from the parent's Investment in Subsidiary balance (under the purchase method) and from the subsidiary's stockholders' equity balances require special treatment. Several such treatments are possible, including worksheet adjustments to combine or reclassify these residual balances and the addition of special columns to collect like items. Probably the simplest, most direct, and most economical approach, however, is to extend the residuals directly to the Balance Sheet column and label them descriptively there. This approach, which is used throughout this book, can be described as follows:

- If the parent's Investment in Subsidiary account yields a debit residual (meaning that the investment was acquired at a cost greater than book value), label the residual "G" for Goodwill from Consolidation.

- If the investment in Subsidiary account yields a credit balance (meaning that the investment was acquired at a cost less than book value), label the residual "A" for Allowance for Overvaluation of Subsidiary Assets. (This amount is subtracted in determining the total amount of assets on the consolidated balance sheet.)
- If the subsidiary is less than 100% owned, label the residuals from its stockholders' equity balances "M" for Minority Interest. (These minority interest elements then are combined and reported as a single amount in the consolidated balance sheet.)

This labeling procedure is illustrated in Exhibit 5-6. The balances that appear in the Balance Sheet column of the consolidation worksheet provide the information necessary to construct the consolidated balance sheet.

In the routine described in the preceding pages and used throughout this book, the schedules in support of the consolidation worksheet are prepared first, following a logical order. The preparation of the consolidation worksheet is the next to last step in the consolidation process, with the preparation of the consolidated financial statements as the final step.

For problem-solving purposes, in which each problem represents a completely new start, this sequence of steps is very efficient. By preparing the supporting schedules first, one is able to anticipate the need to provide extra lines in the worksheet for accounts that will be affected by more than one adjustment or elimination, as well as for the insertion of new accounts. This need will become increasingly apparent as new ingredients are added to the consolidation process and, accordingly, the number of adjustments and eliminations increases.

In actual practice, however, the consolidation process for a given set of affiliates is repetitive, occurring year after year with largely the same components. Thus, the accountant can anticipate easily the need to leave extra lines in the worksheet. If the accountant is using a computer spreadsheet program to perform the consolidation process, the insertion of additional lines is even more easily accomplished. Accordingly, in practice, the trial balances are entered on the worksheet before preparing the supporting schedules. After the schedules are prepared, information is transferred from them to the worksheet, which is then completed.

ILLUSTRATIVE PROBLEM 5.2: COMMON STOCK ACQUISITION

The condensed trial balances of Company C and Company D immediately before their combination on June 30, 1991 are shown below.

	Company C	Company D
Current Assets	$ 325,000	$ 150,000
Plant and Equipment	780,000	520,000
	$1,105,000	$ 670,000
Accumulated Depreciation	$ 280,000	$ 170,000
Liabilities	165,000	60,000
Common Stock ($25 par)	400,000	300,000
Additional Paid-in Capital	30,000	50,000
Retained Earnings	230,000	90,000
	$1,105,000	$ 670,000

Company C issues 15,000 shares of its previously unissued common stock, which has a market value of 30, in exchange for 10,800 of Company D's outstanding shares of common stock.

Case 1: The Purchase Method.   Under the purchase method, Company C records the acquisition of its investment in the Company D common stock as follows:

Investment in Company D	450,000	
Common Stock		375,000
Additional Paid-in Capital		75,000

Instead of recording individual assets and liabilities, as is done in a net asset acquisition, Company C debits Investment in Company D for the cost of the investment, which is the aggregate market value of the common stock issued, $450,000. The newly issued Company C common stock is recorded at par value of $25 per share, with the excess $5 per share credited to Additional Paid-in Capital.

The schedule of the excess of cost over book value and the schedule of eliminations appear in Exhibit 5-3. The cost of Company C's investment in Company D's common stock, $450,000, is compared to Company C's share of the book value of Company D's net assets, which it exceeds by $54,000. The book value of the investment is calculated by multiplying Company C's percentage of ownership, 90%, by Company D's net assets (or total stockholders' equity) at the date of acquisition, $440,000. The excess of cost over book value of $54,000 provides a target figure for the residual from Company C's Investment in Company D balance that should appear in the Balance Sheet column of the consolidation worksheet. This residual will be treated as goodwill from consolidation.

In the Intercompany Ownership Interests set of eliminations, Company C's percentage of ownership, 90%, is eliminated from each of Company D's stockholders' equity balances, with the total of $396,000 credited to Investment in Company D. Notice that the debit eliminations are shown without notation, with the credit eliminations shown in parentheses, as described earlier in this chapter. Notice also that the elimination set balances in terms of debits and credits.

Exhibit 5-4 presents the consolidation worksheet for Case 1 with only the trial balances entered. Company C's trial balance reflects the journal entry shown on page 208, recording its investment in Company D's common stock. The Investment in Company D balance appears among the debits, while Common Stock has increased to $775,000 and Additional Paid-in Capital to $105,000. Company D's trial balance is unchanged. Notice that each affiliate's Common Stock, Additional Paid-in Capital, and Retained Earnings balances appear on separate lines, as described earlier.

Exhibit 5-5 presents the consolidation worksheet with the eliminations entered from the schedule of eliminations, which appears in Exhibit 5-3. Notice that the eliminations appearing in the worksheet are cross-referenced to the schedule of eliminations in Exhibit 5-3. Also, the debit-credit notation used in schedule of eliminations is repeated in the Eliminations column of the worksheet.

The completed worksheet for Case 1 appears in Exhibit 5-6. The balances of the various assets and liabilities of the two companies, which are not affected by eliminations, have been combined and extended to the balance sheet column. When account balances are affected by eliminations, the normal rules of debit and credit apply. A debit balance is increased by a debit elimination and decreased by a credit elimination. Conversely, a credit balance is in-

EXHIBIT 5-3

Illustrative Problem 5.2
Excess of Cost over Book Value and Eliminations
Purchase Method
June 30, 1991

Excess of Cost over Book Value

Cost of Investment	$ 450,000
Book Value (90% × $440,000)	396,000
Excess of Cost over Book Value	$ 54,000

Eliminations

Intercompany Ownership Interests

[1] Common Stock: D	$ 270,000
[2] Additional Paid-in Capital: D	45,000
[3] Retained Earnings: D	81,000
[4] Investment in Company D	$(396,000)

Calculations
[1] 90% × $300,000
[2] 90% × $ 50,000
[3] 90% × 90,000
[4] Sum of Eliminations [1] through [3]

creased by a credit elimination and decreased by a debit elimination. Company C's Investment in Company D balance, a debit, is decreased by the credit in Elimination [4], yielding the $54,000 debit residual targeted in the schedule of the excess of cost over book value in Exhibit 5-3. This amount is extended to the Balance Sheet column and labeled "G" for Goodwill from Consolidation. Company C's stockholders' equity balances are extended to the Balance Sheet column and will be reported as the stockholders' equity of the consolidated entity. Company D's stockholders' equity balances, which are credits, are decreased by the debits in Eliminations [1], [2], and [3], yielding 10% minority interest residuals, which are extended to the Balance Sheet column and labeled "M" for Minority Interest. These minority interest residuals are combined and reported as a single amount in the resulting consolidated balance sheet, as illustrated in Exhibit 5-7.

Reporting Minority Interest.   Although the minority interest resembles both a liability and an element of stockholders' equity with respect to the consolidated entity, it really is neither. That is, the minority stockholders of the subsidiary are neither creditors nor stockholders of the consolidated entity. The minority interest reported in the consolidated balance sheet represents the ownership interest of those minority stockholders in the net assets of the subsidiary, which have been combined with the corresponding assets and liabilities of the parent. Thus, the minority interest constitutes a source of assets of the consolidated entity in addition to creditors and parent company stockholders.

EXHIBIT 5-4

Illustrative Problem 5.2, Case 1
Purchase Method Consolidation Worksheet
Trial Balances Only
June 30, 1991

	Company C	Company D	Eliminations	Balance Sheet
Current Assets	325,000	150,000		
Plant and Equipment	780,000	520,000		
Investment in Company D	450,000			
	1,555,000	670,000		
Accumulated Depreciation	280,000	170,000		
Liabilities	165,000	60,000		
Common Stock: C	775,000			
Common Stock: D		300,000		
Additional Paid-in Capital: C	105,000			
Additional Paid-in Capital: D		50,000		
Retained Earnings: C	230,000			
Retained Earnings: D		90,000		
	1,555,000	670,000		

EXHIBIT 5-5

Illustrative Problem 5.2, Case 1
Purchase Method Consolidation Worksheet
Eliminations Posted
June 30, 1991

	Company C	Company D	Eliminations	Balance Sheet
Current Assets	325,000	150,000		
Plant and Equipment	780,000	520,000		
Investment in Company D	450,000		[4] (396,000)	
	1,555,000	670,000		
Accumulated Depreciation	280,000	170,000		
Liabilities	165,000	60,000		
Common Stock: C	775,000			
Common Stock: D		300,000	[1] 270,000	
Additional Paid-in Capital: C	105,000			
Additional Paid-in Capital: D		50,000	[2] 45,000	
Retained Earnings: C	230,000			
Retained Earnings: D		90,000	[3] 81,000	
	1,555,000	670,000		

EXHIBIT 5-6

Illustrative Problem 5.2, Case 1
Completed Purchase Method Consolidation Worksheet
June 30, 1991

	Company C	Company D	Eliminations	Balance Sheet
Current Assets	325,000	150,000		475,000
Plant and Equipment	780,000	520,000		1,300,000
Investment in Company D	450,000		[4] (396,000)	54,000 G
	1,555,000	670,000		1,829,000
Accumulated Depreciation	280,000	170,000		450,000
Liabilities	165,000	60,000		225,000
Common Stock: C	775,000			775,000
Common Stock: D		300,000	[1] 270,000	30,000 M
Additional Paid-in Capital: C	105,000			105,000
Additional Paid-in Capital: D		50,000	[2] 45,000	5,000 M
Retained Earnings: C	230,000			230,000
Retained Earnings: D		90,000	[3] 81,000	9,000 M
	1,555,000	670,000		1,829,000

How, then, should minority interest be classified in the consolidated balance sheet? *Accounting Research Bulletin No. 51*, the primary source of guidance for the preparation of consolidated financial statements, is silent on this issue. Practice varies in this regard, with some entities reporting minority interest among the noncurrent liabilities and others reporting it as an element of stockholders' equity. An emerging trend appears to be to report minority interest in a separate category between liabilities and stockholders' equity, thus acknowledging that it is a special phenomenon, an additional source of assets, that appears only in the context of consolidated financial statements. This treatment is reflected in the balance sheet in Exhibit 5-7 and is followed throughout this book.

The final step is to use the information in the Balance Sheet column of the consolidation worksheet to prepare the consolidated balance sheet at the date of acquisition, which appears in Exhibit 5-7.

Case 2: The Pooling of Interests Method. Under the pooling of interests method, Company C records the acquisition of its investment in the Company D stock as follows:

Investment in Company D	396,000	
Common Stock		375,000
Additional Paid-in Capital		21,000

Because no new basis of accountability arises in a pooling of interests, the investment in Company D's common stock is recorded at the aggregate book value of Company D's net

EXHIBIT 5-7

Illustrative Problem 5.2, Case 1
Purchase Method Balance Sheet

COMPANY C
Balance Sheet
June 30, 1991

Assets

Current Assets		$ 475,000
Plant and Equipment	$1,300,000	
Less: Accumulated Depreciation	450,000	850,000
Goodwill		54,000
Total Assets		$1,379,000

Liabilities and Stockholders' Equity

Liabilities		$ 225,000
Minority Interest in Subsidiary		44,000
Stockholders' Equity		
Common Stock ($25 par)	$ 775,000	
Additional Paid-in Capital	105,000	
Retained Earnings	230,000	1,110,000
Total Liabilities and Stockholders' Equity		$1,379,000

assets. Again, instead of recording individual assets and liabilities, as is done in a net asset acquisition, Company C debits Investment in Company D for the aggregate book value of Company D's net assets. The newly issued Company C common stock is recorded at par value of $25 per share, with the excess credited to Additional Paid-in Capital. The problem of carrying forward the combined Retained Earnings balances is dealt with in the consolidation worksheet.

No schedule of the excess of cost over book value is constructed under the pooling of interests method. Because no new basis of accountability is present, no difference between cost and book value can exist.

The schedules of eliminations appear in Exhibit 5-8. Under the pooling of interests method, we begin the Intercompany Ownership Interests set of eliminations by eliminating the entire amount of Company C's Investment in Company D balance, $396,000, in Elimination [1]. Then, amounts equal to Company C's percentage of ownership, 90%, are eliminated from Company D's Common Stock and Additional Paid-in Capital balances in Eliminations [2] and [3].

EXHIBIT 5-8

Illustrative Problem 5.2
Eliminations
Pooling of Interests Method
June 30, 1991

Eliminations

Intercompany Ownership Interests

[1] Investment in Company D	$ (396,000)
[2] Common Stock D	270,000
[3] Additional Paid-in Capital: D	45,000
[4] Additional Paid-in Capital: C	51,000
[5] Retained Earnings: D	$ 30,000

Retained Earnings Combination

[6] Retained Earnings: D	$ 54,000
[7] Retained Earnings: C	(54,000)

Calculations
[1] Balance of the account
[2] 90% × $300,000
[3] 90% × $ 50,000
[4] Balance of the account
[5] Sum of Eliminations [1] through [4]
[6] 90% × ($90,000 − $30,000)
[7] Same as [6]

At this point, total credits equal $396,000, while total debits equal $315,000. In order to avoid eliminating any of Company D's Retained Earnings balance, it would be necessary to debit Company C's Additional Paid-in Capital for $81,000. Company C's Additional Paid-in Capital balance (after posting the journal entry to record the acquisition of the Company D common stock), however, is only $51,000. Thus, after debiting Company C's Additional Paid-in Capital for $51,000 in Elimination [4], Company D's Retained Earnings must be debited for $30,000 to complete the Intercompany Ownership Interests set of eliminations.

After applying Elimination [5], the remaining balance of Company D's Retained Earnings is $60,000. In the Retained Earnings Combination set of eliminations, Company D's Retained Earnings is debited and Company C's Retained Earnings is credited for Company C's share, 90%, of that amount, or $54,000. The remainder, $6,000, is extended to the Balance Sheet column as part of Minority Interest, appropriately labeled "M."

As a result of these eliminations, the combined amount of retained earnings (including the minority interest in Company D's retained earnings) will be only $290,000 rather than $320,000. If Company C's Additional Paid-in Capital balance had been at least $81,000, the entire amount of the combined Retained Earnings balances could have been carried forward.

Again, in both sets of eliminations, the debit eliminations are shown without notation, with the credit eliminations shown in parentheses. Also, each set of eliminations balances in terms of debits and credits. Exhibit 5-9 presents the completed consolidation worksheet for Case 2.

EXHIBIT 5-9

Illustrative Problem 5.2, Case 2
Pooling of Interests Method Consolidation Worksheet
June 30, 1991

	Company C	Company D	Eliminations		Balance Sheet
Current Assets	325,000	150,000			475,000
Plant and Equipment	780,000	520,000			1,300,000
Investment in Company D	396,000		[1] (396,000)		
	1,501,000	670,000			1,775,000
Accumulated Depreciation	280,000	170,000			450,000
Liabilities	165,000	60,000			225,000
Common Stock: C	775,000				775,000
Common Stock: D		300,000	[2]	270,000	30,000 M
Additional Paid-in Capital: C	51,000		[4]	51,000	
Additional Paid-in Capital: D		50,000	[3]	45,000	5,000 M
Retained Earnings: C	230,000		[7]	(54,000)	284,000
Retained Earnings: D		90,000	{ [5]	30,000 }	6,000 M
			{ [6]	54,000 }	
	1,501,000	670,000			1,775,000

Company C's trial balance reflects the journal entry given on page 214 to record its investment in Company D's common stock. The Investment in Company D balance appears among the debits, while Common Stock has increased to $775,000 and Additional Paid-in Capital to $51,000. Company D's trial balance is unchanged. The eliminations have been entered from the schedule of eliminations in Exhibit 5-8, using the cross-reference numbers and the debit-credit notation, as discussed earlier in this chapter.

The balances of the various assets and liabilities of the two companies have been combined and extended to the Balance Sheet column. Company C's stockholders' equity balances are extended to the Balance Sheet column and will be reported as the stockholders' equity of the consolidated entity. Company D's stockholders' equity balances yield 10% minority interest residuals, which are extended to the Balance Sheet column and labeled "M" for Minority Interest. These minority interest residuals are combined and reported as a single amount in the resulting consolidated balance sheet, as illustrated in Exhibit 5-10. The final step is to use the information in the Balance Sheet column of the consolidation worksheet to prepare the consolidated balance sheet of the date of acquisition, which appears in Exhibit 5-10.

EXHIBIT 5-10

Illustrative Problem 5.2, Case 2
Pooling of Interests Method Balance Sheet

COMPANY C
Balance Sheet
June 30, 1991

Assets

Current Assets		$ 475,000
Plant and Equipment	$1,300,000	
Less: Accumulated Depreciation	450,000	850,000
Total Assets		$1,325,000

Liabilities and Stockholders' Equity

Liabilities		$ 225,000
Minority Interest in Subsidiary		41,000
Stockholders' Equity		
Common Stock ($25 par)	$ 775,000	
Retained Earnings	284,000	1,059,000
Total Liabilities and Stockholders' Equity		$1,325,000

Alternative Worksheet Structure. In the consolidation worksheets presented thus far, minority interest residuals are extended to the Balance Sheet column and labeled "M" for Minority Interest. These minority interest residuals are then combined and reported as a single amount in the resulting consolidated balance sheet. Some accountants prefer to insert a column entitled Minority Interest immediately to the right of the Eliminations column and use this column to collect the minority residuals. To illustrate this approach, Exhibit 5-11 presents the consolidation worksheet that appears in Exhibit 5-9, with the Minority Interest column added.

Obviously, the inclusion of the Minority Interest column increases the amount of horizontal space required in the consolidation worksheet. We find the labeling device illustrated earlier to be a useful and effective way to streamline the consolidation worksheet. For this reason, it is used consistently throughout the remainder of this text.

FINANCIAL STATEMENT DISCLOSURE

Consolidated financial statements should disclose, either in the body of the financial statements or in notes, the consolidation policy being followed by the reporting entity.[12] Such matters

---

[12]*ARB No. 51,* paragraph 5.

EXHIBIT 5-11

Illustrative Problem 5.2, Case 2
Pooling of Interests Method Consolidation Worksheet
Minority Interest Column Added
June 30, 1991

	Company C	Company D	Eliminations		Minority Interest	Balance Sheet
Current Assets	325,000	150,000				475,000
Plant and Equipment	780,000	520,000				1,300,000
Investment in Company D	396,000		[1]	(396,000)		
	1,501,000	670,000				1,775,000
Accumulated Depreciation	280,000	170,000				450,000
Liabilities	165,000	60,000				225,000
Common Stock: C	775,000					775,000
Common Stock: D		300,000	[2]	270,000	30,000	
Additional Paid-in Capital: C	51,000		[4]	51,000		
Additional Paid-in Capital: D		50,000	[3]	45,000	5,000	
Retained Earnings: C	230,000		[7]	(54,000)		284,000
Retained Earnings: D		90,000	{[5]	30,000}	6,000	
			{[6]	54,000}		
Total Minority Interest					41,000	41,000
	1,501,000	670,000				1,775,000

as the basis for excluding a subsidiary from the consolidated entity, the treatment of minority interests, and the treatment of intercompany profits may fall into the category of consolidation policy.

SUMMARY

In this chapter, we have examined the appropriate accounting for corporate combinations under each of two accounting methods: the purchase method and the pooling of interests method. For corporate combinations in which one corporation acquires the net assets of another, appropriate journal entries to record the combination and the resulting balance sheets at the date of acquisition are illustrated for each of the methods. In addition, in the case of a corporate combination effected through a common stock acquisition, the preparation of consolidated financial statements at the date on which the controlling interest is acquired is discussed and illustrated.

In a purchase, the consolidation process begins with the construction of a schedule of the difference between the cost of the investment and its underlying book value, followed by a schedule showing the eliminations of intercompany ownership balances. The information in these schedules is entered in the consolidation worksheet that, when completed, provides the information from which the consolidated balance sheet is prepared.

In a pooling of interests, no schedule of the difference between the cost of the investment and its underlying book value is necessary because the parent records its investment at the book value of the underlying net assets. Thus, the consolidation process begins with the preparation of schedules showing the eliminations of intercompany ownership balances and the combination of retained earnings balances. As in a purchase, the information in these schedules is entered in the consolidation worksheet, from which the consolidated balance sheet is prepared.

REVIEW PROBLEM

On July 31, 1990, Company P gains control over Company S by issuing 18,000 shares of its previously unissued common stock, which has a market value of 32. Any excess of cost over book value is to be treated as goodwill. The condensed trial balances of Company P and Company S immediately before their combination are

	Company P	Company S
Current Assets	$ 230,000	$ 140,000
Plant and Equipment	890,000	660,000
	$1,120,000	$ 800,000
Accumulated Depreciation	$ 270,000	$ 180,000
Liabilities	190,000	100,000
Common Stock ($25 par)	350,000	300,000
Additional Paid-in Capital	75,000	50,000
Retained Earnings	235,000	170,000
	$1,120,000	$ 800,000

Required
Present (a) the journal entry to record the transaction on Company P's books and (b) either the resulting balance sheet, or consolidation worksheet and supporting schedules, whichever is appropriate, in each of the following cases.

1. Company P acquires Company S's net assets and the combination is treated as a purchase.
2. Company P acquires 95% of Company S's common stock and the consolidated financial statements are prepared under the purchase method.
3. Company P acquires Company S's net assets and the combination is treated as a pooling of interests.
4. Company P acquires 95% of Company S's common stock and the consolidated financial statements are prepared under the pooling of interests method.

QUESTIONS

1. What are the two ways in which one corporation can gain control over another corporation?
2. What is meant by the term *minority interest?*
3. For whom are consolidated financial statements primarily intended?
4. What conditions are necessary for the preparation of consolidated financial statements?
5. What is the meaning of the term *book value* when compared to the cost of the parent's investment in the subsidiary?
6. What does the term *intercompany balances* mean?
7. How are intercompany balances treated in the preparation of consolidated financial statements?
8. What is the essential nature of a business combination accounted for as a purchase?
9. What are the three principal features of the purchase method?
10. What is the essential nature of a business combination accounted for as a pooling of interests?
11. What are the three principal features of the pooling of interests method?
12. Why is an excess of cost over book value schedule not prepared in support of a consolidation worksheet prepared under the pooling of interests method?

EXERCISES

EXERCISE 5-1

Company A invests in the common stock of Companies B, C, D, and E. The following information is available at the date of acquisition of each ownership interest:

	Company B	Company C	Company D	Company E
Common Stock	$500,000	$600,000	$400,000	$300,000
Retained Earnings	200,000	250,000	580,000	460,000
Cost of Investment	580,000	750,000	780,000	550,000
Percentage of Ownership	80%	90%	75%	70%

Required

1. Assuming the use of the purchase method in all cases, determine the excess of cost over book value or vice versa for each of these four investments.
2. Determine the minority interest in each subsidiary that should be reported on a consolidated balance sheet at the date of acquisition.

EXERCISE 5-2

The condensed trial balances of Company F and Company G immediately before their combination are shown below.

	Company F	Company G
Current Assets	$ 210,000	$ 150,000
Plant and Equipment	590,000	380,000
	$ 800,000	$ 530,000

	Company F	Company G
Accumulated Depreciation	$ 200,000	$ 130,000
Liabilities	100,000	50,000
Common Stock ($25 par)	300,000	200,000
Additional Paid-in Capital	50,000	20,000
Retained Earnings	150,000	130,000
	$ 800,000	$ 530,000

On the date of the above trial balances, Company F acquired Company G's net assets by issuing 2,500 shares of its previously unissued common stock, which had a market value of 180. Any excess of cost over book value is attributed to undervaluation of Company G's Plant and Equipment.

Required
Present the journal entry on Company F's books to record the transaction (a) as a purchase and (b) as a pooling of interests.

EXERCISE 5-3
Company H acquired 95% of Company I's common stock by issuing 16,000 shares of its previously unissued common stock, which had a market value of 31. Any excess of cost over book value is attributed to goodwill from consolidation. The condensed trial balances of Company H and Company I immediately before their combination are shown below.

	Company H	Company I
Current Assets	$ 270,000	$ 150,000
Plant and Equipment (net)	530,000	350,000
	$ 800,000	$ 500,000
Liabilities	$ 110,000	$ 20,000
Common Stock ($25 par)	500,000	150,000
Additional Paid-in Capital	50,000	10,000
Retained Earnings	140,000	320,000
	$ 800,000	$ 500,000

Required
Assuming that the purchase method is used, prepare all supporting schedules to the consolidation worksheet at the date of acquisition.

EXERCISE 5-4
Refer to Exercise 5-3. Assuming that the pooling of interests method is used, prepare all supporting schedules to the consolidation worksheet at the date of acquisition.

EXERCISE 5-5
Company J acquired Company K's net assets by issuing 10,000 shares of its previously unissued common stock, which had a market value of 45. Company K's net assets are appropriately valued; therefore, any

excess of cost over book value is attributed to goodwill. The condensed trial balances of Company J and Company K immediately before their combination are shown below.

	Company J	Company K
Current Assets	$ 190,000	$ 110,000
Plant and Equipment (net)	510,000	320,000
	$ 700,000	$ 430,000
Liabilities	$ 80,000	$ 40,000
Common Stock ($25 par)	400,000	200,000
Additional Paid-in Capital	40,000	20,000
Retained Earnings	180,000	170,000
	$ 700,000	$ 430,000

Required

Present Company J's trial balance immediately after the combination if the transaction is treated as (a) a purchase, and (b) a pooling of interests.

EXERCISE 5-6

Company L issued voting common stock with a total par value of $90,000 in exchange for all of the outstanding common stock of Company M. The combination was properly accounted for as a pooling of interests. The stockholders' equity of Company M at the date of acquisition consisted of common stock, $70,000, additional paid-in capital, $7,000, and retained earnings, $50,000. What should be the increase in stockholders' equity of Company L at the date of acquisition as a result of this transaction?
a. Zero
b. $ 37,000
c. $ 90,000
d. $127,000

(AICPA adapted)

EXERCISE 5-7

Which of the following is the best theoretical justification for consolidated financial statements?
a. In form, the affiliates are one entity; in substance, they are separate.
b. In form, the affiliates are separate; in substance, they are one entity.
c. In form and substance, the affiliates are one entity.
d. In form and substance, the affiliates are separate.

(AICPA adapted)

EXERCISE 5-8

Company P acquired Company Q's net assets by issuing 18,000 shares of its previously unissued common stock, which had a market value of 15. Any excess of cost over book value is attributed to undervaluation of Company Q's plant and equipment. The condensed trial balances of Company P and Company Q immediately before their combination are shown below.

	Company P	Company Q
Current Assets	$ 185,000	$ 140,000
Plant and Equipment	323,000	254,000
	$ 508,000	$ 394,000
Accumulated Depreciation	$ 110,000	$ 154,000
Liabilities	58,000	28,000
Common Stock ($10 par)	200,000	100,000
Additional Paid-in Capital	45,000	30,000
Retained Earnings	95,000	82,000
	$ 508,000	$ 394,000

Required

1. Present the journal entry on Company P's books to record the combination as a pooling of interests.
2. How would your answer to part 1 differ if the combination were recorded as a purchase? Answer verbally.

EXERCISE 5-9

Company N was organized to consolidate the resources of Companies O and P in a business combination appropriately accounted for as a pooling of interests. Company N issued 62,000 shares of $10 par value common stock in exchange for all of the outstanding common shares of Companies O and P, whose stockholders' equity balances immediately before the combination are shown below.

	Company O	Company P	Total
Common Stock	$ 200,000	$ 400,000	$ 600,000
Additional Paid-in Capital	25,000	35,000	60,000
Retained Earnings	120,000	210,000	330,000
Totals	$ 345,000	$ 645,000	$ 990,000

Immediately after the combination, Company N's Additional Paid-in Capital balance should be
a. $ 0
b. $ 40,000
c. $ 60,000
d. $390,000

(AICPA adapted)

EXERCISE 5-10

On December 31, 1991, Company R issued 10,000 shares of common stock in exchange for all of Company S's common stock. Condensed trial balances of the two companies immediately before the combination appear below.

	Company R	Company S
Assets	$1,000,000	$ 500,000
Liabilities	$ 300,000	$ 150,000
Common Stock ($10 par)	200,000	100,000
Retained Earnings	500,000	250,000
	$1,000,000	$ 500,000

Company R's common stock had a market price of $60 per share on December 31, 1991. No market price was available for Company S's common stock. If the combination qualifies as a purchase, the balance of Company R's Investment in Company S immediately after the combination will be
a. $100,000
b. $350,000
c. $500,000
d. $600,000

(AICPA adapted)

EXERCISE 5-11
Refer to Exercise 5-10. If the combination qualifies as a pooling of interests, the amount of consolidated retained earnings that would appear in the consolidated balance sheet immediately after the combination will be
a. $500,000
b. $600,000
c. $750,000
d. $850,000

(AICPA adapted)

PROBLEMS

PROBLEM 5-1
Given below are the trial balances of Company A and Company B on September 1, 1990, immediately before Company A acquired Company B's net assets by issuing 10,000 shares of its previously unissued common stock, which had a market value of 39. Any excess of cost over book value is attributed to undervaluation of Company B's plant and equipment.

	Company A	Company B
Current Assets	$ 240,000	$ 165,000
Plant and Equipment	710,000	470,000
	$ 950,000	$ 635,000

	Company A	Company B
Accumulated Depreciation	$ 330,000	$ 160,000
Liabilities	150,000	116,000
Common Stock ($10 par)	300,000	200,000
Additional Paid-in Capital	30,000	25,000
Retained Earnings	140,000	134,000
	$ 950,000	$ 635,000

Required

Present Company A's balance sheet immediately after the combination if the transaction is treated as (a) a purchase, and (b) a pooling of interests.

PROBLEM 5-2

On October 31, 1992, Company C acquired 70% of Company D's common stock and 100% of Company E's common stock, both for cash. Any excess of cost over book value is to be treated as goodwill from consolidation and any excess of book value over cost is to be treated as an aggregate overvaluation of subsidiary net assets. The trial balances of Companies C, D, and E immediately after those transactions appear below.

	Company C	Company D	Company E
Current Assets	$ 180,000	$ 310,000	$ 210,000
Plant and Equipment (net)	710,000	480,000	540,000
Investment in Company D	690,000		
Investment in Company E	580,000		
	$2,160,000	$ 790,000	$ 750,000
Liabilities	$ 380,000	$ 180,000	$ 120,000
Common Stock	1,000,000	400,000	500,000
Additional Paid-in Capital	250,000	70,000	50,000
Retained Earnings	530,000	140,000	80,000
	$2,160,000	$ 790,000	$ 750,000

Required

Prepare a purchase method consolidation worksheet for Company C and its subsidiaries at October 31, 1992, supported by appropriate schedules.

PROBLEM 5-3

On March 31, 1991, Company F acquired 90% of Company G's common stock by issuing 12,000 shares of its previously unissued common stock, which had a market value of 36. The trial balances of Company F and Company G immediately before the combination appear below.

	Company F	Company G
Current Assets	$ 270,000	$ 150,000
Plant and Equipment	720,000	450,000
	$ 990,000	$ 600,000

	Company F	Company G
Accumulated Depreciation	$ 230,000	$ 100,000
Liabilities	100,000	60,000
Common Stock ($25 par)	500,000	200,000
Additional Paid-in Capital	50,000	30,000
Retained Earnings	110,000	210,000
	$ 990,000	$ 600,000

Required

Prepare a consolidation worksheet at March 31, 1991, supported by appropriate schedules, using the pooling of interests method.

PROBLEM 5-4

Given below are the trial balances of Company H and Company I at September 30, 1991, immediately after Company H acquired 80% of Company I's common stock. Any excess of cost over book value is to be treated as goodwill from consolidation.

	Company H	Company I
Current Assets	$ 200,000	$ 100,000
Plant and Equipment	450,000	350,000
Investment in Company I	260,000	
	$ 910,000	$ 450,000
Accumulated Depreciation	$ 310,000	$ 150,000
Liabilities	100,000	50,000
Common Stock ($25 par)	300,000	150,000
Additional Paid-in Capital	110,000	40,000
Retained Earnings	90,000	60,000
	$ 910,000	$ 450,000

Required

1. Prepare a consolidation worksheet at September 30, 1991, supported by appropriate schedules, using the purchase method.
2. Prepare a consolidated balance sheet at September 30, 1991.

PROBLEM 5-5

Given below are the trial balances of Company J and Company K, at April 30, 1992, immediately before Company J acquired 92% of Company K's capital stock by issuing 8,000 shares of its own unissued common stock, which had a market value of 47.

	Company J	Company K
Current Assets	$ 250,000	$ 90,000
Plant and Equipment	450,000	310,000
	$ 700,000	$ 400,000

	Company J	Company K
Accumulated Depreciation	$ 180,000	$ 100,000
Liabilities	170,000	50,000
Common Stock ($25 par)	200,000	100,000
Additional Paid-in Capital	60,000	10,000
Retained Earnings	90,000	140,000
	$ 700,000	$ 400,000

Required

1. Prepare a consolidation worksheet at April 30, 1992, supported by appropriate schedules, using the pooling of interests method.
2. Prepare a consolidated balance sheet at April 30, 1992.

PROBLEM 5-6

Given below are the trial balances of Company L and Company M at August 31, 1991, immediately after Company L acquired 85% of Company M's common stock for cash. Any excess of cost over book value is to be treated as goodwill from consolidation.

	Company L	Company M
Cash	$ 50,000	$ 35,000
Accounts Receivable	78,000	83,000
Inventories	120,000	91,000
Plant and Equipment	610,000	483,000
Investment in Company M	410,000	
Other Assets	52,000	31,000
	$1,320,000	$ 723,000

	Company L	Company M
Accumulated Depreciation	$ 250,000	$ 171,000
Accounts Payable	97,000	112,000
Common Stock ($25 par)	500,000	300,000
Additional Paid-in Capital	30,000	20,000
Retained Earnings	443,000	120,000
	$1,320,000	$ 723,000

Required

1. Prepare a consolidation worksheet at August 31, 1991, supported by appropriate schedules, using the purchase method.
2. Prepare a consolidated balance sheet at August 31, 1991.

PROBLEM 5-7

The condensed trial balances of Company N and Company O immediately before their combination are shown below. On the date of these trial balances, Company N acquired Company O's net assets by issuing 8,000 shares of its previously unissued common stock, which had a market value of 40. Any excess of cost over book value is attributed to undervaluation of Company O's plant and equipment.

	Company N	Company O
Current Assets	$ 161,000	$ 155,000
Plant and Equipment	525,000	339,000
	$ 686,000	$ 494,000
Accumulated Depreciation	$ 200,000	$ 201,000
Liabilities	63,000	42,000
Common Stock ($25 par)	300,000	100,000
Additional Paid-in Capital	25,000	45,000
Retained Earnings	98,000	106,000
	$ 686,000	$ 494,000

Required

1. Present the journal entry on Company N's books to record this combination (a) as a purchase and (b) as a pooling of interests.
2. Present the resulting Company N trial balance assuming that the combination is treated (a) as a purchase and (b) as a pooling of interest.

PROBLEM 5-8

Given below are the trial balances of Company P and Company Q at June 30, 1992, immediately before Company N acquired all of Company Q's common stock by issuing 12,000 shares of its previously unissued common stock, which had a market value of 15. The book values of Company Q's assets and liabilities approximate their fair market values.

	Company P	Company Q
Current Assets	$ 40,000	$ 30,000
Plant and Equipment (net)	150,000	120,000
Other Assets	30,000	
	$ 220,000	$ 150,000
Current Liabilities	$ 35,000	$ 15,000
Long-term Liabilities		50,000
Common Stock ($1 par)	75,000	100,000
Additional Paid-in Capital	40,000	
Retained Earnings	70,000	(15,000)
	$ 220,000	$ 150,000

Required

1. If the acquisition is accounted for as a purchase, the consolidated balance sheet at June 30, 1992 should contain goodwill of
   a. $180,000
   b. $ 95,000
   c. $ 85,000
   d. $120,000

2. If the transaction is accounted for as a pooling of interests, what amount of retained earnings should appear in the June 30, 1992 consolidated balance sheet?
   a. $ 55,000
   b. $ 70,000
   c. $ 35,000
   d. $ 85,000
3. If the transaction is accounted for as a pooling of interests, how should the consolidated net income for the year ended June 30, 1992 be computed?
   a. Use only Company P's net income because the combination occurred on the last day of the fiscal year.
   b. Use only Company Q's net income because the combination occurred on the last day of the fiscal year.
   c. Add together both companies' net incomes even though the combination occurred on the last day of the fiscal year.
   d. Add together both companies' net incomes and subtract the annual amortization of goodwill.

(AICPA adapted)

SOLUTION TO REVIEW PROBLEM

CASE I

Journal Entry

Current Assets	140,000	
Plant and Equipment	480,000	
Goodwill	56,000	
Liabilities		100,000
Common Stock		450,000
Additional Paid-in Capital		126,000

Purchase Method Balance Sheet

COMPANY P
Balance Sheet
July 31, 1990

Assets

Current Assets		$ 370,000
Plant and Equipment	$1,370,000	
Less: Accumulated Depreciation	270,000	1,100,000
Goodwill		56,000
Total Assets		$1,526,000

Liabilities and Stockholders' Equity

Liabilities		$ 290,000
Stockholders' Equity		
Common Stock ($25 par)	$ 800,000	
Additional Paid-in Capital	201,000	
Retained Earnings	235,000	1,236,000
Total Liabilities and Stockholders' Equity		$1,526,000

CASE 2

Journal Entry

Investment in Company S	576,000	
Common Stock		450,000
Additional Paid-in Capital		126,000

Excess of Cost over Book Value

Cost of Investment	$ 576,000
Book Value (95% × $520,000)	494,000
Goodwill from Consolidation	$ 82,000

Eliminations

Intercompany Ownership Interests

[1] Common Stock: S	$ 285,000
[2] Additional Paid-in Capital: S	47,500
[3] Retained Earnings: S	161,500
[4] Investment in Company S	$ (494,000)

Purchase Method Consolidation Worksheet

	Company P	Company S	Eliminations	Balance Sheet
Current Assets	230,000	140,000		370,000
Plant and Equipment	890,000	660,000		1,550,000
Investment in Company S	576,000		[4] (494,000)	82,000 G
	1,696,000	800,000		2,002,000
Accumulated Depreciation	270,000	180,000		450,000
Liabilities	190,000	100,000		290,000
Common Stock: P	800,000			800,000
Common Stock: S		300,000	[1] 285,000	15,000 M
Additional Paid-in Capital: P	201,000			201,000
Additional Paid-in Capital: S		50,000	[2] 47,500	2,500 M
Retained Earnings: P	235,000			235,000
Retained Earnings: S		170,000	[3] 161,500	8,500 M
	1,696,000	800,000		2,002,000

CASE 3

Journal Entry

Current Assets	140,000	
Plant and Equipment	480,000	
Additional Paid-in Capital	75,000	
Liabilities		100,000
Common Stock		450,000
Retained Earnings		145,000

Pooling of Interests Method Balance Sheet

COMPANY P
Balance Sheet
July 31, 1990

Assets

Current Assets		$ 370,000
Plant and Equipment	$1,370,000	
Less: Accumulated Depreciation	270,000	1,100,000
Total Assets		$1,470,000

Liabilities and Stockholders' Equity

Liabilities		$ 290,000
Stockholders' Equity		
Common Stock ($25 par)	$ 800,000	
Retained Earnings	380,000	1,180,000
Total Liabilities and Stockholders' Equity		$1,470,000

CASE 4

Journal Entry

Investment in Company S	494,000	
Common Stock		450,000
Additional Paid-in Capital		44,000

Eliminations

Intercompany Ownership Interests

[1] Investment in Company S	$ (494,000)
[2] Common Stock: S	285,000
[3] Additional Paid-in Capital: S	47,500
[4] Additional Paid-in Capital: P	119,000
[5] Retained Earnings: S	$ 42,500

Retained Earnings Combination

[6] Retained Earnings: S $ 121,125
[7] Retained Earnings: P   (121,125)

Pooling of Interests Method Consolidation Worksheet

	Company P	Company S	Eliminations	Balance Sheet
Current Assets	230,000	140,000		370,000
Plant and Equipment (net)	890,000	660,000		1,550,000
Investment in Company S	494,000		[1] (494,000)	
	1,614,000	800,000		1,920,000
Accumulated Depreciation	270,000	180,000		450,000
Liabilities	190,000	100,000		290,000
Common Stock: P	800,000			800,000
Common Stock: S		300,000	[2] 285,000	15,000 M
Additional Paid-in Capital: P	119,000		[4] 119,000	
Additional Paid-in Capital: S		50,000	[3] 47,500	2,500 M
Retained Earnings: P	235,000		[7] (121,125)	356,125
Retained Earnings: S		170,000	[5] 42,500 [6] 121,125	6,375 M
	1,614,000	800,000		1,920,000

6

DIFFERENCES BETWEEN COST AND BOOK VALUE

As noted in Chapter 5, one corporation can acquire the net assets of another corporation, or a controlling interest in its voting common stock, at a cost equal to, greater than, or less than book value. In a net asset acquisition, book value is the carrying value of the acquired net assets on the books of the acquired company. In a common stock acquisition, book value is the parent company's ownership interest in the net assets of the subsidiary, measured in terms of the aggregate value at which those net assets are carried on the subsidiary's books. Under the pooling of interests method, the parent's "cost" is book value because no new basis of accountability arises for the net assets represented by the parent's investment in the subsidiary. Under the purchase method, on the other hand, a new basis of accountability does arise; therefore, any of the three conditions noted above can apply. Throughout our consideration of the consolidation process, we will assume the use of the purchase method.

In Chapter 5, we temporarily identified any excess of a parent's cost over the book value of its investment in a subsidiary as goodwill from consolidation, and any excess of book value over cost as an aggregate overvaluation of subsidiary assets. In this chapter, we examine more thoroughly the possible causes of differences between cost and book value and the appropriate accounting treatment of each. For an excess of cost over book value, these include

- errors on the subsidiary's books,
- errors in recording the parent's cost,
- undervaluation of specific, recorded subsidiary assets,
- unrecorded subsidiary assets, or
- goodwill from consolidation.

For an excess of book value over cost, the causes include

- errors on the subsidiary's books,
- errors in recording the parent's cost,
- overvaluation of specific, recorded subsidiary assets,
- aggregate overvaluation of subsidiary net assets, or
- an advantageous purchase on the part of the parent company.

ALLOCATION OF THE COST OF THE PARENT'S INVESTMENT

Under the purchase method, the acquisition of the net assets of another company, whether directly or indirectly, requires allocation of the total cost of acquisition among the various assets and liabilities of the acquired company or subsidiary.[1] In the case of a parent–subsidiary relationship, this means allocating the cost of the parent's investment in the subsidiary. The critical factor in this allocation is the identification of the cause or causes of any difference between cost and book value and the resulting accounting treatment of this difference.

Ideally, the accountant, in cooperation with management, should attempt to assign any difference between cost and book value at the date of acquisition to its particular cause or combination of causes. Subsequent accounting treatment, then, would be dictated by that initial identification. Depending on the cause or causes with which the excess is identified, either journal entries on the books of one of the affiliates or worksheet adjustments may be required.

When all or part of the excess is attributed to the undervaluation or overvaluation of subsidiary assets, and the parent owns less than 100 percent of the subsidiary's common stock, the amount of the excess implies a larger amount of undervaluation or overvaluation. This larger amount must be dealt with in the consolidation process through worksheet adjustment.

EXCESS OF COST OVER BOOK VALUE

As noted earlier, an excess of cost over book value might be attributed to any one of the following causes or combinations thereof:

- errors on the subsidiary's books,
- errors in recording the parent's cost,
- undervaluation of specific, recorded subsidiary assets,
- unrecorded subsidiary assets, or
- goodwill from consolidation.

These possible causes are discussed in the following sections and illustrated in Illustrative Problem 6.1.

Each of the possible causes is treated as a separate case within Illustrative Problem 6.1. Although, as noted above, an excess of cost over book value, or vice versa, might be attributed

---

[1] *Accounting Principles Board Opinion No. 16, Business Combinations* (New York: AICPA, 1970), paragraphs 68, 87–88.

to a combination of causes, each is illustrated as if it were the sole cause of the excess of cost over book value in the situation presented in Illustrative Problem 6.1. This is done in order to make the illustration of the accounting treatment as clear as possible. A more elaborate treatment, assuming multiple causes, is demonstrated in Illustrative Problem 6.3.

ILLUSTRATIVE PROBLEM 6.I: EXCESS OF COST OVER BOOK VALUE

The trial balances of Company A and Company B immediately after Company A acquired 80% of Company B's common stock on June 30, 1991 appear below.

	Company A	Company B
Current Assets	$ 290,000	$ 240,000
Plant and Equipment	940,000	650,000
Investment in Company B	640,000	
Other Assets	60,000	70,000
	$1,930,000	$ 960,000
Accumulated Depreciation	$ 310,000	$ 250,000
Liabilities	260,000	110,000
Common Stock ($10 par)	750,000	400,000
Additional Paid-in Capital	290,000	50,000
Retained Earnings	320,000	150,000
	$1,930,000	$ 960,000

Five possible interpretations of the excess of cost over book value are contained in the cases that follow. Notice that the assumption of a single cause in each case implies the assumption that all of the other possible causes are inapplicable.

Case 1. The excess of cost over book value is caused by an error discovered on the subsidiary's books.

Case 2. The excess of cost over book value is caused by an error in recording the parent company's cost.

Case 3. The excess of cost over book value is attributed to the undervaluation of a specific, recorded subsidiary asset.

Case 4. The excess of cost over book value is attributed to the existence of an unrecorded subsidiary asset.

Case 5. The excess of cost over book value is considered to be goodwill from consolidation.

Each case is described more fully, and the appropriate accounting treatment is discussed and illustrated in the following sections.

Case 1. Error on the Subsidiary's Books. Shortly before Company A acquired its investment in Company B's common stock, Company B purchased some machinery for $200,000. Company B's bookkeeper erroneously charged the cost of the machinery to Maintenance

Expense. (Assume that the asset was purchased sufficiently close to the date of acquisition of Company A's investment in Company B that we can ignore depreciation on the machinery.)

The book value of Company A's investment in Company B is $480,000—80% of Comany B's net assets of $600,000. Thus, the excess of cost over book value is $640,000 minus $480,000, or $160,000. This amount of $160,000 represents Company A's share, 80%, of the total amount of the error. The total amount, therefore, must be $200,000.

The easiest, most direct way of dealing with errors on the subsidiary's books is to correct them by journal entry. In this case, Company B should record the following journal entry to correct the error in recording the cost of the machinery:

Plant and Equipment (Machinery)	200,000	
Retained Earnings		200,000

(If the error were discovered during the accounting period in which it was committed, of course, the credit would be to the expense account that had been erroneously debited.)

This journal entry will increase Company B's net assets (and total stockholders' equity) to $800,000, thus making the cost and book value of Company A's investment in Company B equal (80% of $800,000 equals $640,000). Because this is a real journal entry entered on Company B's books, rather than a consolidation worksheet adjustment, it needs to be recorded only once. Thereafter, the asset will be depreciated appropriately on Company B's books.

Case 2. Error on the Parent's Books.   Company A acquired its investment in Company B's capital stock by giving in exchange marketable equity securities that had a market value of $640,000, but were carried on Company A's books at their cost of $800,000. Company A's accountant neglected to recognize the loss on the decline in the market value of the securities and to reduce the carrying value of the securities accordingly.

To correct this error, Company A's accountant should record the following journal entry:

Retained Earnings	160,000	
Investment in Company B		160,000

This journal entry will reduce the balance of Company A's Investment in Company B account to $480,000, the book value of the investment. No further consideration of the initial excess of cost over book value is necessary. Notice that when, as in this case, the excess of cost over book value is attributed to a parent company asset or assets, no implication of a larger amount of excess exists, as appeared in Case 1. This implication is present only in cases in which all or part of the excess is attributed to assets of a partially owned subsidiary.

Case 3. Undervaluation of a Specific, Recorded Subsidiary Asset.   The excess of cost over book value is attributed to the fact that certain intangible assets carried in Company B's Other Assets at their cost of $60,000 have a fair market value of $260,000. Remember that the excess of cost over book value is $640,000 minus $480,000 (80% of Company B's net assets of $600,000), or $160,000. This amount of $160,000 represents Company A's share, 80%, of the total amount of the undervaluation, which is $200,000.

Under the **proprietary theory,** only the parent's share of the undervaluation, $160,000, would be recognized in the consolidated financial statements. Under the **entity theory,** in contrast, the total undervaluation of $200,000 is recognized and the minority interest is increased correspondingly. (In the case of an excess of book value over cost, of course, both assets and minority interest would be reduced.) With regard to asset valuation, we believe that the approach supported by the entity theory more clearly portrays the affiliated corporations as a combined economic entity. Accordingly, it is followed throughout our discussion of consolidated financial statements whenever the difference between cost and book value is attributed, in whole or in part, to undervaluation or overvaluation of subsidiary assets.

In this case, in contrast to Case 1, a journal entry on Company B's books is not appropriate. Generally accepted accounting principles do not permit the upward revaluation of assets in the absence of sufficient objective evidence, usually in the form of a transaction. Company B has not engaged in any transaction that would provide objective evidence of the increase in value of these assets. Therefore, the increase cannot be recognized on Company B's books.

From a consolidated point of view, however, we do have such evidence in the form of Company A's incurred cost of its investment in Company B's common stock. Thus, we can deal with the excess of cost over book value by making a worksheet adjustment that replicates the journal entry that Company B would record to recognize the increase in value of its intangible assets if it were permitted to do so under generally accepted accounting principles. This hypothetical journal entry would be

Other Assets (Intangible Assets)	200,000	
Appraisal Capital		200,000

Four changes in our consolidation process are necessary in order to accommodate this interpretation of the excess of cost over book value. First, the schedule of the excess of cost over book value is modified to show the expansion of the excess, which represents only the parent's share of the amount by which the subsidiary's intangible assets are undervalued, to the full amount of the undervaluation. This is accomplished by dividing the excess of cost over book value by the parent's percentage of ownership. The upward expansion of the excess of cost over book value is necessary whenever the excess is attributed to the undervaluation of assets of a partially owned subsidiary. The revised schedule of the excess of cost over book value for Case 3 is shown in Exhibit 6-1.

EXHIBIT 6-1

Illustrative Problem 6.1, Case 3
Excess of Cost over Book Value
June 30, 1991

Excess of Cost over Book Value

Cost of Investment	$ 640,000
Book Value (80% × $600,000)	480,000
Excess of Cost over Book Value	160,000
Expand to 100%	÷ 80%
Increase in Value of Intangible Assets	$ 200,000

The second change in the consolidation process is to insert a schedule of adjustments between the excess of cost over book value schedule and the schedules of eliminations. Such a schedule will be necessary in any case in which the excess of cost over book value is attributed to the undervaluation of assets of a partially owned subsidiary. The schedule of adjustments for Case 3 is shown in Exhibit 6-2. Although this pair of adjustments exactly replicates the hypothetical Company B journal entry shown on page 237, no actual journal entry is recorded on either affiliate's books. These are worksheet adjustments only and, therefore, must be repeated in successive years.

EXHIBIT 6-2

Illustrative Problem 6.1, Case 3
Adjustments and Eliminations
June 30, 1991

Adjustments

A. Other Assets	$ 200,000
B. Appraisal Capital: B	(200,000)

Eliminations

Intercompany Ownership Interests

[1] Common Stock: B	$ 320,000
[2] Additional Paid-in Capital: B	40,000
[3] Retained Earnings: B	120,000
[4] Appraisal Capital: B	160,000
[5] Investment in Company B	$(640,000)

Calculations
[1] 80% × $400,000
[2] 80% × $50,000
[3] 80% × $150,000
[4] 80% × $200,000
[5] Sum of Eliminations [1] through [4]

The third change in the consolidation process is to retitle the Eliminations column in the consolidation worksheet "Adjustments and Eliminations." We will encounter so few worksheet adjustments in any given situation that it is not worthwhile to include a separate column just for adjustments. In order to be able to distinguish between the adjustments and the eliminations on the worksheet, we will label the adjustments with capital letters, while continuing to label the eliminations by number. The retitled Adjustments and Eliminations column appears in Exhibit 6-3, and the labeling of adjustments appears first in Exhibit 6-2 and is repeated in Exhibit 6-3.

Finally, whenever adjustments or eliminations introduce new accounts, we must save a line or lines following the last account in the debit or credit section of the trial balance, as appropriate, in order to insert the new account or accounts. The new account in Case 3, Appraisal Capital: B, is treated in this manner in Exhibit 6-3.

As noted in Chapter 5, because in actual practice the consolidation process for a given

EXHIBIT 6-3

Illustrative Problem 6.1, Case 3
Consolidation Worksheet
June 30, 1991

	Company A	Company B	Adjustments and Eliminations	Balance Sheet
Current Assets	290,000	240,000		530,000
Plant and Equipment	940,000	650,000		1,590,000
Investment in Company B	640,000		[5] (640,000)	
Other Assets	60,000	70,000	A 200,000	330,000
	1,930,000	960,000		2,450,000
Accumulated Depreciation	310,000	250,000		560,000
Liabilities	260,000	110,000		370,000
Common Stock: A	750,000			750,000
Common Stock: B		400,000	[1] 320,000	80,000 M
Additional Paid-in Capital: A	290,000			290,000
Additional Paid-in Capital: B		50,000	[2] 40,000	10,000 M
Retained Earnings: A	320,000			320,000
Retained Earnings: B		150,000	[3] 120,000	30,000 M
Appraisal Capital: B			{ B (200,000) }	40,000 M
			{ [4] 160,000 }	
	1,930,000	960,000		2,450,000

set of affiliates contains essentially the same components in each successive year, the accountant can anticipate easily the need to leave extra lines in the worksheet. The use of a computer spreadsheet program to perform the consolidation process makes the insertion of additional lines even easier.

The distinction between adjustments and eliminations is important because adjustments usually affect eliminations that follow. For this reason, it is very helpful to make the adjustments first, and then the eliminations. In Case 3, for example, the adjustments shown in Exhibit 6-2 have the following effects on the eliminations at the date of acquisition, which also appear in Exhibit 6-2:

- Because the Appraisal Capital account created in Adjustment B becomes a new Company B stockholders' equity balance for consolidation purposes, 80% of its balance, or $160,000, is eliminated along with 80% of each of the Company B's other stockholders' equity balances. See Elimination [4].
- The presence of Elimination [4] causes the credit to Investment in Company B in Elimination [5] to be $160,000 greater, thus removing the initial excess of cost over book value from that account balance. The amount of Elimination [5], $640,000, equals the Investment in Company B balance appearing in Company A's trial balance and,

therefore, will eliminate that balance entirely. This result is appropriate, however, because we have recognized the asset increment implied by the excess of cost over book value through Adjustment A.

- Elimination [4] also causes Company B's Appraisal Capital balance to yield a $40,000, or 20%, minority interest residual, representing the minority stockholders' share of the increase in the value of the intangible assets.

In addition, amortization on the $200,000 increment in Company B's intangible assets recognized in Adjustment A will be recognized in subsequent worksheets through a special set of eliminations. This type of elimination set is introduced in Chapter 7. The amortization of any increment in a specific, recorded subsidiary asset recognized in the consolidated financial statements should follow the same amortization schedule used by the subsidiary for that asset.

Case 4. Unrecorded Subsidiary Asset.   All or part of the excess of cost over book value might be attributed to the existence of unrecorded subsidiary assets. These might be specific—such as secret processes or secret formulas—or general—goodwill of the subsidiary. Goodwill of the subsidiary can be described as the going concern value of the subsidiary in excess of the aggregate fair market value of its recorded net assets. In this case, we will assume that all of Company B's recorded assets and liabilities are fairly stated and, therefore, that the entire amount of the excess of cost over book value can be attributed to goodwill of Company B.

Recognizing an unrecorded subsidiary asset in the consolidation process is essentially the same as recognizing an increase in the value of a recorded subsidiary asset, as illustrated in Case 3. The only real difference is the starting point—some positive account balance in the case of an increase versus zero in the case of an unrecorded asset.

The schedule of the excess of cost over book value for Case 4 is shown in Exhibit 6-4. Notice that this schedule is identical to that presented for Case 3 in Exhibit 6-1, except for the title of the asset account. Again, the initial excess, representing Company A's share of Company B's goodwill, is expanded to 100% by dividing the initial amount, $160,000, by Company A's percentage of ownership, 80%.

EXHIBIT 6-4

Illustrative Problem 6.1, Case 4
Excess of Cost over Book Value
June 30, 1991

Excess of Cost over Book Value

Cost of Investment	$ 640,000
Book Value (80% × $600,000)	480,000
Excess of Cost over Book Value	160,000
Expand to 100%	÷ 80%
Goodwill of Company B	$ 200,000

Exhibit 6-5 contains schedules of the adjustments and eliminations for Case 4. Company B's Appraisal Capital recognized in Adjustment B becomes one of its stockholders' equity

balances, 80% of which is eliminated in the Intercompany Ownership Interests set of eliminations. The effect of the worksheet adjustments on the subsequent eliminations is the same
as in Case 3, including the fact that amortization of the goodwill will be recognized in a special
set of eliminations in subsequent worksheets. Remember that no actual journal entry is being
recorded on either affiliate's books. Instead, these are merely worksheet adjustments, which
must be repeated in successive years.

EXHIBIT 6-5

Illustrative Problem 6.1, Case 4
Adjustments and Eliminations
June 30, 1991

Adjustments

A. Goodwill	$ 200,000
B. Appraisal Capital: B	(200,000)

Eliminations

Intercompany Ownership Interests

[1] Common Stock: B	$ 320,000
[2] Additional Paid-in Capital: B	40,000
[3] Retained Earnings: B	120,000
[4] Appraisal Capital: B	160,000
[5] Investment in Company B	$(640,000)

Calculations
[1] 80% × $400,000
[2] 80% × $50,000
[3] 80% × $150,000
[4] 80% × $160,000
[5] Sum of Eliminations [1] through [4]

The consolidation worksheet for Case 4 appears in Exhibit 6-6. Notice that Elimination
[5] entirely eliminates Company A's Investment in Company B balance. This result is appropriate because Adjustment A recognizes as goodwill the asset increment implied by the excess
of cost over book value. Notice also the insertion of a new line to accommodate the recognition
of the goodwill.

Case 5. Goodwill from Consolidation.   Finally, all or part of the excess of cost over book
value might be attributed to goodwill from consolidation, which can be described as an amount
in excess of the parent's share of the aggregate fair market value of the subsidiary's net assets
(including any goodwill of the subsidiary) paid by the parent to gain the advantages of control
over the subsidiary. Such advantages may include assurance of a source of supply of a raw
material, securing an outlet for products, product line diversification, geographical expansion,
etc.

EXHIBIT 6-6

Illustrative Problem 6.1, Case 4
Consolidation Worksheet
June 30, 1991

	Company A	Company B	Adjustments and Eliminations	Balance Sheet
Current Assets	290,000	240,000		530,000
Plant and Equipment	940,000	650,000		1,590,000
Investment in Company B	640,000		[5] (640,000)	
Other Assets	60,000	70,000		130,000
Goodwill			A 200,000	200,000
	1,930,000	960,000		2,450,000
Accumulated Depreciation	310,000	250,000		560,000
Liabilities	260,000	110,000		370,000
Common Stock: A	750,000			750,000
Common Stock: B		400,000	[1] 320,000	80,000 M
Additional Paid-in Capital: A	290,000			290,000
Additional Paid-in Capital: B		50,000	[2] 40,000	10,000 M
Retained Earnings: A	320,000			320,000
Retained Earnings: B		150,000	[3] 120,000	30,000 M
Appraisal Capital: B			B (200,000) ⎱	40,000 M
			[4] 160,000 ⎰	
	1,930,000	960,000		2,450,000

Important distinctions exist between goodwill from consolidation and goodwill of the subsidiary, both conceptually and in their treatment in the consolidation process. **Goodwill from consolidation** is a parent company asset—an excess amount paid by the parent in order to gain the advantages of control over the subsidiary. **Goodwill of the subsidiary** is a subsidiary company asset—the value of the subsidiary as a going concern in excess of the aggregate fair market value of its recorded net assets.

The treatment of goodwill of the subsidiary is illustrated in Case 4 above. In the case of a partially owned subsidiary, worksheet adjustments must be used in order to recognize the full amount of goodwill implied by the parent's excess of cost over book value. These worksheet adjustments, in turn, affect the eliminations that follow, including the recognition of amortization in a special set of eliminations. (These observations apply equally to the treatment of the excess of cost over book value as any subsidiary asset or increment therein.)

Goodwill from consolidation can be handled in several ways. It can be isolated by journal entry on the parent company's books or by a set of worksheet adjustments that debit Goodwill and credit Investment in Subsidiary for the amount of the excess of cost over book value. The easiest, most direct way to deal with goodwill from consolidation, however, is to allow it to emerge as a residual from the Investment in Subsidiary balance, extend it to the Balance Sheet column of the worksheet, and label it "G," as illustrated in Chapter 5. In Case 5, we will assume that the entire amount of the excess of cost over book value represents goodwill from consolidation.

Exhibit 6-7 contains the schedule of the excess of cost over book value for Case 5. Notice that the amount of the excess of cost over book value is also the amount of the goodwill from consolidation at the date of acquisition. No upward expansion is necessary when the excess is treated as a parent company asset. Thus, no worksheet adjustments are necessary (although they could be used, as indicated above.)

EXHIBIT 6-7

Illustrative Problem 6.1, Case 5
Excess of Cost over Book Value
June 30, 1991

Excess of Cost over Book Value

Cost of Investment	$ 640,000
Book Value (80% × $600,000)	480,000
Goodwill from Consolidation	$ 160,000

The eliminations for Case 5 are shown in Exhibit 6-8. The amount eliminated from Investment in Company B in Elimination [4], $480,000, when applied to the $640,000 balance of that account yields a $160,000 debit residual. This residual is extended to the Balance Sheet column of the consolidation worksheet and labeled "G."

EXHIBIT 6-8

Illustrative Problem 6.1, Case 5
Eliminations
June 30, 1991

Elminations

Intercompany Ownership Interests

[1] Common Stock: B	$ 320,000
[2] Additional Paid-in Capital: B	40,000
[3] Retained Earnings: B	120,000
[4] Investment in Company B	$(480,000)

> *Calculations*
> [1] 80% × $400,000
> [2] 80% × $50,000
> [3] 80% × $150,000
> [4] Sum of Elminations [1] through [3]

The amortization of goodwill from consolidation also can be recognized in more than one manner. This amortization could be recorded by journal entry on the parent company's books, whether or not the goodwill itself is isolated from the Investment in Subsidiary account on the parent's books. Alternatively, amortization can be recognized on successive worksheets by means of a special set of eliminations, as described in Case 3. For the sake of consistency, the special set of eliminations is used throughout this text.

The consolidation worksheet for Case 5 appears in Exhibit 6-9. Notice that the $160,000 debit residual is extended to the Balance Sheet column of the consolidation worksheet and labeled "G."

EXHIBIT 6-9

Illustrative Problem 6.1, Case 4
Consolidation Worksheet
June 30, 1991

	Company A	Company B	Adjustments and Eliminations	Balance Sheet
Current Assets	290,000	240,000		530,000
Plant and Equipment	940,000	650,000		1,590,000
Investment in Company B	640,000		[4] (480,000)	160,000 G
Other Assets	60,000	70,000		130,000
	1,930,000	960,000		2,410,000
Accumulated Depreciation	310,000	250,000		560,000
Liabilities	260,000	110,000		370,000
Common Stock: A	750,000			750,000
Common Stock: B		400,000	[1] 320,000	80,000 M
Additional Paid-in Capital: A	290,000			290,000
Additional Paid-in Capital: B		50,000	[2] 40,000	10,000 M
Retained Earnings: A	320,000			320,000
Retained Earnings: B		150,000	[3] 120,000	30,000 M
	1,930,000	960,000		2,410,000

EXCESS OF BOOK VALUE OVER COST

As noted earlier, an excess of book value over cost might be attributed to any one of the following causes or combinations thereof:

- errors on the subsidiary's books,
- errors in recording the parent's cost,
- overvaluation of specific, recorded subsidiary assets,
- aggregate overvaluation of subsidiary net assets, or
- an advantageous purchase on the part of the parent company.

These causes are recognizable as the counterparts of the possible causes of an excess of cost over book value discussed and illustrated in the preceding section. Therefore, with the exception of the last item cited, the accounting treatments accorded the possible causes of an excess of book value over cost parallel those applicable to the causes of an excess of cost over book value.

Each of the possible causes of an excess of book value over cost is discussed and the appropriate accounting treatment of each is illustrated in the context of the five independent cases presented in Illustrative Problem 6.2. Again, each is illustrated as if it were the sole cause of the excess of book value over cost in the situation presented in Illustrative Problem 6.2.

ILLUSTRATIVE PROBLEM 6.2: EXCESS OF BOOK VALUE OVER COST

The trial balances of Company C and Company D immediately after Company C acquired 90% of Company D's common stock on April 30, 1990 are shown below.

	Company C	Company D
Current Assets	$ 320,000	$ 130,000
Plant and Equipment	590,000	490,000
Investment in Company D	360,000	
Other Assets	50,000	95,000
	$1,320,000	$ 715,000
Accumulated Depreciation	$ 220,000	$ 170,000
Liabilities	210,000	105,000
Common Stock ($10 par)	700,000	300,000
Additional Paid-in Capital	70,000	60,000
Retained Earnings	120,000	80,000
	$1,320,000	$ 715,000

Case 1. The excess of book value over cost is caused by an error discovered on the subsidiary's books.

Case 2. The excess of book value over cost is caused by an error in recording the parent company's cost.

Case 3. The excess of book value over cost is attributed to the overvaluation of a specific, recorded subsidiary asset.

Case 4. The excess of book value over cost is attributed to the aggregate overvaluation of subsidiary net assets.

Case 5. The excess of book value over cost is attributed to a bargain purchase made by the parent.

Each case is described more fully, and the appropriate accounting treatment is discussed and illustrated in the following sections.

Case 1. Error on the Subsidiary's Books. Company D's current assets include investments in marketable equity securities that are carried at their cost of $57,000, although their market value has declined to $17,000. This decline in market value is presumed to be permanent. Company D's accountant has failed to record the loss on decline in market value and the attendant reduction in the carrying value of the securities.

The book value of Company C's investment in Company D is $396,000—90% of Company D's net assets of $440,000. Thus, the excess of book value over cost is $396,000 minus $360,000, or $36,000. This $36,000 represents Company C's share, 90% of the total amount of the error, which is $40,000.

Company D should record the following journal entry to correct the error:

Retained Earnings	40,000	
Current Assets (Marketable Securities)		40,000

(If the error were discovered during the accounting period in which it was committed, of course, the debit would be to Loss on Decline in Market Value of Securities.) This journal entry will decrease Company D's net assets (and total stockholders' equity) to $400,000, thus making the cost and book value of Company C's investment in Company D equal (90% of $400,000 equals $360,000). Because this is a real journal entry entered on Company D's books, rather than a consolidation worksheet adjustment, it needs to be recorded only once.

Case 2. Error on the Parent's Books.
Company C acquired its investment in Company D's capital stock by issuing 36,000 shares of its previously unissued $10 par value common stock, which had a market value of 11. Company C's accountant recorded the transaction erroneously at the par value of the common stock issued, $360,000, instead of at its market value of $396,000.

To correct this error, Company C's accountant should record the following journal entry:

Investment in Company D	36,000	
Additional Paid-in Capital		36,000

This journal entry will increase the balance of Company C's Investment in Company D account to $396,000, the book value of the investment. No further consideration of the initial excess of book value over cost is necessary.

Case 3. Overvaluation of a Specific, Recorded Subsidiary Asset.
Company D's plant and equipment includes land that is carried at a cost of $84,000, but has a fair market value of $44,000. Exhibit 6-10 presents the schedule of the excess of book value over cost for Case 3. In this schedule, the initial excess, representing Company C's share of the overvaluation of Company D's land, is expanded to 100% by dividing the initial amount, $36,000, by Company C's percentage of ownership, 90%.

Exhibit 6-11 presents schedules of the adjustments and eliminations for Case 3. In this case, in contrast to those for the undervaluation of a subsidiary asset, the adjustments reduce Company D's Retained Earnings rather than creating a new stockholders' equity account, Appraisal Capital. In effect, the asset overvaluation represents a previously unrecognized loss that is being recognized on the consolidation worksheet through the debit to Company D's Retained Earnings. Remember again that no actual journal entry is being recorded on either affiliate's books. Instead, these are merely worksheet adjustments, which must be repeated in successive years.

EXHIBIT 6-10

Illustrative Problem 6.2, Case 3
Excess of Book Value over Cost
April 30, 1990

Excess of Book Value over Cost

Cost of Investment	$ 360,000
Book Value (90% × $440,000)	396,000
Excess of Book Value over Cost	(36,000)
Expand to 100%	÷ 90%
Decrease in Value of Land	$ (40,000)

EXHIBIT 6-11

Illustrative Problem 6.2, Case 3
Adjustments and Eliminations
April 30, 1990

Adjustments

A. Retained Earnings: D	$ 40,000
B. Plant and Equipment (Land)	(40,000)

Eliminations

Intercompany Ownership Interests

[1] Common Stock: D	$ 270,000
[2] Additional Paid-in Capital: D	54,000
[3] Retained Earnings: D	36,000
[4] Investment in Company D	$(360,000)

Calculations
[1] 90% × $300,000
[2] 90% × $60,000
[3] 90% × ($80,000 − $40,000)
[4] Sum of Elimination [1] through [3]

Again, the worksheet adjustments affect the subsequent eliminations. Elimination [3] is applicable only to the balance of Company D's Retained Earnings remaining after the decrease effected by Adjustment A. Thus, Elimination [3] is made for only $36,000. This has the effect, in turn, of reducing the amount credited to Investment in Company D in Elimination [4].

The consolidation worksheet for Case 3 appears in Exhibit 6-12. Notice that Elimination [4] entirely eliminates Company C's Investment in Company D balance. Notice also that both Adjustment A and Elimination [3] reduce Company D's Retained Earnings balance, causing it to yield a $4,000 minority interest residual.

EXHIBIT 6-12

Illustrative Problem 6.2, Case 3
Consolidation Worksheet
April 30, 1990

	Company C	Company D	Adjustments and Eliminations		Balance Sheet
Current Assets	320,000	130,000			450,000
Plant and Equipment	590,000	490,000	B (40,000)		1,040,000
Investment in Company D	360,000		[4] (360,000)		
Other Assets	50,000	95,000			145,000
	1,320,000	715,000			1,635,000
Accumulated Depreciation	220,000	170,000			390,000
Liabilities	210,000	105,000			315,000
Common Stock: C	700,000				700,000
Common Stock: D		300,000	[1]	270,000	30,000 M
Additional Paid-in Capital: C	70,000				70,000
Additional Paid-in Capital: D		60,000	[2]	54,000	6,000 M
Retained Earnings: C	120,000				120,000
Retained Earnings: D		80,000	A 40,000 [3] 36,000		4,000 M
	1,320,000	715,000			1,635,000

Case 4. Aggregate Overvaluation of Subsidiary Net Assets. In this case, we will assume that because the excess of book value over cost cannot be identified with specific subsidiary assets, it results from an aggregate overvaluation of subsidiary net assets. This treatment will be recognized as the same interpretation used in Chapter 5. In Chapter 5, the expansion of the initial excess of book value over cost and the use of worksheet adjustments were avoided by dealing only with wholly owned subsidiaries in illustrations and problems. If this interpretation is used in connection with a partially owned subsidiary, however, these procedures are necessary.

The schedule of the excess of book value over cost for Case 4 is shown in Exhibit 6-13. Again, the initial excess, representing Company C's share of the aggregate overvaluation of Company D's net assets, is expanded to 100% by dividing the initial amount, $36,000, by Company C's percentage of ownership, 90%.

Exhibit 6-14 presents schedules of the adjustments and eliminations for Case 4. In this case, in contrast to that of the undervaluation of a subsidiary asset, the adjustments reduce Company D's Retained Earnings rather than creating a new stockholders' equity account, Appraisal Capital. Remember that no actual journal entry is being recorded on either affiliate's books. Instead, these are merely worksheet adjustments, which must be repeated in successive years.

EXHIBIT 6-13

Illustrative Problem 6.2, Case 4
Excess of Book Value over Cost
April 30, 1990

Excess of Book Value over Cost

Cost of Investment	$ 360,000
Book Value (90% × $440,000)	396,000
Excess of Book Value over Cost	(36,000)
Expand to 100%	÷ 90%
Overvaluation of Subsidiary Assets	$ (40,000)

EXHIBIT 6-14

Illustrative Problem 6.2, Case 4
Adjustments and Eliminations
April 30, 1990

Adjustments

A. Retained Earnings: D	$ 40,000
B. Allowance for Overvaluation of Subsidiary Assets	(40,000)

Eliminations

Intercompany Ownership Interests

[1] Common Stock: D	$ 270,000
[2] Additional Paid-in Capital: D	54,000
[3] Retained Earnings: D	36,000
[4] Investment in Company D	$(360,000)

Calculations
[1] 90% × $300,000
[2] 90% × $60,000
[3] 90% × ($80,000 − $40,000)
[4] Sum of Eliminations [1] through [3]

Again, the worksheet adjustments affect the subsequent eliminations. Elimination [3] is applicable only to the balance of Company D's Retained Earnings remaining after the decrease effected by Adjustment A. Thus, Elimination [3] is made for only $36,000. This has the effect, in turn, of reducing the amount credited to Investment in Company D in Elimination [4]. Because the excess cannot be associated with a specific subsidiary asset, the credit in Adjustment B is made to an account called Allowance for Overvaluation of Subsidiary Assets. The balance of this account is subtracted from what would otherwise be the total of the assets on the consolidated balance sheet. Notice that the eliminations are identical to those presented for Case 3 in Exhibit 6-11. In addition, the balance of the allowance for Overvaluation of Subsidiary assets will be amortized in successive worksheets through a special set of eliminations. The consolidation worksheet for Case 4 appears in Exhibit 6-15.

EXHIBIT 6-15

Illustrative Problem 6.2, Case 4
Consolidation Worksheet
April 30, 1990

	Company C	Company D	Adjustments and Eliminations		Balance Sheet
Current Assets	320,000	130,000			450,000
Plant and Equipment	590,000	490,000			1,080,000
Investment in Company D	360,000		[4]	(360,000)	
Other Assets	50,000	95,000			145,000
	1,320,000	715,000			1,675,000
Accumulated Depreciation	220,000	170,000			390,000
Liabilities	210,000	105,000			315,000
Common Stock: C	700,000				700,000
Common Stock: D		300,000	[1]	270,000	30,000 M
Additional Paid-in Capital: C	70,000				70,000
Additional Paid-in Capital: D		60,000	[2]	54,000	6,000 M
Retained Earnings: C	120,000				120,000
Retained Earnings: D		80,000	{ A	40,000 }	4,000 M
			{ [3]	36,000 }	
Allowance for Overvaluation of Subsidiary Assets			B	(40,000)	40,000
	1,320,000	715,000			1,675,000

Case 5. Bargain Purchase. The interpretation of an excess of book value over cost as a bargain purchase is the counterpart of goodwill from consolidation, sometimes called "negative goodwill." Because *Accounting Principles Board Opinion No. 16* prohibits the use of this interpretation unless all recorded noncurrent subsidiary assets have been reduced to zero carrying values, it is not illustrated here.[2]

In both Illustrative Problem 6.1 and Illustrative Problem 6.2, each case is based on the assumption of a single cause of the difference between cost and book value. As noted earlier, however, an excess of cost over book value, or vice versa, might be attributed to a combination of causes. Illustrative Problem 6.3 is based on the assumption of multiple causes.

[2] *APB Opinion No. 16*, paragraph 91.

ILLUSTRATIVE PROBLEM 6.3: MULTIPLE CAUSES

The trial balances of Company E and Company F immediately after Company E acquired 75% of Company F's common stock on April 30, 1991 appear below.

	Company E	Company F
Current Assets	$ 460,000	$ 210,000
Plant and Equipment	1,250,000	790,000
Investment in Company B	645,000	
Other Assets	75,000	120,000
	$2,430,000	$1,120,000
Accumulated Depreciation	$ 530,000	$ 250,000
Liabilities	310,000	210,000
Common Stock ($10 par)	800,000	400,000
Additional Paid-in Capital	450,000	90,000
Retained Earnings	340,000	170,000
	$2,430,000	$1,120,000

The book value of Company E's investment in Company F's common stock can be calculated as Company E's percentage of ownership, 75%, multiplied by Company F's net assets (or total stockholders' equity), $660,000, or $495,000. A comparison of the cost of Company E's investment, $645,000, and the book value of that investment, $495,000, yields an excess of cost over book value of $150,000. The following causes of that difference are determined through investigation:

- At the end of the year ended April 30, 1991, Company F's accountant failed to record amortization of certain intangible assets included in Other Assets in the amount of $20,000.
- Company F's plant and equipment has a fair market value of $702,000, compared to its net book value of $540,000.
- Company F's other assets have a fair market value of $70,000, compared to a net book value of $100,000 after adjustment for the unrecorded amortization noted above.
- Any remaining difference between the cost and the book value of Comany E's investment in Company F's common stock is attributed to goodwill of Company F.

Before the consolidation process begins, the following journal entry should be recorded on Company F's books to correct the previous failure to record $20,000 of amortization on its intangible assets:

Retained Earnings	20,000	
Other Assets		20,000

This is a real journal entry, not a consolidation worksheet adjustment; thus, it needs to be recorded only once. In Company F's trial balance that appears in the consolidation worksheet in Exhibit 6-18, the effects of this journal entry are shown. Company F's Other Assets balance is reduced to $100,000 and its Retained Earnings is reduced to $150,000.

The above journal entry has the effect of reducing Company F's net assets to $640,000, thus decreasing the book value of Company E's investment in Company F to $480,000, and, in turn, increasing the excess of cost over book value to $165,000. The remaining components of the excess of cost over book value must be recognized through the use of worksheet adjustments.

The schedule of the excess of cost over book value appears in Exhibit 6-16. The initial excess, $165,000, is expanded to 100% by dividing it by Company E's percentage of ownership, 75%, yielding a total of $220,000. The amounts applicable to recorded subsidiary assets, the undervaluation of Plant and Equipment, $162,000, and the overvaluation of Other Assets, $30,000, are applied against that total, yielding remaining goodwill of $88,000.

EXHIBIT 6-16

Illustrative Problem 6.3
Excess of Cost over Book Value
April 30, 1991

Excess of Cost over Book Value

Cost of Investment		$ 645,000
Book Value (75% × $640,000)		480,000
Excess of Cost over Book Value		165,000
Expand to 100%		÷ 75%
Total Undervaluation of Subsidiary Net Assets		220,000
Undervaluation of Plant and Equipment	$ 162,000	
Overvaluation of Other Assets	(30,000)	132,000
Goodwill of Company F		$ 88,000

Exhibit 6-17 contains schedules of the adjustments and eliminations at April 30, 1991. In making Adjustments A, B, and C, Company F's Accumulated Depreciation balance of $250,000 is assumed to apply proportionately to all plant assets. The amount of the under-valuation, $162,000, is 30% of the net book value, $540,000. Thus, increasing both the Plant and Equipment and Accumulated Depreciation balances by 30% yields a net amount of $702,000, the fair market value. The net amount of the increase, $162,000, is credited to Company F's Appraisal Capital in Adjustment C.

In contrast, Adjustment D reduces Company F's Retained Earnings rather than creating a new stockholders' equity account, Appraisal Capital, thus recognizing the previously un-recognized loss of $30,000. Adjustment E reduces the combined Other Assets balances by $30,000, the amount by which Company F's Other Assets balance exceeds fair market value.

Adjustment F recognizes Company F's previously unrecognized asset, Goodwill. As in the case of the undervaluation of Plant and Equipment, the credit in Adjustment G is to Company F's Appraisal Capital.

EXHIBIT 6-17

Illustrative Problem 6.3
Adjustments and Eliminations
April 30, 1991

Adjustments

A. Plant and Equipment	$ 237,000
B. Accumulated Depreciation	(75,000)
C. Appraisal Capital: F	$(162,000)
D. Retained Earnings: F	$ 30,000
E. Other Assets	(30,000)
F. Goodwill	$ 88,000
G. Appraisal Capital: F	(88,000)

Eliminations

Intercompany Ownership Interests

[1] Common Stock: F	$ 300,000
[2] Additional Paid-in Capital: F	67,500
[3] Retained Earnings: F	90,000
[4] Appraisal Capital: F	187,500
[5] Investment in Company F	$(645,000)

Calculations
[1] 75% × $400,000
[2] 75% × $ 90,000
[3] 75% × ($170,000 − $20,000 − $30,000)
[4] 75% × $250,000
[5] Sum of Eliminations [1] through [4]

Remember that no actual journal entries are being recorded on either affiliate's books. Instead, these are merely worksheet adjustments, which must be repeated in successive years.

As noted in the two previous illustrative problems, the worksheet adjustments affect the subsequent eliminations. In this case, Appraisal Capital totaling $250,000 has been recognized in Adjustments C and G, 75% which must be eliminated in Elimination [4]. Also, Elimination [3] is based on a Company F Retained Earnings balance reduced by $30,000 in Adjustment D. (That balance also has been reduced by the journal entry on page 254.)

The consolidation worksheet for Illustrative Problem 6.3 appears in Exhibit 6-18. Notice that Elimination [5] entirely eliminates Company E's Investment in Co. F balance. This result is appropriate because the entire excess of cost over book value has been allocated to appropriate asset categories through Adjustments A, B, E, and F.

EXHIBIT 6-18

Illustrative Problem 6.3
Consolidation Worksheet
April 30, 1991

	Company E	Company F	Adjustments and Eliminations		Balance Sheet
Current Assets	460,000	210,000			670,000
Plant and Equipment	1,250,000	790,000	A	237,000	2,277,000
Investment in Company F	645,000		[5]	(645,000)	
Other Assets	75,000	100,000	E	(30,000)	145,000
Goodwill			F	88,000	88,000
	2,430,000	1,100,000			3,180,000
Accumulated Depreciation	530,000	250,000	B	(75,000)	855,000
Liabilities	310,000	210,000			520,000
Common Stock: E	800,000				800,000
Common Stock: F		400,000	[1]	300,000	100,000 M
Additional Paid-in Capital: E	450,000				450,000
Additional Paid-in Capital: F		90,000	[2]	67,500	22,500 M
Retained Earnings: E	340,000				340,000
Retained Earnings: F		150,000	D [3]	30,000 / 90,000	30,000 M
Appraisal Capital: F			C G [4]	(162,000) / (88,000) / 187,500	62,500 M
	2,430,000	1,100,000			3,180,000

SUMMARY

Although an excess of cost over book value, or vice versa, clearly should be identified with its particular cause or causes and given appropriate accounting treatment, frequently we see the excess attributed to only a single cause. Attributing the difference between cost and book value to a single cause, however, implies that all other possible causes are inapplicable. Although this position is not always justifiable, it does occur. For example, an excess of cost over book value often is reported simply as "Excess of Parent Company's Cost over Equity in Subsidiary," or words to that effect. In such cases, it is virtually impossible to tell whether the amount reported is the initial amount of the excess or if it has been expanded to 100%.

In cases in which the difference between cost and book value is attributed to a single cause and given an explicit title, that title typically is

- either goodwill of the subsidiary or goodwill from consolidation for an excess of cost over book value, and
- aggregate overvaluation of subsidiary assets for an excess of book value over cost.

In order to be able to emphasize new aspects of the consolidation process in each succeeding chapter, beginning in Chapter 7, the illustrative problems treat any excess of cost over book value as either goodwill of the subsidiary or goodwill from consolidation and any excess of book value over cost as an aggregate overvaluation of subsidiary assets. Some of the exercises and problems at the end of each chapter, however, will attribute the difference between cost and book value to other cause or combinations of causes.

The distinction between the two kinds of goodwill is really a distinction between treating the excess of cost over book value as an asset of the subsidiary or a portion thereof (goodwill of the subsidiary) and treating it as an asset of the parent (goodwill from consolidation). Remember that

- Goodwill of the subsidiary (or any other subsidiary asset) requires expansion of the initial excess upward to 100%, while goodwill from consolidation does not.
- Goodwill of the subsidiary (or any other subsidiary asset) is recognized through worksheet adjustments, while goodwill from consolidation emerges as the residual from the Investment in Subsidiary balance.

Worksheet adjustments affect certain subsequent eliminations by introducing new accounts or by changing balances of existing accounts. For this reason, adjustments always should precede eliminations in the consolidation process.

The excess of cost over book value, regardless of the cause or causes to which we attribute it, requires amortization in subsequent years. In our consolidation process, this amortization is recognized on successive worksheets through a special set of eliminations, as explained in Chapter 7.

Remember that worksheet adjustments and eliminations appear only on the worksheet. They are not recorded on either affiliate's books. Therefore, most worksheet adjustments and eliminations must be repeated year after year.

REVIEW PROBLEM

The trial balances of Company P and Company S immediately after Company P acquired 75% of Company S's common stock appear below.

	Company P	Company S
Current Assets	$ 265,000	$ 130,000
Plant and Equipment	430,000	340,000
Investment in Company S	375,000	
Other Assets	40,000	70,000
	$1,110,000	$ 540,000
Liabilities	$ 220,000	$ 120,000
Common Stock ($10 par)	500,000	200,000
Additional Paid-in Capital	100,000	80,000
Retained Earnings	290,000	140,000
	$1,110,000	$ 540,000

Required

Prepare schedules of the excess of cost over book value, adjustments (if necessary), and eliminations in support of the consolidated balance sheet of Company P and Company S at the date of acquisition if the excess of cost over book value is treated (a) as goodwill of Company S, and (b) as goodwill from consolidation.

QUESTIONS

1. What are the possible causes of an excess of cost over book value?
2. What are the possible causes of an excess of book value over cost?
3. What is the appropriate accounting treatment of an error on the subsidiary's books that causes an excess of cost over book value?
4. What effect does the undervaluation of a specific, recorded subsidiary asset have on the schedule of the excess of cost over book value?
5. In what ways do the worksheet adjustments made in connection with goodwill of the subsidiary affect the eliminations at the date of acquisition?
6. Contrast goodwill of the subsidiary and goodwill from consolidation.
7. Contrast the accounting treatments given the two kinds of goodwill in the consolidation process.
8. How do the worksheet adjustments for the overvaluation of a specific, recorded subsidiary asset affect the subsidiary's stockholders' equity?
9. How do the adjustments mentioned in Question 8 affect the eliminations at the date of acquisition?
10. Do the worksheet adjustments for an aggregate overvaluation of subsidiary assets made at the date of acquisition need to be repeated at the end of the next year? Explain.

EXERCISES

EXERCISE 6-1

Company A purchased 30,000 of Company B's 40,000 shares of $10 par value common stock for $427,500 when Company B's Additional Paid-in Capital balance was $75,000 and its Retained Earnings balance was $45,000. The difference between cost and book value is attributed to the unrecorded increase in the market value of Company B's intangible assets.

Required

Prepare schedules of the difference between cost and book value, any necessary worksheet adjustments, and eliminations at the date of acquisition.

EXERCISE 6-2

Company C purchased 80% of Company D's $200,000 of common stock for $260,000 when Company D's Additional Paid-in Capital balance was $80,000 and its Retained Earnings balance was $85,000. The difference between cost and book value is attributed to an aggregate overvaluation of Company D's assets.

Required

What amount should be eliminated from Company D's Retained Earnings balance in the Intercompany Ownership Interests set of eliminations at the date of acquisition?

a. $42,400
b. $36,000
c. $25,600
d. $68,000

EXERCISE 6-3

Company E purchased 9,000 of Company F's 10,000 shares of $10 par value common stock for $171,000 when Company F's Additional Paid-in Capital balance was $20,000 and its Retained Earnings balance was $50,000.

Required

Prepare schedules of the difference between cost and book value, any necessary worksheet adjustments, and eliminations at the date of acquisition, under each of the following assumptions:

1. The difference between cost and book value is considered to be a payment by Company E to gain the advantage of control over Company F.
2. The difference between cost and book value is considered to represent the going concern value of Company F in excess of the aggregate fair market value of its recorded net assets.

EXERCISE 6-4

On February 28, 1990, Company G purchased all of the issued and outstanding shares of Company H's common stock for $1,500,000 in a transaction properly accounted for as a purchase. The book values and fair values of Company H's assets and liabilities at February 28, 1990 are shown below.

	Book Value	Fair Value
Cash	$ 160,000	$ 160,000
Receivables	180,000	180,000
Inventory	290,000	270,000
Plant and Equipment	870,000	960,000
Liabilities	(350,000)	(350,000)

What amount should be reported as goodwill in the February 28, 1990 consolidated balance sheet?
a. Zero
b. $ 70,000
c. $280,000
d. $350,000

(AICPA adapted)

EXERCISE 6-5

Company J purchased 70% of Company K's $300,000 of common stock for $308,000 when Company K's Additional Paid-in Capital balance was $40,000 and its Retained Earnings balance was $60,000. The difference between cost and book value is attributed to goodwill from consolidation.

Required

Prepare schedules of the difference between cost and book value, any necessary worksheet adjustments, and eliminations at the date of acquisition.

EXERCISE 6-6

Company L purchased 6,500 of Company M's 10,000 shares of $10 par value common stock for $75,400 when Company M's Additional paid-in Capital balance was $70,000 and its Retained Earnings balance was $26,000. The difference between cost and book value is attributed to an unrecorded decrease in the market value of various patents owned by Company M.

Required

Prepare schedules of the difference between cost and book value, any necessary worksheet adjustments, and eliminations at the date of acquisition.

EXERCISE 6-7

On April 1, 1990, Company N purchased all of Company O's outstanding common stock for $400,000 cash. The assets and liabilities of Company O at that date consisted of

Cash	$ 40,000
Inventory	120,000
Plant and Equipment (net)	240,000
Liabilities	90,000

On April 1, 1990, it was determined that Company O's inventory had a fair market value of $95,000 and that its plant and equipment had a fair market value of $280,000.

Required

What amount should appear as goodwill on the April 1, 1990 consolidated balance sheet?
a. Zero
b. $75,000
c. $25,000
d. $90,000

(AICPA adapted)

EXERCISE 6-8

Which of the following is the appropriate basis for valuing plant and equipment acquired in a purchase combination accomplished by exchanging cash for common stock?
a. Original acquisition cost of the assets
b. Book value of the assets
c. Cost plus any excess of purchase price over the book value of the assets
d. Fair value of the assets

(AICPA adapted)

EXERCISE 6-9

On April 30, 1990, Company P purchased all 200,000 outstanding shares of Company Q's outstanding common stock for $30 per share. On this date, the book value of Company Q's net assets was $5,000,000 and their fair market value was $5,600,000. In the consolidated balance sheet at April 30, 1990, what amount should be reported as goodwill?
a. Zero
b. $400,000
c. $600,000
d. $1,000,000

(AICPA adapted)

PROBLEMS

PROBLEM 6-1

The trial balances of Company K and Company L immediately after Company K acquired 75% of Company L's common stock are shown below.

	Company K	Company L
Current Assets	$ 180,000	$ 120,000
Plant and Equipment	600,000	400,000
Investment in Company L	255,000	
Other Assets	20,000	30,000
	$1,055,000	$ 550,000
Accumulated Depreciation	$ 200,000	$ 150,000
Liabilities	95,000	80,000
Common Stock ($10 par)	500,000	200,000
Additional Paid-in Capital	100,000	50,000
Retained Earnings	160,000	70,000
	$1,055,000	$ 550,000

The book values of Company L's recorded net assets approximate their fair market values. The excess of cost over book value is attributed to the going concern value of Company L in excess of the aggregate fair market value of its recorded net assets.

Required
Prepare a consolidation worksheet for Company K and Company L at the date of acquisition, supported by appropriate schedules.

PROBLEM 6-2
The trial balances of Company M and Company N immediately after Company M acquired 80% of Company N's common stock appear below.

	Company M	Company N
Current Assets	$ 100,000	$ 80,000
Plant and Equipment	750,000	340,000
Investment in Company N	364,000	
Other Assets	30,000	60,000
	$1,244,000	$ 480,000
	157,000	
Accumulated Depreciation	$ 350,000	$ 140,000
Liabilities	110,000	40,000
Common Stock ($10 par)	500,000	200,000
Additional Paid-in Capital	50,000	10,000
Retained Earnings	234,000	90,000
	$1,244,000	$ 480,000

The book value of Company N's current assets appears to approximate their aggregate fair market value. Company N's plant and equipment has a fair market value of $280,000 and its other assets have a fair market value of $85,000. The remainder of the excess of cost over book value is attributed to goodwill of Company N.

Required

Prepare a consolidation worksheet for Company M and Company N at the date of acquisition, supported by appropriate schedules.

PROBLEM 6-3

The trial balances of Company P and Company Q immediately after Company P acquired 90% of Company Q's common stock appear below.

	Company P	Company Q
Current Assets	$ 320,000	$ 210,000
Plant and Equipment (net)	639,000	630,000
Investment in Company Q	531,000	
Other Assets	110,000	90,000
	$1,600,000	$ 930,000
Liabilities	$ 410,000	$ 240,000
Common Stock ($10 par)	600,000	400,000
Additional Paid-in Capital	150,000	300,000
Retained Earnings	440,000	(10,000)
	$1,600,000	$ 930,000

The difference between cost and book value is attributed to an aggregate overvaluation of Company Q's net assets.

Required

Prepare a consolidation worksheet for Company P and Company Q at the date of acquisition, supported by appropriate schedules.

PROBLEM 6-4

The trial balances of Company R and Company S immediately after Company R acquired 80% of Company S's common stock appear below.

	Company R	Company S
Current Assets	$ 290,000	$ 190,000
Plant and Equipment	760,000	810,000
Investment in Company S	632,000	
Other Assets	30,000	180,000
	$1,712,000	$1,180,000
Accumulated Depreciation	$ 280,000	$ 360,000
Liabilities	302,000	230,000
Common Stock ($10 par)	500,000	350,000
Additional Paid-in Capital	300,000	150,000
Retained Earnings	330,000	90,000
	$1,712,000	$1,180,000

Company S's current assets have an aggregate fair market value of $160,000. Company S's plant and equipment has a fair market value of $530,000 and its other assets have a fair market value of $195,000. The going concern value of Company S in excess of the fair market value of its recorded net asset is determined to be $100,000. The remainder of the excess of cost over book value is attributed to goodwill from consolidation.

Required
Prepare a consolidation worksheet for Company R and Company S at the date of acquisition, supported by appropriate schedules.

PROBLEM 6-5
The trial balances of Company T and Company U immediately after Company T acquired 70% of Company U's common stock are shown below.

	Company T	Company U
Current Assets	$ 180,000	$ 210,000
Plant and Equipment	610,000	480,000
Investment in Company U	490,000	
Other Assets	40,000	120,000
	$1,320,000	$ 810,000
Liabilities	$ 230,000	$ 170,000
Common Stock ($10 par)	500,000	250,000
Additional Paid-in Capital	250,000	200,000
Retained Earnings	340,000	190,000
	$1,320,000	$ 810,000

The book values of Company U's recorded net assets approximate their fair market values. The aggregate fair market value of Company U's recorded net assets, in turn, approximates the going concern value of Company U. Thus, the difference between cost and book value is considered to be an excess amount paid by Company T to gain the advantages of control over Company U.

Required
Prepare a consolidation worksheet for Company T and Company U at the date of acquisition, supported by appropriate schedules.

PROBLEM 6-6
Refer to Problem 6-5. Prepare a consolidation worksheet for Company T and Company U at the date of acquisition, supported by appropriate schedules, if the difference between cost and book value is considered to be the going concern value of Company U in excess of the aggregate fair market value of its recorded net assets.

PROBLEM 6-7
The trial balance of Company W at March 31, 1990, immediately before Company V acquired all of Company W's common stock for $1,500,000 cash, is shown below.

Cash	$ 100,000
Accounts Receivable	200,000
Inventory	500,000
Plant and Equipment (net)	900,000
	$1,700,000

Current Liabilities	$ 300,000
Long-term Debt	500,000
Common Stock ($1 par)	100,000
Additional Paid-in Capital	200,000
Retained Earnings	600,000
	$1,700,000

On March 31, 1990, the fair market value of Company W's inventory was $450,000 and that of its plant and equipment was $1,000,000. The fair market values of Company W's other assets and liabilities were equal to their book values.

Required

1. The consolidated balance sheet at March 31, 1990 should contain goodwill of
   a. $500,000
   b. $550,000
   c. $600,000
   d. $650,000

2. If Company V's March 31, 1990 retained earnings was $2,000,000, what amount of retained earnings should appear in the March 31, 1990 consolidated balance sheet?
   a. $2,000,000
   b. $2,600,000
   c. $2,800,000
   d. $3,150,000

(AICPA adapted)

PROBLEM 6-8

On July 1, 1991, Company X acquires all of the common stock of Company Y by issuing 4,000 shares of its previously unissued common stock, which have a market value of $50 per share. The transaction is treated as a purchase. With the exception of inventory, the book values of Company Y's recorded assets and liabilities approximate their fair market value. The fair market value of Company Y's inventory is $15,000 greater than its book value. The going concern value of Company Y is determined to be $185,000.

The condensed trial balances of Company X and Company Y immediately before Company X acquires Company Y's common stock are

	Company X	Company Y
Current Assets	$ 200,000	$ 100,000
Plant and Equipment	300,000	150,000
	$ 500,000	$ 250,000

	Company X	Company Y
Liabilities	$ 85,000	$ 105,000
Common Stock ($10 par)	100,000	20,000
Additional Paid-in Capital	170,000	10,000
Retained Earnings	145,000	115,000
	$ 500,000	$ 250,000

Required

1. Company X should record its investment in Company Y at a cost of
  a. $185,000
  b. $160,000
  c. $200,000
  d. $145,000

2. The consolidated balance sheet at July 1, 1991 should contain goodwill of Company Y of
  a. $ 25,000
  b. $ 40,000
  c. $ 15,000
  d. Zero

3. The consolidated balance sheet at July 1, 1991 should contain goodwill from consolidation of
  a. $ 25,000
  b. $ 40,000
  c. $ 15,000
  d. Zero

SOLUTION TO REVIEW PROBLEM

CASE A, Goodwill of Company S

Excess of Cost over Book Value

Cost of Investment	$ 375,000
Book Value (75% × $420,000)	315,000
Excess of Cost over Book Value	60,000
Expand to 100%	÷ 75%
Goodwill of Company S	$ 80,000

Adjustments

A. Goodwill	$ 80,000
B. Appraisal Capital: S	(80,000)

Eliminations

Intercompany Ownership Interests

[1] Common Stock: S	$ 150,000
[2] Additional Paid-in Capital: S	60,000
[3] Retained Earnings: S	105,000
[4] Appraisal Capital: S	60,000
[5] Investment in Company S	$(375,000)

CASE B, Goodwill from Consolidation

Excess of Cost over Book Value

Cost of Investment	$ 375,000
Book Value (75% × $420,000)	315,000
Goodwill from Consolidation	$ 60,000

Eliminations

Intercompany Ownership Interests

[1] Common Stock: S	$ 150,000
[2] Additional Paid-in Capital: S	60,000
[3] Retained Earnings: S	105,000
[4] Investment in Company S	$(315,000)

CONSOLIDATED FINANCIAL STATEMENTS AFTER THE DATE OF ACQUISITION

A fter the date of acquisition, each of the affiliates proceeds with its normal, day-to-day operations. In this chapter, we expand our consideration of the parent–subsidiary relationship and
consolidated financial statement preparation to include these operations. First, we consider
the selection of an accounting method under which the parent company accounts for its
investment in the subsidiary, either

- the cost method, or
- the equity method

and the application of each method.

Second, we add several new elements to the consolidation process:

- Selection of the preclosing trial balance form of consolidation worksheet
- Expansion of the consolidation worksheet to include income statement information
- Expansion of the schedule of the difference between cost and book value to recognize amortization
- Addition of sets of eliminations to deal with subsidiary income and dividends and amortization of the difference between cost and book value
- Addition of an income allocation schedule

ACCOUNTING FOR THE INVESTMENT IN THE SUBSIDIARY

A parent company may use either of two methods to account for its investment in a subsidiary:
the **cost method** or the **equity method.** Under the cost method, the balance of the parent's
Investment in Subsidiary accounts reflects the acquisition cost of the investment, unmodified

except in unusual circumstances, which are explained in the next section. The cost method

- respects the legal boundaries between the two corporations, and
- adheres to the accounting principle of realization with regard to recognizing income of the subsidiary.

Under the equity method, the balance of the parent's Investment in Subsidiary account reflects the acquisition cost of the investment, adjusted for changes in the underlying net assets of the subsidiary. The equity method

- treats the affiliates as parts of a single economic entity, and
- relaxes (or perhaps abandons) the accounting principle of realization with regard to recognizing income of the susidiary.

THE COST METHOD

Under the cost method, the parent company records the cost of its investment in the subsidiary at the date of acquisition by debiting Investment in Subsidiary and crediting whatever account or accounts appropriately reflect the consideration given in exchange. After the date of acquisition, the parent records the declaration of dividends by the subsidiary by debiting Dividends Receivable and crediting Dividend Revenue for its share of the subsidiary's dividends. Later, upon receiving the dividends, the parent debits Cash and credits Dividends Receivable. Under the cost method, the parent does not record its share of the subsidiary's net income at the end of each year.

Two exceptions to the cost method as described above may occur. The first occurs if the subsidiary declares dividends based on retained earnings accumulated before the parent acquired its investment in the subsidiary. These dividends, although perfectly legitimate from the standpoint of the subsidiary, represent a return *of* investment rather than a return *on* investment to the parent. To the parent, such dividends constitute **liquidating dividends.** Thus, the parent would credit Investment in Subsidiary rather than Dividend Revenue in recording these dividends.

The second exception occurs if the market value of the parent's investment in the subsidiary's common stock declines materially and permanently. If this happens, a loss should be recognized and the balance of the Investment in Subsidiary account should be reduced accordingly. Journal entries under the cost method are presented in Exhibit 7-1 of Illustrative Problem 7.1.

THE EQUITY METHOD

Under the equity method, the starting point also is acquisition cost; thus, the cost of the investment is recorded as indicated above for the cost method. In contrast with the cost method, the equity method treats all dividends declared by the subsidiary to the parent as the conversion of a part of one asset, the investment in subsidiary, into another, dividends receivable (and, ultimately, cash). Therefore, the parent records the declaration of dividends by the subsidiary by debiting Dividends Receivable and crediting Investment in Subsidiary for its share of the subsidiary's dividends. Later, upon receiving the dividends, the parent debits Cash and credits Dividends Receivable, just as in the cost method.

In addition, under the equity method, the parent records its share of the periodic net income reported by the subsidiary as a debit to Investment in Subsidiary and a credit to Income from Subsidiary. For each full year of ownership, the parent's share of the subsidiary's net income is calculated by multiplying the parent's percentage of ownership by the subsidiary's net income for the entire year. For the year in which the parent acquires its investment in the subsidiary, the parent's percentage of ownership is multiplied by the subsidiary's net income earned from the date of acquisition through the end of the year. In order to allocate susidiary net income to segments of the year, we will assume that it is earned proportionately throughout the year, unless better evidence is available.[1] For example, if the subsidiary is engaged in a highly seasonal business, that fact would be considered in allocating its net income to segments of the year. In addition, information available from the subsidiary's interim financial statements or from a purchase audit could influence that allocation.

This treatment of subsidiary dividends and net income causes the balance of the Investment in Subsidiary account to reflect changes that occur in the underlying net assets of the subsidiary, in proportion to the parent's ownership interest in the subsidiary. Thus, the equity method maintains the same relationship between the parent's Investment in Subsidiary balance and the subsidiary's net assets that existed at the date of acquisition. This relationship often is referred to as **reciprocity.**

The only exception to the equity method as described above is the same as the second exception to the cost method. That is, if the market value of the parent's investment in the subsidiary's common stock declines materially and permanently, a loss should be recognized and the balance of the Investment in Subsidiary account should be reduced accordingly. Journal entries under the equity method are presented in Exhibit 7-1 of Illustrative Problem 7.1.

ILLUSTRATIVE PROBLEM 7.I: ACCOUNTING FOR THE INVESTMENT

Company P acquired 48,000 of Company S's 60,000 outstanding shares of $5 par value common stock for $608,400 on April 1, 1991, when Company S had additional paid-in capital of $120,000. Company S's December 31, 1990 retained earnings balance was $120,250. In 1991, Company S reported net income of $81,000 and declared and paid dividends of $40,000. In 1992, Company S reported net income of $65,000 and declared and paid dividends of $40,000. In each year, the dividends were declared on November 15 and paid on December 15.

Exhibit 7-1 presents the journal entries that would be recorded on Company P's books under both the cost method and the equity method. Notice that in each year, Company P has recorded its share, 80%, of Company S's dividends, crediting Dividend Revenue under the cost method and Investment in Company S under the equity method.

Company S's net income from April 1, 1991 through the end of 1991 is 9/12 of $81,000, or $60,750, which is greater than its 1991 dividends of $40,000. Also, Company S's 1992 net income of $65,000 is greater than its 1992 dividends of $40,000. Thus, none of the dividends could be based on Company S's retained earnings accumulated prior to Company P's acquisition of its investment in Company S. Accordingly, under the cost method, Company

---

[1] *Accounting Research Bulletin No. 51, Consolidated Financial Statements* (New York: AICPA, 1959), paragraph 10.

EXHIBIT 7-I

Illustrative Problem 7.1
Journal Entries under the Cost and Equity Methods

Cost Method			Equity Method		
			4/1/91		
Investment in Company S	608,400		Investment in Company S	608,400	
Cash		608,400	Cash		608,400
			11/15/91		
Dividends Receivable	32,000		Dividends Receivable	32,000	
Dividend Revenue		32,000	Investment in Company S		32,000
			12/15/91		
Cash	32,000		Cash	32,000	
Dividends Receivable		32,000	Dividends Receivable		32,000
			12/31/91		
NO ENTRY			Investment in Company S	48,600	
			Income from Company S		48,600
			11/15/92		
Dividends Receivable	32,000		Dividends Receivable	32,000	
Dividend Revenue		32,000	Investment in Company S		32,000
			12/15/92		
Cash	32,000		Cash	32,000	
Dividends Receivable		32,000	Dividends Receivable		32,000
			12/31/92		
NO ENTRY			Investment in Company S	52,000	
			Income from Company S		52,000

P's share of these dividends is properly recorded as dividend revenue. Under the Equity method, the source of the dividends is irrelevant because Company P treats its share of *all* Company S dividends as a reduction in its Investment in Company S account balance.

Also, at the end of each year, Company P records its share of Company S's net income under the equity method, but not under the cost method. For 1991, Company P's share is 80% of Company S's net income earned from April 1, the date of acquisition, through December 31 (80% × 9/12 × $81,000). For 1992, Company P's share is 80% of Company S's net income for the entire year (80% × $65,000).

The effects of these journal entries on Company P's Investment in Company S account under each of the two methods are summarized in Exhibit 7-2. In 1991, the equity method adds $16,600 more to Company P's Retained Earnings than does the cost method. In 1992, the equity method adds $20,000 more, for a two-year total of $36,600. Similarly, Company

P's Investment in Company S balance increases by $16,600 in 1991 and by $20,000 in 1992 under the equity method, but does not change under the cost method.

EXHIBIT 7-2

Illustrative Problem 7.1
Schedule of Investment in Company S Balances

	Cost Method	Equity Method
Cost of Investment, 4/1/91	$ 608,400	$ 608,400
Dividends, 11/15/91	—	(32,000)
Net Income, 1991	—	48,600
Balance, 12/31/91	608,400	625,000
Dividends, 11/15/92	—	(32,000)
Net Income, 1992	—	52,000
Balance, 12/31/92	$ 608,400	$ 645,000

Liquidating Dividends.   Suppose that Company S had declared and paid dividends of $40,000 in 1991, but reported net income of only $45,000. Under the cost method, 80% of 9/12 of $45,000, or $27,000, of these dividends represents dividend revenue to Company P, but 80% of the remainder of Company S's dividends, or $5,000, represents a return of part of its investment in Company S. As noted earlier, this $5,000 portion constitutes a liquidating dividend to Company P.

If Company P could have known the amount of Company S's 1991 net income at November 15, the dividend declaration date, it would have recorded the following journal entry under the cost method:

Dividends Receivable	32,000	
Dividend Revenue		27,000
Investment in Company S		5,000

Because Company S's net income is not determined until the end of the year, however, Company P actually would have recorded its share of Company S's dividends in exactly the same manner shown in Exhibit 7-1:

Dividends Receivable	32,000	
Dividend Revenue		32,000

At the end of 1991, Company P would adjust its Dividend Revenue account by recording the following journal entry:

Dividend Revenue	5,000	
Investment in Company S		5,000

which would produce the desired result.

WHICH METHOD SHOULD BE USED?

As illustrated later in this chapter, the consolidated financial statements produced using the cost method are identical to those resulting from the equity method. The choice, therefore, is one of approach rather than result.

The equity method maintains reciprocity between the parent's Investment in Subsidiary balance and the subsidiary's net assets in which the parent has invested. This maintenance of reciprocity enables the various worksheet eliminations that affect the parent's Investment in Subsidiary account and the subsidiary's common stockholders' equity accounts to produce the appropriate results without additional adjustment of their balances. Also, because the parent includes in its net income its share of the subsidiary's net income, the equity method also yields the appropriate balance in the parent's Retained Earnings account. Thus, the equity method facilitates the preparation of consolidated financial statements.

The cost method, on the other hand, mantains the parent's Investment in Susidiary account balance at acquisition cost (with the two exceptions noted earlier). Also, the parent's Retained Earnings balance reflects subsidiary net income only to the extent that it has been declared to the parent in the form of dividends. Thus, the parent's Retained Earnings balance under the cost method will be less than that produced under the equity method by the difference between the parent's share of the subsidiary's net income and the parent's share of the subsidiary's dividends since the date of acquisition. Therefore, it is necessary to convert the parent's Investment in Subsidiary and Retained Earnings balances from cost to equity by means of worksheet adjustments before proceeding to the eliminations. Otherwise, the eliminations used under the cost method will be completely different from those used under the equity method. This conversion procedure is shown in Exhibit 7-9 of Illustrative Problem 7.2.

How do the requirements of *Accounting Principles Board Opinion No. 18, The Equity Method of Accounting for Investment in Common Stock* affect the choice between the cost and equity methods? In brief, *APB Opinion No. 18* divides investments in common stock into three categories:

- those in which the investor has *control* over the investee (greater than 50% ownership),
- those in which the investor has *significant influence,* but not control, over the investee (20% to 50% ownership), and
- those in which the investor has *no significant influence* over the investee (less than 20% ownership).[2]

For investments in the control category, *APB Opinion No. 18* reaffirms the presumption that the preparation of consolidated financial statements is appropriate.[3] As noted earlier, either the cost method or the equity method can be used to accomplish this purpose.

For investments in the significant influence category, *APB Opinion No. 18* requires the use of what it calls "the equity method of accounting." This is the equity method as described earlier in this chapter, modified to give effect to the amortization of the difference between cost and book value, however that difference might be interpreted, and of eliminations that would be made for unrealized intercompany profits and losses if consolidated financial state-

---

[2] *Accounting Principles Board Opinion No. 18, The Equity Method of Accounting for Investments in Common Stock* (New York: AICPA, 1971), paragraphs 3.c., 17.

[3] *APB Opinion No. 18,* paragraphs 4, 14.

ments were being prepared. This treatment also is appropriate for unconsolidated subsidiaries, either in consolidated financial statements or in separate parent company financial statements.[4]

For investments in the no significant influence category, *APB Opinion No. 18* requires the use of the cost method of accounting and reporting, which is essentially the same as the cost method described earlier in this chapter.[5]

In summary, *APB Opinion No. 18* is concerned primarily with appropriate reporting by an investor of its ownership interest in an investee when consolidated financial statements are not prepared. It does not dictate the use of either the cost method or the equity method when consolidated financial statements are contemplated. Thus, we must conclude that either method is acceptable.

Under the equity method, the parent company records its share of the changes in the subsidiary's net assets annually in its Investment in Subsidiary and Income from Subsidiary accounts. This allows the accountant to construct the eliminations of intercompany balances in a straightforward manner, without the need for the conversion from cost to equity described above. Thus, the equity method is the more convenient of the two methods.

CONSOLIDATED FINANCIAL STATEMENTS AFTER THE DATE OF ACQUISITION

In preparing consolidated financial statements as of the first reporting date after the parent has acquired its investment in the subsidiary (and, indeed, as of subsequent reporting dates), several changes in and adjustments to the consolidation process presented in Chapters 5 and 6 are necessary. These changes and additions are discussed and illustrated in the remainder of this chapter, as well as in subsequent chapters, in the context of a business combination accounted for as a purchase. The consolidation process for a pooling of interests is presented in Appendix 7-B.

FORMAT OF THE CONSOLIDATION WORKSHEET

First, we must choose the format of the consolidation worksheet that we will use. One popular format arranges the affiliates' account balances in sections corresponding to the major financial statements (balance sheet data in one section, income statement data in another, etc.). This format is illustrated in Appendix 7-A, which follows Chapter 7. An alternative, which is used throughout the remainder of this book, is the preclosing trial balance format. We have chosen this format because

- it resembles the familiar end-of-the-period worksheet used in preparing single-entity financial statements, which tends to make it easier to learn to use, and
- it is economical to use in that it minimizes the number of times that one needs to enter a given account title, a given amount, etc.

---

[4] *APB Opinion No. 18*, paragraphs 14, 17, 19.

[5] *APB Opinion No. 18*, paragraphs 6.b., 17.

For a given set of data, the consolidated financial statements prepared using the different worksheet formats are identical. Therefore, the choice of one format over another is purely a pragmatic one.

The preclosing trial balance worksheet is based on the assumption that each affiliate has recorded its transactions for the accounting period just ended, as well as its normal end-of-the-period adjustments, but has not recorded its closing entries. Thus, the trial balances will contain

- balances for revenues, expenses, and related accounts,
- beginning-of-the-period balances of Retained Earnings for each affiliate,
- a Dividends Declared balance for each affiliate that has declared dividends (assuming that a Dividends Declared account, rather than Retained Earnings, is debited to record the declaration of dividends),
- in the case of a periodic inventory system, beginning-of-the-period inventory balances,
- in the case of a perpetual inventory system, end-of-the-period inventory balances, and
- the end-of-the-period balance of the parent's Investment in Subsidiary account.

The trial balances are arranged in the "over-and-under" format illustrated in Chapter 5. Each affiliate's trial balance is contained in a single column in which all debit balances and their total appear first, followed by all credit balances and their total.

Second, the worksheet must be expanded horizontally to include a pair of columns (debit and credit) to collect the income statement data. These columns, labeled Income Statement, are inserted between the Adjustments and Eliminations column and the Balance Sheet column. Although the "over-and-under" format could be used for a single Income Statement column, separate debit and credit columns are more convenient. This expanded worksheet format is shown in Exhibit 7-6.

SUBSIDIARY INCOME AND DIVIDENDS ELIMINATIONS UNDER THE EQUITY METHOD

When consolidated financial statements are prepared after the date of acquisition, an additional set of eliminations is necessary to deal with the intercompany balances that result from using either the equity method or the cost method to account for the parent's investment in the subsidiary.

If the parent uses the equity method, it will have recorded its share of the subsidiary's net income as a credit to Income from Subsidiary (or to a miscellaneous revenue account such as Other Income). If it is using the cost method, it will have credited Dividend Revenue (or a miscellaneous revenue account such as Other Income) for the dividends declared to it by the subsidiary. (Illustrations of these journal entries appear in Exhibit 7-1). In either case, the amount recorded by the parent represents a portion of the subsidiary's net income. As part of the consolidation process, however, we will combine the subsidiary's revenues and expenses with the corresponding balances of the parent in arriving at total net income. This total net income is allocated between the minority interest in the subsidiary's net income and consolidated net income. Thus, the amount of subsidiary net income previously recorded by the parent must be eliminated in order to avoid double-counting.

The subsidiary's Dividend Declared account is a temporary stockholders' equity account that has not yet been closed to its Retained Earnings account. Its debit balance indicates that it represents a negative component of the subsidiary's stockholders' equity. Therefore, the parent's ownership share must be eliminated from the subsidiary's Dividends Declared balance just as it is from the other subsidiary stockholders' equity balances in the Intercompany Ownership set of eliminations. Any difference is debited or credited to the parent's Investment in Subsidiary account. The Subsidiary Income and Dividends set of eliminations under the equity method is shown in Exhibit 7-4 of Illustrative Problem 7.2.

A Problem-Solving Tip. Sometimes the problem will not state whether the parent is using the cost method or the equity method to account for its investments in the subsidiary, but clues can be gathered from the parent's preclosing trial balance.

- If the parent's Investment in Subsidiary balance is greater than the cost of the investment, the parent must be using the equity method (unless, of course, the parent has purchased additional subsidiary common stock, a topic that is not introduced until Chapter 12).
- If the parent's trial balance contains an Income from Subsidiary account, the parent must be using the equity method. Sometimes this clue is obscured because the parent has recorded its share of the subsidiary's net income in a different account, such as Other Income. If this is true, rely on the previous clue.
- If the balance of the parent's Investment in Subsidiary account is the same as the cost of the investment, the parent almost certainly is using the cost method.
- If the parent's trial balance contains a Dividend Revenue account, the parent probably is using the cost method. (It is possible, however, that the parent owned stock in some other company during the year and that the Dividend Revenue balance resulted from that other investment.) On the other hand, this clue may be obscured because the parent has recorded its share of the subsidiary's dividends in a different account, such as Other Income. If this is true, rely on the previous clue.

AMORTIZATION OF THE DIFFERENCE BETWEEN COST AND BOOK VALUE

After the date of acquisition, the difference between the cost of the parent's investment and its book value, however it is identified, must be amortized over its estimated useful life. If the difference is identified as belonging to the parent (that is, as goodwill from consolidation), it could be amortized either on the parent's books or on successive consolidation worksheets by means of a series of special sets of elminations. If the difference is identified as a positive or negative subsidiary asset element, it must be recognized by worksheet adjustment, as discussed and illustrated in Chapter 6. For the sake of consistency, we will assume throughout the remainder of this book that amortization of the difference between cost and book value always is recognized through worksheet eliminations, regardless of how it is identified. In order to be able to emphasize new aspects of the consolidation process, in Chapter 7 and each succeeding chapter, the illustrative problems treat any excess of cost over book value as either goodwill of the subsidiary or goodwill from consolidation and any excess of book value over cost as an aggregate overvaluation of subsidiary assets.

Two modifications in the consolidation process are necessary in order to recognize amortization of the difference between cost and book value. First, the Excess of Cost over Book Value (or vice versa) schedule is extended beyond the determination of the total amount of the excess to show amortization for all prior years and for the current year, arriving at a year-end balance of the asset element in question. Such a schedule appears in Exhibit 7-3.

Second, a special set of eliminations must be introduced to recognize the amortization of the difference between cost and book value. Amortization for all prior years is debited to one or both Retained Earnings balances, depending on whose asset is being amortized. If goodwill from consolidation (a parent company asset) is being amortized, or if the subsidiary is wholly owned, only the parent's Retained Earnings will be affected. If a partially owned subsidiary asset is being amortized, the prior years' amortization must be allocated between the parent's and the subsidiary's Retained Earnings balances. (This point is discussed more thoroughly in the solution to Illustrative Problem 7.2.)

An appropriate expense account is debited for the current year's amortization of an excess of cost over book value. The total amount of amortization to date is credited to Investment in Subsidiary (for goodwill from consolidation) or to the subsidiary asset or assets debited in the worksheet adjustment to recognize the excess, whichever is appropriate. (If a depreciable asset is involved, the related accumulated depreciation balance would be credited.) If the difference is an excess of book value over cost, of course, the debits and credits are reversed. This special set of eliminations follows the Subsidiary Income and Dividends set, described above, in the consolidation process. It appears in Exhibit 7-4 of Illustrative Problem 7.2.

TREATMENT OF INVENTORIES IN THE WORKSHEET

The treatment of inventories in the consolidation worksheet depends on the inventory system in use by each affiliate, periodic or perpetual. A brief review of these alternative inventory systems is appropriate at this point.

In the periodic inventory system, the beginning inventory of the accounting period is the balance of the Inventory account throughout the period. Purchases of merchandise are debited to a Purchase account. (Related accounts such as Transportation-in, Purchase Returns and Allowances, and Purchase Discounts also are used. In combination with the Purchases account, they measure the net cost of merchandise purchased.) At the end of the accounting period, the ending inventory is determined through a physical inventory count. As part of the closing entries, the beginning balance of the Inventory account (a debit), the net cost of merchandise purchased (a net debit), and the cost of ending inventory (a credit) are combined to determine the cost of goods sold. The ending inventory replaces the beginning inventory as the balance of the Inventory account, and becomes the beginning inventory of the following accounting period. Thus, the preclosing trial balance of an affiliate using the periodic inventory system will contain beginning inventory as the balance of the Inventory account, as well as Purchases (and related accounts).

In the perpetual inventory system, the Inventory account is debited for the cost of each purchase of merchandise. When merchandise is sold, Cost of Goods Sold is debited and Inventory is credited for the cost of that merchandise. At the end of the accounting period, a physical inventory count is conducted only to verify the ending balance of the Inventory account. Thus, the preclosing trial balance of an affiliate using the perpetual inventory system will contain ending inventory as the balance of the Inventory account and Cost of Goods Sold.

When both affiliates use periodic inventory systems, the easiest, most efficient way to handle inventories in the consolidation worksheet is as follows:

- Add together the beginning inventory balances that appear in the trial balance columns and extend the combined amount to the Income Statement debit column, where it becomes an addition in determining cost of goods sold.
- Enter the amount of the combined ending inventories in the Income Statement credit column (a subtraction in determining cost of goods sold) and as a debit in the Balance Sheet column (an asset). (See Exhibit 7-7 of Illustrative Problem 7.2.)

When both affiliates use perpetual inventory systems, their Inventory balances are the ending inventories. Thus, the Inventory balances can be added together and the total extended to the Balance Sheet column as a debit. Also, the affiliates' trial balances contain Cost of Goods Sold balances, which can be added together and extended to the Income Statement debit column.

If the affiliates are using different inventory systems, the Inventory account balances contained in their preclosing trial balances cannot be combined. Instead, the easiest, most efficient way to proceed is as follows:

- When entering the trial balances on the consolidation worksheet, place the Inventory balances on separate lines.
- Extend the Inventory balance of the periodic affiliate (beginning inventory) to the Income Statement debit column.
- Enter the periodic affiliate's ending inventory as a credit in the Income Statement columns and as a debit in the Balance Sheet column.
- Extend the Inventory balance of the perpetual affiliate (ending inventory) to the Balance Sheet column as a debit.
- Bracket the two ending inventory amounts to indicate that they are to be combined in the consoliated balance sheet. (This bracketing device also is useful when two or more adjustments or eliminations affect a given account. It is demonstrated in Exhibit 7-7 of Illustrative Problem 7.2.)

A Problem-Solving Tip. The problem may not state whether the affiliates are using periodic or perpetual inventory systems, but clues are available in the preclosing trial balances.

- If an affiliate's trial balance contains an Inventory balance and a Cost of Goods Sold balance, the affiliate must be using a perpetual inventory system.
- If an affiliate's trial balance contains an Inventory balance and a Purchases balance, and its ending inventory balance also is given, the affiliate must be using a periodic inventory system.

ALLOCATION OF NET INCOME

Finally, it is necessary to allocate the total net income (the combined net incomes of all affiliates) between the **minority interest in the subsidiary's net income** and **consolidated net income.** Consolidated net income consists of

- the parent's net income *from its own operations*, plus or minus any adjustments to it arising from the consolidation process, plus
- the parent's share of the subsidiary's net income, plus or minus any adjustments to it arising from the consolidation process.

The parent's net income from its own operations does not include either income from the subsidiary (under the equity method) or dividend revenue (under the cost method).

One or the other of the net incomes must be adjusted for *any change in total net income caused by worksheet eliminations.* Any elimination that increases or decreases any revenue or expense balance (including cost of goods sold) will change the total amount of net income determined in the Income Statement columns of the consolidation worksheet and, therefore, must be taken into account in allocating that total. So far, the only such item that we have encountered is the additional expense introduced to recognize the amortization of the difference between cost and book value.

Each adjustment is made to the net income of the affiliate that originated the item in question. For example, the current period amortization of goodwill from consolidation would cause an adjustment to the parent's net income. In contrast, the current period amortization of goodwill of the subsidiary would cause an adjustment to the subsidiary's net income.

Obviously, the direction of the adjustment must be the same as the effect of that item on total net income. Eliminations that either increase expenses or decrease revenues will cause a decrease in total net income, whereas those that either decrease expenses or increase revenues will cause an increase in total net income. Adjustments for items that reduce total net income must reduce the originating affiliate's net income, and vice versa.

The amounts of minority interest in the subsidiary's net income and consolidated net income determined in the Income Allocation schedule are entered in the consolidation worksheet as balancing figures in the Income Statement and Balance Sheet columns. This procedure and the Income Allocation schedule are shown in Exhibits 7-7 and 7-4, respectively, of Illustrative Problem 7.2.

ILLUSTRATIVE PROBLEM 7.2: CONSOLIDATION UNDER THE EQUITY METHOD

Illustrative Problem 7.2 is a continuation of Illustrative Problem 7.1, information from which is repeated here. Company P acquired 48,000 of Company S's 60,000 outstanding shares of $5 par value common stock for $608,400 on April 1, 1991, when Company S had additional paid-in capital of $120,000. Company S's December 31, 1990 retained earnings balance was $120,250. In 1991, Company S reported net income of $81,000 and declared and paid dividends of $40,000. In 1992, Company S reported net income of $65,000 and declared and paid dividends of $40,000. In each year, the dividends were declared on November 15 and paid on December 15.

In addition, the following information is available. The excess of cost over book value is being treated as goodwill of Company S, amortized over 10 years. (This treatment implies that the book values of Company S's assets and liabilities are equal to their fair market values and that no other unrecognized Company S assets exist.) Company P uses the equity method to account for its investment in Company S. December 31, 1992 inventories are: Company P, $82,200; Company S, $90,800. Company P's 1992 net income from its own operations was $89,400.

Exhibit 7-3 presents the expanded Excess of Cost over Book Value schedule at December 31, 1992 and the related worksheet adjustments, as discussed above.

Because Company P acquired its investment in Company S on April 1, 1991, it is necessary to update Company S's retained earnings balance from December 31, 1990 through March

EXHIBIT 7-3

Illustrative Problem 7.2
Excess of Cost over Book Value and Adjustments
December 31, 1992

Excess of Cost over Book Value

Cost of Investment		$ 608,400
Book Value (80% × $560,500)		448,400
Excess of Cost over Book Value		160,000
Expand to 100%		÷ 80%
Goodwill, 4/1/91		200,000
Amortization through 12/31/91	$ 15,000	
Amortization, 1992	20,000	35,000
Goodwill, 12/31/92		$ 165,000

Adjustments

A. Goodwill	$ 200,000
B. Appraisal Capital: S	(200,000)

31, 1991 in calculating the book value of the investment. This is done by adding net income for the first three months of 1991 (3/12 of $81,000) to the December 31, 1990 balance of $120,250. (If Company S had declared dividends in 1991 before the date of acquisition, these would have been subtracted.) Company S's total stockholders' equity at April 1, 1991 consists of common stock of $300,000, plus additional paid-in capital of $120,000, plus December 31, 1990 retained earnings of $120,250, plus three months' net income of $20,250, for a total of $560,500.

As explained in Chapter 6, it is necessary to expand the initial excess of cost over book value to 100% because it is identified as an asset element (goodwill) of the partially owned subsidiary, Company S. The initial amount of the excess represents only the parent's share, 80%, of the amount of the subsidiary's unrecorded asset. Therefore, the full amount of the goodwill is determined by dividing the excess of cost over book value by the parent's percentage of ownership. The upward expansion of the excess of cost over book value is necessary whenever the excess is attributed to the undervaluation of assets of a partially owned subsidiary.

Also, the schedule recognizes amortization of the goodwill for nine months of the one prior year, 1991, and for the current year, 1992. The balance of the goodwill at December 31, 1992, $165,000, is the amount that should emerge in the Balance Sheet column of the consolidation worksheet.

The pair of worksheet adjustments, labeled A and B, enable us to recognize both the subsidiary asset, Goodwill, and the ownership interest therein, Company S's Appraisal Capital. Two points noted in Chapter 6 are worth repeating here. First, because these adjustments affect subsequent eliminations, it is important to distinguish between adjustments and eliminations and to make any necessary adjustments before making any eliminations. Second, it is important to remember that worksheet adjustments are made only on the worksheet. They are not recorded on either affiliate's books. Thus, they must be repeated each time a worksheet is prepared.

Exhibit 7-4 presents all worksheet eliminations that we have encountered up to this point. The Intercompany Ownership Interests set of eliminations is affected in two ways by Adjustment B, which recognizes Company S's Appraisal Capital. First, 80% of the balance of Company S's Appraisal Capital is eliminated in Elimination [4], leaving the minority interest therein as a residual. Second, the presence of Elimination [4] increases the amount of Elimination [5] by $9,000, thus removing the initial excess of cost over book value from Company P's Investment in Company S balance. Notice also that the amount of Elimination [3] is based on Company S's Retained Earnings balance at the *beginning* of 1992.

Elimination [8] reestablishes reciprocity between Company P's Investment in Company S balance and the net assets of Company S, as reflected in its stockholders' equity balances, *as of the beginning of 1992.* This is necessary because Company S's Retained Earnings balance, on which Elimination [5] is based in part, is the beginning-of-the-year balance.

The Goodwill Amortization set of eliminations enables us to recognize amortization of the goodwill of Company S in the consolidation worksheet and, hence, in the consolidated financial statements. The prior year's amortization is divided between the two Retained Earnings balances in Eliminations [9] and [10]. Elimination [11] recognizes the current year's amortization expense. Elimination [12] reduces Goodwill to its December 31, 1992 balance.

In every set of eliminations in which allocations between or among Retained Earnings balances are necessary, each affiliate's Retained Earnings should have allocated to it [a] that affiliate's *external ownership percentage,* multiplied by [b] its *share of the quantity being allocated,* multiplied by [c] *the quantity being allocated.* An affiliate's external ownership percentage is the portion of its common stock owned by stockholders outside the affiliate group. An affiliate's share of the quantity being allocated is its ownership interest in that quantity, either directly or indirectly through stock ownership.

In this case, Company P's external ownership percentage is 100%. (Company S, the only other member of the affiliated group, does not own any of Company P's common stock; therefore, all of Company P's common stock is owned externally.) Company P's share of the quantity being allocated (the prior year's amortization of Company S's goodwill) is 80%, because the goodwill belongs to Company S and Company P owns 80% of Company S's common stock.

Company S's external ownership percentage (the portion of its common stock owned by the minority stockholders) is 20%. Its share of the quantity being allocated is 100% because the goodwill being amortized belongs to Company S.

In summary, the allocation can be expressed as

	[a]	×	[b]	×	[c]	=	[d]
	External Ownership Pecentage		Share of Quantity Being Allocated		Quantity Being Allocated		Amount Allocated
Company P	100%	×	80%	×	$15,000	=	$12,000
Company S	20%	×	100%	×	$15,000	=	3,000
Total							$15,000

EXHIBIT 7-4

Illustrative Problem 7.2
Equity Method Eliminations
December 31, 1992

Eliminations

Intercompany Ownership Interests

[1]	Common Stock: S	$ 240,000
[2]	Additional Paid-in Capital: S	96,000
[3]	Retained Earnings: S	129,000
[4]	Appraisal Capital: S	160,000
[5]	Investment in Company S	$(625,000)

Subsidiary Income and Dividends

[6]	Income from Company S	$ 52,000
[7]	Dividends Declared: S	(32,000)
[8]	Investment in Company S	$ (20,000)

Goodwill Amortization

[9]	Retained Earnings: P	$ 12,000
[10]	Retained Earnings: S	3,000
[11]	Operating Expenses	20,000
[12]	Goodwill	$ (35,000)

Calculations

[1]	80% × $300,000
[2]	80% × $120,000
[3]	80% × $161,250
[4]	80% × $200,000
[5]	Sum of Eliminations [1] through [4]
[6]	80% × $65,000
[7]	80% × $40,000
[8]	Elimination [6] minus Elimination [7]
[9]	100% × 80% × $15,000
[10]	20% × 100% × $15,000
[11]–[12]	From Excess of Cost over Book Value Schedule

The allocation of the prior year's amortization between the two Retained Earnings balances also can be explained as follows:

- If Company S somehow could have recorded the goodwill of $200,000 on its books, it would have recorded amortization expense of $15,000 in 1991, thereby reducing its 1991 net income by $15,000.
- Company S's ending balance of Retained Earnings for 1991 (which also is its beginning balance for 1992) would have been $15,000 less. Thus, Elmination [3] would have been $12,000 less and would have yielded a $3,000 smaller minority interest residual.

Elimination [10] reduces the minority interest in Company S's Retained Earnings by $3,000.

- Under the equity method, Company P would have recorded $12,000 less income from Company S in 1991, thereby reducing its ending balance of Retained Earnings for 1991 (also the beginning balance for 1992) by $12,000. Elimination [9] removes this $12,000 from Company P's Retained Earnings balance.

Throughout the schedules of adjustments and eliminations, all stockholders' equity balances are labeled by company name. It is necessary to distinguish the stockholders' equity accounts of each affiliate from those of the other because they will be treated differently in the consolidation process; that is, their balances will not be combined with those of the corresponding accounts of the other affiliate. The parent's stockholders' equity balances become the stockholders' equity of the consolidated entity, whereas those of the subsidiary are modified by worksheet eliminations and yield minority interest residuals. All other accounts either are unique or their balances will be combined with those of the corresponding accounts of the other affiliate; thus, they do not need to be labeled as to company.

Exhibit 7-5 contains the Income Allocation schedule, in which the total net income is allocated between the minority interest in Company S's net income and consolidated net income. Remember that consolidated net income consists of

- the parent's net income from its own operations, plus or minus any adjustments to it arising from the consolidation process, plus
- the parent's share of the subsidiary's net income, plus or minus any adjustments to it arising from the consolidation process.

EXHIBIT 7-5

Illustrative Problem 7.2
Income Allocation Schedule
Year Ended December 31, 1992

Income Allocation

Company P's Own Net Income		$ 89,400
Company S's Own Net Income	$ 65,000	
Less: Goodwill Amortization Expense	20,000	
Company S's Adjusted Net Income	45,000	
Minority Interest (20%)	9,000	
Company P's Share (80%)		36,000
Consolidated Net Income		$ 125,400

Although the two affiliates' 1992 separate net incomes are given in Illustrative Problem 7.2, it is often necessary to calculate the net incomes by reference to the affiliates' preclosing trial balances. Although one could actually construct a separate income statement for each affiliate, the most expedient way to calculate their separate net incomes is to compare the total of each affiliate's income statement credit elements with the total of its income statement debit elements. (Remember that ending inventories in a periodic inventory system will become income statement credits.)

The December 31, 1992 preclosing trial balances of Company P and Company S appear in Exhibit 7-6. Company P's income statement credits consist of Sales of $827,400, Other Income of $20,500, and ending inventory of $82,200, for a total of $930,100. Its income statement debits consist of beginning inventory of $79,600, Purchases of $456,900, and Operating Expenses of $304,200, for a total of $840,700. The difference between the two totals is $89,400, the amount of Company P's own net income. Notice that the Income from Company S balance of $52,000 was omitted from the calculation of Company P's own net income. In order for the Income Allocation schedule to allocate *total* net income between minority interest in the subsidiary's net income and consolidated net income, it must begin with each affiliate's net income *from its own operations,* not including any share of the other affiliate's net income. Thus, income from the subsidiary (under the equity method) or dividend revenue (under the cost method) must be excluded in calculating the parent company's net income.

Company S's income statement credits consist of Sales of $932,800, Other Income of $5,700, and ending inventory of $90,800, for a total of $1,029,300. Its income statement debits consist of beginning inventory of $91,200, Purchases of $519,000, and Operating Expenses of $354,100, for a total of $964,300. The difference between the two totals is $65,000, the amount of Company S's net income.

One or the other of the affiliates' separate net incomes must be adjusted for any changes in total net income caused by worksheet eliminations. So far, the only such item that we have encountered is the additional expense introduced to recognize the amortization of the difference between cost and book value (in this case, Goodwill of Company S). Each adjustment is made to the net income of the affiliate that originated the item causing the adjustment. In this case, Company S's net income is adjusted because it is Company S's goodwill that is being amortized. Finally, the direction of the adjustment must be the same as the effect of that item on total net income. In this case, the recognition of goodwill amortization expense reduces total net income; therefore, it is subtracted from Company S's net income.

Notice that the adjustment to Company S's net income has the effect of allocating the decrease in total net income appropriately between its two components. The minority interest in Company S's net income is reduced by 20% of the adjustment, or $4,000, and consolidated net income is reduced by 80% of the adjustment, or $16,000.

The amounts of minority interest in the subsidiary's net income and consolidated net income determined in the Income Allocation schedule are entered in the consolidation worksheet as balancing figures in the Income Statement and Balance Sheet columns, as shown in Exhibit 7-8.

After preparing the various supporting schedules, we can set up the consolidation worksheet and enter the preclosing trial balances, as shown in Exhibit 7-6. Preparing the supporting schedules first enables us to see how many times each account will be affected by adjustments or eliminations and, accordingly, to provide extra lines where necessary. In this case, extra lines are provided for Investment in Company S and for Company S's Retained Earnings, as well as for the new accounts introduced through the adjustments. For problem-solving purposes, in which each problem represents a completely new start, this sequence of steps is very efficient, as noted in Chapter 5.

EXHIBIT 7-6

Illustrative Problem 7.2
Equity Method Consolidation Worksheet
Trial Balances Only
December 31, 1992

	Company P	Company S	Adjustments and Eliminations	Income Statement	Balance Sheet
Accounts Receivable	127,900	135,400			
Inventories	79,600	91,200			
Plant and Equipment	781,900	1,205,800			
Other Assets	276,800	148,400			
Investment in Company S	645,000				
Purchases	456,900	519,000			
Operating Expenses	304,200	354,100			
Dividends Declared: P	62,500				
Dividends Declared: S		40,000			
Goodwill					
	2,734,800	2,493,900			
Accumulated Depreciation	541,700	290,200			
Current Liabilities	214,900	153,950			
Bonds Payable		500,000			
Premium on Bonds Payable		30,000			
Capital Stock: P	500,000				
Capital Stock: S		300,000			
Additional Paid-in Capital: P	310,000				
Additional Paid-in Capital: S		120,000			
Retained Earnings: P	268,300				
Retained Earnings: S		161,250			
Sales	827,400	932,800			
Income from Company S	52,000				
Other Income	20,500	5,700			
Appraisal Capital: S					
	2,734,800	2,493,900			

In actual practice, however, the consolidation process for a given set of affiliates is repetitive, occurring year after year with largely the same components. Thus, the accountant can anticipate easily the need to leave extra lines in the worksheet. If the accountant is using a computer spreadsheet program to perform the consolidation process, the insertion of additional lines is even more easily accomplished. Accordingly, in practice, the trial balances are entered on the worksheet before preparing the supporting schedules.

Notice that the stockholders' equity balances of the two affiliates appear on separate lines in the worksheet, enabling us to deal with each balance individually. This treatment is not necessary for those accounts whose balances will simply be combined with their counterparts in the other affiliate's trial balance.

Exhibit 7-7 shows the consolidation worksheet after the adjustments, eliminations, and ending inventories have been entered. Notice that all adjustments and eliminations are cross-referenced to the supporting schedules through the identifying letters and numbers.

When adjustments or eliminations introduce new accounts, their titles are inserted in the debit or credit section of the worksheet, as appropriate, and their amounts are entered in the Adjustments and Eliminations column. Goodwill and Company S's Appraisal Capital are examples of this treatment that appear in Exhibit 7-7. In this case, the amount of the new Goodwill Amortization Expense introduced in Elimination [11] was added to the balance of the summary account, Operating Expenses. In a more detailed worksheet, it might also have been entered on a separate line.

The beginning inventories are combined and extended to the Income Statement debit column, where they become an addition in determining cost of goods sold. The amount of the combined ending inventory is entered in the Income Statement credit column, a subtraction in determining cost of goods sold, and as a Balance Sheet debit, an asset.

When two or more adjustments or eliminations affect a given account, it is helpful to use brackets for clarity. Such brackets are shown in Exhibit 7-7 in relation to Investment in Company S, Goodwill, Retained Earnings: S, and Appraisal Capital: S.

Exhibit 7-8 shows the completed consolidation worksheet. The various balances have been extended into the Income Statement and Balance Sheet columns, as appropriate, adding or subtracting the amounts of adjustments and eliminations where applicable. In addition, the minority interest in Company S's net income and the consolidated net income have been entered in the Income Statement debit column, causing the two Income Statement columns to balance. They also appear as credits in the Balance Sheet column, causing its totals to be equal. Notice that the minority interest residuals are labeled "M" so that they easily can be combined into a single amount to be reported on the consolidated balance sheet, as shown in Exhibit 7-14. Also, the components of the ending balance of consolidated Retained Earnings are labeled "R," making it easy to identify them for inclusion in the consolidated statement of retained earnings, as shown in Exhibit 7-13.

ILLUSTRATIVE PROBLEM 7.3: CONSOLIDATION UNDER THE COST METHOD

Illustrative Problem 7.3 is identical to Illustrative Problem 7.2, except that Company P uses the cost method to account for its investment in Company S. The other information from Illustrative Problem 7.2 is repeated here. Company P acquired 48,000 of Company S's 60,000 outstanding shares of $5 par value common stock for $608,400 on April 1, 1991, when Company S had additional paid-in capital of $120,000. Company S's December 31, 1990 retained earnings balance was $120,250.

In 1991, Company S reported net income of $81,000 and declared and paid dividends of $40,000. In 1992, Company S reported net income of $65,000 and declared and paid dividends of $40,000. In each year, the dividends were declared on November 15 and paid on December 15.

The excess of cost over book value is being treated as goodwill of Company S, amortized over 10 years. December 31, 1992 inventories are: Company P, $82,200; Company S, $90,800. Company P's 1992 net income from its own operations was $89,400.

EXHIBIT 7-7

Illustrative Problem 7.2
Equity Method Consolidation Worksheet
Adjustments, Eliminations, and Inventories Entered
December 31, 1992

	Company P	Company S	Adjustments and Eliminations		Income Statement		Balance Sheet
Accounts Receivable	127,900	135,400					
Inventories	79,600	91,200			170,800	173,000	173,000
Plant and Equipment	781,900	1,205,800					
Other Assets	276,800	148,400					
Investment in Company S	645,000		[5]	(625,000)			
			[8]	(20,000)			
Purchases	456,900	519,000					
Operating Expenses	304,200	354,100	[11]	20,000			
Dividends Declared: P	62,500						
Dividends Declared: S		40,000	[7]	(32,000)			
Goodwill			A	200,000			
			[12]	(35,000)			
	2,734,800	2,493,900					
Accumulated Depreciation	541,700	290,200					
Current Liabilities	214,900	153,950					
Bonds Payable		500,000					
Premium on Bonds Payable		30,000					
Capital Stock: P	500,000						
Capital Stock: S		300,000	[1]	240,000			
Additional Paid-in Capital: P	310,000						
Additional Paid-in Capital: S		120,000	[2]	96,000			
Retained Earnings: P	268,300		[9]	12,000			
Retained Earnings: S		161,250	[3]	129,000			
			[10]	3,000			
Sales	827,400	932,800					
Income from Company S	52,000		[6]	52,000			
Other Income	20,500	5,700					
Appraisal Capital: S			B	(200,000)			
			[4]	160,000			
	2,734,800	2,493,900					

EXHIBIT 7-8

Illustrative Problem 7.2
Completed Equity Method Consolidation Worksheet
December 31, 1992

	Company P	Company S	Adjustments and Eliminations	Income Statement		Balance Sheet
Accounts Receivable	127,900	135,400				263,300
Inventories	79,600	91,200		170,800	173,000	173,000
Plant and Equipment	781,900	1,205,800				1,987,700
Other Assets	276,800	148,400				425,200
Investment in Company S	645,000		[5] (625,000) [8] (20,000)			
Purchases	456,900	519,000		975,900		
Operating Expenses	304,200	354,100	[11] 20,000	678,300		
Dividends Declared: P	62,500					62,500 R
Dividends Declared: S		40,000	[7] (32,000)			8,000 M
Goodwill			A 200,000 [12] (35,000)			165,000 G
	2,734,800	2,493,900				3,084,700
Accumulated Depreciation	541,700	290,200				831,900
Current Liabilities	214,900	153,950				368,850
Bonds Payable		500,000				500,000
Premium on Bonds Payable		30,000				30,000
Capital Stock: P	500,000					500,000
Capital Stock: S		300,000	[1] 240,000			60,000 M
Additional Paid-in Capital: P	310,000					310,000
Additional Paid-in Capital: S		120,000	[2] 96,000			24,000 M
Retained Earnings: P	268,300		[9] 12,000			256,300 R
Retained Earnings: S		161,250	[3] 129,000 [10] 3,000			29,250 M
Sales	827,400	932,800		1,760,200		
Income from Company S	52,000		[6] 52,000			
Other Income	20,500	5,700			26,200	
Appraisal Capital: S			B (200,000) [4] 160,000			40,000 M
	2,734,800	2,493,900				
Minority Interest in Company S's Net Income				9,000		9,000 M
Consolidated Net Income				125,400		125,400 R
				1,959,400	1,959,400	3,084,700

If Company P had used the cost method rather than the equity method in accounting for its investment in Company S from the date of acquisition, then at December 31, 1992

- The balance of Company P's Investment in Company S account would have been $608,400 instead of $645,000.
- Company P's trial balance would have included Dividend Revenue of $32,000 instead of Income from Company S of $52,000.
- Company P's Retained Earnings balance would have been $251,700 instead of $268,300.

These balances can be validated by reference to the journal entries shown in Exhibit 7-1 and the schedule appearing in Exhibit 7-2. They also appear in Company P's trial balance contained in the consolidation worksheet in Exhibit 7-11.

Difference between Cost and Book Value.   The treatment of the difference between cost and book value is not affected by whether the parent company accounts for its investment in the subsidiary under the equity method or under the cost method. Thus, under the cost method, the Excess of Cost over Book Value schedule and Adjustments A and B would appear exactly as shown in Exhibit 7-3.

Conversion from Cost to Equity.   If a parent company uses the cost method to account for its investment in a subsidiary, it is necessary before making any worksheet eliminations to reestablish reciprocity between the parent's Investment in Subsidiary balance and the subsidiary's net assets. Otherwise, the eliminations used under the cost method will be completely different from those used under the equity method. This process is accomplished in two steps.

First, the amount of adjustment necessary is determined by preparing a schedule comparing the parent's equity in the subsidiary [a] at the beginning of the current year and [b] at the date of acquisition. The parent's equity at each date equals the parent's percentage of ownership multiplied by the total stockholders' equity of the subsidiary at that date. The difference between the two amounts of the parent's equity is the amount of change (typically, increase) from the date of acquisition of the beginning of the current year. In the sequence of our consolidation process, this schedule appears immediately after the Excess of Cost over Book Value schedule.

This conversion is made from cost to equity as of the beginning, rather than the end, of the current year because we are using preclosing trial balances, which contain beginning-of-the-year Retained Earnings balances. Thus, subsequent eliminations involving both the subsidiary's Retained Earnings and the parent's Investment in Subsidiary will match up chronologically.

Second, a pair of worksheet adjustments is needed in order to bring the change in the parent's equity into the worksheet. If the change is an increase, the amount thereof is debited to Investment in Subsidiary and credited to the parent's Retained Earnings. If the change is a decrease, the debit and credit are reversed. Like the adjustments introduced in Chapter 6 to recognize the difference between cost and book value as a subsidiary asset element, these adjustments appear *only on the consolidation worksheet.* They are not recorded on the parent's books; thus, they must be made at each year end. Both the Conversion from Cost to Equity schedule and the related adjustments are shown in Exhibit 7-9.

EXHIBIT 7-9

Illustrative Problem 7.3
Schedules of Conversion from Cost to Equity and Adjustments
December 31, 1992

Conversion from Cost to Equity

80% of Company S's Total Stockholders' Equity, 1/1/92	$ 465,000 [a]
80% of Company S's Total Stockholders' Equity, 4/1/91	448,400 [b]
Increase in Company P's Equity in Company S	$ 16,600

Adjustments

C. Investment in Company S	$ 16,600
D. Retained Earnings: P	(16,600)

Calculations

[a] 80% × ($300,000 + $120,000 + $161,250)
[b] 80% × ($300,000 + $120,000 + $140,500)

In the Conversion from Cost to Equity schedule, Company P's equity in Company S at the beginning of the current year is compared with its equity at the date of acquisition. The increase in Company P's equity in Company S, $16,600, is the difference between the dividend revenue that Company P recorded under the cost method and the income from Company S, minus Company S dividends, that Company P would have recorded under the equity method, through the end of 1991. Adjustments C and D, shown in Exhibit 7-9, add this increase to Investment in Company S and Retained Earnings balances, converting them to the equity basis as of January 1, 1992.

After making these adjustments, all eliminations are identical to those made under the equity method, except for the Subsidiary Income and Dividends set. Under the cost method, the balance of Company P's Dividend Revenue, rather than Income from Company S, is eliminated against the majority share of Company S's Dividends Declared balance, as shown in Exhibit 7-10.

Exhibit 7-11 presents the completed worksheet prepared under the cost method. Notice that the Income Statement and Balance Sheet columns are identical to those produced under the equity method in Exhibit 7-8.

The consolidated financial statements, of course, are identical whether prepared from the equity method consolidation worksheet in Exhibit 7-8 or the cost method consolidation worksheet in Exhibit 7-11. These financial statements appear in Exhibits 7-12, 7-13, and 7-14.

Consolidated Statement of Cash Flows. In addition to the consolidated income statement, statement of retained earnings, and balance sheet presented in Exhibits 7-12, 7-13, and 7-14, Company P would present a consolidated statement of cash flows for the year ended

EXHIBIT 7-10

Illustrative Problem 7.3
Cost Method Eliminations
December 31, 1992

Eliminations

Intercompany Ownership Interests

[1]	Common Stock: S	$ 240,000
[2]	Additional Paid-in Capital: S	96,000
[3]	Retained Earnings: S	129,000
[4]	Appraisal capital: S	160,000
[5]	Investment in Company S	$(625,000)

Subsidiary Income and Dividends

[6]	Dividend Revenue	$ 32,000
[7]	Dividends Declared: S	(32,000)

Goodwill Amortization

[8]	Retained Earnings: P	$ 12,000
[9]	Retained Earnings: S	3,000
[10]	Operating Expenses	20,000
[11]	Goodwill	$ (35,000)

December 31, 1992. This statement replaces the statement of changes in financial position in the corporate annual reporting package.[6] Once the consolidated income statement and balance sheet information is accumulated in the consolidation worksheet, the consolidated statement of cash flows is prepared in exactly the same manner as a statement of cash flows for a single entity. Because this topic is amply covered in most intermediate accounting texts and courses, we do not discuss and illustrate the process of preparing the statement of cash flows in this text. Based on the information in Illustrative Problem 7.2, and a variety of assumptions as to cash inflows and outflows, Exhibit 7-15 presents the consolidated statement of cash flows for the year ended December 31, 1992 for Company P and its subsidiary, Company S.

Goodwill from Consolidation.   If the excess of cost over book value had been identified as goodwill from consolidation rather than as goodwill of Company S, several elements of the consolidation process would have been different.

Because goodwill from consolidation is a parent company asset, the implication that the initial amount of the excess represents only the parent's share of the amount by which the subsidiary's net assets are undervalued is not present. Therefore, the Excess of Cost over Book Value schedule would not contain the upward expansion of the initial excess of cost over

---

[6] *Statement of Financial Accounting Standards No. 95, Statement of Cash Flows* (Stamford, Connecticut: FASB, 1987).

EXHIBIT 7-11

Illustrative Problem 7.3
Completed Cost Method Consolidation Worksheet
December 31, 1992

	Company P	Company S	Adjustments and Eliminations	Income Statement		Balance Sheet
Accounts Receivable	127,900	135,400				263,300
Inventories	79,600	91,200		170,800	173,000	173,000
Plant and Equipment	781,900	1,205,800				1,987,700
Other Assets	276,800	148,400				425,200
Investment in Company S	608,400		C 16,600			
			[5] (625,000)			
Purchases	456,900	519,000		975,900		
Operating Expenses	304,200	354,100	[10] 20,000	678,300		
Dividends Declared: P	62,500					62,500 R
Dividends Declared: S		40,000	[7] (32,000)			8,000 M
Goodwill			A 200,000			165,000
			[11] (35,000)			
	2,698,200	2,493,900				3,084,700
Accumulated Depreciation	541,700	290,200				831,900
Current Liabilities	214,900	153,950				368,850
Bonds Payable		500,000				500,000
Premium on Bonds Payable		30,000				30,000
Capital Stock: P	500,000					500,000
Capital Stock: S		300,000	[1] 240,000			60,000 M
Additional Paid-in Capital: P	310,000					310,000
Additional Paid-in Capital: S		120,000	[2] 96,000			24,000 M
Retained Earnings: P	251,700		D (16,600)			256,300 R
			[8] 12,000			
Retained Earnings: S		161,250	[3] 129,000			29,250 M
			[9] 3,000			
Sales	827,400	932,800		1,760,200		
Dividend Revenue	32,000		[6]b 32,000			
Other Income	20,500	5,700			26,200	
Appraisal Capital: S			B (200,000)			40,000 M
			[4] 160,000			
	2,698,200	2,493,900				
Minority Interest in Company S's Net Income				9,000		9,000 M
Consolidated Net Income				125,400		125,400 R
				1,959,400	1,959,400	3,084,700

EXHIBIT 7-12

Illustrative Problems 7.2 and 7.3
COMPANY P AND SUBSIDIARY
Consolidated Income Statement
Year Ended December 31, 1992

Sales		$1,760,200
Inventory, January 1	$ 170,800	
Purchases	975,900	
Goods Available for Sale	1,146,700	
Less: Inventory, December 31	173,000	
Cost of Goods Sold		973,700
Gross Profit		786,500
Operating Expenses		678,300
Income from Operations		108,200
Other Income		26,200
Total Net Income		134,400
Minority Interest in Subsidiary Net Income		9,000
Consolidated Net Income		$ 125,400

EXHIBIT 7-13

Illustrative Problems 7.2 and 7.3
COMPANY P AND SUBSIDIARY
Consolidated Statement of Retained Earnings
Year Ended December 31, 1992

Retained Earnings, January 1		$ 256,300
Consolidated Net Income	$ 125,400	
Less: Dividends Declared	62,500	62,900
Retained Earnings, December 31		$ 319,200

book value. Instead, the initial amount of the excess would be the goodwill from consolidation at the date of acquisition. The amounts of prior and current years' amortization and the ending balance would be correspondingly smaller, as shown in Exhibit 7-16. No worksheet adjustments would be necessary; instead, the goodwill would remain as part of the balance of the Investment in Company S account, as described and demonstrated in Chapters 5 and 6.

The eliminations to recognize amortization of goodwill would differ in several respects. First, as noted above, the amounts involved would be smaller. Second, because Company P's asset is being amortized, the prior year's amortization would apply only to Company P's Retained Earnings. Finally, the total amount of amortization would be credited to Investment in Company S rather than to Goodwill. These eliminations appear in Exhibit 7-16.

EXHIBIT 7-14

Illustrative Problems 7.2 and 7.3
COMPANY P AND SUBSIDIARY
Consolidated Balance Sheet
December 31, 1992

Assets

Accounts Receivable		$ 263,300
Inventories		173,000
Plant and Equipment	$1,987,700	
Less: Accumulated Depreciation	831,900	1,155,800
Goodwill		165,000
Other Assets		425,200
Total Assets		$2,182,300

Liabilities and Stockholders' Equity

Liabilities		
Current Liabilities		$ 368,850
Bonds Payable	$ 500,000	
Premium on Bonds Payable	30,000	530,000
Total Liabilities		898,850
Minority Interest in Subsidiary		154,250
Stockholders' Equity		
Common Stock	$ 500,000	
Additional Paid-in Capital	310,000	
Retained Earnings	319,200	1,129,200
Total Equities		$2,182,300

In the consolidation worksheet, the ending balance of goodwill would emerge as a residual from the Investment in Company S balance, extended to the Balance Sheet column and labeled "G", as described and illustrated in Chapter 5.

SUMMARY

At this point, it is useful to review the sequence of the consolidation process as presented and discussed so far. It consists of the following steps:

1. Prepare a schedule of the difference between cost and book value.
2. If the cost method is being used, prepare the Conversion from Cost to Equity schedule.

EXHIBIT 7-15

Illustrative Problems 7.2 and 7.3
COMPANY P AND SUBSIDIARY
Consolidated Statement of Cash Flows
Year Ended December 31, 1992

Cash Flows from Operating Activities

Cash Received from Customers		$1,742,700
Cash Dividends Received		14,100
Cash Provided by Operating Activities		1,756,800
Cash Paid to Employees and Suppliers	$1,490,100	
Interest Paid	5,600	
Income Taxes Paid	50,500	1,546,200
Net Cash Inflow from Operating Activities		210,600

Cash Flows from Investing Activities

Disposal of Operating Assets	$ 250,300	
Collections on Loans	41,200	
Cash Provided by Investing Activities	291,500	
Purchases of Operating Assets	198,000	
Loans to Employees	28,400	
Cash Used by Investing Activities	226,400	
Net Cash Provided by Investing Activities		65,100

Cash Flows from Financing Activities

Proceeds of Long-Term Borrowing	$ 125,000	
Repayment of Long-Term Debt	100,000	
Repayment of Short-Term Debt	8,400	
Dividends Paid	62,500	
Cash Used by Financing Activities	170,900	
Net Cash Used by Financing Activities		(45,900)
Net Increase in Cash		$ 229,800

Reconciliation of Net Income and Cash Flow from Operating Activities

Net Income		$ 125,400
Add: Decrease in Accounts Payable	$ 10,100	
Increase in Accounts Payable	1,300	
Depreciation Expense	91,100	
Less: Increase in Inventories	(12,300)	
Gain on Sale of Operating Assets	(5,000)	85,200
Net Cash Inflow from Operating Activities		$ 210,600

EXHIBIT 7-16

Illustrative Problems 7.2 and 7.3
Schedules of Excess of Cost over Book Value and Eliminations
December 31, 1992

Excess of Cost over Book Value

Cost of Investment		$ 608,400
Book Value (80% × $560,500)		448,400
Goodwill, 4/1/91		160,000
Amortization through 12/31/91	$ 12,000	
Amortization, 1992	16,000	28,000
Goodwill, 12/31/92		$ 132,000

Eliminations

Goodwill Amortization

[8] Retained Earnings: P		$ 12,000
[9] Expenses (Goodwill Amortization)		16,000
[10] Investment in Company S		$ (28,000)

3. If necessary, schedule adjustments to
   a. recognize one or more asset elements of the subsidiary (for example, goodwill of the subsidiary), or
   b. to convert from cost to equity.
4. Schedule the following eliminations:
   a. the Intercompany Ownership Interests set,
   b. the Subsidiary Income and Dividends set,
   c. the set used to recognize amortization of the difference between cost and book value (appropriately titled).
5. Prepare the Income Allocation schedule.
6. Prepare the consolidation worksheet.
7. Prepare the consolidated financial statements.

For problem-solving purposes, in which each problem represents a completely new start, this sequence of steps is very efficient. By preparing the supporting schedules first, one is able to anticipate the need to provide extra lines in the worksheet for accounts that will be affected by more than one adjustment or elimination, as well as for the insertion of new accounts.

In actual practice, however, the consolidation process for a given set of affiliates is repetitive, occurring year after year with largely the same components. Thus, the accountant can anticipate easily the need to leave extra lines in the worksheet. If the accountant is using a computer spreadsheet program to perform the consolidation process, the insertion of additional lines is even more easily accomplished. Accordingly, in practice, the trial balances are entered on the worksheet before preparing the supporting schedules. After the schedules are prepared, information is transferred from them to the worksheet, which is then completed.

     If you are solving a problem using a computer spreadsheet program, you will find it advantageous to follow the sequence commonly used in practice and enter the trial balances in the consolidation worksheet first. As noted above, extra lines can be added easily. In addition, adopting this sequence allows you to use cell addresses in the trial balances in constructing the schedules.

REVIEW PROBLEM

Company J purchased 80% of Company K's common stock for $352,000 on October 1, 1989, when Company K had retained earnings of $90,000. The excess of cost over book value is identified as goodwill of Company K and is to be amortized over 10 years. The September 30, 1992 trial balances of the two companies are shown below.

	Company J	Company K
Inventories, 10/1/91	$ 75,000	$ 90,000
Investment in Company K	377,600	
Other Assets	414,400	427,000
Purchases	325,000	360,000
Expenses	180,000	225,000
Dividends Declared	10,000	8,000
	$1,382,000	$1,110,000
Liabilities	$ 164,000	$ 90,000
Common Stock	400,000	250,000
Additional Paid-in Capital	100,000	50,000
Retained Earnings	172,000	110,000
Sales	530,000	610,000
Income from Company K	16,000	
	$1,382,000	$1,110,000
Inventories, 9/30/92	$ 78,000	$ 85,000

Required

Prepare the September 30, 1992 consolidation worksheet for Company J and Company K, supported by appropriate schedules.

THE FINANCIAL STATEMENT FORM OF CONSOLIDATION WORKSHEET

As noted in Chapter 7, an alternative to the preclosing trial balance form of the consolidation worksheet used throughout this book is a format in which the accounts are arranged in financial statement order. In Appendix 7.A, we demonstrate the financial statement worksheet format by using the information from Illustrative Problem 7.2.

The schedules in support of the financial statement form of worksheet are identical to those presented in Illustrative Problem 7.2. They are reproduced here as Exhibit 7-17 (Excess of Cost over Book Value and Adjustments), Exhibit 7-18 (Equity Method Eliminations), and Exhibit 7-19 (Income Allocation Schedule).

EXHIBIT 7-I7

Appendix 7.A
Excess of Cost over Book Value and Adjustments
December 31, 1992

Excess of Cost over Book Value

Cost of Investment		$ 608,400
Book Value (80% × $560,000)		448,400
Excess of Cost over Book Value		160,000
Expand to 100%		÷ 80%
Goodwill, 4/1/91		200,000
Amortization through 12/31/91	$ 15,000	
Amortization, 1992	20,000	35,000
Goodwill, 12/31/92		$ 165,000

Adjustments

A. Goodwill	$ 200,000
B. Appraisal Capital: S	(200,000)

The completed consolidation worksheet in the financial statement format appears in Exhibit 7-20. The adjustments and eliminations that affect income statement accounts are applied to those account balances in the Income Statement section on the worksheet. In this case, only Eliminations [6] and [11] affect income statement accounts. Total net income is determined by comparing the total credits and total debits in the Consolidated column, from which the minority interest in Company S's net income is subtracted to yield consolidated net income.

EXHIBIT 7-18

Appendix 7.A
Equity Method Eliminations
December 31, 1992

Eliminations

Intercompany Ownership Interests

[1]	Common Stock: S	$ 240,000
[2]	Additional Paid-in Capital: S	96,000
[3]	Retained Earnings: S	129,000
[4]	Appraisal Capital: S	160,000
[5]	Investment in Company S	$(625,000)

Subsidiary Income and Dividends

[6]	Income from Company S	$ 52,000
[7]	Dividends Declared: S	(32,000)
[8]	Investment in Company S	$ (20,000)

Goodwill Amortization

[9]	Retained Earnings: P	$ 12,000
[10]	Retained Earnings: S	3,000
[11]	Operating Expenses	20,000
[12]	Goodwill	$ (35,000)

EXHIBIT 7-19

Appendix 7.A
Income Allocation Schedule
Year Ended December 31, 1992

Income Allocation

Company P's Own Net Income		$ 89,400
Company S's Own Net Income	$ 65,000	
Less: Goodwill Amortization Expense	20,000	
Company S's Adjusted Net Income	45,000	
Minority Interest (20%)	9,000	
Company P's Share (80%)		36,000
Consolidated Net Income		$ 125,400

EXHIBIT 7-20

Appendix 7.A
Completed Equity Method Consolidation Worksheet
December 31, 1992

	Company P	Company S	Adjustments and Eliminations	Minority Interest	Consolidated
Income Statement					
Sales	827,400	932,800			1,760,200
Income from Company S	52,000		[6] 52,000		
Other Income	20,500	5,700			26,200
Inventories (12/31/92)	82,200	90,800			173,000
Total Credits	982,100	1,029,300			1,959,400
Inventories (1/1/92)	79,600	91,200			170,800
Purchases	456,900	519,000			975,900
Operating Expenses	304,200	354,100	[11] 20,000		678,300
Total Debits	840,700	964,300			1,825,000
					134,400
Minority Interest in Company S's Net Income				9,000	9,000
Net Income (carried forward)	141,400	65,000	72,000	9,000	125,400
Retained Earnings Statement					
Retained Earnings: P (1/1/92)	268,300		[9] 12,000		256,300
Retained Earnings: S (1/1/92)		161,250		29,250	
			{ [3] 129,000		
			{ [10] 3,000		
Net Income (brought forward)	141,400	65,000	72,000	9,000	125,400
	409,700	226,250		38,250	381,700
Dividends Declared: P	62,500				62,500
Dividends Declared: S		40,000	[7] (32,000)	8,000	
Retained Earnings (12/31/92) (carried forward)	347,200	186,250	184,000	30,250	319,200
Balance Sheet					
Accounts Receivable	127,900	135,400			263,300
Inventories	82,200	90,800			173,000
Plant and Equipment	781,900	1,205,800			1,987,700
Other Assets	276,800	148,400			425,200
Investment in Company S	645,000		{ [5] (625,000)		
			{ [8] (20,000)		
Goodwill			{ A 200,000		165,000
			{ [12] (35,000)		
	1,913,800	1,580,400			3,014,200

	Company P	Company S	Adjustments and Eliminations		Minority Interest	Consolidated
Accumulated Depreciation	541,700	290,200				831,900
Current Liabilities	214,900	153,950				368,850
Bonds Payable		500,000				500,000
Premium on Bonds Payable		30,000				30,000
Common Stock: P	500,000					500,000
Common Stock: S		300,000	[1]	240,000	60,000	
Additional Paid-in Capital: P	310,000					310,000
Additional Paid-in Capital: S		120,000	[2]	96,000	24,000	
Retained Earnings (12/31/92) (brought forward)	347,200	186,250		184,000	30,250	319,200
Appraisal Capital: S			B	(200,000)	40,000	
			[4]	160,000		
					154,250	154,250
	1,913,800	1,580,400		–0–		3,014,200

The entire last line of the Income Statement section of the worksheet is carried forward into the Retained Earnings section. The adjustments and eliminations that affect retained earnings components are applied to those account balances in the Income Statement section of the worksheet. Notice that the amounts of minority interest in Company S's beginning retained earnings, dividends declared, and net income are collected in the Minority Interest column.

The entire last line of the Retained Earnings section of the worksheet is carried forward into the Balance Sheet section. The adjustments and eliminations that affect balance sheet accounts are applied to those account balances in the Balance Sheet section of the worksheet. Again, the minority interest residuals are collected in the Minority Interest column, the total of which is entered as a credit in the Consolidated column of the Balance Sheet section.

The amounts appearing in the Consolidated columns of the three sections of the worksheet are, of course, the amounts that will appear in the consolidated financial statements. Those financial statements will be identical to the ones that appear in Exhibits 7-12, 7-13, 7-14, and 7-15.

POOLING OF INTERESTS CONSOLIDATION AFTER THE DATE OF ACQUISITION

In Chapter 7, we discuss and illustrate the consolidation process beyond the date of acquisition with respect to a corporate combination accounted for as a purchase. Appendix 7.B applies that process to a pooling of interests, using information first introduced in Illustrative Problem 5.2 in Chapter 5.

The condensed trial balances of Company C and Company D immediately before their combination of June 30, 1991 are

	Company C	Company D
Current Assets	$ 325,000	$ 150,000
Plant and Equipment	780,000	520,000
	$1,105,000	$ 670,000
Accumulated Depreciation	$ 280,000	$ 170,000
Liabilities	165,000	60,000
Common Stock ($25 par)	400,000	300,000
Additional Paid-in Capital	30,000	50,000
Retained Earnings	230,000	90,000
	$1,105,000	$ 670,000

Company C issues 15,000 shares of its previously unissued common stock, which has a market value of 30, in exchange for 10,800 of Company D's outstanding shares of common stock.

Under the pooling of interests method, Company C records the acquisition of its investment in the Company D stock as follows:

Investment in Company D	396,000	
Common Stock		375,000
Additional Paid-in Capital		21,000

Because no new basis of accountability arises in a pooling of interests, the investment in Company D's common stock is recorded at the aggregate book value of Company D's net assets. The newly issued Company C common stock is recorded at par value of $25 per share, with the excess credited to Additional Paid-in Capital. The problem of carrying forward the combined Retained Earnings balances is dealt with in the consolidation worksheet.

Six months later, on December 31, 1991, the two affiliates' preclosing trial balances appear as follows:

	Company C	Company D
Current Assets	$ 308,200	$ 156,500
Plant and Equipment	780,000	520,000
Investment in Company D	397,800	
Cost of Goods Sold	533,200	338,800
Operating Expenses	312,600	198,300
Dividends Declared	50,000	32,000
	$2,381,800	$1,245,600
Accumulated Depreciation	$ 284,700	$ 173,400
Liabilities	164,700	61,100
Common Stock ($25 par)	775,000	300,000
Additional Paid-in Capital	51,000	50,000
Retained Earnings	156,600	56,000
Sales	916,400	603,200
Income from Company D	30,600	
Other Income	2,800	1,900
	$2,381,800	$1,245,600

No schedule of the excess of cost over book value is constructed under the pooling of interests method. Because no new basis of accountability is present, no difference between cost and book value can exist.

The schedules of eliminations appear in Exhibit 7-21. Under the pooling of interests method, we begin the Intercompany Ownership Interests set of eliminations by eliminating the entire cost of Company C's Investment in Company D balance, $396,000, in Elimination [1]. Then, amounts equal to Company C's percentage of ownership, 90%, are eliminated from Company D's Common Stock and Additional Paid-in Capital balances in Eliminations [2] and [3].

At this point, total credits equal $396,000, while total debits equal $315,000. In order to avoid eliminating any of Company D's Retained Earnings balance, it would be necessary to debit Company C's Additional Paid-in Capital for $81,000. Company C's Additional Paid-in Capital balance (after posting the journal entry to record the acquisition of the Company D common stock), however, is only $51,000. Thus, after debiting Company C's Additional Paid-in Capital for $51,000 in Elimination [4], Company D's Retained Earnings must be debited for $30,000 to complete the Intercompany Ownership Interests set of eliminations.

After applying Elimination [5] the remaining balance of Company D's Retained Earnings is $26,000. In the Retained Earnings Combination set of eliminations, Company D's Retained Earnings is debited and Company C's Retained Earnings is credited for Company C's share, 90%, of that amount, or $23,400. The remainder, $2,600, is extended to the Balance Sheet column as part of Minority Interest, appropriately labeled "M."

As a result of these eliminations, the combined amount of beginning retained earnings (including the minority interest in Company D's beginning retained earnings) will be only $180,800 rather than $212,600. If Company C's Additional Paid-in Capital balance had been at least $82,800, the entire amount of the combined Retained Earnings balances could have been carried forward. Again, in both sets of eliminations, the debit eliminations are shown without notation, with the credit eliminations shown in parentheses. Also, each set of eliminations balances in terms of debits and credits.

Exhibit 7-22 presents the Income Allocation schedule for the year ended December 31, 1991. Under the pooling of interests method, of course, no adjustment for amortization of goodwill is present. The

EXHIBIT 7-21

Appendix 7.B
Eliminations
Pooling of Interests Method
December 31, 1991

Eliminations

Intercompany Ownership Interests

[1]	Investment in Company D	$ (396,000)
[2]	Common Stock: D	270,000
[3]	Additional Paid-in Capital: D	45,000
[4]	Additional Paid-in Capital: C	51,000
[5]	Retained Earnings: D	$ 30,000

Retained Earnings Combination

[6]	Retained Earnings: D	$ 23,400
[7]	Retained Earnings: C	(23,400)

Subsidiary Income and Dividends

[8]	Income from Company D	$ 30,600
[9]	Dividends Declared: D	(28,800)
[10]	Investment in Company D	$ (1,800)

Calculations
[1] Balance of the account
[2] 90% × $300,000
[3] 90% × $50,000
[4] Balance of the account
[5] Sum of Eliminations [1] through [4]
[6] 90% × ($56,000 − $30,000)
[7] Same as [6]

net incomes are combined as if the parent–subsidiary relationship has existed throughout 1991 even though Company C acquired its investment in Company D on June 30 of the year.

Exhibit 7-23 presents the completed consolidation worksheet at December 31, 1991.

QUESTIONS

1. How do the cost method and the equity method differ with respect to recording net income of the subsidiary?
2. How do the cost method and the equity method differ with respect to recording dividends declared by the subsidiary?

EXHIBIT 7-22

Appendix 7.B
Income Allocation Schedule
Year Ended December 31, 1991

Income Allocation

Company C's Own Net Income		$ 73,400
Company D's Own Net Income	$ 68,000	
Minority Interest (10%)	6,800	
Company P's Share (90%)		61,200
Consolidated Net Income		$ 134,600

3. Which of the two methods, cost or equity, does *APB Opinion No. 18* require for an investment of greater than 50% ownership?

4. Which two quantities are compared in determining the amount of adjustment needed to convert from cost to equity?

5. Why, when the parent uses the cost method, must the conversion from cost to equity be made at each balance sheet date?

6. How are ending inventories treated in the preclosing trial balance form of the consolidation worksheet when the affiliates use periodic inventory systems?

7. What kind of items require adjustments to the affiliates' individual net incomes in the Income Allocation schedule?

8. In sets of eliminations requiring the allocation of some quantity between or among the affiliates' Retained Earnings balances, how is the amount to be allocated to each Retained Earnings balance determined?

9. What account is credited in the Goodwill Amortization set of eliminations in the case of goodwill from consolidation?

10. What account is credited in the Goodwill Amortization set of eliminations in the case of goodwill of the subsidiary?

11. How are the minority interest in the subsidiary's net income and consolidated net income treated in the preclosing trial balance form of the consolidation worksheet?

EXERCISES

EXERCISE 7-1

On March 1, 1991, Company A purchased 75% of Company B's common stock for $550,000. On that date, Company B had common stock of $500,000. Company B's December 31, 1990 retained earnings balance was $210,000. Company B's net income and dividends through December 31, 1993 were

	1991	1992	1993
Net Income	$52,800	$24,000	$56,000
Dividends Declared	40,000	40,000	40,000

The dividends were declared on October 31 and paid on December 1 of each year.

EXHIBIT 7-23

Appendix 7.B
Pooling of Interests Method Consolidation Worksheet
December 31, 1991

	Company C	Company D	Eliminations		Income Statement	Balance Sheet
Current Assets	308,200	156,500				464,700
Plant and Equipment	780,000	520,000				1,300,000
Investment in Company D	397,800		[1] (396,000)			
			[10] (1,800)			
Cost of Goods Sold	533,200	338,800			872,000	
Operating Expenses	312,600	198,300			510,900	
Dividends Declared: C	50,000					50,000 R
Dividends Declared: D		32,000	[9]	(28,800)		3,200 M
	2,381,800	1,245,600				1,817,900
Accumulated Depreciation	284,700	173,400				458,100
Liabilities	164,700	61,100				225,800
Common Stock: C	775,000					775,000
Common Stock: D		300,000	[2]	270,000		30,000 M
Additional Paid-in Capital: C	51,000		[4]	51,000		
Additional Paid-in Capital: D		50,000	[3]	45,000		5,000 M
Retained Earnings: C	156,600		[7]	(23,400)		180,000 R
Retained Earnings: D		56,000	[5]	30,000		
			[6]	23,400		2,600 M
Sales	916,400	603,200			1,519,600	
Income from Company D	30,600		[8]	30,600		
Other Income	2,800	1,900			4,700	
	2,381,800	1,245,600				
Minority Interest in Company D's Net Income					6,800	6,800 M
Consolidated Net Income					134,600	134,600 R
					1,524,300 1,524,300	1,817,900

Required
In parallel columns, present the journal entries that should be recorded on Company A's books from January 2, 1991 through December 31, 1993 to account for its investment in Company B under [a] the cost method and [b] the equity method.

EXERCISE 7-2
On September 30, 1991, Company C purchased 80% of Company D's common stock for $712,000. On that date, Company D had common stock of $300,000 and additional paid-in capital of $200,000. Company D's December 31, 1990 retained earnings balance was $290,000. Company D reported net income for 1991 of $80,000, but did not declare any dividends during the year. The excess of cost over book value is to be amortized over twenty years.

Required

Prepare schedules showing the goodwill to be reported at December 31, 1993 and any adjustments and/or eliminations directly related to goodwill in support of the December 31, 1993 consolidation worksheet, assuming that the excess of cost over book value is identified as [a] goodwill from consolidation, and [b] goodwill of Company D.

EXERCISE 7-3

On October 1, 1988, Company E paid $622,500 for 7,500 of Company F's 10,000 shares par value common stock, which had been issued originally at 56. On March 31, 1988, Company F had retained earnings of $198,000. Company F reported net income of $84,000 for the year ended March 31, 1989. On August 15, 1988, Company F declared dividends of $30,000, which were paid on September 20, 1988. The excess of cost over book value is attributed to undervaluation of Company F's patents, which had a remaining useful life of 12 years at October 1, 1988.

By March 31, 1992, Company F's retained earnings had increased to $246,000. Company F reported net income of $112,000 for the year ended March 31, 1993 and declared and paid dividends of $5 per share during the year. Company E accounts for its investment in Company F under the equity method.

Required

Prepare schedules of the excess of cost over book value and of all adjustments and eliminations in support of the March 31, 1993 consolidation worksheet.

EXERCISE 7-4

On May 31, 1991, Company G purchased 7,000 of Company H's 10,000 shares of $10 par value common stock for $140,000. On November 30, 1990, Company H had retained earnings of $60,000. Company H reported net income for the years ended November 30, 1991 and 1992 of $60,000 and $18,000, respectively. Company H declared dividends of $2.50 per share on July 31 of each year, payable on the following August 31.

Required

In parallel columns, present the journal entries that should be recorded on Company G's books for the years ended November 30, 1991 and 1992 to account for its investment in Company H under [a] the cost method and [b] the equity mthod.

EXERCISE 7-5

On June 30, 1991, Company I purchaesd 80% of Company J's common stock for $340,000. On that date, Company J had common stock of $200,000 and additional paid-in capital of $100,000. Company J's December 31, 1990 retained earnings balance was $65,000. Company J reported net income of $40,000 for 1991. On November 15, 1991, Company J declared dividends of $20,000, which were paid on December 20, 1991. The excess of cost over book value is attributed to goodwill of Company J and is to be amortized over 10 years.

By December 31, 1993, Company J's retained earnings had increased to $110,000. Company J reported net income of $45,000 for 1994 and declared and paid dividends of $20,000 during the year. Company I accounts for its investment in Company J under the equity method.

Required

Prepare schedules of the excess of cost over book value and of all adjustments and eliminations in support of the December 31, 1994 consolidation worksheet.

EXERCISE 7-6

On January 2, 1990, Company K bought 15% of Company L's common stock for $30,000. Company L reported net income for 1990 and 1991 of $10,000 and $50,000, respectively. Company L declared no dividends in 1990, but declared and paid dividends of $70,000 in 1991. Company K accounts for its investment in Company L under the cost method. How much should Company K report on its 1991 income statement as dividend revenue from Company L?

a. $ 1,575
b. $ 7,500
c. $ 9,000
d. $10,500

[AICPA adapted]

EXERCISE 7-7

When a parent company uses the equity method to account for an investment in the common stock of a subsidiary, the investment account will be increased when the parent recognizes

a. a proportionate interest in the net income of the subsidiary.
b. a cash dividend received from the subsidiary.
c. periodic amortization of the goodwill related to the purchase.
d. depreciation related to the excess of the market value over book value of the subsidiary's depreciable assets at the date of acquisition.

[AICPA adapted]

EXERCISE 7-8

On April 1, 1990, Company M paid $378,000 for 16,000 shares of Company N's 20,000 outstanding shares of common stock. Company N reported net income of $40,000 for 1990, and declared dividends of $25,000 on November 1, 1990. In 1991, Company N reported net income of $18,000, and declared and paid dividends of $25,000.

Required

1. If Company M accounts for its investment in Company N under the equity method, what should be the balance of its Investment in Company N account at December 31, 1991?
   a. $376,000
   b. $376,400
   c. $378,000
   d. $384,400
2. If Company M accounts for its investment in Company N under the equity method, what should it record in its Income from Company N account for 1991?
   a. a $5,600 debit
   b. a $14,400 credit
   c. a $5,600 credit
   d. a $20,000 debit
3. If Company M accounts for its investment in Company N under the cost method, what should be the balance of its Dividend Revenue account at December 31, 1991?
   a. $18,400
   b. $14,400
   c. $20,000
   d. $ 5,600

4. If Company M accounts for its investment in Company N under the cost method, what should be the balance of its Investment in Company N account at December 31, 1991?

a. $376,000
b. $376,400
c. $378,000
d. $384,400

EXERCISE 7-9

On April 30, 1990, Company P purchased 80% of Company Q's common stock for $339,600. On that date, Company Q had common stock of $200,000 and additional paid-in capital of $50,000. Company Q's December 31, 1989 retained earnings balance was $74,500. Company Q reported net income of $35,250 for 1990 and $10,200 for 1991. On November 15 of each year, Company Q declared dividends of $18,000, which were paid on December 20.

Required

Present the journal entries that would be recorded on Company P's books during 1990 and 1991 to account for its investment in Company Q under [a] the cost method and [b] the equity method.

EXERCISE 7-10

On December 31, 1990, Company R purchased 80% of Company S's common stock at a price equal to book value. On this date, Company R and Company S had retained earnings of $500,000 and $200,000, respectively. During 1991, Company R reported net income of $200,000, which included its share of Company S's net income, and declared and paid dividends of $50,000. Also during 1991, Company S reported net income of $40,000 and declared and paid dividends of $20,000. No intercompany transactions other than dividends occurred during 1991. The amount of consolidated retained earnings reported in the December 31, 1991 consolidated balance sheet, assuming the use of the purchase method, should be

a. $650,000
b. $666,000
c. $766,000
d. $770,000

[AICPA adapted]

EXERCISE 7-11

On December 31, 1990, Company T acquired as a long-term investment 25% of Company U's common stock at a price equal to book value. Company T accounts for this investment under the equity method. The balance of Company T's Investment in Company U account at December 31, 1991 was $190,000. During 1991, Company U reported net income of $120,000 and declared and paid dividends of $48,000. How much did Company T pay for its investment in Company U?

a. $172,000
b. $202,000
c. $208,000
d. $232,000

[AICPA adapted]

PROBLEMS

PROBLEM 7-1

Company A purchased 90% of Company B's common stock for $252,000 on December 31, 1990, when Company B had retained earnings of $60,000. The excess of cost over book value is attributed to goodwill of Company B and is to be amortized over 10 years. The December 31, 1992 trial balances of Company A and Company B appear below.

	Company A	Company B
Inventories	$ 80,000	$ 70,000
Investment in Company B	252,000	
Other Assets	338,000	280,000
Cost of Goods Sold	420,000	350,000
Operating Expenses	210,000	160,000
Dividends Declared	12,000	10,000
	$1,312,000	$ 870,000
Liabilities	$ 115,000	$ 50,000
Common Stock	300,000	150,000
Additional Paid-in Capital	100,000	50,000
Retained Earnings	108,000	80,000
Sales	680,000	540,000
Dividend Revenue	9,000	
	$1,312,000	$ 870,000

Required

Prepare the December 31, 1992 consolidation worksheet, supported by all appropriate schedules.

PROBLEM 7-2

The December 31, 1991 trial balances of Company C and Company D appear below.

	Company C	Company D
Accounts Receivable (net)	$ 28,300	$ 37,400
Inventories, 1/1/91	24,800	28,200
Other Current Assets	73,900	101,700
Plant and Equipment (net)	485,300	736,900
Investment in Company D	622,200	
Purchases	243,200	283,100
Operating Expenses	153,300	198,400
Dividends Declared	22,000	16,000
	$1,653,000	$1,401,700

	Company C	Company D
Accounts Payable	$ 98,100	$ 105,300
Other Liabilities	81,600	47,400
Common Stock, $10 par	500,000	200,000
Additional Paid-in Capital	120,000	220,000
Retained Earnings	417,400	318,400
Sales	415,500	510,600
Income from Company D	20,400	
	$1,653,000	$1,401,700

Company C purchased 15,000 shares of Company D's common stock for $618,300 on October 1, 1990. On December 31, 1989, Company D had retained earnings of $297,400. Company D reported net income of $36,000 for 1990. On November 10, 1990, Company N declared dividends of $15,000, which were paid on December 14, 1990. The excess of cost over book value is attributed to the going concern value of Company D in excess of the fair market value of its net assets and is to be amortized over 10 years. Company C and Company D had December 31, 1991 inventories of $28,400 and $26,300, respectively.

Required
Prepare the December 31, 1991 consolidation worksheet, supported by all appropriate schedules.

PROBLEM 7-3
The March 31, 1992 trial balances of Company E and Company F appear below.

	Company E	Company F
Receivables (net)	$ 226,200	$ 122,700
Inventories	317,600	198,600
Other Current Assets	425,100	170,200
Plant and Equipment	1,716,700	1,523,600
Investment in Company F	976,500	
Cost of Goods Solds	1,038,600	483,600
Operating Expenses	613,500	342,100
Dividends Declared	60,000	50,000
	$5,374,200	$2,890,800
Accumulated Depreciation	$ 782,900	$ 723,600
Liabilities	837,300	189,500
Common Stock, $10 par	1,000,000	500,000
Additional Paid-in Capital	318,000	230,000
Retained Earnings	526,200	320,000
Sales	1,827,100	918,400
Other Revenues	82,700	9,300
	$5,374,200	$2,890,800

Company E purchased 37,500 shares of Company F's common stock for $858,000 on June 30, 1988. Company F had retained earnings of $194,000 on March 31, 1988. Company F reported net income of $80,000 for the year ended March 31, 1989. On January 20, 1989, Company F declared dividends of $40,000, which were paid on February 25, 1989. The excess of cost over book value is attributed to the undervaluation of certain of Company F's depreciable assets, which are being depreciated on the straight-line method and which had a remaining useful life at June 30, 1988 of 10 years.

Required

Prepare the March 31, 1992 consolidation worksheet, supported by all appropriate schedules.

PROBLEM 7-4

Company G purchased 7,600 shares of Company H's common stock for $636,000 on June 30, 1989. Company H's outstanding common stock has not changed since that date. Company H's December 31, 1988 retained earnings balance was $85,000. Company H reported net income of $78,000 for 1989. On November 10, 1989, Company H declared dividends of $25,000, which were paid on December 15, 1989. The excess of cost over book value is treated as goodwill from consolidation and is being amortized over 10 years. The December 31, 1992 trial balances of Company G and Company H appear below.

	Company G	Company H
Accounts Receivable (net)	$ 156,800	$ 187,300
Notes Receivable	94,200	73,100
Inventories	87,400	42,000
Other Current Assets	68,900	103,300
Plant and Equipment	1,088,300	962,400
Investment in Company H	636,000	
Purchases	547,200	437,400
Depreciation Expense	161,100	86,200
Other Expenses	125,900	115,600
Dividends Declared	48,000	28,500
Treasury Stock (500 shares, at cost)		29,000
	$3,013,800	$2,064,800
Accumulated Depreciation	$ 419,700	$ 303,100
Notes Payable	102,500	18,200
Accounts Payable	87,400	78,100
Other Liabilities	54,600	37,300
Common Stock, $50 par	800,000	500,000
Additional Paid-in Capital	264,000	120,000
Retained Earnings	318,900	275,500
Sales	937,400	726,500
Other Revenues	29,300	6,100
	$3,013,800	$2,064,800
Inventories, 12/31/92	$ 92,200	$ 35,000

Required

1. Prepare the December 31, 1992 consolidation worksheet, supported by all appropriate schedules.
2. Prepare the consolidated financial statements as of December 31, 1992 and for the year then ended.

PROBLEM 7-5

The April 30, 1993 trial balances of Company J and Company K appear below.

	Company J	Company K
Receivables (net)	$ 101,400	$ 89,100
Inventories	183,600	109,300
Other Current Assets	123,800	188,000
Plant and Equipment	917,300	864,000
Investment in Company K	675,000	
Cost of Goods Sold	526,100	519,300
Other Expenses	392,500	268,300
Dividends Declared	80,000	48,000
Treasury Stock (400 shares, at cost)		24,000
	$2,999,700	$2,110,000
Accumulated Depreciation	$ 292,500	$ 211,900
Liabilities	416,100	204,500
Common Stock, $50 par	800,000	500,000
Additional Paid-in Capital	120,000	140,000
Retained Earnings	314,400	182,000
Sales	1,015,200	863,400
Other Revenues	41,500	8,200
	$2,999,700	$2,110,000

Company J purchased 7,200 shares of Company K's common stock for $675,000 on March 31, 1988. Company K's outstanding common stock has not changed since that date. Company K's April 30, 1987 retained earnings balance was $80,000. Company K reported net income of $72,000 for the year ended April 30, 1988. On February 10, 1988, Company K declared dividends of $42,000, which were paid on March 15, 1988. The excess of cost over book value is attributed to the going concern value of Company K in excess of the fair market value of its recorded net assets and is being amortized over 15 years.

Required

1. Prepare the April 30, 1993 consolidation worksheet, supported by all appropriate schedules.
2. Prepare the consolidated financial statement as of April 30, 1993 and for the year then ended.

PROBLEM 7-6

The December 31, 1992 trial balances of Company L and Company M appear below.

	Company L	Company M
Receivables (net)	$ 89,300	$ 87,200
Inventories	91,600	63,400
Other Current Assets	77,400	102,600
Plant and Equipment	1,925,100	1,605,300
Investment in Company M	775,200	
Cost of Goods Sold	583,600	432,500
Other Expenses	571,300	397,200
Dividends Declared	160,000	30,000
	$4,273,500	$2,718,200

	Company L	Company M
Accumulated Depreciation	$ 721,400	$ 428,200
Current Liabilities	187,700	110,300
Bonds Payable		400,000
Premium on Bonds Payable		21,000
Common Stock, $10 par	1,000,000	500,000
Additional Paid-in Capital	410,000	60,000
Retained Earnings	358,600	280,000
Sales	1,487,300	910,000
Other Revenues	108,500	8,700
	$4,273,500	$2,718,200

Company L purchased 80% of Company M's common stock for $672,000 on June 30, 1989. Company M's December 31, 1988 retained earnings balance was $168,000. Company M reported net income of $84,000 for 1989. On November 1, 1989, Company M declared dividends of $45,000, which were paid on December 5, 1989. The excess of cost over book value is treated as goodwill of Company M and is being amortized over 14 years.

Required

1. Prepare the December 31, 1992 consolidation worksheet, supported by all appropriate schedules.
2. Prepare the consolidated financial statements as of December 31, 1992 and for the year then ended.

PROBLEM 7-7

Company N purchased 7,200 shares of Company O's common stock for $705,300 on June 30, 1989. Company O's outstanding common stock has not changed since that date. Company O had retained earnings of $114,800 on December 31, 1988. Company O reported net income of $76,000 for 1989. On November 12, 1989, Company O declared dividends of $36,000, which were paid on December 15, 1989. The excess of cost over book value is treated as goodwill of Company O and is being amortized over 10 years. The December 31, 1992 trial balances of Company N and Company O appear below.

	Company N	Company O
Accounts Receivable (net)	$ 112,100	$ 84,300
Inventories	87,400	75,700
Other Current Assets	76,900	161,800
Plant and Equipment	833,600	977,900
Investment in Company O	705,300	
Discount on Bonds Payable	31,200	
Purchases	601,300	491,200
Operating Expenses	270,700	226,300
Dividends Declared	22,000	48,000
Treasury Stock (400 shares, at cost)		32,400
	$2,740,500	$2,097,600

	Company N	Company O
Accumulated Depreciation	$ 417,300	$ 254,300
Current Liabilities	125,200	152,700
Bonds Payable	400,000	
Common Stock, $50 par	600,000	500,000
Additional Paid-in Capital	110,000	160,000
Retained Earnings	138,100	216,400
Sales	858,700	796,300
Other Revenues	91,200	17,900
	$2,740,500	$2,097,600
Inventories, 12/31/92	$ 89,300	$ 73,200

Required

1. Prepare the December 31, 1992 consolidation worksheet, supported by all appropriate schedules.
2. Prepare the consolidated financial statements as of December 31, 1992 and for the year then ended.

PROBLEM 7-8

Company P purchased 36,000 shares of Company Q's common stock for $556,800 on March 31, 1989. Company Q's outstanding common stock has not changed since that date. Company Q had retained earnings of $66,200 on December 31, 1988. Company Q reported net income of $52,800 for 1989. On November 1, 1989, Company Q declared dividends of $36,000, which were paid on December 10, 1989. The excess of cost over book value is attributed to the going concern value of Company Q in excess of the fair market value of its recorded net assets and is being amortized over 12 years. The December 31, 1992 trial balances of Company P and Company Q appear below.

	Company P	Company Q
Accounts Receivable (net)	$ 136,200	$ 100,400
Inventories	77,200	99,700
Other Current Assets	98,600	168,100
Plant and Equipment	892,850	700,800
Investment in Company Q	608,550	
Cost of Goods Sold	597,400	458,400
Operating Expenses	363,400	265,800
Dividends Declared	50,000	48,000
Treasury Stock (2,000 shares, at cost)		37,000
	$2,824,200	$1,878,200
Accumulated Depreciation	$ 228,800	$ 186,200
Liabilities	396,800	191,400
Common Stock, $10 par	600,000	500,000
Additional Paid-in Capital	92,000	80,000
Retained Earnings	396,600	136,200
Sales	1,065,400	775,800
Other Revenues	44,600	8,600
	$2,824,200	$1,878,200

Required

1. Prepare the December 31, 1992 consolidation worksheet, supported by all appropriate schedules.
2. Prepare the consolidated financial statements as of December 31, 1992 and for the year then ended.

SOLUTION TO REVIEW PROBLEM

Excess of Cost Over Book Value

Cost of Investment		$ 352,000
Book Value (80% × $390,000)		312,000
Excess of Cost over Book Value		40,000
Expand to 100%		÷ 80%
Goodwill, 10/1/89		50,000
Amortization through 9/30/91	$ 10,000	
Amortization, Y.E. 9/30/92	5,000	
		15,000
Goodwill, 9/30/92		$ 35,000

Adjustments

A. Goodwill	$ 50,000
B. Appraisal Capital: K	(50,000)

Eliminations

Intercompany Ownership Interests

[1]	Common Stock: K	$ 200,000
[2]	Additional Paid-in Capital: K	40,000
[3]	Retained Earnings: K	88,000
[4]	Appraisal Capital: K	40,000
[5]	Investment in Company K	$(368,000)

Subsidiary Income and Dividends

[6]	Income from Company K	$ 16,000
[7]	Dividends: K	(6,400)
[8]	Investment in Company K	$ (9,600)

Goodwill Amortization

[9]	Retained Earnings: J	$ 8,000
[10]	Retained Earnings: K	2,000
[11]	Expenses (Goodwill Amortization)	5,000
[12]	Goodwill	$ (15,000)

Income Allocation

Company J's Net Income		$ 28,000
Company K's Net Income	$ 20,000	
Less: Goodwill Amortization Expense	5,000	
Company K's Adjusted Net Income	15,000	
Minority Interest (20%)	3,000	
Company J's Share (80%)		12,000
Consolidated Net Income		$ 40,000

Equity Method Consolidation Worksheet

	Company J	Company K	Adjustments and Eliminations		Income Statement		Balance Sheet
Inventory	75,000	90,000			165,000	163,000	163,000
Investment in Company K	377,600		[5]	(368,000)			
			[8]	(9,600)			
Other Assets	414,400	427,000					841,400
Purchases	325,000	360,000			685,000		
Expenses	180,000	225,000	[11]	5,000	410,000		
Dividends: J	10,000						10,000 R
Dividends: K		8,000	[7]	(6,400)			1,600 M
Goodwill			A	50,000			
			[12]	(15,000)			35,000
	1,382,000	1,110,000					1,051,000
Liabilities	164,000	90,000					254,000
Common Stock: J	400,000						400,000
Common Stock: K		250,000	[1]	200,000			50,000 M
Additional Paid-in Capital: J	100,000						100,000
Additional Paid-in Capital: K		50,000	[2]	40,000			10,000 M
Retained Earnings: J	172,000		[9]	8,000			164,000 R
Retained Earnings: K		110,000	[3]	88,000			20,000 M
			[10]	2,000			
Sales	530,000	610,000				1,140,000	
Income from Company K	16,000		[6]	16,000			
Appraisal Capital: K			B	(50,000)			10,000 M
			[4]	40,000			
	1,382,000	1,110,000					
Minority Interest in Company K's Net Income					3,000		3,000 M
Consolidated Net Income					40,000		40,000 R
					1,303,000	1,303,000	1,051,000

INTERCOMPANY TRANSACTIONS AND INTERCOMPANY PROFITS IN INVENTORIES

lthough we treat affiliated corporations as parts of a single economic entity in preparing consolidated financial statements, legally they remain separate corporate entities. Therefore, affiliates can and do engage in a variety of transactions with each other. The balances resulting from these *intercompany transactions*, while legitimate with respect to each affiliate separately, must be eliminated in preparing consolidated financial statements to the extent that they

- would otherwise result in double-counting, or
- represent *unrealized intercompany profits*—that is, intercompany profits that have not yet become realized to the consolidated entity through transactions (exchanges) with outside entities.

In general terms, sets of intercompany balances can consist of

- Subsidiary Dividends Declared versus Dividend Revenue (under the cost method) or reduction of the Investment in Subsidiary balance (under the equity method)
- Revenue versus expense
- Asset versus liability
- Intercompany profits

More specifically, this chapter deals with

- Intercompany sales and purchases of merchandise
- Intercompany accounts receivable and accounts payable
- Intercompany profits in beginning and ending inventories

For the sake of clarity, our discussions and illustrations thus far have been based on only two affiliates: a parent and its single subsidiary. We must recognize, however, that a parent may have more than one subsidiary, that subsidiaries may have subsidiaries of their own, etc. Any two affiliates may transact business with each other, with resulting intercompany balances.

INTERCOMPANY BALANCES RESULTING FROM INTERCOMPANY TRANSACTIONS

Without regard to intercompany profits, intercompany transactions can produce the following kinds of intercompany balances:

- Subsidiary Dividends Declared versus Dividend Revenue (under the cost method) or reduction of the Investment in Subsidiary balance (under the equity method)
- Revenue versus expense
- Asset versus liability

These intercompany balances must be eliminated in order to avoid inflating the consolidated financial statements; that is, to avoid double-counting.[1]

Intercompany dividends represent a special case of intercompany balances because of their direct ownership implications. The appropriate treatment of these dividends is presented in Chapter 7 in the Subsidiary Income and Dividends set of eliminations.

Intercompany revenues and expenses can be of many types, including

- Sales and purchases of merchandise
- Sales and purchases of services
- Interest revenue and expense on intercompany receivables and payables
- Rental revenue and expense

If the intercompany portions of these balances are not eliminated, both revenues and expenses will be inflated on the consolidated income statement. Total net income will not be affected, but its components will be overstated.

Examples of intercompany assets and liabilities include

- Dividends receivable and payable
- Accounts or notes receivable and payable arising from sales–purchase transactions
- Notes receivable and payable arising from lending–borrowing transactions
- Investment in an affiliate's bonds and bonds payable of the affiliate
- Interest receivable and payable

If the intercompany portions of these balances are not eliminated, both assets and liabilities will be inflated on the consolidated balance sheet. Stockholders' equity will not be affected and the balance sheet will still balance, but its components will be overstated.

HOW MUCH OF EACH SET OF INTERCOMPANY BALANCES SHOULD BE ELIMINATED?

Arguments can be advanced for eliminating either 100 percent of each set of intercompany balances or only an amount based on the parent company's ownership interest in the subsidiary. The answer lies in the way in which we view the subsidiary: either as a single, intact

---

[1] *Accounting Research Bulletin No. 51, Consolidated Financial Statements* (New York: AICPA, 1959), paragraph 6.

entity or as two entities—the subsidiary itself, represented by the majority ownership interest, and the minority stockholders.

If we view the subsidiary as a single, intact entity, we are led to eliminate 100 percent of the intercompany balances. Under this concept, we are saying, in effect, that the parent has bought from or sold to *the subsidiary,* owes or is owed by *the subsidiary,* etc. In other words, the exchanges that have created intercompany balances have occurred entirely within the consolidated entity. Thus, the entire amount of each intercompany balance should be eliminated.

If we view the subsidiary as consisting of two entities—the subsidiary itself and the minority stockholders—we are led to eliminate only the majority ownership percentage of the intercompany balances. Under this concept, we are saying, in effect, that the parent has bought from or sold to *both the subsidiary and its minority stockholders,* owes or is owed by *both the subsidiary and its minority stockholders,* etc. In such a case, the minority stockholders consitute an outside entity with which the consolidated entity has transacted. Because only the portion resulting from transactions with the subsidiary itself is actually an intercompany balance, only that portion should be eliminated.

The first concept, that of the subsidiary as a single entity, is consistent with the generally accepted method. Accordingly, we will follow it and eliminate 100 percent of all intercompany balances throughout this book. The eliminations of intercompany balances resulting from sales and purchases of merchandise between affiliates are shown in Illustrative Problem 8.1.

INTERCOMPANY PROFITS IN INVENTORY

Because affiliated corporations are separate legal entities, the transfer of merchandise from one affiliate to another is an actual sale by the selling affiliate and an actual purchase by the buying affiliate. Although it is possible for the transfer to be made at the selling affiliate's cost, ordinarily it will be made at a price in excess of that cost. That price could be either an artificially determined transfer price or a market price determined in the same manner as for sales to other customers of the selling affiliate.

When one affiliate sells to another at a price above the selling affiliate's cost, regardless of how that price is determined, an element of **intercompany profit** is included in the intercompany selling price. This intercompany profit might be defined variously as selling price minus cost of goods sold (gross profit), gross profit minus direct selling expenses, gross profit minus direct selling expenses and certain allocated expenses, etc. According to *Accounting Research Bulletin No. 51,* "the concept usually applied for this purpose is gross profit or loss."[2] This approach has the dual advantage of being both conservative and practically expedient.

To the extent that merchandise sold by one affiliate to another has been resold by the buying affiliate to outside entities at a price at least equal to the intercompany selling price, the intercompany profit has become realized to the consolidated entity. Because realized intercompany profit should be recognized in the consolidated financial statements, it is not eliminated in the consolidation process.

To the extent that the merchandise in question has not been resold by the end of a given

[2] *Accounting Research Bulletin No. 51,* paragraph 6.

accounting period, however, it remains, unrealized, in the buying affiliate's ending inventory and must be eliminated in the consolidation process. If unrealized intercompany profit is not eliminated, it will be recognized prematurely in the consolidated income statement and the asset, inventory, will be overstated in the consolidated balance sheet. The ending inventory of one accounting period, of course, becomes the beginning inventory of the following accounting period.

Once more, we face the question addressed in the preceding section—how much of the intercompany profit should be eliminated? To answer this question, we could use the same analysis that was used in reference to intercompany balances other than intercompany profits. In this case, however, *Accounting Research Bulletin No. 51* provides the answer:

> The amount of intercompany profit or loss to be eliminated in accordance with paragraph 6 is not affected by the existence of a minority interest. The complete elimination of the intercompany profit or loss is consistent with the underlying assumption that consolidated financial statements represent the financial position and results of operations of a single business enterprise.[3]

Again, we will follow generally accepted accounting principles and eliminate 100 percent of all unrealized intercompany profits.

INTERCOMPANY PROFITS IN ENDING INVENTORY

At the end of an accounting period in which intercompany sales and purchases of merchandise occur, three kinds of intercompany balances normally appear in the preclosing trial balances of the affiliates:

- Intercompany sales and purchases
- Intercompany receivables and payables
- Intercompany profits (both realized and unrealized)

As explained in the preceding section, the first two sets of intercompany balances must be eliminated completely, without regard to intercompany profits. Indeed, they would be eliminated even if the merchandise had been sold at exactly the selling affiliate's cost. Our consideration of the elimination of intercompany profits begins with unrealized intercompany profit in ending inventory. Remember that an inventory must be the ending inventory of one accounting period before it can become the beginning inventory of the following accounting period.

To the extent that merchandise purchased by one affiliate from another affiliate has not been resold by the end of a given accounting period, an element of unrealized intercompany profit remains in the buying affiliate's ending inventory. Thus, the buying affiliate's ending inventory is overstated; that is, its carrying value is greater than intercompany cost by the amount of the unrealized intercompany profit. In order to report the combined ending inventory on the consolidated balance sheet at a value no greater than intercompany cost, this unrealized intercompany profit must be eliminated from the combined ending inventory.

After the combined ending inventory has been reduced to intercompany cost by eliminating the unrealized intercompany profit, it must be subjected to the lower-of-cost-or-market

---

[3] *Accounting Research Bulletin No. 51*, paragraph 14.

procedure, just as would be done in the case of a single corporation.[4] Because this topic is amply covered in most intermediate accounting texts and courses, we do not discuss and illustrate its application in this text. (In effect, we assume that intercompany cost is less than market in all illustrations, exercises, and problems.)

In addition, the entire amount of the gross profit on the intercompany sales is contained in the selling affiliate's net income and, therefore, in total net income. To the extent that the merchandise acquired from an affiliate has been resold to outside customers by the end of the accounting period, this intercompany profit has become realized to the consolidated entity, and should remain in total net income to be allocated between the minority interest in subsidiary net income and consolidated net income. To the extent that the merchandise acquired from an affiliate has not been sold to an outside entity by the end of the accounting period, however, the intercompany profit remains unrealized and must be eliminated from total net income.

Elimination of unrealized intercompany profit in ending inventory accomplishes two objectives.

- It reduces the combined ending inventory, an asset on the consolidated balance sheet, to *intercompany cost*, its appropriate carrying value (subject, of course, to the lower-of-cost-or-market procedure).
- It shifts the recognition of the intercompany profit out of the current accounting period into the following accounting period or periods when, presumably, it will become realized to the consolidated entity through sale to outside entities. (For our purposes, we will assume that all merchandise on hand at the end of one year has been sold to outside customers by the end of the following year. If for any reason this is not true, the goods in question simply are included in two or more successive ending inventories.)

When the affiliates use perpetual inventory systems, their preclosing trial balances will contain ending inventories (in the Inventory accounts) and Cost of Goods Sold accounts. Thus, the intercompany profit in ending inventory can be eliminated directly from the combined ending inventory and added to the combined cost of goods sold. Removing the unrealized intercompany profit from the combined ending inventory allows that asset to be reported in the consolidated balance sheet at intercompany cost (or market, whichever is lower). Adding the unrealized intercompany profit to combined cost of goods sold reduces the total net income for the period, thus shifting the intercompany profit forward into the following period or periods.

When the affiliates use periodic inventory systems, direct elimination of intercompany profits from ending inventories is not possible, because the ending inventories are not included in the affiliates' preclosing trial balances. In Chapter 7, a worksheet technique is introduced whereby the combined ending inventory amount is entered in the consolidation worksheet as a credit in the Income Statement columns and as a debit in the Balance Sheet column. Using this technique, we can give effect to the elimination of intercompany profit by reducing the combined ending inventory by the amount of the unrealized intercompany profit and then entering the resulting intercompany cost amount in the worksheet. This procedure yields the same results as the direct eliminations used in connection with perpetual inventory systems.

---

[4] *Accounting Research Bulletin No. 43, Restatement and Revision of Accounting Research Bulletins* (New York: AICPA, 1953), Chapter 4, Statement 5 through paragraph 14.

- The asset, inventory, is reported on the consolidated balance sheet at intercompany cost.
- The combined cost of goods sold is increased, thus decreasing total net income.

A schedule showing the reduction of the combined ending inventory to intercompany cost appears in Exhibit 8-1 of Illustrative Problem 8.1.

ILLUSTRATIVE PROBLEM 8.1: INTERCOMPANY PROFITS IN ENDING INVENTORY

Illustrative Problem 8.1 is a continuation of Illustrative Problem 7.2 (in Chapter 7), from which the following information is repeated. Company P acquired 48,000 of Company S's 60,000 outstanding shares of $5 par value common stock for $608,400 on April 1, 1991, when Company S had additional paid-in capital of $120,000. Company S's December 31, 1990 retained earnings balance was $120,250. In 1991, Company S reported net income of $81,000 and declared dividends of $40,000 on November 15, which were paid on December 15. The excess of cost over book value is treated as goodwill of Company S, which is being amortized over 10 years. Comany P uses the equity method to account for its investment in Company S.

In addition, the following information is available. During 1992, Company S sold merchandise that had cost $215,100 to Company P for $358,500. At December 31, 1992, Company P owed Company S $28,600 on open account and $32,500 of the $358,500 of merchandise remained in Company P's inventory. Company P and Company S had December 31, 1992 inventories of $82,200 and $90,800, respectively, and separate net incomes for 1992 of $89,400 and $65,000, respectively. Both affiliates use periodic inventory systems.

Three new sets of intercompany balances must be eliminated in the December 31, 1992 consolidation worksheet.

- The $358,500 of intercompany sales and purchases, which is included in Company S's Sales account balance and in Company P's Purchases account balance (under a perpetual inventory system, it would be included in Company P's Cost of Goods Sold account balance)
- The $28,600 intercompany receivable and payable, which is part of Company S's Accounts Receivable balance and of Company P's Accounts Payable balance
- The unrealized intercompany profit of $13,000, which affects both the combined ending inventory and the combined cost of goods sold

The intercompany profit in ending inventory can be determined as follows. The total intercompany profit for 1992 is intercompany sales of $358,500 minus intercompany cost of $215,100, or $143,400. This intercompany profit expressed as a percent of selling price is $143,400 divided by $358,500, or 40%. Multiplying this intercompany profit percentage, 40%, by the $32,500 of goods remaining in Company P's ending inventory (expressed in terms of intercompany selling price) yields the intercompany profit remaining in ending inventory of $13,000.

Exhibit 8-1 presents the eliminations necessary at December 31, 1992 relative to the intercompany sales and purchases and the resulting balances, under a periodic inventory system. (The other eliminations are not shown here, but are illustrated in Illustrative Problem 8.2 in the context of the consolidation worksheet.)

EXHIBIT 8-1

Illustrative Problem 8.1
Eliminations (Periodic Inventory)
December 31, 1992

Eliminations

Intercompany Sales and Purchases

[13] Sales	$ 358,500
[14] Purchases	(358,500)

Intercompany Receivables and Payables

[15] Accounts Payable	$ 28,600
[16] Accounts Receivable	(28,600)

Intercompany Profit in Ending Inventory

Company P's Ending Inventory	$ 82,200
Company S's Ending Inventory	90,800
Total Ending Inventory	173,000
Less: Intercompany Profit	13,000
[17] Ending Inventory at Intercompany Cost	$ 160,000

Because neither affiliate's Retained Earnings balance is affected, each set of eliminations will be the same regardless of which affiliate is the buyer or the seller and regardless of whether the subsidiary is wholly or partially owned. Also, it is important to note that these eliminations are applied to the *combined* balance of each account (combined Sales, combined Cost of Goods Sold, etc.) regardless of which affiliate's account actually contains each intercompany balance. Each set of account balances will be added together on the consolidation worksheet to form consolidated income statement or balance sheet values. Thus, it is not necessary to identify these accounts by company name.

The Intercompany Sales and Purchases and the Intercompany Receivables and Payables sets of eliminations are made without regard to intercompany profits.

- The $358,500 of intercompany sales and purchases represents the results of transactions with unrelated entities on the part of each affiliate individually, and would be reflected on their individual income statements. From a consolidated point of view, however, this $358,500 represents nothing more than the transfer of merchandise from one location to another within the consolidated entity, and so must be eliminated entirely.
- Similarly, the $28,600 intercompany receivable and payable is a legitimate asset to Company S and a legitimate liability to Company P, and would be so reported in their separate balance sheets. The consolidated entity, however, neither owes nor is owed this amount; thus, it must be eliminated entirely.

Because the ending inventory balances do not appear in the affiliate's preclosing trial balances, we cannot eliminate the unrealized intercompany profit directly from the ending inventories on the consolidation worksheet. The alternative procedure, described earlier in this chapter, is to prepare the schedule shown in Exhibit 8-1 in which the ending inventories are combined and then reduced by the amount of the intercompany profit. The resulting combined ending inventory stated at intercompany cost is entered in the consolidation worksheet in the Income Statement credit column and as a debit in the Balance Sheet column. Both worksheet entries should be cross-referenced to the identifying number in the schedule, in this case, [17].

The net effect of this treatment is as follows:

- It increases the combined cost of goods sold for 1992, which decreases total net income for 1992. This shifts the recognition of this $13,000 of intercompany profit from 1992 into 1993, when it presumably will become realized through resale of the merchandise to outside customers.
- It reduces the asset, Inventory, to intercompany cost.

As indicated in Chapter 7, one of the affiliates' net incomes must be adjusted in the Income Allocation schedule for any change in total net income caused by a worksheet elimination. The addition of unrealized intercompany profit in ending inventory to the combined cost of goods sold is one such change. The affiliate whose income is adjusted is the one that originated the item in question—in this case, the seller, Company S. Exhibit 8-2 presents the 1992 Income Allocation schedule in which the unrealized intercompany profit in ending inventory is subtracted from Company S's net income. If Company P had been the seller, this intercompany profit would have been subtracted from its net income.

EXHIBIT 8-2

Illustrative Problem 8.1
Income Allocation Schedule
Year Ended December 31, 1992

Income Allocation

Company P's Own Net Income		$ 89,400
Company S's Own Net Income	$ 65,000	
Less: Goodwill Amortization Expense	(20,000)	
Intercompany Profit in Ending Inventory	(13,000)	
Company S's Adjusted Net Income	32,000	
Minority Interest (20%)	6,400	
Company P's Share (80%)		25,600
Consolidated Net Income		$ 115,000

In some textbooks, a sale by a subsidiary to its parent is referred to as an "upstream" transaction, whereas a sale by a parent to its subsidiary is referred to as a "downstream" transaction. We prefer to avoid these colorful, but somewhat imprecise, terms. Instead, we describe explicitly the participants in intercompany transactions and their roles therein.

Eliminations under Perpetual Inventory.   If both Company P and Company S had been using perpetual inventory systems, the eliminations for intercompany sales and purchases would have been the same as those appearing in Exhibit 8-1 under the periodic inventory system except that combined Cost of Goods Sold, rather than combined Purchases, would have been credited, as shown in Exhibit 8-3. The eliminations for intercompany receivables and payables would have been identical to those made under the periodic inventory system. The unrealized intercompany profit in ending inventory would have been eliminated directly from Inventory and Cost of Goods Sold, as shown in Exhibit 8-3.

EXHIBIT 8-3

Illustrative Problem 8.1
Eliminations (Perpetual Inventory)
December 31, 1992

Eliminations

Intercompany Sales and Purchases

[13] Sales	$ 358,500
[14] Cost of Goods Sold	(358,500)

Intercompany Receivables and Payables

[15] Accounts Payable	$ 28,600
[16] Accounts Receivable	(28,600)

Intercompany Profit in Ending Inventory

[17] Cost of Goods Sold	$ 13,000
[18] Inventory	(13,000)

The effect of Eliminations [17] and [18] is the same as that of the inventory schedule in Exhibit 8-1. Increasing the combined cost of goods sold for 1992 decreases total net income for 1992, thus shifting the recognition of this $13,000 of intercompany profit from 1992 into 1993. Also, the asset, Inventory, is reduced to intercompany cost.

The Income Allocation schedule under the perpetual inventory system is identical to that under the periodic inventory system shown in Exhibit 8-2. Therefore, it is not repeated here.

INTERCOMPANY PROFITS IN BEGINNING INVENTORY

The buying affiliate's ending inventory of one year, of course, becomes its beginning inventory of the next year. Unless we know otherwise, we will assume that by the end of any year, the buying affiliate has sold its beginning inventory for that year to outside entities at a price at least equal to the intercompany selling price. Accordingly, the intercompany profit in the buying affiliate's beginning inventory, which was unrealized at the end of the preceding year, has become realized to the consolidated entity by the end of the current year.

In the preceding section, we noted that the elimination of unrealized intercompany profit in ending inventory has two results.

- It reduces the combined ending inventory, an asset on the consolidated balance sheet, to intercompany cost.
- It shifts the recognition of the unrealized intercompany profit forward from the year in which it is generated through intercompany sales and purchases of merchandise, into the following year, in which it is assumed to become realized to the consolidated entity through sale to outside entities.

At the end of the second year, we must deal with that same intercompany profit element again, but as a part of the buying affiliate's beginning inventory rather than its ending inventory. Because we are assuming that the goods in question have been resold, the beginning inventory, of course, is no longer an asset. Therefore, we are concerned with only the second of the two results noted above—the forward shift in the recognition of intercompany profit.

The intercompany profit in the buying affiliate's beginning inventory for a given year is included in the selling affiliate's net income of the preceding year. Therefore, it becomes a part of at least the selling affiliate's ending balance of Retained Earnings for that preceding year, which is also its beginning balance of Retained Earnings for the following year. Remember that the preclosing trial balances used in the consolidation worksheet contain beginning of the year retained earnings balances.

- If the parent is the selling affiliate, the intercompany profit in beginning inventory is included in only the parent's beginning Retained Earnings balance, regardless of the parent's percentage of ownership in the subsidiary.
- If a wholly owned subsidiary is the selling affiliate, the intercompany profit in beginning inventory is included in the subsidiary's beginning Retained Earnings balance. The entire amount also is included in the parent's beginning Retained Earnings balance, because the parent has recorded 100 percent of the subsidiary's net income of the preceding year as income from subsidiary under the equity method. (If the parent uses the cost method, we will convert from cost to equity, producing the same result.)
- If a partially owned subsidiary is the selling affiliate, the intercompany profit in beginning inventory is included in the subsidiary's beginning Retained Earnings balance and an amount proportionate to the parent's ownership interest is included in the parent's beginning Retained Earnings balance.

At the end of each year, the intercompany profit in beginning inventory must be removed from the appropriate Retained Earnings balance or balances and added to that year's total net income by reducing the combined cost of goods sold. This completes the forward shifting of the recognition of the intercompany profit. The reduction of the combined cost of goods sold is accomplished by a credit elimination against either

- the combined beginning balance of Inventory under a periodic inventory system, or
- the combined Cost of Goods Sold balance under a perpetual inventory system.

ILLUSTRATIVE PROBLEM 8.2: INTERCOMPANY PROFITS IN BEGINNING AND ENDING INVENTORY

Illustrative Problem 8.2 is a continuation of Illustrative Problem 8.1, from which the following information is repeated. Company P acquired 48,000 of Company S's 60,000 outstanding shares of $5 par value common stock for $608,400 on April 1, 1991, when Company S had additional paid-in capital of $120,000. Company S's December 31, 1990 retained earnings balance was $120,250. In 1991, Company S reported net income of $81,000 and declared dividends of $40,000. In 1992, Company S reported net income of $65,000 and declared and paid dividends of $40,000. In each year, the dividends were declared on November 15 and paid on December 15. The excess of cost over book value is treated as goodwill of Company S, which is being amortized over 10 years. Company P uses the equity method to account for its investment in Company S.

During 1992, Company S sold merchandise that had cost $215,100 to Company P for $358,500. At December 31, 1992, $32,500 of the $358,500 of merchandise remained in Company P's inventory. Company P and Company S had December 31, 1992 inventories of $82,200 and $90,800, respectively. Both affiliates use periodic inventory systems.

The following additional information is available for 1993. During 1993, Company S sold merchandise to Company P for $388,000, which is 60% above Company S's cost. At December 31, 1993, Company P owed Company S $31,700 on open account and $37,600 of the $388,000 of merchandise remained in Company P's inventory. Company P and Company S had December 31, 1993 inventories of $81,800 and $89,900, respectively, and separate net incomes for 1993 of $70,400 and $72,500, respectively.

Exhibit 8-4 presents the schedules of Excess of Cost over Book Value and Adjustments necessary at December 31, 1993. Exhibit 8-5 presents the Intercompany Ownership Interests, Subsidiary Income and Dividends, and Goodwill Amortization sets of eliminations necessary at December 31, 1993.

The three sets of eliminations illustrated in Exhibit 8-1 are repeated in Exhibit 8-6, using the 1993 amounts of intercompany sales and purchases, intercompany receivables and payables, and the unrealized intercompany profit in ending inventory.

EXHIBIT 8-4

Illustrative Problem 8.2
Excess of Cost over Book Value and Adjustments
December 31, 1993

Excess of Cost over Book Value

Cost of Investment		$ 608,400
Book Value (80% × $560,500)		448,400
Excess of Cost over Book Value		160,000
Expand to 100%		÷ 80%
Goodwill, 4/1/91		200,000
Amortization through 12/31/92	$ 35,000	
Amortization, 1993	20,000	55,000
Goodwill, 12/31/93		$ 145,000

Adjustments

A. Goodwill	$ 200,000
B. Appraisal Capital: S	(200,000)

EXHIBIT 8-5

Illustrative Problem 8.2
Eliminations (Periodic Inventory)
December 31, 1993

Eliminations

Intercompany Ownership Interests

[1]	Common Stock: S	$ 240,000
[2]	Additional Paid-in Capital: S	96,000
[3]	Retained Earnings: S	149,000
[4]	Appraisal Capital: S	160,000
[5]	Investment in Company S	$(645,000)

Subsidiary Income and Dividends

[6]	Income from Company S	$ 58,000
[7]	Dividends Declared: S	(36,000)
[8]	Investment in Company S	$ (22,000)

Goodwill Amortization

[9]	Retained Earnings: P	$ 28,000
[10]	Retained Earnings: S	7,000
[11]	Operating Expenses	20,000
[12]	Goodwill	$ (55,000)

Calculations
[1] 80% × $300,000
[2] 80% × $120,000
[3] 80% × $186,250
[4] 80% × $200,000
[5] Sum of Eliminations [1] through [4]
[6] 80% × $72,500
[7] 80% × $45,000
[8] Elimination [6] minus Elimination [7]
[9] 100% × 80% × $35,000
[10] 20% × 100% × $35,000
[11], [12] From Excess of Cost over Book Value Schedule

The intercompany profit in ending inventory can be determined as follows. Company S's profit margin is expressed as a percent of cost, rather than as a percent of selling price, as in Illustrative Problem 8.1. If the profit margin is X% of cost, then selling price must equal X% of cost plus 100% of cost, or (X% + 100%) of cost. To determine cost, we must divide selling price by (X% + 100%). Having determined cost, we can multiply it by X% in order to determine the amount of profit. A convenient way of expressing this series of calculations is

EXHIBIT 8-6

Illustrative Problem 8.2
Additional Eliminations (Periodic Inventory)
December 31, 1993

Eliminations

Intercompany Sales and Purchases

[13] Sales	$ 388,000
[14] Purchases	(388,000)

Intercompany Receivables and Payables

[15] Accounts Payable	$ 31,700
[16] Accounts Receivable	(31,700)

Intercompany Profit in Beginning Inventory

[17] Retained Earnings: P	$ 10,400
[18] Retained Earnings: S	2,600
[19] Inventories	$ (13,000)

Intercompany Profit in Ending Inventory

Company P's Ending Inventory	$ 81,800
Company S's Ending Inventory	89,900
Total Ending Inventory	171,700
Less: Intercompany Profit	14,100
[20] Ending Inventory at Intercompany Cost	$ 157,600

$$\text{Selling Price} \times \frac{\text{Profit Margin}}{1 + \text{Profit Margin}} = \text{Profit}$$

The intercompany profit in ending inventory for 1993 can be determined as

$$\$37,600 \times \frac{60\%}{160\%} = \$14,100$$

The Intercompany Sales and Purchases, Intercompany Receivables and Payables, and Intercompany Profit in Ending Inventory sets of eliminations are essentially the same as those shown in Exhibit 8-1, except that they contain the 1993 amounts. These three sets of eliminations will be the same regardless of which affiliate is the buyer or seller and regardless of whether the subsidiary is wholly or partially owned.

In the Intercompany Profit in Beginning Inventory set of eliminations, the $13,000 of intercompany profit generated in 1992 (see Illustrative Problem 8.1), but realized in 1993, is added to the total net income of 1993 by crediting Inventories, thus reducing the combined cost of goods sold. The balancing debit must be allocated between the two Retained Earnings balances.

In this case, the $13,000 of unrealized intercompany profit in beginning inventory was included in Company S's 1992 net income, and thus is a part of its beginning Retained Earnings balance for 1993. Company P, under the equity method, recorded 80% of Company S's 1992 net income, including the unrealized intercompany profit, as a credit to its Income from Company S account. Thus, 80% of $13,000, or $10,400 of the unrealized intercompany profit in beginning inventory, is included in Company P's beginning Retained Earnings balance for 1993. Elimination [17] removes this $10,400 of intercompany profit from Company P's Retained Earnings.

In the Intercompany Ownership Interests set of eliminations at December 31, 1993, 80% of each of Company S's stockholders' equity balances, including Retained Earnings, has been eliminated, leaving only the minority interest residuals. The portion of the minority interest in Company S's Retained Earnings representing the unrealized intercompany profit in beginning inventory, 20% of $13,000 or $2,600, is eliminated in Elimination [18].

Another way of explaining the allocation of intercompany profit in beginning inventory between the Retained Earnings balances is to refer to the allocation procedure described in Chapter 7. In any set of eliminations in which such allocations are necessary, each affiliate's Retained Earnings should have allocated to it [a] that affiliate's external ownership percentage, multiplied by [b] its share of the quantity being allocated, multiplied by [c] the quantity being allocated. In this case, the results are

$$[a] \times [b] \times [c] = [d]$$

	[a]		[b]		[c]		[d]
Company P:	100%	×	80%	×	$13,000	=	$10,400
Company S:	20%	×	100%	×	$13,000	=	$ 2,600

Exhibit 8-7 presents the 1993 Income Allocation Schedule. Because Company S is the seller, its net income is adjusted for intercompany profits in both beginning and ending inventories. The intercompany profit in beginning inventory, which was generated in 1992, but realized in 1993, is added. The intercompany profit in ending inventory, which was generated in 1993, but will not be realized until 1994, is subtracted. If Company P had been the seller, these intercompany profits would have been added to and subtracted from its net income.

Exhibit 8-8 presents the completed December 31, 1993 consolidation worksheet. Notice the treatment of the inventories when both affiliates are using periodic inventory systems.

The combined ending inventory, from which the unrealized intercompany profit of $14,100 has been eliminated (identified as Elimination [20]), is entered as a credit in the Income Statement columns, thus increasing the combined cost of goods sold and shifting that intercompany profit element into 1994. The same amount of combined ending inventory also is entered as a debit in the Balance Sheet column, causing the asset, Inventory, to be expressed at intercompany cost.

Elimination [19] reduces the amount of combined beginning inventory extended into the Income Statement debit column, reducing the combined cost of goods sold by $13,000, the amount of unrealized intercompany profit at the end of 1992. Thus, the $13,000 of intercompany profit is included in total net income of 1993, when it is assumed to have been realized.

EXHIBIT 8-7

Illustrative Problem 8.2
Income Allocation Schedule
Year Ended December 31, 1993

Income Allocation

Company P's Own Net Income		$ 70,400
Company S's Own Net Income	$ 72,500	
Add: Intercompany Profit in Beginning Inventory	13,000	
Less: Goodwill Amortization Expense	(20,000)	
Intercompany Profit in Ending Inventory	(14,100)	
Company S's Adjusted Net Income	51,400	
Minority Interest (20%)	10,280	
Company P's Share (80%)		41,120
Consolidated Net Income		$ 111,520

Consolidation under Perpetual Inventory. If Company P and Company S had been using perpetual inventory systems, their December 31, 1993 trial balances would include ending inventory balances in their Inventories accounts, as well as Cost of Goods Sold balances. These trial balances are shown in the consolidation worksheet that appears in Exhibit 8-10.

Exhibit 8-9 presents the eliminations necessary at December 31, 1993 relative to the intercompany sales and purchases and the resulting balances, under a perpetual inventory system. Because all the other supporting schedules at December 31, 1993 are the same as those presented in Exhibits 8-4, 8-5, and 8-7, they are not repeated here.

The Intercompany Sales and Purchases set of eliminations is essentially the same as the corresponding set in Exhibit 8-6, except that combined Cost of Goods Sold, instead of combined Purchases, is credited in Elimination [14]. The trial balance of a company using a perpetual inventory system will contain a Cost of Goods Sold account rather than a Purchases account.

The Intercompany Receivables and Payables set of eliminations is not affected by the inventory system in use. Thus, it is exactly the same as that shown in Exhibit 8-6.

As noted above, the trial balance of a company using a perpetual inventory system will contain a Cost of Goods Sold account rather than a Purchases account. In addition, the Inventories account will contain the ending inventory balance. Thus, the intercompany profit in ending inventory is eliminated directly from Cost of Goods Sold and Inventories in Eliminations [17] and [18].

The Intercompany Profit in Beginning Inventory set of eliminations is essentially the same as that shown in Exhibit 8-6. The only difference is that the intercompany profit in beginning inventory is eliminated directly from Cost of Goods Sold when the perpetual inventory system is used. Exhibit 8-10 presents the completed December 31, 1993 consolidation worksheet under the perpetual inventory assumption.

A Problem Solving Hint. What if one affiliate uses a periodic inventory system and the other uses a perpetual inventory system? Because the eliminations are applied to the *combined*

EXHIBIT 8-8

Illustrative Problem 8.2
Completed Equity Method Consolidation Worksheet
Periodic Inventory System
December 31, 1993

	Company P	Company S	Adjustments and Eliminations		Income Statement		Balance Sheet
Accounts Receivable	129,100	141,600	[16]	(31,700)			239,000
Inventories	82,200	90,800	[19]	(13,000)	160,000	[20] 157,600	157,600
Plant and Equipment	848,600	1,285,100					2,133,700
Other Assets	290,400	145,300					435,700
Investment in Company S Stock	667,000		[5]	(645,000)			
			[8]	(22,000)			
Purchases	452,800	523,500	[14]	(388,000)	588,300		
Operating Expenses	311,400	358,700	[11]	20,000	690,100		
Dividends Declared: P	60,000						60,000 R
Dividends Declared: S		45,000	[7]	(36,000)			9,000 M
Goodwill			A	200,000			145,000
			[12]	(55,000)			
	2,841,500	2,590,000					3,180,000
Accumulated Depreciation	589,900	350,900					940,800
Current Liabilities	201,400	152,050	[15]	31,700			321,750
Bonds Payable		500,000					500,000
Premium on Bonds Payable		25,200					25,200
Common Stock: P	500,000						500,000
Common Stock: S		300,000	[1]	240,000			60,000 M
Additional Paid-in Capital: P	310,000						310,000
Additional Paid-in Capital: S		120,000	[2]	96,000			24,000 M
Retained Earnings: P	347,200		[9]	28,000			308,800 R
			[17]	10,400			
Retained Earnings: S		186,250	[3]	149,000			27,650 M
			[10]	7,000			
			[18]	2,600			
Sales	815,200	951,100	[13]	388,000		1,378,300	
Income from Company S	58,000		[6]	58,000			
Other Income	19,800	4,500				24,300	
Appraisal Capital: S			B	(200,000)			40,000 M
			[4]	160,000			
	2,841,500	2,590,000					
Minority Interest in Company S's Net Income					10,280		10,280 M
Consolidated Net Income					111,520		111,520 R
					1,560,200	1,560,200	3,180,000

EXHIBIT 8-9

Illustrative Problem 8.2
Additional Eliminations (Perpetual Inventory)
December 31, 1993

Eliminations

Intercompany Sales and Purchases

[13] Sales	$ 388,000
[14] Cost of Goods Sold	(388,000)

Intercompany Receivables and Payables

[15] Accounts Payable	$ 31,700
[16] Accounts Receivable	(31,700)

Intercompany Profit in Ending Inventory

[17] Cost of Goods Sold	$ 14,100
[18] Inventories	(14,100)

Intercompany Profit in Beginning Inventory

[19] Retained Earnings: P	$ 10,400
[20] Retained Earnings: S	2,600
[21] Cost of Goods Sold	$ (13,000)

balance of each account (combined Sales, combined Cost of Goods Sold, etc.) regardless of which affiliate's account actually contains each intercompany balance, it is possible to use the eliminations for either system.

It is evident that the eliminations and the worksheet treatment of inventories are simpler and more straightforward under a perpetual inventory system than under a periodic inventory system. Therefore, one should use the perpetual inventory system balances whenever they are large enough to absorb the necessary eliminations.

Variation of the Selling Affiliate's Identity. If Company P had been the selling affiliate in 1992 and 1993, only three aspects of the solutions to Illustrative Problems 8.1 and 8.2 would be different. First, in the Intercompany Profit in Beginning Inventory set of eliminations in Exhibits 8-6 and 8-9, the intercompany profit that was unrealized at the end of 1992 would be eliminated from Company P's Retained Earnings balance only, because Comany S's *share* of the intercompany profit would be zero. Exhibit 8-11 presents the Intercompany Profit in Beginning Inventory set of eliminations with Company P as the selling affiliate, assuming that the affiliates use periodic inventory systems. Second, as noted above, Company P's net income would be adjusted in the Income Allocation schedule in Exhibits 8-2 and 8-7. Exhibit 8-12 presents the Income Allocation schedule with Company P as the selling affiliate. Finally, these differences would be reflected in the consolidation worksheets in Exhibits 8-8 and 8-10.

EXHIBIT 8-10

Illustrative Problem 8.2
Completed Equity Method Consolidation Worksheet
Perpetual Inventory System
December 31, 1993

	Company P	Company S	Adjustments and Eliminations		Income Statement	Balance Sheet
Accounts Receivable	129,100	141,600	[16]	(31,700)		239,000
Inventories	81,800	89,900	[18]	(14,100)		157,600
Plant and Equipment	848,600	1,285,100				2,133,700
Other Assets	290,400	145,300				435,700
Investment in Company S Stock	667,000		[5]	(645,000)		
			[8]	(22,000)		
Cost of Goods Sold	453,200	524,400	[14]	(388,000)	590,700	
			[17]	14,100		
			[21]	(13,000)		
Operating Expenses	311,400	358,700	[11]	20,000	690,100	
Dividends Declared: P	60,000					60,000 R
Dividends Declared: S		45,000	[7]	(36,000)		9,000 M
Goodwill			A	200,000		145,000
			[12]	(55,000)		
	2,841,500	2,590,000				3,180,000
Accumulated Depreciation	589,900	350,900				940,800
Current Liabilities	201,400	152,050	[15]	31,700		321,750
Bonds Payable		500,000				500,000
Premium on Bonds Payable		25,200				25,200
Common Stock: P	500,000					500,000
Common Stock: S		300,000	[1]	240,000		60,000 M
Additional Paid-in Capital: P	310,000					310,000
Additional Paid-in Capital: S		120,000	[2]	96,000		24,000 M
Retained Earnings: P	347,200		[9]	28,000		308,800 R
			[19]	10,400		
Retained Earnings: S		186,250	[3]	149,000		27,650 M
			[10]	7,000		
			[20]	2,600		
Sales	815,200	951,100	[13]	388,000	1,378,300	
Income from Company S	58,000		[6]	58,000		
Other Income	19,800	4,500			24,300	
Appraisal Capital: S			B	(200,000)		40,000 M
			[4]	160,000		
	2,841,500	2,590,000				
Minority Interest in Company S's Net Income					10,280	10,280 M
Consolidated Net Income					111,520	111,520 R
					1,402,600	1,402,600 · 3,180,000

EXHIBIT 8-11

Illustrative Problem 8.2
Additional Eliminations (Periodic Inventory)
December 31, 1993

Intercompany Profit in Beginning Inventory

[18] Retained Earnings: P	$ 13,000
[19] Inventories	(13,000)

EXHIBIT 8-12

Illustrative Problem 8.2
Income Allocation Schedule
Year Ended December 31, 1993

Income Allocation

Company P's Own Net Income		$ 70,400
Add: Intercompany Profit in Beginning Inventory		13,000
Intercompany Profit in Ending Inventory		(14,100)
Company P's Adjusted Net Income		69,300
Company S's Own Net Income	$ 72,500	
Less: Goodwill Amortization Expense	(20,000)	
Company S's Adjusted Net Income	52,500	
Minority Interest (20%)	10,500	
Company P's Share (80%)		42,000
Consolidated Net Income		$ 111,300

If Company S had been the selling affiliate, but Company P had owned 100% of Company S's common stock, in the Intercompany Profit in Beginning Inventory set of eliminations in Exhibits 8-6 and 8-9, the intercompany profit would be eliminated from Company P's Retained Earnings balance only, because Company S's *external ownership percentage* would be zero. Therefore, the Intercompany Profit in Beginning Inventory set of eliminations would be exactly the same as that shown in Exhibit 8-11. In this case, of course, no Income Allocation schedule would be necessary. Again, these differences would be reflected in the consolidation worksheets in Exhibits 8-8 and 8-10.

ILLUSTRATIVE PROBLEM 8.3: LONG-LIVED INVENTORIES

The preceding discussions and Illustrative Problems in this chapter are based on the assumption that any units of inventory on hand at the end of one fiscal year will have been sold to outside entities by the end of the following year. Therefore, any unrealized intercompany profit in an affiliate's ending inventory of the first year will have become realized to the consolidated entity by the end of the second year. Although this assumption is applicable to many kinds of inventory, some goods might be carried in inventory over longer periods of time. When this happens, the goods in question simply become part of the beginning inventory of more than one year.

To illustrate the appropriate treatment of long-lived inventories in the consolidation process, we will use the following information taken from Illustrative Problems 8.1 and 8.2, with one change, which is shown in italics. Company P owns 80% of Company S's common stock, which it acquired at the beginning of 1991. During 1992, Company S sold merchandise that had cost $215,100 to Company P for $358,500. At December 31, 1992, $32,500 of the merchandise purchased from Company S during 1992 remained in Company P's inventory. Company P and Company S had December 31, 1992 inventories of $82,200 and $90,800, respectively.

During 1993, Company S sold merchandise to Company P for $388,000, which is 60% above Company S's cost. At December 31, 1993, *$12,500 of the merchandise purchased from Company S during 1992* and $37,600 of the merchandise purchased from Company S during 1993 remained in Company P's inventory. Company P and Company S had December 31, 1993 inventories of $81,800 and $89,900, respectively, and separate net incomes for 1993 of $70,400 and $72,500, respectively. Both affiliates use periodic inventory systems.

The only elements of the consolidation process potentially affected by the revised information are the Intercompany Profit in Ending Inventory sets of eliminations and the Income Allocation schedules. Accordingly, we do not mention the other elements in the following discussion. The December 31, 1992 Intercompany Profit in Ending Inventory set of eliminations would be exactly the same as that appearing in Exhibit 8-1, and is repeated in Exhibit 8-13. The Income Allocation schedule for 1992 also would not be affected by the revised information. It would be identical to the one appearing in Exhibit 8-2; thus, it is not repeated here.

EXHIBIT 8-13

Illustrative Problem 8.3
Eliminations (Periodic Inventory)
December 31, 1992

Eliminations

Intercompany Profit in Ending Inventory

Company P's Ending Inventory	$ 82,200
Company S's Ending Inventory	90,800
Total Ending Inventory	173,000
Less: Intercompany Profit	13,000
[17] Ending Inventory at Intercompany Cost	$ 160,000

The December 31, 1993 Intercompany Profit in Ending Inventory set of eliminations is affected by the revised information, as shown in Exhibit 8-14. In Exhibit 8-6, the $14,100 of unrealized intercompany profit related to intercompany sales and purchases during 1993 is subtracted from the total ending inventory. In addition, in Exhibit 8-14, $5,000 of unrealized intercompany profit ($12,500 × 40%) related to intercompany sales and purchases during 1992 is subtracted from the total ending inventory.

EXHIBIT 8-14

Illustrative Problem 8.3
Additional Eliminations (Periodic Inventory)
December 31, 1993

Eliminations

Intercompany Profit in Ending Inventory

Company P's Ending Inventory		$ 81,800
Company S's Ending Inventory		89,900
Total Ending Inventory		171,700
Less: Intercompany Profit (1992)	$ 5,000	
Intercompany Profit (1993)	14,100	19,100
[17] Ending Inventory at Intercompany Cost		$ 152,600

Finally, the Income Allocation schedule for 1993 would differ from that presented in Exhibit 8-7 in that $19,100, rather than $14,100, of intercompany profit in ending inventory would be subtracted from Company S's own net income. The revised Income Allocation schedule is shown in Exhibit 8-15.

EXHIBIT 8-15

Illustrative Problem 8.3
Income Allocation Schedule
Year Ended December 31, 1993

Income Allocation

Company P's Own Net Income		$ 70,400
Company S's Own Net Income	$ 72,500	
Add: Intercompany Profit in Beginning Inventory	13,000	
Less: Goodwill Amortization Expense	(20,000)	
Intercompany Profit in Ending Inventory	(19,100)	
Company S's Adjusted Net Income	46,400	
Minority Interest (20%)	9,280	
Company P's Share (80%)		37,120
Consolidated Net Income		$ 107,520

SUMMARY

Without regard to intercompany profits, intercompany transactions can produce intercompany balances that must be eliminated in order to avoid inflating the consolidated financial statements; that is, to avoid double-counting. General categories of intercompany balances are

- Subsidiary Dividends Declared versus Dividend Revenue (under the cost method) or reduction of the Investment in Subsidiary balance (under the equity method), which are covered in Chapter 7
- Revenue versus expense
- Asset versus liability

More specifically, Chapter 8 deals with intercompany sales and purchases of merchandise and the resulting intercompany balances:

- Intercompany sales and purchases (or cost of goods sold)
- Intercompany accounts receivable and accounts payable
- Intercompany profits in beginning and ending inventories

The chapter demonstrates the impact of these elements on worksheet eliminations and the income allocation schedule under different assumptions as to the identities of the selling and buying affiliates.

REVIEW PROBLEM

Company P owns 75% of Company S's common stock, which it acquired in 1985. During 1991, one affiliate sold merchandise to the other affiliate for $236,000. At December 31, 1991, the buying affiliate owed the selling affiliate $32,000 on open account. The buying affiliate's beginning and ending inventories for 1991 contained goods purchased from the selling affiliate for $39,000 and $35,100, respectively. The buying affiliate and the selling affiliate had December 31, 1991 inventories of $112,000 and $97,000, respectively. Company P and Company S had separate net incomes for 1991 of $62,000 and $38,000, respectively. During 1991, the selling affiliate sold to the buying affiliate at 30% above cost.

Required

Prepare all supporting schedules to the December 31, 1991 consolidation worksheet that can be determined from the given information [a] if Company P is the seller and both affiliates use periodic inventory systems, and [b] if Company S is the seller and both affiliates use perpetual inventory systems.

QUESTIONS

1. Why must intercompany revenues and expenses be eliminated in preparing consolidated financial statements?
2. What portion of intercompany revenues and expenses should be eliminated in preparing consolidated financial statements? Why?
3. Why must intercompany assets and liabilities be eliminated in preparing consolidated financial statements?

4. What level of profit is referred to in the term, "intercompany profit in inventory"?
5. Why do we not eliminate the entire amount of intercompany profit earned by the selling affiliate during a given year?
6. What is accomplished by eliminating the unrealized intercompany profit in ending inventory?
7. How are the parent's and the subsidiary's Retained Earnings balances affected by the elimination of unrealized intercompany profit in beginning inventory?
8. What is accomplished by eliminating the unrealized intercompany profit in beginning inventory?
9. How is the realized intercompany profit in beginning inventory treated in the Income Allocation schedule?
10. How is the unrealized intercompany profit in ending inventory treated in the Income Allocation schedule?

EXERCISES

EXERCISE 8-1
Company A owns 75% of Company B's common stock, which it acquired in 1982. During 1991, Company A sold merchandise that had cost $90,000 to Company B for $135,000. At December 31, 1991, Company B owed the selling affiliate $18,000 on open account. Company B's beginning and ending inventories for 1991 contained goods purchased from Company A for $12,000 and $9,000, respectively. Company A and Company B had ending inventories for 1991 of $48,000 and $51,000, respectively. Company A's 1990 sales were made at the same average gross profit as its 1991 sales. Both affiliates use periodic inventory systems.

Required
Schedule the eliminations that should be made at December 31, 1991 relative to the information given above.

EXERCISE 8-2
Company C owns 75% of Company D's common stock, which it acquired in 1975. During 1990, Company D sold merchandise to Company C for $180,000, 30% for cash and the remainder on account. At December 31, 1990, Company C owed Company D $9,000 on open account. Company C's beginning and ending inventories for 1990 contained goods purchased from Company D for $10,000 and $12,000, respectively. Company D's gross margin is 25% of selling price. Both affiliates use perpetual inventory systems.

Required
Schedule the eliminations that should be made at December 31, 1990 relative to the information given above.

EXERCISE 8-3
During 1991, Company E sold merchandise to Company F for $240,000. At December 31, 1991, Company F owed Company E $30,000 on open account. Company F's beginning and ending inventories for 1991 contained goods purchased from Company E for $18,000 and $24,000, respectively. Company E sells to Company F at 50% above cost. Both affiliates use perpetual inventory systems. Company E and Company F had individual net incomes of $42,000 and $36,000, respectively, in 1991.

Required
Prepare an Income Allocation schedule to accompany the December 31, 1991 consolidation worksheet [a] if Company E owns 90% of Company F's common stock, and [b] if Company F owns 80% of Company E's common stock.

EXERCISE 8-4

Company G owns 80% of Company H's common stock, which it acquired in 1982. During 1991, Company G purchased merchandise from Company H for $312,400. At December 31, 1991, Company G owed Company H $31,100 on open account. Company G's inventories at December 31, 1990 and December 31, 1991 contained goods purchased from Company H for $31,500 and $32,200, respectively. The December 31, 1991 inventories were: Company G, $96,000; Company H, $60,600. Company H sells to Company G at 40% above cost.

Required

Schedule the eliminations that should be made at December 31, 1991 relative to the information given above [a] if both affiliates use periodic inventory systems, and [b] if both affiliates use perpetual inventory systems.

EXERCISE 8-5

Company I owns 80% of Company J's common stock, which it acquired in 1981. During the year ended September 30, 1991, Company I purchased merchandise from Company J for $575,000. At September 30, 1991, Company I owed Company J $83,000 on open account. Company I's inventories at September 30, 1990 and September 30, 1991 contained goods purchased from Company J for $82,500 and $88,750, respectively. Company J sells to Company I at 25% above cost. Both affiliates use perpetual inventory systems.

Required

1. Schedule the eliminations that should be made at September 30, 1991 relative to the information given above.
2. How would your answer to part **1** above be different if both affiliates used periodic inventory systems? Answer verbally; do not present the periodic inventory eliminations.

EXERCISE 8-6

In addition to the information given in Exercise 8-5, assume that the separate net incomes of Company I and Company J for the year ended September 30, 1991 were $96,800 and $54,500, respectively. Assume also that annual amortization of goodwill from consolidation is $6,400.

Required

Prepare an income allocation schedule for the year ended September 30, 1991.

EXERCISE 8-7

Company K owns 80% of Company L's common stock, which it acquired in 1981. During 1991, Company K purchased merchandise from Company L for $415,300. At December 31, 1991, Company K owed Company L $39,100 on open account. Company K's inventories at December 31, 1990 and December 31, 1991 contained goods purchased from Company L for $32,500 and $35,000, respectively. Company L sells to Company K at 25% above cost. Both affiliates use perpetual inventory systems.

Required

The amount of intercompany profit in inventory to be eliminated from Company K's Retained Earnings balance at December 31, 1991 is
a. Zero
b. $1,300
c. $1,400
d. $5,200

EXERCISE 8-8

Company M owns 70% of Company N's common stock, which it acquired in 1976. During 1991, Company M sold merchandise to Company N for $328,200. At December 31, 1991, Company N owed Company M $25,700 on open account. Company N's inventories at December 31, 1990 and December 31, 1991 contained goods purchased from Company M for $27,300 and $24,700, respectively. Company M sells to Company N at 30% above cost. Both affiliates use perpetual inventory systems.

Required

In allocating total net income for 1991, *realized* intercompany profit will cause

a. $6,300 to be added to Company M's net income.
b. $6,300 to be added to Company N's net income.
c. $5,700 to be added to Company M's net income.
d. $5,700 to be added to Company N's net income.

EXERCISE 8-9

Company P owns 80% of Company Q's common stock, which it acquired in 1986. Company P's inventories at December 31, 1991 and December 31, 1992 contained goods purchased from Company Q for $15,400 and $16,800, respectively. Company Q sells to Company P at 40% above cost. Both affiliates use periodic inventory systems.

Required

The minority interest in the intercompany profit *unrealized* at December 31, 1992 is

a. Zero
b. $ 880
c. $ 960
d. $1,760

EXERCISE 8-10

Company R owns 75% of Company S's common stock, which it acquired in 1983. During 1991, Company R sold merchandise to Company S for $512,100. At December 31, 1991, Company S owed Company R $48,700 on open account. Company S's inventories at December 31, 1990 and December 31, 1991 contained goods purchased from Company R for $43,400 and $40,600, respectively. Company R sells to Company S at 40% above cost. Both affiliates use perpetual inventory systems.

Required

The amount of *realized* intercompany profit to be included in consolidated net income for 1991 is

a. $9,300
b. $8,700
c. $3,100
d. $2,900

PROBLEMS

PROBLEM 8-1

Company K acquired 22,500 shares of Company L's common stock for $576,300 on March 31, 1988. Company L had retained earnings of $132,400 on June 30, 1987. Company L reported net income of $48,000 for the year ended June 30, 1988. On February 15, 1988, Company L declared dividends of

$20,000, which were paid on March 20, 1988. The excess of cost over book value is attributed to goodwill of Company L and is being amortized over 10 years.

During the year ended June 30, 1991, Company K purchased merchandise from Company L for $206,300. At June 30, 1991, Company K owed Company L $18,200 on open account. Company K's inventories at June 30, 1990 and June 30, 1991 contained goods purchased from Company L for $22,400 and $25,200, respectively. Company L sells to Company K at 40% above cost. The June 30, 1991 trial balances of Company K and Company L appear below.

	Company K	Company L
Accounts Receivable (net)	$ 72,100	$ 39,800
Inventories	76,300	44,600
Investment in Company L	618,600	
Other Assets	509,400	840,500
Cost of Goods Sold	436,800	283,100
Other Expenses	309,600	183,300
Dividends Declared	50,000	21,000
	$2,072,800	$1,412,300
Liabilities	$ 406,900	$ 220,100
Common Stock ($10 par)	400,000	300,000
Additional Paid-in Capital	100,000	200,000
Retained Earnings	263,200	173,800
Sales	·863,700	518,400
Income from Company L	39,000	
	$2,072,800	·$1,412,300

Required

Prepare a consolidation worksheet at June 30, 1991, supported by appropriate schedules.

PROBLEM 8-2

Company M acquired 90% of Company N's common stock for $327,000 on July 1, 1988. Company N's retained earnings balance was $54,500 on December 31, 1987. Company N reported net income of $44,000 for 1988. On November 15, 1988, Company N declared dividends of $20,000, which were paid on December 20, 1988. The excess of cost over book value is attributed to goodwill from consolidation and is being amortized over 15 years.

During 1991, Company M purchased merchandise from Company N for $136,200. At December 31, 1991, Company M owed Company N $17,100 on open account. Company M's beginning and ending inventories for 1991 contained goods purchased from Company N for $12,500 and $15,000, respectively. Company N sells to Company M at cost plus 25%. The December 31, 1991 trial balances of Company M and Company N appear below.

	Company M	Company N
Accounts Receivable (net)	$ 53,700	$ 27,200
Inventories	48,100	22,500
Investment in Company N	327,000	
Other Assets	749,400	498,100
Purchases	246,800	140,300
Other Expenses	210,600	134,400
Dividends Declared	25,000	28,000
	$1,660,600	$ 850,500
Liabilities	$ 317,200	$ 180,300
Common Stock ($10 par)	500,000	200,000
Additional Paid-in Capital	120,000	50,000
Retained Earnings	181,300	108,500
Sales	516,900	311,700
Dividend Revenue	25,200	
	$1,660,600	$ 850,500
Inventories, 12/31/91	$ 43,000	$ 25,500

Required
Prepare a consolidation worksheet at December 31, 1991, supported by appropriate schedules.

PROBLEM 8-3
The December 31, 1991 trial balances of Company P and Company Q appear below.

	Company P	Company Q
Accounts Receivable (net)	$ 45,000	$ 32,000
Inventories	37,000	40,000
Investment in Company Q	189,000	
Other Assets	212,000	262,000
Cost of Goods Sold	360,000	
Purchases		330,000
Other Expenses	143,000	105,000
Dividends Declared	12,000	18,000
	$ 998,000	$ 787,000
Liabilities	$ 111,000	$ 97,000
Common Stock ($10 par)	200,000	100,000
Additional Paid-in Capital	15,000	20,000
Retained Earnings	112,000	90,000
Sales	530,000	480,000
Income from Company Q	30,000	
	$ 998,000	$ 787,000

Company P acquired 7,500 shares of Company Q's common stock for $150,000 on December 31, 1988, when Company Q had retained earnings of $60,000. The excess of cost over book value is attributed to goodwill of Company Q and is being amortized over 10 years.

During 1991, Company Q purchased merchandise from Company P for $152,000. At December 31, 1991, Company Q owed Company P $15,000 on open account. Company Q's beginning and ending inventories for 1991 contained goods purchased from Company P for $21,000 and $18,000, respectively. Company P sells to Company Q at 20% above cost. Company Q's December 31, 1991 inventory was $35,000.

Required

Prepare a consolidation worksheet at December 31, 1991, supported by appropriate schedules.

PROBLEM 8-4

The September 30, 1991 trial balances of Company R and Company S appear below.

	Company R	Company S
Accounts Receivable (net)	$ 18,000	$ 87,000
Inventories	47,000	68,000
Investment in Company S	280,000	
Other Assets	140,000	457,000
Cost of Goods Solds	275,000	410,000
Other Expenses	150,000	220,000
Dividends Declared	18,000	20,000
	$ 928,000	$1 ,262,000
Accounts Payable	$ 67,000	$ 94,000
Other Liabilities	84,000	183,000
Common Stock ($10 par)	100,000	200,000
Additional Paid-in Capital	85,000	
Retained Earnings	93,000	105,000
Sales	483,000	680,000
Dividend Revenue	16,000	
	$ 928,000	$ 1,262,000

Company R acquired 16,000 shares of Company S's common stock for $280,000 on October 1, 1987, when Company S had retained earnings of $75,000. The excess of cost over book value is attributed to goodwill from consolidation and is being amortized over 20 years.

During the year ended September 30, 1991, Company S sold merchandise to Company R for $140,000. At September 30, 1991, Company R owed Company S $28,000 on open account. Company R's September 30, 1990 and September 30, 1991 inventories contained goods purchased from Company S for $20,000 and $25,000, respectively. Company S sells to Company R at 25% above cost.

Required

Prepare a consolidation worksheet at September 30, 1991, supported by appropriate schedules.

PROBLEM 8-5

Company T acquired 7,600 shares of Company U's common stock for $653,200 on October 1, 1989. Company U's outstanding common stock has not changed since that date. Company U's December 31, 1988 retained earnings balance was $131,000. Company U reported net income of $54,000 for 1989.

On November 15, 1989, Company U declared dividends of $28,000, which were paid on December 20, 1989. The excess of cost over book value is attributed to goodwill of Company U and is being amortized over 10 years.

During 1992, Company U sold merchandise to Company T for $183,400. At December 31, 1992, Company T owed Company U $16,200 on open account. Company T's beginning and ending inventories for 1992 contained goods purchased from Company U for $18,500 and $21,000, respectively. Company U's December 31, 1992 inventory was $96,300. All of Company U's sales are made at the same average gross margin, which has not changed in recent years. The December 31, 1992 trial balances of Company T and Company U appear below.

	Company T	Company U
Accounts Receivable (net)	$ 53,300	$ 58,400
Inventories	61,400	93,900
Investment in Company U	713,600	
Other Assets	401,600	798,100
Purchases		370,500
Cost of Goods Sold	278,100	
Other Expenses	273,900	201,600
Dividends Declared	26,000	38,000
Treasury Stock (500 shares, at cost)		35,000
	$1,807,900	$1,595,500
Accounts Payable	$ 48,100	$ 63,700
Other Liabilities	144,200	77,100
Common Stock ($50 par)	600,000	500,000
Additional Paid-in Capital	150,000	100,000
Retained Earnings	211,700	222,000
Sales	591,300	613,500
Other Revenue	62,600	19,200
	$1,807,900	$1,595,500

Required
Prepare a consolidation worksheet at December 31, 1992, supported by appropriate schedules.

PROBLEM 8-6
The December 31, 1991 trial balances of Company V and Company W appear below.

	Company V	Company W
Accounts Receivable (net)	$ 136,100	$ 100,400
Inventories	78,000	99,700
Other Current Assets	98,700	176,100
Plant and Equipment	944,500	737,900
Investment in Company W	611,600	
Purchases	597,400	458,500
Other Expenses	363,400	265,800
Dividends Declared	50,000	40,000
	$2,879,700	$1,878,400

	Company V	Company W
Accumulated Depreciation	$ 311,400	$ 186,200
Liabilities	396,800	201,500
Common Stock ($10 par)	500,000	500,000
Additional Paid-in Capital	192,000	80,000
Retained Earnings	369,700	136,200
Sales	1,065,200	765,800
Other Revenue	44,600	8,700
	$2,879,700	$1,878,400
Inventories, 12/31/91	$ 69,400	$ 101,100

Company V acquired 40,000 shares of Company W's common stock for $611,600 on December 31, 1988, when Company W had retained earnings of $94,500. The excess of cost over book value is attributed to the going concern value of Company W in excess of the fair market value of its recorded net assets and is being amortized over 10 years. Both affiliates declared dividends on December 8, 1991, payable on January 15, 1992.

During 1991, Company W purchased merchandise from Company V for $162,400, of which $16,100 remained unpaid at December 31, 1991. Company W's beginning and ending inventories for 1991 contained goods purchased from Company V for $19,500 and $18,850, respectively. Company V sells to Company W at cost plus 30%.

Required
Prepare a consolidation worksheet at December 31, 1991, supported by appropriate schedules.

PROBLEM 8-7
Company X acquired 28,500 shares of Company Y's common stock for $556,800 on December 31, 1988, when Company Y had retained earnings of $79,400. The excess of cost over book value is attributed to the going concern value of Company Y in excess of the fair market value of its recorded net assets and is being amortized over 10 years. Both affiliates declared dividends on December 10, 1991, payable on January 15, 1992.

During 1991, Company Y purchased merchandise from Company X for $312,400, of which $31,100 remained unpaid at December 31, 1991. Company Y's beginning and ending inventories for 1991 contained goods purchased from Company X for $31,500 and $32,200, respectively. Company X sells to Company Y at cost plus 40%. Company X's December 31, 1991 inventory was $75,300.

The December 31, 1991 trial balances of Company X and Company Y appear below.

	Company X	Company Y
Accounts Receivable (net)	$ 136,100	$ 99,400
Inventories	77,200	100,700
Other Current Assets	89,600	168,100
Plant and Equipment	941,900	700,800
Investment in Company Y	556,800	
Purchases	581,400	
Cost of Goods Sold		447,400
Other Expenses	372,600	276,800
Dividends Declared	60,000	48,000
Treasury Stock (2,000 shares, at cost)		37,000
	$2,815,600	$1,878,200

	Company X	Company Y
Accumulated Depreciation	$ 255,800	$ 175,200
Liabilities	389,700	202,400
Common Stock ($10 par)	600,000	400,000
Additional Paid-in Capital	92,000	180,000
Retained Earnings	349,700	136,200
Sales	1,059,200	773,800
Other Revenue	69,200	10,600
	$2,815,600	$1,878,200

Required
Prepare a consolidation worksheet at December 31, 1991, supported by appropriate schedules.

SOLUTION TO REVIEW PROBLEM

CASE I

Eliminations

Intercompany Sales and Purchases

[1] Sales	$ 236,000
[2] Purchases	(236,000)

Intercompany Receivables and Payables

[3] Accounts Payable	$ 32,000
[4] Accounts Receivable	(32,000)

Intercompany Profit in Beginning Inventory

[5] Retained Earnings: P	$ 9,000
[6] Inventory	(9,000)

Intercompany Profit in Ending Inventory

Company P's Ending Inventory	$ 97,000
Company S's Ending Inventory	112,000
Total Ending Inventory	209,000
Less: Intercompany Profit	8,100
[7] Ending Inventory at Intercompany Cost	$ 200,900

Income Allocation

Company P's Net Income		$ 62,000
Add: Intercompany Profit in Beginning Inventory		9,000
Less: Intercompany Profit in Ending Inventory		(8,100)
Company P's Adjusted Net Income		62,900
Company S's Net Income	$ 38,000	
Minority Interest (25%)	9,500	
Company P's Share (75%)		28,500
Consolidated Net Income		$ 91,400

CASE 2

Eliminations

Intercompany Sales and Purchases

[1] Sales	$ 236,000
[2] Cost of Goods Sold	(236,000)

Intercompany Receivables and Payables

[3] Accounts Payable	$ 32,000
[4] Accounts Receivable	(32,000)

Intercompany Profit in Beginning Inventory

[5] Retained Earnings: P	$ 6,750
[6] Retained Earnings: S	2,250
[7] Cost of Goods Sold	$ (9,000)

Intercompany Profit in Ending Inventory

[8] Cost of Goods Sold	$ 8,100
[9] Inventory	(8,100)

Income Allocation

Company P's Net Income		$ 62,000
Company S's Net Income	$ 38,000	
Add: Intercompany Profit in Beginning Inventory	9,000	
Less: Intercompany Profit in Ending Inventory	(8,100)	
Company S's Adjusted Net Income	38,900	
Minority Interest (25%)	9,725	
Company P's Share (75%)		29,175
Consolidated Net Income		$ 91,175

INTERCOMPANY PROFITS IN DEPRECIABLE ASSETS

C hapter 8 introduces the topic of intercompany profits in inventories that are generated through purchases and sales of merchandise between affiliates. One affiliate also can purchase an asset other than merchandise from another affiliate at a price greater than the value at which the asset is carried on the selling affiliate's books, thus creating an element of intercompany profit. This intercompany profit would be expected to be realized not through resale of the asset to an outside entity or entities, but through its use over time by the buying affiliate. In this chapter, we discuss and illustrate the treatment of intercompany profits in assets other than inventory, concentrating on depreciable assets. More specifically, Chapter 9 covers the following topics:

- A review of intercompany profits in inventories
- The nature of assets, leading to the treatment of intercompany profits in depreciable assets in the consolidation process
- A review of depreciation methods
- A three-part analysis to explain the effects of intercompany profits in depreciable assets
- Subsequent sale of a depreciable asset by the buying affiliate
- Intercompany profit in other long-lived assets

In order to place the matter of intercompany profits in long-lived assets in perspective, a brief review of the treatment of intercompany profits in inventories in the consolidation process is presented in the following section.

REVIEW OF INTERCOMPANY PROFITS IN INVENTORIES

Unrealized intercompany profits are present in an affiliate's ending inventory for a given year because that affiliate has bought merchandise from another affiliate at a price greater than the selling affiliate's cost and has not resold all of those goods to outside entities. These intercompany profits, which are unrealized to the consolidated entity, must be eliminated from

- the asset, Inventory, so that it can be reported on the consolidated balance sheet at an amount no greater than intercompany cost, and
- total net income for the year, which is accomplished by increasing the combined cost of goods sold.

The ending inventory of one year, of course, becomes the beginning inventory of the next year. As indicated in Chapter 8, we assume that by the end of each year, the buying affiliate's beginning inventory of that year has been resold to outside entities at a price at least equal to the intercompany selling price and, hence, that the intercompany profit therein has become realized to the consolidated entity. Therefore, the realized intercompany profit in the buying affiliate's beginning inventory must be

- eliminated from one or both of the beginning of the year Retained Earnings balances, and
- added to total net income for the year, which is accomplished by decreasing the combined cost of goods sold.

Because of the relatively short lifetime of inventories (assumed to be less than one year), ordinarily we need to deal with a given element of intercompany profit in inventory only twice—as part of the ending inventory of one year and as a part of the beginning inventory of the following year. If a component of inventory is held by the buying affiliate for longer than one year, however, the unrealized intercompany profit therein is treated as part of ending inventory of each year in which it remains unrealized. This treatment is illustrated in Chapter 8.

INTERCOMPANY PROFITS IN DEPRECIABLE ASSETS

As we shift our attention from inventories to longer-lived assets, the most important factor to consider is the use to which the buying affiliate intends to put the asset acquired from its affiliate. In other words, we must distinguish between an asset that the buying affiliate intends to resell to outside entities (inventory) and one that the buying affiliate intends to use in carrying on its business operations (a noncurrent asset). Whether the asset in question represents inventory to the selling affiliate or is an asset that the selling affiliate has used in its business operations is irrelevant to the way in which we treat the intercompany profit in the consolidation process. How the buying affiliate intends to use the asset is important, because the intended use determines the buying affiliate's accounting for and reporting of the asset, which, in turn, determines the way in which it is treated in the consolidation process.

At this point, it is useful to distinguish between assets and the physical objects in which they sometimes, but not always, are embodied. The Financial Accounting Standards Board defines assets as "probable future economic benefits obtained or controlled by a particular entity as a result of past transactions or events."[1] The Board goes on to point out that tangibility—that is, embodiment in physical property—is a common, but not essential, characteristic of an asset.[2] Later the Board states,

> The common characteristic possessed by all assets . . . is "service potential" or "future economic benefit," the scarce capacity to provide services or benefits to the entities that use them. In a business enterprise, that service potential or future economic benefit eventually results in net cash inflows to the enterprise.[3]

The treatment of intercompany profits in depreciable assets is based on the rationale stated above. The realization of intercompany profits in inventories is measured in terms of the transfer of physical units of inventory from the buying affiliate to outside entities. In the case of depreciable assets, however, the physical property is expected to be resold only at the end of the asset's useful life for a residual salvage value. The true asset, the collection of future economic benefits embodied in the physical property, is expected to be used by the buying affiliate to produce goods and/or services that ultimately will be transferred to outside entities.

In some cases, the transfer of goods or services to outside entities is direct and evident. For example, if the asset in question is a delivery truck that the buying affiliate uses to deliver parcels for customers for a fee, the using up of the service potential of the truck clearly is linked directly to the transfer of services to outside entities.

In other cases, the connection is not nearly so clear. For example, suppose that the asset in question is a computer used in the buying affiliate's office to perform record keeping and billing functions. Although the computer is not directly involved in the transfer of goods or services to outside entities, it is necessary to the conduct of the buying affiliate's business operations. In that sense, it contributes to the generation of revenue.

Because we cannot rely on the transfer of physical units as a means of measuring the realization of intercompany profits in depreciable assets, we need an alternative. Depreciation is a process of systematically allocating the cost of a long-lived asset to the accounting periods that it benefits; that is, a means of approximating the using up of the service potential of the asset, period by period. As such, it provides us with a convenient surrogate measurement of the transfer of goods or services to outside entities, and hence the realization of intercompany profit.

We will use the depreciation schedule already in place on the buying affiliate's books as a means of measuring the realization of intercompany profit in a depreciable asset. In each year of the asset's life, we will recognize a fraction of the total intercompany profit corresponding to the fraction of the buying affiliate's depreciable cost recorded as depreciation in that year. Let us acknowledge that in no sense does the recording of depreciation by the buying affiliate *cause* the realization of intercompany profit. It merely provides a convenient surrogate measure of realization.

---

[1] *Statement of Financial Accounting Concepts No. 6, Elements of Financial Statements* (Stamford, Connecticut: FASB, 1985), paragraph 25.

[2] *SFAC No. 6*, paragraph 26.

[3] *SFAC No. 6*, paragraph 28.

REVIEW OF DEPRECIATION METHODS

Before considering the treatment of intercompany profits in depreciable assets in the consolidation process, students may find it useful to review briefly four common depreciation methods. These methods, all of which appear in the illustrative problems, exercises, and problems in this and subsequent chapters, are

- Straight-line
- Sum-of-the-years'-digits
- Declining balance
- Units of output

To illustrate these methods, assume that a company purchases a machine at a cost of $165,000 on April 1, 1990. The machine is estimated to have a useful life of five years, with a $15,000 residual value at the end of that time. The company's policy is to calculate depreciation beginning on the date of purchase. Its fiscal year ends on December 31.

STRAIGHT-LINE DEPRECIATION

Under the straight-line method, an equal amount of depreciation expense is assigned to each full year of the asset's useful life. The residual value is subtracted from the total cost to obtain the depreciable cost, which is then divided by the number of years of useful life to determine the annual depreciation charge. Depreciation for a partial year is simply the appropriate fraction of the annual amount.

In this case, the depreciable cost is $165,000 minus $15,000, or $150,000, and the straight-line method produces the following depreciation schedule over the useful life of the machine.

Year	Depreciable Cost	Depreciation Rate	Depreciation Expense
1990	$150,000	20% × 9/12	$ 22,500
1991	150,000	20%	30,000
1992	150,000	20%	30,000
1993	150,000	20%	30,000
1994	150,000	20%	30,000
1995	150,000	20% × 3/12	7,500
Total			$150,000

SUM-OF-THE-YEARS'-DIGITS DEPRECIATION

The sum-of-the-years'-digits method produces relatively large amounts of depreciation expense in the early years of the asset's useful life and progressively smaller amounts in the later years. For this reason, it is sometimes referred to as a *diminishing charge* method. As in the straight-line method, the residual value is subtracted from the total cost to obtain the depreciable cost. Then, we literally sum (add together) the digits of the years of the asset's useful life and express each digit as a fraction of the total. Next, the fractions are arrayed in reverse order and multiplied by the depreciable cost to obtain the depreciation charge *for each full year of the asset's useful life*. Depreciation for a partial year is determined as the appropriate fraction of that year's fraction, as illustrated below.

In this case, the sum of the years' digits is calculated as $1 + 2 + 3 + 4 + 5 = 15$. Thus, the fraction for the first full year is 5/15, for the second full year, 4/15, and so forth. A depreciation schedule for five full years would be

Year	Depreciable Cost	Fraction	Depreciation Expense
1	$150,000	5/15	$ 50,000
2	150,000	4/15	40,000
3	150,000	3/15	30,000
4	150,000	2/15	20,000
5	150,000	1/15	10,000
Total			$150,000

Because the depreciation for 1990 begins on April 1, however, the depreciation expense for 1990 is determined as 9/12 of the first full year's amount, or $9/12 \times 5/15 \times \$150,000$. Similarly, the depreciation expense for 1991 is determined as 3/12 of the first full year's amount plus 9/12 of the second full year's amount, etc. Thus, the sum-of-the-years'-digits method produces the following depreciation schedule over the useful life of the machine.

Year	Depreciable Cost	Fraction	Depreciation Expense
1990	$150,000	$9/12 \times 5/15$	$ 37,500
1991	150,000	$(3/12 \times 5/15) + (9/12 \times 4/15)$	42,500
1992	150,000	$(3/12 \times 4/15) + (9/12 \times 3/15)$	32,500
1993	150,000	$(3/12 \times 3/15) + (9/12 \times 2/15)$	22,500
1994	150,000	$(3/12 \times 2/15) + (9/12 \times 1/15)$	12,500
1995	150,000	$3/12 \times 1/15$	2,500
Total			$150,000

DECLINING BALANCE DEPRECIATION

Like the sum-of-the-years'-digits method, the declining balance method produces relatively large amounts of depreciation expense in the early years of the asset's useful life and progressively smaller amounts in the later years. It also is sometimes referred to as a diminishing charge method. Unlike the previous methods, however, the residual value is not subtracted from the total cost to obtain the depreciable cost. Instead, a constant fraction (or percentage), which is a multiple of the straight-line rate, is multiplied by the total cost at the end of the first year, and by the remaining (undepreciated) cost at the end of each following year. Obviously, some portion of the total cost, though not necessarily the estimated residual value, will remain at the end of the asset's useful life. A popular version of this method uses two times the straight-line rate as the constant fraction and, thus, is often called "double declining balance." As in the straight-line method, depreciation for a partial year is simply the appropriate fraction of the annual amount.

In this case, using two times the straight-line rate, or 40%, as the constant fraction, the declining balance method produces the following depreciation schedule over the useful life of the machine.

Year	Remaining Cost	Depreciation Rate	Depreciation Expense
1990	$165,000	40% × 9/12	$ 49,500
1991	115,500	40%	46,200
1992	69,300	40%	27,720
1993	41,580	40%	16,632
1994	24,948	40%	9,979
1995	14,969	40% × 3/12	1,497
Total			$151,528

The total amount depreciated over the useful life of the machine, $151,528, leaves a remaining balance of $13,472, which approximates the originally estimated residual value of $15,000.

UNITS OF OUTPUT DEPRECIATION

In the units of output method, useful life must be estimated, not in years, but in terms of a number of units of output expected from the asset. For an automobile, the appropriate units would be miles; for machinery, units of product produced (or, as a surrogate, machine hours); etc. The residual value is subtracted from the total cost to obtain the depreciable cost, which is then divided by the number of units of useful life to determine the depreciation rate per unit. The annual depreciation expense is determined by multiplying this predetermined rate by the actual number of units for each year. Thus, depreciation for a partial year is determined in the same way as that for a full year.

In this case, the depreciable cost is $165,000 minus $15,000, or $150,000, but the useful life estimate must be expressed in terms of appropriate units of output, which we will assume to be 30,000 machine hours. The depreciation rate, then, is $150,000 divided by 30,000, or $5.00 per machine hour. Because the annual depreciation expense depends on the actual machine hours for each year, it is not possible to produce a depreciation schedule in advance, as shown for the previous methods. To illustrate the method, however, if the machine produced 1,200 machine hours in 1990, the depreciation expense for 1990 would be 1,200 × $5.00, or $6,000. If it produced 5,900 machine hours in 1991, the depreciation expense for 1991 would be 5,900 × $5.00, or $29,500, and so forth for the remaining years.

TREATMENT OF INTERCOMPANY PROFITS IN DEPRECIABLE ASSETS IN THE CONSOLIDATION PROCESS

As in the case of intercompany profits in inventories, we have two goals with respect to intercompany profits in depreciable assets:

- eliminating unrealized intercompany profit from the asset in order to report the asset on the consolidated balance sheet at its unamortized intercompany cost, and

■ including segments of the intercompany profit in the total net incomes of the proper accounting periods.

Unlike inventories, the carrying value of a depreciable asset appears in two account balances—the asset itself and the related accumulated depreciation account. Thus we must eliminate unrealized intercompany profit from both of these balances in order to reduce the carrying value of the asset to undepreciated intercompany cost.

In dealing with intercompany profits in inventories, we use the related expense, cost of goods sold, as a means of shifting the recognition of intercompany profit elements between accounting periods. Here, we also will use the related expense, depreciation, as the means of recognizing intercompany profit. The appropriate fraction of the intercompany profit is recognized each year by reducing the depreciation expense to an amount based on intercompany cost.

In addition, in all years following the year in which the intercompany sale occurs, eliminations must be made from one or both of the beginning Retained Earnings balances so that they will contain only the amount of intercompany profit realized as of the beginning of that year. In the year in which the intercompany sale occurs, the unrealized intercompany profit must be eliminated from total net income. If the asset was carried as inventory by the selling affiliate, combined cost of goods sold must be increased. Otherwise, the selling affiliate will have recorded a gain on the sale of the asset, which must be eliminated.

Obviously, a depreciable asset could be transferred from one affiliate to another at a price below the carrying value of the asset on the selling affiliate's books. In such a case, intercompany loss rather than intercompany profit would result. Intercompany loss, however, is merely negative intercompany profit. Thus, intercompany loss is treated in the consolidation process in the same manner described above for intercompany profit, except that the debit and credit elements are reversed. For the sake of clarity, all further discussions and illustrative problems involve intercompany profit only.

ILLUSTRATIVE PROBLEM 9.1: INTERCOMPANY PROFIT IN MACHINERY

One affiliate sells machinery with a book value of $82,000 to another affiliate for $100,000 on December 31, 1990. The buying affiliate depreciates the asset using the straight-line method, over a three-year life, with a $10,000 salvage value.

Case A: Company A sells to its 80% owned subsidiary, Company C.

Case B: Company B sells to Company A, which owns 100% of Company B's common stock.

Case C: Company C sells to Company A, which owns 80% of Company C's common stock.

In order to see clearly the impact of this transaction on the consolidation process over the lifetime of the machinery, we can perform an analysis showing, for each year, [a] the effect on the accounts of both affiliates, [b] the balances that should appear on the consolidated financial statements, and [c] the additional eliminations needed to accomplish that result. This three-part analysis is intended as an explanatory device only. It is far too cumbersome to use in deriving the additional eliminations necessary for any given year, either in solving textbook problems or in actual practice, and is not recommended for that purpose.

Case A. Sale by Company A to Company C.   Exhibit 9-1 presents the recorded balances produced by the intercompany transaction, the balances that should appear on the consolidated financial statements, and the necessary additional eliminations, at December 31, 1990, 1991, 1992, and 1993, assuming that the machinery was not inventory to Company A. Credits are shown in parentheses.

EXHIBIT 9-1

Illustrative Problem 9.1
Three Part Analysis, Case A

Part 1. Recorded Balances

	12/31/90	12/31/91	12/31/92	12/31/93
Machinery: C	$100,000	$100,000	$100,000	$100,000
Accumulated Depreciation: C	0	(30,000)	(60,000)	(90,000)
Depreciation Expense: C	0	30,000	30,000	30,000
Gain on Sale of Machinery: A	(18,000)	0	0	0
(Beginning) Retained Earnings: A	0	(18,000)	(18,000)	(18,000)

Part 2. Desired Balances

	12/31/90	12/31/91	12/31/92	12/31/93
Machinery	$ 82,000	$ 82,000	$ 82,000	$ 82,000
Accumulated Depreciation	0	(24,000)	(48,000)	(72,000)
Depreciation Expense	0	24,000	24,000	24,000
Consolidated Net Income	0	(6,000)	(6,000)	(6,000)
Consolidated (Beginning) Retained Earnings	0	0	(6,000)	(12,000)

Part 3. Additional Eliminations

	12/31/90	12/31/91	12/31/92	12/31/93
Machinery	$ (18,000)	$ (18,000)	$ (18,000)	$ (18,000)
Accumulated Depreciation	0	6,000	12,000	18,000
Depreciation Expense	0	(6,000)	(6,000)	(6,000)
Gain on Sale of Machinery	18,000	0	0	0
Retained Earnings: A	0	18,000	12,000	6,000

In Part 1, we see that the asset, Machinery, appears in Company C's trial balance at December 31 of each year, stated at Company C's cost of $100,000, which is also intercompany selling price. The annual depreciation expense is one-third of Company C's depreciable cost of $90,000 and, of course, that amount is added to the balance of Company C's Accumulated Depreciation each year. At December 31, 1990, Company A's trial balance contains a Gain on Sale of Machinery balance of $18,000. This gain, along with the rest of Company A's 1990 net income, is closed into Company A's Retained Earnings and appears as part of that balance in subsequent Company A trial balances.

Part 2 shows that the consolidated financial statements should report Machinery and the related depreciation expense and accumulated depreciation in terms of intercompany cost. The consolidated net income for each year of the asset's life should contain one-third of the intercompany profit, or $6,000, the realization of which is measured by reference to the depreciation schedule that Company C is using for the asset. The beginning balance of consolidated Retained Earnings for each year should contain only that portion of the intercompany profit that has become realized as of the beginning of that year.

Part 3 shows the additional set of eliminations necessary to arrive at the desired balances in Part 2. The elimination from the Gain on Sale of Machinery balance at December 31, 1990 is necessary because the entire amount of the gain is unrealized to the consolidated entity at that date. The elimination from Machinery at December 31, 1990 and from Machinery and Accumulated Depreciation at the end of each subsequent year reduce the net carrying value to unamortized intercompany cost. The elimination from Depreciation Expense reduces the amount of expense reported in each year of the asset's life to the appropriate portion of intercompany cost. Also, the $6,000 reduction in Depreciation Expense each year adds $6,000 to total net income of each year. This amount will be allocated to Consolidated Net Income in the Income Allocation Schedule, as shown in Exhibit 9-2. Once the Gain on Sale of Machinery account has been closed at the end of 1990, Company A's Retained Earnings contains the total amount of the intercompany profit at the beginning of each year, as shown in Part 2. At the end of each year, the portion of the intercompany profit *unrealized* as of the beginning of that year is eliminated from Company A's beginning Retained Earnings, leaving in that balance the realized portion. Each year's set of eliminations balances, of course, in terms of debits and credits.

EXHIBIT 9-2

Illustrative Problem 9.1
Income Allocation Schedule, Case A

Income Allocation

Company A's Net Income		$ 55,300
Add: Realized Intercompany Profit on Machinery		6,000
Company A's Adjusted Net Income		61,300
Company C's Net Income	$ 29,400	
Less: Goodwill Amortization Expense	1,000	
Company C's Adjusted Net Income	28,400	
Minority Interest (20%)	5,680	
Company A's Share (80%)		22,720
Consolidated Net Income		$ 84,020

Because Company A is the selling affiliate and thus recorded the intercompany profit initially, its net income must be adjusted each year in the Income Allocation schedule. In 1990, the entire amount of $18,000 is subtracted, and in each subsequent year of the asset's life, $6,000 is added. This causes the $6,000 of intercompany profit realized each year to be included in consolidated net income. Assume that in 1992, Company A and Company C reported separate net incomes of $55,300 and $29,400, respectively, and that amortization of Goodwill of Company C amounted to $1,000. The Income Allocation schedule for Case A appears in Exhibit 9-2.

   Case B. Sale by 100% Owned Company B to Company A.   Exhibit 9-3 presents the recorded balances produced by the intercompany transaction, the desired balances, and the necessary additional eliminations, at December 31, 1990, 1991, 1992, and 1993, again assuming that the machinery was not inventory to the selling affiliate.

EXHIBIT 9-3

Illustrative Problem 9.1
Three Part Analysis, Case B

Part 1. Recorded Balances

	12/31/90	12/31/91	12/31/92	12/31/93
Machinery: A	$100,000	$100,000	$100,000	$100,000
Accumulated Depreciation: A	0	(30,000)	(60,000)	(90,000)
Depreciation Expense: A	0	30,000	30,000	30,000
Investment in Company B: A	18,000	18,000	18,000	18,000
Income from Company B: A	(18,000)	0	0	0
(Beginning) Retained Earnings: A	0	(18,000)	(18,000)	(18,000)
Gain on Sale of Machinery: B	(18,000)	0	0	0
(Beginning) Retained Earnings: B	0	(18,000)	(18,000)	(18,000)

Part 2. Desired Balances

	12/31/90	12/31/91	12/31/92	12/31/93
Machinery	$ 82,000	$ 82,000	$ 82,000	$ 82,000
Accumulated Depreciation	0	(24,000)	(48,000)	(72,000)
Depreciation Expense	0	24,000	24,000	24,000
Consolidated Net Income	0	(6,000)	(6,000)	(6,000)
Consolidated (Beginning) Retained Earnings	0	0	(6,000)	(12,000)

Part 3. Additional Eliminations

	12/31/90	12/31/91	12/31/92	12/31/93
Machinery	$ (18,000)	$ (18,000)	$ (18,000)	$ (18,000)
Accumulated Depreciation	0	6,000	12,000	18,000
Depreciation Expense	0	(6,000)	(6,000)	(6,000)
Gain on Sale of Machinery	18,000	0	0	0
Retained Earnings: A	0	18,000	12,000	6,000

   The analysis becomes a bit more complicated when a subsidiary is the seller because the parent, under the equity method, will record its share of the intercompany profit as part of its share of the subsidiary's net income. Thus, the amount of the gain, $18,000, appears in both trial balances as an income element in the year of the sale, 1990, and as a component of beginning Retained Earnings in subsequent years, as shown in Part 1. It appears in Company B's accounts because Company B is the seller. In this case, because Company A owns 100% of Company B's common stock, the entire $18,000 is included in Company A's 1990 Income from Company B and in its beginning Retained Earnings balances of subsequent years, as well as in its Investment in Company B balance at the end of each year.

Part 2 shows the balances that should appear on the consolidated financial statements at the end of each year. These balances are identical to those in Part 2 of Exhibit 9-1. The reason for including the $6,000 of realized intercompany profit annually in consolidated net income and cumulatively in consolidated beginning Retained Earnings, however, is different. Because Company A owns 100% of Company B's common stock, no minority interest exists. Therefore, even though Company B is the seller, the entire $18,000 of intercompany profit ultimately belongs to Company A. Therefore, no Income Allocation Schedule is necessary.

The additional eliminations presented in Part 3 also are identical to those appearing in Part 3 of Exhibit 9-1, but for different reasons.

- At December 31, 1990, the Subsidiary Income and Dividends set of eliminations will remove the excess $18,000 from Company A's Investment in Company B and Income from Company B balances.
- At December 31, of each of the next three years, the Intercompany Ownership Interests set of eliminations will remove the excess $18,000 from Company A's Investment in Company B balance and from Company B's beginning Retained Earnings balance.

Thus, the additional eliminations are identical to those required when the parent is the seller.

The effects of these additional eliminations on the Machinery, Accumulated Depreciation, Depreciation Expense, and Gain on Sale of Machinery balances are identical to the effects described earlier in relation to Case A. Again, the reduction in Depreciation Expense each year adds $6,000 of realized intercompany profit to total net income, which is included in consolidated net income. Because Company A owns 100% of Company B's common stock, no minority interest exists; therefore, total net income is also consolidated net income. For this reason, no Income Allocation Schedule is necessary.

Case C. Sale by 80% Owned Company C to Company A. Exhibit 9-4 presents the recorded balances produced by the intercompany transaction, the desired balances, and the necessary additional eliminations, at the end of each year, again assuming that the machinery was not inventory to the selling affiliate.

The analysis becomes even more complicated when a partially owned subsidiary is the seller. As shown in Part 1, Company A has recorded its share, 80%, of Company C's net income. Thus, $14,400 of the intercompany profit is included in Company A's 1990 Income from Company C and in its beginning Retained Earnings balances of subsequent years, as well as in its Investment in Company C balance at the end of each year. Company C's Gain on Sale of Machinery for 1990 and its beginning Retained Earnings for each succeeding year contain the entire $18,000 of intercompany profit.

Part 2 shows the balances that should appear on the consolidated financial statements at the end of each year. The Machinery, Accumulated Depreciation, and Depreciation Expense balances are the same as those in Cases A and B. The realized intercompany profit of $6,000 recognized each year is allocated between consolidated net income and the minority interest

EXHIBIT 9-4

Illustrative Problem 9.1
Three-Part Analysis, Case C

Part 1. Recorded Balances

	12/31/90	12/31/91	12/31/92	12/31/93
Machinery: A	$100,000	$100,000	$100,000	$100,000
Accumulated Depreciation: A	0	(30,000)	(60,000)	(90,000)
Depreciation Expense: A	0	30,000	30,000	30,000
Investment in Company C: A	14,400	14,400	14,400	14,400
Income from Company C: A	(14,400)	0	0	0
(Beginning) Retained Earnings: A	0	(14,400)	(14,400)	(14,400)
Gain on Sale of Machinery: C	(18,000)	0	0	0
(Beginning) Retained Earnings: C	0	(18,000)	(18,000)	(18,000)

Part 2. Desired Balances

	12/31/90	12/31/91	12/31/92	12/31/93
Machinery	$ 82,000	$ 82,000	$ 82,000	$ 82,000
Accumulated Depreciation	0	(24,000)	(48,000)	(72,000)
Depreciation Expense	0	24,000	24,000	24,000
Consolidated Net Income	0	(4,800)	(4,800)	(4,800)
Consolidated (Beginning) Retained Earnings	0	0	(4,800)	(9,600)
Minority Interest in Company C's Net Income	0	(1,200)	(1,200)	(1,200)
Minority Interest in Company C's (Beginning) Retained Earnings	0	0	(1,200)	(2,400)

Part 3. Additional Eliminations

	12/31/90	12/31/91	12/31/92	12/31/93
Machinery	$ (18,000)	$ (18,000)	$ (18,000)	$ (18,000)
Accumulated Depreciation	0	6,000	12,000	18,000
Depreciation Expense	0	(6,000)	(6,000)	(6,000)
Retained Earnings: A	0	14,400	9,600	4,800
Gain on Sale of Machinery	18,000	0	0	0
Retained Earnings: C	0	3,600	2,400	1,200

in Company C's net income in the ratio of the ownership interests. The cumulative effect of this allocation appears in the balances of Consolidated (beginning) Retained Earnings and Minority Interest in Company C's (beginning) Retained Earnings.

As in Case B, the additional eliminations presented in Part 3 are affected by two preceding sets of eliminations.

- At December 31, 1990, the Subsidiary Income and Dividends set of eliminations will remove the excess $14,400 from Company A's Investment in Company C and Income from Company C balances.

- At December 31 of each of the next three years, the Intercompany Ownership Interests set of eliminations will remove the excess $14,400 from Company A's Investment in Company C balance and Company A's share, $14,400, of the excess $18,000 in Company C's beginning Retained Earnings balance.

Thus, the additional elimination against Company C's Retained Earnings at the end of each year removes the *minority interest's* share of the unrealized intercompany profit, leaving the *minority interest's* share of the realized intercompany profit to be added in with the other minority interest elements.

Because Company C is the selling affiliate and thus earned the intercompany profit initially, its net income must be adjusted each year in the Income Allocation schedule. In 1990, the entire amount of $18,000 is subtracted, and in each subsequent year of the asset's life, $6,000 is added. This will cause the $6,000 of intercompany profit realized each year to be allocated between consolidated net income and the minority interest in Company C's net income in the ratio of the ownership interests. Based on the assumptions stated in Case A, the Income Allocation schedule for Case C appears in Exhibit 9-5.

EXHIBIT 9-5

Illustrative Problem 9.1
Income Allocation Schedule, Case C

Income Allocation

Company A's Own Net Income		$ 55,300
Company C's Own Net Income	$ 29,400	
Less: Goodwill Amortization Expense	(1,000)	
Add: Realized Intercompany Profit on Machinery	6,000	
Company C's Adjusted Net Income	34,400	
Minority Interest (20%)	6,880	
Company A's Share (80%)		27,520
Consolidated Net Income		$ 82,820

A Practical Way to Construct the Eliminations. As noted earlier, the three-part analysis used in presenting the solutions to Cases A, B, and C, although useful as an explanatory device, is not intended to be used in problem solving. By examining the common characteristics of the sets of eliminations that appear in Exhibits 9-1, 9-3, and 9-4, a more practical approach can be developed. Those characteristics are as follows:

- The amount eliminated from the asset balance at each year end is the total amount of the intercompany profit.
- The amount eliminated from Depreciation Expense in each year is the portion of that year's depreciation based on the intercompany profit component of the buying affiliate's cost. (In Illustrative Problem 9.1, this amount is the same for each full year of the asset's life because the straight-line method is used.)
- The amount eliminated from Accumulated Depreciation in each year equals the cu-

mulative amount eliminated from Depreciation Expense through the end of that year. In other words, it is the difference between [a] the depreciation actually recorded by the buying affiliate through the end of the current year and [b] depreciation based on intercompany cost through the end of the current year.

▪ When the seller is a partially owned subsidiary, the amount eliminated from the Retained Earnings balances is allocated between the parent's and the subsidiary's Retained Earnings balances. In all other cases, the elimination affects only the parent's Retained Earnings.

▪ The total amount eliminated from beginning Retained Earnings balances each year equals the total amount of excess depreciation remaining to be recorded (or the intercompany profit remaining to be recognized) as of the *beginning* of that year.

Based on this information, we easily can construct the Intercompany Profit in Depreciable Assets set of eliminations for any given year. To illustrate, we will construct those eliminations at December 31, 1992 in case C.

Exhibits 9-1, 9-3, and 9-4 demonstrate that the eliminations will take the form shown in Exhibit 9-6. If either the parent or a wholly owned subsidiary were the seller, only the parent's Retained Earnings balance would be debited in this set of eliminations. After structuring the elimination set in this manner, we can proceed to fill in the amounts, ultimately arriving at the completed set of eliminations shown in Exhibit 9-7.

EXHIBIT 9-6

Illustrative Problem 9.1
Structure of Eliminations, Case C

Eliminations

Intercompany Profit in Depreciable Assets

[21] Accumulated Depreciation $
[22] Retained Earnings: A
[23] Retained Earnings: C
[24] Depreciation Expense   (   )
[25] Machinery $(   )

The easiest amount to determine is the credit to the Machinery account in Elimination [25], which is the total amount of the intercompany profit. In this case, Company C sold machinery with a book value of $82,000 to Company A for $100,000, yielding an intercompany profit of $18,000.

The excess depreciation expense is the portion of that expense based on the intercompany profit segment of the buying affiliate's cost. Notice that although the salvage value influences the calculation of the buyer's actual depreciation expense, it has no effect on the determination of the excess depreciation. We are concerned here only with the intercompany profit element. In this case, Company A is depreciating the machinery on the straight-line method, over a three-year life. Thus, the excess depreciation expense is one-third of the total intercompany

EXHIBIT 9-7

Illustrative Problem 9.1
Completed Eliminations, Case C

Eliminations

Intercompany Profit in Depreciable Assets

[21] Accumulated Depreciation	$ 12,000
[22] Retained Earnings: A	9,600
[23] Retained Earnings: C	2,400
[24] Depreciation Expense	(6,000)
[25] Machinery	$(18,000)

profit, or $6,000. This amount is eliminated from Depreciation Expense in Elimination [24], thus adding $6,000 of realized intercompany profit to total net income for 1992.

The amount to be eliminated from Accumulated Depreciation is the total amount of excess depreciation recorded by the buying affiliate through the end of the current year. In this case, two years of the asset's life have expired. Thus, two years' excess depreciation, or $12,000, is eliminated from Accumulated Depreciation in Elimination [21].

The total amount to be debited to one or more Retained Earnings balances can be calculated simply as the amount necessary to balance the set of eliminations in terms of debits and credits. This total also can be verified as representing the excess depreciation remaining to be recorded, or the intercompany profit remaining to be recognized, as of the beginning of the current year. In this case, $12,000 must be allocated between the two Retained Earning balances, because Company C is the seller.

Our previously established allocation formula allocates to each affiliate's Retained Earnings balance an amount equal to [a] that affiliate's external ownership interest, multiplied by [b] its share of the quantity being allocated, multiplied by [c] the quantity being allocated. In this case, the results are

	[a]	×	[b]	×	[c]	=	[d]
Company A:	100%	×	80%	×	$12,000	=	$9,600
Company C:	20%	×	100%	×	$12,000	=	$2,400

These amounts are eliminated from the two Retained Earnings balances in Eliminations [22] and [23].

Using the above approach, we can determine the additional eliminations needed for any year in any depreciable asset's life, regardless of which affiliate is the seller, without going through the entire three-part analysis.

Demonstration of the Realization of Intercompany Profits. The effects of recognizing the realization of intercompany profit in a depreciable asset can be demonstrated as follows. If the machinery in Illustrative Problem 9.1 is used productively by the buying affiliate and, however indrectly, generates revenues over its useful life equal to at least the intercompany selling price of $100,000, the intercompany profit of $18,000 will have become realized to the consolidated entity.

Assume that the machinery generates revenue of $60,000, $75,000, and $80,000 in 1991, 1992, and 1993, respectively. Exhibit 9-8 provides a proof of the intercompany profit included in total net income of each year and of the increase in combined beginning Retained Earnings for each year, as indicated in Exhibits 9-1, 9-3, and 9-4. The allocation of total net income and of the increase in beginning Retained Earnings will depend on which affiliate is the seller.

EXHIBIT 9-8

Illustrative Problem 9.1
Proof of Intercompany Profit Realization

	1991	1992	1993
Before Eliminations			
Revenue	$ 60,000	$ 75,000	$ 80,000
Depreciation Expense	30,000	30,000	30,000
Profit Contribution	$ 30,000	$ 45,000	$ 50,000
After Eliminations			
Revenue	$ 60,000	$ 75,000	$ 80,000
Depreciation Expense	24,000	24,000	24,000
Profit Contribution	$ 36,000	$ 51,000	$ 56,000
Compare Profit Contributions			
Before Eliminations	$ 30,000	$ 45,000	$ 50,000
After Eliminations	36,000	51,000	56,000
Increase	$ 6,000	$ 6,000	$ 6,000
Increase in Beginning Retained Earnings	$ 0	$ 6,000	$ 12,000

Depreciation on the asset provides a convenient means of measuring the realization of the intercompany profit and allocating it to appropriate accounting periods. The realized intercompany profit never appears in the consolidated income statement as "Gain on Sale of Machinery," but is included in total net income through the elimination of the excess depreciation expense.

ILLUSTRATIVE PROBLEM 9.2: INTERCOMPANY ASSET TRANSFERS OTHER THAN AT YEAR END

In Illustrative Problem 9.1, the intercompany sale of the depreciable asset occurs on December 31, 1990, the very last day of the fiscal year. Thus,

- In the year of sale, no depreciation is recorded by the buying affiliate and, therefore, no eliminations are made from either Depreciation Expense or Accumulated Depreciation.

- The entire amount of the intercompany profit is eliminated from Gain on Sale of Machinery and from the Machinery account at December 31, 1990.
- In each successive year of the asset's life, a full year's excess depreciation is eliminated from Depreciation Expense, causing an equal amount to be added to total net income as realized intercompany profit.

Obviously, an intercompany sale and purchase of a depreciable asset might well occur at some other time during the fiscal year. Suppose, for example, that the intercompany transaction in Case C of Illustrative Problem 9.1 had occurred on July 1, 1990. Company C, an 80% owned subsidiary, sold machinery with a book value of $82,000 to Company A for $100,000. Company A began depreciating it as of the purchase date, using the straight-line method, over a three-year life, with a $10,000 salvage value. Exhibit 9-9 shows the three-part analysis.

As shown in Part 1, Company A records six months' depreciation, $15,000, on the machinery in 1990. In 1991 and 1992, Company A records a full year's depreciation, $30,000. In 1993, the last year of the asset's useful life, Company A again records six months' depreciation.

The elimination of $3,000 of excess depreciation from Depreciation Expense in 1990 adds $3,000 of intercompany profit to total net income of 1990. Intercompany profits of $6,000 are recognized in 1991 and again in 1992, leaving only $3,000 to be recognized in 1993.

In addition, in the Income Allocation schedule for 1990, Company C's net income must be adjusted for both the total gain on the sale of the machinery of $18,000 and for the $3,000 of intercompany profit realized in 1990. This can be accomplished either by adding the $3,000 of realized intercompany profit and subtracting the full $18,000 gain, or by subtracting the net amount of $15,000, labeled "Unrealized Intercompany Gain on Machinery."

Assume that in 1990, Company A and Company C reported separate net incomes of $50,200 and $31,600, respectively, and that amortization of Goodwill of Company C amounted to $1,000. The Income Allocation schedule for 1990 is shown in Exhibit 9-10. In this Income Allocation schedule, the net unrealized amount of intercompany profit, $15,000, is added to Company C's net income and is labeled "Unrealized Intercompany Gain on Machinery." If Company A had been the seller, its net income would have been adjusted for the net unrealized gain of $15,000.

SALE OF A DEPRECIABLE ASSET BY THE BUYING AFFILIATE

Illustrative Problems 9.1 and 9.2 are based on the assumption that the buying affiliate holds the asset purchased from the other affiliate through the end of its estimated useful life. Obviously, this does not always happen. If the buying affiliate sells that asset to an outside entity before the end of its useful life, the remaining unrealized intercompany profit becomes realized to the consolidated entity, provided that the selling price equals or exceeds the net book value of the asset at the date of the sale.

To illustrate, we will use Case C of Illustrative Problem 9.1, in which Company C, an 80% owned subsidiary, sells machinery with a book value of $82,000 to its parent, Company A, for $100,000 on December 31, 1990. Exhibit 9-4 shows that the machinery is carried on Company A's books at the intercompany selling price of $100,000 and that the related ac-

EXHIBIT 9-9

Illustrative Problem 9.2
Three-Part Analysis
Sale by Company C on July 1, 1990

Part 1. Recorded Balances

	12/31/90	12/31/91	12/31/92	12/31/93
Machinery: A	$100,000	$100,000	$100,000	$100,000
Accumulated Depreciation: A	(15,000)	(45,000)	(75,000)	(90,000)
Depreciation Expense: A	15,000	30,000	30,000	15,000
Investment in Company C: A	14,400	14,400	14,400	14,400
Income from Company C: A	(14,400)	0	0	0
(Beginning) Retained Earnings: A	0	(14,400)	(14,400)	(14,400)
Gain on Sale of Machinery: C	(18,000)	0	0	0
(Beginning) Retained Earnings: C	0	(18,000)	(18,000)	(18,000)

Part 2. Desired Balances

	12/31/90	12/31/91	12/31/92	12/31/93
Machinery	$ 82,000	$ 82,000	$ 82,000	$ 82,000
Accumulated Depreciation	(12,000)	(36,000)	(60,000)	(72,000)
Depreciation Expense	12,000	24,000	24,000	12,000
Consolidated Net Income	(2,400)	(4,800)	(4,800)	(2,400)
Consolidated (Beginning) Retained Earnings	0	(2,400)	(7,200)	(12,000)
Minority Interest in Company S's Net Income	(600)	(1,200)	(1,200)	(600)
Minority Interest in Company S's (Beginning) Retained Earnings	0	(600)	(1,800)	(3,000)

Part 3. Additional Eliminations

	12/31/90	12/31/91	12/31/92	12/31/93
Machinery	$(18,000)	$(18,000)	$(18,000)	$(18,000)
Accumulated Depreciation	3,000	9,000	15,000	18,000
Depreciation Expense	(3,000)	(6,000)	(6,000)	(3,000)
Retained Earnings: A	0	12,000	6,000	2,400
Gain on Sale of Machinery	18,000	0	0	0
Retained Earnings: C	0	3,000	1,800	600

cumulated depreciation at December 31, 1992 is $60,000. Exhibit 9-1 also shows that $12,000 of the $18,000 of intercompany profit is realized to the consolidated entity by the end of 1992. Assume that on January 1, 1993, Company A sells the machinery to an outside entity for $50,000. Company A would record the following journal entry.

Cash	50,000	
Accumulated Depreciation	60,000	
Machinery		100,000
Gain on Sale of Machinery		10,000

EXHIBIT 9-10

Illustrative Problem 9.2
Income Allocation Schedule
Year Ended December 31, 1990

Income Allocation

Company A's Net Own Income		$ 50,200
Company C's Own Net Income	$ 31,600	
Less: Goodwill Amortization Expense	(1,000)	
Unrealized Intercompany Gain on Machinery	(15,000)	
Company C's Adjusted Net Income	15,600	
Minority Interest (20%)	3,120	
Company A's Share (80%)		12,480
Consolidated Net Income		$ 62,680

Because the selling price is at least equal to the net book value of the machinery at the date of the sale, the remaining intercompany profit of $6,000 is realized to the consolidated entity through this sale transaction. Therefore, the appropriate portions of the $18,000 intercompany profit can remain in the affiliates' respective Retained Earnings balances, as shown in Exhibit 9-4, and no further eliminations are necessary.

INTERCOMPANY PROFIT IN OTHER LONG-LIVED ASSETS

The treatment of intercompany profit in depreciable assets described and illustrated in this chapter also applies to other kinds of amortizable, long-lived assets such as patents, copyrights, franchises, etc. The only real difference, other than the titles of the asset accounts, is that amortization other than depreciation conventionally is credited directly to the asset account rather than to a contra account like Accumulated Depreciation. Thus, no such contra account appears in the eliminations.

Land is a nonamortizable asset. Therefore, intercompany profit arising from the sale of land from one affiliate to another would be eliminated from the asset, Land, and from the appropriate Retained Earnings balance or balances at the end of each year until the land is resold and, thus, the intercompany profit is realized by the consolidated entity. This treatment is demonstrated in Illustrative Problem 9.3.

ILLUSTRATIVE PROBLEM 9.3: INTERCOMPANY PROFIT IN LAND

Company D owns 75% of Company E's common stock. On June 30, 1989, Company E sold land that had cost $60,000 to Company D for $90,000. On September 30, 1993, Company D sold the land to an outside entity for $130,000. The eliminations necessary at December 31, 1990 in regard to the land are shown in Exhibit 9-11.

EXHIBIT 9-11

Illustrative Problem 9.3
Additional Eliminations
December 31, 1989

Eliminations

Intercompany Profit in Land

[21] Retained Earnings: D		$ 22,500
[22] Retained Earnings: E		7,500
[23] Land		$(30,000)

Our previously established allocation formula allocates to each affiliate's Retained Earnings balance an amount equal to [a] that affiliate's external ownership interest, multiplied by [b] its share of the quantity being allocated, multiplied by [c] the quantity being allocated. In this case, the results are

$$\begin{array}{ccccccc} & [a] & \times & [b] & \times & [c] & = & [d] \\ \text{Company D:} & 100\% & \times & 75\% & \times & \$30{,}000 & = & \$22{,}500 \\ \text{Company E:} & 25\% & \times & 100\% & \times & \$30{,}000 & = & \$\ 7{,}500 \end{array}$$

These amounts are eliminated from the two Retained Earnings balances in Eliminations [21] and [22].

Exactly the same set of eliminations is repeated at December 31, 1990, 1991, and 1992. On September 30, 1993, Company D records the sale of the land to a third party in the following journal entry.

Cash	130,000	
Land		90,000
Gain on Sale of Land		40,000

Because the selling price is at least equal to the book value of the land at the date of the sale, the entire intercompany profit of $30,000 is realized to the consolidated entity through this sale transaction. Therefore, the appropriate portions of the $30,000 intercompany profit can remain in the affiliates' respective Retained Earnings balances and no further eliminations are necessary.

ILLUSTRATIVE PROBLEM 9.4: COMPREHENSIVE ILLUSTRATION

To place the treatment of intercompany profits in depreciable assets in the context of the complete consolidation process, we will continue with Illustrative Problems 7.2 and 8.2. Company P acquired 48,000 of Company S's 60,000 outstanding shares of $5 par value common stock for $608,400 on April 1, 1991, when Company S had additional paid-in capital of $120,000. Company S's December 31, 1990 retained earnings balance was $120,250. In 1991, Company S reported net income of $81,000 and declared dividends of $40,000 on November 15 that were paid on December 15. The excess of cost over book value is treated as goodwill of Company S, which is being amortized over 10 years. Company P accounts for its investment in Company S under the equity method. The December 31, 1994 trial balances of the two affiliates appear in the worksheet in Exhibit 9-17.

Exhibit 9-12 shows the schedules of the Excess of Cost over Book Value and the resulting adjustments at December 31, 1994.

EXHIBIT 9-12

Illustrative Problem 9.4
Excess of Cost over Book Value and Adjustments
Year Ended December 31, 1994

Excess of Cost over Book Value

Cost of Investment		$ 608,400
Book Value (80% × $560,500)		448,400
Excess of Cost over Book Value		160,000
Expand to 100%		80%
Goodwill, 4/1/91		200,000
Amortization through 12/31/93	$ 55,000	
Amortization, 1994	20,000	75,000
Goodwill, 12/31/94		$ 125,000

Adjustments

A. Goodwill	$ 200,000
B. Appraisal Capital: S	(200,000)

Exhibit 9-13 presents the Intercompany Ownership Interests, Subsidiary Income and Dividends, and Goodwill Amortization sets of eliminations necessary at December 31, 1994. Eliminations [1] through [5] eliminate Company P's ownership interest, 80%, of each of Company S's stockholders' equity balances and the total thereof, $667,000, against Company P's Investment in Company S balance. Eliminations [6] and [7] eliminate Company P's Income from Company S balance against 80% of Company S's Dividends Declared balance, yielding a $20,000 credit to Investment in Company S.

The 1994 goodwill amortization determined in Exhibit 9-12 is recognized in Elimination [9]. Eliminations [10] and [11] divide the prior years' goodwill amortization, also from Exhibit 9-12, between the two Retained Earnings balances according to the previously established allocation formula, which allocates to each affiliate's Retained Earnings balance an amount equal to [a] that affiliate's external ownership interest, multiplied by [b] its share of the quantity being allocated, multiplied by [c] the quantity being allocated. In this case, the results are

$$[a] \times [b] \times [c] = [d]$$
Company P: $100\% \times 80\% \times \$55,000 = \$44,000$
Company S: $20\% \times 100\% \times \$55,000 = \$11,000$

The total amount of goodwill amortization, of course, is credited to Goodwill in Elimination [12].

EXHIBIT 9-13

Illustrative Problem 9.4
Eliminations
Year Ended December 31, 1994

Eliminations

Intercompany Ownership Interests

[1]	Capital Stock: S	$ 240,000
[2]	Additional Paid-in Capital: S	96,000
[3]	Retained Earnings: S	171,000
[4]	Appraisal Capital: S	160,000
[5]	Investment in Company S	$(667,000)

Subsidiary Income and Dividends

[6]	Income from Company S	$ 60,000
[7]	Dividends Declared: S	(40,000)
[8]	Investment in Company S	$ (20,000)

Goodwill Amortization

[9]	Other Expenses	$ 20,000
[10]	Retained Earnings: P	44,000
[11]	Retained Earnings: S	11,000
[12]	Goodwill	$ (75,000)

During 1994, Company S sold merchandise to Company P for $315,600, of which $28,900 remains unpaid at December 31, 1994. Intercompany profit of $14,100 is included in Company P's January 1, 1994 inventory. Merchandise purchased from Company S for $25,600 is contained in Company P's December 31, 1994 inventory of $79,700. Company S's December 31, 1994 inventory is $90,600. Company S sells to Company P at 60% above cost. Both affiliates use periodic inventory systems.

The additional sets of eliminations required at December 31, 1994 by the intercompany sales and purchases of merchandise and the resulting intercompany balances appear in Exhibit 9-14.

The intercompany profit in ending inventory is calculated as the amount remaining in Company P's inventory, $25,600, multiplied by the fraction, .6/1.6. The intercompany profit in beginning inventory is allocated between the two Retained Earnings balances in the same manner used in Eliminations [10] and [11] in Exhibit 9-13.

On June 30, 1992, Company S sold equipment with a book value of $121,100 to Company P for $163,100. Company P is depreciating the equipment using the sum-of-the-years'-digits method, over a six-year useful life, with a $23,700 salvage value. The resulting additional eliminations necessary at December 31, 1994 appear in Exhibit 9-15.

EXHIBIT 9-14

Illustrative Problem 9.4
Additional Eliminations
Year Ended December 31, 1994

Intercompany Sales and Purchases

[13] Sales	$ 315,600
[14] Purchases	(315,600)

Intercompany Receivables and Payables

[15] Current Liabilities	$ 28,900
[16] Accounts Receivable	(28,900)

Intercompany Profit in Ending Inventory

Company P's Ending Inventory	$ 79,700
Company S's Ending Inventory	90,600
Total Ending Inventory	170,300
Less: Intercompany Profit	9,600
[17] Ending Inventory at Intercompany Cost	$ 160,700

Intercompany Profit in Beginning Inventory

[18] Retained Earnings: P	$ 11,280
[19] Retained Earnings: S	2,820
[20] Inventories	$ (14,100)

EXHIBIT 9-15

Illustrative Problem 9.4
Additional Eliminations
Year Ended December 31, 1994

Intercompany Profit in Depreciable Assets

[21] Accumulated Depreciation	$ 26,000
[22] Retained Earnings: P	20,000
[23] Retained Earnings: S	5,000
[24] Depreciation Expense	(9,000)
[25] Plant and Equipment	$ (42,000)

In the Intercompany Profit in Depreciable Assets set of eliminations, the easiest amount to determine is the credit to Plant and Equipment in Elimination [25], which is the total amount of the intercompany profit. Company S sold equipment that had cost $121,000 to Company P for $163,100, yielding an intercompany profit of $42,000.

Company P is depreciating the equipment over a six-year useful life, using the sum-of-the-years'-digits method. A schedule of the excess depreciation (the portion based on intercompany profit) through December 31, 1994 appears below.

1992: $42,000 × 6/21 × 6/12	$ 6,000
1993: ($42,000 × 6/21 × 6/12) + ($42,000 × 5/21 × 6/12)	11,000
Accumulated Depreciation, 12/31/93	17,000
1994: ($42,000 × 5/21 × 6/12) + ($42,000 × 4/21 × 6/12)	9,000
Accumulated Depreciation, 12/31/94	$ 26,000

The excess depreciation expense for 1994, $9,000, is eliminated from Depreciation Expense in Elimination [24], thus adding $9,000 of realized intercompany profit to total net income for 1994.

The amount eliminated from Accumulated Depreciation is the total amount of excess depreciation recorded by the buying affiliate through the end of the current year. Two and one-half years of the asset's life have expired by the end of 1994. Thus, $26,000 is eliminated from Accumulated Depreciation in Elimination [21].

The total amount to be debited to one or more Retained Earnings balances can be calculated simply as the amount necessary to balance the set of eliminations in terms of debits and credits. This total also can be verified as representing the excess depreciation remaining to be recorded, or the intercompany profit remaining to be recognized, as of the beginning of the current year. In this case, the excess depreciation schedule shows that $17,000 of excess depreciation has been recorded through December 31, 1993. The remaining $25,000 out of the total intercompany profit of $42,000, must be allocated between the two Retained Earnings balances, because Company S is the seller.

Our previously established allocation formula allocates to each affiliate's Retained Earnings balance an amount equal to [a] that affiliate's external ownership interest, multiplied by [b] its share of the quantity being allocated, multiplied by [c] the quantity being allocated. In this case, the results are

	[a]	×	[b]	×	[c]	=	[d]
Company P:	100%	×	80%	×	$25,000	=	$20,000
Company S:	20%	×	100%	×	$25,000	=	$ 5,000

These amounts are eliminated from the two Retained Earnings balances in Eliminations [22] and [23].

Exhibit 9-16 presents the 1994 Income Allocation schedule, in which the $9,000 of intercompany profit in equipment realized in 1994 is added to Company S's own net income in arriving at its adjusted net income. This treatment results in $1,800 being included in the minority interest in Company S's net income and $7,200 being included in consolidated net income.

The December 31, 1994 consolidation worksheet for Company P and Company S appears in Exhibit 9-17. Notice that Eliminations [13] and [17] have the effect of reducing the carrying value of the machinery that Company P purchased from Company S to the remaining undepreciated amount of its intercompany cost. Elimination [16] both causes Depreciation Expense to be reported in terms of intercompany cost and has the effect of adding $6,000 of realized intercompany profit to total net income for 1994. Eliminations [14] and [15] remove appropriate portions of the unrealized intercompany profit from consolidated Retained Earnings and the minority interest in Company S's Retained Earnings.

EXHIBIT 9-16

Illustrative Problem 9.4
Income Allocation
Year Ended December 31, 1994

Income Allocation

Company P's Net Income		$ 69,600
Company S's Net Income	$ 75,000	
Add: Intercompany Profit in Beginning Inventory	14,100	
Intercompany Profit in Equipment	9,000	
Less: Intercompany Profit in Ending Inventory	(9,600)	
Goodwill Amortization Expense	(20,000)	
Company S's Adjusted Net Income	68,500	
Minority Interest (20%)	13,700	
Company P's Share (80%)		54,800
Consolidated Net Income		$ 124,400

SUMMARY

In this chapter, we have discussed and illustrated the following topics:

- A review of intercompany profits in inventories
- The nature of assets
- A review of depreciation methods
- A three-part analysis to explain the effects of intercompany profits in depreciable assets
- The treatment of intercompany profits in depreciable assets in the consolidation process
- Subsequent sale of a depreciable asset by the buying affiliate
- Intercompany profit in other long-lived assets

REVIEW PROBLEM

The July 31, 1992 trial balances of Company P and Company S appear below.

	Company P	Company S
Current Assets	$ 103,400	$ 60,000
Plant and Equipment	284,000	190,000
Investment in Company S	170,200	
Cost of Goods Sold	142,100	91,400
Operating Expenses	41,500	73,600
Dividends Declared	15,000	12,000
	$ 756,200	$ 427,000

EXHIBIT 9-17

Illustrative Problem 9.4
Consolidation Worksheet
December 31, 1994

	Company P	Company S	Adjustments and Eliminations		Income Statement		Balance Sheet
Accounts Receivable	134,100	148,300	[16]	(28,900)			253,500
Inventories	81,800	89,900	[20]	(14,100)	157,600	[17] 160,700	160,700
Plant and Equipment	890,700	1,338,000	[25]	(42,000)			2,186,700
Other Assets	299,500	156,200					455,700
Investment in Company S	687,000		[5]	(667,000)			
			[8]	(20,000)			
Purchases	455,100	525,600	[14]	(315,600)	665,100		
Depreciation Expense	46,300	58,100	[24]	(9,000)	95,400		
Other Expenses	266,400	302,200	[9]	20,000	588,600		
Dividends Declared: P	80,000						80,000 R
Dividends Declared: S		50,000	[7]	(40,000)			10,000 M
Goodwill			A	200,000			125,000 G
			[12]	(75,000)			
	2,940,900	2,668,300					3,271,600
Accumulated Depreciation	622,300	401,300	[21]	26,000			997,600
Current Liabilities	193,500	152,650	[15]	28,900			317,250
Bonds Payable		500,000					500,000
Premium on Bonds Payable		20,400					20,400
Common Stock: P	500,000						500,000
Common Stock: S		300,000	[1]	240,000			60,000 M
Additional Paid-in Capital: P	310,000						310,000
Additional Paid-in Capital: S		120,000	[2]	96,000			24,000 M
Retained Earnings: P	415,600		[10]	44,000			340,320 R
			[18]	11,280			
			[22]	20,000			
Retained Earnings: S		213,750	[3]	171,000			23,930 M
			[11]	11,000			
			[19]	2,820			
			[23]	5,000			
Sales	819,600	955,400	[13]	315,600		1,459,400	
Income from Company S	60,000		[6]	60,000			
Other Income	19,900	4,800				24,700	
Appraisal Capital: S			B	(200,000)			40,000 M
			[4]	160,000			
	2,940,900	2,668,300					
Minority Interest in Company S's Net Income					13,700		13,700 M
Consolidated Net Income					124,400		124,400 R
					1,644,800	1,644,800	3,271,600

	Company P	Company S
Accumulated Depreciation	$ 83,100	$ 42,000
Liabilities	40,300	30,000
Common Stock	300,000	100,000
Additional Paid-in Capital	30,000	20,000
Retained Earnings	67,000	50,000
Sales	217,800	185,000
Income from Company S	18,000	
	$ 756,200	$ 427,000

Company P purchased 90% of Company S's common stock for $154,000 on August 1, 1990, on which date Company S had retained earnings of $40,000. The excess of cost over book value is treated as goodwill from consolidation and is being amortized over 10 years.

On November 1, 1990, Company S sold a truck with a net book value of $7,000 to Company P for $8,800. Company P is depreciating the truck on the basis of a useful life of 60,000 miles and a salvage value of $1,300. The truck was driven 10,000 miles through July 31, 1991 and another 15,000 miles in the year ended July 31, 1992.

Required

Prepare a consolidation worksheet at July 31, 1992, supported by appropriate schedules.

QUESTIONS

1. What is an asset?
2. How does the realization of intercompany profit in depreciable assets differ from the realization of intercompany profit in inventories?
3. How does the measurement of the realization of intercompany profit in depreciable assets differ from the measurement of intercompany profit in inventories?
4. In the Intercompany Profit in Deperciable Assets set of eliminations, what does the total amount eliminated from the affiliates' Retained Earnings balances represent?
5. At what amount should an asset that has been transferred from one affiliate to another be reported in the consolidated balance sheet?
6. In the Intercompany Profit in Depreciable Assets set of eliminations, what does the amount eliminated from Accumulated Depreciation represent?
7. By what means is the intercompany profit in a depreciable asset that is realized in a particular year added to the total net income of that year?
8. How is the intercompany profit in a depreciable asset that is realized in a particular year allocated between consolidated net income and the minority interest in subsidiary net income?
9. How is the intercompany profit in a depreciable asset treated in the Income Allocation schedule of the year in which the asset is sold by one affiliate to another at a date other than the end of the year?

EXERCISES

EXERCISE 9-1

On September 30, 1990, Company A purchased a truck for $22,500. The useful life of the truck was estimated to be 5 years and the salvage value to be $2,500. If Company A used the declining balance

method of depreciation at double the straight-line rate, the depreciation expense on the truck for the year ended December 31, 1991 would be
a. $8,100
b. $7,200
c. $5,400
d. $2,250

EXERCISE 9-2

Refer to Exercise 9-1. If the useful life of the truck had been estimated at 50,000 miles and the truck had been driven 2,800 miles in 1990 and 9,600 miles in 1991, the accumulated depreciation on the truck at the end of 1991 would be
a. $5,580
b. $4,960
c. $4,320
d. $3,840

EXERCISE 9-3

On March 31, 1990, Company B purchased a machine for $225,000. The useful life of the machine was estimated to be 6 years and the salvage value to be $15,000. Under the straight-line method, the accumulated depreciation on the machine at the end of 1992 would be
a. $103,125
b. $ 96,250
c. $ 37,500
d. $ 35,000

EXERCISE 9-4

Refer to Exercise 9-3. If Company B used the sum-of-the-years'-digits method, the depreciation expense on the machine for the year ended December 31, 1991 would be
a. $97,500
b. $60,000
c. $52,500
d. $50,000

EXERCISE 9-5

Company C constructed a small building at a cost of $200,000 and sold it to its affiliate, Company D, for $250,000 on April 1, 1990. Company D is depreciating the building on the straight-line method, over a 25-year useful life beginning on the date of transfer, with an estimated salvage value of $20,000.

Required

In parallel columns, schedule the eliminations relative to the building that are necessary at December 31, 1992 in each of the following independent cases:

1. Company C owns 100% of Company D's common stock.
2. Company C owns 90% of Company D's common stock.
3. Company D owns 100% of Company C's common stock.
4. Company D owns 70% of Company C's common stock.

EXERCISE 9-6

Company E owns 90% of Company F's common stock. On July 1, 1989, the selling affiliate sold a machine with a net book value of $32,000 to the buying affiliate for $42,000. The buying affiliate has depreciated the machine since that date on the straight-line method, over a 10-year useful life, with an estimated salvage value of $2,000.

Required

Schedule the eliminations relative to the machine that are necessary at December 31, 1992 [a] if Company E is the selling affiliate and [b] if Company F is the selling affiliate.

EXERCISE 9-7

Company G owns 75% of Company H's common stock. On September 30, 1990, the selling affiliate sold some equipment with a net book value of $60,000 to the buying affiliate for $75,000. The buying affiliate is depreciating the equipment on the sum-of-the-years'-digits method, over a 5-year useful life, with an estimated salvage value of $3,000.

Required

Schedule the eliminations relative to the equipment that should appear on the consolidation worksheet at September 30, 1992, the fiscal year end, [a] if Company G is the selling affiliate and [b] if Company H is the selling affiliate.

EXERCISE 9-8

Company I owns 75% of Company J's common stock. On July 31, 1990, Company J sold office equipment with a net book value of $9,000 to Company I for $13,000. Company I is depreciating the equipment from that date, over a 5-year useful life, using the declining balance method at 200% of the straight-line rate. Company I and Company J had separate net incomes of $19,500 and $23,000, respectively, for the year ended October 31, 1992.

Required

1. Schedule the eliminations relative to the office equipment that should appear on the October 31, 1992 consolidation worksheet.
2. Prepare an income allocation schedule to accompany that worksheet.

EXERCISE 9-9

Company K owns 80% of Company L's common stock. On October 1, 1988, Company L sold a patent with a net book value of $21,500 to Company K for $29,500. Company K is amortizing the patent from that date, over a remaining useful life of 5 years, using the straight-line method, with no salvage value.

Required

1. Schedule the eliminations relative to the patent that should appear on the December 31, 1992 consolidation worksheet.
2. What adjustments are necessary in the Income Allocation schedule that accompanies that worksheet? Answer verbally; be explicit.

EXERCISE 9-10

Company M owns 80% of Company N's common stock. On July 1, 1990, Company N sold machinery with a net book value of $60,000 to Company M for $102,000. Company M is depreciating the machinery over its remaining useful life of 6 years, using the sum-of-the-years'-digits method and assuming a $21,000 salvage value.

Required

1. In the Intercompany Profits in Depreciable Assets set of eliminations at June 30, 1991, Depreciation Expense is
   a. credited for $12,000
   b. debited for $6,000
   c. debited for $12,000
   d. credited for $10,000

2. In the Intercompany Profits in Depreciable Assets set of eliminations at June 30, 1992, Company M's Retained Earnings is
   a. credited for $6,000
   b. debited for $30,000
   c. credited for $30,000
   d. debited for $24,000

PROBLEMS

PROBLEM 9-1
Company K purchased 16,000 shares of Company L's common stock for $358,800 on October 1, 1987. Company L's March 31, 1987 retained earnings balance was $82,200. Company L reported net income of $52,600 for the year ended March 31, 1988. On January 15, 1988, Company L declared dividends of $28,000, which were paid on February 20, 1988. The excess of cost over book value is treated as goodwill of Company L and is being amortized over 12 years.

On June 30, 1989, Company L sold a machine with a net book value of $19,200 to Company K for $27,600. Company K is depreciating the machine from the date of purchase, using the straight-line method, over a 7-year useful life, with a salvage value of $1,300. The March 31, 1992 trial balances of Company K and Company L appear below.

	Company K	Company L
Current Assets	$ 198,700	$ 313,300
Plant and Equipment	321,400	464,100
Investment in Company L	425,200	
Cost of Goods Sold	301,300	216,700
Depreciation Expense	48,100	21,400
Other Expenses	199,600	121,200
Dividends Declared	38,000	34,500
	$1,532,300	$1,171,200
Accumulated Depreciation	$ 109,600	$ 116,600
Liabilities	238,200	189,300
Common Stock ($10 par)	300,000	200,000
Additional Paid-in Capital	100,000	80,000
Retained Earnings	108,100	162,500
Sales	621,300	419,100
Other Income	55,100	3,700
	$1,532,300	$1,171,200

Required
Prepare a consolidation worksheet at March 31, 1992, supported by appropriate schedules.

PROBLEM 9-2
Company M purchased 22,500 shares of Company N's common stock for $438,600 on June 30, 1989. Company N had retained earnings of $61,900 on December 31, 1988. Company N reported net income

of $45,800 for 1989. On November 5, 1989, Company N declared dividends of $21,000, which were paid on December 10, 1989. The excess of cost over book value is treated as goodwill of Company N and is being amortized over 10 years.

On April 1, 1990, Company M completed construction of a building for $180,400 and sold it to Company N for $236,400. Company N is depreciating the building over 20 years from the date of purchase, using the declining balance method at 200% of the straight-line rate.

The December 31, 1992 trial balances of Company M and Company N appear below.

	Company M	Company N
Current Assets	$ 319,600	$ 261,500
Plant and Equipment	542,100	671,900
Investment in Company N	438,600	
Cost of Goods Sold	261,300	226,700
Depreciation Expense	72,700	63,400
Other Expenses	137,400	146,300
Dividends Declared	33,000	28,000
	$1,804,700	$1,397,800
Accumulated Depreciation	$ 208,300	$ 192,300
Liabilities	269,500	186,700
Common Stock ($10 par)	500,000	300,000
Additional Paid-in Capital	150,000	120,000
Retained Earnings	128,900	117,600
Sales	522,600	478,400
Other Income	25,400	2,800
	$1,804,700	$1,397,800

Required
Prepare a consolidation worksheet at December 31, 1992, supported by appropriate schedules.

PROBLEM 9-3
The June 30, 1992 trial balances of Company P and Company Q appear below.

	Company P	Company Q
Inventories	$ 51,600	$ 32,600
Other Current Assets	262,500	107,800
Plant and Equipment	740,300	384,300
Investment in Company Q	362,000	
Purchases	309,200	198,700
Depreciation Expense	71,900	43,400
Other expenses	146,700	110,600
Dividends Declared	43,000	32,000
	$1,987,200	$ 909,400

	Company P	Company Q
Accumulated Depreciation	$ 194,800	$ 91,100
Liabilities	222,100	82,600
Common Stock ($10 par)	600,000	200,000
Additional Paid-in Capital	100,000	40,000
Retained Earnings	216,600	99,000
Sales	617,300	396,700
Income from Company Q	36,400	
	$1,987,200	$ 909,400
Inventories, 6/30/92	$ 48,700	$ 34,100

Company P purchased 16,000 shares of Company Q's common stock for $322,800 on April 1, 1984. Company Q had retained earnings of $57,300 on June 30, 1983. Company Q reported net income of $41,600 for the year ended June 30, 1984. On February 20, 1984, Company Q declared dividends of $25,000, which were paid on March 25, 1984. The excess of cost over book value is treated as goodwill from consolidation and is being amortized over 20 years.

During the year ended June 30, 1992, Company Q sold merchandise to Company P for $183,400, of which $16,200 remained unpaid at June 30, 1992. Company P's June 30, 1991 and June 30, 1992 inventories contained goods purchased from Company Q of $14,700 and $15,400, respectively. Company Q sells to Company P at cost plus 40%.

On July 1, 1988, Company P purchased equipment from Company Q for $69,600, which had been carried on Company Q's books at a net book value of $48,600. Company P is depreciating the equipment over a 7-year useful life from the date of purchase, using the sum-of-the-years'-digits method, with a $7,700 salvage value.

Required

Prepare a consolidation worksheet at June 30, 1992, supported by appropriate schedules.

PROBLEM 9-4

Company R purchased 8,000 shares of Company S's common stock for $148,000 on December 31, 1988, when Company S had retained earnings of $15,000. The excess of cost over book value is treated as goodwill of Company S and is being amortized over 15 years. The December 31, 1991 trial balances of Company R and Company S appear below.

	Company R	Company S
Inventories	$ 15,000	$ 20,000
Other Assets	235,000	230,000
Investment in Company S	160,000	
Purchases	105,000	60,000
Operating Expenses	60,000	35,000
Dividends Declared	10,000	15,000
	$ 585,000	$ 360,000

	Company R	Company S
Accumulated Depreciation	$ 50,000	$ 35,000
Liabilities	85,000	40,000
Common Stock ($10 par)	150,000	100,000
Additional Paid-in Capital	50,000	40,000
Retained Earnings	62,000	35,000
Sales	180,000	110,000
Income from Company S	8,000	
	$ 585,000	$ 360,000

During 1991, Company R purchased merchandise from Company S for $21,000, of which $5,000 remained unpaid at December 31, 1991. Company R's beginning and ending inventories for 1991 contained intercompany profits of $1,000 and $1,500, respectively. Company R and Company S had December 31, 1991 inventories of $25,000 and $15,000, respectively.

On June 30, 1989, Company R sold equipment with a net book value of $10,600 to Company S for $18,600. Company S is depreciating the equipment over a 10-year useful life from the date of purchase, using the straight-line method, with a $2,000 salvage value.

Required

Prepare a cosolidation worksheet at December 31, 1991, supported by appropriate schedules.

PROBLEM 9-5

The April 30, 1992 trial balances of Company T and Company U appear below.

	Company T	Company U
Receivables (net)	$ 101,400	$ 89,100
Inventories	183,600	109,300
Other Current Assets	123,800	188,000
Plant and Equipment	917,300	864,000
Investment in Company U	675,000	
Cost of Goods Sold	526,100	519,200
Other Expenses	392,500	268,400
Dividends Declared	80,000	48,000
Treasury Stock (400 shares, at cost)		24,000
	$2,999,700	$2,110,000
Accumulated Depreciation	$ 292,500	$ 211,900
Liabilities	416,100	204,500
Common Stock ($50 par)	800,000	500,000
Additional Paid-in Capital	120,000	140,000
Retained Earnings	314,400	182,000
Sales	1,015,200	863,400
Other Revenue	41,500	8,200
	$2,999,700	$2,110,000

Company T purchased 7,200 shares of Company U's common stock for $675,000 on October 31, 1987. Company U had retained earnings of $69,800 on April 30, 1987. Company U reported net income of $68,400 for the year ended April 30, 1988. On March 20, 1988, Company U declared dividends of $32,000, which were paid on April 22, 1988. The excess of cost over book value is attributed to the going concern value of Company U in excess of the fair market value of its recorded net assets and is being amortized over 15 years. Both affiliates declared dividends on April 1, 1992, payable on May 15, 1992.

During the year ended April 30, 1992, Company U purchased merchandise from Company T for $217,400, of which $38,700 remained unpaid at April 30, 1992. Company U's April 30, 1991 and April 30, 1992 inventories contained goods purchased from Company T of $42,100 and $35,400, respectively. Company T sells to Company U at 25% above cost.

On December 31, 1988 Company T purchased equipment from Company U for $158,000, which had been carried on Company U's books at a net book value of $118,000. Company T is depreciating the equipment over a 5-year useful life from the date of purchase, using the declining balance method at 150% of the straight-line rate.

Required
Prepare a consolidation worksheet at April 30, 1992, supported by appropriate schedules.

PROBLEM 9-6
The December 31, 1992 trial balances of Company V and Company W appear below.

	Company V	Company W
Current Assets	$ 223,700	$ 330,900
Plant and Equipment	501,500	456,900
Investment in Company W	495,900	
Cost of Goods Sold	341,700	189,800
Other Expenses	210,200	158,200
Dividends Declared	36,000	28,000
	$1,809,000	$1,163,800
Accumulated Depreciation	$ 172,700	$ 117,200
Liabilities	281,300	189,600
Common Stock ($10 par)	400,000	200,000
Additional Paid-in Capital	80,000	120,000
Retained Earnings	213,300	143,600
Sales	618,500	386,100
Other Income	43,200	7,300
	$1,809,000	$1,163,800

Company V purchased 18,000 shares of Company W's common stock for $427,500 on October 1, 1988. Company W had retained earnings of $48,700 on December 31, 1987. Company W reported net income of $48,400 for 1988. On November 20, 1988, Company W declared dividends of $32,000, which were paid on December 22, 1988. The excess of cost over book value is treated as goodwill of Company W and is being amortized over 10 years. Both affiliates declared dividends on December 15, 1992, payable on January 20, 1993.

On June 30, 1991, Company W sold a truck with a book value of $26,800 to Company V for $38,600. Company V is depreciating the truck on a mileage basis. The truck is estimated to have a useful life of 59,000 miles and is expected to have salvage value of $2,100. The truck was driven a total of 6,000 miles during the remainder of 1991 and a total of 11,000 miles in 1992.

Required
Prepare a consolidation worksheet at December 31, 1992, supported by appropriate schedules.

PROBLEM 9-7
Company X purchased 40,000 shares of Company Y's common stock for $611,600 on June 30, 1989. Company Y had retained earnings of $52,300 on December 31, 1988. Company Y reported net income of $51,900 for 1989. On February 20, 1989, Company Y declared dividends of $25,000, which were paid on March 25, 1989. The excess of cost over book value is treated as goodwill from consolidation and is being amortized over 20 years. The December 31, 1992 trial balances of Company X and Company Y appear below.

	Company X	Company Y
Receivables (net)	$ 136,100	$ 100,400
Inventories	78,000	99,700
Other Current Assets	98,700	176,100
Plant and Equipment	944,500	737,900
Investment in Company Y	611,600	
Purchases	597,400	458,500
Depreciation Expense	42,300	26,100
Other Expenses	321,100	239,700
Dividends Declared	50,000	40,000
	$2,879,700	$1,878,400
Accumulated Depreciation	$ 311,400	$ 186,200
Liabilities	396,800	201,500
Common Stock ($10 par)	500,000	500,000
Additional Paid-in Capital	192,000	80,000
Retained Earnings	369,700	136,200
Sales	1,065,200	765,800
Other Revenue	44,600	8,700
	$2,879,700	$1,878,400
Inventories, 12/31/92	$ 69,400	$ 101,100

During 1992, Company X sold merchandise to Company Y for $162,400, of which $16,100 remained unpaid at December 31, 1992. Company Y's December 31, 1991 and December 31, 1992 inventories contained goods purchased from Company X of $19,500 and $18,850, respectively. Company Y sells to Company X at 30% above cost.

On October 1, 1990, Company X purchased equipment from Company Y for $126,400, which had been carried on Company Y's books at a net book value of $84,400. Company X is depreciating the equipment over a 6-year useful life from the date of purchase, using the sum-of-the-years'-digits method, with a $12,300 salvage value.

Required
Prepare a consolidation worksheet at December 31, 1992, supported by appropriate schedules.

PROBLEM 9-8

The December 31, 1992 trial balances of Company E and Company F appear below.

	Company E	Company F
Receivables (net)	$ 135,400	$ 101,800
Inventories	82,100	70,900
Other Current Assets	88,700	178,100
Plant and Equipment	946,800	716,400
Investment in Company F	557,700	
Cost of Goods Sold	601,200	456,200
Other Expenses	380,100	271,300
Dividends	50,000	40,000
Treasury Stock (2,000 shares, at cost)		38,000
	$2,842,000	$1,872,700
Accumulated Depreciation	$ 264,500	$ 179,200
Liabilities	364,300	196,500
Capital Stock ($10 par)	500,000	300,000
Additional Paid-in Capital	220,000	280,000
Retained Earnings	353,600	129,200
Sales	1,088,400	778,700
Other Revenue	51,200	9,100
	$2,842,000	$1,872,700

Company E purchased 21,000 shares of Company F's capital stock for $557,700 on October 1, 1989. On December 31, 1988, Company F had retained Earnings of $68,400. Company F reported net income for 1989 of $49,600. Company F declared dividends of $35,000 on November 30, 1989 and paid them on December 20, 1989. The excess of cost over book value is attributed to the going concern value of Company F in excess of the fair market value of its recorded net assets and is being amortized over 12 years. Both affiliates declared dividends on December 8, 1992, payable on January 15, 1993.

During 1992, Company F purchased merchandise from Company E for $222,400, of which $21,200 remained unpaid at December 31, 1992. Company F's December 31, 1991 and December 31, 1992 inventories contained goods purchased from Company E of $28,700 and $30,100, respectively. Company E sells to Company F at 40% above cost.

On July 1, 1991, Company E purchased equipment from Company F for $138,500, which had been carried on Company F's books at $93,500. Company E is depreciating the equipment over a 5-year useful life from the date of purchase, using the sum-of-the-years'-digits method, with a $9,500 salvage value.

Required

Prepare a consolidation worksheet at December 31, 1992, supported by appropriate schedules.

SOLUTION TO REVIEW PROBLEM

Excess of Cost over Book Value

Cost of Investment		$ 154,000
Book Value (90% × $160,000)		144,000
Goodwill, 8/1/90		10,000
Amortization through 7/31/91	$ 1,000	
Amortization, Y.E. 7/31/92	1,000	2,000
Goodwill, 7/31/92		$ 8,000

Eliminations

Intercompany Ownership Interests

[1]	Common Stock: S	$ 90,000
[2]	Additional Paid-in Capital: S	18,000
[3]	Retained Earnings: S	45,000
[4]	Investment in Company S	$(153,000)

Subsidiary Income and Dividends

[5]	Income from Company S	$ 18,000
[6]	Dividends: S	(10,800)
[7]	Investment in Company S	$ (7,200)

Goodwill Amortization

[8]	Retained Earnings: P	$ 1,000
[9]	Operating Expenses (Goodwill Amortization)	1,000
[10]	Investment in Company S	$ (2,000)

Intercompany Profit in Depreciable Assets

[11]	Accumulated Depreciation	$ 750
[12]	Retained Earnings: P	1,350
[13]	Retained Earnings: S	150
[14]	Operating Expenses (Depreciation)	(450)
[15]	Plant and Equipment	$ (1,800)

Income Allocation

Company P's Net Income		$ 34,200
Less: Goodwill Amortization Expense		1,000
Company P's Adjusted Net Income		33,200
Company S's Net Income	$ 20,000	
Add: Realized Intercompany Profit on Truck	450	
Company S's Adjusted Net Income	20,450	
Minority Interest (10%)	2,045	
Company P's Share (90%)		18,405
Consolidated Net Income		$ 51,605

Consolidation Worksheet

	Company P	Company S	Eliminations		Income Statement	Balance Sheet
Current Assets	103,400	60,000				163,400
Plant and Equipment	284,000	190,000	[15]	(1,800)		472,200
Investment in Company S	170,200		[4]	(153,000)		8,000 G
			[7]	(7,200)		
			[10]	(2,000)		
Cost of Goods Sold	142,100	91,400			233,500	
Operating Expenses	41,500	73,600	[9]	1,000	115,650	
			[14]	(450)		
Dividends: P	15,000					15,000 R
Dividends: S		12,000	[6]	(10,800)		1,200 M
	756,200	427,000				659,800
Accumulated Depreciation	83,100	42,000	[11]	750		124,350
Liabilities	40,300	30,000				70,300
Common Stock: P	300,000					300,000
Common Stock: S		100,000	[1]	90,000		10,000 M
Additional Paid-in Capital: P	30,000					30,000
Additional Paid-in Capital: S		20,000	[2]	18,000		2,000 M
Retained Earnings: P	67,000		[8]	1,000		64,650 R
			[12]	1,350		
Retained Earnings: S		50,000	[3]	45,000		4,850 M
			[13]	150		
Sales	217,800	185,000			402,800	
Income from Company S	18,000		[5]	18,000		
	756,200	427,000				
Minority Interest in Company S's Net Income					2,045	2,045 M
Consolidated Net Income					51,605	51,605 R
					402,800 402,800	659,800

CHAPTER

10

INTERCOMPANY BONDS

mong the types of intercompany balances introduced in Chapter 8 are intercompany assets and liabilities, and intercompany revenues and expenses. The topic of intercompany bonds involves both of these sets of intercompany balances, as well as a peculiar type of intercompany profit element—gain or loss on the acquisition of intercompany bonds.

Chapter 10 deals with the following topics:

- A review of bond accounting by both the bond issuer and the bondholder
- Consolidation procedures when an affiliate acquires another affiliate's bonds directly from the issuing affiliate
- Gain or loss on retirement of bonds
- Consolidation procedures when an affiliate acquires another affiliate's bonds from other bondholders
- Other long-term intercompany liabilities

REVIEW OF BOND ACCOUNTING

At the outset, it is helpful to acknowledge the true nature of corporate bonds. When a corporation issues bonds, it does not *sell* anything (although we often hear and read references to a corporation's "selling" its bonds). In fact, the corporation is borrowing money from the original bondholders and issuing the bonds as evidence of that borrowing. Conversely, the original bondholders do not *buy* anything from the corporation that issues the bonds; they lend money to it. Corporate bonds, then, originate as borrowing–lending instruments.

After the bonds have been issued, they can be, and frequently are, transferred from one bondholder to another in a purchase–sale transaction. Most corporate bonds are traded in organized bond markets in which investors deal with each other through securities brokers. Thus, one bondholder can *buy* a corporation's bonds from their previous owner, but not from the issuing corporation.

ACCOUNTING FOR BONDS BY THE ISSUER

The bond issuer accounts for its bond liability in two separate accounts: Bonds Payable, which contains the face value of the bonds, and either Discount on Bonds Payable or Premium on Bonds Payable for the difference between the issue price and the face value of the bonds. A more detailed explanation of accounting for bonds by the bond issuer appears below.

To record the issuance of bonds, the issuer debits Cash for the total amount received, debits Discount on Bonds Payable if the bonds are issued at below face value or credits Premium on Bonds Payable if they are issued at above face value, and credits Bonds Payable for the face value of the bonds. If the bonds are issued between interest dates, the total amount of cash received will include accrued interest, the amount of which is credited to Interest Expense. (The accrued interest is credited to Interest Expense rather than Interest Payable so that it will offset against the interest expense recorded at the next interest payment date or in an adjusting entry at year end, whichever occurs first.)

To illustrate, assume that on April 30, 1990, a corporation issues 9% bonds with a face value of $1,000,000 for $1,119,000, plus accrued interest. The bonds mature on March 31, 2000, and interest is payable on March 31 and September 30. The corporation's fiscal year ends on December 31. The accrued interest on the bonds is calculated as $1,000,000 × 9% × 1/12, or $7,500. Notice that the remaining term of the bonds is 9 years and 11 months, or 119 months. The journal entry to record the issuance of the bonds on April 30, 1990 is

Cash	1,126,500	
Bonds Payable		1,000,000
Premium on Bonds Payable		119,000
Interest Expense		7,500

At each interest date, the issuer debits Interest Expense and credits Cash for the amount paid. At the first interest date following an issuance of bonds between interest dates, the accrued interest previously credited to Interest Expense will offset against this debit to Interest Expense, leaving in the account the amount incurred by the issuer. Also at each interest date, the issuer amortizes the issuance premium or discount by debiting Premium on Bonds Payable and crediting Interest Expense or by debiting Interest Expense and crediting Discount on Bonds Payable, as the case may be. This amortization usually is combined in a single journal entry with the recording of the payment of the interest.

Effective interest amortization schedules are both theoretically supportable and widely used in practice. Straight-line amortization, which is procedurally simpler, can be justified only on the basis of immateriality. If the results obtained by using straight-line amortization are not materially different from those yielded by effective interest amortization, straight-line amortization may be used. In order to be able to focus our attention on the consolidation procedures applicable to intercompany bonds, rather than on the construction of amortization schedules, it is convenient to use straight-line amortization. For this reason, we will assume that the difference between effective interest and straight-line amortization is immaterial in all illustrations, exercises, and problems in this text.

To continue our illustration, at September 30, 1990, the first interest date following the issuance of the bonds, the issuing corporation records the following journal entry:

Interest Expense	40,000	
Premium on Bonds Payable	5,000	
Cash		45,000

The corporation pays a full six months' interest, even though the bonds have been outstanding for only five months. Thus, the credit to Cash equals $1,000,000 \times 9\% \times 6/12$, or $45,000. The debit to Premium on Bonds Payable amortizes the issuance premium for the five months that have elapsed since the issuance date. The amortization is calculated as $119,000 \times 5/119$, or $5,000. The difference of $40,000 is debited to Interest Expense. Remember, however, that this amount is partially offset by the previous $7,500 credit, so that the net amount of interest expense reported is $32,500. This amount can be verified as five months' contractual interest, $37,500, minus five months' amortization of the premium, $5,000.

At subsequent interest dates, the issuing corporation records essentially the same journal entry, except that the amortization of the premium is for a full six months. For example, at September 30, 1991, the journal entry would be

Interest Expense	39,000	
Premium on Bonds Payable	6,000	
Cash		45,000

If the issuer's year end falls between bond interest dates, the issuer records a year-end adjustment for the accrued interest, debiting Interest Expense, debiting Premium on Bonds Payable or crediting Discount on Bonds Payable, and crediting Interest Payable. It is also useful to reverse this adjustment after closing the books so that the accrued interest will offset against the interest expense recorded at the next interest date. In this chapter, we assume that the reversing entry is recorded.

To continue our illustration, at December 31, 1990, the issuing corporation's year end, the following adjusting journal entry for three months' accrued interest is recorded:

Interest Expense	19,500	
Premium Bonds Payable	3,000	
Interest Payable		22,500

The credit to Interest Payable equals $1,000,000 \times 9\% \times 3/12$, or $22,500. The debit to Premium on Bonds Payable amortizes the issuance premium for the three months that have elapsed since the last interest date. The amortization is calculated as $119,000 \times 3/119$, or $3,000. The difference of $19,500 is debited to Interest Expense.

Finally, after the last interest payment has been recorded at the maturity date of the bonds, the premium or discount will have been amortized to zero. The payment to retire the bonds at face value is recorded by debiting Bonds Payable and crediting Cash for the face value of the bonds. In our illustration, the journal entry at March 31, 2000 would be

Bonds Payable	1,000,000	
Cash		1,000,000

The bond issuer's accounting for the retirement of bonds before maturity is discussed and illustrated later in this chapter.

ACCOUNTING FOR BONDS BY THE BONDHOLDER

A bondholder accounts for its investment in another entity's bonds in the same manner whether the bonds are acquired from other bondholders or directly from the issuing corporation. The bondholder's accounting for its investment in bonds is essentially the same as the bond issuer's in reverse, with one significant variation—the bondholder's acquisition premium or discount is not recorded in a separate account, but is simply a part of the cost of the investment reflected in an Investment in Bonds account.

The following discussion is based on the assumption that the bond investment is intended to be a long-term investment; that is, the bondholder intends to hold the bonds to maturity.

To record the acquisition of bonds, the bondholder debits the cost thereof to an asset account, Investment in Bonds. If the bonds are acquired between interest dates, the total amount paid includes accrued interest, which is debited to Interest Revenue. The total amount paid, of course, is credited to Cash. (The accrued interest is debited to Interest Revenue rather than Interest Receivable so that it will offset against the interest revenue recorded at the next interest payment date or in an adjusting entry at year end, whichever occurs first.)

To illustrate, assume that on March 1, 1991, a corporation acquires 9% bonds of another corporation (Company X) with a face value of $200,000 for $181,600, plus accrued interest. The investment is acquired at a discount of $18,400, the difference between the face value of the bonds acquired and the cost of the investment. The bonds mature on October 31, 1998 and interest is payable on April 30 and October 31. The acquiring corporation's fiscal year ends on December 31. The accrued interest on the bonds is calculated as $200,000 \times 9\% \times 4/12$, or $6,000. Notice that the remaining term of the bonds is 7 years and 8 months, or 92 months. The journal entry to record the acquisition of the bonds on March 1, 1991 is

Investment in Company X Bonds	181,600	
Interest Revenue	6,000	
Cash		187,600

At each interest date, upon receipt of the interest, the bondholder debits Cash and credits Interest Revenue. At the first interest date following an acquisition of bonds between interest dates, the accrued interest previously debited to Interest Revenue will offset against this credit to Interest Revenue, leaving in the account the amount earned by the bondholder. Also at each interest date, the bondholder amortizes the difference between the cost of the bond investment and the face value of the bonds (the acquisition premium or discount) against Interest Revenue. When bonds are acquired at a premium, the amount amortized is debited to Interest Revenue and credited to the Investment in Bonds account. When bonds are acquired at a discount, the amount amortized is debited to Investment in Bonds and credited to Interest Revenue. This amortization usually is combined in a single journal entry with the recording of the receipt of the interest, which is described above.

To continue our illustration, at April 30, 1991, the first interest date following the acquisition of the bond investment, the bondholder records the following journal entry:

Cash	9,000	
Investment in Company X Bonds	400	
Interest Revenue		9,400

The bondholder receives a full six months' interest, even though it has held the bonds for only two months. Thus, the debit to Cash equals $200,000 \times 9\% \times 6/12$, or $9,000. The debit to Investment in Company X Bonds amortizes the acquisition discount for the two months that have elapsed since the acquisition date. The amortization is calculated as $18,400 \times 2/92$, or $400. The total of $9,400 is credited to Interest Revenue. Remember, however, that this amount is partially offset by the previous $6,000 debit to Interest Revenue, so that the net amount of interest revenue reported is $3,400. This amount can be verified as two months' contractual interest, $3,000, plus two months' amortization of the acquisition discount, $400.

At subsequent interest dates, the bondholder records essentially the same journal entry, except that the amortization of the discount is for a full six months. For example, at April 30, 1992, the bondholder records the following journal entry:

Cash	9,000	
Investment in Company X Bonds	1,200	
Interest Revenue		10,200

If the bondholder's year end falls between bond interest dates, the bondholder records a year-end adjustment for the accrued interest, debiting Interest Receivable, debiting or crediting Investment in Company X bonds to amortize the acquisition discount or premium, and crediting Interest Revenue for the net amount. It is useful to reverse this adjustment after closing the books, so that the accrued interest will offset against the interest revenue recorded at the next interest date. In this chapter, we assume that the reversing entry is recorded.

To continue our illustration, at December 31, 1991, the bondholder's year end, the following adjusting journal entry for two months' accrued interest is recorded:

Interest Receivable	3,000	
Investment in Company X Bonds	400	
Interest Revenue		3,400

The debit to Interest Receivable equals $200,000 \times 9\% \times 2/12$, or $3,000. The debit to Investment in Company X Bonds amortizes the acquisition discount for the two months that have elapsed since the last interest date. The amortization is calculated as $18,400 \times 2/92$, or $400. The total of $3,400 is credited to Interest Revenue.

Finally, after the last interest payment has been recorded at the maturity date of the bonds, the premium or discount will have been amortized to zero and the Investment in Bonds balance will equal face value. The receipt of the payment to retire the bonds at face value is recorded by debiting Cash and crediting Investment in Bonds for the face value of the bonds. In our illustration, the journal entry at October 31, 1988 would be

| Cash | 200,000 | |
| Investment in Company X Bonds | | 200,000 |

The major difference between accounting for bonds by the bondholder and by the issuer (other than direction, of course) is the treatment of premiums and discounts. For some obscure reason, the bondholder conventionally carries the bond investment in a single account, while the issuer conventionally uses two accounts for the bond liability—Bonds Payable for the face value and either a Premium on Bonds Payable or a Discount on Bonds Payable account for the difference between face value and the issue price.

INTERCOMPANY BONDS ACQUIRED FROM THE ISSUING AFFILIATE

When a corporation issues bonds, one of the initial bondholders might well be an affiliate corporation. In other words, this is an intercompany borrowing–lending transaction, resulting in intercompany asset and liability balances that must be eliminated in preparing consolidated financial statements throughout the life of the bonds. Because the bonds bear interest, at least one additional set of intercompany balances is generated. Each of these sets of intercompany balances is discussed in more detail below.

The acquiring affiliate (the bondholder) will have an Investment in Affiliate's Bonds balance, which is exactly offset by a proportionate share of the carrying value of the bond liability on the issuer's books (Bonds Payable plus Premium on Bonds Payable or minus Discount on Bonds Payable). These offsetting intercompany balances must be eliminated. The relationship between the intercompany asset and liability balances, which is created at the issuance-acquisition date, is maintained throughout the life of the bonds as each affiliate amortizes its respective premium or discount.

After the issuance-acquisition date, periodic interest payments by the issuer will create offsetting intercompany Interest Revenue and Interest Expense balances, which must be eliminated. Finally, the year-end adjusting entries for accrued interest recorded by each affiliate will create intercompany balances in Interest Receivable and Interest Payable, which must be eliminated. Also, these adjustments will increase the intercompany Interest Revenue and Interest Expense balances mentioned above. Worksheet eliminations for these intercompany bond balances are presented in Illustrative Problem 10.1.

ILLUSTRATIVE PROBLEM 10.1: INTERCOMPANY BONDS ACQUIRED FROM THE ISSUING AFFILIATE

On December 31, 1990, Company A issued $1,000,000 face value of 9% bonds payable for $1,116,000, plus accrued interest. Company B, an affiliate of Company A, acquired $100,000 face value of those bonds on the same day for $111,600, plus accrued interest. The bonds mature on September 1, 2000 and interest is payable on March 1 and September 1. Thus, the remaining term of the bonds is 9 years and 8 months, or 116 months. Both affiliates report on a calendar year basis.

Company A's journal entry to record the issuance of the bonds is

Cash	1,146,000	
Bonds Payable		1,000,000
Premium on Bonds Payable		116,000
Interest Payable		30,000

The accrued interest on the bonds is calculated as $1,000,000 \times 9\% \times 4/12$, or $30,000. Because the issuance of the bonds occurs exactly at Company A's fiscal year end, the accrued interest is credited to Interest Payable rather than to Interest Expense. In order to obtain the offset against the interest expense recorded at the next interest date, as discussed and illustrated earlier, Company A will record the following reversing entry as of January 1, 1992:

Interest Payable	30,000	
Interest Expense		30,000

Company B's journal entry to record its acquisition of $100,000 face value of the bonds (10% of the total amount issued) is

Investment in Company A Bonds	111,600	
Interest Receivable	3,000	
Cash		114,600

Because the issuance of the bonds occurs exactly at Company B's fiscal year end, the accrued interest is debited to Interest Receivable rather than to Interest Revenue. In order to obtain the offset against the interest revenue recorded at the next interest date, as discussed and illustrated earlier, Company B will record the following reversing entry as of January 1, 1992:

Interest Revenue	3,000	
Interest Receivable		3,000

Exhibit 10-1 presents the eliminations necessary on the December 31, 1990 consolidation worksheet relative to the intercompany bonds, as well as calculations of the amounts included in the eliminations.

EXHIBIT 10-1

Illustrative Problem 10.1
Eliminations
December 31, 1990

Eliminations

Intercompany Bond Investment and Liability

[26] Bonds Payable	$ 100,000
[27] Premium on Bonds Payable	11,600
[28] Investment in Company A Bonds	$(111,600)

Accrued Interest on Intercompany Bonds

[29] Interest Payable	$ 3,000
[30] Interest Receivable	(3,000)

Calculations

[26] 10% × $1,000,000
[27] 10% × $116,000
[28] Given
[29] 10% ($1,000,000 × 9% × 4/12)
[30] $100,000 × 9% × 4/12

Because Company B acquired 10% of the Company A bonds, the Intercompany Bond Investment and Liability set of eliminations offsets 10% of Company A's Bonds Payable and Premium on Bonds Payable balances against Company B's Investment in Company A Bonds balance. These eliminations result in reporting on the consolidated balance sheet the amount of bond liability (Bonds Payable plus Premium on Bonds Payable) held by external bondholders and, thus, owed by the consolidated entity.

The Accrued Interest on Intercompany Bonds set of eliminations eliminates the offsetting amounts of interest payable and interest receivable that appear on the two trial balances at December 31, 1990.

At March 31, 1991, the first interest date following the issuance of the bonds, Company A records the payment of interest in the following journal entry:

Interest Expense	43,000	
Premium on Bonds Payable	2,000	
Cash		45,000

Company A pays a full six months' interest, even though the bonds have been outstanding for only two months. Thus, the credit to cash equals $1,000,000 \times 9\% \times 6/12$, or $45,000. The debit to Premium on Bonds Payable amortizes the issuance premium for the two months that have elapsed since the issuance date. The amortization is calculated as $116,000 \times 2/116$, or $2,000. The difference of $43,000 is debited to Interest Expense. Remember, however, that this amount is partially offset by the $30,000 credit to Interest Expense in the January 1, 1991 reversing entry, so that the net amount of interest expense reported is $13,000. This amount can be verified as two months' contractual interest, $15,000, minus two months' amortization of the premium, $2,000.

Also at March 1, 1991, Company B records the receipt of interest as follows:

Cash	4,500	
Investment in Company A Bonds		200
Interest Revenue		4,300

Company B receives a full six months' interest, even though it has held the bonds for only two months. Thus, the debit to Cash equals $100,000 \times 9\% \times 6/12$, or $4,500. The credit to Investment in Company A Bonds amortizes the acquisition premium for the two months that have elapsed since the acquisition date. The amortization is calculated as $11,600 \times 2/116$, or $200. The difference of $4,300 is credited to Interest Revenue. Remember, however, that this amount is partially offset by the $3,000 debit to Interest Revenue in the January 1, 1991 reversing entry, so that the net amount of interest revenue reported is $1,300. This amount can be verified as two months' contractual interest, $1,500, minus two months' amortization of the acquisition premium, $200.

At September 1, 1991, the next interest date, Company A records the following journal entry in which the issuance premium is amortized for a full six months:

Interest Expense	39,000	
Premium on Bonds Payable	6,000	
Cash		45,000

Also at September 1, 1991, Company B records the following journal entry in which the acquisition premium is amortized for a full six months:

Cash	4,500	
Investment in Company A Bonds		600
Interest Revenue		3,900

At December 31, 1991, Company A records the following adjusting journal entry for four months' accrued interest:

Interest Expense	26,000	
Premium on Bonds Payable	4,000	
Interest Payable		30,000

The credit to Interest Payable equals $1,000,000 × 9% × 4/12, or $30,000. The debit to Premium on Bonds Payable amortizes the issuance premium for the four months that have elapsed since the last interest date. The amortization is calculated as $116,000 × 4/116, or $4,000. The difference of $26,000 is debited to Interest Expense.

Also at December 31, 1991, Company B records the following adjusting journal entry for four months' accrued interest:

Interest Receivable	3,000	
Investment in Company A Bonds		400
Interest Revenue		2,600

The debit to Interest Receivable equals $100,000 × 9% × 4/12, or $3,000. The credit to Investment in Company A Bonds amortizes the acquisition premium for the four months that have elapsed since the last interest date. The amortization is calculated as $11,600 × 4/116, or $400. The difference of $2,600 is credited to Interest Revenue.

By December 31, 1991, each affiliate has amortized its premium for one year (12 months out of the total of 116). Also, intercompany interest has been paid and received, and year-end adjustments have created Interest Receivable and Interest Payable balances. Thus, the following balances appear on the two trial balances:

Company A

Bonds Payable	$1,000,000
Premium on Bonds Payable	104,000
Interest Payable	30,000
Interest Expense	78,000

Company B

Investment in Company A Bonds	$ 110,400
Interest Receivable	3,000
Interest Revenue	7,800

Company A's Premium on Bonds Payable balance of $104,000 is the original issuance premium of $116,000 reduced by one year's amortization, 12/116 of $116,000, or $12,000. Company A's Interest Payable balance of $30,000 represents four months' accrued interest on the face value of the bonds, or $1,000,000 × 9% × 4/12. Company A's Interest Expense balance of $78,000 is composed of one year's contractual interest on the bonds—$1,000,000 × 9% × 12/12, or $90,000—minus one year's amortization of the issuance premium—12/116 × $116,000, or $12,000.

The $110,400 balance of Company B's Investment in Company A Bonds account is the original cost of $111,600 reduced by one year's amortization of the acquisition premium, 12/116 of $111,600 minus $100,000, or $1,200. Company B's Interest Receivable balance of $3,000 represents four months' accrued interest on the face value of the intercompany bonds, or $100,000 × 9% × 4/12. Company B's Interest Revenue balance of $7,800 is composed of one year's contractual interest on the intercompany bonds—$100,000 × 9% × 12/12, or $9,000—minus one year's amortization of the acquisition premium—12/116 × $11,600, or $1,200.

Exhibit 10-2 presents the December 31, 1991 eliminations relative to the intercompany bonds. The Intercompany Bond Investment and Liability set of eliminations offsets 10% of Company A's Bonds Payable balance and 10% of its updated Premium on Bonds Payable balance against Company B's updated Investment in Company A Bonds balance. During 1991, intercompany interest revenue and interest expense has been recorded by the respective affiliates. These intercompany balances are eiminated in the Intercompany Interest Revenue and Expense set of eliminations. The Accrued Interest on Intercompany Bonds set of eliminations eliminates the amounts of intercompany interest payable and interest receivable that have accrued since the last interest date.

EXHIBIT 10-2

Illustrative Problem 10.1
Eliminations
December 31, 1991

Eliminations

Intercompany Bond Investment and Liability

[26] Bonds Payable	$ 100,000
[27] Premium on Bonds Payable	10,400
[28] Investment in Company A Bonds	$(110,400)

Intercompany Interest Revenue and Expense

[29] Interest Revenue	$ 7,800
[30] Interest Expense	(7,800)

Accrued Interest on Intercompany Bonds

[31] Interest Payable	$ 3,000
[32] Interest Receivable	(3,000)

Calculations

[26] 10% × $1,000,000
[27] 10% [116,000 − (12/116 × $116,000)]
[28] $111,600 − [12/116 ($111,600 − $100,000)]
[29] ($100,000 × 9% × 12/12) − (12/116 × $11,600)
[30] 10%[($1,000,000 × 9% × 12/12) − (12/116 × $116,000)]
[31] 10% ($1,000,000 × 9% × 4/12)
[32] $100,000 × 9% × 4/12

At the end of each fiscal year in the remaining life of the bonds, the amounts eliminated from Company B's Investment in Company A Bonds and from Company A's Premium on Bonds Payable will decrease each year because of the amortization of these balances. The other eliminations will remain the same from year to year except, of course, in 2000, when the bonds will be retired before the end of the year.

When the investing affiliate acquires bonds directly from the issuing affiliate, it really is lending money to the issuing affiliate. Because no gain or loss is involved, the affiliates' Retained Earnings balances will not be affected. Therefore, it makes no difference whether the issuer or the investor is the parent or a subsidiary, or whether the subsidiary is wholly or partially owned. Instead, the intercompany transaction results in a set of intercompany asset and liability balances (e.g., Investment in Company A Bonds versus the proportionate amount of Bonds Payable and Premium on Bonds Payable), a set of intercompany revenue and expense balances (Interest Revenue versus a proportionate share of Interest Expense), and an additional set of intercompany asset and liability balances (Interest Receivable versus a proportionate share of Interest Payable), all of which must be eliminated.[1]

GAIN OR LOSS ON EARLY RETIREMENT OF BONDS

If a corporation reacquires its own bonds before their scheduled maturity, the ". . . difference between the reacquisition price and the net carrying amount of the extinguished debt should be recognized currently in income of the period of extinguishment as losses or gains and identified as a separate item."[2] If material, such gain and losses should be classified as extraordinary items and reported in the income statement net of their income tax effect.[3]

To illustrate the determination of a gain or loss on early retirement of bonds, assume that during 1991, a corporation paid $498,200 to retire bonds payable with a face value of $500,000 and an unamortized issuance discount of $18,600. The gain or loss (in this case, loss) on retirement of the bonds would be calculated as follows:

Reacquisition Price		$498,200
Face Value of Bonds Retired	$500,000	
Less: Unamortized Discount	18,600	
Carrying Value of Bonds Retired		481,400
Loss on Retirement of Bonds		$ 16,800

Assuming that the amount of the loss is material, it would be reported on the corporation's 1991 income statement as an extraordinary loss.

INTERCOMPANY BONDS ACQUIRED FROM OTHER BONDHOLDERS

When one affiliate acquires previously issued bonds of another affiliate from other bondholders, the transaction can be viewed as a **constructive retirement** of these intercompany

---

[1] *Accounting Research Bulletin No. 51, Consolidated Financial Statements* (New York: AICPA, 1956), paragraph 6.

[2] *Accounting Principles Board Opinion No. 26, Early Extinguishment of Debt* (New York: AICPA, 1973), paragraph 20.

[3] *Statement of Financial Accounting Standards No. 4, Reporting Gains and Losses from Extinguishment of Debt* (Stamford, Connecticut: FASB, 1975), paragraph 8.

bonds by the consolidated entity. The acquiring affiliate is, in effect, acting as the agent of the issuing affiliate. Therefore, a gain or loss to the consolidated entity can result from this constructive retirement of bonds.

As noted above, if the bonds were retired by the issuing affiliate, a gain or loss on retirement would be measured as the difference between the **reacquisition price** and the **carrying value** of the bonds. Similarly, the gain or loss on an intercompany bond acquisition is measured as the difference between the *cost of the bond investment* to the acquiring affiliate and the *carrying value of the intercompany bonds* on the books of the issuing affiliate.

This gain or loss, however, is not recorded on the books of either affiliate. The acquiring affiliate simply has purchased the bonds from external bondholders, while the issuing affiliate has not engaged in any transaction whatsoever. Instead, the gain or loss must be recognized as a result of eliminating the various intercompany balances related to the intercompany bonds. In a sense, this is just the opposite of our treatment of intercompany profits in inventories and in depreciable assets. Instead of eliminating the *unrealized* portions of intercompany profits included in the affiliates' respective trial balances, we are recognizing the *realized* portion of an intercompany gain or loss that has not been recorded at all.

If the intercompany bond acquisition happens to occur on the last day of the fiscal year, the entire gain or loss is recognized in the Intercompany Bond Investment and Liability set of eliminations. The difference between the intercompany portions of the issuing affiliate's Bonds Payable balance plus its Premium on Bonds Payable balance (or minus its Discount on Bonds Payable balance) and the investing affiliate's Investment in Affiliate's Bonds balance is labeled Gain (or Loss) on Intercompany Bond Acquisition. It also is necessary to save a line on the consolidation worksheet on which to enter this new account. The recognition of the gain or loss is shown in Illustrative Problem 10.2, which follows.

ILLUSTRATIVE PROBLEM 10.2: INTERCOMPANY BONDS ACQUIRED FROM OTHER BONDHOLDERS

Company C owns 75% of Company D's common stock, which it acquired in 1989. Amortization of goodwill from consolidation for 1991 amounts to $1,800. Company C and Company D have individual 1991 net incomes of $69,800 and $48,300, respectively.

On December 31, 1991, Company C acquired $200,000 face value of the 8% bonds of its affiliate, Company D, on the open market for $194,900 plus accrued interest. The bonds mature on April 1, 1996 and interest is payable on April 1 and October 1. Company D's December 31, 1991 trial balance includes Bonds Payable of $1,000,000 and Premium on Bonds Payable of $10,200.

If Company D had reacquired those same bonds, at the same price, on the same date, the gain or loss (in this case, gain) on retirement of the bonds would be calculated as follows:

Reacquisition Price		$ 194,900
Face Value of Bonds Retired	$ 200,000	
Add: Applicable Premium (20%)	2,040	
Carrying Value of Bonds Retired		202,040
Gain on Retirement of Bonds		$ 7,140

This gain would be recorded on Company D's books and reported on its 1991 income statement as an extraordinary item, as discussed earlier.

From the standpoint of the consolidated entity, Company C's acquisition of Company D's bonds from external bondholders constitutes a constructive retirement of bonds payable of the consolidated entity. Thus, the gain must be reflected in the 1991 consolidated income statement. As noted earlier, the gain (or loss) is never recorded on either set of books, but instead is recognized in the process of making worksheet eliminations.

Exhibit 10-3 shows the eliminations needed at December 31, 1991 relative to the intercompany bonds, along with the calculations of the amounts included therein. The amount of gain determined in this manner is exactly the same as the amount that Company D would have recorded if it had reacquired its own bonds.

EXHIBIT 10-3

Illustrative Problem 10.2
Eliminations
December 31, 1991

Eliminations

Intercompany Bond Investment and Liability

[26] Bonds Payable	$ 200,000
[27] Premium on Bonds Payable	2,040
[28] Gain on Intercompany Bond Acquisition	(7,140)
[29] Investment in Company D Bonds	$(194,900)

Accrued Interest on Intercompany Bonds

[30] Interest Payable	$ 4,000
[31] Interest Receivable	(4,000)

Calculations

[26] 20% × $1,000,000
[27] 20% × $10,200
[28] ($200,000 + $2,040) − $194,900
[29] Given
[30] 20%($1,000,000 × 8% × 3/12)
[31] $200,000 × 8% × 3/12

The gain on Intercompany Bond Acquisition recognized in Elimination [28] changes the total amount of net income for 1991. Therefore, it must be treated as an adjustment in the Income Allocation schedule for that year, as shown in Exhibit 10-4. The gain is added to Company D's net income because Company D is the issuing affiliate. (If a loss had occurred instead, it would have been subtracted from Company D's net income.)

EXHIBIT 10-4

Illustrative Problem 10.2
Income Allocation Schedule
Year Ended December 31, 1991

Income Allocation

Company C's Own Net Income		$ 69,800
Less: Goodwill Amortization Expense		1,800
Company C's Adjusted Net Income		68,000
Company D's Own Net Income	$ 48,300	
Add: Gain on Intercompany Bonds	7,140	
Company D's Adjusted Net Income	55,440	
Minority Interest (25%)	13,860	
Company C's Share (75%)		41,580
Consolidated Net Income		$ 109,580

CONSOLIDATION PROCEDURES IN SUBSEQUENT YEARS

Following the date of acquisition of the intercompany bonds, both the issuing and the acquiring affiliate will amortize their respective premiums or discounts over the remaining life of the bonds. Only by coincidence would the bondholder's acquisition premium or discount and the intercompany portion of the issuance premium or discount be the same, with no gain or loss resulting (unless the bonds were acquired directly from the issuing affiliate). Thus, whenever these amounts are different, you can safely assume that the bonds were acquired from other bondholders.

A gain on an intercompany bond acquisition occurs when the acquiring affiliate's cost is *less* than the carrying value of the intercompany bonds on the issuing affiliate's books. Thus, subsequent amortization of the respective premiums or discounts necessarily will yield inter-company interest revenue that is *greater* than intercompany interest expense. A loss on an intercompany bond acquisition occurs when the acquiring affiliate's cost is *greater* than the carrying value of the intercompany bonds on the issuing affiliate's books. Thus, subsequent amortization of the respective premiums or discounts necessarily will yield intercompany interest revenue that is *less* than intercompany interest expense. The difference between the intercompany interest revenue and interest expense resulting from amortizing these different premiums or discounts represents the portion of the gain or loss amortized in each year.

- If a gain is recognized in the intercompany bond acquisition, that gain will be amortized ("used up," if you like) over the remaining life of the bonds through the interaction of the different effective rates of interest. Because the intercompany interest revenue will exceed the intercompany interest expense, the eliminations for these items will *decrease* total net income.
- If a loss is recognized, it will be amortized ("recovered") over the remaining life of the bonds. Because the intercompany interest expense will exceed the intercompany interest revenue, the eliminations for these items will *increase* total net income.

At subsequent balance sheet dates, the eliminations related to intercompany bonds will differ from those made at their date of acquisition in several ways.

- Because each affiliate will have amortized appropriate portions of its respective premium or discount, the amounts eliminated from the issuer's Premium (or Discount) on Bonds Payable and from the investor's investment in Affiliate's Bonds will be different at each year end, as will the gain or loss element recognized in the Intercompany Bond Investment and Liability set of eliminations.
- This gain or loss element, which is the portion of the original gain or loss that is unamortized as of the *end* of the year, will be credited or debited to one or both Retained earnings balances rather than to a Gain or Loss account. If the issuing affiliate is either the parent or a wholly owned subsidiary, the entire amount is allocated to the parent's Retained Earnings. If the issuing affiliate is a partially owned subsidiary, the amount is allocated between its Retained Earnings and the parent's Retained Earnings, using the allocation scheme introduced in Chapter 7.
- As noted earlier, the amounts eliminated from Interest Revenue and Interest Expense in the Intercompany Interest Revenue and Expense set of eliminations will yield a difference representing the portion of the original gain or loss applicable to the current year. This difference also will be allocated to Retained Earnings in the manner indicated above.
- The total amount credited or debited to Retained Earnings balances in the two sets of eliminations represents the portion of the original gain or loss that is unamortized as of the *beginning* of the year.

ILLUSTRATIVE PROBLEM 10.3: CONSOLIDATION PROCEDURES IN SUBSEQUENT YEARS

This is a continuation of Illustrative Problem 10.2. Company C owns 75% of Company D's common stock, which it acquired in 1989. Amortization of goodwill from consolidation for 1992 amounts to $1,800. Company C and Company D have individual 1992 net incomes of $73,400 and $52,100, respectively.

On December 31, 1991, Company C acquired $200,000 face value of the 8% bonds of its affiliate, Company D, on the open market for $194,900 plus accrued interest. The bonds mature on April 1, 1996 and interest is payable on April 1 and October 1. Notice that 51 months remain in the life of the bonds from the date of Company C's acquisition, December 31, 1991, through the maturity date, April 1, 1996. Company D's December 31, 1991 trial balance included Bonds Payable of $1,000,000 and Premium on Bonds Payable of $10,200.

Company C's journal entry to record its acquisition of $200,000 face value of the bonds (20% of the total amount issued) is

Investment in Company D Bonds	194,900	
Interest Receivable	4,000	
Cash		198,900

Because the issuance of the bonds occurs exactly at Company C's fiscal year end, the accrued interest is debited to Interest Receivable rather than to Interest Revenue. In order to obtain the offset against the interest revenue recorded at the next interest date, as discussed and illustrated earlier, Company C will record the following reversing entry as of January 1, 1992:

| Interest Revenue | 4,000 | |
| Interest Receivable | | 4,000 |

At April 1, 1992, Company C records the receipt of interest as follows:

Cash	8,000	
Investment in Company D Bonds	300	
Interest Revenue		8,300

Company C receives a full six months' interest, even though it has held the bonds for only three months. Thus, the debit to Cash equals $200,000 \times 8\% \times 6/12$, or $8,000. The debit to Investment in Company D Bonds amortizes the acquisition discount for the three months that have elapsed since the acquisition date. The amortization is calculated as $5,100 \times 3/51$, or $300. The total of $8,300 is credited to Interest Revenue. Remember, however, this this amount is partially offset by the $4,000 debit to Interest Revenue in the January 1, 1992 reversing entry, so that the net amount of interest revenue reported is $4,300. This amount can be verified as three months' contractual interest, $4,000, plus three months' amortization of the acquisition discount, $300.

At October 1, 1992, the next interest date, Company C records the following journal entry in which the acquisition discount is amortized for a full six months:

Cash	8,000	
Investment in Company D Bonds	600	
Interest Revenue		8,600

At December 31, 1992, Company C records the following adjusting journal entry for three months' accrued interest:

Interest Receivable	4,000	
Investment in Company D Bonds	300	
Interest Revenue		4,300

The debit to Interest Receivable equals $200,000 \times 8\% \times 3/12$, or $4,000. The debit to Investment in Company D Bonds amortizes the acquisition premium for the three months that have elapsed since the last interest date. The amortization is calculated as $5,100 \times 3/51$, or $300. The total of $4,300 is credited to Interest Revenue.

At April 1, 1992, Company D records the payment of interest in the following journal entry:

Interest Expense	38,800	
Premium on Bonds Payable	1,200	
Cash		40,000

The credit to Cash equals $1,000,000 \times 8\% \times 6/12$, or $40,000. The debit to Premium on Bonds Payable amortizes the issuance premium for six months. The amortization is calculated as $10,200 \times 6/51$, or $1,200. The difference of $38,800 is debited to Interest Expense. Remember, however, that this amount is partially offset by a $19,400 credit to Interest Expense in Company D's January 1, 1992 reversing entry, so that the net amount of interest expense reported is $19,400. This amount can be verified as three months' contractual interest, $20,000, minus three months' amortization of the premium, $600.

At October 1, 1992, Company D records the following journal entry in which the issuance premium is amortized for a full six months:

Interest Expense	38,800	
Premium on Bonds Payable	1,200	
Cash		40,000

At December 31, 1992, Company D records the following adjusting journal entry for three months' accrued interest:

Interest Expense	19,400	
Premium on Bonds Payable	600	
Interest Payable		20,000

The credit to Interest Payable equals $1,000,000 \times 8\% \times 3/12$, or $20,000. The debit to Premium on Bonds Payable amortizes the issuance premium for the three months that have elapsed since the last interest date. The amortization is calculated as $10,200 \times 3/51$, or $600. The difference of $19,400 is debited to Interest Expense.

As a result of these two sets of journal entries, the following balances appear in the December 31, 1992 trial balances:

Company C

Investment in Company D Bonds	$ 196,100
Interest Receivable	4,000
Interest Revenue	17,200

Company D

Bonds Payable	$1,000,000
Premium on Bonds Payable	7,800
Interest Payable	20,000
Interest Expense	77,600

The $196,100 balance of Company C's Investment in Company D Bonds is the original cost of $194,900 plus one year's amortization of the acquisition discount, $12/51 \times \$5,100$, or $1,200. Company C's Interest Receivable balance of $4,000 represents three months' accrued interest on the face value of the intercompany bonds, or $200,000 \times 8\% \times 3/12$. Company C's Interest Revenue balance of $17,200 is composed of one year's contractual interest on the intercompany bonds—$200,000 \times 8\% \times 12/12$, or $16,000—plus one year's amortization of the acquisition discount—$12/51 \times \$5,100$, or $1,200.

The $7,800 balance of Company D's Premium on Bonds Payable account results from subtracting one year's amortization—$12/51 \times \$10,200$, or $2,400—from the previous balance of $10,200. Company D's Interest Payable balance of $20,000 represents three months' accrued interest on the face value of the bonds, or $1,000,000 \times 8\% \times 3/12$. Company D's Interest Expense balance of $77,600 is composed of twelve months' contractual interest on the entire bond issue—$1,000,000 \times 8\% \times 12/12$, or $80,000—minus twelve months' amortization of the premium—$12/51 \times \$10,200$, or $2,400.

The eliminations needed at December 31, 1992 in regard to the intercompany bonds appear in Exhibit 10-5. The sum of the amounts credited to Retained Earnings in Eliminations

[28] and [29], $5,460, can be verified as 39/51 of the original gain, the portion unamortized as of the end of 1992. Similarly, the total amount credited to Retained Earnings in Eliminations [32] and [33], $1,680, can be verified as 12/51 of the original gain, the portion applicable to 1992.

EXHIBIT 10-5

Illustrative Problem 10.3
Eliminations
December 31, 1992

Eliminations

Intercompany Bond Investment and Liability

[26] Bonds Payable	$ 200,000
[27] Premium on Bonds Payable	1,560
[28] Retained Earnings: C	(4,095)
[29] Retained Earnings: D	(1,365)
[30] Investment in Company D Bonds	$(196,100)

Intercompany Interest Revenue and Expense

[31] Interest Revenue	$ 17,200
[32] Retained Earnings: C	(1,260)
[33] Retained Earnings: D	(420)
[34] Interest Expense	$ (15,520)

Accrued Interest on Intercompany Bonds

[35] Interest Payable	$ 4,000
[36] Interest Receivable	(4,000)

Selected Calculations

[26] 20% × $1,000,000
[27] 20% × $7,800
[28] 75%[($200,000 + $1,560) − $196,100]
[29] 25%($200,000 + $1,560) − $196,100]
[32] 75% ($17,200 − $15,520)
[33] 25% ($17,200 − $15,520)
[34] 20%[($1,000,000 × 8% × 12/12) − (12/51 × $10,200)]
[35] 20%($1,000,000 × 8% × 3/12)

If Company C had been the issuing affiliate, or if it had owned 100% of Company D's common stock, the amounts credited to Retained Earnings in Eliminations [28] and [29] and in Eliminations [32] and [33] would have been credited entirely to Company C's Retained Earnings.

At the end of each subsequent year of the life of the bonds, the same three sets of eliminations are necessary.

- The continuing amortization of premiums or discounts will change all amounts in the Intercompany Bond Investment and Liability set of eliminations except for the debit to Bonds Payable.
- The Intercompany Interest Revenue and Expense set is the same from year to year when straight-line amortization is used, except for the year in which the bonds mature. The amounts in this set will change, of course, if effective interest amortization is used.
- The Accrued Interest on Intercompany Bonds set of eliminations is the same from year to year except, again, for the year of maturity.

Exhibit 10-6 presents the Income Allocation schedule to accompany the December 31, 1992 consolidation worksheet. Because the net effect of Eliminations [31] and [34] is to reduce total net income of 1992 by $1,680 (the portion of the original gain amortized in 1992), that amount must be subtracted from Company D's net income in allocating total net income. If Company C had been the issuer, the $1,680 would have been subtracted from its net income.

EXHIBIT 10-6

Illustrative Problem 10.3
Income Allocation Schedule
Year Ended December 31, 1992

Income Allocation

Company C's Own Net Income		$ 73,400
Less: Goodwill Amortization Expense		1,800
Company C's Adjusted Net Income		71,600
Company D's Own Net Income	$ 52,100	
Less: Amortization of Gain on Intercompany Bonds	1,680	
Company D's Adjusted Net Income	50,420	
Minority Interest (25%)	12,605	
Company C's Share (75%)		37,815
Consolidated Net Income		$ 109,415

INTERCOMPANY BONDS ACQUIRED DURING THE YEAR

If intercompany bonds are acquired at some date other than the end of the fiscal year, a gain or loss is both recognized as such and amortized during that first year. Because each affiliate will have amortized appropriate portions of its respective premium or discount, the amounts eliminated from the issuer's Premium (or Discount) on Bonds Payable and from the investor's Investment in Affiliate's Bonds in the Intercompany Bond Investment and Liabiilty set of eliminations at the end of the year in which the bonds are acquired will be different from those existing at the date of that acquisition. The difference between the amounts eliminated from these balances, which will be credited (or debited) to a Gain (or Loss) on Intercompany Bond Acquisition, is the portion of the original gain or loss that is unamortized as of the *end* of the year.

In addition, the amounts eliminated from Interest Revenue and Interest Expense in the Intercompany Interest Revenue and Expense set of eliminations will yield a difference representing the portion of the original gain or loss applicable to the current year. This difference also will be credited (or debited) to a Gain (or Loss) on Intercompany Bond Acquisition.

Finally, the fact that different amounts are eliminated from Interest Revenue and Interest Expense in the Intercompany Interest Revenue and Expense set of eliminations either increases or decreases total net income, thus amortizing the portion of the original gain or loss applicable to the current year. These results are shown in Illustrative Problem 10.4, which follows.

ILLUSTRATIVE PROBLEM 10.4: INTERCOMPANY BONDS ACQUIRED DURING THE YEAR

Illustrative Problem 10.4 is based on the same facts as Illustrative Problem 10.3, which are repeated below, except that Company C and Company D both have fiscal years ending on June 30.

Company C owns 75% of Company D's common stock, which it acquired in 1989. Amortization of goodwill from consolidation for the year ended June 30, 1992 amounts to $1,800. Company C and Company D have individual net incomes for the year ended June 30, 1992 of $71,200 and $53,500, respectively.

On December 31, 1991, Company C acquired $200,000 face value of the 8% bonds of its affiliate, Company D, on the open market for $194,900 plus accrued interest. The bonds mature on April 1, 1996 and interest is payable on April 1 and October 1. On December 31, 1991, Company D had a Bonds Payable balance of $1,000,000 and a Premium on Bonds Payable balance of $10,200.

Company C's journal entry to record its acquisition of $200,000 face value of the bonds (20% of the total amount issued) is

Investment in Company D Bonds	194,900	
Interest Revenue	4,000	
Cash		198,900

Notice that the accrued interest is debited to Interest Revenue in order to offset against the interest revenue recorded at the next interest date.

At April 1, 1992, Company C records the receipt of interest as follows:

Cash	8,000	
Investment in Company D Bonds		300
Interest Revenue		8,300

Company C receives a full six months' interest, even though it has held the bonds for only three months. The total of $8,300 credited to Interest Revenue, however, is partially offset by the $4,000 debit to Interest Revenue in the December 31, 1991 journal entry, so that the net amount of interest revenue reported is $4,300.

At June 30, 1992, Company C records the following adjusting journal entry for three months' accrued interest:

Interest Receivable	4,000	
Investment in Company D Bonds		300
Interest Revenue		4,300

At April 1, 1992, Company D records the following journal entry in which the issuance premium is amortized for a full six months, three months of which is applicable to the period following December 31, 1992:

Interest Expense	38,800	
Premium on Bonds Payable	1,200	
Cash		40,000

At June 30, 1992, Company D records the following adjusting journal entry for three months' accrued interest:

Interest Expense	19,400	
Premium on Bonds Payable	600	
Interest Payable		20,000

As a result of these two sets of journal entries, the following balances appear in the June 30, 1992 trial balances:

Company C

Investment in Company D Bonds	$ 195,500
Interest Receivable	4,000
Interest Revenue	8,600

Company D

Bonds Payable	$1,000,000
Premium on Bonds Payable	9,000
Interest Payable	20,000
Interest Expense	77,600

The $195,500 balance of Company C's Investment in Company D Bonds is the original cost of $194,900 increased by six months' amortization of the acquisition discount, 6/51 × $5,100 or $600. Company C's Interest Receivable balance of $4,000 represents three months' accrued interest on the face value of the intercompany bonds, or $200,000 × 8% × 3/12. Company C's Interest Revenue balance of $8,600 represents six months' contractual interest on the intercompany bonds—$200,000 × 8% × 6/12, or $8,000—plus six months' amortization of the acquisition discount—6/51 × $5,100, or $600.

The $9,000 balance of Company D's Premium on Bonds Payable account results from subtracting six months' amortization (6/51 × $10,200) from the previous balance of $10,200. Company D's Interest Payable balance of $20,000 represents three months accrued interest on the face value of the bonds, or $1,000,000 × 8% × 3/12. Company D's Interest Expense balance of $77,600 is composed of twelve months' contractual interest on the entire bond issue—$1,000,000 × 8% × 12/12, or $80,000—minus twelve months' amortization of the premium—12/51 × $10,200, or $2,400.

Exhibit 10-7 presents the eliminations needed at June 30, 1992 in regard to the intercompany bonds. Because this is the end of the year in which Company C acquired the bonds, the gain recognized in Eliminations [28] and [31] is credited to Gain on Intercompany Bond Acquisition rather than being allocated between the Retained Earnings balances. Also, the sum of these two amounts is $7,140, the total amount of the gain. At the same time, the net effect of Eliminations [30] and [32] is to decrease total net income by $840, thus amortizing the portion of the gain applicable to the six months that have elapsed since the intercompany bond acquisition.

EXHIBIT 10-7

Illustrative Problem 10.4
Eliminations
June 30, 1992

Eliminations

Intercompany Bond Investment and Liability

[26] Bonds Payable	$ 200,000
[27] Premium on Bonds Payable	1,800
[28] Gain on Intercompany Bond Acquisition	(6,300)
[29] Investment in Company D Bonds	$(195,500)

Intercompany Interest Revenue and Expense

[30] Interest Revenue	$ 8,600
[31] Gain on Intercompany Bond Acquisition	(840)
[32] Interest Expense	$ (7,760)

Accrued Interest on Intercompany Bonds

[33] Interest Payable	$ 4,000
[34] Interest Receivable	(4,000)

Selected Calculations

[26] 20% × $1,000,000
[27] 20% × $9,000
[28] ($200,000 + $1,800) − $195,500
[31] $8,600 − $7,760
[32] 20% × 6/12 × $77,600

At the end of each subsequent year of the life of the bonds, the same three sets of eliminations are necessary, except that the two affiliates' Retained Earnings balances will be credited instead of Gain on Intercompany Bond Acquisition.

Both the recognition of the full amount of the gain and the amortization of a portion of it require adjustment in the Income Allocation schedule for the year ended June 30, 1992, which appears in Exhibit 10-8. The technique shown there is to adjust the issuing affiliate's (Company D's) net income by adding the unamortized portion of the gain, the net amount of $6,300. As an alternative, we could have added the full amount of the gain, $7,140, and subtracted the amortized portion, $840.

EXHIBIT 10-8

Illustrative Problem 10.4
Income Allocation Schedule
Year Ended June 30, 1992

Income Allocation

Company C's Net Own Income		$ 71,200
Less: Goodwill Amortization Expense		1,800
Company C's Adjusted Net Income		69,400
Company D's Own Net Income	$ 53,500	
Add: Unamortized Gain on Intercompany Bonds	6,300	
Company D's Adjusted Net Income	59,800	
Minority Interest (25%)	14,950	
Company C's Share (75%)		44,850
Consolidated Net Income		$ 114,250

ILLUSTRATIVE PROBLEM 10.5: COMPREHENSIVE ILLUSTRATION

To place the treatment of intercompany bonds in the context of the complete consolidation process, we will continue with Illustrative Problems 7.2, 8.2, and 9.4, which appear in Chapters 7, 8, and 9, respectively. Company P acquired 48,000 of Company S's 60,000 outstanding shares of $5 par value common stock for $608,400 on April 1, 1991, when Company S had additional paid-in capital of $120,000. Company S's December 31, 1990 retained earnings balance was $120,250. In 1991, Company S reported net income of $81,000 and declared dividends of $40,000 on November 15, which were paid on December 15. The excess of cost over book value is treated as goodwill of Company S, which is being amortized over 10 years. Company P accounts for its investment in Company S under the equity method. The December 31, 1995 trial balances of the two affiliates appear in the worksheet in Exhibit 10-15.

Exhibit 10-9 presents the schedules of the Excess of Cost over Book Value and the resulting adjustments. Exhibit 10-10 presents the Intercompany Ownership Interests, Subsidiary Income and Dividends, and Goodwill Amortization sets of eliminations necessary at December 31, 1995. Eliminations [1] through [5] eliminate Company P's ownership interest, 80%, of each of Company S's stockholders' equity balances and the total thereof, $687,000, against Company P's Investment in Company S Stock balance. Eliminations [6] and [7] eliminate Company P's Income from Company S balance against 80% of Company S's Dividends Declared balance, yielding a $14,000 credit to Investment in Company S Stock.

The 1995 goodwill amortization determined in Exhibit 10-9 is recognized in Elimination [9]. Eliminations [10] and [11] divide the prior years' goodwill amortization, also from Exhibit 10-9, between the two Retained Earnings balances according to the previously established allocation formula, which allocates to each affiliate's Retained Earnings balance an amount

EXHIBIT 10-9

Illustrative Problem 10.5
Excess of Cost over Book Value
Year Ended December 31, 1995

Excess of Cost over Book Value

Cost of Investment		$ 608,400
Book Value (80% × $560,500)		448,400
Excess of Cost over Book Value		160,000
Expand to 100%		÷80%
Goodwill, 1/2/91		200,000
Amortization through 12/31/94	$ 75,000	
Amortization, 1995	20,000	95,000
Goodwill, 12/31/95		$ 105,000

Adjustments

A. Goodwill		$ 200,000
B. Appraisal Capital: S		(200,000)

EXHIBIT 10-10

Illustrative Problem 10.5
Eliminations
Year Ended December 31, 1995

Eliminations

Intercompany Ownership Interests

[1] Common Stock: S		$ 240,000
[2] Additional Paid-in Capital: S		96,000
[3] Retained Earnings: S		191,000
[4] Appraisal Capital: S		160,000
[5] Investment in Company S Stock		$ (687,000)

Subsidiary Income and Dividends

[6] Income from Company S		$ 58,800
[7] Dividends Declared: S		(44,800)
[8] Investment in Company S Stock		$ (14,000)

Goodwill Amortization

[9] Other Expenses		$ 20,000
[10] Retained Earnings: P		60,000
[11] Retained Earnings: S		15,000
[12] Goodwill		$ (95,000)

equal to [a] that affiliate's external ownership interest, multiplied by [b] its share of the quantity being allocated, multiplied by [c] the quantity being allocated. In this case, the results are

$$
\begin{array}{lccccccc}
& [a] & \times & [b] & \times & [c] & = & [d] \\
\text{Company P:} & 100\% & \times & 80\% & \times & \$75,000 & = & \$60,000 \\
\text{Company S:} & 20\% & \times & 100\% & \times & \$75,000 & = & \$15,000
\end{array}
$$

The total amount of goodwill amortization is credited to Goodwill in Elimination [12].

During 1995, Company S sold merchandise to Company P for $322,400, of which $29,600 remains unpaid at December 31, 1995. Intercompany profit of $9,600 is included in Company P's January 1, 1995 inventory. Merchandise purchased from Company S for $26,400 is contained in Company P's December 31, 1995 inventory of $80,300. Company S's December 31, 1995 inventory is $89,100. Company S sells to Company P at 60% above cost. Both affiliates use periodic inventory systems. These transactions and the resulting intercompany balances require additional sets of eliminations at December 31, 1995, which appear in Exhibit 10-11.

EXHIBIT 10-11

Illustrative Problem 10.5
Additional Eliminations
Year Ended December 31, 1995

Intercompany Sales and Purchases

[13] Sales	$ 322,400
[14] Purchases	(322,400)

Intercompany Receivables and Payables

[15] Current Liabilities	$ 29,600
[16] Accounts Receivable	(29,600)

Intercompany Profit in Ending Inventory

Company P's Ending Inventory	$ 80,300
Company S's Ending Inventory	89,100
Total Ending Inventory	169,400
Less: Inventory Profit	9,900
[17] Ending Inventory at Intercompany Cost	$ 159,500

Intercompany Profit in Beginning Inventory

[18] Retained Earnings: P	$ 7,680
[19] Retained Earnings: S	1,920
[20] Inventories	$ (9,600)

The intercompany profit in ending inventory is calculated as the amount remaining in Company P's inventory, $26,400, multiplied by the fraction, .6/1.6. The intercompany profit in beginning inventory is allocated between the two Retained Earnings balances in the same manner used in Eliminations [10] and [11] in Exhibit 10-10.

On June 30, 1992, Company S sold equipment with a net book value of $121,100 to Company P for $163,100, yielding an intercompany profit of $42,000. Company P is depreciating the equipment on the sum-of-the-years'-digits method, over a six-year useful life, with a $23,700 salvage value. A schedule of the excess depreciation (the portion based on intercompany profit) through December 31, 1995 appears below.

1992: $42,000 × 6/21 × 6/12	$ 6,000
1993: ($42,000 × 6/21 × 6/12) + ($42,000 × 5/21 × 6/12)	11,000
1994: ($42,000 × 5/21 × 6/12) + ($42,000 × 4/21 × 6/12)	9,000
Accumulated Depreciation, 12/31/94	26,000
1995: ($42,000 × 4/21 × 6/12) + ($42,000 × 3/21 × 6/12)	7,000
Accumulated Depreciation, 12/31/95	$ 33,000

The resulting additional eliminations necessary at December 31, 1995 appear in Exhibit 10-12.

EXHIBIT 10-12

Illustrative Problem 10.5
Additional Eliminations
Year Ended December 31, 1995

Intercompany Profit in Depreciable Assets

[21] Accumulated Depreciation	$ 33,000
[22] Retained Earnings: P	12,800
[23] Retained Earnings: S	3,200
[24] Depreciation Expense	(7,000)
[25] Plant and Equipment	$ (42,000)

The excess depreciation expense for 1995, $7,000, is eliminated from Depreciation Expense in Elimination [24], thus adding $7,000 of realized intercompany profit to total net income for 1995. The amount eliminated from Accumulated Depreciation is the total amount of excess depreciation recorded by Company P through the end of the current year. Three and one-half years of the asset's life have expired by the end of 1995. Thus, $33,000 is eliminated from Accumulated Depreciation in Elimination [21].

The $16,000 needed to balance the set of eliminations in terms of debits and credits must be allocated between the two Retained Earnings balances because Company S is the seller. The previously established allocation formula yields the following results:

$$[a] \times [b] \times [c] = [d]$$
Company P: 100% × 80% × $16,000 = $12,800
Company S: 20% × 100% × $16,000 = $ 3,200

These amounts are eliminated from the two Retained Earnings balances in Eliminations [22] and [23].

Company P owns $200,000 face value of Company S's 8% bonds, which it acquired in 1992. The bonds mature on March 31, 1999 and interest is payable on March 31 and September 30. Exhibit 10-13 contains schedules of the December 31, 1995 eliminations involving the intercompany bonds.

EXHIBIT 10-13

Illustrative Problem 10.5
Additional Eliminations for Intercompany Bonds
Year Ended December 31, 1995

Eliminations

Intercompany Bond Investment and Liability

[26] Bonds Payable	$ 200,000
[27] Premium on Bonds Payable	6,240
[28] Retained Earnings: P	624
[29] Retained Earnings: S	156
[30] Investment in Company S Bonds	$ (207,020)

Intercompany Interest Revenue and Expense

[31] Other Income	$ 13,840
[32] Retained Earnings: P	192
[33] Retained Earnings: S	48
[34] Other Expenses	$ (14,080)

Accrued Interest on Intercompany Bonds

[35] Current Liabilities	$ 4,000
[36] Other Assets	(4,000)

Eliminations [26] and [27] eliminate 40% of Company S's Bonds Payable balance of $500,000 and its Premium on Bonds Payable balance of $15,600, both of which appear in the Company S trial balance included in Exhibit 10-15. Company P's Investment in Company S Bonds balance of $207,020, which appears in the Company P trial balance included in Exhibit 10-15, is eliminated in Elimination [30]. The $780 needed to balance the Intercompany Bond Investment and Liability set of eliminations in terms of debits and credits represents the portion of the loss on the intercompany bond acquisition that is applicable to future years. This amount is allocated between the two Retained Earnings balances according to the previously established allocation formula, yielding the following results:

$$[a] \times [b] \times [c] = [d]$$
$$\text{Company P:} \quad 100\% \times 80\% \times \$780 = \$624$$
$$\text{Company S:} \quad 20\% \times 100\% \times \$780 = \$156$$

The intercompany interest revenue eliminated in Elimination [31] is calculated as the contractual interest on the intercompany bonds, $200,000 \times 8\% \times 12/12$, minus one year's amortization of Company P's acquisition premium, 12/39 × $7,020. Similarly, the intercompany interest expense eliminated in Elimination [34] is calculated as the contractual interest on the intercompany bonds, $200,000 × 8% × 12/12, minus the intercompany portion of one year's amortization of Company S's bond premium, 40% × 12/39 × $15,600. The $240 needed to balance the Intercompany Interest Revenue and Expense set of eliminations represents the portion of the loss on the intercompany bond acquisition that is applicable to the current year. This amount is allocated between the two Retained Earnings balances according to the previously established allocation formula, yielding the following results:

$$[a] \times [b] \times [c] = [d]$$
Company P: 100% × 80% × $240 = $192
Company S: 20% × 100% × $240 = $ 48

Eliminations [35] and [36] eliminate three months' accrued interest on the intercompany bonds, which can be calculated as $200,000 × 8% × 3/12.

Exhibit 10-14 presents the Income Allocation schedule to accompany the December 31, 1995 consolidation worksheet. Because the net effect of Eliminations [31] and [34] is to increase total net income of 1995 by $240 (the portion of the original loss amortized in 1995), that amount must be added to Company S's net income in arriving at Company S's adjusted net income. In addition, Company S's net income is increased for the intercompany profit in beginning inventory, $9,600, and the intercompany profit in depreciable assets, $7,000. It also is decreased for the intercompany profit in ending inventory, $9,900, and the goodwill amortization expense, $20,000.

EXHIBIT 10-14

Illustrative Problem 10.5
Income Allocation
Year Ended December 31, 1995

Income Allocation

Company P's Own Net Income		$ 54,700
Company S's Own Net Income	$ 73,500	
Add: Intercompany Profit in Beginning Inventory	9,600	
Intercompany Profit in Depreciable Assets	7,000	
Amortization of Loss on Intercompany Bonds	240	
Less: Intercompany Profit in Ending Inventory	(9,900)	
Goodwill Amortization Expense	(20,000)	
Company S's Adjusted Net Income	60,440	
Minority Interest (20%)	12,088	
Company P's Share (80%)		48,352
Consolidated Net Income		$ 103,052

The December 31, 1995 consolidation worksheet for Company P and Company S appears in Exhibit 10-15.

EXHIBIT 10-15

Illustrative Problem 10.5
Consolidation Worksheet
December 31, 1995

	Company P	Company S	Adjustments and Eliminations		Income Statement		Balance Sheet
Accounts Receivable	138,200	152,300	[16]	(29,600)			260,900
Inventories	79,700	90,600	[20]	(9,600)	160,700 [17]	159,500	159,500
Plant and Equipment	917,980	1,360,700	[25]	(42,000)			2,236,680
Other Assets	96,500	157,900	[36]	(4,000)			250,400
Investment in Company S Stock	701,000		[5]	(687,000)			
			[8]	(14,000)			
Investment in Company S Bonds	207,020		[30]	(207,020)			
Purchases	458,200	519,400	[14]	(322,400)	655,200		
Depreciation Expense	43,100	56,200	[24]	(7,000)	92,300		
Other Expenses	268,400	299,100	[9]	20,000	573,420		
			[34]	(14,080)			
Dividends Declared: P	80,000						80,000 R
Dividends Declared: S		56,000	[7]	(44,800)			11,200 M
Goodwill			A	200,000			105,000
			[12]	(95,000)			
	2,990,100	2,692,200					3,103,680
Accumulated Depreciation	643,700	422,600	[21]	33,000			1,033,300
Current Liabilities	188,600	145,550	[15]	29,600			300,550
			[35]	4,000			
Bonds Payable		500,000	[26]	200,000			300,000
Premium on Bonds Payable		15,600	[27]	6,240			9,360
Common Stock: P	500,000						500,000
Common Stock: S		300,000	[1]	240,000			60,000 M
Additional Paid-in Capital: P	310,000						310,000
Additional Paid-in Capital: S		120,000	[2]	96,000			24,000 M
Retained Earnings: P	465,200		[10]	60,000			383,904 R
			[18]	7,680			
			[22]	12,800			
			[28]	624			
			[32]	192			
Retained Earnings: S		238,750	[3]	191,000			27,426 M
			[11]	15,000			
			[19]	1,920			
			[23]	3,200			
			[29]	156			
			[33]	48			
Sales	804,200	945,100	[13]	322,400		1,426,900	
Income from Company S	58,800		[6]	58,800			
Other Income	19,600	4,600	[31]	13,840		10,360	
Appraisal Capital: S			B	(200,000)			40,000 M
			[4]	160,000			
	2,990,100	2,692,200					
Minority Interest in Company S's Net Income					12,088		12,088 M
Consolidated Net Income					103,052		103,052 R
					1,596,760	1,596,760	3,103,680

SUMMARY

Chapter 10 begins with a review of bond accounting by both the bond issuer and the bond-holder, which is intended to help the student to understand the treatment of intercompany bonds in consolidated financial statements.

In the remainder of the chapter, we discuss and illustrate the following topics with respect to consolidation financial statement preparation:

- Consolidation procedures when an affiliate acquires another affiliate's bonds directly from the issuing affiliate
- Gain or loss on retirement of bonds
- Consolidation procedures when an affiliate acquires another affiliate's bonds from other bondholders
- Other long-term intercompany liabilities

REVIEW PROBLEM

Company E owns 80% of Company F's common stock. On June 30, 1987, one affiliate acquired 40% of the 8% bonds of the other affiliate on the open market for $852,500 plus accrued interest. The bonds mature on March 31, 1996 and interest is payable on March 31 and September 30. Amortization of goodwill from consolidation for 1991 amounts to $2,300. Company E and Company F have individual 1991 net incomes of $86,400 and $35,700, respectively. The following balances appear in the December 31, 1991 trial balances:

Buying Affiliate

Investment in Affiliate's Bonds	$ 825,500
Interest Receivable	16,000
Interest Revenue	58,000

Issuing Affiliate

Bonds Payable	$2,000,000
Premium on Bonds Payable	40,800
Interest Payable	40,000
Interest Expense	150,400

Required

Schedule the eliminations needed at December 31, 1991 and prepare the Income Allocation schedule for 1991, assuming that [a] Company E is the issuing affiliate, and [b] Company F is the issuing affiliate.

QUESTIONS

1. What really happens when a corporation "sells" bonds?
2. How does the bondholder account for the difference between its acquisition price and the face value of the bonds acquired?

3. How does the issuing corporation account for a discount on the issuance of bonds?
4. When a corporation reacquires its own bonds before their maturity date, how should the gain or loss on retirement of the bonds be reported?
5. When one affiliate acquires bonds of another affiliate directly from that issuing affiliate, how is the gain or loss to the consolidated entity determined?
6. At the end of the third year after an intercompany bond acquisition, how is the difference between the amounts eliminated from Interest Revenue and Interest Expense treated in the eliminations?
7. Refer to Question 6. What does that difference represent?
8. Refer to Question 6. How is that difference treated in the Income Allocation schedule?
9. At the end of the year during which an intercompany bond acquisition occurs, where in the eliminations would a loss on that transaction appear?
10. Refer to Question 9. How is that loss treated in the Income Allocation schedule?

EXERCISES

EXERCISE 10-1
Company A owns 90% of Company B's common stock, which it acquired in 1987. On April 1, 1991, Company A acquired 30% of Company B's $1,000,000 of 9% bonds on the open market for $279,600 plus accrued interest. The bonds mature on November 30, 1996 and interest is payable on May 31 and November 30. The balance of Company B's Premium on Bonds Payable account on December 31, 1990 was $35,500.

Required
Schedule the eliminations required on the December 31, 1991 consolidation worksheet relative to these bonds.

EXERCISE 10-2
Company C acquired 90% of Company D's common stock in 1981. On July 1, 1990, Company C acquired 40% of Company D's $1,000,000 of 7.5% bonds on the open market for $412,300 plus accrued interest. The bonds mature on September 30, 2000 and interest is payable on March 31 and September 30. The balance of Company D's Discount on Bonds Payable account on December 31, 1989 was $43,000. Company C and Company D have separate 1991 net incomes of $80,300 and $35,200, respectively.

Required
1. Schedule the eliminations required on the December 31, 1991 consolidation worksheet relative to the intercompany bonds.
2. Prepare the Income Allocation schedule for 1991.

EXERCISE 10-3
Company E owns 75% of Company F's common stock, which it acquired in 1983. On July 31, 1990, Company F acquired 40% of Company E's 8% bonds, which mature on September 30, 1997 and on which interest is payable on March 31 and September 30. The following balances appear in the December 31, 1990 trial balances:

Company E:	Bonds Payable	
	Discount on Bonds Payable	$1,000,000
	Interest Payable	40,500
	Interest Expense	20,000
		86,000

Company F:	Investment in Company E Bonds	
	Interest Receivable	$ 391,900
	Interest Revenue	8,000
		13,833

Required

Schedule the eliminations required on the December 31, 1990 consolidation worksheet relative to the intercompany bonds.

EXERCISE 10-4

Company G acquired 90% of Company H's common stock in 1984. On July 31, 1990, one affiliate acquired 40% of the other affiliate's $1,000,000 of 6% bonds for $404,850 plus accrued interest. The bonds were issued for $1,030,000 on September 1, 1988 and mature on August 31, 1998. Interest is payable on February 28 and August 31.

Required

Schedule the eliminations required on the December 31, 1992 consolidation worksheet relative to the intercompany bonds [a] if Company G is the issuing affiliate, and [b] if Company H is the issuing affiliate.

EXERCISE 10-5

Company I owns 90% of Company J's common stock and 60% of Company J's 8% bonds. Both investments were acquired before the beginning of 1991. The bonds mature on April 1, 1997 and interest is payable on April 1 and October 1. The following balances appear in the December 31, 1991 trial balances:

Company I:	Investment in Company J Bonds	$ 606,300
	Interest Receivable	12,000
	Interest Revenue	46,800
Company J:	Bonds Payable	$1,000,000
	Discount on Bonds Payable	63,000
	Interest Payable	20,000
	Interest Expense	92,000

Required

Schedule the eliminations required on the December 31, 1991 consolidation worksheet relative to the intercompany bonds.

EXERCISE 10-6

Company K acquired 80% of Company L's common stock in 1985. On April 1, 1986, Company L issued 10% bonds with a $1,000,000 face value for $882,000, plus accrued interest. The bonds pay interest on February 1 and August 1, and mature on February 1, 1996. On August 1, 1988, Company K acquired $300,000 face value of the bonds for $264,000.

Required

1. In the Intercompany Bond Investment and Liability set of eliminations at December 31, 1991, Investment in Company L Bonds is credited for
   a. $280,400
   b. $300,000
   c. $264,000
   d. $279,600
2. In the Intercompany Interest Revenue and Expense set of eliminations at December 31, 1991, Com-

pany L's Retained Earnings is credited for
a. $1,200
b. $ 960
c. $ 240
d. $ 300

EXERCISE 10-7

On December 31, 1991, Company M had outstanding $2,000,000 face value of 7% bonds payable, maturing on December 31, 2001. Interest is payable on June 30 and December 31. The December 31, 1991 balance of the Premium on Bonds Payable account was $25,000. On December 31, 1992, Company M reacquired all of these bonds at 95. What amount of gain or loss should Company M recognize on this transaction?
a. $122,500 gain
b. $122,500 loss
c. $167,500 gain
d. $167,500 loss

PROBLEMS

PROBLEM 10-1

Company K acquired 12,000 shares of Company L's common stock for $240,000 on June 30, 1985. Company L's December 31, 1984 retained earnings balance was $48,000. Company L reported net income of $64,000 for 1985. On November 15, 1985, Company L declared dividends of $40,000, which were paid on December 20, 1985. The excess of cost over book value is treated as goodwill of Company L and is being amortized over 20 years. The December 31, 1991 trial balances of Company K and Company L appear below.

	Company K	Company L
Current Assets	$ 191,400	$ 212,400
Plant and Equipment	543,200	864,700
Investment in Company L Stock	336,000	
Investment in Company L Bonds	202,200	
Cost of Goods Sold	628,000	460,000
Depreciation Expense	62,100	93,400
Other Expenses	529,700	186,600
Dividends Declared	56,000	60,000
Discount on Bonds Payable		22,000
	$2,548,600	$1,899,100
Accumulated Depreciation	$ 108,600	$ 247,100
Bonds Payable		400,000
Other Liabilities	231,200	52,000
Common Stock ($10 par)	350,000	150,000
Additional Paid-in Capital	150,000	50,000
Retained Earnings	316,000	180,000
Sales	1,316,000	816,300
Other Income	76,800	3,700
	$2,548,600	$1,899,100

On August 1, 1989, Company K acquired 50% of Company L's 6% bonds, which mature on October 31, 1993 and on which interest is payable on April 30 and October 31.

Required

Prepare a consolidation worksheet at December 31, 1991, supported by appropriate schedules.

PROBLEM 10-2

The June 30, 1991 trial balances of Company M and Company N appear below.

	Company M	Company N
Investment in Company N Stock	$ 360,000	
Investment in Company M Bonds		$ 103,900
Other Assets	919,400	420,100
Cost of Goods Sold	322,100	218,600
Other Expenses	189,700	126,500
Dividends Declared	30,000	20,000
	$1,821,200	$ 889,100
Bonds Payable	$ 500,000	
Premium on Bonds Payable	11,700	
Other Liabilities	85,400	$ 76,000
Common Stock ($10 par)	400,000	250,000
Additional Paid-in Capital	100,000	50,000
Retained Earnings	172,300	128,000
Sales	530,300	375,900
Other Income	21,500	9,200
	$1,821,200	$ 889,100

Company M acquired 22,500 shares of Company N's common stock for $360,000 on July 1, 1987, when Company N had retained earnings of $90,000. On April 1, 1989, Company N acquired 20% of Company M's 8% bonds, which mature on September 30, 1994 and on which interest is payable on March 31 and September 30. The excess of cost over book value is treated as goodwill of Company N and is being amortized over 10 years.

Required

Prepare a consolidation worksheet at June 30, 1991, supported by appropriate schedules.

PROBLEM 10-3

The December 31, 1991 trial balances of Company P and Company Q appear below.

	Company P	Company Q
Current Assets	$ 505,760	$ 311,200
Plant and Equipment (net)	1,354,200	292,800
Investment in Company Q Stock	713,440	
Investment in Company P Bonds		406,400
Cost of Goods Sold	455,300	362,100
Other Expenses	374,400	310,700
Dividends Declared	56,000	62,000
	$3,459,100	$1,745,200

	Company P	Company Q
Current Liabilities	$ 321,200	$ 218,600
Bonds Payable	1,000,000	
Premium on Bonds Payable	32,000	
Common Stock ($10 par)	600,000	500,000
Additional Paid-in Capital	300,000	150,000
Retained Earnings	223,900	118,800
Sales	910,600	720,300
Other Income	71,400	37,500
	$3,459,100	$1,745,200

Company P acquired 40,000 shares of Company Q's common stock for $663,040 on September 30, 1988. Company Q's December 31, 1987 retained earnings balance was $72,800. Company Q reported net income of $72,000 for 1988. On August 15, 1988, Company Q declared dividends of $48,000, which were paid on September 20, 1988. The excess of cost over book value is treated as goodwill of Company Q and is being amortized over 10 years.

On July 1, 1990, Company Q acquired 40% of Company P's 9% bonds, which mature on September 1, 1994 and on which interest is payable on March 1 and September 1.

Required
Prepare a consolidation worksheet at December 31, 1991, supported by appropriate schedules.

PROBLEM 10-4
The June 30, 1990 trial balances of Company R and Company S appear below.

	Company R	Company S
Current Assets	$ 339,600	$ 311,600
Plant and Equipment (net)	616,390	1,583,400
Investment in Company S Stock	552,410	
Investment in Company S Bonds	222,000	
Cost of Goods Sold	416,200	345,600
Other Expenses	387,600	296,800
Dividends Declared	51,000	45,000
	$2,585,200	$2,582,400
Current Liabilities	$ 279,100	$ 106,300
Bonds Payable		1,000,000
Premium on Bonds Payable		44,000
Common Stock ($10 par)	1,000,000	500,000
Additional Paid-in Capital	250,000	100,000
Retained Earnings	168,900	127,300
Sales	843,700	692,100
Other Income	43,500	12,700
	$2,585,200	$2,582,400

Company R acquired 35,000 shares of Company S's common stock for $552,410 on April 1, 1987. Company S's June 30, 1986 retained earnings balance was $46,700. Company S reported net income of $52,800 for the year ended June 30, 1987. On May 20, 1987, Company S declared dividends of

$36,000, which were paid on June 23, 1987. The excess of cost over book value is treated as goodwill from consolidation and is being amortized over 10 years.

During the year ended June 30, 1990, Company S purchased merchandise from Company R for $216,100, of which $22,400 remained unapid at June 30, 1990. Company S's June 30, 1989 and June 30, 1990 inventories contained goods purchased from Company R for $14,700 and $20,300, respectively. Company R sells to Company S at cost plus 40%.

On January 31, 1989, Company R acquired 20% of Company S's 9% bonds, which mature on March 1, 1994 and on which interest is payable on March 1 and September 1.

Required

Prepare a consolidation worksheet at June 30, 1990, supported by appropriate schedules.

PROBLEM 10-5

Company T acquired 78,400 shares of Company U's common stock for $741,440 on June 30, 1988. Company U's December 31, 1987 retained earnings balance was $255,600. Company U reported net income of $64,000 for 1988. On November 15, 1988, Company U declared dividends of $48,000, which were paid on December 20, 1988. The excess of cost over book value is treated as goodwill from consolidation and is being amortized over 10 years. Both companies declared dividends on December 10, 1990, payable on January 15, 1991.

The December 31, 1990 trial balances of Company T and Company U appear below.

	Company T	Company U
Receivables (net)	$ 127,100	$ 135,400
Inventories	185,600	212,700
Other Current Assets	617,100	496,900
Plant and Equipment	1,681,900	1,105,800
Investment in Company U Stock	801,200	
Investment in Company U Bonds	195,500	
Cost of Goods Sold	455,100	518,400
Other Expenses	304,200	354,100
Dividends Declared	62,500	39,000
Discount on Bonds Payable		22,500
Treasury Stock (2,000 shares, at cost)		180,800
	$4,430,200	$3,065,600
Accumulated Depreciation	$ 941,700	$ 390,600
Current Liabilities	414,900	281,200
Bonds Payable		500,000
Common Stock ($5 par)	1,000,000	500,000
Additional Paid-in Capital	610,000	120,000
Retained Earnings	562,900	335,300
Sales	827,400	932,800
Income from Company U	52,800	
Other Income	20,500	5,700
	$4,430,200	$3,065,600

On December 31, 1988, Company T purchased equipment from Company U for $388,000, which had been carried on Company U's books at a net book value of $260,000. Company T is depreciating the equipment over a five-year useful life from the date of purchase, using the declining balance method at 150% of the straight-line rate.

On September 15, 1989, Company T acquired 40% of Company U's 9% bonds, which mature on September 30, 1994 and on which interest is payable on March 31 and September 30.

Required
Prepare a consolidation worksheet at December 31, 1990, supported by appropriate schedules.

PROBLEM 10-6
Company V acquired 90% of Company W's common stock for $405,000 on December 31, 1990, when Company W had retained earnings of $180,000. The excess of cost over book value is treated as goodwill of Company W and is being amortized over 10 years. The December 31, 1993 trial balances of the two companies appear below.

	Company V	Company W
Receivables (net)	$ 135,590	$ 365,000
Inventories	141,500	136,500
Other Current Assets	451,100	363,700
Plant and Equipment	1,046,400	1,368,100
Investment in Company W Stock	732,510	
Investment in Company W Bonds	262,400	
Cost of Goods Sold	580,000	654,900
Depreciation Expense	85,700	52,400
Other Expenses	392,300	237,300
Dividends Declared	148,000	40,000
	$3,975,500	$3,217,900
Accumulated Depreciation	$ 401,700	$ 125,400
Current Liabilities	332,000	168,000
Bonds Payable		1,000,000
Premium on Bonds Payable		186,000
Common Stock ($10 par)	500,000	100,000
Additional Paid-in Capital	460,000	110,000
Retained Earnings	823,800	354,200
Sales	1,208,000	1,155,400
Other Revenue	250,000	18,900
	$3,975,500	$3,217,900

On July 1, 1991, Company V purchased equipment from Company W for $190,000, which had been carried on Company W's books at a net book value of $130,000. Company V is depreciating the equipment over its remaining 20-year useful life, using the declining balance method at 200% of the straight-line rate.

During 1992, Company V sold merchandise that had cost $180,000 to Company W for $240,000, of which $40,000 remained in Company W's inventory at December 31, 1992. During 1993, Company V sold merchandise that had cost $196,000 to Company W for $280,000, of which $50,000 remained in Company W's inventory at December 31, 1993. Company W owed Company V $42,000 on account at December 31, 1993.

On September 1, 1991, Company V acquired 25% of Company W's 9% bonds, which mature on March 1, 1999 and on which interest is payable on March 1 and September 1.

Required
Prepare a consolidation worksheet at December 31, 1993, supported by appropriate schedules.

PROBLEM 10-7
Company X acquired 80% of Company Y's common stock for $568,400 on June 30, 1987. Company Y's December 31, 1986 retained earnings balance was $98,900. Company Y reported net income of $63,200 for 1987. On November 10, 1987, Company Y declared dividends of $25,000, which were paid on December 15, 1987. The excess of cost over book value is treated as goodwill of Company Y and is being amortized over 10 years.

During 1991, Company Y sold merchandise to Company X for $310,000, of which $33,100 remained unpaid at December 31, 1991. Company X's begininng and ending inventories for 1991 contained goods purchased from Company Y of $33,600 and $32,200, respectively. Company Y sells to Company X at 40% above cost.

On April 1, 1989, Company Y purchased equipment from Company X for $226,400, which had been carried on Company X's books at a net book value of $177,800. Company Y is depreciating the equipment over its remaining six-year useful life, using the straight-line method, assuming a $31,000 salvage value.

On July 1, 1988, Company Y acquired 40% of Company X's 9% bonds on the open market. The bonds mature on September 30, 1994 and interest is payable on March 31 and September 30.

The December 31, 1991 trial balances of the two companies appear below.

	Company X	Company Y
Receivables (net)	$ 78,100	$ 125,100
Inventories	37,600	51,400
Other Current Assets	105,700	374,200
Plant and Equipment	1,018,000	427,400
Investment in Company Y Stock	687,200	
Investment in Company X Bonds		219,800
Cost of Goods Sold	385,600	480,300
Depreciation Expense	82,100	59,600
Other Expenses	182,300	290,300
Dividends Declared	40,000	50,000
	$2,616,600	$2,078,100
Accumulated Depreciation	$ 211,400	186,700
Current Liabilities	188,300	232,200
Bonds Payable	500,000	
Premium on Bonds Payable	33,000	
Common Stock ($10 par)	500,000	300,000
Additional Paid-in Capital	100,000	200,000
Retained Earnings	316,400	220,500
Sales	679,500	926,700
Other Revenue	88,000	12,000
	$2,616,600	$2,078,100

Required

Prepare a consolidation worksheet at December 31, 1991, supported by appropriate schedules.

SOLUTION TO REVIEW PROBLEM

CASE A

Eliminations

Intercompany Bond Investment Liability

[26] Bonds Payable	$ 800,000
[27] Premium on Bonds Payable	16,320
[28] Retained Earnings: E	9,180
[29] Investment in Company E Bonds	$(825,500)

Intercompany Interest Revenue and Expense

[30] Interest Revenue	$ 58,000
[31] Retained Earnings: E	2,160
[32] Interest Expense	$ (60,160)

Accrued Interest on Intercompany Bonds

[33] Interest Payable	$ 16,000
[34] Interest Receivable	(16,000)

Income Allocation

Company E's Net Income		$ 86,400
Less: Goodwill Amortization Expense		(2,300)
Add: Amortization of Loss on Intercompany Bonds		2,160
Company E's Adjusted Net Income		86,260
Company F's Net Income	$ 35,700	
Minority Interest (20%)	7,140	
Company E's Share (80%)		28,560
Consolidated Net Income		$ 114,820

CASE B

Eliminations

Intercompany Bond Investment Liability

[26] Bonds Payable	$ 800,000
[27] Premium on Bonds Payable	16,320
[28] Retained Earnings: E	7,344
[29] Retained Earnings: F	1,836
[30] Investment in Company F Bonds	$(825,500)

Intercompany Interest Revenue and Expense

[31] Interest Revenue	$ 58,000
[32] Retained Earnings: E	1,728
[33] Retained Earnings: F	432
[34] Interest Expense	$ (60,160)

Accrued Interest on Intercompany Bonds

[35] Interest Payable	$ 16,000
[36] Interest Receivable	(16,000)

Income Allocation

Company E's Net Income		$ 86,400
Less: Goodwill Amortization Expense		2,300
Company E's Adjusted Net Income		84,100
Company F's Net Income	$ 35,700	
Add: Amortization of Loss on Intercompany Bonds	2,160	
Company F's Adjusted Net Income	37,860	
Minority Interest (20%)	7,572	
Company E's Share (80%)		30,288
Consolidated Net Income		$ 114,388

CHAPTER
11

SUBSIDIARIES WITH BOTH COMMON AND PREFERRED STOCK

ll of our previous discussions, illustrations, and problems involve subsidiaries that have only common stock. A subsidiary can, of course, have both common and preferred stock. This chapter examines the effects of the presence of subsidiary preferred stock on both the parent company's accounting for its investment on both the subsidiary and the consolidation process.

More specifically, Chapter 11 addresses the following topics:

- Review of the features of preferred stock
- Effects of subsidiary preferred stock on the parent's accounting for its investment in the subsidiary, including
    allocation of subsidiary net income
    allocation of subsidiary dividends
- Effects of subsidiary preferred stock on the consolidation process, including
    allocation of subsidiary retained earnings in determining book value at acquisition
    allocation of subsidiary retained earnings as of the beginning of the current year
    allocation of total net income

Before examining these effects, a brief review of the features of preferred stock is appropriate.

REVIEW OF PREFERRED STOCK FEATURES

Preferred stock usually has preference or priority over the common stock with respect to both assets upon dissolution and dividends. In addition, it may have special features, such as redemption and convertibility. With respect to preferred stock of a subsidiary, our concern is with the dividend preference.

419

Preferred stock has a specified dividend rate, expressed either as a percent of par value or as a number of dollars per share. These preferred dividends are not guaranteed, as is bond interest. Rather, they are subject to the discretion of the corporation's board of directors, as are all dividends. The stipulated preferred stock dividend must be declared, however, before any dividends can be declared to the common stock.

Preferred stock may be **cumulative.** This means that if the preferred dividends are not declared in a given year, no common stock dividends may be declared in that year, and in the following year, two years' preferred dividends must be declared before any common dividends are declared, and so on. Undeclared prior years' dividends on cumulative preferred stock are called **dividends in arrears.**

Preferred stock may be **participating.** This means that after the stipulated current year's preferred stock dividend has been declared, and a matching dividend (in the ratio of the total par values of the two classes outstanding) has been declared to the common stock, the two classes can share in any additional dividends. Any ratio of participation can be specified, but in the absence of any specification, the ratio of the total par values is used.

Four combinations of these dividend preference features are possible. Preferred stock can be

- noncumulative and nonparticipating,
- cumulative and nonparticipating,
- noncumulative and participating, or
- cumulative and participating.

Because participating preferred stock is relatively rare, we will limit our consideration to the first two of these combinations.

EFFECTS OF SUBSIDIARY PREFERRED STOCK ON THE PARENT–SUBSIDIARY RELATIONSHIP

Whether or not the parent owns any of the subsidiary's preferred stock, the dividend preferences of the preferred stock can affect five areas of the parent–subsidiary relationship. These are

- accounting for the parent's investment in the subsidiary,
- determining book value of the investment at the date of acquisition,
- conversion from cost to equity,
- certain worksheet eliminations, and
- the worksheet allocation of net income.

Each of these areas is discussed and illustrated in the following sections.

ACCOUNTING FOR THE INVESTMENT

The presence of subsidiary preferred stock may require allocation of the subsidiary's net income between the preferred and common stockholders, and thus may affect the parent's recording of its share of the subsidiary's net income under the equity method. Therefore, when the subsidiary has preferred stock, one must think in terms of net income to preferred stockholders and net income to common stockholders. The allocation of net income between the two classes of stockholders parallels the allocation that is made in calculating earnings per share.

In approaching the allocation of subsidiary net income (and retained earnings, as discussed later) it is useful to draw a chronological dividing line between the beginning of the current year and all previous years. The current year's preferred dividends can affect only the allocation of the current year's net income; preferred dividends in arrears can affect only the beginning retained earnings of the current year. Subsidiary net income is allocated as follows:

- If the preferred stock is noncumulative, an amount of net income equal to the current year's preferred dividend, *if declared,* is allocated to the preferred stockholders and the remainder is allocated to the common stockholders. If no preferred dividends are declared in the current year, the entire amount of net income is allocated to the common stockholders.
- If the preferred stock is cumulative, an amount of net income equal to the current year's preferred dividend, *whether or not declared,* is allocated to the preferred stockholders and the remainder is allocated to the common stockholders.

Remember that preferred dividends in arrears cannot affect the allocation of the current year's net income.

If the parent acquires an investment at some point during a year, the subsidiary's net income must be apportioned between or among segments of that year in order to record the appropriate amount as the parent's share. Unless better evidence is available, the subsidiary is assumed to have earned its net income proportionately throughout the year. After making the apportionment, it is necessary to allocate the subsidiary's net income between preferred and common stock, as described above. *For this purpose, undeclared cumulative preferred dividends are treated as if they accrue proportionately throughout the year.*

Under the equity method, for each investment that the parent holds in the subsidiary, it debits Investment in Subsidiary and credits Income from Subsidiary for an amount equal to its percentage of ownership multiplied by the net income allocated to that class of the subsidiary's capital stock. When the parent owns both preferred and common stock of the subsidiary, it is convenient to maintain separate Investment in Subsidiary accounts and separate Income from Subsidiary accounts for each investment.

Because the subsidiary declares dividends separately to its preferred and common stockholders, no allocation of subsidiary dividends is necessary. The parent debits Dividends Receivable and credits Investment in Subsidiary (under the equity method) or Dividend Revenue (under the cost method) for the amount actually declared to it by the subsidiary.

The allocation of subsidiary net income and the equity method journal entries to record both subsidiary net income and subsidiary dividends are shown in Illustrative Problem 11.1.

ILLUSTRATIVE PROBLEM 11.1: DIVIDEND DISTRIBUTION, INCOME ALLOCATION, AND EQUITY METHOD JOURNAL ENTRIES

Company P bought 48,000 of Company S's 60,000 shares of $1 par value common stock for $293,200 and 1,200 of Company S's 12,000 shares of 6%, $10 par value preferred stock for $15,400 on April 30, 1991. On December 31, 1990, Company S had the following stockholders' equity balances:

Common Stock	$ 60,000
Additional Paid-in Capital: Common	240,000
Preferred Stock	120,000
Additional Paid-in Capital: Preferred	10,000
Retained Earnings	36,000

Company S had not declared any dividends since December 31, 1989. Company S reported net income of $24,000 for 1991, but declared no dividends for that year. Company S reported net income of $36,000 for 1992. Company S's 1992 dividends were declared on December 10, 1992, payable on January 15, 1993. Company P accounts for its investments in Company S under the equity method.

The distribution of Company S's 1992 dividends, the allocation of its 1991 and 1992 net income between its preferred and common stockholders, and the resulting equity method journal entries are illustrated for four independent cases.

Case 1. The preferred stock is noncumulative and Company S declares total dividends of $25,000 in 1992.

Case 2. The preferred stock is cumulative and Company S declares dividends of $25,000 in 1992.

Case 3. The preferred stock is noncumulative and Company S declares no dividends in 1992.

Case 4. The preferred stock is cumulative and Company S declares no dividends in 1992.

The distribution of Company S's 1992 dividends in Cases 1 and 2 is shown in Exhibit 11-1. (Only Cases 1 and 2 involve the declaration of dividends in 1992.) In Case 1, in which the preferred stock is noncumulative, the fact that Company S did not declare dividends in 1990 and 1991 is irrelevant. These undeclared dividends have been lost forever to the preferred stockholders. In Case 2, however, the undeclared dividends for 1990 and 1991 have accumulated and become dividends in arrears. They must be declared to the preferred stockholders, along with the current year's dividend, before any dividends can be declared to the common stockholders in 1992.

EXHIBIT 11-1

Illustrative Problem 11.1
Distribution of Dividends
Year Ended December 31, 1992

	Case 1	Case 2
Total Dividends	$ 25,000	$ 25,000
Preferred Arrears Dividends	—	14,400
Preferred Current Dividends	7,200	7,200
Total Preferred Dividends	7,200	21,600
Common Dividend	$ 17,800	$ 3,400

The allocation of Company S's 1991 and 1992 net incomes between preferred and common stockholders in Cases 1, 2, 3, and 4 is shown in Exhibit 11-2. Notice that the 1991 net income is apportioned between the periods before and after the date of acquisition before allocating it between preferred and common stock. Four months' net income, or 4/12 of $24,000, is apportioned to the period before the date of acquisition; eight months' net income, or 9/12 of $24,000, is apportioned to the period after the date of acquisition.

EXHIBIT 11-2

Illustrative Problem 11.1
Allocation of Net Income
Years Ended December 31, 1991 and 1992

	Case 1	Case 2	Case 3	Case 4
1991				
Total Net Income	$ 24,000	$ 24,000	$ 24,000	$ 24,000
Net Income through 4/30/91	8,000	8,000	8,000	8,000
Net Income, 5/1/91 through 12/31/91	$ 16,000	$ 16,000	$ 16,000	$ 16,000
Net Income through 4/30/91	$ 8,000	$ 8,000	$ 8,000	$ 8,000
Net Income: Preferred (Undeclared Preferred Current Dividend)	—	2,400	—	2,400
Net Income: Common	$ 8,000	$ 5,600	$ 8,000	$ 5,600
Net Income, 5/1/91 through 12/31/91	$ 16,000	$ 16,000	$ 16,000	$ 16,000
Net Income: Preferred (Undeclared Preferred Current Dividend)	—	4,800	—	4,800
Net Income: Common	$ 16,000	$ 11,200	$ 16,000	$ 11,200
1992				
Total Net Income	$ 36,000	$ 36,000	$ 36,000	$ 36,000
Preferred Current Dividend	7,200	7,200	—	—
Undeclared Preferred Current Dividend	—	—	—	7,200
Net Income: Preferred	7,200	7,200	—	7,200
Net Income: Common	$ 28,800	$ 28,800	$ 36,000	$ 28,800

Although Company S declared no dividends in 1991, an amount of net income equal to the undeclared dividends on the cumulative preferred stock in Cases 2 and 4 is allocated to the preferred stockholders and the remainder is allocated to the common stockholders, both for the first four months and for the last eight months. In performing this allocation, the undeclared cumulative preferred stock dividends are treated as if they accrue proportionately throughout the year. Thus, 4/12 of $7,200 is apportioned to the period before the date of acquisition and 8/12 of $7,200 is apportioned to the period after the date of acquisition.

In 1992, in Cases 1 and 2, Company S declared the current years' dividend to the preferred stockholders; therefore, it does not matter whether the preferred stock is or is not cumulative. An amount of net income equal to the current year's declared preferred stock dividend is allocated to the preferred stockholders. In Case 3, because no dividends are declared in 1992 and the preferred stock is noncumulative, all of the 1992 net income is allocated to the common stockholders. In Case 4, because the preferred stock is cumulative, it does not matter whether or not the 1992 preferred dividend is declared. Even though it is not declared in this case, it accumulates. Therefore, an amount of net income equal to the undeclared current year's preferred dividend is allocated to the preferred stockholders.

The 1991 and 1992 equity method journal entries that would be recorded by Company P in Cases 1, 2, 3, and 4 are shown in Exhibit 11-3. In all cases, the amounts included in the journal entries are based on the amounts of dividends distributed and net income allocated to the two classes of stock in Exhibits 11-1 and 11-2.

EXHIBIT 11-3

Illustrative Problem 11.1
Equity Method Journal Entries
Years Ended December 31, 1991 and 1992

	Case 1	Case 2	Case 3	Case 4
December 31, 1991				
Investment in Company S: Preferred	—	480	—	480
Income from Company S: Preferred	—	(480)	—	(480)
Investment in Company S: Common	12,800	8,960	12,800	8,960
Income from Company S: Common	(12,800)	(8,960)	(12,800)	(8,960)
December 10, 1992				
Dividends Receivable	720	2,160	—	—
Investment in Company S: Preferred	(720)	(2,160)	—	—
Dividends Receivable	14,240	2,720	—	—
Investment in Company S: Common	(14,240)	(2,720)	—	—
December 31, 1992				
Investment in Company S: Preferred	720	720	—	720
Income from Company S: Preferred	(720)	(720)	—	(720)
Investment in Company S: Common	23,040	23,040	28,800	23,040
Income from Company S: Common	(23,040)	(23,040)	(28,800)	(23,040)

For 1991, the amount credited to Income from Company S: Preferred is Company P's share, 10%, of the net income allocated to the preferred stockholders for the last eight months of 1991 in Exhibit 11-2. The amount credited to Income from Company S: Common is

Company P's share, 80%, of the net income allocated to the common stockholders for the last eight months of 1991 in Exhibit 11-2.

For 1992, the amount credited to Income from Company S: Preferred again is Company P's share, 10%, of the net income allocated to the preferred stockholders in Exhibit 11-2. The amount credited to Income from Company S: Common is Company P's share, 80%, of the 1992 net income allocated to the common stockholders in Exhibit 11-2.

The amounts of 1992 Company S preferred stock dividends recorded in Cases 1 and 2 are Company P's share, 10%, of the dividends declared to the preferred stockholders, as shown in Exhibit 11-1. Similarly, the amounts of 1992 Company S common stock dividends recorded in Cases 1 and 2 are 80% of the dividends declared to the common stockholders, as shown in Exhibit 11-1.

If Company P did not own any of Company S's preferred stock, it would not record any of the journal entries involving Investment in Company S: Preferred that appear in Exhibit 11-3. The dividend distributions and allocations of net income that appear in Exhibits 11-1 and 11-2, however, would be exactly the same, and Company P would record the journal entries in Exhibit 11-3 that affect Investment in Company S: Common.

If Company P had used the cost method to account for its two investments in Company S, the journal entries for dividends in Cases 1 and 2 in Exhibit 11-3 would credit Dividend Revenue rather than the respective Investment in Company S accounts. No journal entries would be recorded, of course, for income from the subsidiary.

DETERMINING BOOK VALUE AT ACQUISITION

The first step in the consolidation process is to construct the schedule of the difference between cost and book value. In order to determine the book value of the parent's investment in the subsidiary's common stock (and, if present, its investment in the subsidiary's preferred stock), it may be necessary to allocate the subsidiary's retained earnings balance at the date of acquisition between the two classes of stock. This allocation is made on the basis of a hypothetical distribution of the entire balance of retained earnings in dividends. Thus, if preferred stock dividend are in arrears as of the date of acquisition, an amount of retained earnings equal to the arrears dividends must be allocated to the preferred stock, with the remainder allocated to the common stock.

If the parent acquires an investment at some point during a year, the following steps are necessary to allocate the subsidiary's retained earnings at the date of acquisition.

- First, update total retained earnings from the beginning of the year to the date of acquisition by adding an appropriate portion of net income for the year. In allocating the net income, we assume that it is earned proportionately throughout the year unless better evidence is available. If the subsidiary has declared dividends (either on preferred stock only or on both preferred and common stock) between the beginning of the year and the date of acquisition, the *current year* dividends must be subtracted.
- Second, allocate to Retained Earnings: Preferred an amount equal to any dividends in arrears as of the beginning of the year, plus an appropriate portion of any undeclared cumulative preferred dividends applicable to the year of acquisition. For this purpose, undeclared cumulative preferred dividends are treated as if they accrue proportionately throughout the year.
- The remainder, in each case, is the balance of Retained Earnings: Common.

The book value of the parent's investment in each class of subsidiary capital stock is calculated as the parent's percentage of ownership in that class of stock, multiplied by the total stockholders' equity of that class at the date of acquisition, after allocating retained earnings. These steps are necessary whether or not the parent owns any of the subsidiary's preferred stock. They are demonstrated in Illustrative Problem 11.2.

ILLUSTRATIVE PROBLEM 11.2: RETAINED EARNINGS ALLOCATION AT ACQUISITION

Illustrative Problem 11.2 is a continuation of Illustrative Problem 11.1, in which Company S's Retained Earnings balance is given as $36,000 on December 31, 1990. Company P acquired its 80% interest in Company S's common stock and its 10% interest in Company S's preferred stock on April 30, 1991. Through December 31, 1991, Cases 1 and 3 in Illustrative Problem 11.2 are identical, as are Cases 2 and 4; therefore, we will use only Cases 1 and 2 to illustrate the allocation of Company S's Retained Earnings balance at the date of acquisition and the resulting schedule of Goodwill from Consolidation.

The allocation of Company S's Retained Earnings at April 30, 1991, the date of acquisition, is shown in Exhibit 11-4. The first step in performing the allocation is to update total Retained Earnings from December 31, 1990 to April 30, 1991, the date of acquisition, by adding four months' net income (see Exhibit 11-2). If Company S had declared any dividends between January 1, 1991 and April 30, 1991, the *current* portion of those dividends would have been subtracted.

EXHIBIT 11-4

Illustrative Problem 11.2
Allocation of Retained Earnings
April 30, 1991

	Case 1	Case 2
Total Retained Earnings	$ 44,000 [a]	$ 44,000 [a]
Retained Earnings: Preferred	—	9,600 [b]
Retained Earnings: Common	$ 44,000	$ 34,400

Calculations

[a] $36,000 × (4/12 × $24,000)
[b] $7,200 + (4/12 × $7,200)

Second, it is necessary to allocate to Retained Earnings: Preferred an amount equal to any dividends in arrears as of the beginning of the year, plus an appropriate portion of any undeclared preferred dividends applicable to the year of acquisition, as shown in Case 2. In Case 2, the amount allocated to preferred stock consists of one year's dividend in arrears, $7,200, plus the current year's undeclared preferred dividend "accrued" for the first four months of 1991, 4/12 of $7,200, or $2,400. The remainder, in each case, is the balance of Retained Earnings: Common.

A composite Goodwill from Consolidation Schedule for Cases 1 and 2 at December 31, 1992 appears in Exhibit 11-5. For each investment, the book value at the date of acquisition is calculated as Company P's percentage of ownership, multiplied by the total stockholders' equity of that class of stock at April 30, 1991, taking into consideration the allocation of Company S's Retained Earnings balance in Exhibit 11-4. In Case 1, Company S's total preferred stockholders' equity consists of preferred stock of $120,000 plus additional paid-in capital of $10,000. In Case 2, Company S's total preferred stockholders' equity consists of preferred stock of $120,000, plus additional paid-in capital of $10,000, plus allocated retained earnings of $9,600. In Case 1, Company S's total common stockholders' equity consists of common stock of $60,000, plus additional paid-in capital of $240,000, plus retained earnings of $44,000. In Case 2, Company S's total common stockholders' equity consists of common stock of $60,000, plus additional paid-in capital of $240,000, plus allocated retained earnings of $34,400.

EXHIBIT 11-5

Illustrative Problem 11.2
Composite Goodwill Schedule
December 31, 1992

Goodwill from Consolidation

	Case 1		Case 2	
	Preferred Stock	Common Stock	Preferred Stock	Common Stock
Cost of Investment	$ 15,400	$ 293,200	$ 15,400	$ 293,200
Book Value	13,000	275,200	13,960	267,520
Goodwill, 12/31/90	2,400	18,000	1,440	25,680
Amortization, 1991	(160)	(1,200)	(96)	(1,712)
Amortization, 1992	(240)	(1,800)	(144)	(2,568)
Goodwill, 12/31/92	$ 2,000	$ 15,000	$ 1,200	$ 21,400

CONVERSION FROM COST TO EQUITY

If the parent company elects to account for its investment or investments in the subsidiary under the cost method, it is necessary to convert from cost to equity at the beginning of the current year before making any worksheet eliminations. The amount of this conversion is determined by comparing the parent's equity in each class of the subsidiary's capital stock at the beginning of the current year with its equity in that class of stock at the date of acquisition.

The presence of subsidiary preferred stock may require allocation of the subsidiary's Retained Earnings balance between preferred and common stockholders at either the date of acquisition or the beginning of the current year, or sometimes both dates. If the subsidiary's preferred stock is cumulative and preferred dividends are in arrears at either date, an amount of retained earnings equal to the arrears dividends is allocated to the preferred stock, with the remainder allocated to the common stock. Otherwise, the entire balance is associated with the common stock.

The above steps are necessary whether or not the parent company owns any of the subsidiary's preferred stock. Illustrative Problem 11.3 demonstrates the conversion from cost to equity.

ILLUSTRATIVE PROBLEM 11.3: CONVERSION FROM COST TO EQUITY

Illustrative Problem 11.3 is a continuation of Illustrative Problems 11.1 and 11.2. In Illustrative Problem 11.1, Company S's Retained Earnings balance is given as $36,000 on December 31, 1990. Company P acquired its 80% interest in Company S's common stock and its 10% interest in Company S's preferred stock on April 30, 1991. Company S reported net income of $24,000 for 1991, but declared no dividends for that year. Thus, by December 31, 1991, Company S's Retained Earnings balance had increased to $60,000. Through December 31, 1991, Cases 1 and 3 in Illustrative Problem 11.1 are identical, as are Cases 2 and 4; therefore we will use only Cases 1 and 2 to illustrate the allocation of Company S's Retained Earnings balance at April 30 and December 31, 1991 and the resulting Conversion from Cost to Equity schedule at December 31, 1992.

Exhibit 11-6 shows the allocation of Company S's Retained Earnings at April 30 and December 31, 1991. The April 30, 1991 balances in each case are taken from Exhibit 11-4. The amount allocated to the preferred stock in Case 2 at December 31, 1991 is the amount of preferred dividends in arrears at that date.

EXHIBIT 11-6

Illustrative Problem 11.3
Allocation of Retained Earnings
April 30 and December 31, 1991

	Case 1		Case 2	
	4/30/91	12/31/91	4/30/91	12/31/91
Total Retained Earnings	$ 44,000	$ 60,000	$ 44,000	$ 60,000
Retained Earnings: Preferred	—	—	9,600	14,400
Retained Earnings: Common	$ 44,000	$ 60,000	$ 34,400	$ 45,600

A composite Conversion from Cost to Equity schedule to accompany the December 31, 1992 consolidation worksheet appears in Exhibit 11-7. Each amount of Comany P's equity in Company S's preferred stock is calculated as Company P's percentage of ownership, 10%, multiplied by Company S's total preferred stockholders' equity. In Case 1, Company S's total preferred stockholders' equity at each date consists solely of preferred stock of $120,000 plus additional paid-in capital of $10,000. In Case 2, Company S's total preferred stockholders' equity at April 30, 1991 consists of preferred stock of $120,000, plus additional paid-in capital of $10,000, plus allocated retained earnings of $9,600; at December 31, 1991, it consists of preferred stock of $120,000, plus additional paid-in capital of $10,000, plus allocated retained earnings of $14,400.

EXHIBIT 11-7

Illustrative Problem 11.3
Composite Conversion from Cost to Equity Schedule
December 31, 1992

Conversion from Cost to Equity

	Case 1		Case 2	
	Preferred Stock	Common Stock	Preferred Stock	Common Stock
Company P's Equity, 12/31/91	$ 13,000	$ 288,000	$ 14,440	$ 276,480
Company P's Equity, 4/30/91	13,000	275,200	13,960	267,520
Increase in Equity	$ —	$ 12,800	$ 480	$ 8,960

Similarly, each amount of Company P's equity in Company S's common stock is calculated as Company P's percentage of ownership, 80%, multiplied by Company S's total common stockholders' equity. In Case 1, Company S's total common stockholders' equity at April 30, 1991 consists of common stock of $60,000, plus additional paid-in capital of $240,000, plus retained earnings of $44,000; at December 31, 1991, it consists of common stock of $60,000, plus additional paid-in capital of $240,000, plus retained earnings of $60,000. In Case 2, Company S's total common stockholders' equity at April 30, 1991 consists of common stock of $60,000, plus additional paid-in capital of $240,000, plus allocated retained earnings of $34,400; at December 31, 1991, it consists of common stock of $60,000, plus additional paid-in capital of $240,000, plus allocated retained earnings of $45,600.

WORKSHEET ELIMINATIONS

When the subsidiary has preferred stock, it may be necessary to allocate the subsidiary's beginning Retained Earnings balance between its common and preferred stockholders before preparing the Intercompany Ownership Interests set of eliminations. If the subsidiary's preferred stock is cumulative and preferred dividends are in arrears at the beginning of the current year, an amount of retained earnings equal to the arrears dividends is allocated to the preferred stock, with the remainder allocated to the common stock. Otherwise, the entire balance is assigned to the common stock.

It is very convenient to make this allocation, when necessary, before constructing the worksheet. This allows one to enter the allocated portions of the subsidiary's Retained Earnings balance on two separate lines as Retained Earnings: Preferred and Retained Earnings: Common, so that they can be treated separately throughout the rest of the consolidation process.

The Intercompany Ownership Interests set of eliminations for each of the parent's investments in the subsidiary, then, includes an elimination against the portion of the subsidiary's Retained Earnings balance allocated to that class of subsidiary capital stock. Because the preferred stockholders share in profits and losses only to the extent of their specified dividends, all other eliminations affecting the subsidiary's Retained Earnings balance are made against Retained Earnings: Common only.

The Subsidiary Income and Dividends set of eliminations for each of the parent's investments in the subsidiary is based on the amount of income from the subsidiary (under the equity method) or dividend revenue (under the cost method) recorded by the parent during the current year. The amount of income from subsidiary recorded under the equity method may be influenced by an allocation of the subsidiary's net income between its preferred and common stockholders, as discussed and illustrated earlier in this chapter.

These steps apply whether or not the parent owns any of the subsidiary's preferred stock. They are demonstrated in Illustrative Problem 11.4.

ILLUSTRATIVE PROBLEM II.4: RETAINED EARNINGS ALLOCATION AT YEAR END AND ELIMINATIONS

Illustrative Problem 11.4 is a continuation of Illustrative Problems 11.1, 11.2, and 11.3. In Illustrative Problem 11.1, Company S's Retained Earnings balance is given as $36,000 on December 31, 1990. Company P acquired its 80% interest in Company S's common stock and its 10% interest in Company S's preferred stock on April 30, 1991. Company S reported net income of $24,000 for 1991, but declared no dividends for that year, causing Company S's December 31, 1991 Retained Earnings balance to be $60,000. The following additional information is available.

During 1992, Company P purchased merchandise from Company S for $212,500, of which $19,100 remained unpaid at year end. Company P's beginning and ending inventories for 1992 contained goods purchased from Company S of $18,500 and $17,500, respectively. Company S sells to Company P at 25% above cost. Both affiliates use perpetual inventory systems.

On June 30, 1991, Company S sold some equipment with a net book value of $122,500 to Company P for $162,500. Company P is depreciating the equipment using the straight-line method, over eight years, with a $21,500 salvage value.

Exhibit 11-8 illustrates the allocation of Company S's December 31, 1991 Retained Earnings balance in each of the four cases given in Illustrative Problem 11.1. The amount allocated to Retained Earnings: Preferred in Cases 2 and 4 is the amount of preferred dividends in arrears at December 31, 1991. After allocating Company S's beginning Retained Earnings balance, we are prepared to proceed with the eliminations at December 31, 1992.

Exhibit 11-9 includes the Intercompany Ownership Interests and Subsidiary Income and Dividends sets of eliminations related to Company P's Investment in Company S: Preferred that would appear on the December 31, 1992 consolidation worksheet in each of the four cases. In the Intercompany Ownership Interests set, 10% of Company S's Preferred Stock and, where appropriate, 10% of Company S's Retained Earnings: Preferred (see Exhibit 11-8) are eliminated against Company P's Investment in Company S: Preferred. In the Subsidiary Income and Dividends set, Company P's Income from Company S: Preferred balance in each case (see Exhibit 11-3) is eliminated against 10% of Company S's Dividends Declared: Preferred, where

EXHIBIT 11-8

Illustrative Problem 11.4
Allocation of Retained Earnings
December 31, 1991

	Case 1	Case 2	Case 3	Case 4
Total Retained Earnings	$ 60,000	$ 60,000	$ 60,000	$ 60,000
Retained Earnings: Preferred	—	14,400	—	14,400
Retained Earnings: Common	$ 60,000	$ 45,600	$ 60,000	$ 45,600

EXHIBIT 11-9

Illustrative Problem 11.4
Eliminations
December 31, 1992

	Case 1	Case 2	Case 3	Case 4
Eliminations				
Intercompany Ownership Interests				
[1] Preferred Stock: S	$ 12,000	$ 12,000	$ 12,000	$ 12,000
[2] Additional Paid-in Capital: Preferred: S	1,000	1,000	1,000	1,000
[3] Retained Earnings: Preferred: S	—	1,440	—	1,440
[4] Investment in Company S: Preferred	$(13,000)	$(14,440)	$(13,000)	$(14,440)
Subsidiary Income and Dividends				
[5] Income from Company S: Preferred	$ 720	$ 720	$ —	$ 720
[6] Dividends Declared: Preferred: S	(720)	(2,160)	—	—
[7] Investment in Company S: Preferred	$ —	$ 1,440	$ —	$(720)

appropriate, and the difference, if any, is eliminated against Company P's Investment in Company S: Preferred.

Exhibit 11-10 includes the Intercompany Ownership Interests and Subsidiary Income and Dividends sets of eliminations related to Company P's Investment in Company S: Common that would appear on the December 31, 1992 consolidation worksheet in each of the four cases.

In the Intercompany Ownership Interests set, 80% of the balances of Company S's Common Stock, Additional Paid-in Capital: Common, and Retained Earnings: Common (see Exhibit 11-8) are eliminated against Company P's Investment in Co. S: Common. In the Subsidiary Income and Dividends set, Company P's Income from Company S: Common balance in each case (see Exhibit 11-3) is eliminated against 80% of Company S's Dividends Declared:

EXHIBIT 11-10

Illustrative Problem 11.4
Eliminations
December 31, 1992

	Case 1	Case 2	Case 3	Case 4
Eliminations				
Intercompany Ownership Interests				
[8] Common Stock: S	$ 48,000	$ 48,000	$ 48,000	$ 48,000
[9] Additional Paid-in Capital: Common: S	192,000	192,000	192,000	192,000
[10] Retained Earnings: Common: S	48,000	36,480	48,000	36,480
[11] Investment in Company S: Common	$(288,000)	$(276,480)	$(288,000)	$(276,480)
Subsidiary Income and Dividends				
[12] Income from Company S: Common	$ 23,040	$ 23,040	$ 28,800	$ 23,040
[13] Dividends Declared: Common: S	(14,240)	(2,720)	—	—
[14] Investment in Company S: Common	$(8,800)	$(20,320)	$(28,800)	$(23,040)

Common and the difference is eliminated against Company P's Investment in Company S: Common.

Exhibit 11-11 presents the Goodwill Amortization sets of eliminations needed at December 31, 1992. The goodwill amounts for Cases 1 and 3 are identical, as are those for Cases 2 and 4; therefore, the eliminations for Cases 1 and 2 only are shown. Because the goodwill from consolidation is a parent company asset, Company P's Retained Earnings is debited for the prior year's amortziation in each case.

EXHIBIT 11-11

Illustrative Problem 11.4
Additional Eliminations
December 31, 1992

	Case 1	Case 2
Goodwill Amortization		
[15] Retained Earnings: P	$ 160	$ 96
[16] Goodwill Amortization Expense	240	144
[17] Investment in Company S: Preferred	$(400)	$(240)
[18] Retained Earnings: P	$ 1,200	$ 1,712
[19] Goodwill Amortization Expense	1,800	2,568
[20] Investment in Company S: Common	$(3,000)	$(4,280)

Exhibit 11-12 presents the remaining sets of eliminations needed at December 31, 1992. Because the amounts are identical for all four cases, only one set of eliminations for each purpose is shown. Following the previously established allocation formula, the amount of intercompany profit in beginning inventory allocated to each affiliate's Retained Earnings is [a] its external ownership percentage, multiplied by [b] its share of the quantity being allocated, multiplied by [c] the quantity being allocated, $3,700, yielding the following results:

$$[a] \times [b] \times [c] = [d]$$

Company P: 100% ×   80% × $3,700 = $2,960
Company S: 20% × 100% × $3,700 = $ 740

Company S's allocated amount, however, is eliminated from its Retained Earnings: Common balance.

Applying the same allocation formula to the intercompany profit in equipment, the following results are obtained:

$$[a] \times [b] \times [c] = [d]$$

Company P: 100% ×   80% × $37,500 = $30,000
Company S: 20% × 100% × $37,400 = $ 7,500

Again, Company S's allocated amount is eliminated from its Retained Earnings: Common balance.

WORKSHEET ALLOCATION OF NET INCOME

When the subsidiary has both common and preferred stock, the Income Allocation schedule may include two allocations:

- the allocation of the subsidiary's net income between its common and preferred stock-holders, and
- the allocation of each of the resulting net income amounts between the minority (or external) interest and consolidated net income.

If the subsidiary's preferred stock is noncumulative, the first step is necessary only when the subsidiary has declared the current year's preferred dividend. If the subsidiary's preferred stock is cumulative, it is necessary whether or not the current year's preferred dividends have been declared. The second step, of course, is necessary whenever a minority (or external) interest is present.

In those cases in which subsidiary net income is allocated between·its common and preferred stockholders, three components of total net income emerge:

- minority interest in the subsidiary's net income to common stock,
- minority (or external) interest in the subsidiary's net income to preferred stock, and
- consolidated net income.

If the parent owns all of either class of the subsidiary's stock, of course, the minority or external interest in that class is zero. If the parent does not own any of the subsidiary's preferred stock, the external interest is 100% or all of the subsidiary net income allocated to the preferred stock in the first step. These procedures are demonstrated in Illustrative Problem 11.5.

EXHIBIT 11-12

Illustrative Problem 11.4
Additional Eliminations
December 31, 1992

Intercompany Sales and Purchases

[21] Sales	$ 212,500
[22] Cost of Goods Sold	(212,500)

Intercompany Payables and Receivables

[23] Accounts Payable	$ 19,100
[24] Accounts Receivable	(19,100)

Intercompany Profit in Beginning Inventory

[25] Retained Earnings: P	$ 2,960
[26] Retained Earnings: Common: S	740
[27] Cost of Goods Sold	$(3,700)

Intercompany Profit in Ending Inventory

[28] Cost of Goods Sold	$ 3,500
[29] Inventory	(3,500)

Intercompany Profit in Depreciable Assets

[30] Accumulated Depreciation	$ 7,500
[31] Retained Earnings: P	30,000
[32] Retained Earnings: Common: S	7,500
[33] Depreciation Expense	(5,000)
[34] Plant and Equipment	$(40,000)

ILLUSTRATIVE PROBLEM 11.5: INCOME ALLOCATION SCHEDULE AND CONSOLIDATION WORKSHEET

Illustrative Problem 11.5 is a continuation of Illustrative Problem 11.1, 11.2, 11.3, and 11.4. In Illustrative Problem 11.1, Company S's 1992 net income is given as $36,000. In addition, Company P's 1992 net income from its own operations is $35,000.

Using Case 2 as an illustration, the Income Allocation schedule to accompany the December 31, 1992 consolidation worksheet is shown in Exhibit 11-13. The adjustment for the current year's goodwill amortization is made to Company P's net income because the goodwill from consolidation is Company P's asset. The amount of this adjsutment is the sum of the 1992 amortization amounts included in Eliminations [16] and [19] for Case 2 in Exhibit 11-11.

EXHIBIT 11-13

Illustrative Problem 11.5
Income Allocation Schedule
Year Ended December 31, 1992

Income Allocation

Company P's Own Net Income		$ 35,000
Less: Goodwill Amortization		(2,712)
Company P's Adjusted Net Income		32,288
Company S's Own Net Income	$ 36,000	
Add: Intercompany Profit in Beginning Inventory	3,700	
Intercompany Profit in Depreciable Assets	5,000	
Less: Intercompany Profit in Ending Inventory	(3,500)	
Company S's Adjusted Net Income	41,200	
Less: Net Income to Preferred Stock	(7,200)	
Net Income to Common Stock	34,000	
Minority Interest: Common (20%)	6,800	
Company P's Share (80%)		27,200
Net Income to Preferred Stock	7,200	
Minority Interest: Preferred (90%)	6,480	
Company P's Share (10%)		720
Consolidated Net Income		$ 60,208

The adjustments for intercompany profits in beginning and ending inventories and depreciable assets are made to Company S's Net Income because Company S is the selling affiliate in each instance. These adjustments, however, apply only to Company S's Net Income to Common Stock. Because nonparticipating preferred stock does not participate in profits and losses beyond the stipulated annual dividend, its share of net income is limited to the amount of that stipulated dividend.

Utilizing the information developed for Case 2 in Exhibits 11-5, 11-8, 11-9, 11-10, 11-11, 11-12, and 11-13, the completed December 31, 1992 consolidation worksheet appears in Exhibit 11-14.

REVIEW OF THE CONSOLIDATION PROCESS

At this point, we have encountered all of the basic elements of the consolidation process, and a review of that process seems in order. The routine that has been established consists of the following steps:

1. Prepare a schedule of the difference between cost and book value.
2. Prepare a schedule for the conversion from cost to equity, if necessary.

EXHIBIT 11-14

Illustrative Problem 11.5
Consolidation Worksheet
December 31, 1992

	Company P	Company S	Eliminations		Income Statement	Balance Sheet
Investment in Company S: Common	322,480		[11]	(276,480)		21,400 G
			[14]	(20,320)		
			[20]	(4,280)		
Investment in Company S: Preferred	14,440		[4]	(14,440)		1,200 G
			[7]	1,440		
			[17]	(240)		
Plant and Equipment	328,200	494,600	[34]	(40,000)		782,800
Other Assets	142,600	197,700	[24]	(19,100)		317,700
			[29]	(3,500)		
Cost of Goods Sold	288,100	117,200	[22]	(212,500)	192,600	
			[27]	(3,700)		
			[28]	3,500		
Expenses	121,700	98,800	[16]	144	218,212	
			[19]	2,568		
			[33]	(5,000)		
Dividends Declared: Common: P	18,000					18,000 R
Dividends Declared: Common: S		3,400	[13]	(2,720)		680 MC
Dividends Declared: Preferred: S		21,600	[6]	(2,160)		19,440 MP
	1,235,520	933,300				1,161,220
Accumulated Depreciation	128,100	122,600	[30]	7,500		243,200
Liabilities	176,260	68,700	[23]	19,100		225,860
Common Stock: P	200,000					200,000
Additional Paid-in Capital: P	100,000					100,000
Common Stock: S		60,000	[8]	48,000		12,000 MC
Additional Paid-in Capital: Common: S		240,000	[9]	192,000		48,000 MC
Preferred Stock: S		120,000	[1]	12,000		108,000 MP
Additional Paid-in Capital: Preferred: S		10,000	[2]	1,000		9,000 MP
Retained Earnings: P	162,600		[15]	96		127,832 R
			[18]	1,712		
			[25]	2,960		
			[31]	30,000		
Retained Earnings: Common: S		45,600	[10]	36,480		880 MC
			[26]	740		
			[32]	7,500		
Retained Earnings: Preferred: S		14,400	[3]	1,440		12,960 MP
Sales	444,800	252,000	[21]	212,500	484,300	
Income from Company S: Common	23,040		[12]	23,040		
Income from Company S: Preferred	720		[5]	720		
	1,235,520	933,300				
Minority Interest in Company S's Net Income: Common					6,800	6,800 MC
Minority Interest in Company S's Net Income: Preferred					6,480	6,480 MP
Consolidated Net Income					60,208	60,208 R
					484,300	484,300 1,161,220

3. Prepare schedules of whatever worksheet adjustments are necessary. We have encountered adjustments for
   a. assets (usually goodwill) of the subsidiary, and
   b. conversion from cost to equity.
4. Prepare schedules of the worksheet eliminations, which include
   a. the Intercompany Ownership Interests set,
   b. the Subsidiary Income and Dividends set,
   c. the Goodwill Amortization set (appropriately titled with respect to the treatment of the difference between cost and book value), and
   d. a variety of additional sets of eliminations, including those for
      1) intercompany receivables and payables,
      2) intercompany revenues and expenses,
      3) intercompany profits in inventories,
      4) intercompany profits in depreciable assets, and
      5) intercompany bonds.
5. Prepare the Income Allocation schedule.
6. Set up the consolidation worksheet and enter the trial balances, leaving extra lines where necessary.
7. Enter the adjustments and eliminations on the worksheet.
8. Combine the trial balance balances where appropriate and extend them, plus or minus adjustments and eliminations, to the Income Statement and Balance Sheet columns.
9. Enter the Minority Interest in Subsidiary Net Income and Consolidated Net Income amounts as balancing figures in the Income Statement and Balance Sheet columns.
10. Prepare the consolidated financial statements.

Remember that although we represent sets of adjustments and sets of eliminations in terms of debits and credits, they are not really journal entries. They are recorded only on the consolidation worksheet. Therefore, adjustments and eliminations often must be repeated from year to year.

SUMMARY

The presence of subsidiary preferred stock affects both the parent company's accounting for its investment in the subsidiary and the consolidation process, whether or not the parent owns any of that preferred stock. The chapter begins with a review of the features of preferred stock, particularly dividend preferences.

The effects of subsidiary preferred stock on the parent's accounting for its investment in the subsidiary include the allocation of both subsidiary net income and subsidiary dividends. Illustrative Problem 11.1 demonstrates these allocations and their impact on the parent's equity method journal entries.

The remainder of this chapter is devoted to discussion and illustration of the effects of subsidiary preferred stock on the consolidation process, including

- the allocation of subsidiary retained earnings in determining book value at acquisition,
- the allocation of subsidiary retained earnings as of the beginning of the current year, and
- the allocation of total net income.

REVIEW PROBLEM

Company X purchased 14,000 of Company Y's 20,000 outstanding shares of $10 par value common stock for $272,600 on August 1, 1990, and 4,000 of Company Y's 10,000 outstanding shares of 8%, $10 par value, cumulative preferred stock for $51,200 on December 31, 1991. The common stock had been issued at 14 and the preferred stock at par, both in 1988. Company Y's preferred stock dividends were one year in arrears at December 31, 1990.

Any excess of cost over book value is to be treated as goodwill from consolidation and amortized over 10 years. Company X accounts for both investments under the equity method. Company X's 1992 net income was $35,000. Changes in Company Y's Retained Earnings balance are shown below.

Balance, 1/1/90	$ 41,200
Net Income, 1990	36,800
Balance, 12/31/90	78,000
Net Income, 1991	19,200
Balance, 12/31/91	97,200
Dividends, 12/15/92	(34,000)
Net Income, 1992	49,300
Balance, 12/31/92	$ 112,500

Required
1. Prepare the equity method journal entries for 1992 for both of Company X's investments in Company Y.
2. Prepare all schedules in support of the December 31, 1992 consolidation worksheet.

QUESTIONS

1. Explain the cumulative feature of preferred stock.
2. Explain the participating feature of preferred stock.
3. How can the presence of subsidiary preferred stock affect the parent's recording of subsidiary net income under the equity method?
4. How can the presence of subsidiary preferred stock affect the parent's recording of subsidiary dividends under the equity method?
5. How can the presence of subsidiary preferred stock affect the parent's recording of subsidiary dividends under the cost method?
6. How can the presence of subsidiary preferred stock affect the determination of goodwill from consolidation on the parent's investment in the subsidiary's common stock?
7. Describe the conversion from cost to equity on the parent's investment in the subsidiary's common stock when the subsidiary has cumulative preferred stock.
8. What effect does the presence of noncumulative subsidiary preferred stock have on the Intercompany

Ownership Interests set of eliminations relative to the parent's investment in the subsidiary's common stock?

9. How can the presence of cumulative subsidiary preferred stock with dividends in arrears affect the Intercompany Profits in Beginning Inventory set of eliminations?

10. If the subsidiary has not declared dividends on its preferred stock in a particular year, will any of the subsidiary's adjusted net income be allocated to the preferred stock in the Income Allocation schedule?

EXERCISES

EXERCISE 11-1

Company A owns 80% of Company B's common stock and 30% of Company B's 6% noncumulative preferred stock. Company B reported net income of $28,000 in 1991. The following balances appear on Company B's December 31, 1991 preclosing trial balance.

Preferred Stock	$ 100,000
Common Stock	200,000
Additional Paid-in Capital: Common	25,000
Retained Earnings	80,000
Dividends Declared: Preferred	6,000
Dividends Declared: Common	10,000

Required
1. Present Company A's equity method journal entries for 1991.
2. Schedule the eliminations that would appear on the December 31, 1991 consolidation worksheet.

EXERCISE 11-2

Company C owns 70% of Company D's common stock and 60% of Company D's 6%, cumulative preferred stock. Company C accounts for these investments under the equity method. Company D has outstanding common stock of $500,000 and preferred stock of $200,000. No preferred dividends have been declared since December 31, 1989. Company D's January 1, 1991 Retained Earnings balance is $50,000 and its 1991 net income of $20,000.

Required
Schedule the December 31, 1991 eliminations indicated by the above information.

EXERCISE 11-3

Company E owns 80% of Company F's common stock, which it accounts for under the equity method. The following balances appear in Company F's September 30, 1992 preclosing trial balance.

6% Cumulative Preferred Stock	$ 500,000
Common Stock	1,000,000
Additional Paid-in Capital: Common	80,000
Retained Earnings	120,000

Company F reported net income of $36,000 for the year ended September 30, 1992. Company F's last dividend declaration was in September, 1990.

Required
Schedule the eliminations that would appear on the September 30, 1992 consolidation worksheet.

EXERCISE 11-4

Company G owns 80% of Company H's common stock and 10% of Company H's 6% cumulative preferred stock. Company G accounts for these investments under the equity method. Total par values of Company H's outstanding capital stock are: preferred, $100,000; common, $400,000. Company H has not declared any dividends since December 31, 1988. Company H's January 1, 1991 Retained Earnings balance is $40,000 and its net income for 1991 is $25,000.

Required

Schedule the eliminations that would appear on the December 31, 1991 consolidation worksheet.

EXERCISE 11-5

Company J owns 90% of Company K's common stock and 20% of Company K's 5% cumulative preferred stock. The following balances appear on Company K's December 31, 1991 preclosing trial balance.

Preferred Stock	$ 400,000
Common Stock	800,000
Additional Paid-in Capital: Common	75,000
Retained Earnings	350,000
Dividends Declared: Preferred	40,000
Dividends Declared: Common	20,000

Company K's preferred stock dividends were one year in arrears on December 31, 1990. Company K reported net income of $75,000 in 1991. Company J accounts for its investments in Company K under the equity method.

Required

1. Present Company J's equity method journal entries for 1991.
2. Schedule the eliminations that would appear on the December 31, 1991 consolidation worksheet.

EXERCISE 11-6

Company L purchased 80% of Company M's common stock for $281,600 on December 31, 1991, when Company M had retained earnings of $62,000. Company L accounts for its investment in Company M under the cost method. The following balances appear in Company M's December 31, 1993 preclosing trial balance.

6% Cumulative Preferred Stock	$ 100,000
Common Stock	200,000
Additional Paid-in Capital: Common	40,000
Retained Earnings	104,000

Company M reported net income of $33,000 for 1993. Company M's last dividend declaration was in November 1990.

Required

Prepare schedules of the conversion from cost to equity and the resulting worksheet adjustments at December 31, 1993.

EXERCISE 11-7

Company N owns 75% of Company O's common stock. The following balances appear in Company O's December 31, 1991 preclosing trial balance.

7% Preferred Stock, $50 par	$ 500,000
Common Stock, $10 par	1,000,000
Additional Paid-in Capital: Common	180,000
Retained Earnings	620,000
Dividends Declared: Preferred	105,000
Dividends Declared: Common	60,000

Company O's preferred stock dividends were two years in arrears on December 31, 1990. Company O reported net income of $210,000 for the year ended December 31, 1991. Company N accounts for its investment in Company O under the equity method.

Required
Prepare schedules of the Intercompany Ownership Interests and Subsidiary Income and Dividends sets of eliminations at December 31, 1991.

EXERCISE 11-8
On April 1, 1991, Company P purchased 80,000 of Company Q's 100,000 shares of $5 par value common stock for $554,500 and 2,000 of Company Q's 10,000 shares of $50 par value, 6%, cumulative preferred stock for $165,000. Company Q's preferred stock dividends were one year in arrears at December 31, 1990. Changes in Company Q's retained earnings are shown below.

Balance, 1/1/91	$ 164,000
Net Income, 1991	42,000
Balance, 12/31/91	206,000
Dividends, 11/30/92	(124,000)
Net Income, 1992	176,000
Balance, 12/31/92	$ 258,000

Required
1. The amount of retained earnings included in the book value of Company P's investment in Company Q's preferred stock at the date of acquisition is
   a. $ 30,000
   b. $ 37,500
   c. $ 60,000
   d. $137,000
2. The amount of retained earnings allocated to Company Q's common stock in the December 31, 1992 consolidation worksheet is
   a. $137,000
   b. $144,500
   c. $146,000
   d. $206,000

EXERCISE 11-9
Company R owns 75% of Company S's common stock, but none of Company S's 20,000 shares of $5 par value, 6%, cumulative preferred stock. Company S had retained earnings of $63,400 at December 31, 1990. Company S's preferred stock dividends were two years in arrears at December 31, 1990. Company S reported net income of $38,000 for 1991 and declared and paid dividends totaling $25,000 during that year.

Required

1. The amount of retained earnings allocated to Company S's common stock in the December 31, 1991 consolidation worksheet is
   a. $51,400
   b. $58,400
   c. $63,400
   d. $64,400

2. Under the equity method, Company R records income from its investment in Company S's common stock in 1991 of
   a. $ 5,250
   b. $15,000
   c. $24,000
   d. $28,500

PROBLEMS

PROBLEM 11-1

Company A purchased 80% of Company B's common stock for $3,396,000 on May 1, 1988, when Company B had retained earnings of $510,000. The excess of cost over book value is treated as goodwill from consolidation and is being amortized over 10 years. Company A accounts for its investment in Company B under the equity method. The following balances appear in Company B's April 30, 1991 preclosing trial balance.

8% Cumulative Preferred Stock	$2,000,000
Common Stock	3,000,000
Additional Paid-in Capital: Common	375,000
Retained Earnings	980,000

Company B reported net income of $195,000 for the year ended April 30, 1991. Company B's last dividend declaration was in April 1987.

During the year ended April 30, 1991, Company A purchased merchandise from Company B for $183,300, of which $19,700 remained unpaid at year end. Company A's April 30, 1990 and April 30, 1991 inventories contained goods purchased from Company B of $19,000 and $17,000, respectively. Company B sells to Company A at 25% above cost. Both affiliates use perpetual inventory systems.

Required

Prepare schedules of goodwill and eliminations to accompany the April 30, 1991 consolidation worksheet.

PROBLEM 11-2

On April 1, 1991, Company C purchased 70,000 of Company D's 100,000 shares of $5 par value common stock for $668,100. On December 31, 1991, Company C purchased 1,000 of Company D's 10,000 shares of $50 par value, 6%, cumulative preferred stock for $57,750. Company D's preferred stock dividends were one year in arrears at December 31, 1990. Changes in Company D's retained earnings are shown below.

Balance, 1/1/91	$ 294,000
Net Income, 1991	106,000
Balance, 12/31/91	400,000
Dividends, 11/30/92	(120,000)
Net Income, 1992	184,000
Balance, 12/31/92	$ 464,000

Any excess of cost over book value is treated as goodwill from consolidation, amortized over 10 years. Company C accounts for its investment in Company D under the equity method. Company C reported 1992 net income from its own operations of $203,700.

On September 30, 1991, Company D sold machinery with a net book value of $112,500 to Company C for $172,500. Company C is depreciating the equipment using the straight-line method, over 10 years, with a $10,200 salvage value.

Required

1. Present Company C's equity method journal entries for 1992.
2. Prepare all schedules in support of the December 31, 1992 consolidation worksheet.

PROBLEM 11-3

On July 1, 1991, Company E purchased 36,000 shares of Company F's common stock for $269,400 and 3,000 shares of Company F's 6%, cumulative preferred stock for $34,800. Company F's preferred stock dividends were one year in arrears at December 31, 1990 and its Retained Earnings balance was $72,000 at that date. Company F reported net income of $12,000 in 1991, and did not declare any dividends in that year. Any excess of cost over book value is treated as goodwill from consolidation, amortized over 10 years. The December 31, 1992 trial balances of the two affiliates appear below.

	Company E	Company F
Investment in Company F: Common	$ 317,100	
Investment in Company F: Preferred	32,100	
Other Assets	470,800	$ 438,000
Cost of Goods Sold	192,000	68,000
Expenses	120,000	32,000
Dividends Declared: Common	22,000	20,000
Dividends Declared: Preferred		18,000
	$1,154,000	$ 576,000
Liabilities	$ 176,200	$ 16,000
Common Stock, $5 par	400,000	200,000
Preferred Stock, $10 par		100,000
Retained Earnings	161,000	84,000
Sales	352,000	176,000
Income from Company F: Common	63,000	
Income from Company F: Preferred	1,800	
	$1,154,000	$ 576,000

During 1992, Company F sold merchandise to Company E for $82,100, of which $7,800 remained unpaid at year end. Company E's beginning and ending inventories for 1992 contained goods purchased from Company F of $9,800 and $7,350, respectively. Company F sells to Company E at 40% above cost.

Required
Prepare the December 31, 1992 consolidation worksheet, supported by all appropriate schedules.

PROBLEM 11-4
The December 31, 1993 trial balances of Company G and Company H appear below.

	Company G	Company H
Investment in Company H: Common	$ 277,500	
Investment in Company H Bonds	196,220	
Other Assets	445,780	$ 977,300
Cost of Goods Sold	184,000	91,200
Expenses	171,000	99,800
Discount on Bonds Payable		12,600
Dividends Declared: Common	35,000	22,000
Dividends Declared: Preferred		18,000
	$1,309,500	$1,220,900
Current Liabilities	$ 153,000	$ 49,800
Bonds Payable		500,000
Common Stock, $5 par	500,000	200,000
Additional Paid-in Capital: Common	100,000	50,000
Preferred Stock, $10 par		100,000
Retained Earnings	124,000	72,100
Sales	399,100	249,000
Dividend Revenue	16,500	
Interest Revenue	16,900	
	$1,309,500	$1,220,900

On April 1, 1992, Company G purchased 30,000 shares of Company H's common stock for $277,500. Dividends on Company H's 6%, cumulative preferred stock were one year in arrears at December 31, 1991 and its Retained Earnings balance was $39,300. Company H reported net income of $32,800 for 1992, and did not declare any dividends in 1992. Any excess of cost over book value is treated as goodwill from consolidation, amortized over 10 years.

On July 1, 1992, Company G acquired 40% of Company H's 8% bonds payable, which mature on March 31, 1999 and on which interest is payable on March 31 and September 30.

Required
Prepare the December 31, 1993 consolidation worksheet, supported by all appropriate schedules.

PROBLEM 11-5
On July 1, 1991, Company J purchased 40,000 shares of Company K's common stock for $486,400 and 2,000 shares of Company K's 6%, cumulative preferred stock for $21,800. Company K's preferred stock dividends were one year in arrears at December 31, 1990 and its Retained Earnings balance on that date was $46,000. Company K reported 1991 net income of $36,000, and did not declare any

dividends in 1991. Any excess of cost over book value is treated as goodwill from consolidation amortized over 10 years.

During 1992, Company K sold merchandise to Company J for $62,600, of which $7,100 remained unpaid at year end. Company J's beginning and ending inventories for 1992 contained goods purchased from Company K of $11,000 and $10,000, respectively. Company K sells to Company J at 25% above cost. The December 31, 1992 trial balances of the two affiliates appear below.

	Company J	Company K
Investment in Company K: Common	$ 542,400	
Investment in Company K: Preferred	23,600	
Other Assets	654,000	$ 846,000
Cost of Goods Sold	199,000	93,000
Expenses	143,000	43,000
	$1,562,000	$ 982,000
Liabilities	$ 164,800	$ 103,000
Common Stock, $10 par	800,000	500,000
Preferred Stock, $10 par		100,000
Retained Earnings	139,000	82,000
Sales	413,000	197,000
Income from Company K: Common	44,000	
Income from Company K: Preferred	1,200	
	$1,562,000	$ 982,000

Required

Prepare the December 31, 1992 consolidation worksheet, supported by all appropriate schedules.

PROBLEM 11-6

On August 31, 1991, Company L purchased 16,000 shares of Company M's common stock for $432,800. On December 31, 1991, Company L purchased 3,000 shares of Company M's preferred stock for $51,100. Dividends on Company M's 6%, cumulative preferred stock were one year in arrears at December 31, 1990 and its Retained Earnings balance was $44,800. Company M reported net income of $46,800 for 1991, and did not declare any dividends in 1991. The December 31, 1993 trial balances of Company L and Company M appear below.

	Company L	Company M
Current Assets	$ 313,700	$ 237,400
Plant and Equipment	882,700	1,083,800
Investment in Company M: Common	504,560	
Investment in Company M: Preferred	47,500	
Investment in Company M: Bonds	152,900	
Cost of Goods Sold	254,300	187,600
Depreciation Expense	72,400	66,700
Other Expenses	119,260	102,800
Dividends Declared: Common	35,000	20,000
Dividends Declared: Preferred		24,000
	$2,382,320	$1,722,300

	Company L	Company M
Accumulated Depreciation	$ 188,300	$ 212,800
Current Liabilities	212,100	66,100
Bonds Payable		500,000
Premium on Bonds Payable		11,600
Common Stock, $5 par	500,000	100,000
Additional Paid-in Captial: Common	600,000	150,000
Preferred Stock, $10 par		100,000
Additional Paid-in Capital: Preferred		25,000
Retained Earnings	276,420	134,200
Sales	543,200	422,600
Interest Revenue	12,900	
Income from Company M: Common	47,600	
Income from Company M: Preferred	1,800	
	$2,382,320	$1,722,300

Any excess of cost over book value is treated as goodwill from consolidation, amortized over 10 years.

On September 1, 1992, Company L acquired 30% of Company M's 9% bonds payable, which mature on October 31, 1998 and on which interest is payable on April 30 and October 31.

On June 30, 1992, Company M sold equipment with a net book value of $62,300 to Company L for $102,300. Company L is depreciating the equipment using the straight-line method, over 5 years, with an $11,000 salvage value.

Required
Prepare the December 31, 1993 consolidation worksheet, supported by all appropriate schedules.

PROBLEM 11-7
On November 30, 1986, Company P purchased 24,000 shares of Company Q's common stock for $619,600. Company Q's preferred stock dividends were one year in arrears at May 31, 1986 and its Retained Earnings balance on that date was $109,300. Company Q reported net income of $42,400 for the year ended May 31, 1987. Company Q declared dividends totaling $28,000 on April 12, 1987 and paid them on May 15, 1987. Company Q's preferred stock dividends were not in arrears at May 31, 1990. Any excess of cost over book value is treated as goodwill from consolidation, amortized over 10 years.

During the year ended May 31, 1991, Company Q sold merchandise to Company P for $122,400, of which $10,100 remained unpaid at year end. Company P's May 31, 1990 inventory contained goods purchased from Company Q of $9,800; its May 31, 1991 inventory contained goods purchased from Company Q of $9,100. Company Q sells at Company P at 40% above cost. The May 31, 1991 trial balances of the two affiliates appear below.

	Company P	Company Q
Current Assets	$ 398,700	$ 296,800
Plant and Equipment	980,400	913,600
Investment in Company Q: Common	619,600	
Cost of Goods Sold	493,200	481,600
Depreciation Expense	82,900	71,600
Other Expenses	342,500	274,400
Dividends Declared: Common	65,000	45,000
Dividends Declared: Preferred		6,000
	$2,982,300	$2,089,000
Accumulated Depreciation	$ 382,500	$ 134,900
Liabilities	426,100	256,500
Common Stock, $10 par	500,000	300,000
Additional Paid-in Capital: Common	330,000	200,000
6% Preferred Stock, $10 par		100,000
Additional Paid-in Capital: Preferred		20,000
Retained Earnings	254,800	184,500
Sales	1,052,900	893,100
Dividend Revenue	36,000	
	$2,982,300	$2,089,000

Required

Prepare the May 31, 1991 consolidation worksheet, supported by all appropriate schedules.

PROBLEM 11-8

On August 1, 1990, Company R acquired 80% of Company S's common stock for $400,800. At January 31, 1990, Company S had retained earnings of $44,000 and was one year in arrears on the dividends on its 8%, cumulative preferred stock. Company S's net income for the year ended January 31, 1991 was $38,000. Company S declared no dividends during the years ended January 31, 1991 and January 31, 1992. The following balances appear on Company S's preclosing trial balance at January 31, 1992.

Preferred Stock, $100 par	$ 100,000
Common Stock, $10 par	300,000
Additional Paid-in Capital: Common	75,000
Retained Earnings	82,000

Company S reported net income of $46,000 for the year ended January 31, 1992. Company R accounts for its investments in Company S under the equity method. The excess of cost over book value is attributed to goodwill from consolidation and is being amortized over 10 years.

Required

Prepare schedules of the excess of cost over book value and of all eliminations to accompany the January 31, 1992 consolidation worksheet.

PROBLEM 11-9

On July 1, 1991, Company T purchased 80,000 shares of Company U's common stock for $972,800. Company U's preferred stock dividends were one year in arrears at December 31, 1990 and its Retained Earnings balance on that date was $92,000. Company U reported 1991 net income of $72,000, and did not declare any dividends in 1991. Any excess of cost over book value is treated as goodwill from consolidation, amortized over 10 years.

During 1992, Company T sold merchandise to Company U for $123,600, of which $14,200 remainded unpaid at year end. Company U's beginning and ending inventories for 1992 contained goods purchased from Company T of $22,500 and $19,500, respectively. Company T sells to Company U at 25% above cost.

On September 30, 1991, Company U sold equipment with a book value of $117,400 to Company T for $197,400. Company T is depreciating the equipment over a 5-year life beginning on the date of purchase, using the straight-line method, with a $25,700 salvage value. The December 31, 1992 trial balances of the two affiliates appear below.

	Company T	Company U
Investment in Company K: Common	$1,065,600	
Plant and Equipment	922,100	$1,063,600
Other Assets	402,300	797,500
Cost of Goods Sold	420,300	306,300
Expenses	296,400	166,200
Dividends Declared: Preferred		36,000
Dividends Declared: Common	50,000	24,000
	$3,156,700	$2,393,600
Accumulated Depreciation	$ 332,700	$ 229,800
Liabilities	329,600	204,300
Common Stock, $5 par	700,000	500,000
Additional Paid-in Capital: Common	600,000	500,000
6% Preferred Stock, $10 par		200,000
Retained Earnings	278,100	165,000
Sales	828,300	594,500
Income from Company K: Common	88,000	
	$3,156,700	$2,393,600

Required

Prepare the December 31, 1992 consolidation worksheet, supported by all appropriate schedules.

SOLUTION TO REVIEW PROBLEM

Equity Method Journal Entries

8/1/90	Investment in Company Y: Common		272,600	
	Cash			272,600
12/31/90	Investment in Company Y: Common		8,400	
	Income from Company Y: Common			8,400
	70% × 5/12 × ($36,800 − $8,000)			
12/31/91	Investment in Company Y: Common		7,840	
	Income from Company Y: Common			7,840
	70%($19,200 − $8,000)			

12/31/91	Investment in Company Y: Preferred	51,200	
	Cash		51,200

12/15/92	Dividends Receivable	16,600	
	Investment in Company Y: Common		7,000
	Investment in Company Y: Preferred		9,600
	[70% × ($34,000 − $24,000) = $7,000]		
	[40% × $24,000 = $9,600]		

12/31/92	Investment in Company Y: Preferred	3,200	
	Income from Company Y: Preferred		3,200
	40%($8,000)		

12/31/92	Investment in Company Y: Common	28,910	
	Income from Company Y: Common		28,910
	70%($49,300 − $8,000)		

Goodwill from Consolidation

	Investment in Company Y	
	Preferred Stock	Common Stock
Cost of Investment	$ 51,200	$ 272,600
Book Value	46,400 [a]	236,600 [b]
Goodwill at Acquisition	4,800	36,000
Amortization, 1990	—	(1,500)
Amortization, 1991	—	(3,600)
Amortization, 1992	(480)	(3,600)
Goodwill, 12/31/92	$ 4,320	$ 27,300

[a] 40%[$100,000 + $16,000]
[b] 70%[$200,000 + $80,000 + $41,200 + (7/12 × [$36,800 − $8,000])]

Eliminations

Intercompany Ownership Interests

[1]	Preferred Stock: Y	$ 40,000
[2]	Retained Earnings: Preferred: Y	6,400
[3]	Investment in Company Y: Preferred	$ (46,400)

[4]	Common Stock: Y	$ 140,000
[5]	Additional Paid-in Capital: Common: Y	56,000
[6]	Retained Earnings: Common: Y	56,840
[7]	Investment in Company Y: Common	$(252,840)

Subsidiary Income and Dividends

[8]	Income from Company Y: Preferred	$ 3,200
[9]	Dividends: Preferred: Y	(9,600)
[10]	Investment in Company Y: Preferred	$ 6,400

[11] Income from Company Y: Common	$ 28,910
[12] Dividends: Common: Y	(7,000)
[13] Investment in Company Y: Common	$ 21,910

Goodwill Amortization

[14] Expenses (Goodwill Amortization)	$ 480
[15] Investment in Company Y: Preferred	(480)

[16] Retained Earnings: X	$ 5,100
[17] Expenses (Goodwill Amortization)	3,600
[18] Investment in Company Y: Common	$ (8,700)

Income Allocation

Company X's Net Income		$ 35,000
Less: Goodwill Amortization		(4,080)
Company X's Adjusted Net Income		30,920
Company Y's Net Income	$ 49,300	
Less: Net Income to Preferred Stock	(8,000)	
Net Income to Common Stock	41,300	
Minority Interest: Common (30%)	12,390	
Company X's Share (70%)		28,910
Net Income to Preferred Stock	8,000	
Minority Interest: Preferred (60%)	4,800	
Company X's Share (40%)		3,200
Consolidated Net Income		$ 63,030

CHAPTER
12

CHANGES IN OWNERSHIP

U p to this point, all discussions, illustrations, exercises, and problems have been based on two assumptions: that the parent's percentage of ownership in the subsidiary does not change after its initial acquisition, and that the number of shares of the subsidiary's outstanding common stock does not change over time. Obviously, neither of these assumptions is necessarily true. In this chapter, we consider changes in ownership of four different types.

- More than one acquisition by the parent with control obtained on the first purchase
- More than one acquisition by the parent with less than significant influence obtained on the first purchase
- Sale of subsidiary common stock by the parent
- Transactions by the subsidiary in its own common stock

Each of these types of changes in ownership affects both the parent's accounting for its investment in the subsidiary and the consolidation process.

MULTIPLE ACQUISITIONS—CONTROL ON FIRST PURCHASE

A parent company may acquire a controlling interest in a subsidiary company on its first purchase of the subsidiary's common stock, and then add to that controlling interest through one or more subsequent purchases. The subsequent purchases affect both the parent's accounting for its investment in the subsidiary and the consolidation process. These effects are discussed in the following sections.

RECORDING UNDER THE COST AND EQUITY METHODS

Under both the cost method and the equity method, the parent company records each of its purchases of the subsidiary company's common stock at cost. In addition, the following guidelines apply.

- Under the equity method, the parent records its share of the subsidiary's net income according to the percentages of ownership in force during different segments of the year.[1]
- In order to allocate subsidiary net income to segments of the year, we will assume that it is earned proportionately throughout the year, unless better evidence is available.[2] For example, if the subsidiary is engaged in a highly seasonal business, that fact would be considered in allocating its net income to segments of the year. In addition, information available from the subsidiary's interim financial statements or from a purchase audit could influence that allocation.
- Under both the equity method and the cost method, the parent records its share of dividends declared by the subsidiary according to its percentage of ownership at the effective date of the dividends.

These procedures are demonstrated in Illustrative Problem 12.1.

CONSOLIDATION PROCEDURES

Multiple acquisitions of subsidiary common stock and acquisitions made during the year affect the consolidation process in a number of ways.

First, the Excess of Cost over Book Value (or Goodwill) schedule must be expanded horizontally, as shown in Exhibit 12-1. It contains a column for each block of subsidiary stock purchased by the parent, as well as a total column. An alternative, of course, would be to contruct a separate schedule for each block of subsidiary stock purchased by the parent. The calculation of the book value of each block of subsidiary stock is based on the subsidiary's total stockholders' equity (representing its net assets) at the date of acquisition.[3]

Therefore, the beginning of the year balance of the subsidiary's Retained Earnings must be adjusted for net income and, if applicable, dividends declared, from the first of the year through the date of acquisition, following the guidelines given above for recording changes in the parent's investment under the equity method.

Under both the cost method and the equity method, eliminations from the subsidiary's stockholders' equity balances in the Intercompany Ownership Interests set of eliminations are made at the parent's year-end percentage of ownership.

In the Subsidiary Income and Dividends set of eliminations, the amount eliminated from the parent's Income from Subsidiary (under the equity method) or Dividend Revenue (under the cost method) is the amount recorded for the year. The elimination from the subsidiary's Dividends Declared balance, however, is made at the parent's year-end percentage of ownership, regardless of the amount of subsidiary dividends actually recorded by the parent. The difference is eliminated from the parent's Investment in Subsidiary.

---

[1] *Accounting Research Bulletin No. 51, Consolidated Financial Statements* (New York: AICPA, 1959), paragraph 10.

[2] *ARB No. 51,* paragraph 10.

[3] *ARB No. 51,* paragraph 7.

All other eliminations involving the subsidiary's Retained Earnings are made using the year-end percentages of ownership. The reason for using the year-end percentages of ownership in making all eliminations involving subsidiary stockholders' equity balances (including Dividends Declared) lies in the fact that these balances yield minority interest residuals. The sum of these minority interest residuals is reported on the consolidated balance sheet, dated as of the end of each year. Because the minority interest percentage existing at the end of each year is a matter of fact, the minority interest amounts reported must accord with that precentage of ownership. This result can be accomplished only if we use the year-end percentages of ownership in making these eliminations.

In addition, under the equity method, at the end of any year during which the parent acquires subsidiary common stock, the amount of subsidiary net income that the parent has purchased from previous subsidiary stockholders necessitates a special set of eliminations. Income of Subsidiary Purchased is debited and Investment in Subsidiary is credited, both for an amount equal to (a) the percentage of ownership purchased multiplied by (b) the portion of the subsidiary's net income allocated to the segment of the year preceding the date of acquisition.

The Income of Subsidiary Purchased is entered on a separate added line on the consolidation worksheet and extended to the Income Statement debit column, where it reduces total net income. It is also reported on the consolidated income statement as a reduction in total net income.[4]

In the Income Allocation schedule, the Income of Subsidiary Purchased appears as a subtraction from the amount of subsidiary net income initially allocated to the parent. This treatment is explained in more detail in the solution to Illustrative Problem 12.1.

ILLUSTRATIVE PROBLEM 12.1: MULTIPLE ACQUISITIONS—CONTROL ON FIRST PURCHASE

Company A purchased 14,000 of Company B's 20,000 outstanding shares of $5 par value common stock on January 1, 1990 for $90,000 and an additional 4,000 shares on April 1, 1991 for $27,000. Comany B's common stock was issued at par in 1980. Any excess of cost over book value is treated as goodwill from consolidation and is being amortized over 10 years. Company A accounts for its investment in Company B under the equity method. Company A reported net income from its own operations of $35,000 in 1991. Changes in Company B's Retained Earnings balance for 1990 through 1992 are shown below.

Balance, 1/1/90	$ 20,000
Dividends Declared, 12/1/90	(5,000)
Net Income, 1990	10,000
Balance, 12/31/90	25,000
Dividends Declared, 12/1/91	(6,000)
Net Income, 1991	12,000
Balance, 12/31/91	31,000
Dividends Declared, 12/1/92	(7,500)
Net Income, 1992	15,000
Balance, 12/31/92	$ 38,500

[4] *ARB No. 51,* paragraph 11.

The following information is taken from Company A's Investment in Company B account.

Purchase, 1/1/90	$ 90,000
Dividends from Company B, 12/1/90	(3,500)
Income from Company B, 1990	7,000
Balance, 12/31/90	93,500
Purchase, 4/1/91	27,000
Dividends from Company B, 12/1/91	(5,400)
Income from Company B, 1991	10,200
Balance, 12/31/91	125,300
Dividends from Company B, 12/1/92	(6,750)
Income from Company B, 1992	13,500
Balance, 12/31/92	$132,050

Company A's share of Company B's dividends in each of the three years is based on the percentage of ownership in force at the dividend date—70% for 1990 and 90% for 1991 and 1992. Company A's share of Company B's net income for 1990 is based on the percentage of ownership in force throughout the year, 70%. The calculation for 1992 is similar, using the 90% interest that is effective throughout the year. For 1991, however, Company P's share, $10,200, is calculated as 70% for the first three months of the year plus 90% for the last nine months. This calculation can be expressed as

$$(70\% \times 3/12 \times \$12,000) + (90\% \times 9/12 \times \$12,000)$$

Exhibit 12-1 presents the multicolumn Goodwill from Consolidation schedule described earlier. The calculations of certain critical amounts are explained in more detail in the paragraphs immediately following Exhibit 12-1. The Total column of the schedule not only serves as a device to check arithmetic accuracy, but accumulates the prior and current years' amortization amounts to be included in the Goodwill Amortization set of eliminations.

The book value of the Company B common stock purchased on January 1, 1990 is calculated as Company A's percentage of ownership, 70%, multiplied by Company B's total stockholders' equity at that date (common stock of $100,000 plus retained earnings of $20,000). A full year's goodwill amortization, 12/120 of $6,000, is recognized in each of the three years covered in the schedule—1990, 1991, and 1992.

The book value of Company B common stock purchased on April 1, 1991 is calculated as Company A's percentage of ownership, 20%, multiplied by Company B's total stockholders' equity at that date. Company B's total stockholders' equity at April 1, 1991 consists of common stock of $100,000, plus retained earnings at January 1, 1991, of $25,000, plus 3/12 of Company B's $12,000 of 1991 net income. In 1991, only nine months' amortization, 9/120 of $1,400, is recognized. A full year's amortization, 12/120 of $1,400, however, is recognized in 1992.

The eliminations needed at December 31, 1990, 1991, and 1992 appear in Exhibit 12-2. These eliminations are presented in parallel columns to facilitate comparisons from year to year. In fact, of course, a separate schedule of eliminations would accompany each year's consolidation worksheet. Notice that the eliminations from Company B's Common Stock and Retained Earnings are made at Company A's end of the year percentage of ownership for each year, whether or not that percentage has changed during the year.

EXHIBIT 12-1

Illustrative Problem 12.1
Goodwill from Consolidation
December 31, 1992

Goodwill from Consolidation

	1/1/90 Purchase	4/1/91 Purchase	Total
Cost of Investment	$ 90,000		
Book Value	84,000		
Goodwill, 1/1/90	6,000		$ 6,000
Amortization, 1990	(600)		(600)
Goodwill, 12/31/90	5,400		5,400
Cost of Investment		$ 27,000	
Book Value		25,600	
Additional Goodwill, 4/1/91		1,400	1,400
Amortization, 1991	(600)	(105)	(705)
Goodwill, 12/31/91	4,800	1,295	6,095
Amortization, 1992	(600)	(140)	(740)
Goodwill, 12/31/92	$ 4,200	$ 1,155	$ 5,355

The amount eliminated from Income from Company B in each year is the amount recorded by Company A for that year. The eliminations from Company B's Dividends Declared for each year are made at Company A's end of the year percentage of ownership. Because Company A happened to hold its year-end percentage of ownership at the effective date of Company B's dividends in each year, the amount eliminated is also the amount recorded by Company A in that year. If in any year, however, Company A had purchased Company B common stock *after* the effective dividend date, the amounts recorded and eliminated would have been different. The actual effective date for dividends is the date of record, which falls between the declaration date and the date of payment. For the sake of simplicity, however, only a single dividend date is given in the illustrative problems, exercises, and problems in Chapters 12 and 13.

As noted earlier, the amounts of prior and current years' goodwill amortization appearing in the Goodwill Amortization set of eliminations are taken directly from the Total column of the Goodwill from Consolidation schedule.

The amount debited to Income of Company B Purchased and credited to Investment in Company B at December 31, 1991 is the portion of Company B's 1991 net income that Company A purchased from retiring Company B stockholders on April 1, 1991. It is calculated as 20% × 3/12 × $12,000. As explained earlier, the Income of Company B Purchased reduces total net income for 1991 and, accordingly, must be taken into account in allocating total net income.

In the Income Allocation schedule for the year ended December 31, 1991, which appears

EXHIBIT 12-2

Illustrative Problem 12.1
Eliminations

	12/31/90	12/31/91	12/31/92
Eliminations			
Intercompany Ownership Interests			
[1] Common Stock: B	$ 70,000	$ 90,000	$ 90,000
[2] Retained Earnings: B	14,000	22,500	27,900
[3] Investment in Company B	$(84,000)	$(112,500)	$(117,900)
Subsidiary Income and Dividends			
[4] Income from Company B	$ 7,000	$ 10,200	$ 13,500
[5] Dividends Declared: B	(3,500)	(5,400)	(6,750)
[6] Investment in Company B	$(3,500)	$(4,800)	$(6,750)
Goodwill Amortization			
[7] Retained Earnings: A	$ —	$ 600	$ 1,305
[8] Goodwill Amortization Expense	600	705	740
[9] Investment in Company B	$(600)	$(1,305)	$(2,045)
Income of Subsidiary Purchased			
[10] Income of Company B Purchased		$ 600	
[11] Investment in Company B		(600)	

in Exhibit 12-3, Company B's adjusted net income is allocated initially between the minority interest and consolidated net income on the basis of the end of the year percentages of ownership held by the minority stockholders and by Company A. This approach assures that the minority interest in Company B's net income will be stated properly. On the other hand, this approach allocates to consolidated net income an amount greater than the amount actually earned by Company A. For the first three months of 1991, Company A owned only 70% of Company B's common stock, rather than 90%. Thus, the income of Company B that Company A purchased from retiring Company B stockholders on April 1, 1991 must be subtracted from the amount of Company B's adjusted net income initially allocated to consolidated net income in arriving at Company A's *earned* share of Company B's adjusted net income.

Use of the Cost Method.   If Company A had used the cost method instead of the equity method during 1990, 1991, and 1992, the balance of its Investment in Company B account would have been $90,000 at December 31, 1990 and $117,000 at December 31, 1991 and 1992. At December 31, 1990, no conversion from cost to equity would have been necessary because Company A's Investment in Company B and Retained Earnings balances would have

EXHIBIT 12-3

Illustrative Problem 12.1
Income Allocation Schedule
Year Ended December 31, 1991

Income Allocation

Company A's Own Net Income		$ 35,000
Less: Goodwill Amortization Expense		705
Company A's Adjusted Net Income		34,295
Company B's Own Net Income	$ 12,000	
Minority Interest (10%)	1,200	
Company A's Share (90%)	10,800	
Less: Income of Company B Purchased	600	
Company A's Earned Share		10,200
Consolidated Net Income		$ 44,495

been the same under both methods as of January 1, 1990. The schedules of Conversion from Cost to Equity and the resulting worksheet adjustments needed at December 31, 1991 and 1992 are shown in Exhibit 12-4. In each year, the Conversion from Cost to Equity schedule would have followed the Goodwill from Consolidation schedule.

After making Adjustments A and B, the eliminations would have been the same as those made under the equity method, except for the Subsidiary Income and Dividends set, which appears in Exhibit 12-5.

MULTIPLE ACQUISITIONS—LESS THAN SIGNIFICANT INFLUENCE ON FIRST PURCHASE

A parent company may acquire its ownership interest in a subsidiary company through several purchases, with less than a controlling interest, or, indeed, less than significant influence, being obtained on the first purchase. The effects of such a sequence of purchases on both the parent's (or investor's) accounting for its investment in the subsidiary (or investee) and the resulting financial statements are discussed and illustrated below.

An investment in common stock representing less than a controlling interest in the investee is subject to the provisions of *Accounting Principles Board Opinion No. 18.*[5] Thus the investor's treatment of its investment will vary, depending on the investor's percentage of ownership, as discussed below.

As investor owning between 20% and 50% of the common stock of an investee is presumed to exercise significant influence over the investee and, accordingly, must account for and report its investment under the equity method, as described in *APB Opinion No. 18.*

[5] *Accounting Principles Board Opinion No. 18, The Equity Method of Accounting for Investments in Common Stock* (New York: AICPA, 1959).

EXHIBIT 12-4

Illustrative Problem 12.1
Conversion from Cost to Equity and Adjustments

At December 31, 1991:

Conversion from Cost to Equity

70% of Company B's Stockholders' Equity, 1/1/91	$ 87,500
70% of Company B's Stockholders' Equity, 1/1/90	84,000
Increase in Company A's Equity in Company B	$ 3,500

Adjustments

A. Investment in Company B	$ 3,500
B. Retained Earnings: A	(3,500)

At December 31, 1992:

Conversion from Cost to Equity

90% of Company B's Stockholders' Equity, 1/1/92		$ 117,900
70% of Company B's Stockholders' Equity, 1/1/90	$ 84,000	
20% of Company B's Stockholders' Equity, 4/1/91	25,600	109,600
Increase in Company A's Equity in Company B		$ 8,300

Adjustments

A. Investment in Company B	$ 8,300
B. Retained Earnings: A	(8,300)

EXHIBIT 12-5

Illustrative Problem 12.1
Eliminations

	12/31/90	12/31/91	12/31/92
Eliminations			
Subsidiary Income and Dividends			
[4] Dividend Revenue	$ 3,500	$ 5,400	$ 6,750
[5] Dividends Declared: B	(3,500)	(5,400)	(6,750)

Thus, the subsequent acquisition of a controlling interest would be treated in the same manner as an increase in a controlling interest discussed in the preceding section and demonstrated in Illustrative Problem 12.1. The only differences would be

- consolidated financial statements would not be prepared before control is attained, and
- amortization of the difference between cost and book value would be recorded on the investor's books rather than accomplished on successive consolidation worksheets.

If the investor acquires less than 20% of the investee's common stock, the investment should be accounted for and reported under the cost method. When, through a subsequent purchase, the investor obtains either significant influence or control, the use of the equity method becomes appropriate. At that point, the investor (or parent) would *record* the conversion from cost to equity previously discussed and illustrated as a worksheet adjustment. Alternatively, the investor (or parent) could continue to account for its investment under the cost method and adjust to the equity basis for reporting purposes.

After a controlling interest is acquired, the consolidation worksheet adjustments and eliminations are made in the same manner discussed in the preceding section and shown in Illustrative Problem 12.2.

ILLUSTRATIVE PROBLEM 12.2: MULTIPLE ACQUISITIONS—LESS THAN SIGNIFICANT INFLUENCE ON FIRST PURCHASE

Company C purchased 1,000 of Company D's 10,000 shares of $10 par value common stock on April 1, 1990 for $15,300 and an additional 6,000 shares on July 1, 1992 for $101,400. Company D's common stock was issued originally in 1982 at 11. Changes in Company D's Retained Earnings balance for the period 1990 through 1992 are shown below.

Balance, 1/1/90	$ 20,500
Dividends, 12/1/90	(5,000)
Net Income, 1990	10,000
Balance, 12/31/90	25,500
Dividends, 12/1/91	(6,000)
Net Income, 1991	12,000
Balance, 12/31/91	31,500
Dividends, 12/1/92	(7,500)
Net Income, 1992	15,000
Balance, 12/31/92	$ 39,000

Any excess of cost over book value is considered to be goodwill from consolidation and is to be amortized over 10 years. Until it converts to the equity method after attaining control on the second purchase, Company C does not recognize any amortization.

The journal entries recorded on Company C's books to account for its investment in Company D's common stock for 1990, 1991, and 1992 are shown in Exhibit 12-6. Company C records its share of Company D's 1990 and 1991 dividends under the cost method and, accordingly, credits Dividend Revenue. (Because the problem gives only the single effective dividend date for each year, December 1, the journal entries are presented as if December 1 is the payment date and Company C records dividends when received.) By December 1, 1992, however, Company C has converted to the equity method and the dividends are credited to Investment in Company D.

EXHIBIT 12-6

Illustrative Problem 12.2
Cost and Equity Method Journal Entries

4/1/90	Investment in Company D	15,300	
	Cash		15,300
	Purchase of 1,000 shares of Company D common stock		
12/1/90	Cash	500	
	Dividend Revenue		500
	Dividend from Company D (10% × $5,000)		
12/1/91	Cash	600	
	Dividend Revenue		600
	Dividend from Company D (10% × $6,000)		
7/1/92	Investment in Company D	101,400	
	Cash		101,400
	Purchase of 6,000 shares of Company D common stock		
7/1/92	Investment in Company D	850	
	Retained Earnings		850
	Conversion from the cost method to the equity method [10%($141,500 − $133,000)]		
12/1/92	Cash	5,250	
	Investment in Company D		5,250
	Dividend from Company D (70% × $7,500)		
12/31/92	Investment in Company D	6,000	
	Income from Company D		6,000
	Income from Company D [(10% × 6/12 × $15,000) + (70% × 6/12 × $15,000)]		

As indicated in Exhibit 12-6, the amount of the conversion from cost to equity is calculated as 10% of the change in Company D's total stockholders' equity from the date of acquisition of the original investment, April 1, 1990, to the beginning of the year in which control was obtained, January 1, 1992. Company D's total stockholders' equity at April 1, 1990 consists of common stock of $100,000, plus additional paid-in capital of $10,000, plus retained earnings at January 1, 1990 of $20,500, plus 3/12 of Company D's $10,000 of 1990 net income, for a total of $133,000. Company D's total stockholders' equity at January 1, 1992 consists of common stock of $100,000, plus additional paid-in capital of $10,000, plus retained earnings at January 1, 1992 of $31,500, for a total of $141,500. After making this adjustment, Company

C records its share of Company D's net income for 1992 under the equity method, according to its percentage of ownership held during the different portions of the year.

Assuming that Company C retroactively recognizes amortization for 1990 and 1991 of the goodwill on its first purchase of Company D common stock, the goodwill schedule to accompany the December 31, 1992 consolidation worksheet appears in Exhibit 12-7.

EXHIBIT 12-7

Illustrative Problem 12.2
Goodwill from Consolidation
December 31, 1992

Goodwill from Consolidation

	4/1/90 Purchase	7/1/92 Purchase	Total
Cost of Investment	$ 15,300		
Book Value	13,300		
Goodwill, 4/1/90	2,000		$ 2,000
Amortization, 1990–1991	(350)		(350)
Goodwill, 12/31/91	1,650		1,650
Cost of Investment		$ 101,400	
Book Value		89,400	
Additional Goodwill, 7/1/92		12,000	12,000
Amortization, 1992	(200)	(600)	(800)
Goodwill, 12/31/92	$ 1,450	$ 11,400	$ 12,850

The book value of the Company D common stock purchased on April 1, 1990 is calculated as Company C's percentage of ownership, 10%, multiplied by Company D's total stockholders' equity at that date. Company D's total stockholders' equity at April 1, 1990 consists of common stock of $100,000, plus additional paid-in capital of $10,000, plus retained earnings at January 1, 1990 of $20,500, plus 3/12 of Company D's $10,000 of 1990 net income. Goodwill amortization recognized through the end of 1991 is 21/120 of $2,000. A full year's amortization, 12/120 of $2,000, is recognized in 1992.

The book value of the Company D common stock purchased on July 1, 1992 is calculated as Company C's percentage of ownership, 60%, multiplied by Company D's total stockholders' equity at that date. Company D's total stockholders' equity at July 1, 1992 consists of common stock of $100,000 plus additional paid-in capital of $10,000, plus retained earnings at January 1, 1992 of $31,500, plus 6/12 of Company D's $15,000 of 1992 net income. In 1992, only six months' amortization, 6/120 of $12,000, is recognized.

Consolidated financial statements for Companies C and D are not prepared until 1992, when Company C attains control over Company D. The worksheet eliminations at December 31, 1992 are shown in Exhibit 12-8.

EXHIBIT 12-8

Illustrative Problem 12.2
Eliminations
December 31, 1992

Eliminations

Intercompany Ownership Interests

[1]	Common Stock: D	$ 70,000
[2]	Additional Paid-in Capital: D	7,000
[3]	Retained Earnings: D	22,050
[4]	Investment in Company D	$(99,050)

Subsidiary Income and Dividends

[5]	Income from Company D	$ 6,000
[6]	Dividends Declared: D	(5,250)
[7]	Investment in Company D	$(750)

Goodwill Amortization

[8]	Retained Earnings: C	$ 350
[9]	Goodwill Amortization	800
[10]	Investment in Company D	$(1,150)

Income of Subsidiary Purchased

[11]	Income of Company D Purchased	$ 4,500
[12]	Investment in Company D	(4,500)

SALE OF SUBSIDIARY COMMON STOCK BY THE PARENT

The parent company's ownership interest in a subsidiary company also may change as a result of the sale of subsidiary common stock by the parent. Such a transaction affects both the parent's accounting for its investment in the subsidiary and the consolidation process. These effects are discussed in the following sections.

ACCOUNTING FOR THE INVESTMENT

When the parent sells part of its investment in the subsidiary's common stock, a gain or loss on the sale must be recorded. This gain or loss is determined as the difference between (a) the proceeds from the sale and (b) the net carrying value of the shares sold. Thus, whenever the parent has acquired its investment in the subsidiary through more than one purchase preceding the sale, a cost flow assumption must be adopted in order to determine the net carrying value of the shares sold. Because the first in, first out (FIFO) assumption is common used, it also is used uniformly throughout this book.

Under the equity method, the net carrying value of the shares sold is composed of [a] the cost of the shares (as determined using FIFO), plus or minus [b] the changes in the parent's equity in those shares since the date of acquisition, minus [c] amortization of the difference between cost and book value applicable to those shares. Therefore, if the sale occurs during a year, the net carrying value of the shares sold must be adjusted for subsidiary net income (or net loss) and, when applicable, subsidiary dividends, as well as for amortization of the difference between cost and book value, from the beginning of the year through the date of sale.

Under the cost method, the net carrying value of the shares sold is merely the cost of those shares (as determined under FIFO), adjusted for amortization of the difference between cost and book value through the date of sale. The calculation of the gain or loss on the sale of subsidiary common stock under both methods is shown in Illustrative Problem 12.3.

The parent records its share of the subsidiary's net income and dividends under the equity method (or dividends under the cost method) in essentially the same manner as described and illustrated in the preceding sections, except that a sale of subsidiary common stock causes the parent's percentage of ownership to decrease rather than increase.

CONSOLIDATION PROCEDURES

The sale of subsidiary common stock made during the year affects the consolidation process in a number of ways. First, as noted in the preceding section, the carrying value of shares of subsidiary common stock sold, which is credited to the parent's Investment in Subsidiary account in recording the sale, must be reduced by the amortization of the excess of cost over book value applicable to those shares. Accordingly, in the Goodwill schedule, in the column for the block of subsidiary common stock with which the shares sold are associated, the amortization of goodwill must be recognized to the date of sale. The goodwill related to the shares sold is then subtracted from the resulting balance of goodwill for that block of common stock. All subsequent amortization of goodwill on that block of common stock is calculated in reference to the remainder of that block held by the parent company.

Under both methods, eliminations from the subsidiary's stockholders' equity balances in the Intercompany Ownership Interests set of eliminations are made at the parent's percentage of ownership existing at the end of the year. In the Subsidiary Income and Dividends set of eliminations, the amount eliminated from the parent's Income from Subsidiary (under the equity method) or Dividend Revenue (under the cost method) is the amount recorded for the year. The elimination from the subsidiary's Dividends Declared balance, however, is made at the parent's year-end percentage of ownership, regardless of the amount of subsidiary dividends actually recorded by the parent. The difference is eliminated from the parent's Investment in Subsidiary. All other eliminations involving the subsidiary's Retained Earnings are made using the year-end percentages of ownership.

In addition, under the equity method, at the end of any year during which the parent sells subsidiary common stock, the subsidiary net income that the parent has sold to new subsidiary stockholders necessitates a special set of eliminations. Income of Subsidiary Sold is the counterpart of Income of Subsidiary Purchased, discussed earlier and illustrated in Exhibit 12-2. Investment in Subsidiary is debited and Income of Subsidiary Sold is credited, both for an amount equal to (a) the percentage of ownership sold multiplied by (b) the portion of the subsidiary's net income applicable to the segment of the year preceding the date of sale.

The Income of Subsidiary Sold is entered on a separate added line on the consolidation worksheet and extended to the Income Statement credit column, where it increases total net income. It is also reported on the consolidated income statement as an increase in total net income. In the Income Allocation schedule, the Income of Subsidiary Sold appears as an addition to the amount of subsidiary net income initially allocated to the parent.

ILLUSTRATIVE PROBLEM 12.3: SALE OF SUBSIDIARY STOCK

Illustrative Problem 12.3 is a continuation of Illustrative Problem 12.1, the substance of which is repeated here to refresh your memory. Additional information also is given.

Company A purchased 14,000 of Company B's 20,000 outstanding shares of $5 par value common stock on January 1, 1990 for $90,000 and an additional 4,000 shares on April 1, 1991 for $27,000. Company B's common stock was issued at par in 1982. Any excess of cost over book value is treated as goodwill from consolidation and is being amortized over 10 years. Company A accounts for its investment in Company B under the equity method. In addition, Company A sold 2,800 shares of Company B's common stock for $23,000 on September 30, 1993. Company A reported net income from its own operations of $52,600 in 1993. Changes in Company B's Retained Earnings balance for 1990 through 1993 appear below.

Balance, 1/1/90	$ 20,000
Dividends Declared, 12/1/90	(5,000)
Net Income, 1990	10,000
Balance, 12/31/90	25,000
Dividends Declared, 12/1/91	(6,000)
Net Income, 1991	12,000
Balance, 12/31/91	31,000
Dividends Declared, 12/1/92	(7,500)
Net Income, 1992	15,000
Balance, 12/31/92	38,500
Dividends Declared, 12/1/93	(10,000)
Net Income, 1993	16,000
Balance, 12/31/93	$ 44,500

Using the FIFO cost flow assumption, the gain on the sale of the Company B common stock on September 30, 1993 can be determined as follows:

Proceeds of Sale		$ 23,000
Original Cost	$ 18,000 [1]	
Increase in Equity, 1/1/90–12/31/92	2,590 [2]	
Income of Company B Sold	1,680 [4]	
Less: Amortization of Goodwill, 1/1/90–9/30/93	(450) [3]	
Net Carrying Value		21,820
Gain on Sale		$ 1,180

[1] 28/140 × $90,000
[2] 14% × ($138,500 − $120,000)
[3] 28/140 × 45/120 × $6,000
[4] 14% × 9/12 × $16,000

This calculation is retrospective; that is, it is made after December 31, 1993. Therefore, the amount of Company B's 1993 net income is known and can be included in determining the carrying value of the shares sold. In order to record the transaction at September 30, 1993, Company A's accountant would need either to estimate or to omit the 1993 net income component. The easiest approach is to omit it and record the following journal entry:

Cash	23,000	
Investment in Company B		20,140
Gain on Sale of Company B Stock		2,860

Then, when the amount of Company B's 1993 net income is known, another journal can be made to correct the original one, as follows:

Gain on Sale of Company B Stock	1,680	
Investment in Company B		1,680

The net result is to reduce Company A's Investment in Company B balance by $21,820 and to record a gain of $1,180, as determined in the retrospective calculation.

If Company A had accounted for its investment in Company B under the cost method, the gain on sale would have been calculated as shown below. The difference between the two "gain" amounts is the amount of increase in Company A's equity in Company B already recognized under the equity method, plus the portion of Company B's 1993 net income identified with the shares sold.

Proceeds of Sale		$ 23,000
Original Cost	$ 18,000	
Less: Amortization of Goodwill, 1/1/90–9/30/93	(450)	
Net Carrying Value		17,550
Gain on Sale		$ 5,450

Changes in Company A's Investment in Company B account from January 1, 1990 through December 31, 1993 are shown below.

Purchase, 1/1/90	$ 90,000
Dividends from Company B, 12/1/90	(3,500)
Income from Company B, 1990	7,000
Balance, 12/31/90	93,500
Purchase 4/1/91	27,000
Dividends from Company B, 12/1/91	(5,400)
Income from Company B, 1991	10,200
Balance, 12/31/91	125,300
Dividends from Company B, 12/1/92	(6,750)
Income from Company B, 1992	13,500
Balance, 12/31/92	132,050
Sale of Company B Stock, 9/30/93	(21,820)
Dividends from Company B, 12/1/93	(7,600)
Income from Company B, 1993	13,840
Balance, 12/31/93	$116,470

The determination of Company A's share of Company B's dividends and net income for 1990, 1991, and 1992 is described in Illustrative Problem 12.1. Company A's share of Company B's 1993 dividends is based on the percentage of ownership in force at the dividend date, 76%. Company A's share of Company B's net income for 1993 is based on the percentage of ownership in force during different portions of the year—90% for the first nine months of the year, plus 76% for the last three months. This calculation can be expressed as:

$$(90\% \times 9/12 \times \$16,000) + (76\% \times 3/12 \times \$16,000)$$

Exhibit 12-9 presents the multicolumn Goodwill from Consolidation schedule to accompany the December 31, 1993 consolidation worksheet. Through the balance of goodwill at December 31, 1992, this schedule replicates that appearing in Exhibit 12-1. Beyond that point, the amortization of each of the goodwill amounts is recognized through September 30, 1993 (9/120 of the goodwill at acquisition in each case). The amount related to the Company B shares sold on September 30, 1993 is the fraction of the January 1, 1990 purchase sold, 28/140, multiplied by the September 30, 1993 balance of the goodwill on that block of Company B stock. The amortization of goodwill on the January 1, 1990 block for the remainder of 1993 is based on the fraction of that block remaining (112/140 × 3/120 × $6,000). All subsequent amortization also will be based on that fraction. The amortization of goodwill on the April 1, 1991 purchase for the remainder of 1993 is simply 3/120 of the goodwill at acquisition.

The eliminations needed at December 31, 1993 appear in Exhibit 12-10. The eliminations from Company B's Common Stock and Retained Earnings in the Intercompany Ownership set of eliminations are made at Company A's year-end percentage of ownership, 76%, even though that percentage has changed during the year.

In the Subsidiary Income and Dividends set of eliminations, the amount eliminated from Income from Company B is the amount recorded by Company A for the year. The elimination from Company B's Dividends Declared balance is made at Company A's year-end percentage of ownership. In this case, the amount eliminated from Company B's Dividends Declared balance, $7,600, also is the amount of dividends from Company B recorded by Company A during 1993. If the effective date of the dividends had been before the sale of the Company B common stock, however, these amounts would be different.

EXHIBIT 12-9

Illustrative Problem 12.3
Goodwill from Consolidation
December 31, 1993

Goodwill from Consolidation

	1/1/90 Purchase	4/1/91 Purchase	Total
Cost of Investment	$ 90,000		
Book Value	84,000		
Goodwill, 1/1/90	6,000		$ 6,000
Amortization, 1990	(600)		(600)
Goodwill, 12/31/90	5,400		5,400
Cost of Investment		$ 27,000	
Book Value		25,600	
Additional Goodwill, 4/1/91		1,400	1,400
Amortization, 1991	(600)	(105)	(705)
Goodwill, 12/31/91	4,800	1,295	6,095
Amortization, 1992	(600)	(140)	(740)
Goodwill, 12/31/92	4,200	1,155	5,355
Amortization, 1/1/93–9/30/93	(450)	(105)	(555)
Goodwill, 9/30/93	3,750	1,050	4,800
Amount Related to Shares Sold	(750)		(750)
Amortization, 9/30/93–12/31/93	(120)	(35)	(155)
Goodwill, 12/31/93	$ 2,880	$ 1,015	$ 3,895

As noted earlier, the amounts of prior and current years' goodwill amortization appearing in the Goodwill Amortization set of eliminations are taken directly from the Total column of the Goodwill from Consolidation schedule.

The amount debited to Investment in Company B and credited to Income of Company B Sold is the portion of Company B's 1993 net income that Company A sold on September 30, 1993. It is calculated as $14\% \times 9/12 \times \$16,000$. As explained earlier, the Income of Company B Sold appears in the Income Allocation schedule as an adjustment to the share of Company B's net income initially allocated to Company A, as shown in Exhibit 12-11.

TRANSACTIONS BY A SUBSIDIARY IN ITS OWN COMMON STOCK

Both the parent's percentage of ownership and the book value of its investment in a subsidiary may change as a result of the subsidiary's transactions in its own common stock in which the parent does not participate, either in proportion to its ownership interest or at all. The types of transactions that can cause such a change include

- issuance of new shares of common stock,

- acquisition of shares of common stock from minority interest stockholders, and
- reissuance of common treasury shares.

Such transactions by the subsidiary can affect both the parent's accounting for its investment and the consolidation process. These effects are discussed and illustrated in the following sections.

ACCOUNTING FOR THE INVESTMENT

When the subsidiary engages in a transaction in its own common stock, the following procedures are necessary under the equity method.

- Compare the book value of the parent's ownership interest in the subsidiary immediately before and immediately after the transaction. The difference between these two amounts is an increase or decrease in the parent's equity in the subsidiary.
- Record an increase in the parent's equity as a debit to Investment in Subsidiary and a credit to Gain from Subsidiary Stock Transaction (or a decrease in the parent's equity

---

EXHIBIT 12-10

Illustrative Problem 12.3
Eliminations
December 31, 1993

Eliminations

Intercompany Ownership Interests

[1]	Capital Stock: B	$ 76,000
[2]	Retained Earnings: B	29,260
[3]	Investment in Company B	$(105,260)

Subsidiary Income and Dividends

[4]	Income from Company B	$ 13,840
[5]	Dividends Declared: B	(7,600)
[6]	Investment in Company B	$(6,240)

Goodwill Amortization

[7]	Retained Earnings: A	$ 2,045
[8]	Goodwill Amortization Expense	710
[9]	Investment in Company B	$(2,755)

Income on Subsidiary Sold

[10]	Investment in Company B	$ 1,680
[11]	Income of Company B Sold	(1,680)

EXHIBIT 12-11

Illustrative Problem 12.3
Income Allocation Schedule
Year Ended December 31, 1993

Income Allocation

Company A's Own Net Income		$ 52,600
Less: Goodwill Amortization Expense		710
Company A's Adjusted Net Income		51,890
Company B's Own Net Income	$ 16,000	
Minority Interest (24%)	3,840	
Company A's Share (76%)	12,160	
Add: Income of Company B Sold	1,680	
Company A's Earned Share		13,840
Consolidated Net Income		$ 65,730

as a debit to Loss from Subsidiary Stock Transaction and a credit to Investment in Subsidiary).

Under the cost method, the change in the parent's equity is not recorded, but is taken into account in converting from cost to equity, as discussed in the following section.

The parent records its share of the subsidiary's net income and dividends under the equity method (or dividends under the cost method) in essentially the same manner as described and illustrated in the preceding sections.

CONSOLIDATION PROCEDURES

If the parent company uses the cost method, and the subsidiary engages in a transaction in its own common stock, the conversion from cost to equity is determined in the normal manner, by comparing

- the book value of the parent's investment in the subsidiary at the beginning of the current year (using the parent's percentage of ownership then existing), with
- the book value at the date or dates of acquisition (using the percentage of ownership acquired in each purchase).

At the end of the year in which such a transaction occurs, the transaction does not affect the calculation, of course, because the conversion is being made as of the beginning of that year. At the end of the following year (and of all subsequent years), the calculation automatically includes the change in the parent's equity caused by the subsidiary's common stock transaction.

Under both the cost method and the equity method, eliminations from the subsidiary's stockholders' equity balances in the Intercompany Ownership Interests set of eliminations are made at the parent's percentage of ownership existing at the end of the year.

In the Subsidiary Income and Dividends set of eliminations, the amount eliminated from the parent's Income from Subsidiary (under the equity method) or Dividend Revenue (under the cost method) is the amount recorded for the year. The elimination from the subsidiary's Dividends Declared balance, however, is made at the parent's year-end percentage of ownership, regardless of the amount of subsidiary dividends actually recorded by the parent. The difference, of course, is applied to the parent's Investment in Subsidiary. All other eliminations involving the subsidiary's Retained Earnings also are made using the year-end percentage of ownership.

In addition, under the equity method, at the end of any year during which the subsidiary engages in transactions in its common stock, a special set of eliminations is necessary for the share of the subsidiary's net income gained or lost by the parent company because of the change in its percentage of ownership. Income of Subsidiary Gained is the counterpart of Income of Subsidiary Purchased, discussed earlier and illustrated in Exhibits 12-2 and 12-3. Income of Subsidiary Lost is the counterpart of Income of Subsidiary Sold, discussed earlier and illustrated in Exhibits 12-10 and 12-11. Each is calculated as [a] the percentage of ownership gained or lost, multiplied by [b] the portion of the subsidiary's net income applicable to the segment of the year preceding the date of the subsidiary's common stock transaction. Each is treated in the consolidation process and in the consolidated income statement in the same manner as its counterpart.

ILLUSTRATIVE PROBLEM 12.4: SUBSIDIARY COMMON STOCK TRANSACTION

Company E purchased 7,200 of Company F's 10,000 outstanding shares of $10 par value common stock on January 1, 1991 for $98,400. Company F's common stock was issued at par in 1980. Any excess of cost over book value is treated as goodwill from consolidation and is being amortized over 10 years. Company E accounts for its investment in Company F under the equity method. Company E reported net income from its own operations for 1992 of $42,800. Changes in Company F's Retained Earnings balance for 1991 through 1992 are shown below.

Balance, 12/31/90	$ 25,000
Dividends Declared, 12/1/91	(6,000)
Net Income, 1991	12,000
Balance, 12/31/91	31,000
Dividends Declared, 12/1/92	(7,500)
Net Income, 1992	15,000
Balance, 12/31/92	$ 38,500

On May 1, 1992, Company E acquired 1,000 shares of its own common stock from minority stockholders for $12,000. This stock is to be carried as treasury stock and accounted for at cost on Company F's books. As a result of this transaction, Company E's percentage of ownership in Company F increased from 72% (7,200 of 10,000 shares) to 80% (7,200 of 9,000 shares). The change in the book value of Company E's investment in Company F is calculated by comparing the book value of Company E's ownership interest in Company F immediately before and immediately after the transaction, as shown below.

80% of Company F's Stockholders' Equity after 5/1/92 Transaction	$ 99,200
72% of Company F's Stockholders' Equity before 5/1/92 Transaction	97,920
Increase in Company E's Equity in Company F	$ 1,280

Company F's total stockholders' equity immediately before the May 1, 1992 transaction consists of common stock of $100,000, plus retained earnings at January 1, 1992 of $31,000, plus 4/12 of Company F's $15,000 of 1992 net income. Company F's total stockholders' equity immediately after the May 1, 1992 transaction consists of common stock of $100,000, plus retained earnings at January 1, 1992 of $31,000, plus 4/12 of Company F's $15,000 of 1992 net income, minus the cost of the treasury shares purchased on that date.

Under the equity method, Company E records this increase in its equity in Company F as a debit to Investment in Company F and a credit to Gain from Subsidiary Stock Transaction.

Changes in Company E's Investment in Company F account balance through December 31, 1992 are summarized below.

Purchase, 1/1/91	$ 98,400
Dividends from Company F, 12/1/91	(4,320)
Income from Company F, 1991	8,640
Balance, 12/31/91	102,720
Increase in Equity, 5/1/92	1,280
Dividends from Company F, 12/1/92	(6,000)
Income from Company F, 1992	11,600
Balance, 12/31/92	$ 109,600

Because Company E owned 72% of Company F's common stock throughout 1991, it records 72% of Company F's 1991 net income of $12,000, or $8,640, as its income from Company F. In 1992, however, Company E owned 72% of Company F's common stock for the first four months and 80% for the remainder of the year. Therefore, Company E records as its income from Company F 72% of 4/12 of $15,000, or $3,600, plus 80% of 8/12 of $15,000, or $8,000, for a total of $11,600. In each year, Company E records the dividends actually declared to it by Company F: 72% of $6,000, or $4,320, in 1991 and 80% of $7,500, or $6,000, in 1992.

Exhibit 12-12 presents the Goodwill from Consolidation schedule to accompany the December 31, 1992 consolidation worksheet. The Goodwill from Consolidation schedule is not affected by Company F's acquisition of its treasury stock.

The eliminations needed at December 31, 1992 appear in Exhibit 12-13. The eliminations from Company F's Common Stock and Retained Earnings in the Intercompany Ownership Interests set are made at Company E's end of the year percentage of ownership, 80%, even though that percentage has changed during the year.

The amount eliminated from Income from Company F is the amount recorded by Company E for the year. The elimination from Company F's Dividends Declared is made at Company E's end of the year percentage of ownership.

The amounts of prior and current years' goodwill amortization appearing in the Goodwill Amortization set of eliminations are taken directly from the Goodwill from Consolidation schedule in Exhibit 12-12.

The amount debited to Income of Company F Gained and credited to Investment in Company F is the portion of Company F's 1992 net income that Company E gained from the

EXHIBIT 12-12

Illustrative Problem 12.4
Goodwill from Consolidation
December 31, 1992

Goodwill from Consolidation

Cost of Investment		$ 98,400
Book Value (72% × $125,000)		90,000
Goodwill, 1/1/91		8,400
Amortization, 1991	$ 840	
Amortization, 1992	840	1,680
Goodwill, 12/31/92		$ 6,720

EXHIBIT 12-13

Illustrative Problem 12.4
Eliminations
December 31, 1992

Eliminations

Intercompany Ownership Interests

[1]	Common Stock: F	$ 80,000
[2]	Retained Earnings: F	24,800
[3]	Treasury Stock: F	(9,600)
[4]	Investment in Company F	$(95,200)

Subsidiary Income and Dividends

[5]	Income from Company F	$ 11,600
[6]	Dividends Declared: F	(6,000)
[7]	Investment in Company F	$(5,600)

Goodwill Amortization

[8]	Retained Earnings: E	$ 840
[9]	Goodwill Amortization Expense	840
[10]	Investment in Company F	$(1,680)

Income of Subsidiary Gained

[11]	Income of Company F Gained	$ 400
[12]	Investment in Company F	(400)

minority stockholders from whom Company F purchased its treasury stock. This amount is calculated as 8% × 4/12 × $15,000. As explained earlier, the Income of Company F Gained appears in the Income Allocation schedule as an adjustment to the share of Company F's net income initially allocated to Company E, as shown in Exhibit 12-14.

EXHIBIT 12-14

Illustrative Problem 12.4
Income Allocation Schedule
Year Ended December 31, 1992

Income Allocation

Company E's Own Net Income		$ 42,800
Less: Goodwill Amortization		840
Company E's Adjusted Net Income		41,960
Company F's Own Net Income	$ 15,000	
Minority Interest (20%)	3,000	
Company E's Share (80%)	12,000	
Less: Income of Company F Gained	400	
Company E's Earned Share		11,600
Consolidated Net Income		$ 53,560

STOCK DIVIDENDS AND STOCK SPLITS BY THE SUBSIDIARY

In addition to the types of transactions by the subsidiary in its own common stock discussed above, the subsidiary can declare and issue both stock dividends and stock splits. In both cases, the parent company would receive a number of shares of subsidiary common stock proportionate to its ownership interest in the subsidiary. Furthermore, the underlying net assets of the subsidiary would not change as a result of either of these distributions. Therefore, the impact of either type of distribution on the carrying value of the parent's investment in the subsidiary is zero.

SUMMARY

In this chapter, we have considered four different types of changes in ownership.

- More than one acquisition by the parent with control obtained on the first purchase
- More than one acquisition by the parent with less than significant influence obtained on the first purchase
- Sale of subsidiary common stock by the parent
- Transactions by the subsidiary in its own common stock

The effects of each type of change on both the parent's accounting for its investment in the subsidiary and the consolidation process are discussed and illustrated in separate sections of the chapter.

REVIEW PROBLEM

Company P has made the following purchases and sales of Company S's common stock.

10/31/90	Bought 70,000 shares for $848,400
4/1/91	Bought 20,000 shares for $260,400
4/30/92	Sold 13,000 shares for $182,000

When Company S was organized in 1974, it issued 100,000 shares of $5 par value common stock at 8. These shares remained outstanding until November 1, 1992, when Company S issued 10,000 additional shares at 14½. Company P did not acquire any of these new shares.

Company P accounts for its investment in Company S under the equity method. The excess of cost over book value is treated as goodwill from consolidation and is being amortized over 10 years. Company P's 1992 net income from its own operations was $108,400.

During 1992, Company S sold merchandise that had cost $224,000 to Company P for $320,000, of which $28,000 remained unpaid at December 31, 1992. Company P's beginning and ending inventories for 1992 contained goods purchased from Company S of $30,000 and $33,000, respectively. Both affiliates use perpetual inventory systems. Company S's gross margin on sales to Company P was about the same in 1991 as in 1992.

Changes in Company S's Retained Earnings balance for 1990 through 1992 are shown below.

Balance, 1/1/90	$ 282,000
Dividends Declared, 10/1/90	(40,000)
Net Income, 1990	60,000
Balance, 12/31/90	302,000
Dividends Declared, 10/1/91	(50,000)
Net Income, 1991	80,000
Balance, 12/31/91	332,000
Dividends Declared, 10/1/92	(50,000)
Net Income, 1992	90,000
Balance, 12/31/92	$ 372,000

Required

1. Prepare a schedule showing the changes in Company P's Investment in Company S balance from October 31, 1990 through December 31, 1992.
2. Prepare all schedules in support of the December 31, 1992 consolidation worksheet.

QUESTIONS

1. If a parent company buys or sells subsidiary common stock during a year, on what basis is the subsidiary net income allocated to different segments of the year?
2. Why is it necessary to make the eliminations from the subsidiary stockholders' equity balances in the Intercompany Ownership Interests set of eliminations at the parent's percentage of ownership existing at the end of the year?
3. How is Income of Subsidiary Purchased treated in the Income Allocation schedule?
4. Company A acquires an additional 55% of Company B's common stock after having held 15%

thereof for several years and wishes to change from the cost method to the equity method in its accounts. How will this change be accomplished?

5. In calculating the gain or loss on the sale of subsidiary common stock by a parent using the equity method, how is the net carrying value of the shares sold determined?

6. How is the goodwill associated with shares of subsidiary common stock sold determined and how is it treated in the Goodwill schedule?

7. How is the amortization of goodwill after the sale of subsidiary common stock calculated?

8. How is Income of Subsidiary Sold treated in the consolidation worksheet?

9. When a subsidiary issues additional common stock, none of which is acquired by the parent, how is the effect on the parent's equity in the subsidiary determined?

10. What effect does the issuance of additional common stock in question 9 have on the Goodwill schedule?

EXERCISES

EXERCISE 12-1

On May 1, 1990, Company A purchased 70,000 of Company B's 100,000 shares of $10 par value common stock, which had been issued at 12, for $1,460,000. On October 31, 1991, Company A purchased 10,000 additional shares of Company B's common stock for $214,000. On June 1, 1992, Company A sold 7,000 shares of Company B common stock for $154,000. The excess of cost over book value is treated as goodwill from consolidation and is amortized over 10 years. Company A accounts for its investment in Company B under the equity method. Changes in Company B's Retained Earnings balance for 1990 through 1992 are shown below.

Balance, 1/1/90	$ 520,000
Dividends, 12/1/90	(80,000)
Net Income, 1990	120,000
Balance, 12/31/90	560,000
Dividends, 12/1/91	(90,000)
Net Income, 1991	132,000
Balance, 12/31/91	602,000
Dividends, 12/1/92	(100,000)
Net Income, 1992	144,000
Balance, 12/31/92	$ 646,000

Required
Prepare a schedule showing the goodwill to be reported at December 31, 1990, 1991, and 1992.

EXERCISE 12-2
Refer to Exercise 12-1. Present the equity method journal entries on Company A's books from May 1, 1990 through December 31, 1992.

EXERCISE 12-3
Company C has made the following purchases of Company D's common stock.

1/1/90	Bought 10,000 shares of $16,200
4/1/92	Bought 70,000 shares for $131,800

Changes in Company D's Retained Earnings balance for 1990 through 1992 are shown below.

Balance, 1/1/90	$ 52,000
Dividends, 12/1/90	(10,000)
Net Income, 1990	20,000
Balance, 12/31/90	62,000
Dividends Declared, 12/1/91	(10,000)
Net Income, 1991	18,000
Balance, 12/31/91	70,000
Dividends Declared, 12/1/92	(10,000)
Net Income, 1992	16,000
Balance, 12/31/92	$ 76,000

Company D had 100,000 shares of $1 par value common stock outstanding throughout this entire period. The excess of cost over book value is treated as goodwill from consolidation and is amortized over 20 years. No amortization has been recorded before April 1, 1992.

Required
Present the journal entries to be recorded on Company C's books relative to its investment in Company D for 1990, 1991, and 1992, assuming that Company C adopts the equity method as soon as it is eligible to do so.

EXERCISE 12-4
Refer to Exercise 12-3. Prepare schedules of goodwill and of all eliminations to accompany the December 31, 1992 consolidation worksheet.

EXERCISE 12-5
Company E acquired 8,800 of Company F's 10,000 outstanding shares of $100 par value common stock for $1,253,600 on October 31, 1991, at which date Company F had retained earnings of $370,000. By December 31, 1993, Company F's retained earnings had increased to $425,000. Company F reported net income for 1994 of $36,000 and declared dividends of $12,000 on November 15, 1994. Company E accounts for its investment in Company F under the equity method. The excess of cost over book value is treated as goodwill from consolidation, amortized over 10 years.

On July 31, 1994, Company F issued an additional 1,000 shares of common stock for $150,000. Company E did not acquire any of these new shares.

Required
Prepare a schedule of changes in Company E's Investment in Company F account balance from October 31, 1991 through December 31, 1994.

EXERCISE 12-6
Refer to Exercise 12-5. Present schedules of goodwill and of those eliminations that can be determined from the information given, to accompany the December 31, 1994 consolidation worksheet.

EXERCISE 12-7
Company G acquired 6,000 of Company H's 10,000 outstanding shares of $10 par value common stock for $96,800 on January 1, 1991, at which date Company H had retained earnings of $48,000. By

December 31, 1993, Company H's retained earnings had increased to $68,000. On April 1, 1994, Company H acquired 625 shares of its own common stock (to be held as treasury stock) for $12,500. Company H reported net income for 1994 of $16,000 and declared dividends of $1.00 per share on December 15, 1994, payable on January 15, 1995. Company G accounts for its investment in Company H under the equity method. The excess of cost over book value is treated as goodwill from consolidation and is being amortized over 10 years.

Required
Present schedules of goodwill and of those eliminations that can be determined from the information given, to accompany the December 31, 1994 consolidation worksheet.

EXERCISE 12-8
Refer to Exercise 12-7. Prepare a schedule of changes in Company G's Investment in Company H account balance from January 1, 1991 through December 31, 1994.

EXERCISE 12-9
On April 1, 1990, Company J purchased 80,000 of Company K's 100,000 shares of $10 par value common stock for $533,000. On July 1, 1990, Company J purchased 5,000 additional shares of Company K's common stock for $33,300. On October 1, 1991, Company J sold 8,000 shares of Company K common stock for $56,200. Company K reported net income of $84,000 in 1990.

Required
1. In the Income Allocation schedule for 1990, Income of Company K Purchased of
   a. $17,850 is added to the amount of Company K's net income initially allocated to Company J.
   b. $17,850 is subtracted from the amount of Company K's net income initially allocated to Company J.
   c. $18,900 is added to the amount of Company K's net income initially allocated to Company J.
   d. $18,900 is subtracted from the amount of Company K's net income initially allocated to Company J.
2. In the Income Allocation schedule for 1991, Income of Company K Sold of
   a. $1,680 is added to the amount of Company K's net income initially allocated to Company J.
   b. $1,680 is subtracted from the amount of Company K's net income initially allocated to Company J.
   c. $5,040 is added to the amount of Company K's net income initially allocated to Company J.
   d. $5,040 is subtracted from the amount of Company K's net income initially allocated to Company J.

PROBLEMS

PROBLEM 12-1
On March 1, 1990, Company A purchased 16,000 of Company B's 20,000 shares of $50 par value common stock, which had been issued at 68, for $1,856,000. On May 1, 1991, Company A sold 1,200 shares of Company B common stock for $156,000. The excess of cost over book value is treated as goodwill from consolidation and is amortized over 10 years. Company A accounts for its investment in Company B under the equity method. Company A's 1991 net income from its own operations was $348,000. Changes in Company B's Retained Earnings balance are shown below.

Balance, 1/1/90	$ 620,000
Dividends, 12/1/90	(100,000)
Net Income, 1990	240,000
Balance, 12/31/90	760,000
Dividends Declared, 12/1/91	(110,000)
Net Income, 1991	252,000
Balance, 12/31/91	$ 902,000

During 1991, Company A purchased merchandise from Company B for $412,500, of which $33,100 remained unpaid at year end. Company A's beginning and ending inventories for 1991 contained goods purchased from Company B of $42,000 and $51,500, respectively. Company B sells to Company A at 25% above cost. Both affiliates use perpetual inventory systems.

Required

Prepare all supporting schedules to the December 31, 1991, consolidation worksheet.

PROBLEM 12-2

On April 1, 1990, Company C purchased 9,000 of Company D's 10,000 shares of $50 par value common stock, which had been issued at par, for $548,700. On June 30, 1991, Company C sold 900 shares of Company D common stock for $56,700. On September 30, 1992, Company D acquired 1,000 shares of its own common stock (to be held as treasury stock) for $63,500.

The excess of cost over book value is treated as goodwill from consolidation and is amortized over 10 years. Company C accounts for its investment in Company D under the equity method. Changes in Company D's Retained Earnings balance are shown below.

Balance, 1/1/90	$ 80,000
Dividends, 8/1/90	(8,000)
Net Income, 1990	12,000
Balance, 12/31/90	84,000
Dividends, 8/1/91	(10,000)
Net Income, 1991	16,000
Balance, 12/31/91	90,000
Dividends, 8/1/92	(12,000)
Net Income, 1992	20,000
Balance, 12/31/92	$ 98,000

Required

1. Prepare a schedule of changes in Company C's Investment in Company D account balance from April 1, 1990 through December 31, 1992.
2. Schedule the eliminations that would appear on the December 31, 1992 consolidation worksheet.

PROBLEM 12-3

Company E has made the following purchases and sales of Company F's common stock.

7/1/91	Bought 78,400 shares for $780,960
10/31/92	Bought 4,900 shares for $47,860
8/1/93	Sold 7,840 shares for $78,980

Changes in Company F's Retained Earnings balance are shown below.

Balance, 1/1/91	$ 284,700
Dividends Declared, 10/1/91	(29,400)
Net Income, 1991	54,600
Balance, 12/31/91	309,900
Dividends Declared, 10/1/92	(34,400)
Net Income, 1992	60,600
Balance, 12/31/92	$ 336,100

Trial balances of Company E and Company F at December 31, 1993 are shown below.

	Company E	Company F
Receivables (net)	$ 127,100	$ 135,400
Inventories	185,600	212,700
Other Current Assets	625,353	496,900
Plant and Equipment	1,681,880	1,105,600
Investment in Company F Stock	792,967	—
Investment in Company F Bonds	195,500	—
Discount on Bonds Payable	—	22,500
Dividends Declared	62,500	39,200
Cost of Goods Sold	455,100	518,400
Other Expenses	304,200	354,100
Treasury Stock (2,000 shares at cost)	—	180,800
	$4,430,200	$3,065,600
Accumulated Depreciation	$ 941,900	$ 389,800
Current Liabilities	414,700	281,200
8% Bonds Payable	—	500,000
Common Stock ($5 par value)	1,000,000	500,000
Additional Paid-in Capital	610,000	120,000
Retained Earnings	561,800	336,100
Sales	827,400	932,800
Income from Company F	53,900	—
Other Income	20,500	5,700
	$4,430,200	$3,065,600

Company F's common stock outstanding has not changed since January 1, 1984. Company F's dividends were declared on September 15 and paid on October 25. The excess of cost over book value is treated as goodwill from consolidation and amortized over 10 years.

Company E purchased 40% of Company F's bonds on the open market on September 15, 1992. The bonds mature on September 30, 1997 and interest is payable on March 31 and September 30.

Required

Prepare the December 31, 1993 consolidation worksheet, accompanied by all appropriate supporting schedules.

PROBLEM 12-4

On May 1, 1990, Company G purchased 35,000 of Company H's 50,000 shares of $10 par value common stock, which had been issued at 12, for $730,000. On October 31, 1991, Company G purchased 5,000 additional shares of Company H's common stock for $107,000. On June 1, 1992, Company G sold 3,500 shares of Company H common stock for $77,000.

The excess of cost over book value is treated as goodwill from consolidation and is amortized over 10 years. Company G accounts for its investment in Company H under the equity method. Company G's 1992 net income from its own operations was $78,000. Changes in Company H's Retained Earnings balance are shown below.

Balance, 1/1/90	$ 260,000
Dividends, 10/1/90	(40,000)
Net Income, 1990	60,000
Balance, 12/31/90	280,000
Dividends, 10/1/91	(45,000)
Net Income, 1991	66,000
Balance, 12/31/91	301,000
Dividends, 10/1/92	(50,000)
Net Income, 1992	72,000
Balance, 12/31/92	$ 323,000

Required

Prepare all supporting schedules to the December 31, 1992 consolidation worksheet.

PROBLEM 12-5

On March 1, 1992, Company J purchased 66,500 shares of Company K's $5 par value common stock for $564,900. On October 31, 1992, Company J purchased an additional 19,000 shares of Company K's common stock for $163,800. On July 1, 1993, Company J sold 9,500 shares of Company K common stock for $86,000. From April 30, 1990 through September 30, 1993, Company K had 100,000 shares of common stock issued, of which 5,000 shares had been reacquired and were held as treasury stock at a cost of $35,000. This common stock had been issued originally at 6. On October 1, 1993, Company K reissued the 5,000 treasury shares for $47,500. Company J did not acquire any of these shares.

The excess of cost over book value is treated as goodwill from consolidation and is amortized over 20 years. Company J accounts for its investment in Company K under the equity method. Company J's 1993 net income from its own operations was $92,300. On June 30, 1992, Company K sold some equipment that had cost $378,500 to Company J for $441,500. Company J is depreciating the equipment on the sum-of-the-years'-digits method, over 6 years, with a $21,500 salvage value.

Changes in Company K's Retained Earnings balance are shown below.

Balance, 1/1/92	$ 174,000
Dividends, 8/31/92	(20,000)
Net Income, 1992	48,000
Balance, 12/31/92	202,000
Dividends, 8/31/93	(25,000)
Net Income, 1993	60,000
Balance, 12/31/93	$ 237,000

Required

Prepare all supporting schedules to the December 31, 1993 consolidation worksheet.

PROBLEM 12-6

Company L has made the following purchases and sales of Company M's common stock.

3/31/91	Bought 6,000 shares of $452,800
10/1/91	Bought 3,000 shares for $224,900
6/30/92	Sold 600 shares for $47,400

Company M had 10,000 shares of $50 par value common stock (originally issued at 55) until September 30, 1993, when it issued 1,200 additional shares at 80. Company L did not acquire any of the 1,200 shares. Changes in Company M's Retained Earnings balance for 1991 through 1993 are shown below.

Balance, 1/1/91	$ 128,000
Dividends, 9/1/91	(25,000)
Net Income, 1991	40,000
Balance, 12/31/91	143,000
Dividends, 9/1/92	(36,000)
Net Income, 1992	48,000
Balance, 12/31/92	155,000
Dividends, 9/1/93	(40,000)
Net Income, 1993	60,000
Balance, 12/31/93	$ 175,000

The excess of cost over book value is treated as goodwill from consolidation and is amortized over 10 years. Company L accounts for its investment in Company M under the equity method. Company L's 1993 net income from its own operations was $112,300. During 1993, Company L purchased merchandise from Company M for $418,000, of which $39,500 remained unpaid at year end. Company L's beginning and ending inventories contained goods purchased from Company M of $45,000 and $53,000, respectively. Company M sells to Company L at 25% above cost. Both affiliates use perpetual inventory systems.

Required

Show supporting calculations in answering the following questions.

1. What is the amount of goodwill amortization in 1991?
2. What amount is eliminated from Company L's Investment in Company M balance in the Intercompany Ownership Interests set of eliminations at December 31, 1991?
3. What amount does Company L credit to its Investment in Company M account in recording Company M's 1991 dividends?
4. What amount is eliminated from Company M's Dividends Declared balance at December 31, 1991?
5. What amount does Company L record as a credit to Income from Company M in 1991?
6. What is the amount of Income of Company M Purchased appearing in the December 31, 1991 consolidation worksheet? Is it a debit or a credit?
7. What is the amount of goodwill associated with the Company M shares sold on June 30, 1992?
8. What amount is eliminated from Company M's Retained Earnings balance in the Intercompany Ownership Interests set of eliminations at December 31, 1992?
9. What is the amount of goodwill reported in the December 31, 1992 consolidated balance sheet?
10. What amount is eliminated from Income from Company M at December 31, 1992?
11. What is the amount of Income of Company M Sold in 1992? How is it treated in the Income Allocation schedule?
12. What is the amount of the increase or decrease (tell which) in Company L's equity in Company M resulting from the September 30, 1993 stock issue?

13. What amount is eliminated from Sales at December 31, 1993?
14. What amount is eliminated from Company L's Retained Earnings balance at December 31, 1993 in connection with Company L's 1993 beginning inventory?
15. What is the amount of consolidated net income in 1993?

PROBLEM 12-7

Company N has made the following purchases and sales of Company O's common stock.

4/1/90	Bought 60,000 shares for $631,500
6/30/90	Bought 30,000 shares for $326,700
9/30/91	Sold 9,000 shares for $108,000

Company O had 100,000 shares of $5 par value common stock (originally issued at 7) until November 30, 1992, when it acquired 10,000 shares from minority stockholders for $120,000. These shares are being held as treasury stock. Changes in Company O's Retained Earnings balance for 1990 through 1992 are shown below.

Balance, 1/1/90	$ 136,000
Dividends, 10/31/90	(40,000)
Net Income, 1990	66,000
Balance, 12/31/90	162,000
Dividends, 10/31/91	(44,000)
Net Income, 1991	72,000
Balance, 12/31/91	190,000
Dividends, 10/31/92	(50,000)
Net Income, 1992	78,000
Balance, 12/31/92	$ 218,000

The excess of cost over book value is treated as goodwill from consolidation and is amortized over 10 years. Company N accounts for its investment in Company O under the equity method. Company N's 1992 net income from its own operations was $142,900.

Required

Show supporting calculations in answering the following questions.

1. What amount does Company N record as a credit to Income from Company O in 1990?
2. What is the amount of Income of Company O Purchased appearing in the December 31, 1990 consolidation worksheet? Is it a debit or a credit?
3. What is the amount of goodwill amortization in 1990?
4. What amount is eliminated from Company N's Investment in Company O balance in the Intercompany Ownership Interests set of eliminations at December 31, 1991?
5. What is the amount of goodwill associated with the Company O shares sold on September 30, 1991?
6. What is the amount of gain or loss (tell which) on the sale of Company O stock reported in the 1991 consolidated income statement?
7. What is the amount of goodwill reported in the December 31, 1991 consolidated balance sheet?
8. What is the amount of Income of Company O Sold in 1991? How is it treated in the Income Allocation schedule?
9. What is the amount of the increase or decrease (tell which) in Company N's equity in Company O resulting from the treasury stock acquisition on November 30, 1992?
10. What amount is eliminated from Company O's Retained Earnings balance in the Intercompany Ownership Interests set of eliminations at December 31, 1992?

11. What amount is eliminated from Company O's Dividends Declared balance at December 31, 1992?
12. What is the amount of consolidated net income in 1992?

PROBLEM 12-8

Company P has made the following purchases and sales of Company Q's capital stock.

6/30/90	Bought 133,000 shares for $1,525,200
3/31/91	Bought 38,000 shares for $467,200
9/30/91	Sold 26,600 shares for $425,600

Company Q originally issued 200,000 shares of $5 par value capital stock at 8 on July 1, 1981. On November 1, 1985, it reacquired 10,000 shares at a cost of $120,000. These shares were held as treasury stock until October 1, 1992, when they were reissued at 18.

The excess of cost over book value is treated as goodwill from consolidation and is amortized over 10 years. Company P accounts for its investment in Company Q under the equity method. Company P's 1992 net income from its own operations was $125,600.

Changes in Company Q's Retained Earnings balance for 1990 through 1992 are shown below.

Balance, 1/1/90	$ 284,000
Dividends, 11/15/90	(100,000)
Net Income, 1990	144,000
Balance, 12/31/90	328,000
Dividends, 11/15/91	(120,000)
Net Income, 1991	192,000
Balance, 12/31/91	400,000
Dividends, 11/15/92	(100,000)
Net Income, 1992	216,000
Balance, 12/31/92	$ 516,000

Required

1. Prepare the schedule of the excess of cost over book value to accompany the December 31, 1992 consolidation worksheet.
2. Prepare the income allocation schedule to accompany the December 31, 1992 consolidation worksheet.
3. Prepare a schedule showing the changes in Company P's Investment in Company Q account balance from June 30, 1990 through December 31, 1992. Show supporting calculations.

PROBLEM 12-9

Company R has made the following purchases and sales of Company S's common stock.

4/1/91	Bought 17,500 shares for $768,500
8/1/91	Bought 2,500 shares for $113,100
7/1/92	Sold 3,500 shares for $176,260

From October 1, 1973 until November 30, 1992, Company S had 25,000 shares of $10 par value common stock outstanding. These shares were issued originally at 25. On November 30, 1992, Company S acquired 4,375 shares of its own common stock from minority stockholders at a cost of $227,500, to be held as treasury stock.

The excess of cost over book value is treated as goodwill from consolidation and is amortized over 10 years. Company R accounts for its investment in Company S under the equity method. Company R's 1992 net income from its own operations was $99,300. Changes in Company S's Retained Earnings balance for 1991 through 1992 are shown below.

Balance, 1/1/91	$118,000
Dividends, 10/31/91	(25,000)
Net Income, 1991	48,000
Balance, 12/31/91	141,000
Dividends, 10/31/92	(30,000)
Net Income, 1992	66,000
Balance, 12/31/92	$177,000

Required

Show supporting calculations in answering each of the following questions.

1. What is the amount of goodwill to be reported on the December 31, 1991 consolidated balance sheet?

2. What is the amount of income of Company S Purchased in 1991? How is it shown in the 1991 income allocation schedule?

3. What is the balance of Company R's Investment in Company S account at December 31, 1991?

4. What is the amount of gain or loss (tell which) on the sale of Company S stock reported in the 1992 consolidated income statement?

5. What amount is eliminated from Company S's Dividends balance at December 31, 1992?

6. What is the amount of goodwill associated with the Company S shares sold on July 1, 1992?

7. What amount does Company R record as a credit to Income from Company S in 1992?

8. What is the amount of the increase or decrease (tell which) in Company R's equity in Company S resulting from Company S's acquisition of treasury stock on November 30, 1992?

9. What amount is eliminated from Company R's Investment in Company S balance in the Intercompany Ownership Interests set of eliminations at December 31, 1992?

10. What is the amount of consolidated net income in 1992?

PROBLEM 12-10

Company T has made the following purchases of Company U's common stock.

7/1/90	Bought 1,000 shares for $30,300
3/31/91	Bought 6,000 shares for $181,200

Changes in Company U's Retained Earnings balance for 1990 through 1991 are shown below.

Balance, 1/1/90	$ 84,000
Dividends Declared, 12/1/90	(20,000)
Net Income, 1990	36,000
Balance, 12/31/90	100,000
Dividends Declared, 12/1/91	(20,000)
Net Income, 1991	48,000
Balance, 12/31/91	$128,000

Company U had 10,000 shares of $10 par value common stock outstanding throughout this entire period. These shares had been issued originally at 15. The excess of cost over book value is treated as goodwill from consolidation and is amortized over 10 years. No amortization had been recorded before March 31, 1991. Company T reported net income from its own operations in 1991 of $131,600.

Required

Show supporting calculations in answering each of the following questions.

1. What is the amount of goodwill to be reported on the December 31, 1991 consolidated balance sheet?
2. What is the amount of Income of Company U Purchased in 1991? How is it shown in the 1991 income allocation schedule?
3. Assuming that Company T adopts the equity method to account for its investment in Company U as soon as it is eligible to do so, what amount does it debit to Investment in Company U to accomplish this conversion?
4. What is the balance of Company T's Investment in Company U account at December 31, 1991?
5. What amount is eliminated from Company U's Dividends balance at December 31, 1991?
6. What amount does Company T record as a credit to Income from Company U in 1991?
7. What amount is eliminated from Company T's Investment in Company U balance in the Intercompany Ownership Interests set of eliminations at December 31, 1991?
8. What is the amount of consolidated net income in 1991?

SOLUTION TO REVIEW PROBLEM

Changes in Company P's Investment in Company S Balance

Purchase, 10/31/90	$ 848,400
Income from Company S, 1990	7,000 [a]
Balance, 12/31/90	855,400
Purchased, 4/1/91	260,400
Dividends from Company S, 10/1/91	(45,000) [b]
Income from Company S, 1991	68,000 [c]
Balance, 12/31/91	1,138,800
Sale of Shares, 4/30/92	(164,320) [d]
Dividends from Company S, 10/1/92	(38,500) [e]
Increase in Equity, 11/1/92	20,510 [f]
Income from Company S, 1992	72,150 [g]
Balance, 12/31/92	$ 1,028,640

Calculations

[a] 70% × 2/12 × $60,000

[b] 90% × $50,000

[c] (70% × 3/12 × $80,000) + (90% × 9/12 × $80,000)

[d] 13/70[$848,400 + (13%[(2/12 × $60,000) − $50,000 + $80,000 + (4/12 × $90,000)]) − 13/70($12,600)]

[e] 77% × $50,000

[f] 70%[$550,000 + $395,000 + $332,000 + (10/12 × $90,000) − $50,000] − 77%[$500,000 + $300,000 + $332,000 + (10/12 × $90,000) − $50,000]

[g] (90% × 4/12 × $90,000) + (77% × 6/12 × $90,000) + (70% × 2/12 × $90,000)

Goodwill from Consolidation

	10/31/90 Purchase	4/1/91 Purchase	Total
Cost of Investment	$ 848,400		
Book Value	764,400		
Goodwill, 10/31/90	84,000		$ 84,000
Amortization, 1990	(1,400)		(1,400)
Goodwill, 12/31/90	82,600		82,600
Cost of Investment		$ 260,400	
Book Value		224,400	
Additional Goodwill, 4/1/91		36,000	36,000
Amortization, 1991	(8,400)	(2,700)	(11,100)
Goodwill, 12/31/91	74,200	33,300	107,500
Amortization, 1/1/92–4/30/92	(2,800)	(1,200)	(4,000)
Goodwill, 4/30/92	71,400	32,100	103,500
Amount Related to Shares Sold	(13,260)		(13,260)
Amortization, 4/30/92–12/31/92	(4,560)	(2,400)	(6,960)
Goodwill, 12/31/92	$ 53,580	$ 29,700	$ 83,280

Eliminations

Intercompany Ownership Interests

[1] Capital Stock: S	$ 385,000
[2] Additional Paid-in Capital: S	276,500
[3] Retained Earnings: S	232,400
[4] Investment in Company S	$(893,900)

Subsidiary Income and Dividends

[5] Income from Company S	$ 72,150
[6] Dividends: S	(35,000)
[7] Investment in Company S	$(37,150)

Goodwill Amortization

[8] Retained Earnings: P	$ 12,500
[9] Goodwill Amortization Expense	10,960
[10] Investment in Company S	$(23,460)

Income of Subsidiary Sold

[11] Investment in Company S	$ 3,900
[12] Income of Company S Sold	(3,900)

Income of Subsidiary Lost

[13] Investment in Company S	$ 5,250
[14] Income of Company S Lost	(5,250)

Intercompany Sales and Purchases

[15] Sales	$ 320,000
[16] Cost of Goods Sold	(320,000)

Intercompany Receivables and Payables

[17] Accounts Payable	$ 28,000
[18] Accounts Receivable	(28,000)

Intercompany Profit in Beginning Inventory

[19] Retained Earnings: P	$ 6,300
[20] Retained Earnings: S	2,700
[12] Cost of Goods Sold	$ (9,000)

Intercompany Profit in Ending Inventory

[22] Cost of Goods Sold	$ 9,900
[23] Inventory	(9,900)

Income Allocation

Company P's Net Income		$ 108,400
Less: Goodwill Amortization		10,960
Company P's Adjusted Net Income		97,440
Company S's Net Income	$ 90,000	
Add: Intercompany Profit in Beginning Inventory	9,000	
Less: Intercompany Profit in Ending Inventory	(9,900)	
Company S's Adjusted Net Income	89,100	
Minority Interest (30%)	26,730	
Company P's Share (70%)	62,370	
Add: Income of Company S Sold	3,900	
Income of Company S Lost	5,250	
Company P's Earned Share		71,520
Consolidated Net Income		$ 168,960

13

INDIRECT AND MUTUAL OWNERSHIP

U p to this point, almost all of our discussions, illustrations, and problems have been based on affiliations consisting of a parent company and a single subsidiary company. Obviously, a parent can own common stock interests in more than one subsidiary (or investee). In addition, a parent company can own a common stock interest in one subsidiary (or investee) which, in turn, owns a common stock interest in a second subsidiary (or investee). This type of ownership arrangement gives the parent an **indirect** ownership interest in the second subsidiary (or investee). Finally, affiliates can own common stock interests in each other, giving rise to **mutual** ownership interests.

In this chapter we discuss and illustrate the effect on both the parent's (or investor's) accounting for its investment in its subsidiary (or investee) and the consolidation process of

- multiple ownership interests (briefly)
- indirect ownership interests, and
- mutual ownership interests.

TYPES OF OWNERSHIP CONFIGURATIONS

Diagrams of complex ownership arrangements often are helpful [a] in understanding the relationships between or among affiliates, [b] in accounting for investments under either the equity method or the cost method, and [c] in performing the consolidation process. This section introduces the diagrams and explains further the nature of the various ownership configurations.

As noted earlier, a parent can own common stock interests in more than one subsidiary. An example of such a relationship can be diagramed as

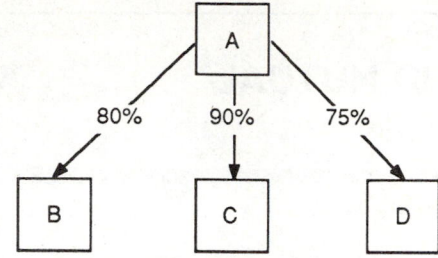

in which the parent company, A, owns 80% of subsidiary B's common stock, 90% of subsidiary C's common stock, and 75% of subsidiary D's common stock.

The presence of more than one subsidiary does not change the application of either the equity or the cost method, or of any of the consolidation procedures that we have dealt with in previous chapters. The only difference is that the process must be repeated for each additional subsidiary.

A parent company also can own stock in one subsidiary (or investee) which, in turn, owns stock in a second subsidiary (or investee). This arrangement gives the parent an **indirect** ownership interest in the second subsidiary.

Many different configurations of indirect ownership arrangements are possible. Of these, however, two general types can be discerned:

- Those in which the parent has only an indirect ownership interest in one or more subsidiaries
- Those in which the parent has both direct and indirect ownership interests in one or more subsidiaries

An example of the first type can be diagramed as

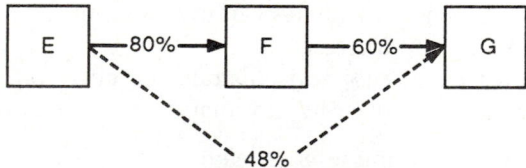

In this diagram, the primary parent, Company E, owns 80% of Company F's common stock and Company F owns 60% of Company G's common stock. Thus, Company E holds an effective indirect ownership interest in Company G of 48% (80% of Company F's 60%), even though Company E owns none of Company G's common stock directly.

An example of the second type can be diagramed as

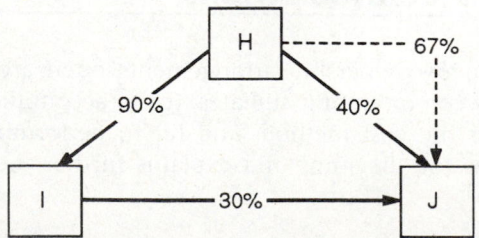

in which the primary parent, Company H, owns 90% of Company I's common stock and 40% of Company J's common stock, and Company I owns 30% of Company J's common stock. Thus, Company H holds a total effective ownership interest in Company J of 67%, the sum of [a] its own directly owned 40% and [b] 90% of Company I's 30%.

Finally, affiliates can own stock in each other. Such an ownership arrangement is called **mutual ownership.** As in the case of indirect ownership, many different configurations are possible, but they can be classified into two general types:

- Those in which a subsidiary owns stock in its parent
- Those in which subsidiaries own stock in each other

An example of the first type can be diagramed as

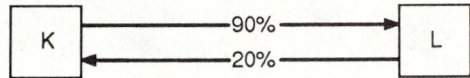

In this diagram, the parent, Company K, owns 90% of Company L's common stock and Company L, in turn, owns 20% of Company K's common stock.

An example of the second type can be diagramed as

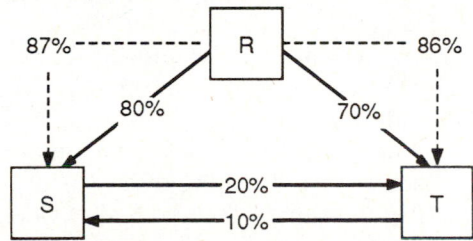

in which the primary parent, Company R, owns 80% of Company S's common stock and 70% of Company T's common stock, Company S owns 20% of Company T's common stock, and Company T owns 10% of Company S's common stock. This configuration can be recognized as being a combination of indirect and mutual ownerships. Company R has a total effective ownership interest in Company S of 87% (its own direct 80%, plus 70% of Company T's 10%) and a total effective ownership interest in Company T of 86% (its own direct 70%, plus 80% of Company S's 20%).

MULTIPLE OWNERSHIP INTERESTS

As noted earlier, the presence of more than one subsidiary does not change the application of either the equity or the cost method, or of any of the consolidation procedures that we have dealt with in previous chapters except to repeat each step for each additional affiliate. For this reason, multiple ownership arrangements are dealt with only briefly in the following paragraphs.

Earlier, an example was presented of a multiple ownership arrangement in which the parent company, A, owns 80% of subsidiary B's common stock, 90% of subsidiary C's common stock, and 75% of subsidiary D's common stock, diagramed as

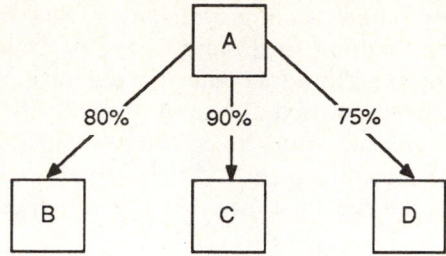

In this example, Company A records separately 80% of Company B's dividends, 90% of Company C's dividends, and 75% of Company D's dividends. Under the equity method, when each subsidiary declares dividends, Company A debits Dividends Receivable and credits the appropriate Investment in Subsidiary account. Under the cost method, the credit in each case is to Dividend Revenue. Upon receiving the dividends, Company A debits Cash and credits Dividends Receivable in each case.

At the end of each year, under the equity method, Company A records separately 80% of Company B's net income, 90% of Company C's net income, and 75% of Company D's net income by debiting the appropriate Investment in Subsidiary account and crediting the appropriate Income from Subsidiary account. Under the cost method, of course, no corresponding journal entry is recorded.

Similarly, each step in the consolidation process is repeated for each additional subsidiary. Rather than preparing separate schedules of the excess of cost over book value, a multicolumn schedule similar to that illustrated in Exhibit 13-1 can be used. Each set of adjustments and eliminations, however, must be repeated for each additional subsidiary. Thus, the ownership arrangement in this example would require three sets of Intercompany Ownership Interests eliminations, three sets of Subsidiary Income and Dividends eliminations, and so forth. A multicolumn Income Allocation schedule similar to that illustrated in Exhibit 13-6 would be appropriate in this example. Finally, the consolidation worksheet obviously would have to be expanded horizontally by adding additional trial balance columns for the additional affiliates.

INDIRECT OWNERSHIP

The presence of indirect ownership affects both [a] the parent's (or investor's) accounting for its investment in an affiliate under either the equity method or the cost method and [b] the consolidation process itself. These issues are discussed and illustrated in the following sections.

RECORDING UNDER THE EQUITY AND COST METHODS

Under the equity method, both direct and indirect ownership interests must be considered in recording each investor's share of its investee's net income. The safest way to proceed is to begin with the affiliate most remote from the primary parent and work upward toward the primary parent, recording each investor's income from its investee using only **direct** ownership percentages. This approach will assure that each investor's *total* net income will include its share of the *total* net income of its investee (or investees).

In contrast, each investor records only the dividends actually declared to it by its investee or investees. Under the equity method, of course, the Investment in Subsidiary (Investee) account would be credited, whereas under the cost method, Dividend Revenue usually would be credited. Because dividends involve an actual, verifiable amount of cash ultimately transferred from one affiliate to another, no indirect ownership interests are considered in recording them.

The accounting procedures under both methods are demonstrated in Illustrative Problem 13.1.

CONSOLIDATION PROCEDURES

The presence of indirect ownership interests also affects the consolidation process in several ways. The first effect is the need to decide which affiliates are to be included in the consolidated financial statements. In general, whenever more than 50% of the common stock of any investee is held within the consolidated group, control of that investee can be said to be present. If the other criteria discussed in Chapter 5 are met, that investee can be included in the consolidated financial statements.

When the consolidation process involves more than just a parent and a single subsidiary, a schedule of the excess of cost over book value is needed for each investment in an affiliate. Rather than prepare a completely separate schedule for each investment, however, we can prepare a composite excess of cost over book value schedule similar to that introduced in Chapter 12, except that no total column is used. This schedule format is illustrated in Exhibit 13-1.

Converting from cost to equity presents a special problem when indirect ownership interests are present. Indirect ownership interests are considered in recording income from the investee under the equity method, but not in recording dividends under either method. Therefore, a simple comparison of the investor's equity in the investee at the beginning of the current year and at the date of acquisition will not yield the correct amount needed to accomplish the conversion from cost to equity. Instead, the amount of the conversion must be calculated as [a] the investor's share of the sum of the investee's *total* net incomes, minus [b] the investor's share of the sum of the investee's dividends, from the date of acquisition to the beginning of the current year. This calculation is shown in Exhibit 13-7.

The Intercompany Ownership Interests set of eliminations is made in the normal manner, using the investor's end of the year percentage of ownership, with resepct to *each* investment in *each* investee qualifying for inclusion in the consolidated financial statements.

Similarly, the Subsidiary (or Investee) Income and Dividends set of eliminations is repeated for each additional investee. Under the equity method, Income from Subsidiary (or Investee) is debited for the amount recorded by the investor, as described in the preceding section. Under the cost method, this debit affects Dividend Revenue. Under both methods, the investee's Dividends Declared balance is credited for the investor's end of the year share of the balance, and the difference is debited or credited to Investment in Subsidiary (or Investee).

In making any other eliminations involving allocations between or among retained earnings balances, indirect as well as direct ownership interests must be considered. Using our previously established allocation formula, the amount allocated to each affiliate's Retained Earnings balance is [a] that affiliate's external ownership percentage, multiplied by [b] its share of quantity being allocated, multiplied by [c] the quantity being allocated. Among the types of items requiring this treatment are prior years' amortization of the difference between cost and book value, intercompany profit in beginning inventory, intercompany profit in depreciable assets, and gain or loss on intercompany bond acquisitions. The effect of indirect ownership interests on eliminations is illustrated in Exhibits 13-2 through 13-5.

The Income Allocation schedule also is affected by the presence of indirect ownership interests. The use of a multicolumn Income Allocation schedule, as illustrated in Exhibit 13-6, provides a convenient way of dealing with multiple investments. The process described earlier for determining the amount to be recorded as Income from Subsidiary (or Investee) by each investor essentially is repeated here, after adjusting the affiliates' own net incomes for elimination items that have changed the grand total of net income.

ILLUSTRATIVE PROBLEM 13.1: INDIRECT OWNERSHIP

On December 31, 1990, Company I purchased 6,000 of Company J's 20,000 shares of $5 par value common stock for $49,000. On April 1, 1991, Company H purchased 9,000 of Company I's 10,000 shares of $10 par value common stock for $156,000 and 8,000 shares of Company J's common stock for $68,000. Company I's common stock was issued at 11 in 1982; Company J's common stock was issued at 6 in 1980. Retained Earnings balances at December 31, 1990 were: Company I, $42,500; Company J, $20,000. All differences between cost and book value are treated as goodwill from consolidation, amortized over 10 years. All investments are accounted for under the equity method.

During 1992, Company J sold merchandise to Company H for $132,000, of which $11,300 remained unpaid at December 31, 1992. Company H's beginning and ending inventories for 1992 contained intercompany profits on goods purchased from Company J of $4,000 and $3,700, respectively. All affiliates use perpetual inventory systems.

The relationship of Companies H, I, and J after April 1, 1991 can be diagramed as

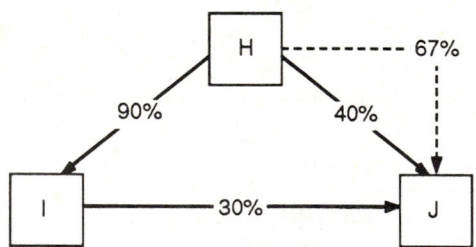

Net incomes of the three affiliates from their own operations and the dividends by each for 1991 and 1992 are given below. All dividends were declared on November 15 and paid on December 20 in each year.

	Net Income	Dividends
Company H, 1991	$ 38,000	$ 12,000
Company I, 1991	24,000	15,000
Company J, 1991	20,000	12,000
Company H, 1992	40,000	10,000
Company I, 1992	30,500	15,000
Company J, 1992	25,000	12,000

Changes in the three Investment account balances through December 31, 1992 are shown below.

	Investment in		
	Company I (H)	Company J (H)	Company J (I)
Cost of Investment	$ 156,000	$ 68,000	$ 49,000
Net Income, 1991	20,250	6,000	6,000
Dividends, 11/15/91	(13,500)	(4,800)	(3,600)
Balance, 12/31/91	162,750	69,200	51,400
Net Income, 1992	34,200	10,000	7,500
Dividends, 11/15/92	(13,500)	(4,800)	(3,600)
Balance, 12/31/92	$ 183,450	$ 74,400	$ 55,300

The safe and convenient approach to recording net income under the equity method indicated earlier is to begin with the affiliate most remote from the primary parent and work upward toward the primary parent, recording each investor's income from its investee using only *direct* ownership percentages. Using this approach, Company I's income from Company J is included in Company I's *total* net income before determining Company H's income from Company I, in each year. In this manner, Company H is able to recognize both its direct and its indirect shares of Company J's net income.

Company I's total 1991 net income consists of its own net income, $24,000, plus its 30% share of Company J's 1991 net income of $20,000, or $6,000. Thus, Company H records 90% of 9/12 of $30,000, or $20,250, as its 1991 income from Company I. Company I's total 1992 net income consists of its own net income, $30,500, plus its 30% share of Company J's 1992 net income of $25,000, or $7,500. Thus, Company H records 90% of $38,000, or $34,200, as its 1992 income from Company I. In each year, Company H records its income from Company J based on its direct ownership interest of 40%—40% of 9/12 of $20,000, or $6,000, in 1991 and 40% of $25,000, or $10,000, in 1992.

The dividends, on the other hand, are simply transfers of assets from investee to investor and, therefore, are not affected by the presence of an indirect ownership interest. Each investor records the actual amount of dividends declared to it by the investee; that is, the investor's direct ownership percentage multiplied by the investee's dividends declared amount.

The Goodwill from Consolidation schedule to accompany the December 31, 1992 consolidation worksheet is shown in Exhibit 13-1. The book value of Company H's investment in Company I's common stock is calculated as Company H's percentage of ownership, 90%, multiplied by Comany I's total stockholders' equity at April 1, 1991, the date of acquisition. On that date, Company I's total stockholders' equity consists of common stock of $100,000, plus additional paid-in capital of $10,000, plus January 1, 1991 retained earnings of $42,500, plus 3/12 of Company I's *total* 1991 net income of $30,000. Company I's total 1991 net income consists of its own net income, $24,000, plus its 30% share of Company J's 1991 net income of $20,000, or $6,000. Only nine months' goodwill amortization, 9/120 of $12,000, is recognized on this investment in 1991, but a full year's amortization, 12/120 of $12,000, is recognized in 1992.

The book value of Company H's investment in Company J's common stock is calculated as Company H's percentage of ownership, 40%, multiplied by Company J's total stockholders'

EXHIBIT 13-1

Illustrative Problem 13.1
Goodwill from Consolidation
December 31, 1992

Goodwill from Consolidation

	Investment in		
	Company I (H)	Company J (H)	Company J (I)
Cost of Investment	$ 156,000	$ 68,000	$ 49,000
Book Value	144,000	58,000	42,000
Goodwill at Acquisition	12,000	10,000	7,000
Amortization, 1991	(900)	(750)	(700)
Amortization, 1992	(1,200)	(1,000)	(700)
Goodwill, 12/31/92	$ 9,900	$ 8,250	$ 5,600

equity at April 1, 1991, the date of acquisition. On that date, Company J's total stockholders' equity consists of common stock of $100,000, plus additional paid-in capital of $20,000, plus January 1, 1991 retained earnings of $20,000, plus 3/12 of Company J's 1991 net income of $20,000. Again, only nine months' goodwill amortization, 9/120 of $10,000, is recognized on this investment in 1991, but a full year's amortization, 12/120 of $10,000, is recognized in 1992.

The book value of Company I's investment in Company J's common stock is calculated as Company I's percentage of ownership, 30%, multiplied by Company J's total stockholders' equity at December 31, 1990, the date of acquisition. On that date, Company J's total stockholders' equity consists of common stock of $100,000, plus additional paid-in capital of $20,000, plus December 31, 1990 retained earnings of $20,000. A full year's goodwill amortization, 12/120 of $7,000, is recognized on this investment in 1991 and again in 1992.

The Intercompany Ownership Interests sets of eliminations that would appear on the December 31, 1992 consolidation worksheet are shown in Exhibit 13-2. In each set of eliminations, the investor's share of ownership is eliminated from each of the investee's stockholders' equity balances, with the total amount eliminated from the appropriate Investment account balance.

The Subsidiary Income and Dividends sets of eliminations that would appear on the December 31, 1992 consolidation worksheet are shown in Exhibit 13-3. In each set of eliminations, the amount recorded by the investor as its share of the investee's total net income is eliminated from the appropriate Income from Affiliate balance, the investor's share of ownership is eliminated from the investee's Dividends Declared balance, and the net amount is eliminated from the appropriate Investment account balance.

The amortization amounts that appear in the December 31, 1992 Goodwill Amortization sets of eliminations in Exhibit 13-4 are taken directly from the Goodwill from Consolidation schedule in Exhibit 13-1. The prior year's amortization amounts in eliminations [22] and [25] are allocated entirely to the Retained Earnings of the investor, Company H, because neither of the other affiliates has any share of ownership in the goodwill being amortized.

EXHIBIT 13-2

Illustrative Problem 13.1
Eliminations
December 31, 1992

Eliminations

Intercompany Ownership Interests

[1]	Common Stock: I	$ 90,000
[2]	Additional Paid-in Capital: I	9,000
[3]	Retained Earnings: I	51,750
[4]	Investment in Company I: H	$(150,750)
[5]	Common Stock: J	$ 40,000
[6]	Additional Paid-in Capital: J	8,000
[7]	Retained Earnings: J	11,200
[8]	Investment in Company J: H	$(59,200)
[9]	Common Stock: J	$ 30,000
[10]	Additional Paid-in Capital: J	6,000
[11]	Retained Earnings: J	8,400
[12]	Investment in Company J: I	$(44,400)

EXHIBIT 13-3

Illustrative Problem 13.1
Additional Eliminations
December 31, 1992

Subsidiary Income and Dividends

[13]	Income from Company I: H	$ 34,200
[14]	Dividends Declared: I	(13,500)
[15]	Investment in Company I: H	$(20,700)
[16]	Income from Company J: H	$ 10,000
[17]	Dividends Declared: J	(4,800)
[18]	Investment in Company J: H	$(5,200)
[19]	Income from Company J: I	$ 7,500
[20]	Dividends Declared: J	(3,600)
[21]	Investment in Company J: I	$(3,900)

EXHIBIT 13-4

Illustrative Problem 13.1
Additional Eliminations
December 31, 1992

Goodwill Amortization

[22] Retained Earnings: H	$ 900
[23] Operating Expenses	1,200
[24] Investment in Company I: H	$(2,100)
[25] Retained Earnings: H	$ 750
[26] Operating Expenses	1,000
[27] Investment in Company J: H	$(1,750)
[28] Retained Earnings: H	$ 630
[29] Retained Earnings: I	70
[30] Operating Expenses	700
[31] Investment in Company J: I	$(1,400)

EXHIBIT 13-5

Illustrative Problem 13.1
Additional Eliminations
December 31, 1992

Intercompany Sales and Purchases

[32] Sales	$ 132,000
[33] Cost of Goods Sold	(132,000)

Intercompany Payables and Receivables

[34] Accounts Payable	$ 11,300
[35] Accounts Receivable	(11,300)

Intercompany Profit in Beginning Inventory

[36] Retained Earnings: H	$ 2,680
[37] Retained Earnings: I	120
[38] Retained Earnings: J	1,200
[39] Cost of Goods Sold	$(4,000)

Intercompany Profit in Ending Inventory

[40] Cost of Goods Sold	$ 3,700
[41] Inventories	(3,700)

The prior year's amortization of the goodwill on Company I's investment in Company J, on the other hand, is affected by the presence of indirect ownership. Because Company H owns 90% of Company I's common stock, it has a share of ownership in the goodwill being amortized. Following the previously established allocation formula, the prior year's amortization allocated to each affiliate's Retained Earnings is [a] its external ownership percentage, multiplied by [b] its share of the quantity being allocated, multiplied by [c] the quantity being allocated, $700, yielding the following results:

$$
\begin{array}{lccccc}
 & [a] & \times & [b] & \times & [c] & = & [d] \\
\text{Company H:} & 100\% & \times & 90\% & \times & \$700 & = & \$630 \\
\text{Company I:} & 10\% & \times & 100\% & \times & \$700 & = & \$\ 70
\end{array}
$$

Exhibit 13-5 contains the December 31, 1992 eliminations resulting from the intercompany sales and purchases of merchandise. The Intercompany Sales and Purchases and Intercompany Receivables and Payables sets of eliminations are not affected by the presence of the indirect ownership interest, because in each case no allocation between or among Retained Earnings balances is necessary. For the same reason, the Intercompany Profit in Ending Inventory set of eliminations is unaffected by the indirect ownership interest.

The Intercompany Profit in Beginning Inventory set of eliminations, in contrast, requires allocation among the Retained Earnings balances. The amount eliminated against each Retained Earnings balance is [a] that affiliate's external ownership percentage, multiplied by [b] its share of the intercompany profit, multipliled by [c] the intercompany profit amount, as follows:

$$
\begin{array}{lccccc}
 & [a] & \times & [b] & \times & [c] & = & [d] \\
\text{Company H:} & 100\% & \times & 67\% & \times & \$4,000 & = & \$2,680 \\
\text{Company I:} & 10\% & \times & 30\% & \times & \$4,000 & = & \$\ \ 120 \\
\text{Company J:} & 30\% & \times & 100\% & \times & \$4,000 & = & \$1,200
\end{array}
$$

The Income Allocation schedule that accompanies the December 31, 1992 consolidation worksheet appears in Exhibit 13-6. The multicolumn format accommodates all three affiliates (or more, if necessary) and also provides a check on arithmetic accuracy through the Total column. The procedure described earlier of beginning with the least owned subsidiary (or investee) and working upward toward the primary parent assures that consolidated net income will include both Company H's direct and indirect shares of Company J's adjusted net income.

The Income Allocation schedule begins by listing the affiliate's individual net incomes, with the total of these amounts entered in the Total column. Then, the individual net incomes are adjusted as necessary. In this case, the intercompany profit in beginning inventory is added to the net income of the selling affiliate, Company J. Also, the current year's amortization of goodwill from consolidation on Company H's investments in Company I and Company J is subtracted from Company H's net income, and the current year's amortization of goodwill from consolidation on Company I's investment in Company J is subtracted from Company I's net income. Finally, the intercompany profit in ending inventory is subtracted from Company J's net income. The totals of these adjustments are entered in the Total column, yielding the total amount of adjusted net income, $92,900. This is the total amount that ultimately must be allocated among the minority interests in Company I's and Company J's net incomes and consolidated net income.

EXHIBIT 13-6

Illustrative Problem 13.1
Income Allocation Schedule
December 31, 1992

Income Allocation

	Company H	Company I	Company J	Total
Individual Net Incomes	$ 40,000	$ 30,500	$ 25,000	$ 95,000
Add: Intercompany Profit in				
Beginning Inventory			4,000	4,000
Less: Goodwill Amortization	(2,200)	(700)		(2,900)
Intercompany Profit in				
Ending Inventory			(3,700)	(3,700)
Adusted Net Incomes	37,800	29,800	25,300	$ 92,900
30% to Company I		7,590	(7,590)	
40% to Company H	10,120		(10,120)	
Company I's Total Net				
Income		37,390		
90% to Company H	33,651	(33,651)		
Minority Interests		$ 3,739	$ 7,590	$ 11,329
Consolidated Net Income	$ 81,571			81,571
Total Net Income				$ 92,900

The adjusted net incomes are allocated by working from Company J, the affiliate most remote from the primary parent, toward the primary parent, Company H. Most importantly, we must be sure to allocate to Company I its share of Company J's adjusted net income, $7,590, before allocating net income from Company I to Company H. As shown in Exhibit 13-6, that $7,590 is added to Company I's adjusted net income in arriving at Company I's total net income, 90% of which is allocated to Company H. Because the allocation of net income from Company J to Company H does not depend on any other allocation, it could be made at any point.

The totals of the Company I and Company J columns represent the minority interests in those affiliates' net incomes. The total of the minority interests is entered in the Total column. The total of the Company H column is consolidated net income; it also is entered in the Total column. The total of the Total column is the same $92,200 determined earlier to be the total of the adjusted net incomes that had to be allocated, thus providing a check on the arithmetic accuracy of the Income Allocation schedule. The completed December 31, 1992 equity method consolidation worksheet appears in Exhibit 13-7.

Use of the Cost Method.　　If Companies H and I had accounted for their respective investments under the cost method, each would have recorded its share of its investee's dividends as Dividend Revenue and the balances of the three Investment accounts would have been their original costs.

Investment in Company I: H	$156,000
Investment in Company J: H	68,000
Investment in Company J: I	49,000

At December 31, 1993, it would have been necessary to convert each Investment balance from cost to equity as of December 31, 1992, as shown in Exhibit 13-8. As noted earlier, the amount of the conversion must be calculated as [a] the investor's share of the sum of the investee's *total* net incomes, minus [b] the investor's share of the sum of the investee's dividends, from the date of acquisition to the beginning of the current year.

Company I's total 1991 net income consists of its own net income, $24,000, plus its 30% share of Company J's 1991 net income of $20,000, or $6,000, for a total of $30,000. Company I's total 1992 net income consists of its own net income, $30,500, plus its 30% share of Company J's 1992 net income of $25,000, or $7,500, for a total of $32,500. Thus, Company H's share of Company I's total net income from April 1, 1991 through December 31, 1992 is 90% of 9/12 of $30,000 plus 90% of $32,500, or $54,450. Company H's share of Company

EXHIBIT 13-7

Illustrative Problem 13.1
Consolidation Worksheet
December 31, 1992

	Company H	Company I	Company J	Eliminations		Income Statement	Balance Sheet
Accounts Receivable	99,100	33,500	41,600	[35]	(11,300)		162,900
Inventories	54,300	25,800	32,400	[41]	(3,700)		108,800
Plant and Equipment	603,900	275,700	316,900				1,196,500
Other Assets	33,200	4,400	4,200				41,800
Investment in Company I: H	183,450			[4]	(150,750)		9,900 G
				[15]	(20,700)		
				[24]	(2,100)		
Investment in Company J: H	74,400			[8]	(59,200)		8,250 G
				[18]	(5,200)		
				[27]	(1,750)		
Investment in Company J: I		55,300		[12]	(44,400)		5,600 G
				[21]	(3,900)		
				[31]	(1,400)		
Cost of Goods Sold	252,800	188,200	171,400	[33]	(132,000)	480,100	
				[39]	(4,000)		
				[40]	3,700		
Operating Expenses	186,400	139,500	135,300	[23]	1,200	464,100	
				[26]	1,000		
				[30]	700		
Dividends Declared: H	10,000						10,000 R
Dividends Declared: I		15,000		[14]	(13,500)		1,500 MI
Dividends Declared: J			12,000	[17]	(4,800)		3,600 MJ
				[20]	(3,600)		
	1,497,550	737,400	713,800				1,548,850

	Company H	Company I	Company J	Eliminations		Income Statement	Balance Sheet
Accumulated Depreciation	245,600	162,400	190,900				598,900
Accounts Payable	81,400	41,800	43,200	[34]	11,300		155,100
Common Stock: H	400,000						400,000
Common Stock: I		100,000		[1]	90,000		10,000 MI
Common Stock: J			100,000	[5]	40,000		30,000 MJ
				[9]	30,000		
Additional Paid-in Capital: H	100,000						100,000
Additional Paid-in Capital: I		10,000		[2]	9,000		1,000 MI
Additional Paid-in Capital: J			20,000	[6]	8,000		6,000 MJ
				[10]	6,000		
				[22]	900		
Retained Earnings: H	147,150			[25]	750		142,190 R
				[28]	630		
				[36]	2,680		
				[3]	51,750		
Retained Earnings: I		57,500		[29]	70		5,560 MI
				[37]	120		
				[7]	11,200		
Retained Earnings: J			28,000	[11]	8,400		7,200 MJ
				[38]	1,200		
Sales	479,200	358,200	331,700	[32]	132,000	1,037,100	
Income from Company I: H	34,200			[13]	34,200		
Income from Company J: H	10,000			[16]	10,000		
Income from Company J: I		7,500		[19]	7,500		
	1,497,550	737,400	713,800				
Minority Interest in Company I's Net Income						3,739	3,739 MI
Minority Interest in Company J's Net Income						7,590	7,590 MJ
Consolidated Net Income						81,571	81,571 R
						1,037,100 1,037,100	1,548,850

I's dividends for 1991 and 1992 is 90% of $30,000, or $27,000. The increase in Company H's investment in Company I, therefore, is $27,450.

Company H's share of Company J's net income from April 1, 1991 through December 31, 1992 is 40% of 9/12 of $20,000 plus 40% of $25,000, or $16,000. Company H's share of Company J's dividends for 1991 and 1992 is 40% of $24,000, or $9,600. The increase in Company H's investment in Company J, therefore, is $6,400.

Company I's share of Company J's net income from January 1, 1991 through December 31, 1992 is 30% of $20,000 plus 30% of $25,000, or $13,500. Company I's share of Company J's dividends for 1991 and 1992 is 30% of $24,000, or $7,200. The increase in Company I's investment in Company J, therefore, is $6,300.

MUTUAL OWNERSHIP

Two approaches to the treatment of mutual ownership are possible. One approach is to ignore the mutuality and treat all ownership interests in affiliates other than those of the primary parent as "treasury stock" in the consolidated financial statements. Under this approach,

EXHIBIT 13-8

Illustrative Problem 13.1
Conversion from Cost to Equity
December 31, 1993

Investment in Company I: H

90% of Company I's Total Net Income, 4/1/91–12/31/92	$ 54,450
90% of Company I's Total Dividends, 1991–1992	27,000
Increase in Equity	$ 27,450

Investment in Company J: H

40% of Company J's Total Net Income, 4/1/91–12/31/92	$ 16,000
40% of Company J's Total Dividends, 1991–1992	9,600
Increase in Equity	$ 6,400

Investment in Company J: I

30% of Company J's Total Net Income, 1991–1992	$ 13,500
30% of Company J's Total Dividends, 1991–1992	7,200
Increase in Equity	$ 6,300

- all investments other than those of the primary parent are accounted for under the cost method,
- eliminations involving allocations between or among Retained Earnings balances are made without regard to mutual ownership, and
- mutual ownership is ignored in allocating net income.

The other appraoch is to deal explicitly with the mutual ownership. Under this approach,

- all investments in affiliates can be accounted for under the equity method,
- mutual ownership is recognized in making eliminations involving allocations between or among Retained Earnings balances, and
- mutual ownership is recognized in allocating net income, both on the books and in the consolidation process.

The first approach can be justified only on grounds of immateriality. For example, if a subsidiary owns 1% of its parent's common stock, we might conclude that the effect of this ownership interest is immaterial to the consolidated financial statements and, therefore, treat the subsidiary's investment as "treasury stock" in those financial statements. Otherwise, the second approach more accurately reflects the underlying economic facts and clearly is preferable. We will follow that approach, respecting mutual ownership when present, throughout the rest of this chapter.

The cross-allocation problems presented by the presence of mutual ownership can be dealt with in several ways, perhaps the most straightforward and precise of which is the use of simultaneous equations. This technique is demonstrated in Illustrative Problem 13.2.

RECORDING UNDER THE EQUITY AND COST METHODS

Under the equity method, both direct and indirect ownership interests, including mutual ownership, must be considered in recording each investor's share of its investee's net income. Again, the safest way to proceed is to begin with the affiliate most remote from the primary parent and work toward the primary parent, recording each investor's share of the *total* net income of its investee(s). At any point along the way, however, we may encounter mutual ownership, requiring cross-allocation through the use of simultaneous equations. In such cases, it is necessary to write an equation for each affiliate's *total* net income and solve these equations simultaneously. The amount that each investor affiliate records as its share of its investee's net income is determined as [a] the investor's percentage of ownership in the investee, multiplied by [b] the investee's *total* net income determined through the simultaneous equation solution.

In contrast, each investor records only the dividends actually declared to it by its investee(s). Under the equity method, of course, the Investment in Subsidiary (Investee) account would be credited, whereas under the cost method, Dividend Revenue usually would be credited. Because dividends involve an actual, verifiable amount of cash ultimately transferred from one affiliate to another, no indirect or mutual ownership interests are considered in recording them.

The accounting procedures under both the cost method and the equity method are demonstrated in Illustrative Problem 13.2.

CONSOLIDATION PROCEDURES

The effects of mutual ownership on the consolidation process are similar to those of indirect ownership, except when the need for cross-allocation arises. These effects are discussed in the following paragraphs.

Again, when the consolidation process involves more than just a parent and a single subsidiary, we will prepare a composite excess of cost over book value schedule, using the format illustrated in Exhibit 13-1 and again in Exhibit 13-9.

Converting from cost to equity when mutual ownership exists presents a problem similar to that encountered when purely indirect ownership interests are present. Because mutual and indirect ownership interests are considered in recording income from the investee under the equity method, but not in recording dividends under either method, the amount of the conversion must be calculated as [a] the investor's share of the sum of the investee's *total* net incomes, minus [b] the investor's share of the sum of the investee's dividends, from the date of acquisition to the beginning of the current year. This calculation is shown in Exhibit 13-15.

The Intercompany Ownership Interest set of eliminations is made in the normal manner, using the investor's end of the year percentage of ownership, with respect to *each* investment in *each* investee qualifying for inclusion in the consolidated financial statements.

Similarly, the Subsidiary (or Investee) Income and Dividends set of eliminations is repeated for each additional investee. Under the equity method, Income from Subsidiary (or Investee) is debited for the amount recorded by the investor, as described in the preceding section.

Under the cost method, this debit affects Dividend Revenue. Under both methods, the investee's Dividends Declared balance is credited for the investor's end of the year share of the balance, and the difference is debited or credited to Investment in Subsidiary (or Investee).

In making any other eliminations involving allocations between or among Retained Earnings balances, direct, indirect, and mutual ownership interests must be considered. Among the types of items requiring this treatment are prior years' amortization of the difference between cost and book value, intercompany profit in beginning inventory, intercompany profit in depreciable assets, and gain or loss on intercompany bond acquisitions. In the previously established allocation formula, the amount allocated to each affiliate's Retained Earnings balance is [a] that affiliate's external ownership percentage, multiplied by [b] its share of the quantity being allocated, multiplied by [c] the quantity being allocated. When mutual ownership is present, however, it is necessary to determine the originating affiliate's *total* share of the quantity being allocated by using the simultaneous equation technique. Then, the allocation formula is applied to that *total* share. The effects of indirect and mutual ownership interests on eliminations are illustrated in Exhibits 13-10 through 13-13.

The multicolumn form of Income Allocation schedule shown in Exhibit 13-6 for indirect ownership interests also is appropriate when mutual ownership is present, but with some modification. After adjusting the affiliate's own net incomes for elimination items that have changed the grand total of net income, the adjusted net incomes of those affiliates involved in mutual ownership are subjected to the simultaneous equation routine. The *total* net incomes determined by solving the equations become the bases for income allocation between or among affiliates. This approach is illustrated in Exhibit 13-14.

ILLUSTRATIVE PROBLEM 13.2: MUTUAL AND INDIRECT OWNERSHIP

Company R purchased 8,000 of Company S's 10,000 shares of $10 par value common stock for $158,000 on April 1, 1990 and 28,000 of Company T's 40,000 shares of $5 par value common stock for $196,300 on June 30, 1990. On January 1, 1991, Company S purchased 8,000 shares of Company T's common stock for $61,400 and Company T purchased 1,000 shares of Company S's common stock for $23,900. At December 31, 1989, Retained Earnings balances were: Company S, $80,000; Company T, $50,000. Both Company S's and Company T's common stock were issued originally at par. The relationship of the three affiliates after June 30, 1990 can be diagramed as

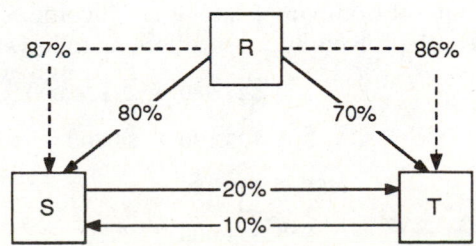

Net incomes and dividends for 1990 through 1992 were

	Net Income	Dividends
Company R, 1990	$ 45,000	$ 20,000
Company S, 1990	20,000	10,000
Company T, 1990	18,000	10,000
Company R, 1991	52,000	25,000
Company S, 1991	25,580	12,000
Company T, 1991	24,000	15,000
Company R, 1992	40,000	16,000
Company S, 1992	28,140	15,000
Company T, 1992	21,000	11,000

All dividends were declared on November 10 and paid on December 15 of each year. All investors account for their investments in affiliates under the equity method.

On July 1, 1991, Company T sold machinery that had cost $17,000 to Company R for $26,800. Company R is depreciating the machinery on the straight-line method, over a useful life of 10 years from the date of purchase, with a $2,000 salvage value.

Because the mutual ownership between Companies S and T did not exist until the beginning of 1991, Company R records its share of each subsidiary's 1990 net income without regard to the other: 80% of 9/12 of Company S's $20,000 net income, or $12,000, and 70% of 6/12 of Company T's $18,000 net income, or $6,300. The mutual ownership, however, affects the allocation of net income for 1991 and 1992. To allocate the 1991 net incomes, we will write equations in which we let

$$S = \text{Company S's } \textit{total} \text{ net income}$$

$$T = \text{Company T's } \textit{total} \text{ net income}$$

These equations read

$$[1]\ S = \$25,580 + .2T$$

$$[2]\ T = \$24,000 + .1S$$

(Because Company R is not a party to the mutual ownership, it is not necessary to write an equation for its total net income.)

Company S's and Company T's net incomes are mutually *interdependent;* that is, each is dependent in part on the other. Therefore, equation [1] states that Company S's total net income equals its own net income of $25,580, plus its share of Company T's total net income. Equation [2], in turn, states that Company T's total net income equals its own net income of $24,000, plus its share of Company S's total net income.

Equation [1] can be solved by substitution, as follows:

$$S = \$25,580 + .2(\$24,000 + .1S)$$

$$S = \$25,580 + \$4,800 + .02S$$

$$.98S = \$30,380$$

$$S = \$31,000$$

Using the value for S obtained above, equation [2] is solved as follows:

$$T = \$24,000 + .1(\$31,000)$$

$$T = \$27,100$$

Based on these solutions, Company R records its share, 80%, of $31,000, or $24,800, as its 1991 income from Company S and its share, 70% of $27,100, or $18,970, as its 1991 income from Company T. Similarly, Company T records its share, 10%, of $31,000, or $3,100, as its 1991 income from Company S and Company S records its share, 20%, of $27,100, or $5,420, as its 1991 income from Company T.

Repeating the process for the 1992 net incomes, we have

$$[1] \ S = \$28,140 + .2T$$

$$[2] \ T = \$21,000 + .1S$$

Equation [1] is solved by substitutions.

$$S = \$28,140 + .2(\$21,000 + .1S)$$

$$.98S = \$32,340$$

$$S = \$33,000$$

Substituting the $33,000 for the term S, equation [2] is solved.

$$T = \$21,000 + .1(\$33,000)$$

$$T = \$24,300$$

Based on these solutions, Company R records its share, 80%, of $33,000, or $26,400, as its 1992 income from Company S and its share, 70%, of $24,300, or $17,010, as its 1992 income from Company T. Similarly, Company T records its share, 10%, of $33,000, or $3,300, as its 1992 income from Company S and Company S records its share, 20%, of $24,300, or $4,860, as its 1992 income from Company T.

In each year, each investor records the amount of dividends actually declared to it by each investee. In each year, Company R records its share of Company S's dividends: 80% of $10,000 in 1990, 80% of $12,000 in 1991, and 80% of $15,000 in 1992. Similarly, Company R records 70% of Company T's dividends in each year: 70% of $10,000 in 1990, 70% of $15,000 in 1991, and 70% of $11,000 in 1992. Because Company T did not acquire its investment in Company S until January 1, 1991, it records dividends from Company S for only the last two years: 10% of $12,000 in 1991 and 10% of $15,000 in 1992. For the same reason, Company S records dividends from Company T for only the last two years: 20% of $15,000 in 1991 and 20% of $11,000 in 1992.

The effects on each Investment account balance of recording investee net income and dividends are summarized below.

	Investment in			
	Company S (R)	Company T (R)	Company S (T)	Company T (S)
Cost of Investment	$ 158,000	$ 196,300	$ 23,900	$ 61,400
Dividends, 11/10/90	(8,000)	(7,000)	—	—
Net Income, 1990	12,000	6,300	—	—
Balance, 12/31/90	162,000	195,600	23,900	61,400
Dividends, 11/10/91	(9,600)	(10,500)	(1,200)	(3,000)
Net Income, 1991	24,800	18,970	3,100	5,420
Balance, 12/31/91	177,200	204,070	25,800	63,820
Dividends, 11/10/92	(12,000)	(7,700)	(1,500)	(2,200)
Net Income, 1992	26,400	17,010	3,300	4,860
Balance, 12/31/92	$ 191,600	$ 213,380	$ 27,600	$ 66,480

Exhibit 13-9 contains the composite Goodwill from Consolidation schedule accompanying the December 31, 1992 consolidation worksheet. The book value of Company R's investment in Company S's common stock is calculated as Company R's percentage of ownership, 80%, multiplied by Company S's total stockholders' equity at April 1, 1990, the date of acquisition. On that date, Company S's total stockholders' equity consists of common stock of $100,000, plus January 1, 1990 retained earnings of $80,000, plus 3/12 of Company S's 1990 net income of $20,000. Only nine months' goodwill amortization, 9/120 of $10,000, is recognized on this investment in 1990, but a full year's amortization, 12/120 of $12,000, is recognized in both 1991 and 1992.

EXHIBIT 13-9

Illustrative Problem 13.2
Goodwill from Consolidation
December 31, 1992

	Investment in			
	Company S (R)	Company T (R)	Company S (T)	Company T (S)
Cost of Investment	$ 158,000	$ 196,300	$ 23,900	$ 61,400
Book Value	148,000	181,300	19,000	51,600
Goodwill at Acquisition	10,000	15,000	4,900	9,800
Amortization, 1990	(750)	(750)	—	—
Amortization, 1991	(1,000)	(1,500)	(490)	(980)
Amortization, 1992	(1,000)	(1,500)	(490)	(980)
Goodwill, 12/31/92	$ 7,250	$ 11,250	$ 3,920	$ 7,840

The book value of Company R's investment in Company T's common stock is calculated as Company R's percentage of ownership, 70%, multiplied by Company T's total stockholders' equity at June 30, 1990, the date of acquisition. On that date, Company T's total stockholders' equity consists of common stock of $200,000, plus January 1, 1990 retained earnings of

$50,000, plus 6/12 of Company T's 1990 net income of $18,000. Only six months' goodwill amortization, 6/120 of $15,000, is recognized on this investment in 1990, but a full year's amortization, 12/120 of $12,000, is recognized in 1991 and 1992.

The book value of Company T's investment in Company S's common stock is calculated as Company T's percentage of ownership, 10%, multiplied by Company S's total stockholders' equity at January 1, 1991, the date of acquisition. On that date, Company S's total stockholders' equity consists of common stock of $100,000, plus January 1, 1990 retained earnings of $80,000, plus Company S's 1990 net income of $20,000, minus Company S's 1990 dividends of $10,000. A full year's goodwill amortization, 12/120 of $4,900, is recognized in both 1991 and 1992.

The book value of Company S's investment in Company T's common stock is calculated as Company S's percentage of ownership, 20%, multiplied by Company T's total stockholders' equity at January 1, 1991, the date of acquisition. On that date, Company T's total stockholders' equity consists of common stock of $200,000, plus January 1, 1990 retained earnings of $50,000, plus Company T's 1990 net income of $18,000, minus Company T's 1990 dividends of $10,000. A full year's goodwill amortization, 12/120 of $9,800, is recognized in 1991 and 1992.

The Intercompany Ownership Interests sets of eliminations that would appear on the December 31, 1992 consolidation worksheet are shown in Exhibit 13-10. In each set of

---

EXHIBIT 13-10

Illustrative Problem 13.2
Eliminations
December 31, 1992

Eliminations

Intercompany Ownership Interests

[1]	Common Stock: S	$ 80,000
[2]	Retained Earnings: S	87,200
[3]	Investment in Company S: R	$(167,200)
[4]	Common Stock: T	$ 140,000
[5]	Retained Earnings: T	49,070
[6]	Investment in Company T: R	$(189,070)
[7]	Common Stock: S	$ 10,000
[8]	Retained Earnings: S	10,900
[9]	Investment in Company S: T	$(20,900)
[10]	Common Stock: T	$ 40,000
[11]	Retained Earnings: T	14,020
[12]	Investment in Company T: S	$(54,020)

eliminations, the investor's share of ownership is eliminated from each of the investee's stockholders' equity balances, with the total amount eliminated from the appropriate Investment account balance. The ownership percentages used are

Company R's Investment in Company S	80%
Company R's Investment in Company T	70%
Company T's Investment in Company S	10%
Company S's Investment in Company T	20%

The Subsidiary Income and Dividends sets of eliminations that would appear on the December 31, 1992 consolidation worksheet are shown in Exhibit 13-11. In each set of eliminations, the amount recorded by the investor as its share of the investee's total net income (as determined earlier, using the simultaneous equations) is eliminated from the appropriate Income from Affiliate balance. Also, the investor's share of ownership is eliminated from the investee's Dividends Declared balance, and the net amount is eliminated from the appropriate Investment account balance. The ownership percentages used are the same as those indicated above for Exhibit 13-10.

EXHIBIT 13-11

Illustrative Problem 13.2
Additional Eliminations
December 31, 1992

Subsidiary Income and Dividends

[13] Income from Company S: R	$ 26,400
[14] Dividends Declared: S	(12,000)
[15] Investment in Company S: R	$ (14,400)
[16] Income from Company T: R	$ 17,010
[17] Dividends Declared: T	(7,700)
[18] Investment in Company T: R	$ (9,310)
[19] Income from Company S: T	$ 3,300
[20] Dividends Declared: S	(1,500)
[21] Investment in Company S: T	$ (1,800)
[22] Income from Company T: S	$ 4,860
[23] Dividends Declared: T	(2,200)
[24] Investment in Company T: S	$ (2,660)

The December 31, 1992 Goodwill Amortization sets of eliminations appear in Exhibit 13-12. The amortization amounts that appear in Exhibit 13-12 are taken directly from the Goodwill from Consolidation schedule in Exhibit 13-9. The prior years' amortization amounts in eliminations [25] and [28] are allocated entirely to the Retained Earnings of the investor, Company R, because neither of the other affiliates has any share of ownership in the goodwill being amortized.

EXHIBIT 13-12

Illustrative Problem 13.2
Additional Eliminations
December 31, 1992

Goodwill Amortization

[25] Retained Earnings: R		$ 1,750
[26] Operating Expenses		1,000
[27] Investment in Company S: R		$ (2,750)
[28] Retained Earnings: R		$ 2,250
[29] Operating Expenses		1,500
[30] Investment in Company T: R		$ (3,750)
[31] Retained Earnings: R		$ 430
[32] Retained Earnings: S		10
[33] Retained Earnings: T		50
[34] Operating Expenses		490
[35] Investment in Company S: T		$ (980)
[36] Retained Earnings: R		$ 870
[37] Retained Earnings: S		100
[38] Retained Earnings: T		10
[39] Operating Expenses		980
[40] Investment in Company T: S		$ (1,960)

The allocation of the prior year's amortization of the goodwill on Company T's investment in Company S, on the other hand, is affected by the presence of the mutual ownership, as is that on Company S's investment in Company T. Thus, these allocation problems must be solved using simultaneous equations. In doing so, however, we must note that the two amounts of prior year's goodwill amortization are unrelated to each other. Unlike the net incomes of mutually related affiliates, which are mutually *interdependent*, these amounts are mutually *independent*. Therefore, two separate sets of equations must be written. In each case, we will let

S = Company S's *total* share of the prior year's amortization

T = Company T's *total* share of the prior year's amortization

With respect to the prior year's amortization of the goodwill on Company T's investment in Company S, the equations read

$$[1] \ T = \$490 + .1S$$

$$[2] \ S = .2T$$

Because the goodwill from consolidation on this investment belongs to Company T, the amortization thereon is attached to Company T (the originating affiliate) in writing this pair of equations.

Equation [1] is solved by substitution as follows:

$$T = \$490 + .1(.2T)$$

$$.98T = \$490$$

$$T = \$500$$

Company T's $500 total share of the prior year's goodwill amortization is then allocated to each affilate's Retained Earnings balance by multiplying [a] that affiliate's external ownership percentage by [b] that affiliate's share of the quantity being allocated by [c] the quantity being allocated. The results are

	[a]	×	[b]	×	[c]	=	[d]
Company R:	100%	×	86%	×	$500	=	$430
Company S:	10%	×	20%	×	$500	=	$ 10
Company T:	10%	×	100%	×	$500	=	$ 50

Notice that the allocation to Company R's Retained Earnings uses Company R's *total effective* ownership interest of 86% in the originating affiliate, Company T.

With respect to the prior year's amortization of the goodwill on Company S's investment in Company T, the equations read

[1] $S = \$980 + .2T$

[2] $T = .1S$

Because the goodwill from consolidation on this investment belongs to Company S, the amortization thereon is attached to Company S (the originating affiliate) in writing this pair of equations.

Equation [1] is solved by substitution as follows:

$$S = \$980 + .2(.1S)$$

$$.98S = \$980$$

$$S = \$1,000$$

Company S's $1,000 total share of the prior year's goodwill amortization is then allocated to each affiliate's Retained Earnings balance as follows:

	[a]	×	[b]	×	[c]	=	[d]
Company R:	100%	×	87%	×	$1,000	=	$870
Company S:	10%	×	100%	×	$1,000	=	$100
Company T:	10%	×	10%	×	$1,000	=	$ 10

The allocation to Company R's Retained Earnings uses Company R's *total effective* ownership interest of 87% in the originating affiliate, Company S.

Exhibit 13-13 contains the December 31, 1992 eliminations resulting from the intercompany sale and purchase of a depreciable asset. The intercompany profit on the intercompany transaction, which is the difference between the selling price of $26,800 and Company T's cost of $17,000, is eliminated from the Plant and Equipment balance in Elimination [46]. The excess depreciation expense for 1992, 1/10 of the intercompany profit of $9,800, is eliminated from Operating Expenses in Elimination [45]. The amount eliminated from Accumulated Depreciation in Elimination [41] is the amount of excess depreciation recorded by Company R through December 31, 1992, 1.5/10 of $9,800. The amount of unrealized intercompany profit as of January 1, 1992, $9,310, must be allocated among the three Retained Earnings balances using simultaneous equations. If we let

S = Company S's *total* share of the intercompany profit

T = Company T's *total* share of the intercompany profit

the equations read

$$[1] \ T = \$9,310 + .1S$$

$$[2] \ S = .2T$$

Because the intercompany profit belongs to the selling affiliate (in this case, Company T), the amortization thereon is attached to Company T (the originating affiliate) in writing this pair of equations. Equation [1] is solved as follows:

$$T = \$9,310 + .1(.2T)$$

$$.98T = \$9,310$$

$$T = \$9,500$$

Company T's $9,500 total share of the intercompany profit is then allocated to each affiliate's Retained Earnings balance by multiplying [a] that affiliate's external ownership percentage by [b] that affiliate's share of the quantity being allocated by [c] the quantity being allocated. The results are

	[a]	×	[b]	×	[c]	=	[d]
Company R:	100%	×	86%	×	$9,500	=	$8,170
Company S:	10%	×	20%	×	$9,500	=	$ 190
Company T:	10%	×	100%	×	$9,500	=	$ 950

EXHIBIT 13-13

Illustrative Problem 13.2
Additional Eliminations
December 31, 1992

Intercompany Profit in Depreciable Assets

[41] Accumulated Depreciation	$ 1,470
[42] Retained Earnings: R	8,170
[43] Retained Earnings: S	190
[44] Retained Earnings: T	950
[45] Operating Expenses	(980)
[46] Plant and Equipment	$ (9,800)

In this case, the primary parent, Company R, has a total effective ownership interest of 86% in the originating affiliate, Company T.

The Income Allocation schedule that accompanies the December 31, 1992 consolidation worksheet appears in Exhibit 13-14. The Income Allocation schedule used here for an arrangement involving both mutual and indirect ownership is similar to that shown earlier in Exhibit 13-6 for indirect ownership only, but differs in the manner in which the allocations are accomplished. It begins by listing the affiliate's individual net incomes, with the total thereof inserted in the Total column. Then, the individual net incomes are adjusted as necessary. In this case, the realized intercompany profit on the sale of machinery is added to the net income of the selling affiliate, Company T. Also, the current year's amortization of goodwill from consolidation on Company R's investments in Company S and Company T is subtracted from Company R's net income, the current year's amortization of goodwill from consolidation on Company S's investment in Company T is subtracted from Company S's net income, and the current year's amortization of goodwill from consolidation on Company T's investment in Company S is subtracted from Company T's net income. The totals of these adjustments are entered in the Total column, yielding the total amount of adjusted net income, $86,150.

EXHIBIT 13-14

Illustrative Problem 13.2
Income Allocation Schedule
Year Ended December 31, 1992

Income Allocation

	Company R	Company S	Company T	Total
Individual Net Incomes	$ 40,000	$ 28,140	$ 21,000	$ 89,140
Add: Intercompany Profit on Machinery			980	980
Less: Goodwill Amortization	(2,500)	(980)	(490)	(3,970)
Adjusted Net Incomes	37,500	27,160	21,490	$ 86,150
70% of $24,700 to Company R	17,290		(17,290)	
20% of $24,700 to Company S		4,940	(4,940)	
80% of $32,100 to Company R	25,680	(25,680)		
10% of $32,100 to Company T		(3,210)	3,210	
Minority Interests		$ 3,210	$ 2,470	$ 5,680
Consolidated Net Income	$ 80,470			80,470
Total Net Income				$ 86,150

The adjusted net incomes of Company S and Company T, however, are allocated in a manner different from that used in Exhibit 13-6 for the net incomes of Company I and Company J. Once the adjusted net incomes of Companies S and T are determined, they must be subjected to the simultaneous equation routine in order to allocate them. The approach is exactly the same as that used to allocate mutually related affiliates' net incomes in order to record them under the equity method. We will write equations in which we let

$$S = \text{Company S's } total \text{ adjusted net income}$$

$$T = \text{Company T's } total \text{ adjusted net income}$$

These equations read

$$[1] \quad S = \$27,160 + .2T$$

$$[2] \quad T = \$21,490 + .1S$$

Equation [1] can be solved by substitution as follows:

$$S = \$27,160 + .2(\$21,490 + .1S)$$

$$.98S = \$31,458$$

$$S = \$32,100$$

Using the value for S obtained above, we can solve equation [2] as follows:

$$T = \$21,490 + .1(\$32,100)$$

$$T = \$24,700$$

Once these values for S and T are determined, they form the bases for the allocations of Company S's and Company T's adjusted net incomes, respectively. Notice that the amount allocated from Company T to Company S, $4,940, is *not* added to Company S's adjusted net income in arriving at Company S's total net income. Nor, in turn, is the amount allocated from Company S to Company T, $3,210, added to Company T's adjusted net income in arriving at Company T's total net income. The total net incomes on which these allocations are based (as well as those from Companies S and T to Company R) already have been determined through the simultaneous equation solutions.

The totals of the Company S column, $3,210, and the Company T column, $2,470, represent the minority interests in those affiliates' net incomes. The total of the Company R column, $80,470, is consolidated net income. The Total column is then used to provide a proof of the accuracy of the income allocation. The total of the minority interests, $5,680, is extended to the Total column, as is the consolidated net income of $80,740. The sum of these two amounts, $86,150, is the amount determined earlier to be the total of the adjusted net incomes, thus verifying the accuracy of the income allocation. The completed December 31, 1992 equity method consolidation worksheet appears in Exhibit 13-15.

Use of the Cost Method. If Companies R, S, and T had accounted for their respective investments under the cost method, each would have recorded its share of its investee's dividends as Dividend Revenue and the balances of the four Investment accounts would have been their original costs.

Investment in Company S: R	$158,000
Investment in Company T: R	196,300
Investment in Company S: T	23,900
Investment in Company T: S	61,400

EXHIBIT 13-15

Illustrative Problem 13.2
Consolidation Worksheet
December 31, 1992

	Company R	Company S	Company T	Eliminations		Income Statement	Balance Sheet
Accounts Receivable	94,800	34,800	50,700	[35]	(11,300)		169,000
Inventories	51,700	27,500	36,800				116,000
Plant and Equipment	599,100	295,300	370,400	[46]	(9,800)		1,255,000
Other Assets	26,300	5,100	8,100				39,500
Investment in Company S: R	191,600			[3]	(167,200)		7,250 G
				[15]	(14,400)		
				[27]	(2,750)		
Investment in Company T: R	213,380			[6]	(189,070)		11,250 G
				[18]	(9,310)		
				[30]	(3,750)		
Investment in Company T: S		66,480		[12]	(54,020)		7,840 G
				[24]	(2,660)		
				[40]	(1,960)		
Investment in Company S: T			27,600	[9]	(20,900)		3,920 G
				[21]	(1,800)		
				[35]	(980)		
Cost of Goods Sold	247,600	177,300	166,600			591,500	
Operating Expenses	192,700	131,700	123,500	[26]	1,000	450,890	
				[29]	1,500		
				[34]	490		
				[39]	980		
				[45]	(980)		
Dividends Declared: R	16,000						16,000 R
Dividends Declared: S		15,000		[14]	(12,000)		1,500 MS
				[20]	(1,500)		
Dividends Declared: T			11,000	[17]	(7,700)		1,100 MT
				[23]	(2,200)		
	1,633,180	753,180	794,700				1,628,360
Accumulated Depreciation	253,700	161,100	178,500	[41]	1,470		591,830
Accounts Payable	90,400	41,080	31,700	[34]	11,300		151,880
Common Stock: R	500,000						500,000
Common Stock: S		100,000		[1]	80,000		10,000 MS
				[7]	10,000		
Common Stock: T			200,000	[4]	140,000		20,000 MT
				[10]	40,000		
Additional Paid-in Capital: R	100,000						100,000
Retained Earnings: R	165,370			[25]	1,750		151,900 R
				[28]	2,250		
				[31]	430		
				[36]	870		
				[42]	8,170		
Retained Earnings: S		109,000		[2]	87,200		10,600 MS
				[8]	10,900		
				[32]	10		
				[37]	100		
				[43]	190		
Retained Earnings: T			70,100	[5]	49,070		6,000 MT
				[11]	14,020		
				[33]	50		
				[38]	10		
				[44]	950		

	Company R	Company S	Company T	Eliminations		Income Statement	Balance Sheet
Sales	480,300	337,140	311,100			1,128,540	
Income from Company S: R	26,400			[13]	26,400		
Income from Company T: R	17,010			[16]	17,010		
Income from Company S: T			3,300	[19]	3,300		
Income from Company T: S		4,860		[22]	4,860		
	1,633,180	753,180	794,700				
Minority Interest in Company S's Net Income						3,210	3,210 MS
Minority Interest in Company T's Net Income						2,470	2,470 MT
Consolidated Net Income						80,470	80,470 R
						1,128,540	1,128,540 1,628,360

At December 31, 1992, it would be necessary to convert each Investment balance from cost to equity as of December 31, 1991, using

- the 1990 individual net incomes of Company S, $20,000, and Company T, $18,000, from the respective dates of acquisition by Company R, and
- the total 1991 net incomes of Company S, $31,000, and Company T, $27,100, as determined on page 528 using the simultaneous equations.

These conversions are shown in Exhibit 13-16.

EXHIBIT 13-16

Illustrative Problem 13.2
Conversion from Cost to Equity
December 31, 1992

Investment in Company S: R

80% of Company S's Total Net Income, 4/1/90–12/31/91	$ 36,800
80% of Company S's Total Dividends, 1990–1991	17,600
Increase in Equity	$ 19,200

Investment in Company T: R

70% of Company T's Total Net Income, 6/30/90–12/31/91	$ 25,270
70% of Company T's Total Dividends, 1990–1991	17,500
Increase in Equity	$ 7,770

Investment in Company S: T

10% of Company T's Total Net Income, 1991	$ 3,100
10% of Company T's Total Dividends, 1991	1,200
Increase in Equity	$ 1,900

Investment in Company T: S

20% of Company T's Total Net Income, 1991	$ 5,420
20% of Company T's Total Dividends, 1991	3,000
Increase in Equity	$ 2,420

Company R's share of Company S's total net income from April 1, 1990 through December 31, 1991 is 80% of 9/12 of $20,000 plus 80% of $31,000, or $36,800. Company R's share of Company S's dividends for 1990 and 1991 is 80% of $22,000, or $17,600. The increase in Company R's investment in Company S, therefore, is $19,200.

Company R's share of Company T's total net income from June 30, 1990 through December 31, 1991 is 70% of 6/12 of $18,000 plus 70% of $27,100, or $25,270. Company R's share of Company T's dividends for 1990 and 1991 is 70% of $25,000, or $17,500. The increase in Company R's investment in Company T, therefore, is $7,770.

Company T's share of Company S's total net income from January 1, 1991 through December 31, 1991 is 10% of $31,000, or $3,100. Company T's share of Company S's dividends for 1991 is 10% of $12,000, or $1,200. The increase in Company T's investment in Company S, therefore, is $1,900.

Company S's share of Company T's total net income from January 1, 1991 through December 31, 1991 is 20% of $27,100, or $5,420. Company S's share of Company T's dividends for 1991 is 20% of $15,000, or $3,000. The increase in Company S's investment in Company T, therefore, is $2,420.

SUMMARY

In this chapter, we have discussed and illustrated the effect on both the parent's (or investor's) accounting for its investment in its subsidiary (or investee) and the consolidation process of

- multiple ownership interests,
- indirect ownership interests, and
- mutual ownership interests,

The presence of more than one subsidiary (multiple ownership) does not change the application of either the equity or the cost method, or of any of the consolidation procedures that we have dealt with in previous chapters except to repeat each step for each additional affiliate.

The presence of indirect ownership interests, mutual ownership interests, or some combination of the two affects the parent's (or investor's) recording of its income from its subsidiary (or investee) under the equity method, the determination of the difference between cost and book value, eliminations affecting retained earnings balances, and the income allocation schedule. Both direct and indirect ownership interests must be considered in each of these cases. When mutual ownership is present, the use of simultaneous equations provides a convenient means of dealing with reciprocal allocations.

REVIEW PROBLEM

On May 1, 1991, Company A purchased 12,000 of Company B's 20,000 shares of $10 par value common stock for $203,400. On September 30, 1991, Company A purchased 8,000 of Company C's 10,000 shares of $25 par value common stock for $280,800. On December 31, 1991, Company B purchased 1,000 shares of Company C's common stock for $35,640 and Company C purchased 6,000 of Company

B's common stock for $102,840. Retained Earnings balances at December 31, 1990 were: Company B, $72,600; Company C, $54,800. All dividends were declared on November 15, payable on December 20, in each year. All investors account for their investments in affiliates under the equity method. Any excess of cost over book value is treated as goodwill from consolidation, amortized over 10 years. Net incomes and dividends for 1991 and 1992 were

	Net Income	Dividends
Company A, 1991	$ 32,600	$ 18,000
Company B, 1991	19,200	9,000
Company C, 1991	21,600	10,000
Company A, 1992	41,300	20,000
Company B, 1992	20,900	10,000
Company C, 1992	23,800	12,000

Required
1. Prepare a schedule showing the changes in each of the investment account balances through December 31, 1992.
2. Prepare all supporting schedules to the December 31, 1992 consolidation worksheet.

QUESTIONS

1. Give an example, other than those in Chapter 13, of a relationship in which a parent company has both direct and indirect ownership interests in two or more susidiaries.
2. Give an example, other than those in Chapter 13, in which both indirect and mutual ownership exists.
3. How does the presence of indirect ownership affect the recording of an investor's share of an investee's net income and dividends under the equity method?
4. How does one determine whether or not a particular affiliate should be included in the consolidated financial statements?
5. When indirect ownership interests are present, how are allocations between or among Retained Earnings balances made in eliminations that require such allocations?
6. What are the two ways in which mutual ownership might be treated in preparing consolidated financial statements?
7. How does the presence of mutual ownership affect the recording of an investor's share of an investee's dividends under the equity method?
8. How is the conversion from cost to equity determined when mutual ownership is present?
9. When mutual ownership interests are involved, how are allocations between or among Retained Earnings balances made in eliminations that require such allocations?
10. How does the presence of mutual ownership affect the Income Allocation schedule?

EXERCISES

EXERCISE 13-1
Company A owns 80% of Company B's common stock and 70% of Company C's common stock. Company B owns 10% of Company C's common stock. On July 1, 1990, Company C sold a machine

with a net book value of $70,000 to Company B for $86,000. Company B is depreciating the machine on the straight-line method, over 10 years, with a $1,500 salvage method.

Required

Schedule the Intercompany Profit in Depreciable Assets set of eliminations at December 31, 1992. Show supporting calculations.

EXERCISE 13-2

Company D owns 70% of Company E's common stock and 60% of Company F's common stock. Company E owns 10% of Company F's common stock and 40% of Company G's common stock. Company F owns 50% of Company G's common stock.

Required

Diagram the ownership configuration described in this exercise.

EXERCISE 13-3

As indicated in Exercise 13-2, Company D owns 70% of Company E's common stock and 60% of Company F's common stock. Company E owns 10% of Company F's common stock and 40% of Company G's common stock. Company F owns 50% of Company G's common stock.

During 1991, Company G sold merchandise that had cost $180,000 to Company E for $240,000. Company E owed Company G $23,700 on account at December 31, 1991. Company E's beginning and ending inventories for 1991 contained mechandise purchased from Company G of $20,000 and $24,000, respectively. All affiliates use perpetual inventory systems.

Required

Schedule all eliminations needed at December 31, 1991 that can be determined from the above information. Show supporting calculations.

EXERCISE 13-4

Company H owns 80% of Company I's common stock and 60% of Company J's common stock. Company J owns 10% of Company I's common stock. On April 1, 1990, Company H bought 25% of Company I's 8% bonds on the open market. The bonds mature on June 30, 1995, and interest is payable on June 30 and December 31. The following balances appear on the trial balances of Companies H and I at March 31, 1992, the fiscal year end:

Company H

Investment in Co. I Bonds	$ 242,200
Bond Interest Receivable	5,000
Miscellaneous Revenue	36,800

Company I

Bonds Payable	$1,000,000
Discount on Bonds Payable	39,000
Bond Interest Payable	20,000
Interest Expense	98,000

Required

Schedule all eliminations related to the intercompany bonds that would appear on the March 31, 1992 consolidation worksheet.

EXERCISE 13-5

Company K owns 80% of Company L's common stock and 60% of Company M's common stock. Company L owns 20% of Company M's common stock. Company M owns 10% of Company L's common stock. On June 1, 1988, Company L bought 20% of Company M's $2,000,000 of 8% bonds on the open market for $268,000, plus accrued interest. Company M's bonds were issued on October 1, 1985 for $2,197,600. They mature on September 30, 1995 and interest payable on March 31 and September 30.

Required

Schedule all eliminations related to the intercompany bonds that should appear on the December 31, 1991 consolidation worksheet. Show supporting calculations.

EXERCISE 13-6

Company P owns 70% of Company Q's common stock and 80% of Company R's common stock. Company Q owns 20% of Company R's common stock. Company R owns 10% of Company Q's common stock.

Required

Diagram the ownership configuration described in this exercise.

EXERCISE 13-7

As indicated in Exercise 13-6, Company P owns 70% of Comany Q's common stock and 80% of Company R's Common stock. Comany Q owns 20% of Company R's common stock. Company R owns 10% of Company Q's common stock.

Company R's beginning inventory for 1992 contains goods purchased from Company Q for $24,500. Company Q sells to Company R at 25% above cost. All three affiliates use periodic inventory systems.

Required

Schedule the Intercompany Profit in Beginning Inventory set of eliminations at December 31, 1992. Show supporting calculations.

EXERCISE 13-8

Company S owns 80% of Company T's common stock and Company T owns 10% of Company S's common stock. In 1991, Company S reported net income from its own operations of $400,000 and declared and paid dividends of $180,000. Also in 1991, Company T reported net income from its own operations of $75,000 and declared and paid dividends of $15,000. Amounts of goodwill from consolidation amortized in 1991 were: on Company S's investment in Company T, $18,400; on Company T's investment in Company S, $4,600. Both affiliates use the equity method.

Required

Prepare the Income Allocation schedule to accompany the December 31, 1991 consolidation worksheet. Show supporting calculations.

EXERCISE 13-9

Company U owns 60% of Company V's common stock and 70% of Company W's common stock. Company V owns 20% of Company W's common stock. Company W owns 20% of Company V's common stock. On December 1, 1990, Company W purchased equipment from Company V for $276,000 which had been carried on Company V's books at $156,000. Company W is depreciating the equipment over a 10-year useful life from the date of purchase, using the declining balance method at 200% of the straight-line rate.

Required

Schedule the eliminations related to this equipment that should appear on the May 31, 1992 consolidation worksheet.

PROBLEMS

PROBLEM 13-1

Company A owns 80% of Company B's common stock and 40% of Company C's common stock. Company B owns 30% of Company C's common stock and 60% of Company D's common stock. Company C owns 30% of Company D's common stock. Individual net incomes (losses) and dividends for 1991 were

	Net Income	Dividends
Company A	$ 86,300	$ 36,000
Company B	19,500	9,000
Company C	(3,200)	—
Company D	48,700	22,000

Amounts of goodwill of the investee amortized in 1991 were

Company A's Investment in Company B	$ 8,400
Company A's Investment in Company C	5,100
Company B's Investment in Company C	3,700
Company B's Investment in Company D	4,300
Company C's Investment in Company D	2,400

Required

1. Present the equity method journal entries on the books of all investor affiliates for 1991. Show supporting calculations.
2. Prepare the income allocation schedule to accompany the December 31, 1991 consolidation worksheet. Show supporting calculations.

PROBLEM 13-2

Company E owns 60% of Company F's common stock and 70% of Company G's common stock. Company F owns 10% of Company G's common stock. Company G owns 20% of Company F's common stock. All investor affiliates account for their investments in affiliates under the equity method. Individual net incomes and dividends for 1992 were

	Net Income	Dividends
Company E	$ 182,000	$ 60,000
Company F	67,500	25,800
Company G	68,200	19,300

Amounts of goodwill from consolidation amortized in 1992 were

Company E's Investment in Company F	$ 3,800
Company E's Investment in Company G	5,100
Company F's Investment in Company G	700
Company G's Investment in Company F	1,200

On June 30, 1989, Company F sold some equipment with a net book value of $38,000 to Company G for $67,400. Company G is depreciating the equipment on the straight-line method, over a six-year life, with a $4,100 salvage value.

Required

1. Schedule the eliminations for intercompany profit required at December 31, 1992. Show supporting calculations.
2. Prepare the income allocation schedule to accompany the December 31, 1992 consolidation worksheet. Show supporting calculations.

PROBLEM 13-3

Company H purchased 2,000 of Company J's 10,000 shares of $10 par value common stock for $49,700 on April 1, 1992 and 14,000 of Company I's 20,000 shares of $10 par value common stock for $270,150 on September 30, 1992. On July 1, 1992, Company I purchased 6,000 shares of Company J's common stock for $151,820. On January 2, 1993, Company J purchased 2,000 shares of Company I's common stock for $37,880. Company I's common stock was issued originally at 12; Company J's common stock was issued originally at 15. At December 31, 1991, Retained Earnings balances were: Company I, $72,600; Company J, $61,700. All dividends were declared on December 15 of each year and paid on January 20 of the following year. Any excess of cost over book value is treated as goodwill from consolidation, amortized over 10 years. All investors account for their investments in affiliates under the equity method. Net incomes and dividends for 1992 and 1993 were

	Net Income	Dividends
Company H, 1992	$ 51,800	$ 23,000
Company I, 1992	25,200	12,000
Company J, 1992	20,000	10,000
Company H, 1993	62,100	25,000
Company I, 1993	27,600	12,000
Company J, 1993	24,500	13,000

Required

1. Schedule all eliminations required at December 31, 1993. Show supporting calculations.
2. Prepare the income allocation schedule to accompany the December 31, 1993 consolidation worksheet. Show supporting calculations.

PROBLEM 13-4

Company K owns 60% of Company L's common stock and 70% of Company M's common stock. Company L owns 80% of Company N's common stock. Company M owns 10% of Company L's common stock and 10% of Company N's common stock. Company N owns 20% of Company M's common stock. Individual net incomes and dividends for 1990 were

	Net Income	Dividends
Company K	$ 51,200	$ 24,500
Company L	34,500	15,000
Company M	44,600	20,000
Company N	22,700	10,000

Amounts of goodwill from consolidation amortized in 1990 were

Company K's Investment in Company L	$ 3,900
Company K's Investment in Company M	1,800
Comany L's Investment in Company N	2,300
Company M's Investment in Company L	680
Company M's Investment in Company N	400
Company N's Investment in Company M	1,200

Required

1. Present the equity method journal entries on the books of all investor affiliates for 1990. Show supporting calculations.
2. Prepare the Income Allocation schedule to accompany the December 31, 1990 consolidation worksheet. Show supporting calculations.

PROBLEM 13-5

The June 30, 1992 trial balances of Companies P, Q, and R are shown below.

	Company P	Company Q	Company R
Investment in Company Q	$ 205,680		
Investment in Company R	146,800	$ 18,800	
Other Assets	210,400	267,800	$ 232,100
Cost of Goods Sold	156,300	130,900	102,700
Operating Expenses	126,700	78,300	70,900
Dividends	14,000	10,000	6,000
	$ 859,880	$ 505,800	$ 411,700
Liabilities	$ 103,200	$ 71,400	$ 56,100
Common Stock, $10 par	300,000	100,000	100,000
Retained Earnings	117,400	106,000	70,000
Sales	312,400	227,200	185,600
Income from Company Q	17,280	—	—
Income from Company R	9,600	1,200	—
	$ 859,880	$ 505,800	$ 411,700

On June 30, 1989, Company P bought 9,000 shares of Company Q's common stock for $174,000 and 8,000 shares of Company R's common stock for $126,000. On that date, Company Q and Company R had retained earnings of $80,000 and $50,000, respectively. On June 30, 1990, when Company R had retained earnings of $60,000, Company Q purchased 1,000 shares of Company R's common stock for $17,200. All differences between cost and book value are treated as goodwill from consolidation and amortized over 10 years.

During the year ended June 30, 1992, Company R sold merchandise to Company P for $78,000, of which $3,200 remained unpaid at year end. Company P's June 30, 1991 and June 30, 1992 inventories contained intercompany profits on goods purchased from Company R of $500 and $600, respectively.

Required

Prepare a consolidation worksheet at June 30, 1992, supported by appropriate schedules. Show calculations where necessary.

PROBLEM 13-6

The July 31, 1992 trial balances of Companies S and T appear below.

	Company S	Company T
Investment in Company T	$ 135,480	
Investment in Company S		$ 41,028
Other Assets	357,800	187,722
Cost of Goods Sold	103,300	74,300
Expenses	86,900	56,858
Dividends	8,000	4,000
	$ 691,480	$ 363,908
Liabilities	$ 92,200	$ 70,900
Common Stock, $10 par	250,000	100,000
Additional Paid-in Capital	50,000	10,000
Retained Earnings	80,000	40,000
Sales	209,800	140,100
Income from Company T	9,480	
Income from Company S		2,908
	$ 691,480	$ 363,908

Company S bought 8,000 shares of Company T's common stock for $121,200 on August 1, 1990, when Company T had retained earnings of $30,000. Company T bought 2,500 shares of Company S's common stock for $38,920 on August 1, 1991. The excess of cost over book value of each investment is treated as goodwill from consolidation and is amortized over 10 years.

Required

Prepare a consolidation worksheet at July 31, 1992, supported by appropriate schedules. Show calculations where necessary.

PROBLEM 13-7

Company V owns 70% of Company W's common stock and 40% of Company X's common stock. Company W owns 40% of Company X's common stock. Company X owns 10% of Company W's common stock. All of these investments were acquired before 1981. All investor affiliates account for their investments in affiliates under the equity method. Individual net incomes and dividends for the year ended June 30, 1991 were

	Net Income	Dividends
Company V	$ 132,600	$ 43,800
Company W	102,600	37,000
Company X	94,448	31,400

Amounts of goodwill from consolidation amortized for the year ended June 30, 1991 were

Company V's Investment in Company W	$ 6,200
Company V's Investment in Company X	4,800
Company W's Investment in Company X	2,600

On February 1, 1989, Company W acquired 40% of Company X's $2,000,000 of 8% bonds for $790,300. The bonds were issued for $1,941,200 on March 1, 1987 and mature on March 1, 1997. Interest is payable on March 1 and September 1.

Required

1. Schedule the eliminations required at June 30, 1991 with respect to the intercompany bonds. Show supporting calculations.
2. Prepare the income allocation schedule to accompany the June 30, 1991 consolidation worksheet. Show supporting calculations.

PROBLEM 13-8

On April 30, 1989, Company A bought 8,000 shares of Company B's common stock for $208,400. On that date, Company B had retained earnings of $80,500. On April 30, 1990, when Company C had retained earnings of $60,700. Company A purchased 6,000 shares of Company C's common stock for $150,400 and Company B purchased 2,000 shares of Company C's common stock for $50,140. All differences between cost and book value are treated as goodwill from consolidation and amortized over 10 years. The April 30, 1992 trial balances of Companies A, B, and C are shown below.

	Company A	Company B	Company C
Investment in Company B	$ 263,120		
Investment in Company C	171,180		
Investment in Company C		$ 57,060	
Plant and Equipment	480,100	277,400	$ 331,200
Other Assets	180,600	174,740	135,600
Cost of Goods Sold	169,700	148,700	122,600
Operating Expenses	136,400	117,200	70,100
Dividends Declared	28,000	30,000	15,000
	$1,429,100	$ 805,100	$ 674,500
Accumulated Depreciation	$ 233,600	$ 132,500	$ 155,400
Liabilities	198,700	71,400	56,100
Common Stock	300,000	100,000	100,000
Additional Paid-in Capital	100,000	50,000	60,000
Retained Earnings	186,400	126,400	78,300
Sales	349,200	318,400	224,700
Income from Company B	42,000		
Income from Company C	19,200	6,400	
	$1,429,100	$ 805,100	$ 674,500

On November 1, 1990, Company A purchased equipment from Company C for $236,000, which had been carried on Company C's books at $156,000. Company A is depreciating the equipment over a 10-year useful life from the date of purchase, using the straight-line method.

Required

Prepare a consolidation worksheet at April 30, 1992, supported by appropriate schedules. Show calculations where necessary.

PROBLEM 13-9

The December 31, 1992 trial balances of Companies D, E, and F are shown below.

	Company D	Company E	Company F
Investment in Company E	$ 311,760		
Investment in Company F		$ 231,440	
Investment in Company E			$ 40,670
Plant and Equipment	515,400	247,630	338,830
Other Assets	189,680	72,530	92,300
Cost of Goods Sold	184,600	164,900	148,700
Operating Expenses	157,800	147,600	112,500
Dividends Declared	35,000	30,000	15,000
	$1,394,240	$ 894,100	$ 748,000
Accumulated Depreciation	199,900	$ 156,300	$ 148,700
Liabilities	171,600	80,600	68,300
Common Stock	300,000	100,000	100,000
Additional Paid-in Capital	100,000	50,000	60,000
Retained Earnings	136,500	88,900	70,800
Sales	401,600	387,100	289,620
Income from Company E	84,640		10,580
Income from Company F		31,200	
	$1,394,240	$ 894,100	$ 748,000

On June 30, 1990, when Company E had retained earnings of $62,400, Company D bought 8,000 shares of Company E's common stock for $229,920 and Company F bought 1,000 shares of Company E's common stock for $30,440. On December 31, 1990, when Company F had retained earnings of $54,500, Company E purchased 8,000 shares of Company F's common stock for $199,200. All differences between cost and book value are treated as goodwill from consolidation and amortized over 10 years.

Required
Prepare a consolidation worksheet at December 31, 1992, supported by appropriate schedules. Show calculations where necessary.

SOLUTION TO REVIEW PROBLEM

Summary of Changes in the Investment Account Balances

	Investment in			
	Company B (A)	Company C (A)	Company C (B)	Company B (C)
Cost of Investment	$ 203,400	$ 280,800	$ 35,640	$ 102,840
Dividends, 11/15/91	(5,400) [a]	(8,000) [b]	—	—
Net Income, 1991	7,680 [c]	4,320 [d]	—	—
Balance, 12/31/91	205,680	277,120	35,640	102,840
Dividends, 11/15/92	(6,000) [e]	(9,600) [f]	(1,200) [g]	(3,000) [h]
Net Income, 1992	14,400 [i]	24,800 [j]	3,100 [k]	7,200 [l]
Balance, 12/31/92	$ 214,080	$ 292,320	$ 37,540	$ 107,040

[a] 60% × $9,000		[g] 10% × $12,000	
[b] 80% × $10,000		[h] 30% × $10,000	
[c] 60% × 8/12 × $19,200		[i] 60% × $24,000	
[d] 80% × 3/12 × $21,600		[j] 80% × $31,000	
[e] 60% × $10,000		[k] 10% × $31,000	
[f] 80% × $12,000		[l] 30% × $24,000	

Equations: Net Income Allocation, 1992

$$[1] \quad B = \$20{,}900 + .1C$$
$$[2] \quad C = \$23{,}800 + .3B$$

Solve [1]:

$$[1] \quad B = \$20{,}900 + .1(\$23{,}800 + .3B)$$
$$B = \$24{,}000$$

Solve [2]:

$$[2] \quad C = \$23{,}800 + .3(\$24{,}000)$$
$$C = \$31{,}000$$

Goodwill from Consolidation

	Investment in			
	Company B (A)	Company C (A)	Company C (B)	Company B (C)
Cost of Investment	$ 203,400	$ 280,800	$ 35,640	$ 102,840
Book Value	167,400 [a]	256,800 [b]	31,640 [c]	84,840 [d]
Goodwill at Acquisition	36,000	24,000	4,000	18,000
Amortization, 1991	(2,400) [e]	(600) [f]		
Amortization, 1992	(3,600) [g]	(2,400) [h]	(400) [i]	(1,800) [j]
Goodwill, 12/31/92	$ 30,000	$ 21,000	$ 3,600	$ 16,200

[a] 60%[$200,000 + $72,600 + (4/12 × $19,200)]
[b] 80%[$250,000 + $54,800 + (9/12 × $21,600)]
[c] 10%[$250,000 + $54,800 + $21,600 − $10,000]
[d] 30%[$200,000 + $72,600 + $19,200 − $9,000]
[e] 8/120 × $36,000
[f] 3/120 × $24,000
[g] 12/120 × $36,000
[h] 12/120 × $24,000
[i] 12/120 × $4,000
[j] 12/120 × $18,000

Eliminations

Intercompany Ownership Interests

[1]	Capital Stock: B	$ 120,000
[2]	Retained Earnings: B	49,680
[3]	Investment in Company B: A	$(169,680)
[4]	Capital Stock: C	$ 200,000
[5]	Retained Earnings: C	53,120
[6]	Investment in Company C: A	$(253,120)
[7]	Capital Stock: C	$ 25,000
[8]	Retained Earnings: C	6,640
[9]	Investment in Company C: B	$(31,640)

[10] Capital Stock: B	$ 60,000
[11] Retained Earnings: B	24,840
[12] Investment in Company B: C	$(84,840)

Subsidiary Income and Dividends

[13] Income from Company B: A	$ 14,400
[14] Dividends: B	(6,000)
[15] Investment in Company B: A	$(8,400)
[16] Income from Company C: A	$ 24,800
[17] Dividends: C	(9,600)
[18] Investment in Company C: A	$(15,200)
[19] Income from Company C: B	$ 3,100
[20] Dividends: C	(1,200)
[21] Investment in Company C: B	$(1,900)
[22] Income from Company B: C	$ 7,200
[23] Dividends: B	(3,000)
[24] Investment in Company B: C	$(4,200)

Goodwill Amortization

[25] Retained Earnings: A	$ 2,400
[26] Goodwill Amortization Expense	3,600
[27] Investment in Company B: A	$(6,000)
[28] Retained Earnings: A	$ 600
[29] Goodwill Amortization Expense	2,400
[30] Investment in Company C: A	$(3,000)
[31] Goodwill Amortization Expense	$ 400
[32] Investment in Company C: B	(400)
[33] Goodwill Amortization Expense	$ 1,800
[34] Investment in Company B: C	(1,800)

Income Allocation

	Company A	Company B	Company C	Total
Individual Net Incomes	$ 41,300	$ 20,900	$ 23,800	$ 86,000
Less: Goodwill Amortization	(6,000)	(400)	(1,800)	(8,200)
Adjusted Net Incomes	35,300	20,500	22,000	$ 77,800
80% of $29,021 to Company A	23,217		(23,217)	
10% of $29,021 to Company B		2,902	(2,902)	
60% of $23,402 to Company A	14,041	(14,041)		
30% of $23,402 to Company C		(7,021)	7,021	
		$ 2,340	$ 2,902	
Minority Interests				$ 5,242
Consolidated Net Income	$ 72,558			72,558
Total Net Income				$ 77,800

Equations: Adjusted Net Income Allocation, 1992

[1] $B = \$20,500 + .1C$
[2] $C = \$22,000 + .3B$

Solve [1]:

[1] $B = \$20,500 + .1(\$22,000 + .3B)$
     $B = \$23,402$

Solve [2]:

[2] $C = \$22,000 + .3(\$23,402)$
     $C = \$29,021$

CHAPTER 14

ACCOUNTING FOR FOREIGN OPERATIONS

U p to this point, all of our discussions, illustrations, and problems have been based on the unstated assumption that all members of an affiliated group are located in the same country (for our purposes, the United States). Not only is this assumption not necessarily true, but it is rather common for U.S. corporations to have subsidiaries in other countries or to be subsidiaries of foreign corporations. In addition, U.S. corporations can and often do engage in a variety of business transactions with foreign entities, whether or not they are affiliated with those entities through stock ownership.

Two major concerns arise from these kinds of relationships:

- accounting for transactions involving foreign currencies, and
- translation of foreign currency financial statements.

This chapter considers these concerns as they affect the parent–subsidiary relationship and the resulting preparation of consolidated financial statements. More specifically, the chapter includes the following topics:

- A brief history of official pronouncements governing accounting for foreign operations
- Accounting for international transactions, including
  —those denominated in the recording entity's functional currency
  —those denominated in a currency other than the recording entity's functional currency
  —hedging transactions
- Translation of foreign currency financial statements
- Parent company accounting for an investment in a foreign subsidiary
- Consolidated financial statements of affiliates operating in different countries

BACKGROUND INFORMATION

Prior to 1976, accounting for foreign operations was governed in the United States by Chapter 12 of *Accounting Research Bulletin No. 43,* as modified by *Accounting Principles Board Opinion No. 6. ARB No. 43,* Chapter 12 calls for the translation of foreign currency financial statements on the basis of a distinction between **current** and **noncurrent** assets and liabilities.[1] *APB Opinion No. 6* introduces the possible use of a distinction between **monetary** and **nonmonetary** assets and liabilities, at least with respect to certain assets and liabilities. Paragraph 18 states in part, "The Board is of the opinion that translation of long-term receivables and long-term liabilities at current exchange rates is appropriate in many circumstances."[2] An **exchange rate** is defined as "the ratio between a unit of one currency and the amount of another currency for which that unit can be exchanged at a particular time."[3] It is often helpful, however, to think of the exchange rate as the number of units of one currency (the price) that must be paid to purchase a unit of another currency.

In October, 1975, the Financial Accounting Standards Board issued *Statement of Financial Accounting Standards No. 8,* which became effective at the beginning of 1976. *SFAS No. 8* required the use of the **temporal** method of translation. Under the temporal method, cash, receivables, liabilities, and any assets carried at market value are translated at the exchange rate in effect at the balance sheet date. All other account balances are translated at the exchange rates in effect at the dates of the transactions that contributed to those balances. The use of historical exchange rates was intended to maintain the original values measured in past transactions and, thus, to report the affected account balances in accordance with the cost principle.[4]

SFAS No. 8 also provides that the net income of an accounting period should include the following types of gains and losses that occur during the period:

- Unrealized exchange gains and losses arising from translation of foreign currency financial statements
- Realized exchange gains and losses arising from transactions involving foreign currencies
- Unrealized exchange gains and losses arising from transactions involving foreign currencies[5]

SFAS No. 8 proved to be a particularly controversial and unpopular pronouncement. Many people in the business and financial community believed that its requirements caused reporting entities to issue financial statements that did not reflect economic reality. In particular, the opponents of *SFAS No. 8* alleged that the temporal method of translation distorted normal relationships among financial statement elements and that the requirement that un-

---

[1] *Accounting Research Bulletin No. 43, Restatement and Revision of Accounting Research Bulletins* (New York: AICPA, 1953), Chapter 12, paragraphs 12–22.

[2] *Accounting Principles Board Opinion No. 6, Status of Accounting Research Bulletins* (New York: AICPA, 1965), paragraph 18.

[3] *Statement of Financial Accounting Standards No. 52, Foreign Currency Translation* (Stamford, Connecticut: FASB, 1981), paragraph 26.

[4] *Statement of Financial Accounting Standards No. 8, Accounting for the Translation of Foreign Currency Transactions and Foreign Currency Financial Statements* (Stamford, Connecticut: FASB, 1975), paragraphs 121.a., 123.

[5] *SFAS No. 8,* paragraph 17.

realized exchange gains and losses be reported currently caused artificial volatility in reported operating results.

In response to this dissatisfaction, the Financial Accounting Standards Board reconsidered the provisions of *SFAS No. 8*. This reconsideration led to the issuance in 1981 of *Statement of Financial Accounting Standards No. 52, Foreign Currency Translation*, which became effective December 15, 1982.[6] This chapter is based on the requirements of *SFAS No. 52*.

ACCOUNTING FOR FOREIGN CURRENCY TRANSACTIONS OTHER THAN HEDGING

The assets and liabilities arising from transactions between entities in different countries are said to be **denominated** in a particular currency if the amounts to be received and paid are fixed in terms of that currency. For example, suppose that a U.S. company purchases merchandise on account from a Japanese company.

- If the U.S. company agrees to pay a fixed number of yen to settle the account, the transaction and the resulting balances are denominated in yen.
- If, instead, the U.S. company agrees to pay a fixed number of dollars, the transaction and the resulting balances are denominated in dollars.

A transaction may be **measured** (and thus, recorded) in terms of either the currency in which it is denominated or another currency. In the above example, the U.S. company normally would measure (record) the transaction in dollars, whether it is denominated in dollars or in yen.

If a transaction between companies in different countries is measured by one of the companies in the same currency in which it is denominated, foreign currency exchange rates have no effect on that company's recording of the transaction. Therefore, that company accounts for the transaction just as if it involved another company in the same country, as shown in Illustrative Problem 14.1.

ILLUSTRATIVE PROBLEM 14.1: TRANSACTIONS DENOMINATED IN DOMESTIC CURRENCY

On April 15, 1991, Company A, a U.S. corporation, purchases merchandise from Company B, located in Canada, agreeing to pay $35,000 (U.S. dollars) within 30 days. On April 24, 1991, Company A sells merchandise to Company C, located in Mexico, and Company C agrees to pay $42,000 (U.S. dollars) within 30 days. Company A pays the amount owed to Company B on May 12, 1991. Company A receives the amount owed from Company C on May 20, 1991.

Company A records these transactions, all in terms of U.S. dollars, as follows:

April 15, 1991

Purchases	35,000	
Accounts Payable		35,000

---

[6] *SFAS No. 52.*

April 24, 1991

Accounts Receivable	42,000	
Sales		42,000

May 12, 1991

Accounts Payable	35,000	
Cash		35,000

May 20, 1991

Cash	42,000	
Accounts Receivable		42,000

The fact that Company B and Company C are located in Canada and Mexico, respectively, has no effect on Company A's accounting for these transactions because Company A measures the transactions in the same currency in which they are denominated, U.S. dollars.

On the other hand, if a transaction between companies in different countries is denominated in one currency, but is measured by one of the companies in a different currency, that company may experience a **transaction gain or loss** either

- upon settlement of the receivable or payable arising from the transaction, or
- at the end of an accounting period, in the case of an unsettled transaction.

The company should record the initial transaction, normally in terms of its **functional currency,** using the exchange rate in effect at the transaction date. *SFAS No. 52* defines an entity's functional currency as "the currency of the primary economic environment in which the entity operates; normally, that is the currency of the environment in which an entity primarily generates and expends cash."[7] Generally speaking, an entity's functional currency is the currency of the country in which it is located and in which it primarily conducts its operations. A notable exception to this generality is the case in which a foreign subsidiary's operations are considered to be an integral part of or an extension of its parent's operations. In such a case, the parent's currency would be the subsidiary's functional currency. *SFAS No. 52* views the functional currency as essentially a matter of fact, but acknowledges that the facts in a particular situation may be difficult to discern.[8]

If the exchange rate changes between the date of the initial transaction and the date of settlement of the resulting receivable or payable, the number of units of the company's functional currency required for settlement will be different from the recorded balance of the receivable or payable. The difference between the balance of the receivable or payable and the amount actually received or paid, expressed in the company's functional currency, is recorded as a **transaction gain or loss.**

If a foreign currency transaction remains unsettled as of a given balance sheet date, the receivable or payable is adjusted for any change in the exchange rate that has occurred and a corresponding transaction gain or loss is recognized. Thus, the balance sheet reflects the amount of functional currency that would be received or paid if the receivable or payable were settled at the balance sheet date. When the subsequent settlement transaction is recorded, any additional transaction gain or loss is measured in reference to the adjusted balance of the receivable or payable rather than its original balance.

---

[7] *SFAS No. 52*, paragraph 5.

[8] *SFAS No. 52*, paragraph 8.

Transaction gains or losses, whether recognized through adjustment of the receivable or payable balances at the balance sheet date (unrealized) or in recording the settlement transaction (realized), are included in determining net income for the period in which they are recorded. Two exceptions to this requirement are to be treated in the same way as **translation adjustments,** which are discussed later in this chapter (that is, as a separate component of stockholders' equity). They are

a. Foreign currency transactions that are designated as, and are effective as, economic hedges of a net investment in a foreign entity, commencing as of the designation date
b. Intercompany foreign currency transactions that are of a long-term investment nature (that is, settlement is not planned or anticipated in the foreseeable future), when the entities to the transaction are consolidated, combined, or accounted for by the equity method in the reporting enterprise's financial statements.[9]

Accounting for nonhedging transactions involving foreign currencies is shown in Illustrative Problem 14.2. Accounting for hedging transactions is shown in Illustrative Problems 14.3, 14.4, and 14.5.

ILLUSTRATIVE PROBLEM 14.2: TRANSACTIONS DENOMINATED IN FOREIGN CURRENCY

On November 1, 1991, Company D, a U.S. company, purchases merchandise from Company E, located in Australia, agreeing to pay $A40,000 (40,000 Australian dollars) within 45 days. On December 1, 1991, Company D buys more mechandise from Company E, agreeing to pay $A50,000 within 45 days. Applicable exchange rates are

November 1, 1991	$A1.00 = $0.89
December 1, 1991	$A1.00 = $0.90
December 15, 1991	$A1.00 = $0.91
December 31, 1991	$A1.00 = $0.93
January 15, 1992	$A1.00 = $0.91

Company D records the November 1, 1991 purchase transaction in terms of the number of U.S. dollars required to buy the promised number of Australian dollars based on the November 1, 1991 exchange rate, as follows:

Purchases	35,600	
Accounts Payable		35,600

($A40,000 × 0.89 = $35,600)

Similarly, Company D records the December 1, 1991 purchase transaction in terms of the number of U.S. dollars required to buy the promised number of Australian dollars based on the December 1, 1991 exchange rates, as follows:

Purchases	45,000	
Accounts Payable		45,000

($A50,000 × 0.90 = $45,000)

[9] *SFAS No. 52*, paragraph 20.

In each case, because the Accounts Payable balance is denominated in Australian dollars, it is subject to the effect of exchange rate fluctuations.

If Company D settles the November 1, 1991 purchase on December 15, 1991, it will record the following journal entry:

Accounts Payable	35,600	
Transaction Loss	800	
Cash		36,400

($A40,000 × 0.91 = $36,400)

Because of the change in the exchange rate, Company D must pay more U.S. dollars than anticipated to acquire the necessary number of Australian dollars, thus incurring a transaction loss.

On December 31, 1991, Company D's year end, the exchange rate has increased to $A1.00 = $0.93. Thus, the value of the account payable created in the unsettled December 1, 1991 purchase expressed in U.S. dollars is $A50,000 × 0.93 or $46,500. Company D must adjust the balance of the account payable and recognize any resulting transaction gain or loss (in this case, a loss). The following journal entry records that adjustment:

Transaction Loss	1,500	
Accounts Payable		1,500

[$45,000 − ($A50,000 × 0.93) = $1,500]

Company D would include both the transaction loss of $800 recorded in the settlement transaction on December 15 and that of $1,500 recorded in the December 31 adjustment, or a total transaction loss of $2,300, in determining its 1991 net income.

When Company D settles the December 1, 1991 purchase on January 15, 1992, it will record the following journal entry:

Accounts Payable	46,500	
Cash		45,500
Transaction Gain		1,000

($A50,000 × 0.91 = $45,500)

Because of the change in the exchange rate, Company D is able to acquire the necessary number of Australian dollars by paying fewer U.S. dollars than anticipated, thus realizing a transaction gain. Notice that the gain is measured as the difference between the required payment and the *adjusted* balance of the account payable, both expressed in U.S. dollars. This transaction gain will be combined with all other transaction gains or losses recognized in 1992 and included in determining Company D's 1992 net income.

ACCOUNTING FOR HEDGING TRANSACTIONS

A company that engages in transactions involving foreign currencies runs a risk of incurring, and thus reporting, transaction losses caused by exchange rate fluctuations, as shown in Illustrative Problem 14.2. Many companies attempt to protect themselves against such losses by **hedging;** that is, entering into offsetting transactions to reduce or eliminate the exposure to risk.

A device commonly used in hedging transactions is the **forward exchange contract.** A forward exchange contract is an agreement to exchange currencies of different countries at a specified future date and at an exchange rate agreed to in advance (called the **forward rate**). A company may contract either to buy or to sell a certain number of units of a foreign currency at a specified future date and at an agreed upon forward rate in order to offset its exposure to risk from exchange rate fluctuation or merely to speculate on changes in exchange rates. More specifically, forward exchange contracts may be used

- to hedge risks related to receivables or liabilities denominated in a foreign currency (often called **exposed foreign currency net asset or net liability positions**),
- to hedge future commitments to pay or receive a fixed amount of a foreign currency,
- for speculation in foreign currencies, or
- to hedge net investments in foreign entities.

Forward exchange contracts are traded by currency brokers in a worldwide market.

Illustrative Problem 14.3 demonstrates accounting for a forward exchange contract used as a hedge in regard to liabilities denominated in a foreign currency (an exposed foreign currency net liability position).

ILLUSTRATIVE PROBLEM 14.3: HEDGE OF AN EXPOSED FOREIGN CURRENCY NET LIABILITY POSITION

Illustrative Problem 14.3 is based on the information given in Illustrative Problem 14.2, which is repeated here. On November 1, 1991, Company D, a U.S. company, purchases merchandise from Company E, located in Australia, agreeing to pay $A40,000 (40,000 Australian dollars) within 45 days. On December 1, 1991, Company D buys more merchandise from Company E, agreeing to pay $A50,000 within 45 days. Applicable exchange rates are

November 1, 1991	$A1.00 = $0.89
December 1, 1991	$A1.00 = $0.90
December 15, 1991	$A1.00 = $0.91
December 31, 1991	$A1.00 = $0.93
January 15, 1992	$A1.00 = $0.91

Anticipating that the exchange rate will continue to rise, Company D's management decides to hedge the account payable created in the December 1, 1991 transaction. As shown in Illustrative Problem 14.2, Company D records the December 1, 1992 purchase transaction, using the December 1, 1991 exchange rate, as follows:

Purchases	45,000	
Accounts Payable		45,000

($A50,000 × 0.90 = $45,000)

Again, because the Accounts Payable balance is denominated in Australian dollars, it is subject to the effect of exchange rate fluctuation. If the exchange rate were to remain the same at January 15, 1992, Company D would have to pay 45,000 U.S. dollars to buy 50,000 Australian dollars, which it would then pay to Company E. If the exchange rate increases, however, Company D will have to pay more than 45,000 U.S. dollars to buy 50,000 Australian dollars on January 15, 1992.

To hedge against this possible transaction loss, Company D enters into a forward exchange contract on December 1, 1991 to buy 50,000 Australian dollars on January 15, 1992 at a forward rate of $A1.00 = $0.92. Company D is agreeing to accept 50,000 Australian dollars from a currency broker in exchange for $46,000 at that future date. Company D records its entry into the forward exchange contract as follows:

Exchange Contract Receivable	45,000	
Premium on Exchange Contract	1,000	
Exchange Contract Payable		46,000

($A50,000 × 0.90 = $45,000
 $A50,000 × 0.92 = $46,000)

The exchange contract receivable is denominated in Australian dollars, and thus is subject to exchange rate fluctuations. The exchange contract payable, in contrast, is denominated in U.S. dollars, and thus will remain constant at $46,000. The premium or discount on the forward exchange contract is the difference between the two amounts. If the amount denominated in the foreign currency is *less* than the amount denominated in U.S. dollars, as in this case, the difference is a **premium.** If the amount denominated in the foreign currency is *greater* than the amount denominated in U.S. dollars, the difference is a **discount.**

On December 31, 1991, Company D's year end, the exchange rate has increased to $A1.00 = $0.93. Thus, the value of the account payable created in the unsettled December 1, 1991 purchase expressed in U.S. dollars is $A50,000 × 0.93 or $46,500. Company D must adjust the balance of the account payable and recognize any resulting transaction gain or loss (in this case, a loss). As shown in Illustrative Problem 14.2, the following journal entry records that adjustment:

Transaction Loss	1,500	
Accounts Payable		1,500

[($A50,000 × 0.93) − $45,000 = $1,500]

In the same manner, Company D must adjust the balance of the exchange contract receivable and recognize any resulting transaction gain or loss (in this case, a gain). The following journal entry records that adjustment:

Exchange Contract Receivable	1,500	
Transaction Gain		1,500

[($A50,000 × 0.93) − $45,000 = $1,500]

Obviously, the $1,500 transaction loss is offset by a $1,500 transaction gain and, as intended, Company D is protected from exposure to risk of loss from exchange rate fluctuation.

In addition, at December 31, 1991, Company D amortizes 30/45 of the premium on the exchange contract recorded on December 1, 1991 as follows:

Currency Hedging Expense	667	
Premium on Exchange Contract		667

As shown in Illustrative Problem 14.2, when Company D settles the December 1, 1991 purchase on January 15, 1992, it will record the following journal entry:

Accounts Payable	46,500	
Cash		45,500
Transaction Gain		1,000

($A50,000 × 0.91 = $45,500)

Because of the change in the exchange rate, Company D is able to acquire the necessary number of Australian dollars by paying fewer U.S. dollars than anticipated, thus realizing a transaction gain. Notice that the gain is measured as the difference between the required payment and the *adjusted* balance of the account payable, both expressed in U.S. dollars. This transaction gain is offset, however, by a transaction loss incurred in the settlement of the forward exchange contract, which is recorded in the following journal entries:

Cash	45,500	
Transaction Loss	1,000	
Exchange Contract Receivable		46,500
Exchange Contract Payable	46,000	
Cash		46,000

In addition, at January 15, 1992, Company D amortizes the remaining 15/45 of the premium on the exchange contract recorded on December 1,1991, as follows:

Currency Hedging Expense	333	
Premium on Exchange Contract		333

Financial Statement Recognition. Although the hedge has accomplished its purpose by offsetting transaction losses with transaction gains, Company D has incurred a total expense of $1,000 in the process. Company D reports these results as follows.

The transaction loss of $1,500 determined by adjusting Accounts Payable and the transaction gain of $1,500 determined by adjusting the Exchange Contract Receivable at December 31, 1991 are reported in Company D's 1991 income statement (although, obviously, they exactly offset each other). The currency hedging expense of $667 recorded at December 31, 1991 also is reported in Company D's 1991 income statement.

Similarly, the transaction gain of $1,000 recognized upon payment of the account payable and the transaction loss of $1,000 recognized upon settlement of the forward exchange contract at January 14, 1992 are reported in Company D's 1992 income statement (although, again, they exactly offset each other), as is the currency hedging expense of $333 recorded at January 14, 1992.

Illustrative Problem 14.4 demonstrates accounting for a forward exchange contract used as a hedge of a future commitment to receive a fixed amount of a foreign currency.

ILLUSTRATIVE PROBLEM 14.4: HEDGE OF A FUTURE COMMITMENT TO RECEIVE FOREIGN CURRENCY

On December 1, 1991, Company F, a U.S. company, contracts to sell merchandise to Company G, located in Belgium, agreeing to accept BF500,000 (500,000 Belgian francs) on March 1,

1992, when the goods are to be delivered. Applicable exchange rates are

December 1, 1991	BF1.00 = $0.0243
December 31, 1991	BF1.00 = $0.0240
March 1, 1992	BF1.00 = $0.0238

To hedge this future commitment, Company F enters into a forward exchange contract on December 1, 1991 to deliver 500,000 Belgian francs on March 1, 1992 at a forward rate of BF1.00 = $0.0231. Company F is agreeing to deliver 500,000 Belgian francs to a currency broker in exchange for $11,550 at that future date. Company F records its entry into the forward exchange contract as follows:

Exchange Contract Receivable	11,550	
Discount on Exchange Contract	600	
Exchange Contract Payable		12,150

(BF500,000 × 0.0231 = $11,550
 BF500,000 × 0.0243 = $12,150)

The exchange contract payable is denominated in Belgian francs, and thus is subject to exchange rate fluctuations. The exchange contract receivable, in contrast, is denominated in U.S. dollars, and thus will remain constant at $11,550.

On December 31, 1991, Company F's year end, the exchange rate has decreased to BF1.00 = $0.0240. Thus, Company F must adjust the balance of the Exchange Contract Payable and recognize any resulting transaction gain or loss (in this case, a gain). The following journal entry records that adjustment:

Exchange Contract Payable	150	
Deferred Transaction Gain		150

[(BF500,000 × 0.0240) − $12,150 = $150)]

Notice that this journal entry adjusts the balance of the Exchange Contract Payable to $12,000.

In addition, at December 31, 1991, Company F amortizes one-third of the discount on the exchange contract recorded on December 1, 1991 as follows:

Currency Hedging Expense	200	
Discount on Exchange Contract		200

When Company F fulfills its contractual obligation to Company G on March 1, 1992, it will record the following journal entries:

Exchange Contract Payable	12,000	
Deferred Transaction Gain		100
Cash		11,900

In this journal entry, the adjusted balance of the Exchange Contract Payable, $12,000, is offset by the delivery of 500,000 Belgian francs at the March 1, 1992 exchange rate of $0.0238, yielding an additional transaction gain of $100.

Cash	11,550	
Exchange Contract Receivable		11,550

This journal entry records the receipt of the 500,000 Belgian francs at the forward contract rate of $0.0231.

Cash	11,900	
Sales		11,900

This journal entry records the fulfillment of the purchase commitment, measured in terms of the March 1, 1992 exchange rate of $0.0238.

Deferred Transaction Gain	250	
Sales		250

This journal entry adjusts the revenue from the sale of the merchandise by the combined amount of deferred transaction gain recorded at December 31, 1991 and at March 1, 1992. Thus, the total revenue from this sale becomes $12,150.

In addition, at March 1, 1992, Company F amortizes the remaining two-thirds of the premium on the exchange contract recorded on December 1, 1991 as follows:

Currency Hedging Expense	400	
Premium on Exchange Contract		400

Financial Statement Recognition. *SFAS No. 52* specifies that gains or losses on a hedge of a future commitment to pay or receive a fixed amount of a foreign currency are to be deferred and included in the measurement of the related transaction, unless this treatment is expected to lead to the recognition of losses in future periods.[10] Thus, the deferred transaction gain amounts recognized at December 31, 1991 and March 1, 1992 become adjustments to the revenue from the sale of the merchandise rather than being reported as gains in either year.

On a hedge of a future commitment to pay or receive a fixed amount of a foreign currency, *SFAS No. 52* permits the premium or discount on the forward contract either [a] to be amortized over the life of the contract or [b] to be included in the measurement of the net result of fulfilling the contract.[11] The first of these alternatives is illustrated here. In this case, the currency hedging expense of $200 recognized at December 31, 1991 would be reported in Company F's 1991 income statement and the $400 amount recognized at March 1, 1992 would be reported in its 1992 income statement.

Illustrative Problem 14.5 demonstrates accounting for a forward exchange contract used for the purpose of speculation.

ILLUSTRATIVE PROBLEM 14.5: FORWARD EXCHANGE CONTRACT USED FOR SPECULATION

On December 1, 1991, Company H, a U.S. company, purchases for the purpose of speculation a forward exchange contract for 100,000 French francs deliverable on January 30, 1992 at a forward rate of F1.00 = $0.150. On December 1, 1991, Company H records the forward contract as follows:

[10] *SFAS No. 52*, paragraph 21.
[11] *SFAS No. 52*, paragraph 18.

| Exchange Contract Receivable | 15,000 | |
| Exchange Contract Payable | | 15,000 |

(F100,000 × 0.150 = $15,000)

The exchange contract receivable is denominated in French francs, and thus is subject to exchange rate fluctuations. The exchange contract payable, in contrast, is denominated in U.S. dollars, and thus will remain constant at $15,000.

On December 31, 1991, Company H's year end, the forward rate for French francs deliverable on January 30, 1992 has increased to F1.00 = $0.156. Thus, Company H must adjust the balance of the Exchange Contract Receivable and recognize any resulting transaction gain or loss (in this case, a gain). The following journal entry records that adjustment:

| Exchange Contract Receivable | 600 | |
| Transaction Gain | | 600 |

[(F100,000 × 0.156) − $15,000 = $600]

Notice that this journal entry adjusts the balance of the Exchange Contract Receivable to $15,600.

On January 30, 1992, when Company H fulfills its contractual obligation to the exchange broker, the exchange rate for French francs has increased to F1.00 = $0.162. Company H records the settlement of the forward contract in the following journal entries:

Cash	16,200	
Exchange Contract Receivable		15,600
Transaction Gain		600

In this journal entry, the adjusted balance of the Exchange Contract Receivable, $15,600, is offset by the receipt of 100,000 French francs at the January 30, 1992 exchange rate of $0.162, yielding an additional transaction gain of $600.

| Exchange Contract Payable | 15,000 | |
| Cash | | 15,000 |

This journal entry records the payment of the promised $15,000 (U.S. dollars).

Financial Statement Recognition. SFAS No. 52 specifies that gains or losses on a forward contract that does not represent a hedge of a foreign currency exposure are to be included in the measurement of net income of appropriate accounting periods.[12] Thus, Company H's 1991 and 1992 income statements each would report a transaction gain of $600.

HEDGE OF A NET INVESTMENT IN A FOREIGN ENTITY

Hedges of net investments in foreign entities are accounted for by the investor (or parent company) in a manner similar to that shown in Illustrative Problem 14.4, except that gains or losses from the hedging transactions become part of the balance of the investor's Cumulative

---

[12] SFAS No. 52, paragraph 17 .

Translation Adjustment account, which is reported as a separate component of stockholders' equity. The derivation and use of the Cumulative Translation Adjustment account is discussed in more detail in the sections of this chapter dealing with translation of foreign currency financial statements and the consolidation of foreign subsidiaries.

TRANSLATION OF FOREIGN CURRENCY FINANCIAL STATEMENTS

When the account balances of a parent company and its subsidiary (or investor and investee) are expressed in different currencies, it is necessary to **translate** the financial information of the subsidiary (or investee) into terms of the currency of the parent (or investor) in order to [a] apply the equity method and [b] prepare consolidated financial statements.

According to *SFAS No. 52*, the objectives of translation are to

    a. Provide information that is generally compatible with the expected economic effects of a rate change on an enterprise's cash flows and equity.

    b. Reflect in consolidated financial statements the financial results and relationships of the individual consolidated entities as measured in their functional currencies in conformity with U.S. generally accepted accounting principles.[13]

Two major types of adjustments to the foreign affiliate's accounts might be necessary in conjunction with, or instead of, translation.

- If the accounting records of the foreign affiliate are based on accounting practices that differ materially from U.S. generally accepted accounting principles, the foreign affiliate's account balances must be brought into conformity with U.S. generally accepted accounting principles before they are translated into U.S. dollars.

- If the foreign affiliate does not keep its records in its functional currency, its account balances must be *remeasured* into the functional currency before they are translated into U.S. dollars. Also, if the foreign affiliate operates in a highly inflationary economy (100% or more cumulative inflation over a three-year period), its account balances must be remeasured into the reporting currency (that of the parent or investor).[14]

The remeasurement process is very similar to the temporal method of translation required under *SFAS No. 8*. Thus, in those cases in which the foreign affiliate's account balances are remeasured into U.S. dollars, no additional translation is necessary.

The remaining illustrative problems in this chapter, as well as the exercises and problems at the end of the chapter, are based on the assumptions [a] that each foreign affiliate maintains its accounting records in accordance with U.S. generally accepted accounting principles and in its functional currency and [b] that it does not operate in a highly inflationary economy. Therefore, we can proceed directly to the translation process.

---

[13] *SFAS No. 52*, paragraph 4.

[14] *SFAS No. 52*, paragraphs 10–11.

EXCHANGE RATES

The translation process under *SFAS No. 52* is based on the use of **current exchange rates.**

> For purposes of translation of financial statements . . . , the current exchange rate is the rate as of the end of the period covered by the financial statements or as of the dates of recognition in those statements in the case of revenues, expenses, gains, and losses.[15]

Under this concept, the appropriate rates to be used to translate the various financial statement elements are[16]

Assets and liabilities	the exchange rate at the balance sheet date.
Revenues, expenses, gains, and losses	a weighted average for the period. (In principle, the exchange rates in effect at the dates of recognition of the various revenues, expenses, gains, and losses should be used, but as a practical matter, the use of a weighted average is permitted.)
Dividends	the exchange rate in effect when the dividends are declared.
Capital stock and additional paid-in capital	the exchange rate(s) in effect when the stock was issued.
Beginning balance of retained earnings	the translated ending balance of retained earnings of the preceding year.

SFAS No. 52 does not address the stockholders' equity items directly, but authorities appear to agree on the use of the rates indicated above for dividends and for capital stock and additional paid-in capital. In addition, the translated ending balance of retained earnings of the preceding year is carried forward as the translated beginning balance of retained earnings for the current year. (If the translated beginning balance of retained earnings cannot be determined, however, translation of the beginning balance at the exchange rate in effect at the end of the preceding year is an acceptable substitute.)

TRANSLATION ADJUSTMENTS

Translation of the accounts as indicated above will give rise to a **translation adjustment.** Under the provisions of *SFAS No. 52*, translation adjustments are not to be included in determining net income. Instead, the cumulative translation adjustment balance should be reported as a separate component of stockholders' equity until disposition of the investment.[17]

The cumulative amount of the translation adjustment can be viewed simply as the amount necessary to make the translated balance sheet balance. The translation adjustment for the current year can be calculated as

[a] net assets at the beginning of the year (expressed in terms of the foreign currency), multiplied by the change in exchange rates from the beginning of the year to the end of the year, plus

---

[15] *SFAS No. 52*, paragraph 162.

[16] *SFAS No. 52*, paragraph 12.

[17] *SFAS No. 52*, paragraphs 13–14.

[b] net income (expressed in terms of the foreign currency), multiplied by the difference between the current exchange rate and the exchange rate used to translate income statement accounts, minus

[c] dividends (expressed in terms of the foreign currency), multiplied by the difference between the current exchange rate and the exchange rate used to translate dividends.

The disclosure requirements of *SFAS No. 52* include the presentation of "an analysis of the changes during the period in the separate component of equity for cumulative translation adjustments . . . in a separate financial statement, in notes to the financial statements, or as part of a statement of changes in equity."[18]

The translation process and a schedule of cumulative translation adjustment changes fulfilling these disclosure requirements are demonstrated in Illustrative Problem 14.6, which follows.

ILLUSTRATIVE PROBLEM 14.6: TRANSLATION OF FOREIGN CURRENCY FINANCIAL STATEMENTS

Comany J, a U.S. corporation, owns 80% of the common stock of Company K, located in France, the primary currency unit of which is the franc (F). Company K's common stock was issued in 1981, when the exchange rate was F1.00 = $0.25. Other applicable exchange rates are

December 31, 1991	F1.00 = $0.14
October 1, 1992	F1.00 = $0.13
1992 average	F1.00 = $0.12
December 31, 1992	F1.00 = $0.11

The translated balance of Company K's December 31, 1991 retained earnings is $44,800. Company K's dividends were declared on October 1, 1991 and paid on November 15, 1991. Company K's December 31, 1992 trial balance is included in the translation worksheet shown in Exhibit 14-1.

Company K's asset and liability balances are translated at the year-end exchange rate of $0.11 per franc, while the 1992 weighted average rate of $0.12 per franc is used to translate its revenue and expense balances. Company K's Dividends Declared balance has been translated at the exchange rate prevailing when the dividends were declared. Company K's Common Stock and Additional Paid-in Capital balances have been translated at the exchange rate prevailing when the stock was issued, $0.25 per franc. Company K's translated beginning Retained Earnings balance is the translated December 31, 1991 balance, as given in the statement of the problem.

The balance of the Cumulative Translation Adjustment at December 31, 1991 is the amount necessary to make the balance sheet balance at that date. Company K's outstanding common stock was the same at December 31, 1991 as it is at December 31, 1992. Also, Company K's preclosing trial balance at December 31, 1992 contains its beginning balance of Retained Earnings, which is the amount that appeared in the December 31, 1991 balance sheet. Because Assets − Liabilities = Stockholders' Equity, the sum of Company K's December 31, 1991 stockholders' equity balances can be used as a surrogate for its net assets at that

---

[18] *SFAS No. 52*, paragraph 31.

EXHIBIT 14-1

Illustrative Problem 14.6
Translation Worksheet
December 31, 1992

	Francs	Exchange Rate	U.S. Dollars
Current Assets	F 280,000	0.11	$ 30,800
Plant and Equipment	920,000	0.11	101,200
Other Assets	30,000	0.11	3,300
Cost of Goods Sold	520,000	0.12	62,400
Depreciation Expense	190,000	0.12	22,800
Other Expenses	210,000	0.12	25,200
Dividends Declared	40,000	0.13	5,200
Cumulative Translation Adjustment			69,900
	F2,190,000		$ 320,800
Accumulated Depreciation	F 220,000	0.11	$ 24,200
Current Liabilities	120,000	0.11	13,200
Long-Term Note Payable	180,000	0.11	19,800
Common Stock	350,000	0.25	87,500
Additional Paid-in Capital	50,000	0.25	12,500
Retained Earnings	280,000	given	44,800
Sales	990,000	0.12	118,800
	F2,190,000		$ 320,800

EXHIBIT 14-2

Illustrative Problem 14.6
Schedule of Cumulative Translation Adjustment Changes
December 31, 1992

Beginning balance		$ 49,600
Beginning net assets, times the change in exchange rates (F680,000 × 0.03)	$ 20,400	
Net income, times the difference between the current and average exchange rates (F70,000 × $0.01)	700	
Dividends declared, times the difference between the current and October 1 exchange rates (F40,000 × $0.02)	(800)	
Translation adjustment, 1992		20,300
Ending balance		$ 69,900

date. Thus, the December 31, 1991 balance of the Cumulative Translation Adjustment, $49,600, can be determined as [a] the sum of the translated stockholders' balances in the December 31, 1992 preclosing trial balance ($144,800), minus [b] the sum of those stockholders' equity balances translated at the December 31, 1991 exchange rate (F680,000 × $.14 = $95,200). The analysis of changes in the balance of the Cumulative Translation Adjustment is shown in Exhibit 14-2.

ACCOUNTING FOR INVESTMENTS IN FOREIGN AFFILIATES

Under the equity method, the parent (or investor) records its share of

- the translated net income of the subsidiary (or investee),
- the current year's translation adjustment, and
- the subsidiary's (or investee's) dividends, translated at the exchange rate in effect when the dividends were declared.

The offsetting debit or credit in each case affects the Investment in Subsidiary (or Investee) account.

Notice that the list above includes a new element, the current year's translation adjustment, which is applicable only in the context of investments in foreign affiliates. Because the cumulative balance of the translation adjustment is treated as a special component of stockholders' equity, the annual amount must be recorded by the parent as indicated above.

Under the cost method, the parent (or investor) records its share of the subsidiary's (or investee's) dividends, translated as indicated above, by debiting Dividends Receivable (or Cash) and crediting Dividend Revenue. These journal entries are shown in Illustrative Problem 14.7.

ILLUSTRATIVE PROBLEM 14.7: ACCOUNTING FOR AN INVESTMENT IN A FOREIGN SUBSIDIARY

Illustrative Problem 14.7 is a continuation of Illustrative Problem 14.6, pertinent information from which is repeated here. Company J, a U.S. corporation, owns 80% of the common stock of Company K, located in France, the primary unit of which is the franc (F). Company K's common stock was issued in 1981, when the exchange rate was F1.00 = $0.25. Other applicable exchange rates are

December 31, 1991	F1.00 = $0.14
October 1, 1992	F1.00 = $0.13
1992 average	F1.00 = $0.12
December 31, 1992	F1.00 = $0.11

By combining the translated balances of Company K's revenues and expenses that appear in Exhibit 14-1, its translated 1992 net income is determined to be $8,400. Also in Exhibit 14-1, the translated amount of Company K's 1992 dividends appears as $5,200. In Exhibit 14-2, the 1992 translation adjustment is determined to be $20,300.

Under the equity method, Company J would record the following journal entries in 1992:

Company K's Net Income

Investment in Company K	6,720	
Income from Company K		6,720

[80% × $8,400]

Company K's Current Translation Adjustment

Cumulative Translation Adjustment	16,240	
Investment in Company K		16,240

[80% × $20,300]

Company K's Dividends

Dividends Receivable	4,160	
Investment in Company K		4,160

[80% × $5,200]

Cash	4,160	
Dividends Receivable		4,160

Under the cost method, Company J would record the following journal entries in 1992:

Company K's Dividends

Dividends Receivable	4,160	
Dividend Revenue		4,160

[80% × $4,400]

Cash	4,160	
Dividends Receivable		4,160

CONSOLIDATED FINANCIAL STATEMENTS WITH FOREIGN SUBSIDIARIES

Before consolidated financial statements involving a foreign subsidiary can be prepared, that subsidiary's preclosing trial balance must be translated into the parent's functional currency (for our purposes, U.S. dollars), as discussed and demonstrated earlier in this chapter. Once translation has been accomplished, the consolidation process is essentially the same as described and illustrated in Chapters 5 through 13, with the exception noted below.

- Because the cumulative translation adjustment is regarded as an element of stockholders' equity, it is subject to elimination in the same manner as the other stockholders' equity balances, and yields a minority interest residual when the subsidiary is partially owned.
- Special consideration is given to the elimination of intercompany profits. These eliminations are to be made using the exchange rates in effect at the dates of the transactions

in which the intercompany profits originated. Reasonable approximations, however, are acceptable.[19]

Mechanically, it is useful to combine the translation and consolidation processes on a single worksheet, as shown in Illustrative Problem 14.8.

ILLUSTRATIVE PROBLEM 14.8: TRANSLATION AND CONSOLIDATION COMBINED

Illustrative Problem 14.8 is a continuation of Illustrative Problems 14.6 and 14.7. The basic information from Illustrative Problem 14.6 is repeated here.

Company J, a U.S. corporation, owns 80% of the common stock of Company K, located in France, the primary currency unit of which is the franc (F). Company K's common stock was issued in 1981, when the exchange rate was F1.00 = $0.25. Other applicable exchange rates are

1991 average	F1.00 = $0.15
December 31, 1991	F1.00 = $0.14
October 1, 1992	F1.00 = $0.13
1992 average	F1.00 = $0.12
December 31, 1992	F1.00 = $0.11

The translated balance of Company K's December 31, 1991 retained earnings is $44,800. Company K's dividends were declared on October 1, 1992 and paid on November 15, 1992.

Company J acquired its investment in Company K for $51,600 on July 1, 1989, when the translated total book value of Company K's net assets was $39,500. The excess of cost over book value is treated as goodwill from consolidation, amortized over 10 years. Company J accounts for its investment in Company K under the equity method.

During 1992, Company K purchased merchandise from Company J for F320,000, of which F40,000 remains unpaid at December 31, 1992. Company K's beginning and ending inventories for 1992 contain intercompany profits of F3,000 and F4,000, respectively.

Company J's and Company K's December 31, 1992 preclosing trial balances are contained in the combined translation and consolidation worksheet shown in Exhibit 14-7. Before the consolidation eliminations can be determined, it is necessary to translate Company K's account balances into U.S. dollars, as shown in Exhibit 14-7.

The Goodwill from Consolidation schedule to accompany the December 31, 1992 consolidation worksheet is shown in Exhibit 14-3. Notice that the book value of Company J's investment in Company K is calculated as Company J's percentage of ownership, 80%, multiplied by the translated book value of Company K's net assets at July 1, 1989, the date of acquisition. Because the translated book value of Company K's net assets is used, all values are expressed in dollars, causing the schedule to appear just as it would in the case of a domestic subsidiary.

Exhibit 14-4 contains the Intercompany Ownership Interests, Subsidiary Income and Dividends, and Goodwill Amortization sets of eliminations that would appear on the December 31, 1992 translation and consolidation worksheet.

---

[19] *SFAS No. 52*, paragraph 25.

EXHIBIT 14-3

Illustrative Problem 14.8
Goodwill from Consolidation Schedule
December 31, 1992

Goodwill from Consolidation

Cost of Investment		$ 51,600
Book Value (80% × $39,500)		31,600
Goodwill, 7/1/89		20,000
Amortization through 12/31/91	$ 5,000	
Amortization, 1992	2,000	7,000
Goodwill, 12/31/92		$ 13,000

EXHIBIT 14-4

Illustrative Problem 14.8
Eliminations
December 31, 1992

Eliminations

Intercompany Ownership Interests

[1]	Common Stock: K	$ 70,000
[2]	Additional Paid-in Capital: K	10,000
[3]	Retained Earnings: K	35,840
[4]	Cumulative Translation Adjustment: K	(55,920)
[5]	Investment in Company K	$ (59,920)

Subsidiary Income and Dividends

[6]	Income from Company K	$ 6,720
[7]	Dividends Declared K:	(4,160)
[8]	Investment in Company K	$ (2,560)

Goodwill Amortization

[9]	Other Expenses (Goodwill Amortization)	$ 2,000
[10]	Retained Earnings: J	5,000
[11]	Investment in Company K	$ (7,000)

All of these eliminations that involve Company K balances are made at 80% of the respective translated balances—that is, in dollars. These translations appear in the translation worksheet in Exhibit 14-1 and again in the combination translation and consolidation worksheet in Exhibit 14-7. Company K's Common Stock and Additional Paid-in Capital balances have been translated at the exchange rate prevailing when the stock was issued, $0.25 per franc. Company K's translated beginning Retained Earnings balance is the translated December 31, 1991 balance, as given in the statement of the problem. Notice that the Intercompany Ownership Interests set of eliminations also includes an elimination [4] against Company K's Cumulative Translation Adjustment for 80% of its balance.

In the Subsidiary Income and Dividends set of eliminations, elimination [6] eliminates Company J's Income from Company K balance. This is the amount recorded by Company J in Illustrative Problem 14.7 and calculated there as 80% of $8,400, Company K's 1992 net income expressed in dollars. Company K's translated 1992 net income is determined by using its revenue and expense balances translated at the 1992 weighted average exchange rate of $0.12 per franc. Elimination [7] eliminates 80% of $5,200, the translated amount of Company K's 1992 dividends. Company K's dividends balance has been translated at the exchange rate of $0.13 per franc that was in effect at the dividend declaration date.

The amounts appearing in the Goodwill Amortization set of eliminations are taken directly from the Goodwill from Consolidation schedule in Exhibit 14-3, where they are expressed in dollars. Thus, they appear just as they would in the case of a domestic subsidiary.

Exhibit 14-5 contains the Intercompany Sales and Purchases, Intercompany Profit in Beginning Inventory, and Intercompany Profit in Ending Inventory sets of eliminations that would appear on the December 31, 1992 translation and consolidation worksheet.

EXHIBIT 14-5

Illustrative Problem 14.8
Additional Eliminations
December 31, 1992

Eliminations

Intercompany Sales and Purchases

[12] Sales	$ 38,400
[13] Cost of Goods Sold	(38,400)

Intercompany Receivables and Payables

[14] Current Liabilities	$ 4,400
[15] Current Assets	(4,400)

Intercompany Profit in Beginning Inventory

[16] Retained Earnings: J	$ 450
[17] Cost of Goods Sold	(450)

Intercompany Profit in Ending Inventory

[18] Cost of Goods Sold	$ 480
[19] Current Assets	(480)

The amount eliminated from Sales and from Cost of Goods Sold in the Intercompany Sales and Purchases set of eliminations has been translated into dollars using the weighted average exchange rate for 1992.

As noted earlier, eliminations of intercompany profits are to be made using the exchange rates in effect when the transactions that gave rise to the intercompany profits occurred, but reasonable approximations are acceptable. Accordingly, the intercompany profit in beginning inventory eliminated in Eliminations [16] and [17], given in the statement of the problem as F3,000 has been translated into dollars using the weighted average exchange rate for 1991, $0.15 per franc. Similarly, the intercompany profit in ending inventory eliminated in Eliminations [18] and [19], given in the statement of the problem as F4,000, has been translated into dollars using the weighted average exchange rate for 1992, $0.12 per franc.

Because all amounts appearing in the Income Allocation schedule in Exhibit 14-6 either were expressed in dollars originally or have been translated into dollars, the schedule looks just as it would if Company K were a domestic subsidiary.

EXHIBIT 14-6

Illustrative Problem 14.8
Income Allocation Schedule
Year Ended December 31, 1992

Income Allocation

Company J's Own Net Income		$ 112,800
Add: Intercompany Profit in Beginning Inventory		450
Less: Intercompany Profit in Ending Inventory		(480)
Goodwill Amortization Expense		(2,000)
Company J's Adjusted Net Income		110,770
Company K's Own Net Income	$ 8,400	
Minority Interest (20%)	1,680	
Company J's Share (80%)		6,720
Consolidated Net Income		$ 117,490

The combined translation and consolidation worksheet is shown in Exhibit 14-7. The first three columns repeat the translation worksheet for Company K that appears in Exhibit 14-1. The remainder of the worksheet is structured in the same manner as the familiar consolidation worksheet, except that the order in which the trial balances appear is reversed.

Notice the treatment of the two Cumulative Translation Adjustment balances. Company J's Cumulative Translation Adjustment balance appears in the Balance Sheet column as a component of the consolidated stockholder's equity, which in this case happens to be negative. Company K's Cumulative Translation adjustment yields a minority interest residual that will be combined with the other minority interest components in the consolidated balance sheet.

EXHIBIT 14-7

Illustrative Problem 14.8
Translation and Consolidation Worksheet
December 31, 1992

	Company K Trial Balance			Company J Trial Balance	Eliminations		Income Statement	Balance Sheet
	Francs	Exchange Rate	U.S. Dollars					
Current Assets	280,000	0.11	30,800	788,320	[15] (4,400) [19] (480)			814,240
Plant and Equipment	920,000	0.11	101,200	1,180,000				1,281,200
Investment in Company K				82,480	[5] (59,920) [8] (2,560) [11] (7,000)			13,000 G
Other Assets	30,000	0.11	3,300	42,000				45,300
Dividends Declared: J				60,000				60,000 R
Dividends Declared: K	40,000	0.13	5,200		[7] (4,160)			1,040 M
Cost of Goods Sold	520,000	0.12	62,400	610,000	[13] (38,400) [17] (450) [18] 480		634,030	
Exchange Loss				3,200			3,200	
Depreciation Expense	190,000	0.12	22,800	107,000			129,800	
Other Expenses	210,000	0.12	25,200	395,000	[9] 2,000		422,200	
Cumulative Translation Adj.: J				55,920				55,920
Cumulative Translation Adj.: K			69,900		[4] (55,920)			13,980 M
	2,190,000		320,800	3,323,920				2,284,68
Accumulated Depreciation	220,000	0.11	24,200	416,000				440,200
Current Liabilities	120,000	0.11	13,200	189,200	[14] 4,400			198,000
Long-Term Notes Payable	180,000	0.11	19,800	248,000				267,800
Common Stock: J				800,000				800,000
Common Stock: K	350,000	0.25	87,500		[1] 70,000			17,500 M
Additional Paid-in Capital: J				200,000				200,000
Additional Paid-in Capital: K	50,000	0.25	12,500		[2] 10,000			2,500 M
Retained Earnings: J				236,000	[10] 5,000 [16] 450			230,550 R
Retained Earnings: K	280,000	given	44,800		[3] 35,840			8,960 M
Sales	990,000	0.12	118,800	1,228,000	[12] 38,400		1,308,400	
Income from Company K				6,720	[6] 6,720			
	2,190,000		320,800	3,323,920				
Minority Interest in Comany K's Net Income							1680	1,680 M
Consolidated Net Income							117,490	117,490 R
							1,308,400	1,308,400 　2,284,680

FINANCIAL STATEMENT DISCLOSURES

SFAS No. 52 requires the following matters related to foreign operations to be disclosed in the financial statements or in the accompanying notes:

- The aggregate amount of transaction gain or loss, including gains and losses on forward exchange contracts, included in the determination of net income.
- An analysis of the changes in the cumulative translation adjustment reported as a separate component of stockholders' equity. This disclosure is discussed and illustrated earlier in this chapter in connection with Illustrative Problem 14.6.
- Significant changes in exchange rates occurring after the balance sheet date and their effects on unsettled balances related to foreign currency transactions.[20]

SUMMARY

This chapter deals with two major topics related to foreign operations by a U.S. corporation:

- accounting for transactions involving foreign currencies, and
- translation of foreign currency financial statements.

It begins with a brief history of official pronouncements governing accounting for foreign operations, including *Accounting Research Bulletin No. 43*, as modified by *Accounting Principles Board Opinion No. 6, Statement of Financial Accounting Standards No. 8*, and *Statement of Financial Accounting Standards No. 52*.

In the section of the chapter devoted to accounting for international transactions, we discuss and illustrate appropriate accounting for and reporting of transactions denominated in the recording entity's functional currency, transactions denominated in a currency other than the recording entity's functional currency, and various types of hedging transactions.

In the section of the chapter devoted to the translation of foreign currency financial statements, we discuss and illustrate the translation of foreign currency financial statements as such, the parent company's accounting for an investment in a foreign subsidiary under both the equity and the cost methods, and the preparation of consolidated financial statements of a U.S. parent company and a foreign subsidiary.

REVIEW PROBLEM

Company G, a U.S. corporation, acquired 80% of Company H's common stock for $54,824 on June 30, 1990, when the translated book value of Company H's net assets was $53,530. Company H is located in Norway, where the principal unit of currency is the Krone (NKr). The excess of cost over book value is treated as goodwill from consolidation, amortized over 10 years. Company G's and Company H's December 31, 1992 trial balances appear below.

---

[20]*SFAS No. 52*, paragraphs 30–32.

	Company G	Company H
Current Assets	$ 473,441	NKr 160,100
Plant and Equipment	868,475	653,900
Investment in Company H	65,944	
Dividends Declared	40,000	20,000
Cost of Goods Sold	425,346	246,300
Other Expenses	213,054	134,700
Transaction Loss	8,100	
Cumulative Translation Adjustment	51,040	
	$ 2,145,400	NKr1,215,000
Accumulated Depreciation	$ 207,408	NKr 111,200
Liabilities	349,620	89,800
Common Stock	500,000	300,000
Additional Paid-in Capital	120,000	30,000
Retained Earnings	218,400	235,000
Sales	742,900	449,000
Income from Company H	7,072	
	$ 2,145,400	NKr1,215,000

Company H's common stock was issued in 1981, when the exchange rate was NKr1.00 = $0.25. Other applicable exchange rates are

December 31, 1991	NKr1.00 = $0.15
1992 average	NKr1.00 = $0.13
November 1, 1992	NKr1.00 = $0.12
December 31, 1992	NKr1.00 = $0.11

The translated balance of Company H's December 31, 1991 retained earnings is $42,290. Company H's dividends were declared on November 1, 1992 and paid on December 10, 1992.

Required
1. Present Company G's equity method journal entries for 1992.
2. Prepare a combined translation and consolidation worksheet at December 31, 1992, supported by appropriate schedules.

QUESTIONS

1. How were unrealized exchange gains and losses reported under *SFAS No. 8*?
2. How are unrealized transaction gains and losses reported under *SFAS No. 52*?
3. Describe a transaction between a U.S. corporation and a foreign corporation in which the resulting assets and liabilities are denominated in a foreign currency.
4. How is a gain or loss on the payment of an account payable denominated in a foreign currency determined under *SFAS No. 52*?

5. If a balance sheet date is reached before an account receivable denominated in a foreign currency is collected, what should be done according to *SFAS No. 52*?

6. According to *SFAS No. 52*, how should gains or losses on a hedge of a future commitment to pay or receive a fixed amount of a foreign currency be reported?

7. According to *SFAS No. 52*, how should gains or losses on a forward contract that does not represent a hedge of a foreign currency exposure be reported?

8. According to *SFAS No. 52*, at what exchange rate should assets and liabilities be translated?

9. According to *SFAS No. 52*, at what exchange rate should revenues and expenses be translated?

10. According to *SFAS No. 52*, how should the cumulative translation adjustment be reported in a corporation's financial statements?

11. Under the equity method, how does the parent company record its share of its subsidiary's current period translation adjustment?

12. How is a subsidiary's cumulative translation adjustment treated in making the eliminations on the consolidation worksheet?

EXERCISES

EXERCISE 14-1

On November 15, 1992, Company A, a U.S. corporation that reports on a calendar year basis, purchased merchandise from Company B, located in Austria. Company A agreed to pay AS400,000 (400,000 Austrian shillings) within 60 days. Company A paid the agreed amount on January 12, 1993. Exchange rates at various dates were

November 15, 1992	AS1.00 = $0.05
December 31, 1992	AS1.00 = $0.03
January 12, 1993	AS1.00 = $0.04

Required

1. Present all journal entries that should appear on Company A's books relative to the above transactions.

2. Present all journal entries that should appear on Company B's books relative to the above transactions.

EXERCISE 14-2

On December 1, 1990, Company C, a U.S. corporation that reports on a calendar year basis, sold merchandise to Company D, located in Angola. Company D agreed to pay Kw500,000 (500,000 kwanzas) within 60 days. Company D paid the agreed amount on January 22, 1991. Exchange rates at various dates were

December 1, 1990	Kw1.00 = $0.034
December 31, 1990	Kw1.00 = $0.036
January 22, 1991	Kw1.00 = $0.038

Required

1. Present all journal entries that should appear on Company C's books relative to the above transactions.

2. Present all journal entries that should appear on Company D's books relative to the above transactions.

EXERCISE 14-3

The translation of a foreign subsidiary's trial balance results in total debits of $402,600 and total credits of $368,200. The parent's share of the difference between these two amounts should be reported in the consolidated financial statements as

a. an extraordinary gain.
b. a gain included in income before extraordinary items.
c. a deferred credit in the balance sheet.
d. a separate component of stockholder's equity.

EXERCISE 14-4

Which of the following items should *not* be included in the 1991 net income of a company engaged in transactions in which receivables and payables are denominated in foreign currencies?

a. A transaction gain recorded upon payment of an account payable on July 8, 1991
b. A transaction loss resulting from a designated hedge of a net investment in a foreign subsidiary
c. A transaction gain resulting from the year-end adjustment of the balance of an account payable
d. A transaction loss recorded upon collection of an account receivable on December 28, 1991

EXERCISE 14-5

Company E, a U.S. corporation, acquired 75% of the common stock of Company F, located in Sweden, in 1989. Company F's December 31, 1991 trial balance, expressed in krona, appears below.

Receivables	SEK	79,000
Other Current Assets		81,000
Plant and Equipment		654,000
Dividends Declared		20,000
Cost of Goods Sold		246,000
Other Expenses		135,000
		SEK1,215,000
Accumulated Depreciation	SEK	127,000
Current Liabilities		89,000
Common Stock		300,000
Additional Paid-in Capital		30,000
Retained Earnings		235,000
Sales		434,000
		SEK1,215,000

Company F's common stock was issued in 1982, when the exchange rate was SEK1.00 = $0.25. Other applicable exchange rates are

December 31, 1990	SEK1.00 = $0.15
November 5, 1991	SEK1.00 = $0.12
1991 average	SEK1.00 = $0.13
December 31, 1991	SEK1.00 = $0.11

The translated balance of Company F's December 31, 1990 retained earnings is $35,250. Company F's dividends were declared on November 5, 1991 and paid on December 15, 1991.

Required

Prepare a translation worksheet as of December 31, 1991.

EXERCISE 14-6

Refer to Exercise 14-5. Calculate independently the 1991 translation adjustment.

EXERCISE 14-7

Refer to Exercise 14-5. Present the equity method journal entries on Company E's books for 1991.

EXERCISE 14-8

Certain December 31, 1991 account balances of Company B, a foreign subsidiary of Company A, have been translated into U.S. dollars as follows:

	Exchange Rates	
	Current	Historical
Long-term Notes Receivable	$120,000	$100,000
Prepaid Insurance	55,000	50,000
Copyright	75,000	85,000
	$250,000	$235,000

The subsidiary's functional currency is the currency of the country in which it is located. At what total amount should these account balances be included in the December 31, 1991 consolidated balance sheet?

a. $225,000
b. $235,000
c. $240,000
d. $250,000

(AICPA adapted)

EXERCISE 14-9

The December 31, 1992 trial balance of Company M, a wholly owned, foreign subsidiary of Company L, contains the following items, expressed in local currency units (LCU):

Depreciation Expense (on equipment purchased on January 15, 1990)	$ 120,000
Bad Debt Expense	80,000
Rent Expense	200,000

The LCU is Company M's functional currency. Exchange rates (U.S. dollar equivalents) of one LCU at various dates are

January 15, 1990	$ .50
1992 average	.44
December 31, 1992	.40

At what total dollar amount should these expenses be reflected in the 1992 consolidated income statement?

a. $160,000
b. $168,000
c. $176,000
d. $183,200

(AICPA adapted)

EXERCISE 14-10

To hedge an exposed net liability position, Company N, a U.S. company, enters into a forward exchange contract. Company N should report the amortization of the premium on the forward exchange contract

a. in the income statement as an expense of the accounting period or periods in which the amortization is recognized.
b. in the income statement as a component of the transaction gain or loss on the related liability.
c. in the balance sheet as a deferred charge.
d. in the balance sheet as a component of stockholders' equity.

PROBLEMS

PROBLEM 14-1

Company A, a U.S. corporation, owns 70% of the common stock of Company B, located in Brunei, the primary currency unit of which is the Brunei dollar (B$). Company A acquired its investment in Company B for $278,900 on December 31, 1989, when the translated book value of Company B's net assets was $327,000. The excess of cost over book value is treated as goodwill from consolidation, amortized over 10 years. Company B's common stock was issued in 1986, when the exchange rate was B$1.00 = $0.30. Other applicable exchange rates are

December 31, 1991	B$1.00 = $0.40
1992 average	B$1.00 = $0.45
October 31, 1992	B$1.00 = $0.47
December 31, 1992	B$1.00 = $0.50

The translated balance of Company B's December 31, 1991 retained earnings is $88,000. Company B's dividends were declared on October 31, 1992 and paid on December 10, 1992. Company A's and Company B's December 31, 1992 trial balances (with Company B's balances expressed in Brunei dollars) are given below.

	Company A	Company B
Receivables	$ 80,000	B$ 150,000
Other Current Assets	110,000	310,000
Plant and Equipment	689,700	1,200,000
Investment in Company B	498,000	
Dividends Declared	40,000	50,000
Cost of Goods Sold	390,000	490,000
Other Expenses	260,000	360,000
	$ 2,067,700	B$2,560,000
Liabilities	$ 298,350	B$ 380,000
Common Stock	600,000	1,000,000
Retained Earnings	236,500	220,000
Sales	740,000	960,000
Income from Company B	34,650	
Cumulative Translation Adjustment	158,200	
	$ 2,067,700	B$2,560,000

Required

Prepare a combined translation and consolidation worksheet at December 31, 1992, supported by appropriate schedules.

PROBLEM 14-2

Company C, a U.S. corporation, owns 75% of the common stock of Company D, located in Qatar. The primary currency unit of Qatar is the riyal (QR). Company C acquired its investment in Company D for $117,100 on July 1, 1988, when the translated book value of Company D's net assets was $102,800. The excess of cost over book value is treated as goodwill from consolidation, amortized over 10 years.

   Company D's common stock was issued in 1986, when the exchange rate was QR1.00 = $0.10. Other applicable exchange rates are

December 31, 1992	QR1.00 = $0.20
1993 average	QR1.00 = $0.25
November 12, 1993	QR1.00 = $0.27
December 31, 1993	QR1.00 = $0.28

   The translated balance of Company D's December 31, 1992 retained earnings is $22,000. Company D's dividends were declared on November 12, 1993 and paid on December 20, 1993. Company C's and Company D's December 31, 1993 trial balances (with Company D's balances expressed in Qatar riyals) are shown below.

	Company C	Company D
Receivables	$ 139,100	QR 38,200
Other Current Assets	102,125	43,700
Plant and Equipment	542,900	534,400
Investment in Company D	142,900	
Dividends Declared	35,000	10,000
Cost of Goods Sold	266,700	182,400
Other Expenses	234,400	112,200
	$1,463,125	QR920,900
Liabilities	$ 119,150	QR126,300
Common Stock	500,000	350,000
Retained Earnings	198,200	110,000
Sales	583,600	334,600
Income from Company D	7,500	
Cumulative Translation Adjustment	54,675	
	$1,463,125	QR920,900

Required

Prepare a combined translation and consolidation worksheet at December 31, 1993, supported by appropriate schedules.

PROBLEM 14-3

Company E, a U.S. corporation, owns 80% of the common stock of Company F, located in Thailand, the primary currency unit of which is the baht (B). Company E's and Company F's December 31, 1991 trial balances (with Company F's balances expressed in bahts) appear below.

	Company E	Company F
Receivables	$ 89,880	B 78,300
Current Assets	101,660	125,600
Plant and Equipment	684,200	715,100
Investment in Company F	361,400	
Dividends Declared	22,000	40,000
Cost of Goods Sold	366,800	250,600
Other Expenses	313,400	107,200
	$1,939,340	B1,316,800
Liabilities	$ 207,300	B 195,500
Common Stock	600,000	500,000
Retained Earnings	260,700	213,500
Sales	714,900	407,800
Income from Company F	18,400	
Cumulative Translation Adjustment	138,040	
	$1,939,340	B1,316,800

Company E acquired its investment in Company F for $310,640 on December 31, 1984, when the translated book value of Company F's net assets was $298,300. The excess of cost over book value is treated as goodwill of Company F, amortized over 10 years.

Company F's common stock was issued in 1982, when the exchange rate was B1.00 = $0.20. Other applicable exchange rates are

December 31, 1990	B1.00 = $0.40
1991 average	B1.00 = $0.46
October 15, 1991	B1.00 = $0.48
December 31, 1991	B1.00 = $0.50

The translated balance of Company F's December 31, 1990 retained earnings is $85,400. Company F's dividends were declared on October 15, 1991 and paid on November 20, 1991.

Required

Prepare a combined translation and consolidation worksheet at December 31, 1991, supported by appropriate schedules.

PROBLEM 14-4

Company G, a U.S. corporation, owns 80% of the common stock of Company H, located in Switzerland. The primary currency unit of Switzerland is the Swiss franc (SwF). Company G acquired its investment in Company H for $248,992 on June 30, 1989, when the translated book value of Company H's net assets was $236,240. The excess of cost over book value is treated as goodwill of Company H, amortized over 10 years. The two corporations' December 31, 1991 trial balances (with Company H's balances expressed in Swiss francs) appear below.

	Company G	Company H
Receivables	$ 54,100	SwF 60,800
Inventories	96,700	118,500
Other Current Assets	102,040	87,300
Plant and Equipment	1,063,200	1,376,200
Investment in Company H	308,832	
Dividends Declared	60,000	80,000
Cost of Goods Sold	542,100	510,300
Depreciation Expense	118,200	79,500
Other Expenses	161,800	114,100
Transaction Loss	13,900	
Cumulative Translation Adjustment	165,464	
	$2,686,336	SwF2,426,700
Accumulated Depreciation	$ 419,300	SwF 395,300
Current Liabilities	89,100	110,700
Long-term Note Payable		100,000
Common Stock	500,000	400,000
Additional Paid-in Capital	350,000	130,000
Retained Earnings	341,776	419,300
Sales	940,600	871,400
Income from Company H	45,560	
	$2,686,336	SwF2,426,700

During 1991, Company H purchased merchandise from Company G for SwF316,600, of which SwF38,400 remained unpaid at December 31, 1991. Company H's beginning and ending inventories contained intercompany profits on goods purchased from Company G of SwF12,600 and SwF11,400, respectively. Company H's common stock was issued in 1981, when the exchange rate was SwF1.00 = $0.60. Other applicable exchange rates are

1990 average	SwF1,00 = $0.45
December 31, 1990	SwF1.00 = $.040
1991 average	SwF1.00 = $0.34
December 1, 1991	SwF1.00 = $0.31
December 31, 1991	SwF1.00 = $0.30

The translated balance of Company H's December 31, 1990 retained earnings is $167,720. Company H's dividends were declared on December 1, 1991 and are payable on January 10, 1992.

Required
Prepare a combined translation and consolidation worksheet at December 31, 1991, supported by appropriate schedules.

PROBLEM 14-5
Company J, a U.S. corporation, owns 80% of the common stock of Company K, located in Saudi Arabia. The primary currency unit of Saudi Arabia is the riyal (SR). Company J acquired its investment in Company K for $295,360 on June 30, 1988, when the translated book value of Company K's net assets was $289,200. The excess of cost over book value is treated as goodwill of Company K, amortized over 10 years.

The two corporations' December 31, 1991 trial balances (with Company K's balances expressed in riyals) appear below.

	Company J	Company K
Accounts Receivable	$ 66,900	SR 93,900
Long-Term Note Receivable		400,000
Inventories	63,600	98,100
Other Current Assets	118,420	84,900
Plant and Equipment	1,111,200	1,146,100
Investment in Company K	378,960	
Dividends Declared	30,000	85,000
Cost of Goods Sold	601,300	510,200
Depreciation Expense	112,600	121,400
Other Expenses	125,200	99,800
Transaction Loss	20,000	
Cumulative Translation Adjustment	15,880	
	$2,644,060	SR2,639,400
Accumulated Depreciation	$ 514,700	SR 364,700
Current Liabilities	111,600	188,300
Long-Term Note Payable	124,000	
Common Stock	500,000	800,000
Additional Paid-in Capital	150,000	120,000
Retained Earnings	288,320	237,500
Sales	911,200	880,900
Income from Company K	44,240	
Interest Revenue		48,000
	$2,644,060	SR2,639,400

On September 30, 1989, when the exchange rate was SR1.00 = $0.25, Company K lent Company J SR400,000 on a 12%, five-year note. Interest on the note is payable each September 30 in riyals. Company K's common stock was issued in 1985, when the exchange rate was SR1.00 = $0.35. Other applicable exchange rates are

December 31, 1990	SR1.00 = $0.26
1991 average	SR1.00 = $0.28
December 5, 1991	SR1.00 = $0.30
December 31, 1991	SR1.00 = $0.31

The translated balance of Company K's December 31, 1990 retained earnings is $61,750. Company K's dividends were declared on December 5, 1991 and are payable on January 10, 1992.

Required
Prepare a combined translation and consolidation worksheet at December 31, 1991, supported by appropriate schedules.

PROBLEM 14-6
Company L, a U.S. corporation, owns 75% of the common stock of Company M, located in West Germany, the primary currency unit of which is the Deutsche Mark (DM). Company L acquired its

investment in Company M for $351,300 on June 30, 1988, when the translated book value of Company M's net assets was $388,400. The excess of cost over book value is treated as goodwill from consolidation and is being amortized over 10 years.

Company M's common stock was issued in 1984, when the exchange rate was DM1.00 = $0.52. Other applicable exchange rates are

1989 average	DM1,00 = $0.45
December 31, 1989	DM1.00 = $0.44
1990 average	DM1.00 = $0.41
October 1, 1990	DM1.00 = $0.40
December 31, 1990	DM1.00 = $0.37

The translated balance of Company M's December 31, 1989 retained earnings is $96,800. Company M's dividends were declared on October 1, 1990 and were paid on November 10, 1990. The two corporations' December 31, 1990 trial balances (with Company M's balances expressed in Deutsche Marks) appear below.

	Company L	Company M
Receivables	$ 129,300	DM 109,100
Other Current Assets	107,650	189,400
Plant and Equipment	550,900	1,170,800
Investment in Company M	331,950	
Dividends Declared	32,000	20,000
Cost of Goods Sold	262,500	363,700
Depreciation Expense	42,300	72,100
Other Expenses	194,300	153,400
Cumulative Translation Adjustment	92,050	
	$1,742,950	DM2,078,500
Accumulated Depreciation	$ 186,300	DM 336,700
Current Liabilities	132,150	152,600
Common Stock	400,000	500,000
Additional Paid-in Capital	100,000	200,000
Retained Earnings	312,100	220,000
Sales	587,800	669,200
Income from Company M	24,600	
	$1,742,950	DM2,078,500

On August 1, 1988, Company M sold equipment with a book value of DM206,400 to Company L for DM342,400. Company L is depreciating the equipment over a 10-year useful life, using the declining balance method at 200% of the straight-line rate.

Required

Prepare a combined translation and consolidation worksheet at December 31, 1990, supported by appropriate schedules.

PROBLEM 14-7

Company P, a U.S. corporation, owns 70% of the common stock of Company Q, located in Malaysia, the primary currency unit of which is the Malaysian Dollar (M$). Company P acquired its investment in Company Q for $283,000 on June 30, 1988, when the translated book value of Company Q's net assets was $310,000. The excess of cost over book value is treated as goodwill from consolidation and is being amortized over 12 years.

Company Q's common stock was issued in 1978, when the exchange rate was M$1.00 = $0.30. Other applicable exchange rates are

Average, Y.E. June 30, 1990	M$1.00 = $0.35
June 30, 1990	M$1.00 = $0.39
Average, Y.E. June 30, 1991	M$1.00 = $0.45
May 15, 1991	M$1.00 = $0.48
June 30, 1991	M$1.00 = $0.50

The translated balance of Company Q's June 30, 1991 retained earnings is $88,000. Company Q's dividends were declared on May 15, 1991 and were paid on June 18, 1991.

The two corporations' June 30, 1991 trial balances (with Company Q's balances expressed in Malaysian Dollars) appear below.

	Company P	Company Q
Receivables	$ 78,200	M$ 125,400
Other Current Assets	105,300	374,800
Plant and Equipment (net)	667,800	1,140,100
Investment in Company Q	514,000	
Dividends Declared	40,000	50,000
Cost of Goods Sold	385,400	479,400
Other Expenses	264,600	350,300
	$2,055,300	M$2,520,000
Liabilities	$ 288,100	M$ 360,300
Common Stock	200,000	800,000
Additional Paid-in Capital	400,000	200,000
Retained Earnings	245,400	220,000
Sales	728,600	939,700
Income from Company Q	34,650	
Cumulative Translation Adjustment	158,550	
	$2,055,300	M$2,520,000

During the year ended June 30, 1991, Company Q sold merchandise to Company P for M$210,000, of which M$27,000 remained unpaid at June 30, 1991. Company P's beginning and ending inventories contained goods purchased from Company Q of M$20,000 and M$25,000, respectively. Company Q sells to Company P at 25% above cost.

Required
Prepare a combined translation and consolidation worksheet at June 30, 1991, supported by appropriate schedules.

PROBLEM 14-8
Company R, a U.S. corporation, owns 80% of the common stock of Company S, located in Singapore, the primary currency unit of which is the Singapore Dollar (S$). Company R acquired its investment in Company S for $308,800 on April 30, 1987, when the translated book value of Company S's net

assets was $311,000. The excess of cost over book value is treated as goodwill from consolidation and is being amortized over 10 years.

Company S's common stock was issued in 1984, when the exchange rate was S$1.00 = $0.30. Other applicable exchange rates are

December 31, 1990	S$1.00 = $0.39
1991 average	S$1.00 = $0.45
October 1, 1991	S$1.00 = $0.47
December 31, 1991	S$1.00 = $0.50

The translated balance of Company S's December 31, 1990 retained earnings is $88,000. Company S's dividends were declared on October 1, 1991 and were paid on November 10, 1991.

On July 1, 1988, Company S purchased 20% of Company R's 9% bonds on the open market. The bonds mature on September 30, 1994 and interest is payable on March 31 and September 30. The two corporations' December 31, 1991 trial balances (with Company S's balances expressed in Singapore Dollars) appear below.

	Company R	Company S
Receivables	$ 78,100	S$ 125,100
Inventories	67,600	51,400
Other Current Assets	204,500	374,200
Plant and Equipment	1,133,200	927,400
Investment in Company S Stock	572,000	
Investment in Company R Bonds		219,800
Dividends Declared	40,000	50,000
Cost of Goods Sold	385,600	480,300
Depreciation Expense	82,300	72,100
Other Expenses	182,100	277,800
	$2,745,400	S$2,578,100
Accumulated Depreciation	$ 236,300	S$ 216,700
Current Liabilities	181,800	201,200
Bonds Payable	500,000	
Premium on Bonds Payable	33,000	
Common Stock	500,000	800,000
Additional Paid-in Capital	100,000	200,000
Retained Earnings	246,000	220,000
Sales	727,900	928,200
Bond Interest Revenue		12,000
Income from Company S	39,600	
Cumulative Translation Adjustment	180,800	
	$2,745,400	S$2,578,100

Required
Prepare a combined translation and consolidation worksheet at December 31, 1991, supported by appropriate schedules.

PROBLEM 14-9
On November 30, 1991, Company T, a U.S. company, sells merchandise to Company U, located in

Uruguay, agreeing to accept N$5,000,000 (5,000,000 new pesos) within 45 days. Applicable exchange rates are

November 30, 1991	N$1.00 = $0.0051
December 31, 1991	N$1.00 = $0.0053
January 14, 1992	N$1.00 = $0.0057

Company T's management decides to hedge the account receivable created in the sales transaction by entering into a forward exchange contract on November 30, 1991 to deliver 5,000,000 new pesos on January 14, 1992 at a forward rate of N$1.00 = $0.0054. On January 14, 1992, Company T receives payment from Company U and settles the forward exchange contract.

Required
Present the journal entries required on Company T's books on November 30, 1991, December 31, 1991, and January 14, 1992.

PROBLEM 14-10
On December 1, 1991, Company V, a U.S. company, contracts to buy merchandise from Company W, located in Luxembourg, agreeing to accept LF800,000 (800,000 francs) on January 31, 1992, when the goods are to be delivered. Applicable exchange rates are

December 1, 1991	LF1.00 = $0.0242
December 31, 1991	LF1.00 = $0.0246
January 31, 1992	LF1.00 = $0.0250

To hedge this future commitment, Company V enters into a forward exchange contract on December 1, 1991 to buy 800,000 francs on January 31, 1992 at a forward rate of LF1.00 = $0.0247. On January 31, 1992, Company V fulfills its contractual obligation to Company W and settles the forward exchange contract.

Required
Assuming that the premium or discount on the forward exchange contract is to be included in the measurement of the net result of fulfilling the contract with Company W, present the journal entries required on Company V's books on December 1, 1991, December 31, 1991, and January 31, 1992.

SOLUTION TO REVIEW PROBLEM

Equity Method Journal Entries

Company H's Net Income

Investment in Company H	7,072	
Income from Company H		7,072

[80% × $8,840]

Company H's Current Translation Adjustment

Cumulative Translation Adjustment	19,008	
Investment in Company H		19,008

[80% × $23,760]

Company H's Dividends

Dividends Receivable	1,920	
Investment in Company H		1,920
[80% × $2,400]		
Cash	1,920	
Dividends Receivable		1,920

Schedule of Cumulative Translation Adjustment Changes

Beginning balance		$ 40,040
Beginning net assets, times the change in exchange rates		
(NKr565,000 × 0.04)	$ 22,600	
Net income, times the difference between the current and average exchange rates (NKr68,000 × $0.02)	1,360	
Dividends declared, times the difference between the current and November 1, exchange rates (NKr20,000 × $0.01)	(200)	
Translation adjustment, 1992		23,760
Ending balance		$ 63,800

Goodwill from Consolidation

Cost of Investment		$ 54,824
Book Value (80% × $53,530)		42,824
Goodwill, 6/30/90		12,000
Amortization through 12/31/91	$ 1,800	
Amortization, 1992	1,200	3,000
Goodwill, 12/31/92		$ 9,000

Eliminations

Intercompany Ownership Interests

[1]	Capital Stock: H	$ 60,000
[2]	Additional Paid-in Capital: H	6,000
[3]	Retained Earnings: H	33,832
[4]	Cumulative Translation Adjustment: H	(51,040)
[5]	Investment in Company H	$ (48,792)

Subsidiary Income and Dividends

[6]	Income from Company H	$ 7,072
[7]	Dividends: H	(1,920)
[8]	Investment in Company H	$ (5,152)

Goodwill Amortization

[9]	Other Expenses (Goodwill Amortization)	$ 1,200
[10]	Retained Earnings: G	1,800
[11]	Investment in Company H	$ (3,000)

Income Allocation

Company G's Net Income		$ 96,400
Less: Goodwill Amortization Expense		(1,200)
Company G's Adjusted Net Income		95,200
Company H's Net Income	$ 8,840	
Minority Interest (20%)	1,768	
Company G's Share (80%)		7,072
Consolidated Net Income		$ 102,272

CONSOLIDATION WORKSHEET

	Company H Trial Balance			Company G Trial Balance	Eliminations		Income Statement		Balance Sheet
	Krone	Exchange Rate	U.S. Dollars	Balance					
Current Assets	160,100	0.11	17,611	473,441					491,052
Plant and Equipment	653,900	0.11	71,929	868,475					940,404
Investment in Company H				65,944	[5] [8] [11]	(48,792) (5,152) (3,000)			9,000 G
Dividends: G				40,000					40,000 R
Dividends: H	20,000	0.12	2,400		[7]	(1,920)			480 M
Cost of Goods Sold	246,300	0.13	32,019	425,346			457,365		
Other Expenses	134,700	0.13	17,511	213,054	[9]	1,200	231,765		
Transaction Loss				8,100			8,100		
Cumulative Translation Adj.: G				51,040					51,040
Cumulative Translation Adj.: H			63,800		[4]	(51,040)			12,760 M
	1,215,000		205,270	2,145,400					1,544,736
Accumulated Depreciation	111,200	0.11	12,232	207,408					219,640
Liabilities	89,800	0.11	9,878	349,620					359,498
Capital Stock: G				500,000					500,000
Capital Stock: H	300,000	0.25	75,000		[1]	60,000			15,000 M
Additional Paid-in Capital: G				120,000					120,000
Additional Paid-in Capital: H	30,000	0.25	7,500		[2]	6,000			1,500 M
Retained Earnings: G				218,400	[10]	1,800			216,600 R
Retained Earnings: H	235,000	given	42,290		[3]	33,832			8,458 M
Sales	449,000	0.13	58,370	742,900				801,270	
Income from Company H				7,072	[6]	7,072			
	1,215,000		205,270	2,145,400					
Minority Interest in Company H's Net Income							1,768		1,768 M
Consolidated Net Income							102,272		102,272 R
							801,270	801,270	1,544,736

INTERIM AND SEGMENT REPORTING

T his chapter discusses two reporting requirements for large publicly held corporations. The first part of the chapter covers the reporting of financial information for periods of less than one year by publicly held corporations—interim reporting. The second part of the chapter discusses the reporting of information by product line or geographic area as supplemental information to the data contained in the annual financial statements for publicly held companies—segment reporting. The interim reporting topics of this chapter are

- Integral and discrete views of interim reporting
- Income statement components including revenue recognition, product and direct costs, and other expenses
- Income tax expense including the computation of the effective annualized combined tax rate and tax savings from loss carrybacks and carryforwards for operating income
- Reporting and income tax expense for unusual or infrequent items, extraordinary items, and discontinued operations
- Reporting of cumulative effects of accounting changes and seasonality of operations
- Disclosure requirements for interim reporting

The topics of segment reporting are

- History of segment reporting
- Three tests to determine a reportable domestic segment and the overall test for adequacy of segments
- Disclosure requirements for segment reporting
- Problems encountered in segment reporting including the definition of a segment, transfer pricing, allocation of common costs, revenues and expenses to be included in operating profit, and allocation of shared assets

- Two tests for foreign segments and the differences between the tests for foreign and domestic segments
- Disclosures regarding export sales and sales to major customers

INTERIM FINANCIAL REPORTING

The reporting of financial information for periods of less than one year is called **interim financial reporting.** The accounting period is usually quarterly, but the period can be monthly, bimonthly, or seminannually. The purpose of interim reporting is to provide the user with more **timely information** than can be obtained from an annual report by reporting information about operating results and balance sheet categories as well as significant changes in the income statement and balance sheet data at more frequent intervals. The interim information is designed to allow investors and creditors to update their predictions regarding a company at intervals throughout the year rather than only once a year.

For many years, the New York Stock Exchange and other securities markets have required the companies listed on their exchanges to report quarterly financial information to their investors. In 1970, the Securities and Exchange Commission began requiring the reporting of quarterly financial information known as a 10-Q filing. In 1973, the Accounting Principles Board issued *Accounting Principles Board Opinion No. 28, Interim Financial Reporting*, which requires quarterly information for publicly held companies.[1]

TWO VIEWS OF INTERIM REPORTING

Interim financial periods can be viewed in two ways, either as an **integral** part of an annual period or as a separate and complete (**discrete**) accounting period. When an interim period is considered part of an annual period, estimates and allocations of revenues and expenses between interim periods are necessary to determine the correct amount of revenue and expense for the period and to properly report assets and liabilities at the end of the period. Expenses usually are recognized in proportion to the revenue earned. When revenue and expense are recognized by this integral approach, income tends to be smoothed and interim period income fluctuations are less pronounced. Thus, the interim data using the integral approach is a good predictor of annual earnings.

When an interim period is considered a discrete accounting period, estimations and allocations are prepared in the same manner as for annual reporting. Annual expenses are recognized in the period regardless of the number of interim periods that may benefit from the expenses. The discrete approach highlights the fluctuations in quarterly earnings and may also point out a change in the trend in earnings more quickly than the integral approach to interim reporting.

---

[1] *Accounting Principles Board Opinion No. 28, Interim Financial Reporting*, (New York, AICPA, 1973).

The approach taken in *Accounting Principles Board Opinion No. 28* is that the interim period is an integral part of the annual reporting period, although expenses directly related to the sale of goods or the provision of services are recognized by the discrete concept.[2] In 1978, the Financial Accounting Standards Board issued a Discussion Memorandum, *Interim Financial Accounting and Reporting,* in an attempt to resolve the inconsistencies in the mixture of the use of the integral and discrete approaches to interim reporting.[3] The standards have not yet been changed as the Discussion Memorandum did not provide any easy solutions to the integral/discrete dilemma.

INCOME STATEMENT COMPONENTS

The condensed income statement information that is required to be disclosed includes gross revenues, provision for income taxes, unusual or infrequent items (material gains and losses), discontinued operations, extraordinary items, cumulative effect of changes in accounting principles, net income, and earnings per share. These disclosures are the minimum information that is required to be disclosed. A company could include a complete income statement rather than simply disclosing the minimum information required. In addition, if revenues and expenses are highly seasonal, this seasonality of income needs to be disclosed. For example, a toy manufacturer will sell the majority of its products during the period prior to Christmas and have very low sales volume during other parts of the year.

REVENUE RECOGNITION

Viewing the interim period as an integral part of the annual period results in revenues being recognized as earned and measurable. Thus, the general accepted accounting principles for recognition of both sales and service revenue (see Chapter 16) are applicable to interim period revenues. Revenue is recognized using the same recognition methods as the company uses in recognizing revenue on an annual basis. Therefore, if a construction company uses the percentage-of-completion method for recognizing its contract revenues, the percentage-of-completion method is used to recognize revenue for the interim information.

PRODUCT AND DIRECT COSTS

Both product costs and costs directly associated with service revenues are recognized by the discrete approach in the same manner that they are recognized in the annual statements. The methods used to determine cost of goods sold, however, either may require data whose cost is greater than the benefit or they may cause misleading results. Therefore, *Accounting Principles Board Opinion No. 28* provides for four integral exceptions to the discrete approach to determining cost of goods sold.[4]

---

[2] *APB No. 28*, paragraph 11.

[3] *Discussion Memorandum, Interim Financial Accounting and Reporting* (Stamford, Connecticut: FASB, 1978).

[4] *APB No. 28*, paragraph 14.

1. The gross profit method may be used to estimate cost of goods sold and ending inventory for interim periods for those companies using a periodic inventory system. This exception eliminates the need for physical inventories for interim reporting.
2. If a company using the LIFO method of valuing inventory liquidates a LIFO layer during an interim period, but expects to replace the layer prior to year end, the cost of replacing the layer is included in cost of goods sold. This exception avoids using a low or high cost layer as compared to current replacement cost in cost of goods sold for the interim period, while the annual cost of goods sold will include current costs as the layer will be replaced during the annual period.
3. If a company that uses the lower of cost or market in valuing its inventory sustains a market decline that is considered to be temporary, the decline is not recognized in the interim period. If a market decline is recognized in one interim period and is followed by a market increase in a following interim period, a gain is recognized only to the extent of the amount of the loss previously recognized.
4. If a company uses a standard cost system, variances are reported in the same manner as they are for the annual reporting period. Planned purchase and volume variances that are expected to be absorbed by year end should be deferred and not recognized in the interim period.

OTHER EXPENSES

Other expenses are usually recognized as incurred. If the costs clearly benefit more than one interim period, the expense is allocated to the periods benefitted. For example, annual property taxes paid in the first interim quarter are allocated equally over the four interim quarters. The allocations can be made on the basis of time, benefits received, or a measure of activity such as sales dollars. The method of allocation should be the same method used in preparing the annual financial information. If an expense is not clearly related to other interim periods, the cost is recognized in the current interim period. Costs subject to year-end adjustment, such as uncollectible accounts expense, bonuses based on net income, and pension expenses, are estimated and allocated to interim periods on some reasonable basis.

INCOME TAX EXPENSE FOR OPERATING INCOME

Income tax expense for operating income or loss is based on the income earned to date in the current year times the company's effective tax rate for the entire fiscal year net of any income tax expense previously reported in the interim income statements for the current year. The approach to determining income tax expense in interim statements is like the estimate of current income taxes payable used in the preparation of personal financial statements illustrated in Chapter 1. Generally accepted accounting principles for accounting for income taxes in interim reporting are included in *Accounting Principles Board Opinion Nos. 11, 23, and 24* and in *Financial Accounting Standards Board Interpretation No. 18, Accounting for Income Taxes in Interim Periods.*[5]

---

[5] *FASB Interpretation No. 18, Accounting for Income Taxes in Interim Periods, An Interpretation of APB Opinion No. 28* (Stamford, Connecticut: FASB, 1977).

ANNUALIZED COMBINED EFFECTIVE TAX RATE

The **effective tax rate** is the percentage that total estimated income tax expense for the current fiscal year is of total expected operating income subject to tax. Thus, the rate used in all interim periods is the effective rate for the entire year. Revenue and expenses not subject to tax, which include state and municipal interest revenue, amortization expense for goodwill, percentage depletion expense, and insurance premium expense for officers' life insurance, are excluded in determining income subject to tax for the fiscal year. The effective income tax rate estimate includes both the federal and state income taxes as well as all the tax planning techniques available, such as tax credits and foreign tax rates. The state income taxes are deductible as expenses on the federal tax return; therefore, the computation of the effective rate includes them as a reduction of the income subject to tax when computing the amount of federal income tax expense.

The 1986 Tax Reform Act eliminated many of the previous tax credits, including the investment tax credit and the special capital gain rates, making the computation of an effective income tax rate simpler and easier than it was prior to the tax reform. However, tax credits, particularly the investment tax credit, have been enacted and repealed several times during the past 30 years. Because Congress is revising the tax code more frequently than in the past and enacting and repealing tax credits, the illustrations in this chapter relating to income taxes are general in nature and apply the principles without attempting to reflect the tax code in effect at any particular point in time.

Any revisions of either federal or state income tax laws that alter items subject to tax, the tax rates, or the tax credits, change the estimated effective tax rate. In addition, if a company revises its estimate of annual income during the year, the revision may also change the effective tax rate. The revision of estimated annual income changes the effective tax rate when the actual tax rate structure contains brackets that tax different levels and amounts of income at different rates. If the actual tax rate is a flat rate, then a revision of the estimate of annual income does not change the effective tax rate.

If an estimate of the effective tax rate changes during the year, any change in the rate is reported in the current interim period, as if it is a change in estimate affecting the current period and future periods. The effective income tax rate does not include income taxes on unusual or infrequent items, discontinued operations, extraordinary items, or cumulative effects of changes in accounting principles. These nonoperating items are reported net of tax in the income statement. In order to determine the tax applicable to these items two approaches are possible: either use the maximum tax rate for the year treating the item as an incremental addition to tax or, if subject to a specific rate, use that rate.

Any revisions in the tax code affecting the estimate of the effective income tax rate are included in the interim period that the revisions are to take effect under the new tax code. The incorporation of a change in the effective tax for the current period is accomplished by computing the total income tax expense for the year to date and subtracting the income tax expense reported in previous quarters during the current year to determine the income tax expense for the current interim quarter.

ILLUSTRATIVE PROBLEM 15.1: COMPUTATION OF INTERIM INCOME TAX EXPENSE FOR OPERATING INCOME

Alpha Company estimates by quarters its annual operating income for the current year to be:

First Quarter	$ 400,000
Second Quarter	600,000
Third Quarter	500,000
Fourth Quarter	1,000,000
Total Estimated Income for the Current Year	$ 2,500,000

The current year's income includes $200,000 of municipal bond interest revenue and $60,000 of insurance premium expense on officers' life insurance, that are not subject to tax. Both the bond interest revenue and the life insurance expense are being allocated ratably to each interim quarter. Alpha Company's income is subject to the following federal tax rates:

First $100,000 of Income	15%
Second $100,000 of Income	25%
Income in Excess of $200,000	34%

In addition, Alpha Company's income is subject to 7.5% Oregon income tax. Alpha Company has $65,220 of tax credits available to offset against its current year's federal income tax liability.

Exhibit 15-1 illustrates the computation of the effective annualized combined income tax rate used to determine income tax expense for the fiscal year. If the first quarter's actual income is the $400,000 estimated, the computation of income tax expense for the first quarter is as shown in Exhibit 15-2.

During the second quarter of the fiscal year, Congress repealed the tax credits and the state of Oregon reduced its tax rate to 6%. Both tax law revisions are effective as of the beginning of the current fiscal year. These revisions must be incorporated into a new effective tax rate before determining the income tax expense for the second quarter. The computation of the new effective tax rate, assuming the estimate of annual income has not changed, is as shown in Exhibit 15-3.

If the actual income for the second quarter is the $600,000 estimated, the income tax expense for the second quarter is computed as shown in Exhibit 15-4. This exhibit illustrates that the effect of the change in the estimate of the effective rate on the income tax expense of the first quarter is an adjustment of the income tax expense of the second quarter.

The increase in the effective tax rate for the year increased the income tax expense for the second quarter by the amount of the underestimation of income tax expense for the first quarter. If the new effective rate of 36.78% had been used in the first quarter, the income tax expense would have been $134,247 ($365,000 × 36.78%) instead of $127,750 or a difference of $6,497. If the income tax expense for the second quarter had been computed on only the second quarter's income at the new effective rate, the tax would be $207,807 ($565,000 × 36.78%) or $6,497 lower. Thus, the change in the estimated effective income tax expense rate is included in the income tax expense of the current period as required by generally accepted accounting principles.

The third quarter's actual income was $200,000 and Alpha Company has revised the estimate of the fourth quarter's earnings to $500,000. The effect of the third quarter's income being less than anticipated and the reduction of the amount of estimated income for the fourth

EXHIBIT 15-1

Illustrative Problem 15.1
ALPHA COMPANY
Computation of the Effective Annualized Combined Income Tax Rate for Operating Income

Computation of Estimated Annual Income Subject to Tax

Estimated Annual Income	$ 2,500,000
Revenue and Expense Not Subject to Tax	
Municipal Bond Interest	(200,000)
Insurance Expense: Officers' Life Insurance	60,000
Estimated Annual Income Subject to Tax	$ 2,360,000

Computation of Combined Estimated Annual Income Tax Expense

Oregon Estimated Income Tax Expense	
Estimated Annual Income Subject to Tax	$ 2,360,000
Oregon Income Tax Rate	× 7.5%
Estimated Oregon Income Tax Expense	$ 177,000

Federal Estimated Income Tax Expense	
Estimated Annual Income Subject to Tax	$ 2,360,000
Less: Oregon Estimated Income Tax Expense	177,000
Estimated Annual Income Subject to Federal Tax	$ 2,183,000

Tax on First $100,000	$ 15,000
Tax on Second $100,000	25,000
Tax on Excess Over $200,000 ($1,983,000 × 34%)	674,220
Total Estimated Gross Federal Income Tax Expense	714,220
Less: Tax Credits	65,220
Estimated Net Federal Income Tax Expense	$ 649,000

Combined Estimated Annual Income Tax Expense	
Estimated Federal Income Tax Expense	$ 649,000
Estimated Oregon Income Tax Expense	177,000
Total Estimated Income Tax Expense	$ 826,000

Computation of Effective Annualized Combined Income Tax Rate

$$\frac{\text{Estimated Annual Income Tax Expense}}{\text{Estimated Annual Income Subject to Tax}} = \frac{\$826,000}{\$2,360,000} = 35.0\%$$

EXHIBIT 15-2

Illustrative Problem 15.1
ALPHA COMPANY
Computation of Income Tax Expense on Operating Income
for the First Quarter

First Quarter Income	$ 400,000
Less: Items Not Subject to Tax ($140,000 × 1/4)	35,000
First Quarter Income Subject to Tax	365,000
Effective Annualized Combined Income Tax Rate	× 35%
Income Tax Expense for First Quarter	$ 127,750

EXHIBIT 15-3

Illustrative Problem 15.1
ALPHA COMPANY
Computation of the Revised Effective Annualized Combined Income Tax Rate

Computation of Combined Estimated Annual Income Tax Expense

Estimated Annual Income Subject to Tax	$ 2,360,000
Oregon Income Tax Rate	× 6.0%
Estimated Oregon Income Tax Expense	$ 141,600

Estimated Federal Income Tax Expense	
Estimated Annual Income Subject to Tax	$ 2,360,000
Less: Estimated Oregon Income Tax Expense	141,600
Estimated Annual Income Subject to Federal Tax	$ 2,218,400

Tax on First $100,000	$ 15,000
Tax on Second $100,000	25,000
Tax on Excess Over $200,000 ($2,018,400 × 34%)	686,256
Estimated Federal Income Tax Expense	$ 726,256

Combined Estimated Annual Income Tax Expense	
Estimated Federal Income Tax Expense	$ 726,256
Estimated Oregon Income Tax Expense	141,600
Total Estimated Income Tax Expense	$ 867,856

Computation of Effective Annualized Combined Income Tax Rate

$$\frac{\text{Estimated Annual Income Tax Expense}}{\text{Estimated Annual Income Subject to Tax}} = \frac{\$867,856}{\$2,360,000} = 36.78\%$$

EXHIBIT 15-4

Illustrative Problem 15.1
ALPHA COMPANY
Computation of Income Tax Expense on Operating Income
for the Second Quarter

First and Second Quarter's Income	$ 1,000,000
Less: Items Not Subject to Tax ($140,000 × 2/4)	70,000
First and Second Quarters' Income Subject to Tax	930,000
Effective Annualized Combined Income Tax Rate	× 36.78%
Effective Tax Expense for Year to Date	342,054
Less: Income Tax Expense, First Quarter	127,750
Income Tax Expense for Second Quarter	$ ⟍214,304

quarter requires a recomputation of the estimated effective income tax rate for the year. The reductions in the total estimated annual income cause the estimated rate to decrease because the tax rate structure is in brackets. Likewise, an increase in estimated annual income causes an increase in the estimated tax rate. Exhibit 15-5 illustrates the recomputation of the estimated effective tax rate and the determination of income tax expense for the third quarter.

EXHIBIT 15-5

Illustrative Problem 15.1
ALPHA COMPANY
Computation Income Tax Expense on Operating Income
for the Third Quarter

Computation of Estimated Annual Income Subject to Tax

Estimated Annual Income	
Actual Income: First Quarter	$ 400,000
Actual Income: Second Quarter	600,000
Actual Income: Third Quarter	200,000
Estimated Income: Fourth Quarter	500,000
Total Estimated Annual Income	1,700,000
Revenue and Expense Not Subject to Tax	
Municipal Bond Interest	(200,000)
Insurance Expense: Officers' Life Insurance	60,000
Estimated Annual Income Subject to Tax	$ 1,560,000

Computation of Combined Estimated Annual Income Tax Expense

Estimated Oregon Income Tax Expense	
Estimated Annual Income Subject to Tax	$ 1,560,000
Oregon Income Tax Rate	× 6.0%
Estimated Oregon Income Tax Expense	$ 93,600

Estimated Federal Income Tax Expense

Estimated Annual Income Subject to Tax	$ 1,560,000
Less: Estimated Oregon Income Tax Expense	93,600
Estimated Annual Income Subject to Federal Tax	$ 1,466,400

Tax on First $100,000	$ 15,000
Tax on Second $100,000	25,000
Tax on Excess Over $200,000 ($1,266,400 × 34%)	430,576
Estimated Federal Income Tax Expense	$ 470,576

Combined Estimated Income Tax Expense

Estimated Federal Income Tax Expense	$ 470,576
Estimated Oregon Income Tax Expense	93,600
Total Estimated Income Tax Expense	$ 564,176

Computation of Effective Annualized Combined Income Tax Rate

$$\frac{\text{Estimated Income Tax Expense}}{\text{Estimated Annual Income Subject to Tax}} = \frac{\$564,176}{\$1,560,000} = 36.17\%$$

Computation of Income Tax Expense for the Third Quarter

Income Earned During First Three Quarters	$ 1,200,000
Less: Items Not Subject to Tax ($140,000 × 3/4)	105,000
Income Subject to Tax	1,095,000
Effective Annualized Combined Income Tax Rate	× 36.17%
Year to Date Income Tax Expense	396,062
Less: Income Tax Expense for First Two Quarters	342,054
Income Tax Expense for Third Quarter	$ 54,008

Just as with the computation of income tax expense for the second quarter, the change in the estimated effective combined income tax rate has altered the income tax expense of the third quarter. The effect of the reduction of the annual effective rate on the first and second quarters has reduced the income tax expense of the third quarter below what it would have been, had the income tax expense been computed on the third quarter's income subject to tax.

TAX SAVINGS FROM OPERATING LOSSES

Income tax savings from net operating losses are recognized only when they can be carried back against income on which tax was previously paid, or when their carryforward is assured. An operating loss carryforward is assured when the loss is caused by a single nonrecurring event and the income of the current period is more than the amount of the loss. For example,

Company A suffered an operating loss of $2,200,000 in 1989 due to the first employee strike in 50 years and has operated profitably every year for 50 years. If, during 1990, Company A signed a 5-year contract with the union, and after the carryback has $1,000,000 of operating loss carryforward and estimated income of $2,500,000 for 1990, the loss carryforward is considered assured. Conversely, if Company A's employees strike every 3 years and the company reports an operating loss in those years, and its income in the nonstrike years varies from little profit to substantial profit, the carryforward is not assured as the loss is not caused by a single nonrecurring event and the income to absorb the carryforward is not assured.

Three types of operating losses situations are possible.

1. An expected loss in the current year that can be carried back against positive operating income of the past on which income tax has already been paid. These loss carrybacks result in a tax benefit as a result of the recovery of income taxes previously paid.
2. A net operating loss of a previous quarter that is being carried forward to an expected operating income quarter within the fiscal year. For example, if a company typically reports operating losses in the first and second quarters of the year, but operating profits in the third and fourth quarters because of a seasonal business, the loss carryforwards are recognized in the interim periods.
3. A quarter results in an operating loss, but the company anticipates positive operating profit for the entire fiscal year.[6]

The effective annual tax rate is used to determine the amount of the tax benefit from a loss carryforward or carryback within the fiscal year, and the tax actually paid is used to determine the effective rate for the tax benefit of a loss carried back to a prior year. The tax benefit of a loss carryback is based on tax paid because the tax refund the company will receive is based on the tax actually paid and not on the tax rates in effect when the refund request is filed. These three possible operating loss carryback and carryforward situations are demonstrated in Illustrative Problem 15.2.

ILLUSTRATIVE PROBLEM 15.2: NET OPERATING LOSS CARRYBACKS AND CARRYFORWARDS

Case 1: Operating Loss for Year With Carryback. Beta Company projects its operating income subject to tax for the current year to be a loss of $400,000. During the first quarter of the current year, Beta Company's operating loss subject to tax is $80,000. Beta Company had $190,000 of taxable operating income in prior years on which tax of $72,000 has been paid that can be used to offset current operating loss carrybacks. Any additional losses will be carried forward to future years, and Beta Company is not certain that operations will be profitable in the future. The effective tax rate of the carryback is

$$\frac{\text{Tax Paid on Prior Year's Operating Income}}{\text{Expected Loss for the Current Year}} = \frac{\$\ 72,000}{\$400,000} = 18\%$$

During the first quarter, Beta Company reports a tax saving from a net operating loss carryback of $14,400 ($80,000 × 18%). Beta Company anticipates more operating losses subject to tax

---

[6]*APB No. 28,* paragraph 20.

in the current year than the company has operating income in the past on which it has paid income taxes. In addition to the tax benefit of the carryback, Beta Company has $210,000 of estimated operating loss carryforwards, which will be included in the computation of its effective tax rates in future years.

Case 2: Operating Loss in First Quarter Carried Forward When Year Is Expected To Be Profitable.   Gamma Company has a highly seasonal business and has operated profitably for a number of years. Gamma Company estimates its operating income, all subject to tax, to be $800,000 and its income tax expense to be $240,000. Therefore, the effective income tax rate is 30%. During the current year, the quarterly operating income subject to tax of Gamma Company is

First Quarter Operating Income	$ (160,000)
Second Quarter Operating Income	(80,000)
Third Quarter Operating Income	440,000
Fourth Quarter Operating Income	600,000

The computations of the tax saving or tax expense for the quarters are

Quarter	Year-to-Date Operating Income	Tax Expense Year to Date	Tax Expense Prior Periods	Tax Expense Current Period
First	$(160,000)	$(48,000)	$ -0-	$(48,000)
Second	(240,000)	(72,000)	(48,000)	(24,000)
Third	200,000	60,000	(72,000)	132,000
Fourth	800,000	240,000	60,000	180,000

This example assumes that the estimated income was equal to the actual income. If the actual income differed from the estimated income, then the effective tax rate may change, and thus alter the computations for some of the quarters.

Case 3: Operating Loss in Quarter, Year Expected To Be Profitable.   Delta Company projects that its operating income subject to tax for the current year will be $800,000 and its effective tax rate is 30%. During the first three quarters, the operating results were

First Quarter Operating Income	$ 160,000
Second Quarter Operating Income	(220,000)
Third Quarter Operating Income	440,000

The computations of the tax saving or tax expense for the quarters are

Quarter	Year-to-Date Operating Income	Tax Expense Year to Date	Tax Expense Prior Periods	Tax Expense Current Period
First	$ 160,000	$ 48,000	$ -0-	$ 48,000
Second	(60,000)	(18,000)	48,000	(66,000)
Third	380,000	114,000	(18,000)	132,000

The entire tax saving from the loss in the second quarter is recognized because the fiscal year is expected to be profitable, and the company expects to offset the tax saving with tax expense before the end of the fiscal year.

UNUSUAL OR INFREQUENT ITEMS, EXTRAORDINARY ITEMS, AND DISCONTINUED OPERATIONS

Unusual or infrequent items, extraordinary items, and discontinued operations are determined in interim statements in the same manner as they are for annual statements and are reported on the income statement as prescribed by generally accepted accounting principles. The income tax expense or tax savings from these nonoperating sources of income are not included in determining the effective income tax rate. These nonoperating items are reported in the interim period in which they occur net of the applicable income tax expense in the same manner as if the interim period were a complete fiscal year.

In computing the income tax expense on these nonoperating items the tax is assumed to be additional tax above the amount already determined as applicable to operating income. If these nonoperating items are positive, the tax on these items is computed starting in the tax bracket where operating income left off. If a company has more than one of these items, the tax is computed in the order they appear in the income statement and moving upward through the brackets as necessary. If one of these nonoperating items is a loss and thus creates a tax benefit, the amount of the benefit is determined by moving downward through the brackets. If a company has more than one loss item, the total amount of all the losses is determined. The tax on the total losses is computed by moving downward through the brackets. The tax savings are then allocated ratably to the loss items. Prior to the Tax Reform Act of 1986, items classified as capital gains and losses were subject to special tax rates. If any of these nonoperating items is subject to a special tax rate, that rate is used to determine the applicable income tax expense or saving. Illustrative Problem 15.3 demonstrates the computation of income tax expense for an unusual or infrequent gain and an extraordinary loss.

ILLUSTRATIVE PROBLEM 15.3: INCOME TAX EXPENSE FOR AN UNUSUAL OR INFREQUENT GAIN AND INCOME TAX SAVING FOR AN EXTRAORDINARY LOSS

The Roberts Company estimates operating income subject to tax of $120,000 for the current year. The current federal tax rates are

First $50,000 of Income	15%
Second $50,000 of Income	20%
Third $50,000 of Income	25%
Income in Excess of $150,000	35%

Case 1: Unusual or Infrequent Gain in Second Quarter. During the second quarter, Roberts had an unusual or infrequent gain of $40,000.

Computation of Estimated Income Subject to Income Taxes

Estimated Operating Income	$ 120,000
Unusual or Infrequent Gain	40,000
Total Income Subject to Income Tax	$ 160,000

Computation of Estimated Income Tax Expense on Total Income Subject to Tax

Tax on First $50,000	$ 7,500
Tax on Second $50,000	10,000
Tax on Third $50,000	12,500
Tax on Excess Over $150,000	3,500
Total Estimated Income Tax Expense	$ 33,500

Computation of Estimated Income Tax Expense on Operating Income Subject to Tax

Tax on First $50,000	$ 7,500
Tax on Second $50,000	10,000
Tax on Remaining $20,000	5,000
Total Estimated Income Tax Expense	$ 22,500

Computation of Estimated Income Tax Expense on Unusual or Infrequent Item

Estimated Income on Expense on Total Income Subject to Tax	$ 33,500
Estimated Income Tax Expense on Operating Income Subject to Tax	22,500
Estimated Income Tax Expense on Unusual or Infrequent Item	$ 11,000
Proof: Tax on $30,000 at 25% =	$ 7,500
Tax on $10,000 at 35% =	3,500
Total Estimated Income Tax Expense	$ 11,000

Case 2: Extraordinary Loss in Third Quarter.   During the third quarter, Roberts Company incurred an extraordinary loss of $60,000 in addition to the unusual or infrequent gain of $40,000 in the second quarter.

Computation of Estimated Income Tax Expense on Total Income Subject to Tax

Tax on First $50,000	$ 7,500
Tax on Second $50,000	10,000
Total Estimated Income Tax Expense	$ 17,500

Computation of Estimated Income Tax Saving on Extraordinary Loss

Estimated Income Tax Expense on Total Income Subject to Tax	$ 17,500
Less: Estimated Income Tax Expense on Operating Income Subject to Tax	22,500
Estimated Income Tax Expense on Unusual or Infrequent Item	11,000
Estimated Income Tax Saving on Extraordinary Loss	$(16,000)
Proof: $10,000 × 35% =	$ 3,500
$50,000 × 25% =	12,500
Estimated Income Tax Saving	$ 16,000

DISCONTINUED OPERATIONS

Discontinued operations are reported net of income tax expense or saving. The discontinued operations component of the income statement consists of the operating results to the measurement date and any gain or loss on the disposal of the net assets. The income tax expense (saving) for the gain or loss component is computed as demonstrated in Illustrative Problem 15.3 for the gain or loss on unusual or infrequent items and extraordinary items. The operating results of the discontinued operation to the measurement date have been included in the determination of the effective tax rate for operating income. When an operation is discontinued, the discontinued operation's operating income or loss is deleted from the previously reported operating income and a new effective tax rate is computed for operating income. The tax on the operating income or loss is the difference between the tax computed with the profit or loss from the discontinued operations and the tax computed without the profit or loss. Illustrative Problem 15.4 demonstrates the recomputation of the effective rate for operating income for continuing operations and the determination of the income tax expense or saving for the discontinued operation.

ILLUSTRATIVE PROBLEM 15.4: INCOME TAX EXPENSE (SAVING) FOR A DISCONTINUED OPERATION

Salsbury Company estimated its operating income for the current year to be $280,000. Salsbury's income is subject to the following federal income tax rates:

First $100,000	16%
Second $100,000	20%
Over $200,000	25%

Salsbury had the following operating income, including the Talbot Division, for the first three quarters of 1990 as originally estimated:

First Quarter	$ 60,000
Second Quarter	50,000
Third Quarter	90,000

During the third quarter, Salsbury discontinued the operations of their Talbot Division and sold the Division's net assets at a $100,000 gain. The operating results of the Talbot Division to the point of sale were

First Quarter	$ 10,000
Second Quarter	(35,000)
Third Quarter	(11,000)

Salsbury estimates its fourth quarter's income will be $100,000. All of Salsbury's income is subject to tax and the company has no tax credits. The original computation of the effective tax rate was

Tax on First $100,000	$ 16,000
Tax on Second $100,000	20,000
Tax on Excess Over $200,000 ($80,000 × 25%)	20,000
Total Estimated Income Tax Expense	$ 56,000

Computation of Original Effective Tax Rate

$$\frac{\text{Estimated Annual Income Tax Expense}}{\text{Estimated Annual Income Subject to Tax}} = \frac{\$\ \ 56,000}{\$\ 280,000} = 20.00\%$$

Computation of Estimated Income Tax Expense Prior to the
Discontinued Operations

First Quarter ($60,000 × 20%)	$ 12,000
Second Quarter ($50,000 × 20%)	10,000

Income Segregated Between Continuing and Discontinued Operations

Quarter	Total Income	Discontinued Income	Continuing Income
First	$ 60,000	$ 10,000	$ 50,000 actual
Second	50,000	(35,000)	85,000 actual
Third	90,000	(11,000)	101,000 actual
Fourth	100,000		100,000 estimated
	$ 300,000	$(36,000)	$ 336,000

Computation of Effective Tax Rate for Operating Income Without the
Discontinued Operations

Tax on First $100,000	$ 16,000
Tax on Second $100,000	20,000
Tax on Excess Over $200,000 ($136,000 × 25%)	34,000
Total Estimated Income Tax Expense	$ 70,000

$$\frac{\text{Estimated Annual Income Tax Expense}}{\text{Estimated Annual Income Subject to Tax}} = \frac{\$\ \ 70,000}{\$\ 336,000} = 20.83\%$$

Computation of Estimated Income Tax Expense (Saving)
on the Discontinued Operations

Quarter	Continuing Income	New Effective Tax Rate	Tax on Continuing Income	Tax as Reported	Tax on Discontinued Income
First	$ 50,000	20.83%	$ 10,415	$ 12,000	$ 1,585
Second	85,000	20.83	17,705	10,000	(7,705)
					$(6,120)

Estimated Income Tax Expense (Saving) for the Discontinued Operations

Discontinued Operating Income	
First and Second Quarters	$ (6,120)
Third Quarter ($11,000 × 25%)	(2,750)
Total Estimated Tax Saving	$ (8,870)
Gain on Sale of Assets ($100,000 × 25%)	$ 25,000

The tax saving from the operating loss of the discontinued Talbot Division for the third quarter is treated incrementally and, therefore, is computed using the maximum tax bracket. The gain on the disposal of the discontinued operation is also treated as an incremental tax and computed at the maximum rate. The $8,870 tax saving is netted against the operating results of the discontinued operation in the income statement and the $25,000 tax expense from the sale of the net assets of the Talbot Division is netted against the gain from the sale of the assets of the discontinued operation.

CUMULATIVE EFFECT OF ACCOUNTING CHANGES

If a cumulative effect of an accounting change occurs during the first interim period, the effect is included in the income of that period. If a cumulative effect occurs beyond the first interim period, the effect of the accounting change is treated as if it had occurred during the first interim period of the current year. Therefore, the first interim period's financial statements are restated to include the cumulative effect and the cumulative effect is not reported in the quarter in which the change in accounting principle occurred.

SEASONALITY OF OPERATIONS

Although some companies have a relatively even sales volume and net profit throughout an annual accounting period, other businesses are very seasonal in nature. For instance, a major toy manufacturer makes the majority of its sales in the late summer and early fall when buyers are purchasing for the anticipated additional sales at Christmastime. When a company has a highly seasonal pattern to its revenues and expenses, *Accounting Principles Board Opinion No. 28* recommends that the prior 12 months be reported in comparative form in addition to the comparable quarter of the previous year.

DISCLOSURE REQUIREMENTS

The following summarized financial information in comparative form with current year-to-date, or preceding 12 months if income is seasonal, is required for interim reporting:

- Sales or gross revenues, provision for income taxes, extraordinary items, cumulative effect of a change in principle, and net income
- Primary and fully diluted earnings per share
- Seasonal revenues, costs, and expenses
- Significant changes in income tax estimates
- Discontinued operations and unusual or infrequently occurring items
- Contingencies
- Changes in accounting principles or estimates
- Significant changes in financial position

SEGMENT REPORTING

Starting in the 1960s, the merger and acquisition of one major corporation by another corporation became commonplace. The results were large, highly diversified conglomerates engaged in many different products and services around the world. For the most part, these corporate giants were reporting financial information only on a consolidated basis, thus obscuring the operations of any one of their product lines or geographic areas. In 1970, the Securities and Exchange Commission began requiring companies under its jurisdiction to include condensed financial information for different product lines in their filings with the Commission, and in 1974, extended that requirement to the companies' annual reports. In addition, financial analysts and the stock exchanges were promoting the reporting of segmented information.

In 1976, the Financial Accounting Standards Board issued *Statement of Financial Accounting Standards No. 14, Financial Reporting for Segments of a Business Enterprise* that provides for the reporting of information relative to a company's industry segments, foreign operations, export sales, and major customers in annual reports.[7] Initially, the standard covered all corporations for both interim and annual reporting. The standard was later amended to include only publicly held enterprises and to exclude interim reporting.

The requirements of segment reporting are a disaggregation of specific information that has been aggregated and consolidated in the annual financial statements. The information required to be disclosed for each segment is the segment's revenues, operating profit or loss, and identifiable assets. In addition, the segmented information is reconciled to the consolidated corporate amounts of the three required disclosures. The purpose of the disaggregation of revenues, operating profit, and identifiable assets is to allow investors and creditors to evaluate the profitability, risk, and growth potential based on the various components that comprise the consolidated entity.

In response to the Discussion Memorandum and the Exposure Draft that preceded the issuance of the standard, the following arguments were advanced against the reporting of segment information:

- Investors and creditors are concerned with a company's overall performance and not with portions of the whole.
- The difference between the nature of a company's operations, the wide choices available for determining segments, and the allocation of common costs and other accounting problems make comparison between companies' segment information invalid.
- Users lack of knowledge will result in misuse or misinterpretations of the information.
- The company's competitive position could be harmed by the detailed information presented.
- Management may not be willing to assume good business risks because of the effect on the profitability of a segment.
- Segment information, although useful, is too analytical or interpretive to be included with financial information.
- Segment information lacks the verifiability of other information contained in the annual report.

---

[7] *Statement of Financial Accounting Standards No. 14, Financial Reporting for Segments of a Business Enterprise* (Stamford: Connecticut: FASB, 1976).

- The cost of preparing the segment information exceeds the benefit of the information to the users.

The Financial Accounting Standards Board provides the following rebuttal to the arguments against segment reporting in *Statement of Financial Accounting Standards No. 14.*[8]

- Investors and creditors find the information useful in analyzing and understanding consolidated statements and overall operating results.
- The statement does caution that comparison between companies' segment information may not be valid.
- The information does not go beyond information that is currently being presented and used.
- The requirements are not any more detailed than a company would present if it operated in a single industry.
- The information is currently being provided by many of the companies that would be required to present the information.
- The information is sufficiently verifiable to be included with the other audited financial information.

DEFINITION OF AN INDUSTRY SEGMENT

An **industry segment** is a component of an enterprise engaged in providing a product or service, or a group of related products or services, primarily to unaffiliated customers for a profit. Management applies this general definition to the business, preferably on a worldwide basis, to determine what are the industry segments that will provide the users with meaningful disaggregated information. The segments selected could be based on geographic areas, product or industry lines, the internal structure of management control, or government versus private operations.

Statement of Financial Accounting Standards No. 14 states that although certain characteristics differentiate among industries, no single set of characteristics fits the industry segments of all businesses.[9] The following factors are to be considered in determining the product or service to be treated as a segment.

- **The nature of the product.** Related products or services have similar purposes or end uses and therefore would be expected to have similar rates of profitability, degree of risk, and opportunity for growth.
- **The nature of the production process.** Sharing of common or interchangeable production or sales facilities, equipment, labor force, or service group, or use of the same or similar basic raw material, can suggest that products or services are related. Likewise, similar degrees of labor intensiveness or similar degreee of capital intensiveness may indicate a relationship among products or services.

[8] *SFAS No. 14,* paragraphs 65–71.
[9] *SFAS No. 14,* paragraph 100.

▪ **The market and marketing methods.** Similarity of geographic market areas, types of customers, or marketing methods may indicate a relationship among products or services. For instance, the use of a common or interchangeable sales force may suggest a relationship among products or services. The sensitivity of the market to price changes and to changes in general economic conditions may also indicate whether products or services are related or unrelated.

The standard also cautions against using broad categories such as manufacturing, wholesaling, and retailing.

TESTS TO DETERMINE REPORTABLE INDUSTRY SEGMENTS

If an industry segment meets any one of three 10% tests of the dollar amount of revenues, operating profit, and identifiable assets of the segment in relation to the total amounts for all segments of the corporate entity, the information required for a segment needs to be disclosed. In addition, an overall test to determine if a majority of a company's business is included in the segments selected may require the inclusion of a segment that does not meet any of the three tests.

THE THREE 10% TESTS

1. **Revenues.** The revenue of the segment (unaffiliated and intersegment) is at least 10% of combined unaffiliated and intersegment revenue of all the segments.
2. **Operating Profit or Loss.** The absolute amount of profit or loss (unaffiliated and intersegment) of the segment is at least 10% of the **greater** of
   1) Combined operating profit of all segments reporting a profit, or
   2) Combined operating losses of all segments reporting a loss.
3. **Identifiable Assets.** The segment's identifiable assets (own and allocated portion of shared assets, but **not** corporate assets) are 10% or more of combined identifiable assets of all segments.[10]

In order to achieve consistency and comparability from year to year of the segments whose information is reported separately, the pronouncement permits two exceptions to the 10% tests. If a segment has been reported on a regular basis, but does not meet any one of the tests during the current year, the segment is included. Conversely, if a segment has not met any of the tests in the past and is not likely to meet the tests in the future, it is excluded.

OVERALL 75% TEST

After applying the 10% tests to all the segments, an overall test of revenue is performed to determine if sufficient segment information is being reported. The test is based **only** on unaffiliated revenues, which is not the same as the 10% revenue test that uses both unaffiliated

---

[10]*SFAS No. 14,* paragraph 15.

and intersegment revenues. The 75% test requires that the combined **unaffiliated** revenue of all reportable segments be at least 75% of combined unaffiliated revenue of all the segments. If the test is not met, then additional segments are added until the test is met.

The maximum number of segments to be reported, as suggested by the pronouncement, is 10. If the number of reportable segments exceeds 10, the assumption is that the information presented is so fragmented that it will be less informative than not reporting any segment information. If the tests determine that the number of reportable segments is more than 10, then either segments are combined or consideration given to whether or not the definition of a segment used by the business is appropriate for determination of the company's segments.

Conversely, if a single segment accounts for 90% or more of the total revenues, operating profit, or identifiable assets as determined by the 10% tests, the company should not report segment information. The company is considered to be operating almost entirely within a single industry and, therefore, the financial statements of the business as a whole are representative of the segment. Illustrative Problem 15.5 demonstrates the application of the 10% tests and the overall 75% test to determine which segment's individual information to report.

ILLUSTRATIVE PROBLEM 15.5: APPLICATION OF REPORTABLE SEGMENT TESTS

Zeta Company is a large conglomerate that operates in a number of different industries. Zeta Company has determined the following revenue, operating profit, and identifiable asset information to decide the segments that will report individual information.

| Segment | Revenues | | | Operating Profit or Loss | Identifiable Assets |
	Unaffiliated	Intersegment	Total		
Alpha	$ 200,000	$ 50,000	$ 250,000	$ 25,000	$ 400,000
Beta	350,000	–0–	350,000	40,000	1,000,000
Colt	800,000	200,000	1,000,000	(100,000)	1,200,000
Delta	1,000,000	40,000	1,040,000	200,000	2,300,000
Evans	550,000	250,000	800,000	(35,000)	1,600,000
Fargo	300,000	35,000	335,000	(40,000)	790,000
Grant	600,000	125,000	725,000	175,000	1,010,000
	3,800,000	700,000	4,500,000	265,000	8,300,000
Corporate	200,000	–0–	200,000	25,000	1,700,000
Total	$ 4,000,000	$ 700,000	$ 4,700,000	$ 290,000	$ 10,000,000

10% Tests

Revenue Test

Total Segment Sales to Unaffiliated Customers	$ 3,800,000
Total Segment Sales to Other Segments	700,000
Total Revenues	4,500,000
Minimum Percentage	× 10%
Minimum Revenues to be Reported as a Segment	$ 450,000

Operating Profit or Loss Test

Segment	Operating Profit	Operating Loss
Alpha	$ 25,000	
Beta	40,000	
Colt		$ 100,000
Delta	200,000	
Evans		35,000
Fargo		40,000
Grant	175,000	
Total	$ 440,000	$ 175,000

Greater of Operating Profits or Losses	$ 440,000
Minimum Percentage	× 10%
Minimum Operating Profit or Loss to be Reported as a Segment	$ 44,000

Identifiable Assets Test

Total Identifiable Assets of the Segements	$ 8,300,000
Minimum Percentage	× 10%
Minimum Identifiable Assets to be Reported as a Segment	$ 830,000

Once the value of the tests has been determined, the revenues, operating profit or loss, and identifiable assets of each segment are compared to the test values. If a segment meets even one of the tests it is included as a reportable segment. The determination of the segments of Zeta Company to be separately included in the company's segment reporting is

Segment	Total Revenue More Than $ 450,000	Operating Profit or Loss More Than $ 44,000	Identifiable Assets More Than $ 830,000	Qualifies as a Reportable Segment
Alpha	No	No	No	No
Beta	No	No	Yes	Yes
Colt	Yes	Yes	Yes	Yes
Delta	Yes	Yes	Yes	Yes
Evans	Yes	No	Yes	Yes
Fargo	No	No	No	No
Grant	Yes	Yes	Yes	Yes

All of the segments except Alpha and Fargo meet at least one of the tests and are reported as separate segments if the revenues from unaffiliated customers of the 5 segments included are at least equal to 75% of the total segment sales to unaffiliated customers.

Overall 75% Test

Total Segment Sales to Unaffiliated Customers		$ 3,800,000
Minimum Percentage Required		× 75%
Minimum Sales to Unaffiliated Customers of Reportable Segments		$ 2,850,000
Total Segment Sales to Unaffiliated Customers		$ 3,800,000
Less: Unaffiliated Customer Sales of Segments Not Qualifying		
Alpha	$ 200,000	
Fargo	300,000	500,000
Total Segment Sales of Qualifying Segments		$ 3,300,000

Total sales to unaffiliated customers meets the overall test and the 5 segments to be reported do not exceed the maximum of 10 segments; therefore, the segment information for Beta, Colt, Delta, Evans, and Grant is separately disclosed as illustrated in Exhibit 15-6. The information for the nonreportable segments, in this example Alpha and Fargo, is summed together and reported as other segments. The segment information regarding unaffiliated and intersegment revenues, operating profits or losses, and identifiable assets can be reported within the financial statements themselves, in the footnotes to the financial statements, or in separate schedules that are an integral part of the financial statements.

DISCLOSURE REQUIREMENTS

In addition to the four disclosures for reportable segments that are reconciled to the consolidated amounts, the following disclosures are required for product or industry segmentation:

- types of products and services produced by each segment,
- specific accounting policies applicable to segments,
- transfer pricing method,
- method of allocating common costs,
- nature and amount of any unusual or infrequent items affecting segment profitability,
- aggregate amounts of depreciation, depletion, and amortization,
- amount of capital expenditures,
- equity in unconsolidated, but vertically integrated subsidiaries and their geographic location, and
- effects of changes in accounting principles on segment income.

PROBLEMS IN DETERMINING SEGMENT INFORMATION

The above discussion of determining which segments to report and the actual reporting assumed that the decision of how a segment is identified, and the determination of segment revenues, operating profits or losses, and identifiable assets, lack complications. In order to

EXHIBIT 15-6

Illustrative Problem 15.5
ZETA COMPANY
Segment Reporting

	Reportable Segments				
	Beta	Colt	Delta	Evans	Grant
Revenues					
Unaffiliated Customers	$ 350,000	$ 800,000	$1,000,000	$ 550,000	$ 600,000
Intersegment Sales	–0–	200,000	40,000	250,000	125,000
Total	$ 350,000	$1,000,000	$1,040,000	$ 800,000	$ 725,000
Operating Profit	$ 40,000	$(100,000)	$ 200,000	$(35,000)	$ 175,000
Equity in Income of High Company					
Interest Revenue					
General Corporate Expenses					
Interest Expense					
Income from Continuing Operations Before Income Taxes					
Identifiable Assets	$1,000,000	$1,200,000	$2,300,000	$1,600,000	$1,010,000
Investment in Net Assets of High Company					
Corporate Assets					
Total Assets					

determine the segments and develop the financial information necessary to meet the reporting requirements, the following problem areas need to be considered: the definition of the segments, the determination of the transfer price used for intercompany sales, the allocation of common costs, the costs excluded in determining segment income, and the allocation of shared assets to determine identifiable assets.

The first problem is determining a definition to use for a segment and the resulting reporting entities. If a conglomerate consists of a number of distinct legal entities, this may be the easiest to use, as the accounting is already in place. However, more than one of the entities may engage in business in the same industry or same geographic area, and thus not accomplish the goal of segment reporting. The use of geographic areas of sales may not achieve the goal, as the company may be operating in the same industry in more than one geographic area. A company could elect to determine industry segments by type of customers, such as government versus nongovernment. This classification may be appropriate for some industries and not for others. The pronouncement specifically cautions against using manufacturing, wholesaling, and retailing as segments. A number of different industry classification codes are available, and these can be used to determine the industries. As stated earlier, no single

Other Segments	Adjustments and Eliminations	Consolidated Totals
$ 500,000		$ 3,800,000
85,000	$ 700,000	–0–
$ 585,000	$ 700,000	$ 3,800,000
$ 10,000	$(30,000)	$ 245,000
		55,000
		145,000
		(135,000)
		(40,000)
		$ 270,000
$1,190,000	$(120,000)	$ 8,180,000
		500,000
		1,200,000
		$ 9,880,000

definition fits all companies, and thus management must ultimately define what constitutes a segment.

The second problem is the transfer price used for intersegment sales. A variety of transfer prices can be used by companies including cost, cost plus a profit percentage, market price, and arbitrarily determined prices. The revenue information required suggests that the transfer price should be the market price of the goods or services transferred. If the market price is used, the combined revenues to unaffiliated and affiliated customers reflect revenues as if the goods had all been sold to unaffiliated customers. In addition, the cost to the acquiring segment reflects the price that would be paid had the goods been purchased from an outside supplier. Practicality dictates, however, that the transfer price that a company uses for intersegment sales is the easiest and least costly method of determining the value of intersegment sales and the method recommended by the standard.

The third problem is how costs that are either for the benefit of two or more segments, or are costs of one or more of the segments and the corporate level of the conglomerate, are apportioned among the reporting elements. The basis of apportionment could be revenue dollars or units, gross profit, operating profit without the common costs, net income without common costs, and tangible assets. Depending on the type of cost being allocated, each of these apportionment bases can be an appropriate method of assigning the costs to the segments. The apportionment basis should be a reasonable one and should reflect the association between the cost incurred and the benefit received by the segments who have shared the expenditure.

The fourth problem is determining the items to exclude in the determination of the operating profit of the segments. *Statement of Financial Accounting Standards No. 14* provides some specific guidance regarding items that are **not** to be included in calculating operating profit or loss. These items include revenue earned at the corporate level, general corporate expenses, interest expense unless the segment activity is financial, income taxes, equity in income of unconsolidated investees, gains or losses on discontinued operations, extraordinary items, minority interests, and cumulative effects of changes in accounting principles.[11] These specific items are excluded so that the revenues and expenses of the segments include only those operating revenues and expenses that are directly traceable to the segment and those revenues and expenses that can be allocated to the segments on a reasonable basis. All corporate revenues and expenses are specifically excluded. The result is operating income that is directly earned by each of the segments.

The last problem is the allocation of the basis of identifiable assets. Assets that are either shared by two or more segments or are assets of one or more segments and the corporate level need to be apportioned between the elements of the entity using the assets. Again, the basis of allocation should be a reasonable one and reflect the benefit received by each element. For example, the cost of a building shared by the corporate level and one of the segments could be allocated based on square footage of use, number of floors occupied, number of employees, or the cost of construction of the portion used.

FOREIGN OPERATIONS

The previous discussion assumed that the segments were domestic operations and the segmentation was determined based on products and services. Many large conglomerates are worldwide enterprises with operations in a number of countries. If a company has both domestic and foreign operations, disclosure of segments is required if the segments are material to the company as a whole. If a company has significant operations in more than one foreign geographic area or country, each of these areas or countries is considered a separate foreign segment.

The determination of how to group foreign operations requires the same judgment as is needed in determining the domestic segments and will differ from company to company depending on the circumstances. The factors to be considered in determining foreign segments are proximity, economic affinity, similarities in business environments, and the nature, scale, and degree of interrelationship of the company's operations in the various countries.[12] The same information as required of domestic segments, unaffiliated and intersegment revenues, operating profit or loss, and identifiable assets, is disclosed for each of the various areas or countries.

The tests to determine if foreign operations are to be considered segments are **not** the

[11] *SFAS No. 14*, paragraph 10.
[12] *SFAS No. 14*, paragraph 34.

same as the tests used to determine if a domestic segment is reported separately. The number of tests is different and the tests themselves are different. Only two 10% tests are used, a revenue test and an identifiable asset test, and the operating profit test for domestic segments is omitted. The two 10% tests are

10% Revenue Test.   The unaffiliated revenues are 10% or more of consolidated revenues.

10% Identifiable Asset Test.   The identifiable assets are 10% or more of total consolidated corporate assets.

The 10% revenue test for a foreign segment compares **only** unaffiliated revenue, rather than the sum of affiliated and intersegment revenues used in the domestic segment test. The unaffiliated revenue of the foreign segment is compared to **total unaffiliated revenue on a consolidated basis,** while the test for domestic segments uses only segment revenues as the denominator. The 10% identifiable asset test compares the foreign segment's identifiable assets to the **total of corporate assets on a consolidated basis,** while the test for a domestic segment uses the total identifiable assets of the segments. Illustrative Problem 15.6 uses the same segments as Illustrative Problem 15.5 to demonstrate determining if a foreign segment is reported separately.

ILLUSTRATIVE PROBLEM 15.6: APPLICATION OF FOREIGN REPORTABLE SEGMENT TESTS

Zeta Company is a large conglomerate that operates in a number of different countries around the world. Zeta Company has determined the following revenue, operating profit, and identifiable asset information to determine which segments will report individual information.

Segment	Country	Revenues			Operating Profit or Loss	Identifiable Assets
		Unaffiliated	Intersegment	Total		
Alpha	Peru	$ 200,000	$ 50,000	$ 250,000	$ 250,000	$ 400,000
Beta	U.S.	350,000	–0–	350,000	40,000	1,000,000
Colt	France	800,000	200,000	1,000,000	(100,000)	1,200,000
Delta	Austria	1,000,000	40,000	1,040,000	200,000	2,300,000
Evans	U.S.	550,000	250,000	800,000	(35,000)	1,600,000
Fargo	Japan	300,000	35,000	335,000	(40,000)	790,000
Grant	U.S.	600,000	125,000	725,000	175,000	1,010,000
		3,800,000	700,000	4,500,000	265,000	8,300,000
Corporate		200,000	–0–	200,000	25,000	1,700,000
Unconsolidated Total		4,000,000	700,000	4,700,000	290,000	10,000,000
Less: Intercompany		–0–	(700,000)	(700,000)	(20,000)	(120,000)
Consolidated Total		$4,000,000	$ –0–	$ 4,000,000	$ 270,000	$ 9,880,000

Foreign Revenue Test

Total Consolidated Sales to Unaffiliated Customers	$ 4,000,000
Minimum Percentage	× 10%
Minimum Unaffiliated Revenues To Be Reported as a Foreign Segment	$ 400,000

Foreign Identifiable Asset Test

Total Consolidated Assets	$ 9,880,000
Minimum Percentage	× 10%
Minimum Identifiable Assets To Be Reported as a Foreign Segment	$ 988,000

Foreign Segment	Unaffiliated Revenue More Than $ 400,000	Identifiable Assets More Than $ 988,000	Qualifies as a Reportable Foreign Segment
Alpha	No	No	No
Colt	Yes	Yes	Yes
Delta	Yes	Yes	Yes
Fargo	No	No	No

A segment may meet the revenue test or the identifiable asset test as an industry segment and not meet the test as a foreign segment or just the opposite may happen. If a domestic segment meets only the operating profit or loss test and not the other tests, the segment may or may not qualify as a foreign segment.

EXPORT SALES AND SALES TO MAJOR CUSTOMERS

In addition to reporting information about the segments of the company, a company must also disclose information about export sales and major customers. The objective is to provide the user with information about the company's heavy reliance on a particular market or a particular customer. If export sales are 10% or more of consolidated revenue, the amount of the export sales is disclosed, regardless of whether or not the company is required to report segment information about either domestic or foreign segments. The foreign sales can be reported as a total amount or may be reported by geographic areas, if that information is considered to be more useful.

A company also must disclose the amount of the revenue, the customer, and the industry segment or segments making the sales if the sales during the year to a single customer are 10% or more of the company's revenue. A group of customers under common control is regarded as a single customer in determining whether or not the reporting requirement applies to the company. If the company does business with domestic and foreign governments, each country's government and each level of government of that country is considered a different customer.

SUMMARY

Interim financial reporting is prepared for publicly held companies to provide users with more timely information about gross revenues, provision for income taxes, unusual or infrequent items, discontinued operations, extraordinary items, cumulative effects of changes in accounting principles, net income, and earnings per share. If a company operates in a highly seasonal environment, the information presented must reflect this seasonality. Interim financial reporting is prepared using the integral approach, which treats the interim period as a portion of the entire year. Revenues and expenses are determined in the same manner as they are for annual reporting purposes except that expenses directly related to the sale of goods or the provision of services are recognized by the discrete approach, which treats the interim period as a complete accounting period. Allocations of expense to interim periods should use a rational basis of allocation such as sales volume. Four integral exceptions to the discrete approach are using the gross profit method for estimating ending inventory if a company uses a periodic inventory system, ignoring temporary erosion of LIFO layers, ignoring temporary market declines if using lower of cost or market, and ignoring planned purchase and volume variances if a standard cost system is used.

Income tax expense for operating income is determined using the combined estimated effective tax rate for the year. The combined estimated effective tax rate is the combined federal and state income tax expense based on the annual estimated income subject to income taxes divided by the estimated annual income subject to income taxes. If the tax laws, tax rates, or estimates of income subject to tax change during the year, a new effective tax rate is computed. The income tax expense for the period of change is the income tax expense for the year to date determined by the new effective tax rate less all previously recognized tax expense.

Income tax savings from operating loss carrybacks are recognized using an effective tax rate based on the tax paid. Tax savings from operating loss carryforwards are recognized if they are caused by a nonrecurring event and the income of the current period is sufficient to absorb the loss. The income tax saving from operating loss carryforwards is computed using the combined estimated effective tax rate for the current year.

Income tax expense on nonoperating items (unusual or infrequent items, discontinued operations, extraordinary gains and losses, and cumulative effects of accounting changes) is assumed to be after the determination of tax on operating income (incremental amount) unless subject to a specific rate. The tax on each item is computed in the order it appears in the income statement. If more than one nonoperating item are loss items, the tax is computed on the total of the losses and allocated ratably among the loss items. If a company has a discontinued operation during the year, the tax on operating income previously reported is recomputed using a new effective tax rate based on operating income without the discontinued operating results. The difference in income tax expense is allocated to the operating income or loss of the discontinued operation.

Large publicly held companies that operate in more than one industry or geographic area are required to disclose the revenues, operating profit or loss, and identifiable assets of their segments reconciled to consolidated information. This disaggregated data is designed to provide users with information to assess the profitability, risk, and growth potential of the various components of a consolidated entity. A business segment is defined as a component of an entity that provides a product or service to unaffiliated customers for a profit.

Three tests are applied to a domestic segment's financial information to determine if it is a reportable segment. These tests are (1) segment's revenue is 10% or more of unaffiliated and intersegment revenue of all segments; (2) segment's operating income is 10% or more of the greater of operating profit or operating loss of all the segments operating either at a profit or at a loss; and (3) segment's identifiable assets are 10% or more of the combined identifiable assets of all the segments. In addition, the unaffiliated revenue of the reportable segments must be at least 75% of the unaffiliated revenue of all of the segments. If the segments are foreign geographic areas, the tests to determine a segment are different from those used for domestic segments. The two foreign segment tests are (1) segment's unaffiliated revenue is 10% or more of total unaffiliated consolidated revenue; and (2) segment's identifiable assets are 10% or more of consolidated identifiable assets. The tests for domestic segments are based on segmental amounts whereas the tests for foreign segments are based on consolidated totals.

In preparing segment reporting information several problems must be solved. These problems include identification of the segments, transfer prices for intersegment sales, allocation of common costs and common assets, and identification of the items to be excluded. All revenues and expenses that are not directly traceable to a segment or allocable to the segment on a reasonable basis are excluded from a segment's operating income, so that it is the segment's operating income. All corporate revenues and expenses, interest expense and income tax expenses, and nonoperating income statement items are specifically excluded in determining segmental operating income.

In addition to the segment information, publicly held corporations need to disclose both exports sales and sales to a single customer that constitute 10% or more of consolidated revenue.

REVIEW PROBLEMS

INTERIM REPORTING

1. Omega Company estimates by quarters its annual operating income for 1990 to be

First Quarter	$ 800,000
Second Quarter	450,000
Third Quarter	325,000
Fourth Quarter	625,000
Total Estimated Income for Current Year	$ 2,200,000

The current year's income includes $60,000 of municipal bond interest revenue and $100,000 of amortization of goodwill. Both the bond interest revenue and the amortization expense are being allocated ratably to each interim quarter. Omega Company's income is subject to the following federal tax rates:

First $50,000 of Income	15%
Second $50,000 of Income	22%
Next $200,000 of Income	28%
Income in Excess of $300,000	35%

In addition, Omega Company's income is subject to state income tax at the rate of 5% on the first $500,000 and 3% on any excess over $500,000.

Required (Compute percentages to the nearest 100th of a percent.)
1) Determine the income tax expense for the first quarter, assuming the income is as estimated.
2) Determine the income tax expense for the second quarter, assuming Omega had a loss of $300,000, but expects that the estimates of income for the remainder of the year are accurate.

3) The investment tax credits were reinstated in the federal tax code effective as of the beginning of Omega's third quarter. Omega estimates it will have $50,130 of tax credits available to offset its current year's tax liability. Determine the income tax expense for the third quarter, assuming Omega earned $350,000 and estimates the fourth quarter earnings to be $450,000.

2. Ignore 1. (3)

Omega Company started in business last year and paid $165,600 of income taxes on $440,000 of operating income subject to tax. Omega suffered a loss of $400,000 for the third quarter and has revised the estimate of the fourth quarter to a loss of $600,000.

Required

Determine the income tax expense for the third quarter.

3. Ignore 2.

In addition to the operating income stated in 1. above, Omega had an extraordinary gain of $130,000 in the second quarter.

Required

Determine the income tax expense on the extraordinary gain.

4. Ignore 2. and 3.

During the second quarter of 1991 Omega discontinued the operations of the Beta Division and sold the net assets of Beta Division at a loss of $65,000. The tax rates for 1991 are the same as 1990 and Omega has the same permanent differences and tax credits as in 1990. The following operating results of the first and second quarters were equal to the estimated income:

Quarter	Continuing Income	Discontinued Operations	Total
First	$ 140,000	$ 20,000	$ 160,000
Second	110,000	(45,000)	65,000

Omega estimates that its third quarter income from continuing operations will be $200,000 and for the fourth quarter the income will be $180,000.

Required

Determine the income tax expense for continuing operations for the first and second quarters and the income tax expense for the operating results and the loss from the discontinued operation.

SEGMENT REPORTING

Global Company is a large multisegmented conglomerate. Global has provided the following information for determining the segments to separately report in a supplemental schedule to its annual financial statements.

Segment	Revenues Unaffiliated	Revenues Intersegment	Revenues Total	Operating Profit or Loss	Identifiable Assets
A	$ 1,000,000	$ 150,000	$ 1,150,000	$ 525,000	$ 2,675,000
B	550,000	550,000	1,100,000	230,000	2,340,000
C	400,000	–0–	400,000	(160,000)	1,890,000
D	1,100,000	440,000	1,540,000	780,000	2,300,000
E	850,000	250,000	1,100,000	475,000	1,400,000
F	420,000	510,000	930,000	(140,000)	2,490,000
G	3,300,000	–0–	3,300,000	1,520,000	5,190,000
H	900,000	–0–	900,000	(820,000)	1,790,000
I	480,000	–0–	480,000	80,000	2,050,000
	9,000,000	1,900,000	10,900,000	2,490,000	22,125,000
Corporate	600,000	–0–	600,000	190,000	2,875,000
Total	$ 9,600,000	$ 1,900,000	$12,500,000	$ 2,680,000	$ 25,000,000

All of the revenue at the corporate level was from interest and dividends. The expenses at the corporate level consisted of general corporate expenses of $320,000 and interest of $90,000. Intercompany eliminations from operating profit totaled $220,000 and intercompany eliminations from identifiable assets totaled $425,000.

Required
1. If all the segments are domestic segments, determine the segments that are to be separately reported.
2. Prepare the schedule of segmental reporting to accompany Global's annual report.
3. If all the segments except Segment G are foreign segments, determine the foreign segments to be separately reported.

QUESTIONS

1. What is the purpose of interim reporting?
2. What are the two views of interim reporting and what approach to revenue and expense recognition is required by these views?
3. What is the general approach of *APB No. 28* to interim reporting?
4. Describe the accounting treatment of revenues, product and direct costs, and other costs and expenses in interim reporting.
5. Describe the four integral exceptions to the discrete approach to determining cost of goods sold.
6. Describe the determination of income tax expense for operating income for an interim period and how revisions in the tax code and changes in estimates of future periods' income for the current year affect the determination of income tax expense.
7. Describe the three types of operation loss situations, and indicate the effect each has on the determination of operating income tax expense or income tax saving.
8. Describe how unusual or infrequent items, extraordinary items, discontinued items, and cumulative effect of accounting changes are treated in interim financial statements.
9. Describe how income tax expense (saving) is determined for unusual or infrequent items, extraordinary items, and cumulative effect of accounting changes.
10. Describe how income tax expense for continuing operations is determined in a period in which a company discontinues an operation.
11. Describe how income tax expense for both the operating results and the gain or loss on the disposal of the net assets of the discontinued operation is computed for a discontinued operation.

12. What are the remedies for reporting meaningful interim information when a company operates in a seasonal industry, such as a fireworks manufacturer?
13. Define an industry segment and give an illustration of each of the different ways that a segment can be determined.
14. What are the three tests to determine if an industry segment is a reportable domestic segment?
15. What is the overall segment test and what is its purpose?
16. What are the problems associated with selecting a segment and determining the necessary information to select the reportable segments and prepare the reporting schedule?
17. How do the tests for a foreign segment differ from the tests for a domestic segment?
18. Describe why the Financial Accounting Standards Board included the requirement of reporting export sales and sales to major customers in *SFAS No. 14* and why this information would be useful to an investor or creditor.

EXERCISES

EXERCISE 15-1

1. For interim financial reporting, which of the following may be accrued or deferred to provide an appropriate cost in each period?

	Property Taxes	Rent
a.	No	No
b.	No	Yes
c.	Yes	Yes
d.	Yes	No

2. In January 1991, Horner Company paid $80,000 in property taxes on its plant for the calendar year 1991. Also in January Horner estimated that its year-end bonus to executives for 1991 would be $320,000. What is the amount of the expenses related to these two items that should be reflected in Horner's quarterly income statement for the three months ended June 30, 1991 (second quarter)?

a. $ −0−
b. $ 20,000
c. $ 80,000
d. $ 100,000

3. On January 15, 1991, Forester Company paid property taxes on its factory building for the calendar year 1991 in the amount of $60,000. The first week of April 1991, Forrester made anticipated major repairs to its plant equipment at a cost of $240,000. These repairs will benefit operations for the remainder of the calendar year. How should these expenses be reflected in Forrester's quarterly income statements?

	Three Months Ended			
	March 31, 1991	June 30, 1991	September 30, 1991	December 31, 1991
a.	$ 15,000	$ 95,000	$ 95,000	$ 95,000
b.	$ 15,000	$255,000	$ 15,000	$ 15,000
c.	$ 60,000	$240,000	$ −0−	$ −0−
d.	$ 75,000	$ 75,000	$ 75,000	$ 75,000

(AICPA adapted)

EXERCISE 15-2

Beaver Company is a publicly traded company with 100,000 shares of voting common stock outstanding. The following information has been compiled to be used in the preparation of the second quarter's interim financial report:

Sales Revenue	$ 4,000,000
Cost of Goods Sold	2,200,000
Selling Expenses	1,600,000
Administrative Expenses	500,000

The following additional information has been determined with regard to the income information:

- Beaver Company uses the installment method of reporting for annual reporting purposes as Beaver sells all of its products to consumers on two-year installment contracts and is not able to accurately estimate the losses from nonpayment. The cash collections on sales totaled $5,000,000 and the gross profit percentage has remained constant over the past three years.
- Selling expenses include a $500,000 payment for an advertising campaign that is to begin in the third quarter.
- Beaver Company decided to change to the straight-line method of depreciation from the double-declining balance method during the quarter. Administrative expenses are $150,000 lower, reflecting the cumulative effect through the first quarter. Beaver Company's depreciation expense for the first quarter would have been $12,000 higher had the double-declining balance method been used.
- Beaver Company estimates its effective tax rate is 40%.

Required

1. Prepare the interim income statement for the second quarter for Beaver Company, assuming Beaver can justify the change in depreciation methods.
2. In addition to the income statement, what additional information is required to be reported in the second quarter's interim report?

EXERCISE 15-3

1. Carver Company, a publicly held company registered with the Securities and Exchange Commission, has determined it cannot prepare interim information since it employs a periodic inventory system. In order to take a physical inventory, Carver would need to shut down its operating plant and, therefore, Carver only takes a physical inventory at the end of the fiscal year. The annual financial statements of Carver indicate the following gross profit margins for the past five years: 1987, 25%; 1988, 26%; 1989, 27%; 1990, 24%; 1991, 25%. Carver had sales of $13,560,000 for the quarter.
2. Durbin, Inc., uses the LIFO method of valuing inventory. During the quarter, Durbin eroded the beginning LIFO layers in the amount of $62,000 with a resulting cost of goods sold of $1,438,000. Durbin anticipates that by the end of the year, the ending inventory will exceed the beginning inventory. If Durbin were to replace the eroded LIFO layers, it would cost $100,000.
3. Erickson Company uses a standard cost system. The cost of goods sold of $4,679,000 included a planned purchase variance of $(235,400) and a planned volume variance of $(342,140). Erickson expects to absorb these planned variances before the end of the current fiscal year.

Required

For each of the above independent situations determine the cost of goods sold to be used in the preparation of the third quarter's interim financial information and support each answer with a brief explanation.

EXERCISE 15-4

1. For interim financial reporting, an inventory loss from a temporary market decline in the first quarter that can reasonably be expected to be restored in the fourth quarter

a. should be recognized as a loss proportionately in each of the first, second, third, and fourth quarters.
b. should be recognized as a loss proportionately in each of the first, second, and third quarters.
c. need **not** be recognized as a loss in the first quarter.
d. should be recognized as a loss in the first quarter.

2. For interim financial reporting, an inventory loss from a market decline in the second quarter that is **not** expected to be restored in the fiscal year should be recognized as a loss

a. in the fourth quarter.
b. proportionately in each of the second, third, and fourth quarters.
c. proportionately in each of the first, second, third, and fourth quarters.
d. in the second quarter.

3. An inventory loss from a market decline occurred in the first quarter that was not expected to be restored in the fiscal year. For interim financial reporting purposes, how would the dollar amount of inventory in the balance sheet be affected in the first and fourth quarters?

	First Quarter	Fourth Quarter
a.	Decrease	No Effect
b.	Decrease	Increase
c.	No Effect	Decrease
d.	No Effect	No Effect

4. An inventory loss from a market price decline occurred in the first quarter. The loss was not expected to be restored in the fiscal year. However, in the third quarter the inventory had a market price recovery that exceeded the market decline that occurred in the first quarter. For interim financial reporting, the dollar amount of net inventory should

a. decrease in the first quarter by the amount of the market price decline and increase in the third quarter by the amount of the market price recovery.
b. decrease in the first quarter by the amount of the market price decline and increase in the third quarter by the amount of decrease in the first quarter.
c. not be affected in the first quarter and increase in the third quarter by the amount of the market price recovery that exceeded the amount of the market price decline.
d. not be affected in either the first quarter or the third quarter.

(AICPA adapted)

EXERCISE 15-5

Felix Company's income is subject to both federal and state income taxes. The state tax rate is 4.5% and the federal graduated tax rates are

First $25,000 of Income	18%
Second $25,000 of Income	24%
Next $100,000 of Income	31%
Excess over $150,000	37%

Felix estimates that its total income before tax for the current fiscal year will be $500,000, which includes $40,000 of expenses not subject to tax and a $70,000 extraordinary gain.

Required

1. If Felix Company has $32,225 of tax credits available to offset income earned in the current year, determine the combined effective tax rate to be used in computing interim income tax expense for the current year.

2. If Felix Company earns $125,000 of operating income in the first quarter and $265,000 of income in the second quarter, which included the extraordinary gain of $70,000, determine the income tax expense for all items to be reported in both quarters' interim income statements.

EXERCISE 15-6

Gable Company estimates that its operating income subject to tax for the current year will be $410,000. The state in which Gable Company is located has no state income tax. Gable Company is subject to the following federal graduated income tax rates:

First $50,000 of Income	17%
Second $50,000 of Income	23%
Next $100,000 of Income	30%
Next $100,000 of Income	38%
Next $100,000 of Income	43%
Excess over $400,000	46%

Required (Compute all percentages to the nearest 100th of a percent.)
1. Determine the estimated effective tax rate for the current year, assuming Gable has $16,700 of tax credits available for use in the current year.
2. During the second quarter, Congress revised the tax rate to a flat tax of 34% on income effective as of the beginning of the fiscal year. Determine the income tax expense for the second quarter, assuming Gable reported $80,000 of income before tax in the first quarter and earned $125,000 in the second quarter.
3. During the third quarter of the year, the state in which Gable Company is located enacted a state income tax of 3% on the first $250,000 of income and 5% on any income over $250,000 effective as of the beginning of the fiscal year. All income earned in the current year is subject to the tax. If Gable earned $90,000 before tax during the third quarter, determine the income tax expense to be reported in Gable's third quarter interim financial statements.

EXERCISE 15-7

Henry Company estimates that its annual operating income for the current year, all subject to tax, will be $380,000. Henry Company is subject to the following graduated federal income tax rate schedule:

First $100,000 of Income	15%
Second $100,000 of Income	25%
Third $100,000 of Income	36%
Excess over $300,000	48%

Required (Compute all percentages to the nearest 100th of a percent.)
1. Determine the effective income tax rate to be used in Henry's interim reporting for the current year.
2. During the first two quarters of the current year, Henry Company had operating income before tax of $168,000. During the third quarter, Henry Company was able to successfully introduce a new product to the market and Henry's third quarter income before tax is $280,000. Henry expects to have operating income before tax in the fourth quarter of $332,000. Determine the income tax expense to be reported in the third quarter of the current year.

EXERCISE 15-8

Indiana Corporation has paid $72,000 of income taxes on $200,000 of net operating income earned in prior years that is available for net operating loss carrybacks. Indiana is subject to a flat combined federal and state tax rate of 40%. All income is subject to tax. The quarterly income for the current year is

First Quarter	$ 52,000
Second Quarter	(156,000)
Third Quarter	(128,000)

Required

1. Determine the income tax expense or saving for the first three quarters of the current year assuming that Indiana projects positive operating income of $300,000 for the year. Indiana is reasonably assured of positive income based on its past history of seasonality.
2. Determine the income tax expense or saving for the first three quarters of the current year if Indiana projects positive operating income of $25,000 for the year.
3. Determine the income tax expense or saving for the first three quarters if Indiana projects negative operating income for the year of $42,000.
4. Determine the income tax expense or saving for the first three quarters if Indiana projects negative operating income for the year of $240,000.
5. Assume this is the first year of operation for Indiana. Determine the income tax expense or saving for the first three quarters if Indiana projects negative operating income for the year of $140,000.

EXERCISE 15-9

Maple Company has been in business for a number of years in several different industries. Maple Company estimated its 1992 operating income to be $645,000. Maple Company is subject to the following federal income tax rates:

First $100,000 of Income	18%
Second $100,000 of Income	24%
Next $100,000 of Income	31%
Excess over $300,000	37%

During the third quarter of 1992, Maple Company disposed of Segment Q's assets at a loss of $235,000. Segment Q had the following operating income to the disposal date:

First Quarter	$ 20,000
Second Quarter	(85,000)
Third Quarter	(62,000)

Maple Company reported operating income of $130,000 for the first quarter and $163,000 of operating income for the second quarter, all subject to tax.

Required (*Compute all percentages to the nearest 100th of a percent.*)

1. Determine the income tax expense to be reported on Maple's first and second quarter interim income statements.
2. Determine the income tax expense for continuing operating income for the third quarter if Maple had continuing operating income of $87,000 and estimates the fourth quarter's operating income will be $400,000.
3. Determine the income tax expense to be reported in the third quarter for all components of the discontinued operations.

EXERCISE 15-10

1. The following information pertains to Hay Corporation and its divisions for the year ended December 31, 1988:

Sales to Unaffiliated Customers	$ 1,000,000
Intersegment Sales of Products Similar to Those Sold to Unaffiliated Customers	300,000
Interest Earned on Loans to Other Industry Segments	20,000

Hay and all of its divisions are engaged solely in manufacturing operations. Hay has a reportable segment if that segment's revenue exceeds

a. $ 100,000
b. $ 102,000
c. $ 130,000
d. $ 132,000

2. Kaycee Corporation's revenues for the year ended December 31, 1992 were as follows:

Consolidated Revenue Per Income Statement	$ 1,200,000
Intersegment Sales	180,000
Intersegment Transfers	60,000
Combined Revenue of All Industry Segments	$ 1,440,000

Kaycee has a reportable segment if that segment's revenues exceed

a. $ 6,000
b. $ 24,000
c. $ 120,000
d. $ 144,000

(AICPA adapted)

EXERCISE 15-11

Kay Corporation and Lemco Company are conglomerates that operate in the same industries and are of approximately the same size and diversity. A financial analyst attempting to assess the future prospects of the two companies cannot understand why the segment reporting of these two very similar companies is not comparable.

Required

Describe how the determination of a segment and the allocation of common factors among segments can result in segment information that is not comparable.

EXERCISE 15-12

Wide Range Company has manufacturing operations in a number of different industries and locations. The following summary information has been determined to decide which industries or locations should be reported as separate segments:

Sales to Unaffiliated Customers	$ 5,000,000
Interunit Sales	500,000
Consolidated Revenues	5,300,000
Total Operating Profit of Profitable Units	650,000
Total Operating Profit of Nonprofitable Units	(700,000)
Consolidated Operating Profit	100,000
Identifiable Assets of Units	8,100,000
Consolidated Assets	7,800,000

Unit Alpha has sales to unaffiliated customers of $460,000, intersegment sales of $100,000, operating profit of $60,000, and identifiable assets of $790,000.

Required

1. Determine which reportable segment tests Unit Alpha meets if Unit Alpha is (a) a domestic segment, and (b) a foreign segment.
2. What additional test is necessary before completing the segment reporting? What is the amount the test requires and why is the test necessary?

EXERCISE 15-13

The following information has been determined to assist in the preparation of the segment reporting for Marble Company:

Segment	Revenues Unaffiliated	Revenues Intersegment	Revenues Total	Operating Profit or Loss	Identifiable Assets
A	$ 630,000	$ 20,000	$ 650,000	$(40,000)	$ 1,500,000
B	720,000	600,000	1,320,000	120,000	1,930,000
C	510,000	370,000	880,000	140,000	1,290,000
D	660,000	160,000	820,000	(100,000)	1,330,000
E	1,710,000	260,000	1,970,000	470,000	4,580,000
F	2,230,000	790,000	3,020,000	785,000	4,820,000
	6,460,000	2,200,000	8,300,000	1,375,000	15,450,000
Corporate Level	400,000	–0–	400,000	75,000	1,450,000
Total	6,800,000	2,200,000	8,700,000	1,450,000	16,900,000
Adjustments and Eliminations		(2,200,000)	(2,200,000)	(450,000)	(1,900,000)
Consolidated Totals	$ 6,800,000	$ –0–	$ 6,500,000	$ 1,000,000	$ 15,000,000

Required

1. Determine the reportable segments of Marble Company.
2. Determine if the reportable segments constiute sufficient information.
3. If segments B and F are domestic segments, and the remainder are foreign segments, determine the reportable segments.
4. Explain how segments that are not separately reportable are included in the schedule of segment information.

EXERCISE 15-14

1. In financial reporting for segments of a business enterprise, the revenue of a segment should include

a. intersegment sales of services similar to those sold to unaffiliated customers.
b. intersegment billings for the cost of shared facilities.
c. equity in income from unconsolidated subsidiaries.
d. extraordinary items.

2. In financial reporting for segments of a business enterprise, the operating profit or loss of a manufacturing segment should include

	Interest Expense	Income Taxes
a.	Yes	Yes
b.	Yes	No
c.	No	Yes
d.	No	No

3. In financial reporting for segments of a business enterprise, the operating profit or loss of a segment should include among other items

a. traceable costs.
b. foreign income taxes.
c. extraordinary items.
d. loss on discontinued operations.

4. In financial reporting for segments of a business enterprise, the operating profit or loss of a segment should include

a. income taxes.
b. expenses that relate to revenue from intersegment transfers.
c. equity in income from unconsolidated subsidiaries.
d. general corporate expenses.

5. In financial reporting for segments of a business enterprise, the operating profit or loss or a segment should include

	Expenses Related to Revenue from Intersegment Sales	Portion of General Corporate Expenses
a.	Yes	Yes
b.	Yes	No
b.	No	No
d.	No	Yes

6. In financial reporting for segments of a business enterprise, which of the following assets should be included as an identifiable asset of industry segment A?

a. An intangible asset used by industry segment A
b. An advance from nonfinancial industry segment A to another industry segment
c. An allocation of a tangible asset used for general corporate purposes, and **not** used in the operations of any particular industry segment
d. An allocation of a tangible asset used by another industry segment that transfers products to industry segment A

7. In Logan Company's financial reporting for segments of a business enterprise, which of the following assets should be included as an identifiable asset of the textile mill product industry segment?

a. A loan from the textile mill product segment to another industry segment
b. An investment by the textile mill product segment in another industry segment
c. An allocated portion of assets maintained for general corporate purposes and **not** used in the operations of the textile mill product segment
d. An allocated portion of intangible assets used jointly by the textile mill product segment and another industry segment

(AICPA adapted)

EXERCISE 15-15

1. Plains, Inc. engages in three lines of business. Each line is considered to be a significant industry segment. Company sales aggregated $1,800,000 in 1991, of which Segment No. 3 contributed 60%. Traceable costs were $600,000 for Segment No. 3 out of a total of $1,200,000 for the company as a whole. In addition, $350,000 of common costs are allocated based on the ratio of a segment's income before common costs to the total income before common costs. What should Plains report as operating profit for Segment No. 3 in 1991?

a. $ 200,000
b. $ 270,000
c. $ 280,000
d. $ 480,000

2. Hines Corporation reports operating profit as to industry segments in its supplementary financial information annually. The following information is available for 1991:

	Sales	Traceable Costs
Segment A	$ 750,000	$ 450,000
Segment B	500,000	225,000
Segment C	250,000	125,000
	$ 1,500,000	$ 800,000

Additional expenses not included above are

Indirect Operating Expenses	$ 240,000
General Corporate Expenses	180,000
Interest Expense	96,000

Hines allocates common costs based on the ratio of a segment's sales to total sales. What should be the operating profit for segment B for 1991?

a. $ 103,000
b. $ 135,000
c. $ 163,000
d. $ 195,000

3. Kee Company has five manufacturing divisions. Each division has been determined to be a reportable segment. Common costs are appropriately allocated on the basis of each division's sales in relation to Kee's aggregate sales. Kee's Sigma division comprised 40% of Kee's total sales in 1991. For the year ended December 31, 1991, Sigma had sales of $1,000,000 and traceable costs of $600,000. In 1991, Kee incurred operating expenses of $100,000 that were not directly traceable to any of the five divisions. In addition, Kee incurred interest expense of $80,000 in 1991. In reporting supplementary segment information, how much should be shown as Sigma's operating income for 1991?

a. $ 300,000
b. $ 328,000
c. $ 360,000
d. $ 400,000

(AICPA adapted)

EXERCISE 15-16

Nottingham Corporation is a large manufacturer of airplanes, including military cargo and fighter planes, and commercial cargo and passenger planes. A competitor of Nottingham's has just released a prototype of a revolutionary new commercial cargo plane. Nottingham has no new designs planned that can compete with this new prototype. Nottingham's commercial cargo plane business accounts for 50% of its sales. Nottingham's commercial cargo plane customers consist of four very large cargo carriers and 16 small airlines.

Required

1. What information about Nottingham would be useful to you if you were attempting to assess the impact of this new prototype on Nottingham's future income?
2. Do the requirements of *SFAS No. 14* provide the type of information you feel you need?
3. Would Nottingham be required to report segment data? What segmentation of the operations would be of the most use to you in assessing the impact of the competitor's edge over Nottingham?
4. If Nottingham issues interim statements, is it likely that the next quarterly report would provide you with adequate information to assess the impact on Nottingham's future income?

PROBLEMS

PROBLEM 15-1

The following statement is an excerpt from Paragraphs 9 and 10 of *Accounting Principles Board Opinion No. 28, Interim Financial Reporting:*

> Interim financial information is essential to provide investors and others with timely information as to the progress of an enterprise. The usefulness of such information rests on the relationship that it has to the annual results of operations. Accordingly, the Board has concluded that each interim period should be viewed primarily as an integral part of an annual period.
>
> In general, the results for each interim period should be based on the accounting principles and practices by an enterprise in the preparation of its latest annual financial statements unless a change in an accounting practice or policy has been adopted in the current year. The Board has concluded, however, that certain accounting principles and practices followed for annual reporting purposes may require modification at interim reporting dates so that the reported results for the interim period may better relate to the results of operations for the annual period.

Required

Listed below are six independent cases on how accounting facts might be reported in an individual company's interim financial reports. For each case, state if the proposed method is acceptable under generally accepted accounting principles applicable to interim financial data. Support each answer with a brief explanation.

1. Able Company wrote inventory down to reflect lower of cost or market in the first quarter of 1991. At year end the market exceeds the original acquisition cost of this inventory. Consequently, management plans to write the inventory back up to its original cost as a year-end adjustment.
2. Baker Company realized a large gain on the sale of investments at the beginning of the second quarter. The company wants to report one-third of the gain in each of the remaining quarters.
3. Carns Company has estimated its annual audit fee. The company plans to prorate this expense equally over all four quarters.
4. Denver Company was reasonably certain it would have an employee strike in the third quarter. As a result, it shipped heavily during the second quarter but plans to defer the recognition of the sales in excess of the normal sales volume. The deferred sales will be recognized as sales in the third quarter

when the strike is in progress. Denver Company's management believes this treatment is representative of normal second quarter and third quarter operations.

5. Edgar Company takes a physical inventory at year end for annual financial statement purposes. Inventory and cost of sales reported in the interim quarterly statements are based on estimated gross profit rates, because a physical inventory would result in a cessation of operations. Edgar does have reliable perpetual inventory records.

6. Farber Company is planning to report one-fourth of its pension expense in each quarter.

(CMA adapted)

PROBLEM 15-2

Monroe Company, a publicly traded company with 5 million shares of common stock outstanding, had the following results of operations for the first three quarters of 1991 in millions of dollars:

	First Quarter	Second Quarter	Third Quarter
Sales Revenue from Continuing Operations	$ 250.0	$ 354.5	$ 280.5
Cost of Goods Sold for Continuing Operations	150.0	200.0	172.0
Selling and Administrative Expenses	50.0	75.0	45.0
Extraordinary Gain	18.0		
Discontinued Operations		(41.0)	
Change in Accounting Principle			25.0

The following additional information has been determined regarding the revenues and expenses of Monroe Company:

■ Included in the selling and administrative expenses of the first quarter is $10 million of amortization of goodwill and $10 million of amortization of goodwill is also included in the selling and administrative expenses of the second quarter. The third quarter does not contain amortization as the business acquired has been discontinued.

■ Included in the selling and administrative expenses of the second quarter is the payment of property taxes in the amount of $14 million for the second, third, and fourth quarters of the current year and the first quarter of the following year.

■ Monroe's employees have a profit-sharing plan that entitles them to 10% of the annual operating profits before profit sharing and income taxes. Monroe has not accrued the profit-sharing expenses in compiling the interim income statement income information. The profit sharing should be recognized in the quarter based on the ratio of quarterly income earned before profit sharing to total expected positive quarterly income before profit sharing for the year.

■ Monroe's federal income tax rate is 34% and its state tax rate is 6% for all items subject to tax.

■ Based on the same accounting principles as the information for the first three quarters, Monroe estimates the fourth quarter will result in an operating loss of $16.5 million.

Required (Make all computations to the nearest $10,000.)

1. Prepare the interim income statements for the first, second, and third quarters for Monroe Company.
2. Describe the additional disclosures that Monroe is required to present in its interim report.
3. Is it necessary for Monroe to present a complete income statement in its interim reports? If not, what income information is required?

PROBLEM 15-3

Jefferson Company is a large publicly traded company that provides it investors with interim financial information. Jefferson Company builds and markets large pleasure boats, both power launches and sail boats. Although the production levels are constant throughout the year, the majority of the sales are concentrated in the months of April through August. Jefferson Company has been in operation for the past 15 years and has operated profitably for all but the first year. Jefferson Company has a fiscal year ending on September 30. The following are the estimated earnings, the actual earnings, and the estimated annual revenues and expenses not subject to tax:

Quarter	Quarterly Estimates of Annual Earnings	Actual Quarterly Earnings	Estimated Annual Revenues Not Subject to Tax	Estimated Annual Expenses Not Subject to Tax
1	$ 600,000	$ (50,000)	$ 10,000	$ 38,000
2	620,000	(85,000)	6,000	35,000
3	595,000	285,000	12,000	36,000

Jefferson Company is subject to the following federal income tax rates in addition to a 9% state income tax:

     16% on the first $100,000
     24% on the second $100,000
     32% on the next $100,000
     35% on income over $300,000

Required *(Compute all percentages to the nearest 100th of a percent.)*

1. Describe the manner of presentation of the interim information that is appropriate for the Jefferson Company and briefly explain why.
2. Determine the income tax expense or saving to be reported in the first three quarters of the current year.
3. During January of the current year, Congress reinstated the investment tax credit, effective April 1. Jefferson estimates that it will have $42,000 of credits for the year ended September 30. Determine the income tax expense for the first three quarters based on this revision.

PROBLEM 15-4

Salem Corporation operates in a volatile industry that has a pattern of high profit years and very low or negative profit years. Due to the excellent management of Salem Corporation, the company has been able to stay in business during the slow periods and has a higher level of profitability than its competitors in the good years. Salem Corporation has net operating income of $1,565,000 on which it has paid income taxes of $497,060 available to absorb current and future years' net operating losses. Salem Corporation estimates the following operating losses for the current year and anticipates that the industry downturn may not reverse for another year or more:

First Quarter	$ 250,000
Second Quarter	471,000
Third Quarter	364,000
Fourth Quarter	629,000
Total Operating Losses	$ 1,714,000

Required

1. What assumption is necessary about Salem Corporation's future profitability in order to report tax savings from all of the operating losses of the current year? Discuss why you would or would not record the tax savings from the operating loss carryforwards.

2. Determine the income tax saving to be reported in Salem Corporation's interim financial statements for the first three quarters, assuming the actual operating results were as estimated and the current prediction is that the industry may never recover from the downturn in business.
3. The following year, Salem Corporation estimated the company's quarterly income to be as follows:

First Quarter	$ 125,000 operating loss
Second Quarter	187,000 operating loss
Third Quarter	243,000 operating profit
Fourth Quarter	465,000 operating profit

Salem Corporation is currently subject to a flat tax of 34% and has tax credits of $28,540 available for use during the year. Determine the income tax expense or saving for the first three quarters, assuming the actual profit or loss equals the estimates.

PROBLEM 15-5

Pebble Company has prior years' income of $500,000 on which tax of $125,000 has been paid to absorb operating loss carrybacks. For 1992, Pebble Company estimates its operating income will be

First Quarter	$ 85,000
Second Quarter	40,000
Third Quarter	50,000
Fourth Quarter	25,000

Pebble Company is subject to a 5% state income tax and to the following graduated federal tax rates:

First $50,000 of Income	15%
Second $50,000 of Income	18%
Third $50,000 of Income	20%
Fourth $50,000 of Income	22%
Excess Over $200,000	25%

Pebble reported first-quarter operating income of $85,000 as estimated and reported a second-quarter operating loss of $(45,000). Pebble earned operating income of $20,000 for the third quarter, which included the operations of the Rock Division. During the third quarter, Pebble sold the net assets of the Rock Division at a loss of $120,000. The Rock Division had the following operating income to the measurement date:

First Quarter	$ (45,000)
Second Quarter	(65,000)
Third Quarter	(35,000)

Required

1. Determine the effective tax rate to be used in the first and second quarters, assuming that the Pebble Company believes its estimate of the third and fourth quarter's income is correct.
2. Determine the income tax expense (saving) for the first two quarters.
3. Determine the income tax expense (saving) for all items in the third quarter, assuming that Pebble now estimates its fourth quarter income will be $110,000.

PROBLEM 15-6

Prior to the issuance of *SFAS No. 14, Financial Reporting for Segments of a Business Enterprise*, the merits of segment reporting were hotly debated, as evidenced by the response to the objections to segment reporting contained in the standard.

Required

1. Present the arguments against segment reporting and defend and refute each of the arguments.

2. Present the arguments for segment reporting and defend and refute each position.

PROBLEM 15-7

Bend Company is a highly diversified publicly owned company operating in five distinctly different industries. The following information regarding the operations of the company for the current year has been developed for use in the company's segment reporting:

	Industry A	Industry B	Industry C	Industry D	Industry E
Sales to Unaffiliated Customers	$ 325,500	$ 279,000	$ 418,500	$ 209,250	$1,092,750
Sales to Other Industries	164,000	–0–	48,000	–0–	–0–
Cost of Goods Sold	189,000	150,000	246,000	115,000	529,000
Selling and Administrative					
Expenses	86,000	37,000	78,000	26,000	214,000
Identifiable Assets	1,100,000	543,000	1,300,000	412,000	3,253,000

The following additional information is determined:

- At the corporate level the revenues are $145,000 and the corporate expenses are $87,600.
- The corporation incurred costs that are considered common to all the industries of $424,000. These costs are not included in the above expenses and are to be allocated to the industry segments based on sales to unaffiliated customers.
- Industry E purchases all the intersegment sales of Industries A and C at a transfer price of 25% above cost. Industry E's beginning and ending inventories of intercompany purchases were approximately equal.
- In addition to the identifiable assets, the corporate assets totaled $346,000.
- Bend Company is subject to a flat income tax rate of 30%.

Required

1. Determine the net income of each of the industries.

2. Determine the industries to be reported as individual segments if Bend Company believes that the best segment division of the company is by industry.

3. Prepare the financial report of the segment information.

4. If the industries are each located in a different country, and only segment E is in the United States, determine the segments that would be reported separately, assuming each country is considered to be a segment.

PROBLEM 15-8

Diversified Inc. has divided the operations of the company into five profit centers. The following information is provided regarding the operations of each of the different profit centers:

	Profit Center A	Profit Center B	Profit Center C	Profit Center D	Profit Center E
Sales to Unaffiliated					
Customers	$ 136,000	$ 724,000	$ 185,000	$ 592,000	$ 106,000
Sales to Other Profit Centers	47,000	268,000	–0–	–0–	108,000
Operating Profit or Loss	(109,000)	178,000	18,000	(62,000)	14,000
Identifiable Assets	540,000	2,067,000	474,000	1,935,000	546,000

The wide variety of products and services that Diversified Inc. sells allows Diversified to determine the segments to be reported in a variety of combinations of the profit centers.

Required

For each of the following combinations of profit centers, determine which segments are reportable as domestic segments:

1. Each profit center is a separate segment.
2. Profit centers A and B are a segment, profit centers C and D are a segment, and profit center E is a segment.
3. Profit centers A and C are a segment, profit centers B and E are a segment, and profit center D is a segment.
4. Profit centers A and D are a segment, profit centers C and E are a segment, and profit center B is a segment.

PROBLEM 15-9

Many Products Company has provided the following information regarding its various industry segments:

Segment	Revenues Unaffiliated	Revenues Intersegment	Total	Operating Profit or Loss	Identifiable Assets
A	$ 630,000	$ 220,000	$ 850,000	$ 48,000	$ 6,130,000
B	720,000	80,000	800,000	113,000	4,590,000
C	1,510,000	–0–	1,510,000	(285,000)	4,463,000
D	660,000	450,000	1,110,000	464,000	4,870,000
E	1,230,000	–0–	1,230,000	209,000	8,940,000
F	2,560,000	–0–	2,560,000	(369,000)	9,620,000
G	940,000	–0–	940,000	(71,000)	4,340,000
H	860,000	–0–	860,000	140,000	4,790,000
I	1,450,000	–0–	1,450,000	485,000	6,310,000
J	1,340,000	498,000	1,838,000	510,000	3,190,000
	11,900,000	1,248,000	13,148,000	1,244,000	57,243,000
Corporate Level	400,000	–0–	400,000	10,000	892,000
Total	12,300,000	1,248,000	13,548,000	1,254,000	58,135,000
Adjustments and Eliminations		(1,248,000)	(1,248,000)	(326,000)	(1,245,000)
Consolidated Totals	$12,300,000	$ –0–	$12,300,000	$ 928,000	$ 56,890,000

The corporate level revenues consist of $265,000 of equity in income of unconsolidated subsidiaries and $135,000 of dividend revenue. The corporate level expenses consist of $100,000 of interest expense and $290,000 of general corporate expenses. The corporate level assets consist of $523,000 of general corporate assets and $369,000 of assets of the unconsolidated subsidiary.

Required

1. Prepare the schedule to disclose the required segment information.
2. In addition to the schedule, what information must also be disclosed with regard to segment reporting?
3. If segments A and B form a foreign geographic area, segments C, D, and E form a foreign geographic area, segments F and G form a foreign geographic area, and the remainder of the segments are in the United States, determine the geographic areas to be reported separately in the segment report.

SOLUTIONS TO REVIEW PROBLEMS

Interim Reporting

1. 1)

Total Estimated Income: Current Year	$ 2,200,000
Municipal Bond Interest Not Subject to Tax	(60,000)
Amortization of Goodwill Not Subject to Tax	100,000
Annual Income Subject to Tax	$ 2,240,000

Estimated Annual Income Tax Expense	
State Income Tax Expense	
Tax on First $500,000 at 5%	$ 25,000
Tax on Excess Over $500,000 at 3% ($1,740,000 × 3%)	52,200
Total State Income Tax Expense	77,200
Federal Income Tax Expense	
Tax on First $50,000 of Income at 15%	7,500
Tax on Second $50,000 of Income at 22%	11,000
Tax on Next $200,000 of Income at 28%	56,000
Tax on Excess Over $300,000 (($1,940,000 − $77,200) × 35%)	651,980
Total Federal Income Tax Expense	726,480
Total Estimated Tax Expense	$ 803,680

Estimated Effective Annual Tax Rate	
$803,680 ÷ $2,240,000 =	35.88%

Estimated Income Tax Expense First Quarter	
Income Earned in First Quarter	$ 800,000
Income Not Subject to Tax ($60,000 × 1/4)	(15,000)
Expenses Not Subject to Tax ($100,000 × 1/4)	25,000
Income Subject to Tax	810,000
Effective Income Tax Rate	35.88%
Estimated Income Tax Expense First Quarter	$ 290,628

2)

Estimated Annual Income Subject to Tax	
Actual First Quarter Income	$ 800,000
Actual Second Quarter Loss	(300,000)
Estimated Third Quarter Income	325,000
Estimated Fourth Quarter Income	625,000
Total Estimated Income	1,450,000
Municipal Bond Interest Not Subject to Tax	(60,000)
Amortization of Goodwill Not Subject to Tax	100,000
Annual Income Subject to Tax	$ 1,490,000

Estimated Annual Income Tax Expense
  State Income Tax Expense

Tax on First $500,000 at 5%	$ 25,000
Tax on Excess Over $500,000 at 3% ($990,000 × 3%)	29,700
Total State Income Tax Expense	54,700

  Federal Income Tax Expense

Tax on First $50,000 of Income at 15%	7,500
Tax on Second $50,000 of Income at 22%	11,000
Tax on Next $200,000 of Income at 28%	56,000
Tax on Excess Over $300,000 (($1,190,000 − $54,700) × 35%)	397,355
Total Federal Income Tax Expense	471,855
Total Estimated Tax Expense	$ 526,555

Estimated Effective Annual Tax Rate

$526,555 ÷ $1,490,000 =	35.34%

Estimated Income Tax Saving Second Quarter

Income Earned in First Two Quarters	$ 500,000
Income Not Subject to Tax ($60,000 × 2/4)	(30,000)
Expenses Not Subject to Tax ($100,000 × 2/4)	50,000
Income Subject to Tax	520,000
Effective Income Tax Rate	35.34%
Estimated Income Tax Expense First Two Quarters	183,768
Income Tax Expense First Quarter	290,628
Income Tax Saving Second Quarter	$(106,860)

3)

Estimated Annual Income Subject to Tax

Actual First Quarter Income	$ 800,000
Actual Second Quarter Loss	(300,000)
Actual Third Quarter Income	350,000
Estimated Fourth Quarter Income	450,000
Total Estimated Income	1,300,000
Municipal Bond Interest Not Subject to Tax	(60,000)
Amortization of Goodwill Not Subject to Tax	100,000
Annual Income Subject to Tax	$ 1,340,000

Estimated Annual Income Tax Expense
  State Income Tax Expense

Tax on First $500,000 at 5%	$ 25,000
Tax on Excess Over $500,000 at 3% ($840,000 × 3%)	25,200
Total State Income Tax Expense	50,200

Federal Income Tax Expense

Tax on First $50,000 of Income at 15%	7,500
Tax on Second $50,000 of Income at 22%	11,000
Tax on Next $200,000 of Income at 28%	56,000
Tax on Excess Over $300,000 (($1,040,000 − $50,200) × 35%)	346,430
Gross Federal Income Tax Expense	420,930
Estimated Tax Credits	50,130
Net Federal Income Tax Expense	370,800
Total Estimated Tax Expense	$ 421,000

Estimated Effective Annual Tax Rate

$421,000 ÷ $1,340,000 =   31.42%

Estimated Income Tax Expense Third Quarter

Income Earned in First Three Quarters	$ 850,000
Income Not Subject to Tax ($60,000 × 3/4)	(45,000)
Expense Not Subject to Tax ($100,000 × 3/4)	75,000
Income Subject to Tax	880,000
Effective Income Tax Rate	31.42%
Estimated Income Tax Expense First Three Quarters	276,496
Income Tax Expense First Two Quarters	183,768
Income Tax Expense Third Quarter	$ 92,728

2.

Estimated Annual Income Subject to Tax

Actual First Quarter Income	$ 800,000
Actual Second Quarter Loss	(300,000)
Actual Third Quarter Loss	(400,000)
Estimated Fourth Loss	(600,000)
Total Estimated Loss	(500,000)
Municipal Bond Interest Not Subject to Tax	(60,000)
Amortization of Goodwill Not Subject to Tax	100,000
Annual Income Subject to Tax	$ (460,000)

Estimated Effective Annual Tax Saving Rate

$165,600 ÷ $460,000 =   36.00%

Estimated Income Tax Saving Third Quarter

Income Earned in First Three Quarters	$ 100,000
Income Not Subject to Tax ($60,000 × 3/4)	(45,000)
Expenses Not Subject to Tax ($100,000 × 3/4)	75,000
Income Subject to Tax	130,000
Effective Income Tax Saving Rate	36.00%
Estimated Income Tax Expense First Three Quarters	46,800
Income Tax Expense First Two Quarters	183,768
Income Tax Saving Third Quarter	$(136,968)

3.

Estimated Income Tax Expense on Extraordinary Gain

State Tax Expense ($130,000 × 3%)	$ 3,900
Federal Tax Expense (($130,000 − $3,900) × 35%)	44,135
Total Estimated Tax Expense	$ 48,035

Note: If the gain had been more than the income remaining in a bracket, a portion of the tax is computed at the higher bracket rate.

4.

Total Estimated Income: Current Year (1)	$ 625,000
Municipal Bond Interest Not Subject to Tax	(60,000)
Amortization of Goodwill Not Subject to Tax	100,000
Annual Income Subject to Tax	$ 665,000

(1) $160,000 + $65,000 + $200,000 + $180,000 = $625,000

Estimated Annual Income Tax Expense	
State Income Tax Expense	
Tax on First $500,000 at 5%	$ 25,000
Tax on Excess Over $500,000 at 3% ($165,000 × 3%)	4,950
Total State Income Tax Expense	29,950
Federal Income Tax Expense	
Tax on First $50,000 of Income at 15%	7,500
Tax on Second $50,000 of Income at 22%	11,000
Tax on Next $200,000 of Income at 28%	56,000
Tax on Excess Over $300,000 (($365,000 − $29,950) × 35%)	117,268
Total Federal Income Tax Expense	191,768
Total Estimated Tax Expense	$ 221,718

Estimated Effective Annual Tax Rate	
$221,718 ÷ $665,000 =	33.34%

Estimated Income Tax Expense First Quarter	
Income Earned in First Quarter	$ 160,000
Income Not Subject to Tax ($60,000 × 1/4)	(15,000)
Expenses Not Subject to Tax ($100,000 × 1/4)	25,000
Income Subject to Tax	170,000
Effective Income Tax Rate	33.34%
Estimated Income Tax Expense First Quarter	$· 56,678

Income Segregated Between Continuing and Discontinued Operations

Quarter	Total Income	Discontinued Income	Continuing Income
First	$ 160,000	$ 20,000	$ 140,000 actual
Second	65,000	(45,000)	110,000 actual
Third	220,000		220,000 estimated
Fourth	180,000		180,000 estimated
	$ 625,000	$(25,000)	$ 650,000

Effective Tax Rate for Operating Income Without Discontinued Operations

Total Estimated Income: Current Year	$ 650,000
Municipal Bond Interest Not Subject to Tax	(60,000)
Amortization of Goodwill Not Subject to Tax	100,000
Annual Income Subject to Tax	$ 690,000

Estimated Annual Income Tax Expense

State Income Tax Expense	
Tax on First $500,000 at 5%	$ 25,000
Tax on Excess Over $500,000 at 3% ($190,000 × 3%)	5,700
Total State Income Tax Expense	30,700
Federal Income Tax Expense	
Tax on First $50,000 of Income at 15%	7,500
Tax on Second $50,000 of Income at 22%	11,000
Tax on Next $200,000 of Income at 28%	56,000
Tax on Excess Over $300,000 (($390,000 − $30,700) × 35%)	125,755
Total Federal Income Tax Expense	200,255
Total Estimated Tax Expense	$ 230,955

Estimated Effective Annual Tax Rate

$230,955 ÷ $690,000 =	33.47%

Estimated Income Tax Expense First Quarter's Continuing Income

Income Earned in First Quarter	$ 140,000
Income Not Subject to Tax ($60,000 × 1/4)	(15,000)
Expenses Not Subject to Tax ($100,000 × 1/4)	25,000
Income Subject to Tax	150,000
Effective Income Tax Rate	33.47%
Estimated Income Tax Expense Continuing Income	50,205
Tax as Originally Computed	56,678
Income Tax Expense Allocated to Discontinued Operation	$ 6,473

Income Tax Expense Second Quarter

Continuing Operating Income ($110,000 × 33.47)	$ 36,817

Discontinued Operation

Operating Loss

Allocated from First Quarter	$ 6,473

Second Quarter Tax Saving

State Tax ($45,000 × 3%)	(1,350)
Federal Tax ($45,000 − $1,350 × 35%)	(15,278)
Total Tax Saving	$(10,155)

Loss on Disposal of Assets

State Tax ($65,000 × 3%)	$(1,950)
Federal Tax ($65,000 − $1,950) × 35%	(22,068)
Total Tax Saving	$(24,018)

Segment Reporting

1.

Total Operating Income of Segments Operating at a Profit	$ 3,610,000

($525,000 + $230,000 + $780,000 + $475,000 + $1,520,000 + $80,000)

Total Operating Loss of Segments Operating at a Loss	$ 1,120,000

10% Tests for Segments

Revenue Test: $10,900,000 × 10% = $ 1,090,000

Operating Income Test: $ 3,610,000 × 10% = $ 361,000

Identifiable Asset Test: $22,125,000 × 10% = $ 2,212,500

Segment	Total Revenue More Than $ 1,090,000	Operating Profit or Loss More Than $ 361,000	Identifiable Assets More Than $ 2,212,500	Qualifies as a Reportable Segment
A	Yes	Yes	Yes	Yes
B	Yes	No	Yes	Yes
C	No	No	No	No
D	Yes	Yes	Yes	Yes
E	Yes	Yes	No	Yes
F	No	No	Yes	Yes
G	Yes	Yes	Yes	Yes
H	Yes	Yes	No	Yes
I	No	No	No	No

Overall Test: $9,000,000 × 75% = $ 6,750,000

The test is met as $9,000,000 − $400,000 − $480,000 = $ 8,120,000

2.

GLOBAL COMPANY
Segment Reporting
(Figures in Thousands of Dollars)

	A	B	D	E	F	G	H	Other Segments	Adjustments and Eliminations	Consolidated Totals
Revenues										
Unaffiliated Customers	$1,000	$ 550	$1,100	$ 850	$ 420	$3,300	$ 900	$ 880		$ 9,000
Intersegment Sales	150	550	440	250	510	–0–	–0–	–0–	$(1,900)	–0–
Total Revenues	$1,150	$1,100	$1,540	$1,100	$ 930	$3,300	$ 900	$ 880	$(1,900)	$ 9,000
Operating Profit	$ 525	$ 230	$ 780	$ 475	$(140)	$1,520	$(820)	$(80)	$(220)	$ 2,270
Dividend and Interest Revenue										
										600
Corporate Expenses										(320)
Interest Expense										(90)
Operating Income Before Income Taxes										
										$ 2,460
Identifiable Assets	$2,675	$2,340	$2,300	$1,400	$ 2,490	$5,190	$ 1,790	$ 3,940	$(425)	$ 21,700
Corporate Assets										2,875
Total Assets										$ 24,575

3. 10% Tests for a Foreign Segment

Revenue Test: $9,600,000 $\times$ 10% = $960,000

Identifiable Assets Test: $24,575,000 $\times$ 10% = $2,457,500

Segments A and D meet the revenue test and segment A meets the identifiable assets test. Therefore, segments A and D are reportable as foreign segments and segment G as a domestic segment. The remaining six segments are added together and reported as other, assuming the overall 75% test is met.

Overall Test

Operating Revenue of Reportable Segments:
$1,000,000 + $1,100,000 + $3,300,000 = $5,400,000

The overall test of revenue is not met. Segments E and H would be included to bring the revenue to $7,150,000.

REVENUE AND EXPENSE RECOGNITION THEORY AND ACCOUNTING FOR RETAIL LAND SALES

This chapter covers the theory of revenue and expense recognition for products and services and then applies the theory to real estate sales. Six methods can be used to account for these sales; accrual method, percentage-of-completion method, installment method, deposit method, reduced profit method, and the cost recovery method. The remainder of the chapter illustrates the accounting for retail land sales. Chapter 17 covers the accounting for other real estate sales and franchising. The topics of this chapter are

- The principles of revenue and expense recognition for both products and services including a discussion of when costs are capitalized
- The characteristics and revenue recognition for real estate sales
- The full accrual method including imputing interest and estimating defaults, the percentage-of-completion method, the accounting for actual defaults and repossessions, and the installment method of accounting for retail land sales
- The balance sheet presentation for the full accrual, percentage-of-completion, and installment methods for retail land sales
- The disclosure requirements for retail land sales
- The deposit method with conversion to the full accrual method
- The accounting for changing from the installment method to the percentage-of-completion method

REVENUE AND EXPENSE PRINCIPLES

The major emphasis of accounting in recent years has been the measurement and reporting of net income. Since the early 1960s, the income statement has been viewed as the most important of the financial statements, and the majority of the development in accounting theory has involved the measurement of net income. Generally accepted accounting principles currently require the following components to be included in determining the income of business enterprises:

- Operating income (operating revenues less operating expenses)
- Material gains and losses (unusual or infrequent items not classified as extraordinary by generally accepted accounting principles)
- Discontinued operations (net income and gains and losses from disposition of the segment)
- Extraordinary gains and losses
- Changes in accounting principles

Statement of Financial Accounting Concepts No. 6 defines comprehensive income as the change in the equity of an entity from transactions and other events and circumstances from nonowner sources.[1] Under this definition, net income, the excess of revenue over expense, includes all changes in equity except the additions of capital by owners and the distributions of assets to owners. Comprehensive income, as defined by *Statement of Financial Accounting Concepts No. 6*, is an "all-inclusive concept of income."[2] *Financial Accounting Concepts No. 5*, in contrast, defines "earnings" as composed of all the same elements as currently included in net income except the cumulative effect on prior years of a change in accounting principle.[3] Therefore, earnings, as defined by *Concepts Statement No. 5*, includes operating income (operating revenues less operating expenses), material gains and losses, net income and gains and losses from disposition of a segment, and extraordinary gains and losses.

At present, other changes in equity exist that are not included in income such as prior period adjustments, unrealized gains and losses from the valuing of long-term investments at the lower of cost or market, and translation adjustments from the consolidation of foreign subsidiaries. The all-inclusive concept of net income as proposed in *Financial Accounting Concept Statement No. 6* has met with opposition from those accountants and users who do not want the items presently excluded to affect the amount reported as net income. At this point in time we do not know if "comprehensive income" or "earnings" as defined by the concept statements will become accepted and used in practice because the concept statements are only advisory to the Financial Accounting Standards Board and not "authoritative pronouncements."

---

[1] *Statement of Financial Accounting Concepts No. 6, Elements of Financial Statements* (Stamford, Connecticut: FASB, 1985), paragraph 70.

[2] *SFAC No. 6*, paragraph 74.

[3] *Statement of Financial Accounting Concepts No. 5, Recognition and Measurement in Financial Statements of Business Enterprises,* (Stamford, Connecticut: FASB, 1984), paragraph 33.

REVENUE PRINCIPLES

Statement of Financial Accounting Concepts No. 6 defines revenue as an increase in assets and/or a decrease in liabilities during an accounting period from delivering goods, rendering services, or other activities constituting the entity's ongoing major or central operations.[4] The Statement defines expenses as a decrease in assets and/or an increase in liabilities during an accounting period from delivering goods, rendering services, or other activities constituting the entity's ongoing major or central operations.[5] Under the realization concept, revenue is recognized (recorded) when the earning process is complete or virtually complete, and revenue is evidenced by the existence of an exchange transaction.[6] *Statement of Financial Accounting Concepts No. 5* states that revenue is recognized when (1) it is realized or realizable and (2) it has been earned.[7] Therefore, the basic revenue recognition principle, called the sales principle, is that revenue from the sale of goods or the provision of services is recognized at the time of sale of the goods or the provision of the services.

The realization and recognition concepts imply that a sale of goods or services to an outside party is an exchange between two unrelated parties that has added either to the cash or to the trade receivables or other assets of the seller. The principles also assume that the exchange between the unrelated parties has resulted in an exchange price, which represents the fair market value of the goods or services. Recognizing revenue when the earning process is complete and an exchange has occurred seems like a very simple process. The application of these basic tenets in practice is difficult, however, as many situations do not precisely fit the assumptions of the basic principles. In addition, differences exist between the recognition of revenue from the sale of a product versus revenue from the provision of services.

PRODUCT REVENUES

Until the 1980s, generally accepted accounting principles primarily established guidelines for the recognition of revenues from the sale of products. Revenues from services were considered either incidental or not material; therefore, principles were unnecessary. In our present economy, service revenues constitute a major portion of all revenues, and generally accepted principles for the recognition of service revenues are just beginning to be developed. Since 1985, standards have been issued that cover such topics as broadcasting, banking, cable television, computer software, futures contracts, regulated enterprises, and stockbrokerage. This list indicates the shift in emphasis from products to services, and also indicates that some of the topics are a combination of products and services.

Beside the general guidelines in the *Financial Accounting Concepts Statements Nos. 5 and 6* of the Financial Accounting Standards Board, and the earlier guidance found in *Accounting*

---

[4] *SFAC No. 6*, paragraph 78.

[5] *SFAC No. 6*, paragraph 80.

[6] *Statement of Accounting Principles Board No. 4, Basic Concepts and Accounting Principles Underlying the Financial Statements of Business Enterprises* (New York: AICPA, 1970), paragraphs 148 and 150.

[7] *SFAC No. 5*, paragraph 83.

Principles Board Statement No. 4 of the American Institute of Certified Public Accountants, a number of pronouncements exist that cover specific product and service situations. The majority of these pronouncements deal with situations where the application of the general recognition principles does not fit the particular situations. *Financial Accounting Concepts Statement No. 5,* paragraph 84, provides examples of the exceptions to the point of sale recognition of revenue.

EXCEPTIONS TO THE RECOGNITION PRINCIPLE

A number of exceptions exist in the practice of accounting to the two requirements for the recognition of revenue: (1) an exchange has taken place and the product has been delivered, and (2) the earning process is either complete or virtually complete.

TRANSACTION COMPLETED

The most common exception to the requirement that a transaction has been completed is the accrual of interest. Interest is recognized as time passes because of the assumption that it is earned ratably over time. Therefore, interest is accrued at the end of the accounting period, assuming reasonable assurance of collectibility, even though a transaction has not taken place for the interest. It can be argued, however, that the transaction that generated the interest, the lending of money, has already taken place. Thus the borrower is legally bound to pay the interest, and the amount and timing of the payments for interest are known.

EARNING PROCESS COMPLETE

A number of exceptions exist to recognizing revenue when the earning process is complete or virtually complete. In some cases, revenue is recognized prior to the completion of the earning process, and in others, the recognition of revenue is postponed beyond the point in time when the earning process is complete. Other exceptions to the recognition of revenue also exist because of the distortion of income that occurs if the recognition of revenue is postponed until the earning process is complete.

For instance, when accounting for long-term construction contracts using the percentage-of-completion method, revenue and expense are recognized throughout the life of the contract, even though the asset is not completed and the purchaser does not have possession of the asset. In this case, the accountant relies on the fact that the contract sets a firm price for the asset so that revenue is measurable, and the purchaser is legally obligated to pay the contract price, and the seller is legally obligated to construct the asset. The method assumes that reasonable estimates can be made of the amount of the asset that is completed and/or yet to be completed.

Some commodities are sold in organized markets where the sale and the selling price are virtually assured and the costs of selling the product are insignificant. These commodities— such as grain, pork bellies, and precious metals—have two characteristics in common: all units of the product are identical, and it is not possible to distinguish one unit from another unit. For example, it is not possible to distinguish one bar of gold from another, or one bushel of rye grass from another. Revenue is recognized at the completion of production and not delayed until the sales transaction occurs.

In some situations, the transaction precedes the recognition of revenue. For instance, a customer may purchase a subscription to a magazine or order a limited series of artwork, such as sculptures, paintings, or prints. The customer has entered into a contract with the seller and paid for the goods, but has not received the product purchased. Revenue is recognized when the goods are completed and delivered. The revenue from the magazine subscription is recognized over time as each edition is printed and mailed to the subscriber.

The opposite situation occurs when uncertainty exists regarding the completion of the transaction that is generating the revenue, and/or the collection of the receivable is questionable and estimation of the losses is unreliable. The recognition of revenue is postponed until the cash is received in order to have reliable evidence that the earning process is complete, or that collection is possible.

For example, the deposit method and the cost recovery method are used for real estate sales because of the inability to predict whether or not realization of the revenue will ultimately occur. In addition, in some situations, the question arises as to whether or not the agreement between the buyer and the seller really constitutes a sale of goods. In these situations, a decision must be reached as to whether the buyer has made a sufficient investment to constitute a purchase of an asset and whether the seller has completed enough of the seller's responsibilities to say that the earning process is complete and that revenue can be recognized. These issues arise in accounting for real estate sales and franchises.

In other situations, the realization has occurred, but the ability to collect the selling price is questionable and reliable estimates of the potential losses are not possible. The installment method is used to recognize revenue. The installment method recognizes a portion of the gross profit from the sale as cash is collected. The installment method is generally used in sales to consumers where payments are received over time, such as with the sale of furniture, appliances, and stereos. In retail land sale developments, the installment method is also used because of the inability to estimate collectibility.

DETERMINATION OF THE TRANSACTION PRICE

Another difficulty in the recognition of revenue is determining the transaction price of the goods being sold. If the payment for goods is to be received over extended periods of time, the question arises as to what portion of the cash to be received is for the asset being sold and what portion is for the use of the seller's funds over the time of payment. If the contract does not specify the portion of the total amount being received that represents the price of the goods or the amount of the interest revenue, the fair market value of the product being sold needs to be determined.

If the measurement of the fair market value is not possible, or if the interest rate is not a reasonable one, *Accounting Principles Board Opinion No. 21* requires that a normal interest rate be imputed.[8] The selling price is assumed to be both the price of the goods sold and the

---

[8] *Opinions of the Accounting Principles Board No. 21, Interest on Receivable and Payables* (New York: AICPA, 1971), paragraph 12.

price to be received for the use of the seller's funds over time. The imputing of the interest rate is the process of allocating the face amount of the debt instrument received between the selling price of the goods and the interest to be earned from the lending of funds using the market rate of interest. In retail land sales, interest is often imputed because the rates of interest charged are below the normal rates that the purchasers would have to pay a lending institution for the money.

SERVICE REVENUES

Until recent years, the rules for the recognition of revenue from the provision of services were really *generally accepted,* as no principles had been promulgated that dealt directly with service revenues other than the general criteria established in *Statement of Accounting Concepts Nos. 5 and 6.* As mentioned earlier, many of the recent pronouncements are dealing with industries that provide services or provide a combination of products and services.

The revenues from the provision of services can be divided into four major categories: specific performance, proportional performance, completed performance, and collection. These groups are similar to the different divisions discussed for product revenues. In specific performance, revenue is recognized at the completion of a single service, which is similar to the point of sale recognition of a product. For example, a broker receives a commission for selling a block of securities, or a physician receives a fee for performing an operation, or an attorney receives a fee for writing a will, or an art gallery receives a commission for selling an artist's painting. Specific performance exists in accounting for the recognition of revenue from franchising.

In proportional performance, the provision of services extends beyond one accounting period with more than one performance act. These multiperformance acts can be classified into three different groups: ongoing similar performance acts, fixed-term similar performance acts, and dissimilar performance acts. If the acts are similar, time is used as the basis for allocating revenue between accounting periods. If the acts are dissimilar, the revenue is allocated based on the value of the various services provided to the customer.

The recognition by the manager of a trust of one-twelfth of the annual fee as revenue each month, even though the fee is paid annually, is an example of an ongoing performance act. An example of a fixed-term similar performance act is a franchisor who agrees to provide management advisory services to a franchisee over the 10-year life of the franchise for a lump-sum price. The franchisor usually allocates the total fee over the 10-year period on the straight-line basis. A third example is one in which a landscaping service contracts to provide total care of a homeowner's property. The services to be provided include planting of trees, shrubs, and lawn; pruning and spraying of trees and shrubbery; mowing of lawn; weeding of flower beds; and layering of mulch to prevent weeds and soil erosion. The landscaper is providing a variety of services that are dissimilar and not of equal value. The landscaper recognizes revenue using some basis other than time. In this case, the price received for the services is recognized as revenue in relation to the direct costs that the landscaper incurred for providing each of the various activities.

If the last act provided as a service is crucial to the purchaser of the service, the service revenue is not recognized until the final act is completed. In completed performance, the various service acts may be similar or they may be different. For example, an accounting firm hires a moving company to pack and load the contents of its present office, deliver them to the new office, and unload and unpack them at the new location. Because the unpacking at the new office is critical to the accounting firm, the moving company does not recognize the revenue until the contents moved are in place at the new location.

If the collection of the cash from the provision of a service is questionable and estimating the loss from uncollectibility is unreliable, then, just as with the sale of a product, the recognition of revenue is postponed until the cash is received. The cash can be a single payment or a series of payments over time. For example, an accounting firm provides audit and tax services to a client whose financial position is precarious and the likelihood that the client will fail and not be able to pay the fee is not determinable. In this case, the accounting firm uses the cash basis to recognize the revenue rather than the accrual method. If the payments are received over time, the installment method is used.

EXPENSE PRINCIPLES

Statement of Financial Accounting Concepts No. 6 defines expense as decreases in assets and/or increases in liabilities during a period from delivering goods, rendering services, or other activities constituting the entity's ongoing major or central operations.[9] The basic characteristics of expenses are

- sacrifices involved in carrying out the earning process,
- actual or expected cash outflows resulting from central operations, and
- gross outflows of net assets.[10]

Therefore, expenses are expired costs or assets that no longer have future value. The primary goal in expense recognition is the matching of expense with revenue. Expenses can be categorized in a number of ways. *Financial Accounting Concepts Statement No. 5* divides expenses into direct expenses, period expenses, and allocated expenses.[11]

EXPENSES RELATED TO SALES OF PRODUCTS

The expenses may be matched because they have a direct association with the product, such as the purchase price of goods sold, freight-in, and warehousing costs. Expenses may be costs of the current period that have no future benefit, such as selling and administrative salaries, and, therefore, are expensed in the current period. Other expenses, such as depreciation, insurance, interest, and rent are expensed in the period in which the benefit is received. The process of recognition of these costs as expenses is one of systematic and rational allocation to expense over time.

---

[9] *SFAC No. 6*, paragraph 74.

[10] *SFAC No. 6*, paragraphs 81 and 87.

[11] *SFAC No. 5*, paragraph 85.

EXPENSES RELATED TO SALES OF SERVICES

Expenses that relate to service revenues can be categorized as either direct expenses or indirect expenses. In addition, the direct expenses are generally divided into two groups: initial direct expenses and other direct expenses. The concept statements do not address the categorization of expenses related to sales of services and this categorization is the one most commonly used in generally accepted accounting principles.

Direct Expenses.   The initial direct expenses are the costs that were incurred to negotiate and consummate a service-type transaction. These expenses can include legal fees, sales salaries and commissions, and employee compensation for negotiating and closing the agreement. The other direct expenses are costs that are incurred to satisfy the conditions of sale. For example, a company develops a computer system for a business, and agrees to provide assistance and problem solving for a period of two years after the installation of the system. The expenses of the assistance and problem solving over the two-year period are necessary to the sale and have a direct association with the original service revenue. Therefore, the costs are classified as other direct expenses.

When the initial and other direct costs are recognized depends on the type of performance method for the recognition of the revenue. If the service revenue is recognized either by the specific performance or the completed performance methods, then the expense is recognized when the revenue is recognized. If costs are incurred prior to the recognition of the revenue, they are recorded as prepayments until the revenue is recognized; then they are recognized as expenses. If the service revenue is not recognized until the cash is collected, all the direct costs are recorded as assets and recognized as expense when the cash is collected. If the service revenue is of a proportional nature, then the initial direct costs are recognized as expense when the revenue is recognized using a comparable proportion. The other direct costs, which are similar to period expenses for the sales of products, are generally expensed as incurred, because this achieves a good matching with the revenue over long periods of time.

Indirect Expenses.   The indirect expenses of providing service revenues, such as general advertising, administrative expenses, and costs associated with unsuccessful efforts are expensed as incurred. These costs are recognized as expense in a systematic and rational manner, which is the same approach that is used when an entity sells a product.

COSTS THAT ARE CAPITALIZED

The recognition of revenue and the matching of expense with that revenue is the emphasis in the discussion of real estate sales and franchising. Another area of concern is when should the cost be expensed and when should the cost remain an asset. In general, the costs are capitalized (recorded as assets), if the revenue they relate to has not been recognized. The costs are capitalized beause they have future service benefit to the entity. For example, interest incurred during the construction of capital assets is capitalized rather than expensed since the issuance of *Statement of Financial Accounting Standards No. 34.*[12] This statement is the result of

---

[12] *Statement of Financial Accounting Standards No. 34, Capitalization of Interest Cost* (Stamford, Connecticut: FASB, 1975).

the determination that the interest incurred is a part of the cost of the asset and not an expense of the period. For a product, the direct costs are included in inventory until the revenue is realized and delivery has been made. For services, the direct costs are recorded as prepayments until the revenue is recognized.

REAL ESTATE SALES

In 1982, the Financial Accounting Standards Board issued Statements of Financial Standards Nos. 66 and 67, which are conversions of previously issued Industry Accounting and Auditing Guides into Statements of Financial Accounting Standards. *Statement No. 66* defines retail land sales as sales, on a volume basis, of lots that are subdivisions of large tracts of land.[13] All other real estate development projects are **nonretail** land sales or other real estate sales. These include housing developments, condominium projects, time-share projects, and mobile home projects. In addition, any sale of real estate other than a retail land sale is covered by the Statements and classified as **other.**

REVENUE RECOGNITION FOR ALL REAL ESTATE SALES

Because of the ingenuity and creativity of developers in marketing and writing contracts for real estate sales, we must analyze the substance of the transaction specified in the sales contract and not rely on the particular form of the terms of sale. Real estate sales are typically characterized by payments over time, often with low down payments, with stated interest rates below the market rates of interest, and promises for improvements and amenities on the part of the developer. The characteristics of real estate sales are reflected in the criteria for revenue recognition established in *Statements of Financial Accounting Standards Nos. 66 and 67.*

From the buyer's standpoint, the questions of whether the substance of the transaction was a sale, and whether the buyer will pay the full amount of the purchase price must be answered. Has the buyer invested sufficient assets and will the buyer continue to invest sufficient assets to assume the real estate was sold or has a deposit been made on the real estate? If the investment is sufficient, then the issue is whether the buyer will complete the payments or default. If the buyer may default, can the developer adequately estimate the amount of uncollectible accounts and/or the losses from repossession? From the seller's standpoint the question of whether the revenue has been realized or is realizable must be answered. Are all the improvements and amenities that the developer is expected to provide complete? If they are not complete, does the developer have the financial resources to complete the obligations to the buyer according to the sales contract?

---

[13] *Statement of Financial Accounting Standards No. 66, Accounting for Sales of Real Estate* (Stamford, Connecticut: FASB, 1982), paragraph 100.

COSTS TO BE CAPITALIZED AND EXPENSE RECOGNITION

Clearly, all costs that are directly associated with the development of a real estate project are capitalized as part of the cost of the project including interest on the debt, insurance, and property taxes incurred during the completion of the project. The indirect costs, that are usually classified as general and administrative expenses in an income statement, are an expense of the period.

Real estate developers frequently include a number of amenities to make a project attractive to the purchaser or renter, which may include a golf course, tennis courts, jogging and bicycle paths, swimming pools, gymnasiums, saunas, boating facilities, restaurants, shopping areas, parking lots, and landscaping. The accounting treatment of the cost of the amenities depends on what the developer intends and has agreed to do with regard to the amenities. In some real estate sales, the development company might say, "They hope to be able to build a golf course, but make no guarantees that it will be built." If and when the golf course is built, it is an expense of the project.

In some cases the development company has committed itself to the completion of certain amenities. The question that needs to be addressed then is, "Who will own the amenities once they are completed?" Will each purchaser own a portion of the amenities when completed, or will the developer sell the amenities separately from the units being sold, or will the developer retain ownership? If the purchaser will have ownership, the costs of construction are capitalized and allocated to each sale. If the developer intends to sell the amenities separately or retain ownership, the costs incurred to develop the amenities, to their fair market value, is the cost of the amenities to the developer. Any costs in excess of the fair market value are recorded as part of the capitalized cost of the units being sold. The logic of this approach is that the developer has incurred the extra costs of the amenity in order to be able to sell the units.

In the process of attempting to sell a real estate development project, be it homesites, homes, condominiums, time-shares, or shopping centers, substantial sums can be spent on promoting the project. The marketing costs might include model units, furnishings and decor items for model units, permanent signs, legal fees, sales salaries, and promotional expenditures such as television and radio commercials, newspaper and magazine advertising, brochures, and free gifts if you just "come and see." *Statement of Financial Accounting Standards No. 67* permits the capitalization of only those costs incurred for tangible assets and/or services to obtain regulatory approval of sale that will be recovered from the sale of the real estate project.[14]

RETAIL LAND SALES

Statement of Financial Accounting Standards No. 66 states that retail land sales are characterized by the following:

- Down payments that are so small that local lending institutions would not loan money on the property at the market rates of interest without substantial discounts.

---

[14] *Statement of Financial Accounting Standards No. 67, Accounting for the Costs and Initial Operations of Real Estate Projects* (Stamford, Connecticut: FASB, 1982), paragraph 17.

- The seller is unable to enforce the sales contract or to collect the buyer's note.
- The buyer has a refund (cancellation) period in which the contract can be canceled and all monies paid are refunded.
- If the buyer defaults after the cancellation period, the only recourse the seller has is repossession of the land and forfeiture of a portion of the principal payments.[15]

In general, revenue is recognized when the earning process is complete or virtually complete and an arm's length exchange has taken place. Expenses are matched with the revenue and recognized during the same period of time that the revenue is recognized. When accounting for retail land sales, the full accrual method (point-of-sale recognition), the percentage-of-completion method, the installment method, or the deposit method may be used depending on the conditions and circumstances of the project and the substance of the terms of sale.

In order to determine the appropriate method, the criteria established by *Statement No. 66* are applied to the methods in the following order: full accrual, percentage-of-completion, installment, and deposit.[16] Therefore, if the criteria for full accrual are met, that method is used; if not, the accountant determines if the percentage-of-completion method can be used. If the percentage-of-completion method cannot be used, the accountant determines if the installment method can be used. If the criteria for use of any of the three methods is not met, then the deposit method, which does not recognize the existence of a sale, is used.

The full accrual, percentage-of-completion, and installment methods all require that the refund period be expired and that the buyer has made sufficient payments on the lot to consider the transaction a sale. The difference between the criteria for full accrual and the percentage-of-completion method is whether or not all the improvements and amenities, such as golf courses, swimming pools, and jogging paths, are complete or not yet constructed. The difference between the criteria for the percentage-of-completion and the installment methods is the inability to estimate collectibility and the status of the improvements and amenities. Because of the ordering of the methods by generally accepted accounting principles, the methods are discussed and illustrated in the above order.

FULL ACCRUAL METHOD OF ACCOUNTING

The full accrual method, which recognizes revenue and expense as soon as the refund period is past, is based on the following five criteria, which *must* all be met to use the full accrual method:

1. **Expiration of Refund Period.** The buyer has made the down payment and all required periodic payments during the refund period. The refund period is the longest of the period required by law, by the sales contract, or by the seller's policy.
2. **Sufficient Periodic Payments.** The total payments made by the buyer, including interest, equal or exceed 10% of the contract price.
3. **Collectibility of Receivables.** Past experience, either of this project or comparable prior projects of the seller, indicates that at least 90% of the contracts that exist after

---

[15] *SFAS No. 66*, paragraph 100.

[16] *SFAS No. 66*, paragraph 100.

the refund period will still be valid six months after the refund period. A contract is valid if the buyer is making the payments and the seller is not repossessing the property. Alternatively a down payment of 20% or more is considered adequate proof of collectibility.

4. **Nonsubordination of Receivables.** The contract is not subject to subordination of new loans, except for loans for the construction of a home.
5. **Completion of the Development.** The seller has completed all the improvements and amenities that are required in the contract of sale and is not obligated to any additional improvements or amenities.[17]

Criteria 1 and 2 answer the question of whether the buyer has made a purchase or only a deposit. Criteria 3 deals with collectibility of the buyer's obligation, and criteria 4 establishes whether or not the seller can repossess the property. Criteria 5 addresses the issue of whether the product has been completed by the seller and, therefore, revenue realized.

IMPUTING INTEREST AND ESTIMATING DEFAULTS

Some states have laws that give the buyer 30 or more days in which to cancel the contract of sale and receive a full refund of all monies paid. These laws are designed to protect "innocent" consumers from high-pressure salesmanship. Some developers, even if not required by law to do so, grant a full or partial refund if the contract is canceled within a specified length of time and/or grant longer refund period than the law requires. Any portion of the payments received during the refund period that is not returned to the purchaser is revenue of the period when the contract was signed. Once the refund period is past, the criteria for use of the full accrual method are tested against the substance of the transaction.

The characteristics of retail land sales result in two complexities in accounting for the retail sale of lots or homesites. In order to sell a land development, a developer typically requires only a small down payment and charges an interest rate for the balance of the contract that is substantially below the normal rate of interest the buyer would pay a lending institution for the purchase of the land. *Accounting Principles Board Opinion No. 21* requires that the sales revenue be the fair market value of the property or, if unknown, a normal rate of interest be imputed to the transaction when the rate contained in the contract is substantially below the normal rate.[18] This procedure results in the net receivable (gross receivable less the valuation discount) from the land sale being equal to the net present value of the contract balance. The interest revenue, from amortizing the valuation discount account and from the interest actually paid in accordance with the contract, is a constant percentage of the net receivable balance.

To illustrate, assume that a lot is sold for $10,000. The contract of sale requires the buyer to make a 10% down payment ($1,000) and to pay the remaining $9,000 plus interest at 8% in four equal annual payments. The annual payment is computed by dividing the balance owing ($9,000) by the present value of an annuity for four periods at 8% (3.3121). Therefore,

---

[17] *SFAS No. 66*, paragraph 45.

[18] *Account Principles Board Opinion No. 21, Interest on Receivables and Payables* (New York: AICPA, 1971), paragraph 12.

the annual payment is $2,717, the total amount to be paid is $10,868 ($2,717 × 4), and the total interest to be paid is $1,868 ($10,868 − $9,000).

   If the buyer had borrowed the money from a local lending institution, the interest rate would have been 12%. To compute the valuation discount that will make interest revenue equal to 12% of the net receivable (gross receivable − valuation discount), the net present value of the annual payments is subtracted from the face amount of the total payments. The net present value of the contract payments at 8% is the contract balance of $9,000. The net present value of the contract payments at the market rate of interest is the annual payment ($2,717) multiplied by the present value of an annuity for the number of payments at the market rate of interest (four payments at 12%). The calculation is

Balance Owing on Retail Land Contract	$ 9,000
Less: Net Present Value of the Annual Payments at the Market Rate of Interest	
($2,717 × 3.0373)	8,252
Valuation Discount	$ 748

The down payment is excluded as interest is charged only on the unpaid balance of the selling price and the present value of the down payment is the dollar amount of the down payment.

   The effect of applying the requirements of *Accounting Principles Board Opinion No. 21* is to divide the total amount to be paid by the buyer between the discounted contract price of the land, which is recognized as sales revenue in the current period, and the revenue from interest, which will be recognized over the life of the contract in the following manner:

	Total Paid	Discounted Contract Price	Interest Revenue
Down Payment	$ 1,000	$ 1,000	
Payments to be Received			
Principal	9,000	8,252	$ 748
Interest	1,868		1,868
Total Cash Paid by the Buyer	$ 11,868	$ 9,252	$ 2,616

The revenue from the sale of the lot is the contract price less the valuation discount or the discounted contract price. The interest revenue to be recognized over the life of the contract is the interest paid according to the terms of the contract plus the amount of the valuation discount.

   The second complexity is the estimation of the expected losses from contract defaults and repossessions after the refund period. The amount of the estimated losses is treated as a reduction of the sales revenue of the period. The estimated loss amount is recorded in an adjusting entry that creates a contra (valuation) sales revenue account and establishes a contract receivable allowance account. When a buyer actually defaults the loss is charged against the allowance account.

   Illustrative Problem 16.1, which is an extension of the previous one-lot example, demonstrates the determination of revenue from a retail land development, the journal entries that are recorded, and Exhibit 16-3 shows the income statement items that are reported over the life of the contract. The effect of actual default, repossession, and resale are omitted and illustrated after all three methods of recognizing revenue are discussed.

ILLUSTRATIVE PROBLEM 16.1: FULL ACCRUAL METHOD FOR RETAIL LAND SALES

Albany Development Company has subdivided a tract of land into 60 homesites. The terms of sale require a $1,000 down payment with the balance of $9,000 plus interest at 8% to be paid in four equal annual installments with the first payment due on the first day of the following year. The market rate of interest is 12%. On January 1, 1991, all the lots are sold, but the developer expects that five buyers will default after the 60-day refund period, based on the company's experience with similar projects. No refunds were paid and no notifications of default were received during the first year.

	Per Lot	60 Lots[a]	55 Lots[a]
Sales Data			
Selling Price	$ 10,000	$ 600,000	$ 550,000
Down Payment	1,000	60,000	55,000
Contract Balance	$ 9,000	$ 540,000	$ 495,000
Cost Data			
Land Cost	$ 2,400	$ 144,000	$ 132,000
Land Improvements, All Complete	1,000	60,000	55,000
Sales Commission Paid on All Lots			
Initially Sold	800	48,000	48,000
Present Value of Payments at 8% Interest			
Contract Balance	$ 9,000	$ 540,000	$ 495,000
Present Value of an Annuity of 4			
Payments at 8%	÷ 3.3121	÷ 3.3121	÷ 3.3121
Annual Payment at 8% Interest	2,717	163,020	149,435
Number of Payments	× 4	× 4	× 4
Present Value of Payments	$ 10,868	$ 652,080	$ 597,740
Present Value of Payments at 12% Interest			
Annual Payment at 8% Interest	$ 2,717	$ 163,020	$ 149,435
Present Value of an Annuity of 4			
Payments at 12%	× 3.0373	× 3.0373	× 3.0373
Present Value of Payments	$ 8,252	$ 495,120	$ 453,860

[a]The values are multiples of the Per Lot column and will not compute precisely.

The journal entries for the costs incurred prior to the sale of the lots are

Land and Improvements Inventory	144,000	
Cash and/or Contract Payable		144,000
To record the purchase of a tract of land		
Land and Improvements Inventory	60,000	
Cash and/or Accounts Payable		60,000
To record the cost of land improvements		

The journal entries for the sale of the lots and the payment of the sales commissions on January 1, 1991 are

Cash	60,000	
Contracts Receivable	540,000	
Sales Revenue		600,000
To record the initial sale of the lots		

Direct Selling Costs	48,000	
Cash		48,000
To record the commissions paid for sales of the lots		

In order to recognize the correct amount of sales revenue, the gross sales revenue is adjusted for both the valuation discount and the allowance for cancellation losses. The calculation of the valuation discount for the 55 estimated valid sales contracts is

Present Value of Collectible Contracts Receivable	
At 8% Stated Rate of Interest	$ 495,000
At 12% Market Rate of Interest	453,860
Valuation Discount	$ 41,140

The calculation of the anticipated losses from five contract cancellations the company expects is

Gross Sales Contracts Expected to be Canceled	$ 50,000
Less: Down Payments Received and Retained (5 × $1,000)	5,000
Losses Expected from Canceled Contracts	$ 45,000

The adjusting journal entry for the valuation discount and expected cancellation losses is

Sales Revenue	86,140	
Discount on Contracts Receivable		41,140
Allowance for Cancellation Losses		45,000
To adjust sales revenue for the market rate of interest and the anticipated losses		

The journal entry to recognize the cost of land and land improvements for the 55 valid sales of lots for 1991, the year of sale, is

Cost of Sales	187,000	
Land and Improvements Inventory		187,000
To record the land costs for the period		
($132,000 + $55,000 = $187,000)		

This entry assumes that the developer incurred equal costs for each lot or elected to allocate costs based on selling price, which in this example is the same for every lot. If lot prices varied, the relative sales value of the lots is used to allocate the total costs between the various lot sales.

The final adjusting entry for the period records the interest revenue on the contracts receivable. For simplicity and to illustrate the recognition of revenue, all the sales were made on the first day of the year and the first installment is due on the first day of the following year. In practice, the interest calculations are made on a contract by contract basis, recognizing interest for the portion of the year each contract had been outstanding.

Interest Receivable (Exhibit 16-1)	39,600	
Discount on Contract Receivable	14,863	
Interest Revenue (Exhibit 16-2)		54,463
To record the interest earned during 1991		

EXHIBIT 16-1

Illustrative Problem 16.1
Schedule to Compute Interest Receivable from Contracts for 55 Lots

Year	Beginning Contract Balance	Interest Revenue @ 8%	Annual Payment Due	Principal Payment	Ending Contract Balance
1991	$ 495,000	$ 39,600	$ 149,435	$ 109,835	$ 385,165
1992	385,165	30,813	149,435	118,622	266,543
1993	266,543	21,323	149,435	128,112	138,431
1994[a]	138,431	11,004	149,435	138,431	–0–

[a]Adjusted for rounding error due to using only whole $ amounts.

EXHIBIT 16-2

Illustrative Problem 16.1
Schedule to Compute Interest Revenue from Contracts for 55 Lots
in Accordance with APB No. 21

Year	Beginning Contract Balance	Unamortized Discount	Net Present Value	Interest Revenue @ 12%	Interest Revenue @ 8%	Discount Amortized
1991	$ 495,000	$ 41,140	$ 453,860	$ 54,463	$ 39,600	$ 14,863
1992	385,165	26,277	358,888	43,067	30,813	12,254
1993	266,543	14,023	252,520	30,302	21,323	8,979
1994[a]	138,431	5,044	133,387	16,048	11,004	5,044

[a]Adjusted for rounding error due to using only whole $ amounts.

The income items that are reported from the sale of the 60 lots with five expected cancellations are as shown in Exhibit 16-3. This presentation excludes any resales of lots beyond 1991 and assumes that the actual cancellations equal the expected cancellations. When the lots are resold, the income from the resales is included.

EXHIBIT 16-3

Illustrative Problem 16.1
Income Statement Items from Retail Land Sales
Full Accrual Method

	1991	1992	1993	1994	Total
Gross Revenue	$ 600,000				$ 600,000
Discount on Contracts Receivable	(41,140)				(41,140)
Estimated Uncollectible Sales	(45,000)				(45,000)
Net Sales Revenue	513,860				513,860
Interest Revenue	54,463	$ 43,067	$ 30,302	$ 16,048	143,880
Total Revenues	568,323	43,067	30,302	16,048	657,740
Expenses					
Land and Improvements	187,000				187,000
Sales Commissions	48,000				48,000
Total Expenses	235,000				235,000
Income from Land Development	$ 333,323	$ 43,067	$ 30,302	$ 16,048	$ 422,740

PERCENTAGE-OF-COMPLETION METHOD

If all the criteria for the accrual method are met except that the improvements and amenities are not complete, the percentage-of-completion method is used if progress has been made on the improvements and the develoment is practical.[19] Progress on improvements is assumed if

- The improvements are beyond the preliminary stages.
- Indications are the work will be finished according to plans.
- Indications are no significant delays will occur.
- Reasonably dependable estimates of costs to complete are available.

That the development is practical implies that the land can be used for the purpose intended. For example, no legal or environmental restrictions exist that prevent a buyer from building a home on the site. When the percentage-of-completion method is used, a portion of the discounted contract price from collectible contracts is deferred and recognized as revenue when the improvements are completed. Illustrative Problem 16.2 is based on the same set of facts as Illustrative Problem 16.1 except for the timing of the completion of the improvements and demonstrates the percentage-of-completion method.

[19] *SFAS No. 66*, paragraph 46.

ILLUSTRATIVE PROBLEM 16.2: PERCENTAGE-OF-COMPLETION METHOD FOR RETAIL LAND SALES

Albany Development Company has subdivided a tract of land into 60 homesites. The terms of sale require a $1,000 down payment with the balance of $9,000 plus interest at 8% to be paid in four equal annual installments with the first payment due on the first day of the following year. The market rate of interest is 12%. On January 1, 1991, all the lots are sold, but the developer anticipates that five buyers will default after the 60-day refund period, based on the company's experience with similar projects. No refunds were paid and no notifications of default were received during the first year.

	Per Lot	60 Lots[a]	55 Lots[a]
Sales Data			
Selling Price	$ 10,000	$ 600,000	$ 550,000
Down Payment	1,000	60,000	55,000
Contract Balance	$ 9,000	$ 540,000	$ 495,000
Cost Data			
Land Cost	$ 2,400	$ 144,000	$ 132,000
Land Improvements, Completed in 1991	100	6,000	5,500
Sales Commission Paid on All Lots			
Initially Sold	800	48,000	48,000
Total Actual Costs 1991	3,300	198,000	185,500
Land Improvements Expected To Be			
Completed in 1992	500	30,000	27,500
Land Improvements Expected To Be			
Completed in 1993	400	24,000	22,000
Total Actual and Expected Costs	$ 4,200	$ 252,000	$ 235,000
Present Value of Payments at 8% Interest			
Contract Balance	$ 9,000	$ 540,000	$ 495,000
Present Value of an Annuity of 4			
Payments at 8%	÷ 3.3121	÷ 3.3121	÷ 3.3121
Annual Payment at 8% Interest	2,717	163,020	149,435
Number of Payments	× 4	× 4	× 4
Present Value of Payments	$ 10,868	$ 652,080	$ 597,740
Present Value of Payments at 12% Interest			
Annual Payment at 8% Interest	$ 2,717	$ 163,020	$ 149,435
Present Value of an Annuity of 4			
Payments at 12%	× 3.0373	× 3.0373	× 3.0373
Present Value of Payments	$ 8,252	$ 495,120	$ 453,860
Gross Collectible Contracts			$ 550,000
Discount on Contracts Receivable			41,140
Discounted Collectible Contracts			$ 508,860

[a]The values are multiples of the Per Lot column and will not compute precisely.

The computation to apportion the discounted contract price between the current period and future periods is based on the costs to date and the total expected costs using the 55 lot sales expected to be collected. For retail land sales, the direct selling costs are also considered to be part of the cost of sales and are included as direct costs. When the five lots are repossessed and resold, the portion of the land and the land improvement costs attributable to those lots is recognized as an expense of the period.

Total Expected Cost of 55 Lots	$ 235,000
Costs Incurred to Date for 55 Lots	185,500
Expected Future Costs of Improvements	$ 49,500

The computation of the discounted contract revenue to be deferred to future periods is

Discounted Contract Price	$ 508,860
Percentage to be Deferred ($49,500/$235,000)	× 21.06%
Discounted Contract Revenue to be Deferred	$ 107,166

The income items reported from the sale of the 60 lots with five expected cancellations are as shown in Exhibit 16-4. This presentation excludes any resales of lots beyond 1991 and assumes that the actual cancellations equal the expected cancellations. When the lots are resold, the income from the resales is included.

EXHIBIT 16-4

Illustrative Problem 16.2
Income Statement Items from Retail Land Sales
Percentage-of-Completion Method

	1991	1992	1993	1994	Total
Gross Revenue	$ 600,000				$ 600,000
Discount on Contracts Receivable	(41,140)				(41,140)
Estimated Uncollectible Sales	(45,000)				(45,000)
Revenue Applicable to Future Improvements	(107,166)				(107,166)
Net Sales Revenue	406,694				406,694
Improvement Revenue(1)		$ 59,537	$ 47,629		107,166
Interest Revenue	54,463	43,067	30,302	$ 16,048	143,880
Total Revenues	461,157	102,604	77,931	16,048	657,740
Expenses					
Land and Improvements	137,500	27,500	22,000		187,000
Sales Commissions	48,000				48,000
Total Expenses	185,500	27,500	22,000		235,000
Income from Land Development	$ 275,657	$ 75,104	$ 55,931	$ 16,048	$ 422,740

(1) 1992: ($27,500/$49,500) × $107,166 = $59,537
    1993: ($22,000/$49,500) × $107,166 = $47,629

The only income statement difference between the full accrual method and the percentage-of-completion method is the timing of the recognition of the discounted contract revenue and the related direct costs. The total of every component of income is the same over the four-year period. The balance sheet items are different, however, due to the differences in timing of the payments for improvements. The balance sheet is also affected by the actual cancellation losses versus the timing and number anticipated by the computation of expected cancellation losses.

DEFAULTS AND REPOSSESSIONS

Illustrative Problems 16.1 and 16.2 ignore the actual default by the buyers and the subsequent repossessions by the developer. The basic characteristics of low down payments and extended periods of time to pay the remaining balance leads to defaults on retail land sales. A buyer may have very little equity in the lot for some period of time, because the down payment is small and the periodic payments of the remaining contract balance are often spread out over 10 or more years. When the buyer's economic situation changes, it is not uncommon for the buyer to simply stop making the payments, because the costs to sell the property often exceed the buyer's equity in the property. These cases are accentuated by economic downturns, particularly if real estate values decline as they did in the early 1980s. At the beginning of the 1980s many developments met the criteria for using either the full accrual or percentage-of-completion methods, but as the economic downturn worsened, these developments experienced far greater cancellations than anticipated, and the selling price of the repossessed lots was frequently below the developer's original costs of the lots. In addition, the developer would have to pay the costs of repossession and resale. These situations caused some accountants and users to question the validity of using the full accrual and percentage-of-completion methods.

The journal entries for the default and repossession are the same for both the full accrual and percentage-of-completion methods as both methods provide for expected cancellation losses. When default and repossession occur, the financial statements are not affected unless the estimated number of defaults and/or the dollar amount of the actual defaults differ from the estimates of cancellation losses. To illustrate, the actual defaults in the Albany Development Company project as demonstrated in Illustrative Problems 16.1 and 16.2 are

Date Annual Payment Due	Number of Defaults	Year of Repossession
January 1, 1992	3	1992
January 1, 1993	2	1993

The journal entries to record the defaults are

	1992		1993	
Allowance for Cancellation Losses	27,000		14,006	
Contracts Receivable		27,000(1)		14,006(2)
To record the defaults on contracts receivable				

(1) $9,000 contract receivable $\times$ 3 defaults = $27,000
(2) $9,000 $-$ [$2,717 $-$ ($9,000 $\times$ .08)] =
     $9,000 $-$ $1,977 = $7,003 $\times$ 2 defaults = $14,006

The repossession of lots is recorded using memorandum entries as the costs of the lots expected to be canceled are still in the Land and Improvements Inventory account. If no additional cancellations occur, the balance in the allowance account will be recognized as income at the end of the life of all the outstanding contracts. If the actual number of defaults exceeds the estimate, the valuation discount is adjusted, and additional losses are recognized when the allowance is not adequate. The inventory of land and improvements is also adjusted if the number of lot repossessions exceeds the estimated number of lots.

When the lots are resold, the sales are recorded in the same manner as the original sales except that a decision is made as to whether or not any of the resales will result in default and if the present allowance is adequate to cover any additional losses from the resale of the lots. The defaulter may be entitled to a refund of any amounts paid that are in excess of the costs of repossession and resale, or the contract may specify that if the developer must repossess, the buyer forfeits any monies paid on the contract.

INSTALLMENT METHOD OF ACCOUNTING FOR RETAIL LAND SALES

The installment method is used if it is not possible to accurately estimate the losses from uncollectibility. The criteria of expiration of the refund period and sufficient cumulative payments must also be met. In addition, the seller must be financially capable of providing the improvements and amenities agreed to in the contracts of sale. Therefore, the seller must have either the assets or the borrowing capacity to finance the land improvements, and thus be able to meet the promises made to buyers in the contracts of sale.

If the installment method is used, revenue and expense recognition differs in two ways from both the full accrual and the percentage-of-completion methods. The contract price is not discounted to make interest revenue equal to the market rate of interest. Instead, interest revenue is recognized based on the stated rate of interest specified in the contracts. The assumption of the method is inability to estimate collectibility; therefore, no allowance for cancellation losses is recorded. Deferred gross profit is the gross selling price less all expected direct costs of the project. The expected direct costs include the land costs, the improvement and amenity costs (even if not yet incurred), and the direct selling costs.

If a developer uses the installment method to recognize the gross profit from a retail land sale, the journal entry for the repossession of the land is the same as any installment sale with one exception: any unpaid future costs that have been accrued in determining the cost of sales are also written off in determining the loss. Illustrative Problem 16.3 is based on the same facts as Illustrative Problem 16.2 except that the developer is unable to estimate the collectibility of the contracts receivable, and the actual defaults are the same as presented in the discussion of the actual defaults for both the full accrual and the percentage-of-completion methods.

ILLUSTRATIVE PROBLEM 16.3: INSTALLMENT METHOD FOR RETAIL LAND SALES

Albany Development Company has subdivided a tract of land into 60 homesites. The terms of sale require a $1,000 down payment with the balance of $9,000 plus interest at 8% to be paid in four equal annual installments. The first payment is due on the first day of the following year. On January 1, 1991, all the lots were sold. No refunds were issued and no notifications of default were received during the first year. The company has sufficient assets and borrowing power to be able to complete the land improvements specified in the contracts of sale.

	Per Lot	60 Lots
Sales Data		
Selling Price	$ 10,000	$ 600,000
Down Payment	1,000	60,000
Contract Balance	$ 9,000	$ 540,000
Cost Data		
Land Cost	$ 2,400	$ 144,000
Land Improvements, Completed in 1991	100	6,000
Sales Commission Paid on All Lots Initially Sold	800	48,000
Land Improvements Expected To Be Completed in 1992	500	30,000
Land Improvements Expected To Be Completed in 1993	400	24,000
Total Direct Costs	$ 4,200	$ 252,000

The computation of the deferred gross profit is

Total Gross Sales Revenue	$ 600,000
Less: Total Direct Costs	252,000
Deferred Gross Profit	$ 348,000
Deferred Gross Profit as a Percentage of Gross Sales	58.00%

ACTUAL DEFAULTS AND REPOSSESSIONS

The installment method is used because an accurate estimate of the number and timing of the cancellations is not possible. Therefore, no allowance can be established, and it is necessary to include the gains or losses from actual defaults in the determination of net income. If we assume that the buyer is not entitled to the return of any amounts already paid, three sales were canceled prior to receipt of the first annual payment, and two sales prior to the receipt of the second annual installment, the computations of the effects of the cancellations are

	1992	1993
Number of Contracts Canceled	three	two
Gross Sales Contracts Canceled	$ 30,000	$ 20,000
Down Payments Retained	(3,000)	(2,000)
First Installment Retained		(3,994) (1)
Unpaid Contract Balances	27,000	14,006
Less: Deferred Gross Profit @ 58.0%	15,660	8,123
Unrecovered Investment in Lots	11,340	5,883
Recoverable Costs		
Land ($2,400 per lot)	(7,200)	(4,800)
Improvements ($1,000 per lot)	(3,000)	(2,000)
Cancellation (Gain) or Loss	$ 1,140	$(917)

(1) $2,717 payment − ($9,000 × 8%) = $1,997 principal × 2 lots = $3,994

If any portion of the payments received is to be returned to the seller, the amount increases the loss or reduces the gain.

The journal entry to record the cancellation losses for 1992 is

Land	7,200	
Land Improvements	300 (1)	
Land Improvement Costs Payable	2,700 (2)	
Deferred Gross Profit	15,660	
Loss on Contract Cancellations	1,140	
Installment Contracts Receivable		27,000

(1) $100 per lot × 3 lots = $300
(2) $500 + $400 = $900 per lot × 3 lots = $2,700

The journal entry to record the gain on repossession in 1993, assuming that the expected improvements of $500 per lot were actually incurred in 1992, is

Land	4,800	
Land Improvements	1,200 (1)	
Land Improvement Costs Payable	800 (2)	
Deferred Gross Profit	8,123	
Installment Contracts Receivable		14,006
Gain on Contract Cancellations		917

(1) $100 + $500 = $600 per lot × 2 lots = $1,200
(2) $400 per lot × 2 lots = $800

Exhibit 16-5 computes the amount of gross profit to be recognized each year.

EXHIBIT 16-5

Illustrative Problem 16.3
Schedule to Compute 58.0% Gross Profit from Cash Payments on Contracts for Sale of Lots

Year	Beginning Contract Balance	Contracts Canceled	Valid Contracts	Interest Revenue @ 8%	Payments Received	Principal Portion	58.0% Gross Profit Realized
1991	$ 600,000	$ −0−	$ 600,000		$ 60,000	$ 60,000	$ 34,800
1992	540,000	27,000	513,000	$ 41,040	154,869[a]	113,829	66,021
1993	399,171	14,006	385,165	30,813	149,435[b]	118,622	68,801
1994	266,543	−0−	266,543	21,323	149,435	128,112	74,305
1995[c]	138,431	−0−	138,431	11,004	149,435	138,431	80,290

[a]60 contracts − 3 canceled = 57 valid contracts × $2,717 = $154,869
[b]57 contracts − 2 canceled = 55 valid contracts × $2,717 = $149,435
[c]Adjusted for rounding error due to using only whole $ amounts

The income statements for the following five years as shown in Exhibit 16-6 contain the following line items based on the computation of realized gross profit in Exhibit 16-5.

EXHIBIT 16-6

Illustrative Problem 16.3
Income Statement Items from Retail Land Sales
Installment Method

	1991	1992	1993	1994	1995	Total
Realized Gross Profit	$ 34,800	$ 66,021	$ 68,801	$ 74,305	$ 80,290	$ 324,217
Cancellation Losses		(1,140)				(1,140)
Cancellation Gains			917			917
Interest Revenue	41,040	30,813	21,323	11,004		104,180
Income from Land Development	$ 75,840	$ 95,694	$ 91,041	$ 85,309	$ 80,290	$ 428,174

COMPARISON OF THE INCOME ITEMS REPORTED USING THE THREE METHODS

The three methods are simply different ways to determine the timing and the character of the various components of income from a retail land development. The total income is the same as all three methods were based on the same set of sales and cost figures, the same actual defaults, and ultimately the same cash flows. As mentioned previously, the income for both the full accrual and percentage-of-completion methods was the same amount, $422,740. The five actual defaults were the same number as estimated, but two contracts did not default until the second payment was due. Thus the estimated losses of $45,000 were overstated by $3,994 ($45,000 − $27,000 − $14,006). The overestimation of the losses is reported as revenue in the last year of the contracts.

In addition, the company received interest revenue from the first installment payment on the two later defaults in the amount of $1,440 ($18,000 × 8%). The interest revenue for 1992 is adjusted to include this additional $1,440 of interest revenue. The adjustments make the net income actually reported $428,174 ($422,740 + $3,994 + $1,440), which is exactly the same as the income shown in Exhibit 16-6 for the installment method. Some accountants believe that the installment method is the preferable method because it does not require estimates of collectibility, which this example shows are not completely accurate. In addition, they favor the method because it results in approximately equal amounts of income per period over the life of the contracts—a smoothing of income.

BALANCE SHEET PRESENTATION FOR THE THREE METHODS

The balance sheet amount of gross contracts receivable is the same for all three methods because the cash received is the same amount. However, because the improvements are not complete when the percentage-of-completion method is used, this method shows a contra account to Contracts Receivable for the deferred revenue until the improvements have been completed. The presentation of the deferral as a contra receivable is in accordance with the recommendation of *Statement of Financial Accounting Concepts No. 6.* The installment method shows different amounts for all the asset items, except gross contracts receivable, over at least a portion of the life of the contracts, depending on when the cancellations occur.

In accordance with *Statement of Financial Accounting Concepts No. 6,* the deferred gross profit is presented as a valuation (contra) account to the contracts receivable, which is considered preferable because deferred gross profit is not a liability of the seller. The land and improvements inventory differs between all three methods, but the full accrual and the percentage-of-completion methods are the same once the improvements and amenities are completed.

The liability for land improvements is recorded only when the installment method is used. If the lots repossessed are sold at some future time, the improvements must be completed. Exhibit 16-7 presents the balance sheet items over the life of the contracts for all three methods. The receivable from the contracts would be divided into current and noncurrent portions if a classified balance sheet were presented.

The amount of the contract receivables for all the methods is from the installment method Percentage of Gross Profit Schedule, Exhibit 16-5. For the full accrual and percentage-of-completion methods, the unamortized valuation discount is from the Schedule to Compute Interest Revenue per APB No. 21, Exhibit 16-2. The interest receivable for the full accrual and percentage-of-completion methods is the amount computed in the Schedule to Compute Interest Revenue per APB 21, Exhibit 16-2, and for the installment method the interest receivable is from the Percentage of Gross Profit Schedule, Exhibit 16-5. For the full accrual method the land and improvements inventory is the total land and improvements cost for five lots (5 × $3,400). For the percentage-of-completion method the amount for 1991 is $2,500 completed times the five lots, for 1992 it is $3,000 completed, and for 1993 and beyond it is the total cost of $3,400 per lot.

The Deferred Gross Profit account, the Land and Improvements Inventory account, and the Land and Improvements Payable account for the installment method show the following entries:

Deferred Gross Profit

12/31/91	34,800	1/1/91	348,000
		Balance	313,200
1992	15,660		
12/31/92	66,021		
		Balance	231,519
1993	8,123		
12/31/93	68,801		
		Balance	154,595
12/31/94	74,305		
		Balance	80,290

Land and Land Improvements Inventory

1992	7,500	
1993	6,000	
Balance	13,500	

Land Improvements Payable

1991	6,000	1/1/91	60,000
		Balance	54,000
1992	2,700		
1992	28,500		
		Balance	22,800
1993	800		
1993	22,000		
		Balance	–0–

The balance sheet items presented in Exhibit 16-7 are based on three actual defaults in 1992 and two in 1993 for all three methods.

SOME CAUTIONS REGARDING THE ILLUSTRATIVE PROBLEMS

The above examples of the three methods demonstrate the basic elements in accounting for retail land sales and their common complexities. In order for the illustrations to bring out the basic points, some assumptions were made that may not be entirely realistic. All the examples ignored the reselling of lots repossessed from canceled contracts, although if the development company could initially sell all the lots, they probably can resell the repossessed lots. When the lots are resold, the income items are reported and the inventory of land and improvements is reduced. All three illustrations assumed that all the sales were made on the first day of the year to simplify the interest computations, although in most developments the sales take place over a span of time and may take several years. Equal periodic payments were used; however, if the contracts require the stated interest rate on the unpaid balance plus an equal portion of the principal on each payment date, a complete payment schedule for each contract is necessary.

In the illustrations of repossessions for both the full accrual and percentage-of-completion methods, the actual number of defaults equaled the estimated number. If the methods are accurate, this result should occur. Because of the extended periods of time for payment, the ability to predict accurately the number of defaults is difficult. The difficulty in predicting potential defaults, both from the initial sales and subsequent resales, is one of the reasons some accountants and users believe that only the installment method should be used.

DISCLOSURE REQUIREMENTS

Statement of Financial Accounting Standards No. 66 requires the following disclosures for retail land sales:

- Maturity value of contracts receivable for each of the five years following the balance sheet date
- Delinquent contracts receivable and method for determining delinquency

EXHIBIT 16-7

Balance Sheet Items for Retail Land Sales
Full Accrual, Percentage-of-Completion, and Installment Methods

	1991	1992	1993	1994
Full Accrual Method				
Assets				
Contracts Receivable	$540,000	$399,171	$266,543	$138,431
Discount on Contracts Receivable	(26,277)	(14,023)	(5,044)	–0–
Allowance for Cancellations	(45,000)	(18,000)	(3,994)	(3,994)
Net Contracts Receivable	468,723	367,148	257,505	134,437
Interest Receivable	39,600	30,813	21,323	11,004
Land and Land Improvements Inventory	17,000	17,000	17,000	17,000
Percentage-of-Completion Method				
Assets				
Contracts Receivable	$540,000	$399,171	$266,543	$138,431
Discount on Contracts Receivable	(26,277)	(14,023)	(5,044)	–0–
Revenue Applicable to Future Improvements	(107,166)	(47,629)		
Allowance for Cancellations	(45,000)	(18,000)	(3,994)	(3,994)
Net Contracts Receivable	331,557	319,519	257,505	134,437
Interest Receivable	39,600	30,813	21,323	11,004
Land and Land Improvements Inventory	12,500	15,000	17,000	17,000
Installment Method				
Assets				
Contracts Receivable	$540,000	$399,171	$266,543	$138,431
Deferred Gross Profit	(313,200)	(231,519)	(154,595)	(80,290)
Net Contracts Receivable	226,800	167,652	111,948	58,141
Interest Receivable	41,040	30,813	21,323	11,004
Land and Land Improvements Inventory (1)	–0–	7,500	13,500	13,500
Liabilities				
Land Improvements Payable	54,000	22,800	–0–	–0–

(1) The amounts assume that improvement costs were not incurred for the repossessed lots. If all the improvement costs were incurred as planned, the expenditures are added to this account.

- The weighted average and range of stated interest rates
- Estimated total costs and estimated dates of expenditures for improvements for major areas from which sales have been made over each of the five years following the balance sheet date
- Recorded obligations for improvements[20]

DEPOSIT METHOD

The deposit method is used if the criteria for use of one of the three revenue recognition methods are not met. Usually, the developer has insufficient assets or borrowing ability to ensure that the land can be paid for or the improvements and amenities can be constructed. In that case, all the payments received, whether they are down payments, principal payments, or interest payments, are recorded in a liability account such as customer deposits.

Frequently a developer is required by the contracts of sale to sell a certain number of lots or reach a minimum dollar amount of gross sales within a specified span of time for the contracts of sale to be executed. The minimum amount is designed to ensure that the developer has sufficient funds to pay for the land and to complete the improvements and amenities. The developer is usually required to keep the monies received separate from other cash and may be required to place the funds with a trustee. In addition, the developer may be required to pay interest to buyers who made payments on prospective purchases if the developer is unable to meet the minimum number of lots sales or gross sales value required.

All the costs associated with the project are capitalized until the criteria are met to employ one of the revenue and expense recognition methods. When the criteria are met, the amount of income earned to the point of conversion is recognized and all the related balance sheet accounts are recorded. Illustrative Problem 16.4 is an extension of the previous land development example and it demonstrates the deposit method and the conversion to the full accrual method when the minimum number of sales required by the contracts of sale is reached.

ILLUSTRATIVE PROBLEM 16.4: CONVERSION FROM THE DEPOSIT METHOD TO THE FULL ACCRUAL METHOD

The 60-lot development is the first retail land development undertaken by Albany Development Company. The lots will sell for $10,000 each with a $1,000 interest at 8% payable in four equal annual installments of $2,717 beginning on the first day of the following year. The current market rate of interest for similar contracts is 12%. The company has paid for the land, but because it does not have sufficient assets or borrowing power to construct the land improvements, the contracts of sale require that the company sell at least 45 lots by January 15, 1991, for the contracts to be executed. If the company is unable to sell at least 45 lots, the cash paid by the buyers must be refunded plus interest at 10%. All of the 1990 buyers made the first installment payment, but two are expected to default before making the second payment. The developer anticipates that three of the 1991 sales will default before the first interest payment.

---

[20] *SFAS No. 66*, paragraph 50.

Sales Information

	1990 Sales	1991 Sales	Total
Number of Lots Sold	25	35	60
Gross Selling Price	$ 250,000	$ 350,000	$ 600,000
Less: Down Payments Received	25,000	35,000	60,000
Contract Balances Receivable	225,000	315,000	540,000
Less: Anticipated Defaults	14,006(a)	27,000(b)	41,006
Collectible Contracts	210,994	288,000	498,994
Less: Present Value of Contracts at 12%	189,804(c)	264,075(d)	453,879
Valuation Discount	$ 21,190	$ 23,925	$ 45,115

(a) $9,000 − $1,997 = $7,003 × 2 = $14,006
(b) $9,000 × 3 = $27,000
(c) $2,717 × 23 valid contracts = $62,491
　　$62,491 × 3.0373 (present value of an annuity of 4 payments at 12% interest) = $189,804
(d) $2,717 × 32 valid contracts = $86,944
　　$86,944 × 3.0373 (present value of an annuity of 4 payments at 12% interest) = $264,075

The journal entries to record the cash received prior to the conversion to the accrual method are

1990 Cash: Lot Sales	25,000	
Deposits from Land Sale Contracts		25,000
1991 Cash: Lot Sales (1)	67,925	
Deposits from Land Sale Contracts		67,925

(1) $2,717 × 25 lots = $67,925

The journal entries to convert from the deposit method to the full accrual method for the 1990 sales, once the 1991 sales occurred are

Deposits from Land Sales Contracts	25,000	
Contracts Receivable: 1990 Sales	225,000	
Sales Revenue		250,000
Sales Revenue	35,196	
Allowance for Cancellation Losses: 1990 Sales		14,006
Discount on Contracts Receivable: 1990 Sales		21,190
Deposits from Land Sales Contracts	67,925	
Discount on Contracts Receivable: 1990 Sales	4,776(2)	
Contract Receivable: 1990 Sales		49,925(3)
Interest Revenue		22,776(1)

(1) $189,804 × 12% = $22,776
(2) $225,000 × 8% = $18,000 interest received
　　$22,776 − $18,000 = $4,776 discount amortization
(3) $67,925 payments − $18,000 interest = $49,925 principal

The sales for 1991 are recorded in the same manner as demonstrated previously for the full accrual method.

Cash	35,000	
Contracts Receivable: 1991 Sales	315,000	
Sales Revenue		350,000
Sales Revenue	50,925	
Allowance for Cancellation Losses: 1991 Sales		27,000
Discount on Contracts Receivable: 1991 Sales		23,925

The costs also are expensed as demonstrated in the example of the full accrual method. These costs are for the 55 valid sales, 23 in 1990 and 32 in 1991.

Direct Selling Costs	48,000	
Cash		48,000
Cost of Sales	187,000	
Land and Improvements Inventory		187,000

The interest revenue for 1991 is derived in the same way except that the interest from the 1990 sales is computed separately from the interest from the 1991 sales, as the 1990 sales include the second installment payment and the 1990 sales are the first installment payment. These entries reflect the actual defaults that occurred and not the estimated number of defaults used in the previous journal entries. If the actual defaults are as estimated, two defaults on 1990 sales and three defaults on 1991 sales, the journal entries to record the receipts of the interest payments are

Cash	62,491(2)	
Discount on Contracts Receivable: 1991 Sales	4,473(3)	
Contract Receivable: 1991 Sales		49,605(4)
Interest Revenue		17,359(1)

(1) $225,000 - $49,925 = $175,075
    $175,075 \times 23/25 = $161,069
    $161,069 - ($21,190 - $4,776) = $144,655
    $144,655 \times 12\% = $17,359
(2) $2,717 \times 23 = $62,491
(3) $161,069 \times 8\% = $12,886 interest received
    $17,359 - $12,886 = $4,473 discount amortization
(4) $62,491 payments - $12,886 interest = $49,605 principal

Cash	86,944(3)	
Discount on Contracts Receivable: 1992 Sales	8,649(2)	
Contract Receivable, 1992 Sales		63,904(4)
Interest Revenue		31,689(1)

(1) $264,075 \times 12\% = $31,689
(2) $288,000 \times 8\% = $23,040 interest received
    $31,689 - $23,040 = $8,649 discount amortization
(3) $2,717 \times 32 = $86,944
(4) $86,944 payments - $23,040 interest = $63,904 principal

If the above illustration were continued for the life of the contracts, the results are the same as previously shown in Illustrative Problem 16.1, except that the timing of the recognition of revenue is different.

CHANGING FROM THE INSTALLMENT METHOD TO THE PERCENTAGE-OF-COMPLETION METHOD

If a company that is using the percentage-of-completion method, because the improvements and amenities are incomplete, completes the required improvements ahead of schedule, the recognition of revenue is moved forward in time. Because the only difference between the full accrual and the percentage-of-completion method is the profit from the initial sales, no change in accounting method occurs. The determination of interest revenue is the same for both methods as illustrated in Illustrative Problems 16.1 and 16.2. However, the inability to estimate collectibility distinguishes the installment method from both the full accrual and the percentage-of-completion methods. A development company may decide part way through the life of the contracts that it can predict collectibility, and elect to change from the installment method to the percentage-of-completion method. If all the improvements and amenities had been completed prior to sale, the conversion is to the full accrual method; if not, the conversion is to the percentage-of-completion method.

The conversion from the installment method to the percentage-of-completion method requires computing all the revenue and expense items as they would have been reported for all prior years using the precentage-of-completion method. All the balances of the related balance sheet accounts also need to be determined. Any difference between the income for all prior years that would have been reported, if the company had used percentage-of-completion method, and the income actually recognized by the installment method, is reported as additional income or loss in the year of the change. *Statement of Financial Accounting Standards No. 66* requires that the change be considered a change in estimate, and the difference be reported as a separate line item in the income statement.[21]

Illustrative Problem 16.5 shows the conversion from the installment method to the percentage-of-completion method using the income statement information presented in Exhibit 16-4 and Exhibit 16-6, and the balance sheet information presented in Exhibit 16-7. The additional interest from the two contracts that did not default until 1993 is included in the 1992 income to completely reflect the actual results under the percentage-of-completion method.

ILLUSTRATIVE PROBLEM 16.5: CONVERSION FROM THE INSTALLMENT METHOD TO THE PERCENTAGE-OF-COMPLETION METHOD

During 1993, Albany Development Company determined that an estimate of future defaults was possible and elected to change from the installment method to the percentage-of-completion method. The income statements for the years 1991 and 1992 would have shown the following revenues and expenses if the percentage-of-completion method had been used, and recognized the following revenues and expenses using the installment method:

[21] *SFAS No. 66*, paragraphs 49 and 97.

	1991	1992	Total
Percentage-of-Completion Method			
Gross Revenue	$ 600,000		$ 600,000
Valuation Discount	(41,140)		(41,140)
Estimated Uncollectible Sales	(45,000)		(45,000)
Revenue Applicable to Future			
Improvements	(107,166)	$ 59,537	(47,629)
Interest Revenue			
Expected from 55 Contracts	54,463	43,067	97,530
Received from 2 Contracts Still Valid		1,440	1,440
Total Revenue	461,157	104,044	565,201
Costs and Expenses			
Land and Improvements	137,500	27,500	165,000
Sales Commissions	48,000		48,000
Total Expenses	185,500	27,500	213,000
Income from Land Development	275,657	76,544	352,201
Installment Method			
Realized Gross Profit	34,800	66,021	100,821
Cancellation Losses		(1,140)	(1,140)
Interest Revenue	41,040	30,813	71,853
Income from Land Development	75,840	95,694	171,534
Difference in Income	$ 199,817	$(19,150)	$ 180,667

The balance sheet at the end of 1992 would have shown the following assets if the percentage-of-completion method had been used and reported the following assets and liabilities using the installment method:

	Percentage-of-Completion Method	Installment Method	Difference
Assets			
Contracts Receivable	$ 399,171	$ 399,171	$ —0—
Discount on Contracts Receivable	(14,023)	—0—	(14,023)
Allowance for Cancellation Losses	(18,000)	—0—	(18,000)
Deferred Revenue for Future			
Improvements	(47,629)	—0—	(47,629)
Deferred Gross Profit		(231,519)	231,519
Net Contracts Receivable	319,519	167,652	151,867
Interest Receivable	30,813	30,813	—0—
Land and Improvements Inventory	15,000	7,500	7,500
Liabilities			
Land Improvements Payable	—0—	21,300	21,300

The journal entry to record the difference in income for 1991 and 1992 and to adjust the balance sheet accounts to the percentage-of-completion method balances at the end of 1992 is

Deferred Gross Profit	231,519	
Land and Improvements Inventory	7,500	
Land Improvements Payable	21,300	
Discount on Contracts Receivable		14,023
Allowance for Cancellation Losses		18,000
Revenue Applicable to Future Improvements		47,629
Income from Change in Accounting Estimate		180,667

SUMMARY

Revenues are increases in assets and/or decreases in liabilities. Expenses are increases in liabilities and/or decreases in assets from delivering goods or providing services. The realization concept states that revenue is recognized when the earning process is complete and an exchange has occurred. *Statement of Financial Accounting Concepts No. 5* states that revenue is recognized when it is realized and earned.

The basic principle for the recognition of revenue is to recognize revenue at the point of sale of goods or when services are provided. A number of exceptions exist to the point of sale principle because the substance of the transaction does not fit point of sale recognition. These exceptions result in revenue recognition either prior to the completion of the earning process and the occurrence of an exchange or after the completion of the earning process and an exchange. The recognition of service revenues is divided into four types, which are similar to the revenue recognition for products: specific performance, proportional performance, completed performance, and collection.

Product costs are matched to the revenue they relate to and recognized as expenses when the revenue is recognized. Period costs, which do not have a direct relationship to the product are either expensed as incurred or recognized as expenses over time in a systematic and rational manner. The direct costs of service revenue, both initial direct and other direct, are recognized when the service revenue is recognized. Indirect costs, which do not have a direct relationship to the service revenue, are either expensed as incurred or recognized as expenses over time in a systematic and rational manner. If costs should not be expensed because the revenue has not been recognized (recorded), then the expenses are recorded as assets until the revenue is recognized for both product and service revenues.

Real estate sales are characterized by low down payments with the balance due over extended periods of time with interest rates well below market. The sellers frequently promise improvements and amenities. Retail land sales are volume sales of subdivisions of large tracts of land. If the refund period has expired, the total payments by the buyer exceed 10% or more of the contract price, the development is completed, no subordination of the buyer's receivables exists, and the seller can estimate collectibility, a retail land sale is accounted for by the full accrual method. The full accrual method recognizes sales revenue equal to the contract price, less the discount for low interest, and the value of estimated uncollectible contracts. Interest revenue is imputed and recognized over the life of the contract.

If the development is not complete and the seller can complete the project, but all the other criteria are met, the percentage-of-completion method is used. A portion of the selling price less the valuation discount and the estimated uncollectible accounts is deferred and recognized as the project is completed. The interest is recognized in the same manner as the full accrual method.

If the seller is unable to estimate collectibility, the installment method is used. Unlike the full accrual and the percentage-of-completion methods, no interest is imputed to the contract and interest revenue is equal to the interest paid by the buyer. Unlike the selling of a product, the selling costs are considered part of cost of goods sold for retail land sales.

If the criteria for the full accrual, percentage-of-completion, or installment methods are not met, the deposit method, which does not recognize revenue, is used. Once the criteria for use of one of the methods is met, then conversion is recorded to one of the methods. During the life of a retail land project, the developer may be able to estimate collectibility and convert from the installment method to either the full accrual or the percentage-of-completion method. Because the cash flow is the same, all three methods result in the same amount of revenue being recognized over time, although the timing and character of the revenue differs between the methods.

REVIEW PROBLEM

Subdivide Inc. has a 100-lot development of homesites adjoining a golf course for sale. Each lot will be sold for $17,000. The terms of sale require the buyer to make a $1,000 down payment and to pay the balance in eight equal semiannual payments including interest at 6% per year. At the beginning of 1990, all the lots were sold and no buyer canceled within the refund period. Subdivide expects five buyers will default prior to making the first installment payment. The semiannual payments of principal and interest are due on June 30 and December 31 of each year. Subdivide's year end is December 31. The current market rate of interest is 10%, but Subdivide charged 6% in order to sell the lots quickly. Subdivide had the following costs for the property:

Land	$ 300,000
Land Improvements	150,000
Golf Course	2,000,000
Direct Selling Costs	286,000

The fair market value of the golf course is $1,750,000. Subdivide will retain title to the golf course and charge buyers for its use.

Required
(All computations are to be to the nearest dollar or the nearest whole percentage.)

1. Determine the income items recognized from the sale of lots for 1990 through 1993, assuming the actual defaults and repossessions equaled the estimated number using the full accrual method.
2. Assume that the golf course is expected to be built in 1992, and that Subdivide has the assets and borrowing capacity to complete the course. Determine the income items recognized from the sale of lots for 1990 through 1993, assuming the actual defaults and repossessions equaled the estimated number using the percentage-of-completion method.
3. Using the additional facts of requirement 2, assume that Subdivide is unable to estimate the number of defaults as this is the first such project they have developed and the community has no other golf

courses. Determine the income items recognized from the sale of the lots for 1990 through 1993, using the installment method and assuming the actual defaults beyond the refund period were four lots prior to the first installment payment.

4. Determine the balance sheet values at the end of 1990 through 1993, using the actual gross contracts receivable from the installment method and assuming the actual cost of the golf course is as estimated.
5. Reconcile the differences in total income determined under each of the three methods.

QUESTIONS

1. Contrast the definitions of net income given in *Statements of Financial Accounting Concepts Nos. 5 and 6.*
2. What are the definitions of revenue and expense according to *Statement of Financial Accounting Concepts No. 6*?
3. What are the conditions necessary to recognize revenue according to the realization concept?
4. What are the assumptions of the revenue realization and recognition concepts?
5. Describe the different exceptions to the revenue recognition principle and give an example of each.
6. Describe the four major categories of service revenues and state when revenue is recognized.
7. Give an example of each of the four major categories of service revenues other than the examples in the text.
8. What are the basic characteristics of product expenses?
9. Describe the two basic categories of service expenses and give an example of each.
10. Describe the problem of expense versus capitalization as an asset.
11. What are the characteristics of real estate sales that are reflected in the criteria for revenue recognition of *Statement of Financial Accounting Standards Nos. 66 and 67*?
12. What costs are capitalized and what costs are expensed in accounting for real estate sales?
13. What are the characteristics of retail land sales?
14. What methods can be used to account for retail land sales?
15. What are the criteria that must be met to use the full accrual method for accounting for retail land sales?
16. Describe the two complexities in revenue recognition and the accounting treatment of each for the full accrual method of accounting for retail land sales.
17. What are the criteria for using the percentage-of-completion method of accounting for retail land sales and how do the criteria differ from the full accrual method?
18. What are the income statement differences between the percentage-of-completion and the full accrual methods for retail land sales?
19. How are defaults and repossessions of retail land sales treated when the full accrual and percentage-of-completion methods are used?
20. When is the installment method of accounting for retail land sales used?
21. How are defaults and repossessions of retail land sales treated when the installment method is used?
22. How do the balance sheet values differ between the full accrual, the percentage-of-completion, and the installment methods?
23. What are the disclosure requirements for retail land sales?
24. What conditions require the use of the deposit method for retail land sales?
25. How are cash receipts recorded when the deposit method is used for retail land sales? How are expenses recorded?
26. When is conversion from the installment method to either the full accrual or the percentage-of-completion method for retail land sales appropriate?

EXERCISES

EXERCISE 16-1

Mr. W has a musical instrument repair business. Mr. W is negotiating with the school district to maintain the district's instruments used by the students who play in the schools' bands and orchestras. Mr. W has asked you to assist him in determining the annual contract amount to quote the school. The records of the school indicate that an average of $50,000 was spent on repairs during each of the prior four years. The repair bills were 60% for replacement parts and 40% for labor. Mr. W's labor cost is $15 per hour and his markup on parts is 35%. The district has decided to replace 20% of the existing instruments during each of the next five years, based on Mr. W's evaluation of the condition of the existing instruments.

Required

1. Discuss the costs that Mr. W should consider in determining the amount to quote as a contract price.
2. Discuss when and how Mr. W should recognize revenue from the contracts.

EXERCISE 16-2

J. Artist is a specialist in wildlife lithographs and produces four new designs each year. J. Artist's lithographs are currently being sold by a gallery for $175 each. Super Sellers have contracted with J. Artist to sell his lithographs on long-term contracts that promise the buyers their choice of two of four new lithographs each year for five years for $100 per lithograph. The buyers may purchase additional lithographs for $125 each. The buyers will pay $250 for the contract and receive one free lithograph. J. Artist is to receive $75 per lithograph including the free one at the signing of the contract.

Required

1. Discuss the amount and the timing of the revenue recognition for J. Artist.
2. Discuss the amount and the timing of revenue and expense recognition for Super Sellers.

EXERCISE 16-3

Seashore Development Co. has purchased one mile of oceanfront property for $1,000,000 and is subdividing the property into 100 homesites. The lots will sell for $25,000 each with a 10% down payment. The balance of the purchase price plus interest at 6% is payable in 20 equal annual installments with the first payment due one year from the date of sale. The current market rate of interest for homesites is 10%.

Required

1. Determine the valuation discount for a lot.
2. Determine the amount to recognize as the contract price and the amount to recognize as interest revenue for a lot.

EXERCISE 16-4

Refer to Exercise 16-3. Seashore spent $500,000 on land improvements and agreed to pay a 7% commission on all lots sold. Seashore estimates that two lots will default each year for five years. All the lots were sold during the first month of the year.

Required

1. Determine the amount of income recognized during the first year from the sale of the lots if Seashore Development has completed all the land improvements.
2. Determine the amount of income recognized during the first year, if only $100,000 of the land improvements are complete, but Seashore had the financial ability to complete the improvements.

EXERCISE 16-5

Rocky Top Development Co. has purchased 100 acres for $500,000 and is subdividing the property into 100 homesites. The lots will sell for $12,000 each with a 20% down payment. The balance of the purchase price plus interest at 6% is payable in 10 equal annual installments with the first payment due one year from the date of sale. The current market rate of interest for homesites is 10%.

Required

1. Determine the valuation discount for a lot.
2. Determine the amount to recognize as the contract price and the amount to recognize as interest revenue for a lot.
3. If Rocky Top estimates that 10 contracts will cancel after the refund period but before the first interest payment, determine the valuation discount for the valid sales and the amount of the allowance for cancellation losses.
4. Rocky Top's cost of subdividing the lots is $600 per lot and the cost of selling the lots is $160,000. If Rocky Top is unable to estimate the number of cancellation losses, determine the amount of deferred gross profit and the gross profit percentage.

EXERCISE 16-6

Able Developers is planning a retirement community and has purchased 80 acres for $200,000, which it plans to subdivide into 100 homesites of 1/2 acre each. Able plans to construct an 18-hole golf course and a clubhouse with swimming pools and covered tennis courts on the remaining 30 acres with a total cost of $1,000,000 for the improvements in addition to the land cost. The lots will sell for $15,500 each with a $1,550 down payment and the balance due in seven equal installments with interest at 8%, although the current market rate of interest is 12%. The selling agency will charge Able $1,000 to sell each lot. Able estimates that eight sales will default within the first year, but after the refund period of 30 days required by state law.

Required

1. State the conditions necessary for Able to use the full accrual method of accounting.
2. Prepare all the journal entries for the first year of the project assuming Able meets the conditions and sells all the lots within the first week of the year.

EXERCISE 16-7

Refer to Exercise 16-6. Assume that prior to the sale the clubhouse with the swimming pools and tennis courts is completed at a cost of $300,000. However, the golf course will not be complete for two more years, although Able has the ability to complete the course. Able estimates that $400,000 will be spent during the year of sale on the golf course and the remaining $300,000 will be spent in the following year.

Required

Determine the amount of income from the land development to be recognized in the year of sale assuming that Able sells all the lots in the first week of the year.

EXERCISE 16-8

Refer to Exercise 16-6. Assume that Able has never been involved in a land development project, and is unable to estimate the number of cancellations that will occur. Therefore, Able will use the installment method of accounting for the retail land sales.

Required

1. Determine the amount and percentage of deferred gross profit.

2. Determine the gain or loss on cancellation if two contracts default before making the first interest payment and an additional four contracts default prior to making the second installment payment.
3. Prepare the journal entries to record the repossessions.

EXERCISE 16-9

Subdivide Inc. has purchased a 30-acre tract of land for $150,000. Subdivide intends to divide the land into 50 half-acre lots and develop the remaining acreage into a park with a lake, nature trails, bike paths, and a jogging trail with intermittent exercise stops. Subdivide estimates that the park will cost $200,000 to complete. Subdivide sold 40 of the lots on the first day of the year for $10,000 each with a $1,000 down payment and the balance in five equal payments due on the last day of the year. The annual payments include interest at 6%, although the market rate of interest for a similar loan is 12%. Subdivide pays a sales commission of 8% only for sales that do not default within the first year.

Required

1. If the park is complete, and Subdivide estimates that four lots will default before making the first interest payment, determine the income recognized in the first year from the sale of the 40 lots and the amount of interest revenue recognized over the life of the contracts.
2. If the park is not complete, but Subdivide has the financial ability to complete the park, and Subdivide estimates that four lots will default before making the first interest payment, determine the income recognized in the first year from the sale of the 40 lots.
3. The park is not complete, but Subdivide has the financial ability to complete the park, and Subdivide is unable to estimate the number of contracts that will be canceled. If no cancellations occur before the first installment payment is due at the end of the year, determine the income recognized in the first year from the sale of the 40 lots.

EXERCISE 16-10

Refer to Exercise 16-9. Assume that the contracts of sale require that Subdivide sell at least 35 lots within one year or the deposits must be refunded to the buyers with interest at 12%. The park is complete and during the first year 25 lots are sold. The cash receipts are recorded by the deposit method as Subdivide is not certain that they will be able to meet the 35-lot requirement. On January 2 of the following year an additional 15 lots are sold. The first installment payment was received at the end of the first year on all 25 lots sold.

Required

1. Prepare the journal entries for the receipt of the cash from the sale of the 25 lots.
2. If Subdivide estimates five lots will default, two before the first installment payment from the current year's sales and three before the second installment payment from the prior year's sales, prepare the journal entries for the conversion to the full accrual method for the 25 lots sold last year.

EXERCISE 16-11

Country Development Inc. is accounting for its retail land development "Scenic Estates" by the installment method, as this is their first land development project and they are unable to estimate the number of cancellations. During the first two years all 200 lots were sold, and only four lots have been repossessed. The amenities are complete except for the last nine holes of the golf course. Because of the few cancellations, Country Development believes they can make a reasonable estimate of future cancellations and, therefore, will convert from the installment method to the percentage-of-completion method. The following income items and balance sheet values were reported under the installment method and would have been reported if the percentage-of-completion method had been used:

	Percentage-of-Completion Method	Installment Method
Income from Land Development	$ 600,000	$ 250,000
Assets		
Contracts Receivable	800,000	800,000
Discount on Contracts Receivable	(30,000)	
Allowance for Cancellation Losses	(40,000)	
Deferred Revenue for Future Improvements	(90,000)	
Deferred Gross Profit		(450,000)
Interest Receivable	65,000	65,000
Land and Improvements Inventory	30,000	15,000
Liabilities		
Land Improvements Payable		45,000

Required

1. What condition is necessary to be able to convert from the installment method to the percentage-of-completion method?
2. Prepare the journal entry to convert from the installment method to the percentage-of-completion method.

PROBLEMS

PROBLEM 16-1

Explain why generally accepted accounting principles have dealt primarily with recognizing revenues from products. Discuss the problems of establishing generally accepted accounting principles for the recognition of revenues and the matching of expenses with those revenues for service revenues. Do you believe that the basic tenets of accounting in the *Statements of Financial Accounting Concepts* provide adequate guidance for the recognition of service revenues? Explain your answer.

PROBLEM 16-2

Rolling Green Builders is planning their first retail land development. The president of Rolling Green has asked you to explain the methods that can be used to account for a retail land development.

Required

Describe the four basic methods, the differences between the methods, and the criteria that must be met to use each of the methods.

PROBLEM 16-3

Describe the similarities and the differences in the income statement and the balance sheet if a retail land developer uses the (1) full accrual method, (2) the percentage-of-completion method, and (3) the installment method.

PROBLEM 16-4

The Wandering Lane Land Developers purchased a tract of land for $300,000. Wandering Lane estimates it will cost $100,000 to subdivide the land into 50 lots and install lanes and underground utilities.

Wandering Lane also has promised to build a recreation facility with covered tennis courts and an indoor pool as well as outdoor courts and an outdoor pool at an estimated cost of $500,000. The lots will sell for $25,000 each with 10% down and the balance in five equal payments beginning one year from the date of sale. The payments will include interest at 6%, although the market rate of interest is 12%. The selling costs are $1,000 per lot sold.

Required

1. On January 2, 1990, Wandering Lane sold all 50 lots. If Wandering Lane estimates that four lots will cancel their contracts before the first installment payment and the amenities are complete, determine the income recognized in each year of the contract.
2. On January 2, 1990, Wandering Lane sold all 50 lots. Wandering Lane has completed the subdividing and the underground utilities. Initial work costing $100,000 has been completed on the other amenities and Wandering Lane estimates $300,000 will be spent in 1991 and the remainder in 1992. If Wandering Lane estimates that four lots will cancel their contracts before the first installment payment and Wandering Lane has the financial ability to complete the amenities, determine the income recognized in each year of the contract.
3. On January 2, 1990, Wandering Lane sold all 50 lots. Wandering Lane is new to the retail land development business and is unable to predict the number of cancellations. Wandering Lane has completed the subdividing and the underground utilities. Initial work costing $100,000 has been completed on the other amenities and Wandering Lane estimates $300,000 will be spent in 1991 and the remainder in 1992. Determine the amount of income recognized in each year of the contract if three contracts default before making the first installment payment and two contracts default before making the second installment payment.

PROBLEM 16-5 (Continuation of Problem 16-4)

On January 1, 1993, Wandering Lane believes that no additional defaults will occur, and elects to convert from the installment method to the full accrual method of accounting. Assume that the actual defaults are as described in requirement (3.), the full accrual income for the period January 1, 1990 through December 31, 1992 would have been $3,629 higher based on the actual defaults, and that interest was accrued when the installment method was used.

Required

Prepare the journal entry on January 1, 1993 to convert to the full accrual method of accounting. (You might want to see if you can compute the $3,629 change in the full accrual income.)

PROBLEM 16-6

The Green Acres Development Company purchased a tract of land for $420,000 containing 100 acres that they intend to subdivide into homesites. The subdivision plans show that 40 acres will be divided into half-acre lots that will sell for $20,000 each. An additional 30 acres will be divided into third-acre lots that will sell for $17,500 each and another 20 acres will be subdivided into quarter-acre lots that will sell for $14,000 each. The remaining 10 acres will be devoted to streets and common park areas. Green Acres estimates that it will cost $240,000 to complete the streets, install the underground utilities, and build the common area parks. The sales staff of Green Acres receives an 8% commission on each sale made that is not canceled within the refund period. The contracts of sale require the purchaser to make a 10% down payment and to pay the balance of the purchase price plus interest at 5% in eight equal annual installments. The current market rate of interest is 10%.

Required

1. Determine the amount of the sales price that is principal and the amount of the sales price that is interest for each lot size.
2. Green Acres sold 25 half-acre lots, 60 third-acre lots, and 50 quarter-acre lots and estimates that 2

lots of each size will default before the first installment payment. Using the full accrual method determine (1) the valuation discount, (2) the allowance for cancellation losses, and (3) the income reported in the year of sale, assuming that land costs are allocated based on acreage, improvement costs, including the land cost used for the improvements are allocated based on relative sales value, and the average interest owing at the end of the year is for six months.

3. Describe the alternative basis other than relative sales value that can be used to allocate the improvement costs.

4. Describe how your solution to requirement (2.) would be different if Green Acres has not yet built the common area parks that will cost $140,000, but has the financial ability to complete the parks.

PROBLEM 16-7

The Metro Development Company has developed a large tract of land into home sites. Metro paid $600,000 for the land, which it subdivided into 100 lots. Metro also agreed in the sales contracts to construct covered tennis courts, an indoor pool, and a golf course, which Metro has the capacity to complete. During the first year Metro spent $350,000 on the land improvements and will spend an additional $100,000 during each of the following two years to complete the amenities. Metro will incur selling costs of $900 per lot for each lot sold. Metro has not developed a retail land project before and, therefore, elected to use the installment method of accounting for the sales. The lots will sell for $20,000 each, with a 10% down payment and the balance due in nine equal payments starting one year from the date of sale, with interest at 8% even though the market rate of interest is 12%. During the first week of Year 1, 40 lots were sold and before the end of Year 1, three contracts defaulted after the cancellation period. During the first week of Year 2, the remainder of the lots were sold, and before the end of Year 2, five contracts from Year 2 sales defaulted after the refund period. Improvements for all 100 lots were paid in Year 2.

Required

1. Determine the income reported for Years 1 and 2, and the balance sheet values at the end of Year 2.

2. Metro expects during the third year that two additional lots will default, one from each year's sales. Because Metro now believes that it can accurately estimate the potential defaults, Metro has elected to change from the installment method to the percentage-of-completion method at the beginning of Year 3.

   1) Determine the income reported for Years 1 and 2, and the balance sheet values at the end of Year 2, assuming that the expected defaults were the actual incurred in Years 1 and 2 and the expected for Year 3, using the percentage-of-completion method. Compute the percentage-of-completion to the nearest whole percentage.

   2) Prepare the journal entry to convert to the percentage-of-completion method at the beginning of Year 3.

SOLUTION TO REVIEW PROBLEM

1. Full Accrual Method

Calculation of Collectible Contracts	
Gross Sales ($17,000 × 100 lots)	$ 1,700,000
Less: Down Payments Received ($1,000 × 100 lots)	100,000
Contracts: Receivable	1,600,000
Less: Expected Defaults ($16,000 × 5 lots)	80,000
Collectible Contracts	$ 1,520,000

Calculation of Equal Semiannual Payments
   $1,520,000 ÷ 7.0197 (Present value of 8 payments at 3% interest as
                 payments are semiannual) $ 216,533

Calculation of Present Value of Payments at 10% Interest
   $216,533 × 6.4632 (Present value of 8 payments at 5% interest) $ 1,399,496

Calculation of the Valuation Discount for Estimated 95 Valid Sales
   Present Value of Collectible Contracts Receivable
      At 6% Stated Rate of Interest $ 1,520,000
      At 10% Market Rate of Interest   1,399,496
   Valuation Discount $ 120,504

Calculation of Anticipated Losses from Five Canceled Contracts
   Gross Sales Contracts Expected to be Canceled $ 85,000
   Less: Down Payment Received (5 lots × $1,000)   5,000
   Losses Expected From Canceled Contracts $ 80,000

Schedule to Compute Interest Revenue
from 95 Estimated Valid Contracts

Period Ending	Beginning Contract Balance	Interest Revenue @ 3%	Semiannual Payment Due	Principal Payment	Ending Contract Balance
6/30/90	$ 1,520,000	$ 45,600	$ 216,533	$ 170,933	$ 1,349,067
12/31/90	1,349,067	40,472	216,533	176,061	1,173,006
6/30/91	1,173,006	35,190	216,533	181,343	991,663
12/31/91	991,663	29,750	216,533	186,783	804,880
6/30/92	804,880	24,146	216,533	192,387	612,493
12/31/92	612,493	18,375	216,533	198,158	414,335
6/30/93	414,335	12,430	216,533	204,103	210,232
12/31/93	210,232	6,301(1)	216,533	210,232	–0–
		$212,264			

(1) Rounded down $6.

Schedule to Compute Interest Revenue
per Accounting Principles Board Opinion No. 21 for 95 Lots

Period Ending	Beginning Contract Balance	Unamortized Discount	Net Present Value	Interest Revenue @ 5%	Interest Revenue @ 3%	Discount Amortized
6/30/90	$ 1,520,000	$ 120,504	$ 1,399,496	$ 69,975	$ 45,600	$ 24,375
12/31/90	1,349,067	96,129	1,252,938	62,647	40,472	22,175
6/30/91	1,173,006	73,954	1,099,052	54,953	35,190	19,763
12/31/91	991,663	54,191	937,472	46,874	29,750	17,124
6/30/92	804,880	37,067	767,813	38,391	24,146	14,245
12/31/92	612,493	22,822	589,671	29,484	18,375	11,109
6/30/93	414,335	11,713	402,622	20,131	12,430	7,701
12/31/93	210,232	4,012	206,220	10,313(1)	6,301	4,012

(1) Rounded up $2.

The income items that are reported from the sale of the 100 lots with five expected cancellations are

	1990	1991	1992	1993	Total
Gross Sales Revenue	$ 1,700,000				$ 1,700,000
Valuation Discount	(120,504)				(120,504)
Estimated Uncollectible Sales	(80,000)				(80,000)
Net Sales Revenue	1,499,496				1,499,496
Interest Revenue	132,622	$ 101,827	$ 67,875	$ 30,444	332,768
Total Revenues	1,632,118	101,827	67,875	30,444	1,832,264
Costs and Expenses					
Land (1)	285,000				285,000
Land Improvements (2)	142,500				142,500
Excess of Cost Over Fair Market Value of Golf Course (3)	237,500				237,500
Direct Sales Costs	286,000				286,000
Total Expenses	951,000	–0–	–0–	–0–	951,000
Income from Land Development	$ 681,118	$ 101,827	$ 67,875	$ 30,444	$ 881,264

(1) $300,000 \times 95/100 = $285,000
(2) $150,000 \times 95/100 = $142,500
(3) $250,000 \times 95/100 = $237,500 The excess is included because Subdivide is retaining title to the golf course.

2. Percentage-of-Completion Method

$$\frac{\text{Excess of Cost of Golf Course Over Fair Market Value}}{\text{Total Expected Costs}} = \frac{\$237,500}{\$951,000} = 25\%$$

Gross Collectible Contracts ($17,000 × 95 lots)	$ 1,615,000
Valuation Discount	120,504
Discounted Collectible Contracts	1,494,496
Percentage to be Deferred	× 25%
Discounted Contract Price to be Deferred	$ 373,624

The income items that are reported from the sale of the 100 lots with five expected cancellations are

	1990	1991	1992	1993	Total
Gross Sales Revenue	$ 1,700,000				$ 1,700,000
Valuation Discount	(120,504)				(120,504)
Estimated Uncollectible Sales	(80,000)				(80,000)
Revenue Applicable to Future Golf Course	(373,624)		$ 373,624		–0–
Net Sales Revenue	1,125,872				1,499,496
Interest Revenue	132,622	$ 101,827	67,875	$ 30,444	332,768
Total Revenues	1,258,494	101,827	441,499	30,444	1,832,264
Costs and Expenses					
Land (1)	285,000				285,000
Land Improvements (2)	142,500				142,500
Excess of Cost Over Fair Market Value of Golf Course (3)			237,500		237,500
Direct Sales Costs	286,000				286,000
Total Expenses	713,500	–0–	237,500	–0–	951,000
Income from Land Development	$ 544,994	$ 101,827	$ 203,999	$ 30,444	$ 881,264

(1) $300,000 × 95/100 = $285,000
(2) $150,000 × 95/100 = $142,500
(1) $300,000 × 95/100 = $285,000
(2) $150,000 × 95/100 = $142,500
(3) $250,000 × 95/100 = $237,500 The excess is included because Subdivide is retaining title to the golf course.

3. Installment Method

Computation of Deferred Gross Profit Percentage

Total Gross Sales	$ 1,700,000
Total Direct Costs	986,000
Gross Profit	$ 714,000
Deferred Gross Profit as a Percentage of Sales	42.00%

Computation of Cancellation Loss

Sales Contracts Canceled ($17,000 × 4)		$ 68,000
Less: Down Payments Retained		4,000
Unpaid Contract Balances		64,000
Less: Deferred Gross Profit @42.00%		26,880
Unrecovered Investment in Lots		37,120
Less: Recoverable Costs		
Land ($300,000 × 4/100)	$ 12,000	
Land Improvements ($150,000 × 4/100)	6,000	
Golf Course ($250,000 × 4/100)	10,000	28,000
Cancellation Loss		$ 9,120

Schedule to Compute 42.00% Gross Profit and Interest Revenue
from Cash Payments Received on Contracts for Sale of Lots

Year	Beginning Contract Balance	Contracts Canceled	Valid Contracts	Interest Revenue @ 3%	(a) Payments Received	Principal Portion	Gross Profit Realized
1990							
1/1	$ 1,700,000		$ 1,700,000		$ 100,000	$ 100,000	$ 42,000
6/30	1,600,000	$ 64,000	1,536,000	$ 46,080	218,813	172,733	72,548
12/31	1,363,267		1,363,267	40,898	218,813	177,915	74,724
Total				86,978			189,272
1991							
6/30	1,185,352		1,185,352	35,561	218,813	183,252	76,966
12/31	1,002,100		1,002,100	30,063	218,813	188,750	79,275
Total				65,624			156,241
1992							
6/30	813,350		813,350	24,401	218,813	194,412	81,653
12/31	618,938		618,938	18,568	218,813	200,245	84,103
Total				42,969			165,756
1993							
6/30	418,693		418,693	12,561	218,813	206,252	86,626
12/31	212,441		212,441	6,372(b)	218,813	212,441	89,225
Total				18,933			175,851

(a) $1,536,000 ÷ 7.0197 = $218,813
(b) Rounded down $1.

The income statements for the following five years contain the following line items from the sale of the lots.

	1990	1991	1992	1993	Total
Realized Gross Profit	$ 189,272	$ 156,241	$ 165,756	$ 175,851	$ 687,120
Cancellation Loss	(9,120)				(9,120)
Interest Revenue	86,978	65,624	42,969	18,933	214,504
Income from Land Development	$ 267,130	$ 221,865	$ 208,725	$ 194,784	$ 892,504

4. Balance Sheets: All Methods

The Allowance for Cancellation Losses account for the full accrual and the percentage-of-completion methods, and the Deferred Gross Profit account for the installment method are

Allowance for Cancellation Losses			
6/30/90	64,000	1/1/90	80,000
		Balance	16,000

Deferred Gross Profit on Installments			
6/30/90	26,880	1/1/90	714,000
1990	189,272		
	216,152		714,000
		Balance	497,848
1991	156,241		
		Balance	341,607
1992	165,756		
		Balance	175,851

The following balance sheet items are based on four actual defaults in 1991:

	1990	1991	1992	1993
Full Accrual Method				
Contracts Receivable (a)	$ 1,185,352	$ 813,350	$ 418,693	$ –0–
Discount on Contracts Receivable (b)	(73,954)	(37,067)	(11,713)	–0–
Allowance for Cancellation Losses	(16,000)	(16,000)	(16,000)	(16,000)
Net Contracts Receivable	1,095,398	760,283	390,980	(16,000)
Land and Improvements Inventory (c)	35,000	35,000	35,000	35,000
Percentage-of-Completion Method				
Contracts Receivable (a)	$ 1,185,352	$ 813,350	$ 418,693	$ –0–
Discount on Contracts Receivable (b)	(73,954)	(37,067)	(11,713)	–0–
Revenue Applicable to Future Improvements (d)	(373,624)	(373,624)	–0–	–0–
Allowance for Cancellation Losses	(16,000)	(16,000)	(16,000)	(16,000)
Net Contracts Receivable	721,774	386,659	390,980	(16,000)
Land and Improvements Inventory (e)	22,500	22,500	35,000	35,000

Continued on following page

	1990	1991	1992	1993
Installment Method				
Assets				
Contracts Receivable (a)	$ 1,185,352	$ 813,350	$ 418,693	$ –0–
Deferred Gross Profit	(497,848)	(341,607)	(175,851)	–0–
Net Contracts Receivable	687,504	471,743	242,842	–0–
Land and Improvements				
Inventory (f)	18,000	18,000	28,000	28,000
Liabilities				
Excess of Cost of Golf Course				
Over Fair Market Value	240,000	240,000	–0–	–0–

(a) From gross profit schedule for the installment method.
(b) From interest income schedule for the full accrual method.
(c) $700,000 − 95/100 ($300,000 + $150,000 + $250,000) =
$700,000 − 95/100 ($700,000) = $35,000
(d) From schedule of deferred contract revenue.
(e) $450,000 × 5/100 = $22,500
(f) $18,000 from loss schedule + $10,000 spent on golf course in 1992.

5. Reconciliation of Income Differences

Income per the Full Accrual and Percentage-of-Completion Methods	$ 881,264
Overestimation of Losses from Contracts Receivable	16,000
Overestimation of Land and Improvements Inventory	(7,000)
Understatement of Interest Revenue (1)	2,240
Income Per Installment Method	$ 892,504

(1) Interest Revenue	
Interest per Installment Method with Four Cancellations	$ 214,504
Interest per Accrual Method with Five Estimated Defaults	212,264
Additional Interest Revenue Actually Received	$ 2,240

The company could have included the additional interest income in its income statements under both the full accrual and the percentage-of-completion methods. The amount is not material, however, and from a practical standpoint might not be recognized until the final payments are received.

OTHER REAL ESTATE SALES AND FRANCHISING

T his chapter illustrates the recognition of revenue and expense and the accounting for other real estate sales and franchising. The topics for other real estate sales include

- The issues involved
- The determination of the sufficiency of the buyer's initial investment
- The determination of the sufficiency of the buyer's continuing investment
- The reduced profit and cost recovery methods
- The sellers continuing involvement

The revenue and expense topics for franchising are

- The definition and description of franchising
- The initial franchise fee
- The continuing franchise fee and bargain sales
- Revenue recognition by the franchisor
- Expense recognition by the franchisee
- The disclosures required for a franchisor

OTHER REAL ESTATE SALES

Real estate contracts often are detailed and complex as a result of the terms that both the buyer and the seller are willing to accept, the terms and conditions specified by any lending agencies involved, and the ingenuity and creativity of the real estate broker. These factors led to the issuance of *Statements of Financial Accounting Standards Nos. 66 and 67*. When the sale of real estate is other than a retail sale of lots, *Statement of Financial Accounting Standards No. 66* requires that the following conditions be met to use the full accrual method for the recognition of revenue and expense:

- The sale is consummated.
- The buyer's initial and continuing investments are adequate to demonstrate a commitment to pay for the property.
- The seller's receivable is not subject to future subordination.
- The seller has transferred to the buyer the usual risks and rewards of ownership in a transaction that is in substance a sale and does not have a substantial continuing involvement with the property.[1]

A sale usually is considered consummated when the escrow company completes the closing of the transaction. At this time, the buyer, the seller, and the lending institutions are all bound to the terms of the contract, the buyer has made a down payment, and the lender has advanced the monies borrowed. These requirements are an extension of the revenue realization principle that an exchange has taken place and the earning process is complete. The criteria for the buyer address the issue of whether an exchange has taken place and the criteria for the seller determine if the earning process is complete.

BUYER'S INITIAL INVESTMENT

Once a real estate transaction has closed, the first step is to determine if the buyer has made an adequate initial investment, so that the transaction is a sale. In other words, was the down payment sufficiently large so that a strong likelihood exists that the buyer has sufficient equity in the property to be willing to continue to make the payments? If so, the possibility of the seller not collecting the selling price is small. An adequate down payment is one that is either

1. the amount required under the usual lending terms for this type of property.
2. or the lesser of
   (1) 25% of the selling price
   (2) the amount by which the sales price exceeds 115% of the amount lent by the primary lender.[2]

In determining if the down payment is adequate, the following types of payments are included as part of the down payment received from the buyer:

- Cash paid
- Notes of the buyer supported by irrevocable letters of credit from a lending institution not involved in the transaction
- Payments to third parties to reduce amounts owed on the property

---

[1] *SFAS No. 66*, paragraph 5.

[2] *SFAS No. 66*, paragraph 53.

- Other amounts paid by the buyer that are part of the sales value, such as prepayment of loan placement fees
- Other notes of the buyer that the seller has converted to cash without recourse[3]

The following items are not included as part of the down payment in applying the sufficient payment test:

- Payment to outside parties for property improvements
- A loan committment by a third party to replace the existing debt on the property
- Any funds the seller will return to the buyer or any loans of the buyer guaranteed or collateralized by the seller[4]

Illustrative Problem 17.1 demonstrates the application of these requirements for the adequacy of the initial down payment.

ILLUSTRATIVE PROBLEM 17.1: ADEQUACY OF BUYER'S INITIAL INVESTMENT

Able Investment Company has agreed to purchase from the BC Construction Company an office building for a total price of $10,000,000 including the delinquent property taxes. Able Investment Company has agreed to pay $1,500,000 in cash plus the delinquent property taxes of $200,000. BC Construction had recently refinanced the property with a first mortgage in the amount of $6,500,000. Able Investment Company will assume the mortgage on the property and issue a second mortgage to BC Construction for the remaining $1,800,000 of the purchase price at the market rate of interest. The maximum amount that the local bank is willing to lend on the property is $8,000,000.

Determination of the Minimum Initial Investment Required

The greater of

1. Down payment under usual loan limits is $2,000,000
   ($10,000,000 − $8,000,000 = $2,000,000).
2. The lesser of
   (1) 25% of the sales value = $2,500,000
       ($10,000,000 × 25%)
   (2) Amount by which the sales value exceeds 115% of the loan by the primary lender is $2,525,000
       ($10,000,000 − ($6,500,000 × 1.15)) =
       ($10,000,000 − $7,475,000 = $2,525,000)

Requirement 2 (1) is less than Requirement 2 (2) and, therefore, is compared to Requirement 1 in applying the test for adequacy of the down payment. Requirement 2 (1) is greater than Requirement 1; therefore, the down payment must equal to or exceed $2,500,000.

[3] *SFAS No. 66,* paragraph 9.

[4] *SFAS No. 66,* paragraph 10.

The down payment received is the sum of the cash paid plus the payment of the delinquent property taxes or $1,700,000. The down payment is not adequate and, therefore, the full accrual method is not used to record the sale.

If the $1,800,000 second mortgage were sold by Able Investment Company for an amount equal to or exceeding the $800,000 deficiency of the initial investment, the full accrual method is used. If the requirements of the initial investment are not met, but the sale has been consummated, the full accrual method is not used because the buyer has not demonstrated a commitment of purchase. If the seller can be reasonably assured of receiving total principal payments in excess of the cost of the property sold, the installment method is used. If the recovery of the seller's investment is questionable, either the cost recovery or the deposit method is used.

BUYER'S CONTINUING INVESTMENT

In addition to making an adequate down payment, the buyer must be committed to paying for the property over a reasonable length of time. In other words, the buyer is really making a purchase of real estate and not simply making a deposit to be able to use the property, and the seller can reasonably expect to be paid for the real estate. Therefore, the terms of sale must require the buyer to pay equal annual payments of principal and interest that are equal to or greater than the amount that an independent lending institution would require of the buyer. In addition, the length of life of the debt cannot exceed the term of a first mortgage loan by an independent lending institution. If the real estate transaction is only for the purchase of land, the length of time of the payments is restricted to 20 years.

All of the above criteria are designed to determine if the buyer has purchased real estaste, and if the seller can assume collectibility as required by the full accrual method. The tests for adequacy of the initial and subsequent payments are cumulative in nature. Therefore, if the tests are not initially met, they may be met at some time in the future and conversion to the accrual method is possible. To illustrate the cumulative nature of the tests, Illustrative Problem 17.2 is an extension of Illustrative Problem 17.1.

ILLUSTRATIVE PROBLEM 17.2: ADEQUACY OF INITIAL AND CONTINUING INVESTMENT

Able Investment Company has agreed to purchase from the BC Construction Company an office building for a total price of $10,000,000 including the delinquent property taxes. Able Investment Company has agreed to pay $1,500,000 in cash plus the delinquent property taxes of $200,000. BC Construction had recently taken out a mortgage on the building in the amount of $6,500,000. Able Investment Company will assume the mortgage on the building and issue a second mortgage to BC Construction for the remaining $1,800,000 of the purchase price at the market rate of interest. The maximum amount that the local bank is willing to lend on the property is $8,000,000.

The first mortgage requires annual payments of $715,000 and the second mortgage requires annual payments of $235,000. In addition, the second mortgage requires an extra principal payment (balloon payment) in the amount of $600,000 at the end of the third year. The maximum bank loan obtainable requires annual payments of $750,000.

	Required by SFAS No. 66	Paid By Buyer	Deficiency
Initial Down Payment	$ 2,500,000	$ 1,700,000	$ 800,000
First Year's Payments	750,000	950,000	(200,000)
Balance	3,250,000	2,650,000	600,000
Second Year's Payments	750,000	950,000	(200,000)
Balance	4,000,000	3,600,000	400,000
Third Year's Payments	750,000	950,000	(200,000)
Balloon Payment		600,000	(600,000)
Requirements Met	$ 4,750,000	$ 5,150,000	$(400,000)

If the continuing investment criterion is not met, but the sale is consummated and the initial investment is adequate, three methods are available for the recording of revenue and expense from the real estate sale: the installment method, the cost recovery method, and the reduced profit method. The reduced profit method is used when the annual payments of the buyer are equal to or exceed the sum of

1. the interest and principal from the maximum amount that can be borrowed against the property, plus
2. the market rate of interest on the amount by which the actual debt exceeds the maximum amount that can be borrowed from an independent lending institution.

The gross profit is reduced by the difference between the face value of the debt with a life in excess of the maximum length of life and the present value of the debt computed at the market rate of interest over the maximum time span. The profit on the maximum debt over the maximum length of time, as determined by the maximum loan amount and term of debt from an independent lending institution, is recognized when the sale occurs. The profit from the amounts and time beyond the maximum is deferred and recognized after the maximum time span has passed.

When the reduced profit method cannot be used, either the installment or the cost recovery method is used. The installment method is demonstrated in Chapter 16. The cost recovery method postpones the recognition of all income until the proceeds received from the buyer exceed the seller's cost of the real estate. The gross profit is deferred and the interest payments received are also deferred. When the total cash received exceeds the seller's cost, then all the principal and interest payments received are income from the sale. The interest revenue previously deferred is recognized first and then the deferred gross profit is recognized. Illustrative Problem 17.3 demonstrates both the reduced profit and the cost recovery methods.

ILLUSTRATIVE PROBLEM 17.3: REDUCED PROFIT AND COST RECOVERY METHODS

On January 1, 1991, BC Construction Company sold DE Development Company a building for $1,000,000. BC Construction's cost of the land and building was $650,000.

Case 1: Reduced Profit Method.   DE Development agreed to the following terms:

Cash Down Payment	$ 300,000
20 Year, 12% First Mortgage from City Bank with Equal Annual Payments of $60,246	450,000
30 Year, 10% Second Mortgage Payable to BC Construction with Equal Annual Payments of $26,520	250,000

The maximum first mortgage loan that can be obtained from an independent lending institution on this property is $600,000 for 20 years at 10% interest with equal annual payments of $70,475. The 10% interest rate is the current market rate for this property and this purchaser. A minimum initial investment for this type of property is a 20% down payment.

The down payment meets the criterion of the initial investment because it exceeds the 25% down payment required. The total annual payments for principal and interest exceed the amount required by the maximum that can be borrowed from a lending institution [($60,246 + $26,520) > $70,475]. The sale does not meet the requirement of adequate continuing investment, however, because the second mortgage exceeds the 20-year term of the maximum loan from an independent lending institution. The first step in determining if the reduced profit method can be used is to ascertain if the annual payments meet the reduced profit test as follows:

Maximum Annual Payment Required by Independent Lending Institution	$ 70,475
Interest on Excess Debt at Market Price of Interest	10,000
[($700,000 − $600,000) × 10%]	
Total Required of Test	$ 80,475
Equal Annual Payment: First Mortgage	$ 60,246
Equal Annual Payment: Second Mortgage	26,520
Total Equal Annual Payments	$ 86,766

The sum of the equal annual payments exceeds the test; therefore, the reduced profit method is used. If the payments had not met the test, either the installment method or the cost recovery method is used. The first mortgage is adequate because the rate of interest exceeds the market rate of interest and the maximum term is the same as the length of life of the maximum loan. However, the second mortgage is inadequate because the term exceeds the maximum term although the rate of interest is the market rate. The computation of the gross profit currently recognized is

Sales Price		$ 1,000,000
Less: Cost of Land and Building		650,000
Gross Profit		350,000
Less: Face Value of Inadequate Debt	$ 250,000	
Less: Present Value for 20 Years	225,781 (1)	24,219
Gross Profit to be Recognized Currently		$ 325,781

(1) $26,520 annual payment × 8.5136 (present value of an annuity for 20 periods at 10% market rate of interest) = $225,781.

The $24,219 of deferred gross profit is recognized in years 21 through 30.

Case 2: Cost Recovery Method. DE Development paid $300,000 down and financed the balance due with a 25-year, 8% first mortgage in the amount of $700,000 payable to the seller. The first mortgage requires annual payments of $65,575 to be paid at the end of each year beginning on December 31, 1991. The maximum amount that a local lending institution will lend is $600,000 at 10% interest for 20 years with annual payments of $70,475.

The initial down payment is adequate because $300,000 exceeds 25% of the selling price. However, the buyer does not meet the continuing investment requirement because the amount of the annual mortgage payment is not more than the amount of the annual payment required for a maximum loan from a local lending institution. In addition, BC Construction questions whether DE Development can pay the annual mortgage payments. Based on these facts, the cost recovery method is the appropriate method to use. The journal entries to record the sale are

Cash	300,000	
First Mortgage Receivable	700,000	
Sales Revenue		1,000,000
Sales Revenue	1,000,000	
Property Inventory		650,000
Deferred Gross Profit: Property Sale		350,000

After the receipt of the initial down payment the unrecovered property cost is

Property Cost	$ 650,000
Less: Down Payment Received	300,000
Unrecovered Property Cost	$ 350,000

Exhibit 17-1 presents the schedule of the cash received as payments over the life of the contract. Until the unrecovered property cost of $650,000 is received in cash, both the interest revenue and the gross profit from the sale are deferred. The journal entry to record the receipt of the first mortgage payment on December 31, 1991 is

12/31/91 Cash	65,575	
Deferred Interest Revenue		56,000
Mortgage Receivable		9,575

Similar entries are recorded on December 31, 1992, 1993, 1994, and 1995.

The schedule in Exhibit 17-1 indicates that when the December 31, 1996 payment is received, all the $650,000 of property cost is recovered. Interest revenue of $43,450 (the mortgage payment of $65,575 less the unrecovered property cost of $22,125) is recognized. The journal entry for the December 31, 1996 payment is

12/31/96 Cash	65,575	
Deferred Interest Revenue	8,056	
Mortgage Receivable	14,069	
Interest Revenue		43,450

In 1997, interest revenue equal to the amount of the cash received is recognized, which includes recognizing both the interest earned for the period plus an amount of deferred interest

EXHIBIT 17-1

Illustrative Problem 17.3
Schedule of Cash Receipts from the Sale of Property

Date	Cash	Interest @ 8%	Deferred Interest Revenue	Mortgage Principal	Mortgage Receivable Balance	Unrecovered Cost	Realized Gross Profit	Realized Interest Revenue
1/1/91	$300,000				$700,000	$350,000		
12/31/91	65,575	$ 56,000	$ 56,000	$ 9,575	690,425	284,425		
12/31/92	65,575	55,234	55,234	10,341	680,084	218,850		
12/31/93	65,575	54,407	54,407	11,168	668,916	153,275		
12/31/94	65,575	53,513	53,513	12,062	656,854	87,700		
12/31/95	65,575	52,548	52,548	13,027	643,827	22,125		
12/31/96	65,575	51,506	8,056	14,069	629,758	–0–		$ 43,450
12/31/97	65,575	50,381	(15,194)	15,194	614,564			65,575
12/31/98	65,575	49,165	(16,410)	16,410	598,154			65,575
12/31/99	65,575	47,852	(17,723)	17,723	580,431			65,575
12/31/00	65,575	46,434	(19,141)	19,141	561,290			65,575
12/31/01	65,575	44,903	(20,672)	20,672	540,618			65,575
12/31/02	65,575	43,249	(22,326)	22,326	518,292			65,575
12/31/03	65,575	41,463	(24,112)	24,112	494,180			65,575
12/31/04	65,575	39,534	(26,041)	26,041	468,139			65,575
12/31/05	65,575	37,451	(28,124)	28,124	440,015			65,575
12/31/06	65,575	35,201	(30,374)	30,374	409,641			65,575
12/31/07	65,575	32,771	(32,804)	32,804	376,837			65,575
12/31/08	65,575	30,147	(26,837)	35,428	341,409		$ 8,591	56,984
12/31/09	65,575	27,313		38,262	303,147		38,262	27,313
12/31/10	65,575	24,252		41,323	261,824		41,323	24,252
12/31/11	65,575	20,946		44,629	217,195		44,629	20,946
12/31/12	65,575	17,376		48,199	168,996		48,199	17,376
12/31/13	65,575	13,520		52,055	116,941		52,055	13,520
12/31/14	65,575	9,355		56,220	60,721		56,220	9,355
12/31/15[a]	65,575	4,854		60,721	–0–		60,721	4,854
	$939,375		$ –0–	$700,000			$350,000	$939,375

[a]Adjusted for rounding due to using whole dollar amounts.

equivalent to the principal portion of the mortgage payment. The journal entry to record the receipt of the December 31, 1997 payment is

12/31/97 Cash	65,575	
Deferred Interest Revenue	15,194	
Mortgage Receivable		15,194
Interest Revenue		65,575

Similar entries are recorded until the year 2008 when all of the previously deferred interest revenue has been recognized.

In 2008, in addition to recognizing a portion of the deferred interest revenue, a portion of the deferred gross profit from the sale of the land is also recognized. The amount of deferred gross profit recognized is the principal portion of the mortgage payment $35,428 less the $26,837 of deferred interest revenue recognized in 2008. The journal entry to record the December 31, 2008 payment is

12/31/08 Cash	65,575	
Deferred Interest Revenue	26,837	
Deferred Gross Profit: Property Sale	8,591	
Mortgage Receivable		35,428
Interest Revenue		56,984
Realized Gross Profit: Property Sale		8,591

Once all of the previously deferred interest revenue is recognized, all of the cash received that is principal is recognized as realized gross profit. The journal entry for the December 31, 2009 payment is

12/31/09 Cash	65,575	
Deferred Gross Profit: Property Sale	38,262	
Mortgage Receivable		38,262
Interest Revenue		27,313
Realized Gross Profit: Property Sale		38,262

SELLER'S CONTINUING INVOLVEMENT

In addition to the obligations and requirements of the buyer, the accountant must determine if the earning process is complete; has the seller transferred the risks and rewards of ownership to the buyer? In other words, has the seller earned the selling price? Frequently a seller of real estate may be committed to additional construction, provision of management services, financing, guarantees of return on investment to the buyer, guarantees against losses by the buyer, and profit participation. When these commitments exist, the seller still is assuming the risks and rewards of ownership and the full accrual method cannot be used. The revenue and expense recognition method used when the seller has unfulfilled commitments to the buyer is the method that matches the continuing involvement. For example, if the involvement is the construction of an additional building over the next three years, the percentage-of-completion method is used to recognize revenue.

FRANCHISING

Franchise operations are part of everyone's daily life and can be found throughout the world. For example, in almost every city in the United States as well as in many foreign countries people are familiar with McDonald's golden arches and the Colonel's Kentucky fried chicken. Some franchise operations are on the scale of McDonald's and Kentucky Fried Chicken, while others are regional or local franchises. Many of the franchises are for goods and services to the ultimate consumer, although franchise operations exist at the manufacturing and wholesale levels as well. A common area for franchising is the fast food industry, but franchises can be granted for any number of products and services including gasoline, auto parts, vacuum cleaners, convenience grocery stores, ice cream and yogurt parlors, beverages, dancing lessons, exercise studios, diet centers, cosmetics, computers, tax services, real estate brokers, and finance companies.

During the 1960s, franchising grew at a rapid rate and many accountants and financial statement users questioned the revenue and expense recognition practices of the franchisors, particularly the recognition of revenue at the signing of the franchise agreement. These concerns led to the issuing of an accounting industry guide in 1973, which the Financial Accounting Standards board later issued as *Statement of Financial Accounting Standards No. 45, Accounting for Franchise Fee Revenue.*

DEFINITION AND DESCRIPTION

Franchising is a system whereby one company grants business rights to another company or individual through a contract to operate a franchised business for a specified period of time. The company granting the business rights is called the **franchisor,** and the company receiving the business rights is called the **franchisee.** The franchisor generally provides a variety of services and products to the franchisee in exchange for fees and charges for products. The franchise fees are partially paid at the signing of the franchise with the remainder often spread out over several succeeding years. The franchisee uses the company name and/or trademark and benefits from the public recognition. In exchange, the franchisee's operations are subject to control by the franchisor.

A typical franchise agreement contains provisions that cover the following areas:

- The outline of the continuing relationship for a specific period of time for the purposes of distribution of a product or service within a specified geographic area.
- The resources to be contributed by both the franchisor and the franchisee. The franchisor may contribute a trademark, company reputation, products, procedures, manpower, equipment, or a process. The franchisee usually contributes operating capital as well as managerial and operating resources for the franchise operation.
- The marketing practices, the contribution of the parties to the operations, and the operating procedures to be followed.
- The specific business entity or entities that are to operate the franchised business.
- The company names, trade names, and trademarks that can be used, and the advertising requirements for both the franchisee and the franchisor.[5]

The franchising of a business provides the franchisor with a wide distribution of the franchisor's product or service without having to provide the working capital or the day to day management. The purchasing of the franchise allows the franchisee to establish a business entity with a known reputation, with less capital, with managerial assistance available, and with less likelihood of failure.

---

[5] *Statement of Financial Accounting Standards No. 45, Accounting for Franchise Fee Revenue* (Stamford, Connecticut: FASB, 1981), paragraph 26.

INITIAL FRANCHISE FEE

A typical franchise requires the payment of an initial franchise fee. This fee is for the use of the trade name or trademark and may also cover the provision of a variety of initial services by the franchisor. The initial services that the franchisor may provide include

- Services related to acquiring land and buildings, such as site selection, architectural and engineering services, construction, and financial assistance
- Services related to promoting the franchise, such as local or national advertising
- Services related to the operations, such as training of the franchisee, training of employees, guidelines for operations and accounting, and quality controls

The initial fee received by the franchisor is recognized as revenue and the related costs as expenses when the franchisee commences business, if all the initial services and conditions have been **substantially performed** and collectibility can be estimated. Substantial performance means that the franchisor

1. has no obligation to refund any payments received or forgive any receivables, and
2. has completed the initial services required by the franchise agreement.[6]

If the franchisor can demonstrate substantial performance prior to the franchisee's commencing business, the revenue and related expense are recognized at that time.

If a franchisor receives payments prior to the time when the initial fee is realized, the amounts received are recorded by the deposit method. If the initial fee is partly paid for by notes from the franchisee, which is a common practice, the notes are recorded at their net present value in accordance with *Accounting Principles Board Opinion No. 21*. If the initial fee is to be paid over a substantial period of time and the franchisor is unable to estimate the possibility of uncollectibility, either the installment method or the cost recovery method is used to recognize the revenue from the initial franchise fee.

Any assets provided to the franchisee, either initially or later, are recognized at their fair market value. Therefore, if the initial fee includes provision of land, buildings, equipment, or inventory at prices below their fair market value, a portion of the initial franchise fee for services is allocated to the tangible assets provided to the franchisee and recorded as a deferred revenue until the asset is sold to the franchisee.

CONTINUING FEES AND BARGAIN SALES

In addition to the initial services provided, the franchisor may continue to supply services to the franchisee, such as management assistance, training of employees, financial and accounting assistance and advice, advertising, and quality control. The revenue from these services is recorded as earned and the expenses are recognized when the costs are incurred. If the franchise agreement specifies a price for these services that is less than their cost plus a normal profit, a portion of the initial fee is deferred and recognized as revenue when the continuing fees are earned. The amount to be deferred is the difference between the cost plus a normal profit and the quoted price.

[6] *SFAS No. 45*, paragraph 5.

If a franchisor agrees to furnish equipment or specific amounts of inventory or supplies to the franchisee at prices below their normal selling prices (bargain purchases), a portion of the initial fee is deferred and allocated to these sales. The amount allocated is the difference between the fair market value of the bargain purchase item and the bargain purchase price. This difference is either the difference between the selling price to other customers and the bargain price, or the difference between the franchisor's cost plus a normal profit and the bargain purchase price. Illustrative Problem 17.4 demonstrates the recognition of revenue for a franchisor and illustrates why the revenue recognition standards were changed.

ILLUSTRATIVE PROBLEM 17.4: REVENUE AND EXPENSE RECOGNITION FOR A FRANCHISE

The Whale O' Burger Company has entered into a 10-year franchise agreement with Ms. Relish for an initial franchise fee of $65,000. Whale O' Burger will rent Ms. Relish a restaurant building, sell her equipment at its cost, assist in selecting furnishings for the restaurant, provide management training for Ms. Relish, provide training for her employees, and provide accounting and financing advice.

In addition, Whale O' Burger will sell Ms. Relish all the necessary food items at market prices and allow her to purchase supplies at 80% of their retail price during the 10 years of the franchise. Whale O' Burger estimates that the supplies will cost Ms. Relish $5,000 per year. Whale O' Burger is to provide Ms. Relish with a restaurant building for 10 years at an annual rental of $12,000, although the fair rental value is $14,000 per year. The equipment sold to Ms. Relish cost Whale O' Burger $22,000 and has a fair market value of $27,500.

Ms. Relish paid an initial deposit of $5,000 when the franchise agreement was signed. When the restaurant was opened nine months later, Ms. Relish paid $10,000 in cash and signed a 10-year, 8% note for the remaining $50,000 of the initial franchise fee. The note requires equal annual payments of $7,451. A local bank would have lent Ms. Relish the $50,000 for 10 years, but would have charged 12% interest. In addition to the cash paid for the initial franchise fee, Ms. Relish paid cash for the equipment, paid three month's rent in advance, and purchased $2,000 worth of supplies for cash.

The journal entry to record the initial deposit is

Cash	5,000	
Unearned Initial Franchise Fee		5,000

The amount of the initial franchise fee recognized as revenue when the restaurant is opened is

Initial Fee		$ 65,000
Less: Difference Between the Fair Market Values and the		
Bargain Prices for		
Equipment Purchases (1)	$ 5,500	
Rental of the Building (2)	20,000	
Supplies (3)	12,500	
Discount from the Note Receivable (4)	7,900	45,900
Initial Franchise Fee Revenue		$ 19,100

(1) $27,500 fair market value − $22,000 cost

(2) $14,000 fair market value − $12,000 rental = $2,000 × 10 years = $20,000

(3) $5,000/.80 = $6,250 − $5,000 = $1,250 × 10 years = $12,500

(4) $50,000 − [$7,451 × 5.6502 (present value of annuity for 10 periods at 12%)] = $50,000 − $42,100 = $7,900 discount on note receivable

The journal entry to record the initial fee revenue is

Cash	10,000	
Note Receivable: Ms. Relish	50,000	
Unearned Initial Franchise Fee	5,000	
Discount on Note Receivable		7,900
Deferred Equipment Revenue		5,500
Deferred Rental Revenue		20,000
Deferred Supplies Revenue		12,500
Initial Franchise Fee Revenue		19,100

Prior to the issuance of *Statement of Financial Accounting Standards No. 45*, the entire $65,000 initial fee, net of the discount of $7,900, or $57,100 would have been recognized as revenue at the signing of the franchise agreement. As illustrated above, the majority of the fee was not earned at the signing of the franchise or even when the restaurant was opened nine months later.

The journal entry to record the sale of equipment is

Cash	22,000	
Deferred Equipment Revenue	5,500	
Equipment		22,000
Gain on Sale of Equipment		5,500

The equipment could have been an inventory item on the books of the franchisor rather than an operating asset. If the equipment is inventory, the entire $27,500 is credited to Sales Revenue.

The journal entry for the sale of supplies is

Cash	2,000	
Deferred Supplies Revenue	500 (1)	
Supplies Revenue		2,500

(1) $2,000/.80 = $2,500 − $2,000 = $500

As Ms. Relish purchases supplies over the life of the franchise similar entries are recorded.

The journal entry to record the rental payment received is

Cash	3,000 (1)	
Deferred Rental Revenue	500 (2)	
Rental Revenue		3,500

(1) $12,000 × 3/12 = $3,000
(2) $ 2,000 × 3/12 = $ 500

As Ms. Relish pays the rent on the restaurant building over the life of the franchise, the remaining deferred rental revenue is recognized.

EXPENSE RECOGNITION BY THE FRANCHISEE

The initial fee is recorded as an intangible asset and amortized over the life of the franchise. The franchisee records the assets and expenses at the same amounts the franchisor used to record the revenues. Just as the franchisor defers a portion of the initial fee when tangible assets and later services are provided at bargain prices, the franchisee defers a portion of the franchise fee and recognizes the deferred portion as an additional cost of the asset or service when it is acquired.

The franchisee's journal entries are

Franchise	19,100	
Discount on Note Payable	7,900	
Deferred Equipment Cost	5,500	
Deferred Rental Expenses	20,000	
Deferred Supplies Expense	12,500	
Cash		10,000
Note Payable: Whale O' Burger		50,000
Franchise Deposit		5,000
To record the payment for the franchise		
Equipment	27,500	
Deferred Equipment Cost		5,500
Cash		22,000
To record the purchase of equipment		
Supplies	2,500	
Deferred Supplies Expense		500
Cash		2,000
To record the purchase of supplies		
Prepaid Rent	3,500	
Deferred Rental Expense		500
Cash		3,000
To record the payment of rent		

The assets and liabilities on the balance sheet of the franchisee, as a result of the transactions of Illustrative Problem 17.4, are shown in Exhibit 17-2. Some accountants would report the entire amount of the Deferred Rental Expense and Deferred upplies Expense as deferred debits. Ms. Relish has paid Whale O' Burger $42,000 ($5,000 initially + $10,000 upon opening of the restaurant + $22,000 for equipment + $3,000 for rent + $2,000 for supplies). The difference of $42,000 between the assets and the liabilities is equal to the cash paid by Ms. Relish.

DISCLOSURE REQUIREMENTS FOR THE FRANCHISOR

A franchisor must disclose

- The nature of all important commitments and obligations from the franchise agreements
- All the services that have been agreed upon, but not yet provided to the franchisees

EXHIBIT 17-2

Illustrative Problem 17.4
Assets and Liabilities of the Franchisee

Assets

Current Assets		
Supplies Inventory	$ 2,500	
Deferred Supplies Expense (1)	750	$ 3,250
Prepaid Rent	3,500	
Deferred Rental Expense (2)	1,500	5,000
Plant and Equipment		
Equipment		27,500
Intangible Assets		
Franchise		19,100
Deferred Debits		
Deferred Supplies Expense (3)	11,250	
Deferred Rental Expense (4)	18,000	29,250
Total Assets Acquired from Whale O'Burger		$ 84,100

Liabilities

Current Liabilities		
Note Payable, Current Portion	$ 5,000	
Less: Discount (5)	1,052	$ 3,948
Long-Term Liabilities		
Note Payable, Noncurrent Portion	45,000	
Less: Discount (6)	6,848	38,152
Total Liabilities		$ 42,100

(1) $5,000 − $2,000 purchased = $3,000 to be purchased in current year
    $3,000/.80 = $3,750 − $3,000 = $750 deferred that is current
(2) $500 × 3 = $1,500 deferred that is current
(3) $12,500 − $500 − $750 = $11,250 that is long-term
(4) $20,000 − $500 − $1,500 = $18,000 that is long-term
(5) ($42,100 × 12%) − ($50,000 × 8%) = $5,052 − $4,000 = $1,052
(6) $7,900 − $1,052 = $6,848

- The amount of franchise revenue that is from initial fees, the amount from continuing services, and the amount from the sales of other assets
- Any revenues that are deferred and when they will be realized
- The amount of fees yet to be collected and their due dates

If a franchisor operates some outlets and franchises some opreations, the income from the franchise operations must be segregated from the amounts earned from the company-operated outlets.

SUMMARY

Other real estate sales are all sales of real estate other than retail land sales. In order to recognize revenue by the full accrual method the sale must be consummated, the buyer's initial and continuing investment must be adequate, the seller holds no obligations of the buyer that are subordinated, and the seller has transferred the risks and rewards of ownership to the buyer. The buyer's initial investment is considered adequate if it is either the amount required under usual lending terms or the lesser of 25% of the selling price or the amount by which the sales price exceeds 115% of the amount loaned by the primary lender.

The buyer's continuing investment must also be adequate to use the full accrual method. The terms of sale must require the buyer to make equal annual payments of principal and interest that are at least equal to the amount an independent lending institution would require of the buyer, and the length of life of the loan cannot exceed the term of a first mortgage from an independent lending institution. If the initial investment is not adequate, the deposit method is used. If the continuing investment is not adequate, but the initial investment is adequate, the installment method, the cost recovery method, and the reduced profit method can be used. The cost recovery method postpones the recognition of any income, either from the sale or from interest, until the cost of the real estate is recovered; then all cash flow is recognized as income. The deferred gross profit method postpones the recognition of a portion of the profit until the maximum life has past.

A franchise is a right to operate a franchised business for a specified period of time. The franchisor (the grantor of the franchise) and the franchisee (the purchaser of the franchise) both agree to conditions that will, hopefully, increase the success and profitability of both the franchisor and the franchisee. The initial franchise fee is not recognized as revenue until the franchisor has substantially completed all the initial services due the franchisee. If the franchisee is not paying a market rate of interest on the balance of the initial franchise fee payments, then interest is imputed at the market rate. If the franchisor is providing products or services to the franchisee at below market prices, a portion of the initial franchise fee is deferred and recognized as revenue from the products or services.

The franchisee records an intangible asset at the same value as the franchisor recorded the revenue from the initial fee. The franchisee records all purchases of goods and services from the franchisor at their fair market value; therefore, if the prices are below the market values, the franchisee allocates a portion of the initial franchise fee to the costs of those products and services.

REVIEW PROBLEMS

OTHER REAL ESTATE SALES

Sweet Home Development Company sold an apartment building for $2,400,000. The cost of the land and the construction was $1,600,000.

1. The buyer paid Sweet Home a cash down payment of $400,000 and financed the balance as follows:

    1) a 12% 20-year first mortgage payable to Lebanon Bank in the amount of $1,500,000. The loan will be repaid with equal annual payments of $200,819.

    2) an 8% 25-year second mortgage payable to Sweet Home Development Company in the amount of $500,000. The loan will be repaid with equal annual payments of $46,839.

The maximum amount that an independent lending institution would lend on the property is $1,750,000 at 12% interest for 25 years. The loan would require equal annual payments of $223,126.

Required
1) Determine if the initial investment is adequate for use of the full accrual method.
2) Determine if the continuing investment is adequate.
3) Determine the length of time necessary before conversion to the full accrual method is possible.

2. The buyer paid Sweet Home a cash down payment of $700,000 and financed the balance as follows:

    1) a 12%, 20-year first mortgage payable to Lebanon Bank in the amount of $1,200,000. The loan will be repaid with equal annual payments of $160,655.

    2) a 12%, 30-year second mortgage payable to Sweet Home Development Company in the amount of $500,000. The loan will be repaid with equal annual payments of $62,072.

The maximum first mortgage loan that an independent lending institution would lend on the property is $1,500,000 at 12% for 25 years. The loan would require equal annual payments of $191,251. The usual down payment is 20% and the market rate of interest is 12%.

Required
1) Determine if the continuing investment is adequate.
2) Determine if the reduced profit method can be used. If the method can be used determine the amount of profit deferred and the point(s) in time when it is recognized as income.
3) Assume that Sweet Home Development Company questions the ability of the buyer to pay the mortgage payments. Determine the point in time when revenue is realized using the cost recovery method. Explain the type of revenue realized and how it is determined.

FRANCHISING

Yummy Yogurt Company franchises retail operations to sell its "just like ice cream" yogurt. The 12-year franchise contract contains the following provisions:
1. An initial fee of $40,000, with a $10,000 payment on the signing of the contract and the balance payable in 10 equal installments at 6% interest.
2. Yummy Yogurt will supply all the equipment necessary to run the yogurt store at cost. The normal selling price of the equipment is $16,500 and Yummy Yogurt's cost is $12,800.
3. Yummy Yogurt will supply all the yogurt needed by the franchisee. The cost of the yogurt is $4.00 per gallon. A typical franchise will sell approximately 12,000 gallons of yogurt per year. If the franchisee were to purchase the yogurt from an outside source the cost would be $4.10 per gallon.
4. Yummy Yogurt agrees to provide management training and assistance to the franchisee over the life of the franchise as is necessary for a successful operation.
5. Yummy Yogurt will actively promote the product on national television and in other appropriate nationwide media. In addition, Yummy Yogurt will assist the franchisee with local advertising.

Required
1. Determine the amount of the initial franchise fee recorded by Yummy Yogurt, if the market rate of interest is 10% and the franchisee is a typical store.

2. Write the journal entries to record the initial franchise fee revenue, the sale of equipment, and the purchase of one month's supply of yogurt assuming Yummy Yogurt manufactures the equipment.
3. Write the journal entries to record the initial franchise fee, the purchase of equipment, and the purchase of one months' supply of yogurt for the franchisee.
4. Draft a footnote to be included in Yummy Yogurt's financial statements, assuming 10 typical franchises were issued during the current year, all purchased the equipment, and 60,000 gallons of yogurt were sold to the franchisees.

QUESTIONS

1. What are the conditions necessary to use the full accrual method for other real estate sales?
2. What is the test to determine if the buyer's initial investment is adequate for an other real estate sale?
3. What items are included and excluded in determining the down payment for an other real estate sale?
4. What is the test to determine if the continuing investment of an other real estate sale is adequate?
5. What methods can be used to account for a nonretail real estate sale if the initial down payment is adequate, but the continuing investment is not adequate?
6. Explain the test to determine if the reduced profit method can be used when the initial and continuing investments are adequate, but the length of life of the debt exceeds the maximum time span of the maximum first mortgage.
7. If the reduced profit method is used, explain how the amount of gross profit realized is determined and when the deferred gross profit is realized.
8. Explain how the cost recovery method for other real estate sales is implemented.
9. What are the typical provisions of a franchise agreement?
10. What are the typical kinds of assets and services that might be paid for with an initial franchise fee?
11. What are the conditions for recognizing the initial franchise fee as revenue?
12. What constitutes substantial performance in a franchising arrangement?
13. What are continuing fees and bargain sales in franchising and how are they accounted for?
14. What disclosures are required of a franchisor?

EXERCISES

EXERCISE 17-1

AB Construction Company has sold an apartment building to Landlord Inc. for $6,000,000. Landlord Inc. has agreed to pay $900,000 as a down payment, to assume the outstanding mortgage on the building of $4,100,000 and to issue a $1,000,000 second mortgage to AB Construction Company with interest at the current market rate of 12%. The local bank will lend $4,750,000 on the property.

Required

1. Determine if the buyer's initial investment is adequate to use the full accrual method of accounting.
2. If AB Construction was able to sell the second mortgage for $665,000, is the initial investment adequate?

EXERCISE 17-2

Refer to Exercise 17-1. The first mortgage requires annual payments of $540,000. The second mortgage requires annual payments of $134,000. A loan from the local bank would require annual payments of $635,000.

Required

1. Determine the contract year in which the initial investment and the continuing payments are adequate, and conversion to the full accrual method is possible.
2. If the second mortgage requires an additional principal payment of $200,000 at the end of the fourth year, determine the contract year in which the initial investment and the continuing investment are adequate to allow conversion to the full accrual method of accounting.

EXERCISE 17-3

Brick Builders, Inc. sold an apartment complex to Happy Haven Investments for $25,000,000. The agreement of sale required Happy Haven to provide the following to purchase the complex:

Cash Down Payment	$ 750,000
Note from Happy Haven Secured by an Irrevocable Letter of Credit from First Security Bank	2,000,000
Payment of the Delinquent Property taxes by Happy Haven	1,000,000
Payment for Landscaping Not Yet Planted	250,000
10%, 20-year First Mortgage from Square One Bank Requiring Equal Annual Payments of $1,762,000	15,000,000
8%, 20-year Second Mortgage Payable to Brick Builders Requiring Equal Annual Payments of $611,200	6,000,000

The maximum that an independent lending institution will lend on the property is $20,000,000 for 20 years at 10% interest. The loan would require equal annual payments of $2,349,200.

Required

1. Determine the amount of the down payment.
2. Determine if the initial investment is adequate.
3. Determine if the continuing investment in adequate.

EXERCISE 17-4

CD Development Company sold a tract of land to EF Construction Company for $2,000,000, which cost CD Development $1,400,000. EF Construction will pay $550,000 down in cash, borrow $1,200,000 from First Mortgage Company at 12% interest payable in 20 equal annual payments of $160,655, and issue a 25-year, 10%, $250,000 second mortgage to CD Development that requires equal annual payments of $27,542. The maximum first mortgage an independent lending institution will lend is $1,350,000 for 20 years at 10% interest with equal annual payments of $158,570. The normal down payment is 25% and the market rate of interest is 10%.

Required

1. Why is it not appropriate to use the full accrual method to account for the sale?
2. Determine if CD Development can use the reduce profit method.
3. What is the amount of gross profit that is recognized in the year of sale and when is the deferred gross profit recognized?

EXERICSE 17-5

Refer to Exercise 17-4. EF Construction paid the down payment of $550,000 and issued a $1,450,000 20-year first mortgage to CD Development with interest at 8% and annual payments of $147,700.

Required

1. Determine if the initial investment and the continuing investment are adequate.
2. Assume that CD Development questions whether or not EF Construction will be able to pay the mortgage payments and, therefore, will use the cost recovery method. Prepare the journal entries to record the receipt of the down payment and the first two annual payments on the mortgage.

3. Determine the length of time necessary for CD Development to recover its costs.
4. Explain the recognition process of the deferrals once the cost is recovered.

EXERCISE 17-6

Smooth as Silk Yogurt Company has entered into a franchise agreement with Mr. and Mrs. Q. The 10-year franchise agreement contains the following provisions:

- Initial Fee of $40,000: $8,000 is payable at the signing of the franchise agreement and the balance of $32,000 is payable in four equal annual installments of $9,662, which include interest at 8%.
- Equipment and furniture for the yogurt shop at a cost of $28,000.
- Yogurt for five years at $1.00 per gallon.

The equipment and furniture have a normal selling price of $31,000. The yogurt cost Smooth as Silk $0.80 per gallon to manufacture and a normal markup is 50% of cost. Smooth as Silk estimates that the Mr. and Mrs. Q's yogurt shop will sell approximately 50,000 gallons over the next five years. A local banker would have lent the money for the franchise, but would have charged 12% interest.

Required

1. Prepare the journal entry to record the revenue from the initial franchise fee, assuming the business began operations five months after signing the franchise.
2. Prepare the journal entry to record the sale of the equipment and furniture for the franchisor.
3. During the first year, Mr. and Mrs. Q's yogurt shop purchased 9,000 gallons. Prepare the journal entry for the purchase of yogurt for the franchisee.
4. Prepare the balance sheet items at the end of the first year, in a current noncurrent format, for Mr. and Mrs. Q's yogurt shop, assuming 8,000 gallons of yogurt are sold, and the equipment and furniture are being depreciated by the straight-line method over the life of the franchise with no salvage value.

EXERCISE 17-7

Super Copy Corp. franchises duplicating stores near college and university campuses. Mr. R has entered into an agreement with Super Copy to franchise a store adjacent to Upstate College. The franchise agreement contains the following provisions:

- An initial fee of $35,000: $5,000 payable immediately, $5,000 upon the opening of the store, and the remainder in five equal annual payments including interest at 6%, even though the local bank would charge interest at 10%.
- Super Copy will sell the duplicating equipment, which it manufactures, for $22,000, which is 10% over cost, although a normal markup is 25% of cost.
- Super Copy agrees to provide repair service on the duplicating equipment for a period of two years at its cost. A typical franchise averages $2,800 of repair costs a year. If the services were purchased from an outside repair company, they would cost $3,500 per year.

Required

1. Prepare all the journal entries for the franchisor for the first year, assuming that the store was opened three months after signing the agreement, Super Copy has performed all the agreed upon services for the initial fee, and the actual repair services totaled $2,200.
2. Prepare all the journal entires for the franchisee for the first year.

EXERCISE 17-8

1. On December 31, 1991, Reed, Inc., authorized Foy to operate as a franchisee for an initial franchise fee of $75,000. Of this amount, $30,000 was received upon signing of the agreement, and the balance, represented by a note, is due in three annual payments of $15,000 each beginning on December 31,

1992. The present value on December 31, 1992 of the three annual payments appropriately discounted is $36,000. According to the agreement, the nonrefundable down payment represents a fair measure of the services already performed by Reed; however, substantial future services are required of Reed. Collectibility of the note is reasonably certain. On December 31, 1991, Reed should record unearned franchise fees in respect of the Foy franchise of

a. $ 0
b. $ 36,000
c. $ 45,000
d. $ 75,000

2. On January 3, 1991, Paterson Services, Inc. signed an agreement authorizing Cobb Company to operate as a franchisee over a 20-year period for an initial franchise fee of $50,000 received when the agreement was signed. Cobb commenced operations on July 1, 1991. As of July 1, 1991, all of the initial services required of Paterson had been performed. The agreement also provided that Cobb must pay Paterson a continuing franchise fee each year equal to 5% of the annual revenue from the franchise. Cobb's franchise revenue for 1991 was $400,000. For the year ended December 31, 1991, how much should Paterson record as revenue from franchise fees in respect of the Cobb franchise?

a. $ 70,000
b. $ 50,000
c. $ 45,000
d. $ 22,500

(AICPA adapted)

EXERCISE 17-9

1. Which of the following is expensed as incurred by the franchisee for a franchise with an estimated useful life of 10 years?

a. Amount paid to the franchisor for the franchise
b. Periodic payments to a company, other than the franchisor, for that company's franchise
c. Legal fees paid to the franchisee's lawyers to obtain the franchise
d. Periodic payments to the franchisor based on the franchisee's income

2. On July 1, 1991, Hart signed an agreement to operate as a franchisee of Ace Printers for an initial franchise fee of $120,000. On the same date Hart paid $40,000 and agreed to pay the balance in four equal annual payments of $20,000 beginning on July 1, 1992. The down payment is not refundable and no future services are required of the franchisor. Hart can borrow at 14% interest for a loan of this type. Present and future value factors are

Present value of 1 at 14% for 4 periods	0.59
Future amount of 1 at 14% for 4 periods	1.69
Presenst value of an ordinary annuity of 1 at 14% for 4 periods	2.91

Hart should record the acquisition cost of the franchise on July 1, 1991 at

a. $ 135,200
b. $ 120,000
c. $ 98,200
d. $ 87,200

3. On December 31, 1991, Wall Company signed an agreement to operate as a franchisee of Fast Food, Inc. for an initial franchise fee of $80,000. Of this amount, $30,000 was paid when the agreement was signed and the balance is payable in five annual payments of $10,000 each beginning December 31, 1992. The present value of the five payments, at an appropriate rate of interest, is $36,000 at December 31, 1991. The agreement provides that the down payment is not refundable and no future services are required of the franchisor. Wall should report the franchise in its December 31, 1991 balance sheet at

a. $ 80,000
b. $ 66,000
c. $ 30,000
d. $ –0–

(AICPA adapted)

PROBLEMS

PROBLEM 17-1
Several revenue recognition methods can be used to record the revenue from other real estate sales.

Required
1. Explain the meaning of the phrase, "substance over form."
2. Discuss the reasons for the criteria that were established for other real estate sales.
3. Describe the basic differences between the methods that can be used and when it is appropriate to use each of the methods.

PROBLEM 17-2
Sports Unlimited has just sold a large covered sports arena to Promotions Inc. for $60 million that has a net book value of $48 million. Promotions Inc. has agreed to make a down payment of $10 million, borrow $40 million by issuing a 20-year, 12% first mortgage that requires equal annual payments of $5,355,182, and to give Sports Unlimited a 20-year second mortgage with interest at 16% for the balance owing. The second mortgage requires equal annual payments of $1,096,343. In addition, Promotions Inc. has agreed to pay the unpaid property taxes totaling $3.5 million. Promotions Inc. expects to spend $8 million refurbishing the arena and has already paid a down payment on the refurbishing of $2 million. A local bank consortium would lend $44 million on a 20-year, 12% first mortgage with equal annual payments of $5,890,700.

Required
1. What is the purpose of the test for the adequacy of the down payment?
2. Determine if the down payment is adequate.
3. Describe the methods that can be used to account for the sale.
4. Determine the year in which conversion to the full accrual method is possible.
5. Assuming that Sports Unlimited is able to sell the second mortgage it received from Promotions Inc. for $5 million without recourse, determine if the buyer's initial investment is adequate.
6. Ignoring part (5), is the continuing investment adequate?
7. If a buyer's continuing investment is not adequate, what methods of accounting for the sale can be used?
8. If the mortgage payments are due on the last day of the year, determine the amount of gross profit that is recognized through Year 5 using the installment method.
9. Prepare the journal entry to convert to the full accrual method from the installment method at the end of Year 5.

PROBLEM 17-3

Land Developers Inc. has sold 10 acres of land adjacent to a large suburban shopping center for $1,250,000 and the purchasers, High Tower Building Contractors, paid a $25,000 deposit when the option was signed. Land Developers paid $50,000 per acre for the land. Land Developers spent an additional $150,000 subdividing the acreage and installing roads and underground utilities. High Tower paid $225,000 down, which is normal for this type of property and agreed to pay the balance as follows:

1) $500,000, 15-year, 12% loan from Land Bank of Boise, payable in equal annual installments of principal and interest
2) $500,000, 25-year, 12% loan from the seller, payable in equal annual installments of principal and interest

The maximum that an independent lending institution will lend on this property is $850,000 for 20 years at 12% interest with equal annual payments.

Required

1. Determine the adequacy of the continuing investment.
2. Determine the income recognized, assuming that Land Developers is reasonably certain it will recover the cost of the property.
3. Determine the income recognized over the life of the contracts if Land Developers is not certain that it will recover the cost of the property. Prepare a single amortization schedule for both mortgages together.

PROBLEM 17-4

Condor Construction Company sold Chain Department Store a building for $1,600,000, which cost Condor $1,250,000 to construct. The terms of sales were

1) Cash Down Payment	$ 500,000
2) 25-year, 8% Mortgage Payable to Condor Construction with Principal and Interest Payable in Equal Annual Payments	$ 1,100,000

The maximum amount that Downtown Bank will lend on this property is $1,200,000 for 20 years at 10% interest.

Required

1. Determine if the full accrual method can be used.
2. Determine if the deferred gross profit method can be used.
3. Condor is concerned about the ability of Chain Stores to pay the payments and, therefore, elected to use the cost recovery method of accounting for the sale. Prepare the journal entries to record the sale.
4. Determine the year in which the deferred gross profit from the sale is recognized.
5. Prepare a schedule for the recognition of interest revenue and deferred gross profit.
6. Prepare the journal entries for the first installment payment, the first payment when interest revenue is recognized, and the first payment when deferred gross profit is recognized.

PROBLEM 17-5

Mr. Small Business has asked you to help him decide whether or not to purchase a franchise for $60,000 from Savoy Realtors, Inc. The representatives from Savoy have advised Mr. Small Business that the entire price paid for the franchise can be capitalized and amortized over the 10-year life of the franchise. Savoy Realtors promises to advertise its trade name, provide training for sales personnel, provide marketing and advertising expertise, and provide accounting assistance over the 10-year life of the franchise at no charge to Mr. Small Business. Savoy Realtors also provides the computer programs for maintenance of the current listings of the office and for mailing of brochures. The cost of the franchise is $10,000 upon signing the contract, an additional $10,000 when the real estate office is opened, and the remaining $40,000 is to be paid in equal annual payments over 5 years with interest at 6%, although the market rate of interest is 10%. Savoy Realtors estimates that the services it is providing to the franchisee would cost $2,500 a year if purchased from other experts. A comparable software package for maintaining listings can be purchased for $300 plus $100 a year for updating. Savoy does not charge the franchisees for the software.

Required

Draft a memo to Mr. Small Business explaining the accounting treatment of all the items that are contained in the franchise agreement including the income statement effects over the life of the franchise. Include in your memo the actual values of the franchise items. Your memo should have exhibits attached to it showing the income statement effects over the life of the franchise, and the balance sheet at the end of each of the first five years.

PROBLEM 17-6

Quik Fix manufactures auto parts and sells the parts through franchised stores. Quik Fix also manufactures the storage units and counters necessary to equip the stores. The franchise agreement that Quik Fix uses for its 10-year franchises contains the following provisions:

- An initial fee of $60,000: $5,000 upon signing the contract, an additional $5,000 when the store is opened, and the balance payable in 5 equal annual payments with interest at 6%.
- Quik Fix provides marketing and location selection aid to the franchisee as part of the initial fee.
- The storage units and counters are sold to the franchisee at 10% above Quik Fix's cost, although a normal markup is 25% of cost. The equipment is estimated to have a useful life of 10 years and a salvage value of $7,500.
- For the first two years, Quik Fix will sell the parts to the franchisee at 60% of the retail selling price, when the normal charge is 75% of selling price. An average franchise will have sales of $250,000 for the first two years.
- Quik Fix agrees to actively promote its products nationwide as well as in local market areas.

On January 1, 1990, Mr. Kay entered into a franchise agreement with Quik Fix. On August 1, 1990, the store opened for business with inventory that retails for $50,000. Quik Fix charged Mr. Kay $33,000 for the storage units and counters. During the remainder of 1990, Mr. Kay had sales of $82,000 and operating expenses of $11,000, exclusive of depreciation and amortization. On December 31, 1990, of Mr. Kay's store has $36,300 of inventory on hand at Mr. Kay's purchase price from Quik Fix.

Required

1. Determine the amount of the initial franchise fee recorded by Quik Fix if Mr. Kay's borrowing rate is 10%.
2. Prepare the journal entries to record the initial franchise fee, the sale and purchase of the storage units and counters, and the sale and purchase of the opening inventory for both the franchisor and the franchisee.
3. Prepare the journal entires to reflect the operating results on the books of the franchisor and the franchisee, assuming Mr. Kay uses a perpetual inventory system.
4. If the income and cash flow for the first five months of operations are good estimates of future income and cash flows, would you invest in one of Quik Fix's franchises? Explain your conclusion.

PROBLEM 17-7

Glamorous Glow sells its cosmetic and perfume products through franchised retail outlets. Glamorous Glow provides location, leasing arrangements, decorating, and store fixture advice for an initial franchise fee of $25,000. During the 10-year life of the franchise, Glamorous Glow provides marketing, and accounting advice and services charging the franchisee the market rate for these services. An average franchise uses $2,500 worth of services during a year.

In addition, Glamorous Glow sells all cosmetics and perfumes to its new franchisees for 80% of the normal selling price for the first two years to enable the franchisee to develop a clientele and still make a profit. Glamorous Glow estimates a normal franchise will purchase $36,000 worth of inventory at the reduced price during the first two years. After two years, Glamorous Glow charges the franchisee the full price for the merchandise. A normal retail outlet will purchase and sell $66,000 of merchandise at the normal selling prices during Years 3 through 5. After five years, Glamorous Glow charges a fee of 5% of gross revenues. A normal retail outlet will sell $150,000 worth of merchandise during Years 6 through 10. The average gross profit margin is 40% of the normal selling price, and the average year-end inventory for a store is $10,000.

Required

1. What is the amount of the initial fee that Glamorous Glow records upon the opening of a franchised store?
2. Determine the amount of revenue that Glamorous Glow records from a normal franchise operation for each of the 10 years of the franchise.
3. If you could lease rental space for $6,000 per year, and estimate that your labor and other overhead will cost $1,500 per month, exclusive of the amortization of the franchise, determine if you would have a profitable operation if you entered into a franchise agreement with Glamorous Glow.
4. Would you advise a client to purchase a Glamorous Glow franchise? Explain your answer and include any warnings you feel are necessary in advising your client.

PROBLEM 17-8

Miracle Carpet Cleaner franchises carpeting cleaning outlets for 15 years. The franchise contracts require an initial franchise fee of $45,000: $5,000 payable upon signing of the franchise and the remaining $40,000 payable in 8 equal annual installments with interest at 8%, although the market rate of interest is 12%. Miracle agrees to furnish each franchisee with brand-name recognition through its national advertising campaign and to provide 1/2-minute spot commercials that can be used on local radio stations at the normal selling price. In addition, Miracle agrees to provide all the equipment, which Miracle manufactures, for 75% of the market price. Miracle will also provide all the cleaning supplies, which Miracle also manufactures, to the franchisee during the life of the franchise at 90% of their market value. The cost of the equipment to the franchisee is $15,000 and its estimated useful life is 15 years. An average franchise will spend $12,000 at the reduced price on supplies during the first year, and its purchases will increase by 20% per year for each of the next 3 years, and then remain constant for the rest of the life of the franchise.

Required

1. Assuming that the franchisor has performed all the services required by the initial fee, determine the amount of franchise revenue recognized in the first year by the franchisor for a normal franchise.
2. Prepare the journal entries for both the franchisor and the franchisee to record the initial franchise fee.
3. Prepare the journal entries for the franchisee for the purchase of equipment and a normal amount of first-year supplies.
4. Assuming that an average franchise maintains an inventory of supplies of $1,800 at the purchase price and the first installment payment of the franchise fee is due on the first day of the following year, determine the balance sheet values at the end of the first year for a franchisee who purchased the normal amount of supplies and equipment.

SOLUTIONS TO REVIEW PROBLEMS

OTHER REAL ESTATE SALES

1. 1) Determination of the Minimum Initial Investment Required
        The greater of
          1. Down payment under usual loan limits is $650,000.
             ($2,400,000 − $1,750,000 = $650,000)
          2. The lesser of
             1) 25% of sales value is $600,000.
                ($2,400,000 × .25 = $600,000)
             2) Amount by which sales value exceeds 115% of the loan by the primary lender is
                $675,000. [$2,400,000 − ($1,500,000 × 1.15)] = $675,000

   Test 2 (1) $600,000 is less than test 2 (2) $675,000, so the value used for test 2 is $600,000. The
   value of test 1 ($650,000) is greater than test 2 (1). Therefore, the initial investment must be at
   least $650,000. The down payment is only $400,000 in cash and, therefore, the initial investment
   is not adequate and the accrual method cannot be used.

1. 2) Adequacy of Continuing Investment
        ($200,819 + $46,839) = $247,658 of equal annual payments. $247,658 > $223,126 and the
        length of life of the mortgages does not exceed the maximum term of a maximum loan from an
        independent lending institution; therefore, the continuing investment is adequate.

1. 3) Computation of Point in Time When Both Initial and Continuing Investment Are Adequate

Total Payments of Principal and Interest	$ 247,658
Payments Required by the Maximum Amount an Independent Lending Institution Will Loan	223,126
Excess to Cover Down Payment Shortage	$ 24,532

Computation of Number of Years Required ($250,000 ÷ $24,532)	10.2 years

   The company can convert to the accrual method during the eleventh year of the contract. Prior
   to that time, it could use the installment method, if collectibility was reasonably assured. If
   collectibility was not reasonably assured, then either the cost recovery method or the deposit
   method would be used.

2. 1) The continuing investment is adequate as the sum of the payments on the two mortgages exceeds
        the amount required by the maximum loan obtainable ($160,655 + $62,072) > $191,251. The
        30-year term of the second mortgage exceeds the 25-year time span of the maximum first mortgage
        loan. When the time spans of the mortgages exceeds the maximum life of a loan from an independent
        lending institution, the full accrual method cannot be used, but the reduced profit method can
        be used if the payments meet the test for its use.

2. 2) Test for Use of the Reduced Profit Method

Payment Required by Maximum First Mortgage Loan		$ 191,251
Interest on the Difference Between Total Amount Borrowed and		
Maximum First Mortgage Loan at the Market Rate of Interest		
($200,000 × 12%)		24,000
Total Equal Annual Payments Required		$ 215,251

Equal Annual Payments Required by Loans		
First Mortgage		$ 160,655
Second Mortgage		62,072
Total Annual Payments		$ 222,727

Selling Price of Property		$ 2,400,000
Cost of Property		1,600,000
Gross Profit		800,000
Less: Excess of Face Value Over Present Value: Second		
Mortgage	$ 500,000	
Less: Present Value at 12% for 25 years (1)	486,837	13,163
Gross Profit Realized at Point of Sale		$ 786,837

(1) $62,072 × 7.8431 = $486,837

The $13,163 of deferred gross profit is recognized in years 26 through 30 of the contract.

2. 3)

Cost of Property		$ 1,600,000
Down Payment Received		700,000
Unrecovered Cost		900,000
Annual Mortgage Payments Required		÷ 222,727
Years Until Revenue Can Be Realized		4.04 years

In Year 5, a portion of the interest revenue deferred in the previous four years is recognized. The amount is equal to the principal payments received less the remainder of the unrecovered cost. In the following years, the remaining deferred interest revenue is recognized in an amount equal to the amount of principal payments received. When all the deferred interest revenue has been recognized, the deferred gross profit from the sale is recognized each year in an amount equal to the principal payments received.

FRANCHISING

1.

Initial Fee		$ 40,000
Less: Discount on Note Receivable		4,955
Net Present Value of Initial Franchise Fee		35,045
Less: Amount Allocated to Equipment		
($16,500 − $12,800)	$ 3,700	
Amount Allocated to Yogurt		
(12,000 gallons × 12 years = 144,000)		
(144,000 × ($4.10 − $4.00))	14,400	18,100
Initial Franchise Fee Revenue		$ 16,945

Computation of Discount on Note Receivable

Face Amount of the 6% Note		$ 30,000
Equal Annual Payments at 6% Interest		
$30,000 ÷ 7.3601 (1) = $4,076		
Present Value of Annual Payments at 10% Interest		
$4,076 × 6.1446 (2)		25,045
Discount on Note Receivable		$ 4,955

(1) Present value of an annuity for 10 years at 6%
(2) Present value of an annuity for 10 years at 10%

2.
Cash	10,000	
Note Receivable	30,000	
Deferred Equipment Revenue		3,700
Deferred Yogurt Revenue		14,400
Initial Franchise Fee Revenue		16,945
Cash and/or Accounts Receivable	12,800	
Deferred Equipment Revenue	3,700	
Sales Revenue: Equipment		16,500
Cash and/or Accounts Receivable (1)	4,000	
Deferred Yogurt Revenue	100	
Sale Revenue: Yogurt (2)		4,100

(1) (12,000 ÷ 12) × $4.00 = $4,000
(2) 1,000 × $4.10 = $4,100

3.
Franchise	16,945	
Discount on Note Payable	4,955	
Deferred Equipment Cost	3,700	
Deferred Inventory Costs	14,400	
Cash		10,000
Note Payable		30,000
Equipment	16,500	
Deferred Equipment Cost		3,700
Cash		12,800
Yogurt Inventory	4,100	
Deferred Inventory Costs		100
Cash		4,000

4. The company is committed to providing its 10 franchise operations with all the yogurt they will need for the 12 years of the franchise contract. In addition, the company is committed to providing management assistance and training as needed by the franchisee. The company has agreed to actively promote the product on national television and in other appropriate national media and to assist the franchisee with local advertising.

Franchise Revenue

Initial Franchise Fees	$ 169,450
Sales of Equipment	165,000
Sales of Yogurt (1)	246,000
Total Franchise Revenue	$ 580,450

Deferred Revenue from the Sales of Yogurt (2) $ 138,000

(1) 60,000 gallons $\times$ $4.10 = $246,000
(2) 144,000 gallons $\times$ 10 franchises = 1,440,000 gallons to be purchased
    1,440,000 $-$ 60,000 purchased = 1,380,000 yet to be purchased
    1,380,000 $\times$ $0.10 = $138,000.

ESTATES AND TRUSTS

T his chapter is the first of six chapters that cover entities that use the fund theory of equity discussed in Chapter 1. This chapter discusses the accounting and reporting for estates and trusts. Chapter 19 discusses the restructuring and dissolution of business entities; Chapters 20, 21, and 22 discuss the accounting and reporting for not-for-profit entities; and Chapter 23 discusses accounting and reporting for governmental units.

The topics of the chapter include

- The operations of estates and trusts, including the people involved, the legal environment, the types of distributable assets, and the application of the fund theory of equity
- The recording of the initial inventory of an estate
- The recording of the transactions that typically are incurred by an estate including the transaction affecting estate principal, estate income, and distributions to devisees and legatees
- The fiduciary's report
- The journal entries for the final distribution of the assets and the closing entries for an estate
- The differences between estates and trusts
- The reporting of transactions for a trust
- The accounting and reporting problems that are unique to trusts

OPERATIONS OF ESTATES AND TRUSTS

The methods of accounting for estates and trusts are the result of the duties and financial reporting required by law of the administrator of an estate or trust. Many of the principles and rules used in financial accounting for profit-making organizations are not followed when accounting for estates and trusts because they differ from the legal requirements for the administration and reporting of a trust or estate by the administrator. The basic thrust of estate and trust accounting is one of accountability by the administrator for the assets of the estate or trust. In accounting for estates and trusts, the approach to the entity is one of sources and uses of assets, and the transactions are usually recorded when cash flows, although some accruals are recorded at the formation of the estate or trust.

The administrator of an estate or trust is called a **fiduciary.** A fiduciary is a person entrusted with another's property for safekeeping, management, and distribution. A fiduciary has a custodial or stewardship role. The fiduciary of an estate or trust is responsible for safeguarding the assets, paying the debts and expenses, collecting the income, distributing the assets to the proper entities, and preparing an accounting of the transactions to the proper legal bodies and to the heirs or beneficiaries. A fiduciary may be either the **executor (executrix** if female) of an estate or the **trustee** of a trust. In some states the fiduciary of an estate is called a **personal representative** rather than an executor or executrix.

When a person dies an executor is appointed by the courts to handle the administration of the estate of the deceased person. A decedent may leave a will that appoints an executor, and the court then approves the appointment, or if the decedent did not have a valid will, the court will appoint an executor. When a person dies and leaves a will, that person is said to die **testate,** and when a decedent does not have a will, that person is said to die **intestate.** A trustee is usually named in the trust document, although occasionally a court may establish a trust and appoint a trustee for a minor child or for a person who is not mentally competent to handle their financial affairs.

LEGAL ENVIRONMENT

The laws of the various states govern the administration and distribution of an estate or trust, and vary from state to state. In addition, states have different laws regarding the transfer of real and personal property. Real property is land and buildings, and *all* other assets are considered personal property. Typically, the laws of the state in which the property is located govern the distribution of real property, and the laws of the state in which the decedent lived govern the distribution of personal property. In some states title to real property passes directly to the beneficiaries of an estate and in others the real property becomes part of the estate and is then distributed to the beneficiaries. Even though some states permit the direct transfer of real property, the property is usually included in the initial inventory of the estate to provide a record of the property and the transaction affecting the transfer of title.

Another set of laws, which are common in the western part of the United States, are the community property laws of states such as Washington and California. The community property laws affect the estates of married decedents. When a state has community property laws, the spouses each own half of all their assets regardless of which one earned the assets, except those assets that a spouse had prior to the marriage or inherited after the marriage and that have been maintained and accounted for separately. Therefore, half of almost all assets are not part of the estate of the deceased, but are the property of the surviving spouse.

DISTRIBUTIONS OF ASSETS TO BENEFICIARIES

If a decedent has a valid will, the executor must follow the provisions of the will regarding the classification of the events and transactions and the distribution of the assets, unless the provisions are in violation of the state's laws governing the administration and distribution of estate assets. When a person dies testate, the provisions of the will covering the distribution of the assets to the heirs or beneficiaries must be followed by the fiduciary. If a person dies intestate, the laws of the state of residence of the decedent govern who receives the assets of the decedent's estate. A number of different types of bequests exist that an individual can provide for in a will or a trust agreement. Real property that is left to a beneficiary of an estate or trust is a **devise** and the recipient is a **devisee.** The personal property left to a beneficiary is referred to as a **legacy** or a **bequest** and the recipient is a **legatee.** Legacies can be classified in a number of ways.

- A **general** legacy is a specific quantity or dollar amount of an asset, for example, 10 bottles of California Cabernet Sauvignon (red wine) or $500 worth of California Cabernet Sauvignon.
- A **specific** legacy is a particular asset, for example, 10 bottles of 1974 Mondavi Special Selection Cabernet Sauvignon stored in bin 5 of wine cellar.
- A **demonstrative** legacy is an exact amount from a specific source, for example, all the Cabernet Sauvignon that is stored in bins 5 through 10 of a wine cellar in residence at Albany, Maine.
- A **residual** legacy is the remainder of the personal property of an estate after all the devises and other legacies have been satisfied and all the debts and expenses have been paid. The person designated to receive a residual legacy is the **remainderman.**
- A **pecuniary** legacy is a bequest of money. The legacy can be general, specific, or demonstrative. For example, a bequest of $5,000 is a general legacy, all the money in savings account number 678-4631 in City Bank is a specific legacy, and $5,000 from savings account number 678-4631 in City Bank is a demonstrative legacy.

Although whether or not a distribution of an asset is a devise or a legacy, and the type of legacy does not alter the accounting for the bequests, these distinctions are important in interpreting a will or trust instrument and in applying the state laws for the administration and reporting for an estate or trust.

When accounting for either a trust or an estate, the fiduciary needs to be fully aware of the state laws applying to property ownership and the laws governing the administration and distribution of estates and trusts. In addition, the fiduciary needs to have a good understanding of the provisions of the will or trust instrument so that the wishes of the decedent of the estate or grantor of the trust are carried out and the accounting complies with the terms of the will or trust instrument.

EQUITY THEORY

In Chapter 1, we discussed the three theories of equity. The fund theory of equity is used to account for the transactions of estates and trusts as profit making is not the objective. Instead, the objective is one of preservation of assets, proper distribution of assets, and accountability for assets. The emphasis is on the sources of assets and the uses of assets: Sources of assets equal uses of assets or assets equal equity. This equation can also be thought of as assets equal accountability for those assets.

A fund is a self-balancing set of accounts designed to record the transactions for a particular set of activities. In estates and trusts the sources and uses of assets are divided into two categories, **Principal** and **Income.** This creates two sets of assets equal equity accounts (funds), and is similar to having two sets of accounts for two different entities. The accounting can be thought of as having two sets of books that are each in balance. The distinction between Principal and Income is critical to the accounting and reporting for estates and trusts as it determines if a transaction is recorded in the set of accounts (fund) for Principal or in the set of accounts for Income.

The principal of an estate or trust consists of the original assets, plus any assets subsequently discovered, plus any gains on the disposition of principal assets, less any principal assets distributed according to the will or trust instrument, and less any losses on the disposition of the principal assets. Typically income is the earnings after death or creation of the trust from the principal assets, less any expenses of earning the income, and less any distribution of the net earnings. Some wills and trust instruments may designate that certain items are to be classified as Principal or as Income. The fiduciary follows this classification unless it is in violation of state law.

The discussion and examples in this chapter are general in nature and do not cover the detailed differences that exist in the laws of the various states. The approach to the accounting for estates and trusts is to use the categorization and recording that is typically used. The chapter emphasizes estates because the accounting for estates and trusts is similar and because trusts are often created from the remaining assets of an estate.

RECORDING THE INITIAL INVENTORY

ACCOUNTING AND REPORTING FOR AN ESTATE

Once the court has approved the appointment of the executor or executrix specified in the decedent's will, or appointed a personal representative if the decedent died intestate, the first responsibility of the fiduciary of an estate is to take possession of the assets of the decedent and to prepare an inventory of the assets of the estate. The inventory and the accounting statements that are prepared during the operation of the estate are submitted to the court. The assets the decedent owned at death comprise the Principal of the estate and are valued at their fair market value at the date of death. This approach is consistent with the accounting for any new entity in which the assets contributed to start the entity are recorded at their fair market value.

The administrator of the estate has the responsibility of establishing the fair market value of the assets. The administrator may need to hire experts to determine the values of some of the assets of the estate. For instance, a real estate appraiser may be used or an expert on art work, antiques, or jewelry. The discussion in Chapter 1 regarding the determination of the estimated current values of personal assets is applicable to the determination of the fair market value of estate and trust assets. Occasionally the administrator may find assets with little intrinsic value, but with great sentimental value to the family members. These assets are usually recorded at a nominal value, so that the administrator can fulfill the fiduciary responsibilities for them. The recording of these assets is particularly important when a will specifically bequeaths these assets to an heir or heirs.

The assets include all the personal property that existed at the date of death and any real property not devised. As previously mentioned, the title to real property devised by a will passes directly to the heirs, but can be included as part of the estate. In some states, the initial inventory includes all the real property, including that transferred by devise, and is subject to court approval (probate) before title can be transferred to the heirs or beneficiaries. For consistency, all of the property, including devised real property, is recorded as part of the initial inventory of the estate in this chapter. To record the initial inventory of the estate, the individual assets are debited with their fair market values and the sum of the fair market values of all the assets in the inventory is credited to the equity account, **Estate Principal.**

Any assets owned at the time of death are part of the estate inventory and classified as Principal. Therefore, any interest accrued, but not received at the date of death, from bond investments, notes receivable, mortgages receivable, or any other debt instruments, that are owned by the decedent at the date of death are included as part of the initial inventory and classified as estate principal. In addition, any dividends that are declared on stocks that are owned by the individual at date of death are included in the initial inventory. In some states the date of record rather than the date of declaration of a dividend is used to determine if the dividend is Principal. The date of declaration is used in this chapter.

Life insurance policies that have the estate of the deceased as the beneficiary are included in the inventory of the estate as the estate will receive the proceeds of the policy less any loans owed the insurance company that are secured by the policy. Those policies insuring the decedent's life that name any other beneficiary are excluded as the payments are remitted directly to the person named as the beneficiary and the estate has no access to the proceeds from the insurance policy. Rents owed the decedent, but not yet received, are included as part of the Principal, while rents earned, but not yet due, are excluded from the initial inventory.

Unlike other entities, the liabilities owed by the decedent are not recorded as part of the initial inventory, regardless of the type of the debt. All liabilities are recorded when paid and only when paid, which follows from the fund theory approach to the estate entity. In accounting for an estate the emphasis is on the assets of the decedent and the use of those assets. In addition, the basic approach of accounting for estates and trusts is the cash basis, except that interest and dividends are accrued in the initial inventory and at the close of the estate if necessary to comply with the terms of distribution.

Assets are often discovered subsequent to the preparation of the initial inventory. Stories abound that tell of money found in mattresses or in coffee cans in backyards, as well as jewelry and stocks and bonds found in unique hiding places and often discovered years later. If an asset is discovered after the preparation of the estate inventory, it is Principal. The asset is debited with its fair market value and credited to a new equity account, **Assets Subsequently Discovered.** This new equity account is used to aid in the preparation of the reports required of the fiduciary.

A stock dividend is another asset that is received subsequent to the preparation of the initial inventory of the estate. In some states the stock dividend is treated as an addition to Principal, while in other states the stock dividend is classified as Income, and in other states an apportionment of the fair market value is required, so that the fair market value of the initial shares is not impaired. For purposes of this chapter, any stock dividend received is treated as Principal and recorded as an asset subsequently discovered.

Illustrative Problem 18.1 demonstrates the determination of the assets to include as Principal and the determination of their fair market values. It also demonstrates the recording of the initial inventory of an estate.

ILLUSTRATIVE PROBLEM 18.1: RECORDING THE INITIAL INVENTORY OF AN ESTATE

On July 1, 1990, Mr. J died, leaving a will that appointed Ms. Q as executrix of his estate. Ms. Q was approved by the court as the executrix. Ms. Q found the following assets:

	Cost	Market
Cash	$ 11,600	$ 11,600
Life Insurance Policy Payable to Mr. J's Estate	10,400	25,000
Life Insurance Policy Payable to JR, Mr. J's Nephew	2,900	10,000
100 Shares of W Company Stock	2,000	5,200
On June 15, 1990, the company declared a $3 per share cash dividend to holders of record on July 7, 1990, payable on July 15, 1990.		
20 12%, $1,000 Face Value Bonds of X Company	20,000	19,600
The bonds pay interest semiannually on February 1 and August 1.		
Residence at 1609 Beach Drive, Albany, Maine	49,500	84,000
Mr. J owes City Bank $29,600 on the 8% mortgage.		
Household Furnishings	7,500	3,100
1984 Ford Automobile	10,400	6,200
Sculptures and Paintings	12,500	8,900

The insurance policy with the nephew as the beneficiary is not included in the inventory as only policies with the estate as beneficiary are included. The mortgage on the home is not recorded since liabilities are not recorded. The interest accrued on the bonds to the date of death is recorded as are the dividends that were declared prior to death. All the assets that

EXHIBIT 18-1

Illustrative Problem 18.1
Estate of Mr. J
Recording the Initial Inventory
July 1, 1990

Principal Cash	11,600
Life Insurance Policy	25,000
W Company Stock	5,200
Dividends Receivable ($3 × 100 shares)	300
X Company Bonds	19,600
Interest Receivable ($20,000 × 12% × 5/12)	1,000
Residence, 1609 Beach Drive, Albany, Maine	84,000
Household Furnishings	3,100
Ford Automobile	6,200
Sculptures and Paintings	8,900
Estate Principal	164,900

To record the initial inventory of the Estate of Mr. J

are included in the initial inventory are recorded at their fair market values. The journal entry to record the initial inventory of the estate is in Exhibit 18-1.

ACCOUNTING FOR THE TRANSACTIONS AFFECTING AN ESTATE

As previously mentioned, the assets and equities of an estate are classified into two sets of accounts called Principal and Income. The distinction between the assets that are Principal and the assets that are Income is critical to the accounting and reporting for an estate. Because of this requirement, account titles that clearly distinguish Principal accounts from Income accounts must be used. The account titles used in this discussion of accounting for the transactions of an estate are intended to be descriptive and meet this requirement. Any account title that accomplishes the objectives of being descriptive and clearly making the distinction between Principal and Income is acceptable.

The emphasis in most accounting is on the accrual basis of accounting and the reporting of net income, but in accounting and reporting for an estate the emphasis is on the protection of the estate principal with the estate income being a secondary consideration. This emphasis on the maintenance of the principal of an estate affects the accounting and reporting for an estate. If a decision needs to be made as to whether a transaction is Principal or Income, the correct choice is the one that ensures that the Principal is not invaded (reduced). The reason is that the primary responsibility of the fiduciary is to protect and preserve the estate principal.

ACCOUNTING FOR TRANSACTIONS AFFECTING ESTATE PRINCIPAL

Any increases or decreases in the principal assets are considered Principal. If an executor sells an asset for less than the recorded value, the loss is a decrease of the estate principal and is recorded in the account, **Loss on Disposition of Principal Assets.** If an executor sells a principal asset at a gain, the gain is an increase in estate principal and is recorded in the account, **Gain on the Disposition of Principal Assets.** If an executor acquires a new asset, it becomes part of the estate principal and is recorded at its acquisition price. An estate often uses a single bank account. However, in the accounting, two ledger accounts must be maintained: one for principal cash and one for income cash.

In the initial recording of an estate, investments in bonds are recorded at their fair market value and no premium or discount is recorded. If an executor purchases bonds, the recording and accounting for any premium or discount differs from the generally accepted methods used in financial accounting. When an executor purchases bonds at a discount, no discount is recorded and when the bonds are purchased at a premium, the premium is recorded and amortized. The amortization of the premium causes the book value of the bonds to decline over time and to be equal to the face value at maturity. If the estate holds the bonds until maturity, no loss is recorded on redemption. Any of the generally accepted methods of amortizing bond premium can be used. In this chapter, the straight-line method is used for ease of computation.

The rationale for amortizing premium and not amortizing discount is that any gain on the sale of bonds purchased at a discount is Principal, but if the premium were not amortized the income beneficiaries would receive more than they should and the principal beneficiaries would receive less, because at maturity the bonds will be redeemed at their par value. Some accountants believe that both premium and discount should be recorded and amortized when a fiduciary purchases bonds. This disagreement has led to wills and trust instruments frequently stating how premium and discount on bonds acquired by the fiduciary are to be recorded and whether Principal or Income is to be charged or credited with the amortization.

Depreciation is usually not recorded in accounting for estates and trusts unless the will or trust instrument specifies that it should be recorded. The rationale for not recording depreciation is that the cash basis of accounting is used and that the preservation of the assets of the estate or trust is the goal. If depreciation is recorded, it is charged to Income. Depletion is recorded as a charge to Income because a principal asset is being consumed.

The majority of the obligations of the estate that are paid are considered charges against Principal. The size and complexity of the obligations determines the number of different accounts that are used to record the payments. Any obligations that existed at the time of death are considered Principal and debited to the account, **Debts of the Decedent,** when paid. These obligations include any income taxes payable on income earned by the decedent prior to death, and any property taxes that were liens at the time of death. If an estate has a large number of debts, separate categories of accounts can be used, with the Debts of Decedent account serving as a control account.

All the expenditures for funeral costs and the administrative expenses of the estate are considered obligations of Principal unless the will specifies that they are to be charged to Income. These expenditures are usually entered in a single account called **Funeral and Administrative Expenses.** However, if the administrative expenses are numerous, they may be placed in separate accounts, or in the case of a very large estate, the **Administrative Expenses** account may function as a control account. The complexity of the situation governs the number of accounts. For the purposes of this chapter the account, **Funeral and Administrative Expenses,** is used for all such expenditures. Any federal or state estate taxes that are paid are considered an obligation of Principal unless directed otherwise by the will. In a small estate, the estate taxes may be included with the funeral and administrative expenses or, if substantial, they are recorded in a separate **Estate Tax Principal** account.

ACCOUNTING FOR TRANSACTIONS AFFECTING INCOME

Any income received after the date of death that was not accrued and recorded as Principal is Income. If an estate has few sources of income, the cash receipts are credited to the account, **Estate Income.** If the sources of income are many, then accounts such as **Estate Dividend Income** and **Estate Interest Income** are used. Any expenses incurred that are necessary to protect the income flow, such as legal fees to protect a patent, and ordinary repairs to income-producing property are debited to the account, **Expenses of Income.**

Income taxes paid by the estate that are on estate income can be complex. If the taxes are for items of income and expenses that are recorded in the Income accounts, they are part of the Expenses of Income. However, the income tax return may also include taxes paid on gains from the sales of principal assets, or the benefit of using losses from the sales of principal assets. Unless the will directs otherwise, those income taxes that relate to the sales of principal assets are charged or credited to Principal.

RECORDING DISTRIBUTIONS TO DEVISEES AND LEGATEES

Any distribution of assets made by an executor is based on the bequests made in the decedent's will or by state law if the decedent died intestate. To record a distribution an account is debited that reduces either the Principal or Income of the estate and the distribution is credited to the account containing the asset being distributed. No gains or losses on the distribution of assets to heirs and beneficiaries are recognized, so the assets are credited with their book values.

A distribution of principal personal assets, when only a few legacies are distributed, is debited to the account, **Principal Legacies Distributed.** If numerous legacies are specified in the will, it may be desirable to use several accounts designating the recipient of the legacy, such as **Principal Legacy Distributed: JR, Nephew.** In some estates, distributions of real property as well as personal property may be specified in the will. If a distribution of real property is made it can be debited to a separate account, **Principal Devises Distributed** or the account Principal Legacies Distributed can be expanded to include both legacies and devises. Distributions of income assets to beneficiaries are debited to the account, **Distributions to Income Beneficiaries.**

SUMMARY OF ESTATE ACCOUNTS AND THEIR NORMAL BALANCES

	Normal Balance	
	Debit	Credit
Principal Accounts		
Principal Cash	X	
Asset Accounts (Initial Assets at Fair Market Value)	X	
Debts of Decedent	X	
Funeral and Administrative Expenses	X	
Losses on Realization of Principal Assets	X	
Principal Legacies and Devises Distributed	X	
Estate Principal (Sum of the Initial Inventory)		X
Assets Subsequently Discovered		X
Gains on Realization of Principal Assets		X
Income Accounts		
Income Cash	X	
Expenses of Income	X	
Distributions to Income Beneficiaries	X	
Estate Income		X

The debits of the Principal accounts are equal to the credits of the Principal accounts. The debits of the Income accounts are equal to the credits. Illustrative Problem 18.2 demonstrates the recording of the transactions of an estate, and is based on the inventory of the estate of Mr. J from Exhibit 18-1.

ILLUSTRATIVE PROBLEM 18.2: RECORDING OF THE TRANSACTIONS OF AN ESTATE

The inventory of the estate that the executrix, Ms. Q, filed with the court is

Estate of Mr. J
Ms. Q, Executrix
Inventory of the Estate
July 1, 1990

Principal Cash	$ 11,600
Life Insurance Policy Receivable	25,000
W Company Stock	5,200
Dividends Receivable: W Company Stock	300
X Company Bonds	19,600
Interest Receivable: X Company Bonds	1,000
Home, 1609 Beach Drive, Albany, Maine	84,000
Household Furnishings	3,100
Ford Automobile	6,200
Sculptures and Paintings	8,900
Total Estate Principal	$ 164,900

The will of Mr. J contained the following provisions:

1. All expenses and taxes normally charged to Principal are to be charged to Principal. My executrix may sell any assets necessary to cover the expenses and may invest any idle cash.
2. I instruct my executrix, Ms. Q, to sell my home and household furnishings. The proceeds from the sale I bequeath to my daughter, BB, together with any income earned during the administration of my estate.
3. I bequeath my sculptures and paintings to the Contemporary Museum, my automobile to my nephew, JR, and $10,000 cash to my brother, SR.
4. The remainder of my estate is to be placed in a trust at the City Bank for the benefit of my granddaughter, CC.

The journal entries to record the transactions and distributions of the estate of Mr. J are as shown in Exhibit 18-2.

EXHIBIT 18-2

Illustrative Problem 18.2
Estate of Mr. J
Transaction and Distribution Entries

July 8	Principal Cash	25,000	
	Life Insurance Policy Receivable		25,000
	To record the receipt of the proceeds from Indemnity Life Company		

July 15	Principal Cash	300	
	Dividends Receivable		300
	To record the receipt of W Company dividend		
July 18	Principal Cash	4,400	
	Assets Subsequently Discovered		4,400
	To record the discovery of a savings account and depositing of the balance in the estate cash account		
July 30	Principal Legacies and Devises Distributed	6,200	
	Ford Automobile		6,200
	To record the transfer of the automobile to nephew, JR, as instructed by the will		
July 31	Debts of Decedent	2,200	
	Principal Cash		2,200
	To record the payment of the outstanding debts of the decedent		
Aug. 1	Principal Cash	1,000	
	Income Cash	200	
	Interest Receivable		1,000
	Estate Income		200
	To record the receipt of the semiannual interest payment on the X Company bonds		
Aug. 1	Y Company Bonds	19,100	
	Principal Cash		19,100
	To record the purchase of Y Company bonds. The bonds have a face value of $20,000, and an interest rate of 10%. The bonds pay interest semiannually on July 31 and January 31.		
Aug. 6	Principal Cash	3,100	
	Household Furnishings		3,100
	To record the proceeds from the sale of the household furnishings		
Aug. 10	Funeral and Administrative Expenses	2,400	
	Principal Cash		2,400
	To record the payment of the funeral expenses		
Sept. 9	Principal Legacies and Devises Distributed	8,900	
	Sculptures and Paintings		8,900
	To record the transfer of the art work to the Contemporary Museum as directed by the will		
Oct. 15	Income Cash	400	
	Estate Income		400
	To record the receipt of the quarterly dividend on W Company stock		
Oct. 20	Principal Cash	6,000	
	W Company Stock		5,200
	Gain on Realization of Principal Assets		800
	To record the sale of W Company stock		

Nov. 1	Principal Legacies and Devises Distributed	10,000	
	Principal Cash		10,000
	To record the distribution of $10,000 cash to brother, SR, as directed by the will		
Nov. 15	Debts of the Decedent	1,300	
	Principal Cash		1,300
	To record the payment of property taxes on the residence which became a lien on June 15, 1990		
Nov. 20	Principal Cash	83,100	
	Loss on Realization of Principal Assets	900	
	Residence		84,000
	To record the sale of the residence		
Dec. 1	Principal Legacies and Devises Distributed	86,200	
	Principal Cash		86,200
	To record the distribution of the proceeds from the sale of the residence and householding furnishings to the daughter, BB, as directed by the will		
Dec. 1	Distributions to Income Beneficiaries	600	
	Income Cash		600
	To record the distribution of income received to date to daughter, BB, as directed by the will		
Dec. 31	Income Cash	1,000	
	Estate Income		1,000
	To record the receipt of the interest received from Y Company Bonds		
Jan. 4	Funeral and Administrative Expenses	4,300	
	Principal Cash		4,300
	To record the payment of the executrix's fee and other expenses of the estate		
Jan. 10	Funeral and Administrative Expenses	1,900	
	Principal Cash		1,900
	To record the payment of Federal Estate taxes		
Jan. 15	Debts of the Decedent	1,100	
	Principal Cash		1,100
	To record the payment of the income taxes owed by Mr. J on income earned prior to his death		
Jan. 15	Expenses of Income	150	
	Income Cash		150
	To record the payment of the income taxes of the estate		

The ledger accounts of the Estate of Mr. J, prior to the final distribution of the estate to the income beneficiary and to the trust for the benefit of the granddaughter, are as shown in Exhibit 18-3.

EXHIBIT 18-3

Illustrative Problem 18-2
Estate of Mr. J
Ledger Accounts
January 15, 1991

Principal Accounts

Principal Cash			
7/ 1	11,600	7/31	2,200
7/ 8	25,000	8/ 1	19,100
7/15	300	8/10	2,400
7/18	4,400	11/ 1	10,000
8/ 1	1,000	11/15	1,300
8/ 6	3,100	12/ 1	86,200
10/20	6,000	1/ 4	4,300
10/20	83,100	1/10	1,900
		1/15	1,100
	134,500		128,500
Balance	6,000		

Life Insurance Policy			
7/ 1	25,000	7/ 8	25,000

W Company Stock			
7/ 1	5,200	10/20	5,200

Dividends Receivable			
7/ 1	300	7/15	300

X Company Bonds	
7/ 1	19,600

Interest Receivable			
7/ 1	1,000	8/1	1,000

Y Company Bonds	
8/ 1	19,100

Residence			
7/ 1	84,000	11/20	84,000

Household Furnishings			
7/ 1	3,100	8/ 6	3,100

Ford Automobile			
7/ 1	6,200	7/30	6,200

Sculptures and Paintings			
7/ 1	8,900	9/ 9	8,900

Estate Principal			
		7/ 1	164,900

Assets Subsequently Discovered			
		7/18	4,400

Debts of Decedent	
7/31	2,200
11/15	1,300
1/15	1,100
Balance	4,600

Funeral and Administrative Expenses	
8/10	2,400
1/ 4	4,300
1/10	1,900
Balance	8,600

Losses on Realization of Principal Assets	
11/20	900

Gains on Realization of Principal Assets		Principal Legacies and Devises Distributed	
	10/20 800	7/30	6,200
		9/ 9	8,900
		11/ 1	10,000
		12/ 1	86,200
		Balance	111,300

Income Accounts

Income Cash				Estate Income		
8/ 1	200	12/ 1	600		8/ 1	200
10/15	400	1/15	150		10/15	400
12/31	1,000				12/31	1,000
	1,600		750		Balance	1,600
Balance	850					

Expenses: Income		Distributions to Income Beneficiaries	
1/15	150	12/ 1	600

FIDUCIARY'S REPORT

Prior to the final distribution of the remaining assets of an estate and occasionally after the final distribution, the fiduciary submits a financial report to the court. In a very complex estate where a substantial period of time is necessary to complete the distributions, a fiduciary will submit several reports to the court at specified intervals. The form of the report varies from state to state, but the content and general format are similar. Just as the accounts are kept in two distinct parts, the report to the court is also prepared with Principal and Income sections. The report is called a **Charge and Discharge Statement,** which consists of charges and credits for both Principal and Income. The **charges** are all of the assets that the fiduciary has been responsible for listed by category of source. The **credits** are all of the uses that have been made of the assets listed by category of use. The difference between the charges and the credits is equal to the assets remaining in the custody and care of the fiduciary. If only a few assets remain, they are reported directly on the charge and discharge statement. If the assets are numerous, an inventory of remaining assets is prepared.

In the Principal section of the charge and discharge statement, the **charges** consist of the inventory of initial assets, which is equal to the **Estate Principal** account; any assets subsequently discovered, which is equal to the **Assets Subsequently Discovered** account; and any additional assets acquired from selling Principal assets at a gain, which is equal to the **Gains on Realization of Principal Assets** account. The **credits** in the Principal section consist of any decreases in assets from selling assets at a loss, which is equal to the **Losses on Realization of Principal Assets** account; the debts of the decedent paid; the funeral and administrative expenses; and any principal legacies or devises distributed, which is equal to the **Principal Legacies and Devises Distributed** account.

In the Income section of the charge and discharge statement, the **charges** consist of all the income earned since the decedent's death. The **credits** consist of the expenses paid out of income cash and any distributions to income beneficiaries. The difference between the income earned and the credits is equal to the income assets, which are typically only cash.

The charge and discharge statement is supported by as many schedules showing the details of transactions as are necessary to clearly reflect the transactions and distributions recorded by the fiduciary. If the estate is relatively simple, few schedules are necessary and the details are included as part of the charge and discharge statement. In some states supporting schedules are prepared because of the requirements of the state laws governing estates. In the examples and problems in this chapter, if more than three items are in a category a schedule is prepared; if less than three times are in a category the details are presented as a line item on the charge and discharge statement. Illustrative Problem 18.3 demonstrates the preparation of a charge and discharge statement and uses the ledger account balances of the Estate of Mr. J from Exhibit 18-3.

ILLUSTRATIVE PROBLEM 18.3: CHARGE AND DISCHARGE STATEMENT

The trial balances of the Estate of Mr. J prepared from the ledger accounts of the Estate of Mr. J in Exhibit 18-3 are

Estate of Mr. J
Trial Balance
January 15, 1991

	Debits	Credits
Estate Principal Accounts		
Principal Cash	$ 6,000	
X Company Bonds	19,600	
Y Company Bonds	19,100	
Estate Principal		$ 164,900
Assets Subsequently Discovered		4,400
Debts of Decedent	4,600	
Funeral and Administrative Expenses	8,600	
Losses on Realization of Estate Assets	900	
Gains on Realization of Estate Assets		800
Principal Legacies Distributed	111,300	
Total	$ 170,100	$ 170,100
Estate Income Accounts		
Income Cash	$ 850	
Expenses of Income	150	
Distributions to Income Beneficiaries	600	
Estate Income		$ 1,600
Total	$ 1,600	$ 1,600

Exhibit 18-4 contains the charge and discharge statement prepared from the above trial balance.

EXHIBIT 18-4

Illustrative Problem 18.3
Estate of Mr. J
Charge and Discharge Statement
January 15, 1991
Ms. Q, Executrix

As to Principal

I Charge Myself With			
Assets per Inventory: Schedule A			$ 164,900
Asset Subsequently Discovered: Savings Account			4,400
Gain on Realization of Principal Asset: Sale of W Company Stock			800
Total Charges			170,100
I Credit Myself With			
Loss on Realization of Principal Asset: Sale of Residence		$ 900	
Debts of Decedent Paid:			
Debts Owed by Decedent	$ 2,200		
Property Taxes	1,300		
Income Taxes	1,100	4,600	
Funeral and Administrative Expenses			
Funeral Costs	2,400		
Executrix Fee	4,300		
Estate Taxes	1,900	8,600	
Principal Legacies Distributed: Schedule B		111,300	
Total Credits			125,400
Estate Principal			
Principal Cash		6,000	
X Company Bonds		19,600	
Y Company Bonds		19,100	$ 44,700

As to Income

I Charge Myself With			
Income Received: Dividends and Interest			$ 1,600
I Credit Myself With			
Expenses of Income Paid		$ 150	
Distributions to Income Beneficiaries		600	750
Estate Income: Income Cash			$ 850

Estate of Mr. J
Ms. Q, Executrix
Schedule A: Inventory of the Estate
July 1, 1990

Principal Cash	$ 11,600
Life Insurance Policy Receivable	25,000
W Company Stock	5,200
Dividends Receivable: W Company Stock	300
X Company Bonds	19,600
Interest Receivable: X Company Bonds	1,000
Home, 1609 Beach Drive, Albany, Maine	84,000
Household Furnishings	3,100
Ford Automobile	6,200
Sculptures and Paintings	8,900
Total Estate Principal	$ 164,900

Estate of Mr. J
Ms. Q, Executrix
Schedule B: Principal Legacies Distributed
July 1, 1990 through January 15, 1991

JR, Nephew: Ford Automobile	$ 6,200
Modern Museum: Sculptures and Paintings	8,900
SR, Brother: Cash	10,000
BB, Daughter: Proceeds from Sale of Residence and Household Furnishings	86,200
Total Principal Legacies Distributed	$ 111,300

FINAL DISTRIBUTION OF ASSETS AND CLOSING JOURNAL ENTRIES

After the court has approved the charge and discharge statement submitted by the fiduciary, the remaining assets are distributed to the beneficiaries. The journal entries for these distributions are exactly the same as those that were prepared for the previous distributions. After all the assets are distributed, the fiduciary prepares the closing entries for the estate. Unlike a going concern entity that has income as the primary motive, an estate has a limited life with asset management as the objective. The closing entries in a profit-making organization are usually recorded annually and have as their goal making the balances in the equity accounts reflect ending balance sheet values. In an estate, however, the closing entries are only recorded at the end of the life of an estate and their purpose is to make all the remaining accounts have zero balances.

For the Principal section of the ledger all of the remaining principal accounts are closed to the **Estate Principal** account. When distributions are made to the heirs the asset account is decreased and the distribution account is increased; therefore, after the final distribution of the assets is made, no balances remain in any of the asset accounts. To close the Income section of the ledger all of the accounts with balances are closed to the **Estate Income** account. To illustrate the entries for the final distribution of the assets and the closing entries for an estate, Illustrative Problem 18.4 uses the Estate of Mr. J and the ledger accounts as presented in Exhibit 18-3.

ILLUSTRATIVE PROBLEM 18.4: FINAL DISTRIBUTION AND CLOSING JOURNAL ENTRIES

Final Distribution Entries

Jan. 15 Principal Legacies and Devises Distributed	44,700	
Principal Cash		6,000
X Company Bonds		19,600
Y Company Bonds		19,100

To record the distribution of the remaining principal assets
to City Bank, the trustee for the trust for the
granddaughter, CC, as instructed by the will

Jan. 15 Distributions to Income Beneficiaries	850	
Income Cash		850

To record the distribution of the remaining income assets
to the daughter, BB, as instructed by the will

Closing Entries

Jan. 15 Estate Principal	164,900	
Assets Subsequently Discovered	4,400	
Gain on Realization of Principal Assets	800	
Loss on Realization of Principal Assets		900
Debts of Decedent Paid		4,600
Funeral and Administrative Expenses		8,600
Principal Legacies and Devises Distributed (1)		156,000

(1) Legacies per charge and discharge statement $111,300
+ legacies from final distribution $44,700 = $156,000

Jan. 15 Estate Income	1,600	
Expenses: Income		150
Distributions to Income Beneficiaries (2)		1,450

(2) Distribution per charge and discharge statement $600
+ final distribution $850 = $1,450

ACCOUNTING AND REPORTING FOR TRUSTS

Trusts can be created by a will or by a living person. A trust that is the result of the provisions of a will is called a **testamentary** trust. A trust created by a living person is called an **inter vivos** trust. Inter vivos is a Latin term meaning between or among the living. Regardless of how the trust is created, the accounting and reporting are the same except for the initial recording of the assets. The assets received by a trust from an estate are recorded at their fair market values at the date of death, or the same values as the estate used. When recording the initial inventory of an inter vivos trust, the assets are recorded at their fair market values at the date the person established the trust.

The accounting for the transaction entries and the reporting are like an estate. The closing entries are similar except that a trust prepares closing entries at least once a year. Unlike estates, which usually have a short life, normally one or two years, a trust may operate for a long period of time. Trusts can have a limited life established by the trust instrument, or they may approach a going concern. For example, a trust may be established for a child that is to end on the child's twenty-first birthday, or a trust may be established for a period of 10 years. Alternately a trust can be established to provide income to a certain class of beneficiaries over a long period of time. For instance, a trust might be established to provide a college education for every direct descendant of the deceased in perpetuity or until the funds are exhausted.

Trust instruments typically contain provisions for the manner in which assets are to be invested and who is to receive the income or assets. The trust instrument can also specify the types of investments that the trustee can purchase and may provide instructions for the handling of bond premium and discount and income taxes. A person who is designated to receive the income of a trust is the **income beneficiary.** If the income beneficiary is to receive the income for a lifetime, the income beneficiary is called a **life tenant.** Just as with an estate, the person who is designated to receive the remaining assets of a trust at its conclusion is the **remainderman.** The trustee must follow the provisions of the trust instrument unless they are in violation of state laws.

Like estates, trusts also maintain two sets of balancing accounts (funds): one for Principal and one for Income. Some trusts allow the trustee to invade the Principal of the trust to satisfy the needs of a beneficiary. For example, a trust may be created to provide for the education and health of a child and permits the use of the Principal for these purposes if the income is not adequate to cover the education and health costs of the child. The discussion of the recording of the initial inventory and the transactions for an estate is equally applicable to trusts. In addition, the trustee is required to make periodic reports, at least annually, to all the beneficiaries regarding the transactions of the trust. The report of a trust can be a charge and discharge statement or a similar document.

Unlike an estate, which only needs closing entries after the final distribution, a trust typically records closing entries annually for both the Principal accounts and the Income accounts. The 1986 Tax Reform Act requires all trusts to operate on a calendar year; thus trusts will, at present, all have years ending on December 31st. The closing entry for Principal is the same as for an estate. If the trust instrument requires periodic distributions of income, the income is typically credited to an individual equity account for each income beneficiary. When the trustee actually distributes the income cash to the income beneficiary, the individual's equity account is debited. Thus the equity account of a beneficiary is like the capital account of a sole proprietor or a partner.

Previously in the chapter, two complex areas, bond premium and discount, and income taxes, were discussed but not illustrated. These problem areas are reviewed and illustrated in Illustrative Problem 18.5. A premium on bonds purchased by a fiduciary is usually recorded and amortized using the straight-line method and discount on bonds purchased is usually not recorded or amortized. Income taxes can be paid on transactions that are classified as Principal such as the gains and losses from the sale of principal assets. If the trust agreement is silent, these taxes are typically treated as Principal. Illustrative Problem 18.5 uses the trust established by the will of Mr. J for his granddaughter, CC, to demonstrate the accounting and reporting for a trust, the handling of bond premium, and the division of income taxes between Principal and Income.

ILLUSTRATIVE PROBLEM 18.5: ACCOUNTING AND REPORTING FOR A TRUST

The will of Mr. J established a trust for the benefit of his granddaughter, CC, with City Bank. The will specified that the granddaughter is to receive the income of the trust to a maximum of $3,000 per year until she is 21, at which time the remainder of the trust is to go to the Modern Museum. The trust instrument specified that the cash basis is to be used and no accruals of income are to be recorded. The trust instrument specified that bond premium is to be recorded and amortized and bond discount is not to be recorded. In addition, income taxes relating to the gains and losses on the sale of principal assets are to be charged to Principal.

The journal entry to record the establishment of the trust is

Jan. 15	Principal Cash	6,000	
	X Company Bonds	19,600	
	Y Company Bonds	19,100	
	Trust Principal		44,700

If the trust instrument had not specified that a strictly cash basis be used to record the transactions of the trust, the trustee could have accrued the interest owing on the bonds in recording the initial inventory of the trust. If the interest is recorded, the entry would include a debit to Interest Receivable in the amount of $2,016.67 computed as follows:

X Company Bonds, $20,000 Face Value, Paying 12% Interest Semiannually		
on February 1 and April 1		
$20,000 \times 12\% \times 5.5/12$		$ 1,100.00
Y Company Bonds, $20,000 Face Value, Paying 10% Interest Semiannually		
on July 31 and January 31		
$20,000 \times 10\% \times 5.5/12$		916.67
Total Interest Receivable		$ 2,016.67

Journal entries for the transactions for the period ending December 31, 1991 are

Feb. 1	Income Cash	2,200	
	Trust Income		2,200
	To record the receipt of the semiannual interest payments:		
	$1,200 from X Company and $1,000 from Y Company		
Feb. 1	Principal Cash	20,400	
	X Company Bonds		19,600
	Gain on Realization of Principal Assets		800
	To record the sale of the X Company bonds		

Feb. 1	Z Company Bonds	25,000	
	Premium on Z Company Bonds	1,200	
	Principal Cash		26,200

To record the purchase of $25,000 face value, 15% Z
Company bonds which mature in 5 years. The bonds pay
interest semiannually on February 1 and August 1

Aug. 1	Income Cash	1,000	
	Trust Income		1,000

To record the receipt of the semiannual interest payment on
the Y Company Bonds

Aug. 1	Principal Cash (1)	120	
	Income Cash (2)	1,755	
	Premium on Z Company Bonds		120
	Trust Income		1,755

To record the receipt of the semiannual interest payment on
the Z Company bonds

(1) $1,200/5 years $\times$ 6/12 = $120
(2) $25,000 $\times$ 15% $\times$ 6/12 − $120 = $1,755

Dec. 31	Expenses: Income	400	
	Income Cash		400

To record the payment of the trustee fee for 1991

Dec. 31	Expenses: Income	85	
	Expenses: Principal	115	
	Income Cash		85
	Principal Cash		115

To record the payment of income taxes for 1991. $115 of
the total tax bill of $200 was paid on the gain on the sale of
X Company bonds.

Income required to be distributed to an income beneficiary by the trust instrument is taxed
to the beneficiary and not to the trust. The income taxes for trust income, therefore, are on
the income earned in excess of the required $3,000 annual distribution to the granddaughter,
CC.

The closing journal entries on December 31, 1991 are

Dec. 31	Gain on Realization of Principal Assets	800	
	Expenses: Principal		115
	Trust Principal		685

To close trust principal accounts

Proof:

Principal Cash ($6,000 + $20,400 − $26,200 + $120 − $115)	$ 205
Y Company Bonds	19,100
Z Company Bonds	25,000
Premium on Z Company Bonds ($1,200 − $120)	1,080
Trust Principal ($44,700 + 685)	$ 45,385

Dec. 31 Trust Income   4,955
        Expenses: Income   485
        Equity in Income: Granddaughter, CC   3,000
        Trust Principal   1,470
    To record the equity payable for the period and to close
    the income accounts to Trust Principal

Proof: Income Cash ($2,200 + $1,000 + $1,755 − $400 − $85) = $4,470

When the cash is distributed to the income beneficiary the Equity in Income account is debited. The trustee prepares a charge and discharge statement similar to the one prepared for the estate of Mr. J as demonstrated in Exhibit 18-4. The above process of recording the transaction entries, the closing entries, and preparing a charge and discharge statement is repeated each year until the granddaughter reaches the age of 21. At that time the trustee would remit any cash payable to the granddaughter to her and distribute the principal assets and any income assets not due the granddaughter to the remainderman, the Modern Museum. The final step is to close the Principal and Income accounts in the same way that the journal entries closed the Principal and Income accounts of the Estate of Mr. J as demonstrated in Illustrative Problem 18.4.

SUMMARY

The accounting and reporting for estates and trusts uses the fund theory of equity and two funds, principal and income, are used for both entities. The emphasis of the accounting is on the protection of the principal of the estate or trust that the personal representative of an estate or the trustee of a trust is responsible for maintaining. The cash basis of accounting is used for both an estate and a trust, except that interest receivable and dividends declared at date of death are accrued and recorded as part of the inventory of the estate and can be accrued for a trust. The original assets of the estate, which are the principal, are recorded at their fair market values and credited to Estate Principal. The original assets of a testamentary trust (created by a will) are recorded at the basis used in the estate and the assets of an inter vivos trust (created by a living person) are recorded at their fair market values when the trust is established.

During the term of a trust or estate, the determination of which transactions are principal and which are income is crucial. For an estate, all transactions involving the sale, purchase, or distribution of the assets contained in the initial inventory or subsequently discovered are principal. For an estate the debts of the decedent, including income taxes owed by the decedent, the funeral expenses, the costs of administering the estate, and estate taxes, are considered uses of principal assets. Income earned and the expenses of earning that income, including income taxes on that income, are classified as income. The same division between principal and income is used for a trust, except that the trust has no debts of the decedent to pay.

The principal of the estate or trust is the initial inventory plus any assets subsequently discovered and any gains from the sale of assets. The principal is reduced by any losses from the sale of assets and by distributions to beneficiaries. A distribution to a beneficiary that is land and buildings is called a devise. All other assets are classified as personal property and a distribution of these assets is called a legacy. A legacy can be a general legacy (a specific quantity or amount of an asset), or it can be specific (a particular asset), or it can be demonstrative (an exact amount from a specific source), or it can be a residual legacy. Legacies can also be pecuniary, which is a gift of money. A person designated to receive a devise or legacy is the beneficiary of an estate or trust. An entity designated to receive only the income of an estate or trust is an income beneficiary, and an entity designated to receive the remaining assets after all other devises and legacies of an estate or trust are satisfied is a remainderman.

An estate operates for a limited period of time and prepares a charge and discharge statement prior to the final distribution of the assets to the remaining beneficiaries. A charge and discharge statement accounts for the sources of assets and the uses of those assets for both the principal and income funds of an estate or trust. A trust, which can have a limited life or a life approaching a going concern, prepares a charge and discharge statement annually for the beneficiaries of the trust.

The accounts of an estate are closed only at the end of the life of an estate and the accounts of a trust are closed each year. Prior to the closing of an estate, all of the assets are distributed so the balances in the asset accounts are zero. The closing entries for an estate have the purpose of making the balances in all the remaining accounts zero as the assets have been accounted for and the measurement of income is not the objective. The closing entries for a trust, which is an ongoing entity, have as the objective the determination of the ending balance of the Trust Principal account and the closing of the income and expense accounts. If any distributions have not been made by a trust, the amounts owing are recorded in separate equity accounts.

REVIEW PROBLEM

On March 1, 1990, Ms. R died. The will of Ms. R provided for the following:

1. Mr. S is to be appointed the executor of my estate and to be paid the normal fee. Mr. S is to use the usual methods of accounting for bonds and income taxes.
2. I bequeath $10,000 to Alma Mater Foundation.
3. I bequeath the proceeds from the sale of my business up to a maximum of $100,000 equally to my sons, R2 and D2.
4. The income from my estate together with 200 shares of my American Telephone and Telegraph stocks and $50,000 face value City of Auburn bonds are to be placed in a trust for my granddaughters, R3 and D3.
5. I bequeath my diaries to my daughter-in-law, D1, because of her interest in the family history.
6. The remainder of my estate I bequeath to my daughter, S1.

1. Mr. S, the executor, determined that the following assets comprised the inventory of Ms. R's estate:

	Cost	Market
Cash	$ 14,100	$ 14,100
Life Insurance Policy Payable to Ms. R's Estate	9,100	35,000
Life Insurance Policy Payable to S1, Ms. R's Daughter	7,200	20,000
500 Shares of American Telephone and Telegraph	12,000	20,400
On February 15, 1990, the company declared a cash dividend of $2.50 per share payable on March 13, 1990, to holders of record on March 8, 1990.		

	Cost	Market
100 9%, $1,000 Face Value, City of Auburn Bonds	$ 91,950	$ 102,300
The bonds pay interest semiannually on January 1 and July 1.		
Ms. R's Nurturing Nursery and Garden Store	39,900	103,000
Ms. R has owned and operated the business for many years and has developed an excellent reputation for healthy plants.		
Household Furnishings	7,500	12,400
Ms. R has furnished her apartment with a number of valuable antiques.		
1989 Mercedes Benz	41,200	40,000
Three Boxes of Diaries	–0–	1

Required

1) Describe the types of legacies that Ms. R has left to her heirs.
2) Prepare the journal entry to record the initial inventory of Ms. R's estate and enter the balances in "T" accounts.

2. During the life of the estate, the executor, Mr. S, entered into the following transactions:

3/13   Received the quarterly dividend from American Telephone and Telegraph.

3/31   Received the proceeds of the life insurance policy.

4/14   Paid the outstanding debts of the decedent in the amount of $3,300.

4/27   Sold the Mercedes Benz for $41,600.

4/30   Distributed the diaries to the daughter-in-law.

4/30   Paid the medical bills from the decedent's final illness in the amount of $2,400 and funeral costs of $3,000.

5/15   Sold the business for $101,000, receiving a $50,000 down payment and a 12% promissory note for the balance, which is payable in three equal installments of principal plus interest on the unpaid balance. The payments are due on July 1, and October 1, 1990 and January 1, 1991.

5/22   Received a dividend check from IBM in the amount of $295. As Mr. S had not located any stock from IBM, he asked the Farm Bank, where Ms. S had her checking account, if she had a safety deposit box. The bank replied yes, but a court order was necessary to open the safety deposit box, since Mr. S was unable to locate the key and only Ms. R had access to the box.

5/25   Received a court order to open the safety deposit box and discovered the following: a diamond ring valued at $5,000, an IRA account passbook with a balance of $8,900, and 25 shares of IBM stock valued at $429 per share.

5/31   Collected the balance of the IRA account and deposited the money in the estate's checking account.

6/30   Distributed the legacy to the Alma Mater Foundation.

7/1   Received the interest on the City of Auburn bonds and the first installment payment from the purchasers of Ms. R's business.

7/10   The daughter, S1, requested that the antique furniture and the diamond ring not be sold. Mr. S agreed as long as the estate had sufficient cash to meet its obligations. The remainder of the furniture with a fair market value of $5,400 was sold for $6,400.

7/13   Received a $3 per share quarterly dividend from American Telephone and Telegraph.

8/24   Received a $4 per share dividend from IBM.

10/1   Received the second installment payment on the sale of the business.

10/15 Received 5 shares of IBM stock as a stock dividend. The stock is currently selling for $412 per share.

11/15 Paid federal estate taxes in the amount of $19,000.

1/1   Received the final installment payment from the sale of the business and the interest on the City of Auburn bonds.

1/15   Distributed the legacies to Ms. R's sons.

1/19   Received a $4 per share dividend from American Telephone and Telegraph.

2/1   Paid the income taxes of the decedent on income earned prior to death in the amount of $7,200 and paid $3,100 of income taxes for the estate, which included $200 of taxes on the sales of principal assets.

2/1   Paid the executor's fee of $5,000.

Required

1) Prepare journal entries for the transactions of the estate and post to the ledger accounts.
2) Prepare a charge and discharge statement using supporting schedules if a category has more than three items.
3) Prepare the journal entries for the distributions to the trust and the remainderman.
4) Prepare the closing journal entries for the estate.
5) Prepare the opening journal entry for the trust for the benefit of the granddaughters.

QUESTIONS

1. Describe the approach used in accounting for estates and trusts and express the appropriate accounting equation for the entity.
2. Explain the difference between a person who dies testate and a person who dies intestate.
3. Explain the difference between a devise and a legacy. Describe the various types of legacies and give an example of each.
4. The accounts of an estate or trust are divided into two sets of accounts called Principal and Income. Describe the types of assets that are Principal and the types of assets that are Income. Also describe the types of transactions that use both Principal and Income assets.
5. Describe the basic steps in accounting and reporting for estates and trusts.
6. Describe the conditions that result in accruing interest, dividends, and rents when recording the initial inventory of an estate.
7. What are the reasons for not recording liabilities for either estates or trusts?
8. Describe the possible ways that a stock dividend can be recorded and indicate the method to be used in the homework.
9. Describe the correct method of accounting for bond premium and discount for (1) bonds that are part of the initial inventory, and (2) bonds that are purchased by the fiduciary.
10. Describe the types of payments that are usually included in the category debts of the decedent, and those that are classified as funeral and administrative expenses.
11. Describe the various types of federal and state taxes that a fiduciary might pay and whether they are charged to Principal or to Income.
12. Describe the types of accounts that have balances after all the distributions as specified in a will are made.
13. Describe the basic differences between an estate and a trust.

EXERCISES

EXERCISE 18-1
Mr. A. died on September 1, 1990. The executor of his estate determined that Mr. A had the following assets at the time of his death:

	Cost	Market
Cash	$ 7,400	$ 7,400
Insurance Policy Payable to Bob A, Mr. A's son	8,975	25,000
100 Shares of Q Company Stock	3,500	6,900
A $2 dividend had been declared on 8/15/90, payable on 9/15/90 to holders of record on 9/10/90.		
100 10% RST Company Bonds	96,000	100,800
Face Value $100,000. The bonds pay interest semiannually on May 1 and November 1.		
1987 Chevrolet		
A $1,060 loan is owed on the car.	10,600	6,100
Pension Plan Benefits Payable to the Estate	–0–	37,400

Required
Prepare the journal entry to record the inventory of the estate.

EXERCISE 18-2: Continuation of Exercise 18-1
Refer to Exercise 18-1. The following transactions occurred during the administration of the estate of Mr. A:

9/15   Received the dividend from Q Company.
9/30   Received the full amount from the pension plan trustee.
9/30   Paid the outstanding debts of the decedent in the amount of $1,840 and funeral costs of $2,100.
10/15 Sold the Q Company stock for $6,500.
11/1   Received the semiannual interest payment from RST Company.
11/1   Sold the RST Company bonds for $101,000.
12/3   Sold the 1987 Chevrolet for $6,500 and paid the outstanding loan secured by the automobile of $1,060.
12/18 Paid personal income taxes of Mr. A of $1,700, estate taxes of $2,200, and an executor's fee of $950.

Required
1. Prepare the journal entries for the transactions of the Estate of Mr. A.
2. Mr. A willed all the principal of his estate to his son and all the income of the estate to his grandson. Using "T" accounts, determine the amount of cash that each beneficiary received.

EXERCISE 18-3
Mr. C died on August 1, 1990. Mr. C was a bachelor and left no heirs. Mr. C's will directed that one-third of the Principal of his estate plus the Income be distributed to his church and the remainder of his estate be distributed to his alma mater, OSU. The church officials question the charge and discharge statement that the executor of Mr. C's estate prepared. The charge and discharge statement prepared by the executor, Mr. Ify, is as follows:

Estate of Mr. C
Mr. Ify, Executor
February 28, 1991

I Charge Myself With

  Inventory I Found

Cash	$ 6,500
Home at price Mr. C paid for house	62,100
Household furnishings at what I would pay for that used stuff	3,000
9% State of Oregon bonds, interest payable semiannually on September 1 and March 1, at value on face of bonds	30,000
10% City of Bend bonds, interest payable semiannually on October 1 and April 1, at value on face of bonds	60,000
1986 Datsun at price Mr. C paid	10,400

  I Also Received

Proceeds of an insurance policy	15,000
Cash from sale of home	91,500
Cash from auction of household furnishings	4,400
Cash from sale of automobile	6,175

  I Paid the Following

Bills Mr. C owed	$ 2,450
Funeral home	2,240
Income taxes owed by Mr. C	4,100
Myself	3,000
Income taxes the accountant said the estate owed	320

The accountants said I should pay $4,970 of estate taxes to the Federal government and $1,230 of estate taxes to the state of Oregon, but I have not bothered to pay these as I think the beneficiaries should pay the taxes. The accountant also submitted a bill for $860, which I did not pay, and Mr. C's attorney sent a bill for $450, which I did pay. I also received two checks marked interest: one was for $1,350 and the other one was for $3,000. I did not know what to do with the checks so I still have them.

On August 1, 1990, the State of Oregon bonds were quoted at 97 1/2 and the City of Bend bonds at 103. The selling prices of the assets were approximately equal to their fair market values at the date of death.

Required

1. Prepare the journal entries for the transactions that the executor failed to complete.
2. Prepare a charge and discharge statement for the estate of Mr. C in good form with supporting schedules as necessary, assuming that any transactions not included in (1.) were correctly recorded.
3. Prepare the journal entries for the distribution of the assets to the beneficiaries.

EXERCISE 18-4

The will of Ms. B contained the following provisions:

1. I bequeath $10,000 to the Salvation Army and $5,000 to UNICEF.
2. I bequeath all my investments in stocks and bonds to my son, Harold.
3. I bequeath my home and household furnishings to my daughter, Susan.
4. The remainder of my estate I leave in trust for my grandchildren, Harold Jr. and Suzette.

The trial balance of Ms. B's estate contained the following assets prior to any distributions to the heirs:

	Debits	Credits
Principal Cash	$ 28,640	
Income Cash	7,100	
Y Company Stock	13,720	
Z Company Bonds	56,300	
City of Albany Bonds	31,900	
Home	73,500	
Household Furnishings	12,100	
Apartment Building	175,000	
Debts of Decedent	4,200	
Funeral and Administrative Expenses	9,300	
Income Expenses	2,700	
Estate Principal		$ 349,000
Gain on Disposition of Principal Assets		4,660
Assets Subsequently Discovered		51,000
Estate Income		9,800

Required

1. Prepare the journal entries for the distribution of the estate assets to the beneficiaries using separate accounts for devises and legacies.

2. Prepare the closing journal entries for the estate of Ms. B.

EXERCISE 18-5: Continuation of Exercise 18-4

The trustee, City Bank of Fayetteville, received the trust assets from the executor. The trust instrument specified that all cash initially received is Principal and that the annual income is to be distributed in equal amounts to the income beneficiaries six weeks after the end of each year. The trust is to continue until the youngest beneficiary reaches the age of 25. During the first year of the trust, the following transactions were entered into by the trustee:

- Purchased $20,000 face value, 12% City of Savannah bonds at 98 on April 1. The bonds pay interest semiannually on April 1 and October 1.
- Received rental income of $18,600 and the October 1 interest payment from the City of Savannah bonds.
- Paid the following expenses related to the apartment house:

Property taxes	$ 6,400
Repairs and maintenance	1,750
Janitorial and gardening service	1,000

Required

1. Prepare the journal entry to establish the trust.

2. Prepare the transaction entries for the trust, assuming the trustee has not distributed the income.

3. Prepare the charge and discharge statement for the trust.

4. Prepare the journal entry to record the income payable to the income beneficiaries.

EXERCISE 18-6

The executor of the estate of Mr. D determined that the following stocks and bonds were part of the inventory of Mr. D's estate:

- $100,000 face value, 8% IQ Company bonds. The bonds pay interest semiannually on April 1 and October 1. Mr. D purchased the bonds at 98 and the bonds were selling at 104 at the date of death.
- $50,000 face value, 10% SAT Company bonds. The bonds pay interest semiannually on March 1 and September 1. Mr. D purchased the bonds at 102 and the bonds were selling at 97 at the date of death.
- 280 shares of $100 par value, 7% GMAT Company preferred stock. Mr. D purchased the stock at $105 per share and the selling price at the date of death was 101. GMAT Company has been paying dividends regularly on its preferred stock in semiannual payments on April 1 and October 1.
- 400 shares of $50 par value ACT Company common stock. Mr. D purchased the stock at 56 and the stock was selling for 61 at the date of death. A $5 per share dividend had been declared on April 15, payable on May 15 to holders of record on May 10.

Required

1. If Mr. D died on May 1, 1990, determine the assets and their values to be included in the initial inventory of the estate of Mr. D to the nearest dollar.
2. If all the interest and dividends payments were paid as indicated, determine the amount of Principal cash and Income cash received from the investments in stocks and bonds during the period ending December 31, 1990 to the nearest dollar.
3. On January 15, 1991, executor received 40 shares of ACT Company stock as a 10% stock dividend. The market price of the stock at that time was 59. Prepare journal entries to record the receipt of the stock dividend as Principal and as Income.

EXERCISE 18-7

John Reed, a wealthy businessman, established an inter vivos trust on January 1, 1991 to provide for the financial needs of his son and wife. The written trust agreement signed by Reed provided for income to his wife, Myrna, for her life with the remainder to his son, Rodney. Reed named Mini Bank as the sole trustee and transferred stocks, bonds, and two commercial buildings to the trust. The accounting period selected for the trust was the calendar year.

During the first year of the trust's existence, Mini made the following allocations to Principal and Income arising out of transactions involving trust property:

- With regard to the sale of $25,000 of stock, $20,000 to Income representing the gain on the sale of stock and $5,000 to Principal representing the cost basis of the stock.
- $95,000 to Income from rental receipts earned and received after the trust was created.
- $6,000 to Income and $2,000 to Principal as a result of a stock dividend of 400 shares of $5 par value common stock at a time when the stock was selling for $20 per share.
- $10,000 to Income for bond interest received and that is payable semiannually on April 1 and October 1.
- $35,000 to Principal as a result of mortgage payments made by the trust on the commercial buildings.

The instrument creating the trust is silent as to the allocation of the trust receipts and disbursements to Principal and Income.

Required

Indicate the proper allocation to Principal and Income of the trust receipts and disbursements described above using the method selected by the text and give your reasons for the allocation. If state laws could permit or require an alternative allocation, describe the allocation.

(AICPA adapted)

EXERCISE 18-8

1. The equity theory and the basis of accounting for an estate or trust is

	Equity Theory	Basis of Accounting
a.	Fund	Accrual
b.	Entity	Accrual
c.	Proprietary	Cash
d.	Fund	Cash

2. The remainderman of an estate or trust is

a. the person who receives the personal property of an estate or trust.
b. the fiduciary of an estate or trust.
c. the person who receives the remaining assets at the end of the term of the estate or trust.
d. the person who receives the real property of an estate or trust.

3. The assets of an estate are recorded at

a. their cost to the decedent.
b. the lower of their cost to the decedent or their fair market value at the date of death.
c. the greater of their cost to the decedent or their fair market value at the date of death.
d. their fair market value at the date of death.

4. A legacy is a bequest

a. of real property.
b. of personal property.
c. to a charitable institution.
d. to a direct heir of the decedent.

5. The premium and discount on bonds purchased by a personal representative of an estate are recorded and amortized.

	Premium	Discount
a.	Yes	Yes
b.	Yes	No
c.	No	Yes
d.	No	No

6. An estate pays a number of different taxes. The following taxes are charged to:

	Income Taxes of the Estate	Income Taxes of the Decedent	Estate Taxes
a.	Principal	Principal	Principal
b.	Income	Income	Principal
c.	Principal	Income	Income
d.	Income	Principal	Principal

EXERCISE 18-9

1. J. Marble died on October 1, 1991. The inventory of her assets at the date of her death consisted of the following:

	Cost	Market Value
Cash	$ 10,000	$ 10,000
A Company Bonds	18,000	20,000
Interest Receivable: A Company Bonds	1,000	1,000
B Company Stock	38,000	40,000
Dividend Declared: B Company Stock	500	500

The amount to be recorded as the value of the estate at the date of death is

a. $ 66,000
b. $ 67,500
c. $ 70,000
d. $ 71,500

2. Alfred Waters died on October 1, 1990. His estate consisted of cash and $300,000 face value, 12% City of Clover bonds, that pay interest semiannually on June 30 and December 31. His will directed that the income of his estate be distributed to the American Red Cross. During the first three months, the executor paid the following:

Executor's Fee	$3,000
Personal Income Taxes of the Decedent	1,000
Estate Income Taxes	2,000

On January 1, 1991, the executor made a distribution to the American Red Cross. The amount to be distributed to the American Red Cross is

a. $ 3,000
b. $ 4,000
c. $ 7,000
d. $ 16,000

INFORMATION FOR QUESTIONS 3 AND 4
During the period August 1, 1990 to October 1, 1990, the estate of Mr. W paid the following expenses:

Property Taxes on Personal Residence Held for Sale	$ 1,300
Professional Fees Relating to the Settlement of the Estate	1,100
Legal Fees to Defend a Copyright of a Book Decedent Published	1,700
Repairs to an Apartment Building Included in the Assets of the Estate	1,500
Federal Estate Taxes	700
Income Taxes Owing at the Date of Death	600
Income Taxes of the Estate	300

3. The amount of these expenses that were paid with Principal cash is

a. $ 2,400
b. $ 3,700
c. $ 3,900
d. $ 4,100

4. The amount of these expenses that were paid with Income cash is

a. $ 1,500
b. $ 3,200
c. $ 3,500
d. $ 4,800

5. The initial inventory of the estate of J. Polly, who died on February 1, 1990, contained $1,000,000 face value, 12% bonds with a market value of $1,067,000. The bonds pay interest semiannually on April 1 and October 1 and mature on October 1, 1995. The journal entry to record the receipt of the semiannual interest payment on April 1, 1990 includes

a. a debit to Income Cash of $60,000.
b. a debit to Principal Cash of $60,000.
c. a debit to Principal Cash of $40,000.
d. a debit to Income Cash of $54,000.

6. The estate of P. Shirley included a personal residence that cost $60,000 and had a fair market value at the date of death of $90,000. The personal representative of the estate sold the residence for $87,000. The journal entry to record the sale of the residence includes

a. a debit to Income Cash of $3,000.
b. a debit to Loss on Sale of Principal Assets of $3,000.
c. a credit to Gain on Sale of Principal Assets of $27,000.
d. a credit to Estate Principal of $3,000.

7. The administrator of the estate of M. Pope distributed a painting to the Bay City Museum as specified by M. Pope's will. M. Pope purchased the painting for $15,000 and the painting had a fair market value at the date of death of $25,000. The administrator of the estate had received an offer of $28,000 for the painting. The journal entry to record the distribution of the painting to the museum includes

a. a debit to Estate Expenses of $25,000.
b. a debit to a Loss on Principal Assets of $3,000.
c. a debit to Legacies Distributed of $25,000.
d. a debit to Legacies Distributed of $15,000.

8. The estate of R. Viceroy contained an insurance policy payable to the estate with a cash surrender value of $22,000 and a face value of $50,000. R. Viceroy had borrowed $6,000 on the policy. The journal entry to record the receipt of $44,000 from the insurance company includes

a. a debit to Debts of the Decedent of $6,000.
b. a debit to Income Cash of $28,000.
c. a credit to Estate Assets: Insurance Policy of $44,000.
d. a credit to Gain on Principal Assets of $28,000.

PROBLEMS

PROBLEM 18-1

Ms. G died on March 15, 1990, leaving an estate consisting of the following assets:

- Household furnishings with a fair market value of $16,300.
- 8% City of Houston bonds, with a face value of $45,000. The bonds pay interest semiannually on January 1 and July 1. The bonds were purchased by Ms. G for $44,100 and have a fair market value of $44,500.
- Cash in interest-bearing checking account in the amount of $28,140.
- Cash found in home in the amount of $525.
- Commercial store building with a fair market value of $81,750. The building is leased at an annual rental of $13,200, that is payable monthly in advance.

- 10% Mortgage receivable from the sale of a personal residence. The principal balance at the date of death was $45,600. The mortgage requires the borrower to pay the interest plus $600 of the principal quarterly on February 1, May 1, August 1, and November 1.
- Ms. G and Ms. H have been partners for many years. The partnership has three boutiques specializing in handmade sweaters. The fair market value of Ms. G's interest in the G & H Partnership was $70,000 at the date of her death.
- 300 Shares of General Motors stock with a cost of $6,000 and a fair market value of $10,300.
- Ms. G has two insurance policies on her life: one for $25,000 payable to her spouse, and one for $50,000 payable to her estate.

Ms. G left a will specifying that her son, Don, and her daughter, Sue, were to act as co-executors of her estate and to receive $3,000 each for their services. Ms. G left her widower $30,000 in cash and the household goods, and she left her two children equal shares of the General Motors stock. The remainder of her estate principal and the estate income is to be placed in a trust. The will provided that Mr. G is to receive $3,000 of the estate income each March 31, June 30, September 30, and December 31, during the term of the estate. The will also provided that Mr. G is to receive the income of the trust quarterly on March 31, June 30, September 30, and December 31.

Ms. G had $4,790 of personal debts at the date of her death and her funeral costs were $2,175. During the term of the estate, the trustee incurred $1,000 of legal fees and $750 of accounting fees. The estate paid $7,950 of personal income taxes for Ms. G as well as $3,100 of property taxes on the commercial building, that became a lien on October 1, 1989.

On May 2, 1990, the executors received the proceeds from the insurance policy. On June 30, 1990, $900 of dividends declared after Ms. G's death were received from the General Motors stock. On October 1, 1990, the executors received $72,465 from the liquidation of Ms. G's partnership interest. All other income was received when due and receivable. All the legacies were distributed except the assets to be placed in the trust. On October 5, 1990, a report was filed with the court.

Required

1. Enter all the transactions of the estate of Ms. G in ledger accounts, using separate accounts for the different types of income and assuming all transactions listed or mentioned occurred. You are not required to prepare journal entries but writing out some entries is helpful.
2. Prepare the report to the court.
3. Prepare the journal entry to transfer the remaining assets to the trust.
4. Prepare the closing entries for the estate of Ms. G.

PROBLEM 18-2

(This is our adaptation of an actual situation that happened recently in a nearby town.)

Mr. H died on February 1, 1990. Mr. H was a bachelor whose only close companions were his cats and his friend, Jim, who lived in a bungalow on property Mr. H owned. Mr. H had operated a local tavern called Harry's Place for a number of years. Mr. H's will contained the following provisions:

- My business is to be sold and the proceeds are to be placed in a trust for the care of my cats. My property is also to be placed in the trust. When the last cat is gone, my good friend, Jim, is to receive the remainder of the trust except for the property.
- My friend, Jim, is to be allowed to live in the bungalow rent-free for the rest of his life in return for caring for my cats. In addition, any income earned by my estate is to go to Jim.
- After the death of my last cat, my property is to go to the City of Sweethome. The city may put the property to any use that will benefit the town, but the city may not sell the property until the death of my friend, Jim.
- I leave $10,000 to the Salvation Army because they helped me when I was down and out.
- I leave the remainder of my estate to my sister, Joan, and my nephew, John, share and share alike (equally).

The inventory of Mr. H's estate consisted of the following:

	Market Value
Cash in Checking Account	$ 4,125
IRA Account	9,120
6% Henry Weinhardt Brewing Company Bonds	38,750
The face value is $40,000. The interest is payable semiannually on March 1 and September 1.	
9% Coors Brewing Company Bonds	26,400
The face value is $25,000. The interest is payable semiannually on April 1 and October 1.	
350 Shares of Anheuser-Busch Brewing Company Common Stock	10,640
A dividend of $425 had been declared on January 20, payable to holders of record on February 15.	
Harry's Place Tavern	55,000
Property with Home and Bungalow	82,150

During the term of the estate, which ended on November 30, 1990, the following transactions occurred:

- Funeral and Administrative Expenses Paid ... $ 6,240
- Debts of Decedent Paid ... 2,450
- Estate Taxes Paid ... 9,130
- Income Taxes on Mr. H's Final Return Paid ... 7,320
- Found Coin Collection in Desk Drawer and sold the Collection for ... 5,400
- Cashed IRA Account and Deposited in Estate checking Account ... 9,120
- Sold the Anheuser-Busch Stock on March 1 for ... 11,100
- Sold Harry's Place for ... 56,150
- Sold the Coors Brewing Company bonds on June 1. The selling price includes the interest to the date of sale. ... 27,100
- Received all the interest and dividend payments due the estate.
- Rented the house to the City of Sweethome on March 1 for an annual rental of $12,000 payable in monthly installments, with the payments due at the beginning of the month. Rental payments in the amount of $9,000 were received.

Required

1. Describe the type of bequest each of the beneficiaries of the estate of Mr. H is to receive either from the estate or from the testamentary trust.
2. Prepare a worksheet showing the effect of the transactions on the assets of the estate, assuming the will provided that no accruals were to be recorded at the close of the estate. Use a four-column worksheet with the first column for the initial inventory, columns two and three for the transactions, and column four for the balances prior to the distributions of any assets.
3. Prepare the journal entries to record the distributions of the assets of the estate.
4. Prepare the closing entries for the estate.

PROBLEM 18-3

Jane Jones died on August 15, 1990. The inventory of her estate consisted of the following:

- Cash ... $ 18,000
- 100 12% State of Oregon Bonds, interest payable April 1, and October 1.
  Face Value ... 100,000

	Acquisition Price	$ 96,000
	Fair Market Value, August 15, 1990	105,000
▪	1,000 shares of Pacific Corp. Stock	
	Par Value Per Share	25
	Acquisition Price	37,000
	Fair Market Value, August 15, 1990	40,000
	Dividend of $1 per share declared on August 1 to holders of record of August 12, payable on August 20.	
▪	Office Building	
	Contains 4 rented offices whose rents are $250 per office, payable monthly. The tenants pay all their own utilities.	
	Acquisition Price	100,000
	Depreciation to August 15, 1990	45,000
	Fair Market Value, August 15, 1990	70,000
	Property Taxes Assessed June 30, 1990, Payable November 15, 1990	3,000
▪	Apartment Furnishings	
	Acquisition Price	20,000
	Fair Market Value, August 15, 1990	10,000
▪	Coin Collection	
	Acquisition Price	21,000
	Fair Market Value, August 15, 1990	50,000
▪	Pension Benefits Payable to the Estate 6 Months after Death	120,000

The estate existed as an entity from August 15, 1990 to March 1, 1991. During this period the following items were received or paid:

8/20/90	Received Pacific Corp. dividend	$	1,000
10/1/90	Paid debts of decedent		5,000
10/1/90	Received interest from State of Oregon		6,000
11/15/90	Paid office building property taxes		3,000
12/31/90	Paid Federal and Oregon income taxes owed by decedent		12,000
1/15/91	Received pension benefits plus interest from date of death		126,000
2/20/91	Received Pacific Corp. dividend		1,000
2/25/91	Sold coin collection		46,000
3/1/91	Paid Federal and Oregon income taxes owed by the estate		2,000
3/1/91	Paid executrix fee		10,000
9/1/90 thru 3/1/91	Received monthly rental of $1,000 per month from all tenants for all months		

On October 1, 1990, the executrix discovered a diamond ring valued at $10,000. The will of Jane Jones stipulated the following distribution of her assets:

▪ City College: State of Oregon bonds
▪ Jack James, nephew: coin collection proceeds and estate income to be placed in a trust
▪ Sonia Grace, daughter: remainder of estate

Required

1. Describe the type of bequest each entity received.
2. Prepare the inventory of the estate.
3. Prepare schedules showing the assets each beneficiary is to receive and the value of the assets in the estate.
4. Prepare the journal entries for transfer of the estate assets to the beneficiaries.
5. Prepare the closing entry for the estate.

PROBLEM 18-4

On May 1, 1990, Helen Heath died testate. Her will contained the following provisions:

- My sister, Maybell, is to receive my Holly Motel stock.
- My roommate, Harry, is to receive my apartment furnishings and my car.
- The remainder of my estate is to be placed in a trust at Bay Bank for the benefit of my niece, Angel. She is to receive the income of the trust until she is 25 years old, and then the trust assets are to be distributed to her. The principal may be invaded to provide for necessary medical care and education costs.

The inventory of Helen's estate contained the following:

- Cash in checking account, $10,000.
- 1,000 shares of Holly Motel stock, acquired at $25 per share, market price on May 1, 1990 is $40 per share. A $2 per share dividend was declared on April 15, payable on June 1 to holders of record on May 20.
- $20,000 face value, 12% Theater Company bonds that pay interest semiannually on January 1 and July 1, acquisition price 98, market price 102 on May 1, 1990.
- Apartment furnishings, cost $15,000, fair market value $12,000.
- 1969 Ford Thunderbird, cost $7,000, fair market value $17,000, since the car has been restored.

The transactions and events of the estate were as follows:

5/20/90	Paid funeral expenses of $2,500 and other debts of $800.
6/1/90	Received Holly Motel dividend.
7/1/90	Received Theater Company interest.
8/1/90	Sold Theater Company bonds for 103 plus accrued interest.
8/5/90	Discovered an insurance policy with a face value of $5,000. The beneficiary of the policy is the Children's Aid Society.
8/15/90	Received the proceeds of the insurance policy and remitted the check to the Children's Aid Society.
8/15/90	Distributed the legacies to Maybell and Harry.
8/31/90	Paid estate taxes of $4,000, estate income taxes of $300, and income taxes of Helen Heath of $2,300.
9/1/90	Submitted the charge and discharge statement to the court.
9/1/90	Distributed the remaining assets to the trust.

Required

1. Prepare the journal entries for the estate.
2. Prepare the charge and discharge statement.
3. Prepare the closing journal entries.

PROBLEM 18-5

The will of J. James, who died on May 1, 1991, appointed B. Kidd as the executor. B. Kidd prepared the following journal entries for the estate of J. James:

5/1	Bank Checking Account		214,100	
	Insurance Policy at Cash Surrender Value		18,000	
	The policy is payable to the estate and the face value is $100,000.			
	United Artists Corp. 12% Bonds at J. James Cost		124,000	
	The interest is payable March 1, and September 1. The face value is $100,000 and the market value on May 1, 1990 is $106,000.			
	James Company Common Stock		1	
	10,000 shares at $10 par value. The stock was quoted at $18 when J. James died. These shares were a gift from his father, the founder of the company, so I've entered them at $1 for a record.			
	Condominium		173,000	
	His condo is just like the one I bought a week before he died which cost me $296,000. J. James only paid $173,000 for his 3 years ago.			
	Paintings			
	I don't understand these, but a dealer valued them at $225,000. J. James paid $90,000 for the paintings.		225,000	
	Gain on Paintings			135,000
	Total Estate			619,000
	I omitted J. James' Jaguar automobile as I intend to keep the car, in lieu of an executor's fee			

5/9	Cash		2,000	
	James Company Dividend			2,000
	Received a check for a dividend declared April 2 to holders of record on April 25			

6/1	Cash		100,000	
	Insurance Policy at Cash Surrender Value			18,000
	Gain on the Death of J. James			82,000
	This is the check from the insurance company			

6/9	Expenses		184,000	
	Cash			184,000
	I issued checks for the following:			
	Funeral Expenses	$ 15,100		
	Medical Bills	300		
	Final Income Tax Payment	117,900		
	American Express Charges	700		
	Partial Payment of Estate Taxes	50,000		
	Total	$184,000		

6/30	Expenses		225,000	
	Paintings			225,000
	The paintings were taken to the Realism Museum as directed by the will			

9/1	Cash		6,000	
	Interest Received			6,000
	Check received from United Artists Corp.			

9/10   Loss on James Company Common Stock   1
      James Company Common Stock   1
The will required the stock be returned to the company

10/1   Cash   290,000
      Condominium   173,000
      Gain on Sale of Condominium   117,000
The sale of the condo. The will states that the proceeds are
to be used to establish a J. James scholarship at Corral
College, his alma mater.

10/3   Cash Turned Over to Corral College   290,000
      Cash   290,000
Check sent to the college

10/31 Expenses   3,000
      Cash   3,000
The court relieved me as executor and said I was to be
paid $3,000 for my work and also made me return the
Jaguar, which I valued at $80,000

Required

1. Prepare correct journal entries for the estate of J. James.
2. Prepare the charge and discharge statement for the court.

PROBLEM 18-6

Mr. F died on January 15, 1990. The court approved Mr. F's son, Lars F, as the executor. The assets owned by the decedent at the time of his death are as follows:

	Market Value
Cash	$ 14,900
Home, Which Cost $34,900 in 1974	70,000
Household Furnishings	14,400
6% Maine Power and Light Company Bonds	123,800
Face Value $120,000, interest payable semiannually on February 1 and August 1	
200 Shares of 7% Vermont Electric Company Preferred Stock	10,750
$50 par value	
500 Shares of Xerox Corporation Common Stock	25,000
A $1.50 per share dividend had been declared on January 10, payable on February 5 to holders of record on January 31.	
1985 Buick Sentra	7,400
Pension Benefit Receivable from Maine Power and Light Company	74,800
Life Insurance Policy Payable to the Widow, Mrs. F	50,000

Mr. F's will stipulated that his widow is to receive the home and its furnishings and the income of the estate. Mr. F's four children are to receive $20,000 each. The remainder of the estate is to be placed in a trust with Mrs. F as the income beneficiary and the children as the remaindermen. During the term of the estate the following transactions occurred:

1/23   Executor filed an inventory of the estate with the court and opened the books of the estate.

2/1   Received the interest from Maine Power and Light Company.

2/8   Received the dividends from Xerox Corporation.

2/25   Paid funeral costs of $2,765.

2/28   Paid medical bills totaling $7,435.

3/1   Received the pension benefits from the pension trustee.

3/10   Transferred the home and the furnishings to Mrs. F.

3/15   Received the quarterly preferred dividend from Vermont Electric Company stock.

3/25   Paid the outstanding bills of Mr. F in the amount of $3,600.

3/30   Received the fair market value of the automobile from Mrs. F.

4/15   Paid the income taxes of the decedent totaling $3,240. While reviewing the tax return, the executor discovered that the accountant had included rental on a safety deposit box and interest from a savings account. An investigation revealed that Mr. F had a savings account in St. Louis Mutual Savings and Loan. The balance in the account at the date of death was $6,900 and $150 of interest had been credited to the account on March 31. An inspection of the safety deposit box revealed gold coins and silver bullion worth $17,400 at the date of death.

4/18   Closed the savings account and deposited the cash in the estate checking account.

5/4   Sold the gold coins and silver bullion for $15,900.

5/8   Received a $2 per share dividend from Xerox Corporation and a 5% stock dividend. The market price of the Xerox stock was $51 per share on the date of the stock dividend.

5/15   Paid $1,820 of property taxes on the home, which became a lien on December 15, 1989.

5/25   Sold the Xerox Corporation stock for $28,620.

6/15   Received another quarterly dividend from Vermont Electric Company.

6/15   Paid estate taxes of $3,200 and income taxes of the estate in the amount of $195.

6/30   Distributed the legacies to Mr. F's children.

6/30   Paid the executor's fee of $3,800.

7/1   Received the interest from Maine Power and Light Company.

7/1   Distributed $5,000 of income to the widow.

7/15   Filed a charge and discharge statement with the court.

Required

1. Prepare the initial inventory of the estate that the executor submitted to the court.
2. Prepare the transaction journal entries for the estate. It is not necessary to prepare the entry to record the initial inventory.
3. Prepare the charge and discharge statement for the court. It is not necessary to prepare ledger accounts, but preparing "T" accounts for cash will be helpful. Use the initial inventory from (1.) as one of the supporting schedules.
4. The court accepted the charge and discharge statement and ordered the estate closed. Prepare the journal entries for the distribution of the income to the widow and the remaining assets to the trust established by the will.
5. Prepare the closing journal entries for the estate.

PROBLEM 18-7: Continuation of Problem 18-6

The trustee, B. Reif, of the testamentary trust established by the will of the late Mr. F accepted the assets from the executor and opened the books of the trust on July 15, 1990. Mr. F's will specified that his widow was to receive the income during her lifetime and that upon her death the remainder of the trust was to be divided equally among his four children or the children's heirs if his children did not survive his widow.

1. During 1990 the trustee entered into the following transactions on behalf of the trust:

7/21   Sold the Vermont Electric Company preferred stock for $11,200.

7/31   Purchased $30,000 face value, 9% City of Portland bonds for $27,100 and also purchased $30,000 face value 10% State of Maine bonds for $30,460. Both bonds pay
interest semiannually on June 30 and December 31 and mature on June 30, 1992.
The above purchase prices do not include accrued interest payable to the sellers of the
bonds.

8/1   Received the semiannual interest payment on the 6% Maine Power and Light Company
bonds.

12/31   Paid the trustee's fee of $500, which the trust instrument specified be charged to income.

12/31   Received the semiannual interest payments from the City of Portland and the State of
Maine bonds.

Required

1) Prepare the journal entry to record the initial inventory of the trust.

2) Prepare the charge and discharge statement for the period ending December 31, 1990.

2. During 1991 the following transactions and events occurred:

2/1   Distributed the 1990 income to the widow.

2/1   Received the semiannual interest payment on the 6% Maine Power and Light Company
bonds.

6/30   Received the semiannual interest on the City of Portland and State of Maine bonds.

8/1   Received the semiannual interest payment on the 6% Maine Power and Light Company
bonds.

8/15   The widow, Mrs. F, and her daughter, Lana, were killed in an automobile accident.

8/15   The trustee was paid $500.

Required

1) Prepare the charge and discharge statement for the period ending August 15, 1991.

2) Prepare the journal entries for distribution of the trust assets, assuming that the trustee closed the
accounts on December 31, 1990. The daughter, Lana, left one heir, Lanette, and Mr. F's other children,
Lars, Larry, and Lorna are living.

PROBLEM 18-8

On October 15, 1990, the executor of the estate of Ms. J, who died on April 1, 1990, asked you to assist
in the preparation of the charge and discharge statement for the court. The only record the executor
kept was a check register. The executor, Mr. Cash, had filed an inventory of assets with the court. The
check register contained the following entries:

Beginning balance	$ 17,325
Receipts	
Quarterly dividends from 1,000 shares of X Company stock	
Received April 25, declared March 24	1,400
Received July 25, declared June 20	1,500
Proceeds of life insurance policy	40,000
Interest on City of Minneapolis bonds	4,000
Proceeds, including interest, from the sale $100,000 face value, 8% City of Minneapolis bonds on August 15. The bonds pay interest semiannually on May 15 and November 15.	98,900
Proceeds from IRA account discovered on September 1. The proceeds included $325 of interest earned since April 1.	12,400
Proceeds from the sale of X Company stock	14,000
Semiannual interest payment from State of Minnesota bonds	6,000

Disbursements

Funeral expense paid on May 10	$ 3,160
Total cost, including interest, of 12% State of Minnesota bonds purchased on August 15. The bonds have a face value of $100,000 and pay interest semiannually on March 15 and September 15.	104,200
Administrative expenses paid	4,200
Income taxes of the decedent paid	2,900
Distribution to college as specified in the will	7,500
Distribution of income to spouse as specified in the will	3,000
Distribution of $10,000 each to two grandchildren as specified in the will	20,000

After reviewing the inventory of the estate that was filed with the court, you determine that only the assets mentioned above existed at the date of death. You also determine that the securities have the following market value per share or per bond:

	4/1/90	10/15/90
X Company stock	$ 13.50	$ 14.50
City of Minneapolis bonds	975.00	950.00
State of Minnesota bonds	1,002.75	1,052.50

Required

1. Prepare the journal entry to record the initial inventory of the estate and all the transaction journal entries.
2. Prepare the charge and discharge statement.
3. The will of Ms. J stipulated that all the remaining assets of her estate are to be placed in a trust with her spouse as the life tenant and her grandchildren as the remaindermen. Prepare the journal entry to transfer the assets to the trust.
4. Prepare the closing journal entries for the estate.

PROBLEM 18-9: Continuation of Problem 18-8

The trustee, First City Bank, received the assets from the executor, Mr. Cash, on October 15, 1990. The trust agreement required the trustee to distribute the trust income to Mr. J every six months, starting 6 months from the date the trust was established. Upon the conclusion of the trust, the trustee is to accrue any income due the income beneficiary.

On November 15, 1990, the trustee purchased $45,000 face value, 10% City of St. Paul bonds at 95 plus accrued interest. The bonds pay interest semiannually on February 15 and August 15. On December 15, 1991, Mr. J died.

Required

1. Prepare the journal entry to record the initial inventory of the trust.
2. Demonstrate how the journal entry of (1.) would be different if the trust were an inter vivos trust rather than a testamentary trust.
3. Prepare the journal entries for the trust, assuming all interest payments were received and the trust was the testamentary trust of (1.).
4. Prepare the journal entry to transfer from Principal Cash to Income Cash the interest accrued at the date of Mr. J's death.
5. Prepare the journal entries for the distribution of the trust assets to the remaindermen.

PROBLEM 18-10

Mr. K, a resident of Seattle, Washington, died on April 1, 1991. His will provided for the following distribution of his assets:

- To my son, Bob, I leave my car, my antique gun collection, and my mining claim.
- To my daughter, Jeanette, I leave the diamond ring and ruby broach that had been her grandmother's favorite jewelry.
- To my wife, Mary, I leave our home and its furnishings.
- The remainder of my assets are to be placed in a trust with my wife as the income beneficiary and my children as the remaindermen.
- All the income of my estate is to go to my wife, Mary.
- I appoint my daughter, Jeanette K., as the personal representative of my estate to serve without bond.

1. Washington is a community property state. All the assets of Mr. K are community property, except the jewelry and the mining claim, which Mr. K inherited from his mother, and he has maintained separate ownership of these assets. An inventory of the assets, at their fair market value, that Mr. K had an ownership interest in at the date of his death are as follows:

Cash in Interest-Bearing Checking Account	$ 34,000
Cash in Time Certificates of Deposit	125,000
Apartment House	300,000
Patented Mining Claim	2,500
Personal Residence	100,000
Household Furnishings	20,000
Diamond Ring	5,000
Ruby Broach	1,500
Antique Gun Collection	7,500
1981 Plymouth Fury	1,500

Required

Prepare the initial inventory of the estate for filing with the court.

2. During the administration of the estate of Mr. K, the following transactions affecting the community property assets occurred, which are for the entire amounts related to these co-owned assets.

• Interest Income from Time Certificates of Deposit	$ 10,000
• Rental Income from Apartment House	16,000
• Rental Expenses Paid	6,500
• Property Taxes on the Apartment House, that became a lien on November 1, 1990	4,000
• Property Taxes on Personal Residence, that became a lien on November 1, 1990	1,800

In addition, the following expenses for the decedent alone were paid:

Funeral Expenses	$ 1,200
Debts of the Decedent	3,500
Income Taxes Owed by the Decedent	2,500
Legal and Administrative Fees	2,100
Property Taxes on Patented Mining Claim, That Became a Lien on March 1, 1991	100

Required

1) Prepare the charge and discharge statement for the court, as of December 31, 1991, assuming that the assets and income left to the wife, son, and daughter have been distributed as instructed by the will.

2) Prepare the journal entry to transfer the assets to the trust.

3) Prepare the closing entries for the estate.

PROBLEM 18-11: Continuation of Problem 18-10

1. Mrs. Mary K decided to establish a trust with her share of the time certificates of deposit, and the apartment house. On January 1, 1992, Mrs. Mary K transferred her interest in those co-owned assets to her trust. The trust instrument specified that she was to receive the income from the trust during her lifetime, and that her children, Bob and Jeanette, were to receive the assets upon her death. Due to a real estate boom, the apartment house had a fair market value of $318,000 on January 1, 1992.

Required

Prepare the journal entries to establish the testamentary trust of Mr. K and the inter vivos trust of Mrs. K.

2. Both trust instruments required the amortization of bond premium and discount and the recording of depreciation to preserve the Principal of the trusts. The trust instruments required that the income be distributed to the income beneficiary, one month after the close of the calendar year. Mr. Moneybags, the trustee of both trusts, decided to operate the trusts as if they were a single trust, due to the indivisibility of the assets, knowing that separate reports would be required for the trusts. During 1992, the following transactions affecting both trusts occurred:

- Interest Income from Time Certificates of Deposit — $ 10,000
- Interest Income from Pacific Power Company Bonds — 2,500
- Proceeds from Time Certificate of Deposit, Which Matured — 50,000
- Rental Income from Apartment House — 25,000
- Rental Expenses Paid — 12,200
- Purchase of $50,000 face value, 10% Pacific Power Company Bonds on June 30, 1992. The bonds pay interest semiannually on March 31 and September 30 and mature 39 months after date of purchase. The purchase price included interest for three months. — 51,640
- Payment of Trustee Fee (Charge Income) — 1,200

Required

Prepare a charge and discharge statement for each trust as of December 31, 1992, assuming the apartment house has an estimated useful life of 30 years, and a total salvage value of $60,000.

SOLUTION TO REVIEW PROBLEM

1. 1) The bequest of $10,000 to Alma Mater Foundation is pecuniary legacy that is also a general legacy. The legacies to the sons, R2 and D2, are pecuniary legacies that are also demonstrative legacies. The trust for the granddaughters has two types of legacies. The stocks and bonds are specific legacies and the income is a pecuniary legacy that is also a specific legacy. The diaries are a specific legacy. The bequest to the daughter S1 is a residual legacy.

1. 2)

3/1	Principal Cash		14,100	
	Life Insurance Policy		35,000	
	AT&T Stock		20,400	
	Dividends Receivable (500 × $2.50)		1,250	
	City of Auburn Bonds		102,300	
	Interest Receivable ($100,000 × 9% × 2/12)		1,500	
	Ms. R's Nurturing Nursery and Garden Store		103,000	
	Household Furnishings		12,400	
	1989 Mercedes Benz		40,000	
	Diaries		1	
	Estate Principal			329,951
	To record the initial inventory of the estate			

2. 1)

3/13	Principal Cash		1,250	
	Dividends Receivable			1,250
	To record the receipt of the AT&T dividend			
3/31	Principal Cash		35,000	
	Life Insurance Policy			35,000
	To record receipt of proceeds of life insurance policy			
4/14	Debts of Decedent		3,300	
	Principal Cash			3,300
	To record the payment of the debts of the decedent incurred prior to death			
4/27	Principal Cash		41,600	
	Gain on the Realization of Principal Assets			1,600
	1989 Mercedes Benz			40,000
	To record the sale of the automobile			
4/30	Principal Legacies Distributed		1	
	Diaries			1
	To record distribution of diaries per will			
4/30	Debts of Decedent		2,400	
	Funeral and Administrative Expenses		3,000	
	Principal Cash			5,400
	To record payment of medical bills and funeral expenses			
5/15	Principal Cash		50,000	
	Note Receivable: Principal		51,000	
	Loss on Disposition of Principal Assets		2,000	
	Ms. R's Nurturing Nursery and Garden Store			103,000
	To record the sale of the decedent's business			
5/22	Income Cash		295	
	Estate Income			295
	To record the receipt of IBM Dividend			

5/25	Diamond Ring	5,000	
	IRA Account	8,900	
	25 Shares IBM Stock	10,725	
	Assets Subsequently Discovered		24,625
	To record assets found in safety deposit box		
5/31	Principal Cash	8,900	
	IRA Account		8,900
	To record receipt of cash from IRA account		
6/30	Principal Legacies Distributed	10,000	
	Principal Cash		10,000
	To record the distribution of cash to the Alma Mater Foundation per will		
7/1	Principal Cash	1,500	
	Income Cash ($100,000 $\times$ 9% $\times$ 4/12)	3,000	
	Interest Receivable		1,500
	Estate Income		3,000
	To record the receipt of the semiannual interest payment from the city of Auburn bonds		
7/1	Principal Cash (($101,000 $-$ $50,000) $\times$ 1/3)	17,000	
	Income Cash ($51,000 $\times$ 12% $\times$ 1.5/12)	765	
	Note Receivable: Principal		17,000
	Estate Income		765
	To record the receipt of the first installment payment on the note receivable from the sale of Ms. R's business		
7/10	Principal Cash	6,400	
	Gain on Realization of Principal Assets		1,000
	Household Furnishings		5,400
	To record the sale of the furniture that was not antiques		
7/13	Income Cash (500 shares $\times$ $3)	1,500	
	Estate Income		1,500
	To record the receipt of AT&T Dividend		
8/24	Income Cash (25 shares $\times$ $4)	100	
	Estate Income		100
	To record receipt of IBM Dividend		
10/1	Principal Cash (($101,000 $-$ $50,000) $\times$ 1/3)	17,000	
	Income Cash [($51,000 $-$ $17,000) $\times$ 12% $\times$ 3/12]	1,020	
	Note Receivable: Principal		17,000
	Estate Income		1,020
	To record the receipt of the second installment payment on the note receivable from the sale of Ms. R's business		
10/15	IBM Stock (5 shares $\times$ $412 per share)	2,060	
	Assets Subsequently Discovered		2,060
	To record the receipt of 5 shares as a stock dividend		
11/15	Funeral and Administrative Expenses	19,000	
	Principal Cash		19,000
	To record the payment of the estate taxes		

Note: Could have used the account, Estate Taxes Principal

1/1	Principal Cash ($101,000 − $50,000) × 1/3		17,000	
	Income Cash [($51,000 − $34,000) × 12% × 3/12)]		510	
	Note Receivable: Principal			17,000
	Estate Income			510

To record the receipt of the final installment payment on the note receivable from the sale of Ms. R's business

1/1	Income Cash		4,500	
	Estate Income			4,500

To record the receipt of the semiannual interest payment on City of Auburn bonds

1/15	Principal Legacies Distributed		100,000	
	Principal Cash			100,000

To record the distribution of cash from the proceeds of the sale of Ms. R's business to her sons R2 and D2. The will stipulated that the amount was limited to $100,000.

1/19	Income Cash (500 shares × $4)		2,000	
	Estate Income			2,000

To record dividend from AT&T

2/1	Debts of Decedent		7,200	
	Funeral and Administrative Expenses		200	
	Expenses: Income		2,900	
	Principal Cash			7,400
	Income Cash			2,900

To record the payment of the income taxes owed by the decedent and the income taxes of the estate

2/1	Funeral and Administrative Expenses		5,000	
	Principal Cash			5,000

To record the payment of the executor fees

Principal Accounts

Principal Cash

3/ 1	14,100	4/14	3,300
3/13	1,250	4/30	5,400
3/31	35,000	6/30	10,000
4/27	41,600	11/15	19,000
5/15	50,000	1/15	100,000
5/31	8,900	2/ 1	7,400
7/ 1	1,500	2/ 1	5,000
7/ 1	17,000		
7/10	6,400		
10/ 1	17,000		
1/ 1	17,000		
	209,750		150,100
Bal.	59,650		

Life Insurance Policy

3/ 1	35,000	3/31	35,000

AT&T Stock

3/ 1	20,400		

Dividends Receivable

3/ 1	1,250	3/13	1,250

City of Auburn Bonds

3/ 1	102,300		

Interest Receivable

3/ 1	1,500	7/ 1	1,500

Household Furnishings

3/ 1	12,400	7/13	5,400
Bal.	7,000		

Diaries

3/ 1	1	4/30	1

Diamond Ring

5/25	5,000

IRA Account

5/25	8,900	5/31	8,900

Estate Principal

		3/ 1	329,951

Gains on Disposition of Principal Assets

		4/27	1,600
		7/10	1,000
		Bal.	2,600

Principal Legacies Distributed

4/30	1
6/30	10,000
1/15	100,000
Bal.	110,001

Funeral and Administrative Expenses

4/30	3,000
11/15	19,000
2/ 1	200
2/ 1	5,000
Bal.	27,200

Ms. R's Nurturing Nursery

3/ 1	103,000	5/15	103,000

1989 Mercedes Benz

3/ 1	40,000	4/27	40,000

Note Receivable Principal

5/15	51,000	7/ 1	17,000
		10/ 1	17,000
		1/ 1	17,000
	51,000		51,000

IBM Stock

5/25	10,725		
10/15	2,060		
Bal.	12,785		

Assets Subsequently Discovered

		5/25	24,625
		10/15	2,060
		Bal.	26,685

Losses on Disposition of Principal Assets

5/15	2,000		

Debts of Decedent

4/14	3,300
4/30	2,400
2/ 1	7,200
	12,900

Income Accounts

Income Cash				Estate Expenses		
5/22	295	2/ 1	2,900	2/ 1	2,900	

		Estate Income	
7/ 1	3,000		
7/ 1	765		
7/13	1,500	5/22	295
8/24	100	7/ 1	3,000
10/ 1	1,020	7/ 1	765
1/ 1	510	7/13	1,500
1/ 1	4,500	8/24	100
1/19	2,000	10/ 1	1,020
	13,690	1/ 1	510
Bal.	10,790	1/ 1	4,500
		1/19	2,000
		Bal.	13,690

(Income Cash credit column: 2/ 1 2,900; total 2,900)

2. 2)

Estate of Ms. R
Charge and Discharge Statement
February 1, 1991
Mr. S, Executor

As To Principal

I Charge Myself With

Assets per Inventory (Schedule A)			$ 329,951
Assets Subsequently Discovered (Schedule B)			26,685
Gain on the Disposition of Assets:			
Sale of 1989 Mercedes Benz		$ 1,600	
Sale of Furniture		1,000	2,600
Total Charges			359,236

I Credit Myself With

Loss on Disposition of Asset: Sale of Business			2,000
Debts of Decedent Paid			
Debts Owed by Ms. R	$ 3,300		
Medical Bills of Ms. R	2,400		
Income Taxes	7,200	12,900	
Funeral and Administrative Expenses (Schedule C)		27,200	
Principal Legacies Distributed			
Diaries: Daughter-In-Law	1		
Cash: Alma Mater Foundation	10,000		
Cash: Sons	100,000	110,001	
Total Credits			152,101
Balance of Estate Principal (Schedule D)			$ 207,135

As to Income

I Charge Myself With

Income Received: Dividends and Interest	$ 13,690
I Credit Myself With: Expenses of Income Paid	2,900
Balance: Income Cash	$ 10,790

Estate of Ms. R
Schedule A
Inventory of Assets
March 1, 1990
Mr. S, Executor

Principal Cash	$ 14,100
Life Insurance Policy	35,000
AT&T Stock	20,400
Dividends Receivable	1,250
City of Auburn Bonds	102,300
Interest Receivable	1,500
Ms. R's Nurturing Nursery and Garden Store	103,000
Household Furnishings	12,400
1989 Mercedes Benz	40,000
Diaries	1
Total Estate Principal	$ 329,951

Estate of Ms. R
Schedule B
Assets Subsequently Discovered
Mr. S, Executor

Diamond Ring	$ 5,000
IRA Account	8,900
IBM Stock: 25 shares	10,725
IBM Stock Dividend: 5 shares	2,060
Total	$ 26,685

Estate of Ms. R
Schedule C
Funeral and Administrative Expenses
Mr. S, Executor

Funeral Costs	$ 3,000
Estate Taxes	19,000
Income Taxes on Gains and Losses from Sales of Principal Assets	200
Executor's Fee	5,000
Total	$ 27,200

Estate of Ms. R
Schedule D
Inventory of Assets
February 1, 1991
Mr. S, Executor

Principal Cash	$ 59,650	
AT&T Stock	20,400	
IBM Stock	12,785	
City of Auburn Bonds	102,300	
Household Furnishings: Antique Furniture	7,000	
Diamond Ring	5,000	
Total Estate Principal	$ 207,135	

2. 3)

Principal Legacies Distributed	59,310	
Distribution to Income Beneficiary	10,790	
AT&T Stock [($20,400 ÷ 500 shares) = $40.80 × 200]		8,160
City of Auburn Bonds ($102,300 ÷ 2)		51,150
Income Cash		10,790

To record the distribution of 200 shares of IBM Stock, $50,000
face value City of Auburn bonds and the income cash to the
trust for the benefit of the granddaughters

Principal Legacies Distributed	147,825	
Principal Cash		59,650
AT&T Stock [($20,400 ÷ 500 shares) = $40.80 × 300)]		12,240
IBM Stock (30 shares)		12,785
City of Auburn Bonds ($102,300 ÷ 2)		51,150
Household Furnishings: Antique Furniture		7,000
Diamond Ring		5,000

To record the distribution of the remaining principal assets to the
daughter S1

2. 4)

Estate Principal	329,951	
Assets Subsequently Discovered	26,685	
Gains on Disposition of Principal Assets	2,600	
Losses on Disposition of Principal Assets		2,000
Principal Legacies Distributed (1)		317,136
Debts of Decedent		12,900
Funeral and Administrative Expenses		27,200

To close the principal accounts to Estate Principal

(1) $110,001 + $59,310 + $147,825 = $317,136

Estate Income	13,690	
Estate Expenses		2,900
Distribution to Income Beneficiaries		10,790

To close the income accounts to Estate Income

2. 5)

Principal Cash	10,790	
AT&T Stock, 200 Shares	8,160	
City of Auburn Bonds	51,150	
Trust Principal		70,100
To record the initial inventory of the trust		

INSOLVENT BUSINESS SOLUTIONS

T his chapter covers the solutions to insolvency or near insolvency of business enterprises. Insolvency has two different meanings, a popular definition and a legal definition. The **accounting** or **popular definition** is that a business does not have sufficient cash to meet its debts as they become due and payable, although the business may have assets well in excess of its liabilities. On the other hand, the **legal definition** is that a business has liabilities that exceed the fair salable value of its assets. When businesses are insolvent, by the popular definition, voluntary arrangements with creditors, troubled debt restructurings, quasi-reorganizations, or legal reorganizations usually are attempted in order to return the business to a going concern status. When a business is insolvent by the legal definition, liquidation usually occurs.

The topics of this chapter include

- Voluntary arrangements with all the creditors
- Troubled debt restructurings with some creditors, including the full settlement of the debt with assets or stock, modification of terms, and settlement of a portion of the debt and modification of terms of the remaining debt for both the debtor and the creditor
- Quasi-reorganizations in which the deficit balance of retained earnings is absorbed by altering the existing capital structure of the company
- Legal reorganizations including the preparation of an accounting statement of affairs
- Role of the fiduciary in reorganizations
- Liquidations including the preparation of a statement of realization and liquidation using both the conventional and net book value approaches

VOLUNTARY ARRANGEMENTS

The creditors of a business may all agree to accept settlement of their claims for less than the face value of the receivables or all agree to extend the due dates of the obligations. For example, each creditor agrees to grant an additional 150 days beyond the due date, or each creditor agrees to accept 85 cents for every dollar owed. The business and the creditors have come to an agreement without the intervention of the law. Both parties, the business and the creditors, believe that either the extension of time or the reduced amounts will allow the once profitable and solvent business to recover. The business is most likely insolvent in the popular sense and not "legally" insolvent.

TROUBLED DEBT RESTRUCTURINGS

A financially troubled business, probably one that is insolvent in the accounting sense, may make an agreement with one or more of its creditors, rather than all of its creditors, to alter the amount or terms of one or more of its outstanding liabilities in order to provide the business with time to solve its existing cash shortfall problems and possibly its temporary unprofitability. Such an arrangement is called a **troubled debt restructuring.** *Statement of Financial Accounting Standards No. 15* states that a troubled debt restructuring occurs when a creditor grants a concession to the debtor for economic or legal reasons that it would otherwise not consider.[1] The concessions can take a variety of forms or combination of forms.

These concessions include reduction of either the amount of the principal or the rate of interest, postponement of interest and principal payments, forgiveness of currently due interest, acceptance of assets other than cash in full or partial payment of the debt, and acceptance of equity shares for payment of the debt. Regardless of the concessions, the objective of the creditor is to either eliminate or reduce potential losses from the inability of the debtor to meet the amounts currently due or amounts that are payable in the near future.

If the creditor accepts assets or stock in the troubled company that have a market value at least equal to the outstanding receivable, the creditor believes that the company may not survive and payment in some form of salable asset is better than not receiving any payment. If the creditor accepts assets or stock that have a market value less than the value of the receivable, the creditor is willing to accept some loss now rather than risk a loss equal to the total amount due now and/or payable in the future. In this situation the creditor has concluded that the best course of action is to accept the maximum amount of assets currently obtainable because it represents the maximum that can ultimately be realized from the debtor.

FULL SETTLEMENT OF DEBT

If a debtor transfers assets other than cash to a creditor in full settlement of an outstanding liability, the debtor recognizes a gain or loss on the asset transferred equal to the difference between the fair market value of the asset transferred and its net book value. The techniques

---

[1] *Statement of Financial Accounting Standards No. 15, Accounting by Debtors and Creditors for Troubled Debt Restructurings* (Stamford, Connecticut: FASB, 1977), paragraph 2.

for determining the fair market value of an asset without a ready market are discussed in Chapter 1, and are equally applicable to assets transferred to settle an outstanding liability. The gain or loss is the same amount that the debtor would have recorded if the asset had been sold and the cash remitted to the creditor.

In addition, the debtor recognizes a gain on restructuring equal to the difference between the net book value of the liability and the fair market value of the asset transferred. The net book value of the liability is the balance of the payable, plus any unpaid interest, plus any unamortized premium or less any unamortized discount, plus any unamortized finance charges, and less any unamortized issue costs. If the restructuring gain is material, it is classified as an **extraordinary gain.** The creditor records the asset received at its fair market value and recognizes a loss equal to the difference between the net book value of the receivable and the fair market value of the asset received. However, unlike the debtor, the loss is classified as an **ordinary business loss** by the creditor. Case 1 of Illustrative Problem 19.1 demonstrates the journal entries for both the debtor and the creditor when assets are transferred in full settlement of the debt.

If the debtor issues its own preferred or common stock to the creditor in full settlement of the outstanding liability, the debtor records the stock at its fair market value. If the net book value of the debt is greater than the fair market value of the shares issued, the debtor records an extraordinary gain and the creditor records an ordinary loss. Case 2 of Illustrative Problem 19.1 illustrates the issuance of shares of stock in satisfaction of a debt.

ILLUSTRATIVE PROBLEM 19.1: TROUBLED DEBT RESTRUCTURING: FULL SETTLEMENT

Troubled Corporation borrowed $10,000,000 at 12% for five years from Alpha Company on January 1, 1988. The terms of the loan require that Troubled Corporation pay the interest annually each January 1 and a principal payment of $2,000,000 each January 1. Troubled Corporation paid the annual interest and principal payments due on January 1, 1989 and paid the interest due on January 1, 1990, but did not pay the required principal payment. Troubled Corporation did not pay either a principal or interest payment on January 1, 1991. During 1989 and 1990, Troubled Corporation had suffered an extended strike by its workers, and had not met the competition for its products from foreign manufacturers.

Case 1: Transfer of Assets in Full Settlement. During January, 1991, Troubled Corporation approached Alpha Company and asked if Alpha would accept a manufacturing plant that Troubled owned in full settlement of the amounts due. The companies agreed to accept the determination of the fair market value of the plant by an independent appraiser. The manufacturing plant originally cost Troubled Corporation $14,000,000, the net book value of the plant is $6,300,000, and the appraised value is $7,100,000. Therefore, Troubled Corporation has an $800,000 gain from the transfer of the assets. Troubled owes $8,000,000 of principal ($10,000,000 − $2,000,000 paid on January 1, 1989) and $960,000 of interest due January 1, 1991 ($8,000,000 × 12%), and thus has a gain of $1,860,000 from the restructuring. Alpha Company's loss is equal to Troubled Corporation's gain. The journal entries that Troubled Corporation records to recognize the gain on the assets transferred and the extraordinary gain from the debt restructuring, and the journal entry that Alpha Company prepares to record the receipt of the asset in settlement of the receivable are

Troubled Corporation: Debtor

Plant Assets	800,000	
Gain on Transfer of Plant Assets		800,000
To record gain on assets to be transferred in settlement of debt		

An alternative to debiting the plant asset account is to debit the accumulated depreciation account.

Loan Payable	8,000,000	
Interest Payable	960,000	
Accumulated Depreciation: Plant Assets	7,700,000	
Plant Assets		14,800,000
Extraordinary Gain: Debt Restructuring		1,860,000
To record the gain on settlement of debt		

Alpha Company: Creditor

Plant Assets	7,100,000	
Loss on Settlement of Receivable	1,860,000	
Note Receivable		8,000,000
Interest Receivable		960,000
To record loss on settlement of receivable		

Case 2: Issuance of Common Stock in Full Settlement. Troubled Corporation issued 100,000 shares of its $25 par value common stock to Alpha Company in full settlement of the $8,960,000 owed to Alpha. Troubled Corporation's common stock is currently selling for $75 per share. Troubled Corporation has 4,900,000 shares outstanding and, therefore, the market price of $75 is a valid measure of the fair market value of the shares issued to Alpha Company. Troubled Corporation has an extraordinary gain of $1,460,000 ($8,960,000 − $7,500,000) and Alpha Company has an ordinary loss of the same amount. The journal entries to record the settlement of the debt with common stock are

Troubled Corporation: Debtor

Loan Payable	8,000,000	
Interest Payable	960,000	
Common Stock		2,500,000
Additional Paid-in Capital: Common Stock		5,000,000
Extraordinary Gain: Debt Restructuring		1,460,000
To record the gain on settlement of debt		

Alpha Company: Creditor

Investment Troubled Corporation Stock	7,500,000	
Loss on Settlement of Receivable	1,460,000	
Note Receivable		8,000,000
Interest Receivable		960,000
To record loss on settlement of receivable		

MODIFICATION OF TERMS OF THE DEBT CONTRACT

If the creditor modifies the terms of the existing receivable, the creditor is hoping that by accepting less than the full amount due that the debtor will recover from the present adverse financial condition, given the relief from current cash outflow requirements and future cash outflow requirements. The creditor may also believe that by not granting any relief, the risk is high that the entire receivable may become worthless. Therefore, the creditor is willing to make concessions in the hope that the company will recover and the creditor will suffer only a partial loss rather than the loss of the entire amount of the receivable should the debtor become insolvent and either elect or be forced into bankruptcy by other creditors. An example of modification of terms and forgiveness of some existing debt was the debt restructuring engineered by Lee Iaccoca for Chrysler Corp. In this case, the company did become economically viable and the creditors, including the government, all received the full amount due under the modified terms.

If the debt is not satisfied, but the terms of the debt are modified, the present net book value of the debt, both principal and interest, must be compared to the total future cash flows, both principal and interest, from the debt under the modified terms. If the total future cash flows are equal to or exceed the carrying value of the debt, the net book value of the debt is not adjusted. A new effective interest rate, however, must be computed that will make the present value of the total future cash flows equal to the present value of the total amount of the debt. The pronouncement has taken a prospective approach to the modification of terms and any gain or loss is reflected in the change (usually decrease) in the amount of interest, rather than being recognized as a gain or loss at the time of the troubled debt restructuring.

If the total future cash to be paid after the restructuring is less than the total net book value of the debt, the debt is written down to an amount equal to the total future cash flows. The debtor recognizes an extraordinary gain from restructuring and the creditor recognizes an ordinary loss equal to the difference between the total carrying value of the debt and the total future cash flows. All future payments of cash are assumed to be payments of principal and, therefore, the debtor will not record any interest expense and the creditor will not record any interest revenue. Illustrative Problem 19.2 is based on the same troubled debt situation as Illustrative Problem 19.1 and demonstrates the determination of whether or not a gain or loss is recognized from the restructuring as well as the journal entries for both the debtor and the creditor when the cash flows exceed the net book value of the debt.

ILLUSTRATIVE PROBLEM 19.2: TROUBLED DEBT RESTRUCTURING: MODIFICATION OF TERMS

Troubled Corporation borrowed $10,000,000 at 12% for five years from Alpha Company on January 1, 1988. The terms of the loan require that Troubled Corporation pay the interest annually each January 1 and a principal payment of $2,000,000 each January 1. Troubled Corporation paid the annual interest and principal payments due on January 1, 1989 and paid the interest due on January 1, 1990, but did not pay the required principal payment. Troubled Corporation did not pay either a principal or interest payment on January 1, 1991. During 1989 and 1990, Troubled Corporation had suffered an extended strike by its workers, and had not met the competition for its products from foreign manufacturers.

Case 1: Modified Future Cash Flows Exceed Net Book Value of Debt.   During January 1991, Alpha Company agreed to forgive the interest owing at January 1, 1991, reduce the interest rate to 8% beginning on January 1, 1991, and require that five equal annual payments of interest and principal be paid beginning on January 1, 1992. The loss to the creditor of the interest forgiven of $960,000 and the gain to the debtor of the interest forgiven is an adjustment of future interest expense/revenue.

Adjusted Interest Expense/Revenue Amount

Future Cash Flows After Restructuring	
Principal	$ 8,000,000
Present Value of an Annuity at 8% for 5 periods	÷ 3.9927
Equal Annual Payments	2,003,657
Number of Payments	× 5
Total Cash to Be Received	10,018,285
Net Book Value of Debt Prior to Restructuring	8,960,000
Interest Expense/Revenue Over Five Years	$ 1,058,285

Effective Interest Rate Computation

$8,960,000/$2,003,657 = 4.4718$, which is between 3% and 4% in the present value of an annuity table. If you are not fortunate enough to have a calculator that will derive the rate, then by interpolation of the table the effective interest rate is 3.84%.

$$.1079 \left\{ \begin{array}{l} 3\% = 4.5797 \\ i = 4.4718 \\ 4\% = 4.4518 \end{array} \right\} .1279$$

$$i = 3\% + [.1079/.1279 \times 1\%] = 3.84\%$$

Schedule to Compute Revised Interest Expense/Revenue

Year	Beginning Liability Balance	Interest Revenue @ 3.84%	Annual Payment Due	Principal Payment	Ending Liability Balance
1992	$ 8,960,000	$ 344,064	$ 2,003,657	$ 1,659,593	$ 7,300,407
1993	7,300,407	280,336	2,003,657	1,723,321	5,577,086
1994	5,577,086	214,160	2,003,657	1,789,497	3,787,589
1995	3,787,589	145,443	2,003,657	1,858,214	1,929,375
1996	1,929,375	74,282[a]	2,003,657	1,929,375	–0–
		$ 1,058,285			

[a]Adjusted to account for error caused by using whole dollar amounts and rounded percentages.

The journal entry to record the January 1, 1992 payment on the books of the debtor is

Loan Payable	1,659,593	
Interest Expense	344,064	
Cash		2,003,657

The journal entry to record the receipt of the payment on January 1, 1992 on the books of the creditor is

Cash	2,003,657	
Loan Receivable		1,659,593
Interest Revenue		344,064

The debtor and the creditor will record similar entries in each of the next four years based on the values in the table, assuming the debt restructuring allows the creditor to survive its present financial difficulties.

Case 2: Modified Future Cash Flows Not Equal to Net Book Value. During January 1991, Alpha Company agreed to forgive the interest owing at January 1, 1991 and the $2,000,000 of principal that was not paid on January 1, 1990, reduce the interest rate to 8% beginning on January 1, 1991, and require that five equal annual payments of interest and principal be paid beginning on January 1, 1992.

Future Cash Flows After Restructuring	
Principal	$ 6,000,000
Present Value of an Annuity at 8% for 5 periods	÷ 3.9927
Equal Annual Payments	1,502,743
Number of Payments	× 5
Total Cash to Be Received	7,513,715
Net Book Value of Debt Prior to Restructuring	8,960,000
Gain/Loss to Be Recognized from Restructuring	$(1,446,285)

The journal entry Troubled Corporation records is

Loan Payable	1,446,285	
Extraordinary Gain: Debt Restructuring		1,446,285

The journal entry Alpha Company records is

Loss on Debt Restructuring	1,446,285	
Loan Receivable		1,446,285

All of the payments are treated as principal and the debtor does not record interest expense and the creditor does not record interest revenue. The journal entry to record the January 1, 1992 payment on the books of the debtor is

Loan Payable	1,502,743	
Cash		1,502,743

The journal entry to record the receipt of the payment on January 1, 1992 on the books of the creditor is

Cash	1,502,743	
Loan Receivable		1,502,743

The debtor and the creditor will record comparable entries in each of the next four years, assuming the debt restructuring allows the creditor to survive its present financial difficulties.

SETTLEMENT OF A PORTION OF THE DEBT AND MODIFICATION OF THE TERMS OF THE REMAINDER OF THE DEBT

A troubled debt restructuring may be accomplished by a settlement of a portion of the debt and a modification of terms of the remainder of the debt. The accounting for this type of restructuring is the same as illustrated above for settlement and modification of terms. In order to correctly determine the gains and or losses, the settlement is recorded at an adjusted basis for the remaining unpaid debt before determining the effect of the modification of the terms on the balance of the debt. Once the settlement has been recorded, the modification of terms is accounted for as previously illustrated, using the adjusted basis of the debt. Illustrative Problem 19.3 demonstrates a combination of settlement and modification of terms, using the same initial debt as Illustrative Problems 19.1 and 19.2.

ILLUSTRATIVE PROBLEM 19.3: TROUBLED DEBT RESTRUCTURING: PARTIAL SETTLEMENT AND MODIFICATION OF TERMS

Troubled Corporation borrowed $10,000,000 at 12% for five years from Alpha Company on January 1, 1988. The terms of the loan require that Troubled Corporation pay the interest annually each January 1 and a principal payment of $2,000,000 each January 1. Troubled Corporation paid the annual interest and principal payments due on January 1, 1989 and paid the interest due on January 1, 1990, but did not pay the required principal payment. Troubled Corporation did not pay either a principal or interest payment on January 1, 1991. During 1989 and 1990, Troubled Corporation had suffered an extended strike by its workers, and had not met the competition for its products from foreign manufacturers.

During January 1991, Alpha Company agreed to accept a parcel of land in payment of the $2,000,000 of principal owing that Troubled Corporation did not pay on January 1, 1990. The land has a fair market value of $1,850,000 and cost Troubled Corporation $1,565,000. In addition, Alpha Company has agreed to forgive the interest owing at January 1, 1991, to reduce the interest rate to 8% beginning on January 1, 1991, and require that five equal annual payments of interest and principal be paid beginning on January 1, 1992.

The first step is to record the transfer of the land. These entries are like the entries shown in Case 1 of Illustrative Problem 19.1 for the transfer of plant assets to a creditor.

Troubled Corporation: Debtor

Land	285,000	
Gain on Transfer of Land		285,000
To record gain on asset to be transferred in settlement of debt		
Loan Payable	2,000,000	
Land		1,850,000
Extraordinary Gain: Debt Restructuring		150,000
To record the gain on settlement of debt		

Alpha Company: Creditor

Land	1,850,000	
Loss on Settlement of Receivable	150,000	
Note Receivable		2,000,000
To record loss from partial settlement of the receivable		

The next step is to determine if the future cash flows from the modified terms of the remaining debt are more than or less than the remaining book value. The computation is

Future Cash Flows After Restructuring	
Principal	$ 6,000,000
Present Value of an Annuity at 8% for 5 periods	÷ 3.9927
Equal Annual Payments	1,502,743
Number of Payments	× 5
Total Cash To Be Received	7,513,715
Net Book Value of Debt Prior to Restructuring (1)	6,960,000
Interest Expense/Revenue Over Next Five Years	$ 553,715

(1) ($8,000,000 − $2,000,000) principal + ($8,000,000 × 12%) interest =
$6,000,000 + $960,000 = $6,960,000

The completion of the solution is similar to Case 1 of Illustrative Problem 19.2 as the cash flow exceeds the net book value of the remaining debt after partial settlement.

Effective Interest Rate Computation

$6,960,000/$1,502,743 = 4.6315, which is between 2% and 3% in the present value of an annuity table. If you are not fortunate enough to have a calculator that will derive the rate, then by interpolation of the table the effective interest rate is 2.61%.

$$.0820 \quad \left\{ \begin{array}{l} ------ \ 2\% = 4.7135 ------ \\ -------- \ i = 4.6315 \\ \quad\quad 3\% = 4.5797 ------ \end{array} \right\} \quad .1338$$

$$i = 2\% + [.0820/.1338 \times 1\%] = 2.61\%$$

Schedule to Compute Revised Interest Expense/Revenue

Year	Beginning Liability Balance	Interest Revenue @ 2.61%	Annual Payment Due	Principal Payment	Ending Liability Balance
1992	$ 6,960,000	$ 181,656	$ 1,502,743	$ 1,321,087	$ 5,638,913
1993	5,638,913	147,176	1,502,743	1,355,567	4,283,346
1994	4,283,346	111,795	1,502,743	1,390,948	2,892,398
1995	2,892,398	75,492	1,502,743	1,427,251	1,465,147
1996	1,465,147	37,596[a]	1,502,743	1,465,147	−0−
		$ 553,715			

[a]Adjusted to account for error caused by using whole dollar amounts and rounded percentages.

The journal entry to record the January 1, 1992 payment on the books of the debtor is

Loan Payable	1,321,087	
Interest Expense	181,656	
Cash		1,502,743

The journal entry to record the receipt of the payment on January 1, 1992 on the books of the creditor is

Cash	1,502,743	
Loan Receivable		1,321,087
Interest Revenue		181,656

The debtor and the creditor will record similar entries in each of the next four years based on the values in the table, assuming the debt restructuring allows the debtor to survive its present financial difficulties.

DISCLOSURE REQUIREMENTS

The following disclosures regarding a troubled debt restructuring are required of the debtor either within the financial statements or in the footnotes:

- A description of the principal changes in terms, the major features of settlement, or both for each restructuring
- Aggregate gain on restructuring and the related income tax effect
- Aggregate net gain or loss on transfer of assets for the period
- Per share amount of the aggregate gain on restructuring, net of the related tax effects[2]

The following disclosures are required of the creditor for receivables whose terms have been modified:

- The aggregate recorded investment
- The gross interest revenue that would have been recorded had the terms not been modified
- The amount of interest revenue recognized in the period[3]

In addition, the creditor must disclose any commitments to lend additional funds to debtors whose loans have been modified under a troubled debt restructuring.[4]

QUASI-REORGANIZATIONS

A company that has been operating unprofitably for some time, and thus has a large deficit in retained earnings, currently may be able to operate profitably. In this situation, the debts are being met, or bankruptcy would have occurred, yet the retained earnings deficit prevents the business from acquiring needed capital in the financial markets either through borrowing or issuance of shares. The business is probably not insolvent under either the accounting or legal definitions of insolvency.

    A **quasi-reorganization** is a reorganization that involves only the company and not the creditors and is permitted under the laws of incorporation in some states. The business restructures its stockholders' equity to eliminate the retained earnings deficit. The elimination of the retained earnings deficit caused by prior losses may enable a company whose prospects

---

[2] *SFAS No. 15*, paragraph 25.

[3] *SFAS No. 15*, paragraph 40 a.

[4] *SFAS No. 15*, paragraph 40 b.

are now profitable to borrow funds, sell additional shares, and pay dividends. The approach in a quasi-reorganization is that of starting a new business; therefore, only balance sheet accounts are involved in the journal entries that accomplish the quasi-reorganization.

Once the company has obtained the approval of its stockholders, three steps are necessary to achieve the reorganization.

1. Revalue all the assets to their net realizable values, recording the change in valuation in the Retained Earnings account. This revaluation can result in either increases or decreases in the present retained earnings deficit.
2. Additional paid-in capital must exist or be created by reducing the dollar amount in the Common Stock account to an amount sufficient to absorb the entire retained earnings deficit after the revaluation of the assets. If the amount in the existing Additional Paid-in Capital account is more than the deficit in Retained Earnings, the deficit is written off against the Additional Paid-in Capital. If the Additional Paid-in Capital is not large enough to absorb the deficit, the par value of the common stock is reduced and the value of the reduction is added to Additional Paid-in Capital in an amount sufficient to absorb the deficit.
3. The deficit balance of Retained Earnings is written off against the Additional Paid-in Capital account.

Illustrative Problem 19.4 demonstrates the journal entries for a quasi-reorganization.

ILLUSTRATIVE PROBLEM 19.4: QUASI-REORGANIZATION

On June 15, 1990, Beta Company had the following net book value and net realizable value of assets, and net book value of liabilities and stockholders' equity prior to undertaking a quasi-reorganization authorized by its stockholders:

	Net Book Value	Net Realizable Value
Current Assets	$ 500,000	$ 500,000
Plant and Equipment	1,300,000	1,100,000
Intangible Assets	200,000	240,000
Total	$ 2,000,000	$ 1,840,000
Liabilities	$ 900,000	
Common Stock, $10 Par Value	1,600,000	
Additional Paid-in Capital	300,000	
Retained Earnings	(800,000)	
Total	$ 2,000,000	

The first step is to record the assets at their net realizable value as follows:

Retained Earnings	160,000	
Intangible Assets	40,000	
Plant and Equipment		200,000

The second step is to create sufficient additional paid-in capital to absorb the adjusted deficit in Retained Earnings account of $960,000 by reducing the par value of the common stock. If the par value is reduced to $5 per share, the journal entry to shift contributed capital from the Common Stock account to the Additional Paid-in Capital account is

Common Stock	800,000	
Additional Paid-in Capital		800,000

The final step is to make the balance of the Retained Earnings account zero, by writing off the deficit as follows:

Additional Paid-in Capital	960,000	
Retained Earnings		960,000

The balance sheet immediately after the quasi-reorganization is

Current Assets	$ 500,000
Plant and Equipment	1,100,000
Intangible Assets	240,000
Total	$ 1,840,000
Liabilities	$ 900,000
Common Stock, $5 Par Value	800,000
Additional Paid-in Capital	140,000
Retained Earnings, June 15, 1990	–0–
Total	$ 1,840,000

In order that the users of the financial statements of a company that has undertaken a quasi-reorganization not be misled as to the past earnings history, the company dates its retained earnings as of the date of quasi-reorganization for a period of 10 years after the change. The total of stockholders' equity is now equal to the total prior to the quasi-reorganization net of the difference between the book value and the net realizable value of the assets. Although the above example uses the account title Additional Paid-in Capital, some accountants might title this account Reorganization Capital or Restructuring Capital to indicate that its value came from an internal change in the balances of the contributed capital accounts of the company and not as a result of the issuance of shares.

LEGAL REORGANIZATIONS

A financially troubled business may voluntarily undertake a legal reorganization in order to remain a viable enterprise or may be forced into a reorganization by its creditors. A reorganization is undertaken with the expectation that the relief granted the business will allow it to again become a profitable business enterprise, without the permanent economic loss to the creditors, investors, and employees from the liquidation of the business entity. A business that is reorganized probably meets the popular definition of insolvency, but not the legal definition. Chapter 11 of The Bankruptcy Reform Act of 1978, which governs reorganizations, does not require that the legal definition be met to have a reorganization.

The purpose of a reorganization is to restructure the liabilities and stockholders' equity of a business so that it may continue to operate, overcome the current insolvency, and again become a going concern. In a reorganization, the officers of the company may continue to operate the business with oversight by the bankruptcy court, or a trustee may be appointed to operate the business. Under Chapter 11 of The Bankruptcy Reform Act of 1978, a plan of reorganization must be formulated and approved by the creditors. The reorganization plan determines the assets and the amount of those assets that a creditor will receive from the debtor once the reorganization has been approved and any changes that are contemplated in the stockholders' equity. The journal entries presented for troubled debt restructurings and quasi-reorganizations are used to record the effects of the reorganization plan once it is approved by the bankruptcy court.

The Bankruptcy Reform Act of 1978 permits reorganizations only when the creditors will receive at least as much as they would receive if the business were liquidated. A **statement of affairs,** which is also used for businesses in liquidation, can be prepared to determine the amount that the various classes of creditors will receive if the business receives the estimated net realizable value of the assets. The statement uses the liquidation values of assets rather than the book values, because the business is being viewed as a going out of business entity rather than as a going concern. Within the statement of affairs, assets are classified by their relationship to the liabilities, and liabilities are classified by the priority they have over the assets.

The Bankruptcy Reform Act of 1978 establishes the first priority of claims (liabilities) called preferred claims. These preferred claims, which are not collateralized, are ranked as follows:

1. **Expenses of administration of the bankruptcy.** This ranking is provided so that the legal, accounting, and trustee services necessary to complete the liquidation will be paid. Without this ranking no incentive exists for professionals to render services in a bankrupt situation.
2. **Claims of creditors that arise between the time a bankruptcy petition is filed and the time it is approved by the bankruptcy court.** Without this protection, creditors are not willing to deal with a failing business that has filed a bankruptcy petition.
3. **Unearned claims for wages, salaries, or commissions** earned by an individual within 90 days prior to the date of filing of the bankruptcy petition or within 90 days prior to the cessation of business. These claims are limited to $2,000 per employee.
4. **Claims for contributions to employee benefit plans,** such as pension plans, health insurance plans, and life insurance plans arising from services rendered within 180 days before the filing for bankruptcy or the cessation of the debtor's business. This claim is limited to $2,000 per employee net of amount paid as a Class 3 preferred claim.
5. **Consumer deposits to a limit of $900 per claim.**
6. **Federal, state, and local government tax claims.**

The ranking of claims (liabilities) used in a statement of affairs is

1. **Preferred claims:** Classes 1–6 listed above.
2. **Fully secured creditors:** The net realizable value of the assets pledged as security for these claims equals or exceeds the amount of the liability.

3. **Partially secured creditors:** The net realizable value of the assets pledged as security for these claims is less than the amount of the liability.
4. **Unsecured creditors:** Claims of general creditors that are not collateralized by the assets of the business or given preference by the bankruptcy code. These are referred to as Class 7 claims in The Bankruptcy Reform Act.

The statement of affairs classifies assets as follows:

1. **Assets pledged with fully secured creditors:** Assets whose net realizable value is equal to or greater than the liability that is secured by those assets.
2. **Assets pledged with partially secured creditors:** Assets whose net realizable value is less than the liability that is secured by those assets.
3. **Unsecured or free assets:** Assets that are not collateral for any liability.

The statement of affairs is prepared with expected net realizable values in order to estimate the amounts that each class of creditors would receive if the business were liquidated. In this case, the statement is prepared to determine if a company qualifies for a reorganization under the bankruptcy laws. This same statement of affairs is prepared to estimate the amount that the various classes of creditors would receive prior to the actual realization of the assets. If the business were actually being liquidated, this same statement of affairs is prepared using actual amounts realized to determine the amounts to be paid to the creditors.

When preparing the statements of affairs, any excess of the expected net realizable value of an asset pledged with a fully secured creditor over the amount of the liability is available to pay unsecured claims, and thus is an unsecured or free asset. The amount of the partially secured claim that is in excess of the expected net realizable value of its collateralized asset is an unsecured liability. The approach is one of liquidation values so all assets are treated net of their contra accounts. The liabilities are gross, as the creditor is owed the gross amount, not the amount net of the discount or the premium.

The steps in the preparation of the statement of affairs are

1. Determine the expected net realizable value of the assets.
2. Determine the amount of unsecured or free assets available to satisfy the claims of the classes 1–6 preferred creditors and the claims of the unsecured (class 7) creditors.
3. Determine the amount of the liabilities without priority or preference.
4. Compute the amount that each unsecured creditor can expect to receive for each dollar owed. This amount is often referred to as the dividend available for general unsecured creditors.

Illustrative Problem 19.5 demonstrates the preparation of an accounting statement of affairs.

ILLUSTRATIVE PROBLEM 19.5: ACCOUNTING STATEMENT OF AFFAIRS

Camel Company is considering applying for reorganization under Chapter 11 of The Bankruptcy Reform Act of 1978. The trial balance of Camel Company just prior to filing on March 15, 1990 is

	Debit	Credit
Cash	$ 3,200	
Accounts Receivable	29,400	
Allowance for Doubtful Accounts		$ 4,500
Inventory	59,000	
Prepaid Expenses	8,000	
Land	43,000	
Building	89,000	
Accumulated Depreciation: Building		34,000
Machinery and Equipment	51,000	
Accumulated Depreciation: Machinery and Equipment		21,500
Goodwill	15,000	
Accounts Payable		48,000
Employee Wages and Benefits Payable		17,900
Note Payable		46,000
Mortgage Payable		75,000
Interest Payable: Mortgage		3,000
Common Stock, $10 Par Value		100,000
Additional Paid-in Capital		35,000
Retained Earnings	87,300	
Totals	$ 384,900	$ 384,900

Additional Information:

1. The expected net realizable value of the accounts receivable is $21,000.
2. The expected net realizable value of the inventory, which is pledged as security for the note payable, is $39,000.
3. The prepaid expenses consist of $3,400 of prepaid insurance, which can be recovered, and the balance is supplies with an estimated net realizable value of $2,135.
4. The expected net realizable value of the land and building, which are the security for the mortgage, is $80,000.
5. The expected net realizable value of the equipment is $13,000.
6. The costs of liquidation are expected to be $5,000.
7. The Employee Wages and Benefits Payable account includes wages of $1,800 due to each of six employees and the remainder is salary owed to the president of the company.

Exhibit 19-1 presents the statement of affairs for the Camel Company as of March 15, 1990.

In Illustrative Problem 19.5, the goodwill is shown with a zero realizable value, as goodwill only has value when a business is a going concern. If a liability is secured or partially secured, as the mortgage in the above illustration, the interest that is owing on the liability is also secured. If a receivable that is pledged as collateral for a liability has interest receivable associated with it, the interest is included with the asset in determining if the liability is fully or partially secured. The costs of the liquidation are included in the liability section and balance of retained earnings is adjusted for these potential expenses.

A company may have an asset without any book value, yet the asset has a net realizable value. For example, a patent may be fully amortized, and therefore, not included in the assets, yet have a market value. If a company has an asset that is not included in the records, but can be sold, the asset is included in the statement of affairs. The company may also have liabilities that have not been recorded in addition to the costs of liquidation. If unrecorded liabilities exist, they are included in the statement.

If the company is a manufacturer, work in process may have to be completed in order to sell the inventory. If completion of work in process is necessary for sale, the costs of completion are added to the net book value of the work in process, and the net realizable value reflects the additional costs of completion as well as the costs of selling the asset. Any raw materials in raw materials inventory that are needed to complete the inventory are deducted from raw materials inventory and included as part of the costs of completion in determining the net book value of work in process. Any liabilities that will be incurred to

EXHIBIT 19-1

Illustrative Problem 19.5
Camel Company
Statement of Affairs
March 15, 1990

Net Book Value	Assets	Expected Net Realizable Value	Estimated Amount for Unsecured Creditors	(Loss) or Gain on Realization
	Assets Pledged with Fully Secured Creditors			
$ 98,000	Land and Building	$ 80,000		$(18,000)
	Less: Mortgage Payable and Interest Payable	78,000	$ 2,000	
	Assets Pledged with Partially Secured Creditors			
59,000	Inventory	39,000		(20,000)
	Note Payable	39,000		
	Free Assets			
3,200	Cash	$ 3,200		
24,900	Accounts Receivable	21,000		(3,900)
8,000	Prepaid Expenses	5,535		(2,465)
29,500	Machinery and Equipment	13,000		(16,500)
15,000	Goodwill	–0–	42,735	(15,000)
	Total Estimated Amount Available		44,735	
	Less: Creditors with Priority		17,600	
	Net Amount Expected for Unsecured Creditors (45 cents on the dollar)		27,135	
	Estimated Deficiency to Unsecured Creditors (55 cents on the dollar)		33,165	
$ 237,600			$ 60,300	$(75,865)

Continued on following page

Camel Company
Statement of Affairs Continued
March 15, 1990

Net Book Value	Equities	Secured Claims	Priority Claims	Unsecured Claims
	Liabilities with Priority			
$ 17,900	Wages and Employee Benefits Payable (1)		$ 12,600	$ 5,300
5,000	Liquidation Costs		5,000	
	Fully Secured Liabilities			
75,000	Mortgage Payable	$ 75,000		
3,000	Interest Payable	3,000		
	Partially Secured Liabilities			
46,000	Note Payable	39,000		7,000
	Unsecured Claims			
48,000	Accounts Payable			48,000
	Stockholders' Equity			
100,000	Common Stock			
35,000	Additional Paid-in Capital			
(92,300)	Retained Earnings (2)			
$ 237,600		$ 117,000	$ 17,600	$ 60,300

(1) $1,800 \times 7 = $12,600
(2) $87,300 + $5,000 of liquidation costs = $92,300

Proof of Results

Net Book Value of Assets			$ 237,600
Less: Estimated Losses			75,865
Total Amount Available for Creditors			161,735
Less: Secured Claims		$ 117,000	134,600
Priority Claims: Classes 1–6		17,600	
Amount Available for Unsecured Creditors			$ 27,135
Or: Total Stockholders' Equity per Statement			$ 42,700
Less: Estimated Losses			75,865
Deficiency to Creditors			$(33,165)

complete the inventory, such as wages and overhead, are included as a Class 2 unsecured claim.

ALTERNATIVE FORMS FOR THE STATEMENT OF AFFAIRS

The statement of affairs presented in Illustrative Problem 19.5 was prepared using a gain or loss column on the asset side. Although not required by the bankruptcy courts, the use of this column provides information and makes proof of the results easier. The use of secured, priority (classes 1–6), and unsecured columns on the equity side facilitates completion of the asset side and also the proof. Frequently these statements are prepared without the gain or loss column in the asset section and with the secured and priority claims combined together in one column in the equity section.

ROLE OF THE FIDUCIARY IN REORGANIZATIONS

A trustee may be appointed to oversee the reorganization or the company management may continue to operate the business. The trustee of a business in reorganization functions like the trustee of a trust as described in Chapter 18. The trustee in a reorganization may continue to use the accounting records of the business, or may establish a new set of books. The establishment of a new set of accounting records is preferable as it separates those assets and liabilities that the trustee is responsible for from the assets and liabilities that have remained with the company.

When the trustee sets up new accounting records, the assets that the trustee has assumed responsibility for are recorded at their net book values by the trustee and the total amount received is credited to an equity account, such as **Camel Company, Trusteeship.** On the books of the business, the assets assumed by the trustee are credited and the total amount assumed by the trustee is entered in an asset account in the name of the trustee, such as **M. E. Phillips, Trustee.**

Generally the trustee does not record the liabilities that exist at the time the reorganization is approved by the bankruptcy court. If the bankruptcy court directs the trustee to pay existing liabilities of the company in reorganization, the payment is usually debited to the equity account, Camel Company, Trusteeship. On the books of the corporation the liability paid by the trustee is debited and the asset account in the name of the trustee is credited.

Any revenues and expenses that are received or incurred by the trustee during the operation of the trusteeship are recorded and accounted for as they normally are under generally accepted accounting principles. At the end of the accounting period or when the reorganization is completed, the revenues and expenses are closed to the trusteeship equity account.

In order to prepare reports to the court and financial statements during the period of the trusteeship, the accounts on the books of the trustee are combined with the accounts on the books of the business in reorganization. This combining of the two sets of records is typically accomplished with a worksheet similar to the worksheet used for the preparation of consolidated financial statements. The equity account of the trusteeship is eliminated against the trustee's account of the business. The periodic report that the trustee prepares for the bankruptcy court to report the activities of the reorganization is called a **realization and liquidation account** or **statement of realization and liquidation.** When an insolvent business is liquidated rather than reorganized, a trustee is appointed and the trusteeship operates exactly like a trusteeship for a reorganization. The trustee in a liquidation also submits periodic statements of realization and liquidation to the bankruptcy court. Illustrative Problem 19.6 following the discussion of liquidations demonstrates the preparation of the statement of realization and liquidation.

LIQUIDATIONS

If the possibility of recovery from insolvency and/or nonprofitability seems unlikely, a company may voluntarily elect bankruptcy or the company's creditors may force the business into bankruptcy. Chapter 7 of the The Bankruptcy Reform Act of 1978 covers the liquidation of businesses. Prior to the 1978 reform of the bankruptcy acts, a business had to be insolvent in the legal sense for creditors to force the business into bankruptcy. The liabilities of the business had to exceed the net realizable value of the assets. Under the revised statutes, however, a company does not have to be legally insolvent for creditors to seek relief under Chapter 7 of the bankruptcy acts. In a liquidation, a trustee is appointed by the bankruptcy court.

The periodic reporting to the court is accomplished with a realization and liquidation account or statement of realization and liquidation whose purpose is to disclose the status of the assets realized and those yet to be realized, the liabilities liquidated and those yet to be liquidated, and any operating events that occurred since the last report. A summary of the cash account, an income statement, and a balance sheet often accompany the statement of realization and liquidation. The statement of realization and liquidation has three basic parts, an asset section, a liability section, and an operating section. The reason that the statement is sometimes referred to as a realization and liquidation account is that the format is like a large "T" account. This format, therefore, classifies events by debits and credits, rather than asset, liability, revenue, and expense.

The three sections of the statement of realization and liquidation are

Debit Side		Credit Side
	Assets	
Assets to Be Realized		Assets Realized
Assets Acquired		Assets Not Realized
	Liabilities	
Liabilities Liquidated		Liabilities to Be Liquidated
Liabilities Not Liquidated		Liabilities Assumed
	Income Statement	
Supplementary Expenses		Supplementary Revenues
Gain for the Period	or	Loss for the Period

The **assets to be realized** are all the assets on hand at the beginning of the period except for cash which, of course, is realized. The **assets acquired** consist of any additional assets discovered, purchased, or received from the sales of other assets. The **assets realized** are the proceeds received from the disposal of any assets during the period. The **assets not realized** are the assets remaining at the end of the period. The **liabilities liquidated** are all the payments to creditors during the period. The **liabilities not liquidated** are the liabilities remaining at the end of the period. The **liabilities to be liquidated** are the unpaid liabilities at the beginning of the period. The **liabilities assumed** are unrecorded liabilities that have been discovered or liabilities incurred in the operation of the trusteeship during the period. The **supplementary expenses and revenues** are those expenses and revenues that the trustee recorded for the period. If the business is continuing to operate, depreciation, depletion, and amortization are recorded and the contra asset accounts are increased by the expense of the period.

The gain or loss is simply the amount that makes the debit side total equal to the credit side total. This loss or gain is a composite of three elements: the gains or losses from changes in assets, the gains or losses from changes in liabilities, and the net income or loss from the income portion of the statement. This approach to the preparation of the statement of realization and liquidation is called the **conventional approach,** and is the one usually required by the courts.

The summing of all the sources of gains and losses is not intuitively appealing to accountants because they are accustomed to disclosing the various sources of gains and losses. An alternative to using the conventional approach is to report the net book value of the asset as the amount of the asset realized rather than the proceeds and show a gain or loss in the income statement section, to report any assets discovered as gains, any liabilities discovered as losses, any liabilities settled for less than book value as gains, and actually compute the income for the period, thus disclosing the sources of gains and losses. This approach is referred to as the **net book value approach.** Illustrative Problem 19.6 demonstrates both the conventional and net book value approaches to the preparation of a statement of realization and liquidation using the Camel Company of Illustrative Problem 19.5.

ILLUSTRATIVE PROBLEM 19.6: STATEMENT OF REALIZATION AND LIQUIDATION

After reviewing the statement of affairs of the Camel Corporation, a decision was made to liquidate the business, as it seemed highly unlikely that a reorganization could restore Camel Company to a going concern position. The trial balance of Camel Company as of March 15, 1990, prior to liquidation, is

	Debit	Credit
Cash	$ 3,200	
Accounts Receivable	29,400	
Allowance for Doubtful Accounts		$ 4,500
Inventory	59,000	
Prepaid Expenses	8,000	
Land	43,000	
Building	89,000	
Accumulated Depreciation: Building		34,000
Machinery and Equipment	51,000	
Accumulated Depreciation: Machinery and Equipment		21,500
Goodwill	15,000	
Accounts Payable		48,000
Employee Wages and Benefits Payable		17,900
Note Payable		46,000
Mortgage Payable		75,000
Interest Payable: Mortgage		3,000
Common Stock, $10 Par Value		100,000
Additional Paid-in Capital		35,000
Retained Earnings	87,300	
Totals	$ 384,900	$ 384,900

Case 1: The Conventional Approach. During the first reporting period the following transactions and events occurred. Following each transaction is an explanation of how the item is reported in the statement of realization and liquidation if the conventional approach is used to prepare the statement.

1. Transaction: Accounts receivable totaling $12,000 were collected and additional receivables of $3,400 were deemed uncollectible.

   Reported: The cash received is treated as the amount of the asset realized. The sum of the collections and the uncollectible accounts is subtracted from accounts receivable to determine the balance of the accounts receivable yet to be realized. The uncollectible accounts are subtracted from the allowance account to determine the balance to use in the assets not realized section of the statement.

2. Transaction: A note receivable from a customer was discovered in the amount of $4,000, with interest owing of $600. The interest was received as well as a payment of $1,000 of the principal balance.

   Reported: The note receivable and the interest receivable are reported as assets acquired. The interest received and the principal received are reported as assets realized. The balance of the note receivable is reported as an asset not realized.

3. Transaction: Inventory with a cost of $28,000 was sold for $30,000. The cash sales totaled $21,000 and the remainder was sales on account.

   Reported: The sales are reported as an asset realized. The accounts receivable are reported as assets acquired. The cost of the merchandise sold is subtracted from the amount of the inventory to determine the amount of inventory to be reported as an asset not realized.

4. Transaction: The cash received from the sale of the inventory in the amount of $21,000 was paid on the note payable plus accrued interest since March 15, 1990 in the amount of $1,400.

   Reported: The payment on the note payable is reported as a liability liquidated and the interest is reported as a supplementary expense.

5. Transaction: Interest owing on the mortgage was paid as well as $5,000 of principal.
   Reported: Both items are reported as liabilities liquidated.

6. Transaction: Inventory with a cost of $6,000 was purchased on account.
   Reported: The inventory is reported as an asset acquired and the account payable as a liability assumed.

7. Transaction: The machinery and equipment were sold for $12,500.
   Reported: The sales price is reported as an asset realized.

8. Transaction: Employees were paid $12,600, representing $1,800 to each of seven employees, which are Class 3 claims.

   Reported: The amount paid is reported as a liability liquidated and the balance of the account is reported as a liability not liquidated.

9. Event: An outstanding account payable in the amount of $2,400 had not been entered in the records, although the inventory is included in the asset account.

   Reported: The amount is reported as a liability assumed.

10. Event: An unrecorded credit memo of $500 from a supplier had not been recorded.

    Reported: The amount is subtracted from initial accounts payable to arrive at the balance not liquidated.

11. Event: Supplies with a cost of $900 were used during the period and prepaid insurance of $500 expired during the period.

    Reported: The amount is subtracted from prepaid expenses to arrive at the balance of assets not realized.

12. Event: Depreciation on the building is $1,000.

    Reported: The accumulated depreciation account is increased to reflect the decrease in value when reporting the building in the assets not realized section.

13. Event: The goodwill has no value.

    Reported: The goodwill is eliminated from the assets not realized.

Exhibit 19-2 presents the statement of realization and liquidation using the conventional approach. Exhibit 19-2 is a statement of realization and liquidation prepared using the conventional approach. The statement shows a loss of $33,300, yet without very careful analysis, the causes of the net loss are almost impossible to discern. The income statement for the period is shown in Exhibit 19-3, which indicates that the total loss is made up of loss from operations, gain from credit memo, loss from the sale of the equipment, and loss from the write-off of the goodwill. Without an income statement, a statement of realization and liquidation, prepared using the conventional approach, does not clearly present the sources of the loss. The balance sheet at the end of the first reporting period is in Exhibit 19-4.

The cash account contains the following entries as a result of the transactions for the first liquidation period:

Cash

Beginning Balance	3,200	Payment of Note	21,000
Collection of Receivables	12,000	Payment of Interest on Note	1,400
Collection of Note	1,000	Payment of Mortgage Interest	3,000
Collection of Interest	600	Payment of Mortgage Principal	5,000
Cash Sales	21,000	Payment of Wages	12,600
Sale of Equipment	12,500		
	50,300		43,000
Balance	7,300		

Because the conventional approach to the preparation of the statement of realization and liquidation does not clearly show the sources of income, most accountants prefer the net book value approach. If the net book value approach is used, the amounts shown as assets realized are the net book values rather than the proceeds. Any adjustments to existing assets are treated as assets realized or assets acquired. For example, depreciation expense or the using up of prepaid items is entered as assets realized. If an asset balance is less than it should be, the addition is treated as an asset acquired. Any adjustments to existing liabilities are treated as

EXHIBIT 19-2

Illustrative Problem 19.6
Camel Company
Statement of Realization and Liquidation
Conventional Approach

Assets

Assets to be Realized			*Assets Realized*		
Accounts Receivable	$ 29,400		Accounts Receivable		$ 12,000
Less: Allowance for			Interest Receivable		600
Doubtful Accounts	4,500	$ 24,900	Note Receivable		1,000
Inventory		59,000	Inventory		30,000
Prepaid Expenses		8,000	Machinery and Equipment		12,500
Land		43,000	*Assets Not Realized*		
Building	89,000		Accounts Receivable	$ 14,000	
Less: Accumulated			Less: Allowance for		
Depreciation	34,000	55,000	Doubtful Accounts	1,100	12,900
Machinery and			Accounts Receivable—new		9,000
Equipment	51,000		Note Receivable		3,000
Less: Accumulated			Inventory—old		31,000
Depreciation	21,500	29,500	Inventory—new		6,000
Goodwill		15,000	Prepaid Expenses		6,600
Assets Acquired			Land		43,000
Note Receivable		4,000	Building	89,000	
Interest Receivable		600	Less: Accumulated		
Accounts Receivable—new		9,000	Depreciation	35,000	54,000
Inventory—new		6,000			

Liabilities

Liabilities Liquidated			*Liabilities to be Liquidated*		
Note Payable		21,000	Accounts Payable		48,000
Interest Payable		3,000	Employee Wages and Benefits Payable		17,900
Mortgage Payable		5,000	Note Payable		46,000
Employee Wages and Benefits Payable		12,600	Mortgage Payable		75,000
Liabilities Not Liquidated			Interest Payable: Mortgage		3,000
Accounts Payable—old		47,500	*Liabilities Assumed*		
Accounts Payable—new		6,000	Accounts Payable—new		6,000
Accounts Payable—unrecorded		2,400	Accounts Payable—unrecorded		2,400
Employee Wages and Benefits Payable		5,300			
Notes Payable		25,000			
Mortgage Payable		70,000			

Income Statement

Supplementary Expenses		*Supplementary Revenues*	
Interest Expense	1,400		
		Loss for the Period	33,300
	$ 453,200		$ 453,200

EXHIBIT 19-3

Illustrative Problem 19.6
Camel Corporation
Income Statement
First Reporting Period

Sales Revenue		$ 30,000
Cost of Sales		28,000
Gross Margin		2,000
Expenses		
Supplies	$ 900	
Insurance	500	
Interest	1,400	
Depreciation	1,000	3,800
Operating Loss		(1,800)
Gain: Unrecorded Credit Memo		500
Losses		
Sale of Equipment	17,000	
Write-off of Goodwill	15,000	(32,000)
Net Loss		$(33,300)

EXHIBIT 19-4

Illustrative Problem 19.6
Camel Company
Balance Sheet
End of First Reporting Period

Assets			Liabilities		
Cash	$ 7,300		Accounts Payable	$ 55,900	
Accounts Receivable: Net	21,900		Wages and Benefits Payable	5,300	
Note Receivable	3,000		Notes Payable	25,000	
Inventory	37,000		Mortgage Payable	70,000	
Prepaid Expenses	6,600		Total Liabilities	156,200	
Land and Building: Net	97,000		Stockholders' Equity		
			Common Stock	100,000	
			Additional Paid-in Capital	35,000	
			Retained Earnings(1)	(118,400)	
Total Assets	$ 172,800		Total Equities	$ 172,800	

(1) Beginning Balance of Retained Earnings	$(87,300)
Asset Subsequently Discovered	4,600
Unrecorded Liabilities	(2,400)
Net Loss	(33,300)
Ending Balance of Retained Earnings	$ 118,400

liabilities liquidated or assumed. For example, a correction to increase an existing liability is a liability assumed, and an unrecorded credit memo is treated as a liability liquidated. Unlike the conventional approach, in which the gain or loss balances the entire statement, in the net book value approach each of the sections is self-balancing.

Case 2: The Net Book Value Approach.   The transactions and events from Illustrative Problem 19.6 that are reported differently on a statement of realization and liquidation prepared using the net book value approach are presented in the following list. The list also contains the manner of reporting these items on the statement.

3.	Transaction:	Inventory with a cost of $28,000 was sold for $30,000. The cash sales totaled $21,000 and the remainder was sales on account.
	Reported:	The sales are reported as supplementary revenues. The accounts receivable are reported as assets acquired. The cost of the merchandise sold is reported as cost of goods sold in supplementary expenses and as an asset realized.
7.	Transaction:	The machinery and equipment were sold for $12,500.
	Reported:	The net book value is reported as an asset realized. The loss is recorded in supplementary expenses.
10.	Event:	An unrecorded credit memo of $500 from a supplier had not been recorded.
	Reported:	The credit memo is reported as a supplementary revenue (or can be subtracted from cost of goods sold, if goods were sold).
11.	Event:	Supplies with a cost of $900 were used during the period and prepaid insurance of $500 expired during the period.
	Reported:	The expenses are reported as supplementary expenses and as assets realized.
12.	Event:	Depreciation on the building is $1,000.
	Reported:	The expense is reported as a supplementary expense and as an asset realized.
13.	Event:	The goodwill has no value.
	Reported:	The net book value is recorded as an assets realized and the loss is reported as a supplementary expense.

Exhibit 19-5 illustrates the statement of realization and liquidation prepared using the net book value approach, with the above transactions reported as indicated and the remainder of the transactions reported exactly as they were when the conventional approach was used.

The cash account, the income statement, and the balance sheet are the same under the conventional approach and the net book value approach, as they are just two different ways to present the same set of transactions and events. The conventional approach is the one often required by the courts, and the net book value approach is the one that intuitively appeals to accountants because it is the usual method of recording transactions for a going concern.

EXHIBIT 19-5

Illustrative Problem 19.6
Camel Company
Statement of Realization and Liquidation
Net Book Value Approach

Assets

Assets to be Realized				*Assets Realized*		
Accounts Receivable	$ 29,400			Accounts Receivable		$ 12,000
Less: Allowance for				Note and Interest Receivable		1,600
Doubtful Accounts	4,500	$ 24,900		Inventory		28,000
Inventory		59,000		Machinery and Equipment		29,500
Prepaid Expenses		8,000		Goodwill		15,000
Land		43,000		Prepaid Expenses		1,400
Building	89,000			Building		1,000
Less: Accumulated				*Assets Not Realized*		
Depreciation	34,000	55,000		Accounts Receivable	$ 14,000	
Machinery and				Less: Allowance for		
Equipment	51,000			Doubtful Accounts	1,100	12,900
Less: Accumulated				Accounts Receivable—new		9,000
Depreciation	21,500	29,500		Note Receivable		3,000
Goodwill		15,000		Inventory—old		31,000
Assets Acquired				Inventory—new		6,000
Note Receivable		4,000		Prepaid Expenses		6,600
Interest Receivable		600		Land		43,000
Accounts Receivable—new		9,000		Building	89,000	
Inventory—new		6,000		Less: Accumulated		
				Depreciation	35,000	54,000
		$ 254,000				$ 254,000

Liabilities

Liabilities Liquidated			*Liabilities to be Liquidated*	
Note Payable	$ 21,000		Accounts Payable	$ 48,000
Interest Payable	3,000		Employee Wages and Benefits Payable	17,900
Mortgage Payable	5,000		Note Payable	46,000
Employee Wages and Benefits Payable	12,600		Mortgage Payable	75,000
Accounts Payable	500		Interest Payable: Mortgage	3,000
Liabilities Not Liquidated			*Liabilities Assumed*	
Accounts Payable—old	47,500		Accounts Payable—new	6,000
Accounts Payable—new	6,000		Accounts Payable—unrecorded	2,400
Accounts Payable—unrecorded	2,400			
Employee Wages and Benefits Payable	5,300			
Notes Payable	25,000			
Mortgage Payable	70,000			
	$ 198,300			$ 198,300

Continued on following page

Camel Company
Statement of Realization and Liquidation Continued
Net Book Value Approach
Income Statement

Supplementary Expenses			*Supplementary Revenues*		
Interest Expense	$	1,400	Sales Revenue	$	30,000
Cost of Goods Sold		28,000	Credit Memorandum		500
Supplies		900			
Insurance		500			
Depreciation		1,000			
Loss on Sale of Equipment		17,000			
Write-off of Goodwill		15,000	Loss for the Period		33,300
	$	63,800		$	63,800

SUMMARY

Insolvency can mean either that a business does not have sufficient cash to meet its current debts as they become due and payable—the accounting or popular definition—or it can mean that a business has liabilities in excess of the net realizable value of its assets—the legal definition. When a business is insolvent according to the accounting definition, the entity may enter into a voluntary arrangement with all creditors, a troubled debt restructuring with some creditors, a quasi-reorganization if permitted by law, or a legal reorganization in order to again become a going concern. When a business is insolvent according to the legal definition, the entity either will voluntarily liquidate or be forced into liquidation by the creditors.

In a voluntary arrangement, all the creditors agree to accept either a lesser amount for the debts owed them, or to postpone the due dates of the amounts owed. In a troubled debt restructuring, a creditor(s) agrees to either accept a noncash asset(s) or the debtor's capital stock in settlement of the debt, or to modify the terms of the debt, or to accept a noncash asset(s) or the debtor's capital stock in partial settlement and modify the terms of the remaining debt. If a debtor gives the creditor a noncash asset, the debtor has a gain or loss on the difference between the fair market value of asset transferred and its net book value. The debtor also has an extraordinary gain for the difference between the net book value of the debt and the fair market value of the asset transferred. The creditor has an ordinary business loss equal to the extraordinary gain of the debtor.

If the debtor issues its capital stock, the stock is valued at its fair market value and the debtor has an extraordinary gain for the difference between the net book value of the debt and the fair market value of the capital stock. The creditor records the investment in the debtor's capital stock at its fair market value and records an ordinary business loss for the difference between the net book value of the receivable and the fair market value of the capital stock.

If a creditor agrees to modify either the amount of the debt, the interest rate, or the terms of repayment, two outcomes are possible. If the total cash to be paid according to the modified terms is more than the net book value of the debt, the difference between the future cash payments and the net book value of the debt is recognized as interest expense/revenue over the term of the repayment. If the total future cash payments are less than the net book value of the debt, no interest is recognized by either party as all the payments are considered principal. The debtor has an extraordinary gain equal to the difference between the net book value of the debt and the total future cash payments and the creditor has an ordinary business loss equal to the debtor's extraordinary gain.

If the debt restructuring is a combination of partial settlement and modification of terms, first the gains and losses on the partial settlement are determined in the same manner as discussed previously for a full settlement. Then the remaining net book value of the debt is used to determine the correct treatment of the modification of terms, which is the same as discussed above when only the terms are modified.

In a quasi-reorganization, which the company undertakes with stockholders' approval, the approach is as if a new business has been formed. The assets and liabilities are adjusted to their fair market values with the difference treated as an adjustment to the Retained Earnings balance. The Retained Earnings deficit balance is written off against the Additional Paid-in Capital account. If the balance of the Additional Paid-in Capital Account is not sufficient, the par value of the common stock is reduced and the reduction is transferred to the Additional Paid-in Capital account in an amount adequate to absorb the deficit balance of Retained Earnings.

A legal reorganization is a restructuring of the liabilities and stockholders' equity of a business so the business can return to a going concern status under Chapter 11 of the Bankruptcy Reform Act. A legal reorganization can only be undertaken if it is estimated that the creditors will receive at least the amount they would be paid from a liquidation. A statement of affairs is prepared to determine the potential dividend payable to the unsecured creditors. The Bankruptcy Reform Act created six classes of preferred claims: expenses of administration, creditor claims after bankruptcy filed, earned employee compensation to a limit of $2,000 per employee, employee fringe benefits to a limit of $2,000 per employee net of the compensation, customer deposits to a limit of $900, and governmental tax claims. Following the six classes of preferred claims are the fully secured creditors whose debt is less than the net realizable value of the assets securing the debt, then the partially secured creditors whose debt exceeds the net realizable value of the assets securing the debt, and lastly the unsecured creditors. Exhibit 19-1 illustrates the statement of affairs.

A liquidation under Chapter 7 of the Bankruptcy Reform Act generally occurs when the liabilities of the debtor exceed the net realizable value of the assets. A statement of realization and liquidation is prepared periodically to report to the bankruptcy court. The statement of realization and liquidation is usually accompanied by an analysis of the cash account, an income statement, and a balance sheet. Two approaches can be used to prepare the statement of realization and liquidation: the conventional approach (Exhibit 19-2) and the net book value approach (Exhibit 19-5).

A statement of realization and liquidation is divided into three debit and credit parts: assets, liabilities, and income. The assets consist of the assets to be realized and the assets acquired as debits, and the assets realized and assets not realized as credits. The liabilities consist of the liabilities liquidated and liabilities not liquidated as debits and the liabilities to be liquidated and the liabilities assumed as credits. The difference between the two approaches results in the statement of realization and liquidation being forced into balance by a gain or loss amount under the conventional approach.

Under the net book value approach, each part is balanced and the income statement contains the usual revenue and expense items. The courts usually prefer the conventional approach, while accountants prefer the net book value approach, because it clearly shows the revenue and expense items for the period and enters transactions and events as if the business were a going concern.

REVIEW PROBLEMS

TROUBLED DEBT RESTRUCTURINGS

Debtor Corporation is in financial trouble and is unable to meet its current obligations, although the assets of Debtor Corporation are substantially in excess of its liabilities. Creditor Corporation holds a three-year, 10%, $250,000 note receivable from Debtor Corporation that requires annual payments of interest and the principal at maturity. Debtor Corporation paid the first interest payment, but is unable to pay the interest payment that is currently due.

Required
For each of the following independent situations prepare the journal entries on the books of both Debtor Corporation and Creditor Corporation.

1. Creditor Corporation has agreed to accept an office building with a fair market value of $210,000 in full settlement of the receivable. The office building cost Debtor Corporation $290,000 and the accumulated depreciation to the present totals $135,000.
2. Creditor Corporation has agreed to accept 2,000 shares of Debtor Corporation's $100 par value, 8%, preferred stock that have a current market value of $115 per share.
3. Creditor Corporation has agreed to reduce the amount of the principal to $200,000, forgive the $25,000 of interest currently owing, and reduce the interest rate to 8%.
4. Creditor Corporation has agreed to accept machinery with a fair market value of $65,000, forgive the interest currently due, reduce the interest rate to 6%, and change the terms to require four equal annual payments of principal and interest beginning one year from the date of the restructuring. The machinery cost Debtor Corporation $88,000 and its accumulated depreciation to the present totals $18,000.

QUASI-REORGANIZATION

Durbin Company has operated unprofitably for the past four years. It has just developed a new product that is expected to generate substantial profits for the company. The following assets have fair market values different from their net book values:

	Fair Market Value	Net Book Value
Land and Buildings	$ 1,600,000	$ 1,890,000
Equipment	600,000	740,000
Patent	360,000	325,000

The stockholders' equity of Durbin Company is

Common Stock, $25 Par Value, 250,000 Shares Issued and Outstanding	$ 6,250,000
Additional Paid-in Capital	125,000
Retained Earnings (deficit)	(2,145,000)

Required

Prepare the journal entries for the quasi-reorganization, assuming that the par value of the common stock is reduced to $12.50 per share.

REORGANIZATION AND LIQUIDATION

Everett Company is having severe liquidity problems and is unable to meet its current obligations. The trial balance of Everett Company as of March 15, 1990 is

	Debit	Credit
Cash	$ 5,100	
Accounts Receivable	39,600	
Allowance for Doubtful Accounts		$ 2,400
Inventory	71,000	
Supplies	4,700	
Land	25,000	
Building	100,000	
Accumulated Depreciation: Building		48,000
Store Fixtures	36,000	
Accumulated Depreciation: Store Fixtures		16,000
Goodwill	9,000	
Accounts Payable		38,000
Employee Wages and Benefits Payable		13,000
State of Washington Business Receipts Tax Payable		6,400
Note Payable: Secured by Accounts Receivable		25,000
Interest Payable: Note		1,500
Mortgage Payable: Land and Building		75,000
Interest Payable: Mortgage		4,200
Common Stock, $25 Par Value		100,000
Additional Paid-in Capital		18,000
Retained Earnings	57,100	
Totals	$ 347,500	$ 347,500

1. Additional Information:

▪ The expected net realizable value of the accounts receivable is $29,000.
▪ The expected net realizable value of the inventory is $40,000.
▪ The supplies can be sold for $2,400.
▪ The expected net realizable value of the land and building is $67,500.
▪ The expected net realizable value of the store fixtures is $8,500.
▪ The costs of liquidation are expected to be $8,500.
▪ The Employee Wages and Benefits Payable account includes wages of $1,500 due to each of five employees, $2,500 due to a sixth employee, and the remainder is unpaid health and life insurance of $500 per employee.

Required

Prepare a statement of affairs to determine the dividend to unsecured creditors, including a proof of the results.

2. Everett Company's creditors have forced the company into liquidation. During the first reporting period of the liquidation, the following transactions and events occurred:

1. The land and building were sold for $70,000. The interest due on the mortgage totaled $5,000 at the time of the sale. The interest and principal to the extent of the available proceeds were paid.
2. Inventory with a cost of $35,000 was sold for $31,500. Cash sales totaled $24,000 and the remainder was on account.
3. Accounts receivable totaling $31,000 were collected and $3,100 of the receivables were determined to be uncollectible.
4. The note payable secured by the accounts receivable plus the interest owing were paid from the collection of the accounts receivable.
5. The supplies were sold for $2,350.
6. The unsecured claims of Class 1–6 priority claims were paid.
7. An unrecorded credit memo from an account payable of $800 was discovered and recorded.
8. Depreciation on the store fixtures totaled $800 for the period.

Required
1) Prepare a statement of realization and liquidation using the conventional approach.
2) Prepare the cash account and the income statement for the reporting period and the balance sheet at the end of the period.
3) List the transactions and events that are treated differently in the statement of realization and liquidation, and explain the treatment if the net book value approach is used to prepare the statement.

QUESTIONS

1. What are the two different definitions of insolvency and what solutions could be used based on these definitions?
2. Describe a voluntary arrangement and the definition of insolvency applicable to a voluntary arrangement.
3. Describe the conditions under which a troubled debt restructuring occurs and the types of concessions the creditor could grant.
4. What value is used by the creditor to record either the assets or debtor's stock received in a troubled debt restructuring?
5. Describe how the two types of gains and losses are determined when assets are transferred in settlement of a debt in a debt restructuring.
6. Why must future cash flows be compared to the net book value of the debt when the terms are modified in a troubled debt restructuring? Describe the difference in the accounting treatment if the future cash flows are (1) more than (2) less than the net book value of the debt.
7. Describe the order of determining gains and losses when a troubled debt is partially repaid, and the terms of the remaining debt are modified.
8. What are the reasons for entering into a quasi-reorganization?
9. What are the steps in recording a quasi-reorganization?
10. How would a user know that a company had undertaken a quasi-reorganization?
11. What requirement must be met in order to have a reorganization under the bankruptcy acts?
12. Describe the unsecured claims with priority and why they were granted priority by the bankruptcy act.
13. What values are used for assets in a statement of affairs?
14. What distinguishes a fully secured claim from a partially secured claim?
15. Describe how the dividend is computed in a statement of affairs.
16. Describe how a fiduciary records assets, liabilities, revenues, and expenses in a reorganization.

17. What definition of insolvency must be met for creditors to force a company into liquidation?
18. Describe the sections of a statement of realization and liquidation.
19. Describe how the net book value method for the preparation of a statement of realization and liquidation differs from the conventional method.

EXERCISES

EXERCISE 19-1

1. Hull Company is indebted to Apex under a $500,000, 12%, three-year note dated December 31, 1988. Because of Hull's financial difficulties developing in 1990, Hull owed accrued interest of $60,000 on the note at December 31, 1990. Under a troubled debt restructuring, on December 31, 1990, Apex agreed to settle the note and accrued interest for a tract of land with a fair market value of $450,000. Hull's acquisition cost of the land is $360,000. Ignoring income taxes, in its 1990 income statement Hull should report the following as a result of the troubled debt restructuring:

	Other Income	Extraordinary Gain
a.	$ 200,000	$ –0–
b.	$ 140,000	$ –0–
c.	$ 90,000	$ 50,000
d.	$ 90,000	$ 110,000

2. During 1989 Mann Company experienced financial difficulties and is likely to default on a $500,000, 15%, three-year note dated January 1, 1988, payable to Summit Bank. On December 31, 1989, the bank agreed to settle the note and unpaid interest of $75,000 for 1989 for $410,000 cash payable on January 31, 1990. Ignoring income taxes, what amount should Mann report as a gain from the debt restructuring in its 1989 income statement?

a. $ 165,000
b. $ 90,000
c. $ 75,000
d. $ –0–

3. Tapscott, Inc., is indebted to Bush Finance Company under a $600,000, 10%, five-year note dated January 1, 1988. Interest, payable annually on December 31, was paid on the December 31, 1988 and 1989 due dates. However, during 1990 Tapscott experienced severe financial difficulties and is likely to default on the note and interest unless some concessions are granted. On December 31, 1990, Tapscott and Bush signed an agreement restructuring the debt as follows:

- Interest for 1990 was reduced to $30,000, payable March 31, 1991.
- Interest payments each year were reduced to $40,000 per year for 1991 and 1992.
- The principal amount was reduced to $400,000.

What is the amount of gain that Tapscott should report on the debt restructuring in its income statement for the year ended December 31, 1990.

a. $ 120,000
b. $ 150,000
c. $ 200,000
d. $ 230,000

(AICPA adapted)

EXERCISE 19-2

1. Grey Company holds an overdue note receivable of $800,000 plus recorded accrued interest of $64,000. As the result of a court-imposed settlement on December 31, 1990, Grey agreed to the following restructuring arrangement:

- Reduced the principal obligation to $600,000.
- Forgave the $64,000 accrued interest.
- Extended the maturity date to December 31, 1992.
- Annual interest of $60,000 to be paid to Grey on December 31, 1991 and 1992.

On December 31, 1990, Grey must recognize a loss from restructuring of

a. $ 144,000
b. $ 200,000
c. $ 204,000
d. $ 264,000

3. On December 31, 1990, Marsh Company entered into a debt restructuring agreement with Saxe Company, which was experiencing financial difficulties. Marsh restructured a $100,000 note receivable as follows:

- Reduced the principal obligation to $70,000.
- Forgave $12,000 of accrued interest.
- Extended the maturity date from December 31, 1990 to December 31, 1992.
- Reduced the interest rate from 12% to 8%.

Interest was payable annually on December 31, 1991 and 1992. In accordance with the agreement, Saxe made payments to Marsh on December 31, 1991 and 1992. How much interest income should Marsh report for the year ended December 31, 1991?

a. $ –0–
b. $ 5,600
c. $ 8,400
d. $11,200

(AICPA adapted)

EXERCISE 19-3

Gilbert Company is having financial problems and lacks sufficient cash to meet its current obligations. The outlook for the industry in which Gilbert operates is good, but Gilbert needs to restructure its current debts in order to avoid bankruptcy before the upturn arrives. Gilbert Company has entered into an agreement with Kraft Company to restructure a three-year, 12%, $3,500,000 outstanding loan that requires annual interest payments, plus a $700,000 principal payment each year. Gilbert Company paid the first annual payment of principal and interest, but is currently in default on second interest and principal payment.

Kraft Company has agreed to accept a shopping center owned by Gilbert Company in full settlement of the amounts due from Gilbert Company. The current market value of the shopping center consists of land valued at $250,000 and a building valued at $2,200,000. Gilbert Company paid $200,000 for the land and incurred construction costs of $3,850,000 for the shopping center. Depreciation in the amount of $1,230,000 has been recorded on the shopping center since its completion.

Required

Prepare the journal entries for both Gilbert Company and Kraft Company for the troubled debt settlement.

EXERCISE 19-4

Harvest Company is having financial problems and lacks sufficient cash to meet its current obligations. The outlook for the industry in which Harvest operates is good, but Harvest needs to restructure its current debts in order to avoid bankruptcy before the upturn arrives. Harvest Company has entered into an agreement with Marne Company to restructure a seven-year, 10%, $2,700,000 outstanding loan that requires annual interest payments, with the principal payable at the end of the seven years. Harvest Company paid the first two annual interest payments, is in default on the third interest payment, and is unable to pay the third interest payment or to pay the fourth interest payment currently due.

Marne Company has agreed to accept the following stocks of Harvest Company in full settlement of the past due interest and principal of the debt:

	Market Value
12,000 Shares of $100 Par Value, 8% Cumulative Preferred Stock	$ 108 per share
25,000 Shares of $25 Par Value Common Stock	$ 68 per share

Required

Prepare the journal entries on the books of Harvest Company and Marne Company to record the settlement of the debt.

EXERCISE 19-5

Monroe Company is having financial difficulties and does not have sufficient cash to meet its current obligations. Monroe Company is indebted to Newberg Company on a $1,300,000, three-year, 12% note that requires annual interest payments and the principal at the end of the three years. Monroe Company paid the first interest payment, but is unable to pay the second interest payment that is currently due. Newberg Company has agreed to reduce the interest rate to 8%, forgive the interest currently due, and extend the maturity date of the note for three years (four years remaining).

Required

1. Prepare the journal entries for the restructuring on the books of Monroe Company and on the books of Newberg Company.
2. If interest is to be recorded, prepare the journal entry to record the first year's interest for both companies.

EXERCISE 19-6

Olympia Company is having financial difficulties and is unable to meet its current obligations. On January 1, 1988, Olympia Company borrowed $2,400,000 from Prine Company for four years at 12% interest. The loan is to be repaid in equal annual installments of principal and interest each January 1. Olympia Company paid the installment payment due January 1, 1989, but the January 1, 1990 payment is past due. Prine Company has agreed to reduce the interest rate to 8% and agreed that the remaining debt is to be repaid in six equal annual installments beginning one year from the date of the restructuring.

Required

1. Determine the interest revenue/expense recognized for each of the six payments after the restructuring of the debt.
2. Prepare the journal entries to record interest for both Olympia Company and Prine Company for the first restructured payment.

EXERCISE 19-7

On January 1, 1990 Pringle Company borrowed $2,000,000 at 14% interest for five years from the Rigby National Bank. The terms of the loan require annual interest payments each January 1 and the principal at the end of five years. Pringle Company paid the interest payments due on January 1, 1991 and 1992, but is unable to pay the interest payment due on January 1, 1993. Rigby has agreed to accept accounts receivable with a net realizable value of $280,000 in settlement of the interest owing. The accounts receivable have a book value of $315,000 with an allowance for doubtful accounts of $15,000. In addition, Rigby has agreed to reduce the interest rate to 9% and extend the due date by two years.

Required

1. Prepare the journal entries for the restructuring on the books of Pringle Company and on the books of Rigby National Bank.
2. If interest is to be recorded, prepare the journal entry to record the first interest payment.

EXERCISE 19-8

1. A company with a substantial deficit undertakes a quasi-reorganization. Certain assets will be written down to their present fair market value. Liabilities will remain the same. How would the entries to record the quasi-reorganization affect each of the following?

	Contributed Capital	Retained Earnings
a.	Increase	Decrease
b.	Decrease	No effect
c.	Decrease	Increase
d.	No effect	Increase

2. A company with a $2,000,000 deficit undertakes a quasi-reorganization on November 1, 1990. Certain assets will be written down by $400,000 to their present fair market value. Liabilities will remain the same. Capital stock was $3,000,000 and additional paid-in capital was $1,000,000 before the quasi-reorganization. How would the entries to accomplish these changes on November 1, 1990 affect each of the following?

	Capital Stock	Total Stockholders' Equity
a.	No effect	No effect
b.	No effect	Decrease
c.	Decrease	Decrease
d.	Decrease	No effect

3. Livingston Corporation has incurred losses from operations for several years. At the recommendation of the newly hired president, the board of directors voted to implement a quasi-reorganization, subject to stockholder approval. Immediately prior to the restatement, On June 30, 1990, Livingston's balance sheet was

Current Assets	$ 550,000
Property, Plant and Equipment: Net	1,350,000
Other Assets	200,000
Total Assets	$ 2,100,000
Liabilities	$ 600,000
Common Stock	1,600,000
Additional Paid-in Capital	300,000
Retained Earnings (deficit)	(400,000)
Total Equities	$ 2,100,000

The stockholders approved the quasi-reorganization effective July 1, 1990 to be accomplished by a reduction in other assets of $150,000, a reduction in property, plant and equipment (net) of $350,000, and an appropriate adjustment to the capital structure. To implement the quasi-reorganization, Livingston should reduce the common stock account in the amount of

a.   −0−
b. $ 100,000
c. $ 400,000
d. $ 600,000

4. Carroll, Inc., accomplished a quasi-reorganization effective December 31, 1990. Immediately prior to the quasi-reorganization the stockholders' equity was

Common Stock, Par Value $10, 400,000 Shares Authorized, Issued, and Outstanding	$ 4,000,000
Additional Paid-in Capital	600,000
Retained Earnings (deficit)	(900,000)
	$ 3,700,000

Under the terms of the quasi-reorganization (1) the par value of the common stock was reduced from $10 per share to $5 per share, and (2) plant and equipment (net) was written down by $1,200,000. Immediately after the quasi-reorganization, the total stockholders' equity should be

a. $ 2,500,000
b. $ 2,000,000
c. $ 1,700,000
d. $ 1,600,000

(AICPA adapted)

EXERCISE 19-9

Ridgeway Corporation has been operating at a deficit for several years. Ridgeway has just completed development of a new product and is attempting to secure additional financing to increase its production capacity and to successfully market the new product. The stockholders of Ridgeway have approved a quasi-reorganization of the corporation. Prior to the reorganization on June 1, 1990, the condensed balance sheet of Ridgeway is

RIDGEWAY CORPORATION
Condensed Balance Sheet
June 1, 1990

Current Assets	$ 350,000	Liabilities	$ 500,000
Plant and Equipment: Net	2,400,000	Common Stock, $10 Par Value	2,400,000
		Additional Paid-in Capital	300,000
		Retained Earnings	(450,000)
	$ 2,750,000		$ 2,750,000

The company has determined that inventories are understated by $40,000, and plant and equipment are overstated by $400,000. The par value of the common stock after the quasi-reorganization is to be $7.50.

Required
1. Prepare the journal entries to effect the quasi-reorganization.
2. Prepare the balance sheet immediately after the reorganization.

EXERCISE 19-10

Senaca Company has been operating at a loss for several years. The demand for its products has risen dramatically in the past year, requiring additions to plant facilities. Senaca is unable to obtain financing because of the retained earnings deficit. The stockholders of Senaca Company have agreed to a quasi-reorganization of the company. The stockholders' equity of Senaca Company on April 1, 1990 just prior to the quasi-reorganization is

Common Stock, $50 Par Value, 100,000 Shares Authorized, Issued, and Outstanding	$ 5,000,000
Additional Paid-in Capital	750,000
Retained Earnings (deficit)	(1,840,000)

The following assets have fair market values different from their net book values:

	Net Book Value	Fair Market Value
Accounts Receivable: Net	$ 429,000	$ 412,000
Inventory	623,000	547,000
Plant and Equipment: Net	2,641,000	2,235,000
Patent	400,000	524,000

In addition, a review of the liabilities indicates that accrued interest in the amount of $60,000 on an outstanding loan has not been recorded. The par value of the stock is to be reduced just enough to cover the deficit.

Required
1. Prepare the journal entries to effect the quasi-reorganization.
2. Prepare the stockholders' equity section of the balance sheet immediately after the reorganization.

EXERCISE 19-11

1. Scott Company filed a voluntary bankruptcy petition on June 25, 1990, and the statement of affairs reflects the following amounts:

	Book Carrying Amount	Estimated Current Value
Assets		
Assets Pledged with Fully Secured Creditors	$ 150,000	$ 185,000
Assets Pledged with Partially Secured Creditors	90,000	60,000
Free Assets	210,000	160,000
Total	$ 450,000	$ 405,000

	Book Carrying Amount	Estimated Current Value
Liabilities		
Liabilities with Priority	$ 35,000	
Fully Secured Creditors	130,000	
Partially Secured Creditors	100,000	
Unsecured Creditors	270,000	
Total	$ 535,000	

Assume that the assets are converted into cash at the estimated current values and the business is liquidated. How much cash will be available to pay unsecured nonpriority claims?

a. $ 240,000
b. $ 180,000
c. $ 160,000
d. $ 125,000

2. Platt Company has been forced into bankruptcy and liquidated. Unsecured claims will be paid at the rate of 50 cents on the dollar. Maga Company holds a noninterest-bearing note receivable from Platt in the amount of $50,000, collateralized by machinery with a liquidation value of $10,000. The total amount to be realized by Maga on this note receivable is

a. $ 35,000
b. $ 30,000
c. $ 25,000
d. $ 10,000

3. Drake Company filed a voluntary bankruptcy petition on July 15, 1990, and the statement of affairs reflects the following amounts:

	Book Carrying Amount	Estimated Current Value
Assets		
Assets Pledged with Fully Secured Creditors	$ 160,000	$ 190,000
Assets Pledged with Partially Secured Creditors	90,000	60,000
Free Assets	200,000	140,000
Total	$ 450,000	$ 390,000
Liabilities		
Liabilities with Priority	$ 20,000	
Fully Secured Creditors	130,000	
Partially Secured Creditors	100,000	
Unsecured Creditors	260,000	
Total	$ 510,000	

Assume that the assets are converted into cash at the estimated current values and the business is liquidated. What total amount of cash should the partially secured creditors receive?

a. $ 60,000
b. $ 84,000
c. $ 90,000
d. $ 100,000

(AICPA adapted)

EXERCISE 19-12

The total expected net realizable value of Topeka Company's assets is $245,000. The following liabilities will be satisfied with the actual cash realized.

Mortgage Payable, Secured by Assets with a Net Realizable Value of $115,000	$ 102,000
Interest Payable: Mortgage	3,240
Note Payable, Secured with Assets with a Net Realizable Value of $40,000	100,000
Interest Payable: Note	2,000
Property Taxes	5,000
Liquidation Costs	6,000
Legal and Accounting Fees Related to the Liquidation	3,000
Wages Payable to Five Employees	8,000
Salaries Payable to Three Executives	10,000
Accounts Payable	72,000

Required
1. Determine the dividend for Class 7 creditors.
2. Determine the dollar amount that will be paid to each of the different creditors.

EXERCISE 19-13

The following information has been determined for the preparation of an accounting statement of affairs for Urbana Company:

	Net Book Value	Net Realizable Value
Assets		
Cash	$ 4,125	$ 4,125
Accounts Receivable: Net	86,400	73,200
Inventory	57,100	43,500
Investment in Wilbur Company	134,300	181,400
Plant: Net	600,000	425,000
Equipment: Net	247,000	126,500
Patent	85,000	102,000
Liabilities		
Accounts Payable	234,000	
Note Payable: Secured by Investment in Wilbur Company	165,000	
Interest Payable: Note	15,000	
Wages and Salaries Payable	82,500	
Property Taxes Payable	18,400	
Employee Benefits Payable	7,350	
Mortgage Payable: Secured by Plant	620,000	
Interest Payable: Mortgage	13,400	

The Wages and Salaries Payable consist of

25 employees @ $1,500 each	$ 37,500
15 employees @ $2,200 each	33,000
3 employees @ $4,000 each	12,000
Total	$ 82,500

The employee benefits consist of $175 per employee. Urbana Company has 10,000 shares of no par common stock outstanding that were issued at $55.

Required
Prepare an accounting statement of affairs and determine the dividend of the Class 7 creditors.

EXERCISE 19-14
The financial condition of Waco Company has deteriorated dramatically during the past months and the creditors of Waco Company have forced the company into liquidation. The trial balance of Waco Company on April 1, 1990, prior to liquidation, is

	Debit	Credit
Cash	$ 4,200	
Accounts Receivable	31,400	
Merchandise Inventory	49,600	
Store Fixtures	60,800	
Accumulated Depreciation: Store Fixtures		$ 36,400
Accounts Payable		92,400
Accrued Expenses Payable		12,700
Common Stock		40,000
Additional Paid-in Capital		7,200
Retained Earnings	42,700	
Totals	$ 188,700	$ 188,700

The following transactions occurred during the first six months of liquidation, ending on September 30, 1990:

1. Merchandise purchased on account was $12,700.
2. Merchandise sold on account was $62,000. The merchandise sold had a net book value of $44,300.
3. Cash received from original receivables totaled $28,340. The remaining original accounts receivable were deemed uncollectible.
4. Cash received from new receivables totaled $52,600.
5. All of the accrued expenses were paid, as they represented claims of Class 1–6 creditors.
6. Operating expenses of $8,400 were incurred and paid.
7. New accounts payable were paid.
8. Store fixtures were sold for $15,000. The store fixtures had a cost of $41,000 and accumulated depreciation of $24,300 at the time of sale.
9. Depreciation on the unsold store fixtures totaled $850 for the period.

Required
Describe how each of the above transactions and events is reported in a statement of realization and liquidation (as demonstrated in Illustrative Problem 19.6) using (1) conventional approach, and (2) net book value approach.

EXERCISE 19-15

Refer to Exercise 19-14. Prepare a statement of realization and liquidation, a cash account, an income statement, and a balance sheet using the conventional approach.

EXERCISE 19-16

Refer to Exercise 19-14. Prepare a statement of realization and liquidation, a cash account, and a balance sheet using the net book value approach.

EXERCISE 19-17

The Yarrow Corporation is being liquidated under the 1978 Bankruptcy Reform Act. Just prior to liquidation, the trial balance of the Yarrow Corporation is

	Debit	Credit
Cash	$ 2,400	
Accounts Receivable	48,700	
Allowance for Uncollectible Accounts		$ 2,700
Inventory	36,900	
Equipment	51,000	
Accumulated Depreciation: Equipment		16,400
Accounts Payable		45,400
Notes Payable		44,000
Accrued Interest Payable: Note Payable		2,200
Common Stock, $100 Par Value		100,000
Additional Paid-in Capital		15,000
Retained Earnings	86,700	
Totals	$ 225,700	$ 225,700

The cash account at the end of the liquidation process is

Cash

Balance, 7/1/90	2,400	Notes Payable	44,000
Equipment	22,000	Interest Payable	2,200
Accounts Receivable	78,000	Liquidation Expenses	5,100

All of the inventory was sold on account for $45,000. The equipment sold had a cost of $42,000, and a net book value of $31,000. Remaining receivables in the amount of $10,000 are deemed collectible. The remaining equipment is old and its scrap value is $2,500.

Required

1. Prepare a statement of realization and liquidation using the conventional approach.
2. Determine the amount of the dividend to the Class 7 creditors and the stockholders.

EXERCISE 19-18

Refer to Exercise 19-17. Prepare a statement of realization and liquidation using the net book value approach.

PROBLEMS

PROBLEM 19-1

The Arion Company has encountered severe financial problems and is attempting to stay solvent by restructuring its outstanding obligations. On July 1, 1990, Arion Company entered into three debt restructurings with its largest creditors. The debt, the settlement, and the changes in the terms of the debt for each of the three debt restructurings are

Debt 1

Five-year, 12%, $2,500,000 note payable to Burns Company, dated January 1, 1989. The principal and interest are payable in five equal annual installments beginning on January 1, 1990. Burns Company was unable to pay a complete payment on January 1, 1990 and paid only the interest portion of the annual payment. Burns Company has agreed to reduce the interest rate to 8% and convert the terms of repayment to eight equal annual installments of the remaining principal plus interest at 8%. The interest paid on the first payment is to be recomputed at 8% interest, and any excess is to be treated as a reduction of principal.

Debt 2

Twenty-year, 12%, $5,000,000 mortgage payable on land and a factory building, dated January 1, 1987, to Commercial Bank. The mortgage requires semiannual payments of interest on the outstanding balance plus $125,000 of principal beginning July 1, 1987. Arion Company paid the first five semiannual payments and is in default on the remaining two payments. Commercial Bank has agreed to accept the land and the factory building in full settlement of the outstanding debt. The current fair market value of the property is $4,700,000. Arion originally spent $7,500,000 on the land and the factory building and the accumulated depreciation to the date of transfer totaled $3,350,000.

Debt 3

A three-year, 10%, $2,000,000 face value note payable to Conroy Corporation, dated July 1, 1988. The note requires annual interest payments beginning July 1, 1989 and the principal is due at the end of the three years. Arion paid the July 1, 1989 interest payment and is unable to pay the July 1, 1990 payment. Conroy Corporation has agreed to accept a patent with a fair market value of $525,000 in partial settlement of the principal. The net book value of the patent transferred is $665,000. In addition, Conroy Corporation has agreed to reduce the interest rate to 6%, forgive the interest payment due July 1, 1990, and extend the maturity date of unpaid principal to July 1, 1994.

Required

1. Determine the type and amount of gains and losses to be reported on income statements of the Arion Company and its creditors from each of the debt restructurings.
2. Prepare the journal entries to record the restructurings on the books of Arion Company and the journal entries to record the first interest payments on the restructured debt.
3. Prepare the journal entries on the books of each of the three creditors as a result of the debt restructuring agreement.

PROBLEM 19-2

Brown Company has been experiencing severe cash flow problems and has entered into two debt restructuring arrangements with its creditors, as well as a direct settlement with its suppliers. On September 1, 1990 the creditors agreed to the following changes in their receivables from Brown Company:

Darwin Corporation holds a $1,500,000, four-year, 12% note receivable from Brown Company dated September 1, 1988. The terms of the note require equal semiannual payments of principal and interest beginning March 1, 1989. Brown Company paid the first two semiannual payments, but did not pay the semiannual payment due March 1, 1990 and cannot pay the semiannual payment due September 1, 1990. Darwin Corporation has agreed to forgive the past due payment, both principal and interest as well as the payment due September 1, 1990. In addition, Darwin has agreed to reduce the interest rate on the remaining principal balance to 10%. The remaining balance is to be paid in six equal semiannual payments beginning on March 1, 1991.

Elder Company holds a five-year, 12%, $2,000,000 note receivable from Brown Company dated December 1, 1988. The terms of the note require quarterly interest payments on the unpaid balance beginning March 1, 1989, and annual principal payments of $400,000 beginning December 1, 1989. Brown Company paid the interest payments due March 1, June 1, September 1, and December 1, 1989. Brown Company also paid the principal payment due December 1, 1989. Brown Company has not remitted any payments to Elder Company since December 1, 1989. Elder Company has agreed to accept a parcel of commercial land with a fair market value of $700,000 in partial settlement of Brown's receivable. The land cost Brown Company $485,000. Elder has also agreed to forgive the interest payments due on March 1, June 1, and September 1, of 1990. In addition, Elder Company has agreed to reduce the interest rate on the quarterly interest payments to 8%, which will begin on December 1, 1990. The remaining restructured principal will be paid in four equal annual installments beginning on September 1, 1991.

Creditors have agreed to accept 80 cents on the dollar for the $65,000 owed them on open accounts payable.

Required

1. Describe why Darwin Company and Elder Company are willing to grant the above concessions to Brown Company.
2. Prepare the journal entries for the Brown Company for the two debt restructurings and the direct settlement.
3. Prepare the journal entries on the books of Darwin Company and the Elder Company for the debt restructurings.
4. Assume that Brown Company paid the remaining payments required for 1990 and 1991. Prepare the journal entries for the required 1990 and 1991 payments (round interest percentage to the nearest 100th of a percent).

PROBLEM 19-3

Calhoun Company, which is in financial trouble, owes Fargo Company $3,250,000 on a five-year, 12% note receivable dated January 1, 1988. The terms of the note require equal annual payments of principal and interest beginning on January 1, 1989. Calhoun Company paid the payment due on January 1, 1989, but is unable to pay the payment due on January 1, 1990. Calhoun Company has approached Fargo Company with the following three options for restructuring its debt to Fargo Company:

Option 1

Accept a 35% interest in Garber Company, which is owned by Calhoun, in full settlement of all amounts owed to Fargo Company. Garber Company has 200,000 shares of common stock outstanding that are currently trading for $39 per share.

Option 2

Accept a parcel of land with a fair market value of $1,000,000 in partial settlement of the debt. Forgive the unpaid interest. Change the terms of the remaining total debt to an interest rate of 10% payable semiannually and the principal due at maturity in three years.

Option 3

Change the terms of the total outstanding debt by reducing the interest rate to 8%, extending the term of the note to January 1, 1997 with annual payments to begin on January 1, 1991, and forgiving any interest currently due.

The net book value of the shares of Garber Company on the books of Calhoun Company is $2,540,000. The cost of the land on the books of Calhoun Company is $865,000.

Required

1. Determine the amount of gain or loss to both Calhoun Company and Fargo Company for each of the options.
2. Discuss the pros and cons of each of the above restructuring arrangements for Fargo Company.
3. Prepare journal entries to record each of the options on the books of both Calhoun Company and Fargo Company.

PROBLEM 19-4

Davis Company has operated at a loss for several years and has a deficit balance in its Retained Earnings account. During the past year, Davis Company developed a new product, which is selling far beyond expectations and Davis Company is again operating profitably. Davis Company's stockholders' have agreed to a quasi-reorganization in order to allow Davis Company to borrow funds for plant expansion to meet the demand for the new product and to allow the company to pay dividends to the stockholders. Just prior to the quasi-reorganization, the trial balance of Davis Company was

	Debit	Credit
Cash	$ 74,600	
Accounts Receivable	62,400	
Allowance for Doubtful Accounts		$ 5,000
Inventory	223,700	
Prepaid Expenses	12,600	
Land	125,000	
Building	650,000	
Accumulated Depreciation: Building		275,000
Equipment	415,000	
Accumulated Depreciation: Equipment		245,000
Accounts Payable		61,300
Accrued Expenses Payable		12,700
Loan Payable, Due January 1, 1992		40,000
Mortgage Payable: Land and Building		350,000
6% Cumulative Preferred Stock, $100 Par Value		200,000
Additional Paid-in Capital: Preferred Stock		10,000
Common Stock, $20 Par Value		500,000
Additional Paid-in Capital: Common Stock		110,000
Retained Earnings	245,700	
Totals	$ 1,809,000	$ 1,809,000

The following assets have fair market values that are different from their net books values:

	Fair Market Value
Inventory	$ 195,000
Land	160,000
Building	350,000
Equipment	75,000

The preferred stock is cumulative and the stockholders' have not received any dividends for the past three years. The reorganization agreement provides that the unpaid preferred dividends are to be recorded as a liability. The preferred stock will be converted into common stock, with each share of preferred stock receiving 4 shares of common stock. The par value of the common stock, after conversion of the preferred stock, will be reduced by a whole dollar amount sufficient to achieve a quasi-reorganization.

Required
1. Prepare the journal entries to record the quasi-reorganization.
2. Prepare the balance sheet of the company immediately after the reorganization.

PROBLEM 19-5
The Farley Company is considering entering into a legal reorganization under The 1978 Bankruptcy Reform Act. Just prior to the reorganization the trial balance of the Farley Company is

	Debit	Credit
Cash	$ 29,400	
Accounts Receivable	328,600	
Allowance for Doubtful Accounts		$ 17,900
Inventory	327,000	
Investment in Harvard Company, 10,000 shares	200,000	
Land	102,600	
Building	890,000	
Accumulated Depreciation: Building		367,000
Equipment	328,000	
Accumulated Depreciation: Equipment		185,000
Accounts Payable		395,300
Wages Payable (equal amounts to 10 employees)		16,800
Loan Payable: Secured by Accounts Receivable		100,000
Interest Payable: Loan		6,000
Note Payable: City Bank		72,000
Mortgage Payable: Land and Building		670,000
Common Stock, $25 Par Value		500,000
Additional Paid-in Capital: Common Stock		250,000
Retained Earnings	374,400	
Totals	$ 2,580,000	$ 2,580,000

A review of the assets and liabilities of the Farley Company reveals the following information:

1. Accounts receivable in the amount of $128,600 are over six months past due and only $50,000 is expected to be realized. Current accounts receivable totaling $100,000 are pledged as security for a $72,000 note with City Bank. The current accounts receivable (total accounts receivable exclusive of the $128,600 old accounts) are considered 90% collectible.
2. The inventory is expected to realize 75 cents per dollar of book value.
3. The selling price of the stock of Harvard Company is $27 per share.
4. The land and building have a current market value of $650,000.
5. The equipment is expected to sell for $100,000.
6. Liquidation costs are expected to be $14,750.

Required
1. Prepare a statement of affairs.
2. Assuming the assets generate the amounts expected to be realized, and all the secured, partially

secured, and priority claims are paid, prepare a statement of realization and liquidation using the conventional approach.

3. Prepare a cash account, an income statement, and a balance sheet to support the statement of realization and liquidation.

PROBLEM 19-6

Gardner Company has been unable to meet its current obligations as they come due and is seeking a reorganization under federal bankruptcy laws. Some of the creditors of Gardner Company believe that the company should be liquidated rather than reorganized. Gardner Company has offered to settle with the unsecured creditors for 40 cents on the dollar, 10 cents payable in 30 days and the remainder in three equal monthly installments beginning 45 days after the initial payment. A statement of affairs is to be prepared to determine if the Class 7 creditors would be better off if Gardner Company were liquidated. The following net book values and estimated realizable values of assets were determined:

	Net Book Value	Estimated Realizable Value
Cash	$ 23,680	$ 23,680
Marketable Securities	64,500	73,528
Accounts Receivable: Net	231,780	189,600
Inventory	317,500	248,700
Supplies	38,900	15,800
Prepaid Insurance	8,400	6,300
Store Fixtures: Net	238,000	159,400

The liabilities of Gardner Company are

Accounts Payable	$ 472,000
Wages and Salaries Payable	
Less Than $2,000 per Employee	41,300
Over $2,000 per Employee (5 employees)	23,100
Customer Deposits	
Less Than $900 per Customer	45,200
Over $900 per Customer (12 customers)	23,700
Property Taxes Payable	35,300
State Gross Business Receipts Tax Payable	54,300
Note Payable: Secured by Accounts Receivable	200,000
Interest Payable: Note	7,200
Loan Payable: Secured by Inventory	86,000
Interest Payable: Loan	4,300

Gardner Company has 20,000 shares of $10 par value common stock outstanding originally issued at $14 per share. In addition, Gardner Company has reacquired 2,000 shares of $22 per share, which is being held as treasury stock. The costs of reorganization or liquidation are estimated to be $18,500.

Required

1. Prepare a statement of affairs.
2. Determine the total amount each class of priority claims will receive, assuming the Gardner Company actually receives the amounts estimated for the assets.

3. If you were a general creditor of Gardner Company, would you allow Gardner Company to proceed with the reorganization or would you force Gardner Company into liquidation? Explain your conclusion.

PROBLEM 19-7

Harold Company is in financial difficulties and has applied for reorganization under federal bankruptcy laws. The balance sheet of Harold Company at March 31, 1990 is

HAROLD COMPANY
Balance Sheet
March 31, 1990

Assets

Current Assets			
Cash			$ 6,100
Marketable Debt Securities			44,600
Accounts Receivable		$ 124,600	
Less: Allowance for Doubtful Accounts		7,500	117,100
Notes Receivable		40,000	
Less: Notes Receivable Discounted		14,000	26,000
Inventories			
Finished Goods		65,300	
Work in Process		12,900	
Raw Materials		17,900	96,100
Supplies			4,650
Prepaid Rent			5,000
Total Current Assets			299,550
Investment in Marrion Corporation (25%)			125,300
Plant and Equipment			
Building	$ 369,000		
Less: Accumulated Depreciation	213,000	156,000	
Equipment	89,000		
Less: Accumulated Depreciation	52,000	37,000	193,000
Total Assets			$ 617,850

Liabilities and Stockholders' Equity

Current Liabilities
   Accounts Payable $ 84,500

Current Liabilities		
Accounts Payable		$ 84,500
Wages Payable		12,430
Property Taxes Payable		6,100
Interest Payable: Square Deal Bank		3,200
Interest Payable: First Savings and Loan		4,100
Interest Payable: Equipment Supply Company		1,700
Note Payable: Equipment Supply Company		22,000
Total Current Liabilities		134,040
Long-Term Debt		
Loan Payable: Square Deal Bank		250,000
Mortgage Payable: First Savings and Loan		250,000
Total Liabilities		634,030
Stockholders' Equity		
Common Stock, $10 Par Value, 10,000 Shares Authorized,		
Issued, and Outstanding	$ 100,000	
Additional Paid-in Capital	30,000	
Retained Earnings (deficit)	(146,180)	(16,180)
Total Liabilities and Stockholders' Equity		$ 617,850

The following information has been determined regarding the balance sheet accounts of Harold Company:

1. The marketable securities and the investment in Marrion Corporation have been pledged as security for the loan payable to Square Deal Bank.
2. The mortgage payable to First Savings and Loan is secured by the land and buildings.
3. The contract payable is for the purchase of equipment and is secured by equipment that cost $45,000, has a net book value of $28,000, and a fair market value of $24,000.
4. The current value of the marketable debt securities is $48,400.
5. The estimated net realizable value of the accounts receivable is 80% of the gross amount.
6. The note receivable discounted was with recourse, and although not yet due, it is probable that the maker will pay the note by the due date. The remaining notes receivable are deemed collectible.
7. The finished good inventory can be sold for 120% of the cost. The work in process requires an additional $5,000 of raw materials and $7,000 of labor to complete. When completed it will sell for 120% above cost. The remaining raw materials can be sold for 60% of their cost.
8. The supplies on hand will be consumed in completing the work in process.
9. The prepaid rent is for rental of the land on which the factory building is located. The rent will be expense by the time the work in process inventory is complete and the building is sold.
10. The investment in Marrion Corporation stock has a fair market value of $135,000.
11. The net realizable value of the building is $225,000.
12. The equipment that is not security for the contract to Equipment Supply Company is old and cannot be sold, but has a scrap value of $2,500.

Required
Prepare a statement of affairs assuming no employee is owed more than $2,000 and that the work in process inventory is to be completed.

PROBLEM 19-8 (Extension of Problem 19-7)
Harold Company's creditors forced the company into liquidation. Harold Company's actual transactions during the liquidation were as follows:

1. The estimated net realizable values predicted in Problem 19-7 were realized for all of the assets.
2. The work in process inventory was completed and all of the inventory was sold on account. All but $17,900 of the accounts receivable from the sales of inventory has been collected. Harold Company estimates that all of the outstanding accounts receivable will be collected within the following months, except for $2,000 that are considered uncollectible.
3. The maker of the discounted note defaulted and Harold Company paid the note plus $400 of interest.
4. Harold Company received $1,200 of interest on the notes receivable when collected.
5. During the liquidation $18,300 was spent on legal, accounting, and trustee fees.
6. Harold Company paid all but Class 7 credit claims.

Required

1. Prepare a statement of realization and liquidation using the conventional approach.
2. Prepare the cash account, the income statement, and the balance sheet to accompany the statement of realization and liquidation.
3. Prepare a statement of realization and liquidation using the net book value approach.

PROBLEM 19-9

Indiana Company has been unable to meet its current obligations as they come due and is being liquidated. The trial balance of Indiana Company prior to liquidation is

	Debit	Credit
Cash	$ 23,680	
Marketable Securities	64,500	
Accounts Receivable	231,780	
Allowance for Doubtful Accounts		$ 23,870
Inventory	317,500	
Supplies	38,900	
Prepaid Insurance	8,400	
Store Fixtures	238,000	
Accumulated Depreciation: Store Fixtures		120,000
Goodwill	60,000	
Accounts Payable		372,000
Wages and Salaries Payable: Less Than $2,000 per Employee		41,300
Customer Deposits: Less Than $900 per Customer		13,400
Note Payable: Secured by Accounts Receivable		200,000
Interest Payable: Note		7,200
Loan Payable: Secured by Inventory		86,000
Interest Payable: Inventory Loan		4,300
Loan Payable: Secured by Store Fixtures		70,000
Common Stock		200,000
Additional Paid-in Capital		40,000
Retained Earnings	195,310	
Totals	$ 1,178,070	$ 1,178,070

Indiana Company entered into the following transactions during the first period of liquidation:

1. Sold the marketable securities for $60,000.
2. Collected $195,000 of the original accounts receivable and determined that the remainder is not collectible. Paid the secured portion of the claim against the accounts receivable.

3. Sold the $300,000 of inventory for $325,000, all on credit. Collected $225,000 of the receivables from the sale of inventory and paid the secured inventory claim.
4. Sold store fixtures with a cost of $175,000 and an accumulated depreciation of $65,000 for $82,400. Paid the secured claim against the store fixtures.
5. Consumed $18,000 of supplies during the period and $4,200 of prepaid insurance expired.
6. Paid the priority (class 1–6) claims.
7. Incurred $12,300 of liquidation costs.

Required

1. Prepare a statement of realization and liquidation using the conventional approach.
2. Prepare the cash account, the income statement, and the balance sheet to accompany the statement of realization and liquidation.
3. Prepare a statement of realization and liquidation using the net book value approach.
4. If the remaining receivables are 100% collectible, the remaining inventory is worth $3,160, the remaining store fixtures have a scrap value of $2,000, and the supplies and prepaid insurance will be consumed in completing the liquidation, what is the dividend that will be paid to the unsecured creditors?

SOLUTIONS TO REVIEW PROBLEMS

TROUBLED DEBT RESTRUCTURINGS

1.

Debtor Corporation

Office Building (1)	55,000	
Gain on Transfer of Plant Assets		55,000
To record gain on assets to be transferred in settlement of debt		

(1) $210,000 − ($290,000 − $135,000) = $55,000

Note Payable	250,000	
Interest Payable	25,000	
Accumulated Depreciation: Office Building	135,000	
Office Building (1)		345,000
Extraordinary Gain: Debt Restructuring		65,000
To record the gain on settlement of debt		

(1) $290,000 + $55,000 = $345,000

Creditor Corporation

Office Building	210,000	
Loss on Settlement of Receivable	65,000	
Note Receivable		250,000
Interest Receivable		25,000
To record loss on settlement of receivable		

2.

Debtor Corporation

Note Payable	250,000	
Interest Payable	25,000	
Preferred Stock		200,000
Additional Paid-in Capital: Preferred Stock		30,000
Extraordinary Gain: Debt Restructuring		45,000
To record the gain on settlement of debt		

Creditor Corporation

Investment Debtor Corporation Preferred Stock	230,000	
Loss on Settlement of Receivable	45,000	
Note Receivable		250,000
Interest Receivable		25,000
To record loss on settlement of receivable		

3.

Future Cash Flows After Restructuring	
Principal	$ 200,000
Interest ($200,000 × 8%)	16,000
Total Cash To Be Received	216,000
Net Book Value of Debt Prior to Restructuring	275,000
Gain or Loss To Be Recognized from Restructuring	$ 49,000

Debtor Corporation

Interest Payable	25,000	
Note Payable	24,000	
Extraordinary Gain on Debt Restructuring		49,000

Creditor Corporation

Loss on Debt Restructuring	49,000	
Note Receivable		24,000
Interest Receivable		25,000

4.

Debtor Corporation

Loss on Disposition of Machinery (1)	5,000	
Machinery		5,000

(1) $65,000 − ($88,000 − $18,000) = ($5,000)

Note Payable	40,000	
Interest Payable	25,000	
Accumulated Depreciation	18,000	
Machinery		83,000

Creditor Corporation

Machinery	65,000	
Note Receivable		40,000
Interest Receivable		25,000

Future Cash Flow After Restructuring

Principal	$ 210,000
Present Value of an Annuity at 6% for 4 periods	÷ 3.4651
Equal Annual Payment	60,604
Number of Payments	× 4
Total Cash To Be Received	242,416
Less: Unpaid Balance of Debt	210,000
Interest Expense/Revenue	$ 32,416

Journal Entries for Payments: No gain or loss will be recorded as the future payments exceed the balance due on the contract.

Debtor Corporation

Year 1	Interest Expense ($210,000 × 6%)	12,600	
	Note Payable ($60,604 − $12,600)	48,004	
	Cash		60,604
Year 2	Interest Expense [($210,000 − $48,004) × 6%]	9,720	
	Note Payable ($60,604 − $9,720)	50,884	
	Cash		60,604
Year 3	Interest Expense [($161,996 − $50,884) × 6%]	6,667	
	Note Payable ($60,604 − $6,667)	53,937	
	Cash		60,604
Year 4	Interest Expense [($111,112 − $53,937) × 6%]	3,429	
	Note Payable ($60,604 − $6,667)	57,175	
	Cash		60,604

Creditor Corporation

Year 1	Cash	60,604	
	Interest Revenue		12,600
	Note Receivable		48,004
Year 2	Cash	60,604	
	Interest Revenue		9,720
	Note Receivable		50,884
Year 3	Cash	60,604	
	Interest Revenue		6,667
	Note Receivable		53,937
Year 4	Cash	60,604	
	Interest Revenue		3,429
	Note Receivable		57,175

QUASI-REORGANIZATION

Patent	35,000	
Retained Earnings	395,000	
Land and Buildings		290,000
Equipment		140,000
To revalue assets to fair market value		

Common Stock		3,125,000		
Additional Paid-in Capital			3,125,000	
To reduce par value to $12.50 per share				
Additional Paid-in Capital (1)		2,540,000		
Retained Earnings			2,540,000	
To eliminate retained earnings deficit				

(1) $2,145,000 + $395,000 = $2,540,000

REORGANIZATION AND LIQUIDATION

1.

EVERETT COMPANY
Statement of Affairs
March 15, 1990

Net Book Value	Assets	Expected Net Realizable Value	Estimated Amount for Unsecured Creditors	(Loss) or Gain on Realization
	Assets Pledged with Fully Secured Creditors			
$ 37,200	Accounts Receivable	$ 29,000		$(8,200)
	Note Payable and Interest Payable	26,500	$ 2,500	
	Assets Pledged with Partially Secured Creditors			
77,000	Land and Building	67,500		(9,500)
	Mortgage Payable and Interest Payable	67,500		
	Free Assets			
5,100	Cash	5,100		
71,000	Inventory	40,000		(31,000)
4,700	Supplies	2,400		(2,300)
20,000	Store Fixtures	8,500		(11,500)
9,000	Goodwill	–0–	56,000	(9,000)
	Total Estimated Amount Available		58,500	
	Less: Creditors With Priority		26,900	
	Net Amount Expected for Unsecured Creditors (62 cents on the dollar)		31,600	
	Estimated Deficiency to Unsecured Creditors (38 cents on the dollar)		19,100	
$224,000			$ 50,700	$(71,500)

Continued on following page

EVERETT COMPANY
Statement of Affairs Continued
March 15, 1990

Net Book Value	Equities	Secured Claims	Priority Claims	Unsecured Claims
	Liabilities with Priority			
$ 13,000	Wages and Employee Benefits Payable		$ 12,000	$ 1,000
6,400	Business Receipts Tax Payable		6,400	
8,500	Liquidation Costs		8,500	
	Fully Secured Liabilities			
25,000	Note Payable	$ 25,000		
1,500	Interest Payable	1,500		
	Partially Secured Liabilities			
75,000	Mortgage Payable	63,300		11,700
4,200	Interest Payable	4,200		
	Unsecured Claims			
38,000	Accounts Payable			38,000
	Stockholders' Equity			
100,000	Common Stock			
18,000	Additional Paid-in Capital			
(65,600)	Retained Earnings (1)			
$ 224,000		$ 94,000	$ 26,900	$ 50,700

(1) $57,100 + $8,500 of liquidation costs = $65,600

Proof of Results

Net Book Value of Assets			$ 224,000
Less: Estimated Losses			71,500
Total Amount Available for Creditors			152,500
Less: Secured Claims		$ 94,000	
Priority Claims: Classes 1–6		26,900	120,900
Amount Available for Unsecured Creditors			$ 31,600
Or: Total Stockholders' Equity per Statement			$ 52,400
Less: Estimated Losses			71,500
Deficiency to Creditors			$(19,100)

2. 1)

EVERETT COMPANY
Statement of Realization and Liquidation
Conventional Approach

Assets

Assets to be Realized			*Assets Realized*		
Accounts Receivable	$ 39,600		Land and Building		$ 70,000
Less: Allowance for			Inventory		31,500
Doubtful Accounts	2,400	$ 37,200	Accounts Receivable		31,000
Inventory		71,000	Supplies		2,350
Supplies		4,700			
Land		25,000	*Assets Not Realized*		
Building	100,000		Accounts Receivable		5,500
Less: Accumulated			Accounts Receivable—new		7,500
Depreciation	48,000	52,000	Inventory		36,000
Store Fixtures	36,000		Store Fixtures	$ 36,000	
Less: Accumulated			Less: Accumulated		
Depreciation	16,000	20,000	Depreciation	16,800	19,200
Goodwill		9,000			
Assets Acquired					
Accounts Receivable—new		7,500			

Liabilities

Liabilities Liquidated		*Liabilities to be Liquidated*	
Interest Payable	4,200	Accounts Payable	38,000
Mortgage Payable	65,000	Employee Wages and Benefits	
Note Payable	25,000	Payable	13,000
Interest Payable	1,500	Business Receipts Tax Payable	6,400
Employee Wages and Benefits		Note Payable	25,000
Payable	12,000	Interest Payable: Note	1,500
Business Receipts Tax Payable	6,400	Mortgage Payable	75,000
		Interest Payable: Mortgage	4,200
Liabilities Not Liquidated		*Liabilities Assumed*	
Accounts Payable—old	37,200		
Employee Wages and Benefits			
Payable	1,000		
Mortgage Payable	10,000		

Income Statement

Supplementary Expenses		*Supplementary Revenues*	–0–
Interest Expense	800		
		Loss for the Period	23,350
	$ 389,500		$ 389,500

2. 2)

		Cash	
Beginning Balance	5,100	Payment of Mortgage Interest	5,000
Sale Land and Building	70,000	Payment of Mortgage Principal	65,000
Sale of Inventory	24,000	Payment of Interest on Note	1,500
Collection of Receivables	31,000	Payment of Note	25,000
Sale of Supplies	2,350	Payment of Wages	12,000
		Payment of Receipts Tax	6,400
	132,450		114,900
Balance	17,550		

EVERETT COMPANY
Income Statement
First Reporting Period

Sales of Inventory		$ 31,500
Sales of Supplies		2,350
Total Sales		33,850
Cost of Sales		
Inventory	$ 35,000	
Supplies	4,700	39,700
Gross Margin		(5,850)
Expenses		
Interest	800	
Bad Debts Not Provided for	700	
Depreciation	800	2,300
Operating Loss		(8,150)
Gain: Unrecorded Credit Memo		800
Losses		
Sale of Land and Building	7,000	
Write-off of Goodwill	9,000	(16,000)
Net Income		$ (23,350)

EVERETT COMPANY
Balance Sheet
End of First Reporting Period

Assets		Liabilities	
Cash	$ 17,550	Accounts Payable	$ 37,200
Accounts Receivable	13,000	Wages and Benefits Payable	1,000
Inventory	36,000	Mortgage Payable	10,000
Store Fixtures: Net	19,200	Total Liabilities	48,200
		Stockholders' Equity	
		Common Stock	100,000
		Additional Paid-in Capital	18,000
		Retained Earnings (1)	(80,450)
Total Assets	$ 85,750	Total Equities	$ 85,750

(1) Beginning Balance of Retained Earnings	$(57,100)
Net Loss	(23,350)
Ending Balance of Retained Earnings	$ 80,450

2. 3)

Transaction 1: The amount for asset realized is $77,000 the net book value of the land and the building. In addition, the loss of $7,000 is recorded in the income statement section as a supplementary expense.

Transaction 2: The $31,500 cash received for the inventory is reported in the income statement section as a supplementary revenue. The amount reported as an asset realized is the cost of the inventory of $35,000 and is reported in the income section as a supplementary expense.

Transaction 3: The $700 of uncollectible accounts in excess of the allowance provided is reported in the income section as a supplementary expense.

Transaction 4: The $2,350 cash from the sale of supplies is reported as a supplementary revenue. The cost of the supplies of $4,700 is reported as an asset realized and as a supplementary expense.

Transaction 6: The $800 from the unrecorded credit memo is reported as a supplementary revenue.

Transaction 7: The $800 of depreciation is reported as a supplementary expense and as an asset realized.

NONBUSINESS ORGANIZATIONS
AND NOT-FOR-PROFIT HOSPITALS

C hapters 20 through 23 discuss and illustrate the accounting and financial reporting for non-business organizations: not-for-profit (nonprofit) organizations and governmental units. The fund theory of equity is applicable to these entities. As discussed in Chapter 1, when the entity is viewed from the fund theory of equity, the emphasis is on assets: custodianship of assets, responsibility for the use of assets, accountability for assets, and restrictions on the use of assets. The method of accounting and reporting is called **fund accounting.** A **fund** is a fiscal and accounting entity with a self-balancing set of accounts used to account for a specific set of activities. A nonbusiness entity typically uses several funds to account for all its activities. In Chapter 18, the use of two funds, Principal and Income, is illustrated in the accounting for estates and trusts.

The approach that we are using in the discussion of nonbusiness organizations is to start with the organizations most like business entities and progress toward those least like business entities. This chapter begins with a general discussion of nonbusiness organizations. Accounting and reporting for not-for-profit hospitals, which are the nonbusiness organizations that are closest to business enterprises in their accounting and reporting, follows the general discussion. Chapter 21 illustrates accounting and financial reporting for voluntary health and welfare organizations and concludes with a discussion of accounting and financial reporting for other not-for-profit organizations, such as churches, fraternal organizations, and trade or professional associations. Chapter 22 covers accounting and financial reporting for not-for-profit colleges and universities. Chapter 23 illustrates accounting and financial reporting for governmental units.

The topics of nonbusiness entities are

- Types of nonbusiness organizations
- Definition of a nonbusiness organization
- Basis of accounting

813

The topics of not-for-profit hospitals are

- Unrestricted or discretionary funds including the general fund and the board-designated funds
- Donor-restricted funds including specific-purpose funds, plant replacement and expansion funds, and endowment funds
- General fund revenues including patient service revenues, other operating revenues, and nonoperating revenues
- General fund expenses
- Depreciable assets and depreciation
- Transfers to and from funds
- Financial statements including a statement of revenues and expenses for the general fund, and the balance sheet and statement of changes in fund balances for all the funds
- Closing journal entry for the general fund

NONBUSINESS ORGANIZATIONS

Nonbusiness organizations are usually divided into five major categories.

1. **Not-for-Profit Hospitals.**
2. **Voluntary Health and Welfare Organizations** (Human Service Organizations). These are organizations that derive their funds from the voluntary contributions of the general public to be used for health, welfare, and community services. Among the organizations in this category are lung and heart associations, hearing and speech centers, halfway houses for runaways, shelters for abused women and children, and mental health clinics.
3. **Not-for-Profit Colleges and Universities.**
4. **Other Not-for-Profit Organizations.** This category includes all the nonbusiness nongovernmental organizations that are not included in the first three categories. These organizations include cemetery associations, civic organizations, fraternal organizations, labor unions, libraries, museums, other cultural institutions, performing arts associations, political parties, private and community foundations, private grade and high schools, professional associations, public broadcasting stations, religious organizations, research and scientific organizations, social and country clubs, trade associations, and zoological and botanical societies.[1]
5. **Governmental Units.** These include federal, state and local governments, school districts, special assessment districts for water, sewers, roads, and other public services, as well as other special districts for ports, industrial development, soil and water conservation, and sanitary districts.

These nonbusiness organizations make up a substantial portion of the economic activity of the United States and other developed nations. Expenditures of these organizations represent approximately 40% of the gross national product of the United States and other developed

---

[1] *Audit and Accounting Guide, Audits of Certain Nonprofit Organizations* (New York: AICPA, 1981), pages 1 and 2.

nations. All of us provide resources, either voluntarily or otherwise, to these nonbusiness enterprises.

DEFINITION OF A NONBUSINESS ORGANIZATION

Statement of Financial Accounting Concepts No. 4 states that the following characteristics distinguish a nonbusiness enterprise from a business enterprise and provide the elements necessary to derive a general definition of a nonbusiness organization:

- Receipts of significant amounts of assets from providers who do not expect to receive either repayment or economic benefits proportionate to the assets provided.
- Operating purposes that are other than to provide goods or services at a profit or a profit equivalent.
- The absence of defined ownership interest that can be sold, transferred, or redeemed, or that conveys rights to a share of the distribution of assets in the event of liquidation.[2]

The general definition of a nonbusiness organization derived from these characteristics is it is an entity that receives assets without having to either repay or provide a reasonable rate of return for the assets, its purposes are not profit oriented, and it lacks defined ownership.

A nonbusiness organization receives assets from a variety of sources. The governing board of the organization can either use the assets at their discretion or use the assets only for the purpose specified by the donor. For example, an alumnus may donate cash to his alma mater to use as the university chooses or an alumna may donate cash to her alma mater for scholarships for accounting majors, in which case the university can only use the cash as scholarships for accounting majors.

A nonbusiness organization is an entity that does not have profit, but the provision of services without profit making, as the prime motive for existence. Within a nonbusiness organization, however, a profit center or business enterprise may exist. For example, a city may provide water and sewer services to its residents and charge a fee for those services that is sufficient to not only cover expenses, but to provide for debt service and capital improvements, thus earning a profit.

It is not possible to determine precisely who the owners are of a nonbusiness organization. For example, who are the owners of the local chapter of the American Red Cross—the donors who contribute assets, or the people who are currently receiving assistance, or the public at large?

BASIS OF ACCOUNTING

Accrual accounting is required for almost all not-for-profit entities even though the determination of income is not the goal of these entities. Instead the goal is to measure the extent to which these entities have met their objectives. Within the governmental units, some of the

---

[2] *Statement of Financial Accounting Concepts No. 4, Objectives of Financial Reporting by Nonbusiness Organizations* (Stamford, Connecticut, FASB, 1980), paragraph 6.

funds use accrual accounting and some use the modified accrual basis of accounting. Governmental units generally use accrual accounting for funds that charge a fee sufficient to cover the cost of the service provided, and the modified accrual basis for the funds that provide services to the public without receiving revenue for the service.

ACCOUNTING AND FINANCIAL REPORTING FOR NOT-FOR-PROFIT HOSPITALS

Hospitals can be investor-owned entities operated for a profit. Hospitals can also be government-owned entities or be affiliated with other not-for-profit entities such as universities, churches, and fraternal organizations that are operated without profit as the objective. Regardless of the ownership, generally accepted accounting principles are the same for all hospitals.

Hospitals are very similar to profit-oriented business entities because they provide products and services to the patients for a fee that frequently is more than the cost of the product or service provided to the patient. Generally accepted accounting principles used for business enterprises are applicable to both profit-oriented and not-for-profit hospitals. Accounting and auditing standards for hospitals, particularly not-for-profit hospitals, are contained in the AICPA's *Hospital Audit Guide* and modified by *Statements of Position 78-1, 78-7, and 85-1*. In addition to the pronouncements of the accounting profession, the American Hospital Association has issued *Chart of Accounts for Hospitals*. The American Hospital Association has recommended that hospitals use price-level accounting for plant and equipment, which is not in accordance with generally accepted accounting principles.

This chapter discusses accounting and financial reporting only for those hospitals that are not-for-profit entities. Not-for-profit hospitals typically use two broad classes of funds: unrestricted funds and donor-restricted funds. **Unrestricted funds** are resources that the board of directors of the hospital can use at its discretion. **Donor-restricted funds** are resources whose use has been specified or restricted by the contributor of the resources. Some hospitals will also have agency funds, in which they collect revenues that belong to another entity, such as collecting the fee for the doctor who interprets the x-rays.

UNRESTRICTED FUNDS

Unrestricted funds are often referred to as discretionary funds because the board of directors of the hospital may use the assets of these funds to operate the hospital in the manner it decides is best. The unrestricted funds are usually classified into two types: a general fund and board-designated funds.[3] If a hospital has donor-restricted funds, they are classified as specific-purpose funds, plant replacement and expansion funds, and endowment funds.

---

[3] *The Exposure Draft, Proposed Audit and Accounting Guide, Audits of Providers of Health Care Services*, issued March 15, 1988 recommends the designation "general fund." The previous standards referred to this fund as an operating fund.

GENERAL FUND

The general fund consists of the operating assets, the liabilities, the revenues, and the expenses needed to operate the hospital. Thus the general fund of a not-for-profit hospital contains the same assets, liabilities, revenues, and expenses as are included in the accounts of a hospital operated for a profit. In addition, a not-for-profit hospital may have revenue accounts that reflect contributions to the hospital in the form of cash, assets, or pledges of cash or assets. Because the various funds are separate fiscal and accounting entities within the reporting entity, the not-for-profit hospital, transfers of assets between the funds are often necessary or desirable. The general fund can have the asset account **Due from Other Funds,** which reflects assets that are to be transferred, but have not yet been transferred to the general fund. The general fund can also have the liability account **Due to Other Funds,** which reflects the amount of the assets of the general fund that are to be transferred to other funds, but have not yet been transferred.

BOARD-DESIGNATED FUNDS

The board of directors of a hospital may, at its discretion, set aside some of the assets of the general fund to be used for a specific purpose or purposes. The assets set aside are usually cash or investments. These board-designated funds can be used for the purchase of equipment, or additions to the hospital building, or research. Because the board has discretionary power over these funds, it can also return the assets or a portion of the assets to the general fund, should it decide that the transfers are necessary. At the board's discretion, the earnings of the board-designated fund's assets may be left in the board-designated fund or transferred to the general fund.

DONOR-RESTRICTED FUNDS

The donor-restricted funds of a hospital consist of three general types: specific-purpose funds, plant replacement and expansion funds, and endowment funds. These funds are called donor-restricted funds because the board of directors and administrators of the hospital may not use the assets of these funds except as specified by the donor of the assets. The entity giving the assets to the hospital has restricted their use to a specific purpose or purposes.

SPECIFIC-PURPOSE FUNDS

The specific-purpose funds are used to account for assets given to the hospital to be used for specific operating purposes. For example, the Women's Auxiliary of the Hospital (an independent entity) earns $2,000, which it donates to the hospital for the purchase of rocking chairs for the nursery. The hospital can use the assets only for this purpose and for no other acquisition. If the hospital can spend only the earnings from the assets contributed and not the assets, the contribution is accounted for in an endowment fund rather than a specific-purpose fund.

PLANT REPLACEMENT AND EXPANSION FUNDS

The plant replacement and expansion funds are used to account for assets given to the hospital specifically for the acquisition of property, plant, and equipment. Thus these assets cannot be used for other purposes by the board of directors of the hospital. Plant replacement and expansion funds are a special type of specific-purpose funds. The property, plant, and equipment of a typical hospital represents the majority of the hospital's assets. Therefore, the funds for replacement and expansion of existing facilities are accounted for separately from other specific-purpose funds. Assets that the board of directors has set aside (designated) for the purpose of acquiring property, plant, and equipment are not included in the plant replacement and expansion fund, but in a board-designated fund, since the board has discretionary power over the assets, and can return the assets to the general fund at any time.

ENDOWMENT FUNDS

Endowment funds are used to account for specific assets donated to the hospital, which cannot be used but must be preserved. The assets donated are accounted for in a manner similar to the principal assets of an estate or trust. The assets donated must be preserved and only the income can be spent. If the principal of the endowment must be maintained in perpetuity, the fund is called a **permanent endowment.** If the endowment has a limited life, at the end of which the principal can be used for the purposes specified by the donor, the endowment is called a **term endowment.**

The donor may not have placed any restrictions on the use of the income. If the income is unrestricted, the income is transferred to the general fund and recognized as revenue in the year earned. On the other hand, the donor may have placed restrictions on the use of the income. If the restriction is for a specific operating purpose, the income is transferred to a specific-purpose fund, or if the restriction is for plant replacement and expansion, the income is transferred to that fund. If the donor has stated that the income cannot be spent for a period of years for any purpose, the income remains in the endowment fund and increases the balance of the fund. Gains and losses from the sale of investments are usually treated as changes in principal and, therefore, change the equity account, **Fund Balance.** When a term endowment matures, the assets are transferred to the appropriate fund and recognized in the same manner as the income from the endowment assets.

HOSPITAL REVENUES

A hospital receives revenue from a wide variety of sources. Hospital revenues are divided into three broad categories or classes:

1. Patient service revenues
2. Other operating revenues
3. Nonoperating revenues

PATIENT SERVICE REVENUES

Patient Service revenues are operating revenues from providing services to patients. These operating revenues come from three major sources: revenue from daily patient services, revenue from other nursing services, and revenue from other professional services. The revenue from daily patient services includes revenue from room, board, and general nursing services. Revenue from other nursing services includes charges for operating rooms, recovery rooms, delivery and labor rooms, and other direct patient care. Revenues for other professional services provided to the patients consist of revenues from x-rays, laboratory work, medications, physical therapy, and other services directly provided to patients.

These revenues are collected from the patients and from third-party payors. **Third-party payments** consist of health insurance company payments for insured medical care, Medicare and Medicaid payments for qualified patients, and state and local welfare agencies' payments for services provided to citizens under the agencies' care. Because these third-party payors place limits on the amounts they will pay for any particular service provided to a patient, payments frequently are for less than the amount of the service billed. If the hospital is unable to collect the difference between the revenue billed and the amount paid by the third-party payor from the patient, the difference is treated as an adjustment of revenues rather than as an expense. This difference is called a **contractual adjustment.**

Just as a profit-making entity incurs bad debts from extending credit, a hospital has uncollectible accounts either from services rendered to patients without a third-party payor, or on the balance owing after payment by a third-party payor. The estimate of bad debt expense for the period is also treated as an adjustment of revenue, rather than as an expense, and the contra asset account, Allowance for Uncollectible Accounts, is credited.

A not-for-profit hospital frequently provides services to patients who neither have the ability to pay nor are covered by any of the third-party payors. Thus the third adjustment to patient service revenues comes from charity care provided to patients. The fourth adjustment to patient services revenues that might be recorded is discounts granted to members of religious orders, volunteers, and employees.

An example of operating revenue recognition, a not-for-profit hospital provided $11,200,000 of services to patients. The hospital made contractual adjustments based on the payments of third-party payors of $235,000, and provided $110,000 of charity care to patients. The hospital estimates that $98,000 of the amounts owed by patients responsible for their own charges for services provided during the current year will not be collected. The summary journal entries to record these patient service revenues are

Accounts and Notes Receivable	11,200,000	
Patient Services Revenues		11,200,000
To record the revenues from services provided to patients during the current year		
Contractual Adjustments	235,000	
Charity Services	110,000	
Provision for Uncollectible Accounts	98,000	
Accounts and Notes Receivable		345,000
Allowance for Uncollectible Accounts		98,000
To record the adjustments to services revenues for the year		

OTHER OPERATING REVENUES

In addition to the patient service revenues, the other operating revenues that a hospital might earn come from a variety of sources. These include transfers from donor-restricted funds for operations, tuition from nursing and medical students, cafeteria revenues, parking fees, gift shop operations, and other activities indirectly related to patient care. Donated medicines and medical supplies are also included in other operating revenues and recorded at their fair market value.

For example, a not-for-profit hospital received $24,000 from meals sold in the hospital cafeteria and $25,000 from tuition from nursing and x-ray technician students, interns, and residents. In addition, the hospital received drugs and other medical supplies with a fair market value of $15,000 that were donated by several different drug companies. The summary journal entry to record these transactions is

Cash	49,000	
Supplies Inventory	15,000	
Other Operating Revenues		64,000

To record other operating revenues received in cash and drugs and supplies donated at their fair market value

Just as a profit-making organization records the receipt of noncash assets at their fair market value, a not-for-profit hospital also records the receipt of noncash assets at their fair market value. Therefore, the drugs and medical supplies donated are recorded at their fair market value.

When a not-for-profit hospital incurs operating expenses for a specific purpose that are to be paid for with restricted use donated assets, a journal entry is prepared that records either the assets that are to be transferred or are transferred and recognizes revenue equal to the amount of the expense incurred. For example, a not-for-profit hospital spent $4,100 on hospice care that is being funded by a specific-purpose fund established to account for donations from the Ladies Auxiliary, an independent entity. The expenses of the hospice care are included with the operating expenses of the hospital. The summary journal entry to record these transactions is

Due from Other Funds: Specific-Purpose Fund	4,100	
Other Operating Revenues		4,100

To record amount due from the specific-purpose fund for hospice care provided by hospital personnel

NONOPERATING REVENUES

In addition to the many sources of operating revenues, a hospital receives revenues from sources that are not directly or indirectly related to patient care. The sources of nonoperating revenue include unrestricted income earned on the assets in the endowment funds, unrestricted expired term endowments, earnings from unrestricted investments in either the general fund or the board-designated fund, gains and losses from the sales of assets, direct donations of both cash and other assets that are unrestricted, pledges of cash and/or assets that are unrestricted, and donated services. Because not all people and other entities who make pledges to not-for-profit organizations pay the entire amount pledged, an allowance for uncollectible pledges is established. Although a pledge to a nonbusiness organization is legally collectible, most not-for-profit institutions are reluctant to press the collection because of the adverse publicity it could create, and they simply write off the pledges they are unable to collect against the Allowance for Uncollectible Pledges.

Some not-for-profit hospitals receive services donated by individuals. These people may be members of the community or members of a church or religious order. These services are recorded as nonoperating revenue based on the fair market value of the services provided to the hospital and as a corresponding expense recorded in the appropriate expense accounts if the following conditions are met:

- The services are material to the hospital's operations and would be performed by salaried personnel if not for the donated services.
- The hospital controls the employment and duties of the volunteers in the same manner as salaried employees.
- The value of the donated services can be measured.[4]

The donated services are classified as both a revenue and an expense to allow the hospital to determine the total cost of patient care and to make the financial statements comparable to a hospital operated as a profit-making entity. The following examples illustrate the types of nonoperating revenues that a not-for-profit hospital might receive during an accounting period.

Unrestricted Revenue Earned by Endowment Funds. The endowment funds earned $27,500 in unrestricted income during the current year and $24,000 of the income was transferred to the general fund. The summary journal entry to record these transactions is

Cash	24,000	
Due from Other Funds: Endowment Funds	3,500	
Nonoperating Revenues: Unrestricted Endowment Fund		
Income		27,500
To record the unrestricted income earned by the endowment funds		
and the amounts transferred from the endowment fund		

Earnings on Investments and Gains and Losses from the Sale of Investments. The board-designated fund earned $56,200 in interest revenue, had a gain of $7,500 on the sale of marketable securities, and none of the board-designated fund's earnings were transferred to the general fund during the year. The summary journal entry to record these transactions is

Due from Other Funds: Board-Designated Fund	63,700	
Nonoperating Revenues: Interest Revenue		56,200
Nonoperating Revenues: Gain on Sale of Securities		7,500
To record the interest revenue and gains of the board-designated fund		

---

[4] *Exposure Draft, Proposed Audit and Accounting Guide, Audits of Providers of Health Care Services* (New York: AICPA, 1988), page 13.

Unrestricted Donations. The hospital received $105,000 in cash from donations during the current year that were not restricted in use.

Cash	105,000	
Nonoperating Revenues: Unrestricted Donations		105,000
To record the donations received during the current year		

Donated Services. The hospital received $60,000 in donated services during the year that meet the recording criteria. The $60,000 in donated services represents the fair market value of the time donated by volunteer help in the emergency room and is considered a nursing services expense. The summary journal entry to record these transactions is

Nursing Services Expenses	60,000	
Nonoperating Revenues: Donated Services		60,000
To record the donated services received during the current year		

HOSPITAL EXPENSES

The expenses of a hospital are usually divided into six broad categories: nursing services expenses, other professional services expenses, general services expenses, fiscal services expenses, administrative service expenses including interest, and provision for depreciation expense. The summary journal entry that a hospital records for its expenses incurred on account during the operating period is

Nursing Services Expenses	4,270,000	
Other Professional Services Expenses	1,230,000	
General Services Expenses	1,280,000	
Fiscal Services Expenses	450,000	
Administrative Services Expenses	514,000	
Accounts Payable		7,744,000
To record the expenses incurred as payables during the current year		

DEPRECIABLE ASSETS AND DEPRECIATION

In addition to land and buildings, hospitals typically classify equipment into three major categories: fixed equipment, major movable equipment, and minor equipment. The fixed equipment and the major movable equipment are depreciated; the minor equipment is not depreciated. Usually this equipment is simply inventoried at the end of the accounting period, and the difference between the beginning balance plus purchases less the inventory of minor equipment on hand at the end of the period is recorded as an expense of the period. Thus minor equipment is accounted for like a supplies account in a profit-making organization.

Prior to January 1990, many not-for-profit organizations were not required to record depreciation for their fixed assets, but now they must record depreciation regardless of how the assets were financed.[5] Hospitals, however, have been required to record depreciation since 1973.

For example, a not-for-profit hospital determined that depreciation expense was $1,040,000 for the year: $410,000 for buildings, $385,000 for fixed equipment, and $245,000 for major movable equipment. The inventory of minor equipment on hand at the end of the fiscal year showed a shrinkage of $136,000. The shrinkage in minor equipment is to be allocated equally between the nursing services and the other professional services. The journal entries to record these adjustments are

Provision for Depreciation Expense	1,040,000	
Accumulated Depreciation: Building		410,000
Accumulated Depreciation: Fixed Equipment		385,000
Accumulated Depreciation: Major Movable Equipment		245,000
To record depreciation expense for the current fiscal year		
Nursing Services Expense	68,000	
Other Professional Services Expense	68,000	
Minor Equipment		136,000
To record the cost of minor equipment lost or damaged during the current year		

TRANSFERS TO AND FROM FUNDS

Because each fund or group of funds is a separate fiscal and accounting entity, cash or other assets transferred from one fund to another are recorded and accounted for in the financial records. The transfers between funds can be either **mandatory** or **nonmandatory**—at the discretion of the board of directors. When a donor contributes assets whose use is restricted, revenue is not recognized. When the expenditure is incurred that meets the donor's restriction, revenue is recognized equal to the expenditure and assets are transferred to the general fund equal to the expenditure—a mandatory transfer. If the use of the income of an endowment fund is not restricted by the donor, the income is recognized in the general fund when earned and assets equal to the income are transferred to the operating fund—a mandatory transfer.

---

[5] *Statement of Financial Accounting Standards No. 93, Recognition of Depreciation by Not-for-Profit Organizations,* (Stamford, Connecticut: FASB), 1987. This pronouncement established the effective date as May 1988. *Statement of Financial Accounting Standards No. 99, Deferral of the Effective Date of Recognition of Depreciation by Not-for-Profit Organizations, an amendment of FASB Statement No. 93* (Stamford, Connecticut: FASB, 1988) delayed the recognition of depreciation to January 1, 1990.

Transfers between the general fund and the board-designated funds are discretionary transfers by the board of directors and are simply transfers of assets with no revenue recognition, as revenue was recognized when the assets were initially received. If cash or assets have been either committed to transfer by the board of directors or are mandatory, but have not been transferred, the asset and liability accounts used are Due from Other Funds and Due to Other Funds.

The journal entries recording the endowment fund income and the revenues for hospice care from the specific-purpose fund in the previous discussion of nonoperating revenue recognition are examples of mandatory transfers to the general fund. The journal entry recording the interest earned and the gain on the sale of securities by the board-designated fund illustrated under nonoperating revenues is an example of a discretionary transfer to the general fund.

FINANCIAL STATEMENTS

The financial statements of a not-for-profit hospital consist of a statement of revenues and expenses, a balance sheet, a statement of changes in fund balances, and a statement of cash flows.[6] Because each of the funds is a separate fiscal and accounting entity with different accountability, the balance sheet and statement of changes in fund balances of a not-for-profit hospital report the assets, liabilities, and fund balance of each of the hospital's funds separately rather than for the entire entity, the hospital.

Illustrative Problem 20.1 demonstrates the summary transaction, adjusting, and closing journal entries that a not-for-profit hospital records for the transactions and events affecting the various funds used by a typical hospital. The previous journal entries illustrating revenue and expense recognition are used in the illustrative problem. The previous entries that are used will not repeat the information necessary to prepare the entry. These entries are presented on a fund by fund basis. Illustrative Problem 20.1 also presents the statement of revenues and expenses for the general fund, and the balance sheet and the statement of changes in fund balances for all the funds. A statement of cash flows is not presented, although a complete set of financial statements would include that statement for the general fund. This illustrative problem uses only the typical control accounts or general categories of accounts previously discussed that are in the general ledger of a not-for-profit hospital.

As hospitals can be very large organizations, substantially more detail regarding receivables, inventory, fixed assets, liabilities, revenues, and expenses are recorded in the accounts of a typical hospital. Some of this detail is designed to provide control over and accountability for assets, liabilities, revenues, and expenses, and some is maintained to enable the hospital to budget, plan, and manage the operations of the institution. For the purpose of understanding the basic accounting and reporting, however, the use of the major control accounts, major

---

[6]*Exposure Draft, Proposed Audit and Accounting Guide, Audits of Providers of Health Care Services* (New York: AICPA, 1988). The exposure draft calls the statement of cash flows a statement of changes in financial position and recommends the cash basis. We have chosen to use the current title, assuming that a statement of cash flows will be the title used when the final version of the audit guide is released.

categories of accounts, and major groups of accounts will enable us to introduce you to accounting and reporting for a not-for-profit hospital.

ILLUSTRATIVE PROBLEM 20.I: ACCOUNTING AND FINANCIAL REPORTING FOR A NOT-FOR-PROFIT HOSPITAL

Monroe Community Hospital is a full-service, not-for-profit hospital serving the town of Monroe and the neighboring small towns.

UNRESTRICTED FUNDS

On July 1, 1990, the beginning of Monroe Community Hospital's fiscal year, the trial balance of the general fund was

	Debit	Credit
Cash	$ 125,000	
Accounts and Notes Receivable	565,000	
Allowance for Uncollectible Receivables		$ 74,000
Due from Other Funds	25,000	
Supplies Inventory	102,000	
Prepaid Expenses	18,000	
Land	1,250,000	
Buildings	12,540,000	
Accumulated Depreciation: Buildings		5,650,000
Fixed Equipment	2,870,000	
Accumulated Depreciation: Fixed Equipment		920,000
Major Movable Equipment	1,840,000	
Accumulated Depreciation: Major Movable Equipment		630,000
Minor Equipment	645,000	
Accounts Payable		1,130,000
Accrued Expenses Payable		104,000
Mortgage Payable		7,100,000
Fund Balance		4,372,000
	$ 19,980,000	$ 19,980,000

GENERAL FUND TRANSACTIONS

The following entries were recorded in the general fund accounts of Monroe Community Hospital for the year ended June 30, 1991:

Summary Revenue Transaction Entries

Accounts and Notes Receivable	11,200,000	
Patient Services Revenues		11,200,000

To record the revenues from services provided to patients during the current year

Contractual Adjustments	235,000	
Charity Services	110,000	
Provision for Uncollectible Accounts	98,000	
Accounts and Notes Receivable		345,000
Allowance for Uncollectible Accounts		98,000

To record the adjustments to services revenues for the year

Cash	49,000	
Supplies Inventory	15,000	
Other Operating Revenues		64,000

To record other revenues received in cash and drugs and supplies donated at their fair market value

Due from Other Funds	4,100	
Other Operating Revenues		4,100

To record amount due from the specific-purpose fund for hospice care provided by hospital personnel

Cash	24,000	
Due from Other Funds	3,500	
Nonoperating Revenues		27,500

To record the unrestricted income earned by the endowment funds and the amounts transferred from the endowment fund

Due from Other Funds	63,700	
Nonoperating Revenues		63,700

To record the interest revenue and gains of the board-designated fund

Cash	105,000	
Nonoperating Revenues		105,000

To record the donations received during the current year

Nursing Services Expenses	60,000	
Nonoperating Revenues		165,000

To record the services donated during the current year

Additional Transfers to the General Fund.   A 10-year endowment fund with a balance of $25,000, which matured at the end of the previous fiscal year and was recorded in the account Due from Other Funds and was recognized as revenue in the previous year, is transferred to the general fund.

Cash	25,000	
Due from Other Funds		25,000

To record the transfer of an endowment fund that expired in the prior year

A transfer of $300,000 was received from the plant replacement and expansion fund to cover a portion of the purchases and is recorded as a Transfer from Plant Replacement and Expansion Fund. An alternative is to record the transfer as an increase in the account, Fund Balance. If the account, Transfer from Plant Replacement and Expansion Fund, is used, it is closed to Fund Balance at the end of the accounting period. Rather than transfer assets to the general fund for purchases of plant and equipment, the purchases could have been made by the Plant Replacement and Expansion Fund and the purchased assets could have been transferred.

Cash	300,000	
Transfer from Plant Replacement and Expansion Fund		300,000
To record the transfer from the plant replacement and expansion fund for expenditures that are according to donors' wishes		

The funds that owe the general fund or have transferred cash to the general fund record comparable entries to reflect the assets due the general fund and the transfer of cash. Assets other than cash can be transferred to the general fund.

Summary Expense and Supplies Inventory Transaction Entries

Nursing Services Expenses	4,270,000	
Other Professional Services Expenses	1,230,000	
General Services Expenses	1,280,000	
Fiscal Services Expenses	450,000	
Administrative Services Expenses	514,000	
Accounts Payable		7,744,000
To record the expenses incurred as payables during the current year		

Supplies totaling $340,000 were purchased on account.

Supplies Inventory	340,000	
Accounts Payable		340,000
To record supplies inventory purchased on account		

Summary Cash Receipts Entries.   During the year ended June 30, 1991, Monroe Community Hospital collected $495,000 of the outstanding accounts and notes receivable at the beginning of the year and $70,000 of accounts and notes receivable were written off. Monroe also collected $10,145,000 of notes and accounts receivable from revenues earned in the current year and $23,000 of the receivables were written off.

Cash	10,640,000	
Allowance for Uncollectible Accounts	93,000	
Accounts and Notes Receivable		10,733,000
To record the collection and write-off of accounts and notes receivable		

Summary Cash Disbursements Entries.   During the year ended June 30, 1991, Monroe Community Hospital paid accrued expenses payable totaling $104,000, accounts payable totaling $8,184,000, and $54,000 for prepaid expenses. In addition, Monroe paid $1,250,000 of principal and $710,000 of interest on the mortgage on the land and building.

Prepaid Expenses	54,000	
Accrued Expenses Payable	104,000	
Accounts Payable	8,184,000	
Cash		8,342,000

To record the payment of accrued expenses payable and
accounts payable for the current year

Administrative Services Expenses	710,000	
Mortgage Payable	1,250,000	
Cash		1,960,000

To record the payments of principal and interest on the
mortgage

Summary Entries for Equipment.   During the year ended June 30, 1991, Monroe Community Hospital purchased $340,000 of fixed equipment, $195,000 of major movable equipment, and $164,000 of minor equipment. Monroe sold major movable equipment with a cost of $87,000 and accumulated depreciation of $63,000 for $19,000. Gains and losses on the sales of assets are nonoperating revenues. If the gains and losses are material in amount, they are reported separately in the statement of revenues and expenses. These transactions are recorded as follows:

Fixed Equipment	340,000	
Major Movable Equipment	195,000	
Minor Equipment	164,000	
Cash		699,000

To record the purchase of equipment during the current year

Cash	19,000	
Nonoperating Revenues	5,000	
Accumulated Depreciation: Major Movable Equipment	63,000	
Major Movable Equipment		87,000

To record the sale of equipment

Transfers From the General Fund.   On June 30, 1991, the board of directors of Monroe Community Hospital decided to transfer $200,000 of general fund cash to a board-designated fund to be used in the future to remodel the maternity wing of the hospital. The board of directors is creating a discretionary fund called a **Board-Designated Fund** that it can use either partially or entirely for the purpose stated or from which it can return the assets to the general fund. The journal entry to record this transfer is

Transfer to Board-Designated Fund	200,000	
Cash		200,000

To record the transfer of cash to a board-designated fund at the
direction of the board of directors minutes

The board-designated fund records the receipt of the cash as a transfer from the general fund.

Summary Adjusting Entries.   Not-for-profit hospitals are required to maintain their accounting records and to prepare their external financial reports on the accrual basis of accounting, just as profit-making hospitals do, using generally accepted accounting principles. At June 30, 1991, therefore, Monroe Community Hospital prepares adjusting entries just as if the hospital were a profit-making hospital.

Monroe Community Hospital used $355,000 worth of supplies during the year ended June 30, 1991: $136,000 for nursing services, $184,000 for other professional services, $15,000 for fiscal services, and $20,000 for administrative services.

Nursing Services Expenses	136,000	
Other Professional Services Expenses	184,000	
Fiscal Services Expenses	15,000	
Administrative Services Expenses	20,000	
Supplies Inventory		355,000
To record the supplies inventory used during the current year		

At June 30, 1991, Monroe Community Hospital accrued the following expenses: interest expense $71,000, nursing services expenses $3,600, other professional services $2,400, general services expenses $6,700, and administrative services $3,100.

Nursing Services Expenses	3,600	
Other Professional Services Expenses	2,400	
General Services Expenses	6,700	
Administrative Services Expenses	74,100	
Accrued Expenses Payable		86,800
To record expenses incurred but not yet recorded at year end		

Prepaid expenses in the amount of $42,000 expired during the current fiscal year. All the prepaid expenses relate to the administrative functions of the hospital.

Administrative Services Expenses	42,000	
Prepaid Expenses		42,000
To record the prepaid expenses that expired during the period		

Provision for Depreciation Expense	1,040,000	
Accumulated Depreciation: Building		410,000
Accumulated Depreciation: Fixed Equipment		385,000
Accumulated Depreciation: Major Movable Equipment		245,000
To record depreciation expense for the current fiscal year		

Nursing Services Expense	68,000	
Other Professional Services Expense	68,000	
Minor Equipment (1)		136,000
To record the cost of minor equipment lost or damaged during the current year		
(1) $645,000 + $164,000 − $673,000 = $136,000		

The adjusted trial balance of the general fund of Monroe Community Hospital for the year ended June 30, 1991 is presented in Exhibit 20-1. Not-for-profit hospitals present a statement of revenues and expenses for the general fund in their financial statements. The statement of revenues and expenses of the general fund is presented in Exhibit 20-2. The balance sheet and statement of changes in fund balances are typically presented showing all of the various funds of the hospital.

EXHIBIT 20-1

Illustrative Problem 20.1
Monroe Community Hospital
Adjusted Trial Balance: General Fund
June 30, 1991

	Debit	Credit
Cash	$ 86,000	
Accounts and Notes Receivable	687,000	
Allowance for Uncollectible Receivables		$ 79,000
Due from Other Funds	71,300	
Supplies Inventory	102,000	
Prepaid Expenses	30,000	
Land	1,250,000	
Buildings	12,540,000	
Accumulated Depreciation: Buildings		6,060,000
Fixed Equipment	3,210,000	
Accumulated Depreciation: Fixed Equipment		1,305,000
Major Movable Equipment	1,948,000	
Accumulated Depreciation: Major Movable Equipment		812,000
Minor Equipment	673,000	
Accounts Payable		1,030,000
Accrued Expenses Payable		86,800
Mortgage Payable		5,850,000
Fund Balance		4,372,000
Patient Services Revenues		11,200,000
Other Operating Revenues		68,100
Nonoperating Revenues		251,200
Transfer from Plant Replacement and Expansion Fund		300,000
Contractual Adjustments	235,000	
Charity Services	110,000	
Provision for Uncollectible Accounts	98,000	
Nursing Services Expenses	4,537,600	
Other Professional Services Expenses	1,484,400	
General Services Expenses	1,286,700	
Fiscal Services Expenses	465,000	
Administrative Services Expenses	1,360,100	
Provision for Depreciation Expense	1,040,000	
Transfer to Board-Designated Fund	200,000	
	$ 31,414,100	$ 31,414,100

EXHIBIT 20-2

Illustrative Problem 20.1
Monroe Community Hospital
Statement of Revenues and Expenses
Year Ended June 30, 1991

Patient Services Revenue		$ 11,200,000
Deductions from Patient Revenue		
Contractual Adjustments	$ 235,000	
Charity Services	110,000	
Provision for Uncollectible Accounts	98,000	443,000
Net Patient Service Revenue		10,757,000
Other Operating Revenue		68,100
Total Operating Revenue		10,825,100
Operating Expenses		
Nursing Services	4,537,600	
Other Professional Services	1,484,400	
General Services	1,286,700	
Fiscal Services	465,000	
Administrative Services	1,360,100	
Provision for Depreciation	1,040,000	10,173,800
Profit from Operations		651,300
Nonoperating Revenue		251,200
Excess of Revenues Over Expenses		$ 902,500

The balance sheet and statement of changes in fund balances report each type of fund separately, as each effectively represents a separate entity within the combined entity Monroe Community Hospital. In addition, the presentation of individual funds provides information regarding the accountability and uses of the resources of the not-for-profit hospital. After the accounting for the board-designated and donor-restricted funds of Monroe Community Hospital is discussed, the combined balance sheet and the combined statement of changes in fund balances are presented in Exhibits 20-3 and 20-4. This statement presentation differs from the concept on which consolidated financial statements are based: that a fairer presentation is made for a group of related business entities presenting its financial statements with the income statement, balance sheet, and statement of cash flows combined into single line items for the consolidated entity as a whole.

BOARD-DESIGNATED FUND TRANSACTIONS

Monroe Community Hospital created a board-designated fund to account for transfers from the general fund for assets set aside to remodel various sections of the hospital building. On July 1, 1990, the beginning of the current fiscal year, the trial balance of the board-designated fund was

	Debit	Credit
Cash	$ 5,200	
Marketable Securities	523,000	
Accrued Interest Receivable	10,600	
Fund Balance		$ 538,800
	$ 538,800	$ 538,800

During the year ended June 30, 1991, the following transactions and events were recorded in the board-designated fund:

Cash	54,500	
Accrued Interest Receivable		10,600
Due General Fund		43,900
To record interest revenue received during the current year		
Cash	91,500	
Marketable Securities		84,000
Due General Fund		7,500
To record sale of securities during the current year		
Cash	200,000	
Fund Balance		200,000
To record cash transferred from the general fund		
Marketable Securities	338,700	
Cash		338,700
To record the purchase of securities		
Accrued Interest Receivable	12,300	
Due General Fund		12,300
To record interest earned but not received at year end		

The entry recording the receipt of the $200,000 is the counterpart of the entry recorded in the general fund for the transfer of the cash. The interest earned on the investment in marketable securities and the gain on the sale of marketable securities are revenues that are to be transferred to and recognized in the general fund.

On June 30, 1991, the end of the current fiscal year, the trial balance of the board-designated fund is

	Debit	Credit
Cash	$ 12,500	
Marketable Securities	777,700	
Accrued Interest Receivable	12,300	
Due General Fund		$ 63,700
Fund Balance		738,800
	$ 802,500	$ 802,500

DONOR-RESTRICTED FUNDS

SPECIFIC-PURPOSE FUNDS

During the prior fiscal year, the Ladies Auxiliary of Monroe Community Hospital, an independent entity, had earned and donated $4,000 to the hospital to be used to provide hospice care by hospital personnel to cancer patients. The Ladies Auxiliary pledged to add $4,000 to the fund each year for the next four years. The administrators of the hospital are confident that the Ladies Auxiliary will be able to meet their pledge and therefore have decided not to provide an allowance for uncollectible pledges. In addition to the hospice care fund, another specific-purpose fund is being created for the revenue from endowments specifying that the income be used for research on weight control. The trial balance of the specific-purpose funds on July 1, 1991, the beginning of the current fiscal year, was

	Debit	Credit
Cash	$ 1,200	
Pledges Receivable	16,000	
Fund Balance		$ 17,200
	$ 17,200	$ 17,200

The following entries were recorded in the specific-purpose funds during the year ended June 30, 1991.

Cash	4,000	
Pledges Receivable		4,000
To record cash received from the Ladies Auxiliary		
Fund Balance	4,100	
Due General Fund		4,100
To record the amount due the general fund for expenses paid in the current year		
Cash	10,000	
Fund Balance		10,000
To record the transfer of income from the endowment fund for weight control research		
Due from Other Funds	1,800	
Fund Balance		1,800
To record the transfer due from the endowment fund for interest earned on endowment for weight control research		

The adjusted trial balance of the specific-purpose funds on June 30, 1991, the end of the current fiscal year, is

	Debit	Credit
Cash	$ 15,200	
Pledges Receivable	12,000	
Due from Endowment Fund	1,800	
Due General Fund		$ 4,100
Fund Balance		24,900
	$ 29,000	$ 29,000

PLANT REPLACEMENT AND EXPANSION FUND

Various citizens and businesses of the city of Monroe have made contributions and pledges to the donor-restricted fund, plant replacement and expansion fund, of the Monroe Community Hospital. These funds can only be used for building and equipment replacements or additions. On July 1, 1991, the beginning of the current fiscal year, the trial balance of the plant replacement and expansion fund was

	Debit	Credit
Cash	$ 427,500	
Marketable Securities	924,600	
Accrued Interest Receivable	32,500	
Pledges Receivable	580,000	
Allowance for Uncollectible Pledges		$ 63,000
Fund Balance		1,901,600
	$1,964,600	$1,964,600

During the year ended June 30, 1991, the following transactions and events were recorded in the plant replacement and expansion fund:

Fund Balance	300,000	
Cash		300,000

To record $300,000 transferred to the general fund for equipment acquisitions that met the donor's specifications

Cash	319,000	
Allowance for Uncollectible Pledges	41,000	
Pledges Receivable		360,000

To record pledges collected and pledges written off because they were not collectible

Cash	117,000	
Accrued Interest Receivable		32,500
Fund Balance		84,500

To record the interest received in cash during the period

Marketable Securities	369,000	
Cash		369,000

To record the purchases of securities during the current year

Cash	59,000	
Fund Balance	4,000	
Marketable Securities		63,000

To record the sale of securities during the current year

Accrued Interest Receivable	25,600	
Fund Balance		25,600

To accrue interest earned at the end of the year but not yet received

The adjusted trial balance of the donor-restricted plant replacement and expansion fund on June 30, 1991, the end of the current fiscal year, is

	Debit	Credit
Cash	$ 253,500	
Marketable Securities	1,230,600	
Accrued Interest Receivable	25,600	
Pledges Receivable	220,000	
Allowance for Uncollectible Pledges		$ 22,000
Fund Balance		1,707,700
	$ 1,729,700	$ 1,729,700

ENDOWMENT FUNDS

Monroe Community Hospital has endowment funds in which it accounts for the assets donated to the hospital. Endowment funds require that principal be maintained and not spent, and only the income can be used by the hospital. The fund balances are divided into assets whose income is unrestricted by the donor and available for current operating purposes at the discretion of the board of directors, and assets whose income is restricted in use by the donor or must be accumulated in the fund until a later date specified by the donor. If the income can be spent currently at the discretion of the board of directors, it is transferred to the general fund and recognized as revenue. If the income has a restricted purpose, it is transferred to either a specific-purpose fund or the plant replacement and expansion fund. If the income cannot be used currently, but must be kept in the endowment fund, the income adds to the Fund Balance until it can be expended.

In Chapter 18, we discussed the accounting for estates and trusts. An endowment fund of a hospital is a type of trust fund and the distinction between principal and income is critical just as it is in accounting for estates and trusts. Gains and losses on the sale of securities are treated as additions to or reductions of the appropriate fund balance. Monroe Community Hospital maintains control accounts over a number of different endowments. For the purposes of this chapter, we will use only the control accounts of both the unrestricted and restricted endowment funds. The trial balance of the endowment funds on July 1, 1990, the beginning of the fiscal year, was

	Debit	Credit
Cash	$ 32,500	
Accrued Interest Receivable	3,000	
Long-term Investments	386,000	
Due General Fund		$ 25,000
Fund Balance: Income Restricted		161,000
Fund Balance: Income Not Restricted		235,500
	$ 421,500	$ 421,500

During the fiscal year ended June 30, 1991, the following transactions and events were recorded in the endowment funds:

Due General Fund	25,000	
Cash		25,000

To transfer to the general fund an expired term endowment, which expired at the end of the prior year, but was not transferred

Cash	38,700	
Accrued Interest Receivable		3,000
Due General Fund		24,000
Due Specific-Purpose Funds		10,000
Fund Balance: Income Restricted		1,700

To record the interest received during the current year: unrestricted endowments $24,000, endowments restricted to a specific purpose $10,000, and term endowments that prohibit the expenditure of the income until the endowment expires $1,700

Due General Fund	24,000	
Due Specific-Purpose Funds	10,000	
Cash		34,000

To transfer income to the appropriate funds

Cash	27,000	
Fund Balance: Income Restricted		15,000
Fund Balance: Income Unrestricted		12,000

To record the receipt of two endowments, one with restrictions on income and one without restrictions

Accrued Interest Receivable	5,300	
Due General Fund		3,500
Due Specific-Purpose Funds		1,800

To accrue interest at year end

The transfers of cash to the general fund and the amounts due the general fund and the specific-purpose funds are reflected in the above entries and have their counterpart in journal entries prepared for the general fund and the specific-purpose funds.

The adjusted trial balance of the endowment funds control accounts on June 30, 1991, the end of the fiscal year, is

	Debit	Credit
Cash	$ 39,200	
Accrued Interest Receivable	5,300	
Long-term Investments	386,000	
Due General Fund		$ 3,500
Due Specific-Purpose Funds		1,800
Fund Balance: Income Restricted		177,700
Fund Balance: Income Not Restricted		247,500
	$ 430,500	$ 430,500

The combined balance sheet and the combined statement of changes in funds balances are presented in Exhibits 20-3 and 20-4. Remember that unlike consolidated statements, each of the funds is a separate set of accounts and is treated like a separate entity; therefore, each is reported separately in the combined statements. The general fund and the board-designated funds are merged, however, because they both represent unrestricted funds and because the board of directors of the hospital can eliminate the board-designated funds at its discretion.

Closing Journal Entry. The hospital prepares only one closing journal entry for the general fund. In the remainder of the funds, either the Fund Balance account was credited directly with the revenue, gains, losses, and expenses, or the revenue was transferred to the general fund. Thus, no other closing entries are necessary. The closing journal entry on June 30, 1991 for the general fund is

Patient Service Revenues	11,200,000	
Other Operating Revenues	68,100	
Nonoperating Revenues	251,200	
Transfer from Plant Replacement and Expansion Fund	300,000	
Contractual Adjustments		235,000
Charity Services		110,000
Provision for Uncollectible Accounts		98,000
Nursing Services Expenses		4,537,600
Other Professional Services Expenses		1,484,400
General Services Expenses		1,286,700
Fiscal Services Expenses		465,000
Administrative Services Expenses		1,360,100
Provision for Depreciation		1,040,000
Transfer to Board-Designated Funds		200,000
General Fund Balance		1,002,500

SUMMARY

Nonbusiness entities use the fund theory of equity and accrual accounting. A fund is a fiscal and accounting entity with a self-balancing set of accounts used to account for a specific activity. A nonbusiness organization is an entity that receives assets without having to repay

EXHIBIT 20-3

Illustrative Problem 20.1
Monroe Community Hospital
Balance Sheet
June 30, 1991

Assets   Liabilities and Fund Balances

UNRESTRICTED FUNDS

Current Assets			Current Liabilities	
Cash		$ 98,500	Accounts Payable	$ 1,030,000
Marketable Securities		777,700	Accrued Expenses Payable	86,800
Accrued Interest Receivable		12,300	Total Current Liabilities	1,116,800
Accounts and Notes Receivable	$ 687,000		Long-term Liabilities	
Less: Allowance for Uncollectible			Mortgage Payable	5,850,000
Receivables	79,000	608,000	Fund Balances	
Due from Other Funds		7,600	General Fund	5,374,500
Supplies Inventory		102,000	Board-Designated Fund	738,800
Prepaid Expenses		30,000		
Total Current Assets		1,636,100		
Property, Plant, and Equipment				
Land		1,250,000		
Buildings	12,540,000			
Less: Accumulated Depreciation	6,060,000	6,480,000		
Fixed Equipment	3,210,000			
Less: Accumulated Depreciation	1,305,000	1,905,000		
Major Movable Equipment	1,948,000			
Less: Accumulated Depreciation	812,000	1,136,000		
Minor Equipment		673,000		
Total Property, Plant and Equipment		11,444,000		
Total Unrestricted Funds		$ 13,080,100	Total Unrestricted Funds	$ 13,080,100

DONOR-RESTRICTED FUNDS

Specific-Purpose Funds

Cash	$ 15,200	Due General Fund	$ 4,100
Pledges Receivable	12,000	Fund Balance	24,900
Due from Endowment Fund	1,800		
Total Specific-Purpose Funds	$ 29,000	Total Specific-Purpose Funds	$ 29,000

Plant Replacement and Expansion Fund

Cash		$ 253,500		
Marketable Securities		1,230,600		
Accrued Interest Receivable		25,600		
Pledges Receivable	$ 220,000			
Less: Allowance for Uncollectible Pledges	22,000	198,000	Fund Balance	$ 1,707,700
Total Plant Replacement and Expansion Fund		$ 1,707,700	Total Plant Replacement and Expansion Fund	$ 1,707,700

Endowment Funds

Cash	$ 39,200	Due General Fund	$ 3,500
Accrued Interest Receivable	5,300	Due Specific-Purpose Funds	1,800
Long-term Investments	386,000	Fund Balance: Income Unrestricted	247,500
		Fund Balance: Income Restricted	177,700
Total Endowment Funds	$ 430,500	Total Endowment Funds	$ 430,500

EXHIBIT 20-4

Illustrative Problem 20.1
Monroe Community Hospital
Statement of Changes in Fund Balances
Year Ended June 30, 1991

Unrestricted Funds

Balance at Beginning of Year	$ 4,910,800
Excess of Revenues Over Expenses	902,500
Transfer from Plant Replacement and Expansion Fund	300,000
Balance at End of Year	$ 6,113,300

Donor-Restricted Funds

Specific-Purpose Funds

Balance at Beginning of Year	$ 17,200	
Transfer from Endowment Fund	10,000	
Transfer from Endowment Fund	1,800	
Transfer to General Fund	(4,100)	
Balance at End of Year		$ 24,900

Plant Replacement and Expansion Fund

Balance at Beginning of Year	1,901,600	
Interest Earned	110,100	
Loss on Sale of Securities	(4,000)	
Transfer to General Fund	(300,000)	
Balance at End of Year		1,707,700

Endowment Funds
  Income Restricted Funds

Balance at Beginning of Year	161,000	
Interest Earned	1,700	
Endowment Received	15,000	
Balance at End of Year		177,700

  Income Not Restricted Funds

Balance at Beginning of Year	235,500	
Endowment Received	12,000	
Balance at End of Year		247,500

Total Donor-Restricted Funds	$ 2,157,800

or provide a reasonable rate of return for the assets, its purposes are not profit oriented, and it lacks defined ownership. Nonbusiness organizations are divided into five categories: not-for-profit hospitals, voluntary health and welfare organizations, not-for-profit colleges and universities, other not-for-profit organizations, and governmental units.

A not-for-profit hospital uses the same generally accepted principles as a profit-oriented hospital. A not-for-profit hospital uses two classes of funds: unrestricted funds and donor-restricted funds. The unrestricted funds are the general fund and the board-designated funds, which are funds the board of directors create, add to, use, or return to the general fund at its discretion. The donor-restricted funds are the specific-purpose funds, the plant replacement and expansion funds, and the endowment funds. The specific-purpose funds are used to account for assets (resources) restricted to a special operating purpose. The plant replacement and expansion funds are used to account for assets that are restricted to acquisitions of plant and equipment. The endowment funds are used to account for assets, which must be maintained either for a definite period of time or indefinitely, and only the income can be spent. If the endowment fund income can be used for any purpose the board of directors selects, it is unrestricted. However, if the use of the income is limited to a specific purpose, the income and the endowment are classified as restricted.

Not-for-profit hospitals use three categories for revenue: patient service revenue, other operating revenue, and nonoperating revenue. Net patient service revenue is the fees charged to patients net of the contractual adjustments from third-party payors, the estimate of uncollectible accounts, the charity care provided to patients who cannot pay and are not covered by third-party payors, and discounts granted to employees. Other operating revenues consist of transfers from donor-restricted funds for operations, tuition charged to students of medicine, cafeteria charges, parking fees, gift shop operations, and other activities indirectly related to patient care. Donated medicines and supplies are also recorded at their fair market value and classified as other operating revenue.

Nonoperating revenues consists of donations, pledges, unrestricted income from endowments, expired term endowments, income from investments of the unrestricted funds, gains and losses on the sale of assets, and donated services. Donated services are recorded at their fair market value and a corresponding expense is recorded.

Income of the specific-purpose funds is recognized in the general fund when the expense is incurred. Income of the plant replacement and expansion fund adds to the fund balance. Income of unrestricted endowments is recognized in the general fund, and the income from restricted endowments is either transferred to the appropriate specific-purpose fund or plant replacement and expansion fund or added to the fund balance if it cannot be spent currently.

Expenses of a not-for-profit hospital are divided into six categories: nursing services expenses, other professional services expenses, general services expenses, fiscal services expenses, administrative services expenses including interest, and provision for depreciation expense. A not-for-profit hospital divides its equipment into three categories: fixed equipment, major movable equipment, and minor equipment. The fixed equipment and major movable equipment are depreciated and the minor equipment is accounted for like supplies. Transfers to and from funds are recorded in both funds.

The financial statements of a not-for-profit hospital consist of a statement of revenues and expenses and a statement of cash flows for the general fund, a balance sheet and a statement of changes in fund balances for all the funds used with each type of funds reported separately.

REVIEW PROBLEM

The Bayshore Hospital is a not-for-profit hospital that serves the town of Lincoln and a number of neighboring towns. The trial balance of Bayshore at January 1, 1990 was

	Debit	Credit
General Fund		
Cash	$ 59,000	
Accounts and Notes Receivable	245,000	
Allowance for Uncollectible Receivables		$ 24,000
Due from Other Funds	12,000	
Supplies Inventory	47,000	
Prepaid Expenses	12,000	
Land	450,000	
Buildings	6,700,000	
Accumulated Depreciation: Buildings		2,500,000
Fixed Equipment	1,800,000	
Accumulated Depreciation: Fixed Equipment		450,000
Major Movable Equipment	1,100,000	
Accumulated Depreciation: Major Movable Equipment		530,000
Minor Equipment	320,000	
Accounts Payable		340,000
Accrued Expenses Payable		28,000
10% Bonds Payable		3,500,000
General Fund Balance		3,373,000
Board-Designated Fund		
Cash	4,000	
Marketable Securities	240,000	
Accrued Interest Receivable	3,000	
Due General Fund		3,000
Board-Designated Fund Balance		244,000
Plant Replacement and Expansion Fund		
Cash	20,000	
Marketable Securities	492,000	
Accrued Interest Receivable	9,000	
Due General Fund		9,000
Plant Replacement and Expansion Fund Balance		512,000
Endowment Funds		
Cash	15,000	
Accrued Interest Receivable: Restricted	2,000	
Long-Term Investments	260,000	
Restricted Fund Balance		210,000
Unrestricted Fund Balance		67,000
	$ 11,790,000	$ 11,790,000

During 1990, the following transactions and events occurred regarding the accounts of Bayshore Hospital:

GENERAL FUND

Operating Revenues consisted of

Patient Services	$ 6,000,000
Cafeteria Revenue	52,000
Parking Fee Revenue	37,000
Donated Drugs and Medical Supplies	32,000

Adjustments to operating revenues consisted of

- payments of third-party payors were $285,000 less than billed, and
- health care in the amount of $140,000 was provided to patients classified as charity patients.

The policy established by Bayshore's board of directors is that all income earned on investments of the board-designated fund is to be recorded as a balance due when earned and transferred to the general fund when the cash is received. The investments of the hospital earned interest as follows:

Marketable Securities: Board-designated Fund	$ 25,000
Marketable Securities: Plant Replacement and Expansion Fund	50,000
Long-term Investments: Unrestricted Endowment Funds	7,000

Services donated by volunteers for patient care had a fair market value of $25,000.

Fund transfers of cash to the general fund consisted of

Board-designated Fund	$ 25,500
Specific-purpose Fund	2,900
Plant Replacement and Expansion Fund	52,800
Unrestricted Endowment Funds	7,000
Expired Term Endowment	9,000

The payables incurred during the year consisted of

Nursing Services Expense	$ 2,300,000
Other Professional Services Expenses	1,020,000
General Services Expenses	640,000
Fiscal Services Expenses	170,000
Administrative Services Expenses	200,000
Interest on Bonds Payable	350,000
Supplies	230,000

Additional cash receipts, exclusive of those previously mentioned, consisted of $5,540,000 of collections on accounts receivable. Accounts receivable totaling $22,000 were written off as uncollectible.

Cash disbursements were

Prepaid Expenses	$ 10,000
Accrued Expenses Payable	28,000
Accounts Payable	4,610,000
Interest Payable	350,000
Fixed Equipment	200,000
Major Movable Equipment	120,000
Minor Equipment	75,000
Refurbishing the Waiting Room (General Services)	2,900

The refurbishing of the waiting room was done with funds donated by the Ladies Auxiliary, an independent entity. The auxiliary is raising funds to refurbish hospital areas used by visitors.

Major movable equipment with a cost of $100,000 and accumulated depreciation of $85,000 was sold for $10,000.

The year-end adjustments consist of the following:

- Bayshore estimates that 10% of outstanding receivables at the end of the year will not be collected.
- The balance of supplies on hand at the end of the year is $44,000. The supplies are used 40% by nursing services, 40% by other professional services, and 20% by fiscal services.
- The balance of prepaid expenses at December 31, 1990 is $9,000; all of the expenses are classified as administrative expenses.
- Accrued expenses at year end totaled $24,000, all attributable to administrative expenses.
- The inventory of minor equipment showed $335,000 on hand at December 31, 1990. The minor equipment is used 50% by nursing services and 50% by other professional services.
- The depreciation for the current year is $167,500 for buildings, $210,000 for fixed equipment, and $165,000 for major movable equipment.

The board of directors of Bayshore Hospital has established the following policies regarding the cash balances of the various funds.

- Any cash in the general fund in excess of $100,000 is to be transferred to a board-designated fund to a limit of $500,000. The cash is to be transferred to a board-designated fund for the retirement of the bonds payable when they come due. If additional cash can be transferred, the cash is to be transferred to a board-designated fund for asset replacement.
- If the cash balance of the endowment funds exceeds $15,000 it is to be invested in long-term investments.
- If the cash balance of the board-designated funds, the plant replacement and expansion funds, or the specific-purpose funds exceeds $20,000 the excess is to be invested in marketable securities.

BOARD-DESIGNATED FUNDS

Cash collected for accrued interest receivable totaled $25,500.

SPECIFIC-PURPOSE FUND

The Ladies Auxiliary of Bayshore contributed $5,000 to be used to refurbish the hospital's surgery waiting room.

PLANT REPLACEMENT AND EXPANSION FUNDS

- Cash collected for interest revenue totaled $54,000.
- Bayshore Hospital launched a major fund-raising campaign to construct and equip an intermediate care center. Cash in the amount of $200,000 was received and an additional $2,500,000 was pledged. Past fund-raising efforts by the hospital indicate that 10% of the pledges will not be collected. Bayshore included the assets in the plant replacement and expansion fund.
- Pledges to the intermediate care center totaling $600,000 were collected and $50,000 of pledges were determined to be uncollectible.
- The plant replacement and expansion fund sold marketable securities with a cost of $37,000 for $40,000. The gain is considered to be part of the fund balance.

ENDOWMENT FUNDS

- Interest totaling $23,000 was earned on restricted endowments.
- Interest totaling $28,600 was received in cash during the current year.
- A $25,000 endowment was received that restricted the use of the income to dietary research.

Required

1. Prepare all the transaction and adjusting entries for each of the funds of Bayshore Hospital assuming that all investment earnings are first recorded as a receivable and assuming excess cash in the funds is invested or transferred according to the board of directors' established policy.
2. Prepare adjusted trial balances for each of the funds.
3. Prepare the financial statements for Bayshore Hospital.

QUESTIONS

1. Describe the five major categories of nonbusiness organizations and give an example of each.
2. Describe the three distinguishing characteristics of a nonbusiness enterprise according to *Statement of Financial Accounting Concepts No. 4*.
3. What is the general definition of a nonbusiness organization?
4. What are the two broad classes of groups of funds used by a not-for-profit hospital?
5. Describe the basic categories of donor-restricted funds of a not-for-profit hospital. Why are these funds called donor-restricted?
6. Describe the three major categories or classes of hospital revenues and give examples of sources of revenue for each major category.
7. What value should be used to record donated medicines and medical supplies? Defend the use of the value.
8. What criteria must be met to record donated services? What value is used to record services donated to a not-for-profit hospital? What ledger accounts are debited and credited in the journal entry to record the donated services?
9. Describe the six broad categories of expenses used by a hospital.
10. What are the three major categories used for equipment by a not-for-profit hospital? Are all three categories depreciated? If not depreciated, how are they accounted for?
11. How are revenues, expenses, gains, and losses recorded in the donor-restricted funds of a not-for-profit hospital?
12. Describe the accounting for a contribution to a not-for-profit hospital that is correctly recorded in (1) the general fund, (2) a specific-purpose fund, (3) a plant replacement and expansion fund, and (4) an endowment fund.
13. Describe the accounting for a transfer to the general fund from (1) a specific-purpose fund, (2) a plant replacement and expansion fund, and (3) an endowment fund.
14. Explain why the major groups of funds of a not-for-profit hospital are reported separately in the financial statements and not consolidated.

EXERCISES

EXERCISE 20-1

1. An unrestricted pledge from an annual contributor to a voluntary not-for-profit hospital made in December 1990 and paid in cash in March 1991 is credited to

a. Nonoperating Revenue in 1990
b. Nonoperating Revenue in 1991
c. Operating Revenue in 1990
d. Operating Revenue in 1991

2. Donated medicines that normally would be purchased by a hospital should be recorded at fair market value and credited directly to

a. Other Operating Revenue
b. Nonoperating Revenue
c. Fund Balance
d. Deferred Revenue

3. A gift to a voluntary not-for-profit hospital that is not restricted by the donor should be credited directly to

a. Fund Balance
b. Other Operating Revenue
c. Operating Revenue
d. Nonoperating Revenue

4. Which of the following would be included in Other Operating Revenues of a voluntary not-for-profit hospital?

a. Unrestricted interest income from an endowment fund
b. An unrestricted gift
c. Donated services
d. Tuition received from an educational program

5. Revenue from the gift shop of a hospital would be included in

a. Other Nonoperating Revenue
b. Other Operating Revenue
c. Patient Service Revenue
d. Professional Services Revenue

6. Revenue from the parking lot operated by a hospital would be included in

a. Patient Service Revenue
b. Ancillary Service Revenue
c. Other Operating Revenue
d. Other Nonoperating Revenue

7. Which of the following would be included in Other Operating Revenues of a hospital?

	Revenues from Educational Programs	Unrestricted Gifts
a.	Yes	No
b.	Yes	Yes
c.	No	Yes
d.	No	No

(AICPA adapted)

EXERCISE 20-2

1. Which of the following would be included in the unrestricted funds of a not-for-profit hospital?

a. Permanent Endowments
b. Term-Endowments
c. Board-Designated Funds
d. Plant Replacement and Expansion Funds

2. The property, plant, and equipment of a not-for-profit hospital should be accounted for as part of

a. Unrestricted Funds
b. Donor-Restricted Funds
c. Specific-Purpose Funds
d. Other Nonoperating Funds

3. Glenmore Hospital's property, plant, and equipment (net of depreciation) consist of

Land	$ 500,000
Buildings	10,000,000
Movable Equipment	2,000,000

What amount should be included in the donor-restricted fund grouping?

a. $ −0−
b. $ 2,000,000
c. $ 10,500,000
d. $ 12,500,000

(AICPA adapted)

EXERCISE 20-3

1. During the year ended December 31, 1990, Melford Hospital received the following donations stated at their respective fair values:

Employee services from members of a religious group	$ 100,000
Medical supplies from an association of physicians. These supplies were restricted for indigent care, and were used for that purpose in 1990.	30,000

How much revenue (both operating and nonoperating) from donations should Melford report in its 1990 statement of revenues and expenses?

a. $ −0−
b. $ 30,000
c. $ 100,000
d. $ 130,000

2. On July 1, 1990, Lilydale Hospital's Board of Trustees designated $200,000 for expansion of outpatient facilities. The $200,000 is expected to be expended in the fiscal year ending June 30, 1991. In Lilydale's balance sheet at June 30, 1990, this cash should be classified as a $200,000

a. Restricted Current Asset
b. Restricted Noncurrent Asset
c. Unrestricted Current Asset
d. Unrestricted Noncurrent Asset

INFORMATION FOR QUESTIONS 3, 4, AND 5. Under Abbey Hospital's established rate structure, the hospital would have earned patient service revenue of $6,000,000 for the year ended December 31,

1990. However, Abbey did not expect to collect this amount because of charity allowances of $1,000,000 and discounts of $500,000 to third-party payors. In May 1990, Abbey purchased bandages from Lee Supply company at a cost of $1,000. However, Lee notified Abbey that the invoice was being canceled and that the bandages were being donated to Abbey. At December 31, 1990, Abbey had board-designated assets consisting of cash $40,000, and investments $700,000.

3. For the year ended December 31, 1990, how much should Abbey report as net patient service revenue?

a. $6,000,000
b. $5,500,000
c. $5,000,000
d. $4,500,000

4. For the year ended December 31, 1990, Abbey should record the donation of bandages as

a. A $1,000 reduction in operating expenses
b. Nonoperating Revenue of $1,000
c. Other Operating Revenue of $1,000
d. A memorandum entry only

5. How much of Abbey's board-designated assets should be included in the unrestricted fund grouping?

a.   −0−
b. $ 40,000
c. $ 700,000
d. $ 740,000

(AICPA adapted)

EXERCISE 20-4

Bend Community Hospital had the following potential sources of revenue and adjustments to revenue during 1990:

Patient Services	$ 2,000,000
Amounts Billed to Patients Estimated Uncollectible	75,000
Tuition and Fees from Nursing Students	200,000
Care Provided to Charity Patients	200,000
Cafeteria Revenue	60,000
Donated Medical Supplies (fair market value)	8,000
Donated Volunteer Services (fair market value)	46,000
Investment Revenue: General Fund	20,000
Investment Revenue: Board-Designated Fund	12,000
Investment Revenue: Specific-Purpose Funds	22,000
Investment Revenue: Plant Replacement and Expansion Fund	15,000
Investment Income: Endowment Fund: Unrestricted	21,000
Investment Income: Endowment Fund: Restricted	16,000
Adjustments to Accounts Paid by Third-Party Payors	350,000
Gains on Sales of Securities: Endowment Fund	22,000
Expired Term Endowment: Unrestricted	40,000
Expired Term Endowment: Restricted	100,000
Loss on Sale of Equipment	(13,000)
Fund-Raising Campaign for Building Addition	
Cash	200,000
Pledges (10% estimated uncollectible)	1,400,000

Required

1. Determine the amounts of the following classes of revenue to be reported on the statement of revenues and expenses of Bend Community Hospital:
   1) Net Patient Service Revenue
   2) Other Operating Revenue
   3) Nonoperating Revenue
2. Explain the reasons for omitting any items you excluded.

EXERCISE 20-5

The Belmont Hospital had the following transactions and events for property, plant, and equipment during the current year:

- A piece of land adjacent to the hospital was purchased for $200,000 with cash of the plant replacement and expansion fund.
- Expenditures of $10,000 were incurred by the general fund to convert the newly acquired land into a parking lot.
- Major movable equipment was sold for $24,000. The equipment originally cost $72,000 and had a net book value of $21,600 at the beginning of the year.
- Fixed equipment was sold for $18,000. The equipment originally cost $48,000 and had a net book value at the beginning of the year of $18,000.
- Minor equipment costing $128,000 was purchased during the year.
- The inventory of minor equipment showed $300,000 on hand at the end of the year. The minor equipment is used in the provision of nursing services.
- The beginning balances of the property, plant, and equipment accounts were

	Cost	Accumulated Depreciation
Land	$ 1,200,000	
Land Improvements	325,000	$ 170,000
Building	6,800,000	3,400,000
Fixed Equipment	2,304,000	1,240,000
Major Movable Equipment	3,690,000	1,460,000
Minor Equipment	280,000	

- The hospital depreciates assets 1/2 year in the year of acquisition and 1/2 year in the year of sale by the straight-line method without salvage value.
- The estimated useful lives of the assets are

Land Improvements	20 years
Buildings	40 years
Fixed Equipment	12 years
Major Movable Equipment	10 years

Required

Prepare the journal entries for the transactions and events affecting the operating assets of Belmont Hospital identifying the fund or funds in which each entry is recorded.

EXERCISE 20-6

The adjusted trial balance of Hanford Hospital's unrestricted funds as of December 31, 1990 is

	Debit	Credit
General Fund		
Cash	$ 30,000	
Accounts and Notes Receivable	120,000	
Allowance for Uncollectible Receivables		$ 12,500
Supplies Inventory	20,000	
Prepaid Expenses	7,500	
Land	125,000	
Buildings	2,250,000	
Accumulated Depreciation: Buildings		1,250,000
Fixed Equipment	1,000,000	
Accumulated Depreciation: Fixed Equipment		200,000
Major Movable Equipment	750,000	
Accumulated Depreciation: Major Movable Equipment		200,000
Minor Equipment	200,000	
Accounts Payable		150,000
Accrued Expenses Payable		15,000
12% Bonds Payable		1,250,000
General Fund Balance		1,362,500
Patient Service Revenues		2,700,000
Donated Medicines and Medical Supplies		25,000
Cafeteria Revenues		15,000
Donated Services		50,000
Unrestricted Current Operating Donations		22,500
Unrestricted Income Endowment Fund		40,000
Income of Board-Designated Investments		15,000
Transfer of Expired Unrestricted Term Endowment		25,000
Contractual Adjustments	45,000	
Charity Services	210,000	
Provision for Uncollectible Accounts	15,000	
Nursing Services Expenses	1,100,000	
Other Professional Services Expenses	400,000	
General Services Expenses	250,000	
Fiscal Services Expenses	100,000	
Administrative Services Expenses	275,000	
Provision for Depreciation	320,000	
Transfer to Board-Designated Funds	40,000	
Transfer to Plant Replacement and Expansion Fund	75,000	
Board-Designated Fund		
Cash	12,000	
Marketable Securities	304,000	
Accrued Interest Receivable	3,000	
Fund Balance		319,000
	$ 7,651,500	$ 7,651,500

Required

1. Prepare the statement of revenues and expenses for Hanford Hospital.
2. Prepare the unrestricted funds sections of the balance sheet and the statement of changes in fund balances for Hanford Hospital.
3. Prepare the closing journal entries for the unrestricted funds.

EXERCISE 20-7

The trial balance of the board-designated fund of Camas General Hospital on January 1, 1990 was

	Debit	Credit
Cash	$ 12,000	
Marketable Securities	300,000	
Accrued Interest Receivable	3,000	
Due from General Fund	4,000	
Fund Balance		$ 319,000
	$ 319,000	$ 319,000

The following transactions and events affected the board-designated fund of Camas General Hospital during 1990:

- Cash in the amount of $22,000 was transferred from the general fund.
- The investments earned $29,000.
- Cash received as earnings on investments totaled $26,000.
- Securities costing $32,000 were sold for $35,000.
- Cash totaling $30,000 was transferred to the general fund.
- Securities costing $51,000 were purchased.

Required

1. Prepare the journal entries to record the transactions and events of the board-designated fund for 1990.
2. Prepare the adjusted trial balance of the board-designated fund at December 31, 1990.
3. Describe how the accounts in the adjusted trial balance are reported in Camas General Hospital's balance sheet.

EXERCISE 20-8

The trial balance of the specific-purpose funds for cancer research of Dwight Hospital as of January 1, 1990 was

	Debit	Credit
Cash	$ 10,000	
Marketable Securities	100,000	
Accrued Interest Receivable	4,000	
Pledges Receivable	215,000	
Allowance for Uncollectible Pledges		$ 21,500
Due General Fund		7,500
Fund Balance		300,000
	$ 329,000	$ 329,000

During 1990, the following transactions and events occurred that affected the specific-purpose funds:

- Cash contributions of $31,000 and pledges of $120,000 were received.
- Pledges totaling $165,000 were collected and $9,000 were determined to be uncollectible.

- Past experience indicates that 10% of the outstanding pledges will not be collected.
- Investments earned $12,000, and $13,000 in cash was received.
- Marketable securities with a cost of $44,000 were sold for $47,000.
- The general fund spent $115,000 for cancer research.
- Cash in the amount of $120,000 was transferred to the general fund.
- Securities with a cost of $142,000 were purchased.

Required

1. Prepare the journal entries to record the transactions and events affecting the specific-purpose funds.
2. Prepare the specific-purpose funds section of Dwight Hospital's balance sheet.
3. Prepare the specific-purpose funds section of Dwight Hospital's statement of changes in fund balances.

EXERCISE 20-9

The trial balance of the plant replacement and expansion fund of Elgin Hospital on January 1, 1990 was

	Debit	Credit
Cash	$ 20,000	
Marketable Securities	300,000	
Accrued Interest Receivable	9,000	
Pledges Receivable	220,000	
Allowance for Uncollectible Pledges		$ 11,000
Due from General Fund	12,000	
Fund Balance		550,000
	$ 561,000	$ 561,000

During 1990, the following transactions events occurred that affected Elgin Hospital's plant replacement and expansion fund:

- Cash contributions of $50,000 and pledges of $340,000 were received.
- Pledges totaling $215,000 were collected and $8,000 were determined to be uncollectible.
- Past experience indicates that 5% of the outstanding pledges will not be collected.
- Investments earned $34,000, and $33,000 in cash was received.
- Marketable securities with a cost of $29,000 were sold for $27,000.
- Land with a cost of $100,000 and major movable equipment with a cost of $57,000 were purchased and transferred to the general fund.
- Cash totaling $85,000 was transferred from the general fund.
- Securities costing $250,000 were purchased during the year.

Required

1. Prepare the journal entries to record the above transactions and events.
2. Prepare the plant replacement and expansion fund section of Elgin Hospital's balance sheet.
3. Prepare the plant replacement and expansion fund section of Elgin Hospital's statement of changes in fund balances.

EXERCISE 20-10

The trial balance of the endowment funds of Faith and Charity Hospital on January 1, 1990 was

	Debit	Credit
Cash	$ 20,000	
Investments	623,000	
Accrued Interest Receivable	11,000	
Due to General Fund		$ 5,000
Due to Plant Replacement and Expansion Fund		6,000
Fund Balance: Restricted		330,000
Fund Balance: Unrestricted		313,000
	$ 654,000	$ 654,000

During 1990, the following transactions and events occurred that affected Faith and Charity Hospital's endowment funds:

- Restricted endowments of $81,000 and unrestricted endowments of $40,000 were received.
- Restricted term endowments of $35,000 for the purchase of equipment, which are to be transferred to the plant replacement and expansion fund, and unrestricted term endowments of $25,000 expired during the year.
- Restricted endowment investments for plant replacement and expansion earned $33,000 and unrestricted endowments earned $37,000.
- Cash in the amount of $68,500 was received as earnings from investments.
- Unrestricted investments with a cost of $23,000 were sold for $21,000.
- Restricted investments with a cost of $34,000 were sold for $38,000.
- Investments totaling $110,000 were purchased.
- Cash totaling $65,000 was transferred to the general fund and $70,000 in cash was transferred to the plant replacement and expansion fund.

Required

1. Prepare the journal entries to record the above transactions and events.
2. Prepare the endowment funds section of Faith and Charity Hospital's balance sheet.
3. Prepare the endowment funds section of Faith and Charity Hospital's statement of changes in fund balances.

PROBLEMS

PROBLEM 20-1

Listed below are four independent transactions or events that relate to a not-for-profit hospital:

1. $25,000 was disbursed from the general fund for the cash purchase of new equipment.
2. An unrestricted cash gift of $100,000 was received from a donor.
3. Listed common stocks with a total carrying value of $50,000, exclusive of any allowance, were sold by an endowment fund for $55,000, before any dividends were earned on these stocks. There are no restrictions on the gain.
4. $1,000,000 face amount of bonds payable were sold at par, with the proceeds required to be used solely for construction of a new building. The building was completed at a total cost of $1,000,000,

and the total amount of bond issue proceeds was disbursed in connection therewith. Disregard interest capitalization.

Required

For each of the above-listed transactions or events, prepare journal entries, with explanations, specifying the affected funds and showing how these transactions or events are recorded by a not-for-profit hospital.

(AICPA adapted)

PROBLEM 20-2

The following transactions were recorded by the bookkeeper of Arnold Hospital for the year ended June 30, 1991. The bookkeeper has never before prepared entries for a not-for-profit hospital.

General Fund

Cash	25,000	
Patient Service Revenue		25,000

To record the receipts of the hospital's cafeteria

Supplies Expense.	33,000	
Nonoperating Revenue		33,000

To record the receipt of donated medical supplies at the donor's cost. The hospital will have to pay $50,000 to replace the supplies.

Allowance for Uncollectible Accounts	82,000	
Accounts Receivable		82,000

To record the difference between the amount that third-party payors were billed and paid that was not paid by patients

Cash	18,000	
Patient Service Revenue		18,000

To record unrestricted donations received from former patients

Cash	50,000	
Pledges Receivable	450,000	
Nonoperating Revenue		500,000

To record cash and pledges received from the building addition fund drive. The hospital normally can collect 85% of the pledges received from fund drives.

Nursing Services Expenses	50,000	
Other Operating Revenue		50,000

To record the amount of volunteer time spent in the emergency room and outpatient surgery at $5 per hour. Nurses aids perform the same functions for the hospital at a cost of $8 per hour.

Cash	25,000	
Other Operating Revenue		25,000

To record the cash received from the estate of J. Johnson. The money cannot be spent, but the earnings can be used for any operating purpose of the hospital.

Specific-Purpose Fund

Lobby Redecorating Expenses   22,500
    Cash   22,500
To record the expenses of redecorating the lobby that is being paid
for by monies earned by volunteer fund-raising projects for lobby
redecoration

Plant Replacement and Expansion Fund

Cash   17,600
    Investment Revenue   17,600
To record the earnings on investments of the plant replacement
and expansion fund

Endowment Fund

Cash   21,400
    Investment Revenue: Unrestricted Endowments   12,800
    Investment Revenue: Restricted Endowments   8,600
To record the earnings of the investments in the endowment funds

Required

Prepare the journal entries that should have been written for each of the above incorrect entries identifying the correct fund for the entry. If an entry affects more than one fund, prepare the entries for all funds affected.

PROBLEM 20-3

Refer to Problem 20-2. Prepare correcting entries for any of the incorrect entries and prepare any omitted entries identifying your entries by fund.

PROBLEM 20-4

The following entries were recorded during the year ended June 30, 1992, the first year of operations, in the unrestricted funds of Newton Hospital. Newton Hospital's accountant did not understand the difference between cash accounting and accrual accounting or the proper accounts to use for hospital accounting; therefore, the entries were not correctly prepared. Newton Hospital's board of directors wants the records of the hospital maintained according to generally accepted accounting principles. The hospital was established with a $5,000,000 cash gift.

General Fund

Cash   2,240,000
    Operating Revenues   2,240,000
To record the cash collected for patient services

Cash	475,000	
Operating Revenues		475,000

To record the cash received from the following activities and
sources:

Cafeteria	$ 80,000
Parking Fees	25,000
Unrestricted Donations	120,000
Restricted Donations for Retirement of	
Mortgage	140,000
Tuition of Nursing Students	80,000
Endowment with Income Restricted to	
Equipment Purchases	30,000

Supplies Expense	160,000	
Cash		160,000

To record the amount paid for supplies during the year

Insurance Expense	450,000	
Cash		450,000

To record the purchase of a two-year comprehensive policy on
July 1, 1991

Nursing Services Expenses	800,000	
Other Professional Services Expenses	500,000	
General Services Expenses	100,000	
Fiscal Services Expenses	150,000	
Administrative Services Expenses	200,000	
Cash		1,750,000

To record the expenses for the year

Administrative Expenses	100,000	
Cash		100,000

To record the amount set aside by the board of directors for
retirement of the mortgage on the building

Additional Information

- Patients were billed $2,925,000 for services provided during the year. Third-party payors paid $185,000 less than billed that was not paid by patients. Patients without third-party payors and the ability to pay received $230,000 of medical care included in the amount billed. Other hospitals in the area have a loss ratio on uncollectible accounts receivable at the end of the year of 20%.
- Drug company donated $38,000 of drugs and medical supplies. Volunteers donated 5,000 hours of time that would have cost the hospital $69,000 had it paid its professional nursing staff to perform the services.
- Unpaid vouchers for supplies totaled $14,000 at year end. The inventory of supplies showed $32,000 on hand at the end of the year. The supplies are used equally by nursing services and other professional services.
- The insurance expense should be allocated equally between nursing services, other professional services, and administrative services.
- Unpaid vouchers at June 30, 1992 totaled $165,000. The vouchers are for the following expenses: nursing services $40,000, other professional services $35,000, general services $25,000, and fiscal services $65,000.
- The hospital initially purchased land for $1,500,000. The hospital building was built for $5,600,000 and financed entirely by a 25-year, 10% mortgage that requires the payment of interest each July 1

and $224,000 of principal. The first payment is due on July 1, 1992. The building is estimated to have a useful life of 40 years and no salvage value.

- The hospital purchased the following equipment with the initial cash gift prior to the opening of the hospital on July 1, 1991: fixed equipment $1,200,000 major movable equipment $900,000, minor equipment $200,000. The equipment is estimated to have a useful life of 10 years and no salvage value.
- The remainder of the initial cash gift, after the purchase of the land and equipment, was used as operating capital for the hospital, which was in accordance with the terms of the gift.
- The inventory of minor equipment shows $180,000 on hand at June 30, 1992. The equipment is used equally by the nursing services and other professional services.

Required

1. Prepare the journal entries that should have been recorded prior to the beginning of operations on July 1, 1991.
2. Prepare all the journal entries that should have been recorded for the unrestricted funds of Newton Hospital for the year ended June 30, 1992.
3. Prepare entries that should have been recorded in the donor-restricted funds but were recorded in the general fund.
4. Prepare the statement of revenue and expense for the year ended June 30, 1992.

PROBLEM 20-5

Refer to Problem 20-4.

Required

1. Prepare the journal entries that should have been prepared prior to the beginning of operations on July 1, 1991.
2. Prepare correcting journal entries for each of the transactions that was incorrectly recorded. Prepare the transaction or adjusting journal entries that were not recorded identifying the entries by fund.

PROBLEM 20-6

Esparanza Hospital's postclosing trial balance at December 31, 1990, is

	Debit	Credit
Cash	$ 60,000	
Investment in U.S. Treasury Bills	400,000	
Investment in Corporate Bonds	500,000	
Interest Receivable	10,000	
Accounts Receivable	50,000	
Inventory	30,000	
Land	100,000	
Building	800,000	
Equipment	170,000	
Allowance for Depreciation		$ 410,000
Accounts Payable		20,000
Notes Payable		70,000
Endowment Fund Balance		520,000
Other Fund Balances		1,100,000
Totals	$ 2,120,000	$ 2,120,000

Esperanza, which is a nonprofit hospital, did not maintain its books in conformity with the principles of hospital fund accounting. Effective January 1, 1991, Esperanza's board of trustees voted to adjust the

December 31, 1990 general ledger balances, and to establish separate funds for the general fund, the endowment fund, and the board-designated plant replacement and expansion fund.

Additional Information

- **Investment in Corporate Bonds** pertains to the amount required to be accumulated under a board policy to invest cash equal to accumulated depreciation until the funds are needed for asset replacement. The $500,000 balance at December 31, 1990 is less than the full amount required because of errors in computation of building depreciation for past years. Included in the Allowance for Depreciation is a correctly computed amount of $90,000 applicable to equipment.
- **Endowment Fund Balance** has been credited with the following:

Donor's bequest of cash	$ 300,000
Gains on sales of securities	100,000
Interest and dividends earned in 1988, 1989, and 1990	120,000
Total	$ 520,000

The terms of the bequest specify that the principal, plus all gains on sales of investments, are to remain fully invested in U.S. government or corporate securities. At December 31, 1990, $400,000 was invested in U.S. Treasury bills. The bequest further specifies that interest and dividends earned on investments are to be used for payment of current operating expenses.

- **Land** comprises the following:

Donation of land in 1950, at appraised value	$ 40,000
Appreciation in fair value of land as determined by an independent appraiser in 1990	60,000
Total	$ 100,000

- **Building** comprises the following:

Hospital building completed in January 1951, when operations were started (estimated useful life 50 years), at cost	$ 720,000
Installation of elevator in January 1971 (estimated useful life 20 years), at cost	80,000
Total	$ 800,000

Required

Using the following headings, set up a worksheet to adjust the general ledger account balances and to establish separate funds for Esperanza Hospital.

Esperanza Hospital
Worksheet to Adjust General Ledger Balances
and to Establish Separate Funds
January 1, 1991

	Trial Balance December 31, 1990		Adjustments		General Fund		Endowment Fund		Board-Designated Plant Replacement and Expansion Fund	
Account	Debit	Credit	Debit	Credit	Debit	Credit	Debit	Credit	Debit	Credit

PROBLEM 20-7

The following selected information was taken from the books and records of Glendora Hospital (a not-for-profit hospital) as of and for the year ended June 30, 1990:

- Patient service revenue total $16,000,000, with allowances and uncollectible accounts amounting to $3,400,000. Other operating revenue aggregated $346,000, and included $160,000 from specific-purpose funds. Revenue of $6,000,000 recognized under cost reimbursement agreements is subject to audit and retroactive adjustment by third-party payors. Estimated retroactive adjustments under these agreements have been included in allowances.
- Unrestricted gifts and bequests of $410,000 were received.
- Unrestricted income from endowment funds totaled $160,000.
- Income from board-designated funds aggregated $82,000.
- Operating expenses totaled $13,270,000, and included $500,000 for depreciation computed on the straight-line basis.
- Gifts and bequests are recorded at fair market values when received.
- Patient service revenue is accounted for at established rates on the accrual basis.

Required

Prepare a formal statement of revenues and expenses for Glendora Hospital for the year ended June 30, 1990.

(AICPA adapted)

PROBLEM 20-8

The adjusted trial balance of Hanover Hospital as of December 31, 1990 is

	Debit	Credit
General Fund		
Cash	$ 60,000	
Accounts and Notes Receivable	240,000	
Allowance for Uncollectible Receivables		$ 25,000
Due from Other Funds	5,000	
Supplies Inventory	40,000	
Prepaid Expenses	15,000	
Land	250,000	
Buildings	4,500,000	
Accumulated Depreciation: Buildings		2,500,000
Fixed Equipment	2,000,000	
Accumulated Depreciation: Fixed Equipment		400,000
Major Movable Equipment	1,500,000	
Accumulated Depreciation: Major Movable Equipment		400,000
Minor Equipment	400,000	
Accounts Payable		285,000
Accrued Expenses Payable		30,000
12% Bonds Payable		2,500,000
General Fund Balance		2,873,000
Patient Service Revenues		5,400,000
Donated Medicines and Medical Supplies		50,000
Donated Services		100,000

	Debit	Credit
Cafeteria Revenues		30,000
Unrestricted Current Operating Donations		45,000
Earnings from Endowment Investments		7,000
Earnings from Board-Designated Funds		30,000
Transfer of Expired Unrestricted Term Endowment		50,000
Parking Lot Fees		35,000
Contractual Adjustments	330,000	
Charity Services	420,000	
Provision for Uncollectible Accounts	30,000	
Nursing Services Expenses	2,200,000	
Other Professional Services Expenses	800,000	
General Services Expenses	500,000	
Fiscal Services Expenses	200,000	
Administrative Services Expenses	550,000	
Provision for Depreciation	620,000	
Transfer to Board-Designated Funds	100,000	
Board-Designated Fund		
Cash	10,000	
Marketable Securities	250,000	
Accrued Interest Receivable	5,000	
Due General Fund		5,000
Board-Designated Fund Balance		260,000
Plant Replacement and Expansion Fund		
Cash	20,000	
Marketable Securities	400,000	
Accrued Interest Receivable	10,000	
Pledges Receivable	110,000	
Allowance for Uncollectible Pledges		10,000
Plant Replacement and Expansion Fund Balance		530,000
Endowment Funds		
Cash	15,000	
Accrued Interest Receivable: Restricted	5,000	
Long-Term Investments	260,000	
Restricted Fund Balance		210,000
Unrestricted Fund Balance		70,000
	$ 15,845,000	$ 15,845,000

The balances of the donor-restricted funds as of January 1, 1990 were as follows:

Plant Replacement and Expansion Fund	$ 157,000
Restricted Endowments	170,000
Unrestricted Endowments	125,000

The following additional information is for the donor-restricted funds:

- Donations totaling $200,000 and $100,000 of net collectible pledges were received by the plant replacement and expansion fund during the current year.

- Securities with a cost of $60,000 were sold for $70,000 by the plant replacement and expansion fund.
- A restricted endowment of $40,000 was received during the year.
- Unrestricted securities with a cost of $40,000 were sold for $35,000 by the endowment fund.
- Plant replacement and expansion fund earned $45,000 on its investments and the restricted endowment investments for plant replacement and expansion earned $18,000.

Required

1. Prepare the statement of revenue and expense of Hanover Hospital for year ended December 31, 1990.
2. Prepare the statement of changes in fund balances for Hanover Hospital for the year ended December 31, 1990 assuming all unrestricted current year's earnings were transferred to the general fund.
3. Prepare the balance sheet of Hanover Hospital as of December 31, 1990.

SOLUTION TO REVIEW PROBLEM

1.

Unrestricted Funds

General Fund

Cash	89,000	
Accounts and Notes Receivable	6,000,000	
Supplies Inventory	32,000	
Patient Services Revenue		6,000,000
Other Operating Revenues		121,000
To record operating revenues for the year		
Contractual Adjustments	285,000	
Charity Services	140,000	
Accounts and Notes Receivable		425,000
To record adjustments to operating revenues		
Due from Other Funds: Board-Designated Fund	25,000	
Due from Other Funds: Unrestricted Endowment Funds	7,000	
Nonoperating Revenues		32,000
To record investment income earned by other funds and due the operating fund		
Nursing Services Expense	25,000	
Nonoperating Revenues		25,000
To record the fair market value of donated services		
Cash	25,500	
Due from Other Funds: Board-Designated Fund		25,500
To record transfer of cash from board-designated fund		
Cash	2,900	
Nonoperating Revenues		2,900
To record transfer of cash from specific-purpose fund for refurbishing the waiting room		

Cash	52,800	
Due from Other Funds		9,000
Transfer from Plant Replacement and Expansion Fund		43,800
To record transfer of cash from plant replacement and expansion fund		
Cash	16,000	
Nonoperating Revenues		9,000
Due from Other Funds: Unrestricted Endowment Fund		7,000
To record transfer of $7,000 of unrestricted income and a $9,000 expired term endowment		
Nursing Services Expense	2,300,000	
Other Professional Services Expenses	1,020,000	
General Services Expenses	640,000	
Fiscal Services Expenses	170,000	
Administrative Services Expenses: Interest	350,000	
Administrative Services Expenses: Other	200,000	
Supplies Inventory	230,000	
Accounts Payable		4,560,000
Interest Payable		350,000
To record the accounts payable for the current year		
Cash	5,540,000	
Allowance for Uncollectible Accounts	22,000	
Accounts and Notes Receivable		5,562,000
To record the cash collected on account and the accounts written off during the year		
Prepaid Expenses	10,000	
Accrued Expenses Payable	28,000	
Accounts Payable	4,610,000	
Interest Payable	350,000	
Fixed Equipment	200,000	
Major Movable Equipment	120,000	
Minor Equipment	75.000	
General Services Expenses	2,900	
Cash		5,395,900
To record the cash disbursements for the year		
Cash	10,000	
Nonoperating Revenues: Loss on Sale of Equipment	5,000	
Accumulated Depreciation: Major Movable Equipment	85,000	
Major Movable Equipment		100,000
To record the sale of equipment		
Provision for Uncollectible Accounts (1)	23,800	
Allowance for Uncollectible Accounts		23,800
To record the estimate of Uncollectible accounts at the end of the year		

(1) $245,000 + $6,000,000 - $425,000 - $5,562,000 = $258,000$ receivables
    $258,000 \times 10\% = $25,800$
    $25,800 - (\$24,000 - \$22,000) = $23,800$

Nursing Services Expenses (2)	106,000	
Other Professional Services Expenses (2)	106,000	
Fiscal Services Expenses (3)	53,000	
Supplies Inventory (1)		265,000
To record the supplies used during the period		

(1) $47,000 + $32,000 + $230,000 - $44,000 = $265,000
(2) $265,000 \times 40\% = $106,000
(3) $265,000 \times 20\% = $53,000

Administrative Expenses (1)	13,000	
Prepaid Expenses		13,000
To record the prepaid expenses during the period		

(1) $12,000 + $10,000 - $9,000 = $13,000

Administrative Expenses	24,000	
Accrued Expense Payable		24,000
To record the expenses incurred but not accrued at year end		

Nursing Services Expenses (2)	30,000	
Other Professional Services Expenses (2)	30,000	
Minor Equipment (1)		60,000
To record the minor equipment no longer available for use		

(1) $320,000 + $75,000 - $335,000 = $60,000
(2) $60,000 \times 50\% = $30,000

Provision for Depreciation	542,500	
Accumulated Depreciation: Buildings		167,500
Accumulated Depreciation: Fixed Equipment		210,000
Accumulated Depreciation: Major Movable Equipment		165,000
To record the depreciation expense for the current year		

Transfer to Board-Designated Funds (1)	299,300	
Cash		299,300
To transfer cash to board-designated fund per board of directors policy		

(1) $59,000 + $89,000 + $25,500 + $2,900 + $52,800 + $16,000
   + $5,540,000 - $5,395,900 + $10,000 = $399,300
   $399,300 - $100,000 = $299,300

Board-Designated Fund

Accrued Interest Receivable	25,000	
Due General Fund		25,000
To record revenue for the year		

Due General Fund	25,500	
Cash		25,500
To record transfer to the operating fund		

Cash	25,500	
Accrued Interest Receivable		25,500
To record collection of accrued interest receivable		

Cash	299,300	
Fund Balance: Board-Designated Fund		299,300
To record transfer from general fund		

Marketable Securities (1)	283,300	
Cash		283,300
To record the purchase of securities according to board of directors policy		

(1) \$4,000 − \$25,500 + \$25,500 + \$299,300 = \$303,300
    \$303,300 − \$20,000 = \$283,300

Donor-Restricted Funds

Specific-Purpose Fund

Cash	5,000	
Fund Balance		5,000
To record receipt of cash from Ladies Auxiliary		

Fund Balance	2,900	
Cash		2,900
To record the transfer of cash to the operating fund		

Plant Replacement and Expansion Fund

Accrued Interest Receivable	50,000	
Fund Balance		50,000
To record revenue for the year		

Due General Fund	9,000	
Transfer to General Fund	43,800	
Cash		52,800
To record transfer of cash due general fund		

Cash	54,000	
Accrued Interest Receivable		54,000
To record interest revenue collected for current year		

Cash	200,000	
Pledges Receivable	2,500,000	
Allowance for Uncollectible Pledges		250,000
Fund Balance		2,450,000
To record the cash and pledges from the fund-raising campaign for an intermediate care center		

Cash	600,000	
Allowance for Uncollectible Pledges	50,000	
Pledges Receivable		650,000
To record the pledges collected and the pledges deemed not collectible		

Cash	40,000	
Marketable Securities		37,000
Fund Balance: Plant Replacement and Expansion Fund		3,000
To record the sale of marketable securities		

Marketable Securities (1)	841,200	
Cash		841,200
To record the purchase of marketable securities		

(1) $20,000 − $52,800 + $54,000 + $200,000 + $600,000
    + $40,000 = $861,200 − $20,000 = $841,200

Endowment Funds

Accrued Interest Receivable	7,000	
Due General Fund		7,000
To record the income for the year from unrestricted endowments		

Due General Fund	7,000	
Restricted Fund Balance: Endowment Fund	9,000	
Cash		16,000
To record transfer of unrestricted income and expired term endowment to the general fund		

Accrued Interest Receivable	23,000	
Restricted Fund Balance: Endowment Fund		23,000
To record earnings of restricted endowment funds		

Cash	28,600	
Accrued Interest Receivable		28,600
To record the collection of accrued interest receivable		

Cash	25,000	
Restricted Fund Balance: Endowment Fund		25,000
To record the receipt of an endowment		

Long-Term Investments (1)	37,600	
Cash		37,600
To record the purchase of investments per the board of directors policy		

(1) $15,000 − $16,000 + $28,600 + $25,000 = $52,600
    $52,600 − $15,000 = $37,600

2.

BAYSHORE HOSPITAL
Adjusted Trial Balance: General Fund
December 31, 1990

	Debit	Credit
Cash	$ 100,000	
Accounts and Notes Receivable	258,000	
Allowance for Uncollectible Receivables		$ 25,800
Due from Other Funds	2,500	
Supplies Inventory	44,000	
Prepaid Expenses	9,000	
Land	450,000	
Buildings	6,700,000	
Accumulated Depreciation: Buildings		2,667,500
Fixed Equipment	2,000,000	
Accumulated Depreciation: Fixed Equipment		660,000
Major Movable Equipment	1,120,000	
Accumulated Depreciation: Major Movable Equipment		610,000
Minor Equipment	335,000	
Accounts Payable		290,000
Accrued Expenses Payable		24,000
10% Bonds Payable		3,500,000
Fund Balance		3,373,000
Patient Service Revenues		6,000,000
Other Operating Revenues		121,000
Nonoperating Revenues		63,900
Transfer from Plant Replacement and Expansion Fund		43,800
Contractual Adjustments	285,000	
Charity Services	140,000	
Provision for Uncollectible Accounts	23,800	
Nursing Services Expenses	2,461,000	
Other Professional Services Expenses	1,156,000	
General Services Expenses	642,900	
Fiscal Services Expenses	223,000	
Administrative Expenses: Interest	350,000	
Administrative Services Expenses: Other	237,000	
Provision for Depreciation	542,500	
Transfer to Board-Designated Funds	299,300	
	$ 17,379,000	$ 17,379,000

BAYSHORE HOSPITAL
Adjusted Trial Balance: Board-Designated Funds
December 31, 1990

	Debit	Credit
Cash	$ 20,000	
Marketable Securities	523,300	
Accrued Interest Receivable	2,500	
Due General Fund		$ 2,500
Fund Balance: Board-Designated Funds		543,300
	$ 545,800	$ 545,800

BAYSHORE HOSPITAL
Adjusted Trial Balance: Specific-Purpose Fund
December 31, 1990

	Debit	Credit
Cash	$ 2,100	
Fund Balance: Specific-Purpose Fund		$ 2,100
	$ 2,100	$ 2,100

BAYSHORE HOSPITAL
Adjusted Trial Balance: Plant Replacement and Expansion Fund
December 31, 1990

	Debit	Credit
Cash	$ 20,000	
Marketable Securities	1,296,200	
Accrued Interest Receivable	5,000	
Pledges Receivable	1,850,000	
Allowance for Uncollectible Pledges		$ 200,000
Fund Balance: Plant Replacement and Expansion Fund		2,971,200
	$ 3,171,200	$ 3,171,200

BAYSHORE HOSPITAL
Adjusted Trial Balance: Endowment Funds
December 31, 1990

	Debit	Credit
Cash	$ 15,000	
Accrued Interest Receivable	3,400	
Long-term Investments	297,600	
Restricted Fund Balance: Endowment Funds		$ 249,000
Unrestricted Fund Balance: Endowment Funds		67,000
	$ 316,000	$ 316,000

BAYSHORE HOSPITAL
Statement of Revenues and Expenses
Year Ended December 31, 1990

Patient Services Revenues		$ 6,000,000
Deductions from Patient Services Revenues		
Contractual Adjustments	$ 285,000	
Charity Services	140,000	
Provision for Uncollectible Accounts	23,800	448,800
Net Patient Service Revenue		5,551,200
Other Operating Revenue		121,000
Total Operating Revenue		5,672,200
Operating Expenses		
Nursing Services	2,461,000	
Other Professional Services	1,156,000	
General Services	642,900	
Fiscal Services	223,000	
Administrative Services: Interest	350,000	
Administrative Services: Other	237,000	
Provision for Depreciation	542,500	5,612,400
Profit from Operations		59,800
Nonoperating Revenue		63,900
Excess of Revenue Over Expenses		$ 123,700

Note: When nonoperating revenues are considered material, the details of the sources are presented in the statement. Since no one item included in nonoperating revenue was material, the revenues are not reported by source.

3.

BAYSHORE HOSPITAL
Balance Sheet
December 31, 1990

Assets   Liabilities and Fund Balances

UNRESTRICTED FUNDS

Current Assets			**Current Liabilities**		
Cash		$ 120,000	Accounts Payable		$ 290,000
Marketable Securities		523,300	Accrued Expenses Payable		24,000
Interest Receivable		2,500	Total Current Liabilities		314,000
Accounts and Notes Receivable (1)	$ 258,000		**Long-term Liabilities**		
Less: Allowance for Uncollectible Receivables	25,800	232,200	10% Bonds Payable		3,500,000
Supplies Inventory		44,000	Total Liabilities		3,814,000
Prepaid Expenses		9,000	**Fund Balances**		
Total Current Assets		931,000	General Fund Balance (2)		3,241,200
Property, Plant, and Equipment			Board-Designated Fund Balance		543,300
Land		450,000	Total Fund Balances		3,784,500
Buildings	6,700,000				
Less: Accumulated Depreciation	2,667,500	4,032,500			
Fixed Equipment	2,000,000				
Less: Accumulated Depreciation	660,000	1,340,000			
Major Movable Equipment	1,120,000				
Less: Accumulated Depreciation	610,000	510,000			
Minor Equipment		335,000			
Total Property, Plant and Equipment		6,667,500			
Total Unrestricted Funds		**$ 7,598,500**	**Total Unrestricted Funds**		**$ 7,598,500**

DONOR-RESTRICTED FUNDS

Specific-Purpose Fund

Cash	$ 2,100	Fund Balance	$ 2,100

Plant Replacement and Expansion Fund

Cash		$ 20,000	Fund Balance	$ 2,971,000
Marketable Securities		1,296,200		
Accrued Interest Receivable		5,000		
Pledges Receivable	$ 1,850,000			
Less: Allowance for Uncollectible Pledges	200,000	1,650,000		
Total Plant Replacement and Expansion Fund		$ 2,971,200	Total Plant Replacement and Expansion Fund	$ 2,971,200

Endowment Funds

Cash	$ 15,000	Fund Balance: Income Not Restricted	$ 249,000
Accrued Interest Receivable	3,400		
Long-term Investments	297,600	Fund Balance: Income Restricted	67,000
Total Endowment Funds	$ 316,000	Total Endowment Funds	$ 316,000

(1) $2,500 receivable and payable between the two funds has been eliminated.
(2) $3,373,000 + $123,700 + $43,800 − $299,300 = $3,241,200

BAYSHORE HOSPITAL
Statement of Changes in Fund Balances
Year Ended December 31, 1990

Unrestricted Funds

Balance at Beginning of Year	$ 3,617,000
Excess of Revenues Over Expenses	123,700
Transfer from Plant Replacement and Expansion Fund	43,800
Balance at End of Year	$ 3,784,500

Donor-Restricted Funds

Specific-Purpose Fund

Balance at Beginning of Year	$ —0—	
Donations Received	5,000	
Transfer to General Fund	(2,900)	
Balance at End of Year		$ 2,100

Plant Replacement and Expansion Fund

Balance at Beginning of Year	512,000	
Donations Received	200,000	
Pledges Received	2,250,000	
Interest Earned	50,000	
Transfer to General Fund	(43,800)	
Gain on Sale of Marketable Securities	3,000	
Balance at End of Year		$ 2,971,200

Endowment Funds
Income Restricted Funds

Balance at Beginning of Year	210,000	
Interest Earned	23,000	
Expired Term Endowment to General Fund	(9,000)	
Endowments Received	25,000	
Balance at End of Year		249,000

Income Not Restricted Funds

Balance at Beginning of Year	67,000	
Interest Earned	7,000	
Transfer to General Fund	(7,000)	
Balance at End of Year		67,000

Total Donor-Restricted Funds	$ 3,289,300

CHAPTER
21

VOLUNTARY HEALTH AND WELFARE ORGANIZATIONS AND OTHER NOT-FOR-PROFIT ORGANIZATIONS

oluntary health and welfare organizations include all the not-for-profit organizations (1) whose primary source of revenue is from voluntary contributions from the public who do not directly benefit from the organization's services, and (2) whose activities are health, welfare, or community service. Many of these organizations are affiliated with national organizations that have the same objectives, such as the local chapter and the national chapter of the Red Cross. The national organization may exert either a minimal amount or substantial amounts of control over the activities of the local organization. The organizations classified as other not-for-profit organizations include all the not-for-profit organizations that are not hospitals, voluntary health and welfare organizations, or colleges and universities. The topics of this chapter for voluntary health and welfare organizations are

- Sources of generally accepted accounting principles for voluntary health and welfare organizations
- Comparison of the funds of a voluntary health and welfare organization with the funds of a not-for-profit hospital including the current unrestricted fund and the restricted funds
- Depreciation
- Financial statements including the statement of support, revenues, expenses, and changes in fund balances; a statement of functional expenses; and a balance sheet
- Public support including contributions in the form of cash, pledges, and donated assets and services; special events; legacies and bequests; and receipts from federated and nonfederated campaigns
- Other revenues
- Expenses including program services expenses and supporting services expenses

The topics of other not-for-profit organizations include

- Types of organizations
- Sources of generally accepted accounting principles
- Comparison to a voluntary health and welfare organization including funds used, financial statements, revenues, and expenses
- Sample set of statements for an other not-for-profit organization

VOLUNTARY HEALTH AND WELFARE ORGANIZATIONS

Generally accepted accounting principles for voluntary health and welfare organizations are contained in an industry audit guide and standards established by the National Health Council. These publications are the industry audit guide, *Audits of Voluntary Health and Welfare Organizations,*[1] and *Standards of Accounting and Financial Reporting for Voluntary Health and Welfare Organizations.*[2]

COMPARISON OF THE FUNDS OF A VOLUNTARY HEALTH AND WELFARE ORGANIZATION WITH THE FUNDS OF A NOT-FOR-PROFIT HOSPITAL

Voluntary health and welfare organizations use fund accounting on the accrual basis the same as do not-for-profit hospitals. Voluntary health and welfare organizations use a current unrestricted fund to account for current operations. In addition, the following restricted funds are typically used: current restricted fund, plant fund (land, building, and equipment fund), and endowment funds. The organizations may also use a custodian fund.

CURRENT UNRESTRICTED FUND

The current unrestricted fund is similar to the general fund of a hospital in that the assets are used at the discretion of the governing board for current operations. The current unrestricted fund differs from a not-for-profit hospital's general fund, however, in that the fund includes only current assets and current liabilities. The fixed assets and the long-term debt are accounted for in the plant fund, rather than in the current unrestricted fund. The governing board of the organization may set aside assets for a specific purpose and thus create a board-designated subgroup of accounts within the current unrestricted fund.

---

[1] *Audits of Voluntary Health and Welfare Organizations* (New York: AICPA), 1974.

[2] *Standards of Accounting and Financial Reporting for Voluntary Health and Welfare Organizations,* National Health Council, National Assembly for Social Policy and Developments, Inc., and United Way of America, revised edition (Washington, D.C.), 1974.

RESTRICTED FUNDS

The current restricted fund assets are used for current operating purposes; however, the voluntary health and welfare organization must use the assets according to the restrictions placed on their use by the donor. The plant fund (land, buildings, and equipment fund) is used to account for these assets as well as assets contributed whose use is restricted to the acquisition or replacement of plant assets. In addition, the long-term debt of the voluntary health and welfare organization is also accounted for in the plant fund, together with the assets donated for the repayment of that debt. The endowment funds are exactly like the endowment funds of a not-for-profit hospital. The income that can be used for general operating purposes is transferred to the current unrestricted fund, and the income that is restricted in use is transferred either to the current restricted fund or to the plant fund if it can currently be used. If not, it is added to the fund balance. The custodian fund is similar to the agency fund of a not-for-profit hospital because the assets are not the assets of the voluntary health and welfare organization. The assets are held or disbursed only on the instructions of the entity who donated the assets.

DEPRECIATION

Since the issuance of the audit guide, *Audits of Voluntary Health and Welfare Organizations,* voluntary health and welfare organizations have been required by generally accepted accounting principles to record depreciation. Depreciation expense is recorded and assigned to the program or service that benefits from the use of the assets. Because depreciable assets are recorded in the plant fund, the accumulated depreciation also is recorded in that fund. The recording of depreciation allows the voluntary health and welfare organization to better assess the total cost of providing a particular program or service.

FINANCIAL STATEMENTS OF A VOLUNTARY HEALTH AND WELFARE ORGANIZATION

The financial statements of a voluntary health and welfare organization consist of a statement of support, revenues, expenses, and changes in fund balances, a statement of functional expenses, and a balance sheet. A statement of cash flows is not required because the information that would be contained in the statement is presented in the other statements.

The statement of support, revenues, expenses, and changes in fund balances includes all the different funds used by the entity. Rather than presenting a statement of changes in fund balances separately as a not-for-profit hospital does, the financial statements of a voluntary health and welfare organization combine these two statements into a single statement. The statement of functional expenses reports the expenses by type, such as salaries and promotion expenses, for each of the different programs or services provided by the voluntary health and welfare organization. Just as not-for-profit hospitals present the balance sheet on a fund by fund basis, the balance sheet of a voluntary health and welfare organization also presents the information on a fund by fund basis.

PUBLIC SUPPORT

Cash donations and pledges from the public constitute the primary source of revenue for a voluntary health and welfare organization. These donations and pledges may be unrestricted or their use may be restricted by the donor. When a contribution is donated without restrictions, the assets and the revenue are recorded in the current unrestricted fund. If the contribution is restricted, the assets and the revenue are recognized in the appropriate restricted fund, unlike a not-for-profit hospital, which recognizes revenue only in the operating fund. In addition, voluntary health and welfare organizations recognize revenue from restricted donations when the contribution is received.

If the donation or pledge is restricted, but for current operations, the assets and revenue are recorded in the current restricted fund. If the contribution is restricted to the acquisition or replacement of land, buildings, or equipment, the contribution is recorded in the plant fund. If the voluntary health and welfare organization must maintain the assets but can use the revenue, the assets are recorded in an endowment fund.

Contributors to a voluntary health and welfare organization may specify the year or years in which the assets contributed can be used by the organization. If a contribution cannot be used in the year in which it is given to the organization, the contribution is not recognized as revenue until the year in which the assets can be used. Until the asset can be used, the amount of the asset received is recorded as a deferred credit (revenue).

Public support is divided into the following categories:

- Contributions
- Special events support
- Legacies and bequests
- Receipts from federated and nonfederated campaigns

CONTRIBUTIONS

Contributions are obtained by the voluntary health and welfare organization by a variety of means. The methods include direct mail campaigns, door-to-door solicitation, radio and television solicitations, and street sales and solicitation. If the contribution is in the form of a pledge of future assets, the receivable is recorded and an allowance is established for uncollectible pledges. The amount that is estimated to be uncollectible is recorded in the account, Provision for Uncollectible Accounts. This account is treated as a contra revenue account instead of as an expense account in the financial statements. The revenue is shown net with the provision parenthetically reported.

For example, a voluntary health and welfare organization received the following unrestricted contributions during the current year:

Cash for Use in the Current Year	$ 47,000
Cash for Use in Future Periods	10,000
Pledges, Estimated 90% Collectible	90,000

In addition, unrestricted contributions totaling $8,000 that were received in prior years can be used in the current year. The journal entries to record the unrestricted contributions are

Unrestricted Current Fund

Cash	57,000	
Public Support		47,000
Contributions Designated for Future Periods		10,000
To record the cash contributions received during the current year		
Pledges Receivable	90,000	
Public Support		90,000
To record the pledges received during the current year		
Provision for Uncollectible Pledges (Public Support)	9,000	
Allowance for Uncollectible Pledges		9,000
To record as uncollectible 10% of the pledges received during the year		
Contributions Designated for Future Periods	8,000	
Public Support		8,000
To record as revenue contributions of prior years that can be used during the current year		

The voluntary health and welfare organization also received cash of $20,000 and pledges of $45,000, which are estimated to be 90% collectible, with use restricted to a counseling center's expenses. The journal entries to record the restricted contributions received during the current year are

Restricted Current Fund

Cash	20,000	
Pledges Receivable	45,000	
Public Support		65,000
To record the contributions received from the fund-raising campaign		
Provision for Uncollectible Pledges	4,500	
Allowance for Uncollectible Pledges		4,500
To record as uncollectible 10% of the pledges received during the current year		

Donated Assets. Voluntary health and welfare organizations receive significant amounts of donated assets and volunteer time. When donated assets are used in the provision of services, they are recorded at their fair market value and a corresponding expense is recorded. If the voluntary health and welfare organization simply receives the donated goods and then distributes them to the recipients without charge, the assets are not recorded. For example, a free health clinic that receives donated medicine recognizes the asset, records the support contributed, and recognizes an expense when the medicine is used. A voluntary health and welfare organization that receives clothing and then distributes the clothing without charge to needy families would neither record an asset nor recognize the support. If the voluntary health and welfare organization receives free use of facilities and other assets, the fair market value is recorded both as a contribution and as an expense.

Donated Services. The amount of services donated to a voluntary health and welfare organization varies from minimal amounts provided by volunteer fund-raisers to active participation in the organization's programs. When the amount of donated services is material, the value of the donated services is recorded if the following three criteria are met:

1. The services would be performed by salaried personnel if not provided by the volunteer.
2. The organization controls the activities of the volunteer.
3. The organization is able to measure the value of the services (usually based on the amount salaried personnel would receive for the same service).

The value of the donated services is recorded as both a contribution and salaries expense of the service or program.

For example, a voluntary health and welfare organization received volunteer professional service in both its rehabilitation center and its counseling center. If the organization had not received the volunteer service, it would have paid comparable professionals $37,000 for the services donated to the rehabilitation center and $13,000 for the services donated to the counseling center. The journal entry to record these volunteer professional services is

Unrestricted Current Fund

Rehabilitation Center Expenses	37,000	
Counseling Center Expenses	13,000	
Public Support		50,000

To record the services provided for by volunteers which would have required the use of professionals without the donated services

If a voluntary health and welfare organization receives two hours of time from 10 volunteers to canvas neighborhoods for contributions, the donated service would not be recorded on the assumption that the organization would not pay someone to do the canvasing.

SPECIAL EVENTS

The revenues net of the direct costs from special activities such as raffles, auctions, bake sales, car washes, fund-raising breakfasts and dinners, bazaars, dances, theater parties, and stage shows are reported in the financial statements as support. All of these activities provide a product or a service to the individual in exchange for the donation. The revenues typically come from the sale of tickets. Some tickets are used for the event and some are purchased as a contribution to the organization (the buyer does not intend to use the ticket).

For example, a voluntary health and welfare organization holds an annual auction to raise additional operating money. The current year's auction grossed $21,000 from purchasers of the auction items and the organization spent $12,000 to hold the auction. The journal entries to record the revenue and expense of holding the auction are

Unrestricted Current Fund

Cash	21,000	
Special Events		21,000

To record the revenue from the annual auction

Special Events: Direct Costs	9,000	
Cash		9,000

To record the direct costs of the annual auction

LEGACIES AND BEQUESTS

Legacies and bequests are assets contributed to the voluntary health and welfare organization according to the will of a deceased person or from either a testamentary or inter vivos trust. These assets typically are substantial in amount compared to the average cash donation, pledge, or fund-raising ticket. Unlike a not-for-profit hospital, the voluntary health and welfare organization treats the assets received as revenue of the appropriate fund. A hospital records the legacy or bequest that creates an endowment fund as a receipt of principal.

For example, a voluntary health and welfare organization received a bequest in the amount of $20,000 whose income can be used for current operations. The journal entry in the endowment fund to record this transaction is

Endowment Funds

Cash	20,000	
Legacies and Bequests		20,000

To record the receipt of a bequest whose income can be used for current operations

RECEIPTS FROM FEDERATED AND NONFEDERATED CAMPAIGNS

The most common example of support from a federated campaign is an allocation of the assets collected by the United Way. A nonfederated campaign is one in which either the local organization or the national affiliate uses either volunteer or professional fund-raising entities to solicit contributions for the voluntary health and welfare organization.

OTHER REVENUES

In addition to the public support provided to a voluntary health and welfare organization, the organization may have revenue either from the fees charged for services or from investments. The fees for services come from three different sources: membership dues, fees charged for program services, and the sales of publications, supplies, and services to the general public. Typically, a voluntary health and welfare organization provides services and asks the recipients of the services to pay a fee equal to the amount they can afford to spend for the service. The revenues from investments include interest, dividends, and rental income, as well as the gains and losses from the sale of investments other than the sale of endowment assets.

EXPENSES

Voluntary health and welfare organizations vary widely from organization to organization. Any one voluntary health and welfare organization may have a single program or service or the organization may provide several programs and services. In both the statement of revenues, expenses, and changes in fund balances and the statement of functional expenses, functional expenses are divided into two categories: program services and supporting services. As previously mentioned, in the statement of support, revenues, expenses, and changes in fund balances, expenses are reported by fund for each program and for supporting services, whereas in the statement of functional expenses, expenses are reported by type for each service or program provided by the voluntary health and welfare organization.

PROGRAM SERVICES EXPENSES

Program services expenses include both the direct expenses of each social service activity and the indirect expenses that can be readily allocated to the activity. For example, if a local health and welfare organization has undertaken a campaign to inform and educate the public about the dangers of driving while intoxicated, indirect costs, such as a portion of the salaries and payroll benefits of executive personnel, are allocated to the campaign.

SUPPORTING SERVICES EXPENSES

Supporting services expenses are categorized into two groups: management and general expenses, and fund-raising expenses. Management and general expenses include the costs of overall operations of the organization as well as indirect costs of programs and services not readily allocable to those programs and services. In addition, the costs of publicity and public relations not associated with a specific fund-raising activity are classified as management and general expenses.

Fund-raising expenses include not only the direct expenses of soliciting contributions but all the indirect expenses of fund-raising. Fund-raising expenses are usually charged to the current unrestricted fund, unless the fund-raising campaign is for a specific purpose such as a building fund campaign or a mortgage retirement campaign.

Illustrative Problem 21.1 presents the accounting and financial reporting for a hypothetical voluntary health and welfare organization. Because voluntary health and welfare organizations vary widely by type of activity and size, other voluntary health and welfare organizations may be quite different from the illustrative problem. The organization in the following illustration has only three programs. Other voluntary health and welfare organizations may have only one program whereas others may provide more than three programs. Just as with not-for-profit hospitals, revenues and expenses are recognized in summary form by major line items that would appear on the statement of support, revenues, expenses, and changes in fund balances.

A voluntary health and welfare organization can record expenses by the major categories of the programs and supporting services or by type of expense. If expenses are recorded by categories of the programs and supporting services, details as to the type of expense contained within each category are necessary in order to prepare the statement of functional expenses by type of expense. If the expenses are recorded by type, then the expenses must be assigned to the categories of programs and supporting services to be able to prepare the statement of support, revenues, expenses, and changes in fund balances. In order to provide continuity in the journal entries throughout the discussion of not-for-profit entities, Illustrative Problem 21.1 is presented on the assumption that expenses are recorded by program and supporting service categories with sufficient supporting detail to prepare the statement of functional expenses. Illustrative Problem 21.1 incorporates the journal entries previously presented in the chapter and the facts to support those journal entries are not repeated. If a new transaction or event is presented, the information for the entry also is presented.

ILLUSTRATIVE PROBLEM 21.1: ACCOUNTING AND FINANCIAL REPORTING FOR A VOLUNTARY HEALTH AND WELFARE ORGANIZATION

The Substance Abuse Association of Albany was formed to provide three programs to the community: a rehabilitation center, a counseling center, and a public education program.

CURRENT UNRESTRICTED FUND

The January 1, 1991 trial balance of the current unrestricted fund was

	Debit	Credit
Cash	$ 40,000	
Pledges Receivable	35,000	
Allowance for Uncollectible Pledges		$ 3,500
Educational Materials Inventory	8,000	
Supplies Inventory	6,000	
Investments	40,000	
Accounts Payable		28,000
Contributions Designated for Future Periods		14,000
Fund Balance: Board-Designated Current Unrestricted Funds for Educational Materials		22,000
Fund Balance: Undesignated Current Unrestricted Fund		61,500
Total Current Unrestricted Fund	$ 129,000	$ 129,000

During the year ended December 31, 1991, the following transactions and events are recorded in the current unrestricted fund.

Cash	57,000	
Public Support		47,000
Contributions Designated for Future Periods		10,000
To record the cash contributions received during the current year		
Pledges Receivable	90,000	
Public Support		90,000
To record the pledges received during the current year		
Provision for Uncollectible Pledges (Public Support)	9,000	
Allowance for Uncollectible Pledges		9,000
To record uncollectible accounts expense as 10% of pledges received during the year		

Contributions Designated for Future Periods	8,000	
Public Support		8,000

To record as revenue contributions of prior years that can be used during the current year

Rehabilitation Center Expenses	37,000	
Counseling Center Expenses	13,000	
Public Support		50,000

To record the services provided by volunteers, which would have required the use of professionals without the donated services

Cash	21,000	
Special Events		21,000

To record the revenue from the annual auction

Special Events: Direct Costs	9,000	
Cash		9,000

To record the direct costs of the annual auction

During the year ended December 31, 1991, the Substance Abuse Society received the following additional support and revenues:

Support	
United Way Allocation	$ 20,000
Revenue	
Fees for Services Provided by the Rehabilitation Center and the	
Counseling Center	41,000
Investment Revenue	5,000

The journal entries to record the additional support and revenue are

Cash	20,000	
Federated Campaign Support		20,000

To record the annual allocation from the United Way

Cash	41,000	
Program Service Fees		41,000

To record the fees charged patients at the rehabilitation center and the counseling center

Cash	5,000	
Investment Revenue		5,000

To record the interest earned on investments

During the year ended December 31, 1991, pledges totaling $67,000 were collected and pledges totaling $8,000 were determined to be uncollectible.

Cash	67,000	
Allowance for Uncollectible Pledges	8,000	
Pledges Receivable		75,000

To record the collection of pledges and the write-off of pledges determined to be uncollectible

The journal entries to record the expenses incurred and paid during 1991 are

Rehabilitation Center Expenses	98,000	
Counseling Center Expenses	30,000	
Educational Program Expenses	12,000	
Management and General Expenses	9,000	
Fund-raising Expenses	5,000	
Educational Materials Inventory	37,000	
Supplies Inventory	8,000	
Salaries and Employee Benefits Payable		120,000
Accounts Payable		79,000
To record the payables for the current year		

Salaries and Employee Benefits Payable	120,000	
Accounts Payable	84,000	
Cash		204,000
To record the payments of salaries and employee benefits payable and accounts payable		

During 1991, the endowment fund transferred cash in the amount of $6,000, which was the unrestricted income from endowments. The board of directors authorized the transfer of $17,000 from the board-designated fund to the current unrestricted fund. The journal entries to record these events are

Cash	6,000	
Investment Revenue		6,000
To record transfer from Endowment Fund of income earned on unrestricted endowments		

This entry has its counterpart in the endowment fund.

Fund Balance: Board-Designated Current Unrestricted Fund for Educational Materials	17,000	
Fund Balance: Current Unrestricted Fund		17,000
To record the transfer from the board-designated fund to the current unrestricted fund per the board of directors minutes		

On December 31, 1991, the following adjusting entry is recorded for the supplies and inventory used during the current year.

Rehabilitation Center Expenses	3,000	
Counseling Center Expenses	8,000	
Educational Expenses	30,000	
Management and General Expenses	5,000	
Fund-raising Expenses	2,000	
Educational Materials Inventory		39,000
Supplies Inventory		9,000
To record the educational materials and supplies used during the period		

The adjusted trial balance of the current unrestricted fund at December 31, 1991 is

	Debit	Credit
Cash	$ 44,000	
Pledges Receivable	50,000	
Allowance for Uncollectible Pledges		$ 4,500
Educational Materials Inventory	6,000	
Supplies Inventory	5,000	
Investments	40,000	
Accounts Payable		23,000
Contributions Designated for Future Periods		16,000
Fund Balance: Board-Designated Current Unrestricted Fund for Educational Materials		5,000
Fund Balance: Undesignated Current Unrestricted Fund		78,500
Public Support		195,000
Special Events		21,000
Federated Campaign		20,000
Program Service Fees		41,000
Investment Revenue		11,000
Provision for Uncollectible Pledges	9,000	
Special Events: Direct Costs	9,000	
Rehabilitation Center Expenses	138,000	
Counseling Center Expenses	51,000	
Educational Program Expenses	42,000	
Management and General Expenses	14,000	
Fund-raising Expenses	7,000	
Total Current Unrestricted Fund	$ 415,000	$ 415,000

CURRENT RESTRICTED FUND

The current restricted fund is used to account for revenues whose use is restricted by the donor to counseling center expenses. The trial balance of the current restricted fund at January 1, 1991 was

	Debit	Credit
Cash	$ 18,000	
Pledges Receivable	5,000	
Allowance for Uncollectible Pledges		$ 500
Accounts Payable		10,000
Fund Balance: Current Restricted Fund for Counseling		12,500
	$ 23,000	$ 23,000

The following summary transactions and events occurred and were recorded in the current restricted fund during the year ended December 31, 1991. A fund-raising compaign raised

$20,000 in cash and received pledges of $45,000. The pledges are estimated to be 90% collectible. The journal entries to record the revenue are

Cash	20,000	
Pledges Receivable	45,000	
Public Support		65,000
To record the contributions received from the fund-raising campaign		
Provision for Uncollectible Pledges	4,500	
Allowance for Uncollectible Pledges		4,500
To record the estimated uncollected pledges expense for the period		

During 1991, the endowment fund transferred cash of $5,000 representing the investment earnings from endowments whose income is restricted to the counseling center. The endowment fund also transferred an expired term endowment in the amount of $3,000. The journal entries to record these transfers from the endowment fund are

Cash	5,000	
Investment Revenue		5,000
To record the investment income transferred from restricted endowment funds		
Cash	3,000	
Transfer from Endowment Fund		3,000
To record the transfer of principal of an endowment fund whose term has expired. The endowment is for the purchase of literature regarding child abuse to be used in the counseling center.		

The above two entries have their counterpart in the endowment fund.

The following entries record the expenses, cash receipts, and cash disbursements for the current restricted fund.

Cash	42,000	
Allowance for Uncollectible Pledges	4,100	
Pledges Receivable		46,100
To record the collection of pledges and the write-off of pledges determined to be uncollectible		
Counseling Expenses	28,000	
Accounts Payable		28,000
To record the cost of educational materials used by the counselors purchased on account that are expected to be used within the current year		
Counseling Expenses	44,000	
Accounts Payable	32,000	
Cash		76,000
To record the cash disbursements for the current year		

The adjusted trial balance of the current restricted fund at December 31, 1991 is

	Debit	Credit
Cash	$ 12,000	
Pledges Receivable	3,900	
Allowance for Uncollectible Pledges		$ 900
Accounts Payable		6,000
Fund Balance: Current Restricted Fund for Counseling		12,500
Public Support		65,000
Investment Revenue		5,000
Provision for Uncollectible Pledges	4,500	
Counseling Center Expenses	72,000	
Transfer from Endowment Fund		3,000
Total Current Restricted Fund	$ 92,400	$ 92,400

PLANT FUND

The plant fund is used to account for the noncurrent assets and liabilities of the organization as well as contributions restricted to the acquisition of noncurrent assets or the payment of long-term debt. The trial balance of the plant fund at January 1, 1991 was

	Debit	Credit
Cash	$ 6,000	
Investments	35,000	
Land, Buildings, and Equipment	242,000	
Accumulated Depreciation		$ 88,000
10% Mortgage Payable		80,000
Fund Balance: Unexpended and Restricted		41,000
Fund Balance: Expended		74,000
Total Plant Fund	$ 283,000	$ 283,000

The following summary transaction and adjusting journal entries are recorded in the plant fund for the year ended December 31, 1991:

Cash	33,000	
Public Support		29,000
Investment Revenue		4,000

To record the contributions to the plant fund and the revenue from investments

Management and General Expenses (Interest)	8,000	
Mortgage Payable	10,000	
Cash		18,000

To record the current year's mortgage payments

Land, Buildings, and Equipment	16,000	
Cash		16,000

To record the purchase of equipment

Rehabilitation Center Expenses	5,000	
Counseling Center Expenses	2,000	
Educational Expenses	1,000	
Management and General Expenses	3,000	
Fund-raising Expenses	1,000	
Accumulated Depreciation		12,000

To record depreciation expense for the current year and allocate the depreciation to expense categories

The following entry adjusts the account, Fund Balance: Expended, making its balance equal to the net book value of the net investment in plant assets or alternatively the account, Fund Balance: Unexpended and Restricted, making its balance equal to the sum of cash and investments:

Fund Balance: Unexpended and Restricted	14,000	
Fund Balance: Expended		14,000

To transfer from Fund Balance: Unexpended to Fund Balance: Expended the increase in the net investment in plant as follows:

Acquisitions of Plant	$ 16,000
Payment of Mortgage Principal	10,000
Increase in Accumulated Depreciation	(12,000)
Increase in Investment	$ 14,000

The adjusted trial balance of the plant fund at December 31, 1991 is

	Debit	Credit
Cash	$ 5,000	
Investments	35,000	
Land, Buildings, and Equipment	258,000	
Accumulated Depreciation		$ 100,000
10% Mortgage Payable		70,000
Fund Balance: Unexpended and Restricted		27,000
Fund Balance: Expended		88,000
Public Support		29,000
Investment Revenue		4,000
Rehabilitation Center Expenses	5,000	
Counseling Center Expenses	2,000	
Educational Program Expenses	1,000	
Management and General Expenses	11,000	
Fund-raising Expenses	1,000	
Total Plant Fund	$ 318,000	$ 318,000

The closing journal entry will close the revenues and expenses to the account, Fund Balance: Unexpended and Restricted. The effect of the previous adjusting entry and the closing entry on the Fund Balance: Unexpended and Restricted account is

Beginning Balance of Fund Balance: Unexpended		$ 41,000
Add: Public Support		29,000
Investment Revenue		4,000
Less: Interest Expense	$ 8,000	
Depreciation	12,000	
Transfer to Fund Balance: Expended	14,000	34,000
Fund Balance: Unexpended		$ 40,000

ENDOWMENT FUNDS

The trial balance of the endowment funds at January 1, 1991 was

	Debit	Credit
Cash	$ 13,000	
Investments	95,000	
Fund Balance: Restricted		$ 35,000
Fund Balance: Unrestricted		73,000
	$ 108,000	$ 108,000

During the year ended December 31, 1991, the following summary transaction and transfer entries are recorded in the endowment funds:

Cash	11,000	
Due to Current Restricted Fund		5,000
Due to Current Unrestricted Fund		6,000
To record the income from investments		

The income received is for current operating purposes and, therefore, is to be transferred and recognized in those funds.

Cash	20,000	
Legacies and Bequests		20,000
To record the receipt of a bequest whose income can be used for current operations		
Due to Current Restricted Fund	5,000	
Due to Current Unrestricted Fund	6,000	
Cash		11,000
To record transfer to current restricted and unrestricted funds of investment income		

Transfer to Current Restricted Fund	3,000	
Cash		3,000

To record transfer of restricted principal of an endowment whose term has lapsed to the current restricted fund for use by the counseling center for literature regarding child abuse according to the donor's restrictions

The two previous entries have their counterparts in the current unrestricted and current restricted funds.

Cash	21,000	
Investments		18,000
Gain on Sale of Investments		3,000

To record the sale of investments held as unrestricted endowments

Investments	50,000	
Cash		50,000

To record the purchase of investments for unrestricted endowments

The adjusted trial balance of the endowment funds at December 31, 1991 is

	Debit	Credit
Cash	$ 1,000	
Investments	127,000	
Fund Balance: Restricted		$ 35,000
Fund Balance: Unrestricted		73,000
Legacies and Bequests		20,000
Gain on Sale of Investments		3,000
Transfer to Current Restricted Fund	3,000	
Total Endowment Funds	$ 131,000	$ 131,000

At the end of the year the balance in the Fund Balance: Restricted account is $32,000 ($35,000 − $3,000 transfer of expired endowment) and the balance in the Fund Balance: Unrestricted account is $96,000 ($73,000 + $20,000 endowment + $3,000 gains).

Exhibits 21-1, 21-2, and 21-3 present the financial statements for the Substance Abuse Association of Albany. Comparative statements are not presented, although in published statements the three statements would be presented in comparative form. Because the journal entries have been presented with expenses recorded by major line items for the statement of support, revenues, expenses, and changes in fund balance, the problem does not contain the detailed information to substantiate the information presented in the statement of functional expenses.

CLOSING JOURNAL ENTRIES

Each of the funds prepares a closing journal entry like the entry prepared for the general fund of a not-for-profit hospital. The prior discussion covered the effect of the closing entries on the funds with more than one balance.

EXHIBIT 21-1

Illustrative Problem 21.1
Substance Abuse Association of Albany
Statement of Support, Revenues, Expenses, and Changes in Fund Balances
Year Ended December 31, 1991

	Current Funds		Plant	Endowment	
	Unrestricted	Restricted	Fund	Fund	Total
Public Support and Revenue					
Public Support					
Contributions Net of Uncollectible Pledges	$ 186,000	$ 60,500	$ 29,000	—	$ 275,500
Special Events Net of Direct Costs	12,000	—	—	—	12,000
Legacies and Bequests	—	—	—	$ 20,000	20,000
Federated Campaign	20,000	—	—	—	20,000
Total Public Support	218,000	60,500	29,000	20,000	327,500
Revenues					
Program Service Fees	41,000	—	—	—	41,000
Investment Revenue	11,000	5,000	4,000	—	20,000
Gain on Sale of Investments	—	—	—	3,000	3,000
Total Revenue	52,000	5,000	4,000	3,000	64,000
Total Support and Revenue	270,000	65,500	33,000	23,000	391,500
Expenses					
Program Services					
Rehabilitation Center	138,000	—	5,000	—	143,000
Counseling Center	51,000	72,000	2,000	—	125,000
Educational Program	42,000	—	1,000	—	43,000
Total Program Services	231,000	72,000	8,000	—	311,000
Supporting Services					
Management and General	14,000	—	11,000	—	25,000
Fund-raising	7,000	—	1,000	—	8,000
Total Supporting Services	21,000	—	12,000	—	33,000
Total Expenses	252,000	72,000	20,000	—	344,000
Excess (Deficiency) of Public Support and Revenues Over Expenses	18,000	(6,500)	13,000	23,000	47,500
Other Changes					
Transfer of Endowment Fund Principal Whose Term Has Expired		3,000		(3,000)	
Fund Balances, Beginning of Year	83,500	12,500	115,000	108,000	319,000
Fund Balances, End of Year	$ 101,500	$ 9,000	$ 128,000	$ 128,000	$ 366,500

SUMMARY

A voluntary health and welfare organization is a not-for-profit organization (1) whose primary source of revenue is from voluntary contributions from the public who do not directly benefit from the organization's services, and (2) whose activities are health, welfare, or community service. A voluntary health and welfare organization uses a current unrestricted fund, a current restricted fund, a plant fund, and endowment funds to account for its transactions and events.

    The current unrestricted fund is used to account for current operations and contains only current assets and current liabilities. If the governing board of the organization sets aside assets

EXHIBIT 21-2

Illustrative Problem 21.1
Substance Abuse Association of Albany
Balance Sheet
December 31, 1991

Assets		Liabilities and Fund Balances	
		CURRENT FUND	
		Unrestricted	
Cash	$ 44,000	Accounts Payable	$ 23,000
Pledges: Net	45,500	Contributions Designated for Future Periods	16,000
Educational Materials Inventory	6,000	Total Liabilities and Deferred Revenues	39,000
Supplies Inventory	5,000	Fund Balance: Board-Designated	5,000
Investments	40,000		
		Fund Balance: Unrestricted	96,500
Total Assets	$ 140,500	Total Liabilities and Fund Balances	$ 140,500
		Restricted	
Cash	$ 12,000	Accounts Payable	$ 6,000
Pledges: Net	3,000	Fund Balance	9,000
Total Assets	$ 15,000	Total Liabilities and Fund Balances	$ 15,000
		PLANT FUND	
Cash	$ 5,000	Mortgage Payable	$ 70,000
Investments	35,000	Fund Balance: Unexpended	40,000
Land, Buildings, and Equipment: Net	158,000	Fund Balance: Expended	88,000
Total Assets	$ 198,000	Total Liabilities and Fund Balances	$ 198,000
		ENDOWMENT FUNDS	
Cash	$ 1,000	Fund Balance: Restricted	$ 32,000
Investments	127,000	Fund Balance: Unrestricted	96,000
Total Assets	$ 128,000	Total Liabilities and Fund Balances	$ 128,000

for a specific purpose, a board-designated subgroup of accounts is created within the current unrestricted fund.

The current restricted fund is used to account for operating assets whose use has been restricted by the donor. The plant fund of a voluntary health and welfare organization accounts for the plant assets, the depreciation of those assets, the debt incurred to acquire plant assets, and contributions for the acquisition of plant assets or the retirement of existing debt from the purchase of plant assets. The voluntary health and welfare organization accounts for its endowment funds in the same manner as a not-for-profit hospital.

The voluntary health and welfare organization accounts for its major source of revenue, public support, in four categories: contributions, special events, legacies and bequests, and

EXHIBIT 21-3

Illustrative Problem 21.1
Substance Abuse Association of Albany
Statement of Functional Expenses
Year Ended December 31, 1991

	Program Services				Support Services			
	Rehabilitation Center	Counseling Center	Educational Center	Total	Management and General	Fund-raising	Total	Total
Salaries and Employee Benefits	$ 75,000	$ 70,000	$ 8,000	$ 153,000	$ 8,000	$ 3,000	$ 11,000	$ 164,000
Professional Fees and Contract Payments	37,000	13,000	—	50,000	—	—	—	50,000
Educational Materials	2,000	35,000	29,000	66,000	—	1,000	1,000	67,000
Supplies	1,000	1,000	1,000	3,000	5,000	1,000	6,000	9,000
Facilities Costs	23,000	4,000	4,000	31,000	1,000	2,000	3,000	34,000
Subtotal	138,000	123,000	42,000	303,000	14,000	7,000	21,000	324,000
Depreciation	5,000	2,000	1,000	8,000	3,000	1,000	4,000	12,000
Interest	—	—	—	—	8,000	—	8,000	8,000
Total	$ 143,000	$ 125,000	$ 43,000	$ 311,000	$ 25,000	$ 8,000	$ 33,000	$ 344,000

receipts from federated and nonfederated campaigns. Unrestricted contributions are accounted for in the current unrestricted fund and restricted operating contributions are accounted for in the current restricted fund. If a contribution is a pledge, any provision required for uncollectible pledges is treated as an adjustment of revenue and not as an expense of the period.

Donated assets are recorded at their fair market value and revenue is recognized. If the donated asset is then used in the provision of services, an expense is recognized. If donated assets are simply passed through the organization, such as donated food for the needy, no entries are recorded. Donated services are recorded at their fair market value with a corresponding expense if the organization would have had to pay personnel to do the job, if the organization controls the activities of the volunteer, and if the organization is able to measure the value of the services.

Special events revenue is recorded gross and reported net of the direct costs of the event. The sources of revenue of a voluntary health and welfare organization are membership dues, fees charged for its programs or services, investment income, and gains and losses from the sales of investments.

The expenses of a voluntary health and welfare organization are divided into program or service expenses and supporting services. The supporting services are further divided into management and general, and fund-raising. The expenses of a voluntary health and welfare organization are reported in two ways: by program or service in the statement of support, revenue, expenses, and changes in fund balances and by type of expense in the statement of functional expenses.

The financial statements of a voluntary health and welfare organization include a statement of support, revenues, expenses, and changes in fund balances; a statement of functional expenses; and a balance sheet. Voluntary health and welfare organizations vary considerably in size and in number of programs and services; thus the complexity of the financial statements varies as well.

OTHER NOT-FOR-PROFIT ORGANIZATIONS

The other not-for-profit organizations category includes a wide range of organizations whose operational objective is not profit making but the provision of services. The following is a list of some of the entities that are classified as other not-for-profit organizations:

Cemetery Organizations	Civic Organizations
Fraternal Organizations	Labor Unions
Libraries	Museums
Other Cultural Organizations	Performing Arts Organizations
Political Parties	Private and Community Foundations
Private Elementary and Secondary Schools	Professional Associations
Religious Organizations	Public Broadcasting Stations
Social and Country Clubs	Research and Scientific Organizations
Trade Associations	Zoological and Botanical Societies

Generally accepted accounting principles for these organizations are contained in *Statement of Position 78-10*[3] and in the audit guide, *Audits of Certain Nonprofit Organizations.*[4]

COMPARISON OF OTHER NOT-FOR-PROFIT ORGANIZATIONS WITH VOLUNTARY HEALTH AND WELFARE ORGANIZATIONS

A voluntary health and welfare organization is a specific type of not-for-profit organization that is very similar to the long list of not-for-profit organizations that are classified as "other." The funds used and the financial statements are very similar for both types of organizations. The wide variety of other organizations, however, results in more diversity in the use of funds and the financial statements within this category of not-for-profit organizations.

FUNDS USED

Generally accepted accounting principles state that fund accounting should be used when an other not-for-profit organization has both restricted and unrestricted funds. The funds used are often comparable to those used by a voluntary health and welfare organization. A current

---

[3] *Statement of Position 78-10, Accounting Principles and Reporting Practices for Certain Nonprofit Organizations* (New York: AICPA, 1978).

[4] *Audits of Certain Nonprofit Organizations* (New York, AICPA), 1981.

fund with both restricted and unrestricted balances as well as board-designated funds within the unrestricted funds can be used. The restricted funds used will vary from organization to organization, but can include plant funds, debt funds, endowment funds, and annuity and life income funds.

FINANCIAL STATEMENTS

The financial statements vary because the organizations differ, but they typically include a balance sheet, an activity statement (often called a statement of support, revenue, expenses, capital additions, and changes in fund balances), and a statement of cash flows. If the changes in fund balances are not included in the activity statement, a separate statement of changes in fund balances is presented.

REVENUES AND EXPENSES

The revenues of the other not-for-profit organizations are usually classified using the same classifications as voluntary health and welfare organizations. Other not-for-profit organizations may or may not use all the categories of revenue that a typical voluntary health and welfare organization reports. Unlike voluntary health and welfare organizations, other not-for-profit organizations do not record revenue from restricted contributions until the expenditure specified by the donor is incurred.

When an other not-for-profit organization receives donated services, they are recorded as both a revenue and an expense if the revenues meet the three conditions used by voluntary health and welfare organizations and if the donated services are not principally intended for the benefit of the members of the organization. Thus, organizations such as religious communities, professional trade associations, labor unions, political parties, fraternal organizations, and social and country clubs usually do not record as revenue and as expense the value of contributed services. Some other not-for-profit organizations may receive third-party reimbursements. The third-party reimbursements are recorded and reported in the same way as a not-for-profit hospital.

The expenses can be classified either by specific program and/or service or by their natural classification such as salaries. Some of the other not-for-profit organizations will classify the activity statement by program or service and supplement this statement with a statement of expenses by natural categories. *Statement of Financial Accounting Standards, No. 93,* as amended by *Statement of Financial Accounting Standards No. 99,* requires that the other not-for-profit organizations record depreciation beginning in January, 1990. *Statement No. 93* explicitly exempts, however, the depreciation of rare works of art and historical treasures because these assets are similar to land in that their loss of value takes place over such a long period of time that the decline in future economic benefit or service potential is extremely small during any one accounting period. If these assets are not depreciated, the assumption is that they have cultural, aesthetic, or historical value that is worth preserving and that the owner has the technological and financial ability to protect and preserve them.

The statement also discusses that many items described as landmarks, monuments, cathedrals, or historical treasures do suffer loss in value over time caused by pollution and vibration as well as wear and tear. These assets need major efforts to protect, clean, and preserve them at significant cost and, therefore, should be depreciated to reflect that loss of value. The restoration of the Statue of Liberty is an excellent example of the enormous cost necessary to restore and preserve a national monument. Exhibit 21-4 contains the financial statements of Oregon Historical Society. These statements are just one example from the many that could be presented for other not-for-profit entity.

EXHIBIT 21-4

Oregon Historical Society
Balance Sheet
June 30, 1987
(Unaudited—See Accountants' Review Report)

ASSETS	Unrestricted Fund	Restricted Fund	Endowment Fund	Total
Current assets:				
Cash	$ 326,261	$	$	$ 326,261
Money market and marketable securities	2,604,730	1,468,986	1,615,495	5,689,211
Receivables, net	164,565			164,565
Inventories—				
Publications	491,215			491,215
Projects in process	13,253	761,328		774,581
Prepaid expenses	21,623			21,623
Total current assets	3,621,647	2,230,314	1,615,495	7,467,456
Due from other funds		30,945		30,945
Property, plant, and equipment	3,357,298			3,357,298
Investment in subsidiary	(232,737)			(232,737)
Note receivable, subsidiary	646,284			646,284
Investment in land	17,820			17,820
Collections (Note 1)				
	$ 7,410,312	$ 2,261,259	$ 1,615,495	$ 11,287,066
LIABILITIES AND FUND BALANCES				
Current liabilities:				
Accounts payable	$ 46,226	$	$	$ 46,226
Accrued expenses	48,625			48,625
Deferred revenue—				
Member dues	179,874			179,874
Projects in process		2,261,259		2,261,259
Rental income	2,500			2,500
Total current liabilities	277,225	2,261,259		2,538,484
Due to other funds	30,945			30,945
Fund balances	7,102,142		1,615,495	8,717,637
Fund balances	$ 7,410,312	$ 2,261,259	$ 1,615,495	$ 11,287,066

The accompanying notes are an integral part of the financial statements.

Oregon Historical Society
Statement of Activity and Changes in Fund Balances
for the biennium ended June 30, 1987
(Unaudited—See Accountants' Review Report)

	Unrestricted Fund	Restricted Fund	Endowment Fund	Total
Support and revenue:				
Program revenue, gifts and grants				
Publishing	$ 251,136	$ 11,700	$	$ 262,836
Bookshop	228,795			228,795
Library	137,239	162,271		299,510
Museum	90,372	622,998		713,370
Member dues	529,537			529,537
Gifts and grants, non-program	1,988,186	850,978		2,839,164
State appropriation	1,073,109			1,073,109
Investment income	988,882	5,578	120,746	1,115,206
Rental income	100,539			100,539
Loss from subsidiary (Note 4)	(161,953)			(161,953)
Total support and revenue	$ 5,225,842	1,653,525	120,746	7,000,113
Expenses:				
Program—				
Publishing	401,166	61,647		462,813
Bookshop	223,589			223,589
Library	866,748	182,989		1,049,737
Museum	900,692	449,897		1,350,589
Member publications	195,549			195,549
Support—				
Administration	937,532	244,103		1,181,635
Membership and development	202,196	20,958		223,154
Investment	33,426			33,426
Rental	28,326			28,326
Total expenses	3,789,224	959,594		4,748,818
Excess of support and revenue over expenses before capital items	1,436,618	693,931	120,746	2,251,295
Capital additions*		100,000	1,487,877	1,587,877
Collections expenditures				
Library	(43,560)			(43,560)
Museum	(74,266)			(74,266)
Excess of support and revenue over expenses after capital items	1,318,792	793,931	1,608,623	3,721,346
Fund Balances, beginning of period	4,392,620	702,730	127,618	5,222,968
Adjustments (Note 10)	(226,677)			(226,677)
Transfers	1,617,407	(1,496,661)	(120,746)	
Fund balances end of period	$ 7,102,142	$	$ 1,615,495	$ 8,717,637

*Capital additions are gifts which, because of donor or legal restrictions, cannot be spent as current program or support expenses.

Oregon Historical Society
Statement of Changes in Financial Positions
for the biennium ended June 30, 1987
(Unaudited—See Accountants' Review Report)

Working capital provided:	
Operations—	
Excess of support and revenue over expenses after capital items	$ 3,721,346
Add depreciation—does not use working capital	246,955
Total writedown of subsidiary investment—does not use working capital	482,737
Total working capital provided	4,451,038
Working capital used:	
Additions to property, plant, and equipment	2,277,271
Addition to note receivable, subsidiary	35,390
Donated land retained	17,820
Adjustments to fund balance	226,677
Total working capital used	2,557,158
Increase in working capital	$ 1,893,880
Changes in components which increased (decreased) working capital	
Cash	$ (407,848)
Money market and marketable securities	1,521,366
Receivables	150,998
Inventories—	
Publications	96,215
Projects in process	(16,475)
Prepaid expenses	21,623
Accounts payable	(28,519)
Accrued expenses	(40,991)
Deferred revenues	
Member dues	(67,709)
Projects in process	667,720
Rental income	(2,500)
Increase in working capital	$ 1,893,880

NOTES TO FINANCIAL STATEMENTS

For the biennium ended June 30, 1987
(Unaudited—See Accountants' Review Report)

1. *The Society and summary of significant accounting policies.*

The Oregon Historical Society is an Oregon nonprofit corporation exempt from income taxes. The financial statements are prepared on the accrual basis. The Society's normal accounting period is a biennium, or two-year period, the same as that of the State of Oregon.

Fund accounting:

Financial amounts are recorded in three funds—unrestricted, restricted, and endowment. Restricted funds are from grants and gifts designated for specific purposes. Endowment funds are from gift or bequest terms requiring permanent investment of principal.

Projects in process:

Costs and revenues of projects in process are normally accumulated as inventory and deferred revenues, respectively, until completion at which time they are closed to revenue and expense (or asset cost, if appropriate).

However, projects with identifiable units of completion are closed on a unit of completion basis. Also, regardless of status of completion, project expenses (as distinguished from asset costs) are expensed at the end of an accounting period with related revenue realized to the extent of such expenses.

Money market and marketable securities:

Such securities are valued at aggregate cost or aggregate market, whichever is lower. Cost basis for donated securities is their market value at the time of receipt. Gains and losses on sale of securities are determined by specific identity cost basis of the items sold.

Inventories:

Projects in process inventories are recorded as indicated above. Publications inventories are recorded at cost or market, whichever is lower, with cost determined by average cost for each publication title.

Property, plant, and equipment:

Property, plant, and equipment are recorded at cost and (except for land) depreciated over their estimated useful lives by the straight-line method. Cost basis for donated items is their market value at the time of receipt.

Investment in subsidiary:

The Society owns all of the common stock of Jefferson-Madison Corp., which is a profit-seeking, real property rental corporation. This investment is recorded by the equity method. Consolidated financial statements are not prepared as such presentation would not be meaningful since the parent corporation, the Society, is nonprofit and the subsidiary's activities are primarily different.

Collections:

Collections, which consist of museum artifacts and exhibits and library materials, are expensed when acquired.

Member dues:

Dues paid but unearned are recorded as deferred revenues at the end of the accounting period.

2. *Receivables*

Receivables are net of $7,183 allowance for uncollectibles.

3. *Property, plant, and equipment.*

Property, plant and equipment at June 30, 1987 consist of the following:

	Cost Basis	Accumulated Depreciation	Book Value
Land	$ 1,073,713	$	$ 1,073,713
Buildings	3,218,021	1,178,478	2,039,543
Furniture and Equipment	626,134	382,092	244,042
	$ 4,917,868	$ 1,560,570	$ 3,357,298

4. *Investment in subsidiary.*

Fund balance at the beginning of the period had been charged $320,784 for subsidiary accumulated losses, consistent with the adoption of the equity method of presentation.

5. *Note receivable, subsidiary.*

Note receivable from subsidiary in the amount of $646,284 at June 30, 1987 is in the form on noninterest bearing demand notes.

6. *Income taxes.*

The Society is exempt from income taxes under Internal Revenue Code Section 501(c)(3) and The Oregon Revised Statutes.

7. *Investment income.*

Investment income for the period is comprised of:

Interest income	$ 1,010,787
Dividends	71
Gain on sale of securities	104,348
	$ 1,115,206

8. *Leased premises.*

The Society previously leased warehouse space under a lease which ran to November 1989. However, the Society purchased this property in February 1986. Rental expense for the period which includes property leased on a month-to-month basis, was $30,326.

9. *Retirement Plan.*

The Society has a retirement plan under 403(b) of the Internal Revenue Code. The plan has Internal Revenue Service approval. Contributions to the plan during the period total $141,324.

10. *Adjustments to unrestricted fund balance.*

For subsidiary (Note 4)	$ (320,784)
Record interest receivable	130,337
Record prepaid expenses	10,289
Accrue vacation pay	(46,519)
	$ (226,677)

REVIEW PROBLEM

The Self Help Society is an organization whose purpose is to provide shelter and counseling to abused mothers and their children. The Society divides its operations into three categories: shelter, counseling, and job placement and referral. On January 1, 1991 the trial balance of the Society was

	Debit	Credit
Current Unrestricted Fund		
Cash	$ 59,000	
Pledges Receivable	65,000	
Allowance for Uncollectible Pledges		$ 6,500
Food Inventory	7,000	
Clothing Inventory	10,000	
Investments	62,000	
Accounts Payable		26,000
Contributions Designated for Future Periods		28,000
Fund Balance: Undesignated Current Unrestricted Fund		132,500
Fund Balance: Board-Designated for Clothing		10,000
Current Restricted Fund		
Cash	14,800	
Pledges Receivable	18,000	
Allowance for Uncollectible Pledges		1,800
Accounts Payable		9,000
Fund Balance: Current Restricted Fund for Children's Counseling		22,000
Plant Fund		
Cash	20,000	
Investments	72,000	
Land, Buildings, and Equipment	250,000	
Accumulated Depreciation: Buildings and Equipment		52,000
Mortgage Payable		100,000
Fund Balance: Unexpended and Restricted		92,000
Fund Balance: Expended		98,000

	Debit	Credit
Endowment Funds		
Cash: Endowment Fund	15,000	
Accrued Interest Receivable: Restricted	2,000	
Long-term Investments	120,000	
Restricted Fund Balance: Endowment Fund		110,000
Unrestricted Fund Balance: Endowment Fund		27,000
	$ 714,800	$ 714,800

The following transactions and events occurred during the current year:

Current Unrestricted Fund

- Received $71,000 in public support in cash of which $14,000 cannot be used in the current year.
- Received $102,000 in pledges during the current year as public support.
- Ten percent of the pledges are estimated to be uncollectible.
- Pledges totaling $21,000 received in prior years can be used in the current year.
- A variety show, the major fund-raising project of the year, earned $24,000 and the direct costs were $8,000.
- Received $38,000 from mothers who stayed in the shelter home.
- The United Way contributed $33,000 to the Society during the current year.
- The investments earned $7,000.
- The following services at their fair market value were received from volunteers. If the Society had not received the voluntary assistance, the Society would have had to hire someone to perform the services.

Shelter Home	$ 25,000
Counseling	16,000
Job Referral and Placement	6,000

- Pledges totaling $101,800 were collected, and pledges of $8,900 were determined to be uncollectible.
- The following expenses were accrued during the current year:

Shelter Home	$ 117,000
Counseling Services	36,000
Job Referral and Placement	25,000
Management and General Expenses	17,000
Fund-raising Expenses	5,000
Inventory of Food	70,000
Inventory of Clothing	13,000
Total	$ 283,000

- Accounts payable totaling $288,000 were paid during the current year.
- Food costing $71,000 and clothing costing $15,000 was used during the current year at the shelter home.
- The board of directors authorized the transfer of $13,000 to the board-designated fund for clothing.
- Endowment income of $9,000 was received during the current year.

Current Restricted Fund

- Cash contributions of $11,000 and $16,000 of pledges were received during the current year from a fund-raising campaign. Pledges are estimated to be 10% uncollectible.
- The endowment fund transferred $3,000.
- Pledges totaling $26,000 were collected and $2,000 were determined to be uncollectible.
- Expenses for counseling totaling $27,000 were incurred during the current year.
- Accounts payable totaling $28,000 were paid.

Plant Fund

- Cash receipts were

Cash Contributions	$ 23,000
Investment Income	8,000
Transfer of Expired Endowment	10,000

- Cash Disbursements were

Land for Parking Lot	$ 12,000
Mortgage Interest	10,000
Mortgage Principal	5,000

- Depreciation totaling $24,000 was recorded and assigned to the following expenses:

Shelter Home	$ 18,000
Counseling Center	2,000
Job Referral and Placement	1,000
Management and General Expenses	3,000

Endowment Funds

- Investment income of $12,000 was earned during the current year: $9,000 was unrestricted and $3,000 was restricted to particular operating activities.
- Cash Receipts consisted of the following:

Accrued Interest Receivable	$ 12,000
Proceeds from Sale of Securities	36,000
Legacy Restricted to Purchase of Furnishings for Shelter Home	15,000

- The book value of the unrestricted investments sold was $32,000.
- Securities costing $47,000 were purchased.
- The following amounts were transferred to other funds during the current year:

Current Unrestricted Fund	$ 9,000
Current Restricted Fund	3,000
Expired Endowment to Plant Fund	10,000

Required

1. Prepare the journal entries to record the transactions and events of the Self Help Society for the year ended December 31, 1991.
2. Prepare the statement of support, revenues, expenses, and changes in fund balances for the year ended December 31, 1991 and the balance sheet as of December 31, 1991.
3. Describe the purpose and the format of the statement of functional expenses.

QUESTIONS

1. What organizations are included in voluntary health and welfare organizations?
2. How does the current unrestricted fund of a voluntary health and welfare organization differ from the general fund of a not-for-profit hospital?
3. Describe what is accounted for in the plant fund of a voluntary health and welfare organization.
4. What are the primary statements of a voluntary health and welfare organization?
5. Describe the major categories used to account for the public support received by a voluntary health and welfare organization.
6. Describe the accounting treatment of donated assets by a voluntary health and welfare organization.
7. What are the criteria that must be met in order for a voluntary health and welfare organization to record the value of donated services and the method of recording the donated services.
8. Describe the sources of revenue, other than public support, of a voluntary health and welfare organization.
9. Describe the accounting for the receipt of a restricted contribution by both voluntary health and welfare organizations and other not-for-profit organizations.
10. Describe the expenses that constitute program services expenses and the expenses that are classified as supporting services expenses by a voluntary health and welfare organization.
11. Describe the purpose of a statement of functional expenses that is prepared by voluntary health and welfare organizations.
12. Explain why a journal entry is prepared at year end to adjust the expended and unexpended balances of the plant fund of a voluntary health and welfare organization.
13. Describe the types of organizations that are classified as other not-for-profit organizations.
14. Describe the use of funds by an other not-for-profit organization.
15. Describe the typical financial statements of an other not-for-profit organization.
16. Describe and contrast the criteria for recording donated services by an other not-for-profit organization with the criteria used by a voluntary health and welfare organization.
17. Describe the types of assets that are not required to be depreciated by an other not-for-profit organization and give the criteria that must be met to not record depreciation.

EXERCISES

EXERCISE 21-1

1. Which basis of accounting should a voluntary health and welfare organization use?

a. Cash basis for all funds
b. Modified accrual basis for all funds
c. Accrual basis for all funds
d. Accrual basis for some funds and modified accrual basis for other funds

2. A voluntary health and welfare organization received a cash donation in 1990 from a donor specifying that the amount donated be used in 1992. The cash donation should be accounted for as

a. support in 1990.
b. support in 1990, 1991, and 1992, and as a deferred credit in the balance sheet at the end of 1991 and 1992.

c. support in 1990 and no deferred credit in the balance sheet at the end of 1990 and 1991.

d. support in 1992 and as a deferred credit in the balance sheet at the end of 1990 and 1991.

3. Securities donated to a voluntary health and welfare organization should be recorded at the

a. donor's recorded amount.

b. fair market value at the date of the gift.

c. fair market value at the date of the gift, or the donor's recorded amount, whichever is lower.

d. fair market value at the date of the gift, or the donor's recorded amount, whichever is higher.

4. In a statement of support, revenue, and expenses and changes in fund balances of a voluntary health and welfare organization, depreciation expense should

a. not be included.

b. be included as an element of support.

c. be included as an element of other changes in fund balances.

d. be included as an element of expense.

(AICPA adapted)

EXERCISE 21-2

INFORMATION FOR QUESTIONS 1 AND 2. Community Service Center is a voluntary welfare organization funded by contributions from the general public. During 1990, unrestricted pledges of $900,000 were received, half payable in 1990, with the other half payable in 1991 for use in 1991. It is estimated that 10% of these pledges are uncollectible. In addition, Selma Zorn, a social worker on Community's permanent staff, earning $20,000 annually for a normal workload of 2,000 hours, contributed an additional 800 hours of her time to Community at no charge.

1. How much should Community report as net contribution revenue for 1990 with respect to the pledges?

a. $ –0–

b. $ 405,000

c. $ 810,000

d. $ 900,000

2. How much should Community record in 1990 for contributed service expense?

a. $ 8,000

b. $ 4,000

c. $ 800

d. $ –0–

3. Cura Foundation, a voluntary health and welfare organization supported by contributions from the general public, included the following costs in its statement of functional expenses for the year ended December 31, 1990:

Fund-raising	$ 500,000
Administrative (including data processing)	300,000
Research	100,000

Cura's functional expenses for 1990 program services included

a. $ 900,000
b. $ 500,000
c. $ 300,000
d. $ 100,000

(AICPA adapted)

EXERCISE 21-3

The current unrestricted fund of the Drydon Mental Health Clinic, a voluntary health and welfare organization, had the following account balances on January 1, 1990:

Pledges Receivable	$ 345,000
Allowance for Uncollectible Pledges	34,500
Unrestricted Contributions Designated for 1990	50,000
Unrestricted Contributions Designated for 1991	28,000
Unrestricted Contributions Designated for 1992	15,000

During the current year the following transactions occurred that affect the current unrestricted fund of Drydon Mental Health Clinic:

- Received $120,000 in unrestricted cash donations and $40,000 in cash donations restricted to operations of a counseling program. Unrestricted cash donations of $25,000 are for the year 1991 and $10,000 are for the year 1992.
- Received unrestricted pledges totaling $185,000 that are estimated to be 10% uncollectible.
- Collected unrestricted pledges totaling $256,000 and determined that $23,000 was not collectible.
- The annual auction earned revenues of $39,000 and incurred direct costs of $14,000.
- Patients of the counseling center paid fees totaling $38,000.
- The United Way remitted $25,000 and $20,000 cash was received from an operating fund campaign run by the Drydon Mental Health Clinic.
- Volunteers donated 2,500 hours to the counseling center. Professional counselors earned $30 per hour.
- The counseling center uses a portion of a downtown office building rent free. If the landlord charged rent, the rental would be $12,000 per year.
- Unrestricted endowment funds earned $10,000 and restricted endowment funds for the counseling center earned $15,000.

On January 1, 1990 the current restricted fund for operations of the counseling center of Drydon Mental Health Clinic had

Pledges Receivable	$ 160,000
Allowance for Uncollectible Pledges	16,000

During the current year the following transactions occurred that affected the current restricted fund of Drydon Mental Health Clinic:

- Received $120,000 in unrestricted cash donations and $40,000 in cash donations restricted to operations of a counseling program.
- Received pledges for the counseling center totaling $85,000 that are estimated to be 10% uncollectible.
- Collected pledges totaling $121,000 and determined that $9,000 were not collectible.
- Unrestricted endowment funds earned $10,000 and restricted endowment funds for the counseling center earned $15,000.
- A restricted term endowment for the counseling center of $32,000 expired during the year.

Required

1. Prepare the public support and revenue section of the statement of support, revenue, expenses, and changes in fund balances for the current unrestricted and current restricted funds for the year ended December 31, 1990.
2. Determine the balances of the following balance sheet accounts: Pledges Receivable, Allowance for Uncollectible Pledges, and Unrestricted Contributions Designated for Future Periods for both the current unrestricted and the current restricted funds.

EXERCISE 21-4

A not-for-profit organization had the following transactions and events during the year ended December 31, 1992:

- Received an unrestricted contribution of $10,000.
- Received a contribution restricted to debt retirement of $25,000.
- Received a contribution restricted to the purchase of equipment of $15,000.
- Received unrestricted pledges of $45,000 for current operations estimated to be 90% collectible.
- Received unrestricted pledges of $30,000 for operations in 1993 and 1994 estimated to be 80% collectible.
- Received $100,000 cash for services provided.
- Received a $20,000 legacy whose principal must be maintained and whose income can be spent for current operations.
- Unrestricted endowments earned $13,000 and restricted endowments whose income can be used only for particular operating purposes earned $15,000.
- The annual charity ball for operating funds earned $22,000 and incurred expenses of $9,000.

Required

Prepare the journal entries by fund for the above transactions assuming the not-for-profit organization is (1) a not-for-profit hospital and (2) a voluntary health and welfare organization.

EXERCISE 21-5

The adjusted trial balance of the current unrestricted and restricted funds of the Child Care Center for Single Parents as of December 31, 1993 is

	Debit	Credit
Current Unrestricted Fund		
Cash	$ 12,000	
Pledges Receivable	30,000	
Allowance for Uncollectible Pledges		$ 3,000
Educational Materials Inventory	11,000	
Supplies Inventory	5,000	
Investments	25,000	
Accounts Payable		13,000
Contributions Designated for Future Periods		14,000
Fund Balance: Board-Designated Current Unrestricted Funds for Educational Materials		11,000
Fund Balance: Undesignated Current Unrestricted Fund		16,500
Public Support		145,000
Special Events		15,000
Federated Campaign		25,000

	Debit	Credit
Program Service Fees		54,000
Investment Revenue		2,500
Provision for Uncollectible Pledges	4,000	
Special Events (Direct Costs)	7,000	
After-School Care Expenses	64,000	
Counseling Center Expenses	34,000	
Day Care Expenses	81,000	
Management and General Expenses	18,000	
Fund-raising	8,000	
Current Restricted Fund		
Cash	9,000	
Pledges Receivable	12,000	
Allowance for Uncollectible Pledges		1,200
Accounts Payable		4,000
Fund Balance: Current Restricted Fund for Clothing for Day Care Children		2,800
Public Support		26,000
Investment Revenue		3,000
Provision for Uncollectible Pledges	2,000	
Clothing Expenses for Day Care Children	19,000	
Transfer of Expired Term Endowment		5,000
Total Current Unrestricted Fund	$ 341,000	$ 341,000

Required

Prepare the statement of support, revenue, expenses, and changes in fund balances for the year ended December 31, 1993 and the balance sheet at December 31, 1993 for the current funds of the Child Care Center for Single Parents.

EXERCISE 21-6

Refer to Exercise 21-6. Prepare the closing journal entries for the current unrestricted fund and the current restricted fund of the Child Care Center for Single Parents.

EXERCISE 21-7

The adjusted trial balance of the plant fund of the Boys and Girls Club of Shedd as of December 31, 1992 is

	Debit	Credit
Cash	$ 10,000	
Investments	65,000	
Land, Buildings, and Equipment	400,000	
Accumulated Depreciation		$ 190,000
10% Mortgage Payable		125,000
Fund Balance: Unexpended and Restricted		77,000
Fund Balance: Expended		85,000

	Debit	Credit
Public Support: Contributions		41,000
Investment Revenue		7,000
Sports Program Expenses	20,000	
Arts and Crafts Program Expenses	4,000	
Educational Program Expenses	6,000	
Management and General Expenses	15,000	
Fund-raising Expenses	5,000	
Total Plant Fund	$ 525,000	$ 525,000

Required

1. Prepare the plant fund section of the statement of support, revenue, expenses, and changes in fund balances for the year ended December 31, 1992 for the Boys and Girls Club of Shedd.
2. Prepare the plant fund section of the balance sheet as of December 31, 1992 for the Boys and Girls Club of Shedd.

EXERCISE 21-8

Refer to Exercise 21-7. During 1992, equipment was purchased with a cost of $19,000, mortgage principal in the amount of $15,000 was paid, and depreciation in the amount of $40,000 was recorded.

Required

1. Prepare the journal entry to adjust the balance of the Fund Balance: Expended account.
2. Prepare the closing journal entry for the plant fund.

EXERCISE 21-9

On January 1, 1990, the trial balance of the plant fund of Glenhaven House, a resident home for troubled youth, was

	Debit	Credit
Cash	$ 20,000	
Investments	60,000	
Land, Buildings, and Equipment	325,000	
Accumulated Depreciation: Buildings and Equipment		$ 101,000
Mortgage Payable		140,000
Fund Balance: Unexpended and Restricted		80,000
Fund Balance: Expended		84,000
	$ 405,000	$ 405,000

The Glenhaven House consists of a large home, a farm operation, and a counseling center. During 1990, the following transactions and events affecting the plant fund occurred:

- A cash contribution of $30,000 was received.
- Investment revenue of $6,200 was earned and received in cash.
- Securities costing $22,000 were sold for $25,000.
- A cash transfer of $40,000 for an expired term endowment was received from the endowment funds.
- A $20,000 legacy restricted to the payment of the principal and interest of the mortgage was received in cash.

- A $20,000 mortgage payment was remitted to City Bank that included $14,000 of interest.
- A new tractor was purchased for the farm for $28,000 cash.
- The kitchen of the home was remodeled for a cost of $35,000, paid in cash. The estimated cost of the existing kitchen is $20,000 and the accumulated depreciation is $8,000. An auction was held to sell the old kitchen cabinets and appliances. The auction netted $2,700 in cash.
- Investments costing $40,000 were purchased.
- Depreciation for the current year is as follows:

Home	$ 9,000
Farm	12,000
Counseling Center	3,000
Management and General	1,500

Required

1. Prepare the journal entries to record the transactions and events affecting the plant fund for the year 1990.
2. Prepare the plant fund section of the statement of support, revenues, expenses, and changes in fund balances for the year ended December 31, 1990 and the plant fund section of the balance sheet as of December 31, 1990 for Glenhaven House.

EXERCISE 21-10

The trial balance of the endowment funds of Glenhaven House, a voluntary health and welfare organization, on January 1, 1990 was

	Debit	Credit
Cash	$ 20,000	
Investments	623,000	
Accrued Interest Receivable	11,000	
Due Current Unrestricted Fund		$ 5,000
Due Current Restricted Fund		6,000
Fund Balance: Restricted		330,000
Fund Balance: Unrestricted		313,000
	$ 654,000	$ 654,000

During 1990, the following transactions and events occurred that affected Glenhaven House's endowment funds:

- Restricted endowments of $51,000 and unrestricted endowments of $50,000 were received.
- Restricted term endowments of $35,000 for the purchase of equipment and unrestricted term endowments of $25,000 expired during the year.
- Investments earned $70,000: $33,000 was from restricted endowments for particular operating purposes and $37,000 was from unrestricted endowments.
- Earnings received in cash from investments totaled $32,000 from restricted investments and $36,500 from unrestricted investments.
- Unrestricted investments with a cost of $23,000 were sold for $21,000.
- Restricted investments with a cost of $34,000 were sold for $38,000.
- Investments totaling $110,000 were purchased.
- The cash received as investment earnings and the expired term endowments were transferred to the appropriate funds.

Required

1. Prepare the journal entries to record the transactions and events affecting the endowment funds of Glenhaven House for the year ended December 31, 1990.
2. Prepare the endowment funds section of the statement of support, revenues, expenses, and changes in fund balances of Glenhaven House for the year ended December 31, 1990.
3. Prepare the endowment funds section of the balance sheet of Glenhaven House as of December 31, 1990.

EXERCISE 21-11

The bookkeeper for Whispering Pines Country Club, an other not-for-profit organization, provided you with the following information for the year ended December 31, 1992:

Cash Received as Dues in 1992	$190,000
Unpaid Dues, January 1, 1992	6,000
Unpaid Dues, December 31, 1992	16,000
Prepaid Dues, January 1, 1992	3,000
Prepaid Dues, December 31, 1992	4,000
Assessments Paid by Members for Clubhouse Renovation	45,000
Contributions to provide golf and tennis lessons and equipment to handicapped children	7,500
Members, who are teachers of golf and tennis, donated 1,000 hours of lessons to the handicapped children's program. The club's professionals are paid $35 per hour.	
Members donated golf clubs and tennis rackets with a fair market value of $4,000, which were given to the handicapped children.	
Members volunteered 500 hours of time as caddies and ball boys for the handicapped children's program. Caddies and ball boys earn $4 per hour.	
Members donated 200 hours to paint the exterior of the club house. The bid from the painting contractor, which was not accepted, included labor of $3,500.	
Pledges received for construction of new indoor tennis courts, estimated to be 90% collectible	80,000
Members donated 200 hours of time to the club's annual golf tournament. The club's staff earn $9 per hour.	
Investment earnings of the building fund	4,500
Gain on sale of land held for future expansion	12,000
Rentals received from outside entities for use of the club house facilities	3,000
Sales of food and beverages	110,000
Sales of the golf and tennis pro shop	62,000
Golf and tennis lesson fees. The pro giving the lessons receives the entire lesson fee.	21,000

Required

Determine the amount of support and revenue reported on the 1992 statement of revenue, expense, and changes in fund balances, identifying the support and revenue by type. If you omitted an item, explain why it is not support or revenue.

PROBLEMS

PROBLEM 21-1

The characteristics of voluntary health and welfare organizations differ in certain respects from the characteristics of other not-for-profit organizations. As an example, voluntary health and welfare organizations derive their revenues primarily from voluntary contributions from the general public, whereas other not-for-profit entities derive a substantial portion of their revenues from services provided.

Required

1. Describe fund accounting and discuss whether its use is consistent with the concept that an accounting entity is an economic unit that has control over resources, accepts responsibilities for making and carrying out commitments, and conducts economic activity.
2. Distinguish between revenue recognition for a voluntary health and welfare organization and revenue recognition for a not-for-profit hospital.
3. Discuss how methods used to account for fixed assets differ between voluntary health and welfare organizations and not-for-profit hospitals.

(AICPA adapted)

PROBLEM 21-2

A not-for-profit organization had the following transactions and events during the year ended December 31, 1992:

1. Received an unrestricted contribution of $20,000.
2. Received a contribution restricted to debt retirement of $15,000.
3. Received a contribution restricted to the purchase of equipment of $10,000.
4. Received unrestricted pledges of $90,000 for current operations estimated to be 90% collectible.
5. Received unrestricted pledges of $60,000 for operations in 1993 and 1994 estimated to be 80% collectible.
6. Received $50,000 of pledges restricted to the purchase of equipment. The pledges are estimated to be 90% collectible.
7. Received $100,000 cash for services provided.
8. Received a $25,000 legacy whose principal must be maintained and whose income can be spent for current operations.
9. Received a $40,000 bequest whose principal must be maintained for 10 years and whose income can only be spent for maintenance of the existing landscaping. During the current year, the endowment earned $4,000 and $3,000 was spent on maintenance of the landscaping.
10. Received $21,000 cash from the annual charity auction and incurred direct costs of $6,000. The auction's proceeds are restricted to health care for the needy.
11. Purchased fixed equipment at a cost of $38,000 with assets donated for the purchase of that particular equipment.
12. Sold fixed equipment with a cost of $41,000 and a net book value of $20,000 for $22,000.
13. Constructed an addition to the building at a cost of $250,000. The not-for-profit organization paid cash of $25,000 from unrestricted cash and financed the balance with a 20-year, 12% mortgage.
14. A term endowment in the amount of $30,000 expired. The endowment is restricted to the purchase of equipment.
15. Depreciation of fixed equipment totaled $30,000 and depreciation of the building totaled $40,000 for the year.
16. Volunteers donated professional services with a fair market value of $40,000.
17. Paid $67,000 of interest and $50,000 of principal on the building's mortgage with cash contributed specifically for debt retirement.

18. Incurred $2,000 of expenses for a fund-raising campaign. The proceeds are to be used to retire the mortgage on the building.
19. Received $21,000 from a fund-raising campaign to raise money for operations. The direct costs of the campaign totaled $5,000.
20. Received a gift of office furniture with a fair market value of $5,000. The donor's basis is $3,000.

Required
1. For each of the above transactions identify the fund(s) of (1) a voluntary health and welfare organization and (2) a not-for-profit hospital in which the transaction or event is recorded.
2. Determine the amount and type of revenue recognized by each of the funds, assuming the not-for-profit organization is (1) a voluntary health and welfare organization and (2) a not-for-profit hospital.
3. Explain the difference in the amount of total revenue recognized by the voluntary health and welfare organization and the revenue recognized by the not-for-profit hospital.

PROBLEM 21-3
Refer to Problem 21-2. The not-for-profit organization is a voluntary health and welfare organization that operates only one program. All facilities costs are assigned 70% to the program, 20% to administration, and 10% to fund-raising.

Required
Prepare journal entries by fund for each of the transactions.

PROBLEM 21-4
Listed below are four independent transactions or events that relate to a voluntary health and welfare organization:

1) $25,000 was disbursed from the general fund (or its equivalent) for the cash purchase of new equipment.
2) An unrestricted cash gift of $100,000 was received from a donor.
3) Listed common stocks with a total carrying value of $50,000, exclusive of any allowance, were sold by an endowment fund for $55,000, before any dividends were earned on these stocks. There are no restrictions on the gain.
4) Bonds payable with a face amount of $1,000,000 were sold at par, with the proceeds required to be used solely for construction of a new building. This building was completed at a total cost of $1,000,000, and the total amount of bond issue proceeds was disbursed in connection therewith. Disregard interest capitalization.

Required
1. For each of the above-listed transactions or events, prepare journal entries, with explanations, specifying the affected funds, and showing how these transactions or events should be recorded by a voluntary health and welfare organization that maintains a separate plant fund.
2. For each of your journal entries to (1.) describe how they would be different if they were prepared for a not-for-profit hospital. Include in your description both the fund and the ledger account titles.

(AICPA adapted)

PROBLEM 21-5
A volunteer has been maintaining the records of a voluntary health and welfare association. The volunteer has had some bookkeeping experience, but has never maintained the records of a voluntary health and welfare organization. During the year ended December 31, 1992, the following entries were recorded by the volunteer:

Current Unrestricted Fund

Cash	100,000	
Contribution Revenue		100,000

To record the receipt of cash contributions that are for current operating use. Contributions totaling $20,000 are for use in 1993, and contributions totaling $10,000 are for use in 1994.

Pledges Receivable	120,000	
Contribution Revenue: Building Fund		120,000

To record the receipt of pledges received during a campaign for pledges to pay the mortgage on the building. The pledges are estimated to be 90% collectible.

Cash	16,000	
Contribution Revenue: Annual Dinner		16,000

To record the receipts of the annual fund-raising dinner for current operations

Fund-raising Expenses	7,000	
Accounts Payable		7,000

To record the direct expenses of the annual fund-raising dinner

Cash	39,000	
Investments		33,000
Fund Balance: Undesignated Current Restricted Fund		6,000

To record the sale of investments purchased with donations for current operations

Cash: Restricted	10,000	
Cash		10,000

To record the setting aside by the board of directors cash for the education program

Fund Balance: Undesignated Current Unrestricted Fund	18,000	
Contribution Revenue: Volunteer Time		18,000

To record the time donated by volunteers in the counseling center at $9.00 per hour. The professionals who work in the counseling center are paid $22 per hour.

Counseling Center Expenses	5,000	
Rehabilitation Center Expenses	5,000	
Cash		10,000

To record the rent charged for the facilities. The owner of the property only charges $10,000 per year, but a normal rental of the space would cost $24,000.

Interest Expense	6,000	
Note Payable	10,000	
Cash		16,000

To record the annual payment on a note payable for the purchase
of equipment

Office Furniture	6,000	
Cash		6,000

To record the purchase of office furniture

Plant Fund

Fund Balance: Unexpended	22,000	
Accumulated Depreciation: Equipment		22,000

To record the depreciation for the year. The equipment is used
40% by the counseling center, 40% by the rehabilitation center,
and 20% by the administrative staff.

Endowment Funds

Cash	50,000	
Fund Balance: Restricted		50,000

To record the receipt of a legacy whose income can be used for
general operating purposes

Cash	17,000	
Interest Revenue: Unrestricted Endowments		10,000
Interest Revenue: Restricted Endowments		7,000

To record the earnings of the endowment funds. The restricted
endowments are for the purchase of equipment and office
furniture.

Required
Prepare the journal entry that should have been recorded for each of the above entries and identify the
fund being used for the entry. If an entry should have been recorded in more than one fund, prepare
the entries for all the funds.

PROBLEM 21-6
Refer to Problem 21-5. Prepare correcting journal entry(s) for each entry that was incorrectly prepared
and prepare the entry for each entry that was omitted. If an entry was correctly prepared but recorded
in the wrong fund, only state the fund that should have been used.

PROBLEM 21-7
Following are the adjusted current funds trial balances of Community Association for Handicapped
Children, a voluntary health and welfare organization, at June 30, 1991:

COMMUNITY ASSOCIATION FOR HANDICAPPED CHILDREN
Adjusted Current Funds Trial Balances
June 30, 1991

	Unrestricted		Restricted	
	Debit	Credit	Debit	Credit
Cash	$ 40,000		$ 9,000	
Bequest Receivable			5,000	
Pledges Receivable	12,000			
Accrued Interest Receivable	1,000			
Investments (at cost, which approximates market)	100,000			
Accounts Payable and Accrued Expenses		$ 50,000		$ 1,000
Deferred Revenue		2,000		
Allowance for Uncollectible Pledges		3,000		
Fund Balances, July 1, 1990				
Designated		12,000		
Undesignated		26,000		
Restricted				3,000
Transfers of Endowment Fund Income		20,000		
Contributions		300,000		15,000
Membership Dues		25,000		
Program Service Fees		30,000		
Investment Income		10,000		
Blind Children's Program	150,000			
Deaf Children's Program	120,000			
Management and General Services	45,000		4,000	
Fund-raising Services	8,000		1,000	
Provision for Uncollectible Pledges	2,000			
	$ 478,000	$ 478,000	$ 19,000	$ 19,000

Required

1. Prepare a statement of support, revenues, expenses, and changes in fund balances, separately presenting each current fund, for the year ended June 30, 1991.
2. Prepare a balance sheet separately presenting each current fund as of June 30, 1991.

(AICPA adapted)

PROBLEM 21-8

The Children's Aid Society is a voluntary health and welfare organization that operates three programs: after-school care, temporary shelter, and counseling. On December 31, 1991, the adjusted trial balances of the funds of the Society are

	Debit	Credit
Current Undesignated Unrestricted Fund		
Cash	$ 12,000	
Pledges Receivable	50,000	
Allowance for Uncollectible Pledges		$ 5,000

	Debit	Credit
Supplies Inventory	5,000	
Investments	25,000	
Accounts Payable		15,000
Contributions Designated for Future Periods		30,000
Fund Balance: Undesignated Current Unrestricted Fund		77,000
Contributions Received		100,000
Pledges Received		70,000
Special Events Proceeds		15,000
Legacies and Bequests Received		25,000
United Way Allocation		20,000
Investment Revenue		7,000
Provision for Uncollectible Pledges	7,000	
Direct Costs of Special Events	9,000	
After-school Care Expenses	24,000	
Temporary Shelter Expenses	144,000	
Counseling Expenses	56,000	
Management and General Expenses	22,000	
Fund-raising Expenses	10,000	
Current Board-Designated Fund for Debt Retirement		
Cash	10,000	
Investments: Board-Designated	90,000	
Fund Balance: Board-Designated for Mortgage Retirement		87,000
Investment Revenue		9,000
Gain on Sale of Investments		4,000
Current Restricted Fund		
Cash	15,000	
Pledges Receivable	30,000	
Allowance for Uncollectible Pledges		3,000
Accounts Payable		10,000
Fund Balance: Current Restricted Fund for Children's Counseling		32,000
Contributions Received		24,000
Legacies and Bequests Received		10,000
Provision for Uncollectible Pledges	4,000	
Counseling Expenses	25,000	
Management and General Expenses	2,000	
Fund-raising Expenses	3,000	
Plant Fund		
Cash	20,000	
Investments	85,000	
Pledges Receivable: Debt Retirement	105,000	
Allowance for Uncollectible Pledges		15,000
Land, Buildings, and Equipment	225,000	
Accumulated Depreciation: Buildings and Equipment		90,000
Mortgage Payable		125,000
Fund Balance: Unexpended and Restricted		142,000

	Debit	Credit
Fund Balance: Expended		10,000
Contributions Received		40,000
Pledges Received		65,000
Investment Revenue		19,000
Provision for Uncollectible Pledges	12,000	
After-school Care Expenses	5,000	
Temporary Shelter Expenses	20,000	
Counseling Expenses	6,000	
Management and General Expenses	23,000	
Fund-raising Expenses	5,000	
Endowment Funds		
Cash: Endowment Fund	10,000	
Accrued Interest Receivable: Restricted	3,000	
Long-term Investments	110,000	
Restricted Fund Balance: Endowment Fund		60,000
Unrestricted Fund Balance: Endowment Fund		43,000
Legacies and Bequests Received		20,000
	$ 1,172,000	$ 1,172,000

During the current year the following transactions and events occurred that affect the endowment funds:

- An unrestricted endowment of $25,000 matured and was transferred to the current unrestricted undesignated fund and the fund balance was reduced.
- Restricted investments were sold at a gain of $4,000.

During the year $20,000 of equipment and furnishings for the shelter home were purchased with current unrestricted funds and transferred to the plant fund and the fund balance reduced.

Required
1. Prepare a statement of support, revenue, expenses, and changes in fund balances for the year ended December 31, 1991.
2. Prepare a balance sheet at December 31, 1991 for the Children's Aid Society.

PROBLEM 21-9
Presented below is the June 30, 1991 adjusted trial balance of Dorn Foundation, a nonprofit research and scientific organization:

	Debit	Credit
Cash: Unrestricted	$ 500,000	
Cash: Restricted to Plant	150,000	
Accounts Receivable	744,000	
Unbilled Contract Revenues and Reimbursable Grant Expenses	976,000	
Prepaid Expenses	80,000	
Investments and Endowment Fund Cash	840,000	
Land and Building	440,000	
Furniture and Equipment	334,000	
Lease Property Under Capital Leases	958,000	

	Debit	Credit
Accumulated Depreciation and Amortization		$ 518,000
Accounts Payable		836,000
Restricted Grant Advances		522,000
Obligations Under Capital Leases		
Current Portion		176,000
Noncurrent Portion		618,000
Fund Balance: Unrestricted		1,114,000
Fund Balance: Net Equity in Property, Plant, and		
Equipment		570,000
Fund Balance: Endowment		780,000
Grant Revenues		5,000,000
Direct Project Expenses	4,300,000	
Interest Expense	400,000	
Depreciation Expense	300,000	
Management and General Expenses	100,000	
Fund-raising Expenses	72,000	
Investment Earnings of Endowment Funds		60,000
	$10,194,000	$10,194,000

The endowment fund, the principal amount of $700,000, was received in 1987. The donor of this fund specified that principal and accumulated interest cannot be expended until 1994, at which time the fund, including accumulated interest, will be used for environmental research projects. Net equity in property, plant, and equipment is the carrying value of all property, plant, and equipment less related depreciation and the liabilities to finance their acquisition. There were no acquisitions or dispositions of property, plant, and equipment during the year.

Required
Prepare a balance sheet by fund for the Dorn Foundation for the year ended June 30, 1991.

(AICPA adapted)

SOLUTION TO REVIEW PROBLEM

1. Journal Entries

Current Unrestricted Fund

Cash	71,000	
Public Support: Contributions		57,000
Contributions: Designated for Future Periods		14,000
To record the cash contributions received during the current year		
Pledges Receivable	102,000	
Public Support: Contributions		102,000
To record the pledges received during the current year		

Provision of Uncollectible Pledges (Public Support)	10,200	
Allowance for Uncollectible Pledges		10,200

To record uncollectible accounts expense as 10% of pledges
received during the year

Contributions Designated for Future Periods	21,000	
Public Support: Contributions		21,000

To record as revenue contributions of prior years that can be used
during the current year

Cash	24,000	
Public Support: Special Events		24,000

To record the revenue from the variety show

Public Support: Special Events	8,000	
Cash		8,000

To record the direct costs of the variety show

Cash	38,000	
Revenues: Fees for Services		38,000

To record the fees charged to women who stayed at the shelter
home

Cash	33,000	
Public Support: Federated Campaign		33,000

To record the annual allocation from the United Way

Cash	7,000	
Revenues: Investment Earnings		7,000

To record the interest earned on investments

Shelter Home Expenses	25,000	
Counseling Center Expenses	16,000	
Job Referral and Placement Expenses	6,000	
Public Support: Contribution of Services		47,000

To record the services provided for by volunteers, which would
have required the use of professionals without the donated services

Cash	101,800	
Allowance for Uncollectible Pledges	8,900	
Pledges Receivable		110,700

To record the collection of pledges and the write-off of pledges
deemed not collectible

Shelter Home Expenses	117,000	
Counseling Center Expenses	36,000	
Job Referral and Placement Expenses	25,000	
Management and General Expenses	17,000	
Fund-raising Expenses	5,000	
Inventory of Food	70,000	
Inventory of Clothing	13,000	
Accounts Payable		283,000

To record the purchases on account during the current year

Accounts Payable	288,000	
Cash		288,000

To record the payment of accounts payable

Shelter Home Expenses	86,000	
Food Inventory		71,000
Clothing Inventory		15,000

To record the food and clothing used by the shelter home during
the current period

Fund Balance: Current Unrestricted Fund	13,000	
Fund Balance: Board-Designated Current Unrestricted Fund		
for Clothing		13,000

To record the transfer to the board-designated fund from the
current unrestricted fund per the board of directors minutes

Cash	9,000	
Revenues: Investment Earnings		9,000

To record transfer from Endowment Fund

Current Restricted Fund

Cash	11,000	
Pledges Receivable	16,000	
Public Support: Contributions		27,000

To record the contribution received from the fund-raising
campaign

Provision for Uncollectible Pledges: Public Support	1,600	
Allowance for Uncollectible Pledges		1,600

To record uncollectible accounts expense as 10% of pledges
received during the year

Cash	3,000	
Revenues: Investment Earnings		3,000

To record the investment revenue from restricted endowment
funds

Cash	26,000	
Allowance for Uncollectible Accounts	2,000	
Pledges Receivable		28,000

To record the collection of pledges and the write-off of pledges
deemed not collectible

Counseling Center Expenses	27,000	
Accounts Payable		27,000

To record the cost of counseling purchased on account

Accounts Payable	28,000	
Cash		28,000

To record the cash disbursements for the current year.

Plant Fund

Cash	41,000	
Public Support: Contributions		23,000
Revenues: Investment Earnings		8,000
Transfer of Expired Term Endowment		10,000
To record the cash receipts of the plant fund		
Land, Buildings, and Equipment	12,000	
Management and General Expenses (Interest)	10,000	
Mortgage Payable	5,000	
Cash		27,000
To record the cash disbursement for the current period		
Shelter Home Expenses	18,000	
Counseling Center Expenses	2,000	
Job Referral and Placement Expenses	1,000	
Management and General Expenses	3,000	
Accumulated Depreciation		24,000
To record depreciation expense for the current year		
Fund Balance: Expended	7,000	
Fund Balance: Unexpended		7,000
To transfer from fund balance expended to fund balance		
unexpended an amount equal to the decrease in net investment		

Assets Purchased	$ 12,000
Long-term Debt Paid	5,000
Depreciation Recorded	(24,000)
Decrease in Net Investment	$ 7,000

Endowment Funds

Accrued Interest Receivable	12,000	
Due to Current Restricted Fund		3,000
Due to Current Unrestricted Fund		9,000
To record the income from investments		
Cash	63,000	
Accrued Interest Receivable		12,000
Public Support: Legacies and Bequests		15,000
Investments		32,000
Revenues: Gain on Sale of Restricted Investments		4,000
To record the cash receipts for the current period		
Investments	47,000	
Cash		47,000
To record the investments purchased during the period		

		Debit		Credit
Due to Current Unrestricted Fund		9,000		
Due to Current Restricted Fund		3,000		
Fund Balance: Restricted		10,000		
Cash				22,000

To record transfers to other funds during the current year

	Debit	Credit
Current Unrestricted Fund		
Cash	$ 46,800	
Pledges Receivable	56,300	
Allowance for Uncollectible Pledges		$ 7,800
Food Inventory	6,000	
Clothing Inventory	8,000	
Investments	62,000	
Accounts Payable		21,000
Contributions Designated for Future Periods		21,000
Fund Balance: Undesignated Current Unrestricted Fund		119,500
Fund Balance: Board-Designated for Clothing		23,000
Public Support: Contributions		227,000
Public Support: Special Events		16,000
Public Support: Federated Campaign		33,000
Revenues: Fees for Services		38,000
Revenues: Investment Earnings		16,000
Provision for Uncollectible Pledges	10,200	
Shelter Home Expenses	228,000	
Counseling Center Expenses	52,000	
Job Referral and Placement Expenses	31,000	
Management and General Expenses	17,000	
Fund-raising Expenses	5,000	
Current Restricted Fund		
Cash	26,800	
Pledges Receivable	6,000	
Allowance for Uncollectible Pledges		1,400
Accounts Payable		8,000
Fund Balance: Current Restricted Fund for Children's Counseling		22,000
Public Support: Contributions		27,000
Revenues: Investment Earnings		3,000
Counseling Center Expenses	27,000	
Provision for Uncollectible Pledges	1,600	
Plant Fund		
Cash	34,000	
Investments	72,000	
Land, Buildings, and Equipment	262,000	
Accumulated Depreciation: Buildings and Equipment		76,000
Mortgage Payable		95,000
Fund Balance: Unexpended and Restricted		99,000
Fund Balance: Expended		91,000
Public Support: Contributions		23,000

	Debit	Credit
Revenues: Investment Earnings		8,000
Transfer of Expired Term Endowment		10,000
Shelter Home Expenses	18,000	
Counseling Center Expenses	2,000	
Job Referral and Placement Expenses	1,000	
Management and General Expenses	13,000	
Endowment Funds		
Cash: Endowment Fund	9,000	
Accrued Interest Receivable: Restricted	2,000	
Long-term Investments	135,000	
Public Support: Legacies and Bequests		15,000
Revenues: Gain on Sale of Restricted Investments		4,000
Restricted Fund Balance: Endowment Fund		100,000
Unrestricted Fund Balance: Endowment Fund		27,000
	$ 1,131,700	$ 1,131,700

2. Financial Statements

SELF-HELP SOCIETY
Statement of Support, Revenues, Expenses, and Changes in Fund Balances
Year Ended December 31, 1990

	Current Funds		Plant Fund	Endowment Fund	Total
	Unrestricted	Restricted			
Public Support and Revenue					
Public Support					
Contributions Net of Uncollectible Pledges	$ 216,800	$ 25,400	$ 23,000	—	$ 265,200
Special Events Net of Direct Costs	16,000	—	—	—	16,000
Legacies and Bequests	—	—	—	$ 15,000	15,000
Federated Campaign	33,000	—	—	—	33,000
Total Public Support	265,800	25,400	23,000	15,000	329,200
Revenues					
Program Service Fees	38,000	—	—	—	38,000
Investment Revenue	16,000	3,000	8,000	—	27,000
Gain on Sale of Investments	—	—	—	4,000	4,000
Total Revenue	54,000	3,000	8,000	4,000	69,000
Total Support and Revenue	319,800	28,400	31,000	19,000	398,200
Expenses					
Program Services					
Shelter Home	228,000	—	18,000	—	246,000
Counseling Center	52,000	27,000	2,000	—	81,000
Job Referral and Placement	31,000	—	1,000	—	32,000
Total Program Services	311,000	27,000	21,000	—	359,000
Supporting Services					
Management and General	17,000	—	13,000	—	30,000
Fund-raising	5,000	—	—	—	5,000
Total Supporting Services	22,000	—	13,000	—	35,000
Total Expenses	333,000	27,000	34,000	—	394,000
Excess (Deficiency) of Public Support and Revenues Over Expenses	(13,200)	1,400	(3,000)	19,000	4,200
Other Changes					
Transfer of Endowment Fund Principal Whose Term Expired			10,000	(10,000)	
Fund Balances, Beginning of Year	142,500	22,000	190,000	137,000	491,500
Fund Balances, End of Year	$ 129,300	$ 23,400	$ 197,000	$ 146,000	$ 495,700

SELF-HELP SOCIETY
Balance Sheet
December 31, 1990

Assets   Liabilities and Fund Balances

CURRENT FUND

Unrestricted

Cash	$ 46,800	Accounts Payable	$ 21,000
Pledges: Net	48,500	Contributions Designated for Future Periods	21,000
Food Inventory	6,000	Total Liabilities and Deferred Revenues	42,000
Clothing Inventory	8,000	Fund Balance: Board-Designated (1)	8,000
Investments	62,000	Fund Balance: Unrestricted (2)	121,300
Total Assets	$ 171,300	Total Liabilities and Fund Balances	$ 171,300

Restricted

Cash	$ 26,800	Accounts Payable	$ 8,000
Pledges: Net	4,600	Fund Balance	23,400
Total Assets	$ 31,400	Total Liabilities and Fund Balances	$ 31,400

PLANT FUND

Cash	$ 34,000	Mortgage Payable	$ 95,000
Investments	72,000	Fund Balance: Unexpended (3)	106,000
Land, Buildings, and Equipment: Net	186,000	Fund Balance: Expended	91,000
Total Assets	$ 292,000	Total Liabilities and Fund Balances	$ 292,000

ENDOWMENT FUNDS

Cash	$ 9,000	Fund Balance: Restricted (4)	$ 119,000
Interest Receivable: Unrestricted	2,000	Fund Balance: Unrestricted	27,000
Investments	135,000		
Total Assets	$ 146,000	Total Liabilities and Fund Balances	$ 146,000

(1) $23,000 − $15,000 = $8,000
(2) $119,500 − ($13,200 − $15,000) = $121,300
(3) $99,000 + $7,000 = $106,000
(4) $100,000 + $15,000 + $4,000 = $119,000

3. The purpose of the statement of functional expenses is to provide information regarding the various types of expenses that were incurred for each of the different programs and services provided by the voluntary health and welfare organization. The statement of support, revenues, expenses, and changes in fund balances does not show the type of expense incurred, but reports expenses by programs and supporting services.

NOT-FOR-PROFIT COLLEGES
AND UNIVERSITIES

 lthough some colleges and universities are operated as profit-making institutions, the majority of colleges and universities are operated as not-for-profit entities. The college or university may be either a private institution and thus a not-for-profit entity in and of itself, or it may be owned and operated as a part of state or local government. The general discussion in the chapter covers both types of not-for-profit colleges and universities. The illustrative problem, review problem, exercises, and problems are only for not-for-profit private colleges and universities. The topics of this chapter are

- Sources of generally accepted accounting principles for not-for-profit colleges and universities
- Comparison of the funds used by not-for-profit colleges and universities to the funds used by not-for-profit hospitals and voluntary health and welfare organizations
- Depreciation expense
- Recording of budgets
- Revenues, expenditures, transfers, and financial statements of the current unrestricted fund and the current restricted fund
- Accounting for the loan funds, endowment funds annuity and life income funds, the four plant funds, and agency funds
- Financial statements of a private not-for-profit college or university

Generally accepted accounting principles for colleges and universities are contained in the publication *College & University Business Administration*, published by the National Association of College and University Business Officers (NACUBO). This is a service that is continually updated as the accounting and financial reporting for colleges and universities changes. In 1973, the Auditing Standards Division of the AICPA issued an audit guide, *Audits of Colleges and Universities,* which was later modified by *Statement of Position 74-8, Financial Accounting and Reporting by Colleges and Universities,* issued by the Accounting Standards Division of the AICPA.

FUNDS USED BY NOT-FOR-PROFIT COLLEGES AND UNIVERSITIES COMPARED TO THE FUNDS USED BY NOT-FOR-PROFIT HOSPITALS AND VOLUNTARY HEALTH AND WELFARE ORGANIZATIONS

Just as not-for-profit hospitals and voluntary health and welfare organizations use unrestricted and restricted funds, not-for-profit colleges and universities also have unrestricted and restricted funds. In addition to the unrestricted current fund, a not-for-profit college or university uses the following restricted funds: restricted current funds, loan funds, annuity and life income funds, plant funds, endowment funds, and agency funds. Note that a not-for-profit college labels the current funds, unrestricted current fund and restricted current fund, whereas a voluntary health and welfare organization reverses the words and labels the current funds, current unrestricted fund and current restricted fund. In addition, colleges may use board-designated funds to permanently set aside unrestricted current fund assets referred to as **quasi-endowment** funds. These quasi-endowment funds are accounted for in the same manner as the other endowment funds of the not-for-profit college or university.

UNRESTRICTED FUNDS

The operations of a not-for-profit college or university are recorded in the unrestricted current fund just like the current unrestricted fund of a voluntary health and welfare organization. A not-for-profit college or university uses the term **expenditure** rather than the term expense used by not-for-profit hospitals and voluntary health and welfare organizations. The term expenditure is used because it denotes the outflow of resources to external entities and because a not-for-profit college or university is interested in the provision of services and not the measurement of income.

A not-for-profit college or university also records mandatory and discretionary (non-mandatory) transfers to other funds in the unrestricted current fund like a voluntary health and welfare organization. The unrestricted current fund of a not-for-profit college and university includes only current assets and current liabilities, the same as the current unrestricted fund of a voluntary health and welfare organization. The not-for-profit college or university may use board-designated funds as a part of the unrestricted current fund as do not-for-profit hospitals and voluntary health and welfare organizations.

RESTRICTED FUNDS

A not-for-profit college or university uses a restricted current fund that is comparable to the specific-purpose funds of a not-for-profit hospital and the current restricted fund of a voluntary health and welfare organization. These academic institutions also have plant funds that are comparable to the plant fund of a voluntary health and welfare organization. Unlike a voluntary health and welfare organization, a not-for-profit college or university creates subfunds or subgroups within the plant fund to account for plant and equipment and debt. A not-for-profit college or university also has endowment funds, which function and are accounted for in the same manner as the endowment funds of a not-for-profit hospital or a voluntary health and welfare organization, and include the board-created quasi-endowment funds.

A not-for-profit college or university uses loan funds to account for assets donated, granted by the federal government, and allocated by the board of regents that are used for loans to students and faculty. A college or university uses annuity and life income funds to account for assets given to the university that provide the donor with income during a period of time or over the lifetime of the donor. Finally, a college or university usually has agency funds like those of a not-for-profit hospital.

RECORDING OF DEPRECIATION EXPENSE

Prior to the issuance of *Statement of Financial Accounting Standards No. 93* in August 1987, not-for-profit colleges and universities were not required by generally accepted accounting principles to record depreciation expense on plant and equipment, although the recording of depreciation was an available option.[1] *Statement of Financial Accounting Standards No. 93* requires all not-for-profit organizations to record depreciation in order to allocate the cost of long-lived assets over time. The standard is based on the assumption that if a not-for-profit entity does not maintain its net assets, its ability to provide services in the future declines over time. In addition, the recording of depreciation will allow a not-for-profit organization to better determine the total cost of providing its services.

For fiscal years ending after January 1, 1990, not-for-profit colleges and universities are required to depreciate their plant and equipment.[2] The original pronouncement required depreciation for fiscal years ending after May 15, 1988.[3] Not-for-profit colleges and universities that are part of a state or local government have been exempted from recording depreciation by *Governmental Accounting Standards Board Statement No. 8.*[4] When this accounting change takes place, the unrecorded accumulated depreciation of all prior years will be recorded in the accounts of the not-for-profit private colleges and universities and the total will be reported as the cumulative effect of an accounting change in the statement of changes in fund balances.[5]

The example problems and exercises and problems in this chapter are based on the assumption that the not-for-profit private college or university has elected early application of the new standards and, therefore, has established the appropriate accounts and amounts

---

[1] *Industry Audit Guide, Audits of Colleges and Universities* (New York: AICPA, Committee on College and University Accounting and Auditing, page 10.

[2] *Statement of Financial Accounting Standards No. 99, Deferral of the Effective Date of Recognition of Depreciation by Not-for-Profit Organizations, an amendment of FASB Statement No. 93* (Stamford, Connecticut: FASB), 1988.

[3] *Statement of Financial Accounting Standards No. 93, Recognition of Depreciation by Not-for-Profit Organizations* (Stamford, Connecticut: FASB), 1987, paragraph 7.

[4] *Statement of Governmental Accounting Standards, No. 8, Applicability of FASB Statement No. 93, Recognition of Depreciation by Not-for-Profit Organizations to Certain State and Local Governmental Entities* (Stamford, Connecticut: GASB), 1988, paragraph 20.

[5] *Industry Audit Guide, Audits of Colleges and Universities,* page 59.

for accumulated depreciation. Because the current funds do not contain the plant assets, which are in the plant funds, both the provision for depreciation and the accumulated depreciation are recorded in the plant funds. The expense is reported in the plant funds section of the statement of changes in fund balances and the accumulated depreciation in the plant funds section of the balance sheet. This treatment of depreciation is suggested in the Audit Guide; *Statement of Financial Accounting Standards No. 93* does not provide guidance for the recording of depreciation expense.

RECORDING OF BUDGETS

Many not-for-profit colleges and universities are state or local government-owned and government-operated institutions and, therefore, have more governmental control than hospitals, even the community hospitals, and voluntary health and welfare organizations. The allocation or appropriation of tax revenues is based on budgets prepared by the college or university. These budgets operate as an authorization to spend and place a ceiling on the amount of funds that can be used for any particular category of expenditure. Therefore, budgets of tax revenue-financed institutions of higher education become the governing instrument for expenditures. To ensure that the not-for-profit public college or university does not spend more than the amounts that it is authorized to spend, budgets are usually recorded within the accounting records. Private colleges and universities may record budgets, but the recording is used for management control purposes and not as spending authorizations.

If a not-for-profit college or university does record its budget, it records the journal entry shown below. The **Unrealized Revenue** account and the **Estimated Expenditures** account are the major control accounts of the budget and represent groups of accounts that are each debited or credited in the entry.

Unrealized Revenues	6,800,000	
Estimated Expenditures		6,500,000
Unallocated Budget Balance		300,000

During the operating period, the budgeted amounts may be adjusted based on new information regarding either revenues or expenditures. The adjustment alters one or more of the unrealized revenue accounts, or one or more of the estimated expenditure accounts, or both unrealized revenue accounts and estimated expenditure accounts, and the fund balance. At the end of the accounting period, the budget entry is reversed.

UNRESTRICTED CURRENT FUND

The unrestricted current fund is used to account for the current operating activities of the not-for-profit college or university. Accrual accounting is used to record the transactions and events of the current funds. The unrestricted current fund assets are expended based on either the discretion of the governing board of the private college or university or the approved budget for a government-owned college or university.

REVENUES OF THE UNRESTRICTED CURRENT FUND

The three following major groups of revenue accounts are used to account for the revenues of the unrestricted current fund:

- Educational and general revenues
- Auxiliary enterprises revenues
- Expired term endowment revenues

The educational and general revenues are further subdivided into the following categories:

- Student tuition and fees
- Governmental appropriations
- Governmental grants and contracts
- Gifts and private grants
- Endowment income
- Other sources

In addition, the governmental appropriations and the governmental grants and contracts categories are further divided by the type of governmental unit—local, state, or federal—providing the revenues.

For example, a not-for-profit private college has the following educational and general revenues all on account during the current year:

Student Tuition and Fees	$ 4,480,000
Governmental Grants and Contracts	1,500,000
Gifts and Private Grants	320,000
Endowment Income	130,000

The journal entry to record the educational and general revenues for the current year is

Accounts Receivable	6,300,000	
Due from Other Funds	130,000	
Student Tuition and Fees Revenue		4,480,000
Governmental Grants and Contracts Revenue		1,500,000
Gifts and Private Grants Revenue		320,000
Endowment Income		130,000
To record the revenues for the current year		

Auxiliary enterprises are entities that furnish goods or services to students, faculty, or staff. These enterprises charge a fee that is directly related to the cost of the goods or services. The fee charged may be more than, less than, or equal to the cost of the goods or services. The sources of revenue of the auxiliary enterprises can include dormitory room fees, food services, intercollegiate athletics (if self-supporting), college stores, faculty clubs, parking fees, and student health services.

For example, a not-for-profit private college has $540,000 of revenues on account from the operations of its auxiliary enterprises during the current year. The journal entry to record the auxiliary revenues is

Accounts Receivable	540,000	
Auxiliary Enterprises Revenue		540,000
To record the revenue earned by the auxiliary enterprises		

EXPENDITURES OF THE UNRESTRICTED CURRENT FUND

Because the major goal of a not-for-profit college or university is the provision of services and, therefore, the measurement of net income is not a concern, colleges and universities use the term **expenditures** rather than expenses. The expenditures of the unrestricted current fund are divided into

- educational and general expenditures, and
- auxiliary enterprises expenditures.

The educational and general expenditures are further divided into the following subgroups:

- Instruction
- Research
- Public service: consulting, seminars, and conferences
- Academic support: libraries, galleries, visual aids, and academic deans
- Student services: admissions, registration, cultural and athletic events
- Institutional support: the cost of central administration
- Operation and maintenance of plant
- Scholarships and fellowships

TRANSFERS TO AND FROM THE UNRESTRICTED CURRENT FUND

In addition to expenditures, the fund balance of the unrestricted current fund is reduced by transfers to other funds. These transfers can be mandatory or they can be nonmandatory. A mandatory transfer is the transfer of funds as a result of a binding contract. For example, the interest and principal payments due on long-term debt are required to be transferred to the plant fund for retirement of long-term debt, or the not-for-profit college or university may have received a grant that requires the institution to provide a certain amount of matching funds.

Nonmandatory transfers are the transfers to other funds that are decided on by the governing body of the not-for-profit college or university. These transfers are like the transfers to the board-designated fund of a not-for-profit hospital. Just as a not-for-profit hospital's board of directors authorizes discretionary transfers of funds from the general fund, the governing body of the not-for-profit college or university can, at its discretion, transfer funds from the unrestricted current fund to other funds.

For example, a not-for-profit private college has an outstanding mortgage that requires the payment of interest and principal in the amount of $210,000 during the current year. In addition, the board of regents has authorized the transfer of $75,000 to the plant funds for purchase of new classroom equipment. The journal entry to record the mandatory and nonmandatory transfers to the plant funds is

Mandatory Transfer to Plant Funds	210,000	
Nonmandatory Transfer to Plant Funds	75,000	
Cash		285,000
To record both the mandatory transfer for the principal and interest on the mortgage and the nonmandatory transfer to the plant funds		

RESTRICTED CURRENT FUND

The assets of the restricted current fund are typically liquid assets that are readily converted into cash. The restricted current fund assets are also available for current operating expenditures, but their use has been either restricted or specified by the person, organization, or entity that provided the assets. The restricted current fund uses the same account groups for revenues, expenditures, and transfers as the unrestricted current fund. The most commonly used revenue accounts are government grants and contracts, gifts and private grants, and endowment income. The most commonly used expenditure accounts are instruction, research, and student aid.

When assets are received by the restricted current fund, they are recorded as an increase in fund balance. The revenue is not considered earned until the assets are expended according to the contributor's instructions. Therefore, revenues and expenditures are recorded in the restricted current fund when the expenditure occurs that meets the restrictions of the donor.

Illustrative Problem 22.1 demonstrates the recording of the budget, the revenues, expenditures, and fund transfers of the current funds of a not-for-profit private college. The entries previously presented are incorporated into this example.

ILLUSTRATIVE PROBLEM 22.1: ACCOUNTING AND REPORTING FOR THE CURRENT FUNDS OF A NOT-FOR-PROFIT PRIVATE COLLEGE

The trial balance of the current funds of Olympus College on July 1, 1990, the beginning of its fiscal year, was

	Debit	Credit
Unrestricted		
Cash	$ 500,000	
Investments	840,000	
Accounts Receivable	615,000	
Allowance for Uncollectible Accounts		$ 15,000
Inventories of Materials	195,000	
Prepaid Expenses	51,000	
Accounts Payable		343,000
Due to Other Funds		40,000
Unrestricted Current Fund Balance		1,803,000
Restricted		
Cash	310,000	
Investments	520,000	
Accounts Receivable	125,000	
Accounts Payable		43,000
Restricted Current Fund Balance		912,000
	$ 3,156,000	$ 3,156,000

The following journal entries are recorded in the unrestricted current fund for the year ending June 30, 1991:

Unrealized Revenues	6,800,000	
Estimated Expenditures		6,500,000
Unallocated Fund Balance		300,000

To record the budget approved by the board of regents of the college

Accounts Receivable	6,300,000	
Due from Other Funds	130,000	
Student Tuition and Fees Revenue		4,480,000
Government Grants and Contracts Revenue		1,500,000
Gifts and Private Grants		320,000
Endowment Income		130,000

To record the revenues for the current year

Provision for Uncollectible Accounts: Student Tuition and Fee Revenue	224,000	
Allowance for Uncollectible Accounts		224,000

To record the estimated amount of uncollectible accounts from charges for tuition and fees

Accounts Receivable	540,000	
Auxiliary Enterprises Revenue		540,000

To record the revenue earned by the auxiliary enterprises

An unrestricted term endowment expired during the year and cash was transferred to the unrestricted current fund.

Cash	30,000	
Expired Term Endowment Income		30,000

To record the receipt of the principal of a term endowment that expired

The cash receipts for the year are recorded as follows:

Cash	6,090,000	
Allowance for Uncollectible Accounts	215,000	
Accounts Receivable		6,175,000
Due from Other Funds		130,000

To record the collection of accounts receivable and due from endowment fund and the write-off of uncollectible accounts

The following entries record the purchase of inventories, prepaid items, and the payment of expenses and accounts payable.

Inventory	758,000	
Prepaid Expenses	69,000	
Accounts Payable		758,000
Cash		69,000

To record the purchases of inventory and prepaid items

Instruction Expenditures	2,800,000	
Research Expenditures	250,000	
Academic Support Expenditures	320,000	
Student Services Expenditures	410,000	
Institutional Support Expenditures	380,000	
Operations and Maintenance of Plant Expenditures	760,000	
Auxiliary Enterprises Expenditures	270,000	
Accounts Payable	743,000	
Cash		5,933,000

To record the cash disbursed for expenses and the payment of accounts payable

Statement of Position 74-8 recommends that waivers of tuition and reductions of tuition be recorded in an expenditure account rather than in a contra revenue account. The following entry records the waivers of tuition and adjustments of tuition.

Scholarships and Fellowships Expenditures	285,000	
Accounts Receivable		220,000
Cash		65,000

To record the cash and tuition credit granted to students

The adjusting journal entries for the inventory and supplies used are

Instruction Expenditures	458,000	
Student Services Expenditures	50,000	
Auxiliary Enterprises Expenditures	270,000	
Inventory		778,000

To record the inventory used during the current year

Institutional Support Expenditures	62,000	
Prepaid Expenses		62,000

To record the prepaid expenses that expired during the current year

The following entries record the mandatory and nonmandatory transfers from the unrestricted current fund and the transfers to the unrestricted current fund:

Due to Other Funds	40,000	
Cash		40,000

To record the transfer of funds authorized by the board of regents in the prior year and transferred in the current year to the loan funds

Mandatory Transfer to Plant Funds	210,000	
Nonmandatory Transfer to Plant Funds	75,000	
Cash		285,000

To record both the mandatory transfer for the principal and interest on the mortgage and the nonmandatory transfer to the plant funds

Nonmandatory Transfer to Loan Funds	80,000	
Due to Other Funds		80,000

To record the board of regents' authorization to transfer funds to the loan funds

At the end of an accounting year, the budget, which is a management control tool in a private college, is reversed as in the following entry:

Unallocated Fund Balance	300,000	
Estimated Expenditures	6,500,000	
Unrealized Revenues		6,800,000

To reverse the budget entry at the end of the current year

The following transactions and events occurred during the year ended June 30, 1991 that affected the restricted current fund and the following summary journal entries are written. As was previously mentioned, the receipt of assets is not recorded as revenue but as an addition to the fund balance. Revenue is recognized when the expenditure is recorded.

Cash	200,000	
Restricted Current Fund Balance		200,000

To record the receipt of a gift restricted to student scholarships and fellowships

Cash	29,000	
Restricted Current Fund Balance		29,000

To record endowment income received for the following purposes:

Research	$ 10,000
Student Scholarships	6,000
Library Operations	13,000

Cash	55,000	
Restricted Current Fund Balance		55,000

To record the investment earnings, $30,000 is for student scholarships and the remainder for cultural activities for students

Cash	125,000	
Accounts Receivable		125,000

To record the collection of accounts receivable

Accounts Payable	43,000	
Cash		43,000

To record the payment of accounts payable

Research Expenditures	45,000	
Academic Support Expenditures	20,000	
Scholarships and Fellowships Expenditures	310,000	
Student Services Expenditures	25,000	
Cash		370,000
Accounts Payable		30,000

To record the expenditures for the current year

Restricted Current Fund Balance	400,000	
Endowment Income		29,000
Gifts and Private Grants Revenue		371,000

To recognize the revenue as expenditures have been recorded for the following purposes:

Research	$ 45,000
Academic Support	20,000
Scholarships and Fellowships	310,000
Student Services	25,000

The prior two entries illustrate that revenues are recognized in the restricted current fund when the related expenditures are incurred and recorded.

Accounts Receivable	80,000	
Restricted Current Fund Balance		80,000
To record a pledge received restricted to student aid		

FINANCIAL STATEMENTS OF NOT-FOR-PROFIT COLLEGES AND UNIVERSITIES

The financial statements of a not-for-profit college or university are the statement of revenues, expenditures, and other changes for the current fund; the balance sheet; and the statement of changes in fund balances. The financial statements for the current funds are similar to the financial statements for the general fund of a not-for-profit hospital. Unlike a voluntary health and welfare organization that records revenue and expenses for all funds, revenues and expenditures are recorded only in the current funds. Therefore, the statement of revenues, expenditures, and other changes is only for the unrestricted and restricted current funds. The balance sheet and the statement of changes in fund balances include all the funds of the not-for-profit college or university on a fund by fund basis.

The statement of revenues, expenditures, and other changes for the current funds of Olympus College from Illustrative Problem 22.1 is presented in Exhibit 22-1 and the balance sheet for only the current funds is presented in Exhibit 22-2. A balance sheet for a not-for-profit college or university is prepared for all funds, and Exhibit 22-2 is only for illustrative purposes. The excess of revenue over restricted receipts is the difference between the revenue recognized during the period because the expenditures were incurred and the revenue that was earned and added to the fund balance.

LOAN FUNDS

The loan funds are assets available for loans to students, faculty, or staff. The donation agreements typically require that the loans operate on a revolving basis. Therefore, as the principal and interest on loans previously granted are collected, the assets received are again lent to others. In some cases, the donor will specify that all or a portion of interest and/or principal be forgiven if the borrower meets certain conditions. For example, a student borrows from the loan fund an amount to be repaid after leaving college. If the student is granted a bachelor's degree, however, only half the loan is required to be repaid and half the principal is forgiven.

The assets of loan funds consist primarily of cash, temporary investments of cash, loans receivable, and interest receivable. The assets of the loan funds come from donations, government grants, repayment of loans and interest, and transfers from the unrestricted current fund. The loan funds do not use revenue and expenditures accounts but credit earnings directly to the fund balance and deduct loans granted, net of allowance for uncollectible loans and interest, from the fund balance. Because revenue and expenditure accounts are not used, the changes in the fund balance from earnings and assets received and disbursed are reported in the statement of changes in fund balances. Illustrative Problem 22.2 demonstrates the recording of transactions for the loan funds of a not-for-profit private college.

EXHIBIT 22-1

Illustrative Problem 22.1
Olympus College
Statement of Revenues, Expenditures, and Other Changes: Current Funds
Year Ended June 30, 1991

	Unrestricted	Restricted	Total
Revenues			
Educational and General			
Student Tuition and Fees	$ 4,256,000		$ 4,256,000
Governmental Grants	1,500,000		1,500,000
Gifts and Private Grants	320,000	$ 371,000	691,000
Endowment Income	130,000	29,000	159,000
Total Educational and General Revenues	6,206,000	400,000	6,606,000
Auxiliary Enterprises	540,000		540,000
Expired Term Endowments	30,000		30,000
Total Revenues	6,776,000	400,000	7,176,000
Expenditures and Mandatory Transfers			
Educational and General			
Instruction	3,258,000		3,258,000
Research	250,000	45,000	295,000
Academic Support	320,000	20,000	340,000
Student Services	460,000	25,000	485,000
Institutional Support	442,000		442,000
Operation and Maintenance of Plant	760,000		760,000
Scholarships and Fellowships	285,000	310,000	595,000
Total Educational and General Expenditures	5,775,000	400,000	6,175,000
Mandatory Transfers to Plant Funds for Mortgage Principal and Interest	210,000		210,000
Auxiliary Enterprises Expenditures	540,000		540,000
Total Expenditures and Mandatory Transfers	6,525,000	400,000	6,925,000
Other Transfers and Additions (Deductions)			
Excess of Revenues over Restricted Receipts		(36,000)	(36,000)
Nonmandatory Transfers			
Transfer to Plant Funds	(75,000)		(75,000)
Transfer to Loan Funds	(80,000)		(80,000)
Net Increase (Decrease) in Fund Balances	$ 96,000	$(36,000)	$ 60,000

EXHIBIT 22-2

Illustrative Problem 22.1
Olympus College
Balance Sheet: Current Funds Only
June 30, 1991

Assets		Liabilities and Fund Balances	
Unrestricted		**Unrestricted**	
Cash	$ 228,000	Accounts Payable	$ 358,000
Investments	840,000	Due to Other Funds	80,000
Accounts Receivable: Net	1,036,000	Unrestricted Current Funds	
Inventory	175,000	Balance	1,899,000
Prepaid Expenses	58,000		
Total Unrestricted Current		Total Unrestricted Current	
Funds	2,337,000	Funds	2,337,000
Restricted		**Restricted**	
Cash	306,000	Accounts Payable	30,000
Investments	520,000	Restricted Current Funds	
Accounts Receivable	80,000	Balance	876,000
Total Restricted Current		Total Restricted Current	
Funds	906,000	Funds	906,000
Total Current Funds	$ 3,243,000	Total Current Funds	$ 3,243,000

ILLUSTRATIVE PROBLEM 22.2: ACCOUNTING FOR THE LOAN FUNDS OF A NOT-FOR-PROFIT PRIVATE COLLEGE

The trial balance of the loan funds of Olympus College on July 1, 1990, the beginning of the fiscal year, was

	Debit	Credit
Cash	$ 32,000	
Loans Receivable	218,000	
Allowance for Uncollectible Loans		$ 25,000
Due from Unrestricted Current Fund	40,000	
Loan Funds Balance		265,000
	$ 290,000	$ 290,000

During the year ended June 30, 1991, the following transactions and transfers were recorded in the loan funds.

Cash	228,000	
Loans Receivable		101,000
Due from Unrestricted Current Fund		40,000
Loan Funds Balance		87,000

To record the cash receipts for the current year: loan repayments of $101,000, interest earned of $19,000, and a $70,000 donation, net of $2,000 of collection fees

Loans Receivable	200,000	
Cash		200,000

To record the loans granted during the current year

Due from Unrestricted Current Fund	80,000	
Loan Funds Balance		80,000

To record the transfer authorized by the board of regents

Allowance for Uncollectible Loans	15,000	
Loans Receivable		15,000

To write off loans deemed uncollectible

Loan Funds Balance	20,000	
Allowance for Uncollectible Loans		20,000

To record the estimate of uncollectible accounts

The adjusted trial balance of the loan funds at June 30, 1991 is

	Debit	Credit
Cash	$ 60,000	
Loans Receivable	302,000	
Allowance for Uncollectible Accounts		$ 30,000
Due from Unrestricted Current Fund	80,000	
Loan Funds Balance		412,000
	$ 442,000	$ 442,000

ENDOWMENT FUNDS

The endowment funds consist of donated assets that must be maintained for either a specified period of time or indefinitely. The income earned by the endowment fund assets can be either restricted or unrestricted. If the income is restricted, it is transferred to the appropriate restricted fund if it can be currently expended, or added to the balance of the endowment fund if the donor has restricted its use for a period of time. Assets received as income that are unrestricted are transferred to the unrestricted current fund and recognized as endowment income by that fund. Illustrative Problem 22.3 demonstrates the recording of the transactions for the endowment funds of Olympus College. If the board of regents of the not-for-profit college or university has created a quasi-endowment fund, these funds are called endowment and similar funds.

ILLUSTRATIVE PROBLEM 22.3: ACCOUNTING FOR THE ENDOWMENT FUNDS
OF A NOT-FOR-PROFIT PRIVATE COLLEGE

The trial balance of the endowment funds of Olympus College on July 1, 1990, the beginning of the fiscal year, was

	Debit	Credit
Cash	$ 45,000	
Interest Receivable	23,000	
Investments	1,350,000	
Fund Balance: Restricted		$ 264,000
Fund Balance: Unrestricted		1,154,000
	$ 1,418,000	$ 1,418,000

During the year ended June 30, 1991, the following transactions are recorded in the endowment funds:

Cash	155,000	
Interest Receivable		23,000
Due Restricted Current Fund		22,000
Due Unrestricted Current Fund		110,000
To record the investment income received during the current year		
Fund Balance: Unrestricted	30,000	
Cash		30,000
To record the transfer of an expired term endowment to the unrestricted current fund		
Interest Receivable	27,000	
Due Restricted Current Fund		7,000
Due Unrestricted Current Fund		20,000
To accrue the interest receivable at year end		
Due Restricted Current Fund	29,000	
Due Unrestricted Current Fund	130,000	
Cash		159,000
To record the transfer of the earnings due the unrestricted current and restricted current funds		

The adjusted trial balance of the endowment funds at June 30, 1991 is

	Debit	Credit
Cash	$ 11,000	
Interest Receivable	27,000	
Investments	1,350,000	
Fund Balance: Restricted		$ 264,000
Fund Balance: Unrestricted		1,124,000
	$ 1,388,000	$ 1,388,000

ANNUITY AND LIFE INCOME FUNDS

Annuity and life income funds consist of assets donated to the college or university. These assets are typically cash, investments, or income-producing property. The donor has required that either the income from the assets or an established amount per period be paid to either the donor or a specified beneficiary for a stipulated period of time or for the lifetime of the recipient.

When annuity assets are donated to the college, the assets are recorded at their fair market value, the actuarially computed present value of the required annuity payments is recorded as a liability, and the remainder contributed is credited to the annuity fund balance. When payments are made to the annuitant, the liability is reduced by the recorded present value and the difference between the cash actually paid and the estimated current value is debited to the annuity fund balance. Alternatively, the liability can be reduced by the amount of the payment and then the liability and the fund balance are periodically adjusted to recognize the change in the life expectancy of the annuitant. The income earned and gains and losses from the sale of annuity investments are adjustments of the fund balance.

The assets of life income funds are recorded at their fair market value and no liability is established. The earnings of the assets are recorded as a liability to the life income beneficiary, and the payments to the life income beneficiary are recorded as a reduction of the liability. Gains and losses on investments are adjustments to the liability.

At the end of the annuity or life income fund, the assets are transferred to the appropriate restricted fund, or if the donor has not specified a use for the assets upon termination, the assets are transferred to the unrestricted current fund. Illustrative Problem 22.4 demonstrates the transactions of the annuity and life income funds of a not-for-profit private college.

ILLUSTRATIVE PROBLEM 22.4: ACCOUNTING FOR THE ANNUITY AND LIFE INCOME FUNDS OF A NOT-FOR-PROFIT PRIVATE COLLEGE

The trial balance of the annuity and life income funds on July 1, 1990, the beginning of the fiscal year, was

	Debit	Credit
Cash: Annuities	$ 77,000	
Cash: Life Income	12,000	
Investments: Annuities	321,000	
Investments: Life Income	144,000	
Annuities Payable		$ 164,000
Life Income Payable		6,000
Annuity Fund Balance		234,000
Life Income Fund Balance		150,000
	$ 554,000	$ 554,000

During the year ending June 30, 1991, the following transactions are entered in the accounts of the annuities and life income funds:

Cash: Annuities	28,000	
Cash: Life Income	15,000	
Life Income Payable		15,000
Annuities Fund Balance		28,000

To record the income earned on the annuity and life income funds

Cash: Annuities	100,000	
Annuities Payable		48,000
Annuity Fund Balance		52,000

To record an annuity received from an alumnus. The alumnus is to receive $8,000 per year for life, and then the fund is to be used for additions to the library. The actuarial computation of the present value of the annuity is $48,000.

Annuities Payable	31,000	
Annuity Fund Balance	5,000	
Cash: Annuities		36,000

To record the payment of annuities whose initial present value was recorded as $31,000

Life Income Payable	18,000	
Cash: Life Income		18,000

To record the payment to life income beneficiaries

Investments: Annuities	156,000	
Cash: Annuities		156,000

To record the purchase of investments with annuity cash

The adjusted trial balance of the annuity and life income funds at June 30, 1991, the end of the fiscal year, is

	Debit	Credit
Cash: Annuities	$ 13,000	
Cash: Life Income	9,000	
Investments: Annuities	477,000	
Investments: Life Income	144,000	
Annuities Payable		$ 181,000
Life Income Payable		3,000
Annuity Fund Balance		309,000
Life Income Fund Balance		150,000
	$ 643,000	$ 643,000

PLANT FUNDS

The plant funds consist of four separate self-balancing sets of accounts or subgroups of accounts.

1. **Unexpended Plant Fund,** which contains assets to be used for acquisition of new property, plant, and equipment
2. **Fund for Renewals and Replacements,** which contains assets to be used to renovate or replace existing plant and equipment

3. **Fund for Retirement of Indebtedness,** which contains assets to be used for the retirement of debt
4. **Investment in Plant,** which includes all the property, plant, and equipment accounts and the liabilities from the acquisitions of those assets.

The unexpended plant fund is used to account for the cash and the investments for future acquisitions of plant assets. If the assets are donated assets, they are recorded in the appropriate asset account and credited to Restricted Fund Balance. Assets that are transferred by discretionary action of the board of regents are recorded in the appropriate asset account and credited to Unrestricted Fund Balance.

The plant fund for renewals and replacements contains assets either donated or transferred as discretionary funds from the unrestricted current fund. The assets are used to maintain and replace existing plant assets. The fund balance is separated into restricted and unrestricted accounts the same as in the unexpended plant fund.

The plant fund for retirement of indebtedness is used to account for the assets to be used for retirement of debt and has both restricted and unrestricted assets. Because the debt is recorded in the investment in plant fund, however, the use of the assets to retire debt is recorded as a reduction of the fund balance.

The investment in plant fund contains all the plant assets of the college, including the investment in library materials, as well as the outstanding debt for the acquisition of the plant assets. The assets come from transfers from the unrestricted current fund—both mandatory and nonmandatory—from donations, and from expenditures of current funds. When the plant fund for retirement of indebtedness pays a long-term liability, the liability is reduced in the investment in plant fund, and the fund balance, Net Investment in Plant, is credited.

As previously mentioned, prior to January, 1990, not-for-profit private colleges and universities were not required by generally accepted accounting principles to depreciate plant and equipment. This chapter assumes that the not-for-profit college or university has elected early application of the standard. The provision for depreciation and the accumulated depreciation accounts are part of the investment in plant fund and are demonstrated in Illustrative Problem 22.5, assuming that the not-for-profit college has already elected early application of the new standard to record depreciation and has entered the cumulative adjustment for the change in accounting principle in a prior year.

Rather than transferring assets for the purchase of plant assets to the plant fund and recording the acquisition of plant assets in the plant fund, a not-for-profit college or university may simply purchase the plant assets with either unrestricted or restricted current fund assets and then transfer the plant assets acquired to the plant fund. The net effect of this approach is exactly the same as if the assets needed for the acquisition are transferred to the plant fund and the plant assets are then purchased with them.

Illustrative Problem 22.5 demonstrates the recording of transactions for the plant funds of a not-for-profit private college.

ILLUSTRATIVE PROBLEM 22.5: ACCOUNTING FOR THE PLANT FUNDS OF A NOT-FOR-PROFIT PRIVATE COLLEGE

The trial balances of the four subfunds of the plant funds of Olympus College at July 1, 1990, the beginning of the fiscal year, were

	Debit	Credit
Unexpended Plant Fund		
Cash	$ 250,000	
Investments	1,500,000	
Fund Balance: Restricted		$ 1,600,000
Fund Balance: Unrestricted		150,000
	1,750,000	1,750,000
Plant Fund for Renewals and Replacements		
Cash	12,000	
Investments	185,000	
Fund Balance: Restricted		165,000
Fund Balance: Unrestricted		32,000
	197,000	197,000
Plant Fund for Retirement of Indebtedness		
Cash	60,000	
Investments	125,000	
Fund Balance: Restricted		45,000
Fund Balance: Unrestricted		140,000
	185,000	185,000
Investment in Plant		
Land	1,500,000	
Land Improvements	2,200,000	
Buildings	17,400,000	
Accumulated Depreciation: Buildings		9,300,000
Equipment	6,600,000	
Accumulated Depreciation: Equipment		3,100,000
Library Books and Materials	300,000	
Notes Payable: Equipment		500,000
Mortgage Payable: Land and Buildings		3,100,000
Net Investment in Plant		12,000,000
	28,000,000	28,000,000
Total	$ 30,132,000	$ 30,132,000

During the year ending June 30, 1991, the following transactions and events are recorded in the four plant subfunds of Olympus College.

Unexpended Plant Fund

Investments	125,000	
Fund Balance: Restricted		125,000

To record the receipt of bonds donated to the college by an alumnus. The assets are to be used to assist in the building of a theater.

Cash	40,000	
Fund Balance: Restricted		40,000

To record the receipt of cash donations that can be used only for plant acquisitions

| Cash | 75,000 | |
| Fund Balance: Unrestricted | | 75,000 |

To record the voluntary transfer from the unrestricted current fund as instructed by the board of regents

This entry has its counterpart in the unrestricted current fund.

Cash	165,000	
Fund Balance: Restricted		150,000
Fund Balance: Unrestricted		15,000

To record the income earned on investments

| Cash | 1,000,000 | |
| Mortgage Payable | | 1,000,000 |

To record the mortgage to be used for the construction of a theater buiding

Theater Building	1,300,000	
Theater Equipment	210,000	
Cash		1,510,000

To record the cost of the theater building completed during the current year and financed with cash and a mortgage. Prior to beginning the building, the college had received $400,000 in donations to construct the building.

If the construction extends over a period of time, the account Construction in Process is used until the building is completed.

Mortgage Payable	1,000,000	
Fund Balance: Restricted	400,000	
Fund Balance: Unrestricted	110,000	
Theater Building		1,300,000
Theater Equipment		210,000

To record the transfer of the asset and the liability to the investment in plant fund

The Fund Balance: Restricted account is debited for $400,000, representing the donations received specifically for the purpose of constructing the theater building.

Plant Fund for Renewals and Replacements

Cash	50,000	
Investments		47,000
Fund Balance: Restricted		3,000

To record the sale of investments

Fund Balance: Restricted	38,000	
Fund Balance: Unrestricted	9,000	
Cash		47,000

To record the expenditures for repairs to buildings and equipment during the current year

Cash	14,000	
Fund Balance: Restricted		11,000
Fund Balance: Unrestricted		3,000

To record the investment earnings for the current period

Plant Fund for Retirement of Indebtedness

Cash	210,000	
Fund Balance: Restricted		210,000

To record the mandatory transfer of cash to pay the mortgage
principal and interest from the unrestricted current fund

This entry has its counterpart in the unrestricted current fund.

Cash	225,000	
Fund Balance: Restricted		225,000

To record the receipt of a contribution restricted to the payment
of mortgage principal and interest

Fund Balance: Restricted	410,000	
Cash		410,000

To record the payment of $310,000 of interest and $100,000 of
principal of the mortgage with restricted assets

Fund Balance: Restricted	40,000	
Fund Balance: Unrestricted	20,000	
Cash		60,000

To record the payment of $50,000 of interest and $10,000 of
principal on the note payable partly with restricted and
unrestricted assets

Cash	14,000	
Fund Balance: Unrestricted		14,000

To record the income from investments

Investment in Plant Fund

Buildings	1,300,000	
Equipment	210,000	
Mortgage Payable		1,000,000
Net Investment in Plant		510,000

To record the completion of the theater and the debt on the
theater

Mortgage Payable	100,000	
Net Investment in Plant		100,000

To record payment of the principal of the mortgage

Note Payable	10,000	
Net Investment in Plant		10,000

To record the payment of the principal of the note

The above three entries reflect the construction of the theater and the purchase of equipment
for the theater from the unexpended plant fund, and the payment of the principal of debt by
the plant fund for retirement of indebtedness.

Net Investment in Plant	1,075,000	
Accumulated Depreciation: Buildings		370,000
Accumulated Depreciation: Equipment		680,000
Library Books and Materials		25,000

To record the depreciation expense for the current year

Colleges and universities typically do not use an accumulated depreciation account for library books and materials, but credit the asset account directly, as a not-for-profit hospital does with minor equipment.

The adjusted trial balances of the four plant subfunds at June 30, 1991 are

	Debit	Credit
Unexpended Plant Fund		
Cash	$ 20,000	
Investments	1,625,000	
Fund Balance: Restricted		$ 1,515,000
Fund Balance: Unrestricted		130,000
	1,645,000	1,645,000
Plant Fund for Renewals and Replacements		
Cash	29,000	
Investments	138,000	
Fund Balance: Restricted		141,000
Fund Balance: Unrestricted		26,000
	167,000	167,000
Plant Fund for Retirement of Indebtedness		
Cash	39,000	
Investments	125,000	
Fund Balance: Restricted		30,000
Fund Balance: Unrestricted		134,000
	164,000	164,000
Investment in Plant		
Land	1,500,000	
Land Improvements	2,200,000	
Buildings	18,700,000	
Accumulated Depreciation: Buildings		9,670,000
Equipment	6,810,000	
Accumulated Depreciation: Equipment		3,780,000
Library Books and Materials	275,000	
Notes Payable: Equipment		490,000
Mortgage Payable: Land and Buildings		4,000,000
Net Investment in Plant		11,545,000
	29,485,000	29,485,000
Total	$ 31,461,000	$ 31,461,000

AGENCY FUNDS

Agency funds are funds held by the college or university for student organizations, individual students, or faculty members. Because the college or university is just acting as the custodian and record keeper of funds that belong to other entities, the funds have no balance, only a liability. Agency funds are not included in the statement of changes in fund balances, but are included in the balance sheet of the college or university. The inclusion in the balance sheet indicates the amount of assets that the college or university has custodianship responsibilities over and a liability to the entity whose assets the college controls. The journal entries to record the transactions of the agency funds are entries that record the receipt of assets and the expenditures of assets that belong to other entities.

Exhibits 22-3 and 22-4 are the statement of changes in fund balances and the balance sheet for all of the funds of Olympus College. The statements have been constructed from the information and the trial balances presented in Illustrative Problems 22.1 through 22.5 and Exhibits 22.1 and 22.2.

EXHIBIT 22-3

Olympus College
Balance Sheet
June 30, 1991

Assets			Liabilities and Fund Balances	

CURRENT FUNDS

Unrestricted			Unrestricted	
Cash		$ 228,000	Accounts Payable	$ 358,000
Investments		840,000	Due to Other Funds	80,000
Accounts Receivable: Net		1,036,000	Unrestricted Current Fund Balance	1,899,000
Inventory		175,000		
Prepaid Expenses		58,000		
Total Unrestricted Current Fund		2,337,000	Total Unrestricted Current Fund	2,337,000
Restricted			Restricted	
Cash		306,000	Accounts Payable	30,000
Investments		520,000	Restricted Current Fund Balance	876,000
Accounts Receivable		80,000		
Total Restricted Current Fund		906,000	Total Restricted Current Fund	906,000
Total Current Funds		$ 3,243,000	Total Current Funds	$ 3,243,000

LOAN FUNDS

Cash		$ 60,000	Fund Balances	$ 412,000
Loans Receivable	$ 302,000			
Less: Allowance for Uncollectible Loans	30,000	272,000		
Due From Unrestricted Fund		80,000		
Total Loan Funds		$ 412,000	Total Loan Funds	$ 412,000

ENDOWMENT FUNDS

Cash		$ 11,000	Fund Balance: Restricted	$ 264,000
Interest Receivable		27,000	Fund Balance: Unrestricted	1,124,000
Investments		1,350,000		
Total Endowment Funds		$ 1,388,000	Total Endowment Funds	$ 1,388,000

Olympus College
Balance Sheet Continued
June 30, 1991

Assets   Liabilities and Fund Balances

ANNUITY AND LIFE INCOME FUNDS

Annuity Funds		Annuity Funds	
Cash	$ 13,000	Annuities Payable	$ 181,000
Investments	477,000	Fund Balances	309,000
Total Annuity Funds	490,000	Total Annuity Funds	490,000
Life Income Funds		Life Income Funds	
Cash	9,000	Income Payable	3,000
Investments	144,000	Fund Balances	150,000
Total Life Income Funds	153,000	Total Life Income Funds	153,000
Total Annuity and Life Income Funds	$ 643,000	Total Annuity and Life Income Funds	$ 643,000

PLANT FUNDS

Unexpended		Unexpended	
Cash	$ 20,00	Fund Balance: Restricted	$ 1,515,000
Investments	1,625,000	Fund Balance: Unrestricted	130,000
Total Unexpended	1,645,000	Total Unexpended	1,645,000
Renewals and Replacements		Renewals and Replacements	
Cash	29,000	Fund Balance: Restricted	141,000
Investments	138,000	Fund Balance: Unrestricted	26,000
Total Renewals and Replacements	167,000	Total Renewals and Replacements	167,000
Retirement of Indebtedness		Retirement of Indebtedness	
Cash	39,000	Fund Balance: Restricted	30,000
Investments	125,000	Fund Balance: Unrestricted	134,000
Total Retirement of Indebtedness	164,000	Total Retirement of Indebtedness	164,000
Investment in Plant		Investment in Plant	
Land	1,500,000	Note Payable	490,000
Land Improvements	2,200,000	Mortgages Payable	4,000,000
Buildings: Net	9,030,000	Net Investment in Plant	11,545,000
Equipment: Net	3,030,000		
Library Books and Materials: Net	275,000		
Total Investment in Plant	16,035,000	Total Investment in Plant	16,035,000
Total Plant Funds	$ 18,011,000	Total Plant Funds	$ 18,011,000

AGENCY FUNDS

Cash	$ 59,000	Deposits Held in Custody for Others	$ 81,000
Marketable Securities	22,000		
Total Agency Funds	$ 81,000	Total Agency Funds	$ 81,000

SUMMARY

Colleges and universities are generally operated as not-for-profit entities. A not-for-profit college or university can be a private institution, and thus a not-for-profit entity in and of itself, or it may be owned and operated as part of a governmental unit. The accounting and financial reporting are the same for both types of not-for-profit colleges and universities except that the government-owned and government-operated colleges and universities are not required to record depreciation, but may elect to depreciate plant assets.

Not-for-profit colleges and universities use an unrestricted current fund and restricted funds to account for their activities. The restricted funds are restricted current funds, loan funds, annuity and life income funds, plant funds, endowment funds, and agency funds. The board of regents may establish board-designated funds with current assets just like a not-for-profit hospital. The board may also establish board-designated funds that are intended to be a permanent setting aside of assets, which are called quasi-endowment funds, that are accounted for like endowment funds.

A not-for-profit college or university that is owned and operated by a governmental unit records a budget, which represents an authorization to spend assets. A not-for-profit private college or university may record a budget that is used for management-control purposes. The operations of the not-for-profit college or university are recorded in the unrestricted current fund, which has only current assets and liabilities, like a voluntary health and welfare organization. The restricted current fund of a not-for-profit college or university is used to account for current operating assets whose use has been restricted by the donor just like a not-for-profit hospital uses specific-purpose funds. All the operating results of a not-for-profit college or university are recognized and recorded in the unrestricted and restricted current funds.

Revenues are recorded in three major categories: educational and general, auxiliary enterprises, and expired term endowments. The educational and general revenues are further divided into student tuition and fees, governmental appropriations, government grants and contracts, gifts and private grants, endowment income, and other sources. Auxiliary enterprises are entities that furnish goods and services to students and faculty for a fee that is directly related to the cost of the goods or services. Revenue is not recognized in the current restricted fund until an expenditure has occurred that meets the donor's restrictions; therefore, when revenue is initially received, it is recorded as an increase in the fund balance.

Not-for-profit colleges and universities use the term expenditure and not the term expense as the major goal of the institutions is the provision of services without profit as the motive. The expenditures of a not-for-profit college or university are divided into two major categories: educational and general expenditures, and auxiliary enterprises expenditures. The educational and general expenditures are further divided into instruction, research, public service, academic support, student services, institutional support, operations and maintenance of plant, and scholarships and fellowships.

A not-for-profit college or university transfers assets between funds just like all the other not-for-profit entities. A not-for-profit college or university, however, has transfers that are mandatory and makes transfers at the discretion of the board of regents, which are nonmandatory transfers. Mandatory transfers are transfers that must be made as a result of a binding contract such as a mortgage. The distinction between mandatory and nonmandatory transfers is reflected in the account titles used in the current funds.

EXHIBIT 22-4

Olympus College
Statement of Changes in Fund Balances
Year Ended, June 30, 1991

	Current Funds		Loan
	Unrestricted	Restricted	Funds
Revenues and Other Additions			
Unrestricted Current Fund Revenues	$ 6,776,000		
Gifts and Private Grants: Restricted		$ 280,000	$ 70,000
Investment Income: Restricted		84,000	
Realized Gains on Sale of Investments: Restricted			
Interest on Loans Receivable			32,000
Expended for Plant Facilities			
Retirement of Indebtedness			
Total Revenues and Other Additions	6,776,000	364,000	112,000
Expenditures and Other Deductions			
Educational and General Expenditures	5,775,000	400,000	
Auxiliary Enterprises Expenditures	540,000		
Loan Cancellations and Write-offs			20,000
Administrative and Collection Costs			2,000
Expired Term Endowments			
Adjustment of Actuarial Liability for Annuities			
Expended for Plant Facilities			
Expended on Plant Maintenance			
Retirement of Indebtedness			
Interest on Indebtedness			
Provision for Depreciation			
Total Expenditures and Other Deductions	6,315,000	400,000	22,000
Transfers Among Funds: Additions (Deductions)			
Mandatory: Principal and Interest	(210,000)		
Other	(155,000)		80,000
Total Transfers	(365,000)		80,000
Net Increase (Decrease) in Fund Balances	96,000	(36,000)	160,000
Fund Balance at Beginning of Year	1,803,000	912,000	265,000
Fund Balance at End of Year	$ 1,899,000	$ 876,000	$ 425,000

The loan funds contain the assets available for loans to students, faculty, and staff that are usually on a revolving basis with new loans being granted from the repayment receipts of old loans. The loan funds do not use revenue and expenditure accounts but report the inflows and outflows of assets as changes in fund balance. The endowment funds of a not-for-profit college or university are accounted for exactly like endowment funds of a not-for-

Endowment Funds	Annuity and Life Income Funds	Plant Funds			
		Unexpended	Renewals and Replacements	Retirement of Indebtedness	Investment In Plant
	$ 52,000	$ 165,000		$ 225,000	
	28,000	165,000	$ 14,000	14,000	
			3,000		
					$ 510,000
					110,000
$ —0—	80,000	330,000	17,000	239,000	620,000
30,000					
	5,000				
		510,000			
			47,000		
				110,000	
				360,000	
					1,075,000
30,000	5,000	510,000	47,000	470,000	1,075,000
				210,000	
		75,000			
—0—		75,000		210,000	
(30,000)	75,000	(105,000)	(30,000)	(21,000)	(455,000)
1,418,000	384,000	1,750,000	197,000	185,000	12,000,000
$ 1,388,000	$ 459,000	$ 1,645,000	$ 167,000	$ 164,000	$ 11,545,000

profit hospital. Annuity and life income funds are assets donated to the college or university that eventually will become its assets. The donor or the beneficiary named by the donor receives either the income or a stipulated amount of the earnings either for a specific period of time or for a lifetime.

If the fund is an annuity, the assets received are recorded at their fair market value, a liability is recorded at the actuarially computed present value of future payments, and the difference is credited to the fund balance. As income is received it is added to the fund balance, and payments to the beneficiary are reductions of the liability. If the fund is a life income fund, the assets received are recorded at their fair market value and the fund balance is credited, with no liability being recorded. As income is received it is recorded as a liability, and payments to the life income beneficiary reduce the liability.

The plant funds consist of four subgroups of funds: the unexpended plant fund, the fund for renewals and replacements, the fund for retirement of indebtedness, and the investment in plant fund. The unexpended plant fund has both unrestricted and restricted assets, whose use has been specified by the donor, for acquisitions of new property, plant, and equipment. The fund for renewals and replacements and the fund for retirement of indebtedness also have unrestricted and restricted assets. The distinction between unrestricted and restricted assets is maintained within these funds. The net investment in plant fund includes all the property, plant, and equipment, and all the debt from the acquisition of those assets. The transactions for acquisitions and dispositions of plant assets and the payment of debt are made in the other three plant funds or the current funds, and only the results are recorded in the net investment in plant fund.

The financial statements of a not-for-profit college or university are a statement of revenues, expenditures, and other changes for only the current funds, a balance sheet, reported on a fund by fund basis, and a statement of changes in fund balances for all the funds used by a not-for-profit college or university.

Exhibit 22-5 contains a summary of the important facts about the not-for-profit organizations discussed in Chapters 20, 21, and 22.

EXHIBIT 22-5

NOT-FOR-PROFIT ENTITIES
SUMMARY OF ACCOUNTING AND REPORTING

Entity	Hospitals	Voluntary Health and Welfare	Other	Colleges and Universities
Sources of GAAP	AICPA: Audit Guide, SOPs AHA: Chart of Accounts FASB: as applicable	AICPA: Audit Guide, SOPs NHC, NASPD, and United Way Standards[a] FASB: as applicable	AICPA: Audit Guide, SOPs, Industry Guides FASB: as applicable	AICPA: Audit Guide, SOPs NACUBO: CUBA FASB: as applicable
Basis of Accounting	Accrual	Accrual	Accrual	Accrual
Measurement Focus	Capital Maintenance	Capital Maintenance	Capital Maintenance	Spending/Capital Maintenance
Funds	Unrestricted General Board-Designated	Current Unrestricted Current Restricted Plant	Unrestricted Restricted at a minimum and as needed	Unrestricted Current Restricted Current Loan

Entity	Hospitals	Voluntary Health and Welfare	Other	Colleges and Universities
	Restricted Endowment Plant Replacement and Expansion Specific-Purpose Agency	Endowment Custodian Loan		Endowment Annuity and Life Income Plant Funds Unexpended Renewals and Replacements Retirement of Indebtedness Investment in Plant Agency
Revenue Recognition Limitations	Current Restricted recognized when unrestricted or expended	Restricted Revenue when available for use	Deferred Revenue recognized when expended	Restricted Revenue recognized when unrestricted or expended
Expenditure Expense	Expenses	Expenses	Expenses	Expenditures/Expense
Depreciation Recorded	Yes	Yes	Yes	Yes if Private No if Government Owned
Property, Plant and Equipment	General Fund if used for hospital operations Appropriate restricted fund if not for hospital operations	Plant Fund	Plant Fund Recommended	Investment in Plant Subfund
Long-term Debt	General Fund	Plant Fund	Plant Fund or Operating Fund if no Plant Fund	Investment in Plant Subfund
Construction Activities	General Fund or Plant Replacement and Expansion Fund	Plant Fund	Plant Fund Recommended	Unexpended Plant Fund or Renewal and Replacement Fund
Major Revenue Sources	User Fees (often third-party paid), Contributions	Contributions, User Fees	Dues, User Fees, Contributions	Tuition, Grants, Contributions
Estimated Bad Debts	Deducted from revenue in Statement of Revenue and Expense	Deducted from support or revenue in operating statement	Deducted from support or revenue in operating statement	Expenditures

Entity	Hospitals	Voluntary Health and Welfare	Other	Colleges and Universities
Interfund Transactions	Transfers are other operating revenue or nonoperating revenue in General Fund	Transfers are changes in fund balances not revenue and expense	Transfers are changes in fund balances not revenue and expense	Mandatory transfers from current funds are changes in fund balances not revenue and expenditures Nonmandatory transfers to or from current funds are changes in fund balances not revenue and expenditures Required transfers to current funds are revenues Required transfers to restricted funds are changes in fund balances not revenues and expenditures
Financial Statements	Balance Sheet Statement of Revenue and Expense Statement of Changes in Fund Balances Statement of Cash Flow for Unrestricted Funds	Balance Sheet Statement of Support, Revenues and Expenses and Changes in Fund Balance Statement of Functional Expenses	Balance Sheet Statement of Revenues, Expenses, and Changes in Fund Balance Statement of Cash Flow	Balance Sheet Statement of Current Fund Revenues and Expenditures and Other Changes Statement of Changes in Fund Balance
Examples	Not-for-Profit Hospitals	Muscular Dystrophy Association, YMCA	Churches, Unions, Cemeteries, Museums, Libraries	Public and Private Not-for-Profit Colleges and Universities

[a]National Health Council, National Assembly for Social Policy and Development, and United Way of America

REVIEW PROBLEM

Benton College is a not-for-profit private college specializing in business and computer science courses, and also offers courses in liberal arts to make its students well-rounded individuals. The trial balance of Benton College on July 1, 1990, the beginning of the college's fiscal year, was

	Debit	Credit
Unrestricted Current Fund		
Cash	$ 259,000	
Marketable Securities	351,000	
Accounts Receivable	422,000	
Allowance for Uncollectible Receivables		$ 21,100
Due from Other Funds	4,000	
Inventory of Materials	163,000	
Prepaid Expenses	34,000	
Accounts Payable		156,000
Due to Other Funds		22,000
Unrestricted Current Fund Balance		1,033,900
Restricted Current Fund		
Cash	184,000	
Marketable Securities	270,000	
Accrued Interest Receivable	6,000	
Accounts Payable		23,000
Restricted Current Fund Balance		437,000
Loan Funds		
Cash	21,000	
Loans Receivable	140,000	
Allowance for Uncollectible Loans		28,000
Due from Unrestricted Current Fund	22,000	
Loan Funds Balance		155,000
Endowment Funds		
Cash	23,000	
Interest Receivable	12,000	
Investments	687,000	
Fund Balance: Restricted		322,000
Fund Balance: Unrestricted		400,000
Annuity and Life Income Funds		
Cash: Annuities	41,000	
Cash: Life Income	8,000	
Investments: Annuities	242,000	
Investments: Life Income	37,000	
Annuities Payable		94,000
Life Income Payable		5,000
Annuity Funds Balance		189,000
Life Income Funds Balance		40,000

	Debit	Credit
Plant Funds		
Unexpended Plant Fund		
Cash	130,000	
Investments	590,000	
Fund Balance: Restricted		340,000
Fund Balance: Unrestricted		380,000
Plant Fund for Renewals and Replacements		
Cash	23,000	
Investments	128,000	
Fund Balance: Restricted		51,000
Fund Balance: Unrestricted		100,000
Plant Fund for Retirement of Indebtedness		
Cash	42,000	
Investments	140,000	
Fund Balance: Restricted		62,000
Fund Balance: Unrestricted		120,000
Investment in Plant		
Land	410,000	
Land Improvements	275,000	
Buildings	6,400,000	
Accumulated Depreciation: Buildings		2,500,000
Equipment	3,800,000	
Accumulated Depreciation: Equipment		1,450,000
Library Books and Materials	190,000	
Notes Payable: Equipment		620,000
Mortgages Payable: Buildings		2,400,000
Net Investment in Plant		4,105,000
	$ 15,054,000	$ 15,054,000

During the year ended June 30, 1991, the following transactions and events occurred that affected the funds of Benton College.

Unrestricted Current Fund

- Revenues were earned from the following sources:

Student Tuition and Fees	$ 3,520,000
Government Grants and Contracts	840,000
Gifts and Private Grants	330,000
Endowment Income	40,000
Auxiliary Enterprises	410,000
Expired Term Endowment	30,000

- Uncollectible accounts are estimated to be 10% of student tuition and fees.
- Cash receipts consisted of $4,700,000 of accounts receivable and $70,000 from the endowment funds. Accounts receivable totaling $360,000 were determined to be uncollectible.

- Scholarships and fellowships of $230,000 were granted. Cash of $30,000 was disbursed to students and the remainder was tuition credit.
- Inventory totaling $510,000 was purchased on account.
- Prepaid expenses totaling $70,000 were purchased for cash.
- Expenditures incurred during the year consisted of

Instructional	$ 2,019,000
Research	320,000
Academic Support	190,000
Student Services	265,000
Institutional Support	289,000
Operation and Maintenance of Plant	624,000
Auxiliary Enterprises	126,000

- Accounts payable totaling $4,200,000 were paid.
- Inventory of materials was used for the following:

Instruction	$ 250,000
Student Services	37,000
Auxiliary Enterprises	233,000

- Prepaid expenses, all for institutional support, of $81,000 expired.
- Cash transferred to other funds consisted of

Nonmandatory transfer to loan fund including prior year's authorization	48,000
Mandatory transfers to plant fund for interest and principal of mortgage and loan	482,000
Nonmandatory transfers for renewals and replacements	52,000

Restricted Current Fund

- Investments earned $28,000.
- Cash receipts consisted of

Interest Receivable	$ 29,000
Gift, restricted to student scholarships	80,000
Endowment funds transfer of investment income	12,000

- Expenditures on account were incurred for

Research	$ 190,000
Academic Support	42,000
Scholarships and Fellowships	60,000

The revenues that supported the expenditures came from

Endowment Income	$ 23,000
Gifts and Private Grants	245,000
Investments	24,000

- Accounts payable totaling $290,000 were paid.

Loan Funds

- Cash was received from

Loans Receivable	$ 59,000
Interest	13,000
Unrestricted Current Fund	48,000
Endowment Funds	10,000
Gifts	100,000

- Loans totaling $197,000 were granted.
- Loans in the amount of $12,000 were determined to be uncollectible.
- The uncollectible loans are estimated to be 20% of the outstanding loans at year end.

Endowment Funds

- Restricted endowments totaling $65,000 were received.
- Investments earned $79,000; $39,000 was from restricted endowments and $40,000 was from unrestricted endowments. The restricted endowment earnings consist of $12,000 restricted for current operations, $10,000 for loan funds, and $17,000 for unexpended plant fund.
- Cash received as earnings on investments totaled $81,000.
- Restricted investments with a cost of $51,000 were sold for $55,000.
- Restricted investments totaling $111,000 were purchased.
- Transfers to other funds consisted of

Unrestricted Current Fund: Income	$ 40,000
Unrestricted Current Fund: Expired Endowment	30,000
Restricted Current Fund	12,000
Loan Funds	10,000
Unexpended Plant Fund	17,000

Annuity and Life Income Funds

- The annuities earned and received in cash $30,000 and the life income funds earned and received in cash $9,000.
- An annuity of $100,000 was received. The actuarially computed present value of the annuity is $61,000.
- A life income fund in the amount of $50,000 was received.
- Annuities totaling $36,000 and life income totaling $10,000 were paid. The present value of the annuities that were paid was $29,000.
- Investments purchased for annuities totaled $110,000 and investments purchased for life income funds totaled $48,000.

Plant Funds

- Gifts and bequests of cash were received for

Acquisitions of Equipment	$ 100,000
Acquisition Restricted to Classrooms	50,000
Acquisition Restricted to Replacement of Out-of-date Computers	33,000

- Investments in the subgroups earned and received in cash the following income:

Unexpended Plant Fund: Restricted	$ 30,000
Unexpended Plant Fund: Unrestricted	32,000
Renewal and Replacement Fund: Restricted	6,000
Renewal and Replacement Fund: Unrestricted	8,000
Retirement of Indebtedness Fund: Restricted	5,000
Retirement of Indebtedness Fund: Unrestricted	11,000

- Transfers from other funds consisted of

Unrestricted Current Fund: Mandatory Transfer for Interest and Principal	$ 482,000
Unrestricted Current Fund: Nonmandatory Transfer for Renewals and Replacements	52,000
Endowment Fund Income: Restricted to Purchases of Equipment	17,000

- A new classroom building was completed at a cost of $2,200,000 with $200,000 paid in cash and the remainder was financed with a mortgage. Cash of $75,000 was restricted in use and cash of $125,000 was not restricted.
- Expenditures for repairs to building and equipment totaled $91,000. The expenditures were paid with $23,000 of restricted cash and $68,000 of unrestricted cash.
- The following long-term liabilities were paid:

Note Payable: Interest	$ 62,000
Note Payable: Principal	60,000
Mortgage Payable: Interest	240,000
Mortgage Payable: Principal	120,000

- Depreciation for the current year consisted of

Buildings	$ 300,000
Equipment	410,000
Library Books and Materials	18,000

Required

1. Prepare the transaction, event, and adjusting journal entries for each of the funds of Benton College for the year ended June 30, 1991.
2. Prepare the adjusted trial balance for all the funds of Benton College as of June 30, 1991.
3. Prepare the statement of revenues, expenditures, and other changes and the statement of changes in fund balances for the year ended June 30, 1991.
4. Prepare the balance sheet of Benton College as of June 30, 1991.

QUESTIONS

1. Describe a quasi-endowment fund and how it is created.
2. Describe how the plant funds of a not-for-profit college differ from the plant fund of a voluntary health and welfare organization.
3. What are the reasons given in *Statement of Financial Accounting Standards No. 93* for a not-for-profit college to record depreciation?

4. Describe how depreciation is being recorded in the examples and problems for not-for-profit colleges in this chapter.

5. Describe the difference between a budget of a state-owned and state-operated college and a private college.

6. What are the three major categories of revenues of the current funds of a not-for-profit college? What are the subcategories used for educational and general revenues of a not-for-profit college?

7. Describe what an auxiliary enterprise is in a not-for-profit college.

8. Explain why a not-for-profit college uses the term expenditure rather than expense.

9. Describe the major categories and subcategories used for expenditures of the current funds of a not-for-profit college.

10. Explain the difference between mandatory and nonmandatory transfers from the unrestricted current fund of a not-for-profit college.

11. Describe how the restricted current fund differs from the unrestricted current fund of a not-for-profit college.

12. When is revenue considered to be earned in the restricted current fund of a not-for-profit college?

13. Describe the purpose of a not-for-profit college's loan funds and how revenue and expenditures are recorded.

14. Describe annuity and life income funds including how contributions to these funds, income, gains and losses, and payments to the beneficiaries are recorded by a not-for-profit college or university.

15. Describe the four subgroups of funds of the plant fund and the purpose of each subgroup used by a not-for-profit college or university.

16. Describe which assets are treated as unrestricted and which are treated as restricted in the unexpended plant fund and the renewal and replacement fund of a not-for-profit college or university.

17. In what plant fund is the payment of long-term debt recorded and in what plant fund is the debt recorded for a not-for-profit college or university?

18. Describe the accounting treatment of the payment of long-term debt in the investment in plant fund of a not-for-profit college or university.

19. In what plant fund is the purchase of plant assets recorded and in what plant fund is the depreciation of plant assets recorded for a not-for-profit private college or university?

20. Explain the accounting for plant assets purchased with unrestricted current fund assets by the unrestricted current fund.

21. Describe agency funds and how they are reported in the financial statements of a not-for-profit hospital or college.

EXERCISES

EXERCISE 22-1

1. Which of the following is used for current expenditures by a not-for-profit university?

	Current Unrestricted Funds	Current Restricted Funds
a.	No	No
b.	No	Yes
c.	Yes	No
d.	Yes	Yes

2. The current funds group of a not-for-profit private university includes which of the following subgroups?

	Term Endowment Funds	Life Income Funds
a.	No	No
b.	No	Yes
c.	Yes	Yes
d.	Yes	No

3. The current funds group of a not-for-profit private university includes which of the following?

	Annuity Funds	Loan Funds
a.	Yes	Yes
b.	Yes	No
c.	No	No
d.	No	Yes

4. The plant funds group of a not-for-profit private university includes which of the following subgroups?

	Investment in Plant Funds	Unexpended Plant Funds
a.	No	Yes
b.	No	No
c.	Yes	No
d.	Yes	Yes

5. Which of the following should be included in the current fund revenues of a not-for-profit private university?

	Tuition Waivers	Unrestricted Bequests
a.	Yes	No
b.	Yes	Yes
c.	No	Yes
d.	No	No

(AICPA adapted)

EXERCISE 22-2

1. During the years ended June 30, 1990 and 1991, Sonata University conducted a cancer research project financed by a $2,000,000 gift from an alumnus. This entire amount was pledged by the donor on July 10, 1989, although he paid only $500,000 at that date. The gift was restricted to the financing of this particular research project. During the two-year research period, Sonata's related gift receipts and research expenditures were

	Year Ended June 30	
	1990	1991
Gift Receipts	$ 1,200,000	$ 800,000
Cancer Research Expenditures	900,000	1,100,000

How much gift revenue should Sonata report in the restricted column of its statement of current fund revenues, expenditures, and other changes for the year ended June 30, 1991.

a. $ –0–
b. $ 800,000
c. $ 1,100,000
d. $ 2,000,000

2. On January 2, 1991, John Reynold donated $500,000 to Manfield University, the income from which is to be used for general operating purposes. What journal entry is required on Manfield's books?

a. Memorandum entry only

b. Cash   500,000
      Endowment Fund Balance: Restricted   500,000

c. Cash   500,000
      Endowment Fund Balance: Unrestricted   500,000

d. Cash   500,000
      Contributions Revenue   500,000

3. For fall semester of 1991, Cranbrook College assessed its students $2,300,000 for tuition and fees. The net amount realized was only $2,100,000 because of the following revenue reductions:

Refunds Occasioned by Class Cancellations and Student Withdrawals	$ 50,000
Tuition Remissions Granted to Faculty Members' Families	10,000
Scholarships and Fellowships	140,000

How much should Cranbrook report for the period for unrestricted fund revenues from tuition and fees?

a. $ 2,100,000
b. $ 2,150,000
c. $ 2,250,000
d. $ 2,300,000

4. For the spring semester of 1991, the Lane University assessed its students $3,400,000 (net of refunds), covering tuition and fees for educational and general purposes. However, only $3,000,000 was expected to be realized because scholarships totaling $300,000 were granted to students, and tuition remission of $100,000 was allowed to faculty members' children attending Lane. How much should Lane include in educational and general current funds revenues from student tuition and fees?

a. $ 3,400,000
b. $ 3,300,000
c. $ 3,100,000
d. $ 3,000,000

5. The following funds were among those on Kery University's books at April 30, 1991:

Funds to be Used for Acquisition of Additional Properties for University Purposes (unexpended at 4/30/91)	$ 3,000,000
Funds Set Aside for Debt Service Charges and for Retirement of Indebtedness on University Properties	5,000,000

How much of the above-mentioned funds should be included in plant funds?

a. $ –0–
b. $ 3,000,000
c. $ 5,000,000
d. $ 8,000,000

(AICPA adapted)

EXERCISE 22-3

The trial balances of the unrestricted current fund and the restricted current fund of Independence College as of July 1, 1990 were

	Debit	Credit
Unrestricted Current Fund		
Cash	$ 100,000	
Marketable Securities	150,000	
Accounts Receivable	250,000	
Allowance for Uncollectible Receivables		$ 25,000
Due from Other Funds	10,000	
Inventory of Materials	160,000	
Prepaid Expenses	30,000	
Accounts Payable		150,000
Due to Other Funds: Loan Fund		25,000
Unrestricted Current Fund Balance		500,000
Restricted Current Fund		
Cash	100,000	
Marketable Securities	200,000	
Accrued Interest Receivable	5,000	
Accounts Payable		20,000
Restricted Current Fund Balance		285,000
Total	$ 1,005,000	$ 1,005,000

During the year ended June 30, 1991, the following transactions and events affecting the current funds of Independence College occurred:

Unrestricted Current Fund

- Revenues were earned from the following sources:

Student Tuition and Fees	$ 2,000,000
Government Grants and Contracts	500,000
Gifts and Private Grants	150,000
Endowment Income	25,000
Auxiliary Enterprises	250,000
Expired Term Endowment	50,000

- Uncollectible accounts are estimated to be 10% of student tuition and fees.
- Cash receipts consisted of $2,800,000 of accounts receivable and $85,000 from the endowment funds.
- Accounts receivable totaling $190,000 are determined to be uncollectible.
- Scholarships and fellowships of $150,000 were granted. Cash disbursed to students totaled $50,000 and the remainder was tuition credit.
- Inventory totaling $300,000 was purchased on account.
- Prepaid expenses totaling $50,000 were purchased for cash.
- Expenditures incurred during the year consisted of

Instructional	$ 1,000,000
Research	200,000
Academic Support	100,000
Student Services	150,000
Institutional Support	200,000
Operation and Maintenance of Plant	400,000
Auxiliary Enterprises	200,000

- Accounts payable totaling $2,400,000 were paid.
- Inventory of materials was used for the following:

Instruction	$ 100,000
Student Services	25,000
Auxiliary Enterprises	100,000

- Prepaid expenses, all for institutional support, of $50,000 were used.
- Cash transferred to other funds consisted of

Loan Funds Including Prior Year's Authorization	$ 50,000
Mandatory Transfers to the Plant Fund for Interest and Principal Mortgage and Loan	250,000
Nonmandatory Transfers for Renewals and Replacements	25,000

Restricted Current Funds

- Investments earned $25,000.
- Cash receipts consisted of

Interest Receivable	$ 30,000
Gift, Restricted to Student Scholarships	50,000
Endowment, Funds, Income	25,000

- Expenditures on account were incurred for

Research	$ 100,000
Academic Support	25,000
Scholarships and Fellowships	50,000

The revenues that supported the expenditures were from

Endowment Income	$ 25,000
Gifts and Private Grants	125,000
Investments	25,000

- Accounts payable totaling $180,000 were paid.

Required

1. Prepare journal entries to record the transactions and events of the unrestricted current fund and restricted current fund for the year ended June 30, 1991.
2. Prepare the statement of revenues, expenditures, and other changes for the current funds for the year ended June 30, 1991.
3. Prepare the balance sheet for the current funds as of June 30, 1991.

EXERCISE 22-4

The trial balance of the loan funds of Kellog College at July 1, 1990 was

	Debit	Credit
Cash	$ 25,000	
Loans Receivable	150,000	
Allowance for Uncollectible Loans		$ 25,000
Due from Unrestricted Current Fund	25,000	
Loan Funds Balance		175,000
	$ 200,000	$ 200,000

During the year ended June 30, 1991, the following transactions and events occurred regarding the loan fund:

- Cash was received from

Loans Receivable	$ 50,000
Interest from Loans Receivable	10,000
Unrestricted Current Fund	50,000
Endowment Funds: Investment Income	25,000
Gifts	40,000

- Loans totaling $185,000 were granted.
- Loans of $10,000 were determined to be uncollectible.
- The uncollectible loans are estimated to be 20% of the outstanding loans at year end.

Required

1. Prepare the journal entries to record the transactions and events of the loan funds of Kellog College for the year ended June 30, 1991.
2. Prepare the loan funds section of the statement of changes in fund balances of Kellog College for the year ended June 30, 1991.
3. Prepare the loan funds section of the balance sheet of Kellog College as of June 30, 1991.

EXERCISE 22-5

The trial balance of the endowment funds of Marion College at July 1, 1990 was

	Debit	Credit
Cash	$ 20,000	
Interest Receivable	10,000	
Investments	700,000	
Due Unrestricted Current Fund		$ 10,000
Fund Balance: Restricted		330,000
Fund Balance: Unrestricted		390,000
	$ 730,000	$ 730,000

During the year ended June 30, 1991 the following transactions and events occurred that affected the endowment funds:

- Income of $70,000 was earned on the investments: $12,000 was from restricted investments for student loans, $20,000 was for plant acquisitions, $8,000 was for scholarships and the remaining $30,000 was unrestricted.
- Income of $75,000 was received in cash.
- A restricted endowment of $50,000 was received.
- An unrestricted endowment of $40,000 was received.
- A restricted term endowment for student loans of $25,000 expired and was transferred to the loan funds.
- Restricted investments with a cost of $35,000 were sold for $40,000.
- Investments totaling $100,000 were purchased with $65,000 of restricted cash and $35,000 of unrestricted cash.
- Unrestricted income totaling $35,000 was transferred to the unrestricted current fund.
- Restricted income of $20,000 was transferred to the plant funds, $8,000 was transferred to the restricted current fund, and $12,000 was transferred to the loan funds.

Required

1. Prepare the journal entries to record the transactions and events of the endowment funds of Marion College for the year ended June 30, 1991.
2. Prepare the endowment fund section of the statement of changes in fund balances of Marion College for the year ended June 30, 1991.
3. Prepare the endowment fund section of the balance sheet of Marion College as of June 30, 1991.

EXERCISE 22-6

The trial balance of the annuity and life income funds of Newton College as of July 1, 1990 was

	Debit	Credit
Cash: Annuities	$ 40,000	
Cash: Life Income	10,000	
Investments: Annuities	250,000	
Investments: Life Income	40,000	
Annuities Payable		$ 100,000
Life Income Payable		5,000
Annuity Fund Balance		190,000
Life Income Fund Balance		45,000
	$ 340,000	$ 340,000

The following transactions and events affecting the annuity and life income funds of Newton occurred during the year ended June 30, 1991:

- Received an annuity of $60,000 with a present value of $35,000.
- Received a life income fund of $30,000.
- Sold annuity investments with a cost of $40,000 for $45,000.
- Purchased annuity investments of $120,000.
- Purchased life income investments of $35,000.
- Annuity investments earned $30,000 and life income investments earned $10,000.
- Cash received from annuity investment earnings totaled $28,000.
- Cash received from life income investment earnings totaled $9,000.
- Annuities of $25,000 were paid. The present value of the annuities paid was $20,000.
- Life income cash of $13,000 was paid to life income beneficiaries.

Required

1. Prepare journal entries to record the transactions and events of the annuity and life income funds of Newton College for the year ended June 30, 1991.
2. Prepare the annuity and life income funds section of the statement of changes in fund balances of Newton College for the year ended June 30, 1991.
3. Prepare the annuity and life income funds section of the balance sheet of Newton College as of June 30, 1991.

EXERCISE 22-7

The trial balances of the plant funds of Oxbow College as of July 1, 1990 were

	Debit	Credit
Unexpended Plant Funds		
Cash	$ 130,000	
Investments	590,000	
Fund Balance: Restricted		$ 380,000
Fund Balance: Unrestricted		340,000
Plant Fund for Renewals and Replacements		
Cash	20,000	
Investments	130,000	
Fund Balance: Restricted		50,000
Fund Balance: Unrestricted		100,000
Plant Fund for Retirement of Indebtedness		
Cash	40,000	
Investments	140,000	
Fund Balance: Restricted		50,000
Fund Balance: Unrestricted		130,000
Investment in Plant		
Land	500,000	
Land Improvements	400,000	
Buildings	10,000,000	
Accumulated Depreciation: Buildings		2,500,000
Equipment	4,800,000	
Accumulated Depreciation: Equipment		1,600,000
Library Books and Materials	200,000	
Notes Payable: Equipment		300,000
Mortgages Payable: Buildings		1,400,000
Net Investment in Plant		10,100,000
Total	$ 16,950,000	$ 16,950,000

During the year ended June 30, 1991 the following transactions and events affecting the plant funds of Oxbow College occurred:

- Gifts and bequests of cash were received for

Acquisitions of Equipment	$ 140,000
Construction of New Buildings	200,000
Renovation of Classroom Buildings	125,000

- During the current year a major fund-raising campaign was launched to provide funds for the retirement of the mortgages for a new administration building and a new classroom building. The campaign resulted in $4,000,000 of pledges and pledges totaling $800,000 were collected in cash during the current year. The pledges require the unpaid portion to be paid in five equal installments over the next five years. The college estimates that 15% of the unpaid pledges will not be collected.
- Investments in the subgroups earned and received in cash the following income:

Unexpended Plant Fund: Restricted	$ 30,000
Unexpended Plant Fund: Unrestricted	35,000
Renewal and Replacement Fund: Restricted	5,000
Renewal and Replacement Fund: Unrestricted	10,000
Retirement of Indebtedness Fund: Restricted	95,000
Retirement of Indebtedness Fund: Unrestricted	10,000

■ Transfers from other funds consisted of

Unrestricted Current Fund: Mandatory Transfer for Interest and Principal	$ 320,000
Unrestricted Current Fund: Nonmandatory Transfer for Renewals and Replacements	40,000
Endowment Fund Income: Restricted to Purchase of Equipment	20,000

■ Restricted investments costing $480,000 were sold for $490,000 by the unexpended plant fund.

■ A new classroom building was completed at a cost of $2,000,000. A down payment of $600,000 cash was paid and the remainder was financed with a 10% mortgage. Cash paid in the amount of $350,000 was restricted in use and the remainder was unrestricted cash.

■ A new administration building was completed at a cost of $3,000,000, financed entirely with a 20-year, 10% mortgage.

■ Equipment costing $390,000 was purchased for the new buildings entirely with restricted cash.

■ Renewals and replacements costing $60,000 were purchased with $20,000 restricted cash and $40,000 unrestricted cash.

■ Investments totaling $920,000 were purchased by the plant fund for retirement of indebtedness.

■ Interest totaling $30,000 and principal of $20,000 were paid on the notes payable.

■ Interest in the amount of $140,000 and principal of $130,000 were paid on the outstanding mortgage at the beginning of the period. No principal or interest payments have been made on the new mortgages for the classroom building and the administration building.

■ Depreciation expense is

Buildings	$ 600,000
Equipment	700,000
Library Books and Materials	30,000

Required

1. Prepare the journal entries for the transactions and events for the plant funds of Oxbow College for the year ended June 30, 1991.
2. Prepare the plant funds section of the statement of changes in fund balances of Oxbow College for the year ended June 30, 1991.
3. Prepare the plant funds section of the balance sheet of Oxbow College as of June 30, 1991, using a separate column for each fund.

EXERCISE 22-8

The following transactions and events occurred during the college year ended May 31, 1993 for Quailrun College, a not-for-profit private college:

1. Billed students $800,000 for tuition. Student loans paid $135,000 and $26,000 was waived. Discounts of $24,000 were granted to faculty and staff.
2. Cash of $245,000 was transferred between funds for the payment of $185,000 of interest and $60,000 of principal on a mortgage.
3. A donation of $20,000 was received for the purchase of new computers.
4. A pledge of $100,000 was received toward the construction of an addition to the library.
5. An unrestricted term endowment of $31,000 expired during the year. The assets have not yet been transferred.
6. An endowment restricted to student loans in the amount of $14,000 expired during the year and was transferred.

7. The auxiliary enterprises had sales of $256,000 and expenses of $268,000.

8. An annuity recipient was paid $35,000, although the actuarially computed value was $36,000.

9. The heating system of the college was replaced at a cost of $367,000. The replacement, which did not add value to the buildings, was paid with unrestricted cash.

10. A life income beneficiary died. The life income fund of $20,000 was restricted to the replacement of classroom furniture.

11. An addition to the library was completed at a cost of $2,400,000. The college paid $600,000 cash for the addition, of which $400,000 had come from a fund-raising campaign and the balance was from previous period transfers of cash generated from operations. The balance of the cost was financed with a 20-year, 10% mortgage.

12. Investments restricted to the operation of the college's experimental farm earned $40,000 that was received in cash. The cost of operating the farm was $38,000.

13. Student loans of $53,000 cash were granted.

14. Restricted endowment investments costing $41,000 were sold for $38,000.

15. Depreciation for the year totaled $126,000: $80,000 for buildings, $40,000 for equipment, and $6,000 for library materials.

16. Former students repaid $25,000 of loans and also paid interest of $2,000 on the loans.

17. The college received a government grant for microbiology research of $75,000. The college must match the grant dollar for dollar with general funds and has made an appropriate transfer. Expenditures for research totaled $65,000, one-half was paid with the government grant assets.

18. Students were granted scholarships of $14,000 as tuition credit.

19. Student loans outstanding of $4,600 were deemed uncollectible.

20. Pledges made to the building fund drive for the addition to the library of $12,000 were determined to be uncollectible.

Required

1. List the fund or funds in which the journal entries to record the above transactions and event are entered.

2. Determine the revenue to be recognized by each of the funds. If a fund has no revenue, explain why.

EXERCISE 22-9

Refer to Exercise 22-8. Prepare journal entries for all funds for each of the transactions and events identifying the fund in which the entry is recorded.

PROBLEMS

PROBLEM 22-1

Colleges and universities and voluntary health and welfare organizations both use fund accounting. Not-for-profit colleges and universities derive a substantial portion of their revenues from services they provide to students and faculty, and voluntary health and welfare organizations derive their revenues primarily from voluntary contributions from the general public.

Required

1. Describe fund accounting and discuss whether its use is consistent with the concept that an accounting entity is an economic unit that has control over resources, accepts responsibilities for making and carrying out commitments, and conducts economic activity.

2. Distinguish between revenue recognition for a voluntary health and welfare organization and revenue recognition for a not-for-profit hospital and revenue recognition for a not-for-profit college.
3. Discuss how the methods used to account for fixed assets differ between voluntary health and welfare organizations, not-for-profit hospitals, and not-for-profit colleges and universities.

(AICPA adapted)

PROBLEM 22-2

The following journal entries were prepared by the new accountant for Pineville College, a not-for-profit private college. The accountant did not understand fund accounting and recorded all the journal entries in the unrestricted current fund and recorded no entries in any other fund.

1. Cash	500,000	
Tuition and Fee Revenue		500,000

To record the amount collected from students for tuition for the current semester. The total tuition billed to students was $790,000. Student loans paid for $180,000, and tuition waivers totaled $40,000, and the remainder was discounts to faculty and faculty's family members.

2. Fund Balance	250,000	
Cash		250,000

To record the transfer to the plant funds the cash necessary to pay the interest of $190,000 and the principal of $60,000 on an outstanding mortgage. The mortgage interest and principal were paid.

3. Cash	75,000	
Fund Balance		75,000

To record the receipt of a donation restricted to loans to students

4. Cash	35,000	
Contribution Revenue		35,000

To record the receipt of a contribution restricted to the operation of the library

5. Cash	40,000	
Due Endowment Fund		40,000

To record the selling price of restricted investments of the endowment fund. The investments had a fair market value of $37,000 when donated to the college.

6. Cash	93,000	
Student Food Service Revenue		93,000

To record the net amount earned by the various dining halls and fast food service centers of the college. The gross revenue earned was $298,000.

7. Addition to Classroom Building	490,000	
Cash: Restricted		90,000
Cash: Unrestricted		60,000
Mortgage Payable		340,000

To record the cost of the new addition to Addison Hall

8. Fund Balance	22,000	
Cash		22,000

To record the payment to a life income beneficiary of the income
from the assets donated to the college

9. Cash	135,000	
Fund Balance		114,000
Interest Revenue		21,000

To record the collections of outstanding student loans from
students who have graduated. Loans and interest in the amount of
$13,000 are not collectible.

10. Cash	24,000	
Contribution Revenue		24,000

To record a contribution for the purchase of library books

Required

Prepare the journal entries that the accountant should have recorded for each of the above transactions including any entries that the accountant did not prepare identifying the fund for the entry. If an entry should be recorded in more than one fund, prepare the entries for all other funds.

PROBLEM 22-3

Refer to Problem 22-2. Prepare correcting entries for each of the incorrectly prepared entries, and prepare any omitted entries for all the funds, assuming all cash paid or received was deposited or withdrawn from the unrestricted current fund.

PROBLEM 22-4

A not-for-profit organization had the following transactions and events during the year ended December 31, 1992.

1. Received an unrestricted contribution of $20,000.
2. Received a contribution restricted to debt retirement of $15,000.
3. Received a contribution restricted to the purchase of equipment of $10,000.
4. Received unrestricted pledges of $90,000 for current operations estimated to be 90% collectible.
5. Received unrestricted pledges of $60,000 for operations in 1993 and 1994 estimated to be 80% collectible.
6. Received $50,000 of pledges restricted to the purchase of equipment. The pledges are estimated to be 90% collectible.
7. Received $100,000 cash for services provided that had not been previously billed.
8. Received a $25,000 legacy whose principal must be maintained and whose income can be spent for current operations.
9. Received a $40,000 bequest whose principal must be maintained for 10 years and whose income can only be spent for landscaping and maintenance of the existing landscaping. During the current year the endowment earned $4,000 and $3,000 was spent on maintenance of the landscaping.
10. Received $21,000 cash from the annual charity auction whose proceeds are to be used for loans for housing needs.
11. Purchased fixed equipment at a cost of $38,000 with restricted cash.
12. Sold fixed equipment with a cost of $41,000 and a net book value of $20,000 for $22,000.
13. Constructed an addition to the building at a cost of $250,000. The not-for-profit organization paid restricted cash of $25,000 and financed the balance with a 20-year, 12% mortgage.

14. A term endowment of $30,000 expired and was transferred to the appropriate fund. The endowment is restricted to the purchase of equipment.

15. Depreciation of equipment totaled $30,000 and depreciation of the building totaled $40,000 for the year.

16. Paid $67,000 of interest and $50,000 of principal on the building's mortgage.

17. Incurred $12,000 of expenses for a fund-raising campaign. The proceeds are to be used to retire the mortgage on the building.

18. Received $21,000 from a fund-raising campaign to raise money for operations.

19. Received a gift of office furniture with a fair market value of $5,000. The donor's basis is $3,000.

Required

1. For each of the above transactions identify the fund(s) of (1) a not-for-profit college, (2) a voluntary health and welfare organization, and (3) a not-for-profit hospital in which the transaction or event is recorded.

2. Determine the amount and type of revenue recognized by each of the funds, assuming the not-for-profit organization is (1) a not-for-profit college, (2) a voluntary health and welfare organization, and (3) a not-for-profit hospital.

PROBLEM 22-5

Refer to Problem 22-4. Prepare journal entries by fund for each of the transactions and events, assuming the not-for-profit organization is a not-for-profit college.

PROBLEM 22-6

Listed below are four independent transactions or events that relate to a not-for-profit college:

1. $25,000 was disbursed from the general fund (or its equivalent) for the cash purchase of new equipment.

2. An unrestricted cash gift of $100,000 was received from a donor.

3. Listed common stocks with a total carrying value of $50,000, exclusive of any allowance, were sold by an endowment fund for $55,000, before any dividends were earned on these stocks.

4. General obligation bonds payable with a face value of $1,000,000 were sold at par, with the proceeds required to be used solely for construction of a new building. This building was completed at a total cost of $1,000,000, and the total amount of bond issue proceeds was disbursed in connection therewith. Disregard interest capitalization.

Required

1. For each of the above-listed transactions or events, prepare journal entries, with explanations, specifying the affected funds, and showing how these transactions or events should be recorded by a not-for-profit college.

2. Describe how each entry would be different from your answer to (1.) if the not-for-profit entity were a hospital, including in your answer both the fund(s) and the account titles.

3. Describe how each entry would be different from your answer to (1.) if the not-for-profit entity were a voluntary health and welfare organization, including in your answer both the fund(s) and the account titles.

(AICPA adapted)

PROBLEM 22-7

The following transactions and events of Marble City College, a not-for-profit private college, occurred during the year ended June 30, 1992.

1. Unrestricted endowment funds earned $45,000 and received cash of $46,000 from earnings.
2. Endowment funds restricted to scholarships and fellowships for students earned $65,000 and collected $63,000.
3. Cash collections of student tuition totaled $4,500,000. Tuition in the amount of $80,000 is deemed uncollectible.
4. The unrestricted current fund made mandatory transfers for principal and interest in the amount of $450,000 to the plant funds. Cash of $20,000, authorized in the prior year to be transferred to restricted funds for renewals and replacements from the unrestricted current fund, was transferred. During the current year the board of regents of the college authorized the transfer of $50,000 for student loans to the loan fund and $100,000 for acquisition of equipment. The transfer for student loans was made in cash, and $75,000 of the transfer authorized for the purchase of equipment was transferred in cash.
5. The restricted current fund spent $200,000 on research, $50,000 on academic support, and $100,000 on student scholarships. The research was funded by a government grant and the academic support and scholarships were funded by private grants.
6. The loan funds granted loans totaling $250,000. Outstanding loans totaling $142,000 were collected, loans totaling $39,000 were forgiven, and loans totaling $15,000 were deemed uncollectible. In addition, $5,000 was spent collecting past due loans.
7. Life income funds totaling $50,000 and annuity funds totaling $100,000 were received in cash. The annuity funds have an actuarially determined present value of $59,000. During the year, $10,000 was earned and received by the life income investments. Beneficiaries of the annuity funds were paid $34,000 for liabilities recorded at $29,000.
8. Cash donations for the purchase of classroom furniture in the amount of $40,000 were received. Pledges totaling $2,000,000 for payment of interest and principal of the mortgage for construction of a new library were also received. Past experience has indicated that 15% will not be collected. Cash of $50,000 was collected from outstanding pledges for the construction of the new library and outstanding pledges of $7,000 were deemed uncollectible.
9. A construction loan of $5,000,000 was obtained for the construction of the new library.
10. A new library costing $5,000,000 was completed during the current school year.
11. The construction loan was replaced by a 40-year, 10% mortgage of $4,800,000, and $200,000 in restricted cash from donations and pledges.
12. Interest payments of $250,000 and principal payments of $200,000 were remitted on outstanding mortgages.
13. The depreciation for the current year consisted of

Buildings	$ 625,000
Equipment	365,000
Library Books	174,000

14. Unrestricted endowment investments with a cost of $41,000 were sold for $45,000 and endowment investments restricted to the purchase of land with a cost of $75,000 were sold for $82,000.

The policy of Marble City College is to transfer income earned by a restricted fund and due to other funds when the cash for the earnings is received.

Required
Prepare the transaction and event entries by fund for each of the above transactions or events for all funds and identifying each entry by its transaction or event number.

PROBLEM 22-8
The partial balance sheet of Rapapo State University as of the end of its fiscal year on July 31, 1991, is

RAPAPO STATE UNIVERSITY
Current Funds Balance Sheet
July 31, 1991

Assets		Liabilities and Fund Balances	
Unrestricted		Unrestricted	
Cash	$ 200,000	Accounts Payable	$ 100,000
Accounts Receivable		Due to Other Funds	40,000
Tuition and Fees, Less		Deferred Revenue	
Allowance for		Tuition and Fees	25,000
Doubtful Accounts of		Fund Balance	435,000
$15,000	360,000		
Prepaid Expenses	40,000		
Total Unrestricted	600,000	Total Unrestricted	600,000
Restricted		Restricted	
Cash	10,000	Accounts Payable	5,000
Investments	210,000	Fund Balance	215,000
Total Restricted	220,000	Total Restricted	220,000
Total Current Funds	$ 820,000	Total Current Funds	$ 820,000

The following information pertains to the year ended July 31, 1992.

1. Tuition and fees charged students for the current year totaled $2,750,000.
2. Cash collected from students' tuition totaled $3,000,000, of which $362,000 represented accounts receivable outstanding at July 31, 1991, $2,500,000 was for the current year's tuition, and $138,000 was for tuition applicable to the semester beginning in August 1992.
3. Deferred revenue at July 31, 1991 was earned during the year ended July 31, 1992.
4. Accounts receivable at July 31, 1991 that were not collected during the year ended July 31, 1992 were determined to be uncollectible and were written off against the allowance account. At July 31, 1992, the allowance account was estimated at $10,000.
5. During the year, an unrestricted appropriation of $60,000 for the 1991–1992 academic year was made by the state. This state appropriation was to be paid to Rapapo sometime in August 1992.
6. During the year, unrestricted cash gifts of $80,000 were received from alumni. Rapapo's board of trustees allocated $30,000 of the gifts to the student loan fund. The gifts were transferred in cash to the student loan fund.
7. During the year, restricted investments costing $25,000 were sold for $31,000. Restricted fund investments were purchased at a cost of $40,000. Restricted investment income of $18,000 was earned and collected during the year.
8. Unrestricted general expenses of $2,500,000 were recorded in the voucher system. At July 31, 1992, the unrestricted accounts payable balance was $75,000.
9. The restricted accounts payable balance at July 31, 1991 was paid.
10. The $40,000 due to other funds at July 31, 1991 was paid to the plant fund as required.
11. One-quarter of the prepaid expenses at July 31, 1991 expired during the current year, and pertained to general education expense. There was no addition to prepaid expenses during the year.

Required

1. Prepare journal entries in summary form to record the foregoing transactions for the year ended July 31, 1992. Number each entry to correspond with the number indicated in the description of its respective transaction. Your answer should be organized as follows:

		Current Funds			
Entry		Unrestricted		Restricted	
Number	Accounts	Debit	Credit	Debit	Credit

2. Prepare a statement of revenues, expenditures, and other changes for the year ended July 31, 1992.

3. Prepare the balance sheet for the current funds as of July 31, 1992.

(AICPA adapted)

PROBLEM 22-9

Shadytown College is a not-for-profit private liberal arts college. The adjusted trial balance of Shadytown College on June 30, 1992 is

	Debit	Credit
Unrestricted Current Fund		
Cash	$ 150,000	
Marketable Securities	225,000	
Accounts Receivable	325,000	
Allowance for Uncollectible Receivables		$ 35,000
Due from Other Funds	10,000	
Inventory of Materials	110,000	
Prepaid Expenses	25,000	
Accounts Payable		75,000
Due to Other Funds		20,000
Unrestricted Current Fund Balance		850,000
Tuition and Fees Revenue		1,700,000
Governmental Grants and Contracts Revenue		325,000
Gifts and Private Grants Revenue		575,000
Endowment Income		210,000
Auxiliary Enterprises Revenues		450,000
Expired Term Endowment		50,000
Instructional Expenditures	1,080,000	
Research Expenditures	300,000	
Academic Support Expenditures	350,000	
Student Services Expenditures	175,000	
Institutional Support Expenditures	315,000	
Operations and Maintenance of Plant Expenditures	285,000	
Scholarships and Fellowships Expenditures	100,000	
Auxiliary Enterprises Expenditures	365,000	
Mandatory Transfer to Plant Fund	385,000	
Nonmandatory Transfer to Loan Fund	50,000	
Nonmandatory Transfer to Unexpended Plant Fund	40,000	

	Debit	Credit
Restricted Current Fund		
Cash	$ 155,000	
Marketable Securities	250,000	
Accrued Interest Receivable	10,000	
Accounts Payable		$ 25,000
Restricted Current Fund Balance		390,000
Governmental Grants and Contracts Revenue		500,000
Gifts and Private Grants Revenue		350,000
Endowment Income		50,000
Investment Income		25,000
Instructional Expenditures	290,000	
Research Expenditures	410,000	
Scholarships and Fellowships Expenditures	225,000	
Loan Funds		
Cash	30,000	
Marketable Securities	90,000	
Loans Receivable	240,000	
Allowance for Uncollectible Loans		40,000
Due from Unrestricted Current Fund	20,000	
Loan Funds Balance		340,000
Endowment Funds		
Cash	25,000	
Interest Receivable	10,000	
Investments	4,250,000	
Due Unrestricted Current Fund		10,000
Fund Balance: Restricted		2,245,000
Fund Balance: Unrestricted		2,030,000
Annuity and Life Income Funds		
Cash: Annuities	15,000	
Cash: Life Income	5,000	
Investments: Annuities	425,000	
Investments: Life Income	185,000	
Annuities Payable		240,000
Life Income Payable		5,000
Annuity Fund Balance		200,000
Life Income Fund Balance		185,000
Plant Funds		
Unexpended Plant Fund		
Cash	130,000	
Investments	590,000	
Fund Balance: Restricted		340,000
Fund Balance: Unrestricted		380,000
Plant Fund for Renewals and Replacements		
Cash	23,000	
Investments	128,000	
Fund Balance: Restricted		51,000
Fund Balance: Unrestricted		100,000

	Debit	Credit
Plant Fund for Retirement of Indebtedness		
Cash	42,000	
Investments	140,000	
Fund Balance: Restricted		62,000
Fund Balance: Unrestricted		120,000
Investment in Plant		
Land	410,000	
Land Improvements	275,000	
Buildings	6,400,000	
Accumulated Depreciation: Buildings		2,500,000
Equipment	3,800,000	
Accumulated Depreciation: Equipment		1,450,000
Library Books and Materials	190,000	
Notes Payable: Equipment		620,000
Mortgages Payable: Buildings		2,400,000
Net Investment in Plant		4,105,000
	$ 23,053,000	$ 23,053,000

The receipts of the restricted current fund exceeded the revenue recognized by $55,000.

Required

1. Prepare a statement of revenues, expenditures, and other changes for Shadytown College for the year ended June 30, 1992.
2. Prepare a balance sheet for Shadytown College as of June 30, 1992.

SOLUTION TO REVIEW PROBLEM

1.   **Unrestricted Current Fund**

Accounts Receivable	5,100,000	
Due from Other Funds	70,000	
Student Tuition and Fees Revenue		3,520,000
Governmental Grants and Contracts Revenue		840,000
Gifts and Private Grants Revenue		330,000
Endowment Income		40,000
Auxiliary Enterprises Revenue		410,000
Expired Term Endowment		30,000
To record the revenues for the current year		
Provision for Uncollectible Accounts	352,000	
Allowance for Uncollectible Accounts		352,000
To record uncollectible accounts expense		

Cash	4,770,000	
Allowance for Uncollectible Accounts	360,000	
Accounts Receivable		5,060,000
Due from Other Funds		70,000

To record the collection of accounts receivable and due from endowment fund and the write-off of uncollectible accounts

Scholarships and Fellowships Expenditures	230,000	
Accounts Receivable		200,000
Cash		30,000

To record the cash and tuition credit granted to students

Inventory	510,000	
Accounts Payable		510,000

To record inventory purchased on account

Prepaid Expenses	70,000	
Cash		70,000

To record the purchases of prepaid items

Instruction Expenditures	2,019,000	
Research Expenditures	320,000	
Academic Support Expenditures	190,000	
Student Services Expenditures	265,000	
Institutional Support Expenditures	289,000	
Operation and Maintenance of Plant Expenditures	624,000	
Auxiliary Enterprises Expenditures	126,000	
Accounts Payable		3,833,000

To record expenditures incurred during the current year

Accounts Payable	4,200,000	
Cash		4,200,000

To record the payment of accounts payable

Instruction Expenditures	250,000	
Student Services Expenditures	37,000	
Auxiliary Enterprises Expenditures	233,000	
Inventory		520,000

To record the inventory used during the current year

Institutional Support Expenditures	81,000	
Prepaid Expenses		81,000

To record the prepaid expenses that expired during the current period

Due to Other Funds	22,000	
Nonmandatory Transfer to Loan Fund	26,000	
Mandatory Transfer to Plant Funds	482,000	
Nonmandatory Transfer to Plant Funds	52,000	
Cash		582,000

To record the transfer of funds authorized by the board of regents

Restricted Current Funds

Interest Receivable	28,000	
Restricted Current Fund Balance		28,000
To record interest earned on investments		
Cash	121,000	
Interest Receivable		29,000
Restricted Current Fund Balance		92,000
To record the cash receipts		
Research Expenditures	190,000	
Academic Support Expenditures	42,000	
Student Aid Expenditures	60,000	
Accounts Payable		292,000
To record the expenditures for the current year		
Restricted Current Fund Balance	292,000	
Endowment Income		23,000
Gifts and Grants Revenues		245,000
Investment Revenue		24,000

To recognize the revenue as expenditures have been made for the following purposes:

Research	$190,000
Academic Support	42,000
Scholarships and Fellowships	60,000

Accounts Payable	290,000	
Cash		290,000
To record the payment of accounts payable		

Loan Funds

Cash	230,000	
Loans Receivable		59,000
Due from Unrestricted Current Funds		22,000
Loan Funds Balance		149,000

To record the cash receipts for the current year, which include
$10,000 of interest earned and transferred from the endowment
fund, gifts of $100,000, interest revenue of $13,000, and
$26,000 transferred from unrestricted current fund

Loans Receivable	197,000	
Cash		197,000

To record the loans granted during the current year

Allowance for Uncollectible Loans and Interest	12,000	
Loans Receivable		12,000

To write off loans determined to be uncollectible

Loan Funds Balance	37,200	
Allowance for Uncollectible Accounts		37,200

To record estimated uncollectible loans at year end
$28,000 − $12,000 − $16,000
$140,000 − $59,000 + $197,000 − $12,000 = $266,000
$266,000 × 20% = $53,200 − $16,000 = $37,200

Endowment Funds

Cash	65,000	
Fund Balance: Restricted		65,000
To record the receipt of an endowment		
Interest Receivable	79,000	
Due Restricted Current Fund		12,000
Due Loan Funds		10,000
Due Unexpended Plant Fund		17,000
Due Unrestricted Current Fund		40,000
To record the investment income earned during the current year		
Cash	81,000	
Interest Receivable		81,000
To record the receipt of interest		
Cash	55,000	
Investments		51,000
Fund Balance: Restricted		4,000
To record the sale of investments		
Investments	111,000	
Cash		111,000
To record the purchase of investments		
Due Unrestricted Current Fund	40,000	
Fund Balance: Unrestricted	30,000	
Due Restricted Current Funds	12,000	
Due Loan Funds	10,000	
Due Unexpended Plant Fund	17,000	
Cash		109,000
To record the transfers to other funds of investment income and a $30,000 expired term endowment		

Annuity and Life Income Funds

Cash: Annuities	30,000	
Cash: Life Income	9,000	
Life Income Payable		9,000
Annuity Fund Balance		30,000

To record the income earned on the annuity life income funds

Cash: Annuities	100,000	
Annuities Payable		61,000
Annuity Fund Balance		39,000

To record annuity received. The actuarial computation of the
present value of the annuity is $61,000.

Cash: Life Income	50,000	
Fund Balance: Life Income		50,000

To record receipt of assets donated with income to be
distributed to the beneficiary for the remainder of her life

Annuities Payable	29,000	
Annuity Fund Balance	7,000	
Cash: Annuities		36,000

To record the payment of annuities whose initial present value
was recorded as $29,000

Life Income Payable	10,000	
Cash: Life Income		10,000

To record the payment to life income beneficiaries

Investments: Annuities	110,000	
Investments: Life Income	48,000	
Cash: Annuities		110,000
Cash: Life Income		48,000

To record the purchase of investments

Plant Funds

Unexpended Plant Fund

Cash	150,000	
Fund Balance: Restricted		150,000

To record the receipt of cash donations that can be used for equipment acquisitions and classroom construction

Cash	62,000	
Fund Balance: Restricted		30,000
Fund Balance: Unrestricted		32,000

To record the income earned on investments

Cash	17,000	
Fund Balance: Restricted		17,000

To record the transfer from the endowment fund of restricted income

Cash	2,000,000	
Mortgage Payable		2,000,000

To record the mortgage for classroom building

Classroom Building	2,200,000	
Cash		2,200,000

To record the cost of a classroom building completed during the current year and financed with cash and a mortgage

Mortgage Payable	2,000,000	
Fund Balance: Restricted	75,000	
Fund Balance: Unrestricted	125,000	
Classroom Building		2,200,000

To record the transfer of the asset and the liability to the investment in plant group of accounts

Plant Fund for Renewals and Replacements

Cash	33,000	
Fund Balance: Restricted		33,000

To record the receipt of a donation restricted to the replacement of computers

Cash	14,000	
Fund Balance: Restricted		6,000
Fund Balance: Unrestricted		8,000

To record the investment earnings for the current period

Cash	52,000	
Fund Balance: Unrestricted		52,000

To record a discretionary transfer from the unrestricted current fund

Fund Balance: Restricted	23,000	
Fund Balance: Unrestricted	68,000	
Cash		91,000

To record the expenditures for repairs to buildings and equipment during the current year

Plant Fund for Retirement of Indebtedness

Cash	16,000	
Fund Balance: Restricted		5,000
Fund Balance: Unrestricted		11,000

To record the income from investments

Cash	482,000	
Fund Balance: Restricted		482,000

To record the transfer of cash to pay loan and mortgage from the unrestricted current fund

Fund Balance: Restricted	122,000	
Cash		122,000

To record the payment of $62,000 of interest and $60,000 of principal on the note payable

Fund Balance: Restricted	360,000	
Cash		360,000

To record the payment of $240,000 of interest and $120,000 of principal of the mortgage

Investment in Plant

Buildings	2,200,000	
Mortgage Payable		2,000,000
Net Investment in Plant		200,000

To record the completion of the classroom building and the mortgage on the building

Note Payable	60,000	
Net Investment in Plant		60,000

To record the payment of the principal of the note

Mortgage Payable	120,000	
Net Investment in Plant		120,000

To record payment of mortgage principal

Net Investment in Plant	728,000	
Accumulated Depreciation: Buildings		300,000
Accumulated Depreciation: Equipment		410,000
Library Books and Materials		18,000

To record the depreciation expense for the current year

2.

BENTON COLLEGE
Adjusted Trial Balance
June 30, 1991

	Debit	Credit
Unrestricted Current Fund		
Cash	$ 147,000	
Marketable Securities	351,000	
Accounts Receivable	262,000	
Allowance for Uncollectible Receivables		$ 13,100
Due from Other Funds	4,000	
Inventory of Materials	153,000	
Prepaid Expenses	23,000	
Accounts Payable		299,000
Unrestricted Current Fund Balance		1,033,900
Tuition and Fees Revenue		3,520,000
Government Grants Revenue		840,000
Private Gifts and Grants Revenues		330,000
Endowment Income		40,000
Auxiliary Enterprises Revenues		410,000
Expired Term Endowment		30,000
Provision for Uncollectible Accounts	352,000	
Scholarships and Fellowships Expenditures	230,000	
Instruction Expenditures	2,269,000	
Research Expenditures	320,000	
Academic Support Expenditures	190,000	
Student Services Expenditures	302,000	
Institutional Support Expenditures	370,000	
Operation and Maintenance of Plant Expenditures	624,000	
Auxiliary Enterprises Expenditures	359,000	
Nonmandatory Transfer to Loan Funds	26,000	
Mandatory Transfer to Plant Funds	482,000	
Nonmandatory Transfer to Plant Funds	52,000	
Restricted Current Fund		
Cash	15,000	
Marketable Securities	270,000	
Accrued Interest Receivable	5,000	
Accounts Payable		25,000
Restricted Current Fund Balance		265,000
Private Gifts and Grants Revenue		245,000
Endowment Income		23,000
Investment Income		24,000
Research Expenditures	190,000	
Academic Support Expenditures	42,000	
Scholarships and Fellowships Expenditures	60,000	
Loan Funds		
Cash	54,000	
Loans Receivable	266,000	
Allowance for Uncollectible Loans		53,200
Loan Funds Balance		266,800

	Debit	Credit
Endowment Funds		
Cash	$ 4,000	
Interest Receivable	10,000	
Investments	747,000	
Fund Balance: Restricted		$ 391,000
Fund Balance: Unrestricted		370,000
Annuity and Life Income Funds		
Cash: Annuities	25,000	
Cash: Life Income	9,000	
Investments: Annuities	352,000	
Investments: Life Income	85,000	
Annuities Payable		126,000
Life Income Payable		4,000
Annuity Funds Balance		251,000
Life Income Funds Balance		90,000
Plant Funds		
Unexpended Plant Funds		
Cash	159,000	
Investments	590,000	
Fund Balance: Restricted		462,000
Fund Balance: Unrestricted		287,000
Plant Fund for Renewals and Replacements		
Cash	31,000	
Investments	128,000	
Fund Balance: Restricted		67,000
Fund Balance: Unrestricted		92,000
Plant Fund for Retirement of Indebtedness		
Cash	58,000	
Investments	140,000	
Fund Balance: Restricted		67,000
Fund Balance: Unrestricted		131,000
Investment in Plant		
Land	410,000	
Land Improvements	275,000	
Buildings	8,600,000	
Accumulated Depreciation: Buildings		2,800,000
Equipment	3,800,000	
Accumulated Depreciation: Equipment		1,860,000
Library Books and Materials	172,000	
Notes Payable: Equipment		560,000
Mortgages Payable: Buildings		4,280,000
Net Investment in Plant		3,757,000
	$ 23,013,000	$ 23,013,000

3.

BENTON COLLEGE
Statement of Revenues, Expenditures, and Other Changes: Current Funds
Year Ended June 30, 1991

	Unrestricted	Restricted	Total
Revenues			
Educational and General			
Student Tuition and Fees	$3,168,000		$3,168,000
Government Grants	840,000		840,000
Private Gifts and Grants	330,000	$ 245,000	575,000
Endowment Income	40,000	23,000	63,000
Total Educational and General Revenues	4,378,000	268,000	4,646,000
Auxiliary Enterprises	410,000		410,000
Investments		24,000	24,000
Expired Term Endowments	30,000		30,000
Total Revenues	4,818,000	292,000	5,110,000
Expenditures and Mandatory Transfers			
Educational and General			
Instruction	2,269,000		2,269,000
Research	320,000	190,000	510,000
Academic Support	190,000	42,000	232,000
Student Services	302,000		302,000
Institutional Support	370,000		370,000
Operation and Maintenance of Plant	624,000		624,000
Scholarships and Fellowships	230,000	60,000	290,000
Total Educational and General Expenditures	4,305,000	292,000	4,597,000
Mandatory Transfers to Plant Funds for Mortgage Principal and Interest	482,000		482,000
Auxiliary Enterprises Expenditures	359,000		359,000
Total Expenditures and Mandatory Transfers	5,146,000	292,000	5,438,000
Other Transfers and Additions (Deductions)			
Excess of Revenues over Restricted Receipts		(172,000)	(172,000)
Discretionary Transfers			
Transfer to Plant Funds	(52,000)		(52,000)
Transfer to Loan Funds	(26,000)		(26,000)
Net Increase (Decrease) in Fund Balances	$(406,000)	$(172,000)	$(578,000)

BENTON COLLEGE
Statement of Changes in Fund Balances
Year Ended, June 30, 1991

	Current Funds		Loan
	Unrestricted	Restricted	Funds
Revenues and Other Additions			
Unrestricted Current Fund Revenues	$ 4,818,000		
Private Gifts and Grants: Restricted		$ 80,000	$ 100,000
Investment Income: Restricted		40,000	10,000
Realized Gains on Sale of Investments: Restricted			
Interest on Loans Receivable			13,000
Expended for Plant Facilities			
Retirement of Indebtedness			
Total Revenues and Other Additions	4,818,000	120,000	123,000
Expenditures and Other Deductions			
Educational and General Expenditures	4,305,000	292,000	
Auxiliary Enterprises Expenditures	359,000		
Loan Cancellations and Write-offs			37,200
Expired Term Endowments			
Adjustment of Actuarial Liability for Annuities			
Expended for Plant Facilities			
Expended on Plant Maintenance			
Retirement of Indebtedness			
Interest on Indebtedness			
Provision for Depreciation			
Total Expenditures and Other Deductions	4,664,000	292,000	37,200
Transfers Among Funds: Additions (Deductions)			
Mandatory: Principal and Interest	(482,000)		
Other	(78,000)		26,000
Total Transfers	(560,000)		26,000
Net Increase (Decrease) in Fund Balances	(406,000)	(172,000)	111,800
Fund Balance at Beginning of Year	1,033,900	437,000	155,000
Fund Balance at End of Year	$ 627,900	$ 265,000	$ 266,800

			Plant Funds		
			Renewals	Retirement	
Endowment	and Life		and	of	Investment
Funds	Income Funds	Unexpended	Replacements	Indebtedness	in Plant
$ 65,000	$ 89,000	$ 150,000	$ 33,000		
	30,000	79,000	14,000	$ 16,000	
4,000					
					$ 200,000
					180,000
69,000	119,000	229,000	47,000	16,000	380,000
30,000					
	7,000				
		200,000			
			91,000		
				180,000	
				302,000	
					728,000
30,000	7,000	200,000	91,000	482,000	728,000
				482,000	
			52,000		
			52,000	482,000	
39,000	112,000	29,000	8,000	16,000	(348,000)
722,000	229,000	720,000	151,000	182,000	4,105,000
$ 761,000	$ 341,000	$ 749,000	$ 159,000	$ 198,000	$ 3,757,000

4.

BENTON COLLEGE
Balance Sheet
June 30, 1991

	Assets			Liabilities and Fund Balances	

CURRENT FUNDS

Unrestricted			Unrestricted	
Cash	$ 147,000		Accounts Payable	$ 299,000
Investments	351,000			
Accounts Receivable: Net	248,900		Unrestricted Current Fund	
Due from Other Funds	4,000		Balance	627,900
Inventory	153,000			
Prepaid Expenses	23,000			
Total Unrestricted Current Fund	926,900		Total Unrestricted Current Fund	926,900
Restricted			Restricted	
Cash	15,000		Accounts Payable	25,000
Investments	270,000		Restricted Current Fund Balance	265,000
Accounts Receivable	5,000			
Total Restricted Current Fund	290,000		Total Restricted Current Fund	290,000
Total Current Funds	$ 1,216,900		Total Current Funds	$ 1,216,900

LOAN FUNDS

Cash		$ 54,000	Loan Fund Balance	$ 266,800
Loans Receivable	$ 266,000			
Less: Allowance for Uncollectible Loans	53,200	212,800		
Total Loan Funds		$ 266,800	Total Loan Funds	$ 266,800

ENDOWMENT FUNDS

Cash	$ 4,000	Fund Balance: Restricted	$ 391,000
Interest Receivable	10,000	Fund Balance: Unrestricted	370,000
Investments	747,000		
Total Endowment Funds	$ 761,000	Total Endowment Funds	$ 761,000

BENTON COLLEGE
Balance Sheet Continued
June 30, 1991

Assets		Liabilities and Fund Balances	

ANNUITY AND LIFE INCOME FUNDS

Annuity Funds		Annuity Funds	
Cash	$ 25,000	Annuities Payable	$ 126,000
Investments	352,000	Fund Balance	251,000
Total Annuity Funds	377,000	Total Annuity Funds	377,000
Life Income Funds		Life Income Funds	
Cash	9,000	Income Payable	4,000
Investments	85,000	Fund Balance	90,000
Total Life Income Funds	94,000	Total Life Income Funds	94,000
Total Annuity and Life Income Funds	$ 471,000	Total Annuity and Life Income Funds	$ 471,000

PLANT FUNDS

Unexpended		Unexpended	
Cash	$ 159,000	Fund Balance: Restricted	$ 462,000
Investments	590,000	Fund Balance: Unrestricted	287,000
Total Unexpended	749,000	Total Unexpended	749,000
Renewals and Replacements		Renewals and Replacements	
Cash	31,000	Fund Balance: Restricted	67,000
Investments	128,000	Fund Balance: Unrestricted	92,000
Total Renewals and Replacements	159,000	Total Renewals and Replacements	159,000
Retirement of Indebtedness		Retirement of Indebtedness	
Cash	58,000	Fund Balance: Restricted	67,000
Investments	140,000	Fund Balance: Unrestricted	131,000
Total Retirement of Indebtedness	198,000	Total Retirement of Indebtedness	198,000
Investment in Plant		Investment in Plant	
Land	410,000	Note Payable	560,000
Land Improvements	275,000	Mortgages Payable	4,280,000
Buildings: Net	5,800,000	Net Investment in Plant	3,757,000
Equipment: Net	1,940,000		
Library Books and Materials: Net	172,000		
Total Investment in Plant	8,597,000	Total Investment in Plant	8,597,000
Total Plant Funds	$ 9,703,000	Total Plant Funds	$ 9,703,000

23

GOVERNMENTAL ACCOUNTING

 governmental unit can be a city, a county, a state, the federal government, a school district, a utility district, a public library, an airport, or a port authority. This chapter uses a city to illustrate the accounting for a governmental unit. The topics of this chapter include

- Funds used by governmental units
- Sources of generally accepted accounting principles
- Comparison between governmental units and business enterprises
- Comparison between the accounting for governmental units and not-for-profit entities with emphasis on basis of accounting and measurement focus, account groups and plant funds, and budgets
- Depreciation expense
- Financial statements of a governmental unit
- General fund including recording budgets, revenue recognition and the property tax system, transfers to and from funds, encumbrances and expenditures, financial statements, and closing journal entries
- Special revenue funds
- Capital projects funds
- Debt service funds
- General fixed asset account group
- General long-term debt account group
- Proprietary funds: enterprise and internal service
- Fiduciary funds including expendable trust funds, unexpendable trust funds, pension trust funds, and agency funds

FUNDS OF A GOVERNMENTAL UNIT

Governmental units, like not-for-profit entities, uses the fund system of accounting. A fund is a fiscal and accounting entity with a self-balancing set of accounts used to account for a specific set of activities. The funds of a governmental unit are classified into three general types: governmental funds, proprietary funds, and fiduciary funds.

The governmental funds consist of the general fund, special revenue funds, capital projects funds, and debt service funds. All governmental units have a general fund, in which all activities that are not identified with a special fund are recorded, and employ as many of the other funds as are needed to account for its activities. Special revenue funds are funds for operational purposes whose assets (resources) have legal restrictions placed on their use. Capital projects funds and debt service funds are restricted to those purposes. The governmental funds have only current assets and current liabilities. In addition, a governmental unit uses self-balancing sets of accounts to control the fixed assets and long-term debt not recorded in other funds. These self-balancing sets of records are called account groups rather than funds, because they do not have revenue inflows but simply account for noncurrent assets and long-term debt.

The proprietary funds, which are like business enterprises, consist of the enterprise funds and the internal service funds. The fiduciary funds are trust funds and agency funds.

SOURCES OF GENERALLY ACCEPTED ACCOUNTING PRINCIPLES

Generally accepted accounting principles for governmental units are promulgated by the Governmental Accounting Standards Board (GASB), established in 1984. The Governmental Accounting Standards Board issues statements, interpretations, and technical bulletins using the same due process procedures as the Financial Accounting Standards Board. In June 1987, the Governmental Accounting Standards Board issued *Codification of Governmental Accounting and Financial Reporting Standards,* which contains all the generally accepted principles for accounting and financial reporting for governmental units through June 15, 1987. If the pronouncements of the Governmental Accounting Standards Board do not include an item, the pronouncements of the Financial Accounting Standards Board are followed.

Prior to the formation of the Governmental Accounting Standards Board, the National Council on Governmental Accounting established the principles of accounting and financial reporting for governmental units. In addition to the principles established by the Governmental Accounting Standards Board, the AICPA audit guide, *Audits of State and Local Governmental Units,* provides guidance in accounting for governmental units. The Governmental Accounting Standards Board, in its first statement, established that the principles previously issued by the National Council on Governmental Accounting or contained in the audit guide were generally accepted until replaced by new pronouncements.

COMPARISON BETWEEN A GOVERNMENTAL UNIT AND A BUSINESS ENTERPRISE

A governmental unit differs from a business enterprise because the environment and objectives of a governmental unit are not the same as those of a business enterprise. A governmental unit does not have profit making as an overall motive; however, a particular governmental unit or portions of a governmental unit may be operated as profit-making enterprises. These enterprises, such as utilities, provide a product or service to the public and charge a price or fee that covers the cost and provides for capital improvements. These profit-making enterprises are like the auxiliary enterprises of a not-for-profit college or university.

In addition to the lack of profit motive, a governmental unit differs from a business enterprise in the following ways:

- A governmental unit has legal restrictions on the raising of revenues and the expenditures of that revenue.
- Revenues come primarily from tax receipts.
- The matching of revenue and expense is generally not possible as the providers of revenues are not the receivers of the governmental unit's services.
- Emphasis is on accountability and stewardship of assets by public employees and elected officials.

COMPARISON BETWEEN THE ACCOUNTING FOR GOVERNMENTAL UNITS AND NOT-FOR-PROFIT ENTITIES

BASIS OF ACCOUNTING/MEASUREMENT FOCUS

All not-for-profit entities use accrual accounting; however, a governmental unit only uses accrual accounting for some funds. The objective of the proprietary funds and the nonexpendable fiduciary funds is cost of services or capital maintenance, and therefore, these funds use the accrual basis of accounting the same as not-for-profit entities whose objective is also capital maintenance. If neither capital maintenance nor the measurement of income is the objective, the modified accrual basis is used. The funds that use the modified accrual basis of accounting have as their objective the reporting of the sources and uses of current financial resources. Therefore, the measurement focus of these funds is on the receipt of financial resources (revenues) and expenditures of those financial resources. The fixed assets and long-term debt are not included in these funds because they are not current financial resources.

The governmental funds—general, special revenue, capital projects, and debt services—the expendable trust funds, and the agency funds use modified accrual accounting. The modified accrual basis of accounting recognizes revenue in the accounting period in which it is both **measurable and available** to finance the expenditures of the period. Expenditures are recognized in the accounting period in which the liabilities are both **measurable and incurred.** If a fund uses the modified accrual basis of accounting, the term expenditures rather than expenses is used, since expenditures refers to the outflow of assets or resources.

ACCOUNT GROUPS AND PLANT FUNDS

The general fixed asset and the general long-term debt account groups are similar to the plant funds of not-for-profit entities in that they are used to account for noncurrent assets and liabilities. The account groups differ from not-for-profit plant funds because they do not have cash or current assets and liabilities, but only have noncurrent assets or liabilities and balancing contra accounts.

BUDGETS

Not-for-profit colleges and universities that are government owned record budgets, and other not-for-profit colleges and universities may use budgets. A governmental unit, however, always records its budget in the general and special revenue funds and may record its budget in the capital projects funds and the debt service fund. Budgets may or may not be recorded in the proprietary and fiduciary funds. The budget establishes the authorization to spend resources (assets) for a particular purpose. The accounting used in preparation of the budgets, and thus the accounting records, may not be the same as required by generally accepted accounting principles for financial reporting.

In addition to the recording of budgets, a governmental unit uses an additional budgetary account called **encumbrances.** Encumbrances are the obligations for products or services that have been ordered. Encumbrances are recorded in all the governmental funds, except the debt service fund. Encumbrances are recorded to prevent spending in excess of the budget authorization.

DEPRECIATION

Depreciation can be but typically is not recorded for the governmental fund assets accounted for in the general fixed asset account group because capital maintenance is not the objective. Depreciation is recorded in the funds that use accrual accounting because capital maintenance and/or income measurement are the primary objectives of these funds. Thus depreciation is recognized in the proprietary funds and the nonexpendable trust funds in order to determine the income earned and to determine if capital is being maintained.

FINANCIAL STATEMENTS

The financial statements of a governmental unit consist of

- A combined balance sheet for all funds
- A combined statement of revenues, expenditures, and changes in fund balances for all governmental funds and expendable trust funds
- A combined statement of revenues, expenditures, and changes in fund balances: budget and actual, for the general fund, the special revenue funds, and similar government-type funds with annual budgets that have been legally adopted
- A combined statement of revenues, expenses, and changes in retained earnings or equity for all proprietary funds and nonexpendable trust funds
- A statement of changes in financial position for all proprietary funds. The cash basis is recommended.

These statements are called the general-purpose financial statements of a governmental unit. Appendix 23-A contains the general-purpose financial statements for the city of Albany, Oregon. The general-purpose financial statements are part of the comprehensive annual financial report (CAFR). In addition to the general-purpose financial statements, the comprehensive annual report includes the auditor's report, individual and combining fund and account group statements and schedules, statistical tables, and component unit financial reports or statements, which are optional. The financial section of the comprehensive report is often portrayed as a reporting pyramid as shown in Exhibit 23-1.[1]

EXHIBIT 23-1

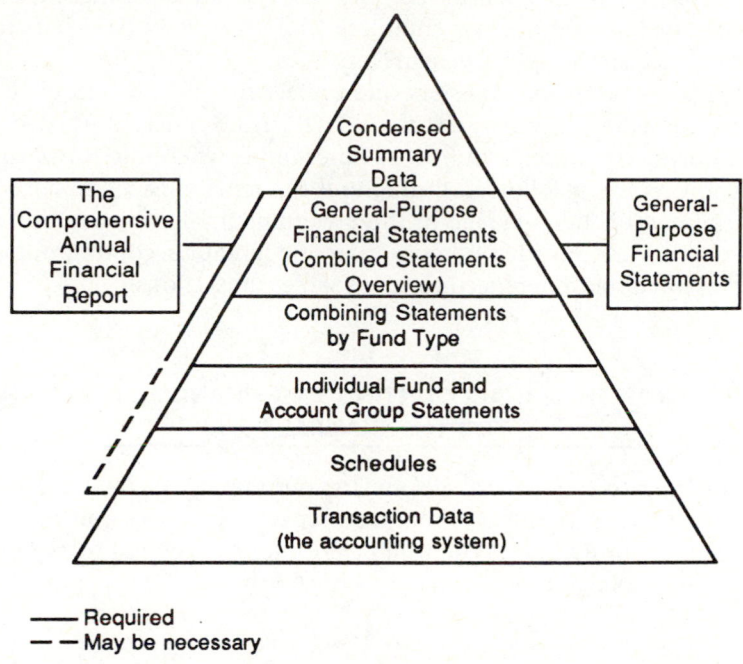

——— Required
— — May be necessary

GOVERNMENTAL FUNDS

GENERAL FUND

The general fund is used to account for all the activities of a governmental unit that are not required to be recorded in another fund. The revenues and expenditures are for general ongoing services provided to the constituents such as administration, maintenance, schools, and police and fire protection. The general fund is considered an expendable fund and, therefore, all purchases including fixed assets acquisitions are recorded as expenditures. In the general fund both the budget and the encumbrances of orders are entered in the accounting records.

The modified accrual basis of accounting is used by the general fund of a governmental unit to record transactions. The sources of revenues of the general fund are property taxes,

[1] *Statement No. 1, National Council on Governmental Accounting and Financial Reporting Principles* (NCGA: Chicago, Illinois), 1979, page 20.

licenses and permits, intergovernmental revenues, charges for services, fines and forfeitures, and interest on investments and delinquent taxes. The expenditures of the general fund are for the major services provided, including general government, public safety, highways and streets, sanitation, health, welfare, culture and recreation, and education.

Illustrative Problem 23.1 demonstrates the budgetary, transaction, adjusting, and closing entries in summary form for a typical city. In addition, the illustrative problem presents the statements of revenues, expenditures, and changes in fund balances: budget and actual and the balance sheet for the general fund.

Transactions and transfers often affect two or more funds and/or account groups. The transactions in Illustrative Problem 23.1 for the general fund are numbered for ease of cross referencing to the same entries in other funds where the transaction numbers are identified. This procedure is followed throughout the remaining discussion of the governmental funds. At the end of the coverage of the governmental funds, a summary of the transactions and events that are recorded in more than one fund or account group in the Illustrative Problems is presented and referenced to these same transactions.

ILLUSTRATIVE PROBLEM 23.I: ACCOUNTING AND FINANCIAL REPORTING FOR THE GENERAL FUND

In addition to the general administration, the city of Railburg provides police and fire protection, schools, streets and roads, sewer services, parks and recreation, and public health for the citizens of Railburg. The trial balance for the general fund of the city of Railburg on July 1, 1990, the beginning of the city's fiscal year, was

	Debit	Credit
Cash	$ 40,000	
Property Taxes Receivable: Delinquent	35,000	
Allowance for Uncollectible Delinquent Property Taxes		$ 5,000
Materials and Supplies Inventory	12,000	
State Road Tax Receivable	8,000	
Vouchers Payable		21,000
Fund Balance: Reserved for Materials and Supplies		12,000
Fund Balance: Reserved for Encumbrances		6,000
Unreserved Fund Balance		51,000
	$ 95,000	$ 95,000

The following is a discussion of the budgetary, transaction, and adjusting entries for the general fund of a governmental unit together with the entries that are recorded in the general fund of the city of Railburg for the fiscal year ended June 30, 1991.

Recording the Budget.   The budgetary control accounts, **ESTIMATED REVENUES** and **APPROPRIATIONS,** are entered in the accounting records to provide control over anticipated revenues and anticipated expenditures and to permit the comparison of budget and actual results. In addition, anticipated transfers from the general fund to other funds are recorded in the account, **ESTIMATED OTHER FINANCING USES,** and anticipated transfers to the general fund are recorded as **ESTIMATED FINANCING SOURCES.** The comparison of budget and actual results is then used to assess how effectively the public employees and elected officials have carried out their stewardship function. Budgetary accounts are **nominal accounts** and, thus, are closed at the end of the accounting period. The journal entry to record the budget is similar to the one used by not-for-profit colleges and universities. A control entry is prepared with the details entered in subsidiary accounts. The entry debits ESTIMATED REVENUES and ESTIMATED OTHER FINANCING SOURCES and credits APPROPRIATIONS and ESTIMATED OTHER FINANCING USES. The difference between these debits and credits is debited or credited to **BUDGETARY FUND BALANCE.** The following entry demonstrates the recording of the budget for the city of Railburg:

1. A budget estimating revenues of $1,100,000, expenditures of $900,000, and transfers to the debt service fund of $160,000 was authorized by voter approval. The details of the budget approved by the voters are

Estimated Revenues	
Property Taxes	$ 875,000
Intergovernmental	60,000
Service Fees	35,000
Licenses and Permits	100,000
Fines and Forfeitures	30,000
Estimated Expenditures and Transfers	
General Government	95,000
Public Safety	325,000
Highways and Streets	70,000
Sanitation	33,000
Health and Welfare	32,000
Culture and Recreation	30,000
Education	315,000
Operating Transfers Out	160,000

The journal entry to record the budget is

ESTIMATED REVENUES	1,100,000	
APPROPRIATIONS		900,000
ESTIMATED OTHER FINANCING USES		160,000
BUDGETARY FUND BALANCE		40,000
To record the budget for the current year		

An alternative to crediting budgetary fund balance is to record the credit in the permanent account, Unreserved Fund Balance.

The capital letters are used to distinguish the budgetary accounts from the real and nominal (transaction) accounts. The use of the capital letters is recommended by the Government Finance Officers Association, although some governmental units may not use the capital letters in their entries, which affect budgetary accounts.

Transfers to and from the General Fund. Just as a not-for-profit entity transfers resources between funds, a governmental unit transfers assets between funds. A governmental unit has required transfers for debt service and transfers designated by the governing body. When the payable is due a transaction entry debiting **Operating Transfers Out** and crediting Due to Other Funds is recorded. The following entry illustrates a transfer authorized by the budget:

2. The budget authorized the transfer of $160,000 to the debt service fund during the current year: $108,000 is for interest and the remaining $52,000 is for principal payments on serial bonds. Because the transfer is payable in the current year, the transfer is recorded at the beginning of the year.

Operating Transfers Out	160,000	
Due Debt Service Fund		160,000
To record the obligation to transfer to the debt service fund an		
amount sufficient to cover the $108,000 interest and $52,000 of		
principal on outstanding serial bonds		

An entry is also recorded in the debt service fund, and an entry is recorded in the general long-term debt account group for the principal.

Recording Revenues.   Revenues from property taxes, firm governmental grants and revenues, interest on investments and delinquent taxes, other taxes collected and not released by intermediary governments (intergovernmental), and regularly billed charges for services are accrued when earned because they are both **measurable** and **available** to the governmental unit. Property tax revenue is considered available for current expenditures if it is collected during the accounting period or will be collected within approximately 60 days after the end of the current period. If these revenues are not measurable and available to finance current period expenditures, including the 60-day rule for property taxes, they are recorded as deferred revenues. No provision for uncollectible accounts is recorded; instead the revenues are recorded net of the expected losses, since the determination of net income is not the objective. An Allowance for Uncollectible Accounts is used, however, to allow the governmental unit to correctly report the amount of receivables that the governmental unit is accountable for to its constituency.

Property Tax System.   A typical property tax system will assess (determine according to city, county, or state policy) the value of real and personal property. The annual amount of the tax on each piece of property is based on the assessed valuation and is the liability of the recorded owner(s) of the property. Property taxes become a lien against the property at a date specified by state law and may not be levied until after the lien date.

The billing of property taxes typically occurs after the levy date. For example, in Oregon property taxes become a lien on July 1, are levied in the fall based on voter-approved budgets, are billed to property owners in October, and are payable on November 15. When unpaid taxes become delinquent, as specified by state law, the receivable, any interest or penalties owing, and the related allowance are reclassified as delinquent. If the delinquent taxes are not paid, the governmental unit follows state law to exercise the tax lien and foreclose (take possession of the property). When the tax lien is exercised, the delinquent taxes and any interest and penalties owing are reclassified as **Tax Liens Receivable** and the related allowance account is also reclassified. The governmental unit then sells the property to recover the outstanding tax lien. If the net proceeds from the sale of the property are less than the amount of the outstanding tax lien, the governmental unit writes off the loss against the Allowance for Uncollectible Tax Liens account, and if sold for more than the lien, state law usually requires that the excess be returned to the former property owner.

Frequently a governmental unit will need operating cash prior to the collection of the current year's tax revenues. For example, in Oregon a governmental unit must operate from July 1 until taxes are payable on November 15 without property tax collections. If cash is needed, the governmental unit may borrow funds on a short-term basis from a local lending institution and pledge the forthcoming tax receipts as security for the loan. The lending institution considers the potential tax receipts valid security for the loan because of the governmental unit's ability to exercise the liens and foreclose against the property to collect delinquent taxes. The loan is secured by a note referred to as a **tax anticipation note.**

The following entry illustrates the recording of property tax revenues:

3. The city levied property taxes of $900,000 and estimates that $30,000 will not be collected.

Property Taxes Receivable: Current	900,000	
Allowance for Uncollectible Property Taxes: Current		30,000
Revenues: Property Taxes		870,000
To record the property tax levy for the current year		

Fees charged for services are recorded by the modified accrual method as are tax revenues collected by other governmental units, which the laws require to be apportioned to constituent governmental units. Entries 4 and 5 illustrate the recording of these revenues.

4. Railburg provides ambulance and rescue service to residents and charges a flat fee of $100 per ambulance run. During the current year, 400 ambulance runs were provided by the fire department.

Ambulance Fees Receivable	40,000	
Revenues: Service Fees		40,000
To record the ambulance fees earned during the current year		

5. Railburg's share of the state road tax for the current year is $65,000.

State Road Tax Receivable	65,000	
Revenues: Intergovernmental		65,000
To record the amounts due from the state for the city's share of the state road tax		

Transactions 3, 4, and 5 demonstrate the recording of the types of revenue that are recognized by the modified accrual method. Revenues from sales taxes, income taxes, fines and forfeitures, and permits and licenses are usually recognized by the cash basis because they are not measurable before the cash is collected. Transaction 6, which follows, illustrates the recording of revenues that are recognized when cash is received.

6. During the year, Railburg received $85,000 from licenses and permits and $45,000 from fines and forfeitures in cash.

Cash	130,000	
Revenues: Licenses and Permits		85,000
Revenues: Fines and Forfeitures		45,000
To record the revenues received in cash for the current year		

Recording Encumbrances and Expenditures.   Encumbrances are a recommended but not required control tool. **ENCUMBRANCES,** a budgetary account, represents restrictions on the balance of the general fund and is the dollar amount of the orders placed for goods and services not yet received by the governmental unit. When an order is placed, the amount of the order is debited to ENCUMBRANCES and credited to **FUND BALANCE RESERVED FOR ENCUMBRANCES** or **RESERVE FOR ENCUMBRANCES.**

A governmental unit may encumber all orders or may only encumber nonroutine orders. If encumbrances are outstanding at the end of the year, they either lapse or are honored in the following year. If they are to be honored, they are included in the appropriations of the next year and recorded as encumbrances in the following year. For example, the city of Railburg had $6,000 of encumbrances from the year ended June 30, 1990, as indicated by the Fund Balance: Reserved for Encumbrances, on the beginning trial balance that the city will honor in the current year. On July 1, 1990, when the budget is recorded, the following entries are also recorded:

Fund Balance Reserved for Encumbrances	6,000	
Unreserved Fund Balance		6,000
To reverse the fund balance reserved for prior year's encumbrances to be honored in the current year		

ENCUMBRANCES: GENERAL GOVERNMENT	6,000	
FUND BALANCE RESERVED FOR ENCUMBRANCES		6,000
To record the encumbrance for office furniture		

Expenditures are recorded when they are incurred with two exceptions. First, the purchase of materials and supplies is recorded either as an expenditure when purchased (purchase method) or when used (consumption method). Second, prepaid items are recognized as an expenditure in the period acquired or in the period consumed. If materials and supplies are recorded by the purchase method, a portion of the fund balance equal to the ending balance of the inventory is reserved, as illustrated in the initial trial balance. When the inventory account is adjusted at year end, the fund balance reserved is also adjusted. The following entries illustrate the recording of encumbrances and expenditures for the city of Railburg:

7. During the year, $700,000 of liabilities were incurred for routine expenditures including salaries, payroll taxes, utilities, rent, repairs, and materials and supplies.

Expenditures: General Government	90,000	
Expenditures: Public Safety	140,000	
Expenditures: Highways and Streets	65,000	
Expenditures: Sanitation	35,000	
Expenditures: Health and Welfare	35,000	
Expenditures: Culture and Recreation	30,000	
Expenditures: Education	305,000	
Vouchers Payable		700,000
To record the liabilities incurred for recurring items for the current year		

The above entry illustrates that the city of Railburg does not record encumbrances for routine items. The materials and supplies purchased are recorded as expenditures rather than assets—the purchase method.

Because the general fund is considered an expendable fund, all purchases regardless of their nature are considered expenditures, even if they are for items that a business enterprise would typically record as noncurrent assets. In order to maintain records of noncurrent assets acquired, they are also entered in the general fixed asset account group.

8. The city of Railburg received office furniture costing $5,900 that had been ordered in the previous fiscal year, encumbered at $6,000, and included in the appropriations of the current year. The encumbrance of $6,000 was recorded at the beginning of the current year. When goods are received that were previously encumbered, the encumbrance entry is reversed and the expenditure is recorded as follows:

FUND BALANCE RESERVED FOR ENCUMBRANCES	6,000	
ENCUMBRANCES: GENERAL GOVERNMENT		6,000
To reverse the encumbrance for office furniture		

Expenditures: General Government	5,900	
Vouchers Payable		5,900
To record the receipt of office furniture		

The office furniture is also recorded in the general fixed asset account group.

9. The city of Railburg budgeted $115,000 for the acquisition of new equipment for the fire department that included $95,000 for a new, fully equipped emergency aid van, and $20,000 for a new car for the fire chief. In addition, $85,000 was budgeted for five new police cars. The emergency aid van was ordered as well as the five police cars. When nonroutine items are ordered the budgetary entry for encumbrances is recorded.

ENCUMBRANCES: PUBLIC SAFETY	180,000	
FUND BALANCE RESERVED FOR ENCUMBRANCES		180,000
To record the ordering of the emergency aid van for the fire department and the five police cars		

Once these items are ordered the maximum amount that can be spent on the new car for the fire chief is $20,000, since the unencumbered portion is only $20,000. The emergency aid van costing $93,000 and five police cars costing $88,000 are received.

FUND BALANCE RESERVED FOR ENCUMBRANCES	180,000	
ENCUMBRANCES: PUBLIC SAFETY		180,000
To reverse encumbrance journal entry as the vehicles ordered were received		

Expenditures: Public Safety	181,000	
Vouchers Payable		181,000
To record the liabilities for vehicles received		

The emergency aid van and the police cars are also recorded in the general fixed asset account group. Only $19,000 remains of the $20,000 that was budgeted for the acquisition of fixed assets for public safety; therefore, the maximum amount without a budget amendment that can be spent on the new car for the fire chief is $19,000.

10. A new car is ordered for the fire chief at a cost of $19,000.

ENCUMBRANCES: PUBLIC SAFETY	19,000	
FUND BALANCE RESERVED FOR ENCUMBRANCES		19,000

To record the order for a new car for the fire chief

Cash Receipts.   The following entries illustrate the typical cash receipts of a governmental unit's general fund:

11. Delinquent property taxes in the amount of $31,000 are collected in addition to $3,000 in interest and penalties. The remaining $4,000 of delinquent property taxes are determined to be uncollectible and the city will not foreclose on the property.

Cash	34,000	
Accounts Receivable: Delinquent Property Taxes		31,000
Revenues: Other		3,000

To record the collection of delinquent property taxes

Allowance for Uncollectible Delinquent Property Taxes	5,000	
Revenues: Property Taxes		1,000
Accounts Receivable: Delinquent Property Taxes		4,000

To write off the delinquent property taxes determined to be uncollectible that will not be collected by foreclosure

Because the allowance provided for uncollectible property taxes is more than the amount of the actual loss, additional property tax revenue equal to the excess is recognized in the current year. If the allowance was not sufficient to cover the losses, the deficiency is charged to current year's property tax revenue because no expense account is used for uncollectible accounts; instead the revenue is recorded at the net amount expected to be collected. This treatment is consistent with the treatment of changes in estimates for business entities.

12. Property taxes totaling $825,000 are collected, ambulance fees of $40,000 are received, and $63,000 is received from the state road fund.

Cash	928,000	
Property Taxes Receivable: Current		825,000
Ambulance Fees Receivable		40,000
State Road Tax Receivable		63,000

To record the cash received as payment of receivables during the current year

Cash Disbursements.   The following entries illustrate the typical cash disbursements of a governmental unit's general fund:

13. Vouchers totaling $870,900 were paid during the current year.

Vouchers Payable	870,900	
Cash		870,900

To record the payment of vouchers outstanding

14. Cash of $160,000 was transferred to the debt service fund.

Due Debt Service Fund	160,000	
Cash		160,000

To record the amount payable to the debt service fund for serial bonds: $108,000 for interest and $52,000 for principal

15. The city council authorized the transfer of $60,000 of cash to the capital projects fund from the general fund.

Transfers Out: Capital Projects Fund	60,000	
Cash		60,000

To record the transfer of funds authorized by the city council

Year-End Adjustments. The following adjusting entries are recorded by the city of Railburg on June 30, 1991:

16. The inventory of materials and supplies shows $15,000 on hand at the end of the year.

Materials and Supplies Inventory	3,000	
Expenditures: General Government		3,000

To adjust the materials and supplies inventory to the actual amount on hand at year end ($15,000 − $12,000 = $3,000 increase)

Unreserved Fund Balance	3,000	
Fund Balance: Reserved for Materials and Supplies		3,000

If the acquisition of the materials and supplies had been recorded as an asset, the journal entry would debit Expenditures and credit Materials and Supplies Inventory for the amount used.

17. The property taxes currently due are now delinquent.

Property Taxes Receivable: Delinquent	75,000	
Property Taxes Receivable: Current		75,000

To record taxes that were current and are now delinquent

Allowance for Uncollectible Property Taxes: Current	30,000	
Allowance for Uncollectible Property Taxes: Delinquent		30,000

To reclassify the allowance as delinquent as the property taxes are past due

When property taxes become delinquent they are transferred from a current receivable to a delinquent receivable, and the related allowance account is also reclassified.

The adjusted trial balance of the general fund on June 30, 1991 is

	Debit	Credit
Cash	$ 41,100	
Property Taxes Receivable: Delinquent	75,000	
Allowance for Uncollectible Delinquent Property Taxes		$ 30,000
State Road Tax Receivable	10,000	
Materials and Supplies Inventory	15,000	
Vouchers Payable		37,000
Fund Balance: Reserved for Materials and Supplies		15,000
Unreserved Fund Balance		54,000
Revenues: Property Taxes		871,000
Revenues: Intergovernmental		65,000
Revenues: Service Fees		40,000
Revenues: Licenses and Permits		85,000
Revenues: Fines and Forfeitures		45,000
Revenues: Other		3,000
Expenditures: General Government	92,900	
Expenditures: Public Safety	321,000	
Expenditures: Highways and Streets	65,000	
Expenditures: Sanitation	35,000	
Expenditures: Health and Welfare	35,000	
Expenditures: Culture and Recreation	30,000	
Expenditures: Education	305,000	
Operating Transfers Out	220,000	
ESTIMATED REVENUES	1,100,000	
APPROPRIATIONS		900,000
ENCUMBRANCES	19,000	
ESTIMATED OTHER FINANCING USES		160,000
FUND BALANCE RESERVED FOR ENCUMBRANCES		19,000
BUDGETARY FUND BALANCE		40,000
	$ 2,364,000	$ 2,364,000

The statement of revenues, expenditures, and changes in fund balances: budget and actual, and the balance sheet of only the general fund of the city of Railburg are presented in Exhibits 23-2 and 23-3. A combined statement of revenues, expenditures, and changes in fund balances for all governmental funds, which is not illustrated, would have the same actual figures as in Exhibit 23-2 for the general fund, because the city of Railburg prepares its budget according to generally accepted accounting principles. If some other basis of accounting were used, the statement of revenues, expenditures, and changes in fund balances would have different values for the actual amounts of some of the line items. Appendix 23-A, which contains the general-purpose financial statements for the city of Albany, Oregon, illustrates the combined statement of revenues, expenditures, and changes in fund balances for the governmental funds.

Closing Journal Entries.   The budgetary entries are reversed at the end of the period. The nominal accounts for revenues, expenditures, and operating transfers in and out are closed to the unreserved fund balance. An entry is recorded to adjust the account, Fund Balance Reserved for Encumbrances, to reflect the balance of outstanding encumbrances at year end. If the outstanding encumbrances at year end are to be honored in the following year, **Un-**

EXHIBIT 23-2

Illustrative Problem 23.1
City of Railburg
Statement of Revenues, Expenditures, and Changes in Fund Balances:
Budget and Actual: General Fund
For the Year Ended June 30, 1991

	Budget	Actual	Variance Over (Under)
Revenues			
Property Taxes	$ 875,000	$ 871,000	$(4,000)
Intergovernmental	60,000	65,000	5,000
Service Fees	35,000	40,000	5,000
Licenses and Permits	100,000	85,000	(15,000)
Fines and Forfeitures	30,000	45,000	15,000
Other	–0–	3,000	3,000
Total Revenues	1,100,000	1,109,000	9,000
Expenditures			
General Government	95,000	92,900	(2,100)
Public Safety	325,000	321,000	(4,000)
Highways and Streets	70,000	65,000	(5,000)
Sanitation	33,000	35,000	2,000
Health and Welfare	32,000	35,000	3,000
Culture and Recreation	30,000	30,000	–0–
Education	315,000	305,000	(10,000)
Total Expenditures	900,000	883,900	(16,100)
Excess of Revenues Over Expenditures	200,000	225,100	25,100
Other Financing Uses: Operating Transfers Out			
Debt Service Fund	160,000	160,000	–0–
Capital Projects Fund		60,000	(60,000)
Excess of Revenues Over Expenditures and Other Financing Uses	40,000	5,100	(34,900)
Fund Balance at the Beginning of the Year	69,000	69,000	–0–
Fund Balance at the End of the Year	$ 109,000	$ 74,100	$(34,900)

reserved Fund Balance is debited and **Fund Balance Reserved for Encumbrances** is credited for the amount to be honored. If the account, Fund Balance Reserved for Encumbrances, has a balance, the closing entry adjusts the balance to the amount of the outstanding encumbrances to be honored in the following year. An alternative to allocating a portion of the fund balance for encumbrances to be honored in the following year is to report the intention in a footnote. As previously discussed, not all governmental units follow the above procedure, but the illustrative problems and homework use this procedure. The closing entries for the city of Railburg are

APPROPRIATIONS	900,000	
ESTIMATED OTHER FINANCING USES	160,000	
BUDGETARY FUND BALANCE	40,000	
ESTIMATED REVENUES		1,100,000

To reverse the entry recording the budget

FUND BALANCE RESERVED FOR ENCUMBRANCES	19,000	
ENCUMBRANCES: PUBLIC SAFETY		19,000

To reverse the balances remaining in the budgetary accounts ENCUMBRANCES and FUND BALANCE RESERVED FOR ENCUMBRANCES

Unreserved Fund Balance	19,000	
Fund Balance Reserved for Encumbrances		19,000

To allocate unreserved fund balance for the amount of outstanding encumbrances at year end to be honored next year

Revenues: Property Taxes	871,000	
Revenues: Intergovernmental	65,000	
Revenues: Service Fees	40,000	
Revenues: Licenses and Permits	85,000	
Revenues: Fines and Forfeitures	45,000	
Revenues: Other	3,000	
Expenditures: General Government		92,900
Expenditures: Public Safety		321,000
Expenditures: Highways and Streets		65,000
Expenditures: Sanitation		35,000
Expenditures: Health and Welfare		35,000
Expenditures: Culture and Recreation		30,000
Expenditures: Education		305,000
Operating Transfers Out		220,000
Unreserved Fund Balance		5,100

To close the revenues, expenditures, and transfer accounts to the unreserved fund balance

---

EXHIBIT 23-3

Illustrative Problem 23.1
City of Railburg
Balance Sheet: General Fund
June 30, 1991

Assets			Liabilities and Fund Balance	
Cash		$ 41,100	Vouchers Payable	$ 37,000
Taxes Receivable: Delinquent	$ 75,000		Fund Balance	
Less: Allowance for Uncollectible Delinquent			Fund Balance: Reserved for Materials and	
Taxes	30,000	45,000	Supplies	15,000
State Road Tax Receivable		10,000	Fund Balance: Reserved for Encumbrances	19,000
Materials and Supplies Inventory		15,000	Unreserved Fund Balance	40,100
			Total Fund Balance	74,100
Total Assets		$ 111,100	Total Liabilities and Fund Balance	$ 111,100

SPECIAL REVENUE FUNDS

Special revenue funds are used to account for revenues from a particular source that are to be used for a specific purpose such as property taxes designated for maintenance of public parks, or using state road tax revenues allocated to the governmental unit for maintenance of streets and roads, or using traffic fines for operation of the traffic court. A special revenue fund differs from an enterprise fund in that the revenues are primarily from taxes and other sources that are not directly related to the services provided. In an enterprise fund the revenue is primarily from fees charged for services provided, and the fees are directly related to the cost of providing the service. A governmental unit may have several special revenue funds or it may not have any. The number of special revenue funds depends on the size of the governmental unit and the particular operations of the governmental unit. If a governmental unit has several special revenue funds, they are combined and reported together in the general-purpose financial statements.

   The accounting for a special revenue fund is the same as the accounting for the general fund including the recording of budgetary accounts and the use of encumbrances. The accounting for the general fund and special revenue funds parallels the accounting for the unrestricted and restricted current funds of a not-for-profit college or university. Because the accounting for a special revenue fund is identical to the accounting for the general fund, the accounting is not demonstrated with an illustrative problem, but the review problem at the end of the chapter has a special revenue fund.

CAPITAL PROJECTS FUNDS

Capital projects funds are used to account for assets (resources) that are for the acquisition or construction of major capital assets used in the operation of general government for the benefit of all the citizens of the governmental unit. A capital project fund may also be used to account for the construction of assets, which are to be paid for by special assessments to the citizens who will primarily benefit from the asset. The capital projects funds are not used to account for the construction of major long-lived assets for either the enterprise or the internal service funds.

   These large and costly projects are typically financed with long-term general obligation bonds, transfers from the general fund, and government grants. The capital projects funds only account for the financing sources and the expenditure of the financing resources, and neither the assets acquired nor the liabilities assumed are recorded in the capital projects funds. The assets acquired or constructed are recorded in the general fixed asset account group and the debt incurred is recorded in the general long-term debt account group. The repayment of the debt, which is usually bonds, is accounted for in the debt service fund.

   An annual budget may be recorded in the capital projects fund. Usually a different fund is used for each project for control purposes; therefore, budgets are seldom recorded in the capital projects fund. For purposes of control over the extended period of time necessary to complete a capital project, additional project-oriented rather than period-oriented budgets are also prepared. The use of encumbrances is optional in capital project funds. The proceeds from the long-term debt and the transfers from the general fund are not recorded as revenues but as **other financing sources.** Government grants and interest on investments are recorded as revenue. The expenditures for the acquisition or construction of fixed assets of the capital projects fund are recorded in the period in which the expenditures occur.

When the bonds are issued, the cash received is recorded in the capital projects fund as bond proceeds and the debt is recorded in the general long-term debt group. If bonds to finance a capital project are issued at a premium, the cash received as a premium is transferred to the debt service fund to help pay future interest and principal. If the bonds are issued at a discount, assets are not transferred from the debt service fund to the capital projects fund. The deficiency from the issuance at a discount is either covered by a transfer from the general fund, or the amount that can be spent on the project is reduced. Illustrative Problem 23.2, which is a continuation of Illustrative Problem 23.1, demonstrates the accounting for a capital projects fund. If a transaction or transfer was recorded in the general fund, the same transaction number used in Illustrative Problem 23.1 is used in this illustrative problem.

ILLUSTRATIVE PROBLEM 23.2: ACCOUNTING FOR A CAPITAL PROJECTS FUND

The voters of the city of Railburg approved the construction of a $1,000,000 addition to the fire station and the issuance of $800,000 of general obligation bonds to finance the project. The remainder of the project is to be financed with a grant of $140,000 from the state government and general fund revenues of $60,000.

The following transactions and transfers are recorded in the capital project fund for the addition to the fire station during the current year. The addition to the fire station is the only capital project of the city of Railburg; therefore, the city has decided not to record a budget in the capital projects fund.

15. The city council authorized the transfer of $60,000 of cash to the capital projects fund from the general fund. The cash is to pay the architectural fee for the addition to the fire station. The cash is received and the architectural firm is paid.

Cash	60,000	
Operating Transfers In: General Fund		60,000
To record the cash transferred from the general fund for architectural fees		

Expenditures: Fire Station Addition	60,000	
Cash		60,000
To record the payment of the architectural fee for the addition to the fire station		

This expense could have been encumbered before being paid. The amount is also recorded as Construction in Process in the general fixed asset account group.

18. The 10% general obligation bonds, with a face value of $800,000, are issued for $815,000.

Cash	815,000	
Proceeds of Bond Issue		815,000
To record the proceeds of the bond issue for the addition to the fire station		

Operating Transfers Out: Debt Service Fund	15,000	
Cash		15,000

To record the transfer of the cash received as bond premium to the debt service fund

The face amount of the bond issue is also recorded in the general long-term debt account group. The transfer of the bond premium is recorded in the debt service fund and the general long-term debt account group.

19. A $140,000 grant is received from the state.

Cash	140,000	
Grant Revenue		140,000

To record the grant received from the state to be used for the fire station addition

20. The city council voted to accept a bid of $935,000 from Able Construction Company.

ENCUMBRANCES	935,000	
FUND BALANCE RESERVED FOR ENCUMBRANCES		935,000

To record the acceptance of the construction contract

21. The bond proceeds are temporarily invested in certificates of deposit. The earnings on investments of the capital projects fund are to be transferred to the debt service fund.

Investments in Certificates of Deposit	800,000	
Cash		800,000

To record the investment of bond proceeds

22. Progress billings in the amount of $230,000 are received from the contractor. Certificates of deposit totaling $135,000 are liquidated to pay the progress billings. The certificates of deposit earned $40,000 of interest, which was received in cash.

Cash	175,000	
Investments in Certificates of Deposit		135,000
Interest Revenue		40,000

To record the receipt of interest revenue and a portion of the principal of the certificates of deposit

Operating Transfers Out: Debt Service Fund	40,000	
Cash		40,000

To record the transfer of interest to the debt service fund

FUND BALANCE RESERVED FOR ENCUMBRANCES	230,000	
ENCUMBRANCES		230,000

To reverse the encumbrance entry for the amount of the progress billings received

Expenditures: Fire Station Addition	230,000	
Cash		230,000

To record the payment of the progress billings from Able Construction Company

The transfer to the debt service fund is recorded in that fund and in the general long-term debt account group. The amount paid to the contractor is recorded as Construction in Process in the general fixed asset account group. The amounts due the contractor could be accrued as a payable prior to payment. Frequently a percentage of the amount of the progress billings is not paid to a contractor until the project is completed. These retainages are recorded as **Contract Payable: Retainage Percentage** until the completion of the project.

The adjusted trial balance of the capital projects fund on June 30, 1991 is in Exhibit 23-4.

EXHIBIT 23-4

Illustrative Problem 23.2
City of Railburg
Adjusted Trial Balance: Capital Projects Fund
June 30, 1991

	Debit	Credit
Cash	$ 45,000	
Investments in Certificates of Deposit	665,000	
Grant Revenue		$ 140,000
Interest Revenue		40,000
Proceeds of Bond Issue		815,000
Operating Transfers In: General Fund		60,000
Expenditures: Fire Station Addition	290,000	
Operating Transfers Out: Debt Service Fund	55,000	
ENCUMBRANCES	705,000	
FUND BALANCE RESERVED FOR ENCUMBRANCES		705,000
	$ 1,760,000	$ 1,760,000

When the addition to the fire station is completed, the capital project fund is terminated. Usually, any cash remaining in the capital project fund at the completion of the project is transferred either to the general fund or to the debt service fund as a **residual equity transfer.** A residual equity transfer is a transfer between funds either when a fund is established or when a fund is eliminated. If the project, due to cost overruns or changes, costs more than the initial estimate, the shortage is usually covered by a transfer from the general fund.

If a governmental unit has more than one capital projects fund, the funds are combined and reported together in the financial statements. The combining statement of revenues, expenditures, and changes in fund balances and the combining balance sheet for the capital projects funds is prepared in columnar form with a separate column for each project. Exhibits 23-5 and 23-6 illustrate the financial statements of the city of Railburg's only capital project fund.

EXHIBIT 23-5

Illustrative Problem 23.2
City of Railburg
Statement of Revenues, Expenditures, and Changes in Fund Balances:
Capital Projects Fund
For the Year Ended June 30, 1991

Revenues		
Grants		$ 140,000
Interest on Investments		40,000
Total Revenues		180,000
Expenditures: Fire Station Addition		290,000
Excess of Expenditures Over Revenues		(110,000)
Other Financing Sources (Uses)		
Proceeds of General Obligation Bonds	$ 815,000	
Operating Transfers In. General Fund	60,000	
Operating Transfers Out: Debt Service Fund	(55,000)	820,000
Excess of Revenues and Other Financing Sources Over		
Expenditures and Other Financing Uses		710,000
Fund Balance at the Beginning of the Year		–0–
Fund Balance at the End of the Year		$ 710,000

EXHIBIT 23-6

Illustrative Problem 23.2
City of Railburg
Balance Sheet: Capital Projects Fund
June 30, 1991

Assets		Fund Balance	
Cash	$ 45,000	Fund Balance	
Investments in Certificates of Deposit	665,000	Reserved for Encumbrances	$ 705,000
		Unreserved	5,000
Total Assets	$ 710,000	Total Fund Balance	$ 710,000

The closing journal entries close the revenues, expenditures, and other financing sources accounts to the unreserved fund balance like the entry closing the revenues, expenditures, and transfers of the general fund. The budgetary accounts, ENCUMBRANCES AND FUND BALANCE RESERVED FOR ENCUMBRANCES, are closed, and the balance of the FUND BALANCE RESERVED FOR ENCUMBRANCES is established as a permanent account. If a budget is recorded in the capital projects fund, the entry is reversed as part of the closing journal entries.

DEBT SERVICE FUNDS

Debt service funds are used to account for the assets (resources) being accumulated for the payment of interest and principal on general obligation debt of the governmental unit, and for the payment of the interest and principal. The funds are also used to account for special assessment debt when the government is obligated in some manner. General obligation debt is a liability that is only secured by the general credit of the governmental unit. Debt incurred by the enterprise funds and the internal service funds is accounted for in those funds and not in the debt service fund. The long-term liabilities serviced by the debt service fund are usually from capital projects.

A budget is not required to be recorded for the debt service fund since the operations are controlled by the terms of the bond indentures, but a budget may be recorded. Encumbrances are seldom used in the debt service fund. When debt is incurred, it is recorded in the general long-term debt account group, and only when it matures and is payable is it recorded in the debt service fund. When the debt matures, it is recorded as an expenditure of the debt service fund. The assets of the debt service fund come primarily from transfers from the general fund and capital projects funds, and from property taxes collected for debt repayment. The debt service fund uses the modified accrual basis of accounting; therefore, expenditures represent the actual cash outlays for principal and interest, and interest is usually not accrued at year end.

Some of the capital projects financed by long-term debt will benefit only a limited number of the citizens. These projects are paid for by a special levy (assessment) on the affected property owners. These special assessments are typically payable over a number of years. The amount of the tax levied plus the interest on the unpaid assessments is the amount needed to pay the principal and the interest on the debt. The financing of these special assessment capital projects may be with debt that is to be paid entirely by the special assessments, or partly with special assessments and partly by the governmental unit. The governmental unit is paying a portion of the debt either because the government is also a property owner or because the government is paying a portion as a public benefit.

The governmental unit may guarantee the payment if property owners default on their assessments—obligated in some manner. If the governmental unit is **obligated in some manner** for the debt, the debt is accounted for in the general long-term debt fund. When the special assessment tax is levied, the entire amount of the levy is recorded in the debt service fund as a receivable and credited to a deferred revenue account. As the assessments become available and measurable, the deferred revenue is recognized as earned. Interest on special assessments is usually recognized when due rather than when earned because it is offset by the interest expense that is recognized when due. Thus, the method of interest revenue recognition results in the matching of interest revenue and interest expense.

Illustrative Problem 23.3, which is a continuation of Illustrative Problems 23.1 and 23.2, demonstrates the accounting for a debt service fund. Transactions that were recorded in either the general fund or the capital projects fund are referenced by the transaction number used in that fund for ease of identifying transactions and events that affect more than one fund and/or account group.

ILLUSTRATIVE PROBLEM 23.3: ACCOUNTING FOR A DEBT SERVICE FUND

The city of Railburg has one outstanding debt issue on July 1, 1990: a $2,000,000 20-year, 8% serial bond issue issued for the construction of a new jail. On July 1, 1990 the trial balance of the debt service fund was

	Debit	Credit
Cash	$ 20,000	
Property Taxes Receivable: Delinquent	50,000	
Allowance for Uncollectible Delinquent Property Taxes		$ 5,000
Fund Balance Reserved for Debt Payment		65,000
	$ 70,000	$ 70,000

The following transaction and transfer entries are recorded in the debt service fund of the city of Railburg during the year ended June 30, 1990:

2. The budget authorized the transfer of $160,000 to the debt service fund during the current year: $108,000 is for interest and the remaining $52,000 is for principal payments on serial bonds. Because the transfer is payable in the current year, the transfer is recorded at the beginning of the year.

Due from General Fund	160,000	
Operating Transfers In: General Fund		160,000
To record the amount due from the general fund for the interest		
and principal on the outstanding serial bonds		

14. Cash of $160,000 was transferred to the debt service fund by the general fund: $52,000 is for principal on the serial bonds and the remainder is interest.

Cash	160,000	
Due from General Fund		160,000
To record the amount received from the general fund for the		
principal and interest on the serial bonds		

The $52,000 cash transferred for the payment of principal on the serial bonds is also recorded in the general long-term debt account group.

18. The 10% general obligation bonds, with a face value of $800,000, are issued for $815,000 and the premium is transferred to the debt service fund to cover future debt payments.

Cash	15,000	
Operating Transfers In: Capital Projects Fund		15,000
To record the transfer of the cash received as bond premium by the		
capital projects fund		

22. Certificates of deposit in the amount of $135,000 are liquidated to pay the progress billings. Interest of $40,000 has been earned and received on the certificates of deposit and transferred to the debt service fund.

Cash	40,000	
Operating Transfers In: Capital Projects Fund		40,000
To record the transfer of interest from the capital projects fund		

The transfers from the capital projects fund are also recorded in the general long-term debt account group.

23. Delinquent property taxes in the amount of $40,000 are collected and the balance is determined to be uncollectible and will not be foreclosed. Property tax assessments for payment of general obligation debt totaled $80,000 and 10% is estimated to be uncollectible. During the current year, $54,000 of the current year's taxes are collected. All the property taxes are for the payment of debt principal.

Cash	40,000	
Revenues: Property Taxes	5,000	
Allowance for Uncollectible Property Taxes	5,000	
Property Taxes Receivable: Delinquent		50,000
To record the collection and write-off of delinquent taxes		
Property Taxes Receivable: Current	80,000	
Allowance for Uncollectible Property Taxes: Current		8,000
Revenues: Property Taxes		72,000
To record the property tax assessments for the current year		
Cash	54,000	
Property Taxes Receivable: Current		54,000
To record the collection of the current year's property taxes		

The property tax revenues, which are all for debt principal payments, are recorded in the general long-term debt account group.

24. Serial bonds with a face value of $1,600,000 are outstanding on July 1, 1990. Principal in the amount of $150,000 is due during the current year. The interest owing on the outstanding bonds of $108,000 plus the principal of $150,000 are paid.

Expenditures	258,000	
Matured Serial Bonds Payable		150,000
Interest Payable: Serial Bonds		108,000
To record the principal of the matured bonds and the interest owing on serial bonds		
Matured Serial Bonds Payable	150,000	
Interest Payable: Serial Bonds	108,000	
Cash		258,000
To record the payment of interest owing on serial bonds and the principal owing on matured serial bonds		

An entry reflecting the matured debt on the serial bonds is also recorded in the general long-term debt account group.

25. The unpaid property taxes are now delinquent.

Property Taxes Receivable: Delinquent	26,000	
Property Taxes Receivable: Current		26,000
To reclassify outstanding property taxes as delinquent		
Allowance for Uncollectible Property Taxes: Current	8,000	
Allowance for Uncollectible Property Taxes: Delinquent		8,000
To reclassify the allowance for uncollectible property taxes that are now delinquent		

The adjusted trial balance of the debt service fund on June 30, 1990 is in Exhibit 23-7.

EXHIBIT 23-7

Illustrative Problem 23.3
City of Railburg
Adjusted Trial Balance: Debt Service Fund
June 30, 1990

	Debit	Credit
Cash	$ 71,000	
Property Taxes Receivable: Delinquent	26,000	
Allowance for Uncollectible Delinquent Property Taxes		$ 8,000
Revenues: Property Taxes		67,000
Operating Transfers In: General Fund		160,000
Operating Transfers In: Capital Projects Fund		55,000
Expenditures	258,000	
Fund Balance Reserved for Debt Payment		65,000
	$ 355,000	$ 355,000

Exhibits 23-8 and 23-9 present the statement of revenues, expenditures, and changes in funds balances and the balance sheet for the debt service fund of the city of Railburg as of June 30, 1990. The transactions in the debt service fund are limited; therefore, the statements for the debt service fund are brief.

ACCOUNT GROUPS: GENERAL FIXED ASSETS AND GENERAL LONG-TERM DEBT

Noncurrent assets acquired and long-term liabilities incurred for general governmental operations by the four governmental funds are accounted for in account groups. The noncurrent assets and long-term liabilities are recorded in account groups because they belong to the governmental unit as a whole and not to a particular fund within the governmental unit. The account groups function like inventory control accounts with neither revenues nor expenditures. All the transactions recorded in the account groups are the result of entries recorded

EXHIBIT 23-8

Illustrative Problem 23.3
City of Railburg
Statement of Revenues, Expenditures, and Changes in Fund Balances: Debt Service Fund
For the Year Ended June 30, 1991

Revenues: Property Taxes		$ 67,000
Expenditures: Debt Principal and Interest		258,000
Excess of Expenditures Over Revenues		(191,000)
Other Financing Sources		
Operating Transfers In: General Fund	$ 160,000	
Operating Transfers In: Capital Projects Fund	55,000	215,000
Excess of Revenues and Other Financing Sources Over		
Expenditures		24,000
Fund Balance at the Beginning of the Year		65,000
Fund Balance at the End of the Year		$ 89,000

EXHIBIT 23-9

Illustrative Problem 23.3
City of Railburg
Balance Sheet: Debt Service Fund
June 30, 1991

Assets		Fund Balance	
Cash	$ 71,000	Fund Balance Reserved for Debt	
Property Taxes Receivable:		Payment	$ 89,000
Delinquent: Net	18,000		
Total Assets	$ 89,000	Total Fund Balance	$ 89,000

for fixed asset acquisition, fixed asset disposition, long-term borrowing, or long-term debt repayment in one of the governmental funds. Thus the recording of a transaction affecting noncurrent assets or the principal of long-term liabilities in one of the governmental funds has its counterpart in one of the account groups.

GENERAL FIXED ASSET ACCOUNT GROUP

The general fixed asset account group is used to account for the permanent assets acquired by the general government. Fixed assets acquired by the enterprise and internal service funds are accounted for in those funds, and not in the general fixed asset account group. The fixed assets are usually reported in five categories: land, buildings, improvements other than buildings, equipment, and construction in process. The assets are represented in the account group by the source of investment, for example, general fund revenues, special revenue fund revenues, capital projects fund revenues, proceeds of general obligation bonds, and grants. Depreciation may be recorded on the assets, but usually is not. The values in the account group represent the original cost of the asset or, if the asset was donated to the governmental unit, its fair market value when donated. Governmental units have not always maintained a general fixed asset account group and have had to estimate the cost of the assets, often acquired many years in the past when the assets were first recorded in the account group.

An asset under construction is recorded as Construction in Process when progress billings are received from contractors. When the asset is completed, it is recorded in the appropriate asset category. When an asset is retired, its cost is removed from the asset account and the related investment account. When an asset is sold, the transaction is usually recorded in the general fund, by debiting Cash and crediting the Proceeds from the Sale of Fixed Assets, an other financing sources account. In the general fixed asset account group, the cost of the asset sold is removed from the asset account and the appropriate investment account.

Among a governmental unit's assets are assets called **public domain** or **infrastructure.** These assets consist of streets, sidewalks, curbs, and bridges. A governmental unit does not have to record these assets, but it is recommended that they be recorded and classified as improvements other than buildings. The reason for not recording these assets is that they have value only to the governmental unit and therefore could not be sold to another entity.

Illustrative Problem 23.4, which is a continuation of Illustrative Problems 23.1, 23.2, and 23.3, demonstrates the recording of transactions previously recorded in the governmental funds that also are recorded in the general fixed asset account group. The transactions are identified by the transaction numbers used in Illustrative Problems 23.1, 23.2, and 23.3.

ILLUSTRATIVE PROBLEM 23.4: ACCOUNTING FOR THE GENERAL FIXED ASSET ACCOUNT GROUP

On July 1, 1990, the trial balance of the general fixed asset account group was

	Debit	Credit
Land	$ 200,000	
Buildings	4,500,000	
Improvements Other Than Buildings	1,800,000	
Equipment	1,200,000	
Investment in General Fixed Assets: General Fund Revenues		$ 4,200,000
Investment in General Fixed Assets: Special Revenue Fund Revenues		900,000
Investment in General Fixed Assets: General Obligation Bonds		2,000,000
Investment in General Fixed Assets: Government Grants		600,000
	$ 7,700,000	$ 7,700,000

8. The city of Railburg received office furniture costing $5,900 that had been ordered and recorded as a $6,000 encumbrance in the previous fiscal year and included in the appropriations of the current year.

Equipment	5,900	
Investment In General Fixed Assets: General Fund Revenues		5,900
To record the purchase of office furniture by the general fund		

9. The city of Railburg budgeted $200,000 for the acquisition of new equipment for public safety. An emergency aid van costing $93,000 and five police cars costing $88,000 are received.

Equipment	181,000	
Investment in General Fixed Assets: General Fund Revenues		181,000
To record the purchase of an emergency aid van and five police cars		

15. The city council authorized the transfer of $60,000 of cash to the capital projects fund from the general fund. The cash is to be used to pay the architectural fee for the addition to the fire station. The cash is received by the capital projects fund and the architectural firm is paid.

Construction in Process: Fire Station Addition	60,000	
Investment in General Fixed Assets: General Fund Revenues		60,000
To record the architectural fees for the fire station addition funded with general fund revenues		

22. Progress billings in the amount of $230,000 are received from the contractor on the $935,000 contract for construction of the addition to the fire station. Government grant revenue of $140,000 and bond proceeds of $90,000 are used to pay the progress billings.

Construction in Process: Fire Station Addition	230,000	
Investment in General Fixed Assets: Government Grants		140,000
Investment in General Fixed Assets: General Obligation Bonds		90,000
To record the progress billing for the construction of the addition to the fire station		

During the course of construction of a major facility a number of progress billings will be received. Therefore, the entry to record construction in process is usually prepared at the end of the accounting period for the entire amount incurred for construction in process during the current year.

The schedule presenting the general fixed asset account group by source at the end of the period is in Exhibit 23-10.

Two additional financial schedules are prepared to report the general fixed asset account group: a schedule of general fixed assets by function and activity and a schedule of changes in general fixed assets by function and activity.

EXHIBIT 23-10

Illustrative Problem 23.4
City of Railburg
Schedule of Fixed Assets
June 30, 1991

Investment in Fixed Assets	
Land	$ 200,000
Buildings	4,500,000
Improvements Other Than Buildings	1,800,000
Equipment	1,386,900
Construction in Process: Fire Station Addition	290,000
Total Investment	$ 8,176,900
Sources of Investment in General Fixed Assets	
General Fund Revenues	$ 4,446,900
Special Revenue Fund Revenues	900,000
General Obligation Bonds	2,090,000
Government Grants	740,000
Total Sources	$ 8,176,900

GENERAL LONG-TERM DEBT ACCOUNT GROUP

The general long-term debt account group is used to account for the **principal only** of the general obligation long-term debt incurred to finance the major general governmental projects of the governmental unit. In addition, the long-term debt account group includes long-term debt from special assessments in which the government is obligated in some manner and long-term liabilities from capital leases, compensated absences, judgments, claims, pensions, and special termination benefits of employees.

When a long-term liability is incurred, the account, **Amount To Be Provided for Retirement of Debt,** is debited with the face amount of the liability and the appropriate liability account is credited. As cash is set aside to pay the principal of the liability in the debt service fund, an entry is recorded in the general long-term debt account group, which debits **Amount Available in Debt Service Fund,** and credits Amount To Be Provided for Retirement of Debt. When the liability is paid, the appropriate liability account is debited and Amount Available in Debt Service Fund is credited. These three types of transactions are the only ones that are recorded in the general long-term debt account group.

Illustrative Problem 23.5, which is a continuation of Illustrative Problems 23.1 through 23.4, demonstrates the recording of the transactions in the general long-term account group, which have their counterparts in the general fund, the capital projects funds, and the debt service fund. As before, the numbers of the entries correspond to the entries recorded in those funds.

ILLUSTRATIVE PROBLEM 23.5: ACCOUNTING FOR THE GENERAL LONG-TERM DEBT ACCOUNT GROUP

The city of Railburg only had one debt issue outstanding at the beginning of the current year: a $2,000,000, 8%, serial bond issue. A serial bond issue is one in which the bonds mature at different points in time rather than on a single date in the future. Prior to the current year, $400,000 of principal had been paid on the serial bond issue. The trial balance of the long-term debt account group on July 1, 1990 was

	Debit	Credit
Amount Available in Debt Service Fund	$ 65,000	
Amount To Be Provided for Retirement of Bonds	1,535,000	
8% Serial Bond Issue Payable		$ 1,600,000
	$ 1,600,000	$ 1,600,000

The following transactions recorded in the capital projects fund and the debt service fund are also recorded in the general long-term debt account group:

14. The general fund transferred $160,000 to the debt service fund. The transfer consisted of $52,000 for principal on the serial bonds and the remainder is interest.

Amount Available in Debt Service Fund	52,000	
Amount To Be Provided for Retirement of Bonds		52,000
To record the transfer from the general fund for the payment of serial bond principal		

18. The 10% general obligation bonds, with a face value of $800,000, were issued for $815,000 and the $15,000 premium was transferred to the debt service fund for future debt payments.

Amount To Be Provided for Retirement of Bonds	785,000	
Amount Available in Debt Service Fund	15,000	
10% General Obligation Bonds Payable		800,000
To record the principal of the bond issue for the addition to the fire station and the transfer of the premium to the debt service fund		

22. Interest earned on investments of the capital projects fund in the amount of $40,000 was transferred to the debt service fund.

Amount Available in Debt Service Fund	40,000	
Amount To Be Provided for Retirement of Bonds		40,000
To record transfer of cash to the debt service fund from the capital projects fund		

23. Delinquent taxes in the amount of $40,000 are collected and the remainder has been determined to be uncollectible. Tax assessments for payment of general obligation debt totaled $80,000 and 10% is estimated to be uncollectible. During the current year $54,000 of the current year's taxes is collected. All property taxes are for the payment of serial bond principal.

Amount Available in Debt Service Fund	67,000	
Amount To Be Provided for Retirement of Bonds		67,000
To record property taxes revenues, which are for the payment of		
serial bond principal ($72,000 − $5,000 = $67,000)		

24. Serial bonds with a face value of $1,600,000 are outstanding on July 1, 1990. Principal in the amount of $150,000 is due during the current year. The $108,000 of interest owing on the outstanding bonds plus the principal of $150,000 are paid.

8% Serial Bond Issue Payable	150,000	
Amount Available in Debt Service Fund		150,000
To record the payment of principal due on the serial bonds		

The reporting for the general long-term debt account group is in Exhibit 23-11. The amount available for the retirement of long-term debt is equal to the fund balance of the debt service fund, just as it was at the beginning of the fiscal year. An alternative to adjusting the Amount Available in Debt Service Fund for each transaction is to record a single summary entry at the end of the period.

EXHIBIT 23-11

Illustrative Problem 23.5
City of Railburg
Schedule of Long-term Debt
June 30, 1991

Amount Available and To Be Provided for Retirement of Long-term Debt	
Amount Available in Debt Service Fund	$ 89,000
Amount To Be Provided for Retirement of Bonds	2,161,000
Total Amount Available and To Be Provided	$ 2,250,000
Long-term Debt Payable	
8% Serial Bonds Payable	$ 1,450,000
10%, 20-year General Obligation Bonds Payable	800,000
Total Long-term Debt Payable	$ 2,250,000

In addition to the above schedule, a statement of changes in long-term debt and a summary of debt service requirements to maturity is required to be presented either separately or in the footnotes to the financial statements.

TRANSACTIONS AFFECTING MORE THAN ONE FUND AND/OR ACCOUNT GROUP

Illustrative Problems 23.1 through 23.5 demonstrated that some transactions are recorded in more than one of the governmental funds and/or account groups. These transactions were identified in the Illustrative Problems by numbers. Exhibit 23-12 is a summary of the transactions and events that affected more than one fund and/or account group for the city of Railburg.

EXHIBIT 23-12

Illustrative Problems 23.1 through 23.5
Summary of Transactions and Events
Affecting More Than One Fund or Account Group

No.	Originating Fund	Transaction or Event	Capital Projects Fund	Debt Service Fund	General Fixed Asset Account Group	General Long-term Debt Account Group
2.	General Fund	Recorded Transfer Budgeted Due Debt Service Fund		Recorded Transfer Due		
8.	General Fund	Recorded Receipt of Office Furniture			Recorded Office Furniture	
9.	General Fund	Recorded Receipt of Emergency Aid Van and Police Cars			Recorded Emergency Aid Van and Police Cars	
14.	General Fund	Recorded Transfer of Bond Principal and Interest to Debt Service Fund		Recorded Receipt of Transfer		Recorded Principal Only
15.	General Fund	Recorded Transfer of Cash to Capital Projects Fund for Police Station Addition	Recorded Receipt of Cash			
15.	Capital Projects Fund	Recorded Payment of Architect's Fee for Fire Station Addition			Recorded Construction in Process	
18.	Capital Projects Fund	Recorded Bond Proceeds as Other Financing Source				Recorded Bond Principal as a Liability

Illustrative Problems 23.1 through 23.5
Summary of Transactions and Events
Affecting More Than One Fund or Account Group Continued

No.	Originating Fund	Transaction or Event	Capital Projects Fund	Debt Service Fund	General Fixed Asset Account Group	General Long-term Debt Account Group
18.	Capital Projects Fund	Recorded Transfer of Bond Premium to Debt Service Fund		Recorded Receipt of Cash		Recorded Amount Available for Debt Principal Payment
22.	Capital Projects Fund	Recorded Transfer of Interest Earned to Debt Service Fund		Recorded Receipt of Cash		Recorded Amount Available for Debt Principal Payment
22.	Capital Projects Fund	Recorded Payment of Progress Billings on Addition to Fire Station			Recorded Construction in Process	
23.	Debt Service Fund	Recorded Revenue from Property Taxes for Payment of Debt Principal				Recorded Amount Available for Debt Principal Payment
24.	Debt Service Fund	Recorded Payment of Serial Bond Principal and Interest				Recorded Payment of Serial Bond Principal

PROPRIETARY FUNDS

The proprietary funds consist of enterprise funds and internal service funds. These funds are called proprietary funds because they function like business entities, charging a price or fee for the product or service that is directly related to the cost of the product or service. The enterprise funds account for activities that serve the general public, charging a fee designed either to cover a portion of the cost of the product or service or to make a profit. If the fee charged is not sufficient to cover the costs and provide for profit, the activity may be accounted for in an enterprise fund to allow the determination of the total amount of the expense of the service and the amount of the subsidy of the service by the governmental unit. For example, a city may operate a public swimming pool and charge an admission fee that only covers 40% of the costs of operation and maintenance. The most common enterprise funds are for utilities such as water, sewer, electricity, and gas. Internal service funds account for activities that serve the other departments in the same governmental unit or other governmental units such as a central motor pool or a central computing center. These internal service funds charge a fee designed to cover costs and provide for capital maintenance.

Proprietary funds use the accrual basis of accounting as the measurement of net income and the maintenance of capital are the objectives of these funds. Revenues and expenses are recorded and measured just as they are in a business enterprise. When an internal service fund provides goods or services to another governmental fund, revenue is recognized. Remember, transfers between the governmental funds are not recognized as revenue or expenditures, but are referred to as other financing sources and uses.

The sale of goods and services by an internal service or enterprise fund to another governmental unit is an example of a **quasi-external transaction.** Because measurement of income is important, these funds use expenses rather than expenditures and record depreciation. The proprietary funds account for their own noncurrent assets and long-term liabilities within the fund, just as business entities record all their assets and liabilities. Budgets are not recorded formally in the records of these funds, just as business enterprises do not record budgets within the formal accounting records. Proprietary funds usually do not use encumbrances.

The financial statements of proprietary funds are the same as the statements of business entities. The financial statements consist of a statement of revenues, expenses, and changes in retained earnings, a balance sheet, and a statement of changes in financial position. The cash basis is recommended for the statement of changes in financial position.

When a proprietary fund is established, cash is transferred from another fund, usually the general fund, or a grant is received from another governmental unit or bonds are issued. The initial cash transferred is entered into an equity account, **Contributed Capital: Governmental Unit** and is treated as a residual equity transfer by the general fund. The proprietary funds use the account, Retained Earnings, to record the accumulation of net income the same as business entities. If funds are loaned (advanced) to a proprietary fund by another fund of the governmental unit, such as the general fund, the loan is recorded as debt in the proprietary fund and recorded as an asset in the fund granting the advance.

ACCOUNTING METHODS OF ENTERPRISE FUNDS

Enterprise funds typically classify both revenues and expenses as either operating or nonoperating. Enterprise funds may receive assets whose use is restricted. If an enterprise fund has restricted assets, they are identified in the accounting records and reported as restricted assets with a corresponding liability or an appropriation of retained earnings. Revenue is not recognized when the assets are received. For example, a public utility may require customers to pay deposits before extending service and must refund the deposits when service is discontinued. These deposits are restricted assets, since they can only be used to pay refunds to customers.

Enterprise funds can also issue revenue bonds that require the principal to be repaid from operating revenues. The bond proceeds are restricted to a particular project and are a restricted asset. The earnings of the project are restricted to the repayment of the principal and interest on the bonds. The retained earnings of the enterprise fund is segregated to indicate the amount of earnings set aside for future interest and principal payments on the revenue bonds. The segregation is recorded as an appropriation of retained earnings.

Enterprise funds may also receive noncurrent assets by gift or contribution or by using funds received as grants from other governmental units. The assets are recorded at their fair market value and the value is credited to separate equity accounts. An enterprise fund can either record or not record depreciation expense for donated assets. An internal service fund has the option of either recording depreciation expense or adjusting the equity account for the depreciation of contributed asset.

ACCOUNTING METHODS OF INTERNAL SERVICE FUNDS

In addition to the purchase of noncurrent assets, an internal service fund may receive fixed assets by gift or contribution or by using funds supplied by other governmental unit's grants. When fixed assets are contributed to an internal service fund, the assets are recorded at their fair market value and a separate equity account such as **Contributions from Private Citizens** is credited. If fixed assets are acquired with monies received as grants, assets are recorded at their acquisition price and credited to a separate equity account such as **Contributions from State Grants.**

The depreciation of assets acquired either by gift or grant can be accounted for differently than the depreciation of assets purchased or constructed. Instead of debiting Depreciation Expense and thus, through the closing journal entry process, reducing Retained Earnings, the debit can be entered directly in the equity account that was credited when the asset was acquired. If the depreciation is charged directly to the equity account, the income of the period does not reflect depreciation on assets either acquired by donation or purchased with grant monies.

FIDUCIARY FUNDS

Fiduciary funds are used to account for assets that a governmental unit is holding and managing for others. The governmental unit is acting as either a trustee or agent for the owner(s) of the assets. Trust funds usually differ from agency funds primarily in the length of time the assets will be held. Agency funds are usually for short periods of time and trust funds are for longer periods of time, often indefinitely. Included in fiduciary funds are expendable trust funds, nonexpendable trust funds, pension trust funds, and agency funds.

EXPENDABLE TRUST FUNDS

An expendable trust fund is one in which both the principal and the income can be spent for the purposes designated by the donor and is like a restricted revenue fund. An expendable trust fund is accounted for by the modified accrual basis as capital maintenance is not the objective. The financial statements consist of a statement of revenues, expenditures, and changes in fund balances and a balance sheet.

UNEXPENDABLE TRUST FUNDS

An unexpendable trust fund is one in which the governmental unit must maintain the principal. An unexpendable trust fund either can permit the earnings to be expended, and is like an endowment fund, or may not permit the earnings to be expended. Just as in the accounting for endowment funds in Chapters 20, 21, and 22, and estates and trusts in Chapter 18, the gains and losses on the sales of assets are considered principal and are not included in income of unexpendable trust funds, but are adjustments to the principal of the trust fund.

An unexpendable trust fund is accounted for by the accrual method because capital maintenance is the goal. The accounting for an unexpendable trust fund whose income can be spent is identical to that illustrated for endowment funds in Chapters 20, 21, and 22. The accounting for unexpendable trust fund whose income cannot be spent is identical to the accounting for a loan fund of a not-for-profit college as illustrated in Chapter 22. The financial statements prepared for unexpendable trust funds consist of a statement of revenues, expenses, and changes in fund balances, a balance sheet, and a statement of changes in financial position on the cash basis. These statements are used because of the capital maintenance approach to accounting for these funds.

PENSION TRUST FUNDS

A pension trust fund is established to account for the contributions of employees and employers toward the retirement benefits of the governmental unit's employees. The pension trust fund can be a public employees' retirement system (PERS) that provides pension benefits to the employees of more than one governmental unit. For example, in Oregon almost all the public employees of the state are covered by a PERS operated at the state level. The equity accounts of a pension trust fund reflect the sources of the assets, such as contributions from employees, contributions from employers, and earnings of the trust fund assets. A pension trust fund is accounted for by the accrual method as capital maintenance is the goal. The financial statements for a pension trust fund are the same as for an unexpendable trust fund: a statement of revenues, expenses, and changes in fund balance, a balance sheet, and a statement of changes in financial position on the cash basis.

AGENCY FUNDS

Agency funds are deposits of cash and other assets that belong to another entity that the governmental unit has control over and responsibility for safekeeping. The most common type of agency fund is the property taxes collected by a county treasurer. The county treasurer places the tax payments received in an agency fund, and then disburses the tax revenues to the various governmental units within the county who were included in the tax levy. Agency funds have only assets and liabilities, and do not record revenues, expenditures, or transfers.

SUMMARY

Governmental units use the fund system of accounting. Governmental units use three general types of funds: governmental funds, proprietary funds, and fiduciary funds. The governmental funds consist of the general fund, the special revenue funds, capital projects funds, and debt service funds. In addition, two accounts groups are used to account for fixed assets and long-term debt that belong to the governmental unit as a whole. The proprietary funds, which are like business enterprises, are the enterprise funds and the internal service funds. The fiduciary funds are trust funds and agency funds.

Some funds of a governmental unit use accrual accounting and some use modified accrual accounting. In modified accrual accounting the emphasis is on financial resources and the use of the resources. When a fund is accounted for using the modified accrual system, the fund has only current assets and liabilities. If measurement of income and capital maintenance is the objective, the fund uses accrual accounting and records fixed assets and long-term debt. Exhibit 23-13 indicates the method of accounting for the various funds.

A governmental unit records budgets in the governmental fund and the special revenue funds because the motive is not profit making and because the emphasis is on the accountability and stewardship functions of public employees and elected officials. The other governmental funds can record budgets. Budgets are not recorded in the proprietary and fiduciary funds. In addition, a governmental unit records encumbrances in the governmental funds. An encumbrance is an order that has been placed and not yet received.

The primary source of revenue of a governmental unit is property taxes. Property taxes are recognized as revenue when they are measurable and available. Property tax revenue is recorded net of the estimated amount of uncollectible taxes and is adjusted for the difference between the amount estimated to be uncollectible and the actual amount of taxes not collected. When property taxes become delinquent according to state law, they and the related allowance are reclassified as delinquent. When, according to state law, a governmental unit forecloses on property for delinquent property taxes, any loss incurred is recognized.

Exhibit 23-13 summarizes the important information about the various funds of a governmental unit presented in the chapter. Appendix 23-A contains a complete set of financial statements for the city of Albany, Oregon for the year ended June 30, 1987.

REVIEW PROBLEM

The trial balances of the governmental fund and account groups of the city of Stevens on July 1, 1990 were

	Debit	Credit
General Fund		
Cash	$ 100,000	
Property Taxes Receivable: Delinquent	275,000	
Allowance for Uncollectible Delinquent Property Taxes		$ 60,000
State Liquor Tax Receivable	22,000	
Materials and Supplies Inventory	20,000	
Vouchers Payable		43,000
Fund Balance: Reserved for Materials and Supplies		20,000
Fund Balance: Reserved for Encumbrances		36,000
Unreserved Fund Balance		258,000

EXHIBIT 23-13

Governmental Units
(Cities, Counties, States, and Federal Government)

Funds and Account Groups	Governmental Funds	Account Groups	Proprietary Funds	Trust Funds	
Sources of GAAP	AICPA Audit Guides and Statements of Position; NCGA Statements and Interpretations; GASB Statements, Technical Bulletins, and Interpretations; FASB as applicable				
Funds and Account Groups Used	General Special Revenue Capital Projects Debt Service	General Fixed Assets General Long-term Debt	Enterprise Internal Service	Expendable	Unexpendable Pension
Basis of Accounting	Modified Accrual		Accrual	Modified Accrual	Accrual
Measurement Focus	Spending		Capital Maintenance	Spending	Capital Maintenance
Revenue Recognition Limitations	Must Be Available	None Recognized	None	Must be Available	None
Major Revenue Sources	Taxes and Grants	None	User Fees	Investments	Investments
Encumbrances	Yes	None	No	No	No
Expenditure/Expense	Expenditure	None Recognized	Expense	Expenditure	Expense
Estimated Bad Debts	Revenue Net of Estimate	None	Expense	Revenue Net of Estimate	Expense
Depreciation Recorded	No	No	Yes	Yes	Yes
Fixed Assets Recorded	No	General Fixed Assets	Yes	Yes	Yes
Construction Activities	Capital Projects Funds	No	Yes	No	No
Long-term Debt	No	General Long-term Debt	Yes	Yes	Yes
Interfund Transfers		No Transfers			
Operating	Other Financial Source/(Use)		Other Financial Source/(Use)	Other Financial Source/(Use)	Other Financial Source/(Use)
Reimbursement	Expenditure of Transferor Reduction of Expenditure of Transferee		Expense of Transferor Reduction of Expense of Transferee	Expenditure of Transferor Reduction of Expenditure of Transferee	Expense of Transferor Reduction of Expense of Transferee
Quasi-External	Expenditure of Transferor Revenue of Transferee		Expense of Transferor Revenue of Transferee	None	None
Residual Equity	Other Financial Source/(Use)		Contributed Capital	None	None
Financial Statements	Revenue, Expenditures, and Changes in Fund Balances Revenues, Expenditures, and Changes in Fund Balances: Budget to Actual Balance Sheet	Schedule of Changes Balance Sheet	Revenue, Expense and Changes in Equity Balance Sheet Statement of Changes in Financial Position on a Cash Basis	Revenue, Expenditures, and Changes in Fund Balances Revenues, Expenditures, and Changes in Fund Balances: Budget to Actual Balance Sheet	Revenue, Expense, and Changes in Equity Balance Sheet Statement of Changes in Financial Position on a Cash Basis

	Debit	Credit
Special Revenue Fund: Traffic and Parking Fines		
Cash	$ 10,000	
Traffic and Parking Fines Receivable	20,000	
Reserved Fund Balance		$ 30,000
Debt Service Fund		
Cash	10,000	
Short-term Investments	300,000	
Reserved Fund Balance		310,000
General Fixed Asset Account Group		
Land	200,000	
Buildings	5,200,000	
Improvements	2,100,000	
Equipment	2,900,000	
Investment in General Fixed Assets: General Fund Revenues		5,500,000
Investment in General Fixed Assets: Special Revenue Fund Revenues		250,000
Investment in General Fixed Assets: General Obligation Bonds		3,800,000
Investment in General Fixed Assets: Government Grants		850,000
Long-term Debt Account Group		
Amount Available in Debt Service Fund	310,000	
Amount To Be Provided for Retirement of General Obligation Bonds	2,040,000	
8% General Obligation Bonds		500,000
10% General Obligation Bonds		1,850,000
	$ 13,507,000	$ 13,507,000

The following summary transactions and events occurred during the fiscal year ended June 30, 1991:

1. A budget estimating revenues of $2,400,000, expenditures of $1,635,000, transfers to the debt service fund of $375,000 for interest and $200,000 for principal, and transfers of $165,000 to the capital projects fund for addition to a school was authorized. The estimated revenues were

Property Taxes	$ 2,000,000
Intergovernmental	160,000
Service Fees	75,000
Licenses and Permits	140,000
Fines and Forfeitures	25,000

The estimated expenditures were

General Government	$ 200,000
Public Safety	425,000
Highways and Streets	150,000
Sanitation	40,000
Health and Welfare	60,000
Culture and Recreation	50,000
Education	710,000

The expenditures include an appropriation for road equipment encumbered in the prior year.

2. The special revenue fund accounts for traffic and parking fines. A city ordinance requires that these fines be spent only for salaries for additional police personnel. The budget estimates that $140,000 of fines will be assessed during the current year, and $100,000 will be expended to cover salaries for additional police personnel.

3. The city levied property taxes of $2,100,000. The city estimates that 1% of the property taxes will not be collected.

4. The city earned revenue from the following sources during the fiscal year:

Revenues: Service Fees	$ 70,000
Revenues: State Liquor Tax	165,000

5. The city received revenue in cash of $148,000 from licenses and permits and $32,000 in cash from fines and forfeitures.

6. Traffic and parking fines of $144,000 were levied and $148,000 was collected in cash.

7. Liabilities of $1,439,000 were incurred by the general fund for routine expenditures that were not encumbered.

General Government	$ 160,000
Public Safety	415,000
Highways and Streets	145,000
Sanitation	38,000
Health and Welfare	59,000
Culture and Recreation	47,000
Education	575,000

Unencumbered expenditures of $110,000 were incurred for the additional police personnel by the special revenue fund.

8. The city of Stevens received road equipment costing $35,000, which had been ordered and recorded as a $36,000 encumbrance in the previous fiscal year.

9. The city of Stevens budgeted $165,000 of general fund revenues for the construction of an addition to the grade school in addition to the planned bond issue of $2,500,000 face value, 12% of general obligation bonds. The proceeds of the bond issue totaled $2,650,000.

10. The general fund's share of the school addition was transferred to the capital projects fund.

11. A contract for $2,665,000 was granted to Super Construction for the addition to the grade school. Equipment costing $125,000 was ordered for the addition and recorded in the general fund.

12. Equipment for the new classroom costing $100,000 was received. The equipment had been encumbered for $102,000.

13. Delinquent property taxes in the amount of $219,000 were collected and $10,000 in interest and penalties were also collected. The remaining taxes were determined to be uncollectible and will not be foreclosed.

14. Property taxes totaling $2,020,000 were collected. Service fees of $70,000 were received and $181,000 was received from the state liquor tax fund.

15. Vouchers totaling $1,560,000 were paid during the current year by the general fund and vouchers totaling $110,000 were paid by the special revenue fund.

16. Debt principal and interest totaling $575,000, as budgeted, was transferred to the debt service fund.

17. The inventory of materials and supplies, used entirely for general government, shows $22,000 on hand at the end of the year.

18. The property taxes currently due are now delinquent.

19. The bond proceeds were temporarily invested in short-term Treasury bills. The earnings on investments of the capital projects fund are to be transferred to the debt service fund.

20. Progress billings in the amount of $480,000 were received from the contractor.
21. Treasury bills totaling $300,000 were liquidated to pay the progress billings. Interest in the amount of $120,000 has been earned and received on the Treasury bills.
22. The progress billings were paid, net of a 5% retainage to be kept by the city of Stevens until the project is complete.
23. The investments of the debt service fund earned $30,000 that was received in cash.
24. Interest of $40,000 and principal of $500,000 were paid on the outstanding 8% general obligation bonds. Interest totaling $185,000 was paid on the outstanding 10% general obligation bonds. The first semiannual interest payment was paid on the bonds issued for the school addition.

Required

1. Prepare the budgetary, transaction, event, and adjusting entries for each of the funds and account groups of the city of Stevens for the year ended June 30, 1991, identifying the fund or account group for each entry and assuming only nonroutine expenditures are encumbered.
2. Prepare adjusted trial balances for the general fund and the special revenue fund.
3. Prepare the following financial statements:
   1) A combined statement of revenues, expenditures, and changes in fund balances: budget and actual for the general fund and the special revenue fund.
   2) A combined balance sheet for the general fund and the special revenue fund.
   3) A statement of revenues, expenditures, and changes in fund balances for both the capital projects fund and the debt service fund.
   4) A balance sheet for both the capital projects fund and the debt service fund.
   5) A schedule of fixed assets.
   6) A schedule of long-term debt.
4. Prepare the closing entries for each of the funds, assuming outstanding encumbrances are to be honored in the following year.
5. Describe the types of proprietary funds and fiduciary funds that the city of Stevens might have used. Indicate in your description the basis of accounting, the reason for the basis of accounting, the types of assets, liabilities, and equity accounts used, and the financial statements that are prepared for each type of fund.

QUESTIONS

1. Define a fund.
2. What are the three general types of funds used by a governmental unit and what are the funds within each type?
3. Explain why governmental funds only have current assets and current liabilities.
4. Why does a governmental unit use account groups and why are they called account groups rather than funds?
5. What are the sources of generally accepted accounting principles for governmental accounting and what body is currently responsible for establishing generally accepted accounting principles?
6. Describe the ways a governmental unit differs from a business enterprise.
7. Define modified accrual accounting. Which funds of a governmental unit use accrual accounting and which use modified accrual accounting?
8. What characteristics of a fund make the use of accrual accounting mandatory?
9. What characteristics of a fund make the use of accrual accounting illogical?

10. Which funds of a governmental unit must record their budgets and why?

11. Describe the funds that record depreciation and why they record depreciation.

12. List the financial statements that are included in general-purpose financial statements of a governmental unit.

13. Describe the statements and other information included in a comprehensive annual financial report (CAFR).

14. Describe the control accounts debited and credited in recording the budget of the general fund.

15. Explain why transfers in and out that are budgeted are recorded as receivables and payables at the beginning of the year.

16. Describe the sources of revenue of the general fund and indicate which are recorded by the modified accrual method and which are recorded by the cash method.

17. Explain why no provision for uncollectible accounts is recorded and how revisions in estimates of uncollectibility are treated and why.

18. Describe an encumbrance and indicate when it is recorded and when it is reversed.

19. Why does the general fund use the term expenditures rather than expenses?

20. When are expenditures recorded in the governmental funds and what are the two common exceptions?

21. What are the two ways that inventories and prepaid items can be recorded and how do the adjusting entries differ?

22. Describe the funds and account groups affected and the entries to be recorded in those funds when equipment is ordered and received by the general fund.

23. Describe the closing journal entries of the general fund.

24. Explain the purpose of special revenue funds.

25. How does a special revenue fund differ from an enterprise fund?

26. What governmental fund does accounting for a special revenue fund replicate? What not-for-profit fund does the accounting for a special revenue fund replicate?

27. Describe how the revenues, expenditures, and changes in fund balances of a special revenue fund are reported.

28. What are capital projects funds used for?

29. Describe how the proceeds from a bond issue are treated in a capital projects fund and the treatment of original issue bond premium and bond discount.

30. Explain why fixed assets are not recorded in a capital projects fund.

31. Explain how interest earned on investments of a capital projects fund is recorded and, if it is transferred to another fund, why the transfer is made?

32. What is the purpose of a debt service fund?

33. Describe when debt is recorded in the debt service fund.

34. Describe the types of entries that are recorded in a debt service fund.

35. Describe the categories used for assets in the general fixed asset account group.

36. Explain the accounting treatment of the sale of fixed assets and the funds in which the transaction is recorded.

37. Explain what infrastructure is and why some governmental units do not record their infrastructure.

38. Describe the typical accounts to be found in the general long-term debt account group and what types of transactions change the balance of those accounts.

39. List two types of transactions for the general fund, the capital projects fund, and debt service fund that would be recorded in at least one other fund or account group and indicate the fund or account group affected.

40. Describe the two types of proprietary funds and differentiate between them.

41. Describe the basis of accounting for proprietary funds, and explain how the basis results in the assets and liabilities being different from governmental funds.

42. Explain a quasi-external transaction and how it is recorded.

43. Explain the equity of each type of proprietary fund.

44. Describe the two most common sources of restricted assets for an enterprise fund and the accounting treatment of the assets.

45. List the types of fiduciary funds and describe the basis of accounting for each type of fund.

EXERCISES

EXERCISE 23-1

1. A debt service fund of a municipality is an example of which of the following types of funds?

a. Fiduciary
b. Governmental
c. Proprietary
d. Internal Service

2. A capital projects fund of a municipality is an example of what type of fund?

a. Internal Service
b. Proprietary
c. Fiduciary
d. Governmental

3. The special revenue fund of a governmental unit is an example of what type of fund?

a. Governmental
b. Proprietary
c. Internal Service
d. Fiduciary

4. Which type of fund can be either expendable or unexpendable?

a. Debt Service
b. Enterprise
c. Special Revenue
d. Trust

(AICPA adapted)

EXERCISE 23-2

1. Which of the following funds of a governmental unit uses the same basis of accounting as an enterprise fund?

a. Special Revenue
b. Internal Service
c. Expendable Trust
d. Capital Projects

2. A state governmental unit should use which basis of accounting for each of the following types of funds?

	Governmental	Proprietary
a.	Cash	Modified Accrual
b.	Modified Accrual	Modified Accrual
c.	Modified Accrual	Accrual
d.	Accrual	Accrual

3. For state and local governmental units, the full accrual basis of accounting should be used for what type of fund?

a. Special Revenue
b. General
c. Debt Service
d. Internal Service

4. Which of the following funds of a governmental unit uses the modified accrual basis of accounting?

a. Debt Service
b. Internal Service
c. Enterprise
d. Unexpendable Trust

5. Which of the following is an appropriate basis of accounting for a governmental fund of a governmental unit?

	Cash Basis	Modified Accrual Basis
a.	Yes	No
b.	Yes	Yes
c.	No	Yes
d.	No	No

6. Which of the following is an appropriate basis of accounting for a proprietary fund of a governmental unit?

	Cash Basis	Modified Accrual Basis
a.	Yes	Yes
b.	Yes	No
c.	No	No
d.	No	Yes

7. Which of the following funds of a governmental unit recognizes revenues and expenditures under the same basis of accounting as the general fund?

a. Debt Service
b. Enterprise
c. Internal Service
d. Nonexpendable Pension Trust

8. Under which basis of accounting for a governmental unit should revenues be recognized in the accounting period in which they are earned and measurable?

	Accrual Basis	Modified Accrual Basis
a.	No	No
b.	No	Yes
c.	Yes	Yes
d.	Yes	No

9. Under the modified accrual basis of accounting for a governmental unit, revenues should be recognized in the accounting period in which they

a. Become available and earned
b. Become available and measurable
c. Are earned and become measurable
d. Are collected

(AICPA adapted)

EXERCISE 23-3

1. Which of the following is most likely to use an encumbrance system?

a. General Fund
b. Internal Service Fund
c. General Fixed Asset Group of Accounts
d. Enterprise Fund

2. Encumbrances would not appear in which fund?

a. General
b. Enterprise
c. Capital Projects
d. Special Revenue

3. Which of the following funds of a governmental unit integrates budgetary accounts into the accounting system?

a. Enterprise
b. Special Revenue
c. Internal Service
d. Unexpendable Trust

4. When the budget of a governmental unit is adopted, and the estimated revenues exceed the appropriations, the excess is

a. Credited to BUDGETARY FUND BALANCE
b. Debited to BUDGETARY FUND BALANCE
c. Credited to Reserve for Encumbrances
d. Debited to Reserve for Encumbrances

5. The ESTIMATED REVENUES account of a governmental unit is credited when

a. The budget is closed out at the end of the year
b. The budget is recorded
c. Property taxes are recorded
d. Property taxes are collected

6. The ESTIMATED REVENUES account of a governmental unit is debited when

a. The budget is closed out at the end of the year
b. The budget is recorded
c. Actual revenues are recorded
d. Actual revenues are collected

7. The ENCUMBRANCE account of a governmental unit is debited when

a. A purchase order is approved
b. Goods are received
c. A voucher payable is recorded
d. The budget is recorded

8. Which of the following accounts of a governmental unit is credited when the budget is recorded?

a. ENCUMBRANCES
b. FUND BALANCE RESERVED FOR ENCUMBRANCES
c. Vouchers Payable
d. APPROPRIATIONS

(AICPA adapted)

EXERCISE 23-4
1. Revenue of a special revenue fund of a governmental unit should be recognized in the period in which the

a. Revenues become available and measurable
b. Revenues become available for appropriation
c. Revenues are billable
d. Cash is received

2. Which of the following types of revenue would generally be recorded directly in the general fund of a governmental unit?

a. Receipts from city-owned parking structure
b. Interest earned on investments held for retirement of employees
c. Revenues from internal service funds
d. Property taxes

3. The Revenues Control account of a governmental unit is debited when

a. The budget is recorded at the beginning of the year
b. The account is closed out at the end of the year
c. Property taxes are recorded
d. Property taxes are collected

(AICPA adapted)

EXERCISE 23-5
1. Which of the following accounts of a governmental unit is credited when a purchase order is approved?

a. FUND BALANCE RESERVED FOR ENCUMBRANCES
b. ENCUMBRANCES
c. Vouchers Payable
d. APPROPRIATIONS

2. If repairs have been made for a governmental unit and a bill has been received, the repairs should be recorded in the general fund as a debit to an

a. Expenditure
b. ENCUMBRANCE
c. Expense
d. APPROPRIATION

3. Which of the following accounts of a governmental unit is credited when supplies previously ordered are received?

a. FUND BALANCE RESERVED FOR ENCUMBRANCES
b. ENCUMBRANCES
c. Expenditures
d. APPROPRIATIONS

4. When goods that have been previously approved for purchase are received by a governmental unit, but have not yet been paid for, what account is credited?

a. FUND BALANCE RESERVED FOR ENCUMBRANCES
b. Vouchers Payable
c. Expenditures
d. APPROPRIATIONS

5. Which of the following accounts of a governmental unit is debited when supplies previously ordered are received?

a. ENCUMBRANCES
b. FUND BALANCE RESERVED FOR ENCUMBRANCES
c. Voucher Payable
d. APPROPRIATIONS

6. When supplies ordered by a governmental unit are received at an actual price less than the estimated price on the purchase order, the ENCUMBRANCE account is

a. Credited for the estimated price on the purchase order
b. Credited for the actual price for the supplies received
c. Debited for the estimated price on the purchase order
d. Debited for the actual price for the supplies received

7. The APPROPRIATIONS account of a governmental unit is credited when

a. Supplies are purchased
b. Expenditures are recorded
c. The budget is recorded
d. The budgetary accounts are closed

8. The expenditures account of a governmental unit is debited when

a. The budgetary accounts are closed
b. The budget is recorded
c. Supplies are purchased
d. Supplies previously encumbered are received

9. At the end of the fiscal year of a governmental unit, the excess of expenditures and encumbrances over appropriations

a. Increases the fund balance
b. Decreases the fund balance
c. Increases the reserve for encumbrances
d. Decreases the reserve for encumbrances

10. The APPROPRIATIONS account of a governmental unit is debited when

a. The budgetary accounts are closed
b. The budget is recorded
c. Supplies are purchased
d. Expenditures are recorded

(AICPA adapted)

EXERCISE 23-6

1. When fixed assets purchased from general fund revenues were received, the appropriate journal entry was recorded in the general fixed asset account group. What account, if any, should have been debited in the general fund?

a. No journal entry should have been made to the general fund
b. Fixed Assets
c. Expenditures
d. Due from General Fixed Asset Account Group

2. When a truck is received by a governmental unit, the truck should be recorded in the general fixed asset account group as a debit to a(an)

a. APPROPRIATION
b. ENCUMBRANCE
c. Fixed Asset
d. Expenditure

EXERCISE 23-7

1. Which of the following funds of a governmental unit would include retained earnings in its balance sheet?

a. Expendable Pension Trust
b. Internal Service
c. Special Revenue
d. Capital Projects

2. Which of the following accounts could be included in the balance sheet of an enterprise fund?

	Reserve for Encumberances	Revenue Bonds Payable	Retained Earnings
a.	No	No	Yes
b.	No	Yes	Yes
c.	Yes	Yes	No
d.	No	No	No

3. Which of the following accounts would be included in the combined balance sheet for the long-term debt account group?

a. Amount To Be Provided for Retirement of General Long-term Debt
b. Unreserved Fund Balance
c. Fund Balance Reserved for Encumbrances
d. Cash

4. Customers' meter deposits, which cannot be spent for normal operating purposes, would be classified as restricted cash in the balance sheet of which fund?

a. Internal Service
b. Trust
c. Agency
d. Enterprise

5. The comprehensive annual financial report (CAFR) of a governmental unit should contain a combined statement of changes in financial position for

	Governmental Funds	Proprietary Funds
a.	No	Yes
b.	No	No
c.	Yes	No
d.	Yes	Yes

6. Which of the following funds of a governmental unit would account for general long-term debt in the accounts of the fund?

a. Special Revenue
b. Capital Projects
c. Internal Service
d. General

7. Which of the following would be included in the Combined Statement of Revenues, Expenditures, and Changes in Fund Balances: Budget and Actual in the comprehensive annual financial report (CAFR) of a governmental unit?

	Enterprise Fund	General Fixed Asset Account Group
a.	Yes	Yes
b.	Yes	No
c.	No	Yes
d.	No	No

8. Proceeds of General Obligation Bonds is an account of a governmental unit that would be included in the

a. Enterprise fund
b. Special Revenue fund
c. Capital Projects fund
d. Debt Service fund

9. Which of the following funds of a governmental unit would include contributed capital in its balance sheet?

a. Expendable Pension Trust
b. Special Revenue
c. Capital Projects
d. Internal Service

(AICPA adapted)

EXERCISE 23-8

1. The comprehensive annual financial report (CAFR) of a governmental unit should contain a combined statement of revenues, expenditures, and changes in fund balances for

	Governmental Funds	Account Groups
a.	Yes	Yes
b.	Yes	No
c.	No	No
d.	No	Yes

2. Which governmental fund or account group would account for fixed assets in a manner similar to a "for-profit" organization?

a. Enterprise
b. Capital Projects
c. General Fixed Asset Account Group
d. General

3. The comprehensive annual financial report (CAFR) of a governmental unit should contain a combined balance sheet for

	Governmental Funds	Proprietary Funds	Account Groups
a.	Yes	Yes	No
b.	Yes	Yes	Yes
c.	Yes	No	Yes
d.	No	Yes	No

4. Fixed assets used by a governmental unit should be accounted for in the

	Capital Projects Fund	General Fund
a.	No	Yes
b.	No	No
c.	Yes	No
d.	Yes	Yes

5. Fixed assets of an enterprise fund should be accounted for in the

a. General fixed asset account group but no depreciation on the fixed assets should be recorded
b. General fixed asset account group and depreciation on the fixed assets should be recorded
c. Enterprise fund but no depreciation on the fixed assets should be recorded
d. Enterprise fund and depreciation on the fixed assets should be recorded

6. The comprehensive annual financial report (CAFR) of a governmental unit should contain a combined statement of revenues, expenses, and changes in retained earnings for

	Governmental Funds	Proprietary Funds
a.	No	Yes
b.	No	No
c.	Yes	No
d.	Yes	Yes

7. How would customers' security deposits, which cannot be spent for normal operating purposes, be classified in the balance sheet of the enterprise fund of a governmental unit?

	Restricted Asset	Liability	Fund Equity
a.	Yes	No	Yes
b.	Yes	Yes	No
c.	Yes	Yes	Yes
d.	No	Yes	No

8. Which of the following funds of a governmental unit would account for depreciation in the accounts of the fund?

a. General
b. Internal Service
c. Capital Projects
d. Special Revenue

9. In the comprehensive annual financial report (CAFR) of a governmental unit, the account groups are included in

a. Both the combined balance sheet and the combined statement of revenues, expenditures, and changes in fund balances
b. The combined statement of revenues, expenditures, and changes in fund balances, but **not** the combined balance sheet
c. The combined balance sheet, but **not** the combined statement of revenues, expenditures, and changes in fund balances
d. Neither the combined balance sheet nor the combined statement of revenues, expenditures, and changes in fund balances

10. Which of the following accounts would be included in the fund equity section of the combined balance sheet of a governmental unit for the general fixed asset account group?

	Investment in General Fixed Assets	Fund Balance Reserved for Encumbrances
a.	Yes	Yes
b.	Yes	No
c.	No	No
d.	No	Yes

(AICPA adapted)

EXERCISE 23-9

1. Which of the following funds of a governmental unit would use the general long-term debt account group to account for unmatured general long-term liabilities?

a. Special Revenue
b. Capital Projects
c. Trust
d. Internal Service

2. Which of the following funds of a governmental unit would use the general fixed assets account group to account for fixed assets?

a. Internal Service
b. Enterprise
c. Unexpendable Trust
d. Special Revenue

3. Fixed assets used by a city-owned utility are accounted for in which of the following?

	Enterprise Fund	General Fixed Assets Group of Accounts
a.	No	No
b.	No	Yes
c.	Yes	No
d.	Yes	Yes

4. Long-term liabilities of an enterprise fund should be accounted for in the

	Enterprise Fund	Long-term Debt Account Group
a.	No	No
b.	No	Yes
c.	Yes	Yes
d.	Yes	No

5. Fixed assets should be accounted for in the general fixed assets account group for

	Governmental Funds	Proprietary Funds
a.	No	Yes
b.	No	No
c.	Yes	No
d.	Yes	Yes

6. Fixed assets should be accounted for in the general fixed assets account group for the

	Capital Projects Fund	Internal Service Fund
a.	Yes	Yes
b.	Yes	No
c.	No	No
d.	No	Yes

(AICPA adapted)

EXERCISE 23-10

1. Which of the following accounts of a governmental unit is (are) closed at the end of a fiscal year?

	ESTIMATED REVENUES	Fund Balance
a.	No	No
b.	No	Yes
c.	Yes	Yes
d.	Yes	No

2. Which of the following accounts of a governmental unit is closed at the end of the fiscal year?

a. Fund Balance
b. Fund Balance Reserved for Encumbrances
c. APPROPRIATIONS
d. Vouchers Payable

(AICPA adapted)

EXERCISE 23-11

1. The following assets are among those owned by the City of Foster:

Apartment building (part of the principal of an unexpendable trust fund)	$ 200,000
City hall	800,000
Three fire stations	1,000,000
City streets and sidewalks	5,000,000

What amount should be included in Foster's general fixed asset account group?

a. $1,800,000 or $6,800,000
b. $2,000,000 or $7,000,000
c. $6,800,000 without election of $1,800,000
d. $7,000,000 without election of $2,000,000

2. The following items were among Kew Township's expenditures from the general fund during the year ended July 31, 1991:

Minicomputer for tax collector's office	$ 22,000
Furniture for Township Hall	40,000

What amount should be classified as fixed assets in Kew's general fund balance sheet at July 31, 1991?

a. $ —0—
b. $ 22,000
c. $ 40,000
d. $ 62,000

3. The following balances are included in the subsidiary records of Burwood Village's Parks and Recreation Department at March 31, 1991:

Appropriations: Supplies	$ 7,500
Expenditures: Supplies	4,500
Encumbrances: Supply Orders	750

What amount does the Department have available for additional purchases of supplies?

a. $ —0—
b. $ 2,250
c. $ 3,000
d. $ 6,750

Items 4 and 5 are based on the following information:

The following events relating to the city of Albury's debt service funds occurred during the year ended December 31, 1991:

Debt principal matured	$ 2,000,000
Unmatured (accrued) interest on outstanding debt at January 1, 1991	50,000
Interest on matured debt	900,000
Unmatured (accrued) interest on outstanding debt at December 31, 1991	100,000
Interest revenue from investments	600,000
Cash transferred from general fund for retirement of debt principal	1,000,000
Cash transferred from general fund for payment of matured interest	900,000

All principal and interest due in 1991 were paid on time.

4. What is the total amount of expenditures that Albury's debt service funds should record for the year ended December 31, 1991?

a. $ 900,000
b. $ 950,000
c. $ 2,900,000
d. $ 2,950,000

5. How much revenue should Albury's debt service funds record for the year ended December 31, 1991?

a. $ 600,000
b. $ 1,600,000
c. $ 1,900,000
d. $ 2,500,000

6. The Board of Commissioners of the City of Rockton adopted its budget for the year ending July 31, 1991, which indicated revenues of $1,000,000 and appropriations of $900,000. If the budget is formally integrated into the accounting records, what is the required journal entry?

a. Memorandum entry only

b. APPROPRIATIONS   900,000
   BUDGETARY FUND BALANCE   100,000   1,000,000
     ESTIMATED REVENUES

c. ESTIMATED REVENUES   1,000,000   900,000
   APPROPRIATIONS   100,000
     BUDGETARY FUND BALANCE

d. REVENUES RECEIVABLE   1,000,000   900,000
   EXPENDITURES PAYABLE   100,000
     BUDGETARY FUND BALANCE

7. Kingsford City incurred $100,000 of salaries and wages for the month ended March 31, 1991. The journal entry at that date is:

a. Expenditures: Salaries and Wages   100,000   100,000
   Vouchers Payable

b. Salaries and Wages Expense   100,000   100,000
   Vouchers Payable

c. Encumbrances: Salaries and Wages   100,000   100,000
   Vouchers Payable

d. Fund Balance   100,000   100,000
   Vouchers Payable

Items 8 and 9 are based on the following information:

During the year ended December 31, 1991, Leyland City received a state grant of $500,000 to finance the purchase of busses, and an additional grant of $100,000 to aid in the financing of bus operations in 1991. Only $300,000 of the capital grant was used in 1991 for the purchase of buses, but the entire operating grant of $100,000 was spent in 1991.

8. If Leyland's bus transportation system is accounted for as part of the city's general fund, how much should Leyland report as grant revenues for the year ended December 31, 1991?

a. $ 100,000
b. $ 300,000
c. $ 400,000
d. $ 500,000

9. If Leyland's bus transportation system is accounted for as an enterprise fund, how much should Leyland report as grant revenues for the year ended December 31, 1991?

a. $ 100,000
b. $ 300,000
c. $ 400,000
d. $ 500,000

10. Ariel Village issued the following bonds during the year ended June 30, 1991:

Revenue bonds to be repaid from admission fees collected from the Ariel Zoo enterprise fund	$ 200,000
General obligation bonds issued for the Ariel water and sewer enterprise fund, which will service the debt	300,000

How much of these bonds should be accounted for in Ariel's general long-term debt account group?

a. $ −0−
b. $ 200,000
c. $ 300,000
d. $ 500,000

(AICPA adapted)

EXERCISE 23-12

Items 1 and 2 are based on the following information:

On December 31, 1991, Madrid Township paid a contractor $2,000,000 for the total cost of a new firehouse built in 1991 on township-owned land. The firehouse was financed with a $1,500,000 general obligation bond issue sold at face amount on December 31, 1991 and $500,000 transferred from the general fund.

1. What should be reported on Madrid's 1991 financial statements for the capital project fund?

a. Revenues, $1,500,000; Expenditures, $1,500,000
b. Revenues, $1,500,000; Other Financing Sources $500,000; Expenditures $2,000,000
c. Revenues, $2,000,000; Expenditures, $2,000,000
d. Other Financing Sources $2,000,000; Expenditures, $2,000,000

2. What should be reported on Madrid's 1991 financial statements for the general fund?

a. Expenditures, $500,000
b. Other Financing Uses, $500,000
c. Revenues, $1,500,000; Expenditures, $2,000,000
d. Revenues, $1,500,000; Other Financing Uses, $200,000

Items 3 and 4 are based on the following information:

The following balances appeared in the City of Reedsbury's general fund at June 30, 1991:

Account	Balance Dr. (Cr.)
Encumbrances: Current Year	$ 200,000
Expenditures: Current Year	3,000,000
Expenditures: Prior Year	100,000
Fund Balance Reserved for Encumbrances: Current Year	(200,000)
Fund Balance Reserved for Encumbrances: Prior Year	None

Reedbury maintains its general fund books on a legal budgetary basis, requiring revenues and expenditures to be accounted for on a modified accrual basis. In addition, the sum of current year expenditures and encumbrances cannot exceed current year appropriations.

3. What total amount of expenditures (and encumbrances, if appropriate) should Reedsbury report in the general fund column of its combined statement of revenues, expenditures, and changes in fund balance for the year ended June 30, 1991?

a. $ 3,000,000
b. $ 3,100,000
c. $ 3,200,000
d. $ 3,300,000

4. What total amount of expenditures (and encumbrances, if appropriate) should Reedsbury report in the general fund "actual" column of its combined statement of revenues, expenditures, and changes in fund balance: budget and actual for the year ended June 30, 1991?

a. $ 3,000,000
b. $ 3,100,000
c. $ 3,200,000
d. $ 3,300,000

5. Fred Bosin donated a building to Palma City in 1991. Bosin's original cost of the property was $100,000. Accumulated depreciation at the date of the gift was $60,000. Fair market value at the date of the gift was $300,000. In the general fixed assets account group, at what amount should Palma record this donated fixed asset?

a. $ 300,000
b. $ 100,000
c. $ 40,000
d. $ –0–

Items 6 and 7 are based on the following data relating to Lely Township:

Printing and binding equipment used for servicing all of Lely's departments and agencies, on a cost-reimbursement basis	$ 100,000
Equipment used for supplying water to Lely's residents	900,000
Cash received from Federal government, dedicated to highway maintenance, which must be accounted for in a separate fund	995,000

6. How much should be accounted for in a special revenue fund or funds?

a. $ 995,000
b. $ 1,050,000
c. $ 1,095,000
d. $ 2,045,000

7. How much could be accounted for in an internal service fund?

a. $ 100,000
b. $ 900,000
c. $ 950,000
d. $ 995,000

Items 8, 9, and 10 are based on the following data:

The Board of Commissioners of Vane City adopted its budget for the year ended July 31, 1991, comprising estimated revenues of $30,000,000 and appropriations of $29,000,000. Vane formally integrates its budget into the accounting records.

8. What entry should be made for budgeted revenues?

a. Memorandum entry only
b. Debit ESTIMATED REVENUES RECEIVABLE $30,000,000
c. Debit ESTIMATED REVENUES $30,000,000
d. Credit ESTIMATED REVENUES $30,000,000

9. What entry should be made for budgeted appropriations?

a. Memorandum entry only
b. Credit ESTIMATED EXPENDITURES PAYABLE $29,000,000
c. Credit APPROPRIATIONS $29,000,000
d. Debit ESTIMATED EXPENDITURES $29,000,000

10. What entry should be made for the budgeted excess of revenues over expenditures?

a. Memorandum entry only
b. Credit BUDGETARY FUND BALANCE, $1,000,000
c. Debit ESTIMATED EXCESS REVENUES $1,000,000
d. Debit EXCESS REVENUES RECEIVABLE $1,000,000

11. Albee Township's fiscal year ends on June 30. Albee uses encumbrance accounting. On April 4, 1991, an approved $1,000 purchase order was issued for supplies. Albee received these supplies on May 2, 1991, and the $1,000 invoice was approved for payment. What journal entry should Albee make on April 4, 1991, to record the approved purchase order?

a. Memorandum entry only

b. ENCUMBRANCES CONTROL   1,000   1,000
      FUND BALANCE RESERVED FOR ENCUMBRANCES

c. Supplies   1,000   1,000
      Vouchers Payable

d. ENCUMBRANCES CONTROL   1,000   1,000
      APPROPRIATIONS CONTROL

(AICPA adapted)

EXERCISE 23-13

The special revenue fund of the city of Brill is used to account for state tax sharing revenues, which must be expended for education according to state law. The budget estimates that $230,000 will be distributed to the city by the state during the current year and $250,000 will be spent for authorized expenditures during the year. The trial balance of the special revenue fund as of July 1, 1990 is

	Debit	Credit
Cash	$ 10,000	
Revenue Sharing Receivable	20,000	
Vouchers Payable		$ 6,000
Restricted Fund Balance		24,000

During the current year, the city of Brill's share of the earned state revenues is $238,000. The state remitted $242,000 to the city. Expenditures meeting the state requirements for education totaled $214,000. Vouchers totaling $215,000 were paid.

Required

1. Prepare the budgetary and transaction entries for the special revenue fund.
2. Prepare the adjusted trial balance of the special revenue fund.
3. Describe how the accounts of the special revenue fund are reported in the financial statements of the city of Brill.

PROBLEMS

PROBLEM 23-1

Governmental accounting gives substantial recognition to budgets, with those budgets being recorded in the accounts of the governmental unit.

Required

1. What is the purpose of a governmental accounting system and why is the budget recorded in the accounts of a governmental unit? Include in your discussion the purpose and significance of appropriations.
2. Describe when and how a governmental unit records its budget and closes the budgetary accounts.

(AICPA adapted)

PROBLEM 23-2

The accounting system of the municipality of Kemp is organized and operated on a fund basis. Among the types of funds used are a general fund, a special revenue fund, and an enterprise fund.

Required

1. Explain the basic differences in revenue recognition between the accrual basis of accounting and the modified accrual basis of accounting as it relates to governmental accounts.
2. Explain the basis of accounting that should be used and the reason for the basis for each of the following funds:
   a. General fund
   b. Special revenue fund
   c. Enterprise fund
3. How should fixed assets and long-term liabilities related to the general fund and to the enterprise fund be accounted for?
4. How should the balance sheets of the general fund, the special revenue fund, and the enterprise fund be handled when preparing the comprehensive annual financial report (CAFR)? Why?

(AICPA adapted)

PROBLEM 23-3

The following information was abstracted from the accounts of the General Fund of the City of Rom after the books had been closed for the fiscal year ended June 30, 1991:

	Postclosing Trial Balance June 30, 1990	Transactions July 1, 1990 to June 30, 1991 Debit	Transactions July 1, 1990 to June 30, 1991 Credit	Postclosing Trial Balance June 30, 1991
Cash	$ 700,000	$ 1,820,000	$ 1,852,000	$ 668,000
Taxes Receivable	40,000	1,870,000	1,828,000	82,000
	$ 740,000			$ 750,000
Allowance for Uncollectible Taxes	$ 8,000	8,000	10,000	$ 10,000
Vouchers Payable	132,000	1,852,000	1,840,000	120,000
Fund Balance Reserved for Encumbrances	–0–	1,000,000	1,070,000	70,000
Unreserved Fund Balance	600,000	140,000	60,000	550,000
			30,000	
	$ 740,000			$ 750,000

Additional Information

The budget for the fiscal year ended June 30, 1991, provided for estimated revenues of $2,000,000 and appropriations of $1,940,000. The city of Rom debits Unreserved Fund Balance in recording the budget entry and closes the budgeted revenues to the actual revenues and the budgeted appropriations and encumbrances to the actual expenditures.

Required

Prepare journal entries to record the budgeted and actual transactions for the fiscal year ended June 30, 1991.

(AICPA adapted)

PROBLEM 23-4

The following financial activities affecting Judbury City's general fund occurred during the year ended June 30, 1991:

1. The following budget was adopted:

Estimated Revenues	
Property Taxes	$ 4,500,000
Licenses and Permits	300,000
Fines	200,000
Total	$ 5,000,000
Appropriations	
General Government	$ 1,500,000
Police Services	1,200,000
Fire Department Services	900,000
Public Works Services	800,000
Acquisition of Fire Engines	400,000
Total	$ 4,800,000

2. Property tax bills totaling $4,650,000 were mailed. It was estimated that $300,000 of this amount will be delinquent, and $150,000 will be uncollectible.
3. Property taxes totaling $3,900,000 were collected. The $150,000 previously estimated to be uncollectible remained unchanged, but $600,000 was reclassified as delinquent. It is estimated that delinquent taxes will be collected soon enough after June 30, 1991 to make these taxes available to finance obligations incurred during the year ended June 30, 1991. There was no balance of uncollected taxes at July 1, 1990.
4. Tax anticipation notes in the face amount of $300,000 were issued.
5. Other cash collections were

Licenses and Permits	$ 270,000
Fines	200,000
Sale of Public Works Equipment (original cost, $75,000)	15,000
Total	$ 485,000

6. The following purchase orders were executed:

	Total	Outstanding at 6/30/91
General Government	$ 1,050,000	$ 60,000
Police Services	300,000	30,000
Fire Department Services	150,000	15,000
Public Works Services	250,000	10,000
Fire Engines	400,000	
Totals	$ 2,150,000	$ 115,000

No encumbrances were outstanding at June 30, 1990.

7. The following vouchers were approved:

General Government	$ 1,440,000
Police Services	1,155,000
Fire Department Services	870,000
Public Works Services	700,000
Fire Engines	400,000
Total	$ 4,565,000

8. Vouchers totaling $4,600,000 were paid.

Required
Prepare journal entries to record the foregoing financial activities in the general fund. Ignore interest accruals.

(AICPA adapted)

PROBLEM 23-5
The general fund trial balance of the city of Solna at December 31, 1990 was

	Debit	Credit
Cash	$ 62,000	
Property Taxes Receivable: Delinquent	46,000	
Allowance for Uncollectible Property Taxes: Delinquent		$ 8,000
Stores Inventory: Program Operations	18,000	
Vouchers Payable		28,000
Fund Balance Reserved for Stores Inventory		18,000
Fund Balance Reserved for Encumbrances		12,000
Unreserved Fund Balance		60,000
	$ 126,000	$ 126,000

Collectible delinquent taxes are expected to be collected within 60 days after the end of the year. Solna used the "purchases" method to account for stores inventory. The following data pertain to 1991 general fund operations:

1. Budget adopted:

Revenue and Other Financing Sources	
Property Taxes	$ 220,000
Fines, Forfeitures, and Penalties	80,000
Miscellaneous Revenues	100,000
Share of Bond Issue Proceeds	200,000
	$ 600,000

Expenditures and Other Financing Uses	
Program Operations	$ 300,000
General Administration	120,000
Stores: Program Operations	60,000
Capital Outlay	80,000
Periodic Transfer to Debt Service Fund	20,000
	$ 580,000

2. Property taxes were assessed at an amount that would result in revenues of $220,800 after deduction of 4% of the tax levy as uncollectible.

3. Orders placed but not received:

Program Operations	$ 176,000
General Administration	80,000
Capital Outlay	48,000
	$ 304,000

4. Cash collection and transfer:

Delinquent Property Taxes	$ 38,000
Current Property Taxes	226,000
Refund of Overpayment of Invoice for Purchase of Equipment	4,000
Fines, Forfeits, and Penalties	88,000
Miscellaneous Revenues	90,000
Share of Bond Issue Proceeds	200,000
Transfer of Remaining Fund Balance of a Discontinued Fund	18,000
	$ 664,000

5. Canceled encumbrances:

	Estimated	Actual
Program Operations	$ 156,000	$ 166,000
General Administration	84,000	80,000
Capital Outlay: Current Year	50,000	50,000
Capital Outlay: Prior Year	12,000	12,000
	$ 302,000	$ 308,000

6. Additional vouchers:

Program Operations	$ 188,000
General Administration	38,000
Capital Outlay	18,000
	$ 244,000

7. Albert, a taxpayer, overpaid his 1991 taxes by $2,000. He applied for a $2,000 credit against his 1992 taxes. The city council granted his request.

8. Vouchers paid totaled $560,000 and $20,000 was transferred to the debt service fund.

9. Stores inventory at December 31, 1991 was $12,000.

10. Current property taxes receivable are now delinquent.

Required

1. Prepare journal entries to record the transactions and events of the city of Solna.

2. Prepare the statement of revenues, expenditures, and changes in fund balance: budget to actual for the year ended December 31, 1991 and the balance sheet at December 31, 1991 for the general fund of the city of Solna. An adjusted trial balance or selected "T" accounts may be helpful.

3. Prepare the closing journal entries for the city of Solna.

(AICPA adapted)

PROBLEM 23-6

The city of Amber accounts for its general fund according to generally accepted accounting principles. The city's policy is to encumber only nonroutine expenditures. On July 1, 1990, the trial balance of the general fund was

	Debit	Credit
Cash	$ 60,000	
Property Taxes Receivable: Delinquent	50,000	
Allowance for Uncollectible Delinquent Property Taxes		$ 20,000
Materials and Supplies Inventory	25,000	
Vouchers Payable		31,000
Fund Balance: Reserved for Materials and Supplies		25,000
Fund Balance: Reserved for Encumbrances		18,000
Unreserved Fund Balance		41,000
	$ 135,000	$ 135,000

The following summary transactions and events occurred during the fiscal year ended June 30, 1991:

1. A budget estimating revenues of $1,500,000, expenditures of $1,200,000, transfers to the debt service fund of $125,000 for interest and $100,000 for principal, and transfers of $220,000 to the capital project fund was authorized by voter approval. The estimated expenditures include the prior year's encumbrances to be honored in the current year. The estimated revenues were

Property Taxes	$ 1,275,000
Intergovernmental	25,000
Service Fees	110,000
Licenses and Permits	55,000
Fines and Forfeitures	35,000

The estimated expenditures were

General Government	$ 160,000
Public Safety	310,000
Highways and Streets	80,000
Sanitation	30,000
Health and Welfare	50,000
Culture and Recreation	25,000
Education	545,000

2. The city levied property taxes of $1,500,000. The city estimates that 15% will not be collected.
3. The city earned revenue from the following sources:

Revenues: Service Fees	$ 108,000
Revenues: County Road Tax	29,000

4. The city received revenue in cash of $56,000 from licenses and permits and $32,000 from fines and forfeitures.
5. Liabilities of $1,122,000 were incurred for routine expenditures that were not encumbered.

General Government	$ 157,000
Public Safety	305,000
Highways and Streets	78,000
Sanitation	29,000
Health and Welfare	47,000
Culture and Recreation	24,000
Education	482,000

6. The city of Amber received two police cars costing $17,700 ordered and encumbered in the prior year and included in the appropriations of the current year.
7. The city budgeted $160,000 of general fund revenues for the construction of a gymnasium for the high school in addition to the planned bond issue of $3,000,000 face value, 10% general obligation bonds. The city also budgeted $60,000 for an addition to the court house, the remainder to be funded with $1,000,000 face value, 10% general obligation bonds. The general fund's share of the gymnasium and addition to the court house was transferred to the capital projects fund.
8. Delinquent taxes in the amount of $41,000 were collected and $4,500 in interest and penalties were also collected. The remaining taxes were determined to be uncollectible and will not be foreclosed.
9. Property taxes totaling $1,295,000 were collected, service fees of $108,000 were received, and $27,000 was received from county road taxes.
10. Equipment for the schools totaling $64,000 was ordered.
11. The equipment ordered was received at a cost of $63,000.
12. Vouchers totaling $1,200,000 were paid during the current year.
13. The $225,000 budgeted for debt principal and interest was transferred to the debt service fund.
14. Equipment costing $78,000 was sold for $24,000. The equipment had originally been purchased with general fund revenues.
15. The inventory of materials and supplies shows $22,000 on hand at the end of the year, all used for general government.
16. The property taxes currently due are now delinquent.

Required
1. Prepare the budgetary, transaction, and adjusting journal entries for the general fund of the city of Amber. In addition, if an entry has a counterpart in another fund and/or account group, also prepare the entry for that fund, indicating the fund or account group.
2. Prepare an adjusted trial balance for the general fund.
3. Prepare the statement of revenues, expenditures, and changes in fund balance: budget and actual for the year ended June 30, 1991 and the balance sheet as of June 30, 1991 for the general fund.
4. Prepare the closing journal entries, assuming outstanding encumbrances will be honored next year.

PROBLEM 23-7
The Village of Dexter was recently incorporated and began financial operations on July 1, 1990, the beginning of its fiscal year. The following transactions occurred during this first fiscal year, July 1, 1990, to June 30, 1991:

1. The village council adopted a budget for general operations during the fiscal year ending June 30, 1991. Revenues were estimated at $400,000. Legal authorizations for budget expenditures were $394,000.
2. Property taxes were levied in the amount of $390,000; it was estimated that 2% of this amount would prove to be uncollectible. These taxes are available as of the date of the levy to finance current expenditures.
3. During the year a resident of the village donated marketable securities valued at $50,000 to the village under the terms of a trust agreement. The terms of the trust agreement stipulated that the principal amount is to be kept intact; use of revenue generated by the securities is restricted to financing college scholarships for needy students. Revenue earned and received on these marketable securities amounted to $5,500 through June 30, 1991.
4. A general fund transfer of $5,000 was made to establish an intragovernmental service fund to provide for a permanent investment in inventory.
5. The village decided to install lighting in the village park with an estimated cost of $75,000. Property

taxes in the amount of $72,000 are to be levied and the remaining $3,000 is to be paid from general fund revenues. The property taxes of $72,000 were levied. All the assessments were collected during the year. The cash was transferred to the capital projects fund including the village's share.

6. A contract for $75,000 was let for installation of the lighting. The village does not record project authorization. At June 30, 1991, the contract was completed but not approved. The contractor was paid, except for 5%, which was retained to ensure compliance with the terms of the contract.
7. During the year the intragovernmental service fund purchased various supplies at a cost of $1,900.
8. Cash collections recorded by the general fund during the year were

Property Taxes	$ 386,000
Licenses and Permits	7,000

9. The village council decided to build a village hall at an estimated cost of $500,000 to replace space occupied in rented facilities. The village decided that general obligation bonds bearing interest at 6% would be issued. On June 30, 1991, the $500,000 face value bonds were issued at $510,000. No contracts were signed for this project and no expenditures were incurred.
10. A fire truck was purchased for $15,000 and the voucher was approved and paid by the general fund. This expenditure was previously encumbered for $15,000.

Required
Prepare journal entries to record each of the above transactions in the appropriate fund(s) or account group(s) of Dexter Village for the fiscal year ended June 30, 1991. Use the following funds and account groups:

- General Fund
- Capital Projects Fund
- Internal Service Fund
- Trust Fund
- General Fixed Asset Account Group
- General Long-term Debt Account Group

Each journal entry is to be numbered to correspond with the transactions described above. Your answer is to be organized as follows:

Transaction Number	Fund or Account Group	Title and Explanation	Amounts	
			Debit	Credit

(AICPA adapted)

PROBLEM 23-8
Listed below are four independent transactions or events that relate to a local government:

1. $25,000 was disbursed from the general fund (or its equivalent) for the cash purchase of new equipment.
2. An unrestricted cash gift of $100,000 was received from a donor.
3. Listed common stocks with a total carrying value of $50,000, exclusive of any allowance, were sold by an endowment fund for $55,000, before any dividends were earned on these stocks. There are no restrictions on the gain.
4. $1,000,000 face amount of general obligation bonds payable were sold at par, with the proceeds required to be used solely for construction of a new building. The building was completed at a total cost of $1,000,000, and the total amount of bond issue proceeds was disbursed in connection therewith. Disregard interest capitalization.

Required

For each of the above-listed transactions or events, prepare journal entries specifying the affected funds and account groups, and showing how these transactions or events are recorded by a local government whose debt is serviced by general tax revenues.

(AICPA adapted)

PROBLEM 23-9

The city of Westgate's fiscal year ends on June 30. During the fiscal year ended June 30, 1990, the city authorized the construction of a new library and the sale of general obligation term bonds to finance construction of the library. The authorization imposed the following restrictions:

- Construction costs not to exceed $5,000,000
- Annual interest rate not to exceed 8.5%

The city does not record project authorizations, but other budgetary accounts are maintained. The following transactions relating to the financing and construction of the library occurred during the fiscal year ended June 30, 1990:

1. On July 1, 1989, the city issued $5,000,000 of 30-year, 8% general obligation bonds for $5,100,000. The semiannual interest dates are December 31 and June 30. The premium of $100,000 was transferred to the library debt service fund.
2. On July 3, 1989, the library capital projects fund invested $4,900,000 in short-term commercial paper. These purchases were at face value with no accrued interest. Interest on cash invested by the library capital projects fund must be transferred to the library debt service fund. During the fiscal year ending June 30, 1990, estimated interest to be earned is $140,000.
3. On July 5, 1989, the city signed a contract with Able Construction Company to build the library for $4,980,000.
4. On January 15, 1990, the library capital projects fund received $3,040,000 from the maturity of short-term notes purchased on July 3. The cost of these notes was $3,000,000. The interest of $40,000 was transferred to the library debt service fund.
5. On January 20, 1990, Able Construction Company properly billed the city $3,000,000 for work performed on the new library. The contract calls for 10% retention until final inspection and acceptance of the building. The library capital projects fund paid Able Construction Company $2,700,000.
6. On June 30, 1990, the library capital projects fund made the proper adjusting entries (including accrued interest receivable of $103,000) and closing entries.

Required

1. Prepare the journal entries to record the transactions and adjustments of the library capital projects fund.
2. Prepare any journal entries that are recorded by the other funds of the city of Westgate.
3. Prepare the statement of revenues, expenditures, and changes in fund balances for the year ended June 30, 1990 and the balance sheet at June 30, 1990 for the capital projects fund of the city of Westgate.

(AICPA adapted)

PROBLEM 23-10

During the current year two capital projects were authorized by the voters of the city of Amber. The first project is an addition to the court house. The project is to be financed by a $60,000 transfer from the general fund and a 10% general obligation bond issue of $1,000,000. The second project is the construction of a gymnasium for the high school. The gymnasium is to be financed by a $160,000 transfer from the general fund and a 10% general obligation bond issue of $3,000,000. During the current year, the following transactions and events affecting the capital projects funds occurred:

1. The budgeted transfers from the general fund were received.
2. The bonds for the construction of the addition to the court house were issued for $1,025,000 and the premium was transferred to the debt service fund.
3. The bonds for the construction of the gymnasium were issued for $2,980,000.
4. Short-term debt securities totaling $3,900,000 were purchased with the bond issue proceeds. The earnings on the securities are to be transferred to the debt service fund.
5. A construction contract for $1,030,000 for the court house addition was awarded to Adams Construction Company and a contract for $3,075,000 was awarded to Baxter Builders Inc. for the construction of the gymnasium.
6. Interest totaling $325,000 was received from the short-term debt securities.
7. Short-term debt securities of $400,000 were liquidated to pay the progress billings received from the contractors.
8. Progress billings of $300,000 for the court house addition were received from Adams Construction Company and $280,000 were paid net of a 5% retainage. Progress billings of $435,000 for the gymnasium were received from Baxter Builders and $400,000 were paid net of a 3% retainage. The cash transferred from the general fund was used first to pay for contracts, and then the proceeds of the bonds were used.

Required
1. Prepare the journal entries for the capital projects funds.
2. Prepare the journal entries for other funds and/or account groups that also record entries based on the transactions of the capital projects funds, identifying the fund or account group.
3. Prepare the adjusted trial balance of the capital projects fund.
4. Prepare the statement of revenues, expenditures, and changes in fund balances for the year ended June 30, 1991 and the balance sheet at June 30, 1991 for the capital projects fund, assuming one-fourth of the interest revenue is attributable to the court house addition and the remainder to the construction of the gymnasium.

PROBLEM 23-11
The city of Amber had the following balances in its debt service fund and its long-term debt account group on July 1, 1990:

	Debit	Credit
Debt Service Fund		
Cash	$ 60,000	
Investments in Debt Securities	400,000	
Property Taxes Receivable: Delinquent	120,000	
Allowance for Uncollectible Delinquent Property Taxes		$ 25,000
Reserved Fund Balance		555,000
General Long-term Debt Account Group		
Amount Available in Debt Service Fund	555,000	
Amount to Be Provided for Retirement of Debt	445,000	
8% General Obligation Bonds, Maturing January 1, 1993		1,000,000

During the current year, the following transactions and events affecting the debt service fund and the long-term account group occurred:

1. Property taxes in the amount of $265,000 for retirement of general obligation bonds were levied and 10% were estimated to be uncollectible. The property taxes were all for the payment of long-term debt.
2. Delinquent property taxes of $95,000 were collected together with interest of $10,000. The remaining taxes were deemed uncollectible and will not be foreclosed.
3. 10% general obligation bonds with a face value of $1,000,000 for the construction of the addition to the court house were issued for $1,025,000 and the premium was transferred to the debt service fund.
4. 10% general obligation bonds with a face value of $3,000,000 for the construction of the gymnasium for the high school were issued for $2,980,000.
5. Property taxes totaling $219,000 were collected.
6. Transfers from the general fund totaled $280,000 for interest.
7. Interest for one year was paid on the 8% general obligation bonds.
8. One semiannual interest payment was remitted on the new bond issues.
9. Interest of $325,000 earned on the capital project funds investments was transferred to the debt service fund.
10. The city of Amber has a standing policy that cash in excess of $60,000 at the end of the fiscal year be invested in debt securities.
11. The unpaid property taxes are now delinquent and 10% are estimated to be uncollectible.

Required

1. Prepare the journal entries for the debt service fund and the general long-term debt account group.
2. Prepare the adjusted trial balances of the debt service fund and the general long-term debt account group as of June 30, 1991.
3. Prepare the statement of revenues, expenditures, and changes in fund balance for the year ended June 30, 1991 and the balance sheet at June 30, 1991 for the debt service fund, and the schedule of long-term debt as of June 30, 1991 for the general long-term debt account group.

PROBLEM 23-12

The City of Merlot operates a central garage through an internal (intragovernmental) service fund to provide garage space and repairs for all city-owned and city-operated vehicles. The central garage fund was established by a contribution of $200,000 from the general fund on July 1, 1988, at which time the building was acquired. The after-closing trial balance at June 30, 1990 was

	Debit	Credit
Cash	$ 150,000	
Due from General Fund	20,000	
Inventory of Materials and Supplies	80,000	
Land	60,000	
Building	200,000	
Allowance for Depreciation: Building		$ 10,000
Machinery and Equipment	56,000	
Allowance for Depreciation: Machinery and Equipment		12,000
Vouchers Payable		38,000
Contribution from General Fund		200,000
Retained Earnings		306,000
	$ 566,000	$ 566,000

The following information applies to the fiscal year ended June 30, 1991:

1. Materials and supplies were purchased on account for $74,000.
2. The inventory of materials and supplies at June 30, 1991 was $58,000, which agreed with the physical count taken.
3. Salaries and wages paid to employees totaled $230,000, including related costs.
4. A billing was received from the enterprise fund for utility charges totaling $30,000 and was paid.
5. Depreciation of the building was $5,000. Depreciation of the machinery and equipment was $8,000.
6. Billings to other departments for services rendered to them were

General Fund	$ 262,000
Water and Sewer Fund	84,000
Special Revenue Fund	32,000

7. Unpaid interfund receivable balances at June 30, 1991 were

General Fund	$ 6,000
Special Revenue Fund	16,000

8. Vouchers payable at June 30, 1991 were $14,000.

Required

1. For the period July 1, 1990 through June 30, 1991 prepare journal entries to record all of the transactions in the central garage fund accounts.
2. Prepare closing entries for the central garage fund at June 30, 1991.

(AICPA adapted)

PROBLEM 23-13

The city of Bendix operates on a fiscal year ending on June 30. The adjusted trial balances of the funds and account groups of the city of Bendix on June 30, 1990 are

CITY OF BENDIX
Adjusted Trial Balance
June 30, 1990

	Debit	Credit
General Fund		
Cash	$ 100,000	
Property Taxes Receivable: Delinquent	400,000	
Allowance for Uncollectible Property Taxes: Delinquent		$ 30,000
State School Tax Receivable	10,000	
Materials and Supplies Inventory	30,000	
Vouchers Payable		60,000
Fund Balance: Reserved for Materials and Supplies		30,000
Unreserved Fund Balance		180,000
ESTIMATED REVENUES	3,825,000	
ESTIMATED OTHER FINANCING SOURCES	75,000	
APPROPRIATIONS		3,150,000
ESTIMATED OTHER FINANCING USES		650,000
BUDGETARY FUND BALANCE		100,000
ENCUMBRANCES	50,000	

CITY OF BENDIX
Adjusted Trial Balance Continued
June 30, 1990

	Debit	Credit
FUND BALANCE RESERVED FOR ENCUMBRANCES		50,000
Revenues: Property Taxes		2,915,000
Revenues: Intergovernmental		665,000
Revenues: Service Fees		145,000
Revenues: Licenses and Permits		125,000
Revenues: Fines and Forfeitures		65,000
Revenues: Other		20,000
Proceeds from Sale of Fixed Assets		95,000
Expenditures: General Government	405,000	
Expenditures: Public Safety	690,000	
Expenditures: Highways and Streets	385,000	
Expenditures: Sanitation	125,000	
Expenditures: Health and Welfare	85,000	
Expenditures: Culture and Recreation	70,000	
Expenditures: Education	1,380,000	
Operating Transfers Out: Capital Projects Fund	390,000	
Operating Transfers Out: Debt Service Fund	260,000	
Special Revenue Fund: State Gasoline Tax for		
Highways and Streets		
Cash	60,000	
State Gasoline Tax Receivable	25,000	
Unreserved Restricted Fund Balance		65,000
ESTIMATED REVENUES	335,000	
APPROPRIATIONS		325,000
BUDGETARY FUND BALANCE		10,000
Revenues: State Gasoline Tax		360,000
Expenditures: Highways and Streets	340,000	
Capital Projects Fund: Jail Addition		
Cash	60,000	
Investments in Government Securities	4,380,000	
Contract Payable: Retainage Percentage		50,000
ENCUMBRANCES	3,905,000	
FUND BALANCE RESERVED FOR ENCUMBRANCES		3,905,000
Interest Revenue		210,000
Proceeds of Bond Issue		5,185,000
Transfers In: General Fund		390,000
Expenditures: Jail Addition	1,000,000	
Transfers Out: Debt Service Fund	395,000	
Debt Service Fund		
Cash	60,000	
Investment in Government Securities	400,000	
Property Taxes Receivable: Delinquent	90,000	
Allowance for Uncollectible Property Taxes: Delinquent		9,000
Reserved Fund Balance		231,000

CITY OF BENDIX
Adjusted Trial Balance Continued
June 30, 1990

	Debit	Credit
Property Tax Revenues		385,000
Other Revenues		20,000
Transfers In: General Fund		260,000
Transfers In: Capital Projects Fund		395,000
Expenditures	750,000	
General Fixed Asset Account Group		
Land	1,200,000	
Buildings	8,400,000	
Improvements Other Than Buildings	1,700,000	
Equipment	3,695,000	
Construction in Process	1,000,000	
Investment in General Fixed Assets: General Fund Revenues		9,895,000
Investment in General Fixed Assets: Special Revenue Fund Revenues		860,000
Investment in General Fixed Assets: General Obligation Bonds		4,200,000
Investment in General Fixed Assets: Government Grants		1,040,000
General Long-term Debt Account Group		
Amount Available in the Debt Service Fund	541,000	
Amount To Be Provided for Retirement of Bonds	6,209,000	
10% General Obligation Serial Bonds Payable		1,750,000
12% General Obligation Bonds Payable		5,000,000
	$42,825,000	$42,825,000

The budget of the city of Bendix for the year ended June 30, 1990 contained the following revenue and expenditure detail:

General Fund

Revenues	
Property Taxes	$ 2,825,000
Intergovernmental	650,000
Service Fees	150,000
Licenses and Permits	125,000
Fines and Forfeitures	60,000
Other	15,000
Other Financing Sources	
Proceeds from Sale of Fixed Assets	75,000
Expenditures	
General Government	408,000
Public Safety	692,000
Highways and Streets	388,000
Sanitation	125,000
Health and Welfare	80,000
Culture and Recreation	75,000
Education	1,382,000

Other Financing Uses: Operating Transfers Out

Capital Projects Fund	390,000
Debt Service Fund	260,000
Special Revenue Fund	
Revenues: State Gasoline Tax	335,000
Expenditures: Highways and Streets	325,000

Required

1. Prepare the following financial statements and schedules:
   1) A combined statement of revenues, expenditures, and changes in fund balances for the general fund and the special revenue fund showing both the budgeted and actual amounts
   2) A statement of revenues, expenditures, and changes in fund for all funds
   3) A combined balance sheet for all funds
   4) A schedule of fixed assets
   5) A schedule of long-term debt
2. Prepare the closing entries for each of the funds, assuming outstanding encumbrances will be honored in the following year.

PROBLEM 23-14

The city of Dexter has two trust funds: an expendable trust fund and an unexpendable trust fund. The expendable trust fund was received from the estate of J. Citizen and the fund is to be used to acquire and maintain city parks. The unexpendable trust fund was received from the estate of C. T. Dweller and the income is to be used to provide playground equipment for the city parks. The trial balances of the two trust funds on June 30, 1991 were

	Debits	Credits
Expendable Trust: J Citizen		
Cash	$ 20,000	
Investments	190,000	
Due General Fund		$ 20,000
Expendable Trust Fund Balance		190,000
Unexpendable Trust: C. T. Dweller		
Cash	5,000	
Investments	60,000	
Expendable Trust Fund Balance		5,000
Unexpendable Trust Fund Balance		60,000
	$ 275,000	$ 275,000

During the year ended June 30, 1991, the following transactions and events affecting the trust funds occurred:

1. The investments of the trust funds earned interest of 10% during the year, which was received in cash.
2. The city of Dexter acquired 10 acres for a new park at a cost of $50,000. Investments costing $45,000 of the J. Citizen trust fund were sold for $50,000 to be used to acquire the park.
3. The city of Dexter spent $24,000 on park maintenance and $38,000 was transferred to the general fund from the J. Citizen trust.

4. The city of Dexter spent $8,000 on playground equipment during the year and prior and current years' earnings of the C. T. Dweller trust were transferred to the general fund to cover the acquisition.
5. Ms. J. Citizen died during the current year and her will specified that $100,000 be given to the city and added to the trust fund established by her husband. The executor of the will transferred cash of $14,000 and investments with a fair market value of $86,000 to the city on June 30, 1991.
6. The C. T. Dweller trust fund sold investments with a cost of $18,000 for $20,000 and purchased $19,000 of investments.

Required

1. Prepare the journal entries for the trust funds.
2. Prepare a statement of revenues, expenditures, and changes in fund balances, and a balance sheet for the trust funds.

SOLUTION TO REVIEW PROBLEM

1.   **General Fund**

1. ESTIMATED REVENUES	2,400,000	
APPROPRIATIONS		1,635,000
ESTIMATED OTHER FINANCING USES		740,000
BUDGETARY FUND BALANCE		25,000
To record the budget for the current year		
Operating Transfers Out: Debt Service Fund	575,000	
Due Debt Service Fund		575,000
To record transfer due debt service fund		
Operating Transfers Out: Capital Projects Fund	165,000	
Due Capital Projects Fund		165,000
To record transfer due capital projects fund		
ENCUMBRANCES	36,000	
FUND BALANCE RESERVED FOR ENCUMBRANCES		36,000
To record the encumbrance of goods ordered in the prior year to be honored in the current year		
Fund Balance Reserved for Encumbrances	36,000	
Unreserved Fund Balance		36,000
To reverse reservation of fund balance		
3. Property Taxes Receivable: Current	2,100,000	
Allowance for Uncollectible Property Taxes: Current		21,000
Revenues: Property Taxes		2,079,000
To record property tax levy for the current year		

4. Service Fees Receivable — 70,000

 State Liquor Tax Receivable — 165,000

   Revenues: Service Fees — — 70,000

   Revenues: State Liquor Tax — — 165,000

 To record revenues earned from service fees

5. Cash — 180,000

   Revenues: Licenses and Permits — — 148,000

   Revenues: Fines and Forfeitures — — 32,000

 To record revenues earned and received in cash during the year

7. Expenditures: General Government — 160,000

 Expenditures: Public Safety — 415,000

 Expenditures: Highways and Streets — 145,000

 Expenditures: Sanitation — 38,000

 Expenditures: Health and Welfare — 59,000

 Expenditures: Culture and Recreation — 47,000

 Expenditures: Education — 575,000

   Vouchers Payable — — 1,439,000

 To record the liabilities incurred for routine expenditures

8. FUND BALANCE RESERVED FOR ENCUMBRANCES — 36,000

   ENCUMBRANCES — — 36,000

 To reverse the encumbrance for road equipment, ordered in the prior year and honored in the current year

 Expenditures: Highways and Street — 35,000

   Vouchers Payable — — 35,000

 To record receipt of road equipment

10. Due Capital Projects Fund — 165,000

   Cash — — 165,000

 To record the transfer to the capital projects fund

11. ENCUMBRANCES — 125,000

   FUND BALANCE RESERVED FOR ENCUMBRANCES — — 125,000

 To record the order placed for equipment for the addition to the school

12. FUND BALANCE RESERVED FOR ENCUMBRANCES — 102,000

   ENCUMBRANCES — — 102,000

 To reverse encumbrance for equipment received

 Expenditures: Education — 100,000

   Vouchers Payable — — 100,000

 To record purchase of equipment for school

13.	Cash	229,000	
	Allowance for Uncollectible Delinquent Property Taxes	60,000	
	Taxes Receivable: Delinquent		275,000
	Revenues: Property Taxes		4,000
	Revenues: Other		10,000

To record collection and write-off of delinquent property taxes

14.	Cash	2,071,000	
	Property Taxes Receivable: Current		1,820,000
	Service Fees Receivable		70,000
	State Liquor Tax Receivable		181,000

To record the collection of receivables

| 15. | Vouchers Payable | 1,560,000 | |
| | Cash | | 1,560,000 |

To record the payment of outstanding vouchers payable

| 16. | Due Debt Service Fund | 575,000 | |
| | Cash | | 575,000 |

To record transfer to debt service fund

| 17. | Materials and Supplies Inventory | 2,000 | |
| | Expenditures: General Government | | 2,000 |

To adjust the inventory of materials and supplies to the actual balance
($22,000 − $20,000 = $2,000)

| | Unreserved Fund Balance | 2,000 | |
| | Fund Balance: Reserved for Materials and Supplies | | 2,000 |

To reclassify fund balance for increase in inventory of materials and supplies

| 18. | Property Taxes Receivable: Delinquent | 280,000 | |
| | Property Taxes Receivable: Current | | 280,000 |

To reclassify property taxes that are now delinquent

	Allowance for Uncollectible Property Taxes: Current	21,000	
	Allowance for Uncollectible Property Taxes:		
	Delinquent		21,000

To reclassify the allowance as the property taxes are now delinquent

Special Revenue Fund: Traffic and Parking Fines

2. ESTIMATED REVENUES	140,000	
APPROPRIATIONS		100,000
BUDGETARY FUND BALANCE		40,000

To record the budget of the special revenue fund to account for traffic and parking fine revenue

6. Traffic and Parking Fines Receivable	144,000	
Revenues: Traffic and Parking Fines		144,000

To record revenues earned during current year from traffic and parking fines

Cash	148,000	
Traffic and Parking Fines Receivable		148,000

To record the traffic and parking fines collected during the current year

7. Expenditures: Public Safety	110,000	
Vouchers Payable		110,000

To record the expenditures for salaries for additional police personnel

15. Vouchers Payable	110,000	
Cash		110,000

To record the payment of vouchers payable

Capital Projects Fund: School Addition

1. Due from General Fund	165,000	
Transfers In: General Fund		165,000

To record transfer due from general fund

9. Cash	2,650,000	
Proceeds of Bond Issue: School Addition		2,650,000

To record proceeds of bond issue for the addition to the school

Transfer Out: Debt Service Fund	150,000	
Cash		150,000

To record the transfer of cash received as bond premium to the debt service fund

10. Cash	165,000	
Due from General Fund		165,000

To record receipt of transfer due from the general fund

11. ENCUMBRANCES: SCHOOL ADDITION	2,665,000	
FUND BALANCE RESERVED FOR		
ENCUMBRANCES: SCHOOL ADDITION		2,665,000

To record acceptance of contract for an addition to the school

19. Investment in Treasury Bills	2,500,000	
Cash		2,500,000

To record the temporary investment of the bond proceeds

20. FUND BALANCE RESERVED FOR ENCUMBRANCES:		
SCHOOL ADDITION	480,000	
ENCUMBRANCES: SCHOOL ADDITION		480,000

To reverse encumbrances for progress billings received

Expenditures: School Addition	480,000	
Contract Payable: School Addition		480,000

To record receipt of progress billings for construction of school addition

21. Cash	420,000	
Investment in Treasury Bills		300,000
Revenues: Interest on Investments		120,000

To record the sale of treasury bills and the collection of interest revenue

Transfer Out: Debt Service Fund	120,000	
Cash		120,000

To record the transfer of investment earnings to the debt service fund

22. Contract Payable: School Addition	480,000	
Contract Payable Retainage Percentage: School		
Addition		24,000
Cash		456,000

To record payment of progress billings net of 5% retainage for school addition

Debt Service Fund

1. Due from General Fund	575,000	
Transfers In: General Fund		575,000

To record transfer due from general fund for payment of debt principal and interest

9. Cash	150,000	
Transfer In: Capital Projects Fund		150,000

To record transfer of bond premium from the capital projects fund

16. Cash   575,000
        Due from General Fund   575,000
     To record the transfer from the general fund

21. Cash   120,000
        Transfer In: Capital Projects Fund   120,000
     To record transfer of interest earned by the capital projects
     fund for renovation of the fire hall

23. Cash   30,000
        Revenues: Investment Earnings   30,000
     To record investment earnings received in cash

24. Expenditures   875,000
        Interest Payable: 8% General Obligation Bonds   40,000
        Matured 8% General Obligation Bonds Payable   500,000
        Interest Payable: 10% General Obligation Bonds   185,000
        Interest Payable: 12% General Obligation Bonds   150,000
     To record the principal and interest due on general
     obligation bonds

     Interest Payable   375,000
     Matured 8% General Obligation Bonds Payable   500,000
        Cash   875,000
     To record the payment of interest on the outstanding
     general obligation bonds and the principal of the general
     obligation bonds that matured

General Fixed Asset Account Group

 8. Equipment   35,000
        Investment in General Fixed Assets: General Fund
           Revenues   35,000
     To record the receipt of road equipment in the schools

12. Equipment   100,000
        Investment in General Fixed Assets: General Fund
           Revenues   100,000
     To record the receipt of the equipment for the addition to
     the school

22. Construction in Process   480,000
        Investment in General Fixed Assets: General Fund
           Revenues   165,000
        Investment in General Fixed Assets: General
           Obligation Bonds   315,000
     To record the progress billings on the school addition
     funded by monies from the general fund and a general
     obligation bond issue

Note: An alternative to using the general fund transfer first is to prorate the amount incurred based on the amount to be funded by general fund revenues and general obligation bonds in relation to the total contract price.

General Long-term Debt Account Group

1. Amount Available in Debt Service Fund   200,000
        Amount To be Provided for Retirement of General
            Obligation Bonds   200,000
    To record the principal due from general fund

9. Amount Available in Debt Service Fund   150,000
        Amount to Be Provided for Retirement of
            General Obligation Bonds   2,350,000
                12% General Obligation Bonds Payable   2,500,000

    To record the issuance of bonds for addition to the school

21. Amount Available in Debt Service Fund   120,000
        Amount to Be Provided for Retirement of General
            Obligation Bonds   120,000
    To record the earnings of capital project investments
    transferred to the debt service fund

21. Amount Available in Debt Service Fund   30,000
        Amount to Be Provided for Retirement of General
            Obligation Bonds   30,000
    To record the earnings of debt service fund investments

24. 8% General Obligation Bonds Payable   500,000
        Amount Available in Debt Service Fund   500,000
    To record the payment of the 8% general obligation bonds
    that matured

CITY OF STEVENS
General Fund: Trial Balance
June 30, 1991

	Debit	Credit
Cash	$ 280,000	
Property Taxes Receivable: Delinquent	280,000	
Allowance for Uncollectible Property Taxes: Delinquent		$ 21,000
State Liquor Tax Receivable	6,000	
Materials and Supplies Inventory	22,000	
Vouchers Payable		57,000
Fund Balance: Reserved for Materials and Supplies		22,000
Unreserved Fund Balance		292,000
ESTIMATED REVENUES	2,400,000	
APPROPRIATIONS		1,635,000
ESTIMATED OTHER FINANCING USES		740,000
BUDGETARY FUND BALANCE		25,000
ENCUMBRANCES	23,000	
FUND BALANCE RESERVED FOR ENCUMBRANCES		23,000
Revenues: Property Taxes		2,083,000
Revenues: Intergovernmental		165,000
Revenues: Service Fees		70,000
Revenues: Licenses and Permits		148,000
Revenues: Fines and Forfeitures		32,000
Revenues: Other		10,000
Expenditures: General Government	158,000	
Expenditures: Public Safety	415,000	
Expenditures: Highways and Streets	180,000	
Expenditures: Sanitation	38,000	
Expenditures: Health and Welfare	59,000	
Expenditures: Culture and Recreation	47,000	
Expenditures: Education	675,000	
Operating Transfer Out: Capital Projects Fund	165,000	
Operating Transfer Out: Debt Service Fund	575,000	
	$ 5,323,000	$ 5,323,000

CITY OF STEVENS
Adjusted Trial Balance: Special Revenue Fund
June 30, 1991

	Debit	Credit
Cash	$ 48,000	
Traffic and Parking Fines Receivable	16,000	
Unreserved Restricted Fund Balance		$ 30,000
ESTIMATED REVENUES	140,000	
ESTIMATED OTHER FINANCING USES		100,000
BUDGETARY FUND BALANCE		40,000
Revenues: Traffic and Parking Fines		144,000
Expenditures: Public Safety	110,000	
	$ 314,000	$ 314,000

3.

CITY OF STEVENS
Statement of Revenues, Expenditures, and Changes in Fund Balances: Budget and Actual:
General Fund and Special Revenue Fund
For the Year Ended June 30, 1991

	General Fund			Special Revenue Fund		
	Budget	Actual	Variance Over (Under)	Budget	Actual	Variance Over (Under)
Revenues						
Property Taxes	$ 2,000,000	$ 2,083,000	$ 83,000			
Intragovernmental	160,000	165,000	5,000			
Service Fees	75,000	70,000	(5,000)			
Licenses and Permits	140,000	148,000	8,000			
Fines and Forfeitures	25,000	32,000	7,000	$ 140,000	$ 144,000	$ 4,000
Other	–0–	10,000	10,000			
Total Revenues	2,400,000	2,508,000	108,000	140,000	144,000	4,000
Expenditures						
General Government	200,000	158,000	(42,000)			
Public Safety	425,000	415,000	(10,000)			
Highways and Streets	150,000	180,000	30,000	100,000	110,000	10,000
Sanitation	40,000	38,000	(2,000)			
Health and Welfare	60,000	59,000	(1,000)			
Culture and Recreation	50,000	47,000	(3,000)			
Education	710,000	675,000	(35,000)			
Total Expenditures	1,635,000	1,572,000	(63,000)	100,000	110,000	10,000
Excess of Revenues Over Expenditures	765,000	936,000	171,000	40,000	34,000	(6,000)
Other Financing (Uses)						
Debt Service Fund	(575,000)	(575,000)	–0–			
Capital Projects Fund	(165,000)	(165,000)	–0–			
Excess of Revenues Over Expenditures and Other Financing Sources (Uses)	25,000	196,000	171,000	40,000	34,000	(6,000)
Fund Balance at the Beginning of the Year	314,000	314,000	–0–	30,000	30,000	–0–
Fund Balance at the End of the Year	$ 339,000	$ 510,000	$ 171,000	$ 70,000	$ 64,000	$(6,000)

CITY OF STEVENS
Combined Balance Sheet: General Fund and Special Revenue Fund
June 30, 1991

Assets

		General Fund	Special Revenue Fund
Cash		$ 280,000	$ 48,000
Property Taxes Receivable: Delinquent	$ 280,000		
Less: Allowance for Uncollectible Delinquent Property Taxes	21,000	259,000	
State Liquor Tax Receivable		6,000	
Traffic and Parking Fines Receivable			16,000
Materials and Supplies Inventory		22,000	
Total Assets		$ 567,000	$ 64,000

Liabilities and Fund Balances

	General Fund	Special Revenue Fund
Vouchers Payable	$ 57,000	
Fund Balances		
Fund Balance: Reserved for Materials and Supplies	22,000	
Fund Balance: Reserved for Encumbrances	23,000	
Reserved Fund Balance		$ 64,000
Unreserved Fund Balance	465,000	
Total Liabilities and Fund Balances	$ 567,000	$ 64,000

CITY OF STEVENS
Statement of Revenues, Expenditures, and Changes in Fund Balances
Capital Projects Fund: School Addition
For the Year Ended June 30, 1991

Revenues: Interest on Investments		$ 120,000
Expenditures: School Addition		480,000
Excess of Expenditures Over Revenues		(360,000)
Other Financing Sources (Uses)		
Proceeds of General Obligation Bonds	$ 2,650,000	
Transfers In: General Fund	165,000	
Transfers Out: Debt Service Fund	(270,000)	2,545,000
Excess of Revenues and Other Financing Sources Over Expenditures and Other Financing Uses		2,185,000
Fund Balance at Beginning of the Year		—0—
Fund Balance at End of the Year		$ 2,185,000

CITY OF STEVENS
Balance Sheet: Capital Projects Fund
June 30, 1991

Assets

Cash (1)	$ 9,000
Investment in Treasury Bills	2,200,000
Total Assets	$ 2,209,000

Liabilities and Fund Balance

Contract Payable: Retainage Percentage	$ 24,000
Fund Balance: Reserved for Encumbrances	2,185,000
Total Liabilities and Fund Balance	$ 2,209,000

(1) $2,650,000 - $150,000 + $165,000 - $2,500,000 + $420,000
   $- $120,000 - $456,000 = $9,000$

CITY OF STEVENS
Statement of Revenues, Expenditures, and Changes in Fund Balances: Debt Service Fund
For the Year Ended June 30, 1991

Revenues: Investment Earnings		$ 30,000
Expenditures: Debt Principal and Interest		875,000
Excess of Expenditures Over Revenues		(845,000)
Other Financing Sources		
Transfers In: General Fund	$ 575,000	
Transfers In: Capital Projects Fund	270,000	845,000
Excess of Revenues and Other Financing Sources Over		
Expenditures		–0–
Fund Balance at the Beginning of the Year		310,000
Fund Balance at the End of the Year		$ 310,000

CITY OF STEVENS
Balance Sheet: Debt Service Fund
June 30, 1991

Assets

Cash (1)	$ 10,000
Investments	300,000
Total Assets	$ 310,000

Fund Balance: Reserved for Debt Principal	$ 310,000

(1) $10,000 + $150,000 + $575,000 + $120,000 + $30,000 − $875,000 = $10,000

CITY OF STEVENS
Schedule of Fixed Assets
June 30, 1991

Investment in Fixed Assets	
Land	$ 200,000
Buildings	5,200,000
Improvements Other Than Buildings	2,100,000
Equipment	3,035,000
Construction in Process	480,000
Total Investment	$11,015,000

Sources of Investment in General Fixed Assets	
General Fund Revenues	$ 5,800,000
Special Revenue Fund Revenues	250,000
General Obligation Bonds	4,115,000
Government Grants	850,000
Total Sources	$11,015,000

CITY OF STEVENS
Schedule of Long-term Debt
June 30, 1991

Amounts Available and To Be Provided

Amount Available in the Debt Service Fund (1)	$ 310,000
Amount To Be Provided for Retirement of General Obligations Bonds	4,040,000
Total	$ 4,350,000

Debt Payable

10% General Obligation Bonds	$ 1,850,000
12% General Obligation Bonds	2,500,000
Total	$ 4,350,000

(1) $310,000 + $200,000 + $150,000 + $120,000 + $30,000 − $500,000 = $310,000

4. 　　　　　　　　　　　　　　　　**General Fund**

APPROPRIATIONS	1,635,000	
ESTIMATED OTHER FINANCING USES	740,000	
BUDGETARY FUND BALANCE	25,000	
ESTIMATED REVENUES		2,400,000

To reverse the entry recording the budget

FUND BALANCE RESERVED FOR ENCUMBRANCES	23,000	
ENCUMBRANCES		23,000

To reverse the balances remaining in the encumbrance accounts

Unreserved Fund Balance	23,000	
Fund Balance Reserved for Encumbrances		23,000

To allocate unreserved fund balance for the amount of
outstanding encumbrances to be honored in the following year

Revenues: Property Taxes	2,083,000	
Revenues: Intergovernmental	165,000	
Revenues: Service Fees	70,000	
Revenues: Licenses and Permits	148,000	
Revenues: Fines and Forfeitures	32,000	
Revenues: Other	10,000	
Expenditures: General Government		158,000
Expenditures: Public Safety		415,000
Expenditures: Highways and Streets		180,000
Expenditures: Sanitation		38,000
Expenditures: Health and Welfare		59,000
Expenditures: Culture and Recreation		47,000
Expenditures: Education		675,000
Operating Transfers Out: Capital Projects Fund		165,000
Operating Transfers Out: Debt Service Fund		575,000
Unreserved Fund Balance		196,000

To close the revenues, expenditures, and transfer accounts to the unexpended fund balance

Special Revenue Fund

APPROPRIATIONS	100,000	
BUDGETARY FUND BALANCE	40,000	
ESTIMATED REVENUES		140,000

To reverse the entry recording the budget

Revenues: Traffic and Parking Fines	144,000	
Expenditures: Public Safety		110,000
Reserved Fund Balance		34,000

To close the revenues and expenditures to the reserved fund balance

Capital Projects Fund

FUND BALANCE RESERVED FOR ENCUMBRANCES	2,205,000	
ENCUMBRANCES		2,205,000

To reverse encumbrances

Unreserved Fund Balance	2,205,000	
Fund Balance Reserved for Encumbrances		2,205,000

To set up fund balance reserved for encumbrances outstanding at year end

Revenues: Interest on Investments	120,000	
Proceeds of Bond Issue: School Addition	2,650,000	
Transfers In: General Fund	165,000	
Expenditures: School Addition		480,000
Transfers Out: Debt Service Fund		270,000
Reserved Fund Balance		2,185,000

To close the revenue, expenditure, and transfer accounts to the reserved fund balance

Debt Service Fund

Revenues: Investment Earnings	30,000	
Transfers In: General Fund	575,000	
Transfers In: Capital Projects Fund	270,000	
Expenditures		875,000
To close revenues, expenditures, and transfer in accounts		

5.

Proprietary funds consist of internal service funds and enterprise funds. An internal service fund provides products and services to other funds for a fee based on cost. Enterprise funds provide products and services to the general public at a price sufficient to cover costs and provide a profit. Proprietary funds use the accrual basis of accounting, since the objectives are the measurement of net income and capital maintenance. Proprietary funds have both current and noncurrent assets and liabilities. The equity consists of contributed capital and retained earnings. The financial statements are a statement of revenues, expenses, and changes in retained earnings; a balance sheet; and a statement of changes in financial position prepared on the cash basis.

Trust funds consist of expendable trust funds, nonexpendable trust funds, and pension trust funds. The expendable trust funds use the modified accrual basis of accounting, since capital maintenance is not the goal. The expendable trust funds can have both current and noncurrent assets and liabilities. The financial statements are the statement of revenues, expenditures, and changes in fund balance, and a balance sheet.

The nonexpendable trust funds and the pension trust funds use the accrual basis of accounting, since capital maintenance is the goal. The funds can have both current and noncurrent assets and liabilities. The equity consists of reserved and unreserved fund balances. The statements prepared are a statement of revenue, expenses, and changes in fund balances, and a balance sheet.

Agency funds account for resources and obligations that belong to other entities. The funds contain the assets of another equity and its liabilities. No revenues or expenses are recorded, and therefore no financial statements are prepared.

APPENDIX 23-A

CITY OF ALBANY, OREGON
COMBINED BALANCE SHEET—ALL FUND TYPES AND ACCOUNT GROUPS
JUNE 30, 1987

Assets and other debits	Governmental Fund Types				Proprietary Fund Types		Fiduciary Fund Types	Account Groups		Total (Memorandum only)
	General Fund	Special Revenue	Debt Service	Capital Projects	Enterprise	Internal Service	Trust and Agency	General Fixed Assets	General Long-term Debt	
Cash and investments	$ 858,452	$ 593,071	$3,595,627	$3,955,288	$ 2,395,989	$ 39,417	$448,814	$	$	$11,886,658
Receivables:										
Property taxes	926,728	151,114	10,616	190,445						1,278,903
Accounts, net	104,436	152,010			532,083					788,529
Assessments		1,219,973		217,689						1,437,662
Interest	12,070	5,482	34,330	41,586	374,964	410	1,036			469,878
Loans		433,357								433,357
Due from other funds		9,275		10,926						20,201
Land held for resale			1,613,049							1,613,049
Other assets	4,049				1,661					5,710
Restricted cash and investments				80,000	2,913,550					2,993,550
Fixed assets, net					12,837,066	242,489		6,294,844		19,374,399
Other debits:										
Amount available for debt service									3,638,370	3,638,370
Amount to be provided for debt service									2,827,954	2,827,954
Total assets and other debits	$1,905,735	$1,344,309	$6,473,595	$4,495,934	$19,055,313	$282,316	$449,850	$6,294,844	$6,466,324	$46,768,220

CITY OF ALBANY, OREGON
COMBINED BALANCE SHEET—ALL FUND TYPES AND ACCOUNT GROUPS (CONTINUED)
JUNE 30, 1987

| Liabilities and fund equity | Governmental Fund Types | | | | Proprietary Fund Types | | Fiduciary Fund Types | Account Groups | | Total |
	General Fund	Special Revenue	Debt Service	Capital Projects	Enterprise	Internal Service	Trust and Agency	General Fixed Assets	General Long-term Debt	(Memorandum only)
Liabilities:										
Accounts payable	$ 154,586	$ 67,733	$ 561	$ 224,324	$ 78,007	$ 12,167	$ 6,668	$	$	$ 544,046
Salaries, withholdings and taxes payable	382,279	28,414			63,285	8,092			179,718	661,788
Matured interest payable			1,162							1,162
Refundable deposits and advances	59,284			66,977	167,504					293,765
Deferred revenue	826,513	1,154,256	2,833,502	406,654			120			5,221,045
Due to other funds		9,275			10,926					20,201
Amounts held in trust							12,015			12,015
Bonds payable					12,291,290				6,286,606	18,577,896
Deferred compensation liability							346,890			346,890
Capital lease obligations						35,449				35,449
Total liabilities	1,422,662	1,259,678	2,835,225	697,955	12,611,012	55,708	365,693		6,466,324	25,714,257
Fund equity:										
Contributed capital					4,402,924	222,318				4,625,242
Investment in general fixed assets								6,294,844		6,294,844
Retained earnings (deficit):										
Reserved for debt service					2,106,412					2,106,412
Unreserved/undesignated					(65,035)	4,290				(60,745)
Fund balances (deficit):										
Unreserved:										
Designated for equipment purchase				1,553,766						1,553,766
Designated for construction				747,850						747,850
Designated for debt service			3,370,034							3,370,034
Undesignated	483,073	84,631	268,336	1,496,363			84,157			2,416,560
Total fund equity (deficit)	483,073	84,631	3,638,370	3,797,979	6,444,301	226,608	84,157	6,294,844		21,053,963
Total liabilities and fund equity	$1,905,735	$1,344,309	$6,473,595	$4,495,934	$19,055,313	$282,316	$449,850	$6,294,844	$6,466,324	$46,768,220

The accompanying notes are an integral part of the combined financial statements.

CITY OF ALBANY, OREGON
COMBINED STATEMENT OF REVENUES, EXPENDITURES AND CHANGES IN FUND BALANCES—
ALL GOVERNMENTAL FUND TYPES
FOR THE YEAR ENDED JUNE 30, 1987

	General Fund	Special Revenue	Debt Service	Capital Projects	Total (Memorandum only)
Revenues:					
Taxes	$4,119,725	$ 766,646	$ 36,108	$ 876,176	$ 5,798,655
Special assessments			279,843	54,000	333,843
Franchise fees, licenses and permits	931,387	74,825			1,006,212
Intergovernmental	899,802	1,551,952		14,496	2,466,250
Charges for services	322,794	269,158		228,703	820,655
Fines and forfeits	131,529				131,529
Miscellaneous	110,295	140,555	204,913	223,650	679,413
Total revenues	6,515,532	2,803,136	520,864	1,397,025	11,236,557
Expenditures:					
Current:					
General government	2,088,810	956,963	55,099	102,887	3,203,759
Public safety	4,302,364				4,302,364
Highways and streets		751,685		269,865	1,021,550
Culture and recreation	403,745	893,074			1,296,819
Capital outlay		239,496		572,839	812,335
Debt service:					
Principal			860,000		860,000
Interest			525,472		525,472
Total expenditures	6,794,919	2,841,218	1,440,571	945,591	12,022,299
Revenues over (under) expenditures	(279,387)	(38,082)	(919,707)	451,434	(785,742)
Other financing sources (uses)					
Bond sale proceeds			21,429	778,571	800,000
Operating transfers in	272,687	380,952	290,767	171,759	1,116,165
Operating transfers out	(323,900)	(442,762)	(171,759)	(327,619)	(1,266,040)
Total other financing sources (uses)	(51,213)	(61,810)	140,437	622,711	650,125
Revenues and other sources over (under) expenditures and other uses	(330,600)	(99,892)	(779,270)	1,074,145	(135,617)
Fund balances, June 30, 1986	813,673	184,523	4,417,640	2,723,834	8,139,670
Fund balances, June 30, 1987	$ 483,073	$ 84,631	$3,638,370	$3,797,979	$ 8,004,053

The accompanying notes are an integral part of the combined financial statements.

CITY OF ALBANY, OREGON

COMBINED STATEMENT OF REVENUES, EXPENDITURES AND CHANGES IN FUND BALANCES (BUDGETARY BASIS)—BUDGET AND ACTUAL
ALL GOVERNMENTAL FUND TYPES
FOR THE YEAR ENDED JUNE 30, 1987

	General Fund			Special Revenue Funds			Debt Service Funds		
	Budget	Actual	Variance favorable (unfavorable)	Budget	Actual	Variance favorable (unfavorable)	Budget	Actual	Variance favorable (unfavorable)
Revenues:									
Taxes	$3,990,000	$4,129,736	$139,736	$ 760,000	$ 769,229	$ 9,229	$ 32,000	$ 36,730	$ 4,730
Special assessments							900,000	806,488	(93,512)
Franchise fees, licenses and permits	915,000	931,387	16,387	81,400	74,825	(6,575)			
Intergovernmental revenues	937,650	899,802	(37,848)	1,619,600	1,551,952	(67,648)			
Charges for services	313,200	322,794	9,594	260,000	269,158	9,158			
Fines and forfeits	117,500	131,529	14,029						
Miscellaneous	140,600	110,295	(30,305)	134,105	140,555	6,450	183,000	221,359	38,359
Total revenues	6,413,950	6,525,543	111,593	2,855,105	2,805,719	(49,386)	1,115,000	1,064,577	(50,423)
Expenditures:									
Current:									
General government	2,573,550	2,080,889	492,661	1,041,200	956,174	85,026	602,500	56,006	546,494
Public safety	4,278,400	4,302,364	(23,964)	443,000		443,000			
Highways and streets				754,400	750,250	4,150			
Culture and recreation				912,800	893,373	19,427			
Capital outlay	405,000	403,745	1,255	254,500	239,496	15,004	721,500	46,260	675,240
Debt service:									
Principal repayment							860,000	860,000	
Interest							527,267	525,472	1,795
Total expenditures	7,256,950	6,786,998	469,952	3,405,900	2,839,293	566,607	2,711,267	1,487,738	1,223,529
Other financing sources (uses):									
Bond sale proceeds							800,000	800,000	
Operating transfers in	278,000	272,687	(5,313)	381,000	380,952	(48)	306,767	290,767	(16,000)
Operating transfers out	(323,900)	(323,900)		(444,100)	(442,762)	1,338	(250,000)	(171,759)	78,241
Total other financing sources (uses)	(45,900)	(51,213)	(5,313)	(63,100)	(61,810)	1,290	856,767	919,008	62,241
Revenues and other sources over (under) expenditures and other uses	(888,900)	(312,668)	576,232	(613,895)	(95,384)	518,511	(739,500)	495,847	1,235,347
Fund balances, July 1, 1986	888,900	888,916	16	613,895	198,038	(415,857)	3,846,500	3,847,544	1,044
Fund balances, June 30, 1987	$	576,248	$576,248	$	102,654	$ 102,654	$3,107,000	4,343,391	$1,236,391

CITY OF ALBANY, OREGON

COMBINED STATEMENT OF REVENUES, EXPENDITURES AND CHANGES IN FUND BALANCES (BUDGETARY BASIS)—BUDGET AND ACTUAL

ALL GOVERNMENTAL FUND TYPES (CONTINUED)

FOR THE YEAR ENDED JUNE 30, 1987

	General Fund			Special Revenue Funds			Debt Service Funds		
	Budget	Actual	Variance favorable (unfavorable)	Budget	Actual	Variance favorable (unfavorable)	Budget	Actual	Variance favorable (unfavorable)
Fund balances, June 30, 1987	$	576,248	$576,248	$	102,654	$ 102,654	$3,107,000	4,343,391	$1,236,391
Adjustments to fund balance on the budgetary basis to reconcile to fund balance on the generally accepted accounting principles basis:									
Excess of revenues over expenditures of items recorded in the Debt Service Funds on a budgetary basis, recorded in the Capital Projects Funds on a generally accepted accounting principles basis								(747,850)	
Taxes recognized, deferred on a budgetary basis		61,998						933	
Vacation liability not recognized on a budgetary basis		(155,173)			10,389				
Assessments recognized, deferred on a budgetary basis					(28,412)			41,896	
Fund balances-generally accepted accounting principles basis, June 30, 1987		$ 483,073			$ 84,631			$3,638,370	

The accompanying notes are an integral part of the combined financial statements.

CITY OF ALBANY, OREGON

COMBINED STATEMENT OF REVENUES, EXPENDITURES AND CHANGES IN FUND BALANCES (BUDGETARY BASIS)—BUDGET AND ACTUAL (CONTINUED)
ALL GOVERNMENTAL FUND TYPES
FOR THE YEAR ENDED JUNE 30, 1987

	Capital Projects Funds			Total (memorandum only)		
	Budget	Actual	Variance favorable (unfavorable)	Budget	Actual	Variance favorable (unfavorable)
Revenues:						
Taxes	$ 935,200	$ 873,705	$ (61,495)	$ 5,717,200	$ 5,809,400	$ 92,200
Special assessments	58,500	81,140	22,640	958,500	887,628	(70,872)
Franchise fees, licenses and permits				996,400	1,006,212	9,812
Intergovernmental revenues	14,500	14,496	(4)	2,571,750	2,466,250	(105,500)
Charges for services	204,900	228,703	23,803	778,100	820,655	42,555
Fines and Forfeitures				117,500	131,529	14,029
Miscellaneous	236,500	207,204	(29,296)	694,205	679,413	(14,792)
Total revenues	1,449,600	1,405,248	(44,352)	11,833,655	11,801,087	(32,568)
Expenditures:						
Current:						
General government	177,730	101,980	75,750	4,394,980	3,195,049	1,199,931
Public safety	473,500	269,865	203,635	4,721,400	4,302,364	419,036
Highways and streets				1,227,900	1,020,115	207,785
Culture and recreation				1,317,800	1,297,118	20,682
Capital outlay	3,011,976	526,579	2,485,397	3,987,976	812,335	3,175,641
Debt service:						
Principal repayment				860,000	860,000	
Interest				527,267	525,472	1,795
Total expenditures	3,663,206	898,424	2,764,782	17,037,323	12,012,453	5,024,870
Other financing sources (uses):						
Bond sale proceeds	250,000	171,759	(78,241)	800,000	800,000	
Operating transfers in				1,215,767	1,116,165	(99,602)
Operating transfers out	(347,767)	(327,619)	20,148	(1,365,767)	(1,266,040)	99,727
Total other financing sources (uses)	(97,767)	(155,860)	(58,093)	650,000	650,125	125
Revenues and other sources over (under) expenditures and other uses	(2,311,373)	350,964	2,662,337	(4,553,668)	438,759	4,992,427
Fund balances, July 1, 1986	2,979,373	2,680,745	(298,628)	8,328,668	7,615,243	(713,425)
Fund balances, June 30, 1987	$ 668,000	3,031,709	$ 2,363,709	$ 3,775,000	8,054,002	$ 4,279,002

Adjustments to fund balance on the budgetary basis to reconcile to fund balance on the generally accepted accounting principles basis:

	Capital Projects	Total
Excess of revenues over expenditures of items recorded in the Debt Service Funds on a budgetary basis, recorded in the Capital Projects Funds on a generally accepted accounting principles basis	747,850	
Taxes recognized, deferred on a budgetary basis	12,285	85,605
Vacation liability not recognized on a budgetary basis		(183,585)
Assessments recognized, deferred on a budgetary basis	6,135	48,031
Fund balances—generally accepted accounting basis, June 30, 1987	$3,797,979	$ 8,004,053

CITY OF ALBANY, OREGON
COMBINED STATEMENT OF REVENUES, EXPENSES AND CHANGES IN RETAINED EARNINGS/FUND BALANCES
ALL PROPRIETARY FUND TYPES AND SIMILAR TRUST FUNDS
FOR THE YEAR ENDED JUNE 30, 1987

| | Proprietary Fund Types | | Fiduciary Fund Type | Total |
| | | | | (Memorandum |
	Enterprise	Internal Service	Nonexpendable Trusts	only)
Operating revenues:				
Service charges and fees	$4,764,404	$565,854	$	$5,330,258
Miscellaneous revenues	24,350	3,281	9,830	37,461
Total operating revenues	4,788,754	569,135	9,830	5,367,719
Operating expenses:				
Salaries, wages and benefits	1,461,432	211,086		1,672,518
Contracted services	111,575	27,008		138,583
Operating supplies		164,485		164,485
Utilities	405,502	12,786		418,288
Depreciation	650,333	43,629		693,962
Repairs and maintenance	848,124	42,632		890,756
Bad debt expense	58,360			58,360
Miscellaneous	299,436	74,376	14,010	387,822
Total operating expenses	3,834,762	576,002	14,010	4,424,774
Operating income (loss)	953,992	(6,867)	(4,180)	942,945
Nonoperating revenues (expenses):				
Interest on investments	1,123,474	2,231		1,125,705
Interest expense	(898,204)	(5,567)		(903,771)
Loss on disposition of fixed assets		(9,261)		(9,261)
Total nonoperating revenues (expenses)	225,270	(12,597)		212,673
Net income (loss) before extraordinary item and operating interfund transfers	1,179,262	(19,464)	(4,180)	1,155,618
Operating transfers in	287,875			287,875
Operating transfers out	(138,000)			(138,000)
Net income (loss) before extraordinary item	1,329,137	(19,464)	(4,180)	1,305,493
Extraordinary item—Loss on defeasance of debt	(358,334)			(358,334)
Net income (loss)	970,803	(19,464)	(4,180)	947,159
Transfer of depreciation on fixed assets constructed with grant receipts to contributed capital	103,043			103,043
Increase (decrease) in retained earnings/fund balances	1,073,846	(19,464)	(4,180)	1,050,202
Retained earnings/fund balances—June 30, 1986	967,531	23,754	88,337	1,079,622
Retained earnings/fund balances—June 30, 1987	$2,041,377	$ 4,290	$84,157	$2,129,824

The accompanying notes are an integral part of the combined financial statements.

CITY OF ALBANY, OREGON
COMBINED STATEMENT OF CHANGES IN FINANCIAL POSITION
ALL PROPRIETARY FUND TYPES AND SIMILAR TRUST FUNDS
FOR THE YEAR ENDED JUNE 30, 1987

	Proprietary Fund Types		Fiduciary Fund Types	Total (Memorandum only)
	Enterprise	Internal Service	Nonexpendable Trusts	
Funds provided (used):				
From operations				
Net income (loss) before extraordinary item	$ 1,329,137	$(19,464)	$(4,180)	$ 1,305,493
Add expenses not requiring outlay of working capital:				
Depreciation	650,333	43,629		693,962
Amortization of bond discount and issue costs	24,704			24,704
Funds provided (used) by operations	2,004,174	24,165	(4,180)	2,024,159
Bond sale proceeds	12,655,000			12,655,000
Loss on disposal of fixed assets		9,261		9,261
Contribution of fixed assets from other funds	96,821	22,474		119,295
Total funds provided	14,755,995	55,900	(4,180)	14,807,715
Funds used:				
Change in current portion of bonds payable	75,000			75,000
Fixed asset additions	511,891	25,545		537,436
Payments under capital lease		31,931		31,931
Bond principal payments	35,000			35,000
Change in current portion of leases payable		3,518		3,518
Establishment of restricted assets for bond payment	1,071,125			1,071,125
Defeasance of bonds	12,267,200			12,267,200
Net change in contributed capital	96,821			96,821
Bond sale expenses	378,446			378,446
Total funds used	14,435,483	60,994		14,496,477
Increase (decrease) in working capital	$ 320,512	$ (5,094)	$(4,180)	$ 311,238
Changes in components which increased (decreased) working capital:				
Cash and investments	$ 135,620	$ 4,550	$ 280	$ 140,450
Accounts receivable	1,317			1,317
Interest receivable	216,973	291	568	217,832
Other assets	(1,522)			(1,522)
Accounts payable	4,409	(3,492)	(5,028)	(4,111)
Due to other funds	(10,926)			(10,926)
Salaries, withholdings, and taxes payable	(9,645)	(2,925)		(12,570)
Refundable deposits and advances	59,286			59,286
Current portion, bonds payable	(75,000)			(75,000)
Current portion, lease obligation		(3,518)		(3,518)
Increase (decrease) in working capital	$ 320,512	$ (5,094)	$(4,180)	$ 311,238

The accompanying notes are an integral part of the combined financial statements.

CITY OF ALBANY, OREGON
NOTES TO COMBINED FINANCIAL STATEMENTS
JUNE 30, 1987

NOTE 1 - SUMMARY OF SIGNIFICANT ACCOUNTING POLICIES:

The following is a summary of significant accounting policies utilized by the City in the preparation of the accompanying combined financial statements:

Basis of accounting

The governmental fund types and agency funds are maintained on the modified accrual basis of accounting. Under the modified accrual basis of accounting, revenues are recorded in the accounting period in which they become measurable and available and expenditures are recorded at the time liabilities are incurred, except for:

- Interfund transactions for services which are recorded on the accrual basis.
- Interest expense on General Long-term Debt which is recorded on its due date.
- Earned but unpaid vacations which are recorded as expenditures to the extent they are expected to be liquidated with expendable available financial resources.

Significant revenues which are measurable and available under the modified accrual basis of accounting are as follows:

- Property taxes collected within sixty days of year end.
- Federal and state grants (to the extent that related expenditures have been incurred).
- Federal revenue sharing entitlements.
- State, county and local shared revenues.
- Current assessments receivable.

The governmental fund measurement focus is on determination of financial position and changes in financial position (sources, uses, and balances of financial resources), rather than on net income determination.

The proprietary fund types of nonexpendable trusts are accounted for on the accrual basis of accounting. Under the accrual basis of accounting, revenues are recorded at the time they are earned and expenses are recorded at the time liabilities are incurred. The measurement focus of the proprietary funds is on determination of net income, financial position and changes in financial position.

The City's agency and nonexpendable trust funds have measurement focuses in accordance with their purpose. The nonexpendable trust funds are accounted for essentially like proprietary funds, and the agency funds are purely custodial (assets equal liabilities) and do not involve the measurement of operations.

The bases of accounting described above are in accordance with generally accepted accounting principles.

Investments

Investments are stated at cost, which approximates market value.

Receivables

Uncollected property taxes receivable for the governmental fund types which are collected within sixty days following year end are considered measurable and available and accordingly are recognized as revenues in the respective funds. All other uncollected property taxes receivable for the governmental fund types are offset by deferred revenues and, accordingly, have not been recorded as revenue. Uncollected property taxes, including delinquent amounts, are deemed to be substantially collectible or recoverable through foreclosure. Property taxes become a lien against the property as of July 1 in the year in which due and are assessed in October through billing by the County to the property owner. Payments are due in three equal installments on November 15, February 15 and May 15 with a 3% discount available for payment in full on November 15.

Assessments receivable in the debt service and capital projects funds are recorded at the time property owners are assessed for property improvements. Assessments receivable not considered measurable and available are offset by deferred revenues and, accordingly, have not been recorded as revenue.

Receivables of the proprietary funds are recorded as revenue as earned, including services earned but not billed.

Receivables for federal and state grants and state, county and local shared revenues are recorded as revenue in all fund types as earned.

Grant receipts unapplied

Amounts received for grant programs in excess of recorded expenditures are shown in the balance sheet as deferred revenue.

Inventories

Inventories of materials and supplies are charged as expenditures as purchased. The value of inventories of year end are considered insignificant to the combined financial statements for all fund types.

Land held for resale

Land held for resale is recorded at the value of the special assessments for which it was foreclosed, or fair market value as indicated by the county assessor at the date of foreclosure, whichever is less. Any interest on foreclosed assessments that may be collected upon the ultimate disposal of the land held for resale is recognized at the time of sale, or as received, whichever is later.

Fixed assets

Fixed assets in the General Fixed Asset Account Group are stated at historical cost, or estimated historical cost if actual historical cost is not available. The total amount of general fixed assets for which estimated historical costs have been used is not significant. Any donated fixed assets would be recorded at the fair market value of such assets at the date of donation. Fixed assets are charged to expenditures in the governmental fund types as purchased and capitalized in the General Fixed Assets Account Group. Maintenance and repairs of fixed assets are charged to expenditures in the governmental fund types as incurred and not capitalized. Expenditures for road and bridge construction, sidewalk, and drainage systems are not capitalized as fixed assets. Upon disposal of fixed assets, the historical cost or estimated historical cost is removed from the General Fixed Assets Account Group, and proceeds from any sales are generally recorded as revenue in the funds originally acquiring the assets. Depreciation is not computed on these fixed assets.

Fixed assets in the proprietary fund types are capitalized at historical cost or estimated historical cost when historical cost is not available (total estimated historical costs of purchased fixed assets are not significant), or the estimated fair market value at the time received in the case of gifts or projects constructed by others and accepted for ownership and maintenance by the City. Maintenance and repairs are expensed as incurred. Replacements which improve or extend the lives of property are capitalized. Depreciation and amortization of fixed assets of the City's proprietary operations are computed on the straight-line method over the estimated useful lives of the related assets. Upon disposal of such assets, the accounts are relieved of the related historical costs and accumulated depreciation, and resulting gains or losses are reflected in operations. Depreciation taken on fixed assets constructed with grant receipts is recorded as an expense of operations and charged to contributed capital.

The estimated useful lives of proprietary fund fixed assets are as follows:

- Buildings and improvements —20 to 50 years
- Sewage system —40 years
- Machinery and equipment —3 to 25 years

Vacation and sick pay

Vacation pay is recorded as an expenditure in the governmental fund types when the amounts, if any, are expected to be liquidated with expendable available resources. Other vacation pay earned is recorded in the General Long-term Debt Account Group. The amount of accumulated vacation pay is considered normal. Vacation pay is recorded as an expense of the proprietary funds when earned. Sick pay is recorded when leave is taken because it does not vest when earned.

Total (Memorandum only) columns

The Total (Memorandum only) columns of the accompanying combined financial statements represent an aggregate of the columnar statements by fund type and account group and are presented only to facilitate financial analysis. Data in these columns do not present financial position, results of operations, or changes in financial position in conformity with generally accepted accounting principles. Such data do not represent consolidated financial information as interfund eliminations have not been made in its aggregation.

Budgets

The City budgets all funds. A City Council order authorizing appropriations for each fund sets the level by which expenditures cannot legally exceed appropriations. Either expenditures by activity within funds or total personal services, materials and services, capital outlay and other expenditures by fund are the levels of control established by the City Council order. The detail budget document, however, is required to contain more specific, detailed information for the above mentioned expenditure categories. Appropriations lapse at the end of each fiscal year.

Unexpected additional resources may be appropriated through the use of a supplemental budget and City Council action. The original and supplemental budgets require budget hearings before the public, publications in newspapers and approval by the City Council. Original and supplemental budgets may be modified during the fiscal year by the use of appropriations transfers between the legal categories. Such transfers require approval by the City Council. The City made several appropriations transfers during the year ended June 30, 1987.

The City budgets all fund types using substantially all of the principles of the modified accrual basis of accounting. The budget is prepared somewhat differently from generally accepted accounting principles as described in Note 4. Therefore, the Combined Statement of Revenues, Expenditures and Changes in Fund Balances (Budgetary Basis) - Budget and Actual - All Governmental Fund Types is presented on the budgetary basis. The Combined Statement of Revenues, Expenditures and Changes in Fund Balances - All Governmental Fund Types is presented in accordance with generally accepted accounting principles.

Capitalizable interest

Fixed assets constructed with tax exempt borrowings issued subsequent to August 31, 1982 include capitalized interest as part of the costs of fixed assets. All interest costs of the borrowing less any interest earned on investments acquired with the proceeds of the borrowing are capitalized from the date of the borrowing until the assets are ready for their intended use. Interest costs prior to the above date on constructed assets was insignificant.

No interest was capitalized during fiscal 1987.

Leases

Leases which meet certain criteria established by the Financial Accounting Standards Board are classified as capital leases and the assets and related liabilities are recorded at amounts equal to the lesser of the present value of minimum lease payments or the fair value of the lease property at the beginning of the respective lease term. Leases which do not meet the criteria of a capital lease are classified as operating leases.

Long-term debt

Unmatured long-term debt directly related to and expected to be paid from proprietary funds is included as a liability of such funds. All other unmatured long-term debt is recorded in the General Long-term Debt Account Group. Repayment of all General Long-term Debt Account Group liabilities is recorded in the debt service funds. Payment of accrued vacation pay will be made from the governmental funds incurring the expenditure.

Bond discount and issuance costs

Bond discount and issuance costs resulting from revenue bond and general obligation bond issues are amortized over the related debt repayment period. Unamortized bond discount and issuance costs are offset against bonds payable.

Contributed capital

Contributed capital in the proprietary funds represents the accumulation of contributions in the form of cash or other assets which generally do not have to be returned to the contributor. Such contributions are recorded directly to contributed capital and, accordingly, are not recognized as revenue (see Note 10). The following transactions are recorded as contributions in the proprietary funds:

- Cash transfers of equity and bond sale proceeds from other funds.
- Receipts of federal and state grants externally restricted for acquisition of fixed assets.
- Fixed assets contributed from other funds or the General Fixed Assets Account Group.
- Contributions from customers for the acquisition of fixed assets.

Designated fund balances

Restriction of fund balances for debt service and the purchase of fixed assets are recorded as designations of fund balances.

Assessments

During the year the City adopted the provisions of the Statement No. 6 of the Governmental Accounting Standards Board (GASB) regarding special assessment funds. Pursuant to that statement, the former special assessment funds were determined to be properly classified as other types of funds. Additionally, the statement requires that the debt formerly recorded in the special assessment funds be transferred to the General Long-term Debt Group of Accounts. Accordingly, the fund balance of the special assessments funds at July 1, 1986 was increased by $3,905,000 related to the transfer of debt and the remaining fund balance was allocated $3,029,208 to a debt service fund entitled the Bancroft Bond Redemption Fund, and $239,025 to the Improvement Fund, a capital projects fund.

NOTE 2 - ORGANIZATION AND OPERATION:

The City of Albany, Oregon (located in Linn and Benton Counties), was incorporated on October 24, 1864. The City Council, composed of the Mayor and Council members, forms the legislative branch of the City government. Administration of the City is vested in the City Manager who is appointed for an indefinite term by the Council. The Manager is responsible for the appointment of the City's employees. Albany's City Manager form of government was initiated in 1949 and operates under a charter approved by the voters in 1956.

The City's financial operations are accounted for in the following funds and account groups:

Governmental Fund Types

General Fund

This fund accounts for the financial resources of the City which are not accounted for in any other fund. Principal sources of revenue are property taxes, franchise fees, licenses and permits, billings for interfund services, and state shared revenues. Primary expenditures are for police, ambulance and fire protection, public works, court, library, planning and general administration.

Special Revenue Funds

These funds account for revenues derived from specific taxes or other designated revenue sources including state gasoline tax, federal and state grants, revenue sharing entitlements, property taxes and fees that are legally restricted to expenditure for specified purposes. When a special revenue fund is not an operating fund, transfers are made from the special revenue fund to the operating funds authorized to make the expenditures. Funds included in this category are:

- Street
- Parks and Recreation
- Transient Room Tax
- Public Transit
- Federal Revenue Sharing
- State Revenue Sharing
- Grants
- Building Inspection
- Economic Improvement District

Debt Service Funds

- The General Obligation Debt Service Fund accounts for the payment of principal and interest on general obligation debt.
- The Bancroft Bond Redemption Fund accounts for the collection of assessments from benefitted property owners and the payment of principal and interest on Bancroft Improvement Serial (special assessment) Bonds.
- The Albany Redevelopment Agency Debt Service Fund accounts for the payment of principal and interest on the Albany Redevelopment Agency Urban Renewal and Redevelopment Bonds.

Capital Projects Funds

These funds account for the financial resources to be used for the acquisition or construction of major capital facilities. The fund type includes:

- Albany Redevelopment Agency Capital Projects Fund—This fund accounts for the construction of infrastructure assets in a designated area of the city. Major financing source was tax increment bonds and is now the collection of the incremental taxes raised by the improvements.
- Equipment Replacement Fund—This fund accounts for monies designated for replacement of equipment used by the City's various operating funds. Major revenue sources are transfers from other funds and interest on investments.
- Improvement Fund—This fund accounts for the construction and financing of specific assessment projects and the collection of assessments from benefitted property owners.
- Senior Center Construction Fund—This is a new fund to account for the construction and financing of a new Senior Center building within the City.

Proprietary Fund Types

Enterprise Funds

- The Sewer Fund accounts for the expansion, operation and maintenance of the City's sanitary sewer system. The system is intended to be self-supporting through charges to customers. The fund includes two budgetary funds: the Sewer Fund and the Sewer Improvement Fund.
- The Water Fund accounts for the expansion, operation and maintenance of the City's water supply system. The system is intended to be self sufficient through charges to customers.

Internal Service Funds

- The Equipment Maintenance Fund accounts for expenditures incurred in maintaining City owned equipment. Primary revenues are charges for services to the various operating funds.
- The Data Processing Services Fund accounts for expenditures incurred in purchasing, maintaining and operating City owned computers, as well as processing the City's financial and other information. The primary revenue source is charges for services to the various operating funds.

Fiduciary Fund Types

These funds account for resources received and held by the City in a fiduciary capacity. Disbursements from these funds are made in accordance with the trust agreement for each particular fund. Funds included in this categroy are:

Agency Funds

- Senior Center Foundation Trust
- Deferred Compensation

Nonexpendable Trust Funds

- Manela Trust
- Library Memorial

Account Groups

General Fixed Assets Account Group

This account group accounts for the City's investment in fixed assets, with the exception of those assets held by the proprietary fund types. Expenditures for the acquisition of general fixed assets are recorded in the various governmental fund types; the costs of such assets are capitalized in this account group. As fixed assets are disposed of, the cost or estimated historical cost is removed from this account group; receipts from sale of general fixed assets are generally accounted for as revenue of the fund which purchased the assets.

General Long-term Debt Account Group

This account group accounts for long-term debt not recorded in the special assessment funds and proprietary funds, and vacation pay not recorded in other funds.

NOTE 3 - GOVERNMENTAL ENTITIES INCLUDED IN THE COMBINED FINANCIAL STATEMENTS:

All significant activities and organizations over which the City exercises oversight responsibility have been included in the City's combined financial statements. The following criteria regarding manifestation of oversight were considered by the City in its evaluation of City organizations and activities:

- Financial interdependency - the City receives financial support or provides financial benefit to the organization, is responsible for or has directly or indirectly guaranteed the organization's debts.
- Authoritative appointment of governing authority - the City Council appoints the organization's governing authority and maintains a significant continuing relationship with the governing authority pertaining to the public functions of the organization.

The City determined that only the Albany Redevelopment Agency met the criteria set forth above and should be included in the financial statements. No other entities were considered but excluded.

NOTE 4 - RECONCILIATION OF GENERALLY ACCEPTED ACCOUNTING PRINCIPLES BASIS TO BUDGETARY BASIS:

The budget of the City is prepared differently from generally accepted accounting principles. Therefore, for purposes of preparing the Combined Statement of Revenues, Expenditures and Changes in Fund Balances (Budgetary Basis) - Budget and Actual - All Governmental Fund Types, the actual results of operations have been adjusted to the budgetary basis. The Combined Statement of Revenues, Expenditures and Changes in Fund Balances—All Governmental Fund Types is presented on the generally accepted accounting principles basis.

The following is a reconciliation of the differences between the budgetary basis and generally accepted accounting principles basis for revenues and other sources over (under) expenditures and other uses for the aforementioned combined financial statements:

	General Fund	Special Revenue	Debt Service	Capital Projects	Total
Revenues and other sources over (under) expenditures and other uses - generally accepted accounting principles basis	$(330,600)	$(99,892)	$(779,270)	$1,074,145	$(135,617)
Revenues:					
Interest revenues budgeted in Debt Service Funds considered Capital Projects Funds revenue under generally accepted accounting principles			16,446	(16,446)	
Tax revenues considered available, recorded as received in cash on budgetary basis	10,011	2,583	622	(2,471)	10,745
Assessment revenues earned, not budgeted			526,645	27,140	553,785
Bond sale proceeds budgeted in General Obligation Debt Service Fund representing an other financing source in Capital Projects Funds under generally accepted accounting principles			778,571	(778,571)	
Expenditures:					
Change in vacation pay accrual	7,921	1,925			9,846
Amounts budgeted in Debt Service Funds representing Capital Projects Funds expenditures under generally accepted accounting principles			(47,167)	47,167	
Revenues and other sources over (under) expenditures and other uses - budgetary basis	$(312,668)	$(95,384)	$ 495,847	$ 350,964	$ 438,759

NOTE 5 - CASH AND INVESTMENTS:

The City of Albany pools virtually all funds for investment purposes. Each fund type's portion of this pool is displayed on the combined balance sheet as "Cash and Investments."

Deposits with financial institutions

At year-end, the carrying amount of the City's deposits was $1,134,325 and the bank balance was $1,422,690. Of the bank balance, $505,000 was covered by federal depository insurance or by collateral held by one or more of the State's authorized collateral pool managers in the name of the City, and $917,690 was uninsured and uncollateralized. The City has, however, met the requirements of Oregon law as to collateralization of bank balances. The State requires collateral be deposited with a value of 25% of the balances over federal depository insurance, but in some instances, the State Banking Commission can require banks and other financial institutions to put up over 25% of the balances of municipal corporations' deposits as collateral. The City cannot, however, determine which, if any, institutions have been required to meet a collateral requirement larger than 25%. The City independently monitors its depository institutions for indications of any situations that could potentially cause loss of City funds. The City was fully collateralized in accordance with State requirements throughout the year.

Investments

Oregon Revised Statutes, Chapter 294, authorize the City to invest in obligations of the U. S. Treasury, U. S. Government agencies and instrumentalities, bankers' acceptances guaranteed by an Oregon financial institution, repurchase agreements, State of Oregon Local Government Investment Pool, and various interest bearing bonds of Oregon municipalities. In addition, the City's investments are governed by a written investment policy. The policy, which is reviewed by the Oregon Short-term Fund Board, the City's Investment Advisory Committee, and the Albany City Council, specifies the City's investment objectives, required diversification, certain limitations, and reporting requirements.

The City's investments are categorized below to give an indication of the level of risk assumed by the City at June 30, 1987. Category 1 includes investments that are insured or registered or for which the securities are held by the City or its agent in the City's name. Category 2 includes uninsured and unregistered investments for which the securities are held by the broker's, banker's or dealer's trust department or agent in the City's name. Category 3 includes uninsured and unregistered investments for which the securities are held by brokers or dealers, or by their trust department or agent, but not in the City's name.

	Category			Carrying	Market
	1	2	3	amount	value
U. S. Government Securities	$1,920,589	$	$	$ 1,920,589	$ 1,941,916
U. S. Government Securities held in escrow		1,304,119		1,304,119	1,292,959
U. S. Government Instrumentality Securities	1,959,469			1,959,469	1,969,058
Bankers' Acceptances		5,387,620		5,387,620	5,473,667
Municipal Bonds		210,500		210,500	210,500
ICMA Deferred Compensation Trust			346,890	346,890	346,890
	$3,880,058	$6,902,239	$ 346,890	11,129,187	11,234,990
State of Oregon Local Government Investment Pool				2,615,834	2,615,834
Total investments				13,745,021	13,850,824
Petty cash				862	862
Deposits with financial institutions				1,134,325	1,134,325
Total cash and investments				$14,880,208	$14,986,011

Cash and investments are shown on the Combined Balance Sheet - All Fund Types and Account Groups as follows:

Cash and investments	$11,886,658
Restricted cash and investments	2,993,550
	$14,880,208

NOTE 6 - DUE FROM/TO OTHER FUNDS:

Interfund accounts at June 30, 1987 comprise:

		Due to	
		Capital Projects	
	Special Revenue Grants	Albany Redevelopment Agency Capital Projects	Totals
Due from:			
Special revenue:			
Parks and Recreation	$9,275		$ 9,275
Enterprise:			
Water		$10,926	10,926
			$20,201

NOTE 7 - FIXED ASSETS:

Changes in General Fixed Assets Account Group for the year ended June 30, 1987 are as follows:

	Land	Buildings and improvements	Machinery and equipment	Total
Balance, June 30, 1986	$1,257,580	$1,986,975	$2,884,372	$6,128,927
Additions and transfers in			291,383	291,383
Disposals and transfers out			(125,466)	(125,466)
Balances, June 30, 1987	$1,257,580	$1,986,975	$3,050,289	$6,294,844

Fixed assets by major classes for the proprietary funds, at June 30, 1987, comprise:

	Land and land improvements	Buildings and improvements	Equipment	Water and Sewer lines	Less accumulated depreciation	Totals
Enterprise Funds:						
Sewer	$ 42,970	$2,177,568	$1,653,925	$2,534,557	$(1,884,777)	$ 4,524,243
Water	109,110	256,403	2,620,806	6,496,690	(1,170,186)	8,312,823
Internal Service Funds:						
Data processing			303,077		(223,219)	79,858
Equipment maintenance	31,260	139,562	49,583		(57,774)	162,631
	$183,340	$2,573,533	$4,627,391	$9,031,247	$(3,335,956)	$13,079,555

NOTE 8 - BONDS PAYABLE:

Bonds payable principal transactions for the year ended June 30, 1987 are as follows:

	Outstanding June 30, 1986	Issued during year net of discounts and issue costs	Defeased or matured and paid during year	Amortization of discounts and issue costs	Outstanding June 30, 1987
General obligation bonds:					
Two serial issues, for sewer system improvements, original amounts $1,300,000, issued in fiscal 1968 and 1969, interest rates from 4.00% to 4.40% payable from general property tax revenues collected in the General Obligation Debt Service Fund	$ 185,000	$	$ (70,000)	$	$ 115,000
1987 Senior Center Bonds, issued in fiscal 1987 to Finance construction of the expansion of City of Albany Senior Center, face amount $800,000, interest rates from 5.4 - 6.0%. Payable from an annual tax which may be levied upon the taxable property within the City		778,571		1,633	780,204
Tax increment bonds:					
1984 Albany Redevelopment Agency Urban Renewal and Redevelopment Bonds, issued in fiscal 1985 to redevelop a special area in the City, face amount $2,400,000, interest rates from 7.25% to 10.875%. Payable from incremental tax receipts from the special area	2,269,253		(50,000)	7,149	2,226,402
Eight Bancroft improvement serial issues special assessments, interest rates from 3.8% to 12.5%, original amounts $7,740,000 issued in fiscal 1977 through 1983, payable first from assessments to benefited properties and second, if necessary, from general property tax revenues	3,905,000		(740,000)		3,165,000
Total General Long-term Debt Account Group	6,359,253	778,571	(860,000)	8,782	6,286,606

	Outstanding June 30, 1986	Issued during year net of discounts and issue costs	Defeased or matured and paid during year	Amortization of discounts and issue costs	Outstanding June 30, 1987
General Obligation/ revenue pledge bonds:					
1985 Advance Refunding Water Bonds issued in fiscal 1985, face amount $9,370,000, for refunding of the 1984 Water Revenue bonds payable first from water system revenues and second, if necessary, from general property tax revenues	$ 9,109,342	$	$(9,117,073)	$ 7,731	$
1987 Advance Refunding General Obligation Water Bonds issued in fiscal 1987, face amount $9,095,000, for refunding the $7,820,000 callable portion only, of the 1985 Advance Refunding General Obligation Bonds payable from monies deposited in the General Obligation Debt Service Fund for the refunded bonds, and water system revenues		8,862,466		7,306	8,869,772
Revenue bonds:					
1984 Sewer System Revenue Bonds recorded in the Sewer Fund issued in fiscal 1985 for development of the City's sewer system, face amount $3,000,000 interest rates from 7% to 9.75% payable from sewer system revenues	2,824,556		(2,826,813)	2,257	
1986 Advance Refunding Sewer Revenue Bonus issued in fiscal 1987, face amount $3,560,000 for refunding all of the City's 1984 outstanding sewer revenue bonds payable from monies deposited in the General Obligation Debt Service Fund and sewer system revenues		3,414,088		7,430	3,421,518
Total proprietary funds	11,933,898	12,276,554	(11,943,886)	24,724	12,291,290
	$18,293,151	$13,055,125	$(12,803,886)	$33,506	$18,577,896

During the year, the City defeased the 1985 Advance Refunding Water Bonds and the 1984 Sewer System Revenue Bonds by placing cash and investments in escrow in such amounts and at such interest rates that the required interest will be fully paid when due and the principal of the bonds will be paid off when first callable. Accordingly, the debt related to these issues is not shown as debt of the City on the Combined Balance Sheet. The City has $21,873,386 in various escrow accounts to meet the obligations of these issues. The face amounts of the defeased bonds, not yet called and cancelled, at June 30, 1987, is $21,825,000 including bonds from the 1984 Water Revenue Bonds defeased in fiscal 1985. The City recognized an extraordinary gain on defeasance of debt of $257,873 in the Water fund, and an extraordinary loss of $616,207 in the Sewer Fund. Each transaction, however, resulted in an economic gain to the City.

Future maturities of unmatured bond principal and interest for the fiscal years ending June 30 are as follows:

Fiscal year	General obligation Principal	General obligation Interest	General obligation/ Senior Center Principal	General obligation/ Senior Center Interest	General obligation/ Tax increment financing Principal	General obligation/ Tax increment financing Interest
1988	$ 70,000	$ 3,481	$	$ 45,300	$ 55,000	$ 236,560
1989	45,000	990		45,300	55,000	231,954
1990				45,300	60,000	226,991
1991				45,300	65,000	221,441
1992				45,300	75,000	215,048
Thereafter			800,000	118,475	1,995,000	1,690,482
Less - unamoritzed discounts and issuance costs			(19,796)		(78,598)	
	$115,000	$ 4,471	$780,204	$344,975	$2,226,402	$2,822,476

Fiscal year	General obligation/ Improvement Principal	General obligation/ Improvement Interest	General obligation/ Revenue pledge bonds Principal	General obligation/ Revenue pledge bonds Interest	Revenue bonds Principal	Revenue bonds Interest
1988	$ 730,000	$227,991	$	$ 588,833	$ 105,000	$ 238,005
1989	710,000	177,302	60,000	587,513	70,000	233,893
1990	605,000	125,895	60,000	584,783	75,000	230,174
1991	545,000	77,040	65,000	581,748	80,000	226,005
1992	375,000	36,812	70,000	578,268	80,000	221,505
Thereafter	200,000	9,500	8,840,000	6,865,435	3,150,000	2,458,423
Less - unamortized discounts and issuance costs			(225,228)		(138,482)	
	$3,165,000	$654,540	$8,869,772	$9,786,580	$3,421,518	$3,608,005

NOTE 9 - CAPITAL LEASE OBLIGATIONS AND ACCRUED VACATION PAY:

The City has entered into a lease/purchase agreement for computer equipment. The interest rate is 10.5%. The changes in the liability and the minimum future lease payments to be made by the City are as follows:

Payments due in fiscal year	June 30, 1986	Payments during year	June 30, 1987
1987	$37,498	$(37,498)	$
1988	37,498		37,498
	74,996	(37,498)	37,498
Less amount attributable to interest	(7,616)	5,567	(2,049)
Present value of minimum lease payments (capital lease obligation)	$67,380	$(31,931)	$35,449

Debt service on the lease obligations is paid by the Data Processing Services Fund, an internal service fund.

Obligation for accrued vacation not to be taken within sixty days of year-end increased by $25,582 during the year ended June 30, 1987 due, primarily, to wage increases.

NOTE 10 - CONTRIBUTED CAPITAL:

Changes in contributed capital in the proprietary funds for the year ended June 30, 1987 are as follows:

	Enterprise Funds	Internal Service Funds	Total
Balances, June 30, 1986	$4,306,103	$199,844	$4,505,947
Net contribution of fixed assets from other funds	49,687		49,687
Fixed assets donated from other funds	150,177	22,474	172,651
Transfer of depreciation expense on contributed fixed asset	(103,043)		(103,043)
Balances, June 30, 1987	$4,402,924	$222,318	$4,625,242

NOTE 11 - RECONCILIATION OF INTERFUND TRANSFERS:

The following reconciles operating transfers out and in on the Combined Statement of Revenues, Expenditures and Changes in Fund Balances, All Governmental Fund Types:

Operating transfers out	$1,266,040
Adjustments to reconcile to operating transfers in:	
Operating transfer out in the Enterprise Funds	138,000
Operating transfers in in the Enterprise Funds	(287,875)
Operating transfers in	$1,116,165

NOTE 12 - PENSION AND DEFERRED COMPENSATION PLANS:

Substantially all City employees are participants in the State of Oregon Public Employees Retirement System (PERS), an agent multiple-employer public employee retirement system that acts as a common investment and administrative agent for governmental units in the State of Oregon. The City's payroll for employees covered by PERS for the year ended June 30, 1987 was $5,522,385; the City's total payroll was $5,527,878.

All City full-time employees are eligible to participate in the PERS. Benefits generally vest after five years of continuous service. Retirement is allowed at age 58 with unreduced benefits, but retirement is generally available after age 55 with reduced benefits. Compulsory retirement age is 70. Retirement benefits are based on salary and length of service, are calculated using a formula and are payable in a lump sum or monthly using several payment options. PERS also provides death and disability benefits. These benefit provisions and other requirements are established by state statutes.

The City is required by the rules applicable to PERS to contribute 9.12% of covered employees' salaries to PERS. The required employee contribution of 6% of covered compensation is paid by the City pursuant to collective bargaining agreements.

The amount shown below as the "pension benefit obligation" required by Governmental Accounting Standards Board Statement No. 5 is a standardized disclosure measure of the present value of pension benefits, adjusted for the effects of projected salary increases estimated to be payable in the future as a result of employee service to date. The measure is intended to help users assess the funding status of PERS on a going-concern basis, assess progress made in accumulating sufficient assets to pay benefits when due, and make comparisons among employers. The measure is the actuarial present value of credited projected benefits, and is independent of the funding method used to determine contributions to PERS.

The pension benefit obligation was computed as part of an actuarial valuation performed as of December 31, 1985 and is the most recent available. Significant actuarial assumptions used in the valuation include (a) a rate of return on the investment of present and future assets of 7.5%, (b) projected salary increase of 6% per year in addition to salary increases due to promotions and longevity, (c) post-retirement benefit increases of 2% per year (the maximum allowable), and (d) a 10% final increase in benefits for members who utilize unused sick leave to increase the final average salary to calculate their pension. No obligation for retirees is attributed to the City as PERS pools the risk related to retired employees among all employers. Accordingly, the City's separate actuarial valuation covers only current employees.

The excess of the actuarial value of assets over the actuarial present value of accrued benefit applicable to the City's employees was $1,052,074 at December 31, 1985, as follows:

Net assets available for benefits at market value for stocks and real estate, at an adjusted yield basis of 7.5% for bonds, mortgages and loans, and at cost for other assets	$8,612,054
Pension benefit obligation - current employees:	
Member account balances	3,136,280
Vested accrued benefits	3,828,895
Non-vested accrued benefits	594,805
	7,559,980
Excess of actuarial value of assets over pension benefit obligation	$1,052,074

PERS policy provides for actuarially determined periodic contributions that are sufficient to pay benefits when due. The contribution rate for normal cost is determined using the "entry age actuarial cost method." A thirty year amortization, which started in 1976, is used to amortize the costs of the unfunded actuarial liabilities. Any ad hoc benefit increases are funded over 30 years.

The significant actuarial assumptions used to compute the actuarially determined contribution requirement are the same as those used to compute the pension benefit obligation described above.

The City's contribution of $865,203 for the year ended June 30, 1987 was made in accordance with the actuarially determined requirements computed through the actuarial valuation performed as of December 31, 1982. No breakdown of the components of the contribution is available. The City's contribution rate will be adjusted beginning January 1, 1988 to 10.37% of covered payroll based on the most current actuarial valuation. The increase is caused by 1985 legislation (0.19%) and 1985 actuarial valuation results (1.06%). Employee's portion (6%) will remain unchanged.

Ten-year and three-year trend information, which is designed to give an indication of the progress made in accumulating sufficient assets to pay benefits when due, as required by Statement No. 5 of the Governmental Accounting Standards Board, is not available because the first actuarial valuation using the required actuarial valuation method was prepared as of December 31, 1985. PERS currently intends to conduct actuarial valuations biennially. At the most recent valuation, the assets exceeded the pension benefit liability by approximately 14%. The excess of the actuarially computed assets over the pension benefit liability approximates 19% of the City's fiscal 1987 payroll. The City's contributions to PERS have been $865,203, $804,009, and $757,254 for fiscal years 1987, 1986 and 1985, respectively.

The City has a deferred compensation plan which is available to all employees wherein they may execute an individual agreement with the City for amounts earned by them to be paid at a future date when certain circumstances are met. Monies accumulated by the City under its deferred compensation plan have been deposited with ICMA Retirement Corporation. The amount deferred since the inception of the plan and investment earnings thereon, net of withdrawals, total $346,890 at June 30, 1987 and is included in cash and investments and offset by a corresponding liability in an agency fund.

The amount accumulated by the City under the deferred compensation plan is excluded from resources for budgetary purposes. Such amount reflects a general liability by the City to its employees whose rights are equal to but not greater than the rights of other general creditors with respect to such amount. Similarly, disbursement of funds to employees under the plan, once circumstances of termination occur, is not included as expenditures for budgetary purposes.

NOTE 13 - OPERATING LEASES:

The City leases office space and photocopiers under operating lease agreements. The total minimum lease payments required under the lease agreements is as follows:

Fiscal year ending June 30	
1988	$ 69,000
1989	69,000
1990	69,000
1991	69,000
1992	69,000
	$345,000

Total lease expense aggregated $69,000 for the year ended June 30, 1987.

NOTE 14 - BUDGETARY OVEREXPENDITURES:

The City overexpended the following number of budgetary activities in the funds indicated during the year ended June 30, 1987. General Fund, 4; Street Fund, 1; Parks and Recreation Fund, 2; Transient Room Tax Fund, 1; Building Inspection Fund, 1; Equipment Replacement Fund, 1; Equipment Maintenance Fund, 1; Senior Center Foundation Trust Fund, 1; Library Memorial Fund, 1.

NOTE 15 - COMMITMENTS AND CONTINGENT LIABILITIES:

The City is contingently liable with respect to lawsuits and other claims incidental to the ordinary course of its operations. Claims are generally covered by insurance. In the opinion of City management, based on the advice of legal counsel with respect to such litigation and claims, the ultimate disposition of these matters will not have a material adverse effect on the financial position or results of operations of the City's funds.

The City has guaranteed half of the borrowings of a private company located within the City by holding $80,000 of certificates of deposit in escrow at a bank. The loan should be repaid by the company over the next four years. City management believes there is little likelihood of a default causing the City to incur costs related to this guarantee.

NOTE 16 - SEGMENT INFORMATION FOR ENTERPRISE FUNDS:

The City maintains two Enterprise Funds which provide water and sewer services, respectively. Segment information for the year ended June 30, 1987 was as follows:

	Water Fund	Sewer Fund	Total Enterprise Funds
Operating revenue	$ 2,808,139	$1,980,615	$ 4,788,754
Depreciation and amortization expense	489,170	185,867	675,037
Operating income	825,955	128,037	953,992
Revenue from other governmental units	—	—	—
Operating transfers in	—	287,875	287,875
Operating transfers out	75,000	63,000	138,000
Net income (loss)	1,155,987	(185,184)	970,803
Current capital contributions and transfers	49,687	47,134	96,821
Property, plant and equipment:			
Additions	374,183	137,708	511,891
Deletions	—	3,500	3,500
Net working capital	492,669	2,387,306	2,879,975
Total assets	10,941,407	8,113,906	19,055,313
Long-term liabilities:			
Payable from operating revenue:			
Current portion	—	105,000	105,000
Long-term portion	8,869,772	3,316,518	12,186,290
Total equity	1,827,217	4,617,084	6,444,301

PRESENT VALUE TABLES

Present Value of $1 Due in *n* Periods

n	1%	2%	3%	4%	5%	6%	7%	8%	9%	10%	12%	14%	16%
1	.9901	.9804	.9709	.9615	.9524	.9434	.9346	.9249	.9174	.9091	.8929	.8772	.8621
2	.9803	.9612	.9426	.9246	.9070	.8900	.8734	.8573	.8417	.8264	.7972	.7695	.7432
3	.9706	.9423	.9151	.8890	.8638	.8396	.8163	.7938	.7722	.7513	.7118	.6750	.6407
4	.9610	.9239	.8885	.8548	.8227	.7921	.7629	.7350	.7084	.6830	.6355	.5921	.5523
5	.9515	.9057	.8626	.8219	.7835	.7473	.7130	.6806	.6499	.6209	.5674	.5194	.4761
6	.9420	.8880	.8375	.7903	.7462	.7050	.6663	.6302	.5963	.5645	.5066	.4556	.4104
7	.9327	.8706	.8131	.7599	.7107	.6651	.6228	.5835	.5470	.5132	.4524	.3996	.3538
8	.9235	.8535	.7894	.7307	.6768	.6274	.5820	.5403	.5019	.4665	.4039	.3506	.3050
9	.9143	.8368	.7664	.7026	.6446	.5919	.5439	.5002	.4604	.4241	.3606	.3075	.2630
10	.9053	.8204	.7441	.6756	.6139	.5584	.5084	.4632	.4224	.3855	.3220	.2697	.2267
11	.8963	.8043	.7224	.6496	.5847	.5368	.4751	.4289	.3875	.3505	.2875	.2366	.1954
12	.8874	.7885	.7014	.6246	.5568	.4970	.4440	.3971	.3555	.3186	.2567	.2076	.1685
13	.8787	.7730	.6810	.6006	.5303	.4688	.4150	.3677	.3262	.2897	.2292	.1821	.1452
14	.8700	.7579	.6611	.5775	.5051	.4423	.3878	.3405	.2993	.2633	.2046	.1597	.1252
15	.8614	.7430	.6419	.5553	.4810	.4173	.3625	.3152	.2745	.2394	.1827	.1401	.1079
16	.8528	.7284	.6232	.5339	.4581	.3936	.3387	.2919	.2519	.2176	.1631	.1229	.0930
17	.8444	.7142	.6050	.5134	.4363	.3714	.3166	.2703	.2311	.1978	.1456	.1078	.0802
18	.8360	.7002	.5874	.4936	.4155	.3503	.2959	.2502	.2120	.1799	.1300	.0946	.0691
19	.8277	.6864	.5703	.4746	.3957	.3305	.2765	.2317	.1945	.1635	.1161	.0829	.0596
20	.8195	.6730	.5537	.4564	.3769	.3118	.2584	.2145	.1784	.1486	.1037	.0728	.0514
21	.8114	.6598	.5375	.4388	.3589	.2942	.2415	.1987	.1637	.1351	.0926	.0638	.0443
22	.8034	.6468	.5219	.4220	.3418	.2775	.2257	.1839	.1502	.1229	.0826	.0560	.0382
23	.7954	.6342	.5067	.4057	.3256	.2618	.2109	.1703	.1378	.1117	.0738	.0491	.0329
24	.7876	.6217	.4919	.3901	.3101	.2470	.1971	.1577	.1264	.1015	.0659	.0431	.0284
25	.7798	.6095	.4776	.3751	.2953	.2330	.1842	.1460	.1160	.0923	.0588	.0378	.0245
26	.7721	.5976	.4637	.3607	.2812	.2198	.1722	.1352	.1064	.0839	.0525	.0332	.0211
27	.7644	.5859	.4502	.3468	.2678	.1609	.1609	.1252	.0976	.0763	.0469	.0291	.0182
28	.7568	.5744	.4371	.3335	.2551	.1956	.1504	.1159	.0896	.0693	.0419	.0255	.0157
29	.7493	.5361	.4244	.3206	.2429	.1846	.1406	.1073	.0821	.0630	.0374	.0224	.0135
30	.7419	.5521	.4120	.3083	.2314	.1741	.1314	.0994	.0754	.0573	.0334	.0196	.0116
31	.7346	.5412	.4000	.2965	.2204	.1643	.1228	.0920	.0692	0521	.0298	.0172	.0100
32	.7273	.5306	.3883	.2851	.2099	.1550	.1147	.0852	.0634	.0474	.0266	.0151	.0087
33	.7201	.5202	.3770	.2741	.1999	.1462	.1072	.0789	.0582	.0431	.0238	.0133	.0075
34	.7130	.5100	.3660	.2635	.1903	.1379	.1002	.0731	.0534	.0391	.0212	.0116	.0064
35	.7059	.5000	.3554	.2534	.1813	.1301	.0937	.0676	.0490	.0356	.0189	.0102	.0055
36	.6989	.4902	.3450	.2437	.1727	.1227	.0875	.0626	.0449	.0324	.0169	.0089	.0048
37	.6920	.4806	.3350	.2343	.1644	.1158	.0818	.0580	.0412	.0294	.0151	.0078	.0041
38	.6852	.4712	.3252	.2253	.1566	.1092	.0765	.0537	.0378	.0267	.0135	.0069	.0036
39	.6784	.4620	3158	.2166	.1492	.1031	.0715	.0497	.0347	.0243	.0120	.0060	.0031
40	.6717	.4529	.3066	.2083	.1420	.0972	.0668	.0460	.0318	.0221	.0107	.0053	.0026
41	.6650	.4440	.2976	.2003	.1353	.0917	.0624	.0426	.0292	.0201	.0096	.0046	.0023
42	.6584	.4353	.2890	.1926	.1288	.0865	.0583	.0395	.0268	.0183	.0086	.0041	.0020
43	.6519	.4268	.2805	.1852	.1227	.0816	.0545	.0365	.0246	.0166	.0077	.0036	.0017
44	.6454	.4184	.2724	.1781	.1169	.0770	.0509	.0338	.0226	.0151	.0068	.0031	.0015
45	.6391	.4102	.2644	.1712	.1113	.0727	.0476	.0313	.0207	.0137	.0061	.0027	.0013
46	.6327	.4021	.2567	.1646	.1060	.0685	.0445	.0290	.0190	.0125	.0054	.0024	.0011
47	.6265	.3943	.2493	.1583	.1010	.0647	.0416	.0269	.0174	.0113	.0049	.0021	.0009
48	.6203	.3865	.2420	.1522	.0961	.0610	.0389	.0249	.0160	.0103	.0043	.0019	.0008
49	.6141	.3790	.2350	.1463	.0916	.0575	.0363	.0230	.0147	.0094	.0039	.0016	.0007
50	.6080	.3715	.2281	.1407	.0872	.0543	.0340	.0213	.0135	.0085	.0035	.0014	.0006

Present Value of an Annuity of $1 per Period

n	1%	2%	3%	4%	5%	6%	7%	8%	9%	10%	12%	14%	16%
1	.9901	.9804	.9709	.9615	.9524	.9434	.9346	.9259	.9174	.9091	.8929	.8772	.8621
2	1.9704	1.9416	1.9135	1.8861	1.8594	1.8334	1.8080	1.7833	1.7591	1.7355	1.6901	1.6467	1.6052
3	2.9410	2.8839	2.8286	2.7751	2.7232	2.6730	2.6243	2.5771	2.5313	2.4869	2.4018	2.3216	2.2459
4	3.9020	3.8077	3.7171	3.6299	3.5459	3.4651	3.3872	3.3121	3.2397	3.1699	3.0374	2.9137	2.7982
5	4.8534	4.7135	4.5797	4.4518	4.3295	4.2124	4.1002	3.9927	3.8897	3.7908	3.6048	3.4331	3.2743
6	5.7955	5.6014	5.4172	5.2421	5.0757	4.9173	4.7666	4.6229	4.4859	4.3553	4.1114	3.8887	3.6847
7	6.7282	6.4720	6.2302	6.0021	5.7864	5.5824	5.3893	5.2064	5.0330	4.8684	4.5638	4.2883	4.0386
8	7.6517	7.3255	7.0197	6.7328	6.4632	6.2098	5.9713	5.7466	5.5348	5.3349	4.9676	4.6389	4.3436
9	8.5660	8.1622	7.7861	7.4353	7.1078	6.8017	6.5152	6.2469	5.9953	5.7590	5.3282	4.9464	4.6065
10	9.4713	8.9826	8.5302	8.1109	7.7217	7.3601	7.0236	6.7101	6.4177	6.1446	5.6502	5.2161	4.8332
11	10.3676	9.7868	9.2526	8.7605	8.3064	7.8869	7.4987	7.1390	6.8052	6.4951	5.9377	5.4527	5.0286
12	11.2551	10.5753	9.9540	9.3851	8.8633	8.3839	7.9427	7.5361	7.1607	6.8137	6.1944	5.6603	5.1971
13	12.1338	11.3484	10.6349	9.9857	9.3936	8.8527	8.3577	7.9038	7.4869	7.1034	6.4235	5.8424	5.3423
14	13.0037	12.1062	11.2961	10.5631	9.8986	9.2950	8.7455	8.2442	7.7862	7.3667	6.6282	6.0021	5.4675
15	13.8651	12.8492	11.9379	11.1184	10.3797	9.7123	9.1079	8.5595	8.0607	7.6061	6.8109	6.1422	5.5755
16	14.7179	13.5777	12.5611	11.6523	10.8378	10.1059	9.4467	8.8514	8.3126	7.8237	6.9740	6.2651	5.6685
17	15.5623	14.2919	13.1661	12.1657	11.2741	10.4773	9.7632	9.1216	8.5436	8.0216	7.1196	6.3729	5.7487
18	16.3983	14.9920	13.7535	12.6593	11.6896	10.8276	10.0591	9.3719	8.7556	8.2014	7.2497	6.4674	5.8179
19	17.2260	15.6785	14.3238	13.1339	12.0853	11.1581	10.3356	9.6036	8.9501	8.3649	7.3658	6.5504	5.8775
20	18.0456	16.3514	14.8775	13.5903	12.4622	11.4699	10.5940	9.8181	9.1285	8.5136	7.4694	6.6231	5.9289
21	18.8570	17.0112	15.4150	14.0292	12.8212	11.7641	10.8355	10.0168	9.2922	8.6487	7.5620	6.6870	5.9732
22	19.6604	17.6580	15.9369	14.4511	13.1630	12.0416	11.0612	10.2007	9.4424	8.7715	7.6446	6.7430	6.0113
23	20.4558	18.2922	16.4436	14.8569	13.4886	12.3034	11.2722	10.3711	9.5802	8.8832	7.7184	6.7921	6.0443
24	21.2434	18.9139	16.9355	15.2470	13.7987	12.5504	11.4693	10.5288	9.7066	8.9847	7.7843	6.8352	6.0726
25	22.0232	19.5234	17.4132	15.6221	14.0940	12.7834	11.6536	10.6748	9.8226	9.0770	7.8431	6.8729	6.0971
26	22.7952	20.1210	17.8768	15.9828	14.3752	13.0032	11.8258	10.8100	9.9290	9.1610	7.8956	6.9061	6.1182
27	23.5596	20.7069	18.3270	16.3296	14.6430	13.2106	11.9867	10.9352	10.0266	9.2372	7.9425	6.9352	6.1364
28	24.3165	21.2813	18.7641	16.6631	14.8981	13.4062	12.1371	11.0511	10.1161	9.3066	7.9844	6.9607	6.1521
29	25.0658	21.8444	19.1885	16.9837	15.1411	13.5908	12.2777	11.1584	10.1983	9.3696	8.0218	6.9831	6.1656
30	25.8077	22.3964	19.6005	17.2920	15.3725	13.7649	12.4091	11.2578	10.2737	9.4269	8.0552	7.0027	6.1772
31	26.5423	22.9377	20.0005	17.5885	15.5928	13.9291	12.5318	11.3498	10.3428	9.4790	8.0850	7.0199	6.1873
32	27.2696	23.4683	20.3888	17.8736	15.8027	14.0841	12.6466	11.4350	10.4062	9.5264	8.1116	7.0350	6.1959
33	27.9897	23.9885	20.7658	18.1477	16.0026	14.2303	12.7538	11.5139	10.4644	9.5694	8.1353	7.0483	6.2034
34	28.7027	24.4986	21.1319	18.4112	16.1929	14.3682	12.8540	11.5870	10.5178	9.6086	8.1565	7.0599	6.2098
35	29.4086	24.9986	21.4872	18.6646	16.3742	14.4983	12.9477	11.6546	10.5668	9.6442	8.1755	7.0701	6.2154
36	30.1075	24.4888	21.8323	18.9083	16.5469	14.6211	13.0352	11.7172	10.6118	9.6765	8.1924	7.0790	6.2201
37	30.7995	25.9694	22.1673	19.1426	16.7113	14.7368	13.1170	11.7752	10.6530	9.7059	8.2075	7.0868	6.2243
38	31.4847	26.4406	22.4925	19.3679	16.8679	14.8461	13.1935	11.8289	10.6908	9.7327	8.2210	7.0937	6.2278
39	32.1631	26.9026	22.8082	19.5845	17.0171	14.9491	13.2650	11.8786	10.7255	9.7570	8.2330	7.0998	6.2309
40	32.8347	27.3555	23.1148	19.7928	17.1591	15.0464	13.3317	11.9246	10.7574	9.7791	8.2438	7.1051	6.2335
41	33.4997	27.7995	23.4124	19.9931	17.2944	15.1381	13.3941	11.9672	10.7866	9.7991	8.2534	7.1097	6.2358
42	34.1581	28.2348	23.7014	20.1857	17.4232	15.2246	13.4525	12.0067	10.8134	9.8174	8.2619	7.1138	6.2377
43	34.8100	28.6615	23.9819	20.3708	17.5459	15.3062	13.5070	12.0432	10.8380	9.8340	8.2696	7.1173	6.2394
44	35.4555	29.0799	24.2543	20.4589	17.6628	15.3833	13.5579	12.0771	10.8605	9.8491	8.2764	7.1205	6.2409
45	36.0945	29.4901	24.5187	20.7201	17.7741	15.4559	13.6055	12.1084	10.8812	9.8628	8.2825	7.1232	6.2422
46	36.7273	29.8923	24.7755	20.8847	17.8801	15.5244	13.6500	12.1374	10.9002	9.8753	8.2880	7.1256	6.2432
47	37.3537	30.2866	25.0247	21.0430	17.9810	15.5891	13.6916	12.1643	10.9176	9.8866	8.2928	7.1277	6.2442
48	37.9740	30.6731	25.2667	21.1952	18.0772	15.6501	13.7305	12.1891	10.9336	9.8969	8.2972	7.1296	6.2450
49	38.5881	31.0521	25.5017	21.3415	18.1687	16.7077	13.7668	12.2122	10.9482	9.9063	8.3010	7.1312	6.2457
50	39.1961	31.4236	25.7298	21.4822	18.2559	15.7619	13.8008	12.2335	10.9617	9.9148	8.3045	7.1327	6.2463

INDEX